ANNUAL REVIEW OF PSYCHOLOGY

ANNUAL REVIEW OF PSYCHOLOGY

VOLUME 37, 1986

MARK R. ROSENZWEIG, *Editor*

University of California, Berkeley

LYMAN W. PORTER, *Editor*

University of California, Irvine

ANNUAL REVIEWS INC.   4139 EL CAMINO WAY   PALO ALTO, CALIFORNIA 94306 USA

ANNUAL REVIEWS INC.
Palo Alto, California, USA

International Standard Serial Number: 0066–4308
International Standard Book Number: 0–8243–0237-0
Library of Congress Catalog Card Number: 50-13143

Annual Reviews Inc. and the Editors of its publications assume no responsibility
for the statements expressed by the contributors to this *Review*.

Typesetting by Kachina Typesetting Inc., Tempe, Arizona; John Olson, President
Typesetting coordinator, Dennis Phillips

PRINTED AND BOUND IN THE UNITED STATES OF AMERICA

PREFACE

From the outset it has been the goal of the *Annual Review of Psychology* to take into consideration research done in all parts of the world. As the Preface to Volume 1 (1950) noted, inaugurating this series was delayed by World War II, in part because the war made it impossible to survey world literature in psychology. Several prefaces in early volumes noted the desirability but also difficulties of recruiting authors from outside of North America, and this has continued to be the case. The present volume includes one review chapter by an author located in Europe, and another such chapter is planned for Volume 38; one or two non-North American authors is typical for recent volumes.

To supplement the information about research abroad furnished in the standard kind of topic-oriented reviews, the Editorial Committees began to run occasional chapters on psychological research in a particular country or region of the world. This practice was regularized in 1972 when we began to publish chapters on psychology in the host countries of the International Congresses of Psychology, sponsored by the International Union of Psychological Science. To date, this has included chapters on psychology in Japan (1972), France (1976), the German Democratic Republic (1980), and Mexico (1984). The present volume takes a further step in this direction by including a chapter on psychology in Israel, as the host country of the International Congress of Applied Psychology. The International Congresses of Psychology and the International Congresses of Applied Psychology are now each held on a four-year basis, one or the other occurring biennially. We plan, therefore, to run in every odd-numbered volume of the *Annual Review of Psychology* a chapter on psychology in the host country of one of the major international congresses.

Readers in several countries are now benefiting from reduced prices for their purchases of the *Annual Review of Psychology* and other publications by Annual Reviews Inc. These are purchases made on group plans set up by various scientific and/or professional organizations with Annual Reviews Inc. At present, these groups include the Australian Psychological Society, Belgian Federation of Psychologists, Canadian Psychological Society, German Society for Psychology, International Council of Psychology, and the Netherlands Institute of Psychology. Interested readers who belong to other organizations and who want to benefit from such a plan may wish to call this to the attention of

(continued) v

their groups. Students of psychology can also benefit from a special student purchase price by having a special form filled out and sending it to Annual Reviews Inc. with their prepaid orders.

The Editors and members of the Editorial Committees are selected only from North America for reasons of rapid communication and economy, but an effort is made to recruit individuals who are well informed about the progress in their fields on an international basis. Members of the Editorial Committee usually serve five-year terms, and we regret that Jeanne S. Phillips has now completed her term on the Committee. Her contributions were both well-informed and enthusiastic, and we will miss her participation in our meetings. We regret that Allan R. Wagner had to withdraw from the Committee without having been able to participate in a meeting. However, we look forward to working with the new Committee members who will replace Jeanne and Allan at the next annual planning meeting.

Finally, the Editors and members of the Editorial Committee are happy to receive comments, suggestions, and questions about the *Annual Review of Psychology* from readers in all parts of the world. (Please do not, however, submit unsolicited manuscripts. Authors of Annual Review articles are selected through deliberations of the Editorial Committee.)

M.R.R.

L.W.P.

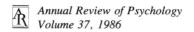

Annual Review of Psychology
Volume 37, 1986

CONTENTS

EVOLVING CONCEPTS OF TEST VALIDATION, *Anne Anastasi*   1

PSYCHOLOGY IN A DEVELOPING SOCIETY: THE CASE OF ISRAEL,
Rachel Ben-Ari and Yehuda Amir   17

SELECTIVE ATTENTION, *William A. Johnston and Veronica J. Dark*   43

THE NEUROCHEMISTRY OF BEHAVIOR, *Jaak Panksepp*   77

THE REGULATION OF BODY WEIGHT, *Richard E. Keesey and Terry
L. Powley*   109

INFANCY, *Dale F. Hay*   135

THE BIOLOGY OF LEARNING, *James L. Gould*   163

PROGRAM EVALUATION: THE WORLDLY SCIENCE, *Thomas D. Cook
and William R. Shadish, Jr.*   193

EXPECTANCIES AND INTERPERSONAL PROCESSES, *Dale T. Miller and
William Turnbull*   233

CONSUMER PSYCHOLOGY, *James R. Bettman*   257

ETIOLOGY AND EXPRESSION OF SCHIZOPHRENIA: NEUROBIOLOGICAL
AND PSYCHOSOCIAL FACTORS, *Allan F. Mirsky and Connie C.
Duncan*   291

INDIVIDUAL PSYCHOTHERAPY AND BEHAVIOR CHANGE, *Morris B.
Parloff, Perry London, and Barry Wolfe*   321

PERSONNEL SELECTION AND PLACEMENT, *Milton D. Hakel*   351

ENVIRONMENTAL PSYCHOLOGY, *Charles J. Holahan*   381

DIAGNOSIS AND CLINICAL ASSESSMENT: THE CURRENT STATE OF
PSYCHIATRIC DIAGNOSIS, *Lee N. Robins and John E. Helzer*   409

UNDERSTANDING THE CELLULAR BASIS OF MEMORY AND LEARNING,
C. D. Woody   433

VISUAL SENSITIVITY, *T. E. Cohn and D. J. Lasley*   495

CULTURE AND BEHAVIOR: PSYCHOLOGY IN GLOBAL PERSPECTIVE,
Marshall H. Segall   523

EMOTION: TODAY'S PROBLEMS, *Howard Leventhal and Andrew J.
Tomarken*   565

INSTRUCTIONAL PSYCHOLOGY, *Paul R. Pintrich, David R. Cross,
Robert B. Kozma, and Wilbert J. McKeachie*   611

INDEXES

Author Index   653
Subject Index   678
Cumulative Index of Contributing Authors, Volumes 33–37   699
Cumulative Index of Chapter Titles, Volumes 33–37   701

SOME ARTICLES IN OTHER *ANNUAL REVIEWS*
OF INTEREST TO PSYCHOLOGISTS

From the *Annual Review of Anthropology,* Volume 14 (1985)

Anthropology, Evolution, and "Scientific Creationism," *James N. Spuhler*
Human Genetic Distance Studies: Present Status and Future Prospects, *L. B. Jorde*
Sexual Dimorphism, *David W. Frayer and Milford H. Wolpoff*
Bioanthropological Research in Developing Countries, *Rebecca Huss-Ashmore and Francis E. Johnston*
Modular Theories of Grammar, *Ann K. Farmer*
Status and Style in Language, *Judith T. Irvine*

From the *Annual Review of Sociology,* Volume 11 (1985)

Ethnicity, *J. Milton Yinger*
Urban Poverty, *William Julius Wilson and Robert Aponte*
New Black-White Patterns: How Best To Conceptualize Them?, *Thomas F. Pettigrew*
Quality of Life Research and Sociology, *K. F. Schuessler and G. A. Fisher*
Sociology of Mass Communication, *Denis McQuail*
The Organizational Structure of the School, *William B. Tyler*
The Impact of School Desegregation: A Situational Analysis, *Douglas Longshore and Jeffrey Prager*
Interorganizational Relations, *Joseph Galaskiewicz*
Organizational Culture, *William G. Ouchi and Alan L. Wilkins*
Social Control of Occupations and Work, *Richard L. Simpson*
White Collar Crime, *John Braithwaite*
Effects of Sibling Number on Child Outcome, *David M. Heer*
Family Violence, *Richard J. Gelles*

From the *Annual Review of Medicine,* Volume 37 (1986)

Behavioral Disturbances Associated with Endocrine Disorders, *Victor I. Reus*

From the *Annual Review of Neuroscience,* Volume 9 (1986)

Invertebrate Learning and Memory: From Behavior to Molecules, *Thomas J. Carew and Christie L. Sanley*
Vertebrate Olfactory Reception, *Doron Lancet*
New Perspectives on Alzheimer's Disease, *Donald L. Price*
Interactions Between Retinal Ganglion Cells During the Development of the Mammalian Visual System, *Carla J. Shatz and David W. Sretavan*
Artificial Intelligence and the Brain: Computational Studies of the Visual System, *Shimon Ullman*

(continued)   ix

x   OTHER ARTICLES OF INTEREST   *(continued)*

From the *Annual Review of Public Health,* Volume 7 (1986)

Occupational Ergonomics: Methods to Evaluate Physical Stress on the Job, *W. Monroe Keyserling and Don B. Chaffin*
Monitoring for Congenital Malformations, *Neil A. Holtzman*
Mediating Solutions to Environmental Risks, *Sam Gusman and Philip J. Harter*

From the *Annual Review of Pharmacology and Toxicology,* Volume 26 (1986)

Potential Animal Models for Senile Dementia of Alzheimer's Type, with Emphasis on AF64A-Induced Cholinotoxicity, *Abraham Fisher and Israel Hanin*

Coming for 1987 . . .

CHAPTERS PLANNED FOR THE NEXT
ANNUAL REVIEW OF PSYCHOLOGY, Volume 38

Prefatory Chapter, *Hans Wallach*
Brain Functions, *Jon H. Kass*
Developmental Psychobiology, *Warren G. Hall and Ronald Oppenheimer*
Auditory Psychophysics, *E. de Boer*
Perception, *James E. Cutting*
Psycholinguistics, *Donald J. Foss*
Thinking and Concepts, *Gregg C. Oden*
Human Learning and Memory, *Marcia K. Johnson and Lynn Hasher*
Social Motivation, *Thane S. Pittman*
Perceptual Development, *Richard N. Aslin and Linda B. Smith*
Gerontology/Life Span, *Nancy Datan, Dean Rodeheaver, and Fergus Hughes*
Personality, *Jerome L. Singer and Marc Mishkind*
Psychopathology of Childhood, *Herbert C. Quay*
Social and Community Interventions, *Ellis L. Gesten and Leonard Jason*
Social Cognition and Perception, *E. Tory Higgins and John Bargh*
Attitudes and Attitude Change, *Shelly Chaiken*
Organizational Behavior, *Robert J. House*
Organizational Change and Development, *Michael Beer and Elise Walton*
Career Counseling, *Samuel Osipow*
New Design in Analysis of Variance, *Rand R. Wilcox*
The Self, *Hazel Markus and Elissa Wurf*
Political Psychology, *David O. Sears*
Contributions of Women to Psychology, *Nancy F. Russo and Florence Denmark*

For the convenience of readers, a detachable order form/envelope is bound into the back of this volume.

Anne Anastasi

Ann. Rev. Psychol. 1986. 37:1-15

EVOLVING CONCEPTS OF TEST VALIDATION[1]

Anne Anastasi

Department of Psychology, Fordham University, Bronx, New York 10458

CONTENTS

THE PLACE OF VALIDITY IN THE TEST CONSTRUCTION PROCESS.............. 2
THE NATURE OF CONSTRUCTS IN TEST VALIDATION 4
TRAITS AND SITUATIONS... 8
VALIDITY GENERALIZATION 10
SUMMARY 12

In the early beginnings of standardized testing, validity was assessed by a diversity of procedures and was called by many names. The type of evidence adduced to demonstrate test validity varied with the purpose of the test, the theoretical orientation of the test author, and—all too often—with the ready availability of the data. Among the earliest empirical approaches to evaluating test items and selecting the most valid was the age-differentiation criterion employed by Binet and Simon (1908). On the assumption that the cognitive skills constituting intelligence increase with age through childhood, they chose tasks whose frequency of correct solution increased with age; they then assigned each task to the age level at which the percentage of children passing it fell within a specified range. This was also a major procedure followed in the construction of the Stanford-Binet and other individual intelligence tests of the period that assessed intelligence in terms of mental age.

Soon total test scores were being evaluated, not only against chronological age but also against judgments of individual achievement, such as teachers' ratings of pupils' performance or other evidence of the quality of behavior in

[1]This chapter is based in part on an invited address presented at the 1984 annual meeting of the American Educational Research Association in New Orleans. This is the seventh in a series of prefatory chapters written by eminent senior psychologists. For more information about this series, see the Preface to Volume 36.

0066-4308/86/0201-0001$02.00

daily life. Case history data and psychiatric diagnoses also served as criteria, especially for personality tests and tests designed for identifying mental retardation. With advances in statistical methodology, techniques of item analysis against total test scores or against external criterion measures came into use. Still later, factor analysis was introduced in test development; it was applied to items, to subtest scores, and to total test scores in combination with scores on other tests. Different investigators and test authors employed a confusing array of names for the validity they reported, ranging from face validity, validity by definition, intrinsic validity, and logical validity to empirical validity and factorial validity.

In 1954, in a major effort to introduce some order into the chaotic state of test construction procedures as a whole, the American Psychological Association (in collaboration with the American Educational Research Association and the National Council on Measurement in Education) published the *Technical Recommendations for Psychological Tests and Diagnostic Techniques*. This publication formally introduced the now familiar classification into content, predictive, concurrent, and construct validity. In subsequent editions of this document (*Standards . . . 1974*), predictive and concurrent validity were subsumed under criterion-related validity, and this tripartite division has survived to the present.

Although initially helping to clarify our thinking about validation procedures, the tripartite categorization of validity has had some adverse side effects on testing practice. Essentially it represents a crude and oversimplified grouping of many data-gathering procedures that contribute to an understanding of what a test measures. Yet there has been a tendency to lean too heavily on this neat, satisfying tripartite classification. The three labels have been reified and endowed with an existence of their own. They first came to be regarded as three distinct *types* of validity and later as three essential *aspects* or *components* of validity. Thus test constructors would feel obliged to tick them off in checklist fashion. It was felt that they should be covered somehow in three properly labeled validity sections in the technical manual, regardless of the nature or purpose of the particular test. Once this tripartite coverage was accomplished, there was the relaxed feeling that validation requirements had been met. This, of course, is a gross distortion of the role of validity in the test development process. It is noteworthy that in the 1985 edition of the *Standards for Educational and Psychological Testing*, some of the apparent rigidities of the earlier editions were eliminated and a more comprehensive and flexible approach to validation procedures was followed.

THE PLACE OF VALIDITY IN THE TEST CONSTRUCTION PROCESS

Let us turn to a basic question: How does one build a valid test? What are the ideal test-construction procedures? What is the general model of test development that the test author endeavors to approximate within the constraints of practical demands and real-life limitations?

More and more we recognize that the development of a valid test requires multiple procedures, which are employed sequentially at different stages of test construction (Jackson 1970, 1973, Guion 1983). Validity is thus built into the test from the outset rather than being limited to the last stages of test development, as in traditional criterion-related validation. The validation process begins with the formulation of detailed trait or construct definitions, derived from psychological theory, prior research, or systematic observation and analyses of the relevant behavior domain. Test items are then prepared to fit the construct definitions. Empirical item analyses follow, with the selection of the most effective (i.e. valid) items from the initial item pools. Other appropriate internal analyses may then be carried out, including factor analyses of item clusters or subtests. The final stage includes validation and cross-validation of various scores and interpretive combinations of scores through statistical analyses against external, real-life criteria.

This multistage process for building validity into a test is illustrated in varying degrees by several recently developed tests. Among them are the Comrey Personality Scales (1970) and the Millon Clinical Multiaxial Inventory (1983). It is most clearly exemplified by the Personality Research Form developed by Jackson (1974), who has contributed substantially to the dissemination of the multistage procedure (Jackson 1970, 1973). In the cognitive domain, the procedure is illustrated by the recently published Kaufman Assessment Battery for Children (1983; see also Anastasi 1984), although the reporting of validity in the interpretive manual still follows the traditional approach. There are separate sections labeled construct, concurrent, and predictive validity; and relevant information from other stages of test development, such as construct formulation and several kinds of item analysis, is scattered through other chapters.

Almost any information gathered in the process of developing or using a test is relevant to its validity. It is relevant in the sense that it contributes to our understanding of what the test measures. Certainly, data on internal consistency and on retest reliability help to define the homogeneity of the construct and its temporal stability. Norms may well provide additional construct specification, especially if they include separate normative data for subgroups classified by age, sex, or other demographic variables that affect test performance. Remember that systematic age increment was a major criterion in the development of early intelligence tests.

If we think of test validity in terms of understanding what a particular test measures, it should be apparent that virtually any empirical data obtained with the test represent a potential source of validity information. After a test is released for operational use, the interpretive meaning of its scores may continue to be sharpened, refined, and enriched through the gradual accumulation of clinical observations and through special research projects. The former was well illustrated by the Stanford-Binet, the latter by the MMPI. Test validity is a living thing; it is not dead and embalmed when the test is released. Obviously, this does not mean that the test is not ready for use until all possible data bearing on its validity are in. Construct validation is indeed a never-ending process. However, that should not preclude using the test operationally to help solve practical problems and reach real-life decisions as soon as the available validity information has reached an acceptable level for a particular application. This level varies with the type of test and the way it will be used. Establishing this level requires informed professional judgment within the appropriate specialty of professional practice.

THE NATURE OF CONSTRUCTS IN TEST VALIDATION

By now it is undoubtedly apparent that I have been talking about what is traditionally known as construct validation. What about the other types, aspects, components, or modifying labels that have become generally associated with test validity? The answer is that what has come to be designated construct validity is actually a comprehensive approach that includes the other recognized validation procedures—and much more besides. This point has been made repeatedly: in the test standards (from the first, 1954 version to the latest), in textbooks, symposium papers, and journal articles. Yet the ambiguity persists. Probably the confusion results from the many usages of the term validity. In a 1980 paper, Messick argued convincingly that the term validity, insofar as it designates the interpretive meaningfulness of a test, should be reserved for construct validity. Other procedures with which the term validity has traditionally been associated, he maintained, should be designated by more specifically descriptive labels. Thus, content validity could be labeled content relevance and content coverage, to refer to domain specifications and domain representativeness, respectively. Criterion-related validity could be labeled predictive utility and diagnostic utility, to correspond to predictive and concurrent validation. These changes in terminology should help, but it may be some time before the old terms can be dislodged.

If we turn from labels to procedures, we can see that content analyses and correlations with external criteria fit into particular stages in the process of construct validation, that is, in the process of both determining and demonstrating what a test measures. Certain procedures may be singled out for special emphasis in order to answer specific practical questions. But constructs are always involved, in both the questions and the answers, even though we may not be aware of it.

Let us consider the nature of the constructs employed in test development. Essentially they are theoretical concepts of varying degrees of abstraction and generalizability which facilitate the understanding of empirical data. They are ultimately derived from empirically observed behavioral consistencies, and they are identified and defined through a network of observed interrelationships. In the description of individual behavior, such a construct corresponds closely to what is generally termed a trait. A simple example, with narrowly limited generalizability, is speed of walking. If we take repeated measurements of an individual's walking speed, we still obtain a whole distribution of speeds, depending upon the person's condition at the time, the context in which the walking occurs, and the purpose of the walking, among other circumstances. Nevertheless, it is likely that an analysis of such varied measures would reveal a substantial common factor that reliably differentiates one person from another in overall walking speed. This common factor would be a construct; it does not necessarily correspond to any single empirical measure.

Another relatively simple example is spelling ability. A test for this ability appears to be a likely candidate for content validation. But as in walking speed, we must guard against overgeneralizing from a behavior sample drawn from a limited domain. There may be several differentiable spelling abilities, and there is evidence that this is the case (e.g. Knoell & Harris 1952, Ahlström 1964). Such diverse spelling behaviors may be illustrated by the recognition of correctly and incorrectly spelled words, as in a multiple-choice or true-false test; frequency of misspellings in spontaneous writing; correctness of spelling when writing from dictation; and sensitivity to one's potential spelling errors, with the associated readiness to verify spelling by consulting sources. In designing a spelling test for a particular purpose, as for inclusion in a job selection battery, one can define the scope and boundaries of the construct that best fits the specific needs. This practice has been followed, to quote another example, in designing tests of functional literacy, or reading ability, for various industrial and military occupational specialties (Sticht 1975, Schoenfeldt et al 1976).

I have deliberately chosen examples of relatively narrow constructs because they can be more readily grasped. If we go to the other extreme of breadth, complexity, and generalizability, many of us would undoubtedly think of intelligence as a construct. I would rather not use that example, however, for at least two reasons. First, the term intelligence has acquired too many excess meanings that obfuscate its nature. Second, the construct measured by tests of intelligence requires some modifying adjectives and delimiting specifications. No test was actually designed to measure universal human intelligence. Some tests could be more accurately described as measures of academic intelligence, or scholastic aptitude, or that cluster of cognitive skills and knowledge demanded and positively reinforced in modern, technologically advanced societies. Even more precise construct definitions would certainly improve the interpretability of scores obtained with most so-called intelligence tests.

When a test author sets out to develop a new test, it is highly unlikely that he or she does so without some idea about the construct or constructs to be assessed, however vaguely defined. Nor did this practice originate with the formal introduction of construct validation into the psychometric lexicon. Binet devoted considerable time to a formulation of his concept of intelligence; the development of his ideas on the subject can be traced through published writings spanning many years (Wolf 1973). At the time when the Binet-Simon tests were prepared, Binet's conception of intelligence included such behavioral qualities as attention control, directed thinking, comprehension, judgment, and self-criticism (Binet 1909/1911). The influence of these constructs in guiding the preparation of the scale can be readily recognized in the test items, many of which have survived in the Stanford-Binet.

Once the testing movement had been fully launched, however, there was a tendency to veer away from theoretical rationale and construct formulation. The knowledge and hypotheses that undoubtedly still guided initial item writing were deemphasized and were rarely discussed in connection with test validity. The test manuals created a general impression of almost blind empiricism. There was heavy reliance on empirical item selection from large, preliminary item pools, followed by ex post facto evaluation of the total test through validation and cross-validation against external criteria. Substantial validity shrinkage was regularly expected in cross-validation because of the large contribution of chance factors to item selection. It is well known that such shrinkage will be largest when the initial item pool is large, the proportion of retained items is small, and the sample of persons is small. Under conditions of blind empiricism, test validity may drop to virtually zero in cross-validation— there are some dramatic demonstrations of this fact in the literature (Kurtz 1948, Cureton 1950). Shrinkage can be drastically reduced, however, when items are prepared to fit clearly formulated hypotheses derived from psychological theory or from previous investigations of criterion requirements (Primoff 1952). It is apparent that clear construct definition as a guide to item writing is not only logically defensible but also efficient.

Empiricism need not be blind. The overemphasis on purely empirical procedures during the early decades of this century arose in part as a revolt against the armchair theorizing that all too often served as the basis for so-called psychological writings of the period. But theory need not be subjective speculation. Theory *can* be derived from an analysis of accumulated research findings and can in turn lead to the formulation of empirically testable hypotheses. The shift toward stronger theoretical orientation discernible in American psychology since midcentury produced a noticeable spinoff in test construction. Tests published in the 1970s and 1980s show increasing concern with theoretical rationales throughout the test development process. A specific example of the integration of empirical and theoretical approaches to test construction is provided by the assignment of items to subtests or scales on the basis of logical as well as statistical homogeneity. In other words, an item is retained in a scale if it was written to meet the specifications of the construct definition of the particular scale and *also* was shown to belong in that scale by the results of factor analysis or other statistical procedures of item analysis (Comrey 1970, Jackson 1974, Millon 1983).

Let us look more closely at the sources of the constructs employed in test development. How are these constructs formulated by the test author? This question actually pertains to criterion analysis, that is, an analysis of *what* the author wants the test to assess. Regardless of the purpose of the test, this is the criterion question.

For the most general types of tests, designed for wide-ranging uses, a major source of guiding constructs is psychological theory and the accumulated store of prior research findings. Among the most common sources actually used by test developers are personality theories, clinical observations, factor-analytic investigations of human abilities, and, more recently, information-processing studies from cognitive psychology.

When tests are designed for use within special contexts, the relevant constructs are usually derived from content analyses of particular behavior domains. Such analyses have varied widely in their thoroughness, fullness, and precision. In educational contexts, the most characteristic tests are the so-called achievement tests, whose purpose is to assess the effects of academic learning and the individual's readiness for further learning of a similar nature. At the broadest level, the constructs for such tests are educational goals, translated into testable behavioral specifications. The sources are essentially consensual judgment data. Ideally, these data are systematically gathered under conditions that are clearly described and amenable to replication. At more specific levels, the criterion analyses are represented by systematic surveys of curricula, course syllabi, and textbooks, as well as judgment data obtained from recognized experts within subject-matter specialities.

In occupational testing, designed for personnel selection and classification, the criterion analysis is generally called a job analysis. To be effective, a job analysis should concentrate on those aspects of performance that differentiate most sharply between the better and the poorer workers. In many jobs, workers of different levels of proficiency may differ little in the way they carry out most parts of their jobs—only certain features of their jobs may bring out the major differences between successes and failures. In his classic book on *Aptitude Testing,* Clark Hull as early as 1928 stressed the importance of these differentiating aspects of job performance which he called "critical part-activities" (p. 286). Later this concept was reemphasized by John Flanagan (1949, 1954), under the name of "critical requirements." To implement the concept of critical requirements, Flanagan proposed the critical incident technique. This technique called for factual descriptions of specific instances of job behavior characteristic of either satisfactory or unsatisfactory workers. The focus on critical job requirements led, through various routes, to the development of the job element method for constructing tests and demonstrating their validity. Variants of this procedure have been applied to a wide diversity of jobs, in industry and in the public sector at the federal, state, and local levels (McCormick et al 1972, Primoff 1975, Menne et al 1976, Tordy et al 1976, Eyde et al 1981).

Essentially, job elements are the units describing critical work requirements. The job element statements are generated and rated by job incumbents and supervisors, chosen because they are thoroughly familiar with the job. Job elements refer to those specific job behaviors that differentiate most clearly between marginal and superior workers. Relying ultimately on the observations and judgment of experienced workers, the job element method provides techniques for systematically collecting and quantifying these judgments. Although various adaptations of the job element method differ in procedural details, all provide for the description of job activities in terms of specific behavioral requirements, from which test items can be directly formulated. The individual behavioral statements can, in turn, be grouped into broader categories or constructs, such as computational accuracy, spatial visualization, manual dexterity, or ability to work under pressure. There is a growing body of research aimed at the development of a general taxonomy of job performance in terms of relatively broad behavioral constructs (Fleishman 1975, Pearlman 1980). The job element method contributes to this goal and thereby facilitates the effective use of a test across many superficially dissimilar jobs.

TRAITS AND SITUATIONS

Any discussion of trait constructs must take into account the question of situational specificity. A long-standing controversy regarding the generalizability of traits versus the situational specificity of behavior reached a peak in the late 1960s and the 1970s. Several developments in the 1960s focused attention on narrowly defined "behaviors of interest" and away from broadly defined traits. In the cognitive domain, this focus is illustrated by individualized instructional programs and criterion-referenced testing and by the diagnosis and treatment of learning disabilities. In the noncognitive or personality domain, the strongest impetus toward behavioral specificity in testing came from social learning theory and the general orientation associated with behavior modification and behavior therapy (Bandura & Walters 1963; Bandura 1969; Goldfried & Kent 1972; Mischel 1968, 1969, 1973). All the advocates of behavioral specificity in both cognitive and noncognitive areas directed their criticisms especially toward the early view of traits as fixed, unchanging, underlying causal entities. This kind of criticism had already been vigorously expressed in earlier writings by several psychologists and had been supported by appropriate psychometric research. In fact, few psychologists today espouse such extreme views of traits with their excess meanings and unwarranted implications.

On the other side of the controversy, the initial emphasis on extreme behavioral specificity, with its accompanying rejection of trait constructs, resulted at least in part from certain methodological constraints. These included predominantly low reliability of measures and failure to aggregate across observations so as to cancel out specific variance (Green 1978; Epstein 1979, 1980; Rushton et al 1983). There is now a growing consensus between the adherents of the opposing views (Mischel 1977, 1979; Anastasi 1983). We are coming to recognize more and more that in order to identify broad traits, we have to assess individuals across situations and aggregate the results. To meet different assessment needs, behavioral observations can be aggregated in different ways and with appropriate degrees of generality or specificity (Mischel & Peake 1982). The focus may be on intraindividual consistencies or on situational categories of varying degrees of breadth.

Both the theoretical discussions and the research on person-by-situation interaction have undoubtedly enriched our understanding of the many conditions that determine individual behavior. They have also contributed to the development of sophisticated research designs such as the application of multimode factor analysis (Tucker 1964, 1966; Levin 1965; Kjerulff & Wiggins 1976). By this technique, one can identify major factors in situations, in response styles, and in persons. In addition, there is a core matrix which integrates the three modes and permits their joint interpretation. For example, in an investigation of graduate student styles for coping with stressful situations (Kjerulff & Wiggins 1976), students who rated themselves as less professionally competent tended to feel anger at themselves for academic failures and anger at others for interpersonal difficulties; they were extremely anxious when facing academic problems, but not at all anxious in stressful situations for which there is no clear source of blame, such as losing subjects in an experiment.

When the heat of the controversy over traits and situations had dissipated, it was clear that situational variance is more conspicuous in analyses of personality traits than in analyses of abilities. For example, a person may be quite sociable and outgoing at the office, but shy and reserved at social gatherings. Or a student who cheats on examinations may be scrupulously honest in handling money. An extensive body of empirical evidence has been assembled by social learning theorists (Mischel 1968, Peterson 1968) showing that individuals exhibit considerable situational specificity in several nonintellective dimensions, such as aggression, social conformity, dependency, rigidity, honesty, and attitudes toward authority.

Part of the explanation for the higher cross-situational consistency of cognitive than of affective functions may be found in the greater uniformity and standardization of the individual's reactional biography in the cognitive domain (Anastasi 1970). Schooling is a major influence in the standardization of cognitive experience. The formal school curriculum, for example, fosters the development of broadly applicable cognitive skills in the verbal and numerical areas. Personality development, in contrast, occurs under far less uniform conditions. Moreover, in the personality domain, the same response may elicit social consequences that are positively reinforcing in one type of situation and negatively reinforcing in another. The individual may thus learn to respond in quite different ways in different contexts.

From the standpoint of personality test development, it should be noted that one can also identify situationally linked traits. This way of categorizing behavior is illustrated by the familiar test anxiety inventories (Spielberger et al 1976, Sarason 1980, Spielberger 1980, Tryon 1980). Such inventories cover essentially a trait construct that is restricted to a specified class of situations, those covering tests and examinations. Individuals high in this trait tend to perceive evaluative situations as personally threatening. The test instructions may be modified to define the anxiety-provoking situations even more specifically by directing examinees to respond, for example, with reference to mathematics tests or essay tests. Constructs such as test anxiety can be identified by aggregating observations within the situationally defined behavior domain, thereby cancelling out error variance as well as specificity that is irrelevant to the construct definition. The behavioral consistencies identified through such aggregation may well prove to be of considerable interest both theoretically and practically.

VALIDITY GENERALIZATION

The concept of situational specificity has played a somewhat different role in research on the validity of ability tests for personnel assessment. When standardized aptitude tests were first correlated with performance on presumably similar jobs in industrial validation studies, the validity coefficients were found to vary widely (Ghiselli 1959, 1966). Similar variability among validity coefficients was observed when the criteria were grades in various school courses (Bennett et al 1984). Such findings led to widespread pessimism regarding the generalizability of test validity across different situations. Until the mid-1970s, "situational specificity" of psychological requirements was generally regarded as a serious limitation in the usefulness of standardized tests in personnel selection (Guion 1976). In a sophisticated statistical analysis of the problem, however, Frank Schmidt, John Hunter, and their associates (Schmidt & Hunter 1977, Schmidt et al 1981) demonstrated that much of the variance among obtained validity coefficients may be a statistical artifact resulting from small sample size, criterion unreliability, and restriction of range in employee samples.

The industrial samples available for test validation are generally too small to yield a stable estimate of the correlation between predictor and criterion. For the same reason, the obtained coefficients may be too low to reach statistical significance in the sample investigated and may thus fail to provide evidence of the test's validity. It has been estimated that about half of the validation samples used in industrial studies include no more than 40 or 50 cases (Schmidt et al 1976). This is also true of the samples often employed in educational settings to compute validity coefficients against grades in particular courses or specialized training programs (Bennett et al 1984). With such small samples, criterion-related validation is likely to yield inconclusive and uninterpretable results within any single study.

Applying their newly developed techniques to data from many samples drawn from a large number of occupational specialties, Schmidt, Hunter, and their coworkers were able to show that the validity of tests of verbal, numerical, and abstract reasoning aptitudes can be generalized far more widely across occupations than had heretofore been recognized (Schmidt et al 1979, 1980, Pearlman et al 1980). The variance of validity coefficients typically found in earlier industrial studies proved to be no greater than would be expected by chance. This was true even when the particular job functions appeared to be quite dissimilar across jobs. Evidently, the successful performance of a wide variety of occupational tasks depends to a significant degree on a common core of cognitive skills. It would seem that this cluster of cognitive skills and knowledge is broadly predictive of performance in both academic and occupational activities demanded in advanced technological societies.

When tests are used for *classification decisions,* whereby individuals are to be matched with the requirements of different types of jobs or different instructional programs, we need to investigate the boundaries of validity generalization for particular tests or combinations of tests. We need to identify the major constructs covered by the tests on the one hand and by the job functions on the other. The procedures used for this purpose can be illustrated by factor analysis of the tests and by job analysis expressed in terms of critical behavioral requirements. Validity generalization can then be investigated within functional job families, consisting of jobs that share major behavioral constructs regardless of superficial task differences.

Such dual analyses of tests and jobs have been applied with promising results in recent research on the validity of the General Aptitude Test Battery (GATB) for some 12,000 jobs described in the Dictionary of Occupational Titles of the U.S. Employment Service (U.S. Department of Labor 1983a,b). For purposes of this analysis, the jobs were classified into five functional job families. Factor analyses of the test battery yielded three broad group factors identified as cognitive, perceptual, and psychomotor. A meta-analysis of data from over 500 U.S. Employment Service validation studies was then conducted with the newly developed validity generalization techniques. This procedure yielded estimated validities of the appropriate aptitude composites for all jobs within each job family.

A more narrowly focused demonstration of the dual identification of behavioral constructs in tests and criteria was also based on analyses of U.S. Employment Service data (Gutenberg et al 1983). The investigators applied a behaviorally oriented job analysis inventory, the Position Analysis Questionnaire (PAQ), to 111 jobs for which validity data were available in the USES files. The object of the research was to investigate the possible moderating effect of certain behavioral demands of a job on the predictive validity of different tests. Three job-analysis dimensions pertaining to decision making and information processing were found to correlate positively with the validities of the cognitive GATB tests (general, verbal, and numerical aptitudes) and negatively with the validities of psychomotor tests (finger and manual dexterity tests). In other words, the more a job called for decision making and information processing, the higher was the correlation of job performance with the cognitive tests and the lower was its correlation with the psychomotor tests. These findings are consistent with the aptitude constructs identified in the previously cited USES research on validity generalization. They also support the desirability of identifying behavioral constructs in both job functions and test performance when investigating the predictive effectiveness of tests.

SUMMARY

The concept of test validation has been undergoing continuing development, clarification, and refinement. Although test authors always begin with some notion, however vague, about the constructs they want to measure, there was an early period of atheoretical empiricism in test development. By the 1970s, the increasing emphasis on theory in American psychology was reflected in test development, with an increasing interest in construct validation. In effect, all validation procedures contribute to construct validation and can be subsumed under it. So-called content validation and criterion-related validation can be more appropriately regarded as stages in the construct validation of all tests. There is a growing recognition that validation extends across the entire test construction process; it encompasses multiple procedures employed sequentially at appropriate stages. Validity is built into a test at the time of initial construct definition and the formulation of item-writing specifications; the hypotheses that guide the early developmental stages are tested sequentially through internal and external statistical analyses of empirical data. Depending upon the purpose of the test, trait constructs may be defined with different degrees of narrowness or breadth and may be linked to specified situational domains. The identification of constructs in both test performance and criterion behavior increases the efficiency of the test construction process and leads to the production of tests that are more valid theoretically, as well as more useful in meeting practical needs. An example of such effects is to be found in reduced item wastage and minimal validity shrinkage in cross-validation. Another example is the broadening of validity generalization through the identification of matching constructs in test performance and criterion behavior.

This approach is not limited to the test developer. Test users, too, can profitably use construct definition in specifying their particular testing needs (as in behaviorally oriented job analyses), and they can choose tests that have been shown to assess the relevant constructs. The same constructs should provide a basis for interpreting test scores. Finally, if it is feasible for the test user to obtain confirmatory follow-up data on the predictive effectiveness of a given test for a particular use, it would be more meaningful to correlate test scores with the relevant and practically significant criterion constructs than with a composite and amorphous assessment of overall criterion performance for each individual.

Literature Cited

Ahlström, K. G. 1964. *Studies in spelling: Analysis of three different aspects of spelling ability*, Rep. No. 20. Uppsala, Sweden: Inst. Educ., Uppsala Univ.

Anastasi, A. 1970. On the formation of psychological traits. *Am. Psychol.* 25:899–910

Anastasi, A. 1983. Traits, states, and situations: A comprehensive view. In *Principals of Modern Psychological Measurement: A Festschrift for Frederic M. Lord*, ed. H. Wainer, S. Messick, pp. 345–56. Hillsdale, NJ: Erlbaum

Anastasi, A. 1984. The K-ABC in historical and contemporary perspective. *J. Spec. Educ.* 18:358–66

Bandura, A. 1969. *Principles of Behavior Modification*. New York: Holt, Rinehart & Winston

Bandura, A., Walters, R. H. 1963. *Social Learning and Personality Development*. New York: Holt, Rinehart & Winston

Bennett, G. K., Seashore, H. G., Wesman, A. G. 1984. *Differential Aptitude Tests: Technical Supplement*. Cleveland: Psychol. Corp.

Binet, A. 1911. *Les idées modernes sur les enfants*. Paris: Flammarion (original work published 1909)

Binet, A., Simon, Th. 1908. Le développement de l'intelligence chez les enfants. *Année Psychol.* 14:1–94

Comrey, A. L. 1970. *Comrey Personality Scales*. San Diego: Educ. Ind. Test. Serv.

Cureton, E. E. 1950. Validity, reliability, and baloney. *Educ. Psychol. Meas.* 10:94–96

Epstein, S. 1979. The stability of behavior: I. On predicting most of the people much of the time. *J. Pers. Soc. Psychol.* 37:1097–1121

Epstein, S. 1980. The stability of behavior: II. Implications for psychological research. *Am. Psychol.* 35:790–806

Eyde, L. D., Primoff, E. S., Hardt, R. H. 1981. *A job element examination for state troopers* (PRR-81-3). Washington, DC: Personnel Res. Dev. Cent., U.S. Off. Personnel Manage. Natl. Tech. Inf. Serv., PB 81 198772

Flanagan, J. C. 1949. Critical requirements: A new approach to employee evaluation. *Personnel Psychol.* 2:419–25

Flanagan, J. C. 1954. The critical incident technique. *Psychol. Bull.* 51:327–58

14   ANASTASI

Fleishman, E. A. 1975. Toward a taxonomy of human performance. *Am. Psychol.* 30:1127–49

Ghiselli, E. E. 1959. The generalization of validity. *Personnel Psychol.* 12:397–402

Ghiselli, E. E. 1966. *The Validity of Occupational Aptitude Tests.* New York: Wiley

Goldfried, M. R., Kent, R. N. 1972. Traditional versus behavioral personality assessment: A comparison of methodological and theoretical assumptions. *Psychol. Bull.* 77:409–20

Green, B. F. Jr. 1978. In defense of measurement. *Am. Psychol.* 33:664–70

Guion, R. M. 1976. Recruiting, selection, and job placement. In *Handbook of Industrial and Organizational Psychology,* ed. M. D. Dunnette, pp. 777–828. Chicago: Rand McNally

Guion, R. M. 1983. Disunity in the trinitarian concept of validity. In *Clearing Away the Cobwebs: A Closer Look at Content Validity.* Symp. meet. Am. Educ. Res. Assoc., Montreal, P. Sandifer, Chair

Gutenberg, R. L., Arvey, R. D., Osburn, H. G., Jeanneret, P. R. 1983. Moderating effects of decision-making/information-processing job dimensions on test validities. *J. Appl. Psychol.* 68:602–8

Hull, C. L. 1928. *Aptitude Testing.* Yonkers, NY: World Book

Jackson, D. N. 1970. A sequential system for personality scale development. In *Current Topics in Clinical and Community Psychology,* ed. C. D. Spielberger, 2:61–96. New York: Academic

Jackson, D. N. 1973. Structured personality assessment. In *Handbook of General Psychology,* ed. B. B. Wolman, pp. 775–92. Englewood Cliffs, NJ: Prentice-Hall

Jackson, D. N. 1974. *Personality Research Form: Manual.* Port Huron, Mich: Res. Psychol. Press

Kaufman, A. S., Kaufman, N. L. 1983. *Kaufman Assessment Battery for Children: Interpretive Manual.* Circle Pines, Minn: Am. Guidance Serv.

Kjerulff, K., Wiggins, N. H. 1976. Graduate student styles for coping with stressful situations. *J. Educ. Psychol.* 68:247–54

Knoell, D. M., Harris, C. W. 1952. A factor analysis of spelling ability. *J. Educ. Res.* 46:95–111

Kurtz, A. K. 1948. A research test of the Rorschach test. *Personnel Psychol.* 1:41–51

Levin, J. 1965. Three mode factor analysis. *Psychol. Bull.* 64:442–52

McCormick, E. J., Jeanneret, P. R., Mecham, R. C. 1972. A study of job characteristics and job dimensions as based on the Position Analysis Questionnaire (PAQ). *J. Appl. Psychol.* 56:347–68

Menne, J. W., McCarthy, W., Menne, J. 1976. A systems approach to the content validation of employee selection procedures. *Public Personnel Manage.* 5:387–96

Messick, S. 1980. Test validity and the ethics of assessment. *Am. Psychol.* 35:1012–27

Millon, T. 1983. *Millon Clinical Multiaxial Inventory: Manual.* Minneapolis: NCS Interpretive Scoring Syst. 3rd ed.

Mischel, W. 1968. *Personality and Assessment.* New York: Wiley

Mischel, W. 1969. Continuity and change in personality. *Am. Psychol.* 24:1012–18

Mischel, W. 1973. Toward a cognitive social learning reconceptualization of personality. *Psychol. Rev.* 80:252–83

Mischel, W. 1977. On the future of personality measurement. *Am. Psychol.* 32:246–54

Mischel, W. 1979. On the interface of cognition and personality: Beyond the person-situation debate. *Am. Psychol.* 34:740–54

Mischel, W., Peake, P. K. 1982. Beyond déjà vu in the search for cross-situational consistency. *Psychol. Rev.* 89:730–55

Pearlman, K. 1980. Job families: A review and discussion of their implications for personnel selection. *Psychol. Bull.* 87:1–28

Pearlman, K., Schmidt, F. L., Hunter, J. E. 1980. Validity generalization results for tests used to predict job proficiency and training success in clerical occupations. *J. Appl. Psychol.* 65:373–406

Peterson, D. 1968. *The Clinical Study of Social Behavior.* New York: Appleton-Century-Crofts

Primoff, E. S. 1952. Job analysis tests to rescue trade testing from make-believe and shrinkage. *Am. Psychol.* 7:386 (Abstr.)

Primoff, E. S. 1975. *How to prepare and conduct job element examinations.* Personnel Res. Dev. Cent., Tech. Study 75–1. Washington, DC: GPO

Rushton, J. P., Brainerd, C. J., Pressley, M. 1983. Behavioral development and construct validity: The principle of aggregation. *Psychol. Bull.* 94:18–38

Sarason, I. G., ed. 1980. *Test Anxiety: Theory, Research, and Applications.* Hillsdale, NJ: Erlbaum

Schmidt, F. L., Gast-Rosenberg, L., Hunter, J. E. 1980. Validity generalization results for computer programmers. *J. Appl. Psychol.* 65:643–61

Schmidt, F. L., Hunter, J. E. 1977. Development of a general solution to the problem of validity generalization. *J. Appl. Psychol.* 62:529–40

Schmidt, F. L., Hunter, J. E., Pearlman, K. 1981. Task differences as moderators of aptitude test validity in selection: A red herring. *J. Appl. Psychol.* 66:166–85

Schmidt, F. L., Hunter, J. E., Pearlman, K., Shane, G. S. 1979. Further tests of the Schmidt-Hunter Bayesian validity generalization model. *Personnel Psychol.* 32:257–81

Schmidt, F. L., Hunter, J. E., Urry, V. W. 1976. Statistical power in criterion-related validation studies. *J. Appl. Psychol.* 61:473–85

Schoenfeldt, L. F., Schoenfeldt, B. B., Acker, S. R., Perlson, M. R. 1976. Content validity revisited: The development of a content-oriented test of industrial reading. *J. Appl. Psychol.* 61:581–88

Spielberger, C. D. 1980. *Test Anxiety Inventory: Preliminary Professional Manual.* Palo Alto, Calif: Consult. Psychol. Press

Spielberger, C. D., Anton, W. E., Bedell, J. 1976. The nature and treatment of test anxiety. In *Emotions and Anxiety: New Concepts, Methods, and Applications,* ed. M. Zuckerman, C. D. Spielberger, pp. 317–45. New York: LEA/Wiley

Standards for Educational and Psychological Testing. 1985. Washington, DC: Am. Psychol. Assoc.

Standards for Educational and Psychological Tests. 1974. Washington, DC: Am. Psychol. Assoc.

Sticht, T. C., ed. 1975. *Reading for Working: A Functional Literacy Anthology.* Alexandria, Va: Human Resources Res. Organ.

Technical Recommendations for Psychological Tests and Diagnostic Techniques. 1954. Washington, DC: Am. Psychol. Assoc.

Tordy, G. R., Eyde, L. D., Primoff, E. S., Hardt, R. H. 1976. *Job Analysis of the Position of New York State Trooper: An Application of the Job Element Method.* Albany: New York State Police

Tryon, G. S. 1980. The measurement and treatment of test anxiety. *Rev. Educ. Res.* 50:343–72

Tucker, L. R. 1964. The extension of factor analysis to three-dimensional matrices. In *Contributions to Mathematical Psychology,* ed. N. Frederiksen, pp. 109–27. New York: Holt, Rinehart & Winston

Tucker, L. R. 1966. Experiments in multimode factor analysis. In *Testing Problems in Perspective,* ed. A. Anastasi, pp. 369–79. Washington, DC: Am. Council Educ.

U.S. Department of Labor, Employment and Training Administration. 1983a. *Overview of validity generalization.* USES Test Res. Rep. No. 43. Washington, DC: GPO

U.S. Department of Labor, Employment and Training Administration. 1983b. *The dimensionality of the General Aptitude Test Battery (GATB) and the dominance of general factors over specific factors in the prediction of job performance.* USES Test Res. Rep. No. 44. Washington, DC: GPO

Wolf, T. H. 1973. *Alfred Binet.* Chicago: Univ. Chicago Press

Ann. Rev. Psychol. 1986. 37:17–41

PSYCHOLOGY IN A DEVELOPING SOCIETY: THE CASE OF ISRAEL[1]

Rachel Ben-Ari and Yehuda Amir

Department of Psychology, Bar-Ilan University, Ramat-Gan 52100, Israel

CONTENTS

HISTORICAL BACKGROUND.. 18
DEVELOPMENT OF PSYCHOLOGY 19
    Embryonic Stages 20
    Coming of Age... 21
    Society and Psychology 23
ORGANIZATIONAL ASPECTS 25
    The Israel Psychological Association... 25
    The Law of Psychologists... 27
PSYCHOLOGISTS AT WORK 29
    Mental Health 29
    Education.. 30
    Rehabilitation.. 30
    Vocational Guidance 30
    Industry and Organizations 31
    The Military.. 31
    Kibbutz.. 32
TRAINING OF PSYCHOLOGISTS 33
RESEARCH IN PSYCHOLOGY... 34
STATE OF PSYCHOLOGY IN SOCIETY 37
    Scientific Contributions 37
    Status in Own Country.. 38
    How was Status Achieved? 39

A number of years ago, on our way to a psychological congress in Japan, we passed through a small kingdom in Asia. At a reception given by the king's psychiatric adviser, we were amazed by a statement he made. In the course of the discussion, he was asked, "How many psychiatrists and psychologists are

[1]This is one of a series of chapters on psychology in the host countries of the International Congress of Psychology and the International Congress of Applied Psychology.

17

0066-4308/86/0201-0017$02.00

practicing in your country?" "None," he answered quietly, "nobody is mentally sick in this country." We looked at each other. "In that case," ventured one of us, "why a chief psychiatric advisor?" "Well," he answered matter of factly, "somebody has to keep the king informed."

What would we reply about the State of Israel, knowing that we have one of the highest per capita ratios of psychologists in the world (Rosenzweig 1982)? Does this mean that Israel's population is infinitely more mentally unhealthy than our former host's people, or is the explanation more complex and related to the interplay of psychology and the political and social history of the Jewish people in Israel?

This article deals with three major themes: 1. it recounts the historical events and development of psychology in Israel; 2. it describes and analyzes the present state of the art of psychology in this country; 3. it tries to evaluate the status of psychology and psychologists here, especially in the light of the unusually high ratio of psychologists to the population.

The chapter includes seven sections. First is an introduction concentrating on the general historical aspects of Israel and its inhabitants, providing some background material for the better understanding of psychology in this country. The second section describes general trends in the development of psychology in Israel during the last 50 to 60 years and indicates how the priorities of this society shaped and paralleled the development of psychology. Sections three to six describe psychology in Israel today. Section three concentrates on structural and organizational aspects; section four deals with work and employment; and sections five and six list centers of research and describe training of psychologists. The last section evaluates the status of Israeli psychology and psychologists.

HISTORICAL BACKGROUND

The development of psychology in Israel reflects the interplay of the more general historical forces—political, social, economic, and the ideological. We therefore offer here some brief general background notes.

The history of the Jewish people in Israel during this century is differentiated into two major periods by the establishment of the State of Israel. These two periods prior to and following this event are clearly distinguishable and reflect diverse strivings and social goals of the people. Major changes took place and were part of a larger and more inclusive process taking place over a period of time.

Israel's preindependence period was shaped by a relatively small group of idealistically oriented people who came to Israel from prerevolutionary Russia with a socialistic and to some extent Marxist-oriented ideology. Their major aims were the establishment of a Jewish state and the shaping of a new type of Jew, both in terms of his general way of life and in terms of his occupational preferences. The synthesis of these aims produced such social structures as labor (or union) owned enterprises, cooperatives, and the kibbutz. The social climate at that time distinctly emphasized social involvement and personal commitment to the well-being of everyone. People, and the youth in particular, were expected to minimize and even suppress personal needs in order to dedicate themselves to the achievement of national goals.

One should realize that many of the Jews coming at that time to Israel (then called Palestine) were to some extent a self-selected, elitist group. They came to Israel primarily of their own choice and in order to fulfill an ideal, knowing full well that life in Israel would be difficult in the extreme.

Drastic changes followed the establishment of the State of Israel in the late 1940s. One of the most salient was in terms of population growth. During the first few years of its existence its population doubled, and since its statehood 38 years ago, it has multiplied no less than sixfold. This population expansion has created a challenge and raised serious problems, especially in the field of human behavior and adjustment. Moreover, in the 1950s, hundreds of thousands of survivors of the Holocaust found their way to Israel, physically impaired, depressed and discouraged, struggling to regain their personal pride and dignity. At the same time, persecution of the Jews in the Moslem countries led to massive emigration from these depressed areas.

These two groups differed enormously in terms of cultural background, social norms, family structures, child-rearing practices, and belief systems. Both groups had to make major efforts to adjust to a new society and way of life. The African and Asian Jews, especially those from the "backwoods" of modern civilization, were suddenly exposed to a Western European-like social milieu for which they were completely unprepared—culturally, mentally, and technologically.

A second change following Israel's early statehood was a switch from social emphasis on idealistic group goals to an orientation geared toward the satisfaction of personal needs. This change probably could be attributed to differences in the makeup of the population during these periods as well as the establishment of the State. It was probably enhanced by the State's taking over many personal and social functions like welfare and education, which reduced the feelings of personal responsibility and encouraged an attitude of "let the government take care of it."

DEVELOPMENT OF PSYCHOLOGY

The overview of the development of psychology in Israel is divided into three parts. The first two parts concentrate on the pre-State period (up to the late 1940s) and then on major developments from the early 1950s until today. The third section attempts to integrate the development of psychology within the context of more global, national, and societal trends.

Embryonic Stages

As early as 1920, some initial signs of psychological work could be detected in Israel. These early "intruders" into Israel's Jewish society were physicians and psychiatrists with a psychoanalytical orientation. They could not be absorbed in the country at that time because little psychiatric work was being done in the hospitals, and the new psychoanalytic idea was far from being acceptable even in the medical community.

The earliest real influence of psychology came from psychoanalysis. In the early 1930s, a group of German psychoanalysts arrived in Israel under the leadership of Max Eitingon, one of Freud's earliest and most loyal disciples. Eitingon had first come in 1910 to start a practice, but he found the population quite unprepared for such a revolutionary idea as psychoanalysis. On his return in the 1930s, he found a much more receptive environment. By 1933 he was able to establish the Palestine Psychoanalytic Society, which was accepted a year later as a "component society" of the International Psychoanalytical Association. By 1936, the Psychoanalytic Institute was founded; it was to a large extent modeled after the Berlin Institute, founded many years previously by Eitingon himself. Immediately upon its establishment, the Jerusalem Institute was accredited as a psychoanalytic teaching institute by the International Psychoanalytical Association, with the following aims: 1. promotion of research in psychoanalysis and its application to related sciences; 2. teaching and training in psychoanalysis; 3. clinical work in the form of counseling and psychoanalytic treatment of needy people.

A stumbling block to the development of psychoanalysis in Israel at that time was the reception to Eitingon's plan to set up a department or chair of psychoanalysis at The Hebrew University in Jerusalem. Freud was one of the governors of The Hebrew University and was actively involved in trying to realize Eitingon's plan. However, the idea of having psychoanalysis at The Hebrew University was strongly opposed by its leadership, who preferred a more general philosophical and experimental orientation. The rejection of Eitingon's plan was not easily forgiven by the world psychoanalytical community. It was only in the late 1970s, with the establishment of the "Sigmund Freud Chair" in psychiatry in the Department of Psychology at The Hebrew University, and with its blessing by Anna Freud, that the breach was healed. Since then Jerusalem has become a major center for the advancement of psychoanalytical thought and research.

To revert to the 1930s—psychoanalytic thinking and to a lesser degree psychoanalytic practice had made inroads in Israeli society. The newly founded Medical School in Jerusalem included psychoanalytic teaching in its curriculum. More impressive was the influence it was having on kibbutz thinking and living, especially with regard to its influence on child-rearing and education.

Early in the 1930s, S. Golan, a graduate of the Psychoanalytic Institute in Berlin and a creator of kibbutz educational ideology, listed five principles for collective education. Four of them related to socialist directives, the fifth to psychoanalytic considerations regarding child development and the upbringing of kibbutz children. His concept of the children's home, still influencing many practices and organizational aspects of Israel's education, is a synthesis between psychoanalytic and socialist theories.

A quite different orientation in psychology also started at that time. Psychometric testing and the attendant educational counseling and vocational guidance began to find their place in the educational system. There were two main purposes for the testing program in the schools: the testing of retarded children and the testing of children who would be discontinuing their studies after graduation from elementary school in order to move into apprenticeship and employment. Initially these functions were performed by professional individuals in the 1940s, but later institutes were established for these purposes in the three main geographical centers of Israel. These institutes were public services, administered by the municipalities or the Workers' Unions.

The final development for this period relates to the attempt to open a department of psychology at The Hebrew University, the only university in the country at that time. While rejecting the psychoanalytical orientation, the university turned to Kurt Lewin to establish the psychology department, but he eventually turned down the idea and went to the United States. In spite of this setback, some courses were given in psychology both in the medical school and in the school of education, but no department materialized. Another attempt was made in the mid 1940s when Enzo Bonaventura, a famous Italian psychologist, came to Palestine and joined the staff of The Hebrew University. At that time, students were eligible for an MA degree when they had completed their studies in one major and two minor subjects. During Bonaventura's time, it was possible to complete the MA degree with psychology as a *minor* subject, but this possibility terminated when Bonaventura was killed in 1947 by a terrorist attack on a university bus.

Up to the late 1940s, then, psychology in this country was hardly visible. Some embryonic signs of a future appearance could be detected, but the bells of birth had not rung out as yet. It was only after Israel gained its independence in 1948 that a new era began for psychology.

Coming of Age

Mass immigration into Israel in the early 1950s increased the need for psychological help and guidance tremendously. At first this assistance could not be provided because psychology in Israel was not yet ready for such a task. However, the demand for psychological work outstripped the supply of professional manpower available. Where were the psychologists to come from?

Attempts were made to attract prominent psychologists from abroad to join The Hebrew University. John Cohen from England and Gregory Razran and David Rapoport from the U.S. came to Jerusalem but only for short periods. Even so, the psychology community expanded slowly and surely as Israelis who had gone abroad to study psychology returned and psychologists from abroad immigrated to Israel.

In 1957 the first department of psychology was opened in Jerusalem, and a year later a department of psychology was also opened at Bar-Ilan University. Another sign of growth was the Israel Psychological Association (IPA), which started functioning is 1957 with an initial membership of 170, including its single section of clinical psychology.

By the end of the 1950s the 200 psychologists in Israel were concentrated in three occupational areas: 1. clinical psychologists working in hospitals and mental health clinics; 2. educational psychologists working in child guidance centers connected with the school system and dealing with the adjustment of children in schools; 3. psychologists in the newly established university departments of psychology. Though small in scope, this last group had a tremendous influence on the development of present-day psychology in Israel.

Psychological services in both clinical and educational fields spread rapidly in the 1960s. Educational psychologists established their own sections in the IPA, followed shortly by social and industrial psychologists who also increased in number and in activity during that period. Tel Aviv and Haifa universities opened psychology departments in 1966, and within a few years they were offering MA and PhD degrees in psychology. The number of applicants grew to such an extent that psychometric and personality techniques were brought into play for the purpose of selecting the most promising students. This made a high level of studies possible and raised the prestige of the profession. Psychology became one of the "hottest" fields of study in Israel, a status it holds to date.

In the 1970s clinical and educational psychology services spread out all over the country, and teaching and research at the universities covered all fields of scientific psychology with emphasis on the applied and socially relevant. Psychological research also continued outside the university in public institutes like Louis Guttman's Institute for Applied Social Research, the Hadassah Institute for Vocational Guidance, the Institute for the Study of Education in the Kibbutz, and the Henrietta Szold Institute for Research in the Behavioral Sciences, which also publishes a scientific journal in Hebrew concentrating on psychological research. The IPA became one of the most active professional organizations in Israel and succeeded in having a licensing law for psychologists passed in the Knesset (Israel's House of Representatives) in 1977.

As a result of continuous military activities, a need arose for rehabilitation psychology to assist maimed soldiers to adjust to the new conditions of their lives. Thus, a fourth section was established in the IPA.

Industry has come to realize that with industrial psychology production can be improved through better selection and understanding of the workers and creating an atmosphere of "team" spirit in the factory. Many Israelis who had studied industrial psychology in the U.S. came home armed with new technological, psychological, and human relations approaches, and they spurred others to do professional work in this area. A growing number of psychologists produced research for industry, the army, and other work settings. Industrial psychologists decided against having a separate section of their own in IPA, preferring to be in the same section with the social and occupational psychologists.

Three developments are taking place in the 1980s: 1. At the Haifa Institute of Technology (Technion), a graduate program in industrial psychology has been approved. At the Ben-Gurion University in Be'er Sheva, the main city in the southern part of Israel, a graduate program in psychology has been implemented though it has not yet been finally accredited. Thus, it is reasonable to assume that before long all six universities in Israel will offer graduate training in psychology and advanced degrees will be given. 2. A fifth section was established in IPA, that of developmental psychology, and a sixth, health psychology, is presently applying and will probably be approved soon. 3. Israel has become a center for international congresses in psychology. These include congresses in clinical psychology, school psychology, child psychology, mental health, and on specific topics in treatment techniques, adjustment to stress, etc. In addition, the 21st International Congress of Applied Psychology, which is expected to host several thousand psychologists from all over the world, will take place in Israel in the summer of 1986.

Society and Psychology

In retrospect, two quite different and even contradictory periods can be observed in this country—one lasting until the late 1940s and the other starting in the 1950s. The first stage is typified by complete stagnation, almost a regression of psychology; in fact, psychology was practically nonexistent at that time. At the later stage, however, psychology flourished and psychologists have increased in number about 100 times in the last 35 years. The standstill of psychology during the first period is especially surprising in terms of the type of people living in the country at that time. These were intellectually superior and culturally sophisticated people who probably were quite familiar with new cultural, philosophical, scientific, and political developments in Europe where psychology had emerged and developed as a new science. Why should these people almost completely ignore psychology? Why should the kibbutz movement be the only exception? Yet later on, when most of Israel's inhabitants were immigrants from Middle-Eastern countries—where psychology was and to a large extent still is nonexistent—and physically and mentally broken refugees from Nazi-occupied Europe or postwar refugee camps—many of whom had been unexposed or unaware of educational, cultural, and scientific events for at least ten years of their lives—why only then did psychology come surprisingly and startlingly to life?

The reasons for the psychological growth following statehood would seem to be intrinsically tied to the wide society in terms of its needs, orientation, and ensuing cultural, political, and social expectations. In this light, it is not surprising that during the pre-State period psychology had little chance in either its scientific-academic or its treatment-oriented aspects. Academically speaking, the general cultural milieu was not particularly inclined toward universities in general or advanced training in particular. The consensus was that science and universities should take a back seat to the achievement of national and social goals. The importance of the treatment or guidance aspects of psychology was also minimized. People were expected to solve their own "little" individual problems so that society would not waste precious time and effort on them.

Why, then, did psychology bloom in the early kibbutz movement of the 1930s? Winnik's (1977) analysis can provide some insight into the phenomenon. He states that:

> The pioneers of the new settlement were attracted, first of all, by the revolutionary aspects of Freud's theory, and they considered him one of history's revolutionaries, like Marx and other groundbreakers of our times. Historical materialism and "Das Kapital" guided them in laying the concrete foundations for the new Israeli society, but in Freud they saw their mentor in everything relating to the psychological structure of the society to be built. In this approach, the pioneers are close to the "leftist" circle around Freud who considered psychoanalysis and Marxism two sides of the same coin, namely, the social revolution. In the eyes of the pioneers, the importance of Freud's work lay mainly in his attempt to illuminate the unconscious, to throw new light on the obscure and irrational in man. . . .if, in the U.S., the circle through which Freud's ideas were disseminated were composed mainly of writers, poets, college teachers, art and theater critics—in Palestine they were the kibbutzim (p. 91).

Thus, in one specific area, psychological theory had a decisive influence as early as the 1930s. The kibbutz, the collective type of settlement in Israel, has always comprised a small percentage of the country's population. Still, its cultural influence on society was much stronger than its numerical representation, partly because of the elitist nature of its membership and its leadership. This phenomenon is weakening lately, but was very salient in the earlier days of Israel. At that time the kibbutz made a most interesting and important experiment in the attempt to use psychoanalytic knowledge for the attainment of improved educational methods, healthy emotional development in children, and better human relationships in general. Educational leaders of the kibbutz believed that coeducation, conducted on scientific lines in the collective framework of living, would help produce a better type of human being, and thus a better humanity in general. At an earlier stage the kibbutz movement rejected

Freud's theory, considering it a bourgeois ideology; but later they accepted its principles, even quite orthodoxly, and for a long time tried to find a synthesis between Marxist ideology and Freudian psychological principles. Only much later, in the late 1960s and the 1970s, did the psychological principles of kibbutz education become more eclectic rather than psychoanalytically oriented.

The mass immigration following the establishment of the State of Israel produced major difficulties in the *personal* adjustment of the newcomers and, consequently, negative group phenomena emerged related to ethnicity, social class, disadvantaged groups, etc. Thus, the need arose for some psychological help to adults and their children and for the involvement in group and community problems. Consequently, clinical, educational and later on social psychology flourished.

Interestingly enough, the necessity to deal with *many* people who were in need of help drove applied psychology into a certain dilemma. Although psychologists at that time preferred individual treatment, because of their emphasis on traditional professional training, it became quite clear that this approach could not satisfy the needs of the many potential clients or the expectations of their public employer and society. These needs required different approaches. Thus, one could find a trend toward "group" techniques such as group and family therapy, community involvement, and work with intermediary agents such as teachers, social workers, and other community agents rather than with the individual client. Though the inclination for a direct client relationship still exists, a strong trend toward group-oriented procedures is evident. Psychologists are quite aware of the fact that the "individual" approach may give them more personal satisfaction, but it is only through "social" orientation that the public's expectation of psychological work can be satisfied.

ORGANIZATIONAL ASPECTS

The Israel Psychological Association

Psychologists in Israel were well organized from the very beginning. As early as 1950, when only a few psychologists were in the country, the Israel Society for Psychology was established. This group comprised psychologists involved in psychometric testing, educational counseling, and vocational guidance. Clinical psychology, including psychodiagnosis and psychotherapy, was somewhat left out, but a few years later a second organization, the Association of Clinical Psychologists, was established, having a small membership but enforcing high standards.

The major controversy between these organizations revolved around standards for membership. The former group accepted academicians who were involved in some way in psychological work even if they had no formal training in psychology. Clinical psychologists required a master's degree in psychology, including a strong background in psychodiagnostics and/or psychotherapy and work under supervision for a number of years by an accredited "trainer" in clinical psychology.

In spite of this limited membership, both groups were quite active, representing psychologists as a professional group and organizing professional meetings and national congresses. In 1955, for instance, 100 members participated in a convention that lasted for three days (as compared to about 1000 who participated in the 20th Convention of the Israel Psychological Association in 1985).

In 1957, the two psychological associations merged, and the Israel Psychological Association (IPA) was established with a membership of about 150. This merger became possible when all psychologists agreed to accept the more severe requirements of the clinical group. An elaborate "Statutes of Psychologists" was written up which included the organization of psychologists, structure of the organization and its activities, membership, code of ethics, etc. These statutes are by and large still in practice.

At present, the membership of IPA has passed the 2000 mark, about two-thirds being women. It is estimated that from 90 to 95 percent of accredited psychologists in Israel are members of the IPA. Although IPA is a voluntary association, most psychologists find it advantageous to belong because this organization determines the professional status of psychologists. This status, in turn, influences in many cases the psychologists' income because, according to the work agreement between the union, government, and employers' association, the advancement of psychologists is partly based on their professional status. We should mention here that practically all psychologists in Israel are salaried, which makes the attainment of professional status even more important. (The only exception to this are the psychologists at the universities who advance according to different procedures set up by the universities themselves.)

The IPA is the only organization of psychologists in Israel, but there is one more organization that can be regarded as a subsidiary of the IPA. That is the Union of Psychologists. This organization was created in the 1960s when the Union of Academicians in the Social Sciences and Liberal Arts was established. The latter invited IPA to join them, and IPA accepted the offer in order to become part of a larger and more powerful union. However, the statutory requirements of the larger union prescribed a membership of salaried people only, and IPA membership could also include self-employed, nonsalaried, or even nonworking psychologists. For this reason, a new entity was created, the Union of Psychologists, whose membership is practically the same as that of the IPA but fulfills the specific function of a union.

In addition to its central representation, IPA is at present divided into five professional sections, namely: Clinical, Educational (i.e. School), Social and Vocational (including Industrial), Rehabilitation, and Developmental Psychology. Health Psychology is the sixth division presently under consideration. Some sections include special interest groups such as the group on Research in Social Psychology, which is part of the section of Social and Vocational Psychology and is primarily comprised of university teachers and researchers in social psychology.

The sections of the IPA fulfill two major functions: (a) accreditation of psychologists for one of the two professional statuses of the IPA, namely, "Expert" and "Supervisor"; (b) organization and furthering of professional training, special seminars, and nationwide meetings of special interest groups.

IPA activities are varied, including the organization of national conventions and sponsorship of international congresses (e.g. IPA together with the International Association of Applied Psychology are sponsoring and organizing the 21st IAAP Congress to be held in Jerusalem in 1986), the organization in conjunction with the departments of psychology of postgraduate courses for certified psychologists, the publication (in Hebrew) of the *Israel Quarterly of Psychology* and of the Directory of Psychologists, the representation of psychologists in various governmental, civil, and international organizations, membership, implementation of professional ethics, etc.

The Law of Psychologists

The law regulating the profession of psychology (1977) was a major achievement for IPA which had been lobbying for it over a number of years. Its main purpose is to protect the public from misuse in psychological practice. Its primary concern is, therefore, the question of who is eligible to practice psychology and what qualifications are needed for the different types of psychological services. Most of the chapters of the law were adopted from the statutes of IPA, including its ethical code. The Law of Psychologists made the public aware that psychological work should be carried out by psychologists. More and more people inquire and make sure before entering into a client-therapist relationship that the "expert" is really an accredited psychologist.

To enforce the law, the Council of Psychologists was established. The Council represents different organizations—the IPA, the departments of psychology of universities, and governmental departments where many psychologists are employed. Almost all the members of the Council are psychologists, and thus members of IPA. Each member of the Council is officially appointed by the Minister (Secretary) of Health who, by governmental decision, has the ministerial responsibility for the "Law of Psychologists."

The Council meets four to five times a year. In addition, subcommittees are established to deal with current issues. The major subcommittees parallel the sections of IPA, and their function is the licensing of psychologists as "experts" or "supervisors." As it turns out, IPA and the Council are at present fulfilling more or less the same task of licensing—one for the Association and one for the Government. This practice seems unnecessary. Thus, suggestions have been made to simplify this duplication in one of two ways: (*a*) The Council will authorize the IPA to decide on licensing. If this is decided, the law will have to be changed. (*b*) The same subcommittee members in each area of licensing will be elected for both the Council and IPA, and their decisions will apply for both. The decision about this will be made in the very near future.

The Law of Psychologists has succeeded in so defining the profession that psychologists know what their duties and privileges are in their fields of work and what is needed for advancement. By and large, psychologists conform to these rules. What has *not* been achieved is preventing other professionals (social workers, educational counselors, industrial consultants, and even non-professionals) from overstepping their own boundaries and encroaching on psychology, even to practicing it. According to the law, they can neither call themselves psychologists nor can they define their work as psychological; still, they give themselves other "titles"—consultants, experts in child-parent relations, educational counselors—and under these guises they actually practice psychology. The difficulty lies in the definition of "psychological work" under the law. At present the Council, with the assistance of government legal advisers, are trying to find ways to overcome the problem by (*a*) introducing acceptable definitions of psychological work, or (*b*) bringing certain cases to court to obtain rulings which in turn may serve as the basis for what may be exclusively defined as psychological practice.

Another activity of the Council relates to psychological testing (intelligence, personality, attitudes, etc) which at present can be administered by anyone. A testing commission has been set up to define what kinds of testing should, by law, be exclusively in the hands of psychologists.

One additional development that concerns psychology and the law refers to recent public interest in Israel concerning experimentation with human beings. A number of members of the Knesset who were involved in this issue were considering passing a law which in many ways was thought to parallel the Helsinki Convention on the experimentation with human beings by the medical profession. After much deliberation, in close cooperation with IPA and with the quite intense involvement of many psychologists, departments of psychology, and the universities, it was decided not to pass a formal law. The main concern was that a rigid law, trying to serve the interest of the public, might unintentionally restrict any meaningful advancement in the psychological study of human beings. Thus, instead of a formal law, the IPA and the universities undertook the responsibility for the ethical conduct of their researchers. Thereafter, IPA established rules and regulations concerning human experimentation which were generally adopted by the universities and their departments of psychology and later by other academic societies in the social sciences.

PSYCHOLOGISTS AT WORK

In this section, we review the major fields in which psychologists in Israel work. These fields are divided into seven settings: mental health, education, rehabilitation, vocational guidance, industry and organizations, the military, and kibbutz.

Mental Health

About one-third of the psychologists in Israel are clinical psychologists. Two national institutions—the Ministry of Health and the Labor Union's Sick Fund—employ most of the clinical psychologists. These institutions are in charge of most of the general and psychiatric hospitals, and they operate a wide variety of mental health clinics for adults and child guidance centers for children. In addition, other public organizations have clinical psychologists on their staffs; these include some of the municipalities, the Youth Immigration Department of the Jewish Agency, the military, student counseling units of the universities, various ministries, and others.

The theoretical and treatment orientations of clinical psychologists are diverse. They include individual and family therapy, Gestalt, behavior therapy, biofeedback techniques, as well as classical psychoanalytical and neo-Freudian approaches. Presently two trends are apparent, one preferring individual treatment, the other emphasizing the community approach including work within the community, preventive psychopathology, and a multidisciplinary approach comprising teamwork with psychiatrists, social workers, anthropologists, etc. It is still too early to predict which direction will be the predominant one. The outcome of the controversy may also determine whether clinical psychology will remain a unique field of psychological treatment or will diffuse into other treatment professions.

One of the recent, unique developments in this field is the emergence of health psychologists. These psychologists, mostly clinical, work in hospitals and clinics but generally not in the psychological or psychiatric departments. They are unique in that their patients are psychologically normal people being treated in hospital departments specializing in heart or lung diseases, terminal illnesses, or requiring mental rehabilitation and support when their physical illness produces psychological problems or maladjustments. Some of the work is with the patients, but a large part is with the physicians, the family, and others who play a major role in the patient's life.

Private practice will not be discussed here since practically all psychologists are employed, and those involved in private practice do so in addition to their regular jobs. The nature of their additional work is similar to that described above.

Education

School psychologists make up about one-third of the psychological community in Israel, and psychological services are presently available in practically every school in the country. School psychologists work in educational child guidance centers which are under the jurisdiction of the local government (municipalities, townships, regional councils). There are about 130 such centers, each one serving the schools in its locality. The Ministry of Education and Culture has a special office in charge of coordination among these centers, which provides them with special professional services.

The work of the school psychologist concentrates on both the school and the center. According to a recent survey on the time allocation of school psychologists (Raviv et al 1981), individual diagnosis of pupils having learning, social, or emotional problems at school amounts to 16%, consultation with teachers 16%, parent counseling 12%, pupil and family therapy 16%, other professional activities 10%, organizational and administrative activities 22%, and in-service training 8%.

Among school psychologists, as with clinicians, a change in orientation can be detected over the years—from individual treatment to a community and social orientation. Their services now include working with the teacher and the administrative staff including the principal, employing preventative techniques and training teachers to implement these tools, implementing ethnic integration, promoting special techniques to assist children from disadvantaged backgrounds to advance scholastically, and utilizing crisis intervention techniques for pupils, their families, the school, and the community. Along with this, they now give special attention to the promotion of special programs and teaching techniques for gifted children.

Rehabilitation

The frequent military activities in the region have channeled a substantial number of psychologists into the field of rehabilitation where they offer psychological support and specific kinds of guidance relevant to the physically handicapped, such as brain-damaged persons, amputees, burn victims, and those otherwise disfigured. Vocational guidance, sex therapy, and retraining are all part of the program to bring the patient to a maximum stage of independence.

Vocational Guidance

Vocational guidance is to some extent implemented by school psychologists within their educational clinics. However, more extensive psychological work and professional service are provided by two major public institutes—the

Center for Vocational Counseling and Information and the Hadassah Vocational Guidance Institute—and a number of smaller private ones.

All these institutions serve similar functions. They provide counseling services to individual clients, helping them in the choice of occupation or in choosing a training path which would best suit the client's aptitude, interests, and personality. A long individual testing program is undertaken, and counselor meets client a number of times for consultation. Group testing is also engaged in, especially before entrance to senior high school, and recommendations are made as to choice of high school or occupation and possibly even on the course of study to follow. Industry, too, uses vocational guidance services in seeking to eliminate wastage in wrong choices for skilled jobs, investment in additional training, and the most advantageous placement of employees. The utilization of services in vocational guidance and placement has been constantly on the rise in the last decade.

Industry and Organizations

Industrial psychologists practice in major industrial plants, in the IDF (Israel Defense Forces), and in private institutions. The function of the industrial psychologist in Israel, as it is elsewhere in industrial countries, consists of establishing criteria for selection, developing training procedures, and assessment. Human relations, organizational development, and management counseling also come within his scope. In large companies, big industries, transportation companies, and some government ministries, departments of industrial psychology or of human resources are part of the total organization, while smaller enterprises hire these services from private institutions. Industrial psychology has become fashionable and is in demand probably because of the openness of managers who had received their academic training in universities where the general attitude towards the utilization of psychology in work settings is positive.

The Military

The nature of the psychological work presented in this subsection and in the following one is quite similar to that described earlier, being a mosaic of clinical, educational, and industrial psychology, but each with a unique slant of its own, especially in terms of extensive amount and the intensive nature of the services provided.

The IDF has two major psychological units at its disposal, one dealing primarily with aspects of industrial psychology and the other with the mental health of its soldiers. Since its very inception, the IDF emphasized certain aspects which required the professional services of psychologists, such as maximizing the quality of the individual and the organization because of the army's numerical paucity compared to the neighboring states, personal well-being of the soldiers, overcoming negative stress factors which may have been produced by continuous war-like activities, etc. In addition, psychological services were needed because the multiethnic population in the armed forces demanded special solutions to the problems of selection, training, living under army discipline, building up an esprit de corps for combat conditions, and eliminating prejudice for the smooth working of the defense machine. Thus, professional services and guidance by psychologists were early deemed necessary and proved to be a critical factor in the IDF complex, respected and appreciated by headquarters and utilized to the maximum.

The functions performed include manpower testing and selection in general and specific diagnoses for special units, development and implementation of unique training techniques including leadership training, assessment of morale and organizational climate in combat units, the development and implementation of crisis-intervention techniques, and the development of special programs and treatment techniques for soldiers with inferior qualifications who in other armies would surely be deferred.

A unique feature of the IDF is the inclusion of psychologists as specialists and advisors at all command levels including brigades, divisions, and armies. Most of these psychologists start their army service and training as soldiers and officers in regular army units and only thereafter start to function as psychologists. This initial experience facilitates their constant contact with the chiefs of staff and heads of these units and their involvement in all aspects of manpower and psychological adjustment. This direct mingling within the army in general and in combat units in particular is also practiced in the mental health corps. Here, too, psychologists serve on the front line. Their major function is to employ preventive mental health techniques and to guide and direct army officers in these respects. During combat activities their major function is to deal as efficiently as possible in close contact with the field of action with the "mentally wounded" (e.g. battle fatigue) and to send them back to the field units as quickly as possible.

In general, the main orientation of mental health in the IDF is the social-community approach, which is meant to reach as many individuals as possible, particularly among the officers, to promote the understanding, acceptance, prevention, and resolving of mental health problems, especially in stress-provoking situations.

Kibbutz

If one could assess the per capita rate of psychological work invested in different groups or societies in the world, the kibbutz would probably top the list. For a relatively small subpopulation (about 3%) of a small country, the psychological work invested there is enormous. As already mentioned, the kibbutz was sensitive and open to the possible contribution of psychology to the welfare of society. Involvement in psychological work started with an emphasis on child-rearing practices and educational psychology. As a matter of fact, many psychological services in these areas presently spread throughout the country had their beginnings at the kibbutz. At present there are a number of centers, located in different geographical areas, serving the kibbutz population and dealing with different psychological aspects such as child guidance, learning disabilities, retardation, psychological adjustment, vocational guidance, etc.

The well-being of the individual in the social setting of the kibbutz in work and industrial situations has given rise to exploration in organizational and industrial psychology. Sensitivity training, organizational development, group dynamics, and organizational training are among the many techniques that the kibbutz has adopted for diagnosis of social-organizational problems and their resolution. Consistent follow-up and evaluation by research has accompanied these efforts. A recently published bibliography (Shur et al 1981) on kibbutz literature bears ample evidence of the interest in this area, including the study of cross-cultural effects, cross-cultural comparisons, and careful evaluation of the psychological phenomena taking place in this environment.

TRAINING OF PSYCHOLOGISTS

The universities, though each has its own individuality, are quite similar in terms of training. Therefore, the following presentation will be general, with only the major differences highlighted. Bachelor's, Master's, and Doctoral degrees in psychology may be obtained at four universities in Israel, namely, Tel-Aviv, Haifa, Bar-Ilan, and The Hebrew University. In addition, in Be'er Sheva, a Master's program in psychology is presently being carried out, and at the Haifa Technion, a Master's program in industrial psychology is being initiated; both are awaiting formal accreditation. Outside of the universities, psychology is taught in schools of education, social work, medicine, sociology, business administration, and criminology, among others.

In order to become a psychologist, a student must overcome quite a few hurdles. First he or she has to be accepted for the BA level, which is difficult because of the large number of applicants. Then an excellent undergraduate study record and further screening are required for acceptance at the graduate level. In clinical psychology and school psychology, the rejection rate is high. In social, industrial, occupational, and rehabilitation psychology, the lower number of applicants makes the acceptance rate somewhat higher. In experimental psychology, where few students seem to show interest, the chances for acceptance are the best. Finally, upon receiving the Master's degree, the title of "Psychologist" is confirmed, although the graduate is as yet not eligible to work independently.

The BA degree requires three years of study with 60 credits in psychology, one credit equaling one semester hour of study. MA studies require, depending on the study area, about 40-50 graduate credits, adding up to 100-110 credits for BA and MA combined. For the granting of the MA degree, the student must pass an examination in his specialty and submit an adequate research thesis. Doctoral studies concentrate primarily on the research dissertation.

Each of the universities accepts up to 100 students a year for a psychology major at the BA level. For Master's applicants, Tel-Aviv and Bar-Ilan Universities accept about 60 each, The Hebrew University about 30, with another 15 in school psychology given as a joint program of the Department of Psychology and the School of Education; Haifa University accepts about 20. Thus, all the universities combined accept about 180. The average length of time required to reach the MA status from university entrance is 7 to 8 years. About one-third of the graduate students go in for clinical psychology, one-third for school or educational psychology, one-sixth for social psychology, and the rest are in other areas of specialization.

Clinical, school, social, and experimental (including cognitive, learning, and physiological) psychology at the graduate level can be studied in all the universities. Besides these, at Bar-Ilan rehabilitation and industrial psychology are offered, and at Tel-Aviv, vocational psychology. At all universities the emphasis in graduate studies is on theory and research as well as on application. For training in application, field settings are arranged for the students where they undergo a kind of "apprenticeship" devoted to training in the field for one full day a week for a period of two years, thus paving the way for a smooth entrance into the working world. About 20 carefully selected students are accepted each year for the PhD program in all the universities together. The average time spent in the PhD program is five to six years, most of the time being devoted to the research dissertation.

To become an independent psychologist after having completed the MA, two additional years of training under a supervisor are required. These requirements are prerequisite for licensing and becoming a member of the relevant section in the IPA.

University faculty members are diversified in their educational backgrounds and in their orientation in psychology. Most of them were educated in Israel but have completed their training abroad, primarily in the United States. The departments have faculties that range from 25 to 40 and are quite eclectic, emphasizing no particular school of psychological thought.

RESEARCH IN PSYCHOLOGY

Most psychological research is conducted at the universities with some research, generally with an applied flavor, undertaken in a number of nonuniversity institutions. All research is supported in one way or another by public funds.

The authors of this article, while surveying the types of research conducted at the universities as well as in other institutions, were struck by its diversity. These studies are in line with the general development of psychological thought and research in the world and the scientific interest and orientation of the researcher. Most of the research is conducted by a single staff member, sometimes with the help of one or two graduate students. Sometimes several staff members will combine forces on a specific topic, but they will not necessarily work together on the next study. Where a special institute does exist at the department, its researchers will generally work on different topics, and the institute only serves as an organizational or fund-raising umbrella. There are only very few exceptions to this rule, a major one being the Institute for the Advancement of Social Integration in the Schools at Bar-Ilan University. The researchers of this institute, almost all of them social psychologists, are involved in the study of ethnicity, particularly ethnic relations and integration in the schools.

Another area of concentration is studies in cross-cultural psychology conducted by researchers at various universities. Evidence indicates that Israeli psychologists have produced a very large amount of cross-cultural research, second only to the U.S. in terms of number of studies and first when the amount is compared to the number of psychologists in each country (Lonner 1980).

Are there other general trends in addition to the diverse and "individualistic" one described above? Two directions which may actually portray two sides of the same coin can be noticed. There is some emphasis on the applied and socially meaningful. Though much of the research deals with basic or theoretical issues, an inherent question to be answered through the research is: What use can be made of this research? How can psychologists, the public, and policymakers utilize this information? On the topic of ethnic integration, for instance, the problem faced was, "How and under what conditions do people from different ethnic groups interact and with what results?" Though this is a general question regarding intergroup behavior, practically all research in this area deals directly or indirectly with applied aspects such as ethnic integration in Israeli schools, the effects of contact between the religious and nonreligious Jews, and Arab-Jewish relations.

Somewhat related to the previous orientation is an interest and an emphasis in research on the socially relevant and salient in Israel such as living under stress, the psychological aftermath of the Holocaust, child-rearing practices, special intervention techniques with disadvantaged groups, intergroup relations, psychological aspects and consequences of life in the kibbutz, and cultural variations. These trends exemplify the notion already advanced in this paper that the development of psychology in general and the directions of psychological research in Israel are strongly related to the interests, trends, and needs of the country and its society, and are influenced by them.

The following are the major institutes of research outside university settings:

1. *The Israel Institute for Applied Social Research in Jerusalem,* established and directed by Louis Guttman, is involved in diverse research projects in the social sciences including psychology, sociology, and social work. Similar to psychological research in other institutions, there is no common direction in these studies, except perhaps for the fact that many of them utilize, test, and develop some of the methodological techniques and new concepts advanced by Guttman. In addition to its research activities, the institute carries out technical and administrative services for studies conducted elsewhere, including the utilization of nonmetric computer programs developed by members of the institute.

2. *The Henrietta Szold Institute in Jerusalem* is involved in research in the behavioral sciences with special emphasis on education and educational psychology. Its main research effort is geared to the study of educational aspects, such as identifying problems in reading and arithmetic, identifying gifted pupils, dealing with stress factors among teachers, and coping with dropouts. It also produces and supervises all matriculation examinations administered to 12th-grade matriculants. The institute also has an information retrieval center which includes all social science research conducted in Israel and by Israelis abroad and publishes a quarterly journal (in Hebrew) entitled *Current Research in the Behavioral Sciences* and a catalog listing the measurement and diagnostic tools utilized in Israel. Another major enterprise of the institute is the publication of *Megamot,* the major social science journal in Israel and the most prestigious publication of psychological research in the Hebrew language.

3. *The Hadassah Vocational Guidance Institute in Jerusalem* devotes part of its activities to research and occupational information retrieval. Its main functions in these repects are: (*a*) the development of diagnostic tools and assessment measures and their evaluation through follow-up studies; (*b*) the compiling of data on occupations and training programs in Israel, their dissemination, and the retrieval of the computer-stored information on these topics.

4. *The Center for Vocational Counseling and Information* has a research division which deals with various aspects of the center's work and its purposes. These include, for instance, the development and evaluation of psychological measures for vocational guidance and assessment, the evaluation of guidance techniques used at the center, and the satisfaction of its clients with the services rendered. In addition, the center collects and summarizes occupational information to help its clients and to facilitate a better and more rational approach to the client's decision when making a vocational choice.

5. *The Institute for the Study of Education in the Kibbutz* along with the newly established *Institute for Research of the Kibbutz* at Haifa University, cover, in regard to research, a wide arena of social and psychological aspects of life in the kibbutz. These include child-rearing practices and socialization patterns, the development of cognitive aspects, personality and interpersonal relations, work structure and management, sex roles, etc. In addition, the institutes coordinate research activities, compile and publish literature related to the kibbutz and research carried out in the kibbutz.

6. *The Psychological Research Division* of the Social Science Department of the IDF from the time of the establishment of the State has conducted widespread research on many psychological aspects of the military. This unit is comparable in its scope and activities to similar institutions in the U.S. armed forces. For obvious reasons, it is not possible to elaborate here on the type of psychological research conducted in this organization.

STATE OF PSYCHOLOGY IN SOCIETY

In the previous sections, the emphasis was on what psychologists in this country do and in which psychological fields they are involved. In this last section, we shall try to evaluate the status of Israeli psychology. Two points of view will be considered: 1. scientific contributions; 2. what people in Israel feel about psychology and how they regard psychologists.

It is quite presumptuous to attempt to evaluate one's own profession objectively, but nevertheless we shall try to be objective, relying as much as possible on facts and observable trends.

Scientific Contributions

Two types of measures seem to be indicative of scientific contributions, namely, the number of papers published and the number of citations received. Studies have demonstrated a positive relationship between the number of citations a paper received in other papers and various other measures of its quality (Narin 1976). On the other hand, it was found that the number of scientific papers produced by a country is not a particularly good predictor of quality of the country's science, and the inference is generally drawn that citation rates are the best indication of scientific quality, impact, or utility.

Qualitative cross-cultural studies of scientific contributions in general and of psychology in particular are almost nonexistent. Only two such studies could be found for psychology which also include data for Israel. Corrigan & Narin (1982) compared 22 countries and larger geographic regions on a number of citation indexes. The comparisons were made on publication data for the 1970s generated from the *Science Citation Index* (SCI) in nine scientific fields, one of them psychology. The analyses showed that in terms of number of papers in psychology, Israel rated tenth. If the size of the population or the number of psychologists in the country had been taken into account, the rank would be higher, either third or fourth out of 22. The rank of Israel on the average quality rating across the 10 indexes developed in the study is fifth and on the index of the top 1% of cited papers, it is first (Table 10, page 57). In their summary, the authors indicate that two countries are especially interesting in the quantitative vs qualitative aspects of their papers. These are Sweden and Israel. Both countries rank average in terms of the number of papers, but high in their overall quality.

An additional item of information on the contribution of Israeli psychologists to psychological research is available in regard to cross-cultural psychology. Lonner (1980) analyzed the citizenship of all the authors who published papers in the *Journal of Cross-Cultural Psychology* from 1970 to 1979. He found that the number of contributions by Israeli psychologists ranked second, preceded only by the U.S. and closely followed by Canada.

These findings can give some indication regarding the involvement of Israeli psychologists in research and their contribution to the advancement of knowledge in this field. Based on that, it seems fair to conclude that their standing in this area is relatively high.

Status in Own Country

Two types of data may serve as indicators for gauging the status of psychology (and probably of psychologists as well) in Israel. One refers to studies on the relative professional status of psychologists compared with other professions, and the other one is the demand for psychologists or psychological services in different areas. On both accounts psychology rates quite high.

A number of studies have been carried out in recent years trying to determine the professional status hierarchy in the eyes of Israel's society (Samuel & Yuchtman-Yaar 1979, Kraus 1981). In general, the picture looks quite similar to what has been found in North America and Europe: Scientists are at the top, followed by professionals and top managers, the white-collared professions, blue-collared and semiskilled workers, and finally nonskilled laborers. Among the professionals, psychologists are in all studies in Israel among the highest, coming after physicians and lawyers.

As to the work demand for psychologists or psychological services, this is quite high in spite of the present depressed economy. In the areas of industrial and rehabilitation psychology, the demand for psychological employees clearly overbalances the supply. This is also true for psychological services in the schools, especially in areas outside the major metropolitan centers. For clinical psychologists, especially those who have recently completed their studies, the picture is a bit more difficult. The clinical field seems to have reached a certain level of saturation. Still, with regard to services required in private practice, they are definitely on the rise. In other more restricted areas of job demand and supply, such as occupational or social psychology, ergonomics, and in the military, there is also a substantial demand for psychological services.

The extremely high number of applicants for psychology at the universities may also be considered an indication of the profession's prestige in the community. As already indicated, the ratio of student applications to the capacity of the psychology departments to accept them is very high. In evaluating this fact one should take into account that the number of students in psychology is quite high as compared with other fields of study. Psychology departments are among the largest in all Israeli universities.

Finally, there is the Law of Psychologists. Many professions have tried throughout the years to apply pressure on the legislative authorities to pass laws protecting their professions from "professional parasites" and only a few have succeeded. For such action to be taken, it would appear that the profession must have achieved a certain status equivalent to those that have already had such protective laws passed, i.e. physicians and lawyers. We still must consider how psychologists achieved this status.

How was Status Achieved?

The final part of this paper is relatively speculative. It is based on interviews with many psychologists, some of whom started their psychological careers in Israel as many as 40 or 50 years ago and have been closely following the development of psychology ever since. Some of their thinking on the subject as well as that of the authors is presented here.

A combination of reasons is probably responsible for the high status attained by psychology in this country. First, there was the tremendous need to deal with the personal adjustment problems of a psychologically difficult immigrant population and their offspring. This problem originated in the 1950s, but has not yet been solved for a part of that population or for their offspring. In addition, there is a strong commitment in society, which has major political implications, to advance these subpopulations and solve their social, psychological, and economic problems in one way or another. All these lead to pressure for additional services, including psychological ones.

Fortunately for psychology, the need for the expansion of services was not accompanied by a reduction in the quality of psychological work. In the early 1950s, psychological services could still be performed by nonpsychologists or psychologists of lesser training. This practice changed categorically at the latter part of the decade when high-level requirements were set up for psychological practice comparable only to that of physicians and lawyers.

These high professional standards generated certain social processes. First, psychology became more prestigious and respected in the public eye. As a consequence, more and more youngsters showed interest in the study of psychology. However, these students could not study psychology because it was only in the late 1950s that the first departments were established. When these departments were opened, the number of applicants far exceeded the number that could be accepted. In turn, only those of the highest scholastic achievement and mental abilities were accepted. Many of those rejected tried again to be accepted, thereby increasing the number of applicants for the following year. This process has permitted the continuous high-level selection up to the present time. As it turned out, there were years when the rejection rate of some departments of psychology reached 14 out of 15 applicants. There can be little doubt that the difficulty in being accepted at the university further increased the demand for psychological studies and the commitment of those accepted to psychology both as a subject of study and a profession. All this took place concurrently with the high demand for psychological work in the labor market and the rising prestige of psychology in the community.

Undoubtedly this high demand for services, followed by high demand for studying psychology which enabled the selection of highly screened students for the BA level and later for additional screening at the graduate level, produced a higher-than-average professional in psychology who turned out high quality work both in its applied and scientific aspects. This, in turn, stabilized the already high prestige level of psychology in society and may even have increased it.

Today pychology in Israel is among the most desirable professions. For a long time, the typical Israeli mother would prefer her son or daughter to become a doctor or at least a lawyer, but now the psychologist has also joined this exclusive club. If this is the case, who are we to question the reliability of the mothers' judgment?

ACKNOWLEDGMENTS

The authors would like to thank Dr. Michael Hoffman for his thoughtful suggestions.

The data for this paper were derived from interviews with prominent figures in various fields of psychology in Israel who have taken leading roles in its development, information received from the Israel Psychological Association, the universities and research centers in Israel, and previous articles published on psychology in Israel (Rosenbaum 1954, Palgi 1963, Shanan & Weiss 1963, Gumbel 1965, Greenbaum & Norman 1966, Miller 1966, Sanua 1971, Kugelmass 1976, Winnik 1977, Greenbaum & Kugelmass 1980, Amir & Ben-Ari 1981, Raviv 1984).

Literature Cited

Amir, Y., Ben-Ari, R. 1981. Psychology and society in Israel. *Int. J. Psychol.* 16:239–47

Corrigan, J. G., Narin, F. 1982. *Relationships Between National Publication Rates and Participation in Highly Cited Papers Within Fields and Within Countries.* Cherry Hill, NJ: Computer Horizons

Greenbaum, C. W., Kugelmass, S. 1980. Human development and socialization in cross-cultural perspective: Issues arising from research in Israel. In *Studies in Cross-Cultural Psychology*, ed. N. Warren, Vol. 2. London: Academic

Greenbaum, C. W., Norman, J. 1966. Israel. In *International opportunities for Advanced Training and Research in Psychology*, ed. S. Ross. Washington, DC: Am. Psychol. Assoc.

Gumbel, E. 1965. Psychoanalysis in Israel. *Isr. Ann. Psychiatry Relat. Discip.* 3:89–98

Kraus, V. 1981. Occupations perception in Israel. *Megamot* 26:283–94 (In Hebrew)

Kugelmass, S. 1976. Israel. In *Psychology Around the World*, ed. V. S. Sexton, H. Misiak. California: Brooks/Cole

Lonner, W. J. 1980. A decade of cross-cultural psychology: JCCP, 1970–1979. *J. Cross-Cult. Psychol.* 11:7–34

Miller, L. 1966. Social change, acculturation and mental health in Israel. *Isr. Ann. Psychiatry Relat. Discip.* 4:1–15

Narin, F. 1976. *Evaluative Bibliometrics: The Use of Publication and Citation Analysis in the Evaluation of Scientific Activity.* Washington, DC: Natl. Sci. Found.

Palgi, P. 1963. Immigrants, psychiatrists, and culture. *Isr. Ann. Psychiatry Relat. Discip.* 1:43–58

Raviv, A. 1984. Psychology in Israel. In *Wiley Encyclopedia of Psychology*, ed. R. S. Corsini. New York: Wiley

Raviv, A., Wiesner, E., Bar-Tal, D. 1981. *A Survey of Psychologists in the School Psychological Services.* Jerusalem: Ministry of Education and Culture (In Hebrew)

Rosenbaum, M. 1954. Freud-Eitingon-Magnes correspondence. *J. Am. Psychoanal. Assoc.* 2:311–17

Rosenzweig, M. R. 1982. Trends in development and status of psychology: An international perspective. *Int. J. Psychol.* 17:117–40

Samuel, Y., Yuchtman-Yaar, E. 1979. The status and situs dimensions as determinants of occupational attractiveness. *Qual. Quant.* 13:485–501

Sanua, V. D. 1971. Psychology in action. *Am. Psychol.* 26:602–5

Shanan, J., Weiss, A. A. 1963. Clinical psychology in Israel. *Isr. Ann. Psychiatry Relat. Discip.* 1:107–11

Shur, S., Beit-Hallahmi, B., Blasi, J., Rabin, A. L., eds. 1981. *The Kibbutz Bibliography of Scientific and Professional Publications in English.* Darby, Pa: Norwood

Winnik, H. Z. 1977. Milestones in the development of psychoanalysis in Israel. *Isr. Ann. Psychiatry Relat. Discip.* 15:85–91

Ann. Rev. Psychol. 1986. 37:43-75

SELECTIVE ATTENTION

William A. Johnston and Veronica J. Dark

Department of Psychology, University of Utah, Salt Lake City, Utah 84112

CONTENTS

INTRODUCTION 43
    Terminology and Basic Concepts 44
    Cocktail-Party Problem 45
    Scope of Review 45
REVIEW OF EMPIRICAL LITERATURE 45
    Priming Effects 46
    Early and Late Selection 47
    Spatial Attention 49
    Processing Outside the Attentional Spotlight 53
    Overview of Spatial Attention 56
    Object-Based Attention 56
    Semantic Processing of Nonselected Objects 59
    Automatic and Controlled Attention 62
    Schema-Based Attention 63
    Summary of Empirical Literature 65
REVIEW OF THEORIES 65
    Cause Theories 66
    Effect Theories 68
    Summary of Theories 70
CONCLUSION 70

INTRODUCTION

In reviewing the literature on attention we were struck by several observations. One was a widespread reluctance to define attention. Another was the ease with which competing theories can accommodate the same empirical phenomena. A third observation was the consistent appeal to some intelligent force or agent in explanations of attentional phenomena. These observations are likely to be causally connected. It is difficult to conceptualize a process that is not well defined, and it is difficult to falsify empirically a vague conceptualization, especially one that relies on a homunculus. As a consequence, the more we

43

0066-4308/86/0201-0043$02.00

read, the more bewildered we became. At a time of despair and panic we turned to William James (1890), where we found new hope and inspiration. The reader will understand, therefore, if from time to time we betray a reverential awe of James. We believe that James understood attention better than most contemporary theorists; he articulated many of the same phenomena with which current theories are concerned, but he managed to avoid some of the pitfalls of many current theories. We consider these pitfalls and how James avoided them after we accomplish our main goal of reviewing the recent empirical literature.

Terminology and Basic Concepts

Attention has several ordinary-language meanings, the most common of which are mental effort and selective processing (Posner & Boies 1971, Johnston & Heinz 1978). The view of attention as mental effort derives from the common assumption that processing capacity is limited in some central mechanism (Kahneman 1973, Shiffrin & Schneider 1977). This mechanism is associated with consciousness and controlled processing and it delimits divided attention, that is, the extent to which different sources of information can be processed at the same time. However, exceptions to this view range from rejecting the whole notion of limited capacity (Neisser 1976) to postulating multiple pools of limited resources (Navon & Gopher 1979, Wickens 1984). On the other hand, there appears to be no disagreement with the view that processing is selective.

This review concentrates on selective attention. We refer to divided attention and the concept of effort or resources only as they may relate to selective attention. Selective attention refers to the differential processing of simultaneous sources of information. In nature these sources are internal (memory and knowledge) as well as external (environmental objects and events). Whereas James considered both of these, we follow the vast majority of contemporary investigators and consider only external sources.

With respect to the processing of environmental information, it is necessary to distinguish between bottom-up or data-driven processing and top-down or internally driven processing (Norman & Bobrow 1975). In data-driven processing a stimulus activates codes at various levels of analysis ranging from simple physical or sensory analysis to complex semantic and schematic analysis. The level to which processing proceeds is determined by the intensity and clarity of the stimulus and the level of analysis at which codes are available (e.g. as a result of learning) for the stimulus. Stimulus processing is data-limited (i.e. restricted to shallow levels of analysis) to the extent that the stimulus is weak, noisy, and unfamiliar. Thus, bottom-up factors alone can lead to selective processing of concurrent stimuli that have different data limits. However, most research has addressed the top-down control of selective processing. In top-down processing, the individual is internally biased toward particular stimuli.

Cocktail-Party Problem

Cherry (1953) framed the principal questions about selective attention in terms of the "cocktail-party problem." One can listen to a particular conversation at a cocktail party and apparently be oblivious to other conversations. This is the focused-attention aspect of the cocktail-party problem. Yet one will sometimes hear important information, such as one's own name, in other conversations. This is the divided-attention aspect of the cocktail-party problem. How can we tune into particular sources of information and, at the same time, remain sensitive to important information from other sources? How can our attention be both focused and divided at the same time? This question has motivated research on attention ever since Cherry raised it, and we shall see to what extent the empirical literature provides an answer.

Scope of Review

Our main objective in this chapter is to review the evidence with respect to the top-down control of selective processing. The next section of the paper is devoted to this review; in the course of it we draw 11 tentative empirical generalizations. These generalizations are intended to capture the current drift of the literature rather than to describe reality. Our secondary objective is to review and evaluate, in the light of our 11 generalizations, extant theories of selective attention. This objective is pursued in a subsequent section.

Our coverage of the literature is quite restricted. First, it is biased toward recent experiments that clearly illustrate important aspects of selective attention. Second, we do not review in a systematic way research with animals (see Riley & Leith 1976), electrophysiological research (see Hillyard & Kutas 1983), neurophysiological research (see Mountcastle 1978, Harter & Aine 1984), neuropsychological research (see Gummow et al 1983, Posner et al 1984), psychophysiological research (see Anthony 1985), or research on individual differences (W. A. Johnston & V. J. Dark, unpublished observations). Several other reviews of the recent literature on selective attention are available. We have been guided in particular by Broadbent (1982), Kahneman & Treisman (1984), Holender (1985), and Shiffrin (1985).

REVIEW OF EMPIRICAL LITERATURE

The following areas of research are reviewed: Priming effects, early and late selection, spatial attention, processing outside the spatial focus of attention, object-based attention, processing of nonselected objects, automatic attention, and schema-based attention.

Priming Effects

Priming effects are reviewed first because they define a possible basis of the top-down control of selective processing, they help to resolve some apparent contradictions and ambiguities in the literature, and they have theoretical implications that we consider later. Priming is said to occur when one stimulus, the prime stimulus, affects the processing of another stimulus, the test stimulus. Priming can be conceived of as either the activation or the establishment of internal codes by the prime stimulus that correspond in some way to the test stimulus. In principle, priming can occur at any level of stimulus analysis, ranging from low-level sensory analysis to high-level semantic analysis (Rabbitt & Vyas 1979). We review evidence for four types of priming: modality, identity, semantic, and schematic.

MODALITY PRIMING   The processing system can be primed toward a specific modality of stimulus input. For example, eye blinks to startle (test) stimuli are larger for stimuli in the modality (e.g. vision) of a prime stimulus on which attention is preengaged than for stimuli in a different modality (e.g. audition). This is found even in infants and is especially pronounced when attention is preengaged on an interesting stimulus (Anthony & Graham 1983). Similarly, very early components of event-related potentials in the brain are greater for stimuli in the modality to which attention is directed than for other stimuli (e.g. Näätänen 1982, Hillyard & Kutas 1983). Priming of one modality may be accompanied by suppression of other modalities. Click-evoked potentials in the auditory nerve are reduced when attention is directed to the visual modality (Oatman 1984). These priming effects occur within 100 msec of presentation of the test stimulus and are thought to result from efferent feedback from prime processing onto afferent pathways needed for test processing.

IDENTITY PRIMING   Jacoby and associates (e.g. Jacoby & Dallas 1981, Jacoby 1983a,b, Johnston et al 1985) have shown that reading a word on one occasion (prime) facilitates its visibility under threshold conditions on a subsequent occasion (test). The effect holds up even when several other words intervene between the prime and test presentations of the word (Dannenbring & Briand 1982). However, the effect is attenuated if the prime and test presentations are in different modalities (e.g. Kirsner & Smith 1974) or in different type fonts (e.g. Jacoby & Witherspoon 1982, Feustel et al 1983), or if they are physically similar but morphologically different (e.g. Kempley & Morton 1982). Thus, identity priming implicates a level of analysis somewhere between modality coding and semantic coding. Identity priming increases up to at least four repetitions of the prime stimulus (Feustel et al 1983). The effect is usually interpreted as the establishment of durable physical codes in memory by the prime presentation that benefits processing of the test presentation (e.g. Jacoby & Dallas 1981, Feustel et al 1983).

SEMANTIC PRIMING   A voluminous literature demonstrates that the process-ing of a test word (e.g. BUTTER) can be speeded up by an immediately preceding and semantically related prime word (e.g. BREAD). Semantic priming shows up in terms of disambiguation of homographic test words (e.g. Conrad 1974, Johnston & Dark 1982), speed and accuracy of identification (e.g. Carr et al 1982, Johnston & Dark 1985) or lexical categorization (e.g. Meyer et al 1975) of test words, latency of repeating (shadowing) test words (Underwood 1977), and latency to match two test stimuli (Posner & Snyder 1975a). Semantic priming is generally attributed to the transitory activation by the prime word of semantic codes that correspond to the test word.

SCHEMATIC PRIMING   A schema refers to an internal representation of a common spatial (Friedman 1979) or temporal (Bower et al 1979) configuration of objects and events (Taylor & Crocker 1981). A schema may comprise a collection of codes at various levels rather than define a single high level of coding. A schema is thought to develop from frequent processing of different instances of a natural category (e.g. kitchens, doctor's offices, restaurants, salespersons, and even one's self). Schemata activated by prime events (e.g. the name of a category) may bias various levels of analysis toward particular test events (e.g. instances of a category). Research has illustrated the biasing effects that active schemata can have on identification of test stimuli (Bieder-man et al 1973, Palmer 1975), memory for test stimuli (Bartlett 1932, Snyder & Uranowitz 1978, Bower 1981), and judgments of test stimuli (Snyder & Swann 1978, Higgins et al 1985).

We can summarize the literature on priming effects in the form of our first empirical generalization: 1. *All levels of stimulus analysis can be primed for particular stimuli.*

Early and Late Selection

We turn now to research that deals more directly with selective attention. We begin by examining the empirical phenomena established by three decades of research on a single theoretical issue: Does selection take place early in stimulus processing, before semantic analysis of any stimulus, as Broadbent (1958) originally proposed, or does it take place only late in stimulus processing, after semantic analysis of all stimuli, as Deutsch & Deutsch (1963) later proposed?

Much of the research on this issue has made use of a dichotic-listening task in which different lists of words or other alphanumeric stimuli are played to the two ears of a subject. We introduce a nomenclature for this task that applies to other (e.g. visual) tasks as well. Instructions are to try to listen either to both lists *(divided attention)* or to just one *(focused attention)*. Any list to which the subject is instructed to attend is called *relevant* and any other is called *irrelevant*. Thus, all stimuli are relevant under divided attention, and only some are relevant under focused attention. The task performed on a relevant list might be to respond to (e.g. repeat or shadow) all stimuli or to respond to (e.g. detect) only particular, *target* stimuli.

EVIDENCE FOR EARLY SELECTION   Initial (see Broadbent 1958) and subsequent research (e.g. Keren 1976, Johnston & Heinz 1978) on this issue have compared selection based on physical differences between relevant and irrelevant stimuli (sensory selection) with selection based on semantic differences (semantic selection). Sensory selection has consistently proved to be both more accurate and less effortful than semantic selection. These and many similar findings are reviewed elsewhere (e.g. Treisman 1969, Moray 1970, Broadbent 1971), and they establish our second empirical generalization: 2. *Selection based on sensory cues is usually superior to selection based on semantic cues.*

    Other evidence in favor of early selection takes a somewhat different form. Ninio & Kahneman (1974) demonstrated that latency of target detection is less when the targets are confined to the relevant list of a focused-attention task than when they are distributed between two lists of a divided-attention task. Treisman & Geffen (1967) and Treisman & Riley (1969) had subjects shadow one of two dichotically presented lists but detect occasional targets in either list. Accuracy of detection was much higher for targets in the shadowed ear than for those in the nonshadowed ear. If selection were not possible until after the semantic analysis of all concurrent stimuli, then why should semantically defined targets be easier to detect under focused-attention instructions or in the shadowed list?

EVIDENCE FOR LATE SELECTION   To the extent that early selection of relevant stimuli implies early rejection of irrelevant stimuli, evidence for semantic analysis of irrelevant stimuli would appear to favor late-selection theories. A considerable amount of evidence of this sort has been reported (Broadbent 1971, 1982, Posner & Snyder 1975b, Shiffrin & Schneider 1977). In dichotic listening, a semantic relationship between coincident relevant and irrelevant words affects latency of shadowing the relevant words (Lewis 1970), shadowing sometimes follows a shift to the irrelevant list of a contextually constrained passage (Treisman 1960), a homophone is disambiguated by a coincident irrelevant word (MacKay 1973), autonomic responses can be elicited by semantically defined conditioned stimuli in the irrelevant list (Corteen & Wood 1972), and one sometimes does hear one's own name in the irrelevant list (Moray 1959). Many of these effects are attributable to semantic or schematic priming of the particular irrelevant words on which they are based (Broadbent

1971, 1982, Logan 1980, Johnston & Dark 1982, Shiffrin 1985). Nonetheless, this line of evidence leads to our third empirical generalization: 3. *Irrelevant stimuli sometimes undergo semantic analysis.*

The foregoing review attempts to capture the gist of the massive literature on the controversy between early- and late-selection theories. Selection on the basis of sensory properties of relevant stimuli is usually superior to selection on the basis of semantic properties, but sensory selection does not preclude semantic analysis of irrelevant stimuli. Sensory priming may form the basis of sensory selection and the focused-attention aspect of the cocktail-party problem. Semantic priming may form the basis of semantic selection, the semantic processing of certain irrelevant stimuli in sensory-selection tasks, and the divided-attention aspect of the cocktail-party problem.

This brief review of early and late selection brings us to the present decade. We now examine more contemporary, but not unrelated, issues. Contemporary theorists whose roots are on different sides of this historical controversy now seem to agree that selection is often guided by sensory cues but that irrelevant stimuli can be processed to semantic levels (e.g. Broadbent 1982, Shiffrin 1985). However, these theorists continue to disagree on some of the issues reviewed below.

Spatial Attention

How are relevant stimuli accorded processing priority? Generalization 2 suggests that sensory priming plays an important role. Among the sensory cues by which attention could be guided, spatial cues seem to be especially effective. We review first evidence that spatial attention is important and second evidence on the spotlight characteristics of attention. Our examination of spatial attention concentrates, as does most of the relevant literature, on visual processing.

THE IMPORTANCE OF SPACE   When a multielement display is followed by a cue that specifies which elements to recall, accuracy of recall is higher if the cue specifies locations (e.g. middle row) than if it specifies other sensory properties (e.g. red items). Accuracy of recall is especially low if the cue specifies semantic properties (e.g. digits) (von Wright 1968, Coltheart 1980). Spatial cues are particularly effective when they are given in advance of the display. Posner et al (1980, Experiment 2) flashed a particular letter at a particular location in the visual field. Speed of detection was facilitated by advance cueing of the location of the target but not by advance cueing of the shape and identity of the target. Hede (1981) reports an auditory analog of this finding. Nissen (1985, Experiment 2) displayed items that varied in location, color, and shape and then provided one dimension as a cue to report the remaining two dimensions. The upshot was that location proved to be more fundamental than color and shape. That is, subjects could not know the color or the shape of an item without knowing its location, but they could know its color without knowing its shape or vice versa. Woods et al (1984) confirmed the relative importance of space (e.g. ear of entry) in attention to auditory stimuli.

Finally, studies of split-brain patients reveal a processing dissociation between spatial information and other sorts of information. For example, a cue presented to one hemisphere can tell the other hemisphere where, but not what, a stimulus will be in a brief display that is presented to the other hemisphere (Holtzman et al 1984a,b). Our fourth empirical generalization is: 4. *Spatial cues are especially effective cues*.

ATTENTIONAL SPOTLIGHT   We now review evidence that spatial attention has the characteristics of a spotlight, that the attentional spotlight is independent of eye fixations, and that the beam of the attentional spotlight can assume various shapes.

Basic findings   Consider first an experiment by LaBerge (1983). In one condition a five-letter word, subtending 1.77° of visual angle, was displayed on a screen and subjects had to categorize the center letter. This condition directed attention to the center position. Occasionally, a single probe character appeared in lieu of (or immediately subsequent to) the string of letters. The probe appeared in one of the five display positions. Reaction time to the probe was a V-shaped function of display position; it was fastest in the center position and slowest in the first and fifth positions. LaBerge suggested that an "attentional spotlight" was focused on the center position and facilitated the processing of any stimulus that appeared in that position. Similar findings are reported by Hoffman et al (1983). In another condition, LaBerge had subjects categorize the whole word. This condition was intended to broaden the beam of the attentional spotlight to cover all five display positions. As expected, reaction time to the probe did not vary with display position in this condition.

Other experiments suggest that the spotlight can be moved across space independently of eye movements (Sperling & Reeves 1980, Tsal 1983, Remington & Pierce 1984). William James (1890) cites an experiment by Helmholtz in which a dark stereoscopic view box could be briefly illuminated by a spark. Before illumination, a tiny beam of light passed through a pinhole in each stereoscopic card, and eye fixation was necessary to keep the beams superimposed and seen as one. Helmholtz reported that in advance of the spark we can " . . . keep our attention voluntarily tuned to any particular portion we please of the dark field, so as then, when the spark comes, to receive an impression only from such parts of the picture as lie in this region. In this respect, then, our attention is quite independent of the position and accommodation of the eyes" (James 1890, p. 438). In more recent studies, Posner had subjects fixate on the center of a screen and then presented targets (e.g. light flashes or alphanumeric characters) in various positions as many as 24° to one or the other side of fixation (Posner et al 1980, Posner & Cohen 1984). Subjects were either precued to the spatial position of an impending target or not precued. When they were precued, the cue usually was correct (valid) but sometimes was incorrect (invalid). Detection of the target was facilitated by valid cues and inhibited by invalid cues. Moreover, if the target did not appear in the precued position, detection performance was higher when it appeared in a position adjacent to the precued position than when it appeared elsewhere.

The above research suggests that attention has the properties of an adjustable-beam spotlight. Other findings indicate that the beam of the attentional spotlight can be split (e.g. Shaw & Shaw 1977, Egly & Homa 1984). Egly & Homa (1984, Experiment 3) had subjects fixate on the center point of a "spider-web" grid consisting of three concentric rings with radii of 1°, 2°, and 3° of visual angle, respectively. Two letters were flashed for 30-60 msec and then followed by a pattern mask. One letter appeared in the center of the display and the other, called the displaced letter, appeared in one of eight "clock" positions on one of the rings. Subjects were to name the center letter, which they did with 95% accuracy, and then localize the displaced letter. As in Posner's studies, accuracy of localization of the displaced letter was facilitated by valid precueing of the ring on which it appeared and inhibited by invalid precueing. The most important findings were generated by invalid precueing. Consider the case in which the middle ring is precued but the displaced letter actually is on either the inner ring or the outer ring. If precueing of the middle ring causes the attentional spotlight to expand just enough to embrace the middle ring, then the miscued letter is going to fall either inside or outside the spotlight and accuracy of localization of the letter should vary accordingly. In fact, the cost of miscueing was just as great when the letter was on the inner ring as when it was on the outer ring. These data suggest that the beam of the spotlight can be split to illuminate both a central region and a satellite ring. The data reviewed above support our fifth empirical generalization: 5. *Attention is independent of eye fixation and can assume the characteristics of an adjustable-beam spotlight.* However, both aspects of this generalization are subject to important qualifications.

Qualifications of basic findings   Although the attentional spotlight may be able to conform to various spatial configurations, the findings of Podgorny & Shepard (1983) suggest that some configurations are easier than others. Subjects classified a dot as being on or off a "figure" that was composed by shading certain cells in a large matrix. Reaction time was not affected by the number of shaded cells but was strongly affected by their compactness. This effect held true for imagined as well as real figures. Thus, selective processing appears to improve with the coherence of the relevant areas of the visual field. Similar findings are reviewed below in connection with object-based attention.

In addition, although the width of the attentional spotlight may be adjustable, there appears to be a minimum width to which it can be constricted. The minimum width of the spotlight has been estimated by determining how far an irrelevant stimulus (e.g. digit) has to be moved away from a relevant stimulus before it ceases to have a disruptive effect on the response to the relevant stimulus. Various studies using this technique estimate the minimum width of the spotlight to be somewhere between .5° and 1° (e.g. Eriksen & Hoffman 1972, Eriksen & Eriksen 1974). However, the disruptive effect of irrelevant stimuli decreases even from .08° to .23° (Estes 1982). Thus, the intensity of a 1° beam seems to diminish from center to periphery.

The independence between eye fixations and spatial attention also must be qualified. Although attention can be moved away from the center of the fovea, it becomes less efficient the farther away that it moves. For example, using the procedure described above, Humphreys (1981a) found that the minimum beam-width of the spotlight increased from less than .5° to more than 1° when attention was shifted from the center of the fovea to just 1° off center. Furthermore, the resolution of the spotlight appears to decrease sharply as it is directed farther away from the center of the fovea. For example, in the Egly & Homa (1984) research, accuracy of both identification and localization of the displaced letter declined from over 80% to less than 40% as eccentricity of the letter increased from 1° to 3°.

The line of research initiated by Rayner and his associates further elucidates the low resolution of parafoveal attention (e.g. Rayner et al 1978, Schiepers 1980, McClelland & O'Regan 1981, Paap & Newsome 1981, Inhoff 1982, Balota & Rayner 1983). In the Rayner et al (1978) study, subjects attended to a letter string that was presented, for at least 165 msec, 1–5° away from the center of the fovea, and then they named a word that was presented to the fovea. The more similar the parafoveal stimulus was to the foveal word in terms of shared letters, the shorter the latency with which the foveal word was named. This sensory-priming effect indicates that some physical information was extracted by parafoveal attention. However, the magnitude of this effect dropped sharply with degree of eccentricity of the parafoveal stimulus and was essentially nil at 5°. On the basis of different estimates of attentional velocity (Tsal 1983, Remington & Pierce 1984), we may assume that the exposure duration of 165 msec was long enough for attention to move at least 5°.

Finally, processing of the parafoveal stimulus even at 1° of eccentricity appears to be minimal when the set from which the stimulus is drawn is large and unconstrained (McClelland & O'Regan 1981, Paap & Newsome 1981). The latter finding points out an important methodological problem with studies that make repeated use of stimuli from the same small pool. The identity-priming effects of earlier presentations of the stimuli can cause these stimuli to be more perceptible on later presentations and receive more semantic process-ing than stimuli presented for the first time. We encounter this problem at various points below.

In short, although spatial attention can be directed away from the fovea and assume various shapes, it can do so only at a considerable sacrifice in process-ing acuity. Processing is most efficient when attention is aligned with the center of the fovea and directed to consolidated regions of space.

Processing Outside the Attentional Spotlight

How much processing takes place for stimuli outside the attentional spotlight? We examine this question with respect to both semantic processing and lower level (nonsemantic) processing. In most of the relevant research, attention is aligned with the fovea so that parafoveal stimuli fall outside the spotlight.

SEMANTIC PROCESSING   Semantic processing of stimuli outside the focus of attention has been measured in terms of both the semantic-interference and semantic-priming effects of these stimuli.

Semantic interference   Responses to relevant stimuli are impeded by the presence of irrelevant stimuli in the visual field, and the magnitude of this effect is dependent (in different ways in different experiments) on the semantic relationship between the relevant and irrelevant stimuli. However, these effects, which reveal the semantic processing of irrelevant stimuli, are sharply curtailed when the attentional spotlight is predirected to the location of the relevant stimulus (e.g. Underwood 1976, Kahneman et al 1983, Allport et al 1985). Indeed, these effects may be eliminated altogether if the irrelevant stimuli are more than 1° away from fixated relevant stimuli and, thus, fall outside the attentional spotlight (Eriksen & Eriksen 1974).

The Stroop effect defines a special kind of semantic interference from irrelevant stimuli. The original effect is that the latency to name the color of ink in which a word is printed is exceptionally long when the word is the name of a different color (Stroop 1935). The effect occurs even when the ink color (e.g. of a rectangle or neutral word) and the conflicting color name are spatially separated by as much as 12.5° (e.g. Kahneman & Henik 1981, Lowe & Mitterer 1982). However, the effect dissipates with the degree of separation and can be completely eliminated when attention is predirected to the location of the ink color (e.g. Iwasaki 1978, Francolini & Egeth 1980, Kahneman & Henik 1981). Furthermore, the Stroop effect that is engendered when a color name is printed above a colored rectangle is nullified, or diluted, when a neutral word, or even a string of Xs, is printed below the rectangle (Kahneman & Chajczyk 1983). Thus, the Stroop effect is quite fragile when the color name is outside the presumed focus of attention.

Semantic priming   In our own laboratory, we have compared words inside and outside the spatial foci of attention in terms of semantic priming (Dark et al 1985, Johnston & Dark 1985). Subjects monitored words presented at relevant locations of a visual display for occasional targets. Both relevant and irrelevant locations fell within 2° of visual angle from the center of the display. On occasion a prime word was inserted in a relevant or irrelevant location. Just after the presentation of the prime word, the attention task was interrupted by a semantically related test word. The test word was severely degraded at first but gradually clarified until it was identified. Priming was measured in terms of speed of identification of the test word. Prime words were exposed for 60–500 msec before being pattern masked. Semantic priming increased directly with exposure duration for words in relevant locations but was nil at all durations for words in irrelevant locations. Semantic processing of all stimuli appears to be data limited when exposure duration is very short. However, when data limits are removed by an increase in exposure duration, semantic processing appears to increase for stimuli inside the spatial foci of attention but remain undetectable for stimuli outside these foci. We have observed similar effects in a study of dichotic listening (Johnston & Dark 1982).

Summary and counterevidence   Semantic-interference and semantic-priming effects support our sixth empirical generalization: 6. *Stimuli outside the spatial focus of attention undergo little or no semantic processing.* How can this generalization be squared with evidence that irrelevant stimuli are sometimes semantically processed (Generalization 3)? One possibility is that irrelevant stimuli might sometimes benefit from semantic- or identity-priming effects, and these top-down effects might yield some semantic analysis even for stimuli outside the attentional spotlight. Indeed, when relevant and irrelevant stimuli have been drawn from the same very small pool so that maximal identity priming of irrelevant stimuli was likely, then both semantic-interference and semantic-priming effects of irrelevant stimuli outside the attentional spotlight have been demonstrated (Van der Heijden et al 1984, Allport et al 1985). Other studies that provide apparent evidence for semantic processing of stimuli outside the attentional spotlight are subject to criticism on other counts. Holender (1985) presents an excellent review and critique of these studies. In any case, Generalization 6 receives additional support in the form of evidence that even physical analysis is attenuated for stimuli outside the spotlight.

NONSEMANTIC PROCESSING   Evidence bearing on lower-level processing of stimuli outside the focus of attention has derived from studies of identity priming and feature integration.

Identity priming   In our own research described above, we also measured the identity priming of words inside and outside the spatial foci of attention. As was the case for semantic priming, identity priming was consistently larger for words in relevant locations than for words in irrelevant locations. However, whereas semantic priming from irrelevant locations was nil at all exposure durations examined (60–500 msec), identity priming from these locations managed to attain significance at the longest duration (500 msec). Eich (1984) observed similar effects in a study of dichotic listening. Although some nonsemantic processing may occur for stimuli outside the attentional spotlight, it appears to be much less than that which occurs inside the spotlight.

Rayner et al (1978, Experiment 3) report additional evidence that even nonsemantic processing is attenuated for stimuli outside the attentional spotlight. They presented different strings of letters to the left and right parafoveas. When the eye started to move toward one of the stimuli (indicating that spatial attention was directed to that stimulus), both stimuli were removed and a test word was presented to the fovea. Only the parafoveal stimulus to which attention had been directed proved to be an effective identity prime for the test word. This is a particularly important finding because it shows that the stimulus to which spatial attention is directed receives more physical analysis than the other stimulus even though the two stimuli are equidistant from the fovea.

Feature integration   Recent research suggests that spatial attention is required at the point in bottom-up processing where simple sensory features are conjoined. Duncan (1979, Experiment 1) had subjects search for the letter Q in a circular array (2.33° in diameter) of 8 locations, only 4 of which were relevant. When the letters O and K served as distractors, latency of detection was increased. This effect is attributable to the formation of an illusory Q by the conjunction of an O with the leg of a K. However, this effect obtained only when O and K appeared in relevant locations. When these distractors appeared outside the foci of attention, they apparently did not undergo a sufficient amount of bottom-up processing to produce an illusory conjunction of their sensory features.

Treisman and her colleagues have examined in detail the relationship between spatial attention and processing of physical features. Treisman & Schmidt (1982) found that simple features were correctly conjoined when the stimuli fell within a narrowly focused spotlight but that illusory conjunctions were found when attention was distributed over a wide area of space. Treisman & Gelade (1980) found that detection of feature conjunctions, but not simple features, was necessarily accompanied by correct localization of the targets. In addition, in a multielement display, detection of simple features appears to involve parallel processing, but detection of feature conjunctions appears to require serial processing (e.g. Hoffman 1979, Treisman & Gelade 1980, Treisman 1982, Egeth et al 1984). Finally, Vaughn (1984) found that accurate processing could occur farther away from fixation for simple features than for feature conjunctions.

The weight of the evidence points toward our seventh empirical generalization: 7. *Stimulus processing outside the attentional spotlight is restricted mainly to simple physical features.* Although a sudden and intense event outside the attentional spotlight may receive enough bottom-up processing to draw the spotlight to its location (e.g. Posner et al 1980), more detailed physical analysis appears to require that spatial attention be directed to the stimulus.

Overview of Spatial Attention

In spatial attention tasks, processing can be selectively focused on a small region of the visual field subtending about 1° of visual angle. Attention can be directed to the parafovea and even to spatially disparate regions, but only by incurring considerable costs in speed and accuracy of stimulus processing. Stimulus processing outside the foci of attention appears to be confined largely to analysis of simple physical features. Processing of feature conjunctions and meaning appear to require spatial attention. We now consider whether selective processing can take place inside the attentional spotlight.

Object-Based Attention

Selective processing is assisted by factors other than spatial attention. James noted that we can selectively perceive different objects in the same spatial array, such as the sound of the oboe in an orchestral performance. In this section we consider selectivity on the basis of *objectness*. First we discuss the influence of perceptual organization on selection. Then we discuss selection between two objects overlapping in space.

PERCEPTUAL ORGANIZATION   Consider the situation in which all stimuli appear around the fixation point but targets are intermixed with distractors. What factors influence selectivity? Selection of targets is strongly determined by Gestalt configuration properties like good continuation and featural similarity (Helson 1933) that produce "good" perceptual groups. These properties are often described as preattentive in the sense that they operate to define objects as candidates for selective processing (Neisser 1967). Identifying a single target is more difficult when the target is embedded among distractors as part of a perceptual group than when it is outside that group (Prinzmetal & Banks 1977, Carter 1982, Treisman 1982, Banks & White 1984). For example, Prinzmetal & Banks (1977) presented a T or F as a target among five similar shapes. Five of the items formed a line while the sixth item was slightly off to the side. Target identification was much faster when the T or F was the odd item than when it was part of the line. Bregman & Rudnicky (1975) showed a similar effect with auditory stimuli. An irrelevant tone interfered with a target sequence when it was perceptually grouped with that sequence but not when it was perceptually grouped with another irrelevant tone.

Similarly, when multiple targets form a perceptual group distinct from distractors, they are easier to identify than when they do not comprise a group (Fryklund 1975, Skelton & Eriksen 1976, Merikle 1980). Treisman et al (1983) presented two targets, a word and a rectangle with a gap in one side, at various positions around fixation. Subjects read the word and reported the position of the gap. When the rectangle surrounded the word and thus formed a single perceptual group, subjects read the word faster and were better able to locate the gap than when the rectangle appeared above or below the word, even though the gap was spatially closer to the word in the latter condition. Treisman et al (1983) interpreted the result as support for object-based attention. If the target information is integrated into one perceptual group, one object, then it will be easily selected. However, if the target information is distributed between two perceptually distinct groups, two objects, then the selection task will be more difficult.

Experience can lead to perceptual segregation based on meaning. A word, for example, appears to be treated as an individual object rather than a string of letters. Prinzmetal (1981) showed that illusory conjunctions are more likely to occur between features from a single perceptual group than between features from two distinct perceptual groups. Prinzmetal & Millis-Wright (1984) argued from that finding that if words are treated as a single object, then there should be more illusory conjunctions between features of words than between features of nonwords. In a series of five experiments, words produced the most illusory conjunctions. Pronounceable nonwords and familiar acronyms also produced more illusory conjunctions than nonwords. These data suggest that familiarity plays a part in parsing stimulus information into perceptual objects.

The controversy concerning local and global features in object perception can be resolved by considering the factors influencing perceptual organization (Hoffman 1980, Ward 1983). Compound letter stimuli (e.g. a large H comprised of small Ss) subtending less than 6° of visual angle produce a perceptual group based on the large letter (Navon 1977, Kinchla & Wolfe 1979) unless the small letters are so widely separated that each one is seen as a separate object (Martin 1979). Compound stimuli subtending more than 6° of visual angle may also produce perceptual groups based on the small letters (Kinchla & Wolfe 1979). Likewise, it is easier to attend to the global features of a triangle than to the component lines because the Gestalt property of closure makes the global figure perceptually more salient (Pomerantz 1983). Ward & Logan (1984) reported that subjects were faster at responding to the level (global vs local) to which they had just responded in a prior stimulus. Thus, the level that produces the quality of objectness appears to be subject to top-down priming effects.

OVERLAPPING OBJECTS   We now turn to a related issue. There is a cost to combining relevant information from two perceptually distinct objects occurring close together in space (Treisman et al 1983). There is also a cost in selecting relevant information under conditions of spatial uncertainty when irrelevant objects/events occur in the visual field (Kahneman et al 1983). Is there a cost associated with selection of one of two overlapping objects in a known spatial location? The answer appears to be "no."

Subjects instructed to attend to one of two overlapping but differently colored line drawings (Goldstein & Fink 1981) or nonsense shapes (Rock & Gutman 1981) reveal very little processing of the irrelevant drawings as measured by a recognition test, but memory for the relevant drawings is equivalent to that produced when only one drawing is presented at a time. Rock & Gutman (1981) attempted to measure perceptual processing by occasionally presenting a familiar shape (a tree or a house) as either the relevant or irrelevant stimulus and requesting subjects to identify any familiar object immediately after stimulus offset. Subjects identified 89% of the relevant familiar shapes but none of the irrelevant familiar shapes. Selection between the two spatially overlapping objects appears to have been complete.

Duncan (1984) compared focused-attention and divided-attention conditions in a task involving a rectangle with a line through it. The entire stimulus subtended less than 1° of visual angle and was presented at fixation. In one experiment the rectangle varied in both size and which side contained a gap and the line varied in both texture and tilt. Subjects had to report two of the four dimensions. The two dimensions could be from the same object (rectangle or line) or from different objects. If both dimensions were from the same object, each dimension was reported as well as if it were the only dimension being reported. However, if the dimensions were from different objects, the second dimension was reported less accurately than in the single-report control. Apparently there is a cost associated with dividing attention between two separate objects even when they overlap and occur within 1° of visual angle.

Selection does not depend on the presence of a simple featural difference, like color or shape, between the stimuli. Neisser & Becklen (1975) simultaneously presented films of a handgame and a ballgame on the same screen and instructed subjects to respond whenever a specified event occurred in the relevant game. There was no performance decrement compared to when just one game was shown. Subjects showed little awareness of either predictable or unpredictable events in the irrelevant game (see also Becklen & Cervone 1983). Subjects instructed to attend to both games showed a severe loss in performance. Selection between games was easy but divided attention was difficult.

Dichoptically presented stimuli of sufficiently similar contours may fuse into a single object with features from each stimulus (e.g. Engel 1958), but dissimilar stimuli lead to binocular rivalry in which one of the two stimuli is selectively perceived while the other stimulus is functionally invisible. There may be switching (rivalry) between the stimuli, but the selection is complete. One or the other is seen but not both (see Walker 1978 for a review).

Considering all the evidence in this section, our eighth empirical generalization is: 8. *Overlapping objects can be selectively processed.*

Semantic Processing of Nonselected Objects

According to Generalization 6, there is not much semantic processing of stimuli outside the attentional spotlight. In the case of object-based attention, the issue becomes one of semantic processing of nonselected objects within the spotlight. As discussed in the previous section, selection between objects appears to be fairly complete as measured by memory and identification. Although subjects in the Neisser & Becklen (1975), Goldstein & Fink (1981), and Rock & Gutman (1981) studies indicated that they were aware of the presence of an irrelevant stimulus, they could report very little about the nonselected stimulus and showed no recognition memory for it. In this section we review and evaluate evidence that objects of which subjects are not aware are semantically processed nonetheless. A stimulus may fail to attain awareness because another stimulus is selected instead of it or because it is exposed too briefly. After presenting the evidence for the semantic processing of nonselected objects we critique the methodologies employed and discuss the counterevidence.

EVIDENCE   Three lines of evidence will be considered in examining this issue: semantic priming from the irrelevant one of two overlapping objects; semantic priming from stimuli presented at threshold durations; and semantic priming from nonreported primes.

Overlapping objects   Allport et al (1985) examined the semantic analysis of the irrelevant member (determined by color) of a pair of overlapping line drawings via its priming effect on the naming of a subsequent test stimulus. Subjects had to attend to the relevant drawing and then recall it after naming the test stimulus. The irrelevant drawing had two semantic-priming effects on latency to name the test stimulus. The priming effect was negative when the relevant drawing was correctly recalled, but it was positive when the relevant drawing was not correctly recalled. Both forms of priming constitute evidence for semantic analysis of nonselected stimuli.

Threshold primes   Several recent investigations have examined the semantic-priming potency of relevant stimuli presented at exposure durations intended to be too brief to allow awareness of the stimuli. For example, Fowler et al (1981, Experiment 5) determined an awareness threshold by reducing the interval between a word or blank field and a subsequent pattern mask until the subject was unable to report reliably the presence/absence of the word. The threshold-setting session was followed by the priming sessions in which the subject made lexical decisions to test stimuli. The primes were presented either below or well above the awareness threshold. The amount of semantic priming was the same in the two conditions. Several other studies using similar procedures have produced similar results (Philpott & Wilding 1979, McCauley et al 1980, Humphreys 1981b, Balota 1983, Marcel 1983a).

Nonreported primes   Another strategy used to show subliminal semantic analysis is to present primes at a duration that only sometimes allows identification and to look at differences in the amount of priming as a function of whether or not the prime is reported. The report of the prime word is requested immediately after the response to the test word. Both McCauley et al (1980) and Carr et al (1982) found that nonreported primes produced just as much priming as reported primes. Fishler & Goodman (1978) examined semantic priming in a lexical decision task and report a curious result: Reliable priming was obtained for the nonreported primes but not for the reported primes. Finally, Evett & Humphreys (1981, Experiment 1) examined semantic priming via increased correct naming of the test word when a prime was presented for about 33 msec and was followed immediately by the test word which was itself masked after 33 msec. Although subjects very rarely reported the prime words, these words increased identification accuracy of the test word by a statistically significant 12%.

CRITIQUE AND COUNTEREVIDENCE   The three lines of evidence described above would seem to present a strong case for semantic processing of objects that fall in the spatial focus of attention but that are not selected into conscious-ness. However, most of the investigations have been severely criticized on methodological grounds. Though varied in nature, the criticisms all suggest that subjects might have been more aware of the primes than was assumed by the investigators.

Overlapping objects   The study by Allport et al (1985) of overlapping objects made repeated use of a small ensemble of objects. A given object was presented many times, sometimes as the relevant object and sometimes as the irrelevant object. Thus, on all but the first few trials, irrelevant objects were likely to have benefitted from massive identity-priming effects. That irrelevant objects can benefit from the identity-priming effects was demonstrated by Wolford & Morrison (1980). Irrelevant words were sandwiched between two relevant digits. Above-chance recognition on a subsequent test was observed for words that had been repeated several times over the course of the experiment (Experiment 1) but not for words that had not been repeated (Experiment 2). The identity-priming problem was obviated in a study of binocular rivalry by Zimba & Blake (1983). A strong semantic-priming effect was observed for dominant (selected) objects but not for suppressed (unselected) objects.

Threshold primes   Most of the threshold studies also made repeated use of the same stimuli. Therefore, it is possible that many of the "threshold" primes were themselves physically primed and rendered perceptible. These studies are subject to three additional criticisms as well. First, the threshold-setting procedures may be questioned on the grounds that the number of observations was insufficient and that subjects may have been conservative in reporting barely perceptible words (Merikle 1982). When a more reliable, forced-choice procedure has been used to establish awareness thresholds, no semantic priming has been observed for threshold stimuli (Cheesman & Merikle 1984). Second, stimuli are apt to be more perceptible on priming trials, especially later ones, than on threshold trials because of general practice effects. Wolford & Marchak (1984) observed a large improvement across trials in the identification of words when duration of exposure was held constant. Third, the extra light introduced on the priming trials by the presentation of test words may allow subjects to become light adapted and, therefore, have better visual acuity than they have on the threshold trials. Purcell et al (1983) showed that an exposure duration that allowed only 38% accuracy of word identification under the light-adaptation levels present on the threshold trials allowed 79% accuracy under the levels present on the priming trials. Furthermore, when Purcell et al used the same level of light adaptation on both threshold and priming trials, semantic priming for threshold words was eliminated.

Nonreported primes   The demonstrations of semantic priming for nonreported primes are also subject to criticism. First, many of these demonstrations are subject to the identity-priming artifact that is introduced by making repeated use of the same stimuli as semantic primes. We controlled for this artifact in several studies in our laboratory. Stimulus presentation parameters allowed for 58% accuracy of prime report. Reported primes produced large semantic-priming effects but nonreported primes were impotent. Second, a prime may be consciously seen when it is presented but be forgotten during the presentation of and response to the test word (Holender 1985). Carr et al (1982) observed that an exposure duration that allowed for 100% report accuracy in a threshold-setting phase of the experiment supported only 32% report accuracy in a subsequent priming phase in which prime report was delayed until after the response to the test word. Thus, some of the semantic priming observed for nonreported words is attributable to primes that had attained awareness but were forgotten during the test trials.

SUMMARY   We agree with Holender (1985) that the evidence on semantic processing of nonselected objects does not warrant rejection of the null hypothesis. Therefore, our ninth empirical generalization is: 9. *Nonselected objects within the spatial foci of attention undergo little or no semantic processing.* However, the evidence is mixed, so this generalization is submitted with some reservation. Indeed, there is evidence that a schema can be activated by repeated subliminal exposures of words that instantiate the schema. Bargh & Pietromonaco (1982) flashed words so briefly that subjects could neither report nor recognize them on a test administered immediately after stimulus presentation. From 0% to 80% of the words connoted hostility. Subsequently, subjects judged an ambiguously described person in terms of hostility and other negative traits. These judgments were a direct function of the number of hostility-related words to which the subjects had been subliminally exposed. It may be that a word exposed subliminally is not sufficient to activate a precise semantic representation of itself but can summate with other such words to activate a general schematic representation that embraces all of the words.

Automatic and Controlled Attention

In the last decade a considerable empirical and theoretical effort has been directed to the distinction between automatic and controlled processing (e.g. LaBerge 1975, Posner & Snyder 1975b, Schneider & Shiffrin 1977, Shiffrin & Schneider 1977). This distinction was well articulated by William James in his chapter on habit in which he provided examples first of controlled processing and then of automatic processing:

> When we are learning to walk, to ride, to swim, skate, fence, write, play, or sing, we interrupt ourselves at every step by unnecessary movements and false notes . . . on the contrary . . . A gleam in his adversary's eye, a momentary pressure from his rapier, and the fencer finds that he has instantly made the right parry and return. A glance at the musical hieroglyphics, and the pianist's fingers have rippled through a cataract of notes (1890, p. 114).

James also brought the distinction to bear on the process of attention: " . . . Attention may be either . . . passive, reflex, nonvoluntary, effortless; or . . . active and voluntary" (1890, p. 416). James noted that attention can be drawn automatically to stimuli by virtue of either their sensory ("immediate") characteristics (e.g. suddeness or intensity) or their semantic ("derived") characteristics. As an example of the latter, James offered the following: "A faint tap per se is not an interesting sound; it may well escape being discriminated from the general rumor of the world. But when it is a signal, as that of a lover on the window-pane, it will hardly go unperceived" (1890, pp. 417–18). Whereas a great deal of research has been directed to the general distinction between automatic and controlled *processing*, relatively little has examined the particular distinction between automatic and controlled *selection*. Much of the work on automaticity of attention has been performed in a series of studies spawned by Schneider & Shiffrin (1977).

In the paradigm developed by Schneider and Shiffrin, subjects detect targets that are embedded among nontargets in briefly exposed displays. In one condition, called consistent matching (CM), the targets and nontargets are always drawn from two different sets of stimuli. In another condition, called variable matching (VM), the targets and nontargets are drawn from the same pool of stimuli such that a stimulus that is a target on one trial can be a distractor on another trial. With sufficient practice at the task, detection of targets can become automatic in the CM condition but not in the VM condition. Among the signs of automatic attention to CM targets are the following (for more thorough reviews see Schneider et al 1984 and Shiffrin 1985): (*a*) detection performance in a CM task is not affected by the number of nontargets on the display (e.g. Schneider & Shiffrin 1977); (*b*) CM training produces severe negative transfer when the target and nontarget stimulus sets are switched (Shiffrin & Schneider 1977); (*c*) detection of a new VM target in relevant locations is disrupted when an old CM target appears nearby in an irrelevant location (Shiffrin & Schneider 1977); and (*d*) performance of a CM task is not disrupted by a concurrent task (Logan 1979, Fisk & Schneider 1983, Schneider & Fisk 1984).

In short, selective processing of CM targets is difficult to either disrupt (e.g. by adding nontargets to the display or imposing a secondary task) or prevent (e.g. by presenting them in irrelevant locations or redefining them as nontargets). By contrast, selective processing of VM targets is slower and less accurate overall, more disruptable, and more preventable. These distinctions hold true only within certain boundary conditions. For example, Hoffman et al (1983) showed that automatic attention to CM targets is diminished to the extent that these targets fall outside the spatial foci of attention. Nonetheless, the distinctions between CM and VM search conditions conform to the distinctions drawn by James between passive and active attention, and they form the basis for our tenth generalization: 10. *Selective processing is sometimes performed passively and sometimes actively.*

Schema-Based Attention

The effects of schemata on stimulus identification, memory, and judgment, and the activation of schemata by subliminal stimuli, were noted earlier. We review here evidence that selective processing can be guided by active schemata. Studies show that stimuli conforming to active schemata are easy to attend to but difficult to ignore.

The Neisser & Becklen (1975) study described in connection with object-based attention demonstrated selective attention to one of two overlapping films of people playing games. Relevant information differed from irrelevant only in terms of the schema to which it belonged. Neisser and Becklen suggest that their subjects selectively processed only information that corresponded to the active schema.

Johnston (1978) measured the effort required to selectively listen to an unfamiliar passage in terms of reaction time to subsidiary visual probes. Subjects had been familiarized with some of the irrelevant passages in a prior phase of the study. The measure of effort increased with the familiarity of the irrelevant passage. One way to interpret this finding is that selective processing of relevant information is difficult when the irrelevant information conforms to active schemata. However, the intrusive effect of familiar irrelevant passages obtained only when they could not be discriminated from the relevant passages on the basis of a simple physical cue (for example, gender of speaker).

Other studies suggest that schemata can render irrelevant material intrusive and disruptive even when subjects can rely on spatial cues (such as ear of entry) to attend to relevant material. Nielsen & Sarason (1981) inserted various classes of words in the irrelevant list of a dichotic listening task. The shadowing performance of their college-student subjects was disrupted when sexually explicit words were presented in the irrelevant list but not when neutral words or words related to hostility, educational evaluation, or university life were presented in the irrelevant list. The disruptive effect of sexually explicit words was correlated with subjects' premeasured level of state anxiety. These results may be diagnostic of the schemata that are most active in college students, especially anxious students.

Bargh (1982) examined the effect of "self schemata" on selective attention. Words related to the personality attribute of independence were inserted in the middle section of either the relevant list or the irrelevant list of a dichotic listening task. Several weeks prior to performing this task, subjects had been categorized as schematic or aschematic with respect to the attribute of independence. Attentional effort was measured in terms of reaction time to subsidiary visual probes. For aschematics, attentional effort was not affected by the presence of independence words in either list. However, for schematics, shadowing required relatively low effort when independence words were presented in the relevant list but relatively high effort when these words were presented in the irrelevant list.

Geller & Shaver (1976) used a color-naming task to study the effect of the self schema on selective attention. Latency to name the ink color in which words were printed was longer when the words were self relevant or self evaluative than when the words were neutral with respect to the self schema. This finding was exaggerated when subjects sat in front of a mirror and thought that their facial expressions were being video recorded, a manipulation designed to elevate the activation of the subjects' self schemata.

Bower (1981) reports two studies by Clore in which subjects were made to feel happy or angry by hypnotic procedures. In the first study, a relevant word was flanked by two irrelevant distractors on a visual display. The task was to classify the relevant word as pleasant or unpleasant. Classification errors were most frequent when the irrelevant words were congruent with the subjects' mood but opposite in emotional tone to the relevant word. In the second study, both happy and angry subjects took longer to name the ink colors of either pleasant words or unpleasant words than to name the ink colors of neutral words. Evidently, active schemata can draw selective processing away from stimuli that are relevant to the task to stimuli that are relevant to the subject. Our eleventh and final empirical generalization is as follows: 11. *Selective attention can be guided by active schemata.*

Summary of Empirical Literature

Our review of the literature can be summarized conveniently by paraphrasing and slightly rearranging our 11 empirical generalizations. Selection on the basis of sensory cues is usually superior to selection on the basis of semantic cues (2); spatial cues comprise a special kind of sensory cue (4); selection on the basis of spatial cues has the properties of an adjustable-beam spotlight (5) that can be focused most sharply at the center of the fovea; processing outside the spotlight is confined mainly to simple sensory features (6 and 7); selection inside the spotlight is based on the configural properties of objects (8); and there is little evidence for semantic processing of nonselected objects inside the spotlight (9). These seven generalizations converge onto the focused-attention aspect of the cocktail-party problem. One can tune into the sensory (especially spatial) and semantic features of a particular conversation and be oblivious to other conversations. However, irrelevant stimuli sometimes receive semantic processing (3), especially if they correspond to active schemata (11). These two generalizations illustrate the divided-attention aspect of the cocktail-party problem. One sometimes hears one's own name when it is mentioned in another conversation.

Both sets of empirical phenomena may be attributable to the priming of various levels of stimulus analysis (1). All levels of stimulus analysis can be biased simultaneously toward the characteristics of most of the relevant stimuli and some of the irrelevant stimuli. In some instances, these biases can be sufficiently strong that attention to the relevant or irrelevant stimuli appears to be automatic (10). Thus, Generalization 1 may help dissolve the apparent contradictions between some of the other generalizations and resolve the cocktail-party problem.

REVIEW OF THEORIES

We now examine and evaluate the major lines of theoretical development in the area of selective attention. A general distinction can be drawn between two classes of theory: those that view attention as a causal mechanism and those that view it as a natural consequence of other processes. We shall follow William James and refer to these as cause theories and effect theories.

Cause Theories

Most contemporary theories of information processing in general and selective attention in particular distinguish between two qualitatively different domains of stimulus processing (e.g. Kahneman 1973, LaBerge 1975, Posner & Snyder 1975b, Shiffrin & Schneider 1977, Lundh 1979, Broadbent 1982, Marcel 1983b). These domains of processing have been assigned various labels including nonconscious and conscious, automatic and controlled, peripheral and central, intraperceptual and extraperceptual, preattentive and attentive, and passive and active. We shall call them Domain A and Domain B. Domain A is the multilevel stimulus-analysis system introduced earlier. It is a relatively large-capacity, nonconscious, and passive system that is responsible for encoding environmental stimuli. Domain B is a relatively small-capacity, conscious, and active system that is responsible for controlling various forms of information processing including selective attention. Domain B can direct some of its limited capacity to the selection of the perceptual products of Domain A for entry or translation into consciousness. Thus, Domain B is, among other things, an attentional mechanism or director, a cause of selective processing.

Theories of this general class differ from one another in terms of the processing fate of nonselected stimuli. A majority of cause theories propose that perceptual encoding of irrelevant stimuli runs to completion regardless of where and how the perceptual records of relevant stimuli have been selected by Domain B. Domain B selects information from Domain A but does not control or modify processing in Domain A. A minority of cause theories propose that Domain B actually controls stimulus analysis in Domain A. Domain B can use its resources to prime different levels of stimulus analysis toward relevant stimuli and away from irrelevant stimuli so that only relevant stimuli undergo complete encoding in Domain A and, as a result, attain consciousness in Domain B. The majority point of view is well represented by Shiffrin & Schneider (1977) and the minority point of view is well represented by Broadbent (1971, 1982). We outline each of these theories and then evaluate the subclasses of cause theory that they represent on both empirical and metatheoretical grounds.

SHIFFRIN AND SCHNEIDER   Shiffrin & Schneider (1977) articulate a cause theory of selective attention in the context of their research on controlled and automatic processing. Stimulus encoding by Domain A proceeds automatically and without interference from Domain B. Domain B expends its limited capacity on various sorts of controlled processing. One kind of controlled processing is the search through the perceptual products of Domain A for VM targets, and this defines one kind of selective attention. By contrast, the perceptual records produced by Domain A of CM targets can yield an "automatic attention response" in Domain B, and this defines another kind of selective attention. In short, Domain B sometimes has to execute a controlled search for the perceptual representations of relevant stimuli (e.g. VM targets) but other times can automatically detect these representations (e.g. CM targets). The focused-attention aspect of the cocktail-party problem is attributable to controlled attention to the relevant conversation bolstered by automatic attention to particular relevant stimuli. The divided-attention aspect is attributable to automatic attention to occasional irrelevant stimuli.

Thus, the variable automaticity with which individuals can attend to relevant stimuli is attributed to the variable automaticity with which Domain B can select the perceptual representations of these stimuli. Similar theories have been proposed by LaBerge (1975), Posner & Snyder (1975b), Hoffman (1979), Duncan (1980), and Marcel (1983b). They have in common the assumption that Domain A runs its full data-driven course even for irrelevant stimuli and that selective processing occurs only in and by Domain B.

BROADBENT   Broadbent (1971, 1982) proposes that Domain B can bias Domain A toward the distinctive physical characteristics of relevant stimuli. This bias is the logical equivalent of an imperfect sensory filter that attenuates irrelevant information but passes relevant information onto the further levels of encoding. Sensory biases accommodate the focused-attention aspect of the cocktail-party problem. Irrelevant information is unlikely to progress through further levels of encoding unless these levels are biased toward, or primed for, this information. These higher-level biases account for the divided-attention aspect of the cocktail-party problem. Selective representation in Domain B of relevant and irrelevant stimuli is a by-product of their selective processing through Domain A.

Similar theories have been proposed by Treisman (1964, Treisman & Gelade 1980) and Kahneman (1973, Kahneman et al 1983). They have in common the assumption that selective processing occurs in Domain A as a result of the top-down operation of Domain B. Even Shiffrin and Schneider have recently hinted at a very similar view. Specifically, Schneider et al (1984) suggest that Domain B may provide " . . . some of the stimulus components necessary for automatic processing to take place. Once the appropriate enabling stimuli occur (both external and internal), the automatic processes may take place without additional control or effort by the subject" (p. 11). If Schneider et al mean by this that Domain B can prime Domain A toward, and thereby facilite the encoding of, relevant stimuli, then they are articulating a view very much like Broadbent's.

EVALUATION   The subclass of cause theory represented by Broadbent can accommodate most of the generalizations with relative ease. The subclass of theory represented by Shiffrin & Schneider is especially well suited to Generalizations 3 and 10 but runs into serious trouble with Generalizations 6, 7, and 9. The assumption that Domain A always runs its full bottom-up course is difficult to square with evidence that stimuli that are successfully kept out of consciousness undergo only low-level sensory analysis. Thus, the view represented by Broadbent appears to survive the empirical evidence somewhat better than the view represented by Shiffrin & Schneider. However, as recent reviews of the literature by Broadbent (1982) and Shiffrin (1985) clearly attest, both subclasses of cause theory can provide post-hoc explanations of all 11 empirical phenomena.

The ease with which Broadbent and Shiffrin can account for the known phenomena of selective attention betrays a serious metatheoretical problem with the view that selection of stimulus information is controlled by an active mental agent. Specifically, Domain B has all the characteristics of a processing homunculus. This is especially evident in the Shiffrin & Schneider theory. The basic explanation given for the variable automaticity with which subjects detect targets (Generalization 10) is that subjects are equipped with a Domain-B "attention director" that detects targets with variable automaticity. This explanation introduces an infinite regress because the same questions that were asked about how individuals pay attention now have to be asked about how the attention director pays attention. In tracing the history of atomic theory, Heisenberg (1958) notes that "Democritus was well aware of the fact that if atoms should . . . *explain* the properties of matter—color, smell, taste—they cannot themselves have these properties" (p. 69). Likewise, if a psychological construct is to explain the intelligent and adaptive selection powers of the organism, then it cannot itself be imbued with those powers. As we shall see below, William James appears to have recognized this metatheoretical problem.

Effect Theories

We review in this section the theory of selective attention articulated by James in 1890 and then note that similar theories have been advanced by more contemporary theorists. These theories have in common the view that selective processing is the passive by-product of natural priming effects.

WILLIAM JAMES   We summarize James's view as much as possible in his own words, beginning with quotations that illustrate the role of sensory and semantic priming in selective attention:

> . . . attention to the idea of a sensible object, is also accompanied with some degree of excitement of the sense organs to which the object appeals . . . The preparation of the

ideational centres exists . . . wherever our interest in the object is derived from, or in any way connected with, other interests, or the presence of other objects, in the mind . . . So that . . . *the two processes of sensorial adjustment and ideational preparation coexist in all our concrete attentive acts"* [p. 434]. . . .When watching for the distant clock to strike, our mind is so filled with its image that at every moment we think we hear the longed-for or dreaded sound. So of an awaited footstep. Every stir in the wood is for the hunter his game; for the fugitive his pursuers. Every bonnet in the street is momentarily taken by the lover to enshroud the head of his idol. The image in the mind is the attention; the preperception . . . is half of the looked-for thing [p. 442].

James dealt directly with the two general classes of attention theory when he asked "Is voluntary attention a resultant or a force?" (p. 447). James went on to articulate in some detail the view of attention as an effect rather than a cause. He explained the focused-attention phenomenon of cocktail parties as follows:

We see how we can attend to a companion's voice in the midst of noises which pass unnoticed though objectively much louder than the words we hear. Each word is *doubly* awakened; once from without by the lips of the talker, but already before that from within by the premonitory processes irradiating from the previous words, and by the dim arousal of all processes that are connected with the "topic" of the talk [p. 450].

Later James stated "The things we attend to *come to us* by their own laws. Attention *creates* no idea; an idea must already be there before we can attend to it" (p. 450);

The stream of thought is like a river. On the whole easy simple flowing predominates in it, the drift of things is with the pull of gravity, and effortless attention is the rule. But at intervals an obstruction, a set-back, a log-jam occurs, stops the current, creates an eddy, and makes things temporarily move the other way. If a real river could feel, it would feel these eddies and set-backs as places of effort . . . Really, the effort would only be a passive index that the feat was being performed [pp. 451–52]. Attention may have to go, like many a faculty once deemed essential, like many a verbal phantom, like many an idol of the tribe . . . No need of it to drag ideas before consciousness or fix them, when we see how perfectly they drag and fix each other there [p. 452].

CONTEMPORARY THEORISTS   James's view is explicitly echoed by Hochberg (1978, pp. 158–211) and Neisser (1976, pp. 33–107). Both theorists articulate, primarily in terms of schema theory, a view of attention as a passive by-product of priming effects. Effect theories attribute both aspects of the cocktail-party problem to chronically active schemata and the natural priming effects of prior processing on subsequent processing.

EVALUATION   Effect theory accommodates all 11 empirical generalizations with relative ease. It makes explicit use of the first and last generalizations. The view of attention as a consequence of natural priming effects has the important advantage of avoiding the homunculus problem. Moreover, this view lends itself well to practical applications and to an understanding of natural phenomena. A few more quotations from James illustrate this point:

> The only general pedagogic maxim bearing on attention is that the more interest the child has in advance in the subject, the better he will attend. Induct him therefore in such a way as to knit each new thing on to some acquisition already there . . . [p. 424]; . . . a teacher who wishes to engage the attention of his class must knit his novelties on to things of which they already have preperceptions [p. 447]. . . . Geniuses are commonly believed to excel . . . in their power of sustained attention . . . the "power" is of the passive sort. Their ideas coruscate, every subject branches infinitely before their fertile minds . . . *But it is their genius making them attentive, not their attention making geniuses of them* [p. 423].

Summary of Theories

The empirical literature, summarized in the form of our 11 empirical generalities, does not discriminate cleanly between the two general classes of theory. Indeed, it is probably not possible to decide empirically between them. As James suggested "The question is of course a purely speculative one . . . As mere *conceptions,* the effect theory and the cause theory of attention are equally clear; and whoever affirms either conception to be true must do so on metaphysical . . . rather than on scientific . . . grounds" (p. 448). It is somewhat ironic that, after his clear articulation of an effect theory, James revealed his private position:

> Under these circumstances, one can leave the question open whilst waiting for light, or one can do what most speculative minds do, that is, look to one's general philosophy to incline the beam. The believers in mechanism do so without hesitation, and they ought not to refuse a similar privilege to the believers in a spiritual force. I count myself among the latter, but as my reasons are ethical they are hardly suited for introduction into a psychological work [p. 454].

CONCLUSION

Our 11 empirical generalities suggest that the investment of three decades of research on selective attention has paid dividends in terms of knowledge. These gains may be illusory, however, since James and other scholars of the late nineteenth century might well have come up with a similar set of generalities. Reflecting on this possibility and on the skepticism of James himself, we are left wondering if the attempt to elucidate the nature of selective attention empirically is ultimately a futile one. Our own inclination is to continue the effort in the context of an effect theory. We suspect that it would be instructive to see how much we can understand about selective attention without appealing to a processing homunculus. Still, a dull, sinking feeling comes with the acknowledgment that James was much brighter than we and that he eventually abandoned psychology altogether.

Literature Cited

Allport, D. A., Tipper, S. P., Chmiel, N. R. J. 1985. Perceptual integration and post-categorical filtering. See Posner & Marin 1985, pp. 107–32

Anthony, B. J. 1985. In the blink of an eye: Implications of reflex modification for information processing. In *Advances in Psychophysiology, Vol. 1*, ed. P. K. Ackles, J. R. Jennings, M. G. H. Coles. Greenwich, CT: JAI Press. In press

Anthony, B. J., Graham, F. K. 1983. Evidence for sensory-selective set in young infants. *Science* 220:742–44

Balota, D. A. 1983. Automatic semantic activation and episodic memory encoding. *J. Verb. Learn. Verb. Behav.* 22:88–104

Balota, D. A., Rayner, K. 1983. Parafoveal visual information and semantic contextual constraints, *J. Exp. Psychol: Hum. Percept. Perform.* 9:726–38

Banks, W. P., White, H. 1984. *Perceptual grouping and lateral masking.* Presented at Ann. Meet. Psychon. Soc., San Antonio

Bargh, J. A. 1982. Attention and automaticity in the processing of self-relevant information. *J. Pers. Soc. Psychol.* 3:425–36

Bargh, J. A., Pietromonaco, P. 1982. Automatic information processing and social perception: The influence of trait information presented outside of conscious awareness on impression formation. *J. Pers. Soc. Psychol.* 43:437–49

Bartlett, F. C. 1932. *Remembering: A Study in Experimental and Social Psychology.* London: Cambridge Univ. Press

Becklen, R., Cervone, D. 1983. Selective looking and the noticing of unexpected events. *Mem. Cognit.* 11:601–8

Biederman, I., Glass, A. L., Stacy, E. 1973. Searching for objects in real world scenes. *J. Exp. Psychol.* 97:22–27

Bower, G. H. 1981. Mood and memory. *Am. Psychol.* 36:129–48

Bower, G. H., Black, J. B., Turner, T. J. 1979. Scripts in memory for text. *Cognit. Psychol.* 11:177–220

Bregman, A. S., Rudnicky, A. I. 1975. Auditory segregation: Stream or streams? *J. Exp. Psychol: Hum. Percept. Perform.* 1:263–67

Broadbent, D. 1958. *Perception and Communication.* London: Pergamon

Broadbent, D. 1971. *Decision and Stress.* London: Academic

Broadbent, D. 1982. Task combination and selective intake of information. *Acta Psychol.* 50:253–90

Carr, T. H., McCauley, C., Sperber, R. D., Parmelee, C. M. 1982. Words, pictures, and priming: On semantic activation, conscious identification, and automaticity of information processing. *J. Exp. Psychol: Hum. Percept. Perform.* 8:757–77

Carter, R. C. 1982. Visual search with color. *J. Exp. Psychol: Hum. Percept. Perform.* 8:127–36

Cheesman, J., Merikle, P. 1984. Priming with and without awareness. *Percept. Psychophys.* 36:387–95

Cherry, E. C. 1953. Some experiments on the recognition of speech, with one and two ears. *J. Acoust. Soc. Am.* 25:975–79

Coltheart, M. 1980. Iconic memory and visible persistence. *Percept. Psychophys.* 27:183–228

Conrad, C. 1974. Context effects in sentence comprehension: A study of the subjective lexicon. *Mem. Cognit.* 1:63–72

Corteen, R. S., Wood, B. 1972. Autonomic responses to shock associated words in an unattended channel. *J. Exp. Psychol.* 94:308–13

Dannenbring, G. L., Briand, K. 1982. Semantic priming and the word repetition effect in a lexical decision task. *Can. J. Psychol.* 36:435–44

Dark, V. J., Johnston, W. A., Myles-Worsley, M., Farah, M. J. 1985. Levels of capacity limitation and selection. *J. Exp. Psychol: Gen.* In press

Deutsch, J. A., Deutsch, D. 1963. Attention: Some theoretical considerations. *Psychol. Rev.* 87:272–300

Duncan, J. 1979. Divided attention: The whole is more than the sum of this parts. *J. Exp. Psychol: Hum. Percept. Perform.* 5:216–28

Duncan, J. 1980. The locus of interference in the perception of simultaneous stimuli. *Psychol. Rev.* 87:272–300

Duncan, J. 1984. Selective attention and the organization of visual information. *J. Exp. Psychol: Gen.* 113:501–17

Egeth, H. E., Virzi, R. A., Garbart, H. 1984. Searching for conjunctively defined targets. *J. Exp. Psychol: Hum. Percept. Perform.* 10:32–39

Egly, R., Homa, D. 1984. Sensitization of the visual field. *J. Exp. Psychol: Hum. Percept. Perform.* 10:778–93

Eich, E. 1984. Memory for unattended events: Remembering with and without awareness. *Mem. Cognit.* 12:105–11

Engel, E. 1958. Binocular fusion of dissimilar figures. *J. Psychol.* 46:53–57

Eriksen, B. A., Eriksen, C. W. 1974. Effects of noise letters upon the identification of a target letter in a nonsearch task. *Percept. Psychophys.* 16:143–49

Eriksen, C. W., Hoffman, J. E. 1972. Temporal and spatial characteristics of selective encoding from visual displays. *Percept. Psychophys.* 12:201–4

Estes, W. K. 1982. Similarity-related channel interactions in visual processing. *J. Exp. Psychol: Hum. Percept. Perform.* 8:353–82

Evett, L. J., Humphreys, G. W. 1981. The use of abstract graphemic information in lexical access. *Q. J. Exp. Psychol.* 33A:325–50

Feustel, T. C., Shiffrin, R. M., Salasoo, A. 1983. Episodic and lexical contributions to the repetition effect in word identification. *J. Exp. Psychol: Gen.* 112:309–46

Fishler, I., Goodman, G. D. 1978. Latency of associated activation in memory. *J. Exp. Psychol: Hum. Percept. Perform.* 4:455–70

Fisk, A. D., Schneider, W. 1983. Category and word search: Generalizing search principles to complex processing. *J. Exp. Psychol: Learn. Mem. Cognit.* 9:177–95

Fowler, C. A., Wolford, G., Slade, R., Tassinary, L. 1981. Lexical access with and without awareness. *J. Exp. Psychol: Gen.* 110:341–62

Francolini, C. M., Egeth, H. 1980. On the non-automaticity of "automatic" activation: Evidence of selective seeing. *Percept. Psychophys.* 27:331–42

Friedman, A. 1979. Framing pictures: The role of knowledge in automatized encoding and memory for gist. *J. Exp. Psychol: Gen.* 108:316–55

Fryklund, I. 1975. Effects of cued-set spatial arrangement and target-background similarity in the partial-report paradigm. *Percept. Psychophys.* 17:375–86

Geller, V., Shaver, P. 1976. Cognitive consequences of self-awareness. *J. Pers. Soc. Psychol.* 12:99–108

Goldstein, E. B., Fink, S. I. 1981. Selective attention in vision: Recognition memory for superimposed line drawings. *J. Exp. Psychol: Hum. Percept. Perform.* 7:954–67

Gummow, L., Miller, P., Dustman, R. E. 1983. Attention and brain injury: A case for cognitive rehabilitation of attentional deficits. *Clin. Psychol. Rev.* 3:255–74

Harter, M. R., Aine, C. J. 1984. Brain mechanisms of visual selective attention. See Parasuraman & Davies 1984, pp. 293–321

Hede, A. J. 1981. Perceptual selection in dichotic listening. *Acta Psychol.* 49:189–200

Heisenberg, W. 1958. *Physics and Philosophy.* New York: Harper

Helson, H. 1933. The fundamental propositions of Gestalt Psychology. *Psychol. Rev.* 40:13–32

Higgins, E. T., Bargh, J. A., Lombardi, W. 1985. Nature of priming effects on categorization. *J. Exp. Psychol: Learn. Mem. Cognit.* 11:59–69

Hillyard, S. A., Kutas, M. 1983. Electrophysiology of cognitive processing. *Ann. Rev. Psychol.* 34:33–61

Hochberg, J. E. 1978. *Perception.* Englewood Cliffs, NJ: Prentice-Hall

Hoffman, J. E. 1979. A two-stage model of visual search. *Percept. Psychophys.* 25:319–27

Hoffman, J. E. 1980. Interaction between global and local levels of a form. *J. Exp. Psychol: Hum. Percept. Perform.* 6:222–34

Hoffman, J. E., Nelson, G., Houck, M. R. 1983. The role of attentional resources in automatic detection. *Cognit. Psychol.* 51:379–410

Holender, D. 1985. Semantic activation without conscious identification in dichotic listening, parafoveal vision, and visual masking: A survey and appraisal. *Behav. Brain Sci.* In press

Holtzman, J. D., Sidtis, J. J., Volpe, B. T., Wilson, D. H., Gazzaniga, M. S. 1984a. Dissociation of spatial information for stimulus localization and the control of attention. *Brain* 104:861–72

Holtzman, J. D., Volpe, B. T., Gazzaniga, M. S. 1984b. Spatial orientation following commissural section. See Parasuraman & Davies 1984, pp. 375–94

Humphreys, G. 1981a. On varying the span of visual attention: Evidence for two modes of spatial attention. *Q. J. Exp. Psychol.* 334:1–15

Humphreys, G. 1981b. Direct vs. indirect tests of the information available from masked displays: What visual masking does and does not prevent. *Br. J. Psychol.* 72:323–30

Inhoff, A. W. 1982. Parafoveal word perception: A further case against semantic preprocessing. *J. Exp. Psychol: Hum. Percept. Perform.* 8:137–45

Iwasaki, S. 1978. The limits of attention and its expansion. *Jpn. Psychol. Res.* 20:133–42

Jacoby, L. L. 1983a. Perceptual enhancement: Persistent effects of an experience. *J. Exp. Psychol: Learn. Mem. Cognit.* 9:21–38

Jacoby, L. L. 1983b. Remembering the data: Analyzing interactive processes in reading. *J. Verb. Learn. Verb. Behav.* 22:485–508

Jacoby, L. L., Dallas, M. 1981. On the relationship between autobiographical memory and perceptual learning. *J. Exp. Psychol: Gen.* 3:306–40

Jacoby, L. L., Witherspoon, D. 1982. Remembering without awareness. *Can. J. Psychol.* 36:300–24

James, W. 1890/1950. *The Principles of Psychology.* New York: Dover

Johnston, W. A. 1978. The intrusiveness of familiar nontarget information. *Mem. Cognit.* 6:38–42

Johnston, W. A., Dark, V. J., 1982. In defense of intraperceptual theories of attention. *J. Exp. Psychol: Hum. Percept. Perform.* 8:407–21

Johnston, W. A., Dark, V. J. 1985. Dissociable domains of selective processing. See Posner & Marin 1985, pp. 567–83

Johnston, W. A., Dark, V. J., Jacoby, L. L. 1985. Perceptual fluency and recognition judgments. *J. Exp. Psychol: Learn. Mem. Cognit.* 11:3–11

Johnston, W. A., Heinz, S. P. 1978. Flexibility and capacity demands of attention. *J. Exp. Psychol: Gen.* 107:420–35

Kahneman, D. 1973. *Attention and Effort.* Englewood Cliffs, NJ: Prentice-Hall

Kahneman, D., Chajczyk, D. 1983. Tests of the automaticity of reading: Dilution of Stroop effects by color-irrelevant stimuli. *J. Exp. Psychol: Hum. Percept. Perform.* 9:497–509

Kahneman, D., Henik, A. 1981. Perceptual organization and attention. In *Perceptual Organization,* ed. M. Kubovey, J. R. Pomerantz, pp. 181–211. Hillsdale, NJ: Erlbaum

Kahneman, D., Treisman, A. 1984. Changing views of attention and automaticity. See Parasuraman & Davies, pp. 29–61

Kahneman, D., Treisman, A., Burkell, J. 1983. The cost of visual filtering. *J. Exp. Psychol: Hum. Percept. Perform.* 9:510–22

Kempley, S. T., Morton, J. 1982. The effects of priming with regularly and irregularly related words in auditory word recognition. *Br. J. Psychol.* 73:441–54

Keren, G. 1976. Some considerations of two alleged kinds of selective attention. *J. Exp. Psychol: Gen.* 105:349–74

Kinchla, R. A., Wolfe, J. M. 1979. The order of visual processing: "Top-down," "bottom-up," or "middle-out." *Percept. Psychophys.* 25:225–31

Kirsner, K., Smith, M. C. 1974. Modality effects in word identification. *Mem. Cognit.* 2:637–40

LaBerge, D. 1975. Acquisition of automatic processing in perceptual and associative learning. See Rabbitt & Dornic 1975, pp. 50–64

LaBerge, D. 1983. Spatial extent of attention to letters and words. *J. Exp. Psychol: Hum. Percept. Perform.* 9:371–79

Lewis, J. 1970. Semantic processing of unattended messages using dichotic listening. *J. Exp. Psychol.* 85:225–28

Logan, G. D. 1979. On the use of concurrent memory load to measure attention and automaticity. *J. Exp. Psychol: Hum. Percept. Perform.* 5:189–207

Logan, G. D. 1980. Attention and automaticity in Stroop and priming tasks: Theory and data. *Cognit. Psychol.* 12:523–53

Lowe, D. G., Mitterer, J. O. 1982. Selective and divided attention in a Stroop task. *Can. J. Psychol.* 36:684–700

Lundh, L. G. 1979. Introspection, consciousness, and human information processing. *Scand. J. Psychol.* 20:223–38

MacKay, D. G. 1973. Aspects of a theory of comprehension, memory and attention. *Q. J. Exp. Psychol.* 25:22–40

Marcel, A. J. 1983a. Conscious and unconscious perception: Experiments on visual masking and word recognition. *Cognit. Psychol.* 15:197–237

Marcel, A. J. 1983b. Conscious and unconscious perception: An approach to the relations between phenomenal experience and perceptual processes. *Cognit. Psychol.* 15:238–300

Martin, M. M. 1979. Local and global processing: The role of sparsity. *Mem. Cognit.* 7:476–84

McCauley, C., Parmelee, C. M., Sperber, R. D., Carr, T. H. 1980. Early extraction of meaning from pictures and its relation to conscious identification, *J. Exp. Psychol: Hum. Percept. Perform.* 6:265–76

McClelland, J. J., O'Regan, J. K. 1981. The role of expectations in the use of parafoveal information in reading. *J. Exp. Psychol: Hum. Percept. Perform.* 7:634–44

Merikle, P. M. 1980. Selection from visual persistence by perceptual groups and category membership. *J. Exp. Psychol: Gen.* 109:279–95

Merikle, P. M. 1982. Unconscious perception revisited. *Percept. Psychophys.* 31:298–301

Meyer, D. E., Schvaneveldt, R. W., Ruddy, M. G. 1975. Loci of contextual effects on visual word-recognition. See Rabbitt & Dornic 1975, pp. 98–118

Moray, N. 1959. Attention in dichotic listening: Affective cues and the influence of instructions. *Q. J. Exp. Psychol.* 11:56–60

Moray, N. 1970. *Attention: Selective Processes in Vision and Hearing.* New York: Academic

Mountcastle, V. B. 1978. Brain mechanisms for directed attention. *J. R. Soc. Med.* 71:14–27

Näätänen, R. 1982. Processing negativity: An evoked-potential reflection of selective attention. *Psychol. Bull.* 92:605–40

Navon, D. 1977. Forest before trees: The precedence of global features in visual perception. *Cognit. Psychol.* 9:353–83

Navon, D., Gopher, D. 1979. On the economy of the human processing system. *Psychol. Rev.* 86:214–55

Neisser, U. 1967. *Cognitive Psychology.* New York: Appleton-Century-Crofts

Neisser, U. 1976. *Cognition and Reality.* San Francisco: Freeman

Neisser, U., Becklen, R. 1975. Selective looking: Attending to visually specified events. *Cognit. Psychol.* 7:480–94

Nielsen, L. L., Sarason, I. G. 1981. Emotion, personality, and selective attention. *J. Pers. Soc. Psychol.* 41:945–60

Ninio, A., Kahneman, D. 1974. Reaction time

in focused and in divided attention. *J. Exp. Psychol.* 103:394–99

Nissen, M. J. 1985. Accessing features and objects: Is location special? See Posner & Marin 1985

Norman, D. A., Bobrow, D. B. 1975. On data-limited and resource-limited processes. *Cognit. Psychol.* 7:44–64

Oatman, L. C. 1984. *Auditory evoked-potential amplitude during simultaneous visual stimulation.* Presented at Ann. Meet. Psychon. Soc., San Antonio

Paap, K. R., Newsome, S. L. 1981. Parafoveal information is not sufficient to produce semantic or visual priming. *Percept. Psychophys.* 29:457–66

Palmer, S. E. 1975. The effects of contextual scenes on the identification of objects. *Mem. Cognit.* 3:519–26

Parasuraman, R., Davies, D. R., eds. 1984. *Varieties of Attention.* Orlando, FL: Academic

Philpott, A., Wilding, J. 1979. Semantic interference from subliminal stimuli in a dichoptic viewing situation. *Br. J. Psychol.* 70:559–63

Podgorny, P., Shepard, R. N. 1983. Distribution of visual attention over space. *J. Exp. Psychol: Hum. Percept. Perform.* 9:380–93

Pomerantz, J. R. 1983. Global and local precedence: Selective attention in form and motion perception. *J. Exp. Psychol: Gen.* 112:516–40

Posner, M. I., Boies, S. W. 1971. Components of attention. *Psychol. Rev.* 78:391–408

Posner, M. I., Cohen, Y. 1984. Components of visual orienting. In *Attention and Performance,* ed. H. Bouma, D. Bowhuis, 10:531–56. Hillsdale, NJ: Erlbaum

Posner, M. I., Marin, O. S. M., eds. 1985. *Mechanisms of Attention: Attention and Performance,* Vol. 11. Hillsdale, NJ: Erlbaum. In press

Posner, M. I., Snyder, C. R. R. 1975a. Facilitation and inhibition in the processing of signals. See Rabbitt & Dornic 1975, pp. 669–82

Posner, M. I., Snyder, C. R. R. 1975b. Attention and cognitive control. In *Information Processing and Cognition: The Loyola Symposium,* ed. R. L. Solso, pp. 55–85. Hillsdale, NJ: Erlbaum

Posner, M. I., Snyder, C. R. R., Davidson, B. J. 1980. Attention and the detection of signals. *J. Exp. Psychol: Gen.* 109:160–74

Posner, M. I., Walker, J. A., Friedrich, F. J., Rafal, R. D. 1984. Effects of parietal injury on covert orienting of attention. *J. Neurosc.* 4:1863–74

Prinzmetal, W. 1981. Principles of feature integration in visual perception. *Percept. Psychophys.* 30:330–40

Prinzmetal, W., Banks, W. P. 1977. Good

continuation affects visual detection. *Percept. Psychophys.* 21:389–95

Prinzmetal, W., Millis-Wright, M. 1984. Cognitive and linguistic factors affect visual feature integration. *Cognit. Psychol.* 16:305–40

Purcell, G., Stewart, L., Stanovich, K. E. 1983. Another look at semantic priming without awareness. *Percept. Psychophys.* 34:65–71

Rabbitt, P. M. A., Dornic, S., eds. 1975. *Attention and Performance,* Vol. 5. New York: Academic

Rabbitt, P. M. A., Vyas, S. 1979. Memory and data-driven control of selective attention in continuous tasks. *Can. J. Psychol./Rev. Can. Psychol.* 33:71–87

Rayner, K., McConkie, G. W., Ehrlich, S. 1978. Eye movements integrating information across fixation. *J. Exp. Psychol: Hum. Percept. Perform.* 4:529–44

Remington, R., Pierce, L. 1984. Moving attention: Evidence for time-invariant shifts of visual selective attention. *Percept. Psychophys.* 35:393–99

Riley, D. A., Leith, C. R. 1976. Multidimensional psychophysics and selective attention in animals. *Psychol. Bull.* 83:138–60

Rock, I., Gutman, D. 1981. The effect of inattention on form perception. *J. Exp. Psychol: Hum. Percept. Perform.* 7:275–85

Schiepers, C. 1980. Response latency and accuracy in visual word recognition. *Percept. Psychophys.* 27:71–81

Schneider, W., Dumais, S. T., Shiffrin, R. M. 1984. Automatic and control processing and attention. See Parasuraman & Davies 1984, pp. 1–27

Schneider, W., Fisk, D. 1984. Automatic category search and its transfer. *J. Exp. Psychol: Learn. Mem. Cognit.* 10:1–15

Schneider, W., Shiffrin, R. M. 1977. Controlled and automatic human information processing: I. Detection, search, and attention. *Psychol. Rev.* 84:1–66

Shaw, M., Shaw, P. 1977. Optimal allocation of cognitive resources to spatial location. *J. Exp. Psychol: Hum. Percept. Perform.* 3:201–11

Shiffrin, R. M. 1985. Attention. In *Stevens' Handbook of Experimental Psychology,* ed. R. C. Atkinson, R. J. Herrnstein, G. Lindsey, R. D. Luce. New York: Wiley. In press

Shiffrin, R. M., Schneider, W. 1977. Controlled and automatic human information processing: II. Perceptual learning, automatic attending, and a general theory. *Psychol. Rev.* 84:127–90

Skelton, J. M., Eriksen, C. W. 1976. Spatial characteristics of selective attention in letter matching. *Bull. Psychon. Soc.* 7:136–38

Snyder, M., Swann, W. B. Jr. 1978. Hypothesis testing processes in social interaction. *J. Pers. Soc. Psychol.* 36:1202–12

Snyder, M., Uranowitz, S. W. 1978. Reconstructing the past: Some cognitive consequences of person perception. *J. Pers. Soc. Psychol.* 36:941–50

Sperling, G., Reeves, A. 1980. Measuring the reaction time of a shift of visual attention. In *Attention and Performance,* ed. R. S. Nickerson, 8:347–60. Hillsdale, NJ: Erlbaum

Stroop, J. R. 1935. Studies of interference in serial verbal reactions. *J. Exp. Psychol.* 18:643–62

Taylor, S. E., Crocker, J. 1981. Schematic bases of social information processing. In *Social Cognition: The Ontario Symposium,* ed. E. T. Higgins, C. P. Heiman, M. P. Zanna, pp. 89–134. Hillsdale, NJ: Erlbaum

Treisman, A. M. 1960. Contextual cues in selective listening. *Q. J. Exp. Psychol.* 12:242–48

Treisman, A. M. 1964. Verbal cues, language and meaning in selective attention. *Am. J. Psychol.* 77:206–19

Treisman, A. M. 1969. Strategies and models of selective attention. *Psychol. Rev.* 76:282–99

Treisman, A. M. 1982. Perceptual grouping and attention in visual search for features and for objects. *J. Exp. Psychol: Hum. Percept. Perform.* 8:194–214

Treisman, A. M., Geffen, G. 1967. Selective attention: Perception or response? *Q. J. Exp. Psychol.* 19:1–17

Treisman, A. M., Gelade, G. 1980. A feature-integration theory of attention. *Cognit. Psychol.* 12:97–136

Treisman, A. M., Kahneman, D., Burkell, J. 1983. Perceptual objects and the cost of filtering. *Percept. Psychophys.* 33:527–32

Treisman, A. M., Riley, J. G. A. 1969. Is selective attention selective perception or selective response? A further test. *J. Exp. Psychol.* 79:27–34

Treisman, A. M., Schmidt, H. 1982. Illusory conjunctions in the perception of objects. *Cognit. Psychol.* 14:107–41

Tsal, Y. 1983. Movements of attention across the visual field, *J. Exp. Psychol: Hum. Percept. Perform.* 9:523–30

Underwood, G. L. 1976. Semantic interference from unattended printed words. *Br. J. Psychol.* 67:327–38

Underwood, G. L. 1977. Facilitation from attended and unattended messages. *J. Verb. Learn. Verb.Behav.* 16:99–106

Van der Heijden, A. H. C., Hagenaar, R., Bloem, W. 1984. Two stages in postcategorical filtering and selection. *Mem. Cognit.* 12:458–69

Vaughn, J. 1984. *Distance of attention switch affects RT only for some stimuli.* Presented at Ann. Meet. Psychon. Soc., San Antonio

von Wright, J. M. 1968. Selection in immediate visual memory. *Q. J. Exp. Psychol.* 20:62–68

Walker, P. 1978. Binocular rivalry: Central or peripheral selective process? *Psychol. Bull.* 85:376–89

Ward, L. M. 1983. On processing dominance: Comment on Pomerantz. *J. Exp. Psychol: Gen.* 112:541–46

Ward, L. M., Logan, G. 1984. *Setting the "focus" parameter of the covert attentional gaze.* Presented at Ann. Meet. Psychon. Soc., San Antonio

Wickens, C. D. 1984. Processing resources in attention. See Parasuraman & Davies 1984, pp. 63–102

Wolford, G., Marchak, F. 1984. *Improvement in a backward masking paradigm.* Presented at Ann. Meet. Psychon. Soc., San Antonio

Wolford, G., Morrison, F. 1980. Processing of unattended visual information. *Mem. Cognit.* 8:521–27

Woods, D. L., Hillyard, S. A., Hansen, J. C. 1984. Event-related brain potentials reveal similar attentional mechanisms during selective listening and shadowing. *J. Exp. Psychol: Hum. Percept. Perform.* 10:761–71

Zimba, L. D., Blake, R. 1983. Binocular rivalry and semantic processing: Out of sight, out of mind. *J. Exp. Psychol: Hum. Percept. Perform.* 9:807–15

Ann. Rev. Psychol. 1986. 37:77–107

THE NEUROCHEMISTRY
OF BEHAVIOR

Jaak Panksepp

Department of Psychology, Bowling Green State University, Bowling Green, Ohio 43403

CONTENTS

THE NEW STOREHOUSE OF NEUROSCIENTIFIC KNOWLEDGE 77
THE QUEST FOR MEANINGFUL RESULTS IN PSYCHOPHARMACOLOGY 83
FUNCTIONS OF MAJOR NEUROCHEMICAL SYSTEMS 86
   Acetylcholine 86
   Serotonin 87
   Norepinephrine 88
   Dopamine 90
   GABA and Other Amino Acids 91
   Nonopioid Peptides 92
   General Function of Brain Opioids 94
   Other Transmitters 96
THE PROMISE OF NEW TECHNIQUES 96
CLOSING REMARKS, WITH A NOTE ON TRANSHYPOTHALAMIC "REWARD"
   CIRCUITS 98

ON THE NEW STOREHOUSE OF NEUROSCIENTIFIC KNOWLEDGE

During the past decade, the quest to understand neurochemical control of behavior has been heading toward paralysis—not a flaccid paralysis, where too few bits of pertinent information are being spilled upon receptive tissues of psychobiologists, but rather, a rigid form, where the outpouring of basic molecular facts has far outstripped the dynamic range of our inductive synapses. In short, it has been a healthy growth period for the accumulation of basic neurochemical and neuroanatomical data, but movement toward neurobehavioral understanding has not kept pace. The aim of this review is to trace the

0066-4308/86/0201-0077$02.00

broad outlines of behaviorally pertinent trends that are emerging from neuroscience research.

From the perspective of an earlier psychobiology, which held out the imminent hope of deriving definitive statements of how neurochemical systems control behavior, it is humbling to view the complex tapestry that modern neuroscience has now revealed. Most neurons contain multiple transmitters (Chan-Palay & Palay 1984), some are of the classic variety that directly control postsynaptic generator potentials, others are of a neuromodulatory sort that act more slowly and indirectly. Multiple receptors also exist for many of the putative transmitters, some (e.g. autoreceptors) which counteract the effects of the classic postsynaptic types (Strange 1983, Snyder 1984). Many synapses exhibit tendencies for homeostatic regulation, developing either subsensitivity or supersensitivity with excessive use or disuse. The complex chemo-architecture of the brain (Björklund & Hökfelt 1983, Emson 1983, Hökfelt et al 1984) is such that all structure-function relationships derived from earlier research are in dire need of reevaluation.

The optimistic manifesto to understanding neurochemical coding of behavior set forth in the 1960s (Miller 1965), the fruits of which were compiled in the early 1970s (Myers 1974, Myers & Drucker-Collin 1974), has come to be tempered by a new reality. The functional neurochemistry of the brain, as revealed largely through receptorology, immunocytochemistry, metabolic imagining, and the chemical analysis of synthetic and degradative pathways for transmitters (Lajtha 1982–1983), has forced a realization that most traditional approaches to understanding the neurochemistry of behavior are simply not robust enough to yield definitive answers.

Now that the complexity of the brain is being visualized in earnest with the tools of modern biochemistry and immunology, new strategies for addressing functional issues must be developed. Toward that end, it can no longer be ignored that more than one brain area and more than one neurochemical system participates in each psychobehavioral process. This is evident from a cursory glance at the widespread dispersion of practically every neurochemical information system that has been characterized. An overview of the brain opioid receptor system (Figure 1) highlights this issue. Opioid receptors, in this case of the δ and μ variety, are widely distributed throughout most of the brain (Panksepp & Bishop 1981, Herkenham & Pert 1982), suggesting that many brain functions are modulated by opioid activity. Similar pictures have been obtained for other receptor systems (Kuhar 1982)—for acetylcholine (Churchill et al 1984), adenosine (Goodman & Snyder 1982, Bisserbe et al 1985), benzodiazepines (Young & Kuhar 1980), bombesin (Zarbin et al 1985), cholecystokinin (Zarbin et al 1983), GABA (Pan et al 1983), glutamate (Green-amyre et al 1984, Halpain et al 1984), substance P (Mantyh et al 1984), and thyrotropin-releasing hormone (TRH) (Mantyh & Hunt 1985), to name a few.

Furthermore, peculiar transmitter-receptor relationships have been detected in many systems. Brain areas that contain high levels of receptors do not routinely have high levels of the appropriate transmitters, and conversely, areas rich in certain transmitters are not necessarily enriched with the pertinent receptors—a finding that has been noted for neurotensin, opioids, Substance P, and TRH, among others (see Mantyh & Hunt 1985 for references). It is not yet clear whether such inverse relationships suggest (*a*) that such transmitters act not only locally but also at long distances, or (*b*) receptor proliferation (i.e. supersensitivity) in terminal areas that have modest levels of transmitter release, or (*c*) merely the distance between cell bodies and synaptic terminal fields. How, then, are we to interpret the behavioral effects of such substances administered directly into pertinent brain sites? In any event, the anatomy of identified systems provides no optimism that unidimensional hypotheses will ever encapsulate the functions of most neurochemical systems.

Just as each neurochemical system influences functions in many different brain areas, many neurochemical systems converge upon a single brain area. Indeed, certain brain regions bind a remarkably large number of distinct ligands. It is becoming almost routine to see the central nucleus of amygdala, the interpeduncular nucleus, and the external layer of the superior colliculus bind practically every radioactive ligand that is applied to rat brain tissue. Likewise, immunocytochemistry has highlighted remarkable hotbeds of peptide activity such as the bed nucleus of the stria terminalis, the paraventricular nucleus of the hypothalamus, and the external layer of the dorsal horn in the spinal cord. Such architectural features appear to be common in the brain. Presumably, at many such convergence points, multimodal neural activity is helping weave key higher-order processes of the nervous system which remain untapped by existing psychobehavioral tools.

Perhaps the most striking example of this at present is that of the septal area, a major way-station between lower brain stem and higher hemispheric processes. This area contains acetylcholine, serotonin, dopamine, norepinephrine, epinephrine, GABA, glutamine, enkephalin, substance P, neurotensin, vasopressin, vasoactive intestinal peptide, somatostatin, cholecystokinin, and others (for references see Costa et al 1983, DeVries & Buijs 1983, Panula et al 1984). On the behavioral side, Grossman (1976) expressed pessimism in understanding the septal area in unitary terms, pointing out that "just about every behavior and/or psychological function which has been investigated to date has shown to be affected in some way by septal lesions, and attempts to account for these diverse effects in term of meaningful neural dysfunctions have become increasingly convoluted and improbable" (p. 361). Still, even in the

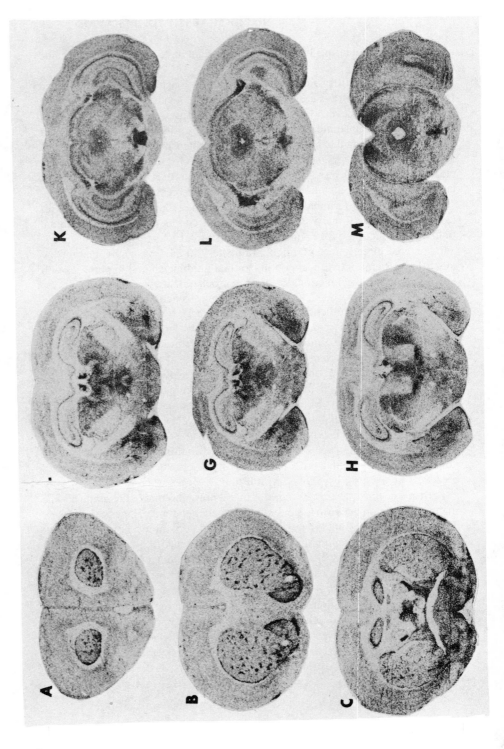

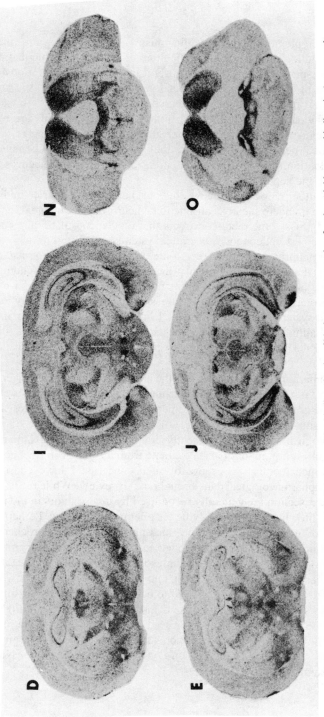

Figure 1   Autoradiographs of in vivo tritiated diprenorphine binding (density of black areas corresponds to δ and μ opioid receptor binding sites) on coronal sections of the rat brain from rostral (upper left) to caudal (lower right) areas (A–O). Anatomical designations can be obtained from Panksepp & Bishop 1981.

midst of such complexity and the prevailing misgivings concerning any unitary theoretical resolution of the existing difficulties, it remains possible that new and broader perspectives may yet prove useful in guiding investigations and organizing findings. For instance, the septal syndrome (DeFrance 1976) may reflect an overall functional dematuration whereby animals regress to earlier phases of behavioral development—explaining why such animals are more active, more emotional, and have shorter attention spans. Of course, such global theoretical perspectives, useful as they may be in guiding behavioral research, do not diminish the need to dissect the diverse neural influences that converge upon the septal area.

Rather than attempting any intensive coverage here of the disparate findings which presently inundate subareas of functional neuroscience, my goal for this chapter is to discuss some meta-constructs that may encapsulate the general functions of the best understood transmitter systems of the brain (e.g. acetylcholine, norepinephrine, dopamine, serotonin, GABA, opioids). For instance, I would suggest that a unitary functional principle underlying opioid function in the brain is the homeostatic reestablishment of baseline conditions in many types of neuronal circuits following stressful perturbations. Many other neurochemical systems, such as adenosine (Snyder 1985), the various amino acid circuits (Lajtha 1983), and most of the recently visualized peptide systems (Krieger et al 1983), will receive little attention in the limited space available here.

Before summarizing empirical work in the area, I will discuss some general methodological issues that need to be considered in drawing inferences about neurochemical control of behavior from psychopharmacological research. These concerns are raised because of the massive amount of psychopharmacological data that are presently available—a substantial amount of it being difficult, if not impossible, to evaluate from the perspective of normal neurophysiological controls. Because of such concerns, I have chosen to emphasize nonpharmacological data throughout this review. While the issues I raise in the next section are generally recognized by investigators in the field, there has been little headway in resolving the dilemmas they pose. Perhaps it is as important to highlight the conceptual sticking-points in the neurochemical analyses of brain systems as to gather together the progress in as integrative a manner as possible. If these problems go unresolved, the signal-to-noise ratio in the literature can only get worse. Although no one can yet prescribe how such problems are to be solved, the areas need to be highlighted boldly for anyone wishing to make sense of the all too abundant literature. Perhaps spotlighting the problems will cause them to be addressed more empirically in the future. The reader who does not want to dwell on such methodological-interpretive, concerns may wish to skip to the section on "Functions of the Major Neurochemical Systems."

THE QUEST FOR MEANINGFUL RESULTS IN PSYCHOPHARMACOLOGY

Considering the complex anatomies of most neurochemical systems, it appears highly likely that traditional psychopharmacological approaches have generated epiphenomena as often as physiologically meaningful results. It is doubtful that all synapses affected by peripherally administered drugs are modulated in unison during ongoing brain transactions of the organism. In addition, synapses work within certain ranges of transmission, but psychoactive drugs surely drive neural activity above or below those normal dynamic ranges. In other words, drugs may all too often disrupt the normal phasic activity of synapses, yielding behavioral effects which may be essentially irrelevant to understanding normal brain functions.

Feeding research is a case in point. Practically any item taken off the drug shelf can reduce food intake, but such effects rarely highlight normal brain mechanisms of energy balance regulation. To distill physiological meaning from such work, a host of behavioral control tests are needed, ranging from the straightforward, such as conditioned taste aversion tests, to the subtle, such as the ability of normal satiety to resurrect complex behaviors (e.g. play) which are markedly reduced by hunger (Siviy & Panksepp 1985).

Even the dictum to collect dose-response data does not assure meaningful results. In fact, such work all too often promotes confusion. For instance, many drug effects reverse as higher doses are used: modest GABA blockade with picrotoxin increases shock-induced fighting while high doses reduce the behavior (Rodgers & DePaulis 1982); morphine has similar biphasic effects on play (Panksepp et al 1985a) and amphetamine on food intake (Blundell & Latham 1978), to name a few. In general, behavioral effects obtained at low drug doses may be physiologically more meaningful than those which require higher doses. From that perspective, I would claim that the higher nervous system function of brain opioids is more likely to be the modulation of negative affect rather than the control of somatic pain. Very low, nonanalgesic doses of morphine can quell separation-induced crying in many species (Panksepp 1981a, Panksepp et al 1985b). It might promote psychobiological understanding more if behavioral studies were directed toward seeking and fully characterizing very low-dose drug effects rather than constructing dose-response curves which all too often can be functionally misleading.

However, since dose-response curves are destined to remain a demand characteristic of most psychopharmacological research, perhaps the shape of such curves could help alert us to especially meaningful results. The most important behavioral findings (considering the limited neurochemical range in which synapses normally operate) may not be reflected in gradual functions, but rather in steep step-functions across narrow dose ranges. For instance, while many norepinephrine receptor antagonists yield shallow dose-response effects on isolation-induced distress vocalizations (DVs), perhaps suggesting nonspecific effects, clonidine provokes a precipitous decline in DVs with only modest increases in the amount of drug administered (Rossi et al 1983). In any event, arguments of behavioral specificity need to be bolstered by demonstrations of opposing effects being induced by opposite manipulations of a neurochemical system, as well as by analysis of drug effects on several distinct types of psychobehavioral processes.

Localized central administration of drugs has similar problems, but in addition, such approaches surely modify neural activity in ways never encountered by the normally functioning brain. The central administration approach permits, however, assessment of a major dilemma of psychopharmacological research—that a single neurochemical system exerts opposing effects in different parts of the brain. Clearly, new strategies are needed to provide a relevant baseline by which the older psychopharmacological findings can be evaluated. The analysis of patterns of transmitter release in the functioning organism (Marsden 1984) and the recording of activity from neurochemically identifed neurons in the waking brain (Jacobs 1984) are especially promising in this regard.

Also, it is desirable to validate that a drug is doing what it is supposed to be doing in the brain. Unfortunately, findings from such molecular studies can all too readily be overgeneralized as causes of observed behavioral effects. The recent case of clonidine is especially poignant in this regard, since the drug has been found to be highly effective in attenuating narcotic (Gold et al 1979) and other withdrawal symptoms (Rossi et al 1983, Glassman et al 1984). Clonidine dramatically reduces the firing of norepinephrine (NE) neurons in the locus coeruleus via autoreceptor inhibition (Aghajanian 1978), and since the same cells contain an abundance of opiate receptors which also inhibit firing, that neural change has been deemed essential for the withdrawal alleviating effects of clonidine. Unfortunately, direct tests [using animals in which NE cells have been destroyed with the neurotoxin 6-hydroxydopamine (6-OHDA)] indicate that clonidine effects are not attenuated and hence the drug alleviates negative emotions by other than NE autoreceptor mechanisms (Rossi et al 1983, Britton et al 1984).

One final complexity is the issue of psychobehavioral taxonomy. Obviously, insights into the neurochemistry of behavior can be no more incisive than our understanding of behavior itself, but unfortunately, there is no agreed-upon taxonomy of basic psychobehavioral systems. Hence, any working hypothesis concerning neurochemical control of behavior must presently be provisional indeed. Many key processes that control animal behavior, such as those that mediate mood and emotions (Panksepp 1982, Plutchik & Kellerman 1985), have received so little systematic psychobiological attention that more conceptual and behavioral-descriptive work needs to be done before any coherent neurochemistry of behavior can be established. The emphasis of several labs toward the analysis of fundamental natural behaviors (Robinson 1983) such as the acoustic startle reflex (M. Davis 1980), animal facial gestures related to gustatory acceptance and rejection (Grill & Norgren 1978), biting reflexes (Hutchinson & Renfrew 1978), natural patterns of aggression (Blanchard et al 1977), and exploratory sniffing (see Panksepp 1981a) is a welcome trend toward the development of simple behavioral systems which are amenable to rigorous analysis.

In our own research of the past decade, we have been guided by the working hypothesis that behaviors related to social separation distress and social play are mediated by robust neuro-affective processes that are very amenable to a psychobiological analysis (Panksepp et al 1984, 1985b). Surely other basic psychobiological processes, such as awareness, curiosity, and greed, will also have to be analyzed (difficult as they may be to operationalize) before a coherent neurochemistry of behavior can emerge. Thus, at present, the weakest link in understanding brain function is, unfortunately, the psychological one. While we may know a great deal about highly concrete behaviors such as feeding, drinking, sexuality, and aggression (as summarized many times before: e.g. Morgane & Panksepp 1980–1981, Pfaff 1982), as well as behaviors related to powerful negative incentives such as foot-shock (Anisman & Bignami 1978), our understanding of the many central states that modulate these behaviors is primitive indeed. Although most of the established transmitter systems can affect most behaviors that are studied in the laboratory, I will not attempt to compile those results here. Rather, my aim is to focus on the possible generalized functions of various neurochemical systems in the control of those global psychobehavioral processes via which many of the more specific effects described in the literature may be mediated.

Since most of the empirical work in mammals has been conducted upon only a few types of laboratory animals, generalizations across species must remain in doubt. However, evolution can only build upon preexisting solutions, and for basic subcortical processes, homologies appear to abound (Panksepp 1982). Many of the neuropeptides that have been revealed recently (Krieger et al 1983) exist in prokaryotes (Le Roith et al 1984), and striking parallels exist between apparent neurochemical functions in mammals and more simple species. For instance, dopamine activates feeding programs in mammals as well as mollusks (Wieland & Gelperin 1983). Opiate receptors, now well established as modulators of appetite (Morley et al 1983), have comparable effects in amoeba (Josefsson & Johansson 1979). Although it may be premature to conclude that functional homologies will be the rule rather than the exception in neurochemical analyses of behavior, the available evidence offers more than modest hope in that direction. Although there are species differences to be cataloged, most psychoactive drugs do have qualitatively similar effects in all mammals. The ability of yohimbine to promote sexual behavior in male rats (Clark et al 1984) and in human males (Morales et al 1982) is only one recent provocative case in point.

FUNCTIONS OF THE MAJOR NEUROCHEMICAL SYSTEMS

For the critical issues and the abundant data that cannot be summarized here, the reader may refer to *The Chemistry of Behavior* (Reinis & Goldman 1982), which can be well supplemented with some *Fundamentals of Neuropsychopharmacology* (Feldman & Quenzer 1984), so one can begin to comprehend the deeper meaning of *Neurotransmitters in Action* (Bousfield 1985). The many-volumed *Handbook of Psychopharmacology* edited by Iversen, Iversen & Snyder (1975–1984, Vols. 1–18) contains chapter upon chapter of indispensable reading in the area, as do the volumes in the *International Review of Neurobiology* (Smythies & Bradley 1959–1984) and *Progress in Psychobiology and Physiological Psychology* (Sprague & Epstein 1976–1983). Work in the area is moving along at such a frenzied pace that in a short time we shall have another *Psychopharmacology: A Generation of Progress* (Lipton et al 1978), and one hopes that each generation to come will be more enriching than the last. The ongoing elucidation of the details of the underlying systems can be found in The *Handbook of Neurochemistry* (Lajtha 1982–1983, Vols. 1–10) and *Advances in Biochemical Psychopharmacology* (Costa & Greengard, 1969–1984, Vols. 1–39).

Acetylcholine

Quite obviously, the study of behavior is the study of the release of acetylcholine (ACh) at the nicotinic neuromuscular junction. If there is a common theme to be extracted from the plethora of data implicating brain ACh in a variety of functions including arousal, attention, and memory as well as a host of more specific motivated behaviors such as aggression, sexuality, and thirst (Goldberg & Hanin 1976), it is that ACh is an action system in the brain (both in motor as well as sensory processing terms)—it helps elaborate the ability to focus on the environment and achieve a coherent behavioral response—a function reminiscent of the basic role of this transmitter at the neuromuscular junction.

The attentional functions of ACh (Cheal 1981, Warburton 1981) help explain the putative functions of this system in establishing memories (Deutsch 1983). In addition, ACh appears to be essential for the elaboration of REM sleep (see McGinty & Drucker-Colin 1982), which further implicates ACh in higher-order associative processes. These perspectives fit well with the finding that a major neurochemical correlate of senile dementia is deficient cholinergic processing in the brain (Bartus et al 1982, Coyle et al 1983).

Whether the diverse motivated and emotional behaviors that are mediated by brain ACh reflect the operation of differentiable circuits or some common shared process—such as a change in mood—remains unknown. Cholinergic activity in the brain appears to trigger several distinct emotions. Defensive and fearful behaviors, often with vocalizations, can be provoked in cats by application of cholinomimetics to widespread subcortical sites (Brudzynksi & Eckersdorf 1984, Myers 1974). Curariform drugs, which presumably act on nicotinic synapses in the brain (whether as agonist or antagonist remains unclear for the CNS), can also evoke highly distressed vocalizations in domestic chicks when applied directly to the brain (Panksepp et al 1983), and increased cholinergic activity in humans can instigate crying with deep despondency (Berger et al 1979).

To the contrary, pleasure has been evoked in humans by localized cholinergic stimulation of the septum (Heath 1972), while self-stimulation in animals can be reduced by antimuscarinic agents placed into the ventral tegmental area (Kofman & Yeomans 1984). The presumably pleasurable activity of social play is also markedly reduced by blockade of muscarinic cholinergic activity (Thor & Holloway 1984), while the nicotinic receptor blocking agent mecamylamine can modestly increase play (Panksepp et al 1984). Thus, it seems evident that the cholinergic system can promote central states with both positive and negative affective attributes, and most peripheral drug strategies probably cannot yield clear answers with regard to the role of cholinergic circuits in normal behavior. Still, the general picture is that cholinergic activity in the brain helps organisms focus better on environmental and internal events and to recruit appropriate behavioral response. Thus, it seems reasonable that certain mood disorders are linked to cholinergic imbalance in the brain (Davis & Berger 1979), and considerable interest has arisen in the preliminary report that depression may be diagnosed by increased cholinergic binding sites on skin fibroblasts (Nadi et al 1984).

Serotonin

The coherent anatomy and electrophysiology of serotonin neurons in the brainstem (Jacobs et al 1984a,b) offers promise for a unified brain function being established for this system, and that function appears to be general inhibition of all behavioral tendencies. The pharmacological literature abundantly demonstrates that practically every type of motivated and emotional behavior (feeding, aggression, play, sexual and maternal behaviors) can be reduced by facilitation of serotonin activity (Vogt 1982) except for sleep, which is, of course, promoted (Jouvet 1972). Although the data with respect to reduction of serotonin activity are not as clear-cut (perhaps partially because the available manipulations are not as definitive), such animals are generally hyperactive, hyperemotional, and hypermotivational, sometimes to the point of not being able to sleep well, with a tendency toward hallucinatory (REM?) activity (Jacobs 1978).

Neural activity of serotonin cells in the raphe presently can be recorded with relative ease. Their activity is slow and regular and state dependent— decreasing from waking to slow wave sleep, with the rostral cell groups generally ceasing activity with REM (McGinty & Drucker-Colin 1982). Although the cells are responsive to environmental stressors, they are best characterized by stable, self-generated rhythms which are impervious to routine environmental changes (Jacobs et al 1984b).

At one time it was proposed that the antianxiety effects of minor tranquilizers were mediated by reduced serotonin turnover in the brain (Stein et al 1975), because both benzodiazepines and drugs that reduce serotonin activity exhibit antipunishment effects. The release of punished behaviors by serotonin antagonists, however, is readily explained by the fact that serotonin is a generalized gain suppressor for all waking activities. If anything, facilitation of serotonin activity tends to inhibit elaboration of all emotions, including negative ones like fear-anxiety.

Norepinephrine

Norepinephrine (NE) systems (Moore & Bloom 1979) have many distinct receptors (Jones et al 1985), some with very strong autoregulatory functions, making psychopharmacological data generally difficult to interpret. The single unit data, however, lend themselves to an elegant simplicity. Because of the tight homogeneous clustering of NE cells in the locus coeruleus of the rat, one can readily obtain NE unit recordings from the waking animal. Definitive work indicates that NE cells are state sensitive just like serotonin cells (neuronal firing decreasing with sleep and ceasing at the onset of REM). In the waking state, such NE cells are exquisitely responsive to all occurrences in the environment to which the organism responds (Aston-Jones & Bloom 1981a,b). This sensitivity is in agreement with a mass of data implicating NE arousal during all stressful circumstances, an effect that is markedly reduced in animals permitted control in the situation (Anisman 1978, Stone 1983).

Although NE generally inhibits neuronal firing in sensory projection areas of the cortex, it simultaneously amplifies signal-to-noise ratios of incoming stimuli (Foote et al 1983). Thus, the traditional assumption that NE mediates attentional processes, especially selective attention (Mason 1981), and hence possibly learning and memory formation (D. Roberts 1981), has generally been supported, but there is no evidence for specificity in the operation of the system. Further, presently it is not clear how the attention-promoting properties of NE and ACh systems differ, nor whether the roles of other NE systems (i.e. the ventral pathways) differ from the dorsal ones. Preliminary evidence suggests that damage to ventral components also attenuates EEG indexes of waking arousal (Panksepp et al 1973).

In any event, older analyses which ascribed highly specific motivational functions to NE circuits should be viewed skeptically. For instance, the extensive evidence of noradrenergic "feeding circuits" (as reviewed by Leibowitz 1980) may need to be revised within the context of how these cells orchestrate overall brain activity. During starvation one would anticipate better information processing in the brain with respect to biologically relevant stimuli, perhaps explaining why NE turnover is increased by food deprivation (Glick et al 1973). The ensuing amplification of signal-to-noise processes may operate on all sensory systems including taste detection so as to facilitate responsivity to relevant foodstuffs, explaining why animals induced to eat by NE application to the brain are unusually responsive to the incentive properties of food (Booth & Quartermain 1965). Further, it has recently been found that neuropeptide Y, which is co-localized in NE cells, can strongly promote feeding (Levine & Morley 1984). Food deprivation may also increase the secretion of this peptide, perhaps yielding specific behavioral effects on the background of a more generalized, NE-mediated sensory arousal. The role of NE systems in reward (e.g. self-stimulation) (German & Bowden 1974) has also become dubious (Corbett & Wise 1979), but it seems quite clear that animals selectively depleted of brain NE do show markedly diminished appetitive behavior (Rossi et al 1982, Zolovick et al 1982).

Of course, brain NE systems operate in concert with a host of interacting neurochemistries, as do all other systems (e.g. Butcher 1978, Garattini et al 1978). Generally, serotonin seems to counteract NE effects in the brain. For instance, the appetite reduction that can be achieved by reduction of brain NE is markedly amplified by facilitation of brain serotonin activity (Rossi et al 1982). More surprisingly, brain NE seems to counteract brain dopamine (DA) activity (Antelman & Caggiula 1977). For instance, unilateral destruction of the locus ceruleus causes increased DA activity in the ipsilateral cerebral hemisphere, suggesting the enhanced DA mechanisms may help compensate for chronic NE denervation of the cortex (Harik 1984). Being neurochemical relatives, it seems perplexing that NE and DA would oppose each other, but maybe that is really not the case in behavioral terms. If one considers the major functions of NE and DA as being sensory and psychomotor arousal, respectively (Panksepp 1981a, Robbins & Everitt 1982), it would be reasonable for the two systems to operate synergistically, albeit in tandem. When an animal is confronted by a new situation, sensory arousal should be amplified and motor arousal momentarily diminished (the orienting response). As the animal becomes accustomed to the situation, psychomotor arousal should increasingly prevail so as to promote success in acquiring available reward in a familiar situation. Thus, dampened activity of DA cells during the orienting response (Steinfels et al 1983), may be, at least partially, a NE-mediated phenomenon. As NE activity diminishes, foraging behaviors and anticipatory eagerness may prevail, with an intensity and persistence dictated by DA activity. Thereby, neurophysiological antagonism of NE and DA may actually represent the normal cascade of sensory and motor arousal in the well-functioning organism.

It has also been suggested that high NE activity in the brain promotes anxiety (Redmond & Huang 1979). As with the serotonin hypothesis of anxiety, this may largely be a case of misplaced emphasis. NE can amplify the sensory response to any situation, and if the environment is already conducive to anxiety, those will be the symptoms amplified by invigorated NE release in the brain. Finally, the fact that NE cells have an intrinsically generated rhythm affirms that they serve to provide background, pacemaker activity for all waking activities (Andrade & Aghajanian 1984). The increasing interest of clinical investigators in the functions of NE in humans (e.g. Zuckerman 1984) should promote identification of the more subtle psychological effects of this neuronally modest but widely ramifying transmitter system in the brain.

Dopamine

Considering the role of altered DA activity in the pathogenesis of Parkinson's disease and schizophrenic disorders, the search for the fundamental behavioral functions of brain DA systems has been intensive. A consensus exists that DA activity promotes a generalized ability for response initiation (Robbins & Everitt 1982), with perhaps a more specific role in triggering species-typical instinctive processes related to positive incentives (pleasure-foraging) (see Wise 1982), as well as negative incentives (Antelman & Chiodo 1984). It appears certain that DA is a key, albeit not the sole, positive influence on self-stimulation behavior (Wise & Bozarth 1984)—an influence that can be depleted by stress (Zacharko et al 1983).

Dopamine cells are anatomically well restricted (Moore & Bloom 1978) and have a unique type of firing pattern by which they can be electrophysiologically identified (Bunney 1979). In anesthetized animals, DA cells increase firing in response to various external stimuli (Chiodo et al 1980). However, unlike NE and serotonin neurons, the basal activity of DA cells is not markedly affected by changing vigilance states (Trulson & Preussler 1984)—only their phasic response tendencies diminish during sleep (Steinfels et al 1983). Since DA cells maintain a tonic level of activity through the sleep-waking cycle (perhaps providing a background state of response readiness), the role of these systems in normal behavior should be premised more on identification of variables that increase firing of DA cells than on pharmacological prevention of DA transmission [as with high doses of neuroleptics, which severely compromise motor abilities, yielding animals that only exhibit vigorous behavior in life-threatening situations such as underwater mazes (Ungerstedt 1979).

Studies in waking animals indicate that DA neurons can respond to both positive incentive cues predicting food (Miller et al 1981) and stressful situations such as the conditioned emotional reaction paradigm (Trulson & Preussler 1984). Two electrophysiologically distinct types of dopamine cells exist in the mesencephalon (Chiodo et al 1980), and it is possible that some are attuned mainly to positive incentives while others respond preferentially to negative ones. In any event, stress-responsive DA systems are directed more toward cortical terminal fields than limbic or striatal ones (Blanc et al 1980).

Although it is generally agreed that brain DA systems promote an animal's ability to interact with both positive and negative incentives, considerable diversity of opinion exists as to the exact psychobehavioral functions they elaborate (see discussion with Wise 1982). The probability that DA arousal participates directly in the registration of reinforcement is remote since secondary reinforcement processes are not consistently dampened by DA receptor blockade (Tombaugh et al 1982). Also, while DA activity promotes goal-directed activity, the cells do not markedly change firing in conjunction with discrete motor movements (DeLong et al 1983). Thus, DA activity appears to be largely permissive for the expression of sensory-motor processing of motivated behaviors (Marshall et al 1981), and the behavioral output loops governened by DA circuits are presently under intense investigation (Chandler & Goldberg 1984, Yang & Mogenson 1984).

In summary, it is the judgment of this writer that the general function of DA activity in appetitive behavior is to promote the expression of motivational excitement and anticipatory eagerness—the heightened energization of animals searching for and expecting rewards (Panksepp 1981a, 1985). Low doses of neuroleptics do not prevent an animal from making appetitive associations, they simply diminish the vitality and vigor animals exhibit in their interactions with the environment. DA activity in the brain appears akin to compression in an internal combustion engine. When it is diminished, the system can do practically everything it did before, it simply does it with less gusto. This aspect of animal behavior, so evident in most appetitive situations, deserves more empirical scrutiny than it has yet received.

GABA and Other Amino acids

GABA is the most ubiquitous inhibitory transmitter in the brain (both behaviorally and electrophysiologically) (Krogsgaard-Larsen et al 1979). Although there are several long-axoned GABA pathways, most serve as interneurons, providing local inhibitory control over action systems of the brain. E. Roberts (1979) has offered a compelling general hypothesis for GABA function in the brain whereby "behavior sequences, innate or learned, are released to function at varying rates and in various combinations largely by the disinhibition of pacemaker neurons whose activities are under the control of tonically active inhibitory command neurons, many of which may use GABA as a transmitter" (p. 535). In other words, most of the brain potential for action has to be under restraint, with well-orchestrated release within restricted subcircuits.

The pharmacological work is generally consistent with such a hypothesis. Most motivated and emotive behaviors, ranging from feeding (Cooper et al 1980, Panksepp & Meeker 1980) to aggression (Rodgers & DePaulis 1982) are reduced by facilitation of GABA activity. Indeed, low GABA activity has been implicated in overaroused states of the nervous system, ranging from epilepsy (Fariello et al 1985) to anxiety (Hoehn-Saric 1982). A close relationship between GABA and benzodiazepine receptor system has been established (Tallman & Gallagher 1985), having substantial implications for understanding anxiety as well as other psychiatric disorders (Lloyd et al 1983).

Being as ubiquitous as it is, normal GABA functions are almost impossible to study credibly using peripheral pharmacological maneuvers, but central studies have yielded some paradoxes for the sweeping generalization that GABA exerts a general inhibitory effect on behavior. For instance, muscimol, a potent GABA receptor agonist, can evoke arousal (Ossowska et al 1984) and self-mutilation (Baumeister & Frye 1984) when placed into extrapyramidal structures. It can also increase feeding when placed into the hypothalamus (Grandison & Guidotti 1977). Perhaps results such as these can be explained via disinhibition (inhibition of inhibition) and autoreceptor inhibition of GABA cell firing. For instance, muscimol applied to the substantia nigra promotes DA cell firing (Scheel-Krüger et al 1979). However, some of the behavioral effects of muscimol are not reversed, but actually simulated, by GABA receptor antagonists (Baumeister & Frye 1984), making interpretation of behavior changes following intracranial muscimol ambiguous indeed.

GABA has been studied more extensively than the other prolific amino acid transmitters of the brain. At least four—glycine, β-alanine, taurine, and proline—have been implicated in mediation of neurophysiological inhibition, while two—glutamic and aspartic acid—appear to serve excitatory functions. Although preliminary data suggest these substances may mediate diverse behavioral functions (including sensory processing, motivational vigor, and memory), it is premature to draw any general conclusions (Lajtha 1982–1983).

Nonopioid Peptides

The recent growth of peptide neurobiology has been well summarized in recent compendia (Iversen et al 1983, Krieger et al 1983, Nemeroff & Dunn 1984). The vast accumulation of basic data is only beginning to be incorporated into behavioral analyses. Most neuroactive peptides, when placed into the brain, can provoke autonomic changes and many promote discrete fixed-action pattern effects such as yawning, stretching, grooming, and changes in activity. Except for a few substances, such as the positive effects of angiotensin on water balance regulation (Phillips 1984) and LH-RH on sexual behavior (Moss & Dudley 1984), the neurobehavioral role of most peptides is poorly understood.

It seems reasonable to expect that the role of most peptides in the brain will be synergistic and consonant with their established peripheral effects, as seems to be the case with angiotensin (facilitation of water conservation and thirst) and LH-RH (preparation of reproductive organs and sexuality). The presence of neuropeptide systems among the independent neural plexuses of the viscera (i.e. the massive enteric nervous system) (Gershon 1981), eventually should provide further clues as to brain functions of such molecules. For instance, a recently identified heart peptide is a credible candidate for a brain mediator of cardiac responsivity (Saper et al 1985). In other words, brain peptides may generally promote psychobehavioral processes consonant with their peripheral homeostatic functions. Just to offer one highly speculative possibility, one might entertain a relationship between the role of vasopressin in the retention of both kidney water and brain memories. Maintenance of body fluid balance is a critical homeostatic demand that should be tightly linked to brain processes which help assure that an animal can find water quickly. Locating water does not typically require much foraging (since water holes typically remain topographically stable), but established sources should be firmly stored in memory. Thus, it may be reasonable for the underlying homeostatic detection of an accruing water imbalance to be strongly linked to associative processes, perhaps of a generalized nature. From such a perspective, the ability of vasopressin to promote memory seems reasonable, at least as far as distal causality is concerned. Why the memory effects of vasopressin and ACTH are mediated via brain opioid systems (De Vito & Brush 1984) is yet another matter.

The role of some other peptides has been inferred from their anatomical localization—for instance, the high dorsal horn concentrations of substance P and bombesin (Panula et al 1983) implicates them in sensory processing. Unfortunately, for many peptides there is little room for empirically guided speculation. Even the true central role of a substance such as choleocystokinin (CCK), which has been studied extensively in the context of energy balance regulation, remains largely unknown since the appetite modulating effects seem explicable by peripheral effects (Smith 1984). CCK is co-localized in DA cells, which may implicate it in the control of motivational excitement, but CCK and its receptors are also highly concentrated in cortical tissues (Van Dijk et al 1984)—brain areas which serve no role in the basic control of appetitive behavior. Since CCK counteracts opioid effects in the brain (Faris et al 1984) perhaps its function is largely related to the control of affect.

In general, circuits that mediate emotional-visceral processes (along the hypothalamic-limbic axis) are especially rich in peptide transmitters while those of the thalamic-somatic axis are comparatively impoverished. Thus, it may be reasonable to expect that many neuropeptides will contribute to our understanding of affective processes, an area of psychobiological inquiry which remains poorly cultivated (Panksepp 1982). Indeed, injection of some substances such as growth hormone-releasing factors can provoke intense arousal (Tannenbaum 1984), as can central administration of corticotrophin-releasing factor (CRF) (Britton et al 1982, Sutton et al 1982). It is noteworthy that the anatomy of CRF-containing neural systems, as revealed by recent immunohistochemical work (Swanson et al 1983), is remarkably similar to the anatomy of distress vocalization systems revealed by localized electrical stimulation of subcortical areas of the brain (Herman & Panksepp 1981). Accordingly, it is possible that the CRF system is a generalized emotive circuit that elaborates various negative emotions typically provoked by stress. More specifically, this neurochemical system may normally mediate emotions such as panic and grief that result from acute social separation.

The proliferation of peptide pathways in the brain is providing many new avenues of inquiry for understanding how emotions and motivations are controlled in the brain. Such pathways may constitute emotive command circuits of the brain (Panksepp 1982), but definitive psychobiological work remains to be done. In any event, the peptide system(s) which has most emphatically highlighted the need of psychobiology to entertain the reality of such central control processes is the ever growing opioid family, of which considerably more is known than any other.

General Functions of Brain Opioids

The role of opioids, as well as several other peptides, in the control of pain is well established and continues to be a vigorous area of inquiry (e.g. Luttinger et al 1984), especially with regard to spinal mechanisms of action (Zieglgänsberger 1984). However, opiate receptor neuroanatomy suggests a much broader function for opioid transmitter systems in higher areas of the brain (Figure 1). Indeed, behavioral effects too numerous to summarize here have been obtained by manipulation of this system (De Wied & Jolles 1982, Henry 1982, Oliverio et al 1984, Olson et al 1984). Further, the diversity of distinct transmitter and receptor systems within the opioid family—endorphins (μ receptors), enkephalins (μ and δ receptors) and dynorphins (κ receptors)—makes it unlikely that a common functional principle will be found to explain the spectrum of established effects.

Since morphine and naloxone act largely through the μ receptor system, more is known about the functions of that opiate-sensitive system than any other. The μ system modulates sensitivity to pain, intensity of emotions related to separation distress (Panksepp et al 1985b), and various attributes of reward (Smith & Lane 1983). It also appears to participate in the elaboration of the placebo response (Grevert et al 1983), and to yield diverse effects such as changes in feeding (Morley et al 1983), consolidation of memory (Martinez et al 1981), and physiological effects ranging from a modulation of growth (Zagon & McLaughlin 1984) to sensitivity to hemorragic shock (Holaday & Faden 1981). Although many of the behavioral effects could be subsumed by the principle that opioids elaborate pleasure or habit processes in the brain (Panksepp 1981b), such a perspective would not explain the peripheral physiological effects of opioids.

Suppose we broaden the scheme and postulate that the global function of opioid systems (μ and perhaps δ) is to counteract the influence of stress. Although stress is a construct beset by serious operational and conceptual difficulties, if we consider any major perturbation of physiological homeostasis to be a stress, with opioid arousal being a cardinal counteracting influence, most effects reported for the opioid system fall into place. For instance, the tendency of opioids to quell negative affect—ranging from separation distress to the generation of placebo effects—could be seen as opioid counterregulation of circuits that have been excessively aroused. The induction of feeding and drinking by opioids could be viewed as responses designed to reachieve homeostasis in those realms. The recruitment of opioids during vigorous exercise (Carr et al 1981, Colt 1981) may help diminish the general bodily consequences of accruing stress by stabilization of breathing rhythms (Pazos & Florez 1983) and amplification of cardiovascular tone (Pfeiffer et al 1983).

In some situations, amplification of antistress effects by increased endogenous opioid activity would be counterproductive. Following severe injury, life function would be better sustained if the recruitment of stress responses is sustained as opposed to being endogenously counteracted; this may explain the ability of naloxone to reverse the autonomic symptoms of various forms of shock (Bereiter et al 1983, Koyama et al 1983), an effect requiring adrenal participation (Patton et al 1983).

Finally, since pleasure appears to be related to stimulus conditions that return organisms to homeostasis (Cabanac 1971), the desirable affective effects of opioids can be understood as the psychic component of a brain process that helps return activity in perturbed neural circuits back to normal. Such a principle could help explicate the addictive properties of opiates. Further, the antistress viewpoint is consistent with the existence of opioid receptors on neural systems that mediate arousal, such as NE and ACh.

However, there is also an arousal component to opioid action in the brain, especially on cells of the mesolimbic DA pathways (Stinus et al 1980), which appears to elaborate the euphoric effects of opioids (Bozarth & Wise 1984). Although this effect seems outwardly contradictory to a global antistress hypothesis, it may be seen as compatible if the arousal components promote homeostasis-sustaining behaviors. Furthermore, "pleasurable" opioid arousal invigorates those active posthomeostatic behavior patterns such as rough-and-tumble play (Panksepp et al 1985a) that are expressed fully only when other bodily needs have been fulfilled (Siviy & Panksepp 1985).

I would add just one final comment regarding the vast literature concerning stress-induced analgesia, which is at least partially opioid mediated (Akil et al 1984, Terman et al 1984). It is generally assumed that it is the applied pain that causes opioid release rather than the relief that follows termination of pain. That is a dubious assumption, for the clearest opioid-based analgesia is produced by intermittent rather than continuous pain (Terman et al 1984). Sustained stress actually impedes opioid-based relief processes from fully engaging. Indeed, intermittent shock yields the highest apparent levels of opioid release within the brain (Seeger et al 1984). Perhaps *stress-induced analgesia* would be more properly called *relief-correlated analgesia*.

Other Transmitters

Snyder (1984) speculated that the brain may harbor more than 200 neuropeptide transmitters, and recent developments (appearing in new journals such as *Peptides* and *Regulatory Peptides*) suggest that prediction just might be borne out in the not too distant future. New molecules and new brain chemistries are being revealed at a remarkable pace. Provocative recent findings include the identification of a peptide that may interact with benzodiazepine receptors to precipitate anxiety (Ferrero et al 1984; also see Ninan et al 1982). The regional distribution of this neural system (see the photomicrograph in Marx 1985 and Alho et al 1985) corresponds well with the putative neuroanatomy of fear systems as delimited by brain stimulation techniques (Panksepp 1981a, 1982). In addition, new nonpeptide systems loom on the horizon, such as the apparent ligand (Rehavi et al 1985) for the recently identified imipramine receptor system (Biegon & Rainbow 1983), which may mediate the rapid emotional (i.e. antipanic) effects of some tricyclic antidepressants. For other systems, such as the phenylcyclidine-sensitive substrate in the brain, interesting cortical patterns of receptor distributions have been identified (Quirion et al 1981), and the neuroscience community awaits the further elucidation of the pertinent ligands and brain functions. An end to the discovery of systems is not yet in sight.

THE PROMISE OF NEW TECHNIQUES

The pace of substantive advance in behavioral neuroscience is set by the development and use of new techniques for evaluating brain functions. Many new approaches of basic neuroscience are beginning to be interfaced with behavioral analyses. The utilization of neural transplant techniques (Björklund & Stenevi 1984, Sladek & Gash 1984) has verified the supposed functions of several neurochemical systems including dopamine (Fray et al 1983, Freed 1983), serotonin (Luine et al 1984), and acetylcholine (Gage et al 1984).

Developments in understanding the energy transactions of neural tissue have led to the metabolic imaging of brain processes (McCulloch 1982, Greitz et al 1985, Sokoloff 1985). Such techniques are still difficult to apply in psychobiological contexts, perhaps because the resolving power of available techniques cannot distinguish between nearby excitatory and inhibitory processes. Still, there have been some major successes such as the analysis of hypothalamic motivational systems with brain stimulation techniques (Roberts 1980) and the recent visualization of the learned association of cues and incentives in the auditory system (Gonzalez-Lima & Scheich 1984).

Of course, one of the key needs in the area is further development and refinement of approaches by which we can determine the conditions under which specific patterns of neurochemicals are released in the brain. Several techniques have been applied to this question, including push-pull cannulae, cortical cups for collecting exudates, and more recently, detection of in situ neurochemical activity with intracranial dialysis and electrochemical detection of the oxidation potentials of certain transmitter metabolites, as of dopamine and serotonin (Marsden 1984). Unfortunately, most such approaches can only sample a limited number of brain loci in a single animal. It would be ideal to evaluate release of a transmitter throughout the behaving brain, and the only economical technique which promises to achieve that in the forseeable future is subtractive autoradiography, where the competition between externally administered receptor ligands and presumed synaptic release of endogenous transmitters is autoradiographically evaluated (Panksepp 1981b, Panksepp & Bishop 1981, Seeger et al 1984).

With regard to direct manipulation of systems, more precise tools are appearing. The use of specific neurotoxins—6-hydroxydopamine to kill catecholamine cells, 5,7-dihydroxytryptamine to kill serotonin neurons, kainic and ibotenic acid to kill cells with glutamate receptors (Fuxe et al 1984)—has set the pace during the past decade, and additional tools have recently been discovered such as DSP4 to selectively destroy NE systems (Delini-Stula et al 1984) and AF64A to destroy ACh neurons (Sandberg et al 1984). Certain receptor systems (e.g. opioid) can by inactivated for extended periods using alkylating agents (Portoghese et al 1979) with clear-cut behavioral results (Panksepp et al 1982).

An array of even more precise manipulative tools should arise from developments in immunology. Polyclonal antibodies have already been used to effectively manipulate brain functions (Rapport et al 1978), and monoclonal technology applied in neuroscience (Valentino et al 1985) should be capable of achieving even higher levels of manipulative precision. Antibodies can be linked to cytotoxic lectins such as ricin (Viteta et al 1983) which may eventually permit exquisite neurochemical microsurgery. Further, generation of antibodies to neural growth gradient governing molecules [perhaps to one such as has been discovered by Trisler and colleagues (1984) in retina] may eventually permit highly selective elimination of neural pathways in the developing nervous system.

The modulation of biochemical events following transmitter-receptor binding should be a spectacular growth area in the future. Characterization of cell-surface architecture may permit development of techniques to modify responsivity of neuronal circuits by many different actions—including the inactivation of iontophores. For instance, Moskal & Schaffner (1985) have cultured monoclonal antibodies derived by using neonatal rat dentate gyrus as the initial immunogen, and one (B6E11) has proved to be an effective inhibitor of long-term potentiation (LTP) in the hippocampus, perhaps through disruption of an ion channel (Stanton et al 1985).

Further characterization of the intracellular events that govern receptor homeostasis and second messenger systems may help solve problems that have long resisted even provisional solution. For instance, specific proteins have been found to be selectively phosphorylated (i.e. indicating enzyme activation) in the hippocampus during LTP (Routtenberg et al 1985). Calcium-dependent thiol proteases (calpains) that appear to regulate glutamate transmission in the hippocampus also appear to participate in the genesis of memory (Lynch & Baudry 1984). Indeed, glutamate receptors are markedly diminished in the brains of individuals with senile dementia (Greenamyre et al 1985).

CLOSING REMARKS, WITH A NOTE ON TRANSHYPOTHALAMIC "REWARD" CIRCUITS

Basic neuroscience continues to reveal an ever more awesome neural landscape in the brain, most of which remains totally undeciphered with respect to functions. What the past 30 years of physiological psychology has achieved, however, is a reasonable familiarity with the generalized functions that most brain areas seem to subserve. Unfortunately, we still do not have a taxonomy that does justice to the basic behavioral control processes of the brain and their interactions. Largely this is because behavioral outputs can only indirectly reflect the actual central processes that presumably occur in the animal brain. The only way out of this dilemma is for psychobiology to become a more theoretical science—more willing to entertain the existence of abstract, higher-order central processes than it has in the past, with provisional conceptual structures being continually honed by accruing advances in neuroscience. The 30-year quest to understand the nature of brain foraging circuits (i.e. transhypothalamic self-stimulation circuits) highlights all this quite nicely.

Emergent understanding of the anatomy and biochemistry of brain catecholamine systems led to the NE hypothesis of self-stimulation reward which yielded many positive results (German & Bowden 1974). This theory ultimately proved to have many deficiencies (Wise 1978), although selective and complete pharmacological depletion of NE certainly does diminish self-stimulation behavior, at least in the short run (Zolovick et al 1982). The DA hypothesis of self-stimulation is proceeding along the same lines, being strongly supported by anatomical and pharmacological data (Wise & Bozarth 1984), providing convergent understanding of other sources of reward such as evoked by psychomotor stimulants and opiates (Wise & Bozarth 1982). However, recent evidence strongly implicates other pathways in such reward, some of which contain acetylcholine synapses (Kofman & Yeomans 1984, Gratton & Wise 1985). Further, the realization that dopamine cells are modulated by a host of other transmitters, including substance P, neurotensin, opioids, vasoactive intestinal peptide, TRH, CCK, and bombesin makes those substances important new candidates in the unfolding analysis of brain "reward" (e.g. Stäubli & Huston 1985).

The next wave of attempts to understand self-stimulation (as well as other brain functions) will arise from simultaneous analysis of the underlying systems through the implementation of the new generation of biochemical and histological techniques (especially via the application of immunocytochemical and new fluorescent retrograde and anterograde tracing techniques in direct conjunction with behavioral studies). Monoclonal antibodies, perhaps linked to neurotoxins such as ricin, may be able to dissect the influences of the various convergent chemistries in neurochemically complex brain areas such as the ventral tegmental area—the apparent neural focus for the most spectacular form of self-stimulation reward. These cells undoubtedly receive a great deal of convergent sensory information from peripheral channels that detect the positive incentive attributes of reward, such as olfactory and gustatory systems, as well as feedback systems of consummatory behavior such as the sensory nuclei of the trigemminal nerve and pertinent deep cerebellar nuclei that regulate the smooth execution of consummatory behaviors. All of these possibilities are suggested by past research, but now they can be evaluated efficiently with new empirical techniques. Likewise, with the gradual liberation of psychobiological theorizing from outmoded traditions, new ways should emerge to address the psychological issues about systems that underlie behavior. This investigator's theoretical views on the topic are summarized elsewhere (Panksepp 1981a, 1982, 1985).

These are optimistic times for behavioral neuroscience. Basic knowledge has grown in quantity and quality to such a degree that we may soon be able to evaluate credibly the subtle attributes of animal mind—curiosity, emotions, play, and greed; perhaps even attributes of consciousness and thought—that have long been forbidding territory in our attempts to understand the nature of the brain empirically. There is no question that the search for such levels of understanding will require risky, theory-guided inferences concerning the meaning of animal actions. This is not to diminish the importance of theory-free analysis of behavior (e.g. see Robinson 1983), but to acknowledge that the penetrating study of psychobehavioral functions is more than the study of patterns of acetylcholine release onto nicotinic neuromuscular receptors. The full neurochemical complexity of the brain beckons us to undertake such endeavors. We have entered an exciting era in the search for the material basis of psychological processes.

ACKNOWLEDGMENTS

I thank Drs. Bob Conner and Olie Smith for their comments on this paper.

Literature Cited

Aghajanian, G. K. 1978. Tolerance of locus coeruleus neurons to morphine suppression of withdrawal by clonidine. *Nature* 276:186–88

Akil, H., Watson, S. J., Young, E., Lewis, M. E., Khachaturian, H., Walker, J. M. 1984. Endogenous opioids: Biology and Function. *Ann. Rev. Neurosci.* 7:223–55

Alho, H., Costa, E., Ferrero, P., Fujimoto, M., Cogenza-Murphy, D., Guidotti, A. 1985. Diazepam-binding inhibitor: A new neuropeptide located in selected neuronal populations of rat brain. *Science* 229:179–82

Andrade, R., Aghajanian, G. K. 1984. Locus coeruleus activity in vitro: Intrinsic regulation by a calcium-dependent potassium conductance but not α_2-adrenoceptors. *J. Neurosci.* 4:161–70

Anisman, H. 1978. Neurochemical changes elicited by stress. See Anisman & Bignami 1978, pp. 119–72

Anisman, H., Bignami, G., eds. 1978. *Psychopharmacology of Aversively Motivated Behavior*. New York: Plenum

Antelman, S. M., Caggiula, A. R. 1977. Norepinephrine-dopamine interactions and behavior. *Science* 195:646–53

Antelman, S. M., Chiodo, L. A. 1984. Stress: Its effect on interactions among biogenic amines and role in the induction and treatment of disease. *Handb. Psychopharmacol.* 18:279–341

Aston-Jones, G., Bloom, F. E. 1981a. Activity of norepinephrine containing locus coeruleus neurons in behaving rats anticipates fluctuations in the sleep-waking cycle. *J. Neurosci.* 8:876–86

Aston-Jones, G., Bloom, F. E. 1981b. Norepinephrine-containing locus coeruleus neurons in behaving rats exhibit pronounced responses to non-noxious environmental stimuli. *J. Neurosci.* 8:117–900

Bartus, R. T., Dean, R. L., Beer, B., Lippa, A. S. 1982. The cholinergic hypothesis of geriatric memory dysfunction. *Science* 217:408–17

Baumeister, A. A., Frye, G. D. 1984. Self-injurious behavior in rats produced by intranigral microinjection of GABA agonists. *Pharmacol. Biochem. Behav.* 21:89–95

Bereiter, D. A., Plotsky, P. M., Gann, D. S. 1983. Selective opiate modulation of the physiological responses to hemorrhage in the cat. *Endocrinology* 113:1439–46

Berger, P. A., Davis, K. L., Hollister, L. E. 1979. Pharmacological investigations of cholinergic mechanisms in schizophrenia and manic psychosis. See Davis & Berger 1979, pp. 15–32

Biegon, A., Rainbow, T. C. 1983. Localization and characterization of [^{3}H]desmethylimipramine binding sites in rat brain by quantitative autoradiography. *J. Neurosci.* 3:1069–76

Bisserbe, J.-C., Patel, J., Marangos, P. J. 1985. Autoradiographic localization of adenosine uptake sites in rat brain using [^{3}H]nitrobenzylthioinosine. *J. Neurosci.* 5:544–50

Björklund, A., Hökfelt, T., eds. 1983. *Handbook of Chemical Neuroanatomy*. New York: Elsevier

Björklund, A., Stenevi, U. 1984. Intracerebral neural implants: Neuronal replacement and reconstruction of damaged circuitries. *Ann. Rev. Neurosci.* 7:279–308

Blanc, G., Herve, D., Simon, H., Lisoprawski, A., Glowinski, J., Tassin, J. P. 1980. Response to stress of mesocortico-frontal dopaminergic neurones in rats after long-term isolation. *Nature* 284:265–67

Blanchard, R. J., Takahashi, L. T., Blanchard, D. C. 1977. The development of intruder attack in colonies of laboratory rats. *Anim. Learn. Behav.* 5:363–69

Blundell, J. E., Latham, C. J. 1978. Pharmacological manipulation of feeding behavior: Possible influences of serotonin and dopamine on food intake. In *Central Mechanisms of Anorectic Drugs*, ed. S. Garattini, R. Samanin, pp. 83–109. New York: Raven

Booth, D. A., Quartermain, D. 1965. Taste sensitivity of eating elicited by chemical stimulation of the rat hypothalamus. *Psychon. Sci.* 3:525–26

Bousfield, D., ed. 1985. *Neurotransmitters in Action*. New York: Elsevier

Bozarth, M. A., Wise, R. A. 1984. Anatomically distinct opiate receptor fields mediate reward and physical dependence. *Science* 224:516–17

Britton, D. R., Koob, G. F., Rivier, J., Vale, W. 1982. Intraventricular corticotropin-releasing factor enhances behavioral effects of novelty. *Life Sci.* 31:363–67

Britton, K. T., Svensson, T., Schwartz, J., Bloom, F. E., Koob, G. F. 1984. Dorsal noradrenergic bundle lesions fail to alter opiate withdrawal or suppression of opiate withdrawal by clonidine. *Life Sci.* 34:133–39

Brudzyński, S. M., Eckersdorf, B. 1984. Inhibition of locomotor activity during cholinergically-induced emotional-aversive response in the cat. *Behav. Brain Res.* 14:247–53

Bunney, B. S. 1979. The electrophysiological pharmacology of midbrain dopaminergic systems. In *The Neurobiology of Dopamine*, ed. A. S. Horn, J. Korf, B. H. C. Westerink, p. 417. New York: Academic

Butcher, L. L., ed. 1978. *Cholinergic-Monoaminergic Interactions in the Brain*. New York: Academic

Cabanac, M. 1971. Physiological role of pleasure. *Science* 173:1103–7

Carr, D., Bullen, B., Krinar, G., Arnold, M. A., Rosenblatt, M., et al. 1981. Physical conditioning facilitates the exercise-induced secretion of beta-endorphin and beta-lipotropin in women. *N. Engl. J. Med.* 305:560–63

Chandler, S. H., Goldberg, L. J. 1984. Differentiation of the neural pathways mediating cortically induced and DA activation of the central pattern generator for rhythmical jaw movements in the anesthetized guinea pig. *Brain Res.* 323:297–301

Chan-Palay, V., Palay, S. L., eds. 1984. *Coexistence of Neuroactive Substances in Neurons*. New York: Wiley

Cheal, M. 1981. Scopolamine disrupts maintenance of attention rather than memory processes. *Behav. Neurol. Biol.* 33:163–87

Chiodo, L., Antelman, S. M., Caggiula, A. R., Lineberry, C. G. 1980. Sensory stimuli alter the discharge rate of dopamine (DA) neurons: Evidence for two functional types of DA cells in the substantia nigra. *Brain Res.* 189:544–49

Churchill, L., Pazdernik, T. L., Jackson, J. L., Nelson, S. R., Samson, F. E., McDonough,

J. H. 1984. Topographical distribution of decrements and recovery in muscarinic receptors from rat brains repeatedly exposed to sublethal doses of soman. *J. Neurosci.* 4:2069–79

Clark, J. T., Smith, E. R., Davidson, J. M. 1984. Enhancement of sexual motivation in male rats by yohimbine. *Science* 225:847–49

Colt, W. D., Wardlaw, S., Frantz, A. 1981. The effect of running on plasma beta-endorphin. *Life Sci.* 28:1637–40

Cooper, B. R., Howard, J. L., White, H. L., Soroko, F., Ingold, K., Maxwell, R. A. 1980. Anorexic effects of ethanolamine-O-sulfate and muscimol in the rat: Evidence that GABA inhibits ingestive behavior. *Life Sci.* 26:1997–2002

Corbett, D., Wise, R. A. 1979. Intracranial self-stimulation in relation to the ascending noradrenergic fibre systems of the pontine tegmentum and caudal midbrain: A moveable electrode study. *Brain Res.* 177:423–36

Costa, E., Greengard, P. 1969–1984. *Advances in Biochemical Psychopharmacology*, Vols. 1–39. New York: Raven

Costa, E., Panula, P., Thompson, H. K., Cheney, D. L. 1983. The transsynaptic regulation of septal-hippocampal cholinergic neurons. *Life Sci.* 32:165–79

Coyle, J. T., Price, D. L., DeLong, M. R. 1983. Alzheimer's disease: A disorder of cortical cholinergic innervation. *Science* 219:1184–90

Davis, K. L., Berger, P. A., eds. 1979. *Brain Acetylcholine and Neuropsychiatric Disease*. New York: Plenum

Davis, M. 1980. Neurochemical modulation of sensory-motor reactivity: Acoustic and tactile startle reflexes. *Neurosci. Biobehav. Rev.* 4:241–63

DeFrance, J. F., ed. 1976. *The Septal Nuclei*. New York: Plenum

Delini-Stula, A., Mogilnicka, E., Hunn, C., Dooley, D. J. 1984. Novelty-oriented behavior in the rat after selective damage of locus coeruleus projections by DSP-4, a new noradrenergic neurotoxin. *Pharmacol. Biochem. Behav.* 20:613–18

DeLong, M. R., Crutcher, M. D., Georgopoulos, A. P. 1983. Relations between movement and single cell discharge in the substantia nigra of the behaving monkey. *J. Neurosci.* 3:1599–1606

Deutsch, J. A., ed. 1983. *The Physiological Basis of Memory*. New York: Academic. 2nd ed.

De Vito, W. J., Brush, F. R. 1984. Effect of ACTH and vasopressin on extinction: Evidence for opiate mediation. *Behav. Neurosci.* 98:59–71

DeVries, G. J., Buijs, R. M. 1983. The origin of the vasopressinergic and oxytocinergic innervation of the rat brain with special reference to the lateral septum. *Brain Res.* 273:307–17

De Wied, D., Jolles, J. 1982. Neuropetides derived from proopiocortin: Behavioral, physiological and neurochemical effects. *Physiol. Rev.* 62:976–1059

Emson, P. C., ed. 1983. *Chemical Neuroanatomy.* New York: Raven

Fariello, R. G., Morselli, P. L., Lloyd, K. G., Quesney, L. F., Engle, J., eds. 1985. *Neurotransmitters, Seizures and Epilepsy II.* New York: Raven

Faris, P. L., McLaughlin, C. L., Baile, C. A., Olney, J. W., Komisaruk, B. R. 1984. Morphine analgesia potentiated but tolerance not affected by active immunization against cholecystokinin. *Science* 226:1215–17

Feldman, R. S., Quenzer, L. F. 1984. *Fundamentals of Neuropsychopharmacology.* Sunderland, Mass: Sinauer

Ferrero, P., Guidotti, A., Conti-Tronconi, B., Costa, E. 1984. A brain octadecaneuropeptide generated by tryptic digestion of DBI (diazepam binding inhibitor) functions as a proconflict ligand of benzodiazepine recognition sites. *Neuropharmacology* 227:1359–62

Foote, S., Bloom, S., Aston-Jones, G. 1983. Nucleus locus ceruleus: New evidence of anatomical and physiological specificity. *Physiol. Rev.* 63:844–914

Fray, P. J., Dunnett, S. B., Iversen, S. D., Björklund, A., Stenevi, U. 1983. Nigral transplants reinnervating the dopamine-depleted neostriatum can sustain intracranial self-stimulation. *Science* 219:416–19

Freed, W. J. 1983. Functional brain tissue transplantation: Reversal of lesion-induced rotation by intraventricular substantia nigra and adrenal medulla grafts, with a note on intracranial retinal grafts. *Biol. Psychiatry* 18:1205–66

Fuxe, K., Roberts, P., Schwarcz, R., eds. 1984. *Exitotoxins.* New York: Plenum

Gage, F. H., Björklund, A., Stenevi, U., Dunnett, S. B., Kelly, P. A. T. 1984. Intrahippocampal septal grafts ameliorate learning impairments in aged rats. *Science* 225:533–36

Garattini, S., Pujol, J. F., Samainin, R., eds. 1978. *Interactions Between Putative Neurotransmitters in the Brain.* New York: Raven

German, D. C., Bowden, D. M. 1974. Catecholamine systems as the neural substrated for intracranial self-stimulation: A hypothesis. *Brain Res.* 73:381–419

Gershon, M. D. 1981. The enteric nervous system. *Ann. Rev. Neurosci.* 4:227–72

Glassman, A. H., Jackson, W. K., Walsh, B. T., Roose, S. P., Rosenfeld, B. 1984. Cigarette craving, smoking withdrawal, and clonidine. *Science* 226:864–66

Glick, S. D., Waters, D. H., Miloy, S. 1973. Depletion of hypothalamic norepinephrine by food deprivation and interaction with *d*-amphetamine. *Res. Commun. Chem. Pathol. Pharmacol.* 6:775–78

Gold, M. S., Redmond, D. E., Kleber, H. D. 1979. Noradrenergic hyperactivity in opiate withdrawal supported by clonidine reversal of opiate withdrawal. *Am. J. Psychiatry* 136:100–2

Goldberg, A. M., Hanin, I., eds. 1976. *Biology of Cholinergic Function.* New York: Raven

Gonzalez-Lima, F., Scheich, H. 1984. Neural substrates for tone-conditioned bradycardia demonstrated with 2-deoxyglucose. I. Activation of auditory nuclei. *Behav. Brain Res.* 14:213–33

Goodman, R. R., Snyder, S. H. 1982. Autoradiographic localization of adenosine receptors in rat brain using [^{3}H]cyclohexyladenosine. *J. Neurosci.* 2:1230–41

Grandison, L., Guidotti, A. 1977. Stimulation of food intake by muscimol and beta endorphin. *Neuropharmacology* 16:533–36

Gratton, A., Wise, R. A. 1985. Hypothalamic reward mechanism: two first-stage fiber populations with a cholinergic component. *Science* 227:545–48

Greenamyre, J. T., Penney, J. B., Young, A. B., D'Amato, C. J., Shoulson, I. 1985. Alterations in L-glutamate binding in Alzheimer's and Huntington's diseases. *Science* 227:1496–97

Greenamyre, J. T., Young, A. B., Penney, J. B. 1984. Quantitative autoradiographic distribution of L-[^{3}H]glutamate-binding sites in rat central nervous system. *J. Neurosci.* 4:2133–44

Greitz, T., Ingvar, D. H., Widen, L., eds. 1985. *The Metabolism of the Human Brain Studied with Positron Emission Tomography.* New York: Raven

Grevert, P., Albert, L. H., Goldstein, A. 1983. Partial antagonism of placebo analgesia by naloxone. *Pain* 16:129–43

Grill, H. H., Norgren, R. 1978. The taste reactivity test. I. Mimetic responses to gustatory stimuli in neurologically normal rats. *Brain. Res.* 143:262–79

Grossman, S. P. 1976. Behavioral functions of the septum: A re-analysis. See DeFrance 1976, pp. 361–422

Halpain, S. C., Wieczorek, C. M., Rainbow, T. C. 1984. Localization of L-glutamate receptors in rat brain by quantitative autoradiography. *J. Neurosci.* 4:2247–58

Harik, S. I. 1984. Locus ceruleus lesion by local 6-hydroxydopamine infusion causes marked and specific destruction of noradrenergic neurons, long-term depletion of norepinephrine and the enzymes that synthesize it, and enhance dopaminergic mechanism in the ipsilateral cerebral cortex. *J. Neurosci.* 4:699–707

Heath, R. G. 1972. Pleasure and brain activity in man. *J. Nerv. Ment. Dis.* 154:3–18

Henry, J. L. 1982. Circulating opioids: possible physiological roles in central nervous function. *Neurosci. Biobehav. Rev.* 6:229–46

Herkenham, M., Pert, C. B. 1982. Light microscopic localization of brain opiate receptors: A general autoradiographic method which preserves tissue quality. *J. Neurosci.* 2:1129–49

Herman, B. H., Panksepp, J. 1981. Ascending endorphin inhibition of distress vocalization. *Science* 211:1060–62

Hoehn-Saric, R. 1982. Neurotransmitters in anxiety. *Arch. Gen. Psychiatry* 39:735–44

Hökfelt, T., Johansson, O., Goldstein, M. 1984. Chemical anatomy of the brain. *Science* 225:1326–34

Holaday, J. W., Faden, A. I. 1981. Naloxone treatment in shock. *Lancet* July 25:201

Hutchinson, R. R., Renfrew, J. W. 1978. Functional parallels between the neural and environmental antecendents of aggression. *Neurosci. Biobehav. Rev.* 2:33–58

Iversen, L. L., Iversen, S. D., Snyder, S. H. 1975–1984. *Handbook of Psychopharmacology*, Vols. 1–18. New York: Plenum

Jacobs, B. L. 1978. Dreams and hallucinations: A common neurochemical mechanism mediating their phenomenological similarities. *Neurosci. Biobehav. Rev.* 2:59–69

Jacobs, B. L. 1984. Single unit activity of brain monoaminergic neurons in freely moving animals: A brief review. In *Modulation of Sensorimotor Activity During Alterations in Behavioral States*, pp. 99–120. New York: Liss

Jacobs, B. L., Gannon, P. J., Azmitia, E. C. 1984a. Atlas of serotonergic cell bodies in the cat brainstem: An immunocytochemical analysis. *Brain Res. Bull.* 13:1–31

Jacobs, B. L., Heym, J., Steinfels, G. F. 1984b. Physiological and behavioral analysis of raphe unit activity. *Handb. Psychopharmacol.* 18:343–95

Jones, L. S., Gauger, L. L., Davis, J. W. 1985. Anatomy of brain α-adrenergic receptors: In vitro autoradiography with [^{125}I]-Heat. *J. Comp. Neurol.* 231:190–208

Josefsson, J.-O., Johansson, P. 1979. Naloxone-reversible effect of opioids on pinocytosis in Amoeba proteins. *Nature* 282:78–80

Jouvet, M. 1972. The role of monoamines and acetylcholine-containing neurons in the regulation of the sleep-waking cycle. *Ergeb. Physiol.* 64:166–307

Kofman, O., Yeomans, J. S. 1984. Dorsal tegmental and lateral hypothalamic self-stimulation are blocked by atropine injected into ventral tegmentum. *Neurosci. Abstr.* 10:308

Koyama, S., Manugian, V., Ammons, W. S., Santiesteban, H. L., Manning, J. W. 1983. Effect of naloxone on baroreflex, sympathetic tone and blood pressure in the cat. *Eur. J. Pharmacol.* 90:367–76

Krieger, D. T., Brownstein, M. J., Martin, J. B. 1983. *Brain Peptides.* New York: Wiley

Krogsgaard-Larsen, P., Scheel-Krüger, J., Kofod, H., eds. 1979. *GABA-Neurotransmitters: Pharmacochemical, Biochemical and Pharmacological Aspects.* Copenhagen: Munksgaard

Kuhar, M. J. 1982. Localization of drug and neurotransmitter receptors in brain by light microscopic autoradiography. See Iversen et al 1982, 15:229–320

Lajtha, A., ed. 1982–1983. *Handbook of Neurochemistry*, Vols. 1–10. New York: Plenum. 2nd ed.

Leibowitz, S. F. 1980. Neurochemical systems of the hypothalamus: Control of feeding and drinking behavior and water-electrolyte excretion. See Morgane & Panksepp 1980, pp. 299–437

Le Roith, D., Shiloach, J., Roth, J. 1984. Coexistence of multiple neuroactive materials in individual neurons: Do recent evolutionary studies provide a rational interpretation. See Chan-Palay & Palay 1984, pp. 411–21

Levine, A. S., Morley, J. E. 1984. Neuropeptide Y: A potent inducer of consummatory behavior in rats. *Peptides* 5:1025–29

Lipton, M. A., DiMascio, A., Killam, K. F., eds. 1978. *Psychopharmacology: A Generation of Progress.* New York: Raven

Lloyd, K. G., Morselli, P. L., Depoortere, H., Fournier, V., Zivkovic, B., et al. 1983. The potential use of GABA agonists in psychiatric disorders: Evidence from studies with progabide in animal models and clinical trials. *Pharmacol. Biochem. Behav.* 18:957–66

Luine, V. N., Renner, K. J., Frankfurt, M., Azmitia, E. C. 1984. Facilitated sexual behavior reversed and serotonin restored by raphe nuclei transplanted into denervated hypothalamus. *Science* 226:1436–39

Luttinger, D., Hernandez, D. E., Nemeroff, C. B., Prange, A. J. Jr. 1984. Peptides and nociception. *Int. Rev. Neurobiol.* 25:186–242

Lynch, G., Baudry, M. 1984. The biochemistry of memory: A new and specific hypothesis. *Science* 224:1057–63

Mantyh, P. W., Hunt, S. P. 1985. Thyrotopin-releasing hormone (TRH) receptors. *J. Neurosci.* 5:551–61

Mantyh, P. W., Hunt, S. P., Maggio, J. E.

1984. Substance P receptors: Localization by light microscopic autoradiography in rat brain using [³H]-SP as the radioligand. *Brain Res.* 307:147–65

Marsden, C. D., ed. 1984. *Measurement of Neurotransmitter Release In Vivo.* Chichester: Wiley

Marshall, J. F., Berrios, N., Sawyer, S. 1981. Neostriatal dopamine and sensory inattention. *J. Comp. Physiol. Psychol.* 94:833–46

Martinez, J. L., Jensen, R. A., Messing, R. B., Rigter, H., McGaugh, J. L., eds. 1981. *Endogenous Peptides and Learning and Memory Processes.* New York: Academic

Marx, J. L. 1985. "Anxiety peptide" found in brain. *Science* 227:934

Mason, S. T. 1981. Norepinephrine and selective attention: A review of the model and evidence. *Life Sci.* 27:617–31

McCulloch, J. 1982. Mapping functional alterations in the CNS with [¹⁴C]deoxyglucose. *Handb. Psychopharmacol.* 15:321–410

McGinty, D. J., Drucker-Colin, R. R. 1982. Sleep mechanisms: Biology and control of REM sleep. *Int. Rev. Neurobiol.* 23:391–436

Miller, J. D., Sanghera, M. K., German, D. C. 1981. Mesencephalic dopaminergic unit activity in the behaviorally conditioned rat. *Life Sci.* 29:1255–63

Miller, N. E. 1965. Chemical coding of behavior in the brain. *Science* 148:328–38

Moore, R. Y., Bloom, F. E. 1978. Central catecholamine neuron systems: Anatomy and physiology of dopamine systems. *Ann. Rev. Neurosci.* 1:129–69

Moore, R. Y., Bloom, F. E. 1979. Central catecholamine neuron systems: Anatomy and physiology of the norepinephrine and epinephrine systems. *Ann. Rev. Neurosci.* 2:113–68

Morales, A., Surridge, D. H., Marshall, P. G., Fenemore, J. 1982. Nonhormonal pharmacological treatment of organic impotence. *J. Urol.* 128:45–47

Morgane, P. J., Panksepp, J., eds. 1980–1981. *Handbook of the Hypothalamus, Vols. 3A, 3B, Behavioral Studies of the Hypothalamus.* New York: Dekker

Morley, J. E., Levine, A. S., Yim, G. K., Lowy, M. T. 1983. Opioid modulation of appetite. *Neurosci. Biobehav. Rev.* 7:281–305

Moskal, J. R., Schaffner, A. E. 1985. A monoclonal antibody to the developing rat dentate gyrus: Identification of a highly restricted cell surface antigen and the isolation of hippocampal newrons that are maintainable in vitro. *Brain Res.* Submitted for publication

Moss, R. L., Dudley, C. A. 1984. The challenge of studying the behavioral effects of neuropeptides. *Handb. Psychopharmacol.* 18:397–454

Myers, R. D. 1974. *Drug and Chemical Stimulation of the Brain.* New York: Van Nostrand Reinhold

Myers, R. D., Drucker-Colin, R. R., eds. 1974. *Neurohumoral Coding of Brain Function.* New York: Plenum

Nadi, N., Nurenberger, J., Gershon, E. S. 1984. Muscarinic cholinergic receptors on skin fibroblasts in familial affective disorder *N. Engl. J. Med.* 311:225–30

Nemeroff, C. B., Dunn, A. J., eds. 1984. *Peptides, Hormones, and Behavior.* New York: SP Medical & Scientific Books

Ninan, P. T., Insel, T. M., Cohen, R. M., Cook, J. M., Skolnick, P., Paul, S. M. 1982. Benzodiazepine receptor-mediated experimental "anxiety" in primates. *Science* 218:1332–34

Oliverio, A., Castellano, C., Puglisi-Allegra, S. 1984. Psychobiology of opioids. *Int. Rev. Neurobiol.* 25:277–338

Olson, G. A., Olson, R. D., Kastin, A. J. 1984. Endogenous opiates: 1983. *Peptides* 5:975–92

Ossowska, K., Wedzony, K., Wolfarth, S. 1984. The role of the GABA mechanisms of the globus pallidus in mediating catalepsy, stereotypy and locomotor activity. *Pharmacol. Biochem. Behav.* 21:825–31

Pan, H. S., Frey, K. A., Young, A. B., Penney, J. B. Jr. 1983. Changes in [³H]muscimol binding in substantia nigra, entopeduncular nucleus, globus pallidus, and thalamus after striatal lesions as demonstrated by quantitative receptor autoradiography. *J. Neurosci.* 3:1189–98

Panksepp, J. 1981a. Hypothalamic integration of behavior: Rewards, punishments, and related psychological processes. See Morgane & Panksepp 1981, pp. 289–431

Panksepp, J. 1981b. Brain opioids—a neurochemical substrate for narcotic and social dependence. In *Theory in Psychopharmacology*, ed. S. J. Cooper, pp. 149–75. London: Academic

Panksepp, J. 1982. Toward a general psychobiological theory of emotions. *Behav. Brain Sci.* 5:407–68

Panksepp, J. 1985. The anatomy of emotions. See Plutchik & Kellerman 1985

Panksepp, J., Bishop, P. 1981. An autoradiographic map of (³H) diprenorphine binding in rat brain: Effects of social interaction. *Brain Res. Bull.* 7:405–10

Panksepp, J., Jalowiec, J., DeEskinazi, F. G., Bishop, P. 1985a. Opiates and play dominance in juvenile rats. *Behav. Neurosci.* 99:441–53

Panksepp, J., Jalowiec, J. E., Morgane, P. J., Zolovick, A. J., Stern, W. C. 1973. Noradrenergic pathways and sleep-waking states in cats. *Exp. Neurol.* 41:233–45

Panksepp, J., Meeker, R. B. 1980. The role of GABA in the ventromedial hypothalamic regulation of food intake. *Brain Res. Bull.* 5 (Suppl. 2):453–60

Panksepp, J., Normansell, L., Siviy, S., Buchanan, A., Zolovick, A., et al. 1983. A cholinergic command circuit for separation distress? *Neurosci. Abstr.* 9:979

Panksepp, J., Siviy, S. M., Normansell, L. A. 1984. The psychobiology of play: Theoretical and methodological perspectives. *Neurosci. Biobehav. Rev.* 8:465–92

Panksepp, J., Siviy, S. M., Normansell, L. A. 1985b. Brain opioids and social emotions. In *The Psychobiology of Attachment and Separation*, ed. M. Reite, T. Fields, pp. 3–49. New York: Academic

Panksepp, J., Siviy, S., Normansell, L., White, K., Bishop, P. 1982. Effects of β-chlornaltrexamine on separation distress in chicks. *Life Sci.* 31:2387–90

Panula, P., Hadjiconstantinou, M., Yang, H.-Y. T., Costa, E. 1983. Immunohistochemical localization of bombesin/gastrin-releasing peptide and substance P in primary sensory neurons. *J. Neurosci.* 3:2021–29

Panula, P., Revuelta, A. V., Cheney, D. L., Wu, J. Y., Costa, E. 1984. An immunohistochemical study of the localization of GABAergic neurons in rat septum. *J. Comp. Neurol.* 222:69–80

Patton, M. L., Gurll, N. J., Reynolds, D. G., Vargish, T. 1983. Adrenalectomy abolishes and cortisol restores naloxone's beneficial effects on cardiovascular function and survival in canine hemorrhagic shock. *Circ. Shock* 10:317–27

Pazos, A., Florez, J. 1983. Interaction of naloxone with μ- and δ-opioid agonists on the respiration of rats. *Eur. J. Pharmacol.* 87:309–14

Pfaff, D. W., ed. 1982. *The Physiological Mechanisms of Motivation.* New York: Springer-Verlag

Pfeiffer, A., Feuerstein, G., Zerbe, R. L., Faden, A. I., Kopin, I. J. 1983. μ-Receptors mediate opioid cardiovascular effects at anterior hypothalamic sites through sympathoadrenomedullary and parasympathetic pathways. *Endocrinology* 113:929–38

Phillips, M. I. 1984. Angiotensin and drinking: A model for the study of peptide action in the brain. See Nemeroff & Dunn 1984, pp. 423–62

Plutchik, R., Kellerman, H., eds. 1985. *Emotion: Theory, Research and Experience, Vol. 3. Biological Foundations of Emotion.* New York: Academic. In press

Portoghese, P. S., Larson, D. L., Jiang, J. B., Caruso, T. P., Takemori, A. E. 1979. Synthesis and pharmacological characterization

of an alkylating analogue (chlornaltrexamine) of naltrexone with ultralong-lasting narcotic antagonist properties. *J. Med. Chem.* 22:168–73

Quirion, R., Hammer, R. P. Jr., Herkenham, M., Pert, C. B. 1981. Phencyclidine (angel dust)/"opiate" receptor: Visualization by tritium-sensitive film. *Proc. Natl. Acad. Sci. USA* 78:5881–85

Rapport, M. M., Karpiak, S. E., Mahadik, S. P. 1978. Biological activities of antibodies injected into the brain. *Fed. Proc.* 38:2391–96

Redmond, D. E. Jr., Huang, Y. H. 1979. New evidence for a locus coeruleus-norepinephrine connection with anxiety. *Life Sci.* 25:2149–62

Rehavi, M., Ventura, I., Sarne, Y. 1985. Demonstration of endogenous "imipramine like" material in rat brain. *Life Sci.* 36:687–93

Reinis, S., Goldman, J. M. 1982. *The Chemistry of Behavior.* New York: Plenum

Robbins, T. W., Everitt, B. J. 1982. Function studies of the central catecholamines. *Int. Rev. Neurobiol.* 23:303–65

Roberts, D. C. S. 1981. An evaluation of the role of noradrenaline in learning. See Cooper 1981, pp. 124–48

Roberts, E. 1979. Status and perspective. See Krogsgaard-Larsen et al 1979, pp. 533–45

Roberts, W. W. 1980. [^{14}C]Deoxyglucose mapping of first-order projections activated by stimulation of lateral hypothalamic sites eliciting gnawing, eating and drinking in rats. *J. Comp. Neurol.* 194:617–38

Robinson, T. E., ed. 1983. *Behavioral Approaches to Brain Research.* New York: Oxford Univ. Press

Rodgers, R. J., DePaulis, A. 1982. GABAergic influences on defensive fighting in rats. *Pharmacol. Biochem. Behav.* 17:451–56

Rossi, J. III, Sahley, T. L., Panksepp, J. 1983. The role of brain norepinephrine in clonidine suppression of isolation-induced distress in the domestic chick. *Psychopharmacology* 79:338–42

Rossi, J. III, Zolovick, A. J., Davies, R. F., Panksepp, J. 1982. The role of norepinephrine in feeding behavior. *Neurosci. Biobehav. Rev.* 6:194–204

Routtenberg, A., Lovinger, D. M., Steward, O. 1985. Selective increase in phosphorylation of a 47-KDa protein (F1) directly related to long-term potentiation. *Behav. Neurol. Biol.* 43:3–11

Sandberg, K., Hanin, I., Fisher, A., Coyle, J. T. 1984. Selective cholinergic neurotoxin: AF64A's effects in rat striatum. *Brain Res.* 293:49–55

Saper, C. B., Standaert, D. G., Currie, M. G., Schwartz, D., Geller, D. M., Needleman, P.

1985. Atriopeptin-immunoreactive neurons in the brain: Presence in cardiovascular regulatory areas. *Science* 227:1047–49

Scheel-Krüger, J., Arnt, J., Braestrup, C., Christensen, A. V., Magelund, G. 1979. Development of new animal models for GABAergic actions using muscimol as a tool. See Krogsgaard-Larsen et al 1979, pp. 447–64

Seeger, T. F., Sforzo, G. A., Pert, C. B., Pert, A. 1984. In vivo autoradiography: Visualization of stress-induced changes in opiate receptor occupancy in the rat brain. *Brain Res.* 305:303–11

Siviy, S. M., Panksepp, J. 1985. Energy balance and play in juvenile rats. *Physiol. Behav.* 35:435–41

Sladek, J. R., Gash, D. M., eds. 1984. *Neural Transplants: Development and Function.* New York: Plenum

Smith, G. P. 1984. Gut hormone and feeding behavior: Intuitions and experiments. See Nemeroff & Dunn 1984, pp. 463–95

Smith, J. E., Lane, J. D., eds. 1983. *The Neurobiology of Opiate Reward Processes.* Amsterdam: Elsevier Biomedical Press

Smythies, J. R., Bradley, R. J., eds. 1959–1984. *International Review of Neurobiology,* Vols. 1–25. New York: Academic

Snyder, S. H. 1984. Drug and neurotransmitter receptors in the brain. *Science* 224:22–31

Snyder, S. H. 1985. Adenosine as a neuromodulator. *Ann. Rev. Neurosci.* 8:103–24

Sokoloff, L., ed. 1985. *Brain Imaging and Brain Function.* New York: Raven

Sprague, J. M., Epstein, A. N. 1976–1983. *Progress in Psychobiology and Physiological Psychology,* Vols. 6–10. New York: Academic

Stanton, P. K., Sarvey, J. M., Moskal, J. R. 1985. A cell surface protein that regulates long term potentiation in the hippocampal slice. *Nature.* Submitted for publication

Stäubli, U., Huston, J. P. 1985. Central action of substance P: Possible role in reward. *Behav. Neurol. Biol.* 43:100–8

Stein, L., Wise, D., Belluzzi, J. D. 1975. Effects of benzodiazepines on central serotonergic mechanisms. *Adv. Biochem. Psychopharmacol.* 14:29–44

Steinfels, G. F., Heym, J., Strecker, R. E., Jacobs, B. L. 1983. Behavioral correlates of dopaminergic unit activity in freely moving cats. *Brain Res.* 258:217–28

Stinus, L., Koob, G. F., Ling, M., Bloom, F. E., LeMoal, M. 1980. Locomotor activation induced by infusion of endorphins into the ventral tegmental area: Evidence of opiate dopamine interactions. *Proc. Natl. Acad. Sci. USA* 77:2323–27

Stone, E. A. 1983. Adaptation to stress and brain noradrenergic receptors. *Neurosci. Biobehav. Rev.* 7:503–9

Strange, P. G. 1983. *Cell Surface Receptors.* New York: Wiley

Sutton, R. E., Koob, G. F., LeMoal, M., Rivier, J., Vale, W. W. 1982. Corticotropin-releasing factor produces behavioral activation in rats. *Nature* 297:331–33

Swanson, L. W., Sawchenko, P. E., Rivier, J., Vale, W. W. 1983. Organization of ovine corticotropin-releasing factor immunoreactive cells and fibers in the rat brain: An immunohistochemical study. *Neuroendocrinology* 36:165–86

Tallman, J. F., Gallager, D. W. 1985. The GABA-ergic system: A locus of benzodiazepine action. *Ann. Rev. Neurosci.* 8:21–44

Tannenbaum, G. S. 1984. Growth hormone-releasing factor: Direct effects on growth hormone, glucose, and behavior via the brain. *Science* 226:464–66

Terman, G. W., Shavit, Y., Lewis, J. W., Cannon, J. T., Liebeskind, J. C. 1984. Intrinsic mechanisms of pain inhibition: Activation by stress. *Science* 226:1270–77

Thor, D. H., Holloway, W. R. Jr. 1984. Social play in juvenile rats: A decade of methodological and experimental research. *Neurosci. Biobehav. Rev.* 8:455–64

Tombaugh, T. N., Grandmaison, L. J., Zito, K. A. 1982. Establishment of secondary reinforcement in sign tracking and place preference tests following pimozide treatment. *Pharmacol. Biochem. Behav.* 17:665–70

Trisler, G. D., Grunwald, G. B., Moskal, J., Darveniza, P., Nirenberg, M. 1984. Molecules that identify cell type or position in the retina. In *Neuroimmunology and Neural Disease,* ed. P. Behan, F. Spreafico, pp. 89–97. New York: Raven

Trulson, M. E., Preussler, D. W. 1984. Dopamine-containing ventral tegmental area neurons in freely moving cats: Activity during the sleep-waking cycle and effects of stress. *Exp. Neurol.* 83:367–77

Ungerstedt, U. 1979. Central dopamine mechanisms and unconditioned behavior. In *The Neurobiology of Dopamine,* ed. A. S. Horn, J. Korf, B. H. C. Westerink, pp. 577–96. New York: Academic

Valentino, K. L., Winter, J., Reichardt, L. F. 1985. Applications of monoclonal antibodies to neuroscience research. *Ann. Rev. Neurosci.* 8:199–232

Van Dijk, A., Richards, J. G., Trzeciak, A., Gillessen, D., Mohler, H. 1984. Cholecystokinin receptors: Biochemical demonstration and autoradiographical localization in rat brain and pancreas using [³H] cholecystokinin as radioligand. *J. Neurochem.* 4:1021–33

Vitetta, E. S., Cushley, W., Uhr, J. W. 1983. Synergy of ricin A-chain-containing immunotoxins and ricin B-chain-containing immunotoxins in vitro killing of neoplastic human B-cells. *Proc. Natl. Acad. Sci. USA* 80:6332–35

Vogt, M. 1982. Some functional aspects of central serotonergic neurones. In *Biology of Serotonergic Transmission,* ed. N. N. Osborne, pp. 299–315. New York: Wiley

Warburton, D. M. 1981. Neurochemistry of behaviour. *Br. Med. Bull.* 37:121–25

Wieland, S. J., Gelperin, A. 1983. Dopamine elicits feeding motor program in Limax Maximus. *J. Neurosci.* 3:1735–45

Wise, R. A. 1978. Catecholamine theories of reward: A critical review. *Brain Res.* 152:215–47

Wise, R. A. 1982. Neuroleptics and operant behavior: The anhedonia hypothesis. *Behav. Brain Sci.* 5:39–88

Wise, R. A., Bozarth, M. A. 1982. Action of drugs of abuse on brain reward systems: An update with specific attention to opiates. *Pharmacol. Biochem. Behav.* 17:239–43

Wise, R. A., Bozarth, M. A. 1984. Brain reward circuitry: Four circuit elements "wired" in apparent series. *Brain Res. Bull.* 12:203–8

Yang, C. R., Mogenson, G. J. 1984. Electrophysiological responses in Accumbens to hippocampal stimulation and the attenuation of the excitatory responses by the mesolimbic DA system. *Brain Res.* 324:69–84

Young, W. S. III, Kuhar, M. J. 1980. Radiohistochemical localization of benzodi-azepine receptors in rats brain. *J. Pharmacol. Exp. Ther.* 212:337–46

Zacharko, R. M., Bowers, W. J., Kokkinidis, L., Anisman, H. 1983. Region-specific reductions of intracranial self-stimulation after uncontrollable stress: Possible effects on reward processes. *Behav. Brain Res.* 9:129–41

Zagon, I. S., McLaughlin, P. J. 1984. Naltrexone modulates body and brain development in rats: A role for endogenous opioid systems in growth. *Life Sci.* 35:2057–64

Zarbin, M. A., Innis, R. B., Wamsley, J. K., Snyder, S. H., Kuhar, M. J. 1983. Autoradiographic localization of cholecystokinin receptors in rodent brain. *J. Neurosci.* 2:877–906

Zarbin, M. A., Kuhar, M. J., O'Donohue, T. L., Wolf, S. S., Moody, T. W. 1985. Autoradiographic localization of $[^{125}I$-Tyr]bombesin binding sites in rat brain. *J. Neurosci.* 5:429–37

Zieglgansberger, W. 1984. Opioid actions on mammalian spinal neurons. *Int. Rev. Neurobiol.* 25:243–76

Zolovick, A. J., Rossi, J. III, Davies, R. F., Panksepp, J. 1982. An improved pharmacological procedure for depletion of noradrenaline: Pharmacology and assessment of noradrenaline-associated behaviors. *Eur. J. Pharmacol.* 77:265–71

Zuckerman, M. 1984. Sensation-seeking: A comparative approach to a human trait. *Behav. Brain Sci.* 7:413–71

Ann. Rev. Psychol. 1986. 37:109–33

THE REGULATION OF BODY WEIGHT

Richard E. Keesey

Department of Psychology, University of Wisconsin, Madison, Wisconsin 53706

Terry L. Powley

Department of Psychology, Purdue University, West Lafayette, Indiana 47907

CONTENTS

BODY WEIGHT—A HOMEOSTATIC PERSPECTIVE 111
ENERGY EXPENDITURE AND BODY WEIGHT REGULATION...................... 112
    The Fate of Ingested Energy.. 112
    Daily Energy Requirements 113
    Energy Expenditure and Body Energy Regulation 113
    Energy Expenditure and Energetic Status 115
VARIATION IN BODY WEIGHT—ITS REGULATORY SIGNIFICANCE.............. 116
    The Case of Obesity.. 118
    Factors Altering the Level of Regulated Energy...................................... 120
MECHANISMS OF BODY WEIGHT REGULATION 123
    Signals and Their Detectors.. 123
    Effectors 125
    Central Nervous Integrative Mechanisms.. 126
SUMMARY AND CONCLUSIONS.. 128

The thesis of this chapter is that body weight, like blood pressure or core temperature, is physiologically regulated. More precisely, body energy is regulated and thus body weight, the most widely employed index of the body's energy stores, is in effect regulated. Being so regulated, weight is normally maintained at a particular level or set-point, not only by the control of food intake, as often assumed, but also by complementary adjustments in energy utilization and expenditure. Such a proposal has broad implications for our understanding of feeding behavior and of body weight, including such disturbances as obesity.

109

0066-4308/86/0201-0109$02.00

In examining this thesis, we attempt to specify what exactly is meant by energy regulation. The concept has been controversial, at least in part because it has been used in a number of different (and at times inappropriate) ways. In some cases, "body weight regulation" is uncritically used and/or mistakenly assumed on the basis that individual body weights are often impressively stable. In other instances, "body weight regulation" is repudiated because, under other conditions, weight can fluctuate dramatically. Stability, however, is neither a necessary nor a sufficient criterion for regulation. Likewise, fluctuation no more refutes regulation than stability establishes it. Thus, so as to specify the defining characteristics of body weight regulation, we first examine the concept of homeostasis. Then we review research of the last decade which has both reinforced the conclusion that body weight is regulated and elucidated certain of the responsible neural and physiological mechanisms.

While the concepts of physiological regulation (Bernard 1878) and homeostasis (Cannon 1932) have played an important role in many areas of biology, their application to body weight and body energy has not won wide acceptance. One argument central to our review is that a careful examination of energy *expenditure* provides some of the most compelling evidence for the regulation of body energy. Yet in the past, neither physiology nor psychology accorded expenditure a significant role in this process. In physiology the prevailing view has been that ingested energy was utilized and expended in a prescribed fashion. Both "basal" metabolism and the increase in whole-body heat production associated with a meal ("SDA") were considered obligatory expenses of internal housekeeping, the first fixed by the organism's mass of metabolically active tissue and the second by the cost of processing ingested food. Such assumptions went largely unchallenged, at least in part because of the technical difficulties involved in sensitively and systematically monitoring expenditure. Thus, when changes in body energy stores did not faithfully follow changes in food intake, it was assumed (incorrectly, we believe) that regulation was lacking. Such a conclusion ignores the role that compensatory adjustments in expenditure can play in modulating the rate at which energy is spent and in providing a defense mechanism complementing food intake in energy homeostasis.

Nor was a role for energy expenditure appreciated in psychology where experimental interest has centered almost exclusively on the control of food intake. Reinforcing this focus on intake while at the same time depreciating its regulatory significance were the views and interpretations formed in the 1950s and 1960s from the widely studied phenomenon of hypothalamic obesity. The diet-dependent nature of the ventromedial hypothalamic (VMH) syndrome, VMH "finickiness," and the apparent dissociation of intake from energy need in this preparation all contributed to the view of obesity as a primary eating disorder. The parallels cited by Schachter (1971) between features of the ventromedial hypothalamic syndrome in rats and the characteristics of obese people contributed to a general acceptance of the view that human obesity too results from a deficiency in behavioral controls unchecked by energy regulation mechanisms.

We attempt in this chapter to show that research in the last decade has radically altered views concerning the processes controlling the expenditure of energy. It has become abundantly clear that expenditure is modulated and that this process thus serves as a key defense mechanism effecting energy balance. The elucidation of these expenditure mechanisms provides evidence critical for the regulation of body energy heretofore lacking in perspectives based primarily upon food intake control. Finally, we will show how changes in an individual's weight, gross weight differences between individuals, and even obesity, each usually presumed to stem from a disordered pattern of intake, can, with an appreciation of body energy homeostasis (and particularly a knowledge of the role played by energy expenditure in this process), all be understood from a regulatory perspective.

BODY WEIGHT—A HOMEOSTATIC PERSPECTIVE

A virtually continuous supply of energy is required by all living creatures. In contrast to this pattern of utilization, however, energy intake in most species is episodic. This results in part from the fact that the feed energy supply is itself unreliable, being subject to seasonal and other natural fluctuations. Organisms that either do not or cannot take in energy continuously must have a reserve of readily mobilizable energy. Functionally, the requirement for continuously available metabolizable fuel dictates that the reservoir be both independent of the stable body tissues (e.g. essential organs and muscle) and be of sufficient size to meet vital needs whenever and for as long as the usual supply of food is interrupted. Conversely, for an animal to remain efficient and maneuverable, the energy reserve, with its obligatory costs in terms of both metabolism and body mass, must be limited. Although glycogen reserves in liver and muscle tissues, as well as partially digested food in the gastrointestinal tract, serve as short-term energy reservoirs, practically, body fat (the densest form of energy) makes up the primary store. When changes occur in the body weight of mature or nongrowing animals, these changes typically reflect alterations in the mass of adipose tissue.

What is meant when it is said that body energy or weight is regulated might be illustrated by a brief examination of the fundamental idea of homeostasis and regulation. *Homeostasis* was introduced by Walter B. Cannon (1932) to refer to "steady" states of the body actively maintained by corrective physiological (and behavioral) mechanisms. The term specifically connotes active defense. The dynamic compensations for some state or level typically—but not necessarily—generate a degree of stability in the regulated factor. Cannon stressed, however, that the term was not used to imply fixity. Rather, body states vary within tolerated limits as a function of circumstance or disturbances, as well as of other necessary regulatory adjustments. Blood pressure and body temperature are prototypical examples of homeostatically maintained variables.

As Brobeck (1965) has noted, the formulation of the principles of homeostasis both created a need for a new terminology and led to the application of systems analysis and control theory, with their specialized vocabularies, to biology. "Feedback," "control," "servomechanism," "regulation," and "setpoint" have all been used to describe the physiological and behavioral processes involved in achieving homeostasis. The term *regulation* is currently used synonymously with homeostasis to denote the process of maintaining such defended equilibria. *Set-point* is frequently used because the term connotes a particular level or value indicative of the null state.[1] We will apply both the principles and terminology of systems analysis in this examination of body energy regulation.

ENERGY EXPENDITURE AND BODY WEIGHT REGULATION

The contributions of energy utilization and expenditure to the achievement of body energy homeostasis provide some of the most compelling evidence for the regulation of body energy. It is for this reason that we begin consideration of body energy regulation by examining the control of energy expenditure.

The Fate of Ingested Energy

Energy, once ingested, is digested, converted to a metabolizable form, and then either expended or stored, but not all ingested calories can be so utilized since some portion cannot be digested. Likewise, the conversion of digested energy into a form the body can use ("metabolizable energy") is less than 100% efficient. Still, these losses are not large, and most ingested energy is eventually utilized in (*a*) meeting the organism's basal or resting metabolic requirements, (*b*) providing the energy necessary for processing newly ingested energy, (*c*) providing energy for motor activity or behavior. In warm-blooded animals (homeotherms), significant amounts of energy are also devoted, particularly during certain times of the year, to the regulation of body core temperature. Any energy remaining after these needs have been met is available for storage in the carcass, usually in the form of fat.

To gain an appreciation of how ingested energy is partitioned among these various processes, consider the following. In studying laboratory rats in energy

---

[1]In systems engineering, a set point is formally the reference signal used by a particular type of controller that achieves stability by employing a comparator to evaluate the controller.

balance (i.e. rats whose energy expenditure exactly equated their intake), we found (Corbett & Keesey 1982) that the diet we used was 80.5% digestable. Of that digested, 92% was converted into a metabolizable form. Thus, approximately 75% of the ingested energy was available for use in various bodily functions.

Of this utilizable energy, by far the largest part (72.7%) went to meeting basal or resting metabolic needs (resting heat production). Just under 11% of this expenditure was associated with the ingestion of a meal ("SDA"). The remaining 16.7% was spent on behavioral processes (activity-related heat production).

Daily Energy Requirements

How much energy do we require to meet our daily needs and what determines this need? In considering this issue, Kleiber (1947) observed that, while the energy needs of animals of different sizes vary, all animals expend energy at a rate proportional to their body weights. Thus, birds, rats, dogs, sheep, man, and cattle ingest and expend markedly different amounts of energy; yet their daily energy requirements all stand in the same relationship to their body size. Kleiber demonstrated that the daily energy needs of animals varying in body mass by a factor of 10,000 times could be accurately predicted from the value obtained by raising body weight (in kilograms) to the 3/4 power ($B.W.^{.75}$). Not only has this remarkable relationship between body mass and energy expenditure stood the test of time, but its generality as a biological principle has been enhanced in two ways. First, it has been shown by Hemmingsen (1956–1960) to apply to an ever greater range of species and body weight—from unicellular organisms to the largest mammals, animals whose body weights range over 18 logarithmic units! Secondly, there are indications (of which more will be said later) that the relationship may also apply to the energy needs of different size members of the same species.

Energy Expenditure and Body Energy Regulation

The stable maintenance of body weight requires that energy intake and expenditure be balanced. While it has been recognized that this balance can be achieved by adjustments in either intake or expenditure, food intake traditionally has been regarded as the factor whose control is critical to this process. Expenditure, on the other hand, has been regarded as obligatory and thus fixed. Resting or "basal metabolism," for example, has commonly been viewed as the irreducible energy cost of maintaining the body's organ systems. Likewise, the heat increment to a meal has been regarded as the necessary energy cost of processing ingested food. Only the energy spent on activity has traditionally been viewed as labile and free to vary in the service of energy regulation. Given these views, it is not surprising that energy expenditure has not, until recently, been regarded as particularly important to body energy homeostasis.

Contributing importantly to the revision in thinking about the role of expenditure in energy regulation, however, were the persistent failures to predict weight gains or losses accurately when individuals increased or decreased their daily intake. Individuals fed in excess of their normal daily intake gain less weight than expected from this "excess" caloric intake. Likewise, calorically restricted individuals consistently lose considerably less weight than predicted from intake-based calculations (see Apfelbaum et al 1971).

These "errors" provided indirect evidence that altered conditions of intake produce altered levels of expenditure. Recently, direct evidence has become available. It is now known that neither the over or underfed organism expends energy at the rate Kleiber's formula would predict. In fact (as will be discussed in greater detail later), Kleiber's formula appears to predict energy needs only for animals or persons in energy balance. This is because weight loss or gain from the level normally maintained brings into play a series of metabolic adjustments which serve both to resist further weight change or to facilitate a return to the original weight. It is these adaptive metabolic adjustments that we now examine.

METABOLIC ADAPTATIONS TO ENERGY DEFICIT   Compensatory adjustments in at least two categories of energy expenditure occur when intake is restricted and weight loss occurs. First, there is a reduction in resting metabolism which exceeds to a significant extent that which would occur were it to result from the loss of metabolically active tissue. In rats, for example, we find that weight declines on the order of 6% will cause a decline in resting heat production of 15% (Keesey & Corbett 1984). Disproportionately large declines in resting metabolism are likewise seen in food-deprived men (Keys et al 1950). Thus, the resting rate of energy expenditure typical of animals and man in energy balance is, strictly speaking, not "basal." Instead, resting energy needs drop substantially below normal (i.e. the level predicted by the Kleiber formula) when body weight is reduced from the normally maintained level.

A second compensatory adjustment in energy expenditure in response to caloric restriction and weight loss occurs in the heat increment to a meal. The normal response of a rat to a meal is a sharp rise in the rate of heat production. Yet when the same meal is administered to animals whose weight has been reduced by caloric restriction, this heat increment is attenuated to the point of being barely detectable (Boyle et al 1981). Evidently, only a small part of the usual heat increment to a meal is actually obligatory or necessary to the processing of the ingested nutrients. The remainder appears instead to vary according to the organism's energy status or need.

Whether activity plays a role in the adjustments in energy expenditure to caloric privation remains unclear. Data bearing on this issue are inconclusive, with some indicating more and others less activity following food deprivation and weight loss. Indeed, it appears that the relationship between caloric restriction and activity is complex, being critically dependent upon both the species under study and the specific measure of activity employed (Cornish & Mrosovsky 1965). It must be recognized, however, that while animals faced with an inadequate food supply could conserve energy by reducing expenditure on activity, such a course would limit opportunities to locate new sources of energy and to secure them. Energy savings derived from reduced activity would thus appear to be of doubtful survival value.

METABOLIC ADAPTATIONS TO ENERGY EXCESS   Numerous reports exist that overconsumption both in animals (Grafe & Graham 1911) and humans (Gulick 1922, Miller & Mumford 1973) fails to produce the weight gain expected on the basis of the caloric excess. Recently, this apparent squandering of energy ("luxuskonsumption") has been assessed directly and an understanding of the responsible physiological mechanisms is emerging.

Animals stimulated to overconsume palatable, calorically dense diets display elevated rates of whole body metabolism (Rothwell & Stock 1982). As with the decline in heat production produced by caloric deficiency, the elevation with overconsumption exceeds that expected from a consideration of the gain in body tissue. Also, like the adaptation to energy deficit, this increased heat production does not appear to be mediated behaviorally. Indeed, while total energy expenditure is elevated during diet-induced weight gain, we find expenditure on activity to be reduced (Vilberg & Keesey 1982).

Energy Expenditure and Energetic Status

These adjustments in energy expenditure in response to over- and undernutrition can be viewed as regulatory in that they tend both to resist weight gain or loss and to facilitate the restoration of body weight to a particular level when it has been previously displaced. As such, they help to explain the relative stability of body weight in the face of variation in food supply, not to mention the dieter's well-known difficulty in losing weight, or the similar (though less commonly encountered) difficulty of people who attempt to gain weight by overeating (Gulick 1922, Sims & Horton 1968).

Conversely, since energy metabolism varies with energy status, rate of expenditure may provide a useful index of when an individual is at his physiologically regulated body weight or set-point (Keesey & Corbett 1984). Since Kleiber's equation relating daily energy expenditure to metabolic body size appears to have been based upon animals in energy balance, it accurately estimates daily energy needs when an animal is at its regulated body weight. But the regulatory adjustments just described cause energy expenditure to be higher than predicted when body weight rises above this level, or to be less than predicted when intake is restricted and weight falls. There is, therefore, only one body weight at which an individual's resting metabolism can be accurately predicted from its metabolic body size according to the Kleiber equation. At only this body weight would the person be in energy balance or at his set-point.[2]

VARIATION IN BODY WEIGHT—ITS REGULATORY SIGNIFICANCE

Variation is a salient feature of body weight, both in individuals and between individuals of the same species. It is not unusual, for example, for the weights of certain adults of the same species (including man) to be two or three times that of others. Since the weight difference between two individuals having the same body build is largely accounted for by body fat, energy stores may easily vary or differ by a factor of five to ten times. Nor is it then unusual for an adult individual to undergo significant weight change at various times in his life.

Inasmuch as stability is often cited as evidence of weight regulation, it is not surprising that instances of variation or change are often used to dispute the claims for regulation (cf Garrow & Stalley 1975). Does such variation in body weight reflect a deficit in regulation? In our view, it does not. As discussed earlier, homeostasis does not imply fixity. Indeed, all regulated physiological variables demonstrate both intraindividual and intraspecific variations. Fluctuation within limits no more refutes regulation than stability (without defense) establishes regulation.

It may be useful in this regard to consider once again the functional significance of body energy stores. As discussed earlier, fat stores provide a reserve

---

[2]This use of the body weight-energy expenditure relationship assumes that Kleiber's formulation, which was based upon interspecific comparisons, applies to different size members of the same species. The few tests of this assumption to date have been inconclusive. The power to which the body weights of mice, rats, rabbits, and dogs must be raised to predict their resting metabolism have been found to differ to some extent (See Kleiber 1975); yet none were greatly different from the .75 value derived from interspecific comparisons. Until more evidence indicates that there are differences, it seems reasonable, as Kleiber (1975) has suggested, to assume that the intra and interspecific relations of body size and metabolic rate are the same. But even if an adjustment in the body weight exponent is required to predict the resting metabolism of individual members of the same species, attempts to characterize the regulated level of body weight by assessing the rate of energy expenditure at different body weights seem both feasible and worthy of further consideration. The regulated or "set-point" weight level indicated by such a procedure would not, of course, be an "ideal" body weight from the standpoint of health risk, cosmetic concern, or other considerations. It would, however, indicate the weight the regulatory machinery of the body is set to maintain. Such information could be of considerable value to the clinician who at present has little more than population norms of the sort provided by the Metropolitan Life Insurance Standards (1983) to inform him of the weight any particular person might reasonably be expected to achieve and maintain.

that ensures a continuous supply of substrates during periods when external sources of energy are not readily available. This essential function of the body energy stores renders them in one sense relatively unique. As a reserve, energy stores must fluctuate, and their size would be expected to covary to some extent with availability of exogenous energy sources. When food is available, an animal can repair its stores; when food is not available, an animal must deplete them. Clearly, maintenance of energy stores must be subsidiary to meeting the essential needs imposed by these dynamic demands facing the organism. If there were no "slack" in the defense mechanisms regulating energy, then body fat, paradoxically, would not be a functional reserve. If the defenses of the reservoir were not relaxed in times of need, an animal would be poorly prepared to mobilize and utilize the energy for essential tissue needs. For these reasons, a certain degree of natural variation in weight is to be expected in response to changing environmental conditions (see Mrosovsky & Powley 1977 for a review of these functional considerations).

In many instances, however, variation in body weight can be shown to be the result of a strict regulation process, not its failure. A most compelling illustration of this point can be found in the case of hibernating ground squirrels (Mrosovsky & Fisher 1970). These rodents display an annual rhythm of steady weight gain in the period preceding hibernation and progressive weight decline during hibernation. Experiments indicate, however, that this annual cycle of weight gain and loss is tightly regulated. Should weight be caused to deviate from the level ordinarily seen at any phase of this annual cycle, either by restricting the squirrels' intake prior to hibernation or by rousing them so as to accelerate weight loss during hibernation, adjustments are subsequently made that quickly restore body weight to the appropriate level. So, even though it is never stable (except from one year to the next), the weight of the ground squirrel is closely and continuously regulated, apparently tracking the course of a constantly changing or sliding "set-point."

Nor is the wide variation in body weight between individuals inconsistent with the strict regulation of body energy. Other physiological variables such as blood pressure, for example, though tightly regulated, display considerable variation between individuals. It is, of course, critical to survival that certain upper and lower limits not be exceeded, and blood pressure thus has a restricted range of biologically acceptable values. Perhaps in this way body weight differs from many other physiological variables in that, while body energy stores have a clear life-threatening lower limit, increasing amounts of the stores provide both advantages and disadvantages. Large fat stores offer a good buffer against the natural seasonal variation in food supply many individuals face [see, for example, Coleman's (1979) discussion of the adaptive significance of "thrifty" genes]. Excessive stores, at the same time, may tend to impair health, reduce mobility, or otherwise impair the individual's ability to survive in competition with other members of the species. The clinical literature stresses, in particular, the various health risks of high body weights. Yet it must be recognized that these risks emerge in middle age and later, substantially beyond the age of peak reproductive activity. Thus, however serious the health risks of large fat stores may be later in life, there is probably little pressure toward selecting those genes transmitting this tendency. The wide natural variation in body weights both in human and many animal populations may thus be, in part, the consequence of there being less stringent selection pressures limiting the upper bound of regulated energy stores.

The Case of Obesity

As the preceding analysis suggests, existence of obesity no more challenges the idea that body weight is regulated than the presence of hypertension in a segment of the population refutes the idea that blood pressure is regulated. The essential question to consider is whether obesity is regulated (albeit at a high body weight), or whether it is an instance of a failure in regulation. Do the obese, for example, fail to display the adjustments in energy expenditure that normally serve so effectively to stabilize body weight at a particular level? Models that tend to treat obesity as stemming from a proper lack of control over intake or a disordered pattern of ingestion favor a regulatory dysfunction interpretation. An alternative hypothesis is that, even at the extremes of the weight continuum, energy regulation can be normal.

Evidence consistent with this latter view can be found in several animal forms of obesity. The Zucker "fatty" rat, a strain in which obesity is transmitted by a single Mendelian recessive gene (Zucker & Zucker 1961), provides one seeming instance of regulation at an elevated set-point. Just as their lean siblings, fatty rats defend their body weight in a way as to suggest that it is actively regulated. Zucker fatties remain obese, for example, even if maintained on unpalatable diets (Cruce et al 1974). Likewise, they defend their obesity metabolically by sharply reducing their rate of resting expenditure when intake is restricted and body weight declines (Keesey et al 1984a). The effectiveness of this metabolic adjustment in sustaining their obesity can be appreciated by the observations from a recent experiment that a modest weight decline (from 610 to 583 grams) caused Zucker fatty rats to reduce their resting metabolism to the level of normal weight lean littermates weighing less than half as much (285 g).

Other genetically obese rodent strains also display a metabolic defense of body energy stores. Both *db/db* and *ob/ob* mice maintain their excessive adiposity by increasing their metabolic efficiency when their characteristic hyperphagia is prevented by experimental pair-feed protocols (Cox & Powley 1977, Coleman 1978).

On the other hand, not all forms of animal obesities appear to be regulated.

One widely studied form, ventromedial hypothalamic (VMH) obesity, provides an apparent instance of a regulatory failure. The obesity of this preparation is diet-dependent. Thus, VMH obesity is expressed with palatable diets but can be prevented entirely by feeding unpalatable diets (Ferguson & Keesey 1975, Sclafani et al 1976). Furthermore, there are indications that VMH-lesioned rats fail to show the expected adjustments in energy expenditure when their weight is experimentally displaced from the maintained level. Across a wide range, their resting metabolism remains proportional to body weight, not, as in the normal rat, becoming disporportionately higher at body weights above a particular level and markedly lower at weights below this level (Vilberg & Keesey 1982, 1984a). These observations suggest the absence of a set-point for body weight in VMH-lesioned rats. Instead, it appears that some aspect of the physiological response to the diet determines the level at which body weight in these rats settles (Powley 1977). However, the level of weight thus generated does not appear to be regulated in that it is defended neither behaviorally nor metabolically.

Which of these animal preparations best model human obesity? Information concerning the metabolic status of obese individuals at the elevated weights they maintain and, in particular, their metabolic response to displacement from this level would provide a key to answering this question. Unfortunately, few observations of this sort have been made. Those that have, however, indicate that the body weights of many obese individuals are metabolically defended. Bray (1969) measured the resting metabolism of 6 obese patients undergoing weight loss and noted that for a weight decline of slightly less than 3%, there was a decline in the group's resting oxygen consumption of 17%. Furthermore, obese persons displaying this metabolic adaptation to weight loss apparently remain hypometabolic for as long as their body weight remains below the formerly maintained level [6 years in one report (Leibel & Hirsch 1984)].

At the same time, it seems that some obese individuals do not regulate normally in that their energy expenditure is not appropriately coupled to the energy regulating system. Garrow & Warwick (1978) measured the changes in resting metabolism of 26 obese women undergoing weight loss. An examination of their findings suggests that approximately 20 of these patients displayed a metabolic resistance to weight loss. That is, they adaptively reduced their resting metabolism at a rate disproportionately faster than their weight loss. The remainder, however, appeared to show no resistance in that their resting metabolism declined at a rate appropriate to the weight loss.

This dichotomous pattern of response to weight loss has prompted the proposal that a clinical distinction be made between "regulated" and "unregulated" obesities (Keesey 1986). To this point, however, there have been no clinical tests of this proposal, and the proportion of each type in the obese population cannot be estimated. Garrow and Warwick's observations suggest that approximately one-fifth to one-fourth of the obese are of the "unregulated" type. A better-informed estimate awaits the systematic measurement of the metabolic response to weight loss in a larger sample of obese individuals.

Factors Altering the Level of Regulated Energy

In the preceding section we considered the differences in maintained body weight between individuals, concluding that these differences in many cases represented different levels of energy regulation. It is also true, however, that the individuals regulating at these different levels display weight change. Individual weights vary with diet, age, lifestyle, health, and other circumstances. Do these factors influence body weight by overriding the normal regulation process, and can the weight changes they produce be taken as evidence of ineffectual regulation of body energy stores? Or do these factors exert their influence upon body weight by directly altering the regulation level or set-point?

DIET INFLUENCES   Without question, diet is a significant factor in determining the level of body weight. It is quite common, in fact, to attribute the presumed tendencies to overweight in our society to the wide availability of various palatable "supermarket" foods, high in both carbohydrate and fat. It is also this influence of diet on body weight that prompts many to question the premise that body energy is regulated.

A frequently encountered observation in both the experimental and popular literatures on body weight is that an individual's weight can be altered by the palatability and/or fat content of the diet. A classic example comes from several rat strains which are particularly susceptible to dietary-induced obesity. These rats will defend normal levels of body fat stores while they are maintained on standard laboratory diets, but will store substantial amounts of energy as fat when they are given access to enriched, calorically dense foods (e.g. Schemmel et al 1970). In a graphic example of this phenomenon, Sclafani & Springer (1976) have demonstrated that some rats maintained on "supermarket" or "junk food" diets often become grossly obese. A variety of factors, including strain or genotype, age, and gender, all influence susceptibility to "dietary obesity."

The critical question to consider, namely, whether dietary-induced hyperphagias and dietary-induced obesities reflect *failures* of regulation or altered regulation levels, can, as in the case of any obesity, only be fully assessed by examining defense of the elevated body weight. One animal form of dietary obesity, that produced by a high sucrose or high carbohydrate diet, provides evidence bearing on this issue. While it appears that such diets do produce overeating and ultimate increases in adipose stores, there is also evidence that this overconsumption concomitantly activates mechanisms that increase expenditure [in this case norepinephrine turnover (Young & Landsberg 1977)].

Similarly, Rothwell & Stock (1982) have observed that animals maintained on a "cafeteria" diet that promotes overeating and weight gain also evidence a regulatory increase in heat production. As a result, such animals gain far less than would be predicted from the very substantial overeating that occurs.

There are instances in which excess intake seems not to be actively resisted by increases in expenditure. The ventromedial hypothalamic rat already discussed offers one such example. More widely studied, however, is a specialized experimental situation not likely to be encountered clinically, but one that may have implications for our understanding of the detector mechanisms of energy regulation. Several research groups have observed that there is little or no evidence for increased expenditure or regulatory compensations when animals are overfed with direct delivery of calories to the stomach (e.g. Rothwell & Stock 1979, Armitage et al 1981, McCracken & McNiven 1983, Walgren & Powley 1985). When animals are hyperalimented directly in the stomach, some signal critical for full regulation seems not to be generated. Typically, when the intragastric feeding is stopped, the animal reestablishes its previous level of energy stores by reducing intake and increasing expenditure.

Excepting these rather special circumstances, the effects of diet on body weight can be appropriately viewed as affecting regulatory systems. It is instructive in this regard to consider the effects of diet upon another regulated variable, namely, blood pressure. Diets high in sodium can result in hypertension, and the hypertension is typically interpreted as an alteration in regulation rather than a failure of homeostasis. Hypertensives regulate their blood pressures, albeit at higher levels. By analogy, when dietary obesity occurs, it is possible that, though weight gain is initially resisted by increased rates of energy expenditure, long-term exposure to such diets may actually change the level or set-point at which body weight is regulated. Several observations support such a conclusion. For example, Rolls and her colleagues (1980) have shown that extended periods of maintenance on enriched diets can establish a higher chronically maintained level of body weight. Other evidence comes from a study of the energy expenditure of dietary obese rats (Keesey et al 1984a). Following six months' maintenance on a high fat diet, obese rats were not hypermetabolic but instead displayed a resting rate of metabolism appropriate to their increased metabolic body size. Furthermore, when the intake of these rats was restricted, their rate of resting energy expenditure actually fell below that of rats maintained on a regular diet and weighing considerably less. These findings again suggest that adaptations can occur in long-term diet-induced obesity that eventuate in the normal regulation of body weight at an obese level. The finding in this experiment that the high-fat diet likewise stimulated a marked increase in fat cell number reinforces the possibility that adipose cell number plays an important role in setting the weight at which these rats achieve energy balance.

ANORECTIC DRUGS   Anorectic drugs, widely used in the clinical management of obesity, have historically been viewed as exerting their effects upon body weight by suppressing appetite. Several observations, however, are not easily reconciled with such an interpretation. One is that such drugs are only temporarily effective in reducing food intake, typically just until body weight declines to a particular level. Even though drug treatment continues, intake then returns to near normal levels and body weight stabilizes at a reduced level. Tolerance has been suggested as the explanation for why the drug fails to continue to suppress intake, but recent observations cast doubt upon this interpretation (Levitsky et al 1981). Prior to administering fenfluramine (or amphetamine), food restriction was used to reduce the body weight of rats to a lower level than they would maintain during drug administration. When fenfluramine was then administered, it had no appetite suppressant effects. In fact, these rats actually gained weight until they reached the reduced level of other rats treated with this drug. Thus, the suppression of food intake ordinarily seen following administration of such drugs is apparently not primary but rather secondary to lowering body weight to a reduced set-point (Stunkard 1982).

EXERCISE   Exercise is also known to promote weight loss and, when used in conjunction with diet, to provide one of the more effective noninvasive clinical means of weight loss (Thompson et al 1982). It appears that upon initiation of an exercise program, the increased energy expenditure it engenders is not initially compensated for by increased intake and weight loss occurs. In time, however, weight stabilizes at a lower level which is then steadily maintained as long as the exercise continues. At this point, resting metabolism is normal, i.e. appropriate to the lower body weight being maintained (Donahoe et al 1984). This contrasts with the sharp reduction in resting metabolism otherwise seen in individuals who lose the same amount of weight but do so by dieting alone. Since exercising individuals thus appear normal, except for their weights, exercise too appears to induce a primary shift in the level of energy regulation.

TOXINS   Some toxins also may exert their effects upon body weight by altering the regulated level of energy stores. TCDD (2,3,7,8-tetracholorodibenzo-p-dioxin) produces a wasting syndrome in rats. When administered in sublethal doses, it lowers the level of maintained body weight in a dose-dependent fashion. Rats so treated display an unimpaired ability to defend this reduced body weight against a variety of challenges (Seefeld et al 1984). Also like normal rats, if stimulated to overconsume, they deposit the excess calories as fat. That is, though their body weight can be restored to control levels, they become obese rather than reassuming a normal body composition (Seefeld et al 1984). TCDD thus appears to exert its influence upon weight by reducing the regulated level of body weight.

ALTERED REGULATION LEVELS: SUMMARY AND CONCLUSIONS   Though less well documented, there are likely many other factors whose effects on body weight are achieved by altering the regulated level of body energy. The changes in adiposity that accompany variation in the gonadal hormones (Wade & Gray 1979), the increases in body weight that follow the cessation of smoking (Carney & Goldberg 1984), and the body composition changes associated with aging (Forbes & Reina 1970) are other factors that appear also to influence the physiological environment so as to alter the level of energy regulation. Thus, set-points are not fixed or invariant. Likewise, just as observations of stability are not sufficient to establish that weight is regulated, neither is the observation of weight change evidence that it is not. Rather, the level of regulated body energy is specific to a given set of internal conditions. Changes produced in these conditions by factors such as diet, drugs, etc cause the regulated energy level to increase or decrease, just as pyrogens cause the regulated level of body temperature to increase, or as diet or exercise can change the level of blood pressure.

MECHANISMS OF BODY WEIGHT REGULATION

In the language of control theory, a system for regulating body energy requires (*a*) detectors or sensors to monitor feedback; (*b*) control mechanisms to produce the output; and (*c*) a controller or comparator for relating input and output (Brobeck 1965). In the terminology of physiology these elements correspond, respectively, to (*a*) adequate stimuli, their receptors, and afferent pathways to detect and signal an organism's energy status; (*b*) effectors to adjust the levels of both energy intake and expenditure; and (*c*) integrative central nervous system mechanisms for coordinating the behavioral and physiological defenses with the energy status. Although engineering theory recognizes a variety of different types of controllers (one of them being a "set-point" controller) that will achieve regulation, too little is known about the neural mechanisms of energy balance to specify the particular form the physiological analog takes. In effect, though, the central nervous system must compare the received and processed input from the sensors to some energy-condition template or "set-point" the system is organized to maintain. Finally, if an imbalance is detected, the effector mechanisms appropriate to reestablishing energy balance will be activated. In this section we describe what is currently known concerning these system components of body energy regulation.

Signals and Their Detectors

At the present time, perhaps less is known about these aspects of energy homeostasis than about any other. Considerable research is available on the nutrients, metabolites, and substrates that influence feeding, but not specifically on the metabolic stimuli that influence ingestion (or expenditure) *qua* energy balance. The lack of more emphasis on the stimuli that provide feedback for the regulation of body weight is also probably reinforced by a recognition that regulation is defined in terms of the system variable (i.e. body energy) and the defense mechanisms (i.e. intake and expenditure), not the particulars of the signals. Nonetheless, some stimulating hypotheses about the signals and their detectors do exist. These ideas suggest directions in which possible answers may be found, and they raise another general issue concerning the thesis that body energy stores are regulated.

There is considerable indirect evidence that some index or correlate of fat cell size is detected. Under a variety of conditions that include different feeding regimens and other experimental and surgical manipulations that change fat cell size or fat cell number, experimenters have found that animals, including humans, seem to defend or maintain an "ideal" adipocyte size (Faust et al 1976, 1977). The signal or (signals) in this case may well be a circulating factor, since several experiments have demonstrated that when one member of a conjoined pair of parabiotic animals is fattened by forced feeding, the partner evidences a "compensatory" reduction in its fat stores (Parameswaran et al 1977, Harris & Martin 1984).

Another candidate signal involved in the detection and regulation of energy stores is insulin, the major hormone of energy storage. Employing an experimental preparation in which the cerebrospinal fluid level of insulin is monitored, Woods & Porte (1983) have found that body weight levels can be chronically decreased by sustained increases in CSF insulin levels. These investigators have also found abnormal levels of endogenous insulin in the CSF of the genetically obese Zucker fatty rat.

In addition to fat cell morphology and insulin, many other substrates, metabolites, and hormones, both in the periphery (in liver and gut, particularly) and in brain, have been demonstrated to influence food intake and/or energy expenditure. The large number and variety of factors influencing energy intake and expenditure raises an issue relevant to the general issue of body energy regulation. Although energy detectors per se have been posited (cf Nicolaidis 1981), it seems that at least some, if not all, of the factors sensed for adjustments of intake and expenditure are not energy as such. Similarly, some or all of the signals may not be body fat per se. The point is relevant because the argument is sometimes made that body weight (or energy or fat) cannot be regulated because an animal has no direct means of measuring weight (or energy or fat). We think this argument is specious, but perhaps it needs to be considered. It is indeed most likely that body weight regulation involves the sensing and transduction of a number of substrates or factors at a number of loci. It is the central integration of these signals into a coordinated response of intake and expenditure that constitutes body weight regulation. To draw again a parallel to other regulatory systems, body weight appears to be regulated in the same manner as blood pressure, another system in which there are multiple indirect signals from multiple detectors at multiple sites organized into an integrated series of defenses.

Effectors

As previously noted, the role of effectors in an energy regulatory system is to produce changes in the intake and expenditure of energy appropriate to the maintenance of homeostasis. With the emphasis on expenditure in this paper, we focus here primarily on the mechanisms responsible for modulating the rate at which energy is spent. Recent reviews of the current work on the mechanisms controlling intake are available elsewhere (Sullivan et al 1983, Le Magnen 1983, Anderson et al 1984, Morley et al 1984).

The rate of energy expenditure appears to be modulated primarily by the autonomic nervous system. Many of the changes in heat production that occur with changes in energy status are executed by the sympathetic branch of the autonomic nervous system. Release of catecholamines enhances a well-known series of physiological responses that liberate substrates from energy stores for metabolic needs. Although this mobilization has been viewed classically in terms of providing additional energy for the demands of "fight or flight" situations, it is now also clear that these sympathetic responses can adaptively increase heat production (and thus energy shunting or energy expenditure) when overconsumption occurs and energy stores exceed the regulated level. Both high levels of catecholamines and enhanced catecholamine turnover have been observed in response to consumption of enriched diets or experimental overfeeding (Landsberg & Young 1982, Rappaport et al 1982).

The parasympathetic branch of the autonomic nervous system, particularly the vagus nerve, likewise participates in various anabolic adjustments modulating expenditure. For example, increases in vagal tone affect the partitioning of endogenous energy stores and this in turn may affect substrate availability. One such example is found in the ventromedial hypothalamic obese animal. This animal exhibits enhanced energy storage and becomes obese even when its food intake is clamped at control levels (Cox & Powley 1981a, Vilberg & Keesey 1984b). Its enhanced metabolic efficiency seems to depend on vagal tone insofar as the efficiency of the lesioned animal is returned to normal levels by vagotomy (Cox & Powley 1981b).

The adaptive adjustments in metabolism that serve to stabilize body energy at the regulated level are usually detected as changes in whole-body heat production. Generally speaking, the brain, heart, and liver are the body's major consumers of energy and they account for a large part of our resting energy expenditure. It should be recognized, however, that adjustments in expenditure in the service of energy homeostasis are not the responsibility of these organs.

Their specific and vital functions would be compromised were their metabolism to be affected each time energy balance was threatened. Required instead is a specific thermogenic organ that can modulate energy expenditure without seriously altering other bodily functions. One organ having such thermogenic capabilities is the sympathetically innervated brown adipose tissue found in a number of subhuman species. Evidence increasingly suggests that this tissue plays a predominant role in the heat production changes associated with shifts in energy intake, in addition to its classically recognized role in nonshivering thermogenesis in the service of body core temperature regulation (see Seydoux 1983). Brown adipose tissue thermogenesis is elevated after overconsumption of palatable diets, and it has been estimated that this organ has the thermogenic potential to dissipate as heat essentially all the excess calories consumed by cafeteria-fed rats (Rothwell & Stock 1981). Further, brown adipose tissue thermogenesis has been shown to be reduced or absent in several rodent models of obesity (Thurlby & Trayhurn 1980, Wickler et al 1982), thus reinforcing the speculation that the impairment of a physiological defense normally involved in body weight regulation may contribute to these forms of obesity (James & Trayhurn 1981).

It is less clear whether the brown adipose tissue can account for the conservation of energy that occurs with caloric restriction and weight loss. Reduced sympathetic activity in brown adipose tissue has been noted in fasting rats (Young et al 1982), but the normal or resting rates of thermogenesis in this organ are not sufficiently high to account for the decline (20% or more) seen with whole-body expenditure of deprived animals. It may be worth noting that energy savings can be realized from compromises in other regulations. The normally strict regulation of body core temperature is, for example, relaxed in energy-deprived organisms (Heim & Mestyán 1964, Vigersky et al 1977). The energy normally expended on the menstrual cycle can likewise provide a source of savings. The amenorrhea of the anorexia nervosa patient (Crisp & Stonehill 1971) or of the highly trained female athlete (Schwartz et al 1981) or ballet dancer (Frisch et al 1980) whose adipose stores have been sharply reduced appear to be examples of such an adaptation.

Central Nervous Integrative Mechanisms

Analyses of the central nervous mechanisms integrating these receptor and effector elements into an energy-regulating system have focused on the hypothalamus. The rich and unique afferent and efferent organization of this area includes reciprocal connections with brainstem and spinal autonomic mechanisms that modulate energy expenditure, projections to medullary and pontine areas that integrate ingestive responses, and control over the hypophysiotropic area of the basomedial hypothalamus that can modulate energy expenditure. Two specific regions attract particular attention in this regard.

VENTROMEDIAL HYPOTHALAMUS   The ventromedial hypothalamic syndrome has been the object of intensive study ever since the pioneering work of Hetherington & Ransom (1942). Animals with ventromedial hypothalamic lesions allowed *ad libitum* access to food exhibit a dramatic overeating or hyperphagia and often become extraordinarily obese (cf Powley et al 1980 for a review). However, as discussed earlier, this obesity appears not to be defended either behaviorally or metabolically, though under some dietary conditions VMH-lesioned animals do modify their patterns of ingestion to reestablish a given level of obesity if their weights are experimentally displaced.

A variety of observations implicate the ventromedial hypothalamic area in the defense of body energy stores. Lesions of this area are known to produce a pattern of effects associated with reductions in expenditure (Nishizawa & Bray 1978, Seydoux et al 1981, Vander Tuig et al 1982). Reductions in expenditure both on resting metabolism and activity are part of this pattern (Vilberg & Keesey 1984b). The role of the autonomic nervous system in this syndrome has been the subject of several thorough reviews (see Powley 1977, Powley & Opsahl 1976, Bray & York 1979).

Recent investigations provide an important link between the ventromedial hypothalamus and the control of brown adipose tissue thermogenesis. Direct electrical stimulation of this hypothalamic area activates brown adipose tissue thermogenesis (Perkins et al 1981). Conversely, lesions of this area appear to "disconnect" control of the brown adipose tissue from energy-related variables which otherwise cause it to be activated (Seydoux et al 1981). Although still displaying increased brown adipose tissue thermogenesis when cold-stressed, rats with ventromedial hypothalamic lesions apparently fail to do so following overconsumption of a cafeteria diet (Triandafillou & Himms-Hagen 1983).

LATERAL HYPOTHALAMUS   The lateral hypothalamus appears to play both a critical and unique role in energy regulation. As we have summarized elsewhere (Powley & Keesey 1970, Keesey & Powley 1975), bilateral lesions of the lateral hypothalamic area that produce the classical lateral hypothalamic feeding syndrome (Teitelbaum & Epstein 1962) are also associated with a chronically reduced level of body weight maintenance. A series of experiments designed to determine whether this lowered weight level reflected a failure or an alteration in energy regulation has shown that the reduced body weight of LH-lesioned animals is a regulated maintenance level, i.e. it reflects a lowered set-point. Animals with lateral hypothalamic lesions employ appropriate behavioral strategies to defend their reduced energy stores. When experimentally displaced above or below the reduced body weight maintained following lesioning, the animals become anorexic or hyperphagic respectively (Powley & Keesey 1970, Keesey et al 1976). Indeed, the aphagia and anorexia, commonly viewed as pathognomonic for the lateral hypothalamic syndrome, can instead be viewed as behavioral compensation to achieve energy balance at the lesion-lowered level.

LH-lesioned animals likewise display the full array of metabolic responses appropriate to the regulation of body weight at a reduced set-point. In the immediate postlesion period, when lateral hypothalamic animals are aphagic or anorexic, they display elevated rates of energy expenditure (Keesey et al 1984b). Once weight has declined to the new (reduced) level, however, their resting rate of energy expenditure is normal for the amount of tissue they now maintain (Corbett & Keesey 1982). This stands in contrast to the sharply reduced resting metabolic rate of nonlesioned rats whose weights are reduced to this same level by caloric restriction and supports the conclusion that LH-lesioned rats are in energy balance at the reduced body weight they now maintain. Further supporting this view are recent observations that, just as nonlesioned animals defend a normal body weight by appropriately increasing or decreasing energy expenditure when challenged, so do LH-lesioned rats respond when their reduced body weights are challenged (Corbett et al 1985).

In this normal intake and expenditure of energy at a reduced body weight, in their hypophagia and elevated rates of energy expenditure following over-consumption and weight gain from this reduced level, and in their hyperphagia and depressed rates of metabolism following caloric restriction and weight loss, LH-lesioned rats give every indication of defending a reduced body weight. It thus appears that this hypothalamic area plays a primary role in determining the set-point for regulated body weight. It is likewise conceivable, though still undemonstrated, that it is by way of this lateral hypothalamic mechanism that the known genetic and developmental influences upon the level of regulated body weight are expressed, thereby producing the rather substantial weight differences between adult members of the same species.

SUMMARY AND CONCLUSIONS

The argument for body energy regulation has, in our judgment, been significantly enhanced by research of the past decade. Work demonstrating the role of energy expenditure in this process has been pivotal. It now seems clear that both "basal" metabolism and the heat increment to a meal are sharply reduced when an organism falls into negative energy balance. In a similar fashion energy expenditure is sharply elevated by excess intake and weight gain. These observations not only demonstrate an important role for energy expenditure in stabilizing body energy at the regulated level but they also relieve food intake of the exclusive responsibility it has historically borne for this function. Because changes in intake often fail to produce corresponding changes in body weight, and because many factors affecting food intake appear to have little or no regulatory significance, this prior reliance on food intake as the primary energy effector gave an unconvincing picture of body energy regulation. Conversely, the demonstrated capacity of energy expenditure to compensate for those instances in which food intake is not consistent with energy needs revitalizes the regulatory thesis.

More speculatively, we might argue that it is primarily through the control of expenditure rather than through adjustments in intake that weight stability is ordinarily achieved. Unlike the intake of energy, which is episodic (occurring only every several days in some species), expenditure of energy is continuous and thereby amenable to uninterrupted control and continual adjustment. Certainly from this standpoint, control of expenditure is better suited than intake for maintaining stable energy stores. Another consideration favoring expenditure for this function is the observation that even small displacements in weight from the regulated level, sometimes too small to produce a compensatory adjustment in intake, produce substantial changes in energy expenditure. Thus, it may well be that the fine tuning required for the maintenance of body weight at the regulated level is accomplished by adjusting energy expenditure. Only when an energy excess or deficit exceeds the capacity of these expenditure adjustments to compensate fully would it be necessary for adjustments in food intake come into play.

Discussed throughout the chapter are observations concerning body weight that have been cited as evidence inconsistent with the regulation of body energy. The wide differences in maintained body weight between individuals and the prevalence of obesity are two such examples. Another is the observation that individual body weights are often not stable but subject to influences such as the taste, texture, and macronutrient composition of diets, drugs, exercise, and hormones. We have attempted in each case to demonstrate that these observations are not in conflict with the regulation of body energy and in many cases can, upon closer examination, be taken as evidence of its presence. Evidence is cited that body weights, even at the extreme represented by the obese, can be regulated. So was it shown that many factors altering body weight do so not by disrupting or overriding the regulation process but by changing the system's set-point. Finally, it was possible in some cases to cite the specific physiological or neural mechanisms participating in this regulation process.

We have attempted to summarize these points in Table 1 where the features and operating characteristics of the system regulating body energy are explicitly compared to those involved in the regulation of another physiologically regulated variable, blood pressure. Listed on the left side of this table are certain operating characteristics of the system regulating blood pressure. To the right are two columns pertaining to the system for energy regulation. The first considers whether the energy regulating system also exhibits each of these features or operating characteristics. The second indicates where in the present chapter the observations supporting such a conclusion can be found.

Table 1 Comparison of energy regulation with blood pressure regulation

SYSTEM CHARACTERISTICS FOR BLOOD PRESSURE REGULATION[a]	BODY ENERGY REGULATION	
	Exhibits same characteristics	Where discussed
1. Level can vary considerably between individuals.	Yes	pp. 117–18
2. Level affected by diet.	Yes	pp. 120–21
3. Level affected by drugs.	Yes	p. 122
4. Level influenced by hormones (e.g. estrogens).	Yes	p. 123
5. Level affected by life style (e.g. exercise).	Yes	p. 122
6. Multiple detector mechanism and inputs.	Yes	pp. 123–24
7. Detector mechanisms sense *correlates* of the regulated variable, not the variable per se.	Yes	pp. 124–25
8. Multiple effector mechanisms defend the system variable.	Yes	pp. 125–26
9. The regulation is cross-lined with other regulatory systems.	Yes	p. 126
10. Individuals may defend levels too high for optimal health.	Yes	pp. 118–20

[a]Based on material from *Handbook of Physiology: The Cardiovascular System, Vol. 3: Peripheral Circulation and Organ Blood Flow, Part 2.* 1983, T. T. Shepherd, F. M. Abbond, eds. Bethesda: Am. Physiol. Soc. See particularly chapters by Abbond, F. M., Thames, M. D. "Interactions of cardiovascular reflexes in circulatory control," pp. 675–753; Mancia, G., Mark, A. L. "Arterial baroreflexes in humans." pp. 755–93.

The table both summarizes the major points of the chapter and concludes the discussion. An inspection of the parallels between body energy and blood pressure regulation and a careful consideration of the observations and arguments upon which each of these comparisons rests provides, we believe, a compelling case for the regulation thesis espoused here.

Literature Cited

Anderson, G. H., Li, E. T. S., Glanville, N. T. 1984. Brain mechanisms and the quantitative and qualitative aspects of food intake. *Brain Res. Bull.* 12:167–73

Apfelbaum, M., Bostsarron, J., Lacatis, D. 1971. Effect of caloric restriction and excessive caloric intake on energy expenditure. *Am. J. Clin. Nutr.* 24:1405–9

Armitage, G., Hervey, G., Tobin, G. 1981. Energy expenditure in rats overfed by tube-feeding. *J. Physiol.* 312:58

Bernard, C. 1878. *Lecons Sur Les Phenomenes De La Vie Communs Aux Animaux Et Aux Vegetaux* 1:67, 111–14, 123–24. Paris: Balliere

Boyle, P. C., Storlien, L. H., Harper, A. E., Keesey, R. E. 1981. Oxygen consumption and locomotor activity during restricted feeding and realimentation. *Am. J. Physiol.* 241:R392–97

Bray, G. A. 1969. Effect of caloric restriction on energy expenditure in obese patients. *Lancet* 2:397–98

Bray, G. A., York, D. A. 1979. Hypothalamic and genetic obesity in experimental animals: An autonomic and endocrine hypothesis. *Physiol. Rev.* 59:719–809

Brobeck, J. R. 1965. Exchange, control, and regulation. *Physiological Controls and Regulation*, ed. W. S. Yamamoto, J. R.

Brobeck, pp. 1–13. Philadelphia/London: Saunders

Cannon, W. B. 1932. *The Wisdom of the Body.* New York: Norton

Carney, R. M., Goldberg, A. P. 1984. Weight gain after cessation of cigarette smoking: A possible role for adipose-tissue lipoprotein lipase. *N. Engl. J. Med.* 310:614–16

Coleman, D. L. 1978. Obese and diabetes: Two mutant genes causing diabetes-obesity syndromes in mice. *Diabetologia* 14:141–48

Coleman, D. L. 1979. Obesity genes: Beneficial effects in heterozygous mice. *Science* 203:663–65

Corbett, S. W., Keesey, R. E. 1982. Energy balance of rats with lateral hypothalamic lesions. *Am. J. Physiol.* 242:E273–79

Corbett, S. W., Wilterdink, E. J., Keesey, R. E. 1985. Resting oxygen consumption in over and underfed rats with lateral hypothalamic lesions. *Physiol. Behav.* 35: In press

Cornish, E. R., Mrosovsky, N. 1965. Activity during food deprivation and satiation of six species of rodent. *Anim. Behav.* 13:242–48

Cox, J. E., Powley, T. L. 1977. Development of obesity in diabetic mice pair-fed with lean siblings. *J. Comp. Physiol. Psychol.* 91:347–58

Cox, J. E., Powley, T. L. 1981a. Intragastric pair feeding fails to prevent VMH obesity or hyperinsulinemia. *Am. J. Physiol.* 240:E566–72

Cox, J. E., Powley, T. L. 1981b. Prior vagotomy blocks VMH obesity in pair-fed rats. *Am. J. Physiol.* 240:E573–83

Crisp, A. H., Stonehill, D. 1971. Relation between aspects of nutritional disturbances and menstrual activities in primary anorexia nervosa. *Br. Med. J.* 3:149–51

Cruce, J. A. F., Greenwood, M. R. C., Johnson, P. R., Quartermain, D. 1974. Genetic versus hypothalamic obesity: Studies of intake and dietary manipulations in rats. *J. Comp. Physiol. Psychol.* 87:295–301

Donahoe, C. P., Lin, D. H., Kirschenbaum, D. S., Keesey, R. E. 1984. Metabolic consequences of dieting and exercises in the treatment of obesity. *J. Consult. Clin. Psychol.* 52(5):827–36

Faust, I. M., Johnson, P. R., Hirsch, J. 1976. Noncompensation of adipose mass in partially lipectomized mice and rats. *Am. J. Physiol.* 231:538–44

Faust, I. M., Johnson, P. R., Hirsch, J. 1977. Surgical removal of adipose tissue alters feeding behavior and the development of obesity in rats. *Science* 197:393–96

Ferguson, N. B. L., Keesey, R. E. 1975. Effect of a quinine-adulterated diet upon body weight maintenance in male rats with ventromedial hypothalamic lesions. *J. Comp. Physiol. Psychol.* 89:478–88

Forbes, G. B., Reina, J. C. 1970. Adult lean body mass declines with age: Some longitudinal observations. *Metabolism* 19:653–63

Frisch, R. E., Wyshak, G., Vincent, L. 1980. Delayed menarche and amenorrhea in ballet dancers. *Med. Intell.* 303:17–19

Garrow, J. S., Stalley, S. 1975. Is there a "set-point" for human body weight? *Proc. Nutr. Soc.* 37:84–85a

Garrow, J. S., Warwick, P. M. 1978. Diet and obesity. In *The Diet of Man: Needs and Wants,* ed. J. Yudkin, pp. 127–44. Barking: Appl. Sci. Publ.

Grafe, E., Graham, D. 1911. Uber die anpassungsfahigkeit des tierschen organisms an uberreichliche nahringzufuhr. *Hoppe-Seyler's Z. Physiol. Chem.* 73:1–67

Gulick, A. 1922. A study of weight regulation in the adult human during overnutrition. *Am. J. Physiol.* 60:371–95

Harris, R. S., Martin, R. 1984. Specific depletion of body fat in parabiotic partners of tube-fed obese rats. *Am. J. Physiol.* 247:R380–86

Heim, T., Mestyán, J. 1964. Undernutrition and temperature regulation in adult rats. *Acta Physiol. Acad. Sci. Hung.* 25:305–12

Hemmingsen, A. M. 1956–60. Energy metabolism as related to body size and respiratory surfaces, and its evolution. *Copenhagen Steno Mem. Hosp. Rep.* 6–9

Hetherington, A. W., Ranson, S. W. 1942. Hypothalamic lesions and adiposity in the rat. *Anat. Rec.* 78:149–72

James, W. P. T., Trayhurn, P. 1981. Obesity in mice and men. In *Nutritional Factors: Modulating Effects of Metabolic Processes,* ed. R. F. Beers Jr., E. G. Basset, pp. 123–38. New York: Raven

Keesey, R. E. 1986. A set-point theory of obesity. In *Physiology, Psychology, and Treatment of the Eating Disorders,* ed. K. D. Brownell, J. P. Foreyt. New York: Basic Books. In press

Keesey, R. E., Boyle, P. C., Kemnitz, J. W., Mitchel, J. S. 1976. The role of the lateral hypothalamus in determining the body weight set-point. In *Hunger: Basic Mechanisms and Clinical Implications,* ed. D. Novin, W. Wyricka, G. A. Bray, pp. 243–55. New York: Raven

Keesey, R. E., Corbett, S. W. 1984. Metabolic defense of the body weight set-point. In *Eating And Its Disorders,* ed. A. J. Stunkard, E. Stellar, pp. 87–96. New York: Raven

Keesey, R. E., Corbett, S. W., Stern, J. S. 1984a. Resting metabolism of calorically-restricted rats with genetic or dietary obesity. Poster presented at satellite symp. 1984 Neurosci. Soc. Meet. titled "The Neural and Metabolic Bases of Feeding." Napa, Calif.

Keesey, R. E., Corbett, S. W., Hirvonen, M. D., Kaufman, L. N. 1984b. Heat production and body weight changes following lateral hypothalamic lesions. *Physiol. Behav.* 32: 309–17

Keesey, R. E., Powley, T. L. 1975. Hypothalamic regulation of body weight. *Am. Sci.* 63:558–65

Keys, A., Brozek, J., Henschel, A. 1950. *The Biology of Human Starvation.* Minneapolis: Univ. Minn. Press

Kleiber, M. 1947. Body size and metabolic rate. *Physiol. Rev.* 15:511–41

Kleiber, M. 1975. *The Fire of Life.* New York: Krieger

Landsberg, L., Young, J. B. 1982. Effects of nutritional status on autonomic nervous system function. *Am. J. Clin. Nutr.* 35:1234–40

Leibel, R. L., Hirsch, J. 1984. Diminished energy requirements in reduced-obese patients. *Metabolism* 33:164–70

Le Magnen, J. 1983. Body energy balance and food intake: A neuroendocrine regulatory mechanism. *Physiol. Rev.* 63:314–86

Levitsky, D. A., Strupp, B. J., Lupoli, J. 1981. Tolerance to anorectic drugs: Pharmacological or artifactual? *Pharmacol. Biochem. Behav.* 73:311–22

McCracken, K. J., McNiven, M. A. 1983. Effects of overfeeding by gastric intubation on body composition of adult female rats and on heat production during fasting and feeding. *Br. J. Nutr.* 49:193–202

Metropolitan Life Insurance Co. 1983. *Stat. Bull.* 64:1–9

Miller, D. S., Mumford, P. 1973. Luxuskonsumption. In *Energy Balance in Man,* ed. M. Apfelbaum, pp. 195–207. Paris: Masson et Cie

Morley, J. E., Levine, A. S., Gosnell, B. A., Bellington, C. J. 1984. Which opioid receptor mechanism modulates feeding? *Appetite* 5:61–68

Mrosovsky, N., Fisher, K. C. 1970. Sliding set points for body weight in ground squirrels during the hibernation season. *Can. J. Zool.* 48:241–47

Mrosovsky, N., Powley, T. L. 1977. Set points for body weight and fat. *Behav. Biol.* 20:205–33

Nicolaides, S. 1981. Lateral hypothalamic controls of metabolic factors relating to feeding. *Diabetologia* 20:426–34

Nishizawa, Y., Bray, G. A. 1978. Ventromedial hypothalamic lesions and the mobilization of fatty acids. *J. Clin. Invest.* 61:714–21

Parameswaran, S. V., Steffens, A. B., Hervey, G. R., DeRuiter, L. 1977. Involvement of a humoral factor in regulation of body weight in parabiotic rats. *Am. J. Physiol.* 232:R150–57

Perkins, N., Rothwell, N. J., Stock, M. J., Stone, T. W. 1981. Activation of brown adipose tissue thermogenesis by the ventromedial hypothalamus. *Nature* 289:401–2

Powley, T. L. 1977. The ventromedial hypothalamic syndrome, satiety, and a cephalic phase hypothesis. *Psychol. Rev.* 84:89–126

Powley, T. L., Keesey, R. E. 1970. Relationship of body weight to the lateral hypothalamic feeding syndrome. *J. Comp. Physiol. Psychol.* 70:25–36

Powley, T. L., Opsahl, C. A. 1976. Autonomic components of the hypothalamic feeding syndromes. See Keesey et al 1976, pp. 313–26

Powley, T. L., Opsahl, C. A., Cox, J. E., Weingarten, H. P. 1980. The role of the hypothalamus in energy homeostasis. In *Handbook of the Hypothalamus,* Vol. 3: *Behavioral Studies On The Hypothalamus,* ed. P. J. Morgane, J. Panksepp. New York: Dekker

Rappaport, E. B., Young, J. B., Landsberg, L. 1982. Initiation, duration and dissipation of diet-induced changes in sympathetic nervous system activity in the rat. *Metabolism* 31:143–46

Rolls, B. J., Rowe, E. A., Turner, R. C. 1980. Persistent obesity in rats following a period of consumption of a mixed high energy diet. *J. Physiol.* 298:415–27

Rothwell, N. J., Stock, M. J. 1979. A role for brown adipose tissue in diet-induced thermogenesis. *Nature* 281:31–35

Rothwell, N. J., Stock, M. J. 1981. Influence of noradrenaline on blood flow to brown adipose tissue in rats exhibiting diet-induced thermogenesis. *Pflügers Arch.* 389:237–42

Rothwell, N. J., Stock, M. J. 1982. Energy expenditure of 'cafeteria'-fed rats determined from measurements of energy balance and indirect calorimetry. *J. Physiol.* 328:371–77

Schachter, S. 1971. Some extraordinary facts about obese humans and rats. *Am. Psychol.* 26:129–44

Schemmel, R., Mickelsen, O., Gill, J. L. 1970. Dietary obesity in rats: Body weight and body fat accretion in seven strains of rats. *J. Nutr.* 100:1041–48

Schwartz, B., Cumming, D. C., Riordan, E., Selye, M., Yen, S. S. C., Rebar, R. W. 1981. Exercise-associated ammenorrhea: A distinct entity. *Am. J. Obstet. Gynecol.* 141:662–70

Sclafani, A., Springer, D. 1976. Dietary obesity in adult rats: Similarities to hypothalamic and human obesity syndromes. *Physiol. Behav.* 17:461–71

Sclafani, A., Springer, D., Kluge, L. 1976. Effects of quinine adulterated diets on the food intake and body weight of obese and non-obese hypothalamic hyperphagic rats. *Physiol. Behav.* 16:631–40

Seefeld, M. D., Keesey, R. E., Peterson, R. E. 1984. Body weight regulation in rats treated with 2,3,7,8-tetrachlorodibenzene-*p*-dioxin. *Toxicol Appl. Pharacol.* 76:526–36

Seydoux, J. 1983. Recent evidence for the involvement of brown adipose tissue in body weight regulation. *Diabete Metab.* 9:141–47

Seydoux, J., Rohner-Jeanrenaud, F., Assimacopoulos-Jeannet, F., Jeanrenaud, B., Girardier, L. 1981. Functional disconnection of brown adipose tissue in hypothalamic obesity in rats. *Pflügers Arch.* 390:1–4

Sims, E. A. H., Horton, E. S. 1968. Endocrine and metabolic adaptation to obesity and starvation. *Am. J. Clin. Nutr.* 21:1455–70

Stunkard, A. J. 1982. Anorectic agents lower a body weight set point. *Life Sci.* 30:2043–55

Sullivan, A. C., Triscari, J., Cheng, L. 1983. Appetite regulation by drugs and endogenous substances. In *Nutrition and Drugs*, ed. M. Winick. New York: Wiley

Teitelbaum, P., Epstein, A. N. 1962. The lateral hypothalamic syndrome: Recovery of feeding and drinking after lateral hypothalamic lesions. *Psychol. Rev.* 69:74–90

Thompson, J. K., Jarvie, G. J., Lahey, B. B., Cureton, K. J. 1982. Exercise and obesity: Etiology, physiology, and intervention. *Psychol. Bull.* 91:55–79

Thurlby, P. L., Trayhurn, P. 1980. Regional blood flow in genetically obese (ob/ob) mice. *Pflügers Arch.* 385:193–201

Triandafillou, J., Himms-Hagen, J. 1983. Brown adipose tissue in genetically obese (fa/fa) rats: Response to cold and diet. *Am. J. Physiol.* 244:E145–50

Vander Tuig, J. G., Knehans, A. W., Romsos, D. R. 1982. Reduced sympathetic nervous system activity in rats with ventromedial hypothalamic lesions. *Life Sci.* 30:913–20

Vigersky, R. A., Anderson, A. E., Thompson, R. H., Loriaux, M. D. 1977. Hypothalamic dysfunction in secondary amenorrhea associated with simple weight loss. *N. Engl. J. Med.* 297:1141–45

Vilberg, T. R., Keesey, R. E. 1982. Metabolic contributions to VMH obesity. *Types of Obesity: Animal Models and Clinical Applications.* NIH Workshop on the Characterization of Obesities and 1st Meet. Am. Assoc. Study of Obesity. Poughkeepsie, NY

Vilberg, T. R., Keesey, R. E. 1984a. Caloric restriction does not reduce resting metabolic rate in static-obese VMH lesioned rats. See Keesey et al 1984a

Vilberg, T. R., Keesey, R. E. 1984b. Reduced energy expenditure after ventromedial hypothalamic lesions in female rats. *Am. J. Physiol.* 247:R183–88

Wade, G. N., Gray, J. M. 1979. Gonadal effects on food intake and adiposity: A metabolic hypothesis. *Physiol. Behav.* 22:583–93

Walgren, M. C., Powley, T. L. 1985. Effects of intragastric hyperalimentation on pair-fed rats with ventromedial hypothalamic lesions. *Am. J. Physiol.* 248:E172–80

Wickler, S. J., Horowitz, B. A., Stern, J. S. 1982. Regional blood flow in genetically-obese rats during nonshivering thermogenesis. *Int. J. Obesity* 6:481–90

Woods, S. C., Porte, J. D. 1983. The role of insulin as a satiety factor in the central nervous system. In *CNS Regulation Of Carbohydrate Metabolism: Advances In Metabolic Disorders*, Vol. 10, ed. A. J. Szabo. New York: Academic

Young, J. B., Landsberg, L. 1977. Stimulation of the sympathetic nervous system during sucrose feeding. *Nature* 269:615–17

Young, J. B., Saville, E., Rothwell, N. J., Stock, M. J., Landsberg, L. 1982. Effect of diet and cold exposure on norepinephrine turnover in brown adipose tissue in the rat. *J. Clin. Invest.* 69:1061–71

Zucker, L. M., Zucker, T. F. 1961. Fatty, a new mutation in the rat. *J. Hered.* 52:275–78

Ann. Rev. Psychol. 1986. 37:135–61

INFANCY

Dale F. Hay

Departments of Child and Adolescent Psychiatry and Psychology, Institute of Psychiatry, University of London, London SE5 8AF, United Kingdom

CONTENTS

INTRODUCTION 135
THE INFANT AS INFORMATION PROCESSOR 138
    Inventing vs Perceiving the World 138
    Attention, Discrimination, and Preference 139
    Emotion 139
    Learning and Memory 140
    Search and Exploration 141
    Understanding Relations in Space and Time 142
THE INFANT AS PART OF THE NATURAL WORLD 142
    Locomotion 143
    Speech and Communication 143
    Forming Social Relationships 144
    The Emergence of Self 145
THE INFANT AS EVENTUAL ADULT 145
    Continuity Studies 146
    Studies of Biological Risk 148
    Studies of Rearing Environments 148
    Intervention Studies 149
THE INFANT AS DEVELOPING SYSTEM 150
    Stages and Shifts in Development 150
    The Question of Precursors 151
    Bidirectional Influences of Genes and Environments 152
    The Timing of Experience 152
    Infants' Contributions to their Own Development 153
    Reversibility of Development 154
CONCLUSIONS 155
SUMMARY 156

INTRODUCTION

Nearly 200 years have passed since Tiedemann published his observations of his infant son in 1787 (Murchison & Langer 1927), which marked the beginning of psychological research on infants. The purpose of this chapter is to reflect on the state of the field on the occasion of its bicentennial. To do so, I shall highlight four general perspectives on the study of infancy, which is arbitrarily defined here as the first two years of human life and as the period prior to weaning for other young mammals.

Infancy research was last reviewed in this series nearly a decade ago (Haith & Campos 1977). Since then there has been a remarkable surge of interest in the topic. For example, a new journal, handbook, and international conference on infant studies have appeared, and almost an entire volume of the influential *Handbook of Child Psychology* (Mussen 1983) is devoted to research on infants. In 1983, infancy research even was featured on the cover of *Time* magazine! It thus seems appropriate to ask, why are so many adults studying babies, and what exactly are they trying to find out? What new facts, models, and theories are emerging from all this activity?

The current interest in infancy is partly the result of demographic and historical factors. The cohort of infants studied in the research reviewed here was born at a time of technological and social changes that have greatly affected infants' chances for survival and many dimensions of their lives. The effects of these changes cried out for study. Demographic factors also determined the sheer number of developmental psychologists plying their trade in the 1980s. Many members of the so-called "baby boom" generation entered the field, and many of them were themselves parents of infants; perhaps, like Tiedemann, their interest in infancy was sparked by the captivating behavior of their own progeny.

What about developments within the field of psychology itself that promoted the study of infants? In general, the current research, while prolific and interesting, does not seem ground-breaking, particularly in comparison with the earlier wave of interest in infants that occurred in the 1960s. In developmental psychology as a whole, the 1980s might be characterized as a time of latent theory—theory that is not articulated formally, but rather exists in an individual scientist's underlying view of a domain of research that constrains the questions he or she asks and the methods taken to answer those questions. Grand theories of development are definitely on the decline, particularly the approaches of the learning theorists and of Piaget. There is renewed interest in the thoughts of James Mark Baldwin, Sigmund Freud, George Herbert Mead, Myrtle McGraw, James and Eleanor Gibson, and Lev Vygotsky—but no dominating, grand vision can be said to be directing the energies of most developmentalists. Moreover, the traditional topical boundaries within psychology are themselves shifting and disappearing; old barriers between perception and cognition, cognition and emotion, individual skills and social processes, basic and applied research no longer seem impermeable. Infancy research is especially interesting in this regard, as it represents a microcosm of psychology as a whole.

Because the entire discipline is in the midst of growth and change, I have not organized my review in terms of traditional topics or theories. Rather, I have asked, what are some different reasons why adults might study infants? More than one such reason might have stimulated a particular investigation, and at times the distinctions being made will seem forced. Nonetheless, infants are studied in quite different ways, with quite different objectives, which is the main reason why the field as a whole lacks coherence. The four following perspectives illustrate the diversity of approaches taken to the study of infants:

1. *The infant as information processor*—Psychologists who are interested in fundamental abilities such as sensation and perception, attention, learning, memory, and problem solving have turned to infancy to seek the origins and chart the early development of such abilities. The assumption underlying their research is that one may better understand psychological phenomena by studying their origins. Research in this perspective falls squarely into the tradition of experimental psychology, and is greatly influenced by the theories, paradigms, and research questions used in the study of adult information processing.

2. *The infant as part of the natural world*—In a somewhat different perspective, infants have been studied in their own right, as infants, that is, as intrinsically interesting organisms within the natural world, much as natural historians have studied streams and elm trees. Here the investigator asks, what are infants like and what kinds of lives do they lead? In particular, what important developmental milestones characterize the period of infancy? This research is typically marked by careful, detailed description of infants' behavior in environments in which an unrestricted range of behavior is possible.

3. *The infant as eventual adult*—Yet a third perspective is one that looks at infants with an eye to the future. Infants' capabilities, deficits, and experiences are assessed in an effort to predict later developmental outcomes. Cronbach (1957) once distinguished between "two disciplines of scientific psychology," namely, the nomothetic search for general principles vs the idiographic analysis of individual differences; the third perspective exemplifies the latter. Infants are studied longitudinally into later periods of childhood and adolescence. Issues of the reliability and validity of measurement are critical.

4. *The infant as developing system*—In the fourth perspective, the central interest is not infants per se, but the process of development. Infancy is studied because it is a period of rapid and important changes and thus provides a convenient arena in which to chart developmental pathways and seek general principles that transcend particular topics and domains. In the course of such analyses, the grand old dichotomies of nature and nurture, mind and body, disposition and situation, continuity and discontinuity once again loom into view. Attempts to grapple with these issues frequently require experimental manipulations of development, and thus much pertinent work within this perspective concerns the development of nonhuman infants.

I now present some illustrative ideas being set forth within each perspective. The review necessarily is selective, not exhaustive, and the reader may consult the many excellent articles that discuss each of the topics mentioned here in considerably more detail (e.g. Mussen 1983). In my attempt to blaze an intelligible trail through this forest, no doubt I have ignored many interesting and valuable trees.

THE INFANT AS INFORMATION PROCESSOR

Inventing vs Perceiving the World

The search for the origins of human knowledge has always led psychologists to study babies. For example, Tiedemann's search for "acquired ideas" led him to record his son's first encounters with the world. Similar questions about what infants perceive and know continue to be asked today. The recent work follows from that of the past two decades in terms of paradigms and procedures, but not in terms of theoretical climate. In a word, researchers in the 1980s are studying "information processing in infancy," not "sensorimotor intelligence." Piaget's grand vision of genetic epistemology no longer dominates the study of the development of thought.

Most of the research in this perspective is frankly empirical, and rightly so, insofar as there remains much to learn about infants' basic abilities to acquire information. There is, however, renewed interest in J. J. Gibson's (1979) "ecological" theory of "direct perception," which is seen by many as an alternative to Piaget's constructivist theory of development (see Wilcox & Katz 1981, Butterworth 1983). Like Piaget, Gibson took note of organisms' propensity to see the world in personal terms. However, Gibson's proposal that organisms perceive what the environment affords for them refers to the perception of veridical conditions, not the construction of a personal reality. His concept of affordances implies a relationship between the perceiving organism and its world, but not one that is an egocentric creation.

Gibson's views are the subject of much controversy in the adult literature (see Ullman 1980, and commentaries). Moreover, J. J. Gibson's theory is not explicitly developmental, and E. J. Gibson's account of perceptual development is not universally accepted by those espousing allegiance to "ecological" theory (see Wilcox & Katz 1981). Where then is the developmental alternative to genetic epistemology? Has the decline of faith in Piaget's formulations signaled a decline of interest in the general problem of development? There certainly seems to be considerable interest in assessing the commonalities in, as well as the differences between, infant and adult information processing.

Beyond these general theoretical concerns, there are numerous debates, controversies, and flurries of research activity. Some illustrative topics follow.

Attention, Discrimination, and Preference

The key to an infant's perception of the world lies in its motivation to perceive. Like adults, infants do not attend to everything they might; unlike adults, their attention cannot be easily channeled by instructions. Hence questions about perception are inextricably linked to questions about attention, motivation, and liking. The tools used to assess infants' attention continue to be the differential fixation of paired stimuli and, most commonly, habituation. All sensory modalities are studied, but vision remains of paramount interest.

Infants are asked to compare all sorts of shapes, arrangements, and locations of stimuli; however, there continues to be special interest in the general problem of species identification, that is, infants' responses to the faces and voices of conspecifics. In the comparative literature, there is currently much interest in determining whether young organisms can identify not just conspecifics in general but their particular kin (e.g. Frederickson & Sackett 1984). Similar concerns are raised about young humans' responsiveness to their parents' faces and voices. For example, newborns reportedly can discriminate their mothers' but not their fathers' voices, a finding attributed to prenatal experiences (De-Casper & Prescott 1984).

Insofar as many conclusions about what infants can discriminate and comprehend rest on attention data, some recent conceptual and methodological analyses of attention tasks are particularly worthy of note. For example, investigators are asking, under what circumstances do infants attend to familiar rather than novel stimuli (Hunter et al 1982, Rheingold 1985)? Can infants' natural preferences always be modified by habituation procedures (Slater et al 1985)? How may we distinguish psychological habituation from sensory adaptation (Dannemiller & Banks 1983)? Others note that misleading conclusions have been drawn about attention in infancy because of statistical artifacts (see Cohen & Menten 1981, Mendelson 1983, Dannemiller 1984). Those artifacts derive from systematic individual differences among habituators that become especially problematic when infants themselves control the timing and length of habituation trials. Thus, the measurement issues that preoccupy investigators who study infants as eventual adults are also beginning to be raised by those who study normative information processing.

Emotion

Questions about infants' attention to events are closely related to questions about how the infants feel about those events, and emotional expression has been used to index discrimination. For example, facial expressions of disgust have been used to measure taste perception at least since Tiedemann recorded his son's reactions to medicine. In the 1980s, however, there has been increased focus on infants' emotions as developmental phenomena in their own right. Much interest has been shown in the extent to which facial expressions thought to index particular emotions in adults are shown by infants. For example, characteristic signs of anger are recorded when adults yank teething biscuits out of the mouths of babes (Stenberg et al 1983).

Infants' display of particular emotions appears to depend on the intensity and predictability of the events that confront them (Field 1981, Gunnar et al 1984a), and especially on the extent to which infants can exert control over those events (Gunnar 1980, Horner 1983). Comparative work suggests that the felicitous effects of control may be mediated by a modulation of the pituitary-adrenal response to stress (Davis & Levine 1982).

Emotion shown by others seems to be one of the first things an infant notices and talks about (Bretherton & Beeghly 1982). Very young infants match the emotions of others, imitating facial expressions (Field et al 1982), crying when peers cry (Hay et al 1981, Martin & Clark 1982), and depressing their own responding when their mothers act depressed (Cohn & Tronick 1983). The salience of emotion may decline with age: 2-month olds respond to expression changes in holograms of faces, but 5-month-olds do not (Nelson & Horowitz 1983).

Older infants in ambiguous situations appear to use other people's emotions as cues to their own, a phenomenon termed "social referencing" (e.g. Feinman 1982). There is considerable debate about what social referencing entails and implies. It is not clear whether infants are truly appraising a situation from the point of view of another's feelings or whether they are simply matching the emotions of others, as younger infants would do. Longitudinal analyses of infants' responsiveness to others' emotions and comprehension of their own may clarify this point.

Learning and Memory

Hardly any difference between the newborn and the two-year-old is more striking than the fact that the elder has learned a great deal in the past two years. Learning in infancy was once the focus of much study, both as a phenomenon undergoing development and an explanation of development in other domains; it no longer is. Those studies of infants' learning that are still conducted are only rarely discussed in terms of the classic theories of learning.

Consider, for example, the lively controversy about whether newborns can imitate, which has been discussed almost entirely with respect to Piagetian theory and not in terms of the vast, relevant literature on observational learning. The initial claim that newborns can imitate adults' facial contortions (Meltzoff & Moore 1977) was refuted by other data (e.g. Hayes & Watson 1981), but defended and replicated by the original investigators (Meltzoff & Moore 1983). Recent work suggests that the evidence for early imitation is most convincing with respect to one category of behavior, sticking out one's tongue, and that this form of imitation does not increase with age (Abravanel & Sigafoos 1984).

A theme running through this controversy is whether early matching be-havior qualifies as "true" imitation. Some confusion might be eliminated if these data were viewed in terms of broader theories of learning and develop-ment, in which distinctions between response facilitation and acquisition have always been made (see Bandura & Walters 1963). The imitation of tongue protrusions represents the facilitation of an existing response, not the acquisi-tion of a new one. The more interesting question of when infants begin to learn new things by observing others remains in need of study. By the second year, observational learning of novel actions is clearly taking place (Hay et al 1985, Meltzoff 1985), but when does it begin? Prolonged debate about the abilities of newborns has prevented a more encompassing analysis of the development of observational learning.

The study of learning seems to remain respectable when questions are framed in terms of memory for things learned in the past. Habituation performance is traditionally taken as evidence for recognition memory, though some scholars have challenged that assumption (Sophian 1980, Rovee-Collier & Fagen 1981). Attention has also been given to quite young infants' recall of their past conditioning experiences. Rovee-Collier and her colleagues have extensively investigated young infants' retention of learning in a conjugate reinforcement paradigm in which infants must kick their feet to move a mobile. Three-month-olds show free recall of the learned response days after it was taught, and can be reminded of it by noncontingent movement of the mobile weeks later (see Rovee-Collier & Fagen 1981). To the extent that infants' performance in this paradigm reveals their expectations as well as their recall (Fagen et al 1984), we see that even very young humans have at least rudimentary awareness of their pasts and futures.

Search and Exploration

Attention, perception, learning, and memory are all at work when infants explore environments in search of the resources they afford. One of the most striking signs of the decline of influence of Piagetian views of sensorimotor intelligence is the fact that the classic object permanence task is now most often spoken of as a search problem, and thereby integrated with broader concerns addressed by classic psychological theories of place learning and ecological theories of optimal foraging. In addition, the study of search may also be integrated with the study of infants' self-directed manual and locomotor ex-ploration of their environments (see Rheingold 1985). The distinction between studies of search and those of exploration may be construed as one between intentional and incidental learning, respectively.

Reconceptualizing the object permanence task as a search problem implies that developmental limitations are not the only factors that constrain per-formance; so do various components of the task, such as the number of choices offered the infant to search (Cummings & Bjork 1981), characteristics of the hiding place (Cornell 1981), the presence of landmarks (Presson & Ihrig 1982), and opportunities for practice (Corrigan 1981). Furthermore, integrating the study of search and exploration allows for the examination of motivational factors. For example, infants who have not learned all there is to learn in a familiar environment may return to it rather than going on to explore a new environment (Hunter et al 1982); something akin to this may be going on when infants make the Stage 4 error of returning to original hiding places in an object permanence experiment. In general, search provides an important domain in which to examine infants' emerging abilities to process information. For example, early memory strategies can be observed when young children are asked to delay their search for hidden objects (DeLoache et al 1985).

Understanding Relations in Space and Time

With the resurgence of interest in Gibsonian theory, questions about knowledge become questions about the perception of environmental order. Relevant information is provided by the many studies documenting infants' perception of relationships across stimulus events and across sensory modalities. For example, infants are reported to perceive visual symmetry (Bornstein & Krinsky 1985), melodic patterns (Trehub et al 1984), and the number of items present in an array (Treiber & Wilcox 1984). Like the psychologists who study them, older infants are attuned to correlations and causal relations in stimulus events (Younger & Cohen 1983, Golinkoff et al 1984). The comprehension of abstract relationships seems to develop gradually over the first year; very young infants seem more like pointillists, perceiving the world as discrete units of information (Cohen & Younger 1984). To the extent that all these results rest on habituation performance, however, attentional as well as perceptual differences may distinguish age groups.

Of special concern for the Gibsons' theory are infants' abilities to perceive environmental affordances that hold across modalities (e.g. E. Gibson & Walker 1984). There has been much recent interest in intermodal perception, both within and without the Gibsonian perspective. Even newborns reportedly are sensitive to intermodal relations (e.g. Crassini & Broerse 1980). The task now in order is the systematic study of intermodal perception, both in its own right and in terms of its role in other domains of development, such as language acquisition and social relations, which are most frequently studied within the next perspective to be described.

THE INFANT AS PART OF THE NATURAL WORLD

The studies just reviewed indicate that much is learned by focusing on infants' performance on experimental tasks. Much is also learned when infants are studied under less constrained conditions, in the naturalistic tradition begun by Tiedemann. Indeed, it may be that Piaget's grand vision of sensorimotor intelligence as a set of parallel, stage-like attainments could only have been arrived at through his observation of his own infants, in their own home, with the experiments he made integrated into a stream of father-child interaction. Some of the differences between Piagetian views and the current work on information processing may derive from this basic difference in perspective.

To illustrate the perspective, I shall now review some recent findings concerning four "developmental milestones" that parents and psychologists alike perceive as uniquely characterizing the period of infancy: walking, talking, forming relationships, and acquiring a sense of self.

Locomotion

The study of locomotor development has been more controversial than one might expect, largely because of some new attention to a perplexing phenomenon: the disappearance of the neonatal "stepping reflex" and the later reemergence of full-blown walking. Careful analyses of the topography of neonatal stepping have shown that it is virtually identical to kicking, which does not disappear in the same way (see Thelen 1984). The disappearance of stepping and its later reemergence can be attributed to the process of physical growth; infants' legs simply become too heavy to move when the infant is held in an upright position, although they can still be kicked when the infant is supine and gravity is aiding the task. Physical growth has also been implicated in the changing patterns of gait as children grow older (Hennessey et al 1984). There is still debate, however, over the role of higher order psychological functioning in inducing the infant to walk (see Zelazo 1984).

One can also ask about the impact of walking on the rest of infants' lives. It is clear that infants' psychological and social lives change when they begin to crawl and then to walk. That such effects result from locomotion itself rather than associated maturational changes is attested to by the fact that nonlocomoting infants placed in mechanical "walkers" show similar changes in their behavior (Gustafson 1984).

Speech and Communication

The literal definition of an infant is "one who cannot speak"; the acquisition of language is thus the developmental milestone that marks the end of infancy. Studies of language development fall firmly within the tradition of studying infants as part of the natural world; many report the detailed, lengthy observation of a small sample of children who are learning to talk in familiar settings. Investigators in the 1980s have been especially concerned with what young children acquiring language have to say—that is, with the relationship between language and thought as revealed in speech and action.

Children learning language talk about thought itself; words about thought and feeling appear in children's vocabularies as early as the second year (Bretherton & Beeghly 1982). In addition, the words young children produce evince their abilities to think and reason, for example, to plan (Gopnik 1982) and to understand the truth and falsehood of verbal statements (Pea 1982). Some investigators report parallels between language development and other forms of representational activity such as symbolic play (see McCune-Nicholich 1981); the parallels to be observed depend on the nature of the tasks and on the scales of measurement and statistical techniques that are used (Smolak & Levine 1984). In general, all of these studies on the relations between language and thought serve to integrate the naturalistic study of language learning with the experiments on information processing.

Forming Social Relationships

Development in infancy follows a paradoxical course; as the months go by, infants become more self-sufficient and more truly social. They proceed from a state of utter yet impersonal dependence on others to a capacity for independence and mature interdependence. A host of studies have charted infants' developing interactive skills and their formation of distinct personal relationships with mothers, fathers, siblings, and peers.

During the 1970s a number of claims were made about infants' interactive abilities; recently, more conservative statistical procedures are being recommended for determining that nonrandom interaction between infants and others is in fact taking place (e.g. Martin et al 1981). In addition, rather than simply noting the occurrence of any sort of interaction, there is increased interest in the content of infants' social encounters, especially in terms of their resemblance to prosocial exchanges and conflicts among older persons. For example, one-year-olds are reported to help their mothers with household tasks (Rheingold 1982) and to quarrel with their siblings and peers (Hay & Ross 1982; Kendrick & Dunn 1983). Finally, increased attention is being paid to infants' participation in triadic interactions and to indirect as well as direct social influence (e.g. Lewis & Feiring 1981).

The primary theoretical perspective taken to social development in infancy derives from Freud's speculations about human relations, as evidenced in the extensive clinical interest in theories of object relations (see Greenberg & Mitchell 1983) and in the influence of the psychoanalyst John Bowlby's "ethological" theory of infant-mother attachment. However, most researchers espousing allegiance to Bowlby's views do not in fact test his nomothetic theory of attachment formation; rather, their work follows more closely from Mary Ainsworth's analysis of differences among individual attachment relationships (Ainsworth et al 1978), and thus falls into the third perspective to be discussed in the next section. There has been surprisingly little attention given to the problem of how infants in general become attached to parents, and little consensus about the signs that indicate when an attachment has been formed. Discrete indexes of attachment like proximity-seeking have been found to be multiply determined and to serve multiple functions (Hay 1980); instead, more general patterns of "exploration from a secure base" are sought. However, the secure base phenomenon itself deserves a closer look. It has been suggested that the mere presence of the mother is not sufficient to induce the infant to explore; rather, she must signal her "emotional availability" (Sorce & Emde 1981). At the same time, this form of social facilitation is not unique to the attachment relationship; the presence of siblings or peers also reduces infants' stress and facilitates their exploration (e.g. Samuels 1980, Ispa 1981, Gunnar et al 1984b). In general, the normative processes underlying attachment formation are in need of specification. The extent to which such processes influence the establishment of other relationships as well is of particular interest.

The Emergence of Self

Parents frequently report that, as an infant grows older, he or she seems to have become "more of a person." Over the months, infants become independent social agents and objects of their own reflections. There are many strands in the development of self; unfortunately, they are only rarely examined in relation to each other. In the first year, infants' activities become more intentional (see Bruner 1981) and independent. The emerging sense of self as effective agent is seen in infants' motivation to master their environments (e.g. Yarrow et al 1984). The sense of self as object of one's reflection develops over the second year of life, as revealed by the ability to recognize one's features in mirrors and photographs (Brooks-Gunn & Lewis 1984).

A particularly important part of the development of self from a parent's point of view is the infant's ability to control its own behavior, both in the presence and absence of commands and reminders (see Kopp 1982). One might say that the true end of infancy, at least in Western culture, is when infants are able to control their elimination of wastes; young humans who do not need diapers are viewed as children, not infants. Social changes, including the availability of paper diapers, seem to have infantilized two-year-olds in recent years, and much lore surrounds the issue. Toilet training is of theoretical interest, insofar as it demands that infants view their own behavior in the light of adult standards. Unfortunately, infancy researchers have not turned their attention to this socially relevant form of self-control.

THE INFANT AS EVENTUAL ADULT

A third perspective on infancy is one that focuses on infants as proto-adults and attempts to divine what sorts and conditions of adults they will turn out to be.

Most such studies employ longitudinal, correlational designs. Nonetheless, psychologists, like most humans, are wont to speculate about causes and effects. One of the most important recent developments is a change in the statistical techniques used when trying to ask about causal relations in correlational data. Infancy researchers no longer seem sanguine about the use of cross-lagged designs, which have been extensively criticized. Rather, they are devising structural equation models. In general, discussions of measurement and design issues dominate the third perspective on infancy.

In reviewing the work, it seems that almost every imaginable characteristic of infants and their experience is being correlated with almost every imaginable later outcome. However, four general types of investigations are currently being pursued: studies of continuity, risk, rearing environments, and interventions, respectively.

Continuity Studies

Development implies continuity as well as change; a developing organism or system retains its basic integrity in the face of change. Those who seek continuities from infancy to adulthood in a sense are seeking formal causes, in Aristotelian terms—latent, unseen essences of individuality that organize and explain outward manifestations at any given age. There are several domains where such essences are the matter of much debate: intellectual ability, temperament, social competence, and psychopathology.

No search for continuity has been pursued with as much vigor and ingenuity as the quest for the antecedents of intelligence. It has been established that standard scales of infant development do not adequately predict later measures of intelligence. Infancy researchers react to this fact by either questioning the idea of intellectual continuity from infancy to childhood, or by questioning the standard scales. The former reaction is exemplified by McCall's (1981) "scoop" model of development, which posits infancy to be a period of highly canalized species-typical development, buffered from environmental upsets and from genetically determined individual variation. The alternative reaction is exemplified by attempts to predict IQ from recognition abilities in infancy (see Fagan & Singer 1983). Fagan argues that, unlike the conventional developmental scales, the visual fixation task used in studies of infants' information processing demands the same basic discrimination and retention abilities called for in later tests of intelligence. He reports significant correlations between infants' fixation of novel stimuli and their intellectual performance several years later.

An infant's reaction to novel and untoward events is also used as an index of temperament (e.g. Kagan et al 1984), another construct thought to organize development throughout life. Temperament is variously defined, but usually implies an individual's characteristic activity and reactivity, mood and emotionality. Infancy may indeed be somewhat canalized, but infants, even siblings, are clearly not all alike; for that matter, neither are all members of litters of mountain lions or wolf cubs (Pfeifer 1980, MacDonald 1983). The extent to which such temperamental differences are heritable is a matter of much current interest (see Goldsmith 1983).

Evidence for continuity is also sought within the domain of social relations, where a primary focus has been the antecedents and sequelae of infant-parent attachment. Here the concern is with dyadic continuity over time, which is influenced by but not reducible to temperamental characteristics of children. Individual attachment relationships have been distinguished along a general dimension of security, as measured in Ainsworth's "strange situation" (Ainsworth et al 1978), which is best viewed as a stress interview for babies, or in the home (Waters 1985). Patterns of attachment security are predictable from earlier patterns of mother-infant interaction (Antonucci & Levitt 1984, Belsky et al 1984), and in turn predict differences in children's subsequent social and emotional development (Waters & Sroufe 1983). The observed correlational data of course prove nothing about the causal role of attachment per se; such data could be accounted for by consistent patterns of parent-child interaction that independently facilitate a secure attachment in infancy and the child's subsequent social adjustment. At present, this literature has been marked by disagreements about the degree of observed continuity and the merits of Ainsworth's "strange situation"; it is now time for researchers to assess dimensions of parent-child relationships beyond security and to search for the maturational and experiential processes underlying the patterns of correlations they observe.

Problems in attachment relations are of central concern for the growing field of "developmental psychopathology" (Sroufe & Rutter 1984). For example, boys who experience insecure attachment in infancy are also more likely to show signs of psychopathology at six years; however, this outcome was not observed for girls and was not characteristic of all insecure boys (Lewis et al 1984). Other antecedents of childhood psychopathology must also be sought.

In general, the search for continuity from infancy to adulthood has been impeded by the maintenance of distinctions made in psychology as a whole. The observed continuities in the intellectual, temperamental, and social realms may reflect a general trend rather than parallel developments. Consider, for example, the attempts to predict IQ from visual fixation data (Fagan & Singer 1983). In common with many investigators, Fagan interprets infants' fixation of novel stimuli as evidence for recognition of familiar ones. However, infants' reactivity to novelty also reveals a motivation to engage in new experiences that may predict later testability as well as intellectual skill. Intolerance of new experiences is also a defining component of temperament, distinguishes secure from anxious attachment relations, and, in the extreme, is a hallmark of psychopathology. It would seem profitable to study infants' reaction to familiar and unfamiliar social and nonsocial events as a fundamental developmental progression spanning domains (see Rheingold 1985). Indeed, the concepts of assimilation and accommodation discussed by Baldwin and Piaget are at the heart of the matter and could well be studied from an idiographic as well as a nomothetic perspective.

Studies of Biological Risk

One of the most striking features of the infancy literature in recent years is the study of children born at risk for later development. Recent advances in medical technology have permitted more infant lives to be saved; what are the prospects for infants who in earlier decades would have died? Gloomy prognostications of a terribly high incidence of gross anomalies have happily not been confirmed; nevertheless, there are many domains in which infants born at risk show some problems.

The risk factors investigated include parental age, genetic and chromosomal conditions, prenatal teratogens, the timing of birth, events surrounding the birth process, such as maternal anaesthetic and Caesarian delivery, and conditions arising immediately after birth, such as neonatal jaundice. An enormous number of facts about the impact of these risk factors is being gathered. In addition, several important conceptual and methodological issues are being raised: Are there genetic or experiential differences among individuals that mediate which among the possible effects of a teratogenic agent will be observed (Jacobson et al 1984)? Can the direct effects of a risk factor be distinguished from other experiences associated with its presence? For example, the effects of preterm birth itself are different from those of associated respiratory illness and extended hospitalization (Holmes et al 1982). Are there occasions when risk factors are associated with positive outcomes? For example, infants delivered by Caesarian section were performing less optimally than comparison infants on some measures later in infancy, but more optimally on others (Field & Widmayer 1980). And does the labeling of an infant "at risk" lead to self-fulfilling prophecies, mediated by attitudes such as the stereotypes adults hold about infants labeled "premature" (Stern & Hildebrandt 1984)? This latter issue underscores the need to integrate studies of biological risk with investigations of the effects of infants' social environments, another important topic within the third perspective.

Studies of Rearing Environments

One apparently distinctive feature of the cohort of infants studied in the 1980s is the diversity of conditions under which they were being reared, related to social changes throughout the world. For example, in Western countries, factors such as the elimination of some discrimination against women, and, more importantly, economic forces, have facilitated mothers' paid employment, which in turn necessitates shared care arrangements. Increased urbanization and mobility have decreased contact with grandparents. The availability of contraception and abortions and the increased likelihood of unmarried women to rear their own infants have led to fewer infants being reared in orphanages and by adoptive parents.

Nonetheless, what seems like rapid and radical change in infants' lives must be examined in historical context. Consider, for example, Tiedemann's son, born over 200 years ago. Like many infants of the 1980s, his care was shared by a mother, who breast-fed and played with him, and a nurse, who seems to have been responsible for a great deal of his other needs. In addition, he obviously had an "involved," concerned father, who, by all reports, spent a great deal of time observing him, entertaining and being entertained by him, and recording his behavior! At the same time, unlike a child of the 1980s, Tiedemann's son was swaddled and was served alcohol. Such comparisons across historical eras underscore the impossibility of determining a single, "natural" standard of infant care.

The dimensions of infants' rearing environment examined in the recent empirical literature include the encompassing influences of culture (e.g. Anisfeld 1982) and social class (e.g. Farran & Ramey 1980). They also include general characteristics of the home environment (see Elardo & Bradley 1981); parental psychopathology (e.g. Zahn-Waxler et al 1984); and shared care arrangements, including paternal involvement (e.g. Lamb et al 1982) and day care (e.g. Clarke-Stewart 1984). The studies of day care illustrate some of the issues that need to be considered in this entire domain of research, including the choice of social or cognitive dependent variables, the choice of care arrangements to be compared in terms of quality and structure, the characteristics of the sample, and the general model of development to be tested. Is day care presumed to have direct effects, or ones that are mediated by parental satisfaction with the existing arrangements? Is day care thought to produce unique developmental outcomes or simply to adjust the usual course of development? For example, a study of upper-middle class children indicated that day care experience accelerated the usual course of cognitive and social development, but did not distort it (Clarke-Stewart 1984). However, that study illustrates two difficulties in the entire research area, unforeseen sampling bias and the propensity of parents to respond to their own needs and change their day care arrangements in the middle of a study.

Intervention Studies

The problems just alluded to might be dealt with if infants were assigned randomly to rearing conditions. Such experiments are possible with nonhuman infants, and thus there exists a vast comparative literature on the effects of isolation, crowding, deprivation, and enrichment on later development. Experiments on human lives are conducted only when the experimental treatments are presumed to benefit the children whose lives are being manipulated, and even in such cases questions are raised about the ethics of depriving control subjects of comparable benefits. This concern, along with the costs of such research, and the current social climate, may be reasons why relatively few intervention studies seem to have been published in the 1980s.

The interventions whose effects have been reported recently include both short-term and long-term stimulation programs. An example of the first is the use of demonstrations of the Brazelton neonatal assessment exam to facilitate mother-infant interaction (Anderson & Sawin 1983). Other, more extended interventions include parental visitations to preterms in intensive care (Zeskind & Iacino 1984), nutritional supplementation (Barrett et al 1982), and comprehensive enrichment programs (Slaughter 1983, Ramey et al 1984). The latter studies illustrate some of the general complexities in intervention research, for example, the facts that mothers' lives as well as children's test scores may be changed by mother-centered intervention programs, and that conclusions drawn about an intervention's effects will differ, depending on whether the focus of analysis is average trends or individual differences.

THE INFANT AS DEVELOPING SYSTEM

Theories of development require both careful description and testable explanations. Yet development itself is an unseen, dynamic process that must be inferred from static observations; even a description of development demands inference. In addition, the theorist must seek determinants and functions at several levels of analysis—within developing organisms, in their immediate situations, in their past histories, and in the evolutionary heritage of their species. Furthermore, the theorist must try to determine all the factors that induce, accelerate, maintain, retard, or arrest development; those forces that start an organism along a developmental trajectory are not necessarily identical to those that maintain its path (e.g. Johnston & Gottlieb 1985). Given the complexity of the task, it is to the credit of infancy researchers that so many are asking searching questions about the process of development.

Stages and Shifts in Development

One question faced by those who try to describe development concerns shifts and stages in development. Put simply, is development a discrete or continuous variable? Infancy researchers continue to describe development in terms of stages, phases, or levels. However, developmental theorists are reexamining the concepts of stage and sequence (e.g. Fischer 1980) and debating the utility of the distinction between continuous and discontinuous development (see

Hinde & Bateson 1984). Even the most extreme case of discrete stages in development, metamorphosis in insects, seems not completely discontinuous (Oppenheim 1980). The effects of such reformulations on empirical studies of infants is yet to be clearly seen. However, interesting questions about stage-like performance are being asked, such as whether there are conditions under which adults make the same kinds of errors that infants do (Chromiak & Weisberg 1981), and whether experimentally created differences in frontal lobe functioning among primates mimic stage differences in human infants (Diamond & Goldman-Rakic 1985).

One matter of continued concern is the relationship of spurts in nervous system development to apparent shifts and changes in psychological ability. One example is Epstein's (1974) concept of "phrenoblysis," which posits that periods of rapid brain growth, including one between 3 and 10 months of age, foster learning. However, recent studies of brain growth in infancy, either as measured directly in mice (Hahn et al 1983) or indirectly from head circumference in humans (McCall et al 1983), provide little support for the phenoblysis hypothesis.

Another example is Bronson's (1974) hypothesis that a shift around 2 months of age in infants' visual abilities derives from maturation of the fovea, which permits central vision. However, other researchers claim to have documented the use of central vision by newborns (Lewis & Maurer 1980), and some of the components of the proposed shift have analogs in the auditory system (see Aslin et al 1983). It has been suggested that the shift is a matter of increased efficiency of processing (Cohen & Younger 1984). Thus, it may indeed be useful to speak of an early developmental shift in perceptual ability, but the determinants of the shift require further specification.

The Question of Precursors

There are of course instances when, on the face of it, development seems discontinuous. New abilities emerge that either seem qualitatively different from what has gone before or were preceded by early, primitive manifestations that have since disappeared. In both cases, one may ask whether early attainments qualify as precursors to later ones. For example, are nonverbal gestures or the symbolic use of objects precursors to language? Is the newborn stepping reflex a precursor to mature walking?

There are differing understandings of the meaning of "precursor" and different methods for specifying the relations between early attainments and later ones. One may try to approach the question by charting the stability of individual differences, but correlations may be misleading if development really follows a progression of discrete stages (Smolak & Levine 1984), or if the range of scores at either age is truncated. One may also look for evidence of topographical similarity and shared determinants and functions (e.g. Thelen

1984). However, this raises issues similar to the distinction between homologies and analogies in evolution. Infancy researchers use the term "precursor" loosely; it deserves more theoretical attention.

Bidirectional Influences of Genes and Environments

Most developmentalists, if questioned, would probably say that the classic nature/nurture issue is unresolvable as posed, and that the task is to determine exactly how genetic endowment interacts with experience in the course of development. In practice, however, that worthy epigenetic task seems seldom undertaken. Developmental psychologists persist in misconceptions about genetic influences, such as the notion that genetic contributions are made only at the outset of development, while behavioral geneticists often attribute entire lumps of unexplained variance to diffuse, unspecified environmental effects (see Plomin 1983 for a discussion of this issue). One helpful approach is to view a developing system as including both "open" and "closed" genetic programs (Mayr 1974). For example, experimental analyses of the development of cowbird song have shown that learning processes influence the male's ability to produce the song of the species, but the female's ability to perceive his song and respond accordingly seems buffered from the effects of experience (e.g. King & West 1983). In general, there is need for increased examination of the bidirectional influences between the genetic heritage of species and individuals and their experiences during ontogeny. Rearing environments can affect biological structures and processes as well as behavioral outcomes; for example, crowding during infancy can affect dendrite formation in fish (Burgess & Coss 1982). At the same time, genetic selection processes such as domestication can modify the effectiveness of experience (Miller & Gottlieb 1981).

When ascribing developmental change to experiential factors, it is important to examine exactly how experience exerts its effects and what types of experiences are especially effective. Some factors considered recently include the timing of experience, the developing organism's contribution to its own experience, and the extent to which early experiences are reversible.

The Timing of Experience

Many questions about the effects of experiences during infancy continue to be asked, as seen in the literature concerning the effects of rearing environments reviewed in the preceding section. More specific questions can be asked about the precise timing of such experiences. For example, are experiences during infancy more powerful than those that occur at later points in childhood? Within infancy, are there particular points at which the organism is especially vulnerable to the effects of experience?

Evidence for such "critical periods" of development derives from experimental studies of nonhuman species and correlational studies of humans; the latter may be either retrospective or prospective (see Colombo 1982). The notion of critical periods has been entertained even when development is viewed as fundamentally discontinuous. For example, periods in which learning abilities are especially fostered have been identified in grain beetles undergoing metamorphosis in a series of discrete stages (Sheimann et al 1980). The onset of critical periods is not necessarily abrupt, and may be influenced by rearing history as well as maturational factors (Colombo 1982). Thus experience itself affects susceptibility to early experience.

When documenting the effects of experiences during infancy, it is not sufficient to compare infants who receive certain experiences with control infants. Rather, one must also examine the effects of similar experiences administered at other ages. For example, it appears that enriched environments improve the lot of aging as well as infant mice (Warren et al 1982).

One area in which the issue of critical periods in human life has loomed large is the study of mother-infant "bonding," which concerns the timing of maternal, not infant experience. It was proposed that the mother's early, unconstrained contact with her infant is a critical determinant for her forming an emotional attachment with the infant (Klaus & Kennell 1976). The bonding hypothesis caught the fancy of the public in the 1980s; it is invoked in child custody disputes and has promoted changes in obstetrical practices. Given these far-reaching implications, it is especially important to note that the existence of a critical period for bonding is not supported by most of the relevant data (see Myers 1984).

Infants' Contributions to their Own Development

Bidirectional influences between infants and their environments have been greatly emphasized during the past two decades. It is assumed that the distinctive characteristics and needs of infants promote their care and stimulation; it is further suggested that differences among infants traceable to genetic conditions, preterm birth, illness, or the like, may lead to differences in the care received. For example, characteristics of the cry that differentiate individual infants (Gustafson et al 1984) and risk groups (Zeskind 1980) affect parental responsiveness.

Infants in general stimulate older persons to respond in distinctive ways; the most obvious example of this is the characteristic "baby talk" directed to infants. This might be viewed as a means by which infants acquire the precise sort of environmental input they need for further development. Nonetheless, the distinctive features of "baby talk" are not shown in every culture (Ratner & Pye 1984), and appear when adults speak to dogs as well as to babies (Hirsh-Pasek & Treiman 1982). Nor is adult speech to infants always clear and intelligible (Bard & Anderson 1983). For these reasons and others, the precise contribution of infant-stimulated linguistic experience to language learning is still the matter of much debate (see Shatz 1984).

To what extent does an infant's developmental status constrain the experiences he or she receives? How good a match must there be between current attainments and new inputs? A theme running through many disparate theories is the importance of stimulation that is a bit more complex than an organism is currently able to process. The notion that such experience promotes growth is central to Piaget's concept of accommodation and to Vygotsky's notion of the "zone of proximal development." In Vygotsky's view, caregivers are sensitive to their infants' current abilities and stimulate the infants accordingly, asking them to do just a bit more than they are able. It is certainly true that, as infants mature, the stimulation provided and the demands made by their parents change as well; for example, maternal speech to younger infants stresses prosodic features whereas that to older infants underscores meaning (Fernald 1984).

A final question about infants' contributions to their own development concerns the infant's role as active producer vs passive recipient of experience, which has been studied with respect to perceptual learning. Self-produced movement promotes infants' successful search for hidden objects (Hay 1977, Acredolo et al 1984); passive exposure to imprinting objects leads to preferences that are easily extinguished (Kertzman & Demarest 1982). However, parents spontaneously try to compensate for their infants' enforced passivity by increasing the stimulation that they provide (Hay 1977), and additional perceptual information can compensate for the effects of passive exposure (Acredolo et al 1984).

Reversibility of Development

The issue of compensation for passive exposure to the environment raises the more general question of whether the effects of experience can be eliminated, reversed, or recovered from. Developmental systems have self-righting properties, but the extent of self-righting that occurs of course depends on the nature and extent of the impairment in development. Several recent experiments on nonhumans have documented reversals of or compensations for early experiences. For example, rats can recover from generations of malnutrition (Galler 1981), and squirrel monkeys' experience with kitten companions ameliorates some of the effects of isolate rearing (Huebner & King 1984). In addition, a case study of one human family documents remarkable recovery from a grossly deprived early rearing history (Skuse 1984). The ability to recover from deleterious experience seems to differ among individuals and groups. For example, male rats suffer more than females from intergenerational malnutrition, and recovery for males, but not females, takes more than a single generation (Galler 1981). The case study of the human family revealed that recovery was possible only where biological insult was lacking; the one member of the family who recovered did not have severe biological anomalies and showed remarkable persistence in seeking even minimal social stimulation wherever she could (Skuse 1984).

CONCLUSIONS

In sum, the current state of infancy research is one of almost feverish inductive activity. Many facts are being garnered, many ideas are being set forth; classic theories and standard procedures are being questioned. The first half of this decade has been a time of stock taking, not theory building.

When developmental psychology was reviewed in this series at the beginning of the decade (Masters 1981), it was remarked that infancy research was the last remaining subfield defined in terms of the age of the organism, not the topics studied. This is more true in terms of the professional identification of infancy researchers than in terms of the actual coherence of the field. Investigators working within any one or more of the four perspectives identified here, and on any topic within any perspective, draw on differing parts of the general psychological literature. A comprehensive understanding of infancy would require not only mastery of the diverse literature on the psychology of infants, but ideally total knowledge of all relevant theory and data, i.e. psychology as a whole. It is no wonder that investigators specialize.

The four perspectives identified here differ in terms of assumptions, methods, and even the populations of infants that are sampled. For example, the information-processing perspective encounters severe problems of attrition of subjects that are systematically confounded with age (Richardson & McCluskey 1983). The longitudinal studies that trace infants' development into later childhood also suffer from attrition, but for other reasons. The developmental perspective necessitates difficult cross-species comparisons. All of these factors work against synthesis across perspectives.

To what extent, then, is it even reasonable that infancy research continue to be identified as a distinctive subarea of psychology? The merit, I think, is that the study of infancy is one place where the naturalistic tradition begun by Tiedemann is honored, and a holistic view of the organism is retained. Adults who study infants must constantly face the fact that convenient distinctions between social and cognitive development, perception and attention, individual temperament and dyadic relations, are not easily maintained. They are forced to look beyond traditional lines of demarcation. Furthermore, they must cope with a whole organism who displays immense charm, but frequently intractable behavior. Even those investigators who borrowed the basic paradigms of experimental psychology have had to take into account the state of the organism; such an appreciation of the receptivity of organisms to experimentation would prove useful for studies of adults as well. Thus the study of infancy leads to insights that have considerable significance for psychology as a whole.

To the extent that infancy researchers meet together, read the same journals, and consider themselves part of the same discipline, synthesis across perspectives, while difficult, remains possible. Several examples of attempted synthesis were identified in the preceding review. For example, the paradigms used in studies of information processing may help elucidate the puzzling developmental course of intellectual ability. Attention to measurement issues prevents false conclusions about infants' perceptual abilities. Naturalistic studies of infants learning language reveal important attainments in the development of thought. These attempts at synthesis would not be possible if investigators studying various topics did not retain a general view of the organism they were observing. Two hundred years ago, Tiedemann set out to answer grand questions about the nature of mind by observing details of the life of the human infant. His approach to psychology is still not such a bad idea.

SUMMARY

Research on the psychology of infancy in the 1980s was prolific and diverse. At least four different perspectives have been taken. The first views the infant as information processor, adopts the methods and assumptions of experimental psychology, and focuses on such fundamental processes as attention, perception, emotion, learning and memory, search and exploration, and cognition. The second views the infant as an infant, as part of the natural world, and focuses on the important developmental milestones that uniquely characterize the period of infancy, such as walking, talking, forming relationships, and developing a sense of self. The third perspective views the infant as an eventual adult, emphasizes differences among individuals, and focuses on continuities across age and experiences such as biological risk factors, characteristics of rearing environments, and planned intervention that influence the kinds of adults infants will turn out to be. The fourth perspective focuses not on the infant per se, but on the general process of development; the issues examined concern the description and explanation of development, in terms of the existence of shifts and stages, the relationship of early attainments to later ones, the bidirectional influence of genes and environments, the timing of experience, individuals' contributions to their own experiences, and the reversibility of development. Synthesis across perspectives is difficult, but remains possible. The field of infancy research is a microcosm of psychology, but one that retains a view of the organism as holistic being. As such, the study of infancy produces insights of considerable relevance to psychology as a whole.

ACKNOWLEDGMENTS

This review was prepared while the author was a member of the Department of Psychology, State University of New York at Stony Brook. I thank Harriet L. Rheingold for all that she has taught me about the study of infancy and for her advice about this project.

Literature Cited

Abravanel, E., Sigafoos, A. D. 1984. Exploring the presence of imitation during early infancy. *Child Dev.* 55:381–92

Acredolo, L. P., Adams, A., Goodwyn, S. W. 1984. The role of self-produced movement and visual tracking in infant spatial orientation. *J. Exp. Child Psychol.* 38:312–27

Ainsworth, M. D. S., Blehar, M., Waters, E., Wall, S. 1978. *Patterns of Attachment.* Hillsdale, NJ: Erlbaum

Anderson, C. J., Sawin, D. B. 1983. Enhancing responsiveness in mother-infant interaction. *Infant Behav. Dev.* 6:361–68

Anisfeld, E. 1982. The onset of social smiling in preterm and full-term infants from two ethnic backgrounds. *Infant Behav. Dev.* 5:387–95

Antonucci, T. C., Levitt, M. J. 1984. Early prediction of attachment security: A multivariate approach. *Infant Behav. Dev.* 7:1–18

Aslin, R. N., Pisoni, D. B., Jusczyk, P. W. 1983. Auditory development and speech perception in infancy. See Mussen 1983, pp. 573–687

Bandura, A., Walters, R. H. 1963. *Social Learning and Personality Development.* New York: Holt, Rinehart & Winston

Bard, E. G., Anderson, A. H. 1983. The unintelligibility of speech to children. *J. Child Lang.* 10:265–92

Barrett, D. E., Radke-Yarrow, M., Klein, R. E. 1982. Chronic malnutrition and child behavior: Effects of early caloric supplementation on social and emotional functioning at school age. *Dev. Psychol.* 18:541–56

Belsky, J., Rovine, M., Taylor, D. G. 1984. The Pennsylvania Infant and Family Development Project, III: The origins of individual differences in infant-mother attachment: Maternal and infant contributions. *Child Dev.* 55:718–28

Bornstein, M. H., Krinsky, S. J. 1985. Perception of symmetry in infancy: The salience of vertical symmetry and the perception of pattern wholes. *J. Exp. Child Psychol.* 39:1–19

Bretherton, I., Beeghly, M. 1982. Talking about internal states: The acquisition of an explicit theory of mind. *Dev. Psychol.* 18:906–21

Bronson, G. W. 1974. The postnatal growth of visual capacity. *Child Dev.* 45:873–90

Brooks-Gunn, J., Lewis, M. 1984. The development of early visual self-recognition. *Dev. Rev.* 4:215–39

Bruner, J. S. 1981. Intention in the structure of action and interaction. *Adv. Infancy Res.* 1:41–56

Burgess, J. W., Coss, R. G. 1982. Effects of chronic crowding stress on midbrain development: Changes in dendritic spine density and morphology in jewel fish optic tectum. *Dev. Psychobiol.* 15:461–70

Butterworth, G. 1983. Structure of the mind in human infancy. *Adv. Infancy Res.* 2:1–29

Chromiak, W., Weisberg, R. W. 1981. The role of the object concept in visual tracking: Child-like errors in adults. *J. Exp. Child Psychol.* 32:531–43

Clarke-Stewart, A. 1984. Day care: A new context for research and development. *Minn. Symp. Child Psychol.* 17:61–100

Cohen, L. B., Menten, T. G. 1981. The rise and fall of infant habituation. *Infant Behav. Dev.* 4:269–80

Cohen, L. B., Younger, B. A. 1984. Infant perception of angular relations. *Infant Behav. Dev.* 7:37–47

Cohn, J. F., Tronick, E. Z. 1983. Three-month-old infants' reactions to simulated maternal depression. *Child Dev.* 54:185–93

Colombo, J. 1982. The critical period concept: Research, methodology, and theoretical issues. *Psychol. Bull.* 91:260–75

Cornell, E. H. 1981. The effects of cue distinctiveness on infants' manual search. *J. Exp. Child Psychol.* 32:330–42

Corrigan, R. 1981. The effects of task and practice on search for invisibly displaced objects. *Dev. Rev.* 1:1–17

Crassini, B., Broerse, J. 1980. Auditory-visual integration in neonates: A signal detection analysis. *J. Exp. Child Psychol.* 29:144–55

Cronbach, L. 1957. The two disciplines of scientific psychology. *Am. Psychol.* 12:671–84

Cummings, E. M., Bjork, E. L. 1981. The search behavior of 12 to 14 month-old infants on a free-choice invisible displacement hiding task. *Infant Behav. Dev.* 4:47–60

Dannemiller, J. L. 1984. Infant habituation criteria: I. A Monte Carlo study of the 50%

decrement criterion. *Infant Behav. Dev.* 7:147–66

Dannemiller, J. L., Banks, M. S. 1983. Can selective adaptation account for early infant habituation? *Merrill-Palmer Q.* 29:151–58

Davis, M., Levine, S. 1982. Predictability, control, and the pituitary-adrenal response in rats. *J. Comp. Physiol. Psychol.* 96:393–404

DeCasper, A. J., Prescott, P. A. 1984. Human newborns' perception of male voices: Preference, discrimination, and reinforcing value. *Dev. Psychobiol.* 17:481–91

DeLoache, J. S., Cassidy, D. J., Brown, A. L. 1985. Precursors of mnemonic strategies in very young children's memory. *Child Dev.* 56:125–37

Diamond, A., Goldman-Rakic, P. S. 1985. *Evidence that maturation of the frontal cortex of the brain underlies behavioral changes during the first year of life. I. The AB task.* Presented at Bienn. Meet. Soc. Res. Child Dev., Toronto, Canada

Elardo, R., Bradley, R. H. 1981. The home observation for measurement of the environment (HOME) scale: A review of research. *Dev. Rev.* 1:113–45

Epstein, H. T. 1974. Phrenoblysis: Special mind and brain growth periods. II. Human mental development. *Dev. Psychobiol.* 7:217–24

Fagan, J. F. III, Singer, L. T. 1983. Infant recognition memory as a measure of intelligence. *Adv. Infancy Res.* 2:31–78

Fagen, J. W., Morrongiello, B. A., Rovee-Collier, C., Gekoski, M. J. 1984. Expectancies and memory retrieval in three-month-old infants. *Child Dev.* 55:936–43

Farran, D. C., Ramey, C. T. 1980. Social class differences in dyadic involvement during infancy. *Child Dev.* 51:254–57

Feinman, S. 1982. Social referencing in infancy. *Merrill-Palmer Q.* 28:445–70

Fernald, A. 1984. *The perceptual, affective, and linguistic salience of mothers' speech to infants.* Presented at Int. Conf. Infant Stud., New York

Field, T. M. 1981. Infant arousal, attention, and affect during early interactions. *Adv. Infancy Res.* 1:57–100

Field, T. M., Widmayer, S. M. 1980. Developmental follow-up of infants delivered by Caesarian section and general anesthesia. *Infant Behav. Dev.* 3:253–64

Field, T. M., Woodson, R., Greenberg, R., Cohen, D. 1982. Discrimination and imitation of facial expressions by neonates. *Science* 146:668–70

Fischer, K. W. 1980. A theory of cognitive development: The control and construction of hierarchies of skills. *Psychol. Rev.* 87:477–531

Frederickson, W. T., Sackett, G. A. 1984. Kin preferences in primates *(Macaca nemestrina)*: Relatedness or familiarity? *J. Comp. Psychol.* 98:29–34

Galler, J. R. 1981. Visual discrimination in rats: The effects of rehabilitation following intergenerational malnutrition. *Dev. Psychobiol.* 14:229–36

Gibson, E. J., Walker, A. S. 1984. Development of knowledge of visual-tactual affordances of substance. *Child Dev.* 55:453–60

Gibson, J. J. 1979. *The Ecological Approach to Visual Perception.* Boston: Houghton Mifflin

Goldsmith, H. H. 1983. Genetic influences on personality from infancy to adulthood. *Child Dev.* 54:331–55

Golinkoff, R. M., Uzgiris, I. C., Gibson, E. J., Harding, C. G., Carlson, V., et al. 1984. The development of causality in infancy: A symposium. *Adv. Infancy Res.* 3:127–65

Gopnik, A. 1982. Words and plans: Early language and the development of intelligent action. *J. Child Lang.* 9:303–18

Greenberg, J. R., Mitchell, S. A. 1983. *Object Relations in Psychoanalytic Theory.* Cambridge, MA: Harvard Univ. Press

Gunnar, M. R. 1980. Control, warning signals, and distress in infancy. *Dev. Psychol.* 16:281–99

Gunnar, M. R., Leighton, K., Peleaux, R. 1984a. Effects of temporal predictability on the reactions of 1-year-olds to potentially frightening toys. *Dev. Psychol.* 20:449–58

Gunnar, M. R., Senior, K., Hartup, W. W. 1984b. Peer presence and the exploratory behavior of eighteen- and thirty-month-old children. *Child Dev.* 55:1103–9

Gustafson, G. E. 1984. Effects of the ability to locomote on infants' social and exploratory behavior: An experimental study. *Dev. Psychol.* 20:397–405

Gustafson, G. E., Green, J. A., Tomic, T. 1984. Acoustic correlates of individuality in the cries of human infants. *Dev. Psychobiol.* 17:311–24

Hahn, M. E., Walters, J. K., Lavooy, J., Deluca, J. 1983. Brain growth in young mice: Evidence on the theory of phrenoblysis. *Dev. Psychobiol.* 16:377–83

Haith, M. M., Campos, J. J. 1977. Human infancy. *Ann. Rev. Psychol.* 28:251–93

Hay, D. F. 1977. Following their companions as a form of exploration for human infants. *Child Dev.* 48:1624–32

Hay, D. F. 1980. Multiple functions of proximity-seeking in infancy. *Child Dev.* 51:636–45

Hay, D. F., Murray, P., Cecire, S., Nash, A. 1985. Social learning of social behavior in early life. *Child Dev.* 56:43–57

Hay, D. F., Nash, A., Pedersen, J. 1981. Responses of six-month-olds to the distress of their peers. *Child Dev.* 52:1071–75

Hay, D. F., Ross, H. S. 1982. The social nature of early conflict. *Child Dev.* 53:105–13

Hayes, L. A., Watson, J. S. 1981. Neonatal imitation: Fact or artifact? *Dev. Psychol.* 17:655–60

Hennessey, M. J., Dixon, S. D., Simon, S. R. 1984. The development of gait: A study in African children ages one to five. *Child Dev.* 55:844–53

Hinde, R. A., Bateson, P. 1984. Discontinuities versus continuities in behavioral development and the neglect of process. *Int. J. Behav. Dev.* 7:129–43

Hirsh-Pasek, K., Treiman, R. 1982. Doggerel: Motherese in a new context. *J. Child Lang.* 9:229–37

Holmes, D. L., Nagy, J. N., Slaymaker, F., Sosnowski, R. J., Prinz, S. M., et al. 1982. Early influences of prematurity, illness, and prolonged hospitalization on infant behavior. *Dev. Psychol.* 18:744–50

Horner, T. M. 1983. On the formation of personal space and self-boundary structures in early human development: The case of infant stranger reactivity. *Dev. Rev.* 3:148–77

Huebner, D. K., King, J. E. 1984. Kittens as therapists: Social behavior sequences in isolated squirrel monkeys after exposure to young non-conspecifics. *Dev. Psychobiol.* 17:233–42

Hunter, M. A., Ross, H. S., Ames, E. W. 1982. Preferences for familiar or novel toys: Effects of familiarization time in 1-year-olds. *Dev. Psychol.* 18:519–29

Ispa, J. 1981. Peer support among Soviet day care toddlers. *Int. J. Behav. Dev.* 4:255–69

Jacobson, J. L., Jacobson, S. W., Fein, G. G., Schwartz, P. M., Dowler, J. K. 1984. Prenatal exposure to an environmental toxin: A test of the multiple effects model. *Dev. Psychol.* 20:523–32

Johnston, T. D., Gottlieb, G. 1985. Effects of social experience on visually imprinted maternal preferences in Peking ducklings. *Dev. Psychobiol.* 18:261–71

Kagan, J., Reznick, S., Clarke, C., Snidman, N., Garcia-Coll, C. 1984. Behavioral inhibition to the unfamiliar. *Child Dev.* 55:2212–25

Kendrick, C., Dunn, J. 1983. Sibling quarrels and maternal responses. *Dev. Psychol.* 19:62–70

Kertzman, C., Demarest, J. 1982. Irreversibility of imprinting after active vs. passive exposure to the object. *J. Comp. Physiol. Psychol.* 96:130–42

King, A. P., West, M. J. 1983. Female perception of cowbird song: A closed developmental program. *Dev. Psychobiol.* 16:335–42

Klaus, M. H., Kennell, J. H. 1976. *Maternal-Infant Bonding*. St. Louis: Mosby

Kopp, C. B. 1982. Antecedents of self-regulation: A developmental perspective. *Dev. Psychol.* 18:199–214

Lamb, M. E., Frodi, A. M., Frodj, M., Hwang, C-P. 1982. Characteristics of maternal and paternal behavior in traditional and nontraditional Swedish families. *Int. J. Behav. Dev.* 5:131–41

Lewis, M., Feiring, C. 1981. Direct and indirect interactions in social relationships. *Adv. Infancy Res.* 1:129–61

Lewis, M., Feiring, C., McGuffog, C., Jaskir, J. 1984. Predicting psychopathology in six-year-olds from early social relations. *Child Dev.* 55:123–36

Lewis, T. L., Maurer, D. 1980. Central vision in the newborn. *J. Exp. Child Psychol.* 29:475–80

MacDonald, K. 1983. Stability of individual differences in behavior of a litter of wolf cubs *(Canis lupus)*. *J. Comp. Psychol.* 97:99–106

Martin, G. B., Clark, R. D. III. 1982. Distress crying in neonates: Species and peer specificity. *Dev. Psychol.* 18:3–9

Martin, J. A., Maccoby, E. E., Baran, K. W., Jacklin, C. N. 1981. Sequential analysis of mother-child interaction at 18 months: A comparison of microanalytic methods. *Dev. Psychol.* 17:146–57

Masters, J. 1981. Developmental psychology. *Ann. Rev. Psychol.* 32:117–51

Mayr, E. 1974. Behavioral programs and evolutionary strategies. *Am. Sci.* 62:650–59

McCall, R. B. 1981. Nature-nurture and the two realms of development: A proposed integration with respect to mental development. *Child Dev.* 52:1–12

McCall, R. B., Meyers, E. D. Jr., Hartman, J., Roche, A. F. 1983. Developmental changes in head-circumference and mental-performance growth rates: A test of Epstein's phrenoblysis hypothesis. *Dev. Psychobiol.* 16:457–68

McCune-Nicholich, L. 1981. Toward symbolic functioning: Structure of early pretend games and potential parallels with language. *Child Dev.* 52:785–97

Meltzoff, A. N. 1985. Immediate and deferred imitation in fourteen- and twenty-four-month-old infants. *Child Dev.* 56:62–72

Meltzoff, A. N., Moore, M. K. 1977. Imitation of facial and manual gestures by human neonates. *Science* 198:75–78

Meltzoff, A. N., Moore, M. K. 1983. Newborn infants imitate adult facial gestures. *Child Dev.* 54:702–9

Mendelson, M. J. 1983. Attentional inertia at 4 and 7 months? *Child Dev.* 54:677–85

Miller, D. B., Gottlieb, G. 1981. Effects of domestication on production and perception of mallard maternal alarm calls: Developmental lag in behavioral arousal. *J. Comp. Physiol. Psychol.* 95:205–19

Murchison, C., Langer, S. (Transl.) 1927.

Tiedemann's observations on the development of the mental faculties of children. *Pedagog. Semin.* 34:205–30

Mussen, P. H., ed. 1983. *Handbook of Child Psychology.* New York: Wiley

Myers, B. J. 1984. Mother-infant bonding: The status of this critical period hypothesis. *Dev. Rev.* 4:240–74

Nelson, C. A., Horowitz, F. D. 1983. The perception of facial expressions and stimulus motion by two- and five-month-old infants using holographic stimuli. *Child Dev.* 54:868–77

Oppenheim, R. W. 1980. Metamorphosis and adaptation in the behavior of developing organisms. *Dev. Psychobiol.* 13:353–56

Pea, R. D. 1982. Origins of verbal logic: Spontaneous denials by two- and three-year-olds. *J. Child Lang.* 9:597–626

Pfeifer, S. 1980. Role of the nursing order in social development of mountain lion kittens. *Dev. Psychobiol.* 13:47–53

Plomin, R. 1983. Developmental behavioral genetics. *Child Dev.* 54:253–59

Presson, C. C., Ihrig, L. H. 1982. Using mother as a spatial landmark: Evidence against egocentric coding in infancy. *Dev. Psychol.* 18:699–703

Ramey, C. T., Yeates, K. O., Short, E. J. 1984. The plasticity of intellectual development: Insights from preventive intervention. *Child Dev.* 55:1913–25

Ratner, N. B., Pye, C. 1984. Higher pitch in BT is not universal: Acoustic evidence from Quiche Mayan. *J. Child Lang.* 11:515–22

Rheingold, H. L. 1982. Little children's participation in the work of adults, a nascent prosocial behavior. *Child Dev.* 53:114–25

Rheingold, H. L. 1985. Development as the acquisition of familiarity. *Ann. Rev. Psychol.* 36:1–17

Richardson, G. A., McCluskey, K. A. 1983. Subject loss in infancy research: How biasing is it? *Infant Behav. Dev.* 6:235–39

Rovee-Collier, C. K., Fagen, J. W. 1981. The retrieval of memory in early infancy. *Adv. Infancy Res.* 1:225–54

Samuels, H. R. 1980. The effect of an older sibling on infant locomotor exploration of a new environment. *Child Dev.* 51:607–9

Shatz, M. 1984. Contributions of mother and mind to the development of communicative competence: A status report. *Minn. Symp. Child Psychol.* 17:33–59

Sheimann, I. M., Khutzian, S. S., Ignatovitch, G. S. 1980. Periodicity in the behavior of grain beetle larvae. *Dev. Psychobiol.* 13:585–90

Skuse, D. H. 1984. Extreme deprivation in early childhood. I. Diverse outcomes for three siblings from an extraordinary family. *J. Child Psychiatry Psychol.* 25:523–41

Slater, A., Earle, D. C., Morison, V., Rose, D. 1985. Pattern preferences at birth and their interaction with habituation-induced novelty preferences. *J. Exp. Child Psychol.* 39:37–54

Slaughter, D. T. 1983. Early intervention and its effects on maternal and child development. *Monogr. Soc. Res. Child Dev.* 48, no. 202

Smolak, L., Levine, M. P. 1984. The effects of differential criteria on the assessment of cognitive-linguistic relationships. *Child Dev.* 55:973–80

Sophian, C. 1980. Habituation is not enough: Novelty preferences, search, and memory in infancy. *Merrill-Palmer Q.* 26:239–57

Sorce, J. F., Emde, R. N. 1981. Mother's presence is not enough: Effect of emotional availability on infant exploration. *Dev. Psychol.* 17:737–45

Sroufe, L. A., Rutter, M. 1984. The domain of developmental psychopathology. *Child Dev.* 55:17–29

Stenberg, C. R., Campos, J. J., Emde, R. N. 1983. The facial expression of anger in seven-month-old infants. *Child Dev.* 54:178–84

Stern, M., Hildebrandt, K. A. 1984. Prematurity stereotype: Effects of labeling on adults' perceptions of infants. *Dev. Psychol.* 20:360–62

Thelen, E. 1984. Learning to walk: Ecological demands and phylogenetic constraints. *Adv. Infancy Res.* 3:213–50

Trehub, S. E., Bull, D., Thorpe, L. A. 1984. Infants' perception of melodies: The role of melodic contour. *Child Dev.* 55:821–30

Treiber, F., Wilcox, S. 1984. Discrimination of number by infants. *Infant Behav. Dev.* 7:93–100

Ullman, S. 1980. Against direct perception. *Behav. Brain Sci.* 3:373–415

Warren, J. M., Zerweck, C., Anthony, A. 1982. Effects of environmental enrichment on old mice. *Dev. Psychobiol.* 15:13–18

Waters, E. 1985. *A Q-sort instrument for assessing attachment in infancy and early childhood.* Presented at Bienn. Meet. Soc. Res. Child Dev., Toronto, Canada

Waters, E., Sroufe, L. A. 1983. Social competence as a developmental construct. *Dev. Rev.* 3:79–97

Wilcox, S., Katz, S. 1981. The ecological approach to development: An alternative to cognitivism. *J. Exp. Child Psychol.* 32:247–63

Yarrow, L. J., MacTurk, R. H., Vietze, P. M., McCarthy, M. E., Klein, R. P., et al. 1984. Developmental course of parental stimulation and its relationship to mastery motivation during infancy. *Dev. Psychol.* 20:492–503

Younger, B. A., Cohen, L. B. 1983. Infant perception of correlations among attributes. *Child Dev.* 54:858–67

Zahn-Waxler, C., Cummings, E. M., McKnew, D. H., Radke-Yarrow, M. 1984. Altruism, aggression, and social interactions in young children with a manic-depressive parent. *Child Dev.* 55:112–22

Zelazo, P. 1984. "Learning to walk": Recogni-tion of higher order influences? *Adv. Infancy Res.* 3:251–56

Zeskind, P. S. 1980. Adult responses to cries of low and high risk infants. *Infant Behav. Dev.* 3:167–77

Zeskind, P. S., Iacino, R. 1984. Effects of maternal visitation to preterm infants in the neonatal intensive care unit. *Child Dev.* 55:1887–93

Ann. Rev. Psychol. 1986. 37:163–92

THE BIOLOGY OF LEARNING

James L. Gould

Department of Biology, Princeton University, Princeton, New Jersey 08544

CONTENTS

INTRODUCTION 163
CONCEPTS FROM EARLY ETHOLOGY 164
    Cue Recognition 164
    Effector Organization 165
    Terminology 167
    Endogenous Control 167
    Selective Learning 168
    "Genetic Constraints" 170
LEARNING IN THE FIELD 171
    Food Acquisition 171
    Reproduction 176
    Parental Care 177
    Defense 177
    Navigation 179
    Social Behavior, Social Communication, and "Culture" 180
ETHOLOGICAL PERSPECTIVES ON LEARNING IN THE LABORATORY 182
    Nonassociative Learning 182
    Classical Conditioning 183
    Trial-and-Error Learning 184
    Anomalies and Biases 185
    Alpha Conditioning 187
COGNITIVE TRIAL AND ERROR 187
CONCLUSION 189

INTRODUCTION

Ethologists are usually seen as preoccupied with innate behavior, an interest succinctly described by the title of Tinbergen's famous book, *The Study of Instinct* (1951). Yet the Nobel prize-winning trio of early ethologists—von Frisch, Tinbergen, and Lorenz—all began with and frequently returned to studies of learning: von Frisch's earliest work (von Frisch 1967) was on

163

0066-4308/86/0201-0163$02.00

classical conditioning of goldfish to sound and honey bees to color; Tinbergen's earliest study was on landmark memory in hunting wasps (Tinbergen 1972); Lorenz began his career investigating imprinting and learned social recognition (Lorenz 1970). What distinguishes these studies (excepting, presumably, that with goldfish) is the use of natural problems in natural or seminatural situations. Ethologists have generally found little of interest in behavioristic studies—experiments involving a very limited number of species facing what appear to be for the most part unnatural problems in artificial environments. Behaviorists, in turn, have often found little of value in studies of species-specific learning in largely uncontrolled, naturalistic settings. The goal of this review is to examine the increasing evidence that the research from these two different perspectives together provides a useful and coherent picture of learning. The review first defines some standard ethological terminology, then looks at some examples of (and the need for) animal learning in the wild, and finally examines the connections between laboratory studies of learning and field studies.

CONCEPTS FROM EARLY ETHOLOGY

Cue Recognition

From the early work of Lorenz and Tinbergen came the four general concepts that still provide a conceptual framework for many ethologists. The first is the idea of innate recognition by animals of important objects or individuals in the environment. Ethologists have cataloged an almost endless list of such "releasers." The egg-retrieval behavior of ground-nesting birds such as the Greylag goose is a cogent example (Lorenz & Tinbergen 1938). The sight of an egg outside the nest captures the attention of the incubating parent, and results in the goose's standing, extending its neck toward and over the egg, and then gently rolling it back with the bottom of the bill. The recognition of the egg is innate and highly schematic: geese will readily retrieve batteries, beer bottles, and baseballs. The basic, schematic features of the stimulus object which effect recognition are usually called "sign stimuli."

Although there was a time when many ethologists thought complex patterns could be genetically encoded in minute detail and act as sign stimuli, our growing understanding of the mechanics of sensory processing makes this unlikely. It seems more reasonable to believe that most sign stimuli are the relatively simple sorts of cues for which ensembles of visual, acoustic, and olfactory feature-detector cells in the CNS are known to code (Gould 1982a). This is particularly obvious in the case of behavioral specialists such as toads and bats (Ewert 1981), where even the hyper-complex feature detectors serve relatively clear-cut functions, identifying prey, predators, and conspecifics. The existence of similar detectors in generalists like cats (as opposed, say, to a simple dot-by-dot representation of the retina on the visual cortex) argues that here too they serve an essential function. Since learning often supplements or replaces innate mechanisms, and because generalists frequently depend on learning more than innate recognition, it seems reasonable to think that schematic-recognition elements can play a role in learning. Perhaps they could be used (in the manner of olfactory coding) such that the pattern of output of a variety of high-order feature detectors with differing "personalities" can uniquely define any object, independent of its apparent size or even (with a little clever wiring) preserving lateral relationships. Thus, through learning, an animal could form an enormous library of subconscious, automatic recognition circuits out of novel combinations of feature detectors.

To return to the use of releasers in innate recognition, it is frequently the case that several relatively simple cues are effective simultaneously, together making the response potentially more specific; but the various relevant feature detectors, whether simple or complex, most often appear to act independently and additively—a phenomenon known as "heterogeneous summation." When a baby herring gull, for instance, pecks at its parent's bill, it is reacting independently to a vertical bar moving horizontally (the parent's bill) and a moving high-contrast spot (the red spot on the parent's yellow bill) (Hailman 1967; J. Dollinger, J. Gordon, S. Mariscal, and J. L. Gould, unpublished observations); the response to a model combining these features is the sum of responses to two models each with only one feature. Since both stimuli correspond to well-known classes of feature detectors, even to the extent of displaying optimum responses to particular rates of angular motion, it seems reasonable to believe that the circuitry may be as simple as it looks.

The consequence of the sign-stimulus strategy is that animals can be prewired to recognize important and predictable objects, individuals, and events with a reasonable degree of certainty, at least so long as they are not transported into environments (or laboratory situations) which are "unnatural" to the species.

Effector Organization

The second of the concepts crucial to ethology's exploration of behavior, and a natural outgrowth of the idea of sign stimuli, is the fixed-action pattern of Lorenz (1970). The goose's egg-retrieval behavior is again a good example. Most of this behavior is highly stereotyped, and once triggered, proceeds to completion even if the egg is removed. Other parts depend on specific proprioceptive feedback to tune the behavior. The sight of a goose delicately rolling the ghost of an egg which had been removed as the bird was extending its neck makes it clear that at the heart of this highly coordinated piece of motor activity is a prewired behavioral unit. These units are often called "motor programs," a name that emphasizes their neural basis while removing the implication that the units need to be innate or immune to sensory feedback

(Gould 1982a). Indeed, the ability to wire up novel behavioral units with all the characteristics of innate motor programs plays a very large role in the behavior of many animals. Many song birds, for example, must have auditory feedback to learn a new song, but once their song "crystallizes," they can be deafened without effect (Konishi 1965, Marler 1970): although they can no longer hear themselves sing, they produce normal songs. Similarly, since the song is produced by two bilaterally separate sets of muscles in the syrinx, when the neural connections to one set are cut, the other side continues to sing its part (and only its part) of the duet just as before (Nottebohm 1971).

Not only can novel behavior become virtually automatic in this way, but learning can serve to put several innate motor programs together into the proper order (Gould & Marler 1984). For instance, it appears that though male rhesus monkeys reared in isolation are equipped innately with all of the critical components for copulation behavior—the sign stimulus recognition circuits and the various motor programs—and "know" that the various components belong to this behavioral situation, they assemble them in an inappropriate way (Mason 1968). The idea that there can be an innately directed trial-and-error ordering of motor program subroutines may be applied to a wide variety of behaviors, like the maturation of food-burying behavior in squirrels (Eibl-Eibesfeldt 1961, Ewer 1965), song learning in birds (Marler 1984), and many other behaviors (Grillner 1985). The consequence of the motor-program strategy is that animals can be prewired to perform certain sorts of predictable behavior correctly; or, after learning to perform a motor task, transform the task into a more-or-less automatic behavioral unit.

The concept of behavioral units has helped explain many kinds of complex but largely innate feats. Research on animals as diverse as orb-weaving spiders, digger wasps, and nest-building birds (e.g. Collias & Collias 1962) appears to point to a hierarchical strategy in which one unit or series of units is cycled through repeatedly until some criterion is reached, whereupon another unit is triggered. An Australian digger wasp, for example, builds a funnel to protect its nest from parasites in just this way (A. W. Smith 1978). The wasp begins by constructing a mud cylinder perpendicular to the ground, whether the substrate it is building on is horizontal, oblique, or vertical. Once she has begun, however, the angle of the substrate or tunnel can be changed but the wasp will continue to build a straight tube. The wasp works on the cylinder until it is 3 cm long, and then begins the curving neck. If an experimenter repeatedly buries the bottom of the cylinder so the 3 cm criterion is never met, the wasp can be made to build indefinitely, but once the 3 cm criterion *is* reached and work on the curved neck begins, burying has no effect. The wasp continues the neck until the plane of its opening is roughly 20° from the horizontal. Experimental manipulation of the angle of the tube can determine how much neck must be constructed before the 20° criterion is reached, but once the wasp begins the next stage of the task, further changes have no effect. And so it goes for the construction of the flange and then the bell of the funnel, each unit an independent step with its own set of releasers and motor programs that allow the animal to perform this very complex task.

A similar hierarchical arrangement appears to underlie the processing of information in at least certain types of complex navigation behavior. In these cases, the various "units" are often arranged hierarchically as alternatives, with a primary system backed up by one or more secondary systems. Foraging honey bees, for instance, choose the sun over other directional cues if it is available, but automatically resort to polarized light when the sun is not available (Gould 1982a, Dyer & Gould 1983). Many birds also choose the sun first, but can use the earth's magnetic field if necessary (Gould 1982b)

Terminology

I should point out at this stage that the use of sign stimulus and motor program here are purposely broad. On the motor side, dividing behavioral gestures into motor programs and reflexes is artificial—to the extent that they can be reliably distinguished at all. The distinction is merely quantitative. Moreover, the endogenously coordinated performances of simple motor programs doubtless evolved from simple reflexive gestures. On the sensory side, I use sign stimuli when the stimulus, however crude, differentially triggers a specific response that other perceptible stimuli do not. From this crude but organized relationship between stimulus and response, evolution has evolved more precise sensory filtering to optimize the specificity of sign stimuli.

Endogenous Control

Endogenously generated motivation, often referred to as "drive," is used in many different senses. Motivation, as used here, refers only to endogenous, innately prearranged behavioral switchings. If we take for granted for the moment that much of behavior, particularly in lower animals, is triggered and directed by sign stimuli and accomplished by motor programs, it becomes clear that some behaviors are performed only during certain periods of an animal's life. Egg rolling, for instance, is a behavioral unit that occurs seasonally, appearing about a week before incubation begins and lasting until about a week after hatching. The drive or "motivation" to respond to the sign stimulus for eggs in this way appears to be absent at other times. It is easy to think of behavioral units of this sort as subroutines whose availability is controlled by day length, hormone level, social or environmental signals, or other stimuli. Hence, the long-term responsiveness to particular cues is shifted in a predictable and adaptive way as an animal's needs change on the basis of innately recognized endogenous and exogenous "priming stimuli" (e.g. Klinghammer & Hess 1964, Harding & Follett 1979, Brzoska & Obert 1980).

Attempts to understand the mechanisms underlying most shorter-term changes in motivation, even at this qualitative level, have not been very successful, though the work that has been done on hunger and thirst is an obvious exception. Unfortunately, motivation is extremely difficult to sort out: recent performance of a behavior, deprivation, displacement activity, the "quality" of the sign stimuli, the motivation associated with other "needs," competition for the use of shared final common pathways, and other physiological mechanisms all affect it in some tangential but significant way. One of the more promising approaches to the study of motivation envisions currently available behavioral alternatives as competing for (or "time sharing") an animal's "attention" on the basis of the levels of drive associated with each (McFarland & Lloyd 1973, Heiligenberg 1974). There is a preordained system of priorities, so that responses to threatening stimuli, for example, always tend to take precedence; but in addition, behavioral priorities can be adjusted to balance the urgency of an animal's needs against the quality of the opportunities available. When honey bees, for instance, evaluate the "quality" of food sources (von Frisch 1967), recruit bees take into account the needs of the colony for pollen (protein for brood rearing) vs nectar (carbohydrates to fuel adults and to store for the winter). Their readiness to follow dances to these two sources varies with the internal condition of the hive. Also, recruits weigh the sugar concentration of the nectar being advertised against the distance being indicated: more dilute nectar must be closer, to allow the calories gathered per unit time to balance out. Finally, the bees' preference for more concentrated nectar can reverse itself as the hive temperature increases (Lindauer 1959). When coolant is needed, nectar with a low sugar content, which can be spread out and fanned to provide evaporative cooling for the hive, becomes more desirable.

Selective Learning

"Imprinting" is another concept preserved from early ethology. We propose to consider it here as a subset of a more general class of "selective learning" processes. The general characteristics of most selective learning include its frequent temporal specificity (the "sensitive phase"); the innate triggering of learning by specific sign stimuli [innate learning triggers (ILT), as defined by Marler (1984)]; its context-dependent cue specificity (a specificity that often dictates that particular, frequently multimodel features of a stimulus will be more easily remembered than others); its frequent resistance to reversal (especially in imprinting); and (again particularly in imprinting) its usual lack of obvious external reward.

The adaptive role of selective learning seems clear enough. It helps a naive animal surrounded by a world full of potentially learnable stimuli to "decide" what it should remember and what to do with the information subsequently. A baby herring gull, as we saw, is born knowing to peck at a horizontally moving vertical bar and at a moving red spot—both sign stimuli. They also know to memorize the details of the other features of this stimulus complex such as the head, beak shape, and so on, if the stimulus object feeds them. Interestingly, the chick will not learn the characteristics of a wholly inappropriate stimulus even if it is fed by it (J. Dollinger, J. Gordon, S. Mariscal, and J. L. Gould, unpublished observations). The same pattern is evident in laughing gulls (Margolis et al 1986). This particular example of parental imprinting is unusual, since food reinforcement is rarely involved in selective learning, but it unequivocably demonstrates that different sign stimuli can be involved at different stages in the learning sequence.

The result for gull chicks in the wild is that the reliable but schematic, innately recognized stimuli are replaced eventually by a detailed visual, and/or acoustic (and, for all we know, olfactory) picture of the parents which is then used for individual as well as species recognition. In short, information too detailed or insufficiently generalized across the environments encountered by the species, or otherwise too unpredictable to be prewired, can be specifically acquired and used.

This is not to say that animals necessarily memorize and use complex pictures in all instances. Indeed, Lashley (1938), studying form discrimination by rats on his jumping stand apparatus, pointed out that "with very complex, irregular figures, the basis of discrimination is a part figure; the response is to some limited cue and the remainder of the figure is ignored." Different rats focused on different parts of the figures, choosing some simple but sufficient dichotomy between the choices. Lea (1984) reports a similar phenomenon in pigeons. The "part figures" are very like sign stimuli, and it is tempting to wonder whether, when possible, learning might employ such basic units as simple or complex feature detectors to make essential distinctions. Certainly this inductive abstraction of a reliable distinction or correlation makes sense in the context of associative learning, to be discussed below. Perhaps when the distinctions to be made are more subtle, more complex configurational details must be remembered than can be accounted for by a simple collection of independently active feature detectors, and learning performance is often improved. As a result, a multimodel set or even something like a true mental picture must be involved. Examples of photographic-like selective learning that develop around innate responsiveness to simple sign stimuli are virtually endless, and include some aspects of bee learning (see Gould 1985); song learning (Marler 1984); parental, sibling, and sexual imprinting (Immelmann 1984); enemy learning by birds (Curio & Vieth 1978); and face learning by human infants (Cary 1981, Marler 1985). The probability of a relationship between selective learning and the predictability and elaborateness of what must be known by an animal to survive and reproduce provides a conceptual basis for examining selective learning in general, as we shall see.

"Genetic Constraints"

Before looking at the likely need for learning in the wild, a point should be made about the frequently heard phrase "genetic constraints on learning." It derives from the overwhelming commitment of most psychologists to general process learning theory, a concept that is now outdated (Jenkins 1984). The implication of the term is that animals would be smart if their genes did not constrain their general ability to learn and thereby make them selectively stupid. If one is inclined (as many ethologists are) to think of selective learning as specialized behavioral units analogous to motor programs and navigational information-processing subroutines, then evolution would be expected to act to *create* specific learning abilities where needed rather than specifically edit out the general ability to learn everything (or even anything) from specific contexts. It is unlikely that an ability to learn anything and everything would be adaptive. Consider the pattern of egg and offspring learning in birds (Burtt 1977, Birkhead 1978, Rothstein 1978, 1982). Most birds do not learn to recognize their eggs, even though they see them many times a day, frequently turn them, and otherwise care for them. Species that do memorize the number and/or appearance of their eggs (and, given the opportunity, can do so in remarkable detail) are either subject to brood parasites or nest so close to other birds that the possibility of a mixup is realistic. We could suppose that originally birds learned everything about the world around them, including what their eggs looked like, but that evolution acted to "constrain" the species for whom this learning was not essential. But for evolution to weed out a behavior with such thoroughness, the behavior would probably have to be actively maladaptive. It is not easy to see how the battery-rolling goose would be a less fit parent if it were able to remember what its eggs looked like. This point is underscored by the subset of parasitized host species that do *not* imprint on their eggs. It seems more reasonable to suppose that they have, for a variety of possible reasons, not evolved this learning program, than to suppose that having it, they lost the ability through some sort of "constraining" process.

Nor does it seem reasonable to suppose that the species which memorize egg appearance are just somehow generally smarter than others. Herring gulls, for instance, who seem unable to learn even the color of their eggs, *do* learn to recognize their young individually within three days (Tinbergen 1972). This is just the time at which the chicks begin to wander about and the possibility of confusing one nest's chicks with another's becomes a potentially serious problem. Birds that nest in trees generally do not learn what their young look like until the offspring begin to fledge—again, just the time when the potential for confusion begins. Species such as the cliff-nesting kittiwakes who do not face brood parasites, the possibility of foreign chicks wandering into the nest, nor the need to feed their fledged young, never learn to recognize their offspring at all (Cullen 1957). Again, it is not easy to see that there has been any adaptive edge to insouciance that could easily explain these "constraints."

The counterintuitive logic of this "constraint" position is perhaps more tellingly obvious when we look at our own species. Have our genes constrained us from memorizing the locations of hundreds of buried seeds (Shettleworth 1983), or from readily learning to compensate for the sun's movement, or from easily distinguishing all the eggs in an oriole's nest, and so on? The idea that evolution has built selective learning routines where necessary seems far more consistent with both the field data and our present understanding of how natural selection operates. The use of "constraints," then, is both misleading and potentially confusing.

LEARNING IN THE FIELD

Food Acquisition

From this perspective on selective learning, we can make some predictions about the likely need for learning (as opposed to preordained "hardwiring") as a function of the behavioral context and an animal's niche or life history. Consider foraging, for example. Different species may make their livings by being specialists perfectly adapted for harvesting one kind of food, or by being generalists, able to gather or capture a wide range of food, or by adopting a strategy falling anywhere along the continuum in between. Some basic prewiring of behavior might seem adaptive for a specialist, with its constant, narrow food preferences. The very predictability from generation to generation of its food's characteristic appearance, defense, preferred habitat, and behavior (if it is animate), should make it a prime candidate for some sort of encoding. We would expect specialists, then, as a rule to be less willing and/or able to learn about food sources than generalists. Digger wasps, for instance, are born able to recognize, capture, and paralyze particular prey, with one species specialized for honey bees, another for crickets, and so on. Bees, on the other hand, though innately able to recognize the sign stimuli for flowers, come programmed to memorize the odor, color, and shape (among other things) of each specific species they forage, as well as the most efficient way in which to harvest each blossom.

FINDING A FLOWER   The ways in which honey bees learn about food sources illustrate the role of selective learning in dealing with the predictably unpredictable—a situation in which only broad, innate floral predispositions (as opposed to a prewired set of specific details of a series of flowers) are practicable and adaptive, and learning of specific details based on experience is necessary. Indeed, a bee searching for a food source, whether she is a scout or a recruit, does not land at random. Instead, she has innate guidance—what we could call behavioral biases or spontaneous preferences. Hence it is that bees know innately that flowers usually have dark UV centers and bright surrounds (Daumer 1958); normally possess nectar guides (Anderson 1977a); are often finely divided (Hertz 1929, 1931); frequently have points (Anderson 1977b,c); and so on. Targets with these features attract both naive and experienced searching bees. None of these are absolute behavioral criteria any more than they correlate perfectly with flowers. Instead, the bees' choice of targets to land on and explore is a probabilistic combination of variables. This principle of probabilistic control of behavior is particularly obvious in the case of spontaneous color and odor preferences (Menzel 1985). Of all colors, for instance, naive recruit bees prefer to land on violet. This preference is probabilistic rather than absolute, so that even in the presence of a violet flower, a naive bee will sometimes choose a blue or yellow or white blossom. This makes sense evolutionarily, because not all flowers are violet. As Maynard Smith (1976) and others have shown in the context of evolutionary stable strategies, distributing behavior probabilistically is highly adaptive so long as the probabilities assigned to the various alternatives correspond well to the likely distribution of correct choices in the real world. Many cases of selective learning should be thought of as mechanisms by which experience serves to tune an animal's behavior from the spontaneous distribution of choices to the actual odds in the world around it (Gould & Gould 1982).

Once a bee lands on a potential food source and finds a sufficient reward, she makes repeated visits and memorizes its location, odor, color, shape, nearby landmarks, time of nectar production, and how to harvest it. If there are enough flowers with nectar or pollen to allow the bee to exploit the source during several trips, the forager will probably become a temporary specialist on this species of flower.

COLOR LEARNING   The first aspect of bee learning investigated by von Frisch was the ability of bees to learn the color of a food source. Using simple associative conditioning, he demonstrated that bees could memorize any color from yellow to ultraviolet (UV) (von Frisch 1967). Later, Opfinger (1931) showed that the color was learned only during the bees' approach to the flower before the innately recognized US of sugar could tell the bees that the color was worth learning.

Menzel and his colleagues have vastly extended our knowledge about this episode (Menzel 1985). They have shown that this learning is restricted to the color seen in the final two or three seconds before landing and not the color seen while feeding or hovering near the flower before departing. This seems reasonably consistent with the usual pairing relationship seen in associative learning. The Menzel group has also shown that the rate at which bees learn color depends on the color used, so that innately preferred colors like violet are learned more readily.

Bees require about three to five trials to select a particular color with 90% certainty in a two-color choice test. Regardless of the amount of training, bees rarely get beyond the 95% level. According to Menzel (1985), neither a polarized nor a flashing light can be remembered. Bees forget colors they have been trained to only once over about a week, but they seem never to forget a food source they have visited three times. Color learning is subject to disruption by electroconvulsive shock, chilling, and CO_2 just after training, which implies to many researchers that there is a short-term memory phase followed by consolidation. Subsequent work on the short-term memory phase of color learning suggests that information from separate trials can interact during the first moments of short-term processing, but that as consolidation begins the input of new information is temporarily blocked (Menzel 1979).

ODOR LEARNING   Von Frisch (review 1967) demonstrated over half a century ago that bees learn odors quickly and accurately. Menzel and his colleagues have expanded our understanding greatly (Menzel 1985). Odor learning is virtually one-trial learning and takes place the instant before the nectar is tasted. Using a supercooled needle to "anesthetize" one locus at a time, Menzel & Erber (1978) have traced the site of active processing in the bee brain as a function of the time after the pairing of odor and sugar takes place. The neural activity essential to later storage of the odor association begins in the antennal lobe of the brain and proceeds about two minutes later to the alpha lobe of the mushroom body. Roughly two minutes later still, activity has shifted to the calyx. After another two minutes or so, chilling no longer has any effect anywhere. By training only one antenna, Menzel and his colleagues showed that the processing is initially unilateral, but the information leaving the alpha lobe is sent to both calyxes.

SHAPE LEARNING   After considerable controversy (e.g. Anderson 1972, 1977b, Cruse 1972, Gould 1984a), convincing evidence now indicates that bees remember flower shapes as low-resolution photographs or eidetic images (Gould 1985).

TIME LEARNING   Von Frisch (1967) demonstrated the link between time and food location in the first half of the century, and pointed out the adaptive nature of this learning: particular species of flowers produce nectar only during particular parts of the day. Individual bees, then, will specialize on different flowers at different times of day and maintain their periodicity indefinitely. In exploring this invertebrate version of the Kamin effect—the spontaneous assumption that a particular food source will reappear roughly 24 hours later—Koltermann (1974) succeeded in training bees to remember nine different times of day; he reports that he could show temporal discrimination of two separate food sources down to an interval of 20 minutes (this required the temporal equivalent of differential conditioning). The discrimination was sharp only when nearby times had different food cues. In theory, bees might be capable of storing 40 or even 50 different times. It would be extraordinarily difficult to test the limits of the time learning of bees by the usual free-flying training techniques. It may be that a laboratory approach would succeed in defining the size and resolution of this system.

LANDMARK LEARNING   Anyone who has ever trained bees knows that three-dimensional landmarks near a food source strongly affect where bees search for the target (von Frisch 1967). This learning takes place during departure (Opfinger 1931), thereby violating the normal US/CS relationship. Bees appear to remember the direction of landmarks around a food source (Cartwright & Collett 1982, 1983; but see Anderson 1977d; the controversy is reviewed by Gould 1984a), but whether they remember the color or shape of landmarks is not known.

CUE HIERARCHIES   Bees do not value all information equally. After bees are trained to a food source until their accuracy in choice tests reaches its maximum level, the component cues can be separated to see which are more potent. Hence, a violet, orange-scented, triangular target can be removed and the returning bee offered a target with the correct scent but the wrong color and shape, one with the training color but a different odor and shape, and so on. The preference for a higher ranking cue is very strong, and the rank order is odor, color, and then shape (Gould 1984). Oddly enough, the position of landmark cues in this hierarchy varies between races. For the German race, *Apis mellifera carnica,* landmarks are more important than shape, whereas for the Italian race, *A. M. ligustica,* shapes outweigh landmarks. Moreover, the learning curves for odor, color, shape, and landmarks, though quite consistent among bees of a particular race, are distinctly different between races, as are some elements in the spontaneous preference behavior. These observations underscore how evolution has acted to orchestrate and fine tune virtually every aspect of the learning behavior of bees to meet the challenges posed by their niche.

ORGANIZATION OF MEMORY   In the process of investigating how time is linked to other cues, Bogdany (1978) has uncovered a fascinating pattern of organization in flower learning. Consider the following experiment: we train a group of foragers to a blue, peppermint-scented, triangular target from 9:00–

10:00, and then to a yellow, orange-scented, star-shaped target from 10:00–11:00. We repeat this sequence for a few days. On the next day, we set out both targets together, each supplied with sugar solution. The foragers appear at about 8:45 and land almost exclusively on the triangle. At about 9:45, they begin to switch from the triangular target, which still has food, to the star-shaped feeder. By 10:00, all the trained bees have abandoned the perfectly good triangle for the star. It is as though the bees have organized their daily activities by means of a mental appointment book listing all of the relevant cues for each time of day.

Bogdany also showed that if one component of an expected combination was changed, all of the components had to be relearned. For example, if we were to substitute rose for peppermint in the blue triangular target to which bees had been trained at 9:00, we would find that after landing, feeding, and returning to the hive, the forager on her next visit would be able to choose rose odor over a new odor at the 90% level, but would be very poor at selecting the color blue or the triangle shape in a similar choice test. The bee also loses and must relearn the precise beginning and ending times for the food source. Apparently, the bee must start over and relearn each cue if any one is changed, each cue at its own specific rate.

This picture of storage in terms of sets of independently acquired cues is reinforced by the observation that if a cue—color or odor, for instance—is omitted initially but then added later, the set does *not* have to be relearned. Apparently the blank space for, say, odor can be filled in after the time-linked slots for color and shape have been filled. Clearly there is no hint of classical "blocking" here. It is tempting to think of flower memory organized as a matrix, with the "rows" perhaps prelabeled for time of day (which would account for the exclusivity of time in flower memory) and the "columns" assigned to color, odor, and so on.

FLOWER HANDLING   In addition to all of the associative tasks by which a bee memorizes the information necessary for efficient foraging, bees also face an operant task: how best to land on the flower and extract the nectar or pollen. There are many different flower morphologies, and most require very different strategies for harvesting the reward. Recruits to an artificial food source are remarkably incompetent at getting the food, but soon perfect a technique. This technique can differ between bees, so that one individual may always land at the periphery of the feeder and walk directly up to one of the feeding grooves where she feeds until full; another will always land on the food reservoir, feeding in an awkward head-down posture; still another will land directly on the grooves and move counterclockwise from groove to groove around the circular feeder, and so on. At flowers a similar pattern is clear, though the range of behavioral choices is much restricted. Through experimentation, then, bees discover the motor behavior necessary to exploit blossoms, and so handling time goes down (Heinrich 1979). This is probably one of the reasons bees tend so strongly to specialize.

COSTS AND BENEFITS   Although the generalist strategy provides more flexibility for an animal to adapt to a new environment or switch between food types as conditions change, a generalist must apparently sacrifice to some extent the benefit of highly efficient morphological and behavioral specializations. But a generalist must be able to recognize the general class of objects and individuals in its cluttered environment which *might* qualify as suitable food (as bees recognize flowers as a class), but then it must experiment with each.

Specialized learning sequences which help solve these problems are well known. Some animals, for instance, imprint on salient aspects of the food they are fed pre- or postnatally (e.g. Burghardt & Hess 1966). Others learn from social experience with their parents or other members of their group (Bonner 1980). The broad predispositions of animals of other species are focused and refined by purely personal experiences, based on some innate (presumably chemical) recognition (before and/or after tasting) that a particular food item is acceptable. The well-known phenomenon of food-avoidance learning (Revusky 1984) probably represents a specific safeguard for such essential experimentation.

Reproduction

In addition to finding food, an animal must be able to locate, identify, court, and mate with the best "quality" reproductively ready member of the opposite sex of its species available. In this context all species can be considered as specialists, and examples of prewired recognition and motor behavior abound (Gould 1982a). But in many cases the specialization is so extreme (and crucial) that complete reliance on innate cues seems to have been insufficient. To the extent that sign stimuli really are functionally equivalent to the cues abstracted by ensembles of feature detectors (rather than elaborate innate "photographs"), they may be inadequate to distinguish reliably between morphologically similar species. The role of sexual imprinting (including song learning) is probably to use the sign stimuli available from parents and/or siblings early in life, when social experience is adequately restricted, to direct the formation of a more precise image (Immelmann 1984, Marler 1984). The well-studied case of song learning in birds (Marler 1984) illustrates the kinds of specializations frequently evident in sexual imprinting. The general pattern for song birds is that individuals reared in isolation sing very simple songs which, upon close analysis, are often schematic versions of the normal song heard in the wild. The same result is often obtained even if the bird is exposed to songs of other species. But there are one or more sensitive periods during which exposure to a conspecific song leads to production of a virtual copy when song development subsequently occurs. It seems clear that several independent acoustic features can contribute (Marler & Peters 1986), and the song model copied by a young bird has one or more key features—sign stimuli—which trigger learning. Apparently heterogeneous summation may be at work, since visual stimuli from a socially interacting companion can be an effective trigger as well (Babtista & Petrinovich 1984).

In many species, an interval of weeks or months passes between the sensitive period and the beginning of vocal experimentation. Experimentation in the form of subsong and plastic song—the avian equivalent of "babbling"—is necessary for normal song development; it occurs only in birds that learn to sing. Birds deafened after training but before singing produce disorganized, nonmelodic songs, but after mature song has "crystallized," deafening often has little effect. Apparently song, through a process of feedback matching, becomes a permanent motor program (Konishi 1965). Careful analysis of conspecific song learning in swamp sparrows reveals an apparently innate set of syllable elements common to all young swamp sparrows, with mature song consisting of a particular ordering of a subset of these gestures to match the song heard in the sensitive period (Marler & Pickert 1984).

Parental Care

Caring for an animal's units of fitness would be a risky context for learning and experimentation—except, of course, for learning to recognize offspring when that knowledge is useful. Critical aspects of the parenting process can include choosing a nest site, recognizing suitable construction materials, building the nest, recognizing the young (discussed above briefly under the heading of "genetic constraints"), feeding and otherwise caring for them. Although there are several established cases of nest-site imprinting, and although in some cases building and parental care behavior (particularly in primates) improves with practice, most of the rest of parenting appears to be relatively immune to learning in most species. Even in primates, it is difficult to assess the role of learning accurately: the behavior of parent monkeys reared in isolation is grossly atypical, and it is difficult to separate this from the pharmacopoeia of abnormal behavior traits they display. Nevertheless, many primatologists believe that the parenting play that young monkeys of many species engage in with the infants of other individuals *does* contribute to the proper development of skillful parenting when they mature.

Defense

Escape and defensive behaviors are also important facets of an animal's repertoire. Animals need to recognize danger and react appropriately to the particular threat. There is evidence that many animals react to the paired, forward-looking eyes typical of predators (Gallup 1977), recognize species-specific dangers such as coral snakes or starfish (S. M. Smith 1975, Kandel 1976), or possess a general suspicion of unfamiliar animals; but the details of enemy recognition in general seem surprisingly dependent on experience. Perhaps danger, like a generalist's food supply, comes in too many unpredictable or morphologically complex forms to be adequately cataloged genetically in most cases.

Curio's discovery that the innately recognized mobbing call triggers what one might call species-avoidance learning may provide a general model for the selective learning of threats (Curio & Vieth 1978). Curio and his colleagues used a rotating, 4-compartment box arranged so that birds in cages on either side of the box could see only the compartment facing them and not the compartment visible to birds on the other side. When one cage of birds was shown a stuffed owl in the rotating box, its occupants began directing the characteristic mobbing call at the box, and the birds in the other cage attempted to mob the object that *they* could see. In most cases what the second group of birds was shown was something as innocuous as a stuffed honey guide (which they had previously ignored), yet they produced the mobbing call on each subsequent exposure. This aversion could then be passed to other naive birds, and from them to others, all without any bird ever having been attacked by a honey guide. The automatic nature of this kind of adaptive learning subroutine is most tellingly illustrated by the success with which Curio transferred the mobbing behavior to an empty milk bottle.

It is particularly interesting that animals can learn to modulate and modify their normal escape or attack responses to suit the particular stimulus. Birds and prairie dogs (Leger et al 1980), for instance, appear to differentiate (both by their alarm calls and their subsequent behavior) at least two general classes of predators, while vervet monkeys differentiate at least three (and probably four) (Seyfarth et al 1980). Different species within any one danger category may be further discriminated, as seems clear in the way herds of antelope judge how close to permit various carnivores to approach. Young vervets appear to recognize the classes of potential threat innately, but only in a very general way; they learn from social experience—that is, the behavior of older vervets— which members of the class really do constitute threats. A young vervet will deliver the aerial predator alarm call for storks and even falling leaves, but slowly learns to restrict it to a particular species of eagle. Adult alarm calling may again be the tutorial vehicle. Playbacks of tape-recorded alarm calls in the absence of predators elicit escape behavior that lacks the normal escape vocalizations. Perhaps escaping adults add this vocalization only when they have actually seen the predator themselves, thereby providing this feedback only when the alarm call is appropriately directed. Obviously, animals must strike a balance between forever escaping and hiding to be safe and pursuing their many other essential, risk-incurring activities such as foraging, courting, rearing young, and so on. Similarly, many animals clearly learn where safety is to be found as well as how to modify their escape behavior to match the threat. It may be that learning to recognize predators and learning when to escape are the optimal answers in the face of relatively unpredictable, context-specific risks.

Navigation

The point that animals can learn where to find safety should remind us that members of many species from bees to primates learn the location of their home and the geography of their range as well as how to navigate around the home range. The process, and its heavy dependence on internally directed learning, is best understood in honey bees.

SUN ORIENTATION   Scout bees keep track of each leg of their outward search flight. The direction of each leg is determined relative to the sun's azimuth. Since the sun moves from east to west, bees must compensate for this motion if they are to make accurate calculations. There is abundant evidence that they do so (Gould 1980). The actual rate of movement depends on the season, latitude, and time of day, and the direction of movement is also an essential variable (left to right in the northern temperate zone, right to left in the southern temperate zone, and either direction in the tropics depending on the time of year). Bees appear to learn the direction of movement when they begin to fly (about 10 days into their lifespan of 4–6 weeks in summer), and this learning may not be reversible (Lindauer 1959).

The actual rate of movement at each time of day is derived from two alternative systems. In the absence of usable landmarks, bees extrapolate the most recent rate of the sun's azimuth movement (Gould 1980)—which rate they must be constantly measuring and remembering. [Actually, they use a running average of several measurements, though whether each measurement is remembered separately or weighted and added into the existing running-average value is not yet known (Gould 1984b).]

If useful landmarks are available, however, bees memorize the azimuth movement of the sun over the course of the day (Dyer & Gould 1981, 1983). This requires some sort of time-linked memory array which must be periodically updated. Under most contemporary situations, this is probably the most heavily used system. However, bees evolved in (and frequently still reside in) forests, where the multiplicity of similar looking trees, combined with the low visual resolution (1–4° depending on the part of the eye) of these insects (corresponding to about 20/2000 vision in humans), may severely limit their use of landmarks.

LANDMARK NAVIGATION   In the absence of both sun and blue sky, bees attempt to use prominent landmarks that they have memorized (Dyer & Gould 1983). Indeed, bees experienced with the route to and from a food source prefer prominent landmarks over celestial cues, at least on the outward journey. There is some evidence to suggest that bees even form "maps" of their home range.

A particularly apt set of examples is described by Brines (1978). He could capture departing foragers at the hive entrance and carry them in total darkness several hundred meters to locations well out of sight of the hive and its nearby landmarks. These displaced bees would be permitted to feed and then depart. Two general patterns of behavior were commonly observed: young foragers (recognizable by their furry backs and undamaged wings) would usually circle and either land back on the feeder or drift off in random directions; many older bees, however, would circle and then depart directly toward the unseen hive. Flight times indicated that the return path must have been virtually direct, and, because of the serious need for food in the hive, the returning bees would sometimes perform dances. These dances were quite accurate.

Presumably the experienced bees knew where they were, based on the landmarks they saw upon departure from the food source. It is unlikely that the transported foragers were operating on the basis of any memory of a specific food source in the close vicinity since most of the releases were from a large, empty, perfectly barren parking lot at least 50 meters from the nearest vegetation (grassy playing fields). Reviewing the hymenoptera literature in general, Wehner (1981) concludes that insects store a set of "snapshots" from along familiar foraging paths and consult this neural "album" when lost. He also believes that the pictures are arranged in serial order along the flight paths. Evidence exists (Gould 1984) to suggest that a two-dimensional, landmark-based cognitive map, rather than route-specific snapshot strategy, is at work. The definitive experiment remains to be performed.

The general pattern of navigational learning in bees is clear: specific information is gathered in specific, innately recognized behavioral contexts, fed into specific information-processing circuits, almost certainly stored in temporally defined memory arrays, and retrieved and used in an appropriate way at the correct time. All this specialized learning behavior is possible because the processing strategy can be innately programmed and the important variables specified in advance. Neither the pure use of innately stored information nor unguided learning could work in this context.

As nearly as one can tell, the pattern in bird navigation is similar. Pigeons, for example, are programmed to calibrate their navigational systems, the local magnetic field, solar arc, and (perhaps) odors (Gould 1982b). Similarly, nocturnally migrating birds appear to imprint on constellation patterns (Emlen 1975).

Social Behavior, Social Communication, and "Culture"

All animals must understand the social signals of their species and, in many cases, recognize other individuals and their status. Most social signals appear to be produced and decoded innately, but the facial and postural gestures seen in many birds and mammals are so strikingly intricate that either the recognition wiring must have become unusually complex, or only the dynamic components of the gesture must be attended to, or a kind of social imprinting must be taking place. This ambiguity arises because most sign-stimulus recognition systems are demonstrably crude (e.g. recognition of conspecific adults and infants), and at least the primordia for the recognition of facial expression and body posture appears to be innate (e.g. Sackett 1966). However, it seems likely that adult animals are sensitive to the complexities of facial expressions as well as to their simpler features. Innate recognition of such complexities is probably not feasible, but there may well be some highly correlated visual components or associated auditory cue which would trigger detailed memorization of these gestures and expressions. In short, there may be more learning in this context than meets the eye, and in any case this is a subject ripe for experimentation.

An indisputable function of learning in many social animals is individual or group recognition, often accompanied by memorization of various relationships such as dominance orders, alliances, pairings, and so on. Many social animals provide extended care for their young, giving them an opportunity for play and social learning. Play allows animals a safe opportunity to practice behavior that will later be crucial, and in many species play marks the beginning of the future dominance hierarchy. Social learning includes most obviously cultural practices in foraging such as fishing for termites by chimpanzees and harvesting mussels by oyster catchers, although there is considerable controversy over the degree to which observational learning plays a major role outside of the higher primates. Chimpanzees' use of toothpicks (McGrew & Tutin 1973) and rocks (Boesch & Boesch 1983) are fairly convincing examples of social learning, and other, less well-documented cases such as operating drinking fountains are well known (Bonner 1980). We must be careful here, however, since most if not all of these behaviors involve innate motor elements. Laboratory-reared chimpanzees, for instance, spontaneously poke sticks in holes as though searching for termites. Some supposedly learned social behaviors may even depend on sign stimuli. The famous blue tits who learned to peel off milk bottle tops or drum holes in them to get at the cream actually harvest food in the wild by peeling bark from trees, and the stimulus and motor program for the bottle-opening behavior are probably very similar. Indeed, even hand-reared tits spontaneously peel wallpaper from the walls of their foster homes (Hinde 1982). Bolles (1984) goes so far as to wonder if any motor learning is truly novel.

In short, though it is tempting to think of social learning as entirely free from innate aid and guidance, I suspect that a strict application of such a distinction might ultimately be empty of examples. Human language acquisition, for instance, would certainly no longer qualify as a totally learned behavior (Chomsky 1967, Gould 1982a, Eimas 1984, Gleitman 1984).

ETHOLOGICAL PERSPECTIVES ON LEARNING IN THE LABORATORY

Several general functional categories of learning have traditionally been distinguished, such as habituation, sensitization, classical conditioning, trial-and-error learning (operant conditioning), and higher-order learning which Gould & Gould (1982) have called cognitive trial and error. Although these distinctions are frequently attacked, they provide a useful organization for comparing ethological and behavioristic observations. Biologists are interested in underlying mechanisms rather than in superficial "laws" which beg both physiological and evolutionary questions. In an attempt to move from words to wiring, the discussion will focus on quite a different level of analysis than that used, for example, by Terrace (1984).

Nonassociative Learning

Habituation is the stimulus-specific waning of an individual behavioral response as a result of repeated stimulation, as in the well-studied case of *Aplysia,* whose gill-withdrawal response (motor program) becomes ever more difficult to elicit after it has been repeatedly triggered by a jet of water (a crude sign stimulus) (Kandel 1976). The decline of responsiveness is not for the most part a result of sensory adaptation (which we can think of as sensory fatigue, and which is brief and usually confined to the sensory cell itself). Although the *Aplysia* circuit is probably atypical—the sensory neurons send processes directly to the motor neurons so that habituation is not entirely mediated centrally by interneurons—there seems little doubt that the phenomenon is essentially the same as that seen in other animals (Quinn 1984). The role of this very simple sort of learning in the lives of animals seems clear: the threshold for triggering individual units of behavior adjusts to the time-averaged "background level" of the relevant stimuli. Hence the gill of an *Aplysia* in calm water is very sensitive to mechanical stimulation, but that of an *Aplysia* in rough water is sufficiently less sensitive so that it is not continually "withdrawn"—only something really out of the ordinary will trigger this defensive behavior. This behavior-specific threshold-tuning function is crucial, and helps animals avoid what can be called behavioral do-loops (Gould 1982a) by becoming adaptively "bored."

Sensitization, of course, serves to reduce or eliminate habituation when a novel stimulus is encountered, and even to heighten an unhabituated animal's responsiveness. Hence, an *Aplysia* with a habituated gill withdrawal response will, after being poked in the tail or startled with a light, begin to respond to a previously ignored water jet. This sensitization, though pathway-specific in many cases, can serve as a relatively generalized alerting mechanism. The various curiosities of its time course and so on are probably inevitable (but not necessarily optimal) consequences of its wiring and biochemistry (Quinn 1984). Mechanistically, habituation and sensitization appear to be combined to create associative learning, at least in *Aplysia*.

Classical Conditioning

Classical conditioning, as described by Pavlov (1927), involves taking a stimulus-response "reflex" and presenting a novel training stimulus (the CS) immediately before the normal stimulus (the US). In time the response (UR) can be elicited to the novel stimulus alone. As has been shown repeatedly, the CS does not need to be perfectly correlated with the US: as long as it has substantial predictive value, it will be learned. One of the first persons to put Pavlov's discovery to use in naturalistic studies was von Frisch, who used associative learning to demonstrate that fish can hear and honey bees have color vision.

Because of the work of von Frisch, Tinbergen, and other early researchers, ethologists have little trouble in restating classical conditioning in ethological terms. The UR "reflex" is, for ethologists, a motor program; the innately recognized US is a sign stimulus; the learned CS is a search image. The adaptive value of this prewired form of inductive reasoning seems clear: relatively crude and schematic but diagnostic sign stimuli are replaced through associative learning with what is potentially a far more detailed picture of the appropriate stimulus, (although, as we pointed out earlier, something very like a sign stimulus may still dominate some learned responses in which a minimum of discrimination is needed). The sign stimulus defines the context, while the inductive programming of the learning routine abstracts from a world full of stimuli the ones which best correlate with and predict the context. As Hollis (1984) points out, the CS in some cases also allows animals to anticipate the arrival of an individual of interest, as would be the case when an animal hears or smells a predator. (There are, inevitably, some difficulties in this relatively simple interpretation, but most seem to arise from the frequent intrusion of trial-and-error learning which is discussed below.)

Viewed from this perspective, most of the selective learning studied by ethologists is probably simple or slightly elaborated (e.g. two-step) associative learning. Enemy learning in birds, for instance, depends on the mobbing call (the US or sign stimulus) to define the context; virtually all forms of imprinting are directed by sign stimuli (such as the species-typical exodus call in ducks which leads the ducklings from the nest and initiates imprinting); flower learning in bees is triggered by the taste of sugar water; and so on. The frequent restriction of learning to critical periods and the facilitated recall of learned information to particular contexts or times of day (the Kamin effect) probably represent adaptive, context-specific programming. The same is clearly the case for food-avoidance learning (Revusky 1984).

In this light, the widespread existence of contextual triggering and cue biases in associative learning seems of a piece with the general pattern of selective learning: the danger-avoidance system (which in pigeons, for example, is prewired to attend more to sounds than to visual cues) can be independent of the food-learning system (which in pigeons focuses instead on visual information to the near exclusion of auditory cues) (Forse & LoLordo 1973). In most natural cases of classical conditioning we should probably expect to find an innate recognition of behavioral contextual triggers so that the animal "knows" when learning is appropriate. Moreover, we probably ought to expect to find (where it would be useful) some degree of reliance on cue-specific biases in the learning which are correlated with the situation and the species' associated behavioral repertoire, although the generality of many of the basic features of learning argues for the optimistic view that we are looking at many variations on a fairly small set of themes.

Trial-and-Error Learning

Trial-and-error learning, first investigated by Thorndike (1898), is generally distinguished from classical conditioning in that the animal must perform behavioral experiments by which it modifies (i.e. shapes) its behavior into the most adaptive (i.e. rewarding) form. This kind of self-imposed modification obviously depends on environmental feedback and an animal's ability to recognize when a new behavioral variant, whether intentional or not, is more or less successful at obtaining the particular goal. (It is important to keep in mind that the goal need not be food or even an overt positive reward: avoiding danger or punishment or obtaining internalized rewards can be an adaptive goal in many contexts.) Trial-and-error learning, then, is in many ways analogous to deductive reasoning, and is a very common strategy among animals. Bees, as described earlier, must solve the problem posed by the distinctive morphology of each new species of flower, improving slowly with every visit to a particular type of blossom. Indeed, it is almost certainly the dramatic increase in foraging efficiency that results from trial-and-error learning which accounts for the strong tendency of individual bees to specialize on one or a few species of flower (Heinrich 1984).

In the case of bees (and, we suspect, most other animals), the behavioral solution frequently becomes a highly efficient, relatively stereotyped, and almost automatic motor program (Bolles 1984, Gould 1984a). Even rats running mazes can become so used to a particular route that they will run into newly erected barriers or stop after having run the usual distance down an alley to a food dish even though the dish has been plainly moved a few steps farther along

(Schwartz 1978). As mentioned earlier, the adaptive value of this automation of learned but routine behavior is most likely that it frees the attention of the animal for other concerns—a finch, having solved the problem of how to handle and open sunflower seeds, can devote its attention to watching for predators rather than to the intricacies of cracking open seeds and separating the heart from the husk. Beyond introspective evidence, Squire (1984) and Mishkin (1982) note that in both monkeys and humans, procedural/habitual tasks like shoe tying (which, once learned, become unconscious) and declarative/associative tasks are anatomically segregated.

In both the bee and the bird example, and many others besides, we note that associative and trial-and-error learning can work in concert to provide first recognition and then response. The response, obviously, is specific to the particular contingency—the kind of seed—as well as to the general context—feeding vs fleeing or courting. Hence, particular associative and trial-and-error "subroutines" will often be tightly linked, as we will mention again shortly. Just as in the case of associative learning, any anomalies may represent species-specific, context-dependent programming.

Anomalies and Biases

Anomalies in both associative and trial-and-error learning seem to fall into several well-studied categories (Schwartz 1978, Staddon 1983, Bolles 1984, Jenkins 1984, Revusky 1984) such as the problems with omission schedules and the like. It seems reasonable that animals ought to have associative and response biases, and the economically logical behavior on variable schedules as opposed to that on fixed schedules suggests that the behavior may be pretuned to the more natural "probabilistic" nature of the real world. Indeed, I predict that the response pattern of relatively unselective herbivores like rabbits to a food reward ought to be less probabilistically adapted than that of a rat.

Other examples of response biases are to be seen in the familiar phenomena of autoshaping in which animals perform spontaneous, unrewarded but contextually logical behavior (Hearst 1984), the reward-specific associative biases seen in pigeon pecking (Jenkins 1984), learned helplessness, adjunctive behavior, and in differential conditionability (Schwartz 1978). The latter category includes the observation that pigeons, for instance, learn more readily to peck than to bar-press for food, but can be trained to bar-press to avoid danger more easily than to peck. Rats, on the other hand, seem able to learn bar-pressing for food rather quickly, but they are difficult to instruct to bar-press when the goal is to avoid danger; running away, on the other hand, is easily taught. It is difficult to avoid the suspicion that there may be context-specific motor biases—that rats, who manipulate food with the forepaws, and pigeons, who handle food with the beak, in some sense "expect" to learn with these tools in the context of foraging (i.e. food-rewarded tasks). Similarly, the apparently preferred modes of escape behavior seem at least roughly related to the realities of each species' niche (Gould & Marler 1984).

Each of these anomalies may hint that there exists an innate motor bias, a "default routine" (to use programming jargon) which may serve to guide an animal's initial motor experimentation. (Judging from the nearly universal use of word processors in preparing manuscripts, an example from these special-purpose machines might be apropos: most programs take for granted that you want, say, a 12-space margin, double spacing, page numbering at the top right, and so on. These are the default values, parameters that are assumed in the absence of information to the contrary.) Indeed, it is tempting to place a default-value interpretation on the associative biases of animals. As mentioned earlier, although bees can learn that a flower is any color from yellow to ultraviolet, they learn the color of violet most readily (Gould 1984a). At the same time, bees prefer violet silhouettes to all other colors on a spontaneous-preference test. It is as though violet is the default parameter—a probabilistic bias that helps guide bees when they experiment with various flowers while searching for food. A similar pattern is seen in shape and odor learning.

I suspect, then, that innate, context-specific behavioral predispositions may play a role in trial-and-error learning by providing animals with a degree of adaptive (but by no means absolute) guidance. Deafened birds seem to know to experiment with their syrinxes rather than their wings or feet in order to shape their singing behavior to match the song on which they have imprinted [although even here there is a default program—the crude "innate song" mentioned earlier (Marler 1984)]. It is also interesting to note that many cases of quite complex motor learning appear to involve the liberal use of innate behavioral elements. The elaborate shell-harvesting behavior of oyster catchers, learned from the parents over the course of several months (and of which there are two very different forms), is composed almost entirely of innate behavioral gestures which are reordered, coordinated, and directed on the basis of learning (Norton-Griffiths 1969). Such a strategy, which involves building up complex motor behavior out of a "library" of innate elements, has obvious advantages for certain tasks. The possibility that at least some other cases of trial-and-error learning exploit this sort of organization seems worthy of serious consideration. For example, certain songbirds "invent" new song themes by recombining both innate and learned song elements (see Marler 1984). It may also be that the subset of easily reorganized elements may be context specific (as we suggested could be the case with response biases), so that here too there could be the sort of specific prewired links between associative and trial-and-error learning to which we alluded earlier. The apparently learned ordering and orientation of nut-opening and of burying behavior by squirrels (Eibl-Eibelsfeldt 1961, Ewer 1965) and copulation by rhesus macaques (Mason

1968), mentioned earlier, appear to fall into this pattern since the motor elements are for the most part unique to the behavioral situation.

Another interesting example was described by Thorpe (1950). He gave birds the problem of retrieving food hung on a string inside a glass tube. It is easy for birds with innate beak/foot coordination to solve this problem by pulling up hanks of string with the beak and catching them in a foot, thus reaching the food. Great tits, for instance, solve the problem quickly and all in the same way. Canaries, on the other hand, lack useful innate motor-program elements, and so they slowly solve the problem by creating novel behavior. Each individual canary solves the problem in a slightly different way.

Alpha Conditioning

The phenomenon of alpha conditioning suggests a possible mechanistic rationale for many of the biases just discussed. Alpha conditioning is the tendency of some animals in some situations to show a slight UR to a CS before pairing (Schwartz 1978); even Pavlov's dogs salivated slightly to novel stimuli (Pavlov 1927). As a result of pairing the CS with the US, the spontaneous salivation response was greatly amplified. It seems reasonable to suppose that the animals were prepared to make the association—that, in short, the neural pathways from various potential CSs are wired weakly to the circuit for the UR from birth, and that the input from the feature detector(s) responsible for recognizing the releaser(s), or US(s), both trigger the response and interact with the inputs from potential CSs. This interaction would presumably serve to strengthen the CS-UR connections when the CS and US pathways are active simultaneously. Just this sort of wiring appears to underlie the associative learning of *Aplysia* (Quinn 1984), in which classical conditioning arises from an interaction between habituation and sensitization. The step from alpha conditioning to the widespread learning biases of animals is not very imposing; we need only make the reasonable assumption, amply borne out by neurophysiological studies, that the preexisting wiring need not trigger an overt response. Biases in learning, as a result, could be thought of as resulting from covert alpha conditioning. Gould (1984) and Marler (1984) have analyzed honey bee flower learning and bird-song learning from this perspective, and conclude not only that covert alpha conditioning is the most likely explanation, but that the memory for these tasks must be prewired as a specialized array.

COGNITIVE TRIAL AND ERROR

Although habituation, sensitization, associative learning, and trial-and-error learning seem to account for most of what is seen in the laboratory and field, a considerable part of the behavior of many animals is difficult to interpret along these lines. We find it both convenient and useful to distinguish these cases of what is often called higher-order learning by the term "cognitive trial and error" (Gould 1982a). The most familiar manifestations of this phenomenon, exemplified by the rats in Olton's radial mazes, are usually interpreted to imply that animals have the ability to use "cognitive maps"—neural constructs by which animals in some sense "think" about the problem, evaluating behavioral alternatives or formulating a "plan" of sorts (Olton 1978). The rat may be thought of as solving the maze problem by mapping its previous behavior and then referring to (and subsequently modifying) this map in the process of making later behavioral choices so as not to visit the same area of the maze twice. Cognitive maps may underlie the abilities of animals even down to the level of honey bees which, as we have seen, learn their home range and navigate in it as though they have an internalized map. Other sorts of problem-solving behavior in which overt motor experimentation plays a relatively minor role also seem to fall into the same general category. Animals sometimes appear to evaluate behavioral possibilities internally, as though neural "pictures" of objects could be manipulated mentally and potential consequences imagined.

One difficulty with cognitive trial-and-error is that it resists easy experimental manipulation. The mind is a relatively private organ, and much high-level processing goes on subconsciously anyway. Another problem is that conscious cognitive trial-and-error is the major mental process of which each of us is introspectively aware. As Griffin (1981) has pointed out, this may raise the thorny question of animal consciousness. One can rather easily imagine a prewired two-dimensional array for home-range information in the brain of the honey bee, and the appropriate programming for filling it in on the basis of foraging experience. Indeed, if the range of potential inputs to the hypothetical grid points on such a map are sufficiently predictable, it might even be possible to imagine this process involving nothing more than covert alpha conditioning. Suitable programming to enable bees to use landmarks or return home from more-or-less familiar spots on the basis of such a map would be relatively easy to design.

None of this would seem to require consciousness, though awareness might on the one hand facilitate it, or, on the other, create behavior which, though as automatic as egg-rolling or stinging, might be easily mistaken for consciousness. The adaptive role of such maps for both long- and short-distance spatial navigators like bees and rats is too obvious to require comment, and the potential advantage of prewiring the predictable aspects of acquisition, transformation, storage, recall, and use of map information is also clear. Whether map abilities are so organized is another question, one probably well worth further exploration.

The analogous ability (obvious at least in our species) to learn by conjuring up and manipulating mental representations is more difficult to study in animals (Lea 1984). Still more difficult is determining whether such abilities might depend on particular sorts of specialized, preordained wiring. It is tempting to imagine that genetic predispositions and specific neural organization rather than some general, nebulous factor such as "increased size" or "greater complexity" is responsible, and that the many inter- and intrahemispheric processing specializations known or suspected in our species are consonant with the specialization perspective. Piaget's idea that the sort of cognitive abilities we are describing develop in humans in a stereotyped, apparently innately directed way, but require building on information already acquired and formed into "concepts," should remind us that the mechanistic basis of cognitive trial and error in at least our species is probably *very* complex. Even here, however, there is evidence that some sort of elaborate preordained organization is at work recognizing speech elements (Peterson & Jusczyk 1984) and generating language (Gleitman 1984). One evolutionary perspective on human language would see specialized, "dedicated" memory arrays as an essential preadaptation for language. The program for loading, manipulating, reorganizing, and accessing these arrays could be imagined as evolving from the programming of other more modest cognitive abilities.

CONCLUSION

I have tried to examine laboratory learning studies from an ethological point of view and to restate field observations in terms of the principles uncovered by laboratory work. I have argued that to see learning as for the most part consisting of specialized, dedicated, but well-integrated subroutines, based on a small number of general learning strategies that have been "customized" as appropriate for each context and each species, is particularly helpful when considering learning under naturalistic conditions and some apparent laboratory anomalies. Learning theorists may have made a fundamental mistake when they gave up their attempt to explain all behavior in terms of classical and operant conditioning in favor of a search for a "general theory" from which all learning behavior, conditioning included, is to be explained. Both the biological perspective and the laboratory evidence argue that associative and trial-and-error learning, along with habituation and sensitization, are the building blocks of learning rather than the consequences. By analogy with the Kandel model in which sensitization and habituation are wired to generate associative learning, a relatively straightforward consideration of how natural selection has wired up these various components to create more complex, species-typical behavior is likely to be far more fruitful than a search for a "general theory." For example, imprinting looks very like a two-step associative learning sequence, so that a well-informed building-block approach immediately suggests tests not apparent either to ethologists or learning theorists. With this overly theoretical predisposition aside, the evidence suggests that a synergistic collaboration of ethology and psychology should be to understand the mechanistic basis of learning and memory, with a view to comprehending the evolution of the strategies of specialized learning which play such a crucial role in the adaptive, well-tuned behavior of animals in their world.

ACKNOWLEDGMENT

I thank Peter Marler for many suggestions and criticisms of an earlier draft of this review. Work of the author was supported by NSF grants BNS 85-06797 and BNS 82-01004.

Literature Cited

Anderson, A. M. 1972. The ability of honey bees to generalize visual stimuli. In *Information Processing in the Visual System of Arthropods*, ed. R. Wehner, pp. 207–12. Berlin: Springer-Verlag

Anderson, A. M. 1977a. Parameters determining the attractiveness of stripe patterns in the honey bee. *Anim. Behav.* 25:80–87

Anderson, A. M. 1977b. Shape perception in the honey bee. *Anim. Behav.* 25:67–69

Anderson, A. M. 1977c. The influence of pointed regions on the shape preference of honey bees. *Anim. Behav.* 25:88–94

Anderson, A. M. 1977d. A model for landmark learning in the honey bee. *J. Comp. Physiol.* 114:335–55

Babtista, L. F., Petrinovich, L. 1984. Social interaction, sensitive phases, and the song-template hypothesis in the white-crowned sparrow. *Anim. Behav.* 32:172–81

Birkhead, T. R. 1978. Behavioral adaptations to high-density nesting in the common guillemot. *Anim. Behav.* 26:321–31

Boesch, C., Boesch, H. 1983. Optimization of nut-cracking with natural hammers by wild chimpanzees. *Behaviour* 83:265–86

Bogdany, F. J. 1978. Linking of learning signals in honey bee orientation. *Behav. Ecol. Sociobiol.* 3:323–36

Bolles, R. C. 1984. Species-typical response predispositions. See Marler & Terrace 1984, pp. 435–46

Bonner, J. T. 1980. *The Evolution of Culture in Animals*. Princeton: Princeton Univ. Press

Brines, M. 1978. *Skylight polarization patterns as cues for honey bee orientation: Physical measurements and behavioral experiments.* PhD thesis. Rockefeller Univ., New York, NY

Brzoska, J., Obert, H-J. 1980. Acoustic signals influencing hormone production of the testes in the grass frog. *J. Comp. Physiol.* 140:25–29

Burghardt, G. M., Hess, E. H. 1966. Food imprinting in the snapping turtle. *Science* 151:108–9

Burtt, E. H. 1977. Some factors in the timing of parent-chick recognition in swallows. *Anim. Behav.* 25:231–39

Cartwright, B. A., Collett, T. S. 1982. How honey bees use landmarks to guide their return to a food source. *Nature* 295:560–64

Cartwright, B. A., Collett, T. S. 1983. Landmark learning in bees. *J. Comp. Physiol.* 161:521–43

Cary, S. 1981. The development of face perception. In *Perceiving and Remembering Faces*, ed. G. Davies, H. Ellis, J. Shepherd, pp. 41–61. New York: Academic

Chomsky, N. 1967. The formal nature of language. In *Biological Foundations of Language*, ed. E. H. Lennenberg. New York: Wiley

Collias, N. E., Collias, E. C. 1962. An experimental study of the mechanisms of nest building in a weaver bird. *Auk* 79:568–95

Cruse, H. 1972. A qualitative model for pattern discrimination in the honey bee. In *Information Processing in the Visual System of Arthropods*, ed. R. Wehner, pp. 201–6. Berlin: Springer-Verlag

Cullen, E. 1957. Adaptations in the kittiwake to cliff-nesting. *Ibis* 99:275–302

Curio, E., Vieth, W. 1978. Cultural transmission of enemy recognition. *Science* 202:899–901

Daumer, K. 1958. Blumenfarben, wie sie die Bienen sehen. *Z. Vgl. Physiol.* 41:49–110

Dyer, F. C., Gould, J. L. 1981. Honey bee orientation: A backup system for cloudy days. *Science* 214:1041–42

Dyer, F. C., Gould, J. L. 1983. Honey bee navigation. *Am. Sci.* 71:587–97

Eibl-Eibesfeldt, I. 1961. The interactions of unlearned behavior patterns and learning in mammals. In *Brain Mechanisms and Learning*, ed. J. F. Delafresnaye, pp. 53–73. Berlin: Springer-Verlag

Eimas, P. D. 1984. Infant competence and the acquisition of language. In *Biological Perspectives on Language*, ed. D. Caplan, A. R.

Lecours, A. Smith, pp. 109–29. Cambridge, MA: MIT Press

Emlen, S. 1975. The stellar-orientation system of migratory birds. *Sci. Am.* 233(2):102–11

Ewer, R. F. 1965. Food burying in the African ground squirrel. *Z. Tierpsychol.* 22:321–27

Ewert, J-P. 1981. *Neuroethology.* Berlin: Springer-Verlag

Forse, D. D., LoLordo, V. M. 1973. Attention in the pigeon: Differential effects of food-getting vs. shock-avoidance procedures. *J. Comp. Physiol. Psychol.* 88:551–58

Gallup, G. G. 1977. Tonic immobility: The role of fear and predation. *Psychol. Rec.* 27:41–61

Gleitman, L. C. 1984. Biological predispositions to learn language. See Marler & Terrace 1984, pp. 553–84

Gould, J. L. 1980. Sun compensation by bees. *Science* 207:545–47

Gould, J. L. 1982a. *Ethology: The Mechanisms and Evolution of Behavior.* New York: Norton

Gould, J. L. 1982b. The map sense of pigeons. *Nature* 296:205–11

Gould, J. L. 1984a. Natural history of honey bee learning. See Marler & Terrace 1984, pp. 149–80

Gould, J. L. 1984b. Processing of sun-azimuth information by honey bees. *Anim. Behav.* 32:149–52

Gould, J. L. 1985. How bees remember flower shapes. *Science* 227:1492–94

Gould, J. L., Gould, C. G. 1982. The insect mind: physics or metaphysics? In *Animal Mind,* ed. D. R. Griffin, pp. 269–98. Berlin: Springer-Verlag

Gould, J. L., Marler, P. 1984. Ethology and the natural history of learning. See Marler & Terrace 1984, pp. 47–74

Griffin, D. R. 1981. *The Question of Animal Awareness.* New York: Rockefeller Univ. Press. Rev. ed.

Grillner, S. 1985. Neurobiological bases of rhythmic motor acts in vertebrates. *Science* 228:143–49

Hailman, J. 1967. The ontogeny of an instinct. *Behav. Suppl.* 15:1–159

Harding, C. F., Follett, B. K. 1979. Hormone changes triggered by aggression in a natural population of blackbirds. *Science* 203:918–20

Hearst, E. 1984. Signals, conditioned directed movements, and species-typical response predispositions in nonmammalian vertebrates. See Marler & Terrace 1984, pp. 341–56

Heiligenberg, W. 1974. Processes governing behavioral states of readiness. *Adv. Study Behav.* 5:173–200

Heinrich, B. 1979. *Bumble Bee Economics.* Cambridge, MA: Harvard Univ. Press

Heinrich, B. 1984. Learning in invertebrates. See Marler & Terrace 1984, pp. 135–48

Hertz, M. 1929. Die Organisation des optischen Feldes bei der Biene, II. *Z. Vgl. Physiol.* 11:107–45

Hertz, M. 1931. Die Organisation des optischen Feldes bei der Biene, III. *Z. Vgl. Physiol.* 14:629–74

Hinde, R. A. 1982. *Ethology: Its Nature and Relations with Other Sciences.* Oxford: Oxford Univ. Press

Hollis, K. L. 1984. Cause and function of animal learning processes. See Marler & Terrace 1984, pp. 357–72

Immelmann, K. 1984. The natural history of bird learning. See Marler & Terrace 1984, pp. 271–88

Jenkins, H. M. 1984. The study of animal learning in the tradition of Pavlov and Thorndike. See Marler & Terrace 1984, pp. 89–114

Kandel, E. R. 1976. *Cellular Basis of Behavior.* San Francisco: Freeman

Klinghammer, E., Hess, E. H. 1964. Parental feeding in ring doves: innate or learned? *Z. Tierpsychol.* 21:338–47

Koltermann, R. 1974. Periodicity in the activity and learning performance of the honey bee. In *Experimental Analysis of Insect Behavior,* ed. L. B. Brown, pp. 218–27. Berlin: Springer-Verlag

Konishi, M. 1965. The role of auditory feedback in the control of vocalization in the white-crowned sparrow. *Z. Tierpsychol.* 22:770–85

Lashley, K. S. 1938. Conditional reactions in the rat. *J. Psychol.* 6:311–24

Lea, S. E. G. 1984. Complex general process learning in mammalian vertebrates. See Marler & Terrace 1984, pp. 373–98

Leger, D. W., Owings, D. H., Gelfand, D. L. 1980. Single-rate vocalizations of California ground squirrels: Graded signals and situation specificity of predator and socially evoked calls. *Z. Tierpsychol.* 52:227–46

Lindauer, M. 1959. Angeborene und erlernte Komponenten in der Sonnenorientierung der Bieren. *Z. Vgl. Physiol.* 42:43–62

Lorenz, K. Z. 1970. *Studies in Animal and Human Behavior.* Cambridge, MA: Harvard Univ. Press

Lorenz, K. Z., Tinbergen, N. 1938. Taxis und Instinktbegriffe in der Eirollbewegung der Graugans. *Z. Tierpsychol.* 2:1–29

Margolis, R., Mariscal, S., Gordon, J., Dollinger, J., Gould, J. L. 1986. Ontogeny of pecking and parental recognition in laughing gull chicks. *Anim. Behav.* In press

Marler, P. 1970. Song development in white-crowned sparrows. *J. Comp. Physiol. Psychol.* 71:1–25

Marler, P. 1984. Song learning: Innate species

differences in the learning process. See Marler & Terrace 1984, pp. 289–310

Marler, P., Peters, S. 1986. The role of different song features in vocal learning preferences in the song sparrow. Z. Tierpsychol. In press

Marler, P., Pickert, R. 1984. Species-universal microstructure in the learned songs of the swamp sparrow. Anim. Behav. 32:673–99

Marler, P., Terrace, H., eds. 1984. The Biology of Learning. Berlin: Springer-Verlag

Mason, W. A. 1968. Early social deprivation in the non-human primates: Implications for human behavior. In Environmental Influences, ed. D. C. Glass, pp. 70–100. New York: Rockefeller Univ. Press

Maynard Smith, J. 1976. Evolution and the theory of games. Am. Sci. 64:41–45

McFarland, D. J., Lloyd, I. H. 1973. Time-shared feeding and drinking. Q. J. Exp. Psychol. 25:48–61

McGrew, W. C., Tutin, C. E. G. 1973. Chimpanzee tool use in dental grooming. Nature 241:477–78

Menzel, R. 1979. Behavioural access to short-term memory in bees. Nature 281:368–69

Menzel, R. 1985. Learning in honey bees in an ecological and behavioral context. In Experimental Behavioral Ecology and Sociobiology, ed. B. Holldobler, H. Lindauer, pp. 55–74. Stuttgart: Fischer Verlag

Menzel, R., Erber, J. 1978. Learning and memory in bees. Sci. Am. 239(1):102–10

Mishkin, M. 1982. A memory system in the monkey. Philos. Trans. R. Soc. London Ser. B 298:85–95

Norton-Griffiths, M. N. 1969. Organization, control, and development of parental feeding in the oystercatcher. Behavior 34:55–114

Nottebohm, F. 1971. Neural lateralization of vocal control in a passerine bird. J. Exp. Zool. 177:229–62

Olton, D. S. 1978. Characteristics of spatial memory. In Cognitive Processes in Animal Behavior, ed. S. H. Hulse, H. Fowler, W. K. Honig, pp. 341–73. Hillsdale, NJ: Erlbaum

Opfinger, E. 1931. Uber die Orientierung der Biene an der Futterqueulle. Z. Vgl. Physiol. 15:431–87

Pavlov, I. 1927. The Conditioned Reflex. New York: Norton

Peterson, M. R., Jusczyk, P. W. 1984. Perceptual predispositions for human speech and monkey vocalizations. See Marler & Terrace 1984, pp. 585–616

Quinn, W. G. 1984. Work in invertebrates on the mechanisms underlying learning. See Marler & Terrace 1984, pp. 197–248

Revusky, S. 1984. Associative predispositions. See Marler & Terrace 1984, pp. 447–60

Rothstein, S. I. 1978. Mechanisms of avian egg-recognition: Additional evidence for learned components. Anim. Behav. 26:671–77

Rothstein, S. I. 1982. Successes and failures in avian egg and nestling recognition. Am. Zool. 22:547–60

Sackett, G. P. 1966. Monkeys reared in visual isolation with pictures as visual input: Evidence for an innate releasing mechanism. Science 154:1468–72

Schwartz, B. 1978. Psychology of Learning and Behavior. New York: Norton

Seyfarth, R. M., Cheney, D. L., Marler, P. 1980. Vervet monkey alarm calls: Semantic communication in a free-ranging primate. Anim. Behav. 28:1070–94

Shettleworth, S. J. 1983. Memory in food-hoarding birds. Sci. Am. 248(3):102–10

Smith, A. W. 1978. Investigation of the mechanisms underlying nest construction in a mud wasp. Anim. Behav. 26:232–40

Smith, S. M. 1975. Innate recognition of a coral snake by a possible avian predator. Science 187:759–60

Squire, L. R. 1984. The neuropsychology of memory. See Marler & Terrace 1984, pp. 667–86

Staddon, J. E. R. 1983. Adaptive Behavior and Learning. New York: Cambridge Univ. Press

Terrace, H. S. 1984. Animal learning, ethology, and biological constraints. See Marler & Terrace 1984, pp. 15–46

Thorndike, E. L. 1898. Animal intelligence: An experimental study of the associative processes in animals. Psychol. Rev. Monogr. Suppl. 2:1–109

Thorpe, W. 1950. The concepts of learning and their relationship to instinct. Symp. Soc. Exp. Biol. 4:387–408

Tinbergen, N. 1951. The Study of Instinct. Oxford: Oxford Univ. Press

Tinbergen, N. 1972. The Animal in its World. Cambridge, MA: Harvard Univ. Press

von Frisch, K. 1967. The Dance Language and Orientation of Bees. Cambridge, MA: Harvard Univ. Press

Wehner, R. 1981. Spatial vision in arthropods. In Handbook of Sensory Physiology, ed. H. Autrum, pp. 287–616. Berlin: Springer Verlag

Ann. Rev. Psychol. 1986. 37:193–232
Copyright © 1986 by Annual Reviews Inc. All rights reserved

PROGRAM EVALUATION: THE WORLDLY SCIENCE

Thomas D. Cook

Department of Psychology and Center for Urban Affairs and Policy Research, Northwestern University, Evanston, Illinois 60201

William R. Shadish, Jr.

Center for Applied Psychological Research, Department of Psychology, Memphis State University, Memphis, Tennessee 38152

CONTENTS

INTRODUCTION 193
KNOWLEDGE BASE ABOUT SOCIAL PROGRAMS 195
    Concepts 195
    Social Programming Methods 198
KNOWLEDGE BASE ABOUT EVALUATION USAGE 200
    Concepts 200
    Methods to Stimulate Usage 204
KNOWLEDGE BASE ABOUT VALUING 208
    Concepts 208
    Methods for Valuing 210
KNOWLEDGE BASE ABOUT CONSTRUCTING VALID KNOWLEDGE 217
    Concepts 217
    Knowledge Methods 220
THEORIES OF EVALUATION PRACTICE 224
CONCLUSION 230

INTRODUCTION

Social program evaluation produces knowledge about the value of social programs and their constituent parts, knowledge that can be used in the short term to make the programs more responsive to the social problems they are

0066-4308/86/0201-0193$02.00

meant to ameliorate. In the title of this chapter we call program evaluation the worldly science. We have several reasons for this. Unlike many other sciences, evaluation makes no distinction between applied and basic research. The real world of social programs is its only home; there is no laboratory into which to return; and even theoretical work is concerned with constructing better guides to evaluation practice. Because evaluators are paid to improve social programs, they must interact with programs on the latter's terms. They have to embrace the whole messy world of social programming, knowing that its boundaries do not respect those of the disciplines in which they were trained, while also realizing that they will have to learn practical lessons they could not have been taught, or would not have appreciated, during their training.

The ways in which the real world has returned the evaluator's embrace have resulted in some embarassment and a considerable loss of naivete when compared to the state of affairs 20 years ago when systematic program evaluation began. Evaluators have emerged from the 20-year embrace more sophisticated about the complexity of their task and more realistic about the political realities that exist in social programs and about how social science information is used in social problem solving. Evaluators now find themselves addressing an expanded list of theoretical and practical issues, most of which were identified as lessons learned from the earlier years of evaluation practice. Debates in the field have now acquired a remarkably catholic, interdisciplinary, and grounded character, some of which we hope to capture as we summarize the theoretical literature on evaluation.

Briefly, we will suggest that accumulated experiences have indicated that at least four knowledge bases are needed for a comprehensive theory of evaluation. First, evaluators should understand social programs so as to identify where they are most and least amenable to productive change; second, they need to know how social science knowledge is and is not used to influence social programming; third, they need an explicit theory of *value* so as to distinguish good from bad programs; and finally, they need ways of constructing valid knowledge about programs.

But these four bases are not enough. They have to feed into a theory of evaluation practice that guide' question and method choice within the limits set by budget, time, and staff constraints and in light of the trade-offs that inevitably follow once particular issue or method choices have been made. While only a theory of practice is essential to evaluation, our assumption is that such a theory will not be useful if it is naive or wrong in its underlying assumptions about any of the four knowledge bases. Consequently, the present chapter seeks to describe the lessons learned over the last 20 years in each of the areas. We begin with the lessons learned about social programs because, more than anything else, it was these that robbed evaluators of their early innocence.

KNOWLEDGE BASE ABOUT SOCIAL PROGRAMS

Concepts

The 1960s were characterized by optimism about ameliorating significant social problems through large social programs such as Job Corps, the Community Mental Health Center Program, Aid to Families with Dependent Children, and Model Cities, to name just a few. In these early years, program evaluators made many optimistic assumptions about solving social problems through social programs, believing 1. that social science theory would point to clear causes of target problems and would suggest interventions for overcoming them; 2. that these interventions would be implemented and then evaluated in ways that provided unambiguous answers; 3. that the evaluated "successes" would be welcomed by policy makers, service deliverers, and program managers who would willingly adopt them; so that 4. a significant amelioration of the original social problem would occur (Suchman 1967). But the world of social programming proved greatly inconsistent with these early assumptions, and within the policy-making community in general, optimism about social reform gave way to disillusionment about the efficacy of most federal efforts at social change other than the provision of income support and health services to the elderly and poor.

The reasons for this disappointment are complex. Some relate to intrinsic difficulties in creating major changes in "advanced" societies where many of the problems less fortunate societies now face have already been solved to a generally satisfactory degree. The problems that remain are the stubborn ones for which inexpensive solutions do not yet exist. Also, multiple groups have a stake in how most "advanced" societies are organized and changed. In the United States, such groups include Congress, officials from federal, state, and local agencies, and organizations representing professional service providers and social groups in need. Most of these groups are politically active but differ both in the priority they assign to various problems and in the preferences they hold for proposed solutions. Hence, most plans for action have to be watered down as a political precondition for being implemented as policy. To be implemented also requires that a proposed change be consistent with majority beliefs about the kind of society that is desirable and the kinds of changes that are feasible. Consequently, few policies are approved if they call for more than marginal changes in the status quo (Shadish 1984), further predisposing social change attempts toward those that are less conceptually bold.

To be acted upon, every policy has to be embodied as a program. However strong aspirations to standardize programs might be, the reality in the United States is that most federal programs are implemented in heterogeneous fashion across the 50 states and 78,000 local governments that make up the nation's administrative structure (Lindblom 1977). With the exception of income support programs such as Social Security, social "programs" are little more than administrative umbrellas for distributing funds and issuing regulations aimed at managing the many local "projects" that are physically located in city or county agencies where service provision actually takes place. Even when they receive funds from the same program, local projects differ from each other in the mix of services provided, in local traditions about service provision, in client characteristics, in the training staff members have had, and in the mix of other state and federal programs from which operating funds have been received. Social programs are diffuse, heterogeneous, and ever-changing entities, usually composed of a central program staff and many local projects that receive funds and directives from program personnel but that administer the services themselves.

Each project is itself not much more than a set of service "elements" presumed to be useful for ameliorating a social problem. Thus, the Women Infant Children program of the U.S. Department of Agriculture has many local project offices where the elements of service include medical checkups, nutrition counseling, and well-baby care, and where the elements of management include outreach, intake, record keeping, and service coordination. Since elements make up projects and projects make up programs, a complex chain of relationships connects the central program officials who are accountable for project performance to the many managers and service providers at the local level whose practice has to change if clients are to be better helped and programs improved. But the vast majority of project personnel have established ways of doing things, enjoy considerable discretion in what they do, and are only loosely coupled to program headquarters.

All social programs need political constituencies to be funded initially; and once implemented, they tend to develop even larger constituencies of those who benefit from the program through employment, power, or services. This leads to a political impactedness that makes nearly all social programs permanent features of the policy world. Local projects are subject to similar entrenchment dynamics; even so, they are not as impacted as programs. Some projects do close down for want of human energy or because of budget changes, while new projects may be added to a program as budgets expand. Such project turnover creates the opportunity to modify the mix of program-funded projects in ways that might improve the program as a whole. But since any one local project reaches only a small fraction of a program's total pool of clients, its potential for program improvement is necessarily limited. Elements are not as impacted as programs or projects, so more latitude exists to add or remove elements from projects so as to improve their functioning and that of the social programs of which they are a part. Though some elements have the advantage of being manipulable and capable of transfer across projects, most suffer from the disadvantage that they have only a puny potential to influence individual lives and are often only a small part of the total set of services a client receives.

Here we see one of the great paradoxes of evaluation. Programs reach more people than projects and promise larger individual effects than elements, but they are so politically entrenched that they cannot be modified easily by evaluation results. Projects turn over more than programs, and by influencing the number and mix of projects in a program one can influence the program itself. Yet project turnover is presumably a slow process that can only be speeded within limits. Elements have potentially the most leverage if they can be added to the repertoires of those who deliver or manage services without much disruption of routine. Unfortunately, most elements that meet these specifications will usually promise little change in the lives of individual clients. There is a mismatch here between (a) the ability to introduce new practices—lowest with programs and highest with elements; (b) the number of people who receive new or improved services—lowest with individual projects and highest with programs; and (c) the degree of anticipated influence on individual lives—lowest with individual elements and highest with programs and projects.

Being concerned with ameliorating social problems, evaluation would seem to have a well-ordered place in any rational problem-solving model which requires that: 1. problems are first clearly defined; 2. then a wide array of potential solutions is generated; 3. some of these potential solutions are then implemented and 4. *eventually evaluated.* 5. Knowledge of the successful solutions is then widely disseminated with the expectation that 6. policy makers will use the knowledge in making decisions. Unfortunately, the real world of social programming is not as rational as this decision-making model requires. In the real world, problems are ill defined and stakeholders disagree about the priority each definition deserves (Bryk 1983); program objects can be vague or contradictory (Wholey 1983); the change attempts actually implemented are marginal (Shadish 1984); program structures involve long chains of communication that hinder the accurate dissemination of information between program and project staff (McLaughlin 1985); and sources of authority for local decision making are typically diffuse, with directives from a program central office often playing only a minor role in determining the decisions made (Weiss 1978). Such realities make problematic each step in the formal problem-solving model above, forcing evaluators out of the cool world of pure analysis into a maelstrom of political and administrative complexity. With the exception of Weiss (1972), early evaluators were not very aware of the intransigence of social programs, of the descriptive inaccuracy of normative theories of decision making, and of the limited role evaluation plays as only one of the many steps in formal models of social problem solving.

As this contextual complexity became more salient, it influenced most of the social scientists who had hoped that their substantive input would improve program functioning. They gained a new appreciation of the rationality and tenacity with which policy makers, program officials, and project employees pursue their primary goals of keeping or improving their jobs and of promoting their beliefs, assigning these a higher priority than the evaluator's goal of identifying technically superior options for problem definition, program design, or problem amelioration. These same lessons also influenced many evaluators. They came to realize that because of the way programs are embedded in the world of politics, they would rarely be called upon to evaluate bold new programs or fundamental changes that had been made in existing programs. Hence, "large" effects could not be expected. Moreover, since projects are so different from each other and respond so variably to requests for change from central program authorities, most evaluators also came to realize that they could not expect the effects obtained in some projects to be consistent across all the projects in a program. Of all effects, probably the most difficult to uncover are those that are both small on the average and variable in where they are manifest.

Social Programming Methods

We might posit three action strategies for creating social changes to ameliorate social problems, each of which has different implications for program evaluation. The most frequent strategy involves creating incremental modifications in existing social programs so as to improve their functioning, usually through adding projects to a program or changing some elements in the package of services provided. The need for such change is usually felt when budgets shift, clients complain, service providers seek better ways to do things, or managers and auditors detect specific troubles.

One crucial assumption of this incrementalist approach is that by modifying projects or programs at the margin, they will become more effective and will eventually contribute to ameliorating some target social problem. Yet if the basic assumptions of a program or project are flawed, evaluation may help make a project function more efficiently without improving clients' lives. A major challenge to those who advocate incrementalism is to identify the types of programmatic change that are most likely to result in nontrivial improvements in programs that have a significant potential for ameliorating a particular problem. Such changes might require combining many novel elements or identifying the attributes of those single elements that are most likely to create significant change. While presumably rare, some elements with these attributes do exist. In mental health, for example, we can point to phenothiazine medications for treating psychotic disorders and to systematic desensitization procedures for treating phobias. We might surmise that their importance depends on a number of factors that various theorists of evaluation have emphasized in their search for approaches to evaluation that might "make a difference"— namely, each is a manipulable practice (Campbell 1969), difficult to implement incorrectly (Sechrest et al 1979), consonant with the values of the professionals who use it (Fullan 1982), keyed to an easily identified problem (Williams 1980), and robust in its effects across different types of clients and service providers (Cronbach 1982). Moreover, each is inexpensive, can be used to influence many lives, and through significantly reducing symptoms will demonstrably lead to enhanced individual functioning by criteria which everyone would agree are important (F. L. Cook 1982).

A second strategy of social change involves the use of demonstration projects to test the efficacy of planned innovations before deciding whether to introduce them as approved policy. Many things can be demonstrated, although in the later 1960s and early 1970s the emphasis seems to have been on new philosophies of service with different assumptions from the then dominant practice. Thus, experimental demonstrations of a negative income tax were launched, predicated on the notion that in times of need every citizen ought to be able to rely on a guaranteed income rather than be provided with social services (Rossi & Lyall 1976). Also, Fairweather (1980) experimented with a demonstration predicated on the assumption that chronic mental patients can look after themselves in small group living arrangements without the help of hospitals and mental health professionals. Largely because options are explored in highly circumscribed settings and are not advocated as current policy, demonstrations can be more bold than incremental changes. They are most likely to be funded when existing programs are widely acknowledged to be ineffective and difficult to improve at the margin, and our impression is that demonstrations of novel projects reached their zenith in the early 1970s. They have declined in frequency since then, as a more laissez-faire approach to social welfare came to predominate that ascribed less importance to bold innovation and preferred to use demonstrations as clinical trials of new elements that might be added to existing philosophies of service.

Demonstrations have their drawbacks. They have never been initiated as often as program or project elements have been changed. They can never convincingly indicate what would happen if an intervention were to become policy because the time frame of a demonstration is limited and the staff's commitment usually exceeds that of the persons who would implement the demonstrated activities if they became bureaucratically routinized. The utility of demonstrations is also reduced because, with the rapid turnover of federal officials and "hot" policy issues, demonstration results are sometimes provided when windows of opportunity have closed or the persons receiving the results are not those who fought to set up the demonstration. Also, although demonstrations are labeled as "tentative" or "experimental," they occur in the real world and are affected by it. In the first negative income tax experiment, for example, implementation of a minimum guaranteed income was hampered by local welfare authorities who wanted to ensure that the households receiving benefits from the demonstration were reporting them in full when filing for their regular welfare entitlements. Finally, the transition from a successful demonstration to a fully funded social program is strewn with obstacles, as the fate of Fairweather's Lodge illustrates. Despite positive evaluation results and many recommendations to implement the concept widely, we still do not have many Lodges, probably because its assumptions are too radically different for most mental health professionals (Shadish 1984). Though successful evaluation results may raise the likelihood that a demonstration's activities will be used as a basis for policy, this felicitous outcome is not at all guaranteed.

The third strategy of social change involves changes in basic social structures and beliefs that touch on such fundamental matters as the nature and locus of political authority, the form of the economy, and the distribution of income and wealth. Such system change is rare, although during the Depression major changes did occur in many American beliefs and in the structure and responsibilities of the federal government. However, such changes are not part of the routine government functioning that evaluators aspire to improve and so are more properly the purview of historians, sociologists, and political scientists.

KNOWLEDGE BASE ABOUT EVALUATION USAGE

Concepts

With the wisdom of hindsight, we can now see the naivete of early conceptions of how evaluation results would improve social programs. The dominant notion in the 1960s was that evaluative feedback about which programs did and did not work would be used to maintain or expand effective programs and to discontinue or radically change ineffective ones (Suchman 1967). But discontinuing social programs is rare, and discontinuing them because of evaluation results is unheard of. This is partly because evaluations are never so compelling, and their findings usually lead to dispute rather than consensus (Lindblom & Cohen 1979). It is also because evaluation is in many ways just another political act that occurs in a context where power, ideology, and interests are more powerful determinants of decision making than feedback about programs.

It is not clear how often evaluation results influence program budgets, increasing them when effectiveness is indicated and decreasing them when it is not. This is a less stringent criterion than discontinuance, although it retains the same connotation of evaluation results being used to shape the decisions made by formal decision makers. Claims have been made that some past evaluations did influence funding levels, as with the decision to phase out the small summer component of Head Start (Weiss & Rein 1970). However, it is difficult to attribute any single decision to evaluation findings alone, given the complexity of the world of politics. Nonetheless, the consensus among evaluators is that in the short term, evaluations rarely influence program budget levels.

Somewhat stronger, but still indirect, evidence suggests that evaluation findings can influence the internal priorities of programs, affecting the mix of services made available, the manner of their provision, the target beneficiaries of preference, how regulations are enforced, etc. While obviously political, such changes are less so when compared to changes in budget levels, for the latter transmit powerful symbolic messages about the social problems being addressed on a priority basis and about the client groups and professional guilds that are to benefit from a program's provisions. Still, we know little that is systematic about the frequency with which evaluation results lead to short-term changes in internal program priorities.

The foregoing discussion has emphasized the instrumental use of evaluations designed to summarize the achievements of national programs and demonstrations that might later become national programs. This is not the only model of short-term instrumental usage. A small number of federal programs mandated self-evaluation by local projects under the assumption that evaluators employed by a project are more trusted than external evaluators and know the project and its operations better. The expectation was such that in-house evaluators would be better at identifying where evaluative results might have leverage, at collecting high-quality data, and at getting evaluation results used. Self-evaluation was mandated for all the projects receiving program funds so that the feedback provided would improve each project and in so doing would enhance the overall program to which each project belonged.

Unfortunately, there is little empirical support for this project-level theory of instrumental usage, except with some types of educational television (Cook & Curtin 1986). In community mental health (Cook & Shadish 1982), community crime prevention (Feeley & Sarat 1980), and local Title I projects in education (David 1982), the theory seems to have run afoul of several realities. First, project managers rarely want systematic information based on social science methods and instead prefer ammunition to help with their project's public relations. Second, in-house evaluators tend to have little power and multiple responsibilities, and are named as the "evaluator" only because someone has to have this title and they know something about social science methodology. Finally, in-house evaluators are sometimes seen as allies of project management. Hence, if factions are competing for power within a project, the evaluator may be seen as taking sides and may lose the very advantages she or he is supposed to have over external evaluators. While some exceptions undoubtedly exist, the administrative conditions required by the local project model of instrumental usage may not occur often.

The emphasis on immediate instrumental usage by elected officials or the managers of programs and projects is now less salient than it used to be in evaluation. This is probably because disappointingly few large effects have been discovered, and because few clear incidences of instrumental usage have been documented. It is not easy to document such usage, for when results and decisions coincide, the evaluation results could have been used to justify decisions already made on other (and more political) grounds. As currently practiced, few evaluations seem to be of a clearly demonstrated, short-term instrumental utility, though exceptions exist (see Leviton & Boruch 1984).

Empirical attacks on the instrumental conception of evaluation use were accompanied by some evaluators beginning to ask: What should the role of evaluative information be in an open, democratic society (Cook 1983)? Should decisions not be influenced by enduring cultural values and the give and take of political compromise every bit as much as by the type of feedback that evaluation provides? Normative reflections like these were probably partly responsible for decoupling the definition of evaluation usage from an exclusive emphasis on results constituting decisions and for enlarging the definition to include evaluations being cited in policy deliberations where they might function as just one of many inputs and not have any clear link to a particular decision. The dissociation of usage from decision making was also furthered by the realization that prior decisions often leave decision makers with little freedom for present action (Weiss 1980). To label the choices they eventually make as "decisions" suggests a greater freedom to select among options than is actually warranted, and to believe that evaluation results influence such pre-empted "decisions" is naive. If many political decisions are preempted, and if theories of democracy do not imply that evaluation feedback should determine political decisions, no rationale exists for defining the use of evaluation results solely in terms of results causing decisions.

A second shift in the conceptualization of usage followed from learning that individuals in decision-making groups are exposed to many different sources of information, some of which use evaluation findings in ways that suit their own purposes but are not closely linked to the evaluator's major stated conclusions. Thus, lobbyists or journalists might sometimes refer to findings about one program in deliberations about other programs, or they might cite results to help make points about the needs of a particular social group or about the length of time it might take for a new program to impact on national-level statistics. They might do this, even though none of these points was explicitly made in the evaluation report they cite and though none of these uses speaks directly to short-term instrumental usage. Rather, they concern a more diffuse and indirect type of use called "enlightenment" (Weiss 1977), that deals with the influences knowledge has on cognitive frameworks. For instance, enlightenment occurs when knowledge clarifies the theoretical assumptions undergirding a program, when it highlights relationships among the values of various stakeholder groups, or when it illuminates the priorities that different problems deserve. In altering cognitive frameworks rather than uncovering and teaching specific "facts," enlightenment decouples usage both from a dependence on reports about a single program and from the notion that usage should occur soon after an evaluation is completed. For Cronbach and his associates (1980, 1982) and Guba & Lincoln (1981), enlightenment came to replace short-term decision making as the ultimate justification for evaluation.

Another shift decoupled the definition of evaluation usage from usage by particular decision makers. Pluralist conceptions of evaluation stress that multiple groups have a stake in programs. Of these, program managers and funders originally received most attention, and some theories of evaluation were specifically tailored to meeting their information needs (e.g. Patton 1978, Wholey 1983). But with time other stakeholders came to be seen as equally important, especially service deliverers (Cronbach et al 1980) and consumers of services (Scriven 1980). Their importance increased even more after it was realized that while evaluations might be used to modify the regulations coming from a program central office, these regulations did not always influence local practices that are shaped by many other forces, some more immediately pressing than program regulations. Growing awareness of the partial independence of local practitioners also led to an interest in how they learn about evaluation findings—through in-service training, books and journals that cite evaluations, or observing colleagues whose own practice has been influenced by evaluations (Leviton & Boruch 1983). Congruent with this was a growing interest in how evaluations are used to train future professionals who will later deliver services in local projects as teachers, social workers, nurses, and the like (Leviton & Cook 1984). These themes all reject the notion that the use of evaluations should be expected only from senior program and project managers.

A further shift decoupled usage from dependence on the formal conclusions presented in an evaluation report. Research suggested that potential users sometimes raise issues with evaluators that transcend the information gained from a single study (Leviton & Hughes 1981, Mielke & Chen 1981). Instead, the issues require knowledge synthesized from the total body of prior studies, from the incidental observations made by evaluators during their work, or even from their own reflections on the program, project, or element they have studied. Being able to respond on the basis of such incidental knowledge can prove helpful in ways that transcend the major conclusions explicitly drawn in a particular evaluative study.

By 1985 the concept of usage was much broader than in 1965. It encompassed evaluations constituting decisions, playing a codeterminative role in constituting decisions, being cited in formal and informal debates, being used in the in-service training of working professionals, being used in the education of future practitioners, and being used to enhance the enlightenment of all stakeholders so that they might conceptualize past and future social programs and problems in a different manner. The agent of influence was no longer a single evaluation report presented to formal decision makers. Literature reviews were also involved, as was knowledge gained from incidental reading and interactions with substantive experts and practitioners. Even the sources for disseminating knowledge were now more broadly understood. Instead of being restricted to evaluation reports and briefings targeted at funders, they now included reports aimed at audiences of scholars and practitioners, ad hoc media presentations of findings, and even unanticipated conversations with important persons at informal events.

Methods to Stimulate Usage

Empirical and conceptual work suggests that the usage of evaluations is promoted in three major and related ways: through the choice of issues addressed; through the roles the evaluator adopts regarding potential users; and through the communication channels chosen for disseminating evaluation results.

To help create a descriptive language for discussing how evaluation issues are framed, Cook et al (1985) distinguished between issues framed at the program, project, or element level and issues framed around issues of (a) targeting (who receives or distributes services?); (b) implementation (what are the program inputs, processes, and cost, and how can the treatment be specified?); (c) effectiveness (what changes have occurred in the units receiving services?); and (d) impacts (how do the services influence the social and other systems with which persons in need interact—e.g. their families, neighborhoods, other service projects?). Cook et al (1985) also distinguished between issues framed in a more descriptive or explanatory mode. The former would be involved when one asks: "Which types of clients received services more often?," or "What are the program's effects?" The more explanatory mode would be involved when one asks: "Why did this group receive more services than another?", or "Why did the intervention have the effects attributed to it?" We now use these distinctions to discuss how methods for stimulating usage depend on the framing of an evaluative issue.

Since programs rarely die, the powerful consensus in more recent evaluation theory is that orienting evaluation exclusively toward the description of program effects and impacts provides little leverage for short-term usage. More utility is assigned to describing and explaining the targeting and implementation of program services on the dual grounds that describing program operations (a) will help identify problems of implementation that occur widely across the projects in a program, and (b) will generate practical suggestions for improving projects, with the suggestions coming from common sense, current professional practice, and knowledge of what has been implemented at the superior sites among those studied. The ultimate hope is that once a source of improvement has been identified, knowledge of it will be disseminated throughout a program and will be adopted (or adapted) by a significant number of projects (Wholey 1983).

A second source of leverage at the program level is presumed to come from explanatory studies that model the theoretical and operational logic behind a program. The hope is to trace all the time-bound relationships through which program inputs are supposed to influence project processes that in their turn are supposed to bring about effects on clients' lives and ultimately impact on indicators of a social problem. Once such models have been made explicit, they can be critically examined prior to data collection to estimate whether the financial, human, and material resources they postulate as necessary are available and whether the hypothesized relationships between inputs, processes, and outcomes are congruent with relevant, substantive theory. It is surprising how often such preevaluative model building reveals failures of program planning, even though no primary data have been collected. Nonetheless, collecting such data is crucial for assessing the correspondence between program operations and planners' assumptions. Although armchair analysis and ad hoc reports from practitioners provide useful preevaluative knowledge, they cannot be relied upon for a comprehensive or veridical description of what actually happens within a program (Rossi & Freeman 1982).

A third source of leverage at the program level involves the description of effects attributable to elements that central program administrators can control. (These will be quite different from the elements that local project officials can control.) While many program elements are puny in the effects anticipated on individuals, their potential to reach so many clients can make their aggregate impact considerable. Thus, a minor change in the application forms for free and reduced-price school lunches that was sponsored by central program authorities reduced fraudulent applications by a small percentage; but since about a billion lunches of these types are served each year, the savings in the first year were estimated to be about seven million dollars (Applied Management Services 1984). The need is to identify the types of program element that can be changed and are most likely to result in improving program operations in socially significant ways.

If we move from the program to the project level, we note that considerable leverage was once anticipated from evaluations describing the targeting, implementation, and effects achieved in each of the individual projects making up a program. Indeed, the payoff anticipated from this source was once enough to justify mandating local project evaluations for many programs. However, for reasons mentioned earlier, this path to program improvement now appears less promising. More emphasis is now placed on identifying projects that are particularly successful by the most important effect criteria in the hope that such knowledge will eventually influence program managers to modify the mix of projects funded and will persuade local project personnel to change the mix of service elements they provide. However, research on this leverage point has not had an auspicious history, since (*a*) most past procedures for identifying successful projects concentrated on *single* exemplary instances even though many were unique in ways that precluded effective transfer elsewhere—often because of the charisma of project developers; (*b*) active disagreement emerged about the criteria of success and standards of methodological adequacy that should be used to identify exemplary projects; and (*c*) the identification procedures rarely emphasized those elements within projects that were responsible for success, even though such explanatory knowledge might facilitate transfer to other projects.

Because of these limitations, it has been suggested that evaluation should be directed at identifying the *types* of projects that are so effective by major outcome criteria that they deserve to be more widely distributed throughout a program (Cook et al 1985). The logic behind this is that the number of projects in a program does wax and wane since projects terminate voluntarily, program budgets change, and projects occasionally seek to change their operating philosophy. However, it would be naive to pretend either that project-level turnover is high or that evaluators can easily identify the more successful types of projects in a program. The latter task requires constructing a typology of project types and then sampling some individual projects from within each type. Inevitably there will be considerable variability within each type, and the more there is the less useful is the concept of type.

If we turn to the level of project elements, there are undoubtedly some novel elements of practice that, if introduced into projects, would improve many of them and thus enhance the overall program of which they are a part. In these current times of fiscal stringency, much leverage is attributed to identifying manipulable practices that practitioners can adopt (or adapt) into their repertoire without changing the essence of their practice (McLaughlin 1985). Some theorists emphasize locating such practices through identifying the elements to which the success of exemplary projects can be attributed. However, there is no need to focus only on exemplary projects, and our guess is that much of the research aimed at identifying successful elements occurs in evaluations of more ordinary projects where data on the implementation of services is used to try to explain the pattern of obtained results.

Causal explanation is not the only source of knowledge about transferrable project manipulanda. Many developers gear their work to improving the tools practitioners use; some practitioners actively experiment in their own work in the hope of identifying better procedures; and in each policy sector new substantive theories develop from which implications for practice are abstracted. Each of these instances can lead to a clinical trial (or demonstration) in which a particular element serves as the independent variable in a focused study designed to identify successful elements that deserve to be made available for general practice or even reimbursement (Pacht et al 1980, Bunker 1985).

Clinical trials of possible future practices do not link reimbursement to current professional practice and so are less threatening than clinical trials of elements of present practice. Indeed, many professional associations will resist the latter type of study, but such instances do occur. However, when clinical trials are used to identify successful elements of local practice, it is difficult for program authorities to monitor practitioner compliance with any specific behaviors that might be recommended because of clinical trials. If such monitoring is conducted independently and on site, it tends to be expensive and obtrusive; but if it is done through fellow professionals employed at the same agency or through self-reports from practitioners, the monitoring is likely to be biased toward obtaining exaggerated levels of compliance with the recommendations or prescriptions of program personnel.

The degree of leverage for getting evaluation results used does not depend solely on how evaluation issues are framed. It is also associated with the nature of the persons setting evaluative questions and with the role relationships evaluators adopt regarding these persons. For instance, Wholey (1983) assigns a major role to program managers, reasoning that their job puts them in a special position to suggest and enforce changes in program guidelines. Hence, Wholey believes that evaluators should look to program managers to provide the guiding evaluation questions. However, he believes that evaluators should not be passive in doing this. They need to help managers formulate questions that are clear, important, and answerable within the constraints of time and budget, and they also need to keep regular contact with managers. Indeed, almost all theorists of evaluation agree that usage is stimulated by frequent, close contact between evaluators and prospective users.

The type of contact they recommend varies somewhat. Campbell (1969) favors the evaluator as servant to the honest administrator, but as a "whistle blower" to the dishonest administrator; Wholey (1983) sees him or her as a faithful retainer who also seeks to educate managers about how to evaluate more usefully; Cronbach (Cronbach et al 1980) also favors an educator role, but one that takes theory and past research findings into greater account than is the case with Wholey and that tilts more toward representing the needs of those who directly deliver or manage services at the local level; Berman & McLaughlin (1977) see the evaluator as an information broker; while Scriven (1983) sees him as a consumer consultant who tells prospective purchasers about the best buys from among the competing alternatives. A few case studies suggest that short-term usage is associated with the evaluator playing more of a proactive than reactive role, responding flexibly if the information needs of potential users change during a study and, when required, invoking background knowledge of the social problem and social program under analysis instead of sticking only to preformulated evaluative issues (Leviton & Hughes 1981, Leviton &

Boruch 1983). Thus, the pendulum has now swung closer to the conception of Cronbach and of Berman and McLaughlin, or perhaps even of Wholey, than to the conception of Campbell or Scriven.

Roles have to do with communication, and we assume that some ways of communicating are more likely than others to lead to the dissemination and eventual utilization of evaluative results. All theorists are agreed that communication should be informal and cast in simple language devoid of jargon. Many theorists also contend that evaluation reports might be in several different forms tailored to the unique information needs and communication patterns of different stakeholder groups. All except Campbell argue that the action implications of the evaluation findings should be spelled out and defended but without obscuring the basic findings or inadvertently promoting the evaluators' values. The theorists also believe that evaluators should do all they can to get publicity for their findings in the mass media and professional outlets. The assumption is that such exposure will increase the number of stakeholder groups that learn of the evaluation findings and hence might use them for their own enlightenment even if they do not use them as guides to immediate changes in what they do.

KNOWLEDGE BASE ABOUT VALUING

Concepts

In its early years, evaluation gave little explicit attention to the role of values. Scriven (1983) suggests that this was because evaluators naively believed that their activities could and should be value-free. But many evaluators learned from experience that it was impossible in the political world of social programming to make most of the choices they had to make without values becoming salient, perhaps most clearly when evaluative criteria were being selected and justified. While evaluators have increasingly come to acknowledge that values deserve more attention, they have not known how to proceed in this delicate task, for most evaluators were trained to believe that values are not part of "science."

To address issues of value, a few evaluators have used metatheoretical approaches to construct frameworks from which statements about the value, merit, or "goodness" of any entity can be deduced. Scriven's (1980) approach is the best known, and his general logic involves four steps. First, justifiable criteria of merit have to be developed that specify what an evaluand has to influence as a condition for being labeled good. Second, justifiable standards of performance have to be selected for each criterion that specify how well the evaluand ought to perform in order to attain a specified level of merit. Third, performance has to be measured on each criterion so as to estimate whether specified standards of quality performance have been reached. And finally, where multiple criteria are involved, the measured results have to be integrated into a single statement about the overall goodness or value of the evaluand.

A form of logic like Scriven's is heavily used in several areas. Consider product evaluations. In evaluating automobiles, the criteria of merit would include purchase price, gas mileage, passenger capacity, and comfort. Standards of performance might specify minimal standards of safe handling under emergency conditions which, if not met, would lead to a car not being recommended. Yet standards can also be relative, as when several automobile models in the same size and price range are compared because they are the alternatives from which potential consumers will actually have to choose. After performance standards have been set comes the measurement of performance, which can involve test drives, owner surveys, interviews with automobile engineers, or laboratory tests. Finally, the results are somehow synthesized across the various measures to recommend the "best buy" from among the standards considered. Traditional quantitative research practice follows the same metatheoretic logic. Criteria are called dependent variables; standards of performance are called comparison or control groups; data collection retains the same name; while global synthesis is achieved through decision-making statistical procedures. However, in social science the object being evaluated is usually a theoretical hypothesis rather than an automobile or a social program.

Metatheoretic approaches do not specify which criteria or standards to use or how to measure and synthesize. Prescriptive ethical theories could be a source of such criteria, on the rationale that evaluators participate in a moral act by providing data to improve social programs aimed at poverty, racism, crime, and the like (Warnock 1971). One such prescriptive theory is Rawls's (1971) egalitarian theory of justice, which states that social goods and services ought to be distributed to alleviate those material needs of the disadvantaged that, if not met, will result in unacceptable harm. In suggesting how to operationalize his otherwise apparently neutral metatheoretic logic of valuing, Scriven (1980) adopts a similar position, suggesting that a program or element is good to the extent it meets needs, with the latter being inferred when an unacceptably high cost is incurred in the absence of the service being evaluated. House (1980) is even more explicit than Scriven, arguing that Rawls's theory should be used to guide the selection and weighting of evaluative criteria and performance standards.

However, few evaluators are willing to rely on prescriptive ethics for criteria selection. This is largely because no compelling reason currently exists for preferring one prescriptive theory over another. In the case of theories of justice, a number of credible alternatives to Rawls have been constructed, most notably Nozick's (1974) libertarian theory. Moreover, while justice is a central moral concern in evaluation, it is not the only relevant concern. Criteria can also be justified in terms of their relationship to human rights, equality, liberty, utility, and many other such abstract concepts. Evaluators may also be unwilling to endorse particular prescriptive ethics because few data have been advanced thus far to support particular philosophers' claims that a better society will result if one ethic is followed rather than another and because the American political system has traditionally preferred to foster a pluralism of values. Promoting a single prescriptive ethic is therefore inconsistent with the political context in which evaluation occurs. While evaluators will benefit from being generally informed about the prescriptive implications of criteria selections so that they can help others reason about the values and kind of society that particular choices seem to imply, it is difficult to justify a more extensive role than this.

A descriptive approach to valuing is better suited to the political context in which evaluators actually function, since decision making depends more on the values held by relevant legislators, managers, voters, lobbyists, etc, than on any single prescriptive calculus of value. Hence, knowledge of stakeholder values can be used to help select criteria so that no criteria are overlooked that are of crucial importance to particular groups. More is at issue here than conformity with a pluralist ethic. Without an understanding of stakeholder values the process of conducting an evaluation may be more difficult. Stakeholders may not be cooperative with data collection and may even challenge the eventual evaluation findings on grounds of evaluator partisanship.

Descriptive approaches are now popular in evaluation, but are limited by the wisdom of the values held by the various participants in the political process. Many participants do not have the time, interest, or experience to express their values with the degree of articulation found among theorists of ethics or among organized stakeholders who seek to clothe their self-interest with ethical-sounding rationales for or against particular government programs. Descriptive approaches are also limited because, although values are interrelated in complex ways, many Americans have been socialized to believe in the special priority of certain values—e.g. life, liberty, and the pursuit of happiness—and may have a limited understanding of how promoting these values could hinder the attainment of others. Moreover, while knowing the values of different groups may be enlightening, it cannot easily generate specific principles for justifying the selection of some criteria and standards over others. The description of values generates a list and not a justified procedure for setting priorities.

Methods for Valuing

As Scriven's first step in his metatheoretic logic of valuing suggests, to know how good a program is requires criteria of merit. In the early years of evaluation, it was standard practice to use program goals to set criteria. This was not unreasonable. Programs have goals, and since they are usually formulated through give-and-take in the political arena, they presumably reflect some conjunction of the many interests participating in the democratic process. Nonetheless, exclusive reliance on program goals proved to be an error because 1. goals are often vague, contradictory, or latent (Weiss 1977, Scriven 1983); 2. program implementation is so heterogeneous and locally controlled that the goals of program officials do not overlap heavily with the goals of local officials and service deliverers; and 3. programs have unintended effects that sometimes turn out to be just as important as planned goals. Also, 4. if they have enough control over goal specification, program managers are often tempted to specify excessively modest goals on the grounds that it is better to succeed at something less important than to fail at something more important. And 5. when they have less control over goal specification, managers are likely to find themselves stuck with unrealistically high goals that mirror the overpromises that program advocates gave to secure initial funding. Finally, 6. to know that a program or project reached its goals says nothing about whether it represents the most efficient available way of meeting these goals.

Although goals have been rejected as the sole source of criteria of merit, no replacement has yet been agreed upon. Candidates for criteria now include: 1. examining the claims that clients, service deliverers, and program managers make about what a program is achieving and about the factors that led to success or failure (Guba & Lincoln 1981); 2. studying factors that will feed into decisions that policy makers or managers have to make in the near future (Weiss 1972); 3. assessing any substantive system models that have been developed to explain how program inputs should be related to subsequent processes and outcomes (Chen & Rossi 1983); 4. estimating the degree to which the material needs of clients have been met (Scriven 1980); and 5. catering to the information needs of multiple stakeholder groups (Bryk 1983) or of just managers and policy makers (Wholey 1983). By itself, none of these options results in a neat set of criteria or priority judgments. Procedures for prioritizing do exist, of which the most noteworthy are decision-theoretic in their origins (see Edwards et al 1975). But these procedures are more easily implemented with fewer stakeholder groups, and have been used most often in the management-centered evaluations that Wholey prefers. When multiple stakeholder interests are taken into account and no a priori reason exists for weighting some interests more than others, no perfect method currently exists for generating a prioritized list of criteria of merit.

Once a goal-based approach to valuing is rejected, the value of an evaluand must depend on the total set of effects it achieves, whether intended or not, harmful or beneficial. A serious practical problem is to know how to identify the unintended effects that might occur. Chen & Rossi (1983) suggest that substantive social science theories will often provide clues to such effects if the theories are used to help articulate the links relating program inputs to subsequent processes, effects, and impacts. Scriven (1980) suggests that potential side effects may be discovered if evaluators come to know the evaluand in detail before collecting more formal evaluation data. Interviews with clients, service providers, and program managers might be used for this purpose, with particular attention being paid to passionate advocates and opponents of the program, since no one is more likely than they to have thought about potential beneficial or harmful side effects. However, no perfect method exists for informing evaluators about unplanned effects.

The second step in Scriven's metatheoretic logic of valuing concerns the construction of standards for ranking performance. Two possibilities are suggested. Absolute standards link evaluative rankings to prespecified levels of performance, as when criterion-referenced tests are used in education to assign letter grades or to certify competency for graduation from high school. Since the results of such tests do not depend on how classmates perform, they differ from the results that follow from using comparative performance standards, as when school grades are assigned on a curve or alternative automobile models are directly compared. These last examples are instructive, for with grading on a curve students can perform very well and still receive a D; and an automobile can be totally satisfactory but not be recommended for purchase because it performs less well than an alternative.

Although social programs can be held to either absolute or comparative standards, the latter are more easily justified and in fact predominate in evaluation practice. Of the five comparative standards used to date, Campbell (1969) is most closely identified with the selection of *no-treatment control group* standards that represent what would have happened to respondents in the absence of the evaluand. Evaluators hope to learn from this standard whether exposure to a program, project, or element is better than no such exposure, even though receiving no exposure does not prevent control group members from exercising their initiative and receiving comparable services from nonprogram sources.

A *no-services baseline* restricts the counterfactual conditions to those where it can be presumed that the controls receive no ameliorative services whatsoever. A precondition for this is a measure of service implementation that includes measures of help from sources other than those being evaluated, so that a group can be constructed of persons with no sources of help at all. The preference for no-service controls is often associated with a preference for purified treatment groups that are restricted to those persons who demonstrably received more or better services. This permits a "high or maximal dosage" group to be constructed that can be contrasted with the "no-service" or "no-dosage" control group.

Scriven (1980) suggests that comparisons should be with the *available alternatives* among which the "consumers" of programs, projects, or elements have to choose in determining how to act. He argues that no consumer needs to choose between a particular automobile model and having no car at all, and that decision makers in the social policy world rarely have to choose between a program or no program, or even between a current program and a single alternative. Campbell's work on evolutionary epistemology (1974) also implies the same preference for identifying the better performers among multiple viable alternatives, and it buttresses his advocacy that evaluations are particularly useful if they are linked to demonstration studies that examine multiple "planned variations" and are not restricted to a single program or a single plan for a program.

Cronbach (1963) opposes the use of comparative standards from outside a program or project, arguing that social problem solving is best facilitated by improving the evaluand relative to itself in the past. He argues that studies of variants cannot identify how to improve current practices, and he further maintains that the variants examined rarely pursue the same set of goals, rarely prioritize their shared goals the same way, and rarely postulate the same time frames in which effects and impacts should be expected. Hence, he believes it is misleading to treat social variants as though they were functionally equivalent, and he cautions anyone who commissions an evaluation with this premise that they are likely to engender in project developers and personnel an apprehension about being evaluated that may be counterproductive. This is because project personnel tend to see the services they provide as unique, and they fear that their work will be insensitively tested if evaluation activities are limited to those consequences that the evaluators believe all the projects under analysis should achieve.

Light (1983) has added another relative standard of performance to the list. He notes that in many areas of social welfare the planned interventions involve attention being paid to clients, and he suggests that the marginal contribution of an evaluand be assessed over and above any results attributable to such attention. His rationale is presumably that while attention is an intrinsic component of many interventions, it is a less expensive form of treatment than the total package of services provided, it may not have the same long-term effects, and it does not define what is unique about a program or project. At issue here is a *placebo control group*.

In selecting relative standards: 1. a concern for maximizing the likelihood of obtaining some treatment effects impels evaluators toward the strategy of contrasting maximally implemented services with the total absence of such services; 2. a concern for comparing future alternatives with current ones impels evaluators toward the comparison of treatments-as-implemented with no-treatment controls who are free to seek out alternative services; 3. a concern for comparing the major alternatives available for service provision impels evaluators toward studies of planned variations; 4. a concern to attribute effects to the specific services that define a treatment's uniqueness impels the evaluator toward the use of placebo controls; and 5. a concern to improve an evaluand on its own terms impels an evaluator toward before-after measurement on the evaluand, especially if there is no reason to believe that maturation or testing will increase performance over time. Since so much depends on the choice of comparative standards, since so many standards exist, and since they have not been well discussed to date in the evaluation literature, our guess is that much more debate on standards of comparison will occur in the future. Two issues might then be worth developing.

First, no algorithm yet exists for helping evaluators select among the various relative standards. Yet the choice of a standard can have profound implications, for it is not unreasonable to assume that the likelihood of effects will generally be lowest when an evaluand is compared to an alternative, next lowest when compared to a placebo control group, and next lowest when compared to a no-treatment group. Effectiveness is more likely when no-services baselines are used or when before-after changes are contrasted, particularly when treatment groups are defined in terms of the subgroup of persons manifestly receiving high-quality services. Fortunately, the choice of comparison standards does not require selecting a single option, and evaluations can be designed with multiple controls. When resources permit, this is clearly the preferred strategy (Light 1983), but no choice algorithm yet exists.

Second, the comparison standards that are most likely to result in "effects" seem to be more heavily advocated by evaluation theorists today. This probably reflects their belief that past evaluations chronically underestimated the potential of treatments because of inadequate evaluation designs (Cronbach 1982, Light & Pillemer 1984), suboptimally implemented program activities (Sechrest et al 1979), and operational plans that were not well linked to the social science theory undergirding program design (Chen & Rossi 1983). From such concerns arises the recent attention to implementation and its emphasis on no-service baselines and before-after changes. However, it is important to distinguish between impediments to implementation that are the result of inherent structural constraints and those that result from temporary problems that might be corrected with better knowledge, more resources, or keener commitment. To select standards of performance assessing what services might achieve if they were implemented well makes sense if past impediments to high-quality implementation are likely to be corrigible. Evaluators can then orient future work to probing ways to improve the implementation of those factors that improve performance, while ceasing work on those elements of practice that are ineffective even when evaluated by standards designed to maximize effectiveness. However, if evidence strongly suggests that the impediments to high-quality implementation are structural, it makes little sense to evaluate a program under conditions that maximize the contrast between no services and services implemented at their best, for it will not be possible to implement on a routine basis those conditions associated with highest quality implementation.

As for measuring performance—the third step in his metatheoretical logic—Scriven cautions evaluators that this is a limited task. It does not include for him the preevaluative tasks of describing the evaluand or assessing opinions about its value. Nor does it include postevaluative analyses of why an evaluand was effective or of how the evaluation results might be used. While all of these tasks result in knowledge useful for the program improvement that Cronbach prefers, Scriven contends that such measurements are not necessary for the evaluative purpose he most prizes—summarizing the value of an entity. For this purpose, Scriven contends that only measurement of each alternative on each pre-specified criterion is required, provided that the measurement is sensitive enough to permit strong inferences about whether absolute standards were reached or true comparative differences detected. Although measurement is a restricted concept for Scriven, it does entail more than performance assessment alone. To make statements about an evaluand's value, it must be clear that it was the evaluand, and not some force correlated with it, that caused the changes observed in the criteria of merit (see Campbell 1969). Hence, inferences about causal connections are necessarily implied by Scriven's concept of measurement.

For Scriven (1980), valuing is not complete until a fourth step has been made and a final synthesis about merit has been achieved. Since all synthesis requires weighting criteria and then summing them, measurements have to be converted into a common metric. Benefit-cost analysis attempts to do this by converting all program inputs and outputs into money terms so that the ratio of costs to benefits can be computed. However, it is difficult to assign a monetary value to outcomes such as increased marital happiness, decreased fear of crime, or higher self-concept, and so the weighting schemes used in benefit-cost analysis are especially assumption-riddled at their core. Consequently, some economists in evaluation prefer cost-effectiveness analysis (Levin 1983). This also requires converting program inputs into monetary terms; but unlike with benefit-cost analysis, effects and impacts are left in the original metric so that statements can be made about how much financial input is required to cause a particular unit of change in any outcome. Syntheses of individual studies can also be achieved through descriptive weighting techniques that measure the values of the persons who might eventually use the evaluation results and then using these values to assign different weights to different patterns of results. The most common methods for doing this are Bayesian but are rarely used today (Edwards et al 1975).

It would be wrong to think of synthesis as being restricted to a single evaluation. Because it puts all effect size estimates onto the same standardized scale, metaanalysis (Glass et al 1981) has been widely used in recent years to synthesize results across multiple evaluations of a program, project, or element. Metaanalysis permits evaluators to escape from the limitations of statistical power and contextual uniqueness that attend single studies, but it also requires assumptions about weights, especially as concerns weighting effect sizes by the sample sizes used to achieve them and weighting studies by the quality of their methodology. Considerable interest has been shown recently in techniques for qualitatively integrating single evaluative studies into the findings from earlier research and into the knowledge base of professional wisdom (see Cronbach et al 1980). Like metaanalysis, qualitative integration techniques can help in drawing conclusions about the robustness of findings, in identifying situational or personological factors on which effect sizes might depend, and in providing a more comprehensive picture of an evaluand's total influence by adding information about important variables that were left out of a particular evaluation.

Evaluators do not seem to be very concerned with methods for synthesizing results, particularly across different outcome constructs. Cronbach (1982) argues that separate conclusions should be presented for each criterion, because different conclusions warrant different degrees of confidence, and individual conclusions are less likely to be challenged if they stand alone than if they are part of a criterion synthesis that depends on a weighting system with which some stakeholders will disagree. Moreover, letting each conclusion stand by itself gives readers the chance to assign their own weights to findings, perhaps eventually coming to an overall conclusion that differs from the evaluator's. After all, very tall readers of automobile evaluations in *Consumer Reports* are likely to weight front leg room more highly than the magazine's staff, and so are likely to buy different cars! Evaluators can reduce the problem of parochial weighting by constructing multiple value positions—often representing different stakeholder groups—from which different sets of weights can be generated. For example, Cook et al's (1975) review of data on *Sesame Street* resulted in the conclusion that if one values learning about two or three letters of the alphabet in six months, and if one does not object to the fact that economically advantaged children learn more from *Sesame Street* in the aggregate than disadvantaged children, then *Sesame Street* is good; but if one objects to either of these premises, then the program is not good.

Yet despite these reasons for not constructing a single system of weights and summing across criteria, it is worth noting that both benefit-cost and metaanalysis have proven spectacularly appealing in the world of public policy, probably because they lead to simple, quantified results that are general in application, can be readily remembered, and are not hindered by multiple caveats. Perhaps the lesson to be learned is that while a good overall synthesis may be compatible with the political system's struggle for simple answers to complex issues, individual findings need nonetheless to be respected so that those who can justify a unique weighting system can construct their own syntheses.

KNOWLEDGE BASE ABOUT CONSTRUCTING VALID KNOWLEDGE

Concepts

Like most social science, evaluation originally looked to versions of logical positivism to justify method choices. Congruent with this was a preference for using program goals to formulate causal hypotheses which could then be tested using experiments (Suchman 1967, Campbell 1969). This strategy assumes that programs are relatively homogeneous, have goals that are totally explicit, postulate effects that can be validly measured, and can be assessed using feasible experimental designs that rule out all spurious interpretations of a treatment effect. All these assumptions have come under attack, not only in evaluation, but also in science at large. Of special importance are three themes that Kuhn (1962, 1970) has popularized: 1. since all observations are theory-laden, no "objective" measurement is possible; 2. since all theories are incommensurable and "squishy," disconfirming evidence can always be rejected; and 3. being conducted by humans, science relies heavily on intuition and background knowledge, sometimes preferring theories on aesthetic or social grounds rather than strictly logical ones.

These attacks were especially relevant to evaluation. Realization of the vague, contradictory, and latent nature of program goals made it questionable to assume that goals could function like theoretical hypotheses. Of the alternative sources of evaluative issues that were forwarded, some did not necessarily imply the primacy of causal analysis that is built into the hypothetico-deductive model. For instance, from a pluralist perspective on question formulation, multiple stakeholders should be consulted to learn of their information needs. Program managers constitute one relevant stakeholder group, and because they are held accountable for the smooth operation of programs, they are more likely to be interested in the more descriptive issues of targeting and implementation than in the more inferential and causal issues associated with assessing effects and impacts. A further justification for deemphasizing the description of causal connections came from the ambiguity of results from evaluations of the early Great Society programs. Did these programs achieve so little because of 1. deficiencies in the substantive theories that buttressed program design, 2. the operational activities constituted poor representation of core theoretical constructs, or 3. the evaluations were too insensitive to detect the smaller-than-expected effects that actually occurred? Such uncertainty led to more emphasis on describing program and project activities, justifying the wider use of implementation measures and of theoretical excursions into the "black box."

While experiments probe causal connections between manipulanda and outcomes, they cannot by themselves explain why a treatment is or is not effective. Causal explanation requires a description of program process and the identification of those factors that are necessary and sufficient for the causally efficacious components of a program to influence the causally affected components of effect and impact measures. Full explanation of why a program achieves its effects is extremely useful because it specifies the factors that have to be present if a program or project is to be effective when transferred elsewhere (Cronbach 1982). As program descriptions revealed more variability than had been expected both within and between projects, the need for explanatory knowledge as a guide to transfer became all the more obvious. By 1985, explaining effects (or non-effects) had a higher profile than describing them, especially for Cronbach (1982), Guba & Lincoln (1981), and Rossi & Freeman (1982).

More sensitivity also developed to the utility of letting evaluation issues emerge from intensive on-site knowledge as opposed to formulating them prior to data collection. While such openness is obviously beneficial for detecting unanticipated side effects, the advocacy of grounded discovery went beyond this (Patton 1978, Guba & Lincoln 1981). Since programs are evolving entities characterized by considerable local discretion in the form and scheduling of services, it is presumptuous of evaluators either to maintain they know in advance the most useful research questions to ask or to believe that the issues of greatest importance at the beginning of a study will remain so by its end. Since they assume a nonstationary target for evaluation, some evaluation theorists have rejected quantitative research altogether and have turned to qualitative methods. Their expectation is that intensive on-site observation and interviews will lead to the formulation of explanatory hypotheses about process and effects that can be iteratively tested and reformulated in the field until a satisfactory fit is achieved between the data and the explanation. This rationale is based on the use of both ethnographic and hermeneutic techniques (Habermas 1972, Dunn 1982), with the latter being particularly used to provide closure on the interpretations of events. Ethnographers and hermeneuticists make quite different epistemological assumptions from those of quantitative social scientists who prefer a hypothetico-deductive research strategy based on prespecified program goals and formal experimental designs.

By 1985, the world evaluators assumed what they were studying was no longer universally considered to be real and consisting of simple causal connections from programs to outcomes, as the work of Suchman (1967) and Campbell (1969) had implied. Some evaluators abjured realism in favor of an idealism which emphasized how humans cognitively create their own worlds and, in communicating their creations to others, help generate a shared social reality whose links to the outside world are unclear. Indeed, if one assumes humans respond to social constructions of the world rather than to the world itself (Patton 1978, Guba & Lincoln 1981), then the whole issue of how these cognitive links relate to reality is of no practical interest. Even among those scholars who retained realist assumptions, their ontological world view changed. It came to encompass a multivariate world of complex, interdependent causal forces rather than a simpler world of bivariate pushes and pulls. As with epistemological options, the ontological options from which evaluators had to select in 1985 were far more numerous and diverse than 20 years earlier.

New options for knowledge construction also followed from attacks on the positivist assumption that theory-neutral measurement is possible. The attacks came mainly from those historians and sociologists of science who illustrated how scientific observation is theory-impregnated 1. in the choice of constructs, 2. in the way constructs are conceptually "defined," 3. in the theoretical irrelevancies operational representations contain, 4. in the theory components particular operational instances fail to include, and 5. in the weights implicitly assigned to factors in the multidimensional measures that social scientists invariably use. These attacks led nearly all evaluators into some form of fallibilism, often taking the form of a critical multiplism that justified the selection of multiple operations, multiple methods, and the integration of any one study into the (usually) multiple relevant studies that had preceded it (Cook 1985). In cases where observational practice did not change because of the attacks on theory-neutral measurement, many evaluators must have felt less certain about their results, especially after receiving commentary on them, for the commentary often occurred in a context of cacophonous dispute about the constructs selected (and not selected) for measurement and about the ways particular measures were constructed (Lindblom & Cohen 1979). The attacks on "objective" measurement also caused some evaluators to firm their belief that anthropology and journalism, rather than experimental psychology (Guba & Lincoln 1981), should provide the appropriate models for constructing knowledge in evaluation.

Claims also began to surface that evaluation should abjure not only positivist forms of constructing knowledge but also traditional scientific standards of inference. Cronbach (1980, 1982) asserted that the potential users of evaluation are less concerned than academics with reducing the final few grains of uncertainty about knowledge claims; that prospective users are also more willing to trust their own experience and tacit knowledge for ruling out validity threats; and that they also expect to act upon whatever knowledge base is available, however serious its deficiencies. Like Rossi & Freeman (1982), Cronbach maintained that each evaluation should seek to generate many findings, even at the cost of achieving less certainty about any one of them. In his own terminology, "bandwidth" should be preferred over "fidelity."

Cronbach particularly objected to the traditional scientific preference for resolving method trade-offs in favor of enhancing internal validity or external validity defined as generalizing from the samples of persons, settings, times, and constructs studied to the target universes they are meant to represent. Cronbach favors making method trade-offs so as to enhance his own conception of external validity which is based on generalizing from the samples achieved in a study to populations with different characteristics from those of the samples studied. Cronbach justifies this preference on two grounds. First, social programs are so heterogeneous that sampling plans cannot by themselves provide knowledge that is demonstrably applicable to the unique characteristics of single projects, particularly those not yet studied. Second, evaluation results tend to be used in mostly unexpected ways that speak less to "instrumental usage" than to the "enlightenment" associated with generalized explanatory knowledge about practical procedures and substantive theories that are more or less successful and that might therefore guide transfer to other projects and programs.

Knowledge Methods

In the 1960s the methods for acquiring knowledge from evaluation could have been laid out according to something like the following schema: 1. The most important questions in evaluation concern the causal consequences of programs or projects. To examine such consequences, randomized experiments should be used or, failing this, strong quasi-experiments based on interrupted time-series or regression-discontinuity designs. 2. Since it is sometimes important to make general causal statements, evaluators should try to sample people and settings at random. If this is not possible—as will often be the case—the samples should at least be heterogeneous in composition so that final inferences are not restricted to a small range of settings and persons. 3. For those who insist on causal explanation—as opposed to descriptive causal connections—substantive theory should be used to identify the constructs worth measuring and then some form of causal modeling should be carried out. If such modeling is not possible, one should at least "correlate" each potential explanatory construct with the degree of change obtained on major effect and impact measures.

By 1985, the experiment had lost its hegemony. In part this was because of the increased importance of noncausal issues and of questions about causal explanation for which the experiment was not designed. The loss in hegemony was also the result of a growing awareness of the limitations of experimentation. Randomized experiments came under attack because (a) they are only relevant to causal forces that can be manipulated; (b) ethical and political concerns sometimes preclude assignment by lottery in favor of assignment by need, merit, or "first come, first served"; (c) because most social programs are ameliorative in intent and provide valued treatments, attrition is often treatment-related and so violates the most critical assumption of all experimentation that the various treatment groups are probabilistically equivalent on all characteristics other than treatment assignment; and (d) respondents in one group may sometimes compare the treatment they receive with what others receive, leading to compensatory rivalry, resentful demoralization, treatment diffusion, or compensatory equalization (Cook & Campbell 1979). Quasi-experiments also came under attack, mostly from advocates of randomized experimentation who focused on the quasi-experimental design most used in evaluation that requires pretest and posttest data from treatment groups that are initially nonequivalent. Critics maintained that equivocal causal inferences usually result from this design because the processes leading to treatment-related selection are rarely, if ever, completely understood and so cannot be statistically modeled with confidence. The disturbing possibility was also noted that in some substantive areas a single source of selection bias may plague all the evaluations conducted, creating an impressive convergence of results on the same wrong answer (Campbell & Boruch 1975)!

Probably as important as awareness of the limitations of experimental methods were claims that alternative methods existed that could fulfill the experiment's function of probing causal connections while simultaneously probing other evaluation-relevant issues. Within quantitative traditions, the challenge to experiments came principally from causal modeling, especially in the latent trait models exemplified by LISREL and in the econometric methods developed by Heckman (1980) that have recently come under attack (Lalonde 1985, Murnane et al 1985). Within the more qualitative tradition, the challenge came from case studies (Yin 1985), especially after Campbell (1975) pointed out that a case study with multiple dependent variables could under certain (rare) conditions achieve a pattern of results fit by only one causal explanation. The desirability of alternatives to the experiment increased because they seemed more generally applicable, more flexible in the types of knowledge achieved, and hardly worse for facilitating inferences about causal connections.

The preference for functionally plastic methods also influenced how causal explanations came to be studied. Primitive forms of causal modeling were espoused in the late 1960s, principally multiple regression. More sophisticated, maximum-likelihood models came to be preferred later, partly because they are sensitive to issues of unreliability and partial invalidity of measurement and partly because they are capable of simultaneously interrelating client characteristics, program inputs, program processes, third variable spurious causes, and intended outcomes measured at different points along a distal time chain (Flay & Cook 1982). However, quantitative causal modeling does not provide the only means for explaining program results. Advocates of qualitative research emphasize the explanatory knowledge that can emerge from juxtaposing prior knowledge, expert opinion, practitioner belief, logical analysis, and qualitative knowledge acquired on site, and to these Cronbach adds knowledge gained from quantitative studies relating input, process, and outcome variables. It is also possible to extend the sampling and measurement frameworks of most experiments so as to probe issues of process in addition to issues of causal connections. Ironically, the form of analysis that results from such an extension involves the very same explanatory modeling techniques that are advocated for nonexperimental data! Since multiple method options are now available for studying causal explanation, the formerly preferred option based on the quantitative causal modeling of process and other forms of contingency has lost its hegemony, though not to the same extent that experiments have lost theirs in the area of probing causal connections.

We turn now to the task of constructing generalized knowledge. The initially preferred techniques required sampling with known probability from some clearly designated universe, but it is difficult to define some types of universe, particularly when historical times or physical situations are at issue. Also, the variability between projects, and between clients and practitioners within projects, requires that samples have to be "large" (and hence more expensive) if formal representativeness is to be achieved within "reasonable" limits.

For both reasons, the respectability of various forms of purposive sampling increased, particularly those that emphasize selecting instances from within a population that is either presumptively modal or manifestly heterogeneous. The rationale for selecting modal instances is to ascertain whether causal relationships can be generalized to the most frequently occurring types of persons or settings. One rationale for selecting heterogeneous instances is to probe whether a causal relationship can be inferred despite the heterogeneity in respondents and settings; the other is to analyze whether similar findings are obtained when different subgroups of persons and settings are separately examined (Cook & Campbell 1979). It is only a small step from haphazard heterogeneous sampling within individual studies to metaanalysis and its unsystematic sampling of studies that are heterogeneous on many important attributes. Formally, metaanalysis assumes that the achieved effect sizes under review constitute a random sample of all the effect sizes that could have been achieved with a particular class of treatment. Since this assumption cannot be sensitively tested, metaanalysts actually operate on the less restrictive assumption that the effect sizes under review come from a less formally representative set of studies with considerable heterogeneity in the populations and settings sampled. This makes the generalization metaanalysis achieves more like a product of purposive sampling than of formal random sampling.

Generalization is not only a product of sampling strategies. As Cronbach (1982) emphasizes, it is also a product of causal explanation. The more we know about the plethora of contingencies on which program or project effectiveness depends, the more likely it is that we will be able to transfer successful practices to other sites that have not yet been studied. As the realization grew that generalization can follow from a number of different sampling procedures and from theoretical explanation, so it became clearer that multiple methods exist for generalizing. As a result, the initially favorite method based on random selection lost its hegemony.

When we turn to a fourth research function—discovering novel issues and questions—the degree of functional blurring between methods is not as noticeable as it is with causal issues and generalization. Intensive on-site observation and interviews have always been preferred for gaining knowledge that could not have been preformulated as hypotheses. These methods remained the distinct favorites. What changed with time were attitudes about the priority that discovery deserved, probably because of the demise of the goal-centered approaches to evaluation that had implicitly devalued discovery in favor of hypothesis testing. What also changed was appreciation of the functional plasticity of the methods advocated for discovery, given the way Yin (1985) and Campbell (1975) linked intensive on-site knowledge to causal connections and the way Cronbach (1982) linked it to the causal explanation he favors for evaluation.

It would be wrong to leave the impression that over the 20 years since Suchman's (1967) advocacy of causal questions and experimental designs, the only changes in thinking about methods has been to blur former certainties about question and method preferences and to raise the priority accorded to discovery and causal explanation. Two other changes are worth comment. First, growing consciousness of the inevitable fallibility of observation is reflected, not only in the growth of multiplist methods of data collection, but also in the advocacy of multiple investigators analyzing the same data set and in the advocacy of data analysis in more of an exploratory than confirmatory mode. In this last regard, a philosophy of data analysis akin to Tukey's (1977) seems to be taking hold in the more quantitative tradition within evaluation, with individual substantive issues being approached several different ways predicated upon different methodological and substantive assumptions. While the popularity of confirmatory factor analytic models like LISREL seems to be an exception, even here the advocated strategy is to pit multiple models against each other and to measure each construct in several different ways, creating a more exploratory flavor than when the data are used to generate a single best-fit model and there is only one measure for most of the constructs in the model. An analogous development in the more qualitative tradition is that multiple observers are now advocated for each site instead of single observers, and in some research where this has been done the observers have honestly struggled to reconcile the different interpretations that resulted (e.g. Stake & Easley 1978). There are even some cases where both qualitative and quantitative methods were used in the same study and at first seemed to generate results that had different implications for the overall evaluation conclusion, leading to a creative tension that was only resolved after many iterations (Trend 1978). Whatever the data collection mode, multiple tentative probes seem now to be the watchword, replacing older and more positivist conceptions based on theory-free observation, single definitive tests, and crucial single studies.

The recognition that evaluation has both social and logical components and is built upon necessarily fallible methods has been associated with increased interest in methods for making evaluations more critical in the questions and methods selected for study. Among the methods advocated to increase the critical component are commentaries on research plans by heterogeneous groups of experts and other stakeholders; more extensive monitoring of the implementation of evaluations by federal program officers and scientific advisory groups; calls for the simultaneous funding of several independent evaluations of the same program, project, or element; recommendations to conduct secondary analyses of collected data; and the advocacy of including in final evaluation reports comments by personnel from the program evaluated (Hennigan et al 1980). Also heard have been calls to force out the latent assumptions behind evaluation designs and the interpretations offered for results, usually through some form of adversarial legal process or through a committee of substantive experts (Cronbach 1982). All evaluations can be evaluated according to publicly justifiable criteria of merit and standards of performance, and data can be collected to determine how good an evaluation is. The need for metaevaluation (Cook 1974) implies a frank recognition of the limitations of all social science methods, including evaluation.

THEORIES OF EVALUATION PRACTICE

At a minimum, a theory of evaluation practice should use logic and the last 20 years of experience with evaluation to specify and justify the types of knowledge that are supposed to have leverage because it is presumed they will help improve social programs and ameliorate social problems. A theory of practice should also use the 20 years of experience to specify critically assessed and practical methods that are relevant to the types of knowledge presumed to have most leverage. Such a theory should also detail the most productive roles evaluators can play in furthering the conduct of evaluations that are likely to be used in one of the many ways usage is now understood. But that is not enough. A theory of practice should also use past experience to highlight the constraints under which evaluators will most likely have to work—constraints of budget, time, staff capabilities, and sponsor sophistication about evaluation—for these constraints independently influence the issues, methods, and roles that can be selected for a particular evaluation assignment. Finally, a theory of evaluation practice has to be detailed about the steps to follow in physically conducting an evaluation once issues with leverage have been determined, general stances about methods and roles have been adopted, and constraints have been fully understood. All evaluations require that plans for sampling, measurement, and data collection have to be implemented, and a theory of practice should describe the options available for each of these tasks. In particular, it should outline the strengths and weaknesses of each option, the trade-offs between them, the signs that indicate when a preferred option is being inadequately implemented, and the fallback positions that are available should a breakdown occur in implementing some option. Since we cannot discuss all these issues in the space available, we will concentrate only on the most general level of discussion of evaluation practice in the literature. Fortunately, many of the lower-order issues can be inferred from the more general.

All the theorists discussed here agree that evaluation should help ameliorate social problems; but they disagree about what evaluators ought to do to achieve that purpose. All seem to take one of three general approaches to prescribing evaluation practice, which we might call approaches based on 1. "identifying manipulable solutions," 2. "identifying generalizable explanations," and 3. "providing stakeholder service." Most of the differences among the approaches are related to specific disagreements about one or more of the knowledge bases covered in this chapter, although the differences are sometimes more implicit than explicit in the writings of particular theorists. Nonetheless, we will attempt to make the most important differences explicit so that they can be publicly scrutinized on logical and empirical grounds, for this should eventually help assess their relative strengths and weaknesses as guides to evaluation practice.

Campbell's (1969, 1971) experimenting society and Scriven's (1983) consumer model of evaluation epitomize the "manipulable solution" approach. This mounts a frontal assault on social problems by orienting evaluation toward the discovery of manipulable solutions, postulating that it is far less important to know how and why purported solutions work than to know to what extent they work. Campbell and Scriven view evaluation as a service in the "public interest" more than in the interests of specific stakeholders; they place a premium on studying multiple potential solutions to a problem so as to increase the chances of discovering one that works or of discovering the most efficient; they emphasize truth about effects over reducing uncertainty about elements that might improve a program; and their concern with effectiveness leads them to be most explicit about methods for causal inference and about the selection of criteria that speak to obvious social needs. Finally, they believe that the political and economic system should determine how an effective solution is used, with the evaluator playing only a small role in this process.

The "manipulable solution" approach was dominant in the early years of social program evaluation, but its popularity is currently on the wane. This is largely because of the purported disconfirmation of its most crucial single assumption: that novel solutions to problems can be readily identified through the use of evaluative techniques. Randomized experiments and planned variation studies were advocated for this purpose, but early experience suggested that they were fundamentally flawed as models for evaluation practice. A second crucial assumption of the manipulable solution approach is that, once identified, novel solutions will be widely disseminated through society. Once again, experience indicated that dissemination and adoption are not so easy in the real world of social programming. The approach also tends to relegate analyses of program implementation and causal mediation to a subordinate position; but some interpretations of experience during the past 20 years suggest that analyses of implementation and causal mediation are crucial in evaluation for they promote explanation, and explanation may be crucial for the transfer of evaluation findings to new settings and populations. Moreover, empirical studies of use suggest that the restricted role evaluators are urged to adopt by Campbell and Scriven may not facilitate evaluation results being used, especially in the short term. By the middle 1970s, the assumptions buttressing the "manipulable solution" approach were under heavy attack, and alternative models for social program evaluation were beginning to be formulated.

Cronbach (1982) and the later writings of both Rossi (Chen & Rossi 1980, 1983) and Weiss (1977, 1978) represent the generalized explanation alternative. Where manipulability theorists believe that many solutions will be robust enough in their effects that it will be rare to discover negative relationships within any of the subpopulations of relevance, explanatory theorists believe that the world is so ontologically complex that it is best described, not in terms of simple main effects, but in terms of higher-order statistical interactions which indicate that a particular effect may be present under some conditions but absent or reversed under others. Hence, knowledge of the complex interrelationships among multiple causal determinants is believed necessary for generalizability and for transferring findings from the samples studied to other projects in a program. Where manipulability theorists believe that the implementation of identified solutions can proceed smoothly, explanatory theorists contend that such instrumental usage is far less likely than enlightenment and that if it is to be useful, instrumental use must occur at the site of local service delivery rather than in the offices of central program officials.

Where manipulability theorists believe that summative questions about effects and impacts are sufficient to justify evaluation, generalizability theorists seek to achieve some uncertainty reduction about many questions of many different forms. Descriptions of causal connections constitute only one such form. Thus, they also tend to deal with issues of implementation, targeting, or costs in both an explanatory and descriptive mode, preferring methods that are functionally plastic over methods developed for highly specific purposes. Above all, theorists of generalizable explanation seek to test the substantive theory that underlies the program so as to achieve a complete understanding of all its operations and consequences. This emphasis on "enlightenment" and "demystification" favors external validity in Cronbach's sense over internal validity, and it stresses multivariate causal models over simple causal connections from a program variable to effects.

The generalizable explanation approach requires great fath in our ability to construct social theories that relate program inputs, processes, and effects. It also assumes that generalizable knowledge facilitates the transfer of knowledge to such an extent that social problems are eventually ameliorated. Moreover, in placing a higher premium on explanation than description, evaluators may expend considerable effort explaining complex causal relationships in which the basic causal connection between the evaluand and a major outcome is not itself well justified. And Cronbach's exhortation—which Rossi does not seem to share—that evaluators should adopt lower inferential standards than academics flies in the face of some case study findings which suggest that decision makers at the federal level ask social scientists for findings that are beyond reproach, believing these to be the only findings they can effectively use in the political process (Boeckman 1974).

As represented by Wholey's (1983) management-centered evaluation, Stake's (Stake & Easley 1978) responsive evaluation, and Patton's (1978) utilization-focused evaluation, proponents of the "stakeholder service" approach postulate that evaluations will ameliorate social problems only if they are explicitly tailored to the information needs of stakeholders who have close relationships with the specific projects or programs being evaluated. Theorists who take this approach subordinate all other aspects of evaluation to producing usable information for stakeholders, although they differ as to who those stakeholders should be. Wholey and Patton focus mostly on program managers, probably reasoning that they have more responsibility for changes in social programming than any other actors. But Stake, and Guba & Lincoln (1981), try to serve a broader array of stakeholders that includes managers, program clients, service providers, and local boards. However, all the theorists who adopt a stakeholders service approach agree that evaluations should not be concerned with generalizing evaluation findings to other programs or projects. The priority is on the particular program or project under highly particularistic study. Theorists who favor this approach want stakeholders to play the major role in deciding on problems, questions, and interventions, with the evaluator serving as a consciousness-raising educator. They also prefer methods that provide quick answers to a wide array of questions rather than methods that might provide higher quality answers to a narrower set of questions. They also seek to maintain close contact with the evaluation clients at all times so as to be responsive to their changing needs and to maximize the eventual use of the results.

Adherents of the stakeholder service approach criticize other theorists on several grounds. One is for being too concerned with traditional social science theory and methodology at the expense of serving individuals and groups with a direct stake in a program or project. Another is for concocting an ephemeral "public interest" that serves to justify particular evaluator stances but is divorced from real people with real information needs. A third is for being insufficiently concerned with providing rapid results that can be profitably used in the short term. And a final criticism is for presuming that they can construct better understandings of social problems and social programs than service-providers who have much more frequent and direct contact with clients and with the social world from which these clients come.

Several criticisms of the "stakeholder service" approach can be made. First, its connection to social problem solving is dependent on locating a stakeholder who wants information about important social problems and their solution. But stakeholders may ask uninformed, trivial, or self-centered questions, and the resulting information, while usable, may have minimal relevance to important social problems. Second, the idea that the evaluator will often educate stakeholders to ask better questions and want better methodology will sometimes be inconsistent with political and economic realities. Practicing evaluators make their living by securing contracts, and those who contract with evaluators are free to give future work to other evaluators if they do not like the education current contractors are providing. Finally, the trade-offs between the accuracy, timeliness, and comprehensiveness of results are not yet well known, but adherents of the stakeholders service approach run the risk of providing timely information that is wrong in its claims or is misleading because of its incompleteness.

It is not yet possible to judge the merit of these three approaches to evaluation practice. For one thing, proponents often speak as if they were inevitably distinct. However, the manipulable solution approach comes close to the generalized explanation approach once evaluation uses formal sampling, metaanalysis, simultaneous replications, or other methods yet being developed (Cook et al 1985) in order to identify main effects that are demonstrably robust. Similarly, the stakeholder service approach can regain a focus on social problem solving through an informed choice of stakeholders, for some stakeholders are more actively concerned with social problem solving than others. For instance, when members of Congressional committees request evaluations from the General Accounting Office, the resulting work will often have a clearer link to acts that might help ameliorate important social problems on a broad scale than would be the case if a local project manager asked an evaluator to upgrade his record-keeping system for billing purposes.

It is also difficult to choose between these three approaches to evaluation practice because data-based argumentation is still sadly lacking. Advocates of the generalizable explanation approach depend heavily on the assumption that short-term instrumental usage is rare, but there is some empirical evidence to the contrary (Leviton and Boruch 1983). The techniques that Wholey has promoted for so long rely heavily on stimulating short-term use by program managers. Would they have continued funding such work for so long if it were not useful in some immediate way? Advocates of both the generalized solution and the stakeholder service approaches write as though failures of randomized experiments and planned variation studies are well documented. While their arguments are well taken, it may nonetheless be premature to conclude that the experimental option in evaluation is dead, especially if the early failures of social experiments were due as much to inexperience in implementing the research designs as to any intrinsic limitations randomized experiments are supposed to have. Indeed, recent successful experiments with multiple planned variations warrant more study than they have had in order to determine the conditions under which such efforts can be undertaken fruitfully (Cook 1986). A similar need for data applies to most other arguments in the field. Do case studies really foster use in readers, and if so, of what kind? What loss in accuracy is incurred from the use of "quick and dirty" methods for providing fast feedback? How educable are evaluation clients in the question formation process? Where does nontrivial social change take place in social systems, and how can it be catalyzed by evaluation? How accurate are the inferences about causal connections produced by different methods? Evaluation theorists should be no different from other social science theorists in subjecting their claims and counterclaims to logical and empirical scrutiny.

Our brief discussion of the relative merits of these three approaches should not mislead the reader into thinking that evaluators ought to be choosing from among them. Proponents of each approach provide intelligent and often persuasive arguments in favor of their different positions on the same issue. Indeed, it is sometimes easy to believe that all of them may be correct and that the positions appear inconsistent only because our theories of evaluation are not yet complex enough to specify the contingencies that will eventually lead to integrating the apparent disagreements. It may be that our classification scheme overlooked some more integrative approaches to evaluation that go beyond the theories we analyzed, although the partial similarity of our scheme to others (e.g. Stufflebeam & Shinkfield 1985) leads us to be optimistic that our sins of omission are few and minor. Rather than encouraging evaluators to choose any one approach, we hope that the present discussion will encourage them to get to know each approach on its own terms; to explore how well each is grounded in the knowledge bases we outlined; to seek ways to resolve apparent differences between the approaches; and to base their practice choices on considerations from each approach instead of relying exclusively on a single one.

CONCLUSION

Our review of the field of evaluation leaves us impressed with the intellectual vigor and yield of the many debates in which evaluation theorists are currently engaged. To be sure, the simplicity of the early years of evaluation has been replaced by a complexity that must seem bewildering to some, by a keen sense of the limitations of evaluation and social programming, and by an active search for novel evaluation approaches. All this is consonant with the major lesson of the last 20 years: that program evaluation should be predicated on knowledge about how social programs really operate and use social science information.

In taking this important lesson to heart, our hope is that evaluators will not forget the tasks of knowledge construction and value analysis that loom less salient today because of the emphasis on fitting evaluation into the world of social programs. Evaluation does indeed need to be worldly in the sense of seeing the world of social programs as it really is. However, it also needs to be worldly in the second sense of the term that connotes responding to the world by working hard to achieve such grace and style that, in evaluation's case, it would be rare to generate inaccurate knowledge or place a wrong set of values on research findings. Evaluators must be careful lest knowledge construction and value analysis are drowned in the sea of accommodation to the complexity and intransigence of social programs and to the ways in which program officials do and do not use evaluation findings.

ACKNOWLEDGMENTS

The authors would like to thank the Center for Applied Psychological Research at Memphis State University for providing a congenial and supportive setting in which to write this paper.

Literature Cited

Applied Management Services Inc. 1984. Income verification pilot project Phase II: Results of the quality-assurance evaluation, 1982–1983 school year. 962 Wayne Ave., Silver Spring, MD

Berman, P., McLaughlin, M. W. 1977. *Federal programs supporting educational change.* Vol. 8: *Factors affecting implementation and continuation.* Santa Monica, CA: Rand Corp.

Boeckmann, M. E. 1974. Policy impacts of the New Jersey income maintenance experiment. *Policy Sci.* 7:53–76

Bryk, A. S., ed. 1983. *Stakeholder-Based Evaluation.* San Francisco: Jossey-Bass

Bunker, J. P. 1985. When doctors disagree. *NY Rev. Books* 32:7–12

Campbell, D. T. 1969. Reforms as experiments. *Am. Psychol.* 24:409–28

Campbell, D. T. 1974. Evolutionary epistemology. *The Philosophy of Karl Popper,* ed. P. A. Schilpp, 14:413–63. LaSalle, IL: Open Court Pub.

Campbell, D. T. 1975. "Degrees of freedom" and the case study. *Comp. Polit. Stud.* 8: 178–93

Campbell, D. T., Boruch, R. F. 1975. Making the case for randomized assignment to treatments by considering the alternatives: Six ways in which quasi-experimental evaluations in compensatory education tend to underestimate effects. In *Evaluation and Experiments: Some Critical Issues in Assessing Social Programs*, ed. C. A. Bennett, A. A. Lumsdaine, pp. 195–296. New York: Academic

Chen, H., Rossi, P. H. 1980. The multi-goal, theory-driven approach to evaluation: A model linking basic and applied social science. *Soc. Forces* 59:106–22

Chen, H., Rossi, P. H. 1983. Evaluating with sense: The theory-driven approach. *Eval. Rev.* 7:283–302

Cook, F. L. 1982. Assessing age as an eligibility criterion. In *Age or Need? Public Policies for Older People*, ed. B. L. Neugarten. Beverly Hills, CA: Sage

Cook, T. D. 1974. The potential and limitations of secondary evaluations. In *Educational Evaluation: Analysis and Responsibility*, ed. M. W. Apple, M. J. Subkoviak, H. S. Lufler Jr. Berkeley, CA: McCutchan

Cook, T. D. 1983. Evaluation: Whose questions should be answered? In *Making and Managing Policy: Formulation, Analysis, Evaluation*, ed. G. R. Gilbert. New York: Dekker

Cook, T. D. 1986. Evaluating health education curricula: An exemplary planned variations study that should have failed. *Int. J. Educ.* In press

Cook, T. D. 1985. Post-positivist critical multiplism. In *Social Science and Social Policy*, ed. R. L. Shotland, M. M. Mark. Beverly Hills, CA: Sage

Cook, T. D., Appleton, H., Conner, R. F., Shaffer, A., Tamkin, G., Weber, S. J. 1975. *"Sesame Street" Revisited*. New York: Sage Found.

Cook, T. D., Campbell, D. T. 1979. *Quasi-experimentation: Design and Analysis Issues for Field Settings*. Boston: Houghton Mifflin

Cook, T. D., Curtin, T. R. 1986. An evaluation of the models used to evaluate educational television series. In *Public Communication and Behavior*, ed. G. A. Comstock, New York: Academic. In press

Cook, T. D., Leviton, L. C., Shadish, W. R. 1985. Program evaluation. In *Handbook of Social Psychology*, ed. G. Lindzey, E. Aronson. New York: Random House. 3rd ed.

Cook, T. D., Shadish, W. R. 1982. Metaevaluation: An evaluation of the congressionally-mandated evaluation system for community mental health centers. In *Innovative Approaches to Mental Health Evaluation*, ed. G. Stahler, W. R. Tash. New York: Academic

Cronbach, L. J. 1963. Evaluation for course improvement. *Teachers Coll. Bull.* 64:672–83

Cronbach, L. J. 1982. *Designing Evaluations of Educational and Social Programs*. San Francisco: Jossey-Bass

Cronbach, L. J., Ambron, S. R., Dornbusch, S. M., Hess, R. D., Hornik, R. C., et al. 1980. *Toward Reform of Program Evaluation*. San Francisco: Jossey-Bass

David, J. L. 1982. Local uses of Title I evaluations. In *Evaluation Studies Review Annual*, Vol. 7, ed. E. House. Beverly Hills, CA: Sage

Dunn, W. 1982. Reforms as arguments. *Knowledge: Creation, Diffusion, Utilization* 3:293–326

Edwards, W., Guttentag, M., Snapper, K. 1975. A decision theoretic approach to evaluation research. In *Handbook of Evaluation Research*, Vol. 1. Beverly Hills, CA: Sage

Fairweather, G. W. 1980. *The Fairweather Lodge: A Twenty-five-year Retrospective*. San Francisco: Jossey-Bass

Feeley, M. M., Sarat, A. D. 1980. *The Policy Dilemma: Federal Crime Policy and the Law Enforcement Assistance Administration*. Minneapolis: Univ. Minn. Press

Flay, B. R., Cook, T. D. 1982. The evaluation of mass media prevention campaigns. In *Public Communication Campaigns*, ed. R. E. Rice, W. J. Paisley. Beverly Hills, CA: Sage

Fullan, M. 1982. *The Meaning of Educational Change*. New York: Teachers College Press

Glass, G. V., McGaw, B., Smith, M. L. 1981. *Meta-analysis in Social Research*. Beverly Hills, CA: Sage

Guba, E. G., Lincoln, Y. S. 1981. *Effective Evaluation: Improving the Usefulness of Evaluation Results Through Responsive and Naturalistic Approaches*. San Francisco: Jossey-Bass

Habermas, J. 1972. *Knowledge and Human Interests*. London: Heinemann

Heckman, J. J. 1980. Sample selection bias as a specification error. In *Evaluation Studies Review Annual*, Vol. 5, ed. E. W. Stromsdorfer, G. Farkas. Beverly Hills, CA: Sage

Hennigan, K. M., Flay, B. R., Cook, T. D. 1980. "Give me the facts": The use of social science evidence in formulating national policy. In *Advances in Applied Social Psychology*, Vol. 1, ed. R. F. Kidd, M. J. Saks. Hillsdale, NJ: Erlbaum

House, E. R. 1980. *Evaluating with Validity*. Beverly Hills, CA: Sage

Kuhn, T. S. 1962. *The Structure of Scientific Revolutions*. Chicago: Univ. Chicago Press. 1st ed.

Kuhn, T. S. 1970. *The Structure of Scientific Revolutions*. Chicago: Univ. Chicago Press. 2nd ed.

Lalonde, R. J. 1985. Evaluating the econometric evaluations of training programs with experimental data, Working Pap. 183, Industrial Relations Section. Princeton, NJ: Princeton Univ.

Levin, H. M. 1983. *Cost-effectiveness: A Primer*. Beverly Hills, CA: Sage

Leviton, L. C., Boruch, R. F. 1983. Contributions of evaluation to education programs and policy. *Eval. Rev.* 7:563–98

Leviton, L. C., Boruch, R. F. 1984. Why compensatory education evaluation was useful. *J. Policy Anal. Manage.* 3:299–305

Leviton, L. C., Cook, T. D. 1984. Use of evaluations in textbooks in education and social work. *Eval. Rev.* 7:497–518

Leviton, L. C., Hughes, E. F. X. 1981. Research on the utilization of evaluations: Review and synthesis. *Eval. Rev.* 5:528–48

Light, R. J. 1983. *Evaluation Studies Review Annual*, Vol. 8. Beverly Hills, CA: Sage

Light, R. J., Pillemer, D. B. 1984. *Summing Up: The Science of Reviewing Research*. Cambridge, MA: Harvard Univ. Press

Lindblom, C. E. 1977. *Politics and Markets: The World's Political and Economic Systems*. New York: Basic Books

Lindblom, C. E., Cohen, D. K. 1979. *Usable Knowledge: Social Science and Social Problem Solving*. New Haven, CT: Yale Univ. Press

McLaughlin, M. W. 1985. Implementation realities and evaluation design. In *Social Science and Social Policy*, ed. R. L. Shotland, M. M. Mark. Beverly Hills, CA: Sage

Mielke, K. W., Chen, M. 1981. *Children, Television and Science: An overview of the formative research for 3-2-1 contact*. New York: Children's Television Workshop

Murnane, R. J., Newstead, S., Olsen, R. J. 1985. Comparing public and private schools: The puzzling role of selectivity bias. *J. Bus. Econ. Stat.* 3:23–35

Nozick, R. 1974. *Anarchy, State, and Utopia*. New York: Basic Books

Pacht, A. R., Bent, R., Cook, T. D., Klebanoff, L. B., Rodgers, D. A., et al. 1980. Continuing evaluation and accountability controls for a national health insurance program. *Am. Psychol.* 33:305–13

Patton, M. Q. 1978. *Utilization-Focused Evaluation*. Beverly Hills, CA: Sage

Rawls, J. 1971. *A Theory of Justice*. Cambridge, MA: Harvard Univ. Press

Rossi, P. H., Freeman, H. E. 1982. *Evaluation: A Systematic Approach*. Beverly Hills, CA: Sage. 2nd ed.

Rossi, P. H., Lyall, K. C. 1976. *Reforming Public Welfare: A Critique of the Negative Income Tax Experiment*. New York: Sage Found.

Scriven, M. S. 1980. *The Logic of Evaluation*. Inverness, CA: Edgepress

Scriven, M. S. 1983. Evaluation ideologies. In *Evaluation Models: Viewpoints on Educational and Human Services Evaluation*, ed. G. F. Madaus, M. Scriven, D. L. Stufflebeam. Boston, MA: Kluwer-Nijhoff

Sechrest, L., West, S. G., Phillips, M. A., Redner, R., Yeaton, W. 1979. Some neglected problems in evaluation research: Strength and integrity of treatments. In *Evaluation Studies Review Annual*, Vol. 4, ed. L. Sechrest, S. G. West, M. A. Phillips, R. Redner, W. Yeaton. Beverly Hills, CA: Sage

Shadish, W. R. 1984. Policy research: Lessons from the implementation of deinstitutionalization. *Am. Psychol.* 39:725–38

Stake, R. E. 1982. A peer response: A review of "Program Evaluation in Education": When? How? To what ends? In *Evaluation Studies Review Annual*, Vol. 7, ed. E. R. House. Beverly Hills, CA: Sage

Stake, R. E., Easley, J. A. 1978. *Case Studies in Science Education*. Champaign: Univ. Ill. Cent. Instruct. Res. Curriculum Eval., and Comm. on Cult. Cognit.

Stufflebeam, D. L., Shinkfield, A. J. 1985. *Systematic Evaluation*. Boston, MA: Kluwer-Nijhoff

Suchman, E. 1967. *Evaluative Research*. New York: Sage Found.

Trend, M. G. 1978. On the reconciliation of qualitative and quantitative analyses: A case study. *Hum. Organ.* 37:345–54

Tukey, J. W. 1977. *Exploratory Data Analysis*. Reading, MA: Addison-Wesley

Warnock, G. J. 1971. *The Object of Morality*. London: Methuen

Weiss, C. H. 1972. *Evaluation Research: Methods for Assessing Program Effectiveness*. Englewood Cliffs, NJ: Prentice-Hall

Weiss, C. H. 1977. Research for policy's sake: The enlightenment function of social research. *Policy Anal.* 3:531–45

Weiss, C. H. 1978. Improving the linkage between social research and public policy. In *Knowledge and Policy: The Uncertain Connection*, ed. L. E. Lynn. Washington, DC: Natl. Acad. Sci.

Weiss, C. H. 1980. Knowledge creep and decision accretion. *Knowledge: Creation, Diffusion, Utilization* 1:381–404

Weiss, R. S., Rein, M. 1970. The evaluation of broad-aim programs: Experimental design, its difficulties, and an alternative. *Admin. Sci. Organ.* 15:97–113

Wholey, J. S. 1983. *Evaluation and Effective Public Management*. Boston, MA: Little Brown

Williams, W. 1980. *The Implementation Perspective*. Berkeley: Univ. Calif. Press

Yin, R. K. 1985. *Case Study Research: Design and Methods*. Beverly Hills, CA: Sage

Ann. Rev. Psychol. 1986. 37:233-56

EXPECTANCIES AND INTERPERSONAL PROCESSES

Dale T. Miller and William Turnbull

Department of Psychology, Simon Fraser University, Burnaby, British Columbia, Canada, V5A 1S6

CONTENTS

INTRODUCTION 233
BEHAVIORAL INFLUENCES 234
    Self-Fulfilling Prophecies 234
    Self-Disconfirming Prophecies 238
MEDIATING LINKS 238
    Perceiver Expectancy and Behavior 238
    Target Response 241
    Summary 243
PROCESSING TARGET BEHAVIOR 244
    Perceptual and Behavioral Combinations 244
    Perceptual Confirmation 246
SELF-CONCEPT CHANGE 248
    Psychological Model 249
    Sociological Model 250
CONCLUSION 250
    Interaction and Coaction Effects 251
    Limits of Expectancy Effects 251

INTRODUCTION

We rarely interact with others without at least some expectancies about how they will act or perform. Expectancies derive from beliefs about demographic characteristics, such as age, gender, and ethnicity, and more individuating characteristics, such as personality traits, previous actions, and past experiences. Social psychologists' interest in interpersonal expectancies stems largely from their interest in the perseverance of stereotypes. The term *stereotype* refers to those interpersonal beliefs and expectancies that are both widely shared and generally invalid (Ashmore & Del Boca 1981). The question of why

0066-4308/86/0201-0233$02.00

false interpersonal beliefs are so pervasive and resistant to change has led to considerable research on the effects that expectations have on interpersonal processes generally (Jones 1977, Darley & Fazio 1980, Snyder 1984). In this chapter we focus on how the expectancy that one person (the perceiver) holds concerning another (the target) affects three phenomena: 1. the target's behavior, 2. the processing of the target's behavior by the perceiver, and 3. the target's perception of him or herself.

The most widely studied expectancy effect is what Merton (1948) termed the *self-fulfilling prophecy*. In Merton's words, "a self-fulfilling prophecy is, in the beginning, a *false* definition of the situation evoking a new behavior which makes the originally false conception come *true*" (p. 195). As an illustration of the self-fulfilling prophecy effect, Merton described how the expectancy of war can lead one nation to interact with another in a manner that actually provokes war.

Prophecies or expectancies do not always fulfill themselves, of course. They can also disconfirm themselves. Merton referred to *self-disconfirming prophecies* as "suicidal prophecies." To illustrate the difference between a self-fulfilling and a self-disconfirming prophecy imagine that you expected another to be nervous. If this expectancy led you to act in an uncomfortable and nervous manner, your behavior might well induce the other to act more nervously than he or she might have otherwise. In this case your prophecy would have fulfilled itself. On the other hand, if this expectancy led you to act in an especially solicitous and reassuring manner, your behavior might well induce the other to act more calmly than he or she might have otherwise. In this case, your prophecy would have disconfirmed itself. Despite the ease of generating examples of self-disconfirming prophecies, researchers have focused almost exclusively on self-fulfilling prophecies. Merton himself relegated his discussion of self-disconfirming prophecies to a footnote.

BEHAVIORAL INFLUENCES
Self-Fulfilling Prophecies

Most research on the effects of expectancies on targets' behavior can be organized in terms of four categories of social interaction: 1. experimenter-subject interactions, 2. teacher-student interactions, 3. casual interactions, and 4. bargaining and negotiation.

EXPERIMENTER-SUBJECT INTERACTIONS   A well-known research program by Rosenthal and his colleagues (Rosenthal 1963, 1966, Rosenthal & Fode 1963a,b, Rosenthal & Lawson 1964) demonstrated that an experimenter's expectation about the outcome of a study can unwittingly influence both animal and human performance. In an illustrative study, Rosenthal & Fode (1963a) informed students assisting in a maze learning experiment that the rat they were responsible for was either "maze bright" or "maze dull." Although these labels had been applied randomly, the performance of "maze bright" rats was superior to that of "maze dull" rats. Apparently, the expectancies conveyed by the labels affected the students' behavior which, in turn, affected the rats' behavior.

Despite the failure to specify the precise preconditions for the effect as well as various other problems (Rosenthal et al 1966, Barber & Silver 1968, Zegers 1968, Minor 1970), the *experimenter expectancy effect,* as it has come to be known, would seem to be an established phenomenon in social psychology. Virtually all contemporary texts in research methods and social psychology cite the phenomenon as a serious threat to experimental validity, and researchers are expected to go to considerable lengths to ensure that the experimenter's knowledge of the hypothesis does not influence the experimental results.

TEACHER-STUDENT INTERACTIONS   Rosenthal & Jacobson's (1968) investigation of the effects of teacher expectancies on student performance—the *Pygmalion effect*—is one of the best known and most controversial studies in all of social science. In the initial study, teachers in an elementary school were told that a new IQ test administered to their students indicated that certain students, "bloomers," should show a marked increase in intellectual competence over the course of the school year. In actuality, the label "bloomer" was assigned randomly by the researchers. All students were given an IQ test at both the beginning and the end of the school year. The results indicated that students labeled "bloomers" showed a significantly greater gain in IQ than other pupils.

Attempts to replicate the Pygmalion effect have yielded inconsistent results. Expectancy effects are most easily demonstrated on measures of academic performance such as mathematics and reading tests (Meichenbaum et al 1969, Palardy 1969, Beez 1970, Seaver 1973, Zanna et al 1975, Crano & Mellon 1978, Taylor 1979). It has proved more difficult to replicate the Pygmalion effect on IQ measures (Conn et al 1968, Claiborn 1969, Fleming & Anttonen 1971, Jose & Cody 1971, Mendels & Flanders 1973, O'Connell et al 1974, Sutherland & Goldschmid 1974). Nevertheless, in a review of 15 years of research, Rosenthal & Rubin (1978) concluded that some sort of teacher expectancy effect occurred in approximately two-thirds of the 345 studies they reviewed.

A few studies have examined teacher-student interactions in nonschool settings. King (1971) manipulated welding instructors' expectancies about certain students in a vocational training program. Compared to men about whom instructors were given no expectancies, men believed to have a high aptitude acquired basic welding skills faster and scored higher on a welding test. Eden & Shani (1982) manipulated instructors' expectancies about the performance of military trainees. Trainees expected to do well performed better on objective achievement tests than did "less promising" trainees.

In summary, there is relatively strong evidence that teacher expectancies can influence student performance. The effect is strongest when teachers form their own expectancies and when there is a discrepancy between the student's actual level of ability and teachers' perceptions of the student's ability (Sutherland & Goldschmid 1974, Cooper 1979). Furthermore, teachers' expectancies influence students' academic performance to a greater degree than students' performance influences teachers' expectancies (Crano & Mellon 1978). More comprehensive discussions of the data and controversies pertaining to teacher expectancy effects can be found in various sources (e.g. Thorndike 1968, Elashoff & Snow 1971, Brophy & Good 1974, Braun 1976, Rosenthal & Rubin 1978, Cooper 1979, Jensen 1980, Rogers 1982, Dusek et al 1984).

CASUAL INTERACTIONS   In an influential study by Snyder et al (1977), male subjects were told that they would engage in a getting acquainted telephone conversation with a female subject. Prior to the conversation, each male viewed a picture of either an attractive or unattractive female whom he was told would be his partner. It was assumed that the males' stereotypic beliefs about female attractiveness would lead them to certain expectations about the sociability of their partner. Conversations were recorded and the female partners' responses were presented to naive judges. As predicted, judges rated women whose partners believed them to be attractive as more friendly, likable, and sociable than women whose partners believed them to be unattractive.

A study by Farina et al (1968) manipulated the expectancy of friendliness in an especially ingenious manner. Rather than provide perceivers with information about the characteristics of the target, these researchers provided perceivers with information about the expectancies that targets allegedly held about them. Specifically, the perceiver was told that the target believed that the perceiver was a former mental patient, a homosexual, or a "normal" person. In fact, the target received no information about the perceiver. Subsequently, the perceiver and target collaborated on a manual dexterity task during which they were allowed to converse only about task-relevant issues. Conversations were recorded and scored for the number of times each subject initiated discussion. Perceivers who believed they were viewed as belonging to a stigmatized category were spoken to significantly less than were perceivers who believed they were perceived as "normal." Apparently, the perception that they were stigmatized led perceivers to interact with targets in a manner that actually induced stigmatization.

Under the guise of a simulated interview, Christensen & Rosenthal (1982) assigned subjects randomly to the roles of interviewer or interviewee. Each interviewer was given the expectancy that the interviewee was either a highly sociable or highly unsociable individual. The interviews were videotaped and the responses of the interviewees were presented to naive judges. The judges rated the "sociable" interviewees as more enthusiastic than the "unsociable" interviewees.

BARGAINING AND NEGOTIATION   Studies of bargaining and negotiation indicate that beliefs about one's opponent's cooperativeness, gender, and even age can influence that opponent's behavior. Kelley & Stahelski (1970a,b) demonstrated in the context of the prisoner's dilemma game that the expectation that another is competitive leads individuals to act competitively which, in turn, induces competitiveness in their partners. A similar finding was reported by Snyder & Swann (1978a). In this study subjects competed in a reaction time task which involved a noise weapon that could be set at one of six levels of noxiousness. Prior to the competition, perceivers were falsely informed that their opponent was either very hostile or nonhostile. The procedure dictated that the setting of the noise weapon was to be decided upon by the perceiver on the first three trials, by the target on the next three trials, and so on for a total of 24 trials. The results indicated that the average setting of the noise weapon chosen by both the perceiver and the target was significantly higher when the target was believed to be hostile.

Skrypnek & Snyder (1982) conducted a study in which male subjects were required to negotiate a division of tasks with another person whom they could not see or talk to directly. In one condition the other, who was always a female, was identified as a male, in a second condition as a female, and in a third condition no gender label was given. The tasks had been chosen by the researchers to be either stereotypically masculine or feminine. As predicted, male subjects induced female targets labeled "female" to choose a greater number of feminine tasks than female targets in either the "male" or "no label" conditions.

Musser & Graziano (1983) investigated the effects that expectancies about age have on task performance. The perceivers and targets in this study were second- and fourth-grade children. Perceivers were told that their partner was either two years older or two years younger than themselves. Musser and Graziano predicted that stereotypes about age would lead perceivers to expect lower competence on the part of younger partners. The perceiver and the target were each provided with pieces for two puzzles. The task required the perceiver and the target to produce identical puzzles using a procedure that permitted discussion but no visual contact. Audiotapes of the children's conversations were content-analyzed by naive judges who rated each child's contribution in terms of number of influence attempts, solicitations, acquiescence responses, and neutral responses. Although the age label had no effect on these measures, there was an expectancy effect on the nature of the tasks that the targets chose to work on next. Targets labeled "younger" selected significantly easier tasks than those labeled "older."

Self-Disconfirming Prophecies

In the literature on the behavioral effects of interpersonal expectancies we could locate very few studies that found evidence of a self-disconfirming prophecy. Farina & Ring (1965) found that perceivers who believed that a coworker was mentally ill actually induced a more competent performance from their coworker than did perceivers who believed their coworker was "normal." Bond (1972) reported that subjects led to believe that they would be interacting with a "cold" other induced the other to act in a warmer manner than subjects led to expect a "warm" other. Similarily, Ickes et al (1982) found that targets expected to be "unfriendly" were induced to behave in a more friendly manner than either "friendly" or unlabled targets. Finally, Swann & Snyder (1980) found that students expected to have "Lo ability" learned to do a card trick more proficiently than students expected to have "High ability" when teachers believed that success with the card trick was largely a matter of intrinsic ability.

We now take a closer look at behavioral expectancy effects. Our analysis of the sequence by which one person's expectancies influence another's behavior focuses on two links, that between a perceiver's expectancy and his or her behavior and that between the perceiver's behavior and the behavior of the target.

MEDIATING LINKS

Perceiver Expectancy and Behavior

Is it more probable that a person's expectancy about another will fulfill or disconfirm itself? According to the weight of research we have just reviewed, the answer would appear to be obvious: self-fulfilling effects are much more probable than self-disconfirming effects. But why should the influence that an expectancy has on a perceiver's behavior most commonly be such that it induces the target to confirm the expectancy? Descriptions of self-fulfilling prophecies suggest one reason. According to many analyses, self-fulfilling prophecies are the rule and self-disconfirming prophecies the exception, because self-fulfilling prophecies emerge when perceivers act "consistent" with or "congruent" with or "in accordance" with their expectancies. Self-disconfirming prophecy effects presumably only arise when perceivers act "inconsistent" with or "not in accordance" with their expectancies. When coupled with the additional assumption that people prefer consistency to inconsistency, this logic would seem to offer a sensible explanation for the predominance of self-fulfilling prophecies.

Is it reasonable to describe behaviors as being consistent or inconsistent with expectancies? For example, are teachers who give special encouragement to students of supposedly low ability acting any less consistent with their expectancies than teachers who give reduced encouragement to such students? Similarly, are people who act in a particularly friendly manner in the presence of others who are expected to be unfriendly behaving any less in accordance with their expectancy than people who respond to expected unfriendliness with unfriendliness of their own? We do not think so (see also Hilton & Darley 1985). In neither of these examples is one expectancy-behavior link any more scripted or inevitable than the other. Liberation from the assumption that one expectancy-behavior link, and hence one type of prophecy effect, is more natural or inevitable leads to an interesting question: When do perceivers respond to an expectancy in a manner that fulfills it and when do they respond in a manner that disconfirms it? Two of the many factors that probably moderate the expectancy-behavior link are (*a*) the perceiver's interaction goals (Jones & Thibaut 1958, Showers & Cantor 1985) and (*b*) the perceiver's belief in the target's modifiability.

INTERACTION GOALS   The literature suggests that people who expect another to be antisocial sometimes act in a hostile fashion (Kelley & Stahelski 1970a,b) and sometimes act in an especially friendly fashion (Ickes et al 1982). It may not be surprising that the former reaction leads to a self-fulfilling prophecy and the latter to a self-disconfirming prophecy. But why do perceivers with the same expectation act in different ways? One possibility is that people who act in a friendly manner when they expect unfriendliness are motivated by a different goal than people who meet anticipated unfriendliness with unfriendliness of their own. Behaving in a friendly manner when unfriendliness is expected is consistent with the goal of trying to establish a harmonious interaction with the other. Such a goal might well arise when the relationship is destined to be a long-term one or when the target has some power over the perceiver. Behaving in an unfriendly manner when unfriendliness is expected is consistent with the goal of trying to avoid being taken advantage of by the other. A number of conditions might be expected to foster this goal.

Evidence consistent with the hypothesis that perceivers with different goals often react to the same expectancies differently was provided by Andersen & Bem (1981). These researchers employed the "get-acquainted" procedure of Snyder et al (1977) with subjects who had been previously categorized as sex-typed or androgynous. Sex-typed females were more friendly to "attractive" targets than to "unattractive" targets. Androgynous females, on the other hand, were more friendly to "unattractive" than "attractive" targets. As a result, "unattractive" targets who interacted with androgynous females actually were more sociable than "attractive" targets. The fact that androgynous females shared the sex-typed females' beliefs about the characteristics of attractive people suggests that they may have been influenced by different goals. For example, they may have been motivated to act supportively or to avoid appearing prejudiced (Dutton 1976).

A similar interpretation can be applied to the findings of Babad et al (1982). Subjects in this study were first classified as "biased" or "unbiased" on the basis of their willingness to endorse various stereotypes. Next, they were given the opportunity to assist a student whom they expected to do well or poorly on a task. The results revealed that only the "biased" subjects were influenced by their expectancies. One interpretation of the fact that "unbiased" perceivers did not act upon their expectancy is that they were motivated to act in a nondiscriminatory manner.

The importance of interaction goals was demonstrated even more directly in a study by Fleming (1985). Perceivers were led to expect that the person with whom they were to interact was overly emotional and had difficulty under pressure. Before encountering the target, perceivers were provided with one of two interaction goals—to consider the target as a possible teammate for a cooperative game or simply to have a time-passing conversation. The responses available to targets also were manipulated, such that they either refuted or supported the perceiver's expectancy. When given the opportunity to ask questions of the target, perceivers instructed to have a time-passing conversation opted mainly for expectancy-irrelevant questions. On the other hand, perceivers who were required to assess the teammate potential of the target opted mainly for expectancy-relevant questions. The different strategies adopted by perceivers in the two conditions yielded different outcomes. Expectancy-irrelevant questions produced self-fulfilling outcomes regardless of the responses available to the target. Expectancy-relevant questions also produced self-fulfilling outcomes when confirming responses were available to the target, but produced self-disconfirming outcomes when disconfirming responses were available to the target.

TARGET MODIFIABILITY   The importance of the perceiver's belief in the modifiability of the target was demonstrated in a study by Swann & Snyder (1980). These researchers manipulated both the perceiver's expectancy about the target's ability and the perceiver's belief about the relationship between ability and performance on the experimental task. In one condition, perceivers were led to believe that task performance was primarily related to intrinsic factors such as ability, and in another, to extrinsic factors such as practice. Perceivers who were led to believe that practice would not help the "Hi ability" targets treated the targets in a manner that resulted in a self-disconfirming prophecy. On the other hand, perceivers who were led to believe that practice would help the "Hi ability" targets treated them in a manner that resulted in a self-fulfilling prophecy.

The context in which perceivers confront targets is also likely to affect perceivers' beliefs that they can modify targets' performance or behavior. If the interaction is anticipated to be very brief or constrained, perceivers often will be inhibited from trying to modify the performance or behavior of the target, even if they are motivated to do so (Jones et al 1984).

Target Response

Not only is there no one-to-one relationship between a perceiver's expectancy and behavior but there is no one-to-one correspondence between the behavior of the perceiver and the behavior of the target. Even when a perceiver responds to a "cold" person with coldness it is not inevitable that the perceiver's coldness will be reciprocated. There is evidence that certain classes of behavior elicit some responses more readily than others (Coppella 1981), but there is little evidence to suggest that humans routinely display fixed patterns of interdependent behaviors. Nevertheless, a reader of the expectancy literature could be forgiven for concluding that targets of erroneous expectations are powerless to alter or resist the behavioral confirmation sequence once it has begun. Neither the phenomenology nor the resources of the target have generated much interest among psychologists. This neglect appears to be part of a general tendency of psychological formulations to view targets of influence as passive. Admittedly, many of the targets studied are low in power relative to the perceiver but this is not inevitable. Furthermore, it is inappropriate to equate low power with passivity. This point was forcefully made by Moscovici and his colleagues (Moscovici & Faucheux 1972, Moscovici & Nemeth 1974) in their rebuke of social psychology for neglecting minority influence. It is also implicit in Ralph Ellison's caustic accusation that psychologists, and social scientists generally, tend to view blacks as "nothing more than reactions to oppression" (Jones et al 1984).

Myriad factors likely influence how targets react to the perception that others hold false beliefs about them. Two factors that have received experimental attention are: (a) the nature of the discrepancy between perceivers' and targets' conceptions and (b) the perceived cost and rewards of modifying the perceivers' false beliefs.

BELIEFS ABOUT SELF   The direction of the discrepancy between the target's self-concept and the conception reflected in the perceiver's behavior is one variable that may affect the target's reaction. Specifically, targets can be expected to be more strongly motivated to modify an erroneous negative conception than an erroneous positive conception. Consistent with this hypothesis, Jones et al (1984) report that disabled individuals are more strongly inclined to "educate" a perceiver the more unflattering they judge that perceiver's expectancy to be. It is important to distinguish in this regard between the negativity of perceivers' behavior and the negativity of their expectancy. As Gibbons et al (1979) report, even "positive" behaviors can provoke reactance if they are judged to be patronizing.

There appear to be occasions on which targets will challenge positive as well as negative misconceptions of themselves. Swann & Read (1981) found that targets who considered themselves dislikable acted more unpleasantly when they believed that their partners might find them likable than when they believed that their partners would find them dislikable. In this instance, targets' desire to verify their self-concepts apparently dominated their desire to enhance their public or private image. A fuller understanding of how self-verification and self-enhancement processes relate to one another must await further research.

Targets' confidence in their self-concept can also influence their responses to the false beliefs of others. Swann & Ely (1984) manipulated targets' certainty about an aspect of their self-concept as well as perceivers' certainty about their conception of the target. Certainty was operationalized as the degree of consistency characterizing the evidence received about the self (or other). Perceivers and targets then engaged in an interaction in which the perceiver tried to get to know the target by asking questions. Targets resisted incongruent and accepted congruent conceptions of themselves when they were relatively certain about their self-conceptions (regardless of the certainty of perceivers) and when both targets and perceivers were uncertain. Perceivers only induced targets to accept incongruent conceptions of themselves when perceivers were certain of their conceptions and targets were uncertain of theirs.

CONSEQUENCES OF DISAVOWAL   Knowing that a perceiver holds an inaccurate expectancy will not invariably lead to a challenge to that expectancy. Targets are often inhibited from disabusing perceivers of their beliefs because it is advantageous for targets to conform to these expectancies. The tendency to conform willingly to the expectancy of another has been referred to variously as "fictional acceptance" (Davis 1961) and "acquiescence" (Humphreys 1972) and was demonstrated impressively in two studies by Zanna and his colleages. Zanna & Pack (1975) found that females conformed to the stereotypes of males if they found the males to be attractive but not if they found them unattractive. This finding presumably reflects both the greater desire of females to be liked by attractive males and the females' belief that conforming to the stereotypes of attractive males would elicit liking from them. In a subsequent study, von Baeyer et al (1981) reported a tendency for women to conform to the stereotypes of male job interviewers, even though the women generally rejected these stereotypes. Since perceivers often will react negatively to targets who disconfirm their expectancies, targets risk incurring costs whenever they attempt to disavow the expectancy of another. When the costs associated with disconfirmation are greater than those associated with confirmation, targets can be expected to be reluctant to challenge the perceiver's false expectancy. When the balance of costs and rewards are reversed targets can be expected to attempt disavowal.

Whether another succeeds in resisting the behavioral confirmation cycle depends on the opportunity as well as the motivation to resist. A student may be motivated to resist a teacher's unflattering perception, but unless the student has the resources to compensate for the lack of support he or she is receiving from the teacher, behavioral confirmation may be unavoidable. The bargaining study of Miller & Holmes (1975) illustrates the importance of behavioral opportunity. Pairs of subjects played one of two bargaining games. The first game provided only two responses: a cooperative response and a competitive response. The second game provided a cooperative response, a competitive response and an additional, "defensive" response which served to protect the player from exploitation without simultaneously threatening the resources of the other. Players who expected their partners to be competitive, and who thus tended to play competitively themselves, were much less likely to produce a self-fulfilling prophecy when the other player had access to the defensive response option.

Summary

We have argued that it may be no more probable for expectancies to lead to self-fulfilling prophecies than it is for them to lead to self-disconfirming prophecies. But if this is true, why are there so many more demonstrations of self-fulfilling than self-disconfirming effects? The answer, we think, is that researchers have been more interested in demonstrating the range of contexts in which self-fulfilling prophecies can occur than in investigating the expectancy process more generally. For the most part, experimental situations have been designed to maximize the likelihood of finding self-fulfilling prophecies. The prevalent practice of keeping targets ignorant of the perceivers' expectancy is perhaps the best example of a design feature that favors fulfilling over defeating effects (Hilton & Darley 1985). Which prophecy effect will emerge depends on both how perceivers react to their expectancies and how targets react to the behavior of perceivers. Perceivers are not constrained to react to a particular expectancy in a particular way, and targets are not constrained to confirm the image of themselves that is communicated by perceivers. Rather than generating further demonstrations of the self-fulfilling prophecy, future research might more profitably seek a better understanding of the factors that moderate the relationship between perceivers' expectancies and behavior and between behaviors of perceivers and targets.

PROCESSING TARGET BEHAVIOR

The influence of erroneous expectancies is not only manifest in the behavior of targets. In spite of objective evidence to the contrary, perceivers may conclude that their expectancies have been confirmed. To the extent that confirmation is "in the eye of the beholder," stereotypes and other false expectancies will persist even in the face of objective disconfirmation. Perceivers do not need to induce expectancy-consistent behavior in order to perpetuate their expectancies. They need only to see the behavior as expectancy-consistent.

Perceptual and Behavioral Combinations

The fact that the perceiver's expectancy can be confirmed or disconfirmed perceptually as well as behaviorally gives rise to four possible outcome combinations: 1. behavioral confirmation/perceptual confirmation, 2. behavioral disconfirmation/perceptual disconfirmation, 3. behavioral confirmation/ perceptual disconfirmation, and 4. behavioral disconfirmation/perceptual confirmation. We now review the literature relevant to each of these four categories. To be included in this review a study had to assess both behavioral and perceptual responses.

BEHAVIORAL CONFIRMATION—PERCEPTUAL CONFIRMATION   There are a number of studies in which targets' behavior both objectively confirmed the perceivers' expectancy and was interpreted by perceivers as confirming their original expectation. Rosenthal & Fode (1963a) reported that "maze bright" rats not only outperformed "maze dull" rats, but they were perceived by expectancy holders to be brighter, more pleasant, and likable. Similarily, Rosenthal & Jacobson (1968) found that "bloomers" not only gained significantly more in IQ than control students, but were perceived by their teachers to have a better chance of a successful future and to be more interesting, curious, and happy. A similar pattern was found in Feldman & Prohaska's (1979) study of students' expectancies of teachers. Teachers whom students expected to be competent both behaved in a more capable manner and were perceived to be more competent than teachers whom students expected to be incompetent. In four additional studies previously discussed (Farina et al 1968, Kelley & Stahelski 1970a, Snyder et al 1977, Christensen & Rosenthal 1982), evidence of both behavioral and perceptual confirmation was also found.

BEHAVIORAL DISCONFIRMATION—PERCEPTUAL DISCONFIRMATION   Virtually no published studies report evidence of both perceptual and behavioral disconfirmation. An obvious reason for this is that such a pattern would ordinarily constitute a null effect and be unlikely to become part of the published literature. An interesting study by Hilton & Darley (1985) provides one relevant exception. In this study both the perceiver's expectancy concerning the target's warmth/coldness and the target's awareness of this expectancy were manipulated. In the "target aware" condition, the perceiver's expectancy did not affect the behavior of the target. Moreover, targets whom perceivers expected to be cold were actually judged by perceivers to be warmer than control targets. Here we have a case of a nonsignificant behavioral effect accompanied by a self-disconfirming perceptual effect.

BEHAVIORAL CONFIRMATION—PERCEPTUAL DISCONFIRMATION   We could find only one study in which targets' behavior confirmed and perceivers' ratings disconfirmed perceivers' expectancies. In this study, Zanna et al (1975) manipulated teachers' expectancies about the academic potential of students participating in a seven-week summer enrichment program in mathematics and English. Teachers were told that certain students would "bloom" and were given no expectations about other students. Three weeks into the course, and again at the course's conclusion, teachers graded students' potential and performance. Scores on mathematics and reading tests revealed a self-fulfilling prophecy at both the third and seventh week. A self-fulfilling prophecy effect was also observed in the teachers' perceptions of the students at three weeks, but this effect was not present in the seventh-week ratings. In other words, "bloomers" performed better than nonlabeled students throughout the course, but teachers ceased to see them as superior after three weeks.

BEHAVIORAL DISCONFIRMATION—PERCEPTUAL CONFIRMATION   There are a number of studies in which expectancy manipulations failed to produce statistically significant behavioral effects, although perceivers' ratings of targets' behavior confirmed perceivers' expectancies. Jones & Panitch (1971) studied expectations about opponents' likability in the context of the prisoner's dilemma game. Perceivers were told that their opponent was either likable or unlikable and then played 15 trials of the game with him. There were no significant effects of the manipulation on the number of cooperative moves made by targets. However, perceivers rated "likable" targets as more compatible and likable than "unlikable" targets. In a similar vein, Andersen & Bem (1981) found that while both male and female targets' telephone conversations were not significantly influenced by male perceivers' beliefs about targets' attractiveness, perceivers did report liking the "attractive" targets more than "unattractive" targets. Hilton & Darley (1985) also found evidence of perceptual confirmation in the absence of behavioral confirmation in a condition in which targets were unaware of perceivers' expectancies.

A few studies even have reported self-fulfilling perceptual effects accompanying self-disconfirming behavioral effects. Farina & Ring (1965) induced perceivers to believe that targets were either mentally ill or normal. The subsequent task performance of "mentally ill" targets was actually superior to that of "normals," yet the "mentally ill" targets were perceived by their partners as having contributed less to the task. Bond (1972) told subjects they would interact with either a cold or warm partner. Targets labeled "cold" actually behaved more warmly than those labeled "warm," but "cold" targets were judged by their partners to be colder. Similarily, Ickes et al (1982) found that although targets who were expected to be unfriendly actually behaved in a more friendly fashion, they were seen by their partners to be less friendly than either "friendly" or control targets. A final example is Swann & Snyder's (1980) study in which "Lo ability" students achieved greater proficiency at a card trick than "Hi ability" students when teachers believed that success with the card trick was largely a matter of intrinsic ability. Despite the performance superiority of "Lo ability" targets, teachers judged their performance to be inferior to that of "Hi ability" targets.

Perceptual Confirmation

There are at least two explanations for the occurrence of perceptual confirmation in the absence of behavioral confirmation. One explanation involves the measurement of behavioral effects. In some studies the instrument used to measure behavioral effects may not have been sufficently sensitive. Consistent with this possibility, evidence suggests that the perceiver's influence may be reflected primarily in subtle behaviors, such as the target's nonverbal and paralinguistic behaviors (Rosenthal 1966, Word et al 1974).

On the other hand, perceptual confirmation in the absence of behavioral confirmation also has been reported in contexts where the target's behavioral repertoire is highly circumscribed (e.g. responses in a prisoner's dilemma game). In these situations it is difficult to believe that perceivers can discern objective cues not captured by the scoring system. The measurement explanation is particularly weak in those situations in which judgments of naive observers do not correspond with judgments of perceivers. In sum, measurement difficulties do not seem to be a sufficient explanation for all instances in which perceptual confirmation occurs.

The second and more likely explanation is that perceivers "see" what they expect to see regardless of the objective evidence (Darley & Fazio 1980, Snyder 1984). The hypothesis that expectancies can lead to the perceptual distortion of social behavior has received considerable support (Hastorf & Cantril 1954, Zadny & Gerard 1974, Duncan 1976, Darley & Gross 1983). The possibility of perceptual distortion on the part of perceivers is especially great in those studies in which a self-disconfirming behavioral effect emerges but the perceiver nevertheless interprets the target's behavior as confirming the expectancy (Farina & Ring 1965, Rosenthal & Jacobson 1968, Jones & Panitch 1971, Bond 1972, Rosenhan 1973, Swann & Snyder 1980, Andersen & Bem 1981, Ickes et al 1982, Hilton & Darley 1985).

Perceivers' expectancies can lead to distortion at two different stages in the processing of targets' behavior—either at the stage in which the perceivers encode the behavior of targets or at the stage in which perceivers explain targets' behavior. Expectancies affect the encoding process by leading perceivers to see or attend to behaviors consistent with their expectancies (Rothbart et al 1979). We are more likely to attend to, and thus remember, the warm behaviors of a person we expect to be warm than one we expect to be cold. Hamilton (1981) cleverly describes the influence of expectancies on the encoding process in his witticism ". . . If I didn't believe it, I wouldn't have seen it." Expectancies can also affect the encoding process by leading perceivers to label behaviors in a manner consistent with their expectancies (Jones et al 1984). The same facial expression might be encoded as a smirk or a smile depending on whether the target is expected to be cold or warm.

In addition to affecting how perceivers encode targets' behavior, perceivers' expectancies can affect how they explain the behavior (Strenta & Kleck 1984). There are at least three reasons why perceivers might explain behaviors which they encoded as disconfirming their expectancies in a manner which makes the behavior appear consistent. First, perceivers may discount the reliability or diagnostic value of unexpected behavior. An unexpected level of performance, for example, is more likely to be attributed to chance, and less likely to be attributed to ability, than is an expected level of performance (Miller & Ross 1975). Second, perceivers may attribute the unexpected behavior of another to their own behavior. This is especially likely if targets deviate from expectancies in a direction consistent with perceivers' interaction goals (Ickes et al 1982). Third, perceivers may discount the unexpected behavior of others by focusing on motives of concealment that they may attribute to targets (Hilton 1985). Jones et al (1984) note, for example, that it is difficult for a blind person to convince a sighted person that he or she is actually cheerful because sighted people tend to attribute cheerfulness on the part of the blind to impression management or self-deception.

In short, even when unexpected behavior is encoded objectively it may still be interpreted by perceivers as consistent with their expectancy. For example, if a student's performance exceeds a teacher's expectancy, the teacher might attribute it to (a) the good luck of the student, (b) the teacher's own efforts or competence, or (c) the overachieving personality of the student.

Despite the many cognitive processes that contribute to perceptual confirmation, perceivers sometimes are surprised. We all have encountered people whose actions or performances deviated from our expectancies. Unfortunately, we know very little about the factors that affect the relative likelihood of confirmation and disconfirmation. One obvious factor is the nature of the expectancy. Interpersonal expectancies vary in many respects. For one thing, they vary in the degree and nature of the evidence on which they are based (Darley & Fazio 1980, Jones et al 1984). Expectancies can be based on experience with the target, the target's social category, or the context in which the interaction is to occur (Holmes & Miller 1976, Jones & McGillis 1976). We hope that future research will address the question of how differences in the evidential basis of expectancies affect the perceptual and behavioral confirmation process.

The content of the trait or attribute on which the expectancy is based is another factor that merits further consideration. Jones et al (1984) have identified four aspects of trait content which they believe affect the likelihood of expectancy disconfirmation. One factor is the extent to which the target is believed to have control over the expression of the relevant attribute. It is easier for people to control the expression of some attributes (e.g. attitudes) than others (e.g. athletic prowess). The more difficult perceivers believe it is for targets to misrepresent their true standing on an attribute, the more willing perceivers will be to modify their expectancies in the face of behavioral disconfirmation. A second factor involves the link between the trait and its behavioral expression (Reeder & Brewer 1979). Some characteristics (e.g. disposition toward dishonesty) are defined by the most extreme behavioral expression, others (e.g. disposition toward friendliness) by the most typical behavioral expression. Expectancies based on traits defined by typical behaviors will be easier to disconfirm than expectancies based on traits defined by extreme behaviors. It is more surprising to see an unfriendly person act friendly than it is to see a dishonest person act honestly.

A third factor is the opportunity for disconfirmation afforded by social interaction (Rothbart 1981). Some attributes (e.g. extraversion) can be expressed in virtually all situations, other attributes (e.g. courage) in only a few situations. The more opportunities there are for the expression of an attribute, the more disconfirmable is an expectancy based on that attribute. A final factor is the extent to which the trait is defined by internal as opposed to external referents. Some attributes (e.g. nervousness) are defined mainly in terms of observable, external features, while other attributes (e.g. machiavellianism) are defined primarily in terms of unobservable, internal features, such as motives. Expectancies based on traits defined by external referents will be easier to disconfirm than expectancies based on traits defined by internal referents.

SELF-CONCEPT CHANGE

The self-concept is widely believed to be an important determinant of a person's behavior (Felson 1984). Two influences on self-concept formation are one's own behaviors and the behaviors of others. Psychologists, inspired by Bem's (1972) self-perception theory, have emphasized the role of one's own actions in self-concept formation. Sociologists, on the other hand, especially the followers of Cooley and Mead, have preferred to emphasize the reactions of others in self-concept formation. These two models, which we term the psychological and sociological models, respectively, differ in the relative weight they attach to the perceiver's versus the target's behavior in the development of the target's self-concept.

Psychological model

According to the psychological model, one of the consequences of a perceiver holding an erroneous expectancy is that this expectancy may lead the target not only to behave consistently with the expectancy but to conclude on the basis of this behavior that he or she is actually that type of person (Darley & Fazio 1980). The study of Fazio et al (1981) provides the most directly relevant evidence. This study was built upon Snyder & Swann's (1978b) finding that perceivers who were searching for evidence of either introversion or extraversion in another tended to ask questions designed to elicit confirmatory evidence. Fazio et al (1981) employed the Snyder and Swann procedure to determine if targets would come to perceive themselves in a manner consistent with the nature of the questions they were asked, and hence with the nature of the responses they gave. The results were clear. First, targets who were asked extravert questions (e.g. "What would you do if you wanted to liven things up at a party?") sounded more extraverted in their answers than did targets asked neutral or introverted questions (e.g. "What things do you dislike about loud parties?"). Second, when asked to describe themselves, targets in the extravert condition described themselves as more extraverted, and those in the introvert condition described themselves as more introverted, than did targets in the neutral condition. The Fazio et al (1981) study supports other research (e.g. Salancik & Conway 1975, Jones et al 1981) which has found that making certain behaviors in a person's repertoire salient can affect the person's self-descriptions. It falls short, however, of demonstrating that perceiver-induced behavior that is not typically expressed can influence targets' self-perception. For example, a student induced by a teacher to perform poorly on an exam might not incorporate this performance into his or her self-concept if it is strikingly inconsistent with past performances.

Self-perception theory contends that only behavior that is not explained situationally will provide information about the self (Bem 1972, Ross & Fletcher 1985). Accordingly, it can be predicted that targets will be hesitant to see their behavior as informative about the self to the extent they believe it was caused by the perceiver. A study by Snyder & Swann (1978b) bears on this point. These researchers manipulated the attributions that targets made for the behaviors that perceivers had induced in them. Targets who were induced by perceivers to act in a hostile manner continued to act in a hostile manner with a "naive" perceiver if they had been encouraged to explain their hostility dispositionally but not if they had been induced to explain it situationally. In sum, the general proposition that people's own behavior contributes to the formation of their self-concept appears to generalize to the case where the relevant behavior is induced by another's erroneous expectations.

Sociological model

The psychological model emphasizes the *indirect* influence that a perceiver's behavior, by virtue of its impact on the target's behavior, can have on a target's self-concept. The sociological model, on the other hand, emphasizes the *direct* impact that a perceiver's behavior can have on a target's self-concept. For example, the psychological model points to the effect that being induced to act stupidly can have on a student's self-concept, whereas the sociological model points to the effect that being labeled and treated as stupid can have on a student's self-concept. There is little empirical research bearing on the sociological model. Most relevant are those few studies that have looked at the effects of labels on a target's behavior (Kraut 1973, Miller et al 1975, Steele 1975, Gurwitz & Topol 1978). In one of the earliest studies in this tradition, Kraut (1973) found that labeling children on the basis of their donation behavior had an impact on their subsequent donation behavior. Children who had previously donated to charity *and* had been labeled as charitable subsequently donated more than an unlabeled control group; and children who had not previously donated *and* had been labeled as uncharitable subsequently donated less than a control group. Apparently, the experimenter's interpretation of the children's behavior had affected their self-images and, in turn, their behavior. In some of the studies that have employed negative labels, targets have acted in a label-inconsistent manner (e.g. Steele 1975, Gurwitz & Topol 1978). One interpretation of these results is that the negative labels aroused self-presentational concerns in targets which led them to attempt to discredit the label.

The sociological perspective serves to remind psychologists that a perceiver can influence a target's self-concept without first influencing the target's behavior. A person who is mistakenly labeled as fat need not become fat to feel fat and develop the identity of a fat person. Of course, in many instances it is likely that targets' self-concepts are a joint function of their interpretation of perceivers' behavior and their own behavior.

CONCLUSION

This chapter has reviewed research on the effects of interpersonal expectancies on three phenomena: 1. the target's behavior, 2. the perceiver's processing of the target's behavior, and 3. the target's self-concept. Although the self-fulfilling prophecy has been the focal concept in the literature, this review has argued for a broader conceptualization of interpersonal expectancy effects. Our review has emphasized three points. First, there is no empirical or logical justification for the assumption that an expectancy is more likely to lead perceivers to act in a manner which will fulfill the expectancy than it is to lead them to act in a manner which will disconfirm it. Second, the target can often defeat the perceiver's prophecy, irrespective of the actions taken by the perceiver. Third, the perceiver's behavior can affect the target's self-concept either directly or indirectly through its effect on the target's behavior. There are two additional issues pertaining to expectancy effects that merit consideration. The first concerns the need to distinguish between interaction and coaction based expectancy effects. The second concerns the need to establish limits of expectancy effects.

Interaction and Coaction Effects

The various examples of self-fulfilling prophecies provided by Merton (1948, 1957) fall into one of two general categories: *interaction* and *coaction* effects. The literature has focused almost exclusively on interaction effects. From this perspective, a self-fulfilling prophecy occurs when a perceiver's expectancy about a target affects the perceiver's interaction with the target in a manner that leads the target to fulfill the perceiver's expectancy. A second type of self-fulfilling prophecy occurs when an expectancy shared by a collectivity leads to independent *coactions* that collectively fulfill the initial expectancy. A self-fulfilling coaction effect is illustrated by Merton's example of a bank that failed in 1932 because the initially false rumor that the bank was insolvent led the fearful depositors to remove their money, thereby causing the bank actually to become insolvent.

Self-disconfirming prophecies can occur in coaction as well as interaction contexts. An example of a self-disconfirming coaction effect occurred in our city a few years ago during the visit of Pope John Paul II. A midafternoon outdoor mass was one of the major events on the Pope's schedule, and the police prophesied that the traffic jam created by this event would be "monumental." However, as a result of the precautionary coactions taken by those attending the mass and other citizens (most of whom stayed home or took public transportation), the traffic flow that day was the lightest in many years. Neither Merton nor subsequent authorities have distinguished between interaction- and coaction-based expectancy effects, but the dynamics underlying each would seem quite distinct. For one thing, an analysis of coaction effects is likely to benefit substantially from a consideration of the literature on social traps and related collective phenomena (Platt 1973, Dawes 1980).

Limits of Expectancy Effects

What are the limits to the effects of interpersonal expectancies? Specifically, are some target characteristics more susceptible to expectancy effects than others? Consider target sociability as an example. Remember that Snyder et al (1977) found that male subjects who had a telephone conversation with women whom they believed to be attractive induced the women to respond in a more friendly manner than men who believed their partners to be unattractive. Target sociability is only one of a number of dependent measures that could have been used in this study. For example, the study could have assessed target attractiveness. Indeed, since it was expectancies about target attractiveness that were manipulated, it might be argued that target attractiveness was the most appropriate measure to employ. Of course, many people would doubt that a perceiver's belief about another's attractiveness could actually affect that person's attractiveness. On the other hand, this possibility would not seem fanciful to those who adopt a radical perspective on the social construction of reality (Becker 1963, Scott 1969, Schur 1980). Thus, investigating the sensitivity of different variables to expectancy effects would expand both our knowledge of expectancy effects and our general understanding of the constraints on the social construction of reality.

A related issue concerns the degree of influence that expectancies can exert on any particular characteristic. Specifically, is the influence of perceivers' expectancies about target characteristics constrained by targets' actual characteristics? Consider intelligence as an example. Research has demonstrated that people's intellectual performance will improve if they are around people who think they are smart. But will everyone treated as though he or she has an IQ of 150 perform at a level commensurate with this expectancy? Different assumptions about the malleability of human behavior and performance lead to different answers to this question. A radical perspective assumes that if people are treated as though they had similar abilities or traits, they will perform or act similarily to one another. A less radical perspective assumes that each ability of an individual can give rise to only a limited range of performance levels and that each personality trait of an individual can be manifested in only a limited range of behavioral expressions. At present there is no evidence to assist in the adjudication of these two perspectives. It is possible that the applicability may vary across behavioral and performance domains. Identifying the limits of expectancy effects remains a challenge for future researchers.

ACKNOWLEDGMENTS

The preparation of this chapter was facilitated by a President's Research Grant from Simon Fraser University. The authors are indebted to Brenda Salter for her invaluable assistance in the preparation of the chapter and to John Darley, Ned Jones, Cathy McFarland, Carol Porter, and Mark Zanna for their helpful comments.

Literature Cited

Andersen, S. M., Bem, S. L. 1981. Sex typing and androgyny in dyadic interaction: Individual differences in responsiveness to physical attractiveness. *J. Pers. Soc. Psychol.* 41:74–86

Ashmore, R. D., Del Boca, F. K. 1981. Conceptual approaches to stereotypes and stereotyping. In *Cognitive Processes in Stereotyping and Intergroup Behavior,* ed. D. L. Hamilton, pp. 1–35. Hillsdale, NJ: Erlbaum

Babad, E. Y., Inbar, J., Rosenthal, R. 1982. Pygmalion, Galatea, and the Golem: Investigations of biased and unbiased teachers. *J. Educ. Psychol.* 74:459–74

Barber, T. X., Silver, M. J. 1968. Fact, fiction, and the experimenter bias effect. *Psychol. Bull. Monogr. Suppl.* 70(6, Pt. 2): 1–29

Becker, H. 1963. *Outsiders: Studies in the Sociology of Deviance.* New York: Free Press

Beez, W. 1970. Influence of biased psychological reports on teacher behavior and pupil performance. In *Learning in Social Settings,* ed. M. W. Miles, W. W. Charters Jr., pp. 71–94. Boston: Allyn & Bacon

Bem, D. J. 1972. Self-perception theory. *Adv. Exp. Soc. Psychol.* 6:1–62

Bond, M. 1972. Effect of an impression set on subsequent behavior. *J. Pers. Soc. Psychol.* 24:301–5

Braun, C. 1976. Teacher expectation: Social psychological dynamics. *Rev. Educ. Res.* 46:185–213

Brophy, J. E. 1983. Research on the self-fulfilling prophecy and teacher expectations. *J. Educ. Psychol.* 75:631–61

Brophy, J. E., Good, T. 1974. *Teacher-Student Relationships: Causes and Consequences.* New York: Holt, Rinehart & Winston

Christensen, D., Rosenthal, R. 1982. Gender and nonverbal decoding skill as determinants of interpersonal expectancy effects. *J. Pers. Soc. Psychol.* 42:75–87

Claiborn, W. 1969. Expectancy effects in the classroom: A failure to replicate. *J. Educ. Psychol.* 60:377–83

Conn, L. K., Edwards, C. N., Rosenthal, R., Crowne, D. P. 1968. Perception of emotion and response to teachers' expectancy by elementary school children. *Psychol. Rep.* 22:27–34

Cooper, H. 1979. Pygmalion grows up: A model for teacher expectation, communication, and performance influence. *Rev. Educ. Res.* 49:389–410

Coppella, J. W. 1981. Mutual influence in expressive behavior: Adult-adult and infant-adult interaction. *Psychol. Bull.* 89:101–32

Crano, W. D., Mellon, P. M. 1978. Causal influence of teachers' expectations on children's academic performance: A cross-lagged panel analysis. *J. Educ. Psychol.* 70: 39–49

Darley, J. M., Fazio, R. H. 1980. Expectancy confirmation processes arising in the social interaction sequence. *Am. Psychol.* 35:867–81

Darley, J. M., Gross, R. H. 1983. A hypothesis-confirming bias in labeling effects. *J. Pers. Soc. Psychol.* 44:20–33

Davis, F. 1961. Deviance disavowal: The management of strained interaction by the visibly handicapped. *Soc. Probl.* 9:120–32

Dawes, R. M. 1980. Social dilemmas. *Ann. Rev. Psychol.* 31:169–83

Duncan, S. L. 1976. Differential social perception and attribution of intergroup violence: Testing the lower limits of stereotyping blacks. *J. Pers. Soc. Psychol.* 34:590–98

Dusek, J. B., Hall, V. C., Neger, W. J. 1984. *Teacher Expectancies.* Hillsdale, NJ: Erlbaum

Dutton, D. G. 1976. Tokenism, reverse discrimination, and egalitarianism in interracial behavior. *J. Soc. Issues* 32:93–197

Eden, D., Shani, A. B. 1982. Pygmalion goes to boot camp: Expectancy, leadership and trainee performance. *J. Appl. Psychol.* 67:194–99

Elashoff, J. D., Snow, R. E. 1971. *Pygmalion Reconsidered.* Worthington, OH: Jones

Farina, A., Allen, J. G., Saul, B. B. 1968. The role of the stigmatized person in affecting social relationships. *J. Pers.* 36:169–82

Farina, A., Ring, K. 1965. The influence of perceived mental illness on interpersonal relations. *J. Appl. Soc. Psychol.* 70:47–51

Fazio, R. H., Effrein, E. A., Falender, V. J. 1981. Self-perception following social interaction. *J. Pers. Soc. Psychol.* 41:232–42

Feldman, R. S., Prohaska, T. 1979. The student as Pygmalion: Effect on student expectation of the teacher. *J. Educ. Psychol.* 71:485–93

Felson, R. B. 1984. The effect of self-appraisals of ability on academic performance. *J. Pers. Soc. Psychol.* 47:944–52

Fleming, E. S., Anttonen, R. G. 1971. Teacher expectancy as related to the academic and personal growth of primary-age children. *Monogr. Soc. Res. Child Dev.* 36(5):1–32

Fleming, J. H. 1985. *When (self-fulfilling) prophecy fails: An interaction goals analysis of the expectancy confirmation process.* MA thesis. Princeton Univ. Princeton, NJ

Gibbons, F. X., Sawin, L. S., Gibbons, B. N.

1979. Evaluations of mentally retarded persons: "Sympathy" is patronization? *Am. J. Ment. Defic.* 84:124–31

Gurwitz, S. B., Topol, B. 1978. Determinants of confirming and disconfirming responses to negative social labels. *J. Exp. Soc. Psychol.* 14:31–42

Hamilton, D. L. 1981. Illusory correlation as a basis for stereotyping. In *Cognitive Processes in Stereotyping and Intergroup Behavior*, ed. D. L. Hamilton, pp. 115–44. Hillsdale, NJ: Erlbaum

Hastorf, A., Cantril, H. 1954. They saw a game: A case study. *J. Appl. Soc. Psychol.* 49:129–34

Hilton, J. L. 1985. *Discounting and expectancy confirmation.* PhD thesis. Princeton Univ. Princeton, NJ

Hilton, J. L., Darley, J. M. 1985. Constructing other persons: A limit on the effect. *J. Exp. Soc. Psychol.* 21:1–18

Holmes, J. G., Miller, D. T. 1976. *Interpersonal Conflict.* Morristown, NJ: General Learning Press

Humphreys, L. 1972. *Out of the Closets.* Englewood Cliffs, NJ: Prentice Hall

Ickes, W., Patterson, M. L., Rajecki, D. W., Tanford, S. 1982. Behavioral and cognitive consequences of reciprocal versus compensatory responses to pre-interaction expectancies. *Soc. Cognit.* 1:160–90

Jensen, A. R. 1980. *Bias in Mental Testing.* New York: Free Press

Jones, E. E., Farina, A., Hastorf, A. H., Markus, H., Miller, D. T., Scott, R. A. 1984. *Social Stigma: The Psychology of Marked Relationships.* New York: Freeman

Jones, E. E., McGillis, D. 1976. Correspondent inferences and the attribution cube: A comparative reappraisal. In *New Directions in Attribution Research*, Vol. 1, ed. J. H. Harvey, W. J. Ickes, R. F. Kidd, pp. 389–420. Hillsdale, NJ: Erlbaum

Jones, E. E., Rhodewalt, F., Berglass, S., Skelton, J. A. 1981. Effects of strategic self-presentation on subsequent self-esteem. *J. Pers. Soc. Psychol.* 41:407–21

Jones, E. E., Thibaut, J. W. 1958. Interaction goals as bases of human inferences in interpersonal perception. In *Person Perception and Interpersonal Behavior*, ed. R. Tagiuri, L. Petrullo, pp. 151–78. Stanford, CA: Stanford Univ. Press

Jones, R. A. 1977. *Self-Fulfilling Prophecies: Social, Psychological and Physiological Effects of Expectancies.* Hillsdale, NJ: Erlbaum

Jones, S. C., Panitch, D. 1971. The self-fulfilling prophecy and interpersonal attraction. *J. Exp. Soc. Psychol.* 7:356–66

Jose, J., Cody, J. J. 1971. Teacher-pupil interaction as it relates to attempted changes in teacher expectancy of academic ability and achievement. *Am. Educ. Res. J.* 8:39–49

Kelley, H. H., Stahelski, A. J. 1970a. Errors in perception of intentions in a mixed-motive game. *J. Exp. Soc. Psychol.* 6:379–400

Kelley, H. H., Stahelski, A. J. 1970b. Social interaction basis of cooperators' and competitors' beliefs about others. *J. Pers. Soc. Psychol.* 16:6–91

King, A. S. 1971. Self-fulfilling prophecies in training the hard-core: Supervisors' expectations and the underprivileged worker's performance. *Soc. Sci. Q.* 52(1):369–78

Kraut, R. E. 1973. Effects of social labeling on giving to charity. *J. Exp. Soc. Psychol.* 9:551–62

Meichenbaum, D. H., Bowers, K. S., Ross, R. R. 1969. A behavioral analysis of the teacher expectancy effect. *J. Pers. Soc. Psychol.* 13:306–16

Mendels, G. E., Flanders, J. P. 1973. Teachers' expectations and pupils' performance. *Am. Educ. Res. J.* 10:203–12

Merton, R. K. 1948. The self-fulfilling prophecy. *Antioch Rev.* 8:193–210

Merton, R. K. 1957. *Social Theory and Social Structure.* New York: Free Press

Miller, D. T., Holmes, J. G. 1975. The role of situational restrictiveness on self-fulfilling prophecies: A theoretical and empirical extension of Kelley and Stahelski's triangle hypothesis. *J. Pers. Soc. Psychol.* 31:661–73

Miller, D. T., Ross, M. 1975. Self-serving biases in the attribution of causality: Fact or fiction? *Psychol. Bull.* 82:213–25

Miller, R. L., Brickman, P., Bolen, D. 1975. Attribution versus persuasion as a means for modifying behavior. *J. Pers. Soc. Psychol.* 31:430–41

Minor, M. W. 1970. Experimenter-expectancy effect as a function of evaluation apprehension. *J. Pers. Soc. Psychol.* 15:326–32

Moscovici, S., Faucheux, C. 1972. Social influence, conformity bias, and the study of active minorities. *Adv. Exp. Soc. Psychol.* 6:149–202

Moscovici, S., Nemeth, C. 1974. Social influence: Minority influence. In *Social Psychology: Classic and Contemporary Integrations*, ed. C. Nemeth, pp. 217–49. Chicago: Rand McNally

Musser, L. M., Graziano, W. G. 1983. *Self-fulfilling prophecies in children's interactions with peers.* Presented at bienn. meet Soc. Res. Child Dev., Detroit

O'Connell, E. J., Dusek, J. B., Wheeler, R. J. 1974. A follow-up study of teacher expectancy effects. *J. Educ. Psychol.* 606:325–28

Palardy, J. 1969. What teachers believe— What children achieve. *Elem. Sch. J.* 69:370–74

Platt, G. 1973. Social traps. *Am. Psychol.* 28:641–51

Reeder, G. D., Brewer, M. B. 1979. A schematic model of dispositional attribution in interpersonal perception. *Psychol. Rev.* 86:61–79

Rogers, C. 1982. *A Social Psychology of Schooling.* London: Routledge & Kegan Paul

Rosenhan, D. L. 1973. On being sane in insane places. *Science* 179:250–58

Rosenthal, R. 1963. On the social psychology of the psychological experiment: The experimenter's hypothesis as an unintentional determinant of experimental results. *Am. Sci.* 51:268–83

Rosenthal, R. 1966. *Experimenter Effects in Behavioral Research.* New York: Appleton-Century-Crofts

Rosenthal, R., Fode, K. L. 1963a. The effect of experimenter bias on the performance of the albino rat. *Behav. Sci.* 8:183–89

Rosenthal, R., Fode, K. L. 1963b. Three experiments in experimental bias. *Psychol. Rep.* 12:491–511

Rosenthal, R., Jacobson, L. 1968. *Pygmalion in the Classroom.* New York: Holt, Rinehart & Winston

Rosenthal, R., Kohn, P., Greenfield, P. M., Carota, N. 1966. Data desirability, experimenter expectancy, and the results of psychological research. *J. Pers. Soc. Psychol.* 3:20–27

Rosenthal, R., Lawson, R. 1964. A longitudinal study of the effects of experimenter bias on the operant conditioning of laboratory rats. *J. Psychol. Res.* 2:61–72

Rosenthal, R., Rubin, D. B. 1978. Interpersonal expectancy effects: The first 345 studies. *Behav. Brain Sci.* 3:377–415

Ross, M., Fletcher, G. 1985. Social perception and attribution. In *Handbook of Social Psychology*, ed. G. Lindzey, E. Aronson, pp. 73–122. New York: Random House

Rothbart, M. 1981. Memory processes and social beliefs. In *Cognitive Processes in Stereotyping and Intergroup Behavior*, ed. D. L. Hamilton, pp. 145–81. Hillsdale, NJ: Erlbaum

Rothbart, M., Evans, M., Fulero, S. 1979. Recall for confirming events: Memory processes and the maintenance of social stereotypes. *J. Exp. Soc. Psychol.* 15:343–55

Salancik, G. R., Conway, M. 1975. Attitude inference from salient and relevant cognitive content about behavior. *J. Pers. Soc. Psychol.* 32:829–40

Schur, E. M. 1980. *The Politics of Deviance.* Englewood Cliffs, NJ: Prentice Hall

Scott, R. A. 1969. *The Making of Blind Men.* New York: Sage Found.

Seaver, W. B. 1973. Effects of naturally induced teacher expectancies. *J. Pers. Soc. Psychol.* 28:333–42

Showers, C., Cantor, N. 1985. Social cognition: A look at motivated strategies. *Ann. Rev. Psychol.* 36:275–305

Skrypnek, B. J., Snyder, M. 1982. On the self-perpetuating nature of stereotypes about women and men. *J. Exp. Soc. Psychol.* 18:277–91

Snyder, M. 1984. When belief creates reality. *Adv. Exp. Soc. Psychol.* 18:62–113

Snyder, M., Swann, W. B. Jr. 1978a. Behavioral confirmation in social interaction: From social perception to social reality. *J. Exp. Soc. Psychol.* 14:148–62

Snyder, M., Swann, W. B. Jr. 1978b. Hypothesis-testing processes in social interaction. *J. Pers. Soc. Psychol.* 36:1202–12

Snyder, M., Tanke, E. D., Berscheid, E. 1977. Social perception and interpersonal behavior: On the self-fulfilling nature of social stereotypes. *J. Pers. Soc. Psychol.* 35:656–66

Steele, C. M. 1975. Name calling and compliance. *J. Pers. Soc. Psychol.* 31:361–69

Strenta, A. C., Kleck, R. E. 1984. Physical disability and the perception of social interaction: It's not what you look at but how you look at it. *Pers. Soc. Psychol. Bull.* 10:279–88

Sutherland, A., Goldschmid, M. 1974. Negative teacher expectation and IQ change in children with superior intellectual ability. *Child Dev.* 45:852–56

Swann, W. B. Jr., Ely, R. J. 1984. A battle of wills: Self-verification versus behavioral confirmation. *J. Pers. Soc. Psychol.* 46:1287–1302

Swann, W. B. Jr., Read, S. J. 1981. Self-verification processes: How we sustain our self-conceptions. *J. Exp. Soc. Psychol.* 17:351–72

Swann, W. B. Jr., Snyder, M. 1980. On translating beliefs into action: Theories of ability and their applications in an instructional setting. *J. Pers. Soc. Psychol.* 38:879–88

Taylor, M. C. 1979. Race, sex and the expression of self-fulfilling prophecies in a laboratory teaching situation. *J. Pers. Soc. Psychol.* 37:897–912

Thorndike, R. L. 1968. Review of *Pygmalion in the Classroom*. *Am. Educ. Res. J.* 5:708–11

von Baeyer, C. L., Sherk, D. L., Zanna, M. P. 1981. Impression management in the job interview: When the female applicant meets the male chauvinist interviewer. *Pers. Soc. Psychol. Bull.* 7:45–52

Word, C. O., Zanna, M. P., Cooper, J. 1974. The nonverbal mediation of self-fulfilling prophecies in inter-racial interaction. *J. Exp. Soc. Psychol.* 10:109–20

Zadny, J., Gerard, H. B. 1974. Attributed intentions and informational selectivity. *J. Exp. Soc. Psychol.* 10:34–52

Zanna, M. P., Pack, S. J. 1975. On the self-fulfilling nature of apparent sex differences in behavior. *J. Exp. Soc. Psychol.* 11:583–91

Zanna, M. P., Sheras, P. L., Cooper, J., Shaw, C. 1975. Pygmalion and Galatea: The interactive effects of teacher and student expectancies. *J. Exp. Soc. Psychol.* 11:279–87

Zegers, R. A. 1968. Expectancy and the effects of confirmation and disconfirmation. *J. Pers. Soc. Psychol.* 9:67–71

Ann. Rev. Psychol. 1986. 37:257–89

CONSUMER PSYCHOLOGY

James R. Bettman

Fuqua School of Business, Duke University, Durham, North Carolina 27706

CONTENTS

INTRODUCTION 257
INDIVIDUAL DECISION MAKING 258
    Attention and Perception 258
    Information Acquisition and Search 260
    Memory 261
    Decision Processes 263
    Persuasion and Attitudes 267
    The Relationship between Cognition and Affect 273
    The Processing of Advertising 274
    Learning 277
GROUP AND SOCIAL INFLUENCES.. 278
    Family Decision Making... 278
    Consumption Symbolism 278
POLICY ISSUES AND CONSUMER SATISFACTION 279
    Policy Issues 279
    Consumer Satisfaction... 280
CONCLUSION 281

INTRODUCTION

Behaviors related to the choice, purchase, and use of products and services are ubiquitous in everyday life. Whether it is selection of a brand of toothpaste, a new automobile, a graduate school, or a political candidate, individuals constantly make choices among arrays of alternatives that can be broadly categorized as services or products. The individual often receives persuasive communications about the various alternatives and may possess a good deal of knowledge from previous experience.

The individual may also be subject to forces ranging from factors influencing the details of information processing to the influence of other individuals to the broad impact of culture. The focus of consumer psychology is on understanding

257

0066-4308/86/0201-0257$02.00

and explaining the psychological factors that influence these choice, purchase, and usage behaviors.

This review generally covers research in the years 1981–1984 and focuses on topics that are mainly psychological in nature. One set of topics includes areas related to individual decision making: attention and perception, information acquisition and search, decision processes, persuasion and attitudes, the relationship between cognition and evaluations, the processing of advertising, and learning. Group and social influences on consumer behavior are examined next, followed by a consideration of policy issues and consumer satisfaction research. Areas that are not primarily psychological in nature have been excluded, even though they are important within consumer research. Other areas such as research on energy consumption have been excluded because of space limitations and because surveys exist elsewhere (e.g. Winett & Kagel 1984).

Several issues have assumed particular importance in consumer psychology in the past few years, reflecting common themes that recur across many different areas of research. The first issue concerns the relationship of prior knowledge to current information processing. Consumers often are provided with a good deal of information via advertising, the package, brochures, and so on. In addition, consumers may have had prior experience with a product. Hence, prior knowledge is usually available. In many areas of consumer research, understanding how such knowledge affects and is affected by ongoing processing is a major concern. This relationship between prior expectations and beliefs and current processing is also an important focus within psychology in general (e.g. Alba & Hasher 1983).

A second important theme concerns the relationship between affect and cognition. In particular, the recent emphasis on information processing and cognitive approaches has led researchers to ask about the proper role for affect in such models. As a result, the relative emphasis and precedence of affect and cognition have been the subject of much debate (e.g. Zajonc 1980).

Finally, recent work in consumer psychology has focused on understanding the processes underlying various effects rather than merely describing such effects. All three of these issues appear in a variety of areas within consumer psychology and will be considered where appropriate in the following discussions.

INDIVIDUAL DECISION MAKING

Attention and Perception

PRIOR KNOWLEDGE AND PERCEPTION   One recurrent issue in understanding consumer behavior is how to account for the role of prior knowledge. Consumer psychologists have noted that organized knowledge structures such as schemas, scripts, or categories play an important role in perception. While there have been a reasonable number of conceptual discussions, empirical work has been limited to attempts to measure scripts in consumer settings (Bozinoff & Roth 1983, Leigh & Rethans 1983, Whitney & John 1983) and to examine how scripts may affect memory. However, such issues as when a particular script is elicited or how scripts affect the perception of discrepant events have not yet been addressed.

Alba & Hasher (1983) note that there are problems in attempting to apply the notion of organized prior knowledge structures. They argue there is not one schema theory and that memory for events is often more detailed than schema theories would predict. Thus, one cannot assume that prior expectations override processing of the details of current experience. The schema and script notions applied in consumer psychology have tended to be fairly loosely specified. What is needed is more empirical work with carefully specified versions of these theories.

ASSESSMENT OF COVARIATION   Assessment of covariation refers to the processes by which individuals judge the relationships between events. Such judgments are important in helping to explain prior events, control current outcomes, and predict future contingencies. Covariation judgments have relevance for consumer behavior. For example, consumers may have beliefs about the relationship between price and quality or the relationship between using fluoride toothpaste and having fewer cavities.

Bettman et al (1985, John et al 1985) have carried out a series of studies related to consumers' assessment of price-quality relationships. This research examined the relationship between prior beliefs about price and quality and the processing of current data. The pattern of results across the several studies is quite interesting. Crocker (1981) outlines six steps in the process of covariation assessment: (a) deciding what data are relevant; (b) sampling cases; (c) interpreting cases; (d) recalling the data; (e) integrating the evidence; and (f) using the estimates. Consumers appear to be biased in the early steps (a and b), but not the later ones (d and e). That is, consumers with higher prior beliefs that price and quality are related tend to sample higher-priced brands (John et al 1985) when they are attempting to gather data about price and quality. However, consumers' assessments of covariation for a given set of price and quality data tend to be quite accurate (Bettman et al 1985) and are generally unaffected by prior price-quality beliefs. Hence, consumers appear to assess relationship data accurately if such data are provided for them, but they may gather biased samples of such data. These studies have *not* examined the interpretation of cases (Step c), however. Rather, subjects have been given price and quality data to assess. There may also be substantial biases in interpretation.

PERCEPTIONS OF RISK   Perceived risk, the notion that a consumer's choice may have unpleasant consequences that cannot be foreseen with certainty, has been of interest in consumer research for a long time (Bauer 1960). However, prior research has been plagued with measurement difficulties and lack of a conceptual framework (Ross 1975). There has been a recent resurgence of interest in this area from the perspective of behavioral decision theory.

Slovic et al (1981) and Rethans & Albaum (1981) found that consumers could estimate risks and that these estimates included factors other than estimates about probability of injury. For example, the likelihood of user error and the degree of foreseeability of the consequences are related to perceptions of risk (e.g. for power mowers; Rethans & Albaum 1981). Other research has examined factors affecting such risk assessments. Johnson & Tversky (1983) find that bad mood leads to increased estimates of risk, while a positive mood leads to decreased estimates. Rethans & Hastak (1982) found that memory for specific high imagery instances of accidents was quite prevalent. Hence, such incidents may play a disproportionate role in risk assessments because of their potentially greater availability (Lichtenstein et al 1978).

This approach appears to be an encouraging direction for research on the perception of risk. One promising research direction would be to integrate this work on estimates of risk with recent theories of risky choices. Kahneman & Tversky's (1979) prospect theory may provide a conceptual framework for understanding consumer choices under risk. An individual's choice among prospects or gambles is viewed as having two stages: an editing phase and an evaluation phase. In the editing phase, individuals simplify the prospects. A crucial simplification is coding the outcomes of the gamble as gains or losses relative to some reference point. In the evaluation phase, the prospects are assigned a value and compared. The important principles in valuing prospects are that the value function is convex for losses, concave for gains, and steeper for losses than gains.

One can postulate that consumers perceive of given potential choices as prospects with some overall potential gain and some overall potential loss relative to some reference point (see Shimp & Kavas 1984, p. 806). The reference point might be the current situation (e.g. the current brand being used) or the consumer's current expectations for product performance. However, as Payne et al (1980) point out, the selection of the reference point is crucial, so factors affecting what is used as a reference point are important areas for study. Thaler (1983) presents some related ideas for applying prospect theory and extensions to consumer choice.

Information Acquisition and Search

EFFECTS OF PRIOR KNOWLEDGE   In general, empirical results show decreased search for external information (i.e. information available from sources outside of the consumer) with increases in prior knowledge (Kiel & Layton 1981, Biehal 1983, Punj & Staelin 1983). Reilly & Conover (1983) report a meta-analysis of seven previous studies which shows a high degree of support for a negative relationship between familiarity with a product category and the amount of external search.

While these results seem fairly consistent, several authors have noted that their explanation is not as simple as it might appear. Individuals with greater prior knowledge should have greater ability to process current information (Johnson & Russo 1981, 1984, Srull 1983b), and hence may acquire more in some circumstances (Brucks 1985). However, they may have less need for such information and may be less motivated to process it. Thus, an inverted U shaped relationship between prior knowledge and information acquisition may arise in some cases, with consumers with moderate knowledge acquiring the most information (Bettman and Park 1980).

COST-BENEFIT APPROACHES   The motivational argument above is one example of the general cost-benefit framework applied in studies of consumer search. It is argued that consumers trade off the expected benefits and costs of search (Schaninger & Sciglimpaglia 1981, Duncan & Olshavsky 1982, Midgley 1983, Punj & Staelin 1983, Furse et al 1984). Meyer (1982) develops a formal cost-benefit model of search that is particularly interesting in that it includes a component for making inferences from prior information if an alternative is unfamiliar.

INDIVIDUAL DIFFERENCES   Some very interesting work attempts to relate cognitive abilities to search. Calcich & Blair (1983) report that the time required for consumers to acquire specified information by looking at a package is significantly correlated with scores on the Embedded Figures Test (Witkin 1950). Capon & Davis (1984) find that measures that tap systematic combination abilities (Inhelder & Piaget 1958) are correlated with more complex patterns of information acquisition and integration. Hence, measures of basic cognitive abilities may prove useful in characterizing consumer information processing skills.

Memory

Research on memory has become a strong focus in recent consumer research, reflecting the realization that prior knowledge plays a major role in consumer behavior. Hence, memory has major interactions with many other components of choice processes such as perception, information acquisition, and decision processes. The interaction of memory with these components is discussed with each component. In the following, research specific to memory functioning per se is the focus.

Several features of the consumer environment imply that an extended view of memory might be useful. Consumers often make choices in a store where there is an external memory available. That is, there is information available on the packages, price information is present, and so on. If such information is available externally, the consumer may not need to store that information in memory. Thus, a functional view of consumer memory may be appropriate, noting that consumers may remember only that which is functional or necessary to remember (Russo & Johnson 1980, Hastie 1982, Zeithaml 1982).

Two factors that affect consumer memory have been examined: prior knowledge and mood. Prior knowledge and experience have been found to have strong effects on consumer memory. Subjects with more knowledge show different clustering patterns in recall than subjects with less knowledge. In particular, more knowledgeable subjects tend to cluster information by brand (Srull 1983b, Johnson & Russo 1984) and to cluster brands by functional equivalence (Hutchinson 1983). Thus, prior knowledge effects the structure of memory for current information.

Johnson & Russo (1984) provide a framework for understanding these effects of prior knowledge on memory. They outline three skills that should develop with increased knowledge: superior knowledge of existing products, greater ability to encode new information, and greater ability to select relevant information. The impact of prior knowledge on memory will depend on the relative importance of these three skills. The greater ability to encode will tend to increase memory, while the superior knowledge of existing products and greater ability to be selective may actually lead to fewer items of information recalled if new information is presented. Given tasks may emphasize these skills to differing degrees, allowing one to predict differential effects of such tasks on memory. A specific example is discussed below in the section on decision processes.

Mood effects have also been of interest in examining consumer memory. To the extent that the television show or other vehicle in which an advertisement is placed has effects on the consumer's mood, or to the extent that the advertisement itself may affect mood, there can be mood effects on memory for the advertisement. Earlier work had shown state-dependent memory: events learned in a particular mood state are remembered better when in that state (Bower 1981, Gardner & Vandersteel 1984). Positive mood can also lead to increased cognitive organization (Isen 1984a). However, the findings in consumer settings have been more complex. Srull (1983a) examined mood effects on memory for print advertisements and found the opposite of mood congruence effects. His subjects recalled more positive information when in a negative mood, and more negative information when in a positive mood. While these results have not yet been replicated, they suggest that the interactions between mood and memory for advertising stimuli may not be simple. Srull

(1983b) also found that high familiarity subjects showed less effect of format and mood on memory.

In general, studying memory effects in consumer settings provides a challenge for memory researchers. The stimuli are fairly complex, the typical consumer environment is potentially subject to a great deal of interference, and consumers often have a wealth of prior knowledge. While these aspects can all be eliminated experimentally, the interaction of such aspects with other factors affecting memory potentially can provide interesting new issues for memory research.

Decision Processes

THE INTERACTION BETWEEN MEMORY AND DECISION PROCESSES   One of the major developments in research on consumer decision processes is the realization that memory and decision processes interact. Earlier work on consumer decision making had implicitly assumed that all the information needed to implement various decision rules was available, either externally or in memory. The purest case of this assumption is stimulus-based choice, where all of the information is available in a display of the alternatives. However, if choices are made based only on information in memory, then information may be incomplete, inferences may be made about missing information, and the information available for choice may also be a function of salience and other factors that influence memory. Thus, memory-based choices are much more dependent upon retrieval cues in the choice environment (Lynch & Srull 1982).

Most consumer choices are probably a mixture of memory- and stimulus-based processes, where some data are available in the choice environment and some are in memory. This mix of memory- and stimulus-based aspects is probably enhanced when choice strategies are constructed on the spot (Bettman 1979, Hayes-Roth 1982). If the decision process is being built at the time of choice, there will tend to be missing information, prior knowledge brought to bear, and interactions between memory and the stimulus information available (e.g. information on packages).

Several studies have examined the interactions between memory and choice and have found effects both of memory on choices and of choice on subsequent memory traces. Biehal & Chakravarti (1982) placed subjects in conditions where they either learned information and then made choices or made choices and then were asked to recall the information. Subjects who learned the information first tended to organize that information in memory by brand and showed a greater tendency to process information by brand when they made choices than subjects who made choices first. The subjects who made choices first, on the other hand, processed more by attribute and showed much greater attribute organization in memory than the subjects who learned information first. The choice-first subjects also showed much better recall for the chosen brand than rejected brands (also found in Johnson & Russo 1981).

Biehal & Chakravarti (1983) also show how the interactions between memory and choice can influence choices over time. They examine a situation where subjects initially either learn information or make a choice. Then information on new alternatives and new attributes is added, and a second choice is made. The added attribute information makes one of the original alternatives more attractive. The results show that if a choice is made first, the decreased memory for rejected alternatives makes it harder to reevaluate an alternative that had been rejected, even if that alternative would be attractive if processed.

Johnson & Russo (1981, 1984) studied the effects of type of decision task, judgment or choice, on memory. Work in behavioral decision theory has emphasized that judgment and choice are not equivalent (Einhorn & Hogarth 1981). In a judgment task, the subject is asked to make an overall evaluation of each alternative. In a choice task, the subject is asked to choose the alternative they most prefer. A judgment task encourages the subject to examine all of the information on an alternative, whereas a choice task allows the subject to be much more selective (e.g. some alternatives may be virtually ignored if they have a bad value on one attribute). Johnson & Russo show that prior knowledge is positively related to memory for information about the alternatives for a judgment task, but that the subjects with the greatest prior knowledge show decreased memory for information about current alternatives in the choice task. If subjects process all information, as in the judgment task, greater knowledge aids memory. However, in the choice task, subjects with greater knowledge appear to process information more selectively, and hence remember less (for related results see Bettman & Park 1980).

Thus, memory and choice show interactions in both directions. What is in memory can influence future choice processes, and current choice processes can affect subsequent memory.

PRIOR KNOWLEDGE AND TYPE OF PROCESSING   Fiske (1982, Fiske & Pavelchak 1986) has proposed that individuals may evaluate stimuli in two basic modes. In piecemeal processing, the evaluation of a stimulus is the combination of the evaluations of the individual elements or attributes of that stimulus. In category-based processing, if a stimulus is successfully categorized in an existing category, the evaluation associated with that category is associated with the stimulus. Fiske & Pavelchak hypothesize a two-stage process. If the first categorization stage succeeds, then category-based evaluation processing ensues. If categorization fails, piecemeal processing is invoked.

The categorization approach has been examined by Sujan (1985) in a consumer setting. Sujan shows that when the information in a print advertisement matches expectations, there is evidence of category-based processing: faster impression times, more category verbalizations, and fewer attribute verbalizations. When the information does not match expectations, there is evidence for piecemeal processing. These effects are more pronounced for experts than for novices in the product category used (cameras). Thus, there is some very interesting evidence that prior knowledge can affect the basic type of evaluative processing carried out.

THE EFFECTS OF EXPERTISE   Several of the results described above imply that characterizing consumer expertise and its effects could be an extremely important contribution. The early search for the supposedly more powerful problem-solving heuristics of experts has yielded to the study of the different knowledge structures of experts (Chi 1983). It is felt that the content and organization of knowledge is the crucial factor underlying expertise. For example, Hutchinson (1983) shows that subjects with higher expertise tend to group items more by their functional equivalence than by their surface similarities. As noted above, Sujan has also shown how experts process information differently depending on the degree to which it matches or mismatches their existing knowledge. Finally, Beattie (1982, 1983) provides some interesting hypotheses about the effect of expertise. However, much more empirical work needs to be done.

INFERENCES   If a consumer does not know the value of a particular attribute for some alternative, he or she may infer that attribute's value from other available information. Meyer (1981) developed a model that accounts for consumer uncertainty about attribute values and assumes that consumers make inferences if no information is available. His results showed that consumers infer a discounted value for a missing attribute value (i.e. a value which is less than the average value of that attribute across other alternatives). Huber & McCann (1982) and Yates et al (1978) get similar results.

MEASUREMENT OF PRIOR KNOWLEDGE   The sections above document that understanding the interaction between prior knowledge and decision processes has assumed a major role in recent consumer research. This implies that measurement of prior knowledge is of utmost importance. Broad categorizations of familiarity are inadequate (Bettman & Park 1980). To make more precise predictions, measures of the content and structure of knowledge are needed. This has proved to be a very difficult endeavor. Despite some interesting conceptual and empirical work (Brucks & Mitchell 1981, Kanwar et al 1981, Marks & Olson 1981, Mitchell 1982, Olson & Reynolds 1983), there has as yet been no convincing empirical demonstration of a measurement scheme that can provide the necessary framework.

CONTINGENCY RESEARCH ON DECISION PROCESSES   As pointed out by Payne (1982) and Punj & Stewart (1983), decision processes are contingent on many factors. In particular, three areas of research have seen significant results: task effects, context effects, and accuracy/effort tradeoffs.

Task effects refer to factors describing the general structure of a problem, such as number of alternatives or response mode (Payne 1982). Several researchers investigated the effects of number of alternatives and number of attributes per alternative on information overload. Malhotra et al (1982) reanalyzed data from earlier studies and found that there was little evidence of a decrease in decision accuracy as the number of attributes per alternative increased (see Staelin & Payne 1976 for a similar analysis). Malhotra (1982) performed a study with a much larger number of alternatives and attributes and demonstrated overload.

Johnson & Meyer (1984) also studied the effects of number of alternatives, replicating earlier findings that an increased number of alternatives leads to increased elimination of alternatives early in the choice process. They also found, somewhat surprisingly, that compensatory choice models maintained high predictive accuracy across differing numbers of alternatives.

A final task effect, response mode, was studied by Levin & Johnson (1984). They found that a price cue had the greatest effect on judgments when price judgments were to be made and that a quality cue had the greatest effect on quality judgments, a response mode compatibility effect.

Context effects refer to factors describing a particular set of alternatives, such as similarity (Payne 1982). Huber et al (1982), Huber & Puto (1983), and Huber (1983) examine the effects of adding a new alternative to a set. Huber et al (1982) find that adding a dominated alternative to the set can increase choice of the alternative which is dominant, a violation of the principle of regularity fundamental to most choice models. Huber & Puto (1983) and Huber (1983) extend these findings to nondominated alternatives and document the existence of an attractive effect (a new item can lead to increased choice of similar items) as well as the normal substitution effects (a new item takes choice from those items to which it is most similar). These findings provide important new constraints which viable choice models must meet.

Another context effect that has been examined is whether the importance weights given an attribute depend on the variation in scores on that attribute across the set of alternatives. Meyer & Eagle (1982) report that weights did shift as a function of variance, with attributes with greater variance receiving more weight. In contrast, Curry & Menasco (1983) find that weights do not depend on the variation in scores. The difference in results may be partially due to the fact that Curry and Menasco used a judgment task, whereas Meyer and Eagle get their strongest results for a choice task.

Ofir & Lynch (1984) attempt to characterize context effects on the use of base-rate and specific case information in judgments. They find that the utilization of base-rate information depends upon the levels of base and case cues, their relative specificity, and subjects' knowledge of the content area of the judgment problem. They also show relatively high usage of base-rate information relative to prior research.

M. Johnson (1984) considers how the degree of comparability of alternatives affects choice processing. He shows that consumers make more comparisons on abstract attributes (e.g. necessity) as alternatives become more noncomparable.

Finally, significant research efforts have been directed at understanding accuracy/effort tradeoffs in decision processes. Several authors (e.g. Olshavsky & Granbois 1979, Formisano et al 1982) have argued that most consumer choices are unimportant and the result of low effort. However, observing low effort does not necessarily mean accuracy is being sacrificed. Johnson & Payne (1985) develop a simulation model based on production-system representations of various decision strategies. They measure effort by counting the number of operations necessary to make a choice for a particular rule. They find that in a given situation, there may be a rule that provides relatively accurate decisions for relatively low effort.

Grether & Wilde (1984) also consider accuracy/effort tradeoffs. They undertake a theoretical analysis of the conjunctive choice model and note that an optimal approach would require difficult computations. They derive a simplified version of the model and note that subjects generally behave in accord with that simpler version.

Finally, Isen (1984a,b) also reports that positive mood leads to less effort and less search in decision tasks. However, the results also show that the positive mood subjects are equally accurate and hence more efficient.

Persuasion and Attitudes

The general area of persuasion and attitudes is one of the classic areas of consumer research, and interest in it is substantial. Because of the volume of research in this area, the discussion is split into two major parts: consideration of general research on persuasion, and a discussion of specific research related to the processing of advertising stimuli. It should be noted that the approaches discussed are cognitive, focusing on manipulation of beliefs or cognitive responses. Zajonc & Markus (1982) argue that such theories may not apply to attitudes or preferences that have a primarily affective rather than cognitive base. We will return to this notion of the relation between affect and cognition below.

THE FISHBEIN AND AJZEN MODEL   The concept of multiattribute models of attitude is well established in consumer research (Lutz 1982). The most influential conceptualization for more than the past decade has undoubtedly been the model of Fishbein & Ajzen (1975). In the period from 1981–1984, several challenges to the model have appeared.

The sufficiency assumption of the Fishbein-Ajzen model has been the subject of a great deal of research during the past several years. Fishbein & Ajzen (1975, Ajzen & Fishbein 1980) claim that all effects on behavioral intentions are mediated by attitude toward the behavior (A_B) and subjective norm (SN), and that all effects on behavior are mediated by intentions. Hence, if one can show direct effects of some factor on behavioral intentions or behavior, that result is inconsistent with Fishbein and Ajzen's theory.

Bentler & Speckart (1979, 1981) reported that prior behaviors directly affect intentions and present behavior, and that attitude directly affects behavior as well as having an indirect affect through intentions. Bagozzi (1981, 1982) argues that Bentler and Speckart's results are suspect because they used a self-report of behavior and because the domains used (alcohol, marijuana, and hard drugs in the 1979 study and dating, studying, and exercise in the 1981 study) may not be totally under volitional control. Bagozzi, using data on blood donation, found that attitudes influence behavior only through intentions. However, past behavior influenced current behavior directly, and in the 1982 paper, expectancy-value judgments influenced intentions directly as well as indirectly through attitude. Saltzer (1981) found that individual difference variables (weight locus of control and value placed on health and appearance) influenced the strength of the relationship between behavioral intentions and behavior for the domain of weight loss. However, it is not clear that weight loss is totally subject to volitional control. Fredricks & Dossett (1983) reported for class attendance data that prior behavior directly affected intention and present behavior, but that attitude affected behavior only through intention. Finally, Shimp & Kavas (1984) found that intentions mediated the effects on coupon usage.

These results do not provide a simple picture. The weight of evidence appears to be that attitude generally affects behavior indirectly through intentions, in accord with Fishbein and Ajzen. However, there appear to be systematic direct affects of past behavior on intentions and/or current behavior which are not consistent with the Fishbein-Ajzen approach.

A second area subject to some controversy pertains to the normative component of the Fishbein and Ajzen model. Miniard & Cohen (1981) argue that the normative and attitudinal components are not clearly separated in the Fishbein-Ajzen approach and that some forms of influence could appear in both the attitudinal and normative components, thus leading to double counting in the model. Manipulations of variables intended to affect one component also affected the other in their study, so they conclude that the normative and attitudinal components have conceptual difficulties. Fishbein & Ajzen (1981) argue strongly that the Miniard and Cohen results do not support such conclusions. Miniard & Cohen (1983) develop and test a model which attempts to divide the salient consequences at a particular point in time into normative and personal consequences. Manipulations generally affect their measures for these components in the proper way. However, they note that separating the normative and personal components is likely to be very difficult.

Other researchers have also examined the normative and attitudinal components. Ryan (1982) finds complex interrelationships among his normative and attitudinal measures. Burnkrant & Page (1982) find that the normative and attitudinal components are correlated. Finally, Miniard & Page (1984) and Shimp & Kavas (1984) report complex patterns of interrelationships that differ from those found by Ryan.

Once again the results do not form a simple pattern. It is clear that there is a great deal of disagreement over the conceptualization of the normative component, its measurement, and its relationship with the attitudinal component. It appears that achieving separability of the two components is unlikely. However, better theorizing about the relationships between the two components under various conditions would be extremely valuable.

A third challenge to Fishbein and Ajzen concerns the conceptualization and measurement of behavioral intentions. Warshaw et al (1986) extend the Fishbein and Ajzen conceptualization to include other aspects of intentions. In particular, Warshaw and colleagues propose a model for the determination of intention when choosing among several alternative behaviors, expand the model to include intentions to pursue goals (outcomes not completely under volitional control), and distinguish the concepts of behavioral intention and behavioral prediction.

Other researchers have examined issues concerning the measurement of intentions. Warshaw (1980a,b) proposed that behavioral intention could be best predicted by measuring intentions, given certain contexts and the probabilities of those contexts, and then summing the corresponding products of intentions given contexts times the probabilities. Warshaw (1980b) found that his contextual measure provided better predictions than a standard single question measure. Miniard et al (1983) attempted to replicate and extend these findings, but did not find significant differences between the conditional contextual measure and standard direct measures of intentions. Warshaw (1980a) also proposes an alternative model of behavioral intentions that compares favorably to Fishbein and Ajzen's model.

In general, the Fishbein-Ajzen approach has stood up well to its challenges. The most serious issues are the role of prior behavior in the model and specifying the particular relationships to be expected between the normative and attitudinal components under different conditions.

TWO MODELS OF COGNITIVE MESSAGE REACTIONS   Cognitive response approaches argue that it is not the message itself that is important, but rather thoughts, ideas, and reactions brought about by the message which mediate persuasion (Brock & Shavitt 1983). Two new approaches to cognitive message reactions have been the focus of research in consumer behavior: Cacioppo and Petty's Elaboration Likelihood Model and Kiselius and Sternthal's Availability-Valence Model.

Cacioppo & Petty (1984; Petty & Cacioppo 1983, 1984; Petty, Cacioppo & Schumann 1983) have proposed the Elaboration Likelihood Model (ELM) of attitude change. The elaboration likelihood of a communication situation is a function of the motivation and ability of the communication recipients. If conditions are such that people are motivated and able to process the communication message, then elaboration likelihood is high and recipients will scrutinize and process message arguments. On the other hand, when elaboration likelihood is low for lack of motivation and/or lack of ability to process, recipients will form attitudes based not on processing of message arguments but on processing of simple cues associated with the message (e.g. the source). The ELM predicts that cognitive responses related to careful message processing, such as counterarguments and support arguments, will occur more often under high elaboration likelihood. Such cognitive responses as source derogations or source supports should occur under low elaboration likelihood.

Petty and Cacioppo argue there are two main routes to attitude change: the central route, where recipients diligently consider message arguments; and the peripheral route, where attitude change is based upon positive or negative cues associated with the message. The central route would occur under high elaboration likelihood, while the peripheral route would be associated with low elaboration likelihood. Although they focus on these two modes of attitude change, they note that these modes are positions on a continuous scale of elaboration likelihood. Attitude change resulting from the central route is felt to be more enduring and more predictive of future behaviors.

Various factors can affect elaboration likelihood. Elaboration likelihood will be greater under greater involvement (Petty et al 1983), greater need for cognition (Cacioppo & Petty 1981), less distraction (Petty et al 1976), and when the message is less quantitative (Yalch & Elmore-Yalch 1984). Hence, Cacioppo and Petty propose a contingent model of attitude change where different processes are invoked under different conditions.

The availability-valence model proposed by Kisielius & Sternthal (1984) does not directly consider typical cognitive responses (i.e. counterarguments, support arguments, source derogations). However, it is classed as a cognitive response approach because its central premise is that attitudes are based on cognitive reactions to the message. In particular, Kisielius & Sternthal argue that recipients process message information by relating that message information to information they have stored in memory, especially that which is most available. The favorableness (valence) of that available information will then be the major determinant of the attitudinal response. Availability of information, Kisielius and Sternthal hypothesize, increases with the degree of cognitive elaboration of information and with the recency of the information.

Several studies report results consistent with the above interpretation. Kisielius & Sternthal (1984) use several manipulations thought to stimulate cognitive elaboration of relatively unfavorable information. The results showed decreases in persuasion, as predicted by the availability-valence model. Hannah & Sternthal (1984) use availability-valence arguments to predict sleeper effects in two experiments. Tybout et al (1983), in a series of studies on behavioral compliance, also report four experiments consistent with availability-valence notions. Finally, Tybout et al (1981) support the availability-valence model. Both their retrieval and storage strategies attempt to make more positive information available. In all of this research, the proposed role of cognitive elaboration and the pattern of cognitive reactions it implies have not been examined directly. As Kisielius & Sternthal (1984) note, development of adequate measures of the cognitive mediation process hypothesized by the availability-valence model should be a priority for future research on this approach.

CONTINGENCY APPROACHES TO PERSUASION PROCESSES   Recent theorizing in consumer psychology has emphasized contingent approaches to persuasion. The major contingency variable has been degree of involvement; however, some approaches have also postulated contingencies based upon prior knowledge.

Several different theories have postulated differing persuasion processes under low and high involvement. As noted above, Cacioppo & Petty have proposed that persuasion occurs via diligent message processing under high involvement (the central route), but via positive or negative cues associated with the message under low involvement (the peripheral route).

Batra & Ray (1983) discuss three different processes of advertising effects, which they label the high involvement, low involvement, and dissonance-attribution hierarchies. In the high involvement sequence, message processing may lead to belief change, then to attitude change, and finally to behavior change. The attitude formed is thus cognitively based and enduring. In low involvement, on the other hand, messages create awareness and mere-exposure affect (Zajonc 1968), which then leads to behavior, which then can lead to more firmly held attitudes. The Batra and Ray conceptualization appears to be quite compatible with that of Cacioppo and Petty. In both cases there is message processing under high involvement and use of a cue (e.g. frequency of exposure) under low involvement.

Deighton (1983) also proposes that advertisements may be processed in two ways: highly involved processing of the message, or a low involvement mode he calls "schematic inquiry." Under this latter process, advertising provides a hypothesis about the advertised product which may be casually accepted, and confirmatory biases in search may tend to ensure confirmation of that hypothesis. Trial is limited to those products one expects to perform well, so there is a tendency to confirm. The hypothesized processes are fascinating, and Deighton cites research in social cognition (e.g. Lord et al 1979, Gilovich 1981) that supports his conceptions. Initial research in a consumer context (Deighton 1984) is also supportive.

While there seems to be some agreement about the basic nature of the different processes involved by high (message processing) vs low (nonmessage cues) involvement, there is not as much agreement about the nature of involvement itself. Mitchell (1981) defines involvement as an internal state variable with the motivational properties of direction and intensity. Cohen (1983) describes involvement as a state of activation directed to some portion of the psychological field. Finally, Greenwald & Leavitt (1984) describe four levels of involvement: preattention, focal attention, comprehension, and elaboration. These levels are associated with allocation of increasing cognitive capacity and produce increasingly durable memory traces. Greenwald & Leavitt attempt to relate their conception to those of other researchers. Although the above conceptualizations appear to embody two slightly different notions of involvement, involvement as motivation (Mitchell, Cohen) and involvement as the degree of processing resulting from some level of motivation (Greenwald & Leavitt), the notions seem generally compatible.

In addition to persuasion processes contingent on involvement, other researchers have postulated that the road to persuasion may also depend upon the degree of prior knowledge. Tybout & Scott (1983) find that when well-defined internal knowledge is available, persuasion occurs via a standard information integration model of attitude. However, when such knowledge is not available, self-perception processes occur.

ATTITUDE-BEHAVIOR RELATIONS   Cooper & Croyle (1984) discuss the attitude-behavior relationship for persuasion research in general. Hence, only specific consumer research studies are considered. As noted above, Bagozzi (1981, 1982) found that attitudes were related to behavior through intentions within the context of the Fishbein-Ajzen model. Other researchers have adopted a contingency approach, focusing on the conditions under which attitude-behavior consistency can be expected to occur (Fazio & Zanna 1981). Smith & Swinyard (1983) find that attitudes formed on the basis of trial predict subsequent behavior better than attitudes based upon advertising. Roedder et al (1983) find that children behave in an attitude-consistent fashion when their abilities to process information are not exceeded. When the situation overtaxes their processing abilities, children may make choices inconsistent with their attitudes.

The Relationship between Cognition and Affect

MEMORY AND EVALUATIVE JUDGMENTS   Several models of persuasion and decision making have been discussed above. In many of these cases, it was noted that decisions can have effects on memory and vice versa. Hence, it might seem that there would be a simple relationship between memory and evaluative judgments, namely that those items recalled from memory about an alternative should predict evaluative judgments about that alternative. Surprisingly, this does not seem to be the case. In many studies, recall and evaluations are weakly related (see Srull 1984 for a review; Petty et al 1983, Gardner 1983). These results refer to recall of the original stimulus information; these results do not imply that the reactions to incoming messages will not be related to persuasion (Kisielius & Sternthal 1984).

Srull (1984) notes that in some cases recall and judgment are related. He argues that the degree of relationship depends upon how the evaluations are made. If evaluations are constructed when information is acquired, the evaluation will be stored independently of the information on which it is based. Later evaluations will be based on retrieval of this original judgment and will not necessarily have any relationship to recall of the specific information. On the other hand, if an evaluation is not formed at the time of information acquisition, any later evaluation will have to be constructed based upon recall of the original information and there will be a relationship between recall and evaluation in this case. For research that supports this conception, see Lichtenstein & Srull (1985).

Bettman (1982) discusses conditions under which evaluations may or may not be formed at the time of information acquisition. His framework could be used to generate hypotheses about recall-evaluation correlations in various conditions. Bettman notes that the conditions likely to foster evaluations at the time of information acquisition (e.g. information presented sequentially, information not easily comparable across brands, format encouraging processing by brand) are likely to characterize most consumer choices. Hence, the recall-evaluation relationship may be low in many consumer situations.

COGNITIVE VERSUS AFFECTIVE PRECEDENCE   The preceding discussion raises the more general issue of the relationship between affect and cognition in consumer choice. Many of the models discussed thus far assume cognitive precedence: cognition → affect → choice. Some low involvement models differ, but still assume cognitive precedence: cognition → behavior → affect. Zajonc (1980), in a provocative analysis, disputes these sequences. He argues that affective reactions to stimuli always occur and generally occur prior to cognitions. Affect and cognitions, he argues, are independent systems, and affect is often predominant. In Zajonc & Markus (1982), the argument is also made that there are many cases where affective preferences precede cognitive appraisals. Zajonc's views have not been without their strong critics (Lazarus

1981, Mandler 1982). However, these views raise important issues with which any conceptualization must deal.

Several consumer researchers have argued for a contingent view of the extent of cognitive participation in choice. Bagozzi (1983) proposes that there are several circumstances under which affect could precede cognition (e.g. intense emotionality, high pressure communication). Batra & Ray (1983) argue that under low involvement mere exposure affect may occur prior to cognition. As noted earlier, categorization models (Fiske 1982, Fiske & Pavelchak 1986, Sujan 1985) argue that a very rapid affective response occurs if input matches a category. Otherwise, more cognitive piecemeal processing occurs. However, if the initial categorization process requires cognition, this model still assumes cognitive precedence. This rapid categorization part of the model appears very similar to Lazarus's (1981) view of cognitive appraisal. Cacioppo & Petty (1981) note that electromyogram measures of muscular activity might be useful in testing the temporal sequencing of affect and cognition. Coyne (1982), however, argues that affect and cognition will be extremely hard to separate.

NEW EMPHASES   The debate about cognitive or affective precedence, even if difficult (if not impossible) to resolve, has been useful in focusing interest on the affective component in consumer behavior. Much-needed effort has been devoted to understanding the role played by affect in consumer choice. Holbrook & Hirschman (1982, Hirschman & Holbrook 1982) have argued that affect, feelings, and emotions should be the subject of more study in consumer research. They argue that the experiential view of consumer behavior has been neglected to date. Nonverbal, hedonic, physiological, and multisensory responses have been studied very little. While this emphasis appears to be appropriate and important, little work has as yet been reported. In two of the first efforts of this sort, Unger & Kernan (1983) examine determinants of the subjective experience of leisure and Holbrook et al (1984) examine some of the experiential aspects of playing games.

The Processing of Advertising

There has been a great deal of research on the details of the processing of advertisements. Several edited books have appeared (Harris 1983, Percy & Woodside 1983) and interest seems to be growing. This area of research is an example of the tendency to examine the processes underlying consumer response in greater detail (Mitchell 1983a).

THE EFFECT OF ATTITUDE TOWARD THE ADVERTISEMENT   Although the notion that a consumer's like or dislike of an advertisement might affect that individual's response to the advertised brand is not new (Lucas & Benson 1929, Silk & Vavra 1974), examination of the mediating role of attitude toward the advertisement (A_{Ad}) has been of more recent origin. Mitchell & Olson (1981) examined the effects of visual stimuli in ads for facial tissues and found that brand attitudes were not only a function of brand beliefs, but also of A_{Ad}. Shimp (1981) showed that A_{Ad} also affected behavior. Further research has attempted to clarify the role of A_{Ad}.

MacKenzie & Lutz (1983) proposed four models of the relationship between A_{Ad} and attitude toward the brand itself (A_B). Their research supported the notion that $A_{Ad} \rightarrow A_B \rightarrow$ intentions. Moore & Hutchinson (1983) examined both immediate and delayed effects and found that A_{Ad} and A_B were directly related immediately after exposure. However, after a one-week delay, both positively and negatively evaluated advertisements had stronger A_B than neutral advertisements.

Lutz et al (1983) hypothesize that A_{Ad} will play a more important role in low involvement/low knowledge situations, arguing that A_{Ad} may function as a positive or negative cue in the peripheral route to persuasion (Petty et al 1983). Their results show that A_{Ad} does have stronger effects than brand cognitions under low involvement and low knowledge. However, A_{Ad} also has greater effects under high involvement and high knowledge, contrary to prediction. Park & Young (1983) examine three involvement conditions: high cognitive involvement (an informational focus), high affective involvement (a focus on the brand's image), and low involvement. They showed that A_{Ad} was related to A_B for low involvement and affective involvement, but not for cognitive involvement. Cognitive responses were related to A_B for cognitive involvement and affective involvement, but not low involvement. An expectancy-value index was related to A_B only under cognitive involvement. Finally, Mitchell (1983b) reports studies which show that A_{Ad} can lead to attitudes which persist; that A_{Ad} effects can occur with verbal copy, not just visual copy; and that A_{Ad} is mediated only partly by verbal responses. He argues that A_{Ad} mediates visual and emotional responses to the advertisement.

Although there has been a reasonable amount of research, the processes underlying the effects of A_{Ad} are still not well understood. Edell & Burke (1984) argue that examining the relationship between A_{Ad} and A_B over time provides leverage for distinguishing the various models proposed.

PROCESSING OF VISUAL STIMULI IN ADVERTISING   There has been a great increase in research interest in how the visual stimuli in advertisements are processed. Such knowledge is important for policy concerns, as policy makers have become more concerned with the communication effects of the nonverbal portions of advertisements (Beales et al 1981).

Edell & Staelin (1983) directly examined the relationship between the visual and verbal components of an advertising message. They distinguish two cases: (a) the message is either totally verbal or is a "framed" picture (i.e. the verbal information is a restatement of the picture); (b) the message is an "unframed" picture (i.e. the verbal information does not relate the picture to the brand). The study shows that framed pictures and verbal messages elicit equivalent reactions. Unframed pictures, on the other hand, are characterized by fewer brand evaluative thoughts, fewer brand items recalled, and longer response times to questions about brand items. The Edell & Staelin (1983) results are an important demonstration that the degree of congruence between the visual and verbal components of a message has a major impact on the processing of the message.

Kisielius & Sternthal (1984) also examine the effect of visual and verbal stimuli. However, the results obtained differ from those of Edell & Staelin (1983). Kisielius & Sternthal find that verbal information alone is responded to more favorably than (a) verbal information accompanied by pictures in the "control" conditions of their three experiments; (b) verbal information with instructions to image; and (c) verbal information with additional information about other favorable alternatives. The results support their availability-valence model. The reason for the difference between the results and those of Edell & Staelin (1983) is not clear. One possibility may be that the pictures in Kisielius and Sternthal's study were not "framed" according to Edell and Staelin's terms. That is, it appears from the description of the stimuli that the verbal and pictorial components were only partially related in Kisielius and Sternthal's experiments. If true, this explanation for the difference in results reemphasizes the importance of the congruence between the visual and verbal components.

Childers & Houston (1984) consider the effect of verbal (words only) and visual (pictures plus words) advertising stimuli on recall. They find that for immediate recall, verbal stimuli perform as well as visual stimuli under semantic processing (instructions to focus on the information content of the ad). Under sensory processing (instructions to focus on appearance), however, visual stimuli showed superior recall. When delayed recall (after two days) was tested, visual stimuli were better recalled for both types of processing, although this effect was more pronounced for sensory processing. Hence, Childers and Houston argue that the relative memorability of visual and verbal advertising material depends on the motivation and capability of the audience to engage in semantic processing.

Other work has also examined the effect of visual stimuli on responses. Percy & Rossiter (1983) report several studies where use of concrete words in an advertisement leads to more favorable responses. The effects of picture size on response varied across two studies. In one study, greater picture size led to more favorable response. In a second, size had an effect only for color pictures, not for black and white.

Despite the importance of the issue of visual processing, relatively little empirical work has been done. This is an area of research that deserves much more emphasis. In addition, the effects of stimuli in other sensory modes (taste, smell, touch) have been subject to even less research (Holbrook 1983). There is a major need for research on the effects of nonverbal stimuli on consumer judgments.

EFFECTS OF LINGUISTIC STRUCTURE   Responses to advertising may also be affected by the linguistic structure of the verbal portion of the advertisement. Percy (1982) and Alesandrini (1983) outline the potential effects of various linguistic properties of the message on memory for the message (e.g. concrete copy should be more memorable). Two studies have used the text comprehension model of Kintsch & van Dijk (1978) to develop a model called the Ad Language Model (ALM) (Thorson & Rothschild 1983, Thorson & Snyder 1984). In Thorson & Snyder (1984), the ALM was able to predict recall of ideas, richness of detail in the recall protocols, recall of executional characteristics, how viewers referred to the product, and day-after recall scores. Thorson & Rothschild (1983) use the ALM to predict recognition data as well as recall. They find that the recall data are generally predicted better than the recognition data, and that the best predictors for recall are more global measures, while the best for recognition are more specific measures of propositional structure.

Linguistic factors may also be important in examining deception in advertising. Several researchers have examined the effect of linguistic features on the inferences drawn from advertisements (Coleman 1983, Harris et al 1983, Monaco & Kaiser 1983). The results show that consumers do make inferences and that they often remember these inferences as having been directly stated. Hence, linguistic properties can affect the degree to which advertisements may mislead consumers.

Learning

Learning is a crucial process in understanding consumer behavior that has seen a recent resurgence in research interest. Several cognitive frameworks for examining consumer learning have been proposed. Bettman et al (1984) propose a hypothesis testing view of learning. They argue that consumers assess current hypotheses, acquire and interpret information, and revise and use hypotheses. However, they note that each of these steps is subject to biases in the way information is processed. They also argue that assessment of covariation is central to this process. Hoch (1984) discusses how individuals may learn or change hypotheses or rules and considers factors affecting the persistence of rules. Finally, Crocker (1984) discusses schema change as a form of learning. She considers the aspects of schemas that are subject to change and the factors that affect them. These discussions provide a variety of hypotheses based on cognitive views of consumer learning. Empirical research is now necessary to fuel advances in our understanding of learning processes.

While the above work represents a focus on cognitive approaches, noncognitive principles have also been considered. Rothschild & Gaidis (1981) and Peter & Nord (1982) discuss the application of operant conditioning principles to consumer behavior, and McSweeney and Bierley (1984) outline the implications for consumer research of recent developments in classical conditioning.

GROUP AND SOCIAL INFLUENCES

Family Decision Making

Research in family decision making has shown an increased emphasis on studies of the decision making process and on the interrelationships among the choice processes of family members. Park (1982) examined the relationship over time between spouses' decision processes in a home-buying decision. He found relatively low initial similarity between the decision plans of the spouses, and this similarity did not increase over time. Perceived similarity was a function of the degree of agreement on those dimensions that could lead to rejecting a house, and there was more agreement on the role of objective dimensions (e.g. number of bedrooms) in the choice process than on the role played by subjective dimensions (e.g. appearance). Spiro (1983) examined the types of strategies used when disagreements arose in purchases. She found that spouses did not agree in their perceptions of the type of influence used by the other. Thus, these studies take a more detailed look at family decision making than earlier studies.

Rudd & Kohout (1983) and Zimmer & Jacoby (1984) examine information acquisition processes in family decision making. Rudd and Kohout find that couples take less time and acquire less information in the search task than do ad hoc dyads. Whether this results from shared prior knowledge or differences in interaction patterns is not examined. Zimmer and Jacoby find that spouses' search patterns are similar with respect to both amount and content for information about birth control devices. However, their choices disagreed, implying differences in information evaluation or integration. These studies also represent promising approaches to examining the details of family decision processes. Additional process-tracing studies of such decisions appear warranted.

Consumption Symbolism

Belk, Bahn & Mayer (1982) and Belk, Mayer & Driscoll (1984) examine the degree to which consumption choices communicate the nature of the consumer to others. In particular, they examined the extent to which children possessed stereotypes of the owners of both adults' and children's products. They found that children did have such stereotypes if they were older than preschool age.

Thus, products do appear to communicate something about the owner to children. Kehret-Ward & Yalch (1984) also examine what item selection can communicate. They found that females labeled as unique and younger children were more likely to take the only one of a particular item. Thus, labeling seemed to affect the meaning ascribed to taking the only one by the older children (i.e. as a reward for uniqueness vs possibly being selfish). Finally, Solomon (1983) argues that product symbolism can help one define one's role or one's self-image. Product symbolism can be used to assign meaning to oneself, a process Solomon terms reflexive evaluation. Thus, it is evident that products can communicate properties of the owner to others or even to the owner him- or herself.

POLICY ISSUES AND CONSUMER SATISFACTION

Policy Issues

INFORMATION PROVISION AND CONSUMER EDUCATION   Researchers have continued to examine the effects of providing additional information to consumers. Zeithaml (1982) examined the effect of providing prices in several different formats in the store. Consumers were less able to recall prices when prices were removed from individual items and were only available on the shelf. Consumers were also less certain about price recall if the item prices were removed. Recall of the average unit price paid was lower with an ordered list of unit prices posted on the shelf. Muller (1984) provided different amounts of nutritional data on signs in supermarkets. He found no differences in brand choices as a function of the amount of information presented. However, merely making any nutritional information available, regardless of amount, led to more nutritional brand choices over the course of the experiment. Russo et al (1985) found no effects of in-store nutrition listings on purchases if positive nutrients (e.g. vitamins) were presented, but did find effects if negative nutrients (e.g. sugar) were disclosed. Finally, Anderson & Claxton (1982) provided energy labels for refrigerators and found a small effect on purchases only in the small-size refrigerator segment.

Two studies reported effects of consumer education programs. Crosby & Taylor (1981) found very little effect of education. However, their education program was of limited duration and comprehensiveness. On the other hand, Kourilsky & Murray (1981) found that an eight-week program of education in consumer economic reasoning resulted in increased levels of economic reasoning in family budgetary decisions and increased family satisfaction with the family budgetary decision process.

DECEPTION IN ADVERTISING   Russo et al (1981) develop a procedure for identifying misleading advertising. They argue that "an advertisement is misleading if it creates, increases, or exploits a false belief about expected product performance" (Russo et al 1981, p. 128). They test whether an advertisement is misleading by comparing the beliefs held by consumers exposed to the ad to those held by consumers exposed to a corrected ad or to no ad at all. They tested the procedure on ten advertisements and found that it appeared to work as hoped for.

Jacoby and his colleagues (Jacoby & Hoyer 1982, Jacoby et al 1982) have raised some provocative questions about misleading advertising, however. They argue that all forms of communication are subject to miscomprehension and show that not only advertisements but many other communications appear to be miscomprehended. Thus, they argue, evidence of miscomprehension is not sufficient evidence for policy intervention. While fault might be found with the specific measures used in the studies (Ford & Yalch 1982, Mizerski 1982), Jacoby and his coresearchers do provide a stimulating thesis that should be examined carefully in future research.

RESEARCH ON CHILDREN   Research on the abilities of children has been carried out during the period of the review. Roedder (1981, 1982) argues that one must consider whether any processing deficits observed in children result from lack of ability (limited processors) or lack of knowledge of the appropriate strategy (cued processors). The performance of cued processors can be improved by providing them with the appropriate strategy. However, limited processors may require regulation of their information input. Roedder et al (1983) find that children's abilities to compare alternatives can be exceeded, resulting in a lack of attitude-behavior consistency. Knowing that comparison skills are the locus of the deficit suggests education in decision making strategies as a possible remedy.

Consumer Satisfaction

Most of the research on consumer satisfaction has focused on the model of consumer satisfaction proposed by Oliver (1980). He argues that satisfaction is a function of both performance expectations and degree of disconfirmation (i.e. the degree to which actual performance departs from expectations). His model also includes effects of expectations and satisfaction on attitudes and intentions. In the many studies that have tested this model, the results generally support Oliver's conceptualization (Oliver & Linda 1981, Bearden & Teel 1983, LaBarbera & Mazursky 1983, Oliver & Beardon 1983). However, there are minor discrepancies in most applications that indicate potential problems. Churchill & Surprenant (1982) report more serious discrepancies, finding that there is no link from disconfirmation or expectations to satisfaction in the case of a durable product. Instead, perceived performance influences satisfaction.

This implies that perhaps absolute level of performance is more important for durables, and expectations and disconfirmation are not as crucial.

Results by Churchill & Surprenant (1982) and theorizing by others (LaTour & Peat 1979, Woodruff et al 1983) suggest that there may be a problem in using expectations as the standard. Thus, the major issue facing research on this approach to consumer satisfaction is how to determine an appropriate norm for performance or a reference point. The problem of the selection of reference point in prospect theory (Kahneman & Tversky 1979) is a very similar issue. The framework provided by prospect theory might be useful in conceptualizing satisfaction. Note that the Oliver approach implies that satisfaction is a linear function of departures from the reference point (i.e. disconfirmation), whereas prospect theory assumes a nonlinear response, as noted above.

A second stream of research has examined consumers' responses to dissatisfaction. Complaint behavior seems to be a function of the attributions made about the cause of dissatisfaction and consumer complaint styles. Folkes (1984) uses the attributional framework of Weiner (1980), categorizing attribution for the causes of product failure along the causal dimensions of stability (stable or unstable), locus (firm-related or consumer-related), and controllability (controllable or uncontrollable). She finds that stable attributions are associated with expectations of future product failure and desire for a refund rather than an exchange; when product failure is firm-related, the consumer is perceived to be owed a refund and an apology; and when failure is firm-related and controllable consumers feel angry and desire revenge. This attributional approach seems particularly appropriate for investigating how consumers interpret and respond to product outcomes (see also Richins 1983b). Richins (1983a) develops scales for aggression and assertion in a consumer context. She finds that aggression and assertion are associated with favorable attitudes toward complaining, with more prior complaint behaviors, and with resistance to attempts to gain compliance.

CONCLUSION

A great deal of progress has been made in consumer research in the past few years. Understanding of the interaction between consumers' knowledge and their decision processes has been greatly enhanced. It is now clear that prior knowledge focuses current search and information acquisition on a subset of the available information; knowing that focus can lead to specific predictions regarding potential biases in information processing and future choices. It is also evident that choice processes exert an influence on what is remembered. This influence can also be selective in nature.

Further progress in comprehending the prior knowledge-decision process interaction will require more detailed models and better measures of memory structure (e.g. Anderson 1983). Such detailed models of memory linkages would enable better predictions of consumers' reactions to and subsequent memory for available information. Detailed memory models would also be particularly valuable for furthering understanding of the effects of the structure of advertisements (e.g. verbal and visual structure) and of properties of the advertising environment (e.g. interference from other advertisements) on response to those persuasive messages. More detailed empirical studies of expert consumers would also be extremely useful in clarifying the effects of prior knowledge. Studies using highly expert (as opposed to relatively more knowledgeable) consumers have simply not been done.

A second area where progress has been made is the attempt to clarify the relationship between affect and cognition. While there are fewer answers here, the right questions appear to have emerged. The current focus on effects of mood, the relationship between memory and evaluative judgments, and cognitive versus affective precedence is encouraging. However, further progress will require careful theorizing about the nature of affect and its control processes. Given such a conceptualization, the relationship with cognition can be more easily explored. It appears likely that no uniform relationship exists; rather, contingency notions appear most plausible and should be a focus for theoretical efforts.

Insight into the processes of persuasion continues to grow. Despite ever-increasing scrutiny, multiattribute models of beliefs, attitude, intention, and behavior continue to receive substantial support. Research over the period of the review has continued to clarify the areas most in need of further work. The relationship between personal and normative beliefs and the impact of prior actions on current behaviors are the two areas most in need of research. Cognitive response approaches also continue to provide new understanding. The attempts to specify those factors that influence the nature and amount of responding represent substantial progress. Detailed models of memory structure would allow even further progress here. Specifically, models that predict which aspects of prior knowledge will be activated in interpreting current information would be invaluable (see Anderson 1983 for a production system approach to this issue).

In many of the instances cited above, progress has been made by attempting to focus on the details of the processes underlying the effects observed, and the suggestions for further progress argue for even more specific models. Specifying processing details is useful because it allows more detailed and precise predictions to be made. This allows for easier falsification and revision of current conceptualizations. As an example, a great deal of specification is needed before schema concepts can make precise predictions regarding consumers' use of existing knowledge to interpret incoming information. Invocation of schema concepts in broad terms is not sufficient (Alba & Hasher 1983).

Finally, it has become increasingly apparent that the issues involved in consumer research present an intriguing and demanding laboratory for developing and testing psychological theory. The nature of the consumer choice task implies that prior knowledge, information presented through different media and with different structure, other consumers, and many other factors interact in their effects. This forces the researcher more and more to consider such interactions. Such consideration is not only fascinating in its own right, but can lead to significant progress in the underlying theories that might not be likely if such interactions were ignored. The complex problems of consumer psychology can provide important leverage in deepening psychological theory.

Literature Cited

Ajzen, I., Fishbein, M. 1980. *Understanding Attitudes and Predicting Social Behavior*. Englewood Cliffs, NJ: Prentice-Hall. 278 pp.

Alba, J. W., Hasher, L. 1983. Is memory schematic? *Psychol. Bull.* 93:203–31

Alesandrini, K. L. 1983. Strategies that influence memory for advertising communications. See Harris 1983, pp. 65–82

Anderson, C. D., Claxton, J. D. 1982. Barriers to consumer choice of energy efficient products. *J. Consum. Res.* 9:163–70

Anderson, J. R. 1983. *The Architecture of Cognition*. Cambridge, MA: Harvard Univ. Press. 345 pp.

Bagozzi, R. P. 1981. Attitudes, intentions, and behavior: A test of some key hypotheses. *J. Pers. Soc. Psychol.* 41:607–26

Bagozzi, R. P. 1982. A field investigation of causal relations among cognitions, effect, intentions, and behavior. *J. Market. Res.* 19:562–83

Bagozzi, R. P. 1983. A holistic methodology for modeling consumer response to innovation. *Oper. Res.* 31:128–76

Batra, R., Ray, M. L. 1983. Advertising situations: The implications of differential involvement and accompanying affect responses. See Harris 1983, pp. 127–51

Bauer, R. A. 1960. Consumer behavior as risk taking. In *Risk Taking and Information Handling in Consumer Behavior*, ed. D. F. Cox, pp. 23–33. Boston: Harvard Grad. Sch. Bus. Adm.

Beales, H., Mazis, M. B., Salop, S. C., Staelin, R. 1981. Consumer search and public policy. *J. Consum. Res.* 8:11–22

Bearden, W. O., Teel, J. E. 1983. Some determinants of consumer satisfaction and complaint reports. *J. Market. Res.* 20:21–28

Beattie, A. E. 1982. Effects of product knowledge on comparison, memory, evaluation, and choice: A model of expertise in consumer decision-making. *Adv. Consum. Res.* 9:336–41

Beattie, A. E. 1983. Product expertise and advertising persuasiveness. *Adv. Consum. Res.* 10:581–84

Belk, R. W., Bahn, K. D., Mayer, R. N. 1982. Developmental recognition of consumption symbolism. *J. Consum. Res.* 9:4–17

Belk, R., Mayer, R., Driscoll, A. 1984. Children's recognition of consumption symbolism in children's products. *J. Consum. Res.* 10:386–97

Bentler, P. M., Speckart, G. 1979. Models of attitude-behavior relations. *Psychol. Rev.* 86(5):452–64

Bentler, P. M., Speckart, G. 1981. Attitudes "cause" behaviors: A structural equation analysis. *J. Pers. Soc. Psychol.* 40:226–38

Bettman, J. R. 1979. *An Information Processing Theory of Consumer Choice*. Reading MA: Addison-Wesley. 402 pp.

Bettman, J. R. 1982. A functional analysis of the role of overall evaluation of alternatives in choice processes. *Adv. Consum. Res.* 9:87–93

Bettman, J. R., John, D., Scott, C. A. 1984. Consumers' assessment of covariation. *Adv. Consum. Res.* 11:466–71

Bettman, J. R., John, D., Scott, C. A. 1985. Consumer assessment of covariation between price and quality. Submitted for publication

Bettman, J. R., Park, C. W. 1980. Effects of prior knowledge and experience and phase of the choice process on consumer decision processes: A protocol analysis. *J. Consum. Res.* 7:234–48

Biehal, G., Chakravarti, D. 1982. Information-presentation format and learning goals as determinants of consumers' memory retrieval and choice processes. *J. Consum. Res.* 8:431–41

Biehal, G., Chakravarti, D. 1983. Information accessibility as a moderator of consumer choice. *J. Consum. Res.* 10:1–14

Biehal, G. J. 1983. Consumers' prior experiences and perceptions in auto repair choice. *J. Market.* 47:82–91

Bower, G. H. 1981. Mood and memory. *Am. Psychol.* 36:129–48

Bozinoff, L., Roth, V. J. 1983. Recognition memory for script activities: An energy conservation application. *Adv. Consum. Res.* 10:655–60

Brock, T. C., Shavitt, S. 1983. Cognitive-response analysis in advertising. See Percy & Woodside 1983, pp. 91–116

Brucks, M. 1985. The effects of product class knowledge on information search behavior. *J. Consum. Res.* 12:1–16

Brucks, M., Mitchell, A. A. 1981. Knowledge structures, production systems and decision structures. *Adv. Consum. Res.* 8:750–57

Burnkrant, R. E., Page, T. J. 1982. An examination of the convergent, discriminant, and predictive validity of Fishbein's behavioral intention model. *J. Market. Res.* 19:550–61

Cacioppo, J. T., Petty, R. E. 1981. Electromyograms as measures of extent and affectivity of information processing. *Am. Psychol.* 36:441–56

Cacioppo, J. T., Petty, R. E. 1984. The elaboration likelihood model of persuasion. *Adv. Consum. Res.* 11:673–75

Calcich, S., Blair, E. 1983. The perceptual task in acquisition of product information. *Adv. Consum. Res.* 10:222–51

Capon, N., Davis, R. 1984. Basic cognitive ability measures as predictors of consumer information processing strategies. *J. Consum. Res.* 11:551–63

Chi, M. T. H. 1983. The role of knowledge on problem solving and consumer choice behavior. *Adv. Consum. Res.* 10:569–71

Childers, T. L., Houston, M. J. 1984. Conditions for a picture-superiority effect on consumer memory. *J. Consum. Res.* 11:643–54

Churchill, G. A., Surprenant, C. 1982. An investigation into the determinants of consumer satisfaction. *J. Market. Res.* 19:491–504

Clark, M. S., Fiske, S. T., eds. 1982. *Affect and Cognition: The 17th Annual Carnegie Symposium.* Hillsdale, NJ: Erlbaum. 357 pp.

Cohen, J. B. 1983. Involvement and you: 1000 great ideas. *Adv. Consum. Res.* 10:325–28

Coleman, L. 1983. Semantic and prosodic manipulation in advertising. See Harris 1983, pp. 217–40

Cooper, J., Croyle, R. T. 1984. Attitudes and attitude change. *Ann. Rev. Psychol.* 35:395–426

Coyne, J. C. 1982. Putting Humpty Dumpty back together: Cognition, emotion, and motivation reconsidered. *Adv. Consum. Res.* 9:153–55

Crocker, J. 1981. Judgment of covariation by social perceivers. *Psychol. Bull.* 90:272–92

Crocker, J. 1984. A schematic approach to changing consumers' beliefs. *Adv. Consum. Res.* 11:472–77

Crosby, L. A., Taylor, J. R. 1981. Effects of consumer information and education on cognition and choice. *J. Consum. Res.* 8:43–56

Curry, D. J., Menasco, M. B. 1983. On the separability of weights and scale values: Issues and empirical results. *J. Consum. Res.* 10:83–92

Deighton, J. 1983. How to solve problems that don't matter: Some heuristics for uninvolved thinking. *Adv. Consum. Res.* 10:314–19

Deighton, J. 1984. The interaction of advertising and evidence. *J. Consum. Res.* 11:763–70

Duncan, C. P., Olshavsky, R. W. 1982. External search: The role of consumer beliefs. *J. Market. Res.* 19:32–43

Edell, J. A., Burke, M. C. 1984. The moderating effect of attitude toward an ad on ad effectiveness under different processing conditions. *Adv. Consum. Res.* 11:644–49

Edell, J. A., Staelin, R. 1983. The information processing of pictures in print advertisments. *J. Consum. Res.* 10:45–60

Einhorn, H. J., Hogarth, R. M. 1981. Behavioral decision theory: Processes of judgment and choice. *Ann. Rev. Psychol.* 32:53–88

Fazio, R. H., Zanna, M. P. 1981. Direct experience and attitude-behavior consistency. *Adv. Exp. Soc. Psychol.* 14:161–202

Fishbein, M., Ajzen, I. 1975. *Belief, Attitude, Intention and Behavior: An Introduction to Theory and Research.* Reading, MA: Addison-Wesley. 578 pp.

Fishbein, M., Ajzen, I. 1981. On construct validity: A critique of Miniard and Cohen's paper. *J. Exp. Soc. Psychol.* 17:340–50

Fiske, S. T. 1982. Schema-triggered affect. See Clark & Fiske 1982, pp. 55–78

Fiske, S. T., Pavelchak, M. A. 1986. Category-based versus piece meal-based effective responses: Developments in schema-triggered affect. In *The Handbook of Motivation and Cognition: Foundations of Social Behavior,* ed. R. M. Sorrentino, E. T. Higgins. New York: Guilford. In press

Folkes, V. S. 1984. Consumer reactions to product failure: An attributional approach. *J. Consum. Res.* 10:398–409

Ford, G. T., Yalch, R. 1982. Viewer miscomprehension of televised communication: A comment. *J. Market.* 46:27–31

Formisano, R. A., Olshavsky, R. W., Tapp, S. 1982. Choice strategy in a difficult task environment. *J. Consum. Res.* 8:474–79

Fredricks, A. J., Dossett, D. L. 1983. Attitude-behavior relations: A comparison of the Fishbein-Ajzen and Bentler-Speckart models. *J. Pers. Soc. Psychol.* 45:501–12

Furse, D. J., Punj, G. N., Stewart, D. W. 1984. A typology of individual search strategies among purchasers of new automobiles. *J. Consum. Res.* 10:417–31

Gardner, M. P. 1983. Advertising effects on attributes recalled and criteria used for brand evaluations. *J. Consum. Res.* 10:310–18

Gardner, M. P., Vandersteel, M. 1984. The consumer's mood: An important situational variable. *Adv. Consum. Res.* 11:525–29

Gilovich, T. 1981. Seeing the past in the present: The effect of association to familiar events on judgments and decisions. *J. Pers. Soc. Psychol.* 40:797–808

Greenwald, A. G., Leavitt, C. 1984. Audience involvement in advertising: Four levels. *J. Consum. Res.* 11:581–92

Grether, D., Wilde, L. 1984. An analysis of conjunctive choice: Theory and experiments. *J. Consum. Res.* 10:373–85

Hannah, D. B., Sternthal, B. 1984. Detecting and explaining the sleeper effect. *J. Consum. Res.* 11:632–42

Harris, R. J., ed. 1983. *Information Processing Research in Advertising.* Hillsdale, NJ: Erlbaum. 322 pp.

Harris, R. J., Dubitsky, T. M., Bruno, K. J. 1983. Psycholinguistic studies of misleading advertising. See Harris 1983, pp. 241–62

Hastie, R. 1982. Consumers' memory for product knowledge. *Adv. Consum. Res.* 9:72–73

Hayes-Roth, B. 1982. Opportunism in consumer behavior. *Adv. Consum. Res.* 9:132–35

Hirschman, E. C., Holbrook, M. B. 1982. Hedonic consumption: Emerging concepts, methods and propositions. *J. Market.* 46:92–101

Hoch, S. J. 1984. Hypothesis testing and consumer behavior: "If it works, don't mess with it". *Adv. Consum. Res.* 11:478–83

Holbrook, M. B. 1983. Product imagery and the illusion of reality: Some insights from consumer esthetics. *Adv. Consum. Res.* 10:65–71

Holbrook, M. B., Hirschman, E. C. 1982. The experiential aspects of consumption: Consumer fantasies, feelings, and fun. *J. Consum. Res.* 9:132–40

Holbrook, M. B., Chestnut, R. W., Oliva, T. A., Greenleaf, E. A. 1984. Play as a consumption experience: The roles of emotions, performance, and personality in the enjoyment of games. *J. Consum. Res.* 11:728–39

Huber, J. 1983. The effect of set composition on item choice: Separating attraction, edge aversion, and substitution effects. *Adv. Consum. Res.* 10:298–304

Huber, J., McCann, J. 1982. The impact of inferential beliefs on product evaluations. *J. Market. Res.* 19:324–33

Huber, J., Payne, J. W., Puto, C. 1982. Adding asymmetrically dominated alternatives: Violations of regularity and the similarity hypothesis. *J. Consum. Res.* 9:90–98

Huber, J., Puto, C. 1983. Market boundaries and product choice: Illustrating attraction and substitution effects. *J. Consum. Res.* 10:31–44

Hutchinson, J. W. 1983. Expertise and the structure of free recall. *Adv. Consum. Res.* 10:585–99

Inhelder, B., Piaget, J. 1958. *The Growth of Logical Thinking from Childhood to Adolescence.* New York: Basic Books

Isen, A. M. 1984a. The influence of positive affect on decision making and cognitive organization. *Adv. Consum. Res.* 11:534–37

Isen, A. M. 1984b. Positive affect as a factor in decision-making. *APA Div. 23 Proc.*, pp. 7–10

Jacoby, J., Hoyer, W. D. 1982. Viewer miscomprehension of televised communication: Selected findings. *J. Market.* 46:12–26

Jacoby, J., Nelson, M. C., Hoyer, W. D. 1982. Corrective advertising and affirmative disclosure statements: Their potential for confusing and misleading the consumer. *J. Market.* 46:61–72

John, D., Scott, C. A., Bettman, J. R. 1985. Sampling data for covariation assessment: The effect of prior beliefs on search patterns. Submitted for publication

Johnson, E. J., Meyer, R. J. 1984. Compensatory choice models of noncompensatory processes: The effect of varying context. *J. Consum. Res.* 11:528–41

Johnson, E. J., Payne, J. W. 1985. Effort and accuracy in choice. *Manage. Sci.* 31:395–414

Johnson, E. J., Russo, J. E. 1981. Product familiarity and learning new information. *Adv. Consum. Res.* 8:151–55

Johnson, E. J., Russo, J. E. 1984. Product familiarity and learning new information. *J. Consum. Res.* 11:542–50

Johnson, E. J., Tversky, A. 1983. Affect, generalization, and the perception of risk. *J. Pers. Soc. Psychol.* 45:20–31

Johnson, M. D. 1984. Consumer choice strategies for comparing noncomparable alternatives. *J. Consum. Res.* 11:741–53

Kahneman, D., Tversky, A. 1979. Prospect theory: An analysis of decision under risk. *Econometrica* 47:263–91

Kanwar, R., Olson, J. C., Sims, L. S. 1981. Toward conceptualizing and measuring cognitive structures. *Adv. Consum. Res.* 8:122–27

Kehret-Ward, T., Yalch, R. 1984. To take or not to take the only one: Effects of changing the meaning of a product attribute on choice behavior. *J. Consum. Res.* 10:410–16

Kiel, G. C., Layton, R. A. 1981. Dimensions of consumer information seeking behavior. *J. Market Res.* 18:233–39

Kintsch, W., van Dijk, T. A. 1978. Toward a model of text comprehension and production. *Psychol. Rev.* 85:363–94

Kisielius, J., Sternthal, B. 1984. Detecting and explaining vividness effects in attitudinal judgments. *J. Market. Res.* 21:54–64

Kourilsky, M., Murray, T. 1981. The use of economic reasoning to increase satisfaction with family decision making. *J. Consum. Res.* 8:183–88

LaBarbera, P. A., Mazursky, D. 1983. A longitudinal assessment of consumer satisfaction/dissatisfaction: The dynamic aspect of the cognitive process. *J. Market. Res.* 20:393–404

LaTour, S. A., Peat, N. C. 1979. Conceptual and methodological issues in consumer satisfaction research. *Adv. Consum. Res.* 6:431–37

Lazarus, R. S. 1981. A cognitivist's reply to Zajonc on emotion and cognition. *Am. Psychol.* 36:222–23

Leigh, T. W., Rethans, A. J. 1983. Experiences with script elicitation within consumer decision making contexts. *Adv. Consum. Res.* 10:667–72

Levin, I. P., Johnson, R. D. 1984. Estimating price-quality tradeoffs using comparative judgments. *J. Consum. Res.* 11:593–600

Lichtenstein, M., Srull, T. K. 1985. Conceptual and methodological issues in examining the relationship between consumer memory and judgment. In *Psychological Processes and Advertising Effects: Theory, Research, and Application*, ed. L. F. Alwitt, A. A. Mitchell. Hillsdale, NJ: Erlbaum

Lichtenstein, S., Slovic, P., Fischhoff, B., Layman, M., Combs, B. 1978. Judged frequency of lethal events. *J. Exp. Psychol: Hum. Learn. Mem.* 4:551–78

Lord, C., Ross, L., Lepper, M. 1979. Biased assimilation and attitude polarization: The effects of prior theories on subsequently considered evidence. *J. Pers. Soc. Psychol.* 37:2098–2109

Lucas, D. B., Benson, C. E. 1929. The relative values of positive and negative advertising appeals as measured by coupons returned. *J. Appl. Psychol.* 13:274–300

Lutz, R. J. 1982. Lessons learned from a decade of multiattribute attitude research in marketing. *Proc. Conv. Market. Symp.*, pp. 107–23

Lutz, R. J., MacKenzie, S. B., Belch, G. E. 1983. Attitude toward the ad as a mediator of advertising effectiveness: Determinants and consequences. *Adv. Consum. Res.* 10:532–39

Lynch, J. G., Srull, T. K. 1982. Memory and attentional factors in consumer choice: Con-

cepts and research methods. *J. Consum. Res.* 9:18–37

MacKenzie, S. B., Lutz, R. J. 1983. Testing competing theories of effectiveness via structural equation models. *Proc. Winter Conf.*, Am. Market. Assoc., pp. 70–75.

Malhotra, N. K. 1982. Information load and consumer decision making. *J. Consum. Res.* 8:419–30

Malhotra, N. K., Jain, A. K., Lagakos, S. W. 1982. The information overload controversy: An alternative viewpoint. *J. Market.* 46:27–37

Mandler, G. 1982. The structure of value: Accounting for taste. See Clark & Fiske 1982, pp. 3–36

Marks, L. J., Olson, J. C. 1981. Toward a cognitive structure conceptualization of product familiarity. *Adv. Consum. Res.* 8:145–50

McSweeney, F. K., Bierley, C. 1984. Recent developments in classical conditioning. *J. Consum. Res.* 11:619–31

Meyer, R. J. 1981. A model of multiattribute judgments under attribute uncertainty and information constraint. *J. Market. Res.* 18:428–41

Meyer, R. J. 1982. A descriptive model of consumer information search behavior. *Market. Sci.* 1:93–121

Meyer, R. J., Eagle, T. C. 1982. Context-induced parameter instability in a disaggregate-stochastic model of store choice. *J. Market. Res.* 19:62–71

Midgley, D. F. 1983. Patterns of interpersonal information seeking for the purchase of a symbolic product. *J. Market. Res.* 20:74–83

Miniard, P. W., Cohen, J. B. 1981. An examination of the Fishbein-Ajzen behavioral intentions model's concepts and measures. *J. Exp. Soc. Psychol.* 17:309–39

Miniard, P. W., Cohen, J. B. 1983. Modeling personal and normative influences on behavior. *J. Consum. Res.* 10:169–80

Miniard, P. W., Obermiller, C., Page, T. J. 1983. A further assessment of measurement influences on the intention-behavior relationship. *J. Market. Res.* 20:206–12

Miniard, P. W., Page, T. J. 1984. Causal relationships in the Fishbein behavioral intention model. *Adv. Consum. Res.* 11:137–42

Mitchell, A. A. 1981. The dimensions of advertising involvement. *Adv. Consum. Res.* 8:25–30

Mitchell, A. A. 1982. Models of memory: Implications for measuring knowledge structures. *Adv. Consum. Res.* 9:45–51

Mitchell, A. A. 1983a. Cognitive processes initiated by exposure to advertising. See Harris 1983, pp. 13–42

Mitchell, A. A. 1983b. The effects of visual and emotional advertising: An information processing approach. See Percy & Woodside 1983, pp. 197–217

Mitchell, A. A., Olson, J. C. 1981. Are product attribute beliefs the only mediator of advertising effects on brand attitude? *J. Market. Res.* 18:318–32

Mizerski, R. W. 1982. Viewer miscomprehension findings are measurement bound. *J. Market.* 46:32–34

Monaco, G. E., Kaiser, D. 1983. Effects of prior preference, inferences, and believability in consumer advertising. See Harris 1983, pp. 263–87

Moore, D. L., Hutchinson, J. W. 1983. The effects of ad affect on advertising effectiveness. *Adv. Consum. Res.* 10:526–31

Muller, T. E. 1984. Buyer response to variations in product information load. *J. Appl. Psychol.* 69:300–6

Ofir, C., Lynch, J. G. 1984. Context effects on judgment under uncertainty. *J. Consum. Res.* 11:688–79

Oliver, R. L. 1980. A cognitive model of the antecedents and consequences of satisfaction decisions. *J. Market. Res.* 17:460–69

Oliver, R. L., Bearden, W. O. 1983. The role of involvement in satisfaction processes. *Adv. Consum. Res.* 10:250–55

Oliver, R. L., Linda, G. 1981. Effect of satisfaction and its antecedents on consumer preference and intention. *Adv. Consum. Res.* 8:88–93

Olshavsky, R. W., Granbois, D. H. 1979. Consumer decision-making—fact or fiction? *J. Consum. Res.* 6:93–100

Olson, J. C., Reynolds, T. J. 1983. Understanding consumers' cognitive structures: Implications for advertising strategy. See Percy & Woodside 1983, pp. 77–90

Park, C. W. 1982. Joint decisions in home purchasing: A muddling-through process. *J. Consum. Res.* 9:151–62

Park, C. W., Young, S. M. 1983. Types and levels of involvement and brand attitude formation. *Adv. Consum. Res.* 10:320–24

Payne, J. W. 1982. Contingent decision behavior. *Psychol. Bull.* 92(2):382–402

Payne, J. W., Laughhunn, D. J., Crum, R. 1980. Translation of gambles and aspiration level effects in risky choice behavior. *Manage. Sci.* 26(10):1039–60

Percy, L. 1982. Psycholinguistic guidelines for advertising copy. *Adv. Consum. Res.* 9:107–11

Percy, L., Rossiter, J. R. 1983. Mediating effects of visual and verbal elements in print advertising upon belief, attitude, and intention responses. See Percy & Woodside 1983, pp. 171–96

Percy, L., Woodside, A. G., eds. 1983. *Advertising and Consumer Psychology.* Lexington, MA: Lexington Books. 400 pp.

Peter, J. P., Nord, W. R. 1982. A clarification and extension of operant conditioning principles in marketing. *J. Market.* 46(3):102–7

Petty, R. E., Cacioppo, J. T. 1983. Central and peripheral routes to persuasion: Application to advertising. See Percy & Woodside 1983, pp. 3–23

Petty, R. E., Cacioppo, J. T. 1984. Source factors and the elaboration likelihood model of persuasion. *Adv. Consum. Res.* 11:668–72

Petty, R. E., Cacioppo, J. T., Schumann, D. 1983. Central and peripheral routes to advertising effectiveness: The moderating role of involvement. *J. Consum. Res.* 10:135–46

Petty, R. E., Wells, G. L., Brock, T. C. 1976. Distraction can enhance or reduce yielding to propaganda: Thought disruption versus effort justification. *J. Pers. Soc. Psychol.* 34:874–84

Punj, G. N., Staelin, R. 1983. A model of consumer information search behavior for new automobiles. *J. Consum. Res.* 9:366–80

Punj, G. N., Stewart, D. W. 1983. An interaction framework of consumer decision making. *J. Consum. Res.* 10:181–96

Reilly, M. D., Conover, J. N. 1983. Meta-analysis: Integrating results from consumer research studies. *Adv. Consum. Res.* 10:510–13

Rethans, A. J., Albaum, G. S. 1981. Towards determinants of acceptable risk: The case of product risks. *Adv. Consum. Res.* 8:506–10

Rethans, A. J., Hastak, M, 1982. Representation of product hazards in consumer memory. *Adv. Consum. Res.* 9:487–93

Richins, M. L. 1983a. An analysis of consumer interaction styles in the marketplace. *J. Consum. Res.* 10:73–82

Richins, M. L. 1983b. Negative word-of-mouth by dissatisfied consumers: A pilot study. *J. Market.* 47:68–78

Roedder, D. L. 1981. Age differences in children's responses to television advertising: An information processing approach. *J. Consum. Res.* 8:144–53

Roedder, D. L. 1982. Understanding and overcoming children's processing deficits. *Adv. Consum. Res.* 9:148–52

Roedder, D. L., Sternthal, B., Calder, B. J. 1983. Attitude-behavior consistency in children's responses to television advertising. *J. Market. Res.* 20:337–49

Ross, I. 1975. Perceived risk and consumer behavior: A critical review. *Adv. Consum. Res.* 2:1–19

Rothschild, M. L., Gaidis, W. C. 1981. Behavioral learning theory: Its relevance to marketing and promotions. *J. Market.* 45:70–78

Rudd, J., Kohout, F. J. 1983. Individual and group consumer information acquisition in brand choice situations. *J. Consum. Res.* 10:303–9

Russo, J. E., Johnson, E. J. 1980. What do consumers know about familiar products? *Adv. Consum. Res.* 7:417–23

Russo, J. E., Metcalf, B. L., Stephens, D. 1981. Identifying misleading advertising. *J. Consum. Res.* 8:119–31

Russo, J. E., Staelin, R., Nolan, C., Russell, G. J., Metcalf, B. L. 1985. Nutrition information in the supermarket. *J. Consum. Res.* 12:In press

Ryan, M. J. 1982. Behavioral intention formation: The interdependency of attitudinal and social influence variables. *J. Consum. Res.* 9:263–78

Saltzer, E. B. 1981. Cognitive moderators of the relationship between behavioral intentions and behavior. *J. Pers. Soc. Psychol.* 41:260–71

Schaninger, C. M., Sciglimpaglia, D. 1981. The influence of cognitive personality traits and demographics on consumer information acquisition. *J. Consum. Res.* 8:208–16

Shimp, T. A. 1981. Attitude toward the ad as a mediator of consumer brand choice. *J. Advert.* 10:9–15

Shimp, T. A., Kavas, A. 1984. The theory of reasoned action applied to coupon usage. *J. Consum. Res.* 11:795–809

Silk, A. J., Vavra, T. G. 1974. The influence of advertising's affective qualities on consumer response. See Hughes & Ray 1974, pp. 157–86

Slovic, P., Fischhoff, B., Lichtenstein, S. 1981. Facts and fears: Societal perception of risk. *Adv. Consum. Res.* 8:497–502

Smith, R. E., Swinyard, W. R. 1983. Attitude-behavior consistency: The impact of product trial versus advertising. *J. Market. Res.* 20:257–67

Solomon, M. R. 1983. The role of products as social stimuli: A symbolic interactionism perspective. *J. Consum. Res.* 10:319–29

Spiro, R. L. 1983. Persuasion in family decision-making. *J. Consum. Res.* 9:393–402

Srull, T. K. 1983a. Affect and memory: The impact of affective reactions in advertising on the representation of product information in memory. *Adv. Consum. Res.* 10:520–25

Srull, T. K. 1983b. The role of prior knowledge in the acquisition, retention, and use of new information. *Adv. Consum. Res.* 10:572–76

Srull, T. K. 1984. The effects of subjective affective states on memory and judgment. *Adv. Consum. Res.* 11:530–33

Staelin, R., Payne, J. W. 1976. Studies of the information seeking behavior of consumers. In *Cognition and Social Behavior*, ed. J. S. Carroll, J. W. Payne, pp. 185–202. Hillsdale, NJ: Erlbaum

Sujan, M. 1985. Consumer knowledge: Effects on evaluation strategies mediating consumer judgments. *J. Consum. Res.* 12:31–46

Thaler, R. 1983. Transaction utility theory. *Adv. Consum. Res.* 10:229–32

Thorson, E., Rothschild, M. L. 1983. Recognition and recall of commercials: Prediction from a text-comprehension analysis of commercial scripts. See Percy & Woodside 1983, pp. 287–302

Thorson, E., Snyder, R. 1984. Viewer recall of television commercials: Prediction from the propositional structure of commercial scripts. *J. Market. Res.* 21:127–36

Tybout, A. M., Calder, B. J., Sternthal, B. 1981. Using information processing theory to design marketing strategies. *J. Market. Res.* 18:73–79

Tybout, A. M., Scott, C. A. 1983. Availability of well-defined internal knowledge and the attitude formation process: Information aggregation versus self-perception. *J. Pers. Soc. Psychol.* 44:474–91

Tybout, A. M., Sternthal, B., Calder, B. J. 1983. Information availability as a determinant of multiple request effectiveness. *J. Market. Res.* 20:280–90

Unger, L. S., Kernan, J. B. 1983. On the meaning of leisure: An investigation of some determinants of the subjective experience. *J. Consum. Res.* 9:381–92

Warshaw, P. R. 1980a. A new model for predicting behavioral intentions: An alternative to Fishbein. *J. Market. Res.* 17:153–72

Warshaw, P. R. 1980b. Predicting purchase and other behaviors from general and contextually specific intentions. *J. Market. Res.* 17:26–33

Warshaw, P. R., Sheppard, B. H., Hartwick, J. 1986. The intention and self-prediction of goals and behavior. In *Advances in Marketing Communication*, ed. R. P. Bagozzi. Greenwich, CT: JAI Press. In press

Weiner, B. 1980. *Human Motivation.* New York: Holt, Rinehart & Winston. 480 pp.

Whitney, J. C., John, G. 1983. An experimental investigation of intrusion errors in memory for script narratives. *Adv. Consum. Res.* 10:661–6

Winett, R. A., Kagel, J. H. 1984. Effects of information presentation format on resource use in field settings. *J. Consum. Res.* 11:655–67

Witkin, H. A. 1950. Individual differences in ease of perception of embedded figures. *J. Pers.* 19:1–15

Woodruff, R. B., Cadotte, E. R., Jenkins, R. L. 1983. Modeling consumer satisfaction processes using experience-based norms. *J. Market. Res.* 20:296–304

Yalch, R. F., Elmore-Yalch, R. 1984. The effect of numbers on the route to persuasion. *J. Consum. Res.* 11:522–27

Yates, J. F., Jagacinski, C. J., Faber, M. D. 1978. Evaluation of partially described multi-attribute options. *Organ. Behav. Hum. Perform.* 21:240–51

Zajonc, R. B. 1968. Attitudinal effects of mere exposure. *J. Pers. Soc. Psychol. Monogr.* 9(pt. 2):1–28

Zajonc, R. B. 1980. Feeling and thinking: Preferences need no inferences. *Am. Psychol.* 35:151–75

Zajonc, R. B., Markus, H. 1982. Affective and cognitive factors in preferences. *J. Consum. Res.* 9:123–31

Zeithaml, V. A. 1982. Consumer response to in-store price information environments. *J. Consum. Res.* 8:357–69

Zimmer, M. R., Jacoby, J. 1984. The selection of a contraceptive method as a joint decision of married couples. *APA Div. 23 Proc.*, pp. 25–28

Ann. Rev. Psychol. 1986. 37:291–319

ETIOLOGY AND EXPRESSION OF SCHIZOPHRENIA: Neurobiological and Psychosocial Factors[‡]

Allan F. Mirsky and Connie C. Duncan

Laboratory of Psychology and Psychopathology, National Institute of Mental Health, Bethesda, Maryland 20892

CONTENTS

INTRODUCTION 291
NEUROLOGICAL AND NEUROANATOMICAL STUDIES 294
    Disturbances in Regional Cerebral Blood Flow 295
    Alterations in Ventricular Size and/or Cortical Atrophy 296
    Abnormalities in Glucose Metabolism 297
    Viral Brain Infections 298
    Disturbed Hemispheric Function or Interhemispheric Relations 298
    Delayed Nervous System Maturation or Deficient Neurointegration—Pre- and Peri-
        natal Disturbances 299
COGNITIVE PSYCHOPHYSIOLOGICAL STUDIES 300
    Attentional Deficit 300
    Cognitive Psychophysiology 302
    Application of Cognitive Psychophysiology to Research on Schizophrenia 304
STUDIES OF FAMILIAL AND SOCIOENVIRONMENTAL FACTORS 307
VULNERABILITY TO SCHIZOPHRENIA: SOME WORKING HYPOTHESES 310
CONCLUSION 313

INTRODUCTION

One of us noted 17 years ago in this forum (Mirsky 1969) that every major advance in methodology in biological science is accompanied by an effort to apply the new technique to the study of schizophrenia. This trend, which we

---

[‡]The US Government has the right to retain a nonexclusive royalty-free license in and to any copyright covering this paper.

support with enthusiasm, has continued. To the brief, informal list compiled in 1969, we can now add a series of brain-imaging techniques, including computerized axial tomography (CT),[1] regional cerebral blood flow (RCBF), and positron emission transaxial tomography (PET). The emerging field of cognitive psychophysiology—with the identification of event-related brain potentials (ERPs) as markers of specific aspects or stages of information processing—has also been applied to the study of schizophrenia.

The etiology of schizophrenia is accepted by all to be multifactorial; however, whereas most schizophrenologists would agree that a particular combination of biological predisposition and environmental circumstance is necessary for a schizophrenic disorder to develop, there is disagreement as to the relative weighting of biological as opposed to environmental factors.

In this paper, we highlight some factors that may play a significant role in the etiology of schizophrenia. We cannot be comprehensive given the constraints of this format; our selection reflects our assessment of the importance of certain factors and, to some extent, our biases.

Since the prior review was published (Mirsky 1969), there has been another major class of variables added to etiological investigations of schizophrenia, namely, psychological stressors acting through parents, family, or community. Allegations of the importance of such variables have been made for many years (Fromm-Reichmann 1948). However, recent studies reviewed here provide evidence from controlled investigations that the external family-community milieu interacts with the internal neuropsychological-neurobiological milieu to produce psychiatric disorder in vulnerable persons. Therefore, no current model of etiological factors in schizophrenia can be considered complete without an attempt to integrate some of the psychosocial findings.

There are two illustrious examples of this type of effort: Kety's Maudsley Lecture (Kety 1980) and Zubin's Hoch Lecture (Zubin et al 1985). While similar in the broad scope of factors they reviewed, these authors differed in their emphasis. A primary difference was whether schizophrenia is to be viewed as a chronic, lifetime disorder (Kety 1980) or as an episodic disorder from which substantial recovery is possible (Zubin et al 1985). Kety emphasized neurobiological aspects of the disorder while agreeing that psychosocial factors play a role; Zubin, while acknowledging the role of neurobiological factors, emphasized the role of psychosocial factors in modifying the course, severity, and longevity of the disorder. The authors agreed on the principle of a "heterogenous etiology" (Kety 1980), but genetics, according to Zubin, "is neither sufficient nor necessary as an etiological agent."

---

[1]The following abbreviations are used in this chapter: AS, affective style; CD, communication deviance; CPT, continuous performance test; CT, computerized axial tomography; EE, expressed emotion; ERP, event-related brain potential; NID, neurointegrative deficit; PBC, pregnancy and birth complications; PDM, pandysmaturation; PET, positron emission transaxial tomography; RCBF, regional cerebral blood flow; SBA, schizophrenogenic brain abnormalities.

These issues lead us to consider "sporadic" or "symptomatic" (nongenetic?) schizophrenia, a type of schizophrenia in which there is no discernible family history of the disorder. The existence of such a group of patients emphasizes that our research strategies—and our ultimate understanding—must take into account multiple etiological paths to the disorder. Opinions vary concerning the existence of sporadic schizophrenia. Gottesman & Shields (1982) stated without equivocation that "no environmental causes have been found that will invariably or even with moderate probability produce a genuine schizophrenia in persons who are unrelated to a schizophrenic index case" (p. 243). This is in contrast to the view of Zubin et al (1985), noted above, that it is unnecessary to posit a genetic basis for schizophrenia. Neurological factors may differentiate sporadic from genetic schizophrenia. The eventual correct classification and description of these two forms of the disorder will require extensive biological as well as psychiatric-genetic information. In our view, there is a continuum of vulnerability to schizophrenia in which biological (derived from genetic or environmental causes) and life experience factors play a role.

Family history, twin, and adoption studies are the chief methods of determining the importance of genetic factors in psychiatric disorders. With respect to the question of family history in sporadic schizophrenia, the issue is unresolved, since data are sparse. It may be that data gathered only from first-degree relatives are not sufficient to rule out genetic factors; studies of second-degree relatives may reveal evidence of genetic influence that would otherwise escape detection. L. Erlenmeyer-Kimling (personal communication 1985) recently noted that whereas only a small proportion of diagnosed schizophrenics may have an identifiable first-degree relative with the disorder, the percentage could increase substantially when second-degree relatives are included.

The main body of our text presents selected findings in three areas of schizophrenia research: (a) neurological and neuroanatomical studies, (b) cognitive psychophysiological studies, and (c) studies of familial and socioenvironmental factors. Our paper concludes with some hypotheses concerning vulnerability to schizophrenia.

For detailed discussions of related aspects of research, we refer the reader to the recently published, comprehensive reviews of neuropsychological (Seidman 1983), attentional and information processing (Gjerde 1983, Nuechterlein & Dawson 1984), and psychophysiological (Zahn 1985) factors in schizophrenia. Some recent reviews of neurochemical research in schizophrenia are provided by Bowers (1980), Berger (1981), Haracz (1982), and Lewis (1980).

Among the current issues and controversies in schizophrenia research, one that is important to our review is that of a schizophrenia "spectrum." This refers to a distribution or "spectrum" of schizophreniform disorders ranging from relatively mild disturbances of personality (schizoid, borderline, and paranoid personality disorders) through the more serious types of disorder, such as schizotypal personality and the various manifestations of schizophrenia itself.

The concept of schizophrenia spectrum disorder was stimulated by the landmark adoption study of Rosenthal and associates conducted in Denmark in the 1960s (Rosenthal et al 1968). It was found that the prevalence of schizophrenia in adopted-away offspring of schizophrenic patients was similar to that in nonadoptive offspring. The stimulus for the spectrum concept was, in part, the low incidence of schizophrenia in the adopted-away offspring of schizophrenic mothers. Kety et al (1968) speculated that the mild form of the disorder seen in their study was a reflection of the state-supported program of euthenic abortion once promulgated in Denmark: thus, women known to be schizophrenic or to have been impregnated by a schizophrenic man were encouraged to have abortions. The gene pool was thus altered in Denmark, resulting in late-onset schizophrenia (and presumably milder forms) and a variety of spectrum disorders that *looked like* schizophrenia but were less virulent. The existence of spectrum disorders, related in some as yet unspecified way to schizophrenia itself, poses a challenge to research and theory on the etiology of the disorder. We return to this question.

One further note: in this paper, we use the term "high-risk" or "at-risk" to refer to individuals who are more likely, on a statistical basis, to develop a schizophrenic disorder than the general population (Mednick & McNeil 1968, Garmezy & Streitman 1974). Thus, 10–15% of the children of a schizophrenic parent develop some form of schizophrenia as compared to 1% or less of the children of normal parents (Rosenthal 1970, Gottesman & Shields 1982, Mirsky et al 1985).

NEUROLOGICAL AND NEUROANATOMICAL STUDIES

Both Kraepelin (1913) and Bleuler (1911) believed that central nervous system disease plays a role in the etiology of schizophrenia. During the more than 70 years since these men published their influential works, numerous studies have been conducted on neurological damage and brain disease in schizophrenia. The existence of such damage is beyond dispute. Kety (1980) recently stated:

> I find it difficult to avoid the conclusion that in a substantial fraction of typical chronic schizophrenics there is an underlying neurological disturbance. That fraction has not diminished with increasingly rigorous observations and it is augmented by each new technique as it is applied. It is not unlikely that the actual fraction so affected is considerably larger than thus far has been demonstrated (p. 428).

In this section, we review briefly some of the more recent research findings on neurological disease or disturbance in schizophrenia. They are included under the following headings:

1. Disturbances in regional cerebral blood flow;
2. Alterations in ventricular size and/or cortical atrophy;

3. Abnormalities in glucose metabolism;
4. Viral brain infections;
5. Disturbed hemispheric function or interhemispheric relations;
6. Delayed nervous system maturation or deficient neurointegration—pre- and perinatal disturbances.

The studies of neural variables included in this list range from relatively simple microscopic examination of brain tissue from schizophrenic patients through very complex brain visualization with imaging systems requiring nuclear-medical installations (PET). Midway between these extremes are CT scans, based on focused X-ray image reconstructions, and RCBF measurements.

The special advantage of the RCBF and PET methods lies in their measurement of *functional* changes in the brains of subjects as opposed to the structural data revealed by CT scans. However, since these methods are sensitive to the functional state of the brain, a host of psychological variables must be considered that are not of concern to the structuralist. Thus, a difference between patients and controls cannot be attributed to a difference in brain function unless differences in such factors as cooperation, motivation, attention, and comprehension of the task instructions can be ruled out. Sutton (1969) recommended using unambiguous tasks that are easy to follow as the only way of maintaining constancy within a test and across subjects. The more classes of psychological variables there are that influence the measure, the more rigorous the experimental controls must be to reduce the role of "subject option" (Sutton 1969).

The studies reported below exemplify some current approaches to the study of brain dysfunction in schizophrenia.

Disturbances in Regional Cerebral Blood Flow

Ingvar and coworkers applied the method of radioactive xenon to study RCBF in chronic schizophrenia (Ingvar & Franzen 1974, Franzen & Ingvar 1975). Their method involves injection of a radioactive isotope of xenon (Xe^{133}) into the carotid artery; the distribution of the isotope, as measured by radioactivity detectors, correlates well with the blood flow in various cortical and subcortical regions. Schizophrenic patients showed reduced blood flow in frontal regions of the brain under passive as well as active conditions.

A less invasive version of the xenon technique involves inhalation of a gaseous form of the isotope. Studies with this method have yielded mixed results. For example, Ariel et al (1983) found reduced blood flow in all brain regions in their schizophrenic subjects, although there was relatively greater reduction in anterior regions. In contrast, in a carefully controlled comparison of unmedicated patients and controls, Gur et al (1985) reported that resting blood flow in the left hemisphere was higher in schizophrenic patients than in controls. Moreover, unlike the schizophrenic patients, the controls tended to show symmetric RCBFs. They also reported a reversal of the activation pattern seen in normal subjects, in which the largest increase on RCBF was seen in the right hemisphere during a spatial task. That is, the schizophrenic patients showed the greatest increase in blood flow during a verbal task. This reversal was more pronounced in more disturbed patients. Gur et al related their findings of relative inactivity in the right hemisphere to the attentional deficit often described in schizophrenia. The left hemisphere hyperactivity was seen as compatible with the hypothesis of left hemisphere overactivation in the disorder (e.g. Flor-Henry 1983). They suggested that the difference between their results and those of prior investigators stemmed from such factors as task demands, chronicity, sex of subject, and medication. D. Weinberger (personal communication 1985) reported that schizophrenic patients did not show the normal pattern of increased blood flow observed during performance of the frontal-lobe-dependent Wisconsin Card Sorting Test (Grant & Berg 1948, Milner 1963).

Thus, there is no consensus regarding disturbance of cerebral blood flow in schizophrenia. Additional studies with behavioral paradigms, however, appear to hold promise for illuminating some of the pathophysiology associated with this disorder. It will also be necessary to establish whether the changes seen in schizophrenic subjects are specific and not shared by subjects with other psychiatric disorders.

Alterations in Ventricular Size and/or Cortical Atrophy

At least six groups of investigators have studied abnormalities in cerebral ventricular size and/or atrophy of cerebral structures in patients with schizophrenia (Johnstone et al 1976, Golden et al 1980, 1981, Andreasen et al 1982b,c, Jernigan et al 1982a,b, Nasrallah et al 1982, Weinberger et al 1979, 1980, 1982). With the exception of Jernigan et al (1982a,b), each group reported evidence of enlarged ventricles, cerebral atrophy, cranial asymmetry, or some combination of these abnormalities in schizophrenic patients. The first two abnormalities tend to be highly correlated (Rieder et al 1983). The finding of no difference by Jernigan and coworkers could possibly be reconciled with the other reports on the basis of sampling: the Weinberger group suggested that only 40–50% of patients have increased ventricular size and other abnormalities.

Some of the investigators attempted to relate ventricular enlargement to diagnoses or other characteristics of their patients. Nasrallah et al (1982) found the greatest enlargements in chronic schizophrenics. The results of Weinberger et al (1979, 1980, 1982) tended, in general, to support that finding, although there is some suggestion that ventricular enlargement may predate the psychosis (Weinberger et al 1982). They also reported that enlarged ventricles tended to be associated with poor response to neuroleptic treatment (Weinberger et al 1980). Andreasen et al (1982b,c) reported that patients characterized as having primarily "negative" symptoms (e.g. flattened affect, withdrawal, apathy) had larger ventricles than those with more "positive" (hallucinations, delusions, excitement) or mixed symptoms (Andreasen 1982, Andreasen & Olsen 1982). The negative symptom group, in addition, was found to be more impaired intellectually and to have had a poorer premorbid history. Johnstone et al (1976) and Golden et al (1980) also demonstrated a correlation between intellectual impairment and enlarged ventricles.

Luchins et al (1979) described more frequent reversed brain asymmetry in schizophrenic patients than in normal persons—normal right-handed persons were more likely to show larger left than right hemispheres on CT scans; schizophrenics (especially those with normal ventricles) showed the reverse of the normal asymmetry in frontal and occipital areas. This finding was not replicated by Jernigan et al (1982a,b) nor by Andreasen et al (1982a). Ventricular enlargement is of interest because it can reflect a variety of neuropathological conditions, such as hydrocephalus, infection, injury, or anoxia, thus raising the issue of the possible contribution of such agents to the etiology of the disorder. The question arises as to whether sporadic schizophrenia is more likely than familial schizophrenia to be associated with ventricular enlargement; there are at present insufficient data to answer this question.

There does seem to be some consensus that perhaps up to 50% of chronic schizophrenic patients exhibit abnormalities on the CT scan. The differences in methods used from study to study, coupled with the large range in ventricular sizes reported, underscore the conclusion that the CT scan is still a research tool and not a diagnostic test for schizophrenia. Further, it should be noted that CT scan abnormalities probably occur as frequently among schizoaffective and bipolar patients as among chronic schizophrenic patients (Rieder et al 1983), limiting further the diagnostic specificity of this marker.

Abnormalities in Glucose Metabolism

PET involves computer-assisted reconstructions of sections or "slices" of the brains of living subjects. Cerebral structures are defined on the basis of their differential uptake of a radioactively tagged material and their subsequent differential emission of radioactive particles (positrons). The density of emissions is detected by a scanning device, and the pattern is used to create a "functional" brain image. Virtually all of the human studies have been done with a tagged form of fake glucose (deoxyglucose) that cannot be completely metabolized by the brain (Sokoloff 1979, Sokoloff et al 1985). The PET brain image is formed during a 30–40-min period during which the isotope "sets" in the brain at the point where its metabolic dissolution stops.[2] The image reflects

[2]The metabolism of deoxyglucose cannot proceed further since it is not true glucose.

functional glucose use and relative degrees of activity of brain regions. The lengthy period of image formation limits the types of psychological processes that can be studied by means of deoxyglucose, since it is difficult to conceive of a uniform psychological state over such a time interval (cf Sutton 1969). Other tagged, metabolically active substances that depend on isotopes of oxygen or carbon will undoubtedly be developed that will allow image formation during much shorter intervals, compatible with the study of psychological processes involving attention, learning, and memory.

Despite the limitations of the deoxyglucose method, a number of PET studies have been conducted with schizophrenic and other psychotic patients. Buchsbaum and associates (1984a,b) reported that schizophrenics showed relatively less metabolic activity in their frontal lobes, as compared with posterior cortical regions, than normal subjects. However, Buchsbaum's technique required continuous delivery of electric shock to the forearm of the subject during the 30–40-min induction period. This experimental condition (designed to investigate altered pain sensation in schizophrenia) may limit the generality of the results. It should also be emphasized that schizophrenic patients may show more *absolute* metabolic activity than controls; it is the *ratio* of anterior/posterior activity that is lower in schizophrenic patients than in normal control subjects. Moreover, recent studies indicate that "hypofrontality," as it has been labeled, is also found in patients with severe affective disorder and not exclusively in schizophrenic patients (Buchsbaum et al 1984a,b).

At present, the results of PET studies on schizophrenic patients seem to be consistent with those of CT scan studies: there may be changes associated with schizophrenia, but they are not specific to the disorder.

Viral Brain Infections

The search for consistent and reliable lesions in the brains of schizophrenic patients continues. Some investigators noted the coincidence between the periods of the year when certain viral brain infections were most likely to occur (winter months) and the increased incidence of winter births in persons who later develop schizophrenia (see review by Torrey & Peterson 1976). There is evidence from immunological as well as neuropathological studies that changes compatible with prior viral infections are found in the brains of some schizophrenic patients (Weinberger et al 1983); however, Stevens et al (1984) recently reported failure to find evidence of herpes and cytomegalovirus antigens in brain tissue from schizophrenic patients. The viral hypothesis of schizophrenia remains an attractive one, since viral infections could account for enlarged ventricles and other neuropathological brain changes seen in the disorder.

Disturbed Hemispheric Function or Interhemispheric Relations

In recent years, a number of investigators have promoted the view that the signs of the major psychiatric disorders are localizable in one cerebral hemisphere.

Flor-Henry (1983) is perhaps the most fervent current advocate of the view that schizophrenia is the result of pathological processes in the left cerebral hemisphere. His position developed from earlier studies on the relation between laterality of temporal lobe dysfunction and psychotic manifestations in patients suffering from complex partial epilepsy. The dichotomy he proposed suggests that "the endogenous syndrome of schizophrenia is associated with dominant hemisphere disorganization . . .," whereas "the depressive syndrome complex is derivative of right hemisphere lesions" (Flor-Henry 1983, pp. 159–61). On the basis of a review of the literature on lateralization of abnormalities in schizophrenia as assessed by electrophysiological and psychophysiological methods, Myslobodsky and associates concluded that there is no "common laterality denominator" of schizophrenia and "In dealing with such a nebulous pathological condition as schizophrenia, this left-right polarization . . . may be insufficient" (Myslobodsky et al 1983, p. 373).

Delayed Nervous System Maturation or Deficient Neurointegration—Pre- and Perinatal Disturbances

The concept of early neurological disturbance in the offspring of schizophrenic women was noted by Fish (1975, 1977, Fish & Hagin 1973). Her concept of pandysmaturation (or PDM) found in children at genetic risk for schizophrenia refers to a generalized neurointegrative disorder. This disorder includes a transient lag in physical growth, the presence of irritability, and delays and disorganization of gross motor and/or visual-motor development between birth and two years. One of the patterns of special interest seen in these infants involved unusually quiet behavior including hypotonia, absence of crying, and underactivity. It is conceivable that such behaviors represent the earliest manifestations of attentional disturbances in high-risk subjects.

Fish studied a group of 12 such subjects as well as 12 controls from birth through adulthood. Although the original neurological examinations of these subjects were not conducted on a "blind" basis, subsequent evaluations were done by raters ignorant of the original group classifications. Fish (1985) recently reported significant correlations between PDM and later psychiatric status in the 24 subjects. Seven of the 12 high-risk subjects (and one of the 12 controls) showed PDM: 5 of the 7 received the diagnosis at age 27 of schizotypal personality disorder, one of schizophrenia, and one of paranoid personality disorder. There was no schizophrenia spectrum disorder in the control group; psychiatric disorder was limited to personality disorders in 6 subjects. There was one control subject with "mild paranoid traits," but this was not the one with PDM.

Marcus and coworkers reported data from two groups of children at genetic risk for schizophrenia. One of these groups, examined first at a mean age of 11 and later at a mean age of 17, showed more "soft" neurological signs than a group of matched controls. These soft signs included disturbances in the perceptual-sensory domain, motor coordination, right-left orientation, balance, and motor control. Twenty-two of the 50 high-risk subjects, as opposed to 3 of the 50 controls, exhibited multiple manifestations of neurological dysfunction on at least one of the two examinations (Marcus et al 1985); 7 of these 22 cases developed a schizophrenia spectrum disorder as compared to none of the controls (Mirsky et al 1985; J. Marcus, personal communication 1985).

The other group of children at risk was studied as infants (Marcus et al 1981). A subgroup of 13 of the 19 high-risk infants repeatedly performed more poorly than controls in motor and sensorimotor functions during their first year of life. The authors concluded that there may be a genetic susceptibility to neurointegrative deficit (NID) (Marcus et al 1981).

The presence of NID as well as other brain abnormalities in many schizophrenic patients has led to speculation as to whether such abnormalities were acquired during the pre- and/or perinatal period. For example, Mednick and coworkers pointed to the interaction between pregnancy and birth complications (PBC) and increased risk for schizophrenia (Mednick et al 1971). Some data indicate that, compared with controls, the offspring of schizophrenic women are likely to have lower birth weights, more PBCs, and to suffer more damage as a result of such PBCs (Mednick et al 1971, Rieder et al 1975, Sameroff & Zax 1978, Marcus et al 1981; see summary by McNeil & Kaij 1978). McNeil & Kaij (1985) also reported recently significant correlations between obstetrical complications and various measures of functioning in 6-year-old high-risk children. None of these correlations was found in a group of control children. To the extent that PBCs result in asphyxia neonatorum, there may be reason to suspect diffuse and widespread lesions in the brain, the nature and extent of which depend on the stage of gestation when the asphyxic insult occurred and the type and severity of the asphyxia (Myers 1972). The work of Windle (1969) and Myers (1972) with primate models established the vulnerability of cortical and subcortical structures to the asphyxia occasioned by difficult labor and delivery and emphasized the special vulnerability of the brain at or near term. It may be, therefore, that a major portion of the schizophrenic brain damage diathesis seen with the CT and PET techniques is acquired during the birth process. The possibility also exists that the brain changes associated with sporadic schizophrenia are acquired in this way.

COGNITIVE PSYCHOPHYSIOLOGICAL STUDIES

Attentional Deficit

Matthysse (1978) noted that deficits in attention and information processing are generally more consistent than neurochemical findings in schizophrenia. These results have led many theorists to view faulty attention as the fundamental cognitive deficit and have led them to suggest that study of the neurobiological mechanisms of attention may provide keys to understanding schizophrenia.

Perhaps the first experimental study of impaired attention in schizophrenic patients was that conducted by Shakow and coworkers beginning in the 1930s (Huston et al 1937). These pioneering investigators showed that schizophrenic patients had slower reaction times than normal controls (Rodnick & Shakow 1940, Zahn et al 1963); they were affected more adversely than normals by conditions that distract attention (Zahn et al 1961); and they benefited more than normals by conditions that help focus attention (Lang 1959). These findings, which have been replicated in a number of laboratories, were linked by Shakow (1962) to the concept of "segmental-set" in schizophrenia. This concept refers to the schizophrenic's inability to attend appropriately and to maintain a flexible and efficient information processing strategy on such tasks.

Other techniques, in addition to reaction time, have been applied to the study of attentional impairment in schizophrenic patients and in persons at risk for the disorder. These include vigilance tasks, such as the Continuous Performance Test (CPT) (Rosvold et al 1956, Stammeyer 1961, Orzack & Kornetsky 1966, Wohlberg & Kornetsky 1973, Grunebaum et al 1974) and versions of the CPT with high processing load (Rutschmann et al 1977, Nuechterlein 1983, Asarnow & MacCrimmon 1978, Walker & Shaye 1982, Erlenmeyer-Kimling & Cornblatt 1978). A forced-choice span of apprehension task for large stimulus arrays has also been used extensively (Neale 1971, Asarnow et al 1977, 1983, Asarnow & MacCrimmon 1982) as has a serial recall task for items that involve active rehearsal (Oltmanns 1978, Harvey et al 1981, Frame & Oltmanns 1982).

Evidence that persons at risk for schizophrenia show deficits on these tasks similar to those of schizophrenic patients suggests that these measures index genetic vulnerability to the disorder (Nuechterlein & Dawson 1984). However, the precise explanation for the deficits is still a matter of conjecture and controversy. Hypotheses that have been proposed to account for the nature of the schizophrenic attentional disturbance include defective filtering or screening of incoming information (Payne et al 1959, Callaway & Stone 1960, McGhie et al 1965, Broen 1968, Hemsley & Richardson 1980), information loss in short-term memory (Yates 1966, Korboot & Damiani 1976, Neale & Oltmanns 1980), a disorder in the control and maintenance of a selective processing strategy (Shakow 1962), a deficit in the amount of available processing capacity (Gjerde 1983, Nuechterlein & Dawson 1984), and an impairment in effortful, controlled processing (Callaway & Naghdi 1982). No consensus has been reached. Nuechterlein & Dawson noted that the variety of tasks and measures within tasks on which performance deficits have been found suggests that dysfunction of a variety of processes rather than a single process may be involved. The technique reviewed in the next section has the potential to provide additional insight into the nature of the deficit.

Cognitive Psychophysiology

In recent years, psychophysiological researchers have sought to apply ERPs to the study of attention and information processing as these processes are defined by cognitive psychology. The aim of the field of "cognitive psychophysiology" is to identify ERP components as indexes of specific aspects or stages of information processing (Donchin 1982).

A widely studied ERP component, the P300, is a manifestation of cognitive activity invoked by task-relevant stimuli. The discovery of the P300 component was a direct result of the study of attentional deficit in schizophrenia. Response

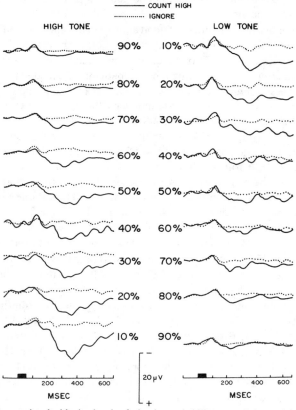

Figure 1   ERPs associated with nine levels of stimulus probability, recorded over the parietal (Pz) scalp area and averaged over 10 subjects. High and low frequency tones were presented in random order at complementary probabilities. Data are superimposed for two task conditions in which subjects either counted the high tones (solid lines) or ignored the tones and performed a word puzzle (dotted lines). Stimulus occurrence is indicated by a black bar on the time scale. It is apparent that when the stimuli were task relevant, the amplitude of P300 was inversely related to probability. Note, however, that when the tones were irrelevant to the subject's task, no P300 was elicited even by low probability tones. (Copyright © 1977, The Society for Psychophysiological Research. Reprinted with permission of the publisher from Duncan-Johnson & Donchin, 1977.)

time increases when the modality of a stimulus differs from that of the immediately preceding stimulus in the sequence, and the effect of this "cross-modality shift" was found to be exaggerated in schizophrenic patients (Sutton et al 1961). The newly developing ERP technique was applied to an investigation of the cause of this increase in latency. Sutton et al (1965) observed a previously unreported phenomenon in the ERP elicited by a shift in modality—a large positive wave that varied in amplitude as an inverse function of stimulus probability. This wave was not related to the modality of the stimulus nor to its physical attributes, but to the informational characteristics of the stimulus. Thus was born the "P300" component.

A series of studies since that time has shown that the P300 is highly responsive to manipulations of event probabilities (Sutton et al 1967, Tueting et al 1970, Duncan-Johnson & Donchin 1977, 1982, Johnson & Donchin 1978) and task relevance (Duncan-Johnson & Donchin 1977, Squires et al 1977, Johnson & Donchin 1980). The P300 has been shown to be an extremely sensitive index of the brain's response to "surprising" stimuli (Figure 1). These characteristics suggest that the process manifested by P300 is associated with the updating of the schema of the environment (Donchin 1981).

The P300 component has been found to vary in peak latency from less than 300 to nearly 1000 msec poststimulus, depending on the complexity of the stimuli and the task. P300 latency is proportional to the time required to classify and evaluate a stimulus, independent of response-production factors (Kutas et al 1977, Donchin et al 1978, Duncan-Johnson 1981, McCarthy & Donchin 1981).

Using ERPs, it is also possible to get a measure of selective attention (i.e. a selective allocation of processing resources to the relevant stimuli in the environment) distinct from general attentiveness (i.e. changes in the overall amount of processing capacity). When a subject is instructed to attend in a selective fashion to certain stimuli, there are characteristic ERP effects. Hillyard and coworkers (1973, 1978) presented subjects with multiple "channels" (defined by such characteristics as ear of delivery or frequency of tone) of auditory stimuli and required them to listen selectively and respond to one channel or category of stimuli at a time. The channel to which attention is directed has been shown to yield ERPs with a prolonged negative component beginning as early as 50 msec[3] (Näätänen et al 1978).

---

[3]Initially, this early selection effect was viewed as an enhancement of the evoked N100 component to stimuli in the attended channel (Hillyard et al 1973). Recent studies, however, have shown that the effect is due to a negativity that overlaps in time with the N100 but is primarily endogenous in nature (Näätänen & Michie 1979, Okita 1979). That is, the "N100 effect" comprises a broad negativity, termed the "processing negativity" (Näätänen et al 1978), which begins as early as 50 msec poststimulus and lasts as long as several hundred msec, depending on the complexity of the relevant cues (Hansen & Hillyard 1980, Okita 1981). The negativity appears to index the continued processing of a stimulus identified as a member of a relevant category (Näätänen 1982, Hansen & Hillyard 1983).

Application of Cognitive Psychophysiology to Research on Schizophrenia

The techniques of cognitive psychophysiology appear to hold promise for the study of the attentional or information processing deficit in schizophrenia, since they can help to clarify the timing and order of neural events involved in information processing activities (Hillyard & Kutas 1983). Moreover, the functional significance of the P300 and processing negativity are sufficiently well established to make them viable candidates for the study of disturbed attention that is characteristic of schizophrenia.

STUDIES OF SCHIZOPHRENIC PATIENTS   Most electrophysiological investigations of schizophrenic patients have been limited to ERPs evoked by simple stimuli such as sound, light, or shock in passive, no-task situations (Buchsbaum 1977, Roth 1977, Shagass 1977). These empirical studies of sensory ERP differences between schizophrenic patients and normal controls were a necessary first step. The next step has involved the use of cognitive psychophysiological indexes, which are being used increasingly in studying the nature of the attentional deficit in schizophrenia (Pfefferbaum 1985). We focus on two ERP measures, the P300 and the processing negativity.

Experimental procedures used to elicit ERPs in schizophrenic patients have included five paradigms: (a) the "oddball" paradigm, in which a random sequence of two or more stimuli is presented and either no task is assigned (Roth & Cannon 1972, Roth et al 1979, 1980a, 1981, Shagass et al 1977, 1978) or the subject is required to count one of them (Cohen et al 1981, Steinhauer & Zubin 1982, Morstyn et al 1983) or to press a button to one or more of them (Roth et al 1980b, 1981, Duncan-Johnson et al 1982, 1984, Pfefferbaum et al 1984); (b) the "prediction" paradigm, in which the subject is required to guess which of a set of stimuli will occur next in a sequence; the presentation of the stimulus disconfirms or confirms the subject's prediction and may or may not elicit a P300 (Levit et al 1973, Verleger & Cohen 1978); (c) the "CPT" paradigm, a type of oddball task in which a random series of letters is presented with and without irrelevant, distracting stimuli, and the subject is required to press a button to a target stimulus (Pass et al 1980); (d) "selective attention" paradigms based on Broadbent's (1971) model of information processing, including the "dichotic listening" task, in which the subject has to focus attention and detect a subset of auditory signals presented to one channel and ignore all signals presented to the other channel (Baribeau-Braun et al 1983, Hiramatsu et al 1983, Saitoh et al 1983) and the "somatosensory selection" task, in which fingers on both hands are randomly stimulated and the subject has to detect the shocks presented to one finger (Josiassen et al 1981, 1984); and (e) the "incentive" paradigm, in which the oddball paradigm is used with incentives to improve task performance (Brecher & Begleiter 1983).[4]

Despite differences in paradigms, stimulus modalities, instructional sets, diagnostic criteria, medication status, matching of patient and control groups, and data analysis techniques, there has been remarkable consistency in the finding of reduced amplitude of P300 in schizophrenic patients as compared with normal controls. If we assume that the amplitude of P300 is an index of orienting or allocating processing capacity to task-relevant stimuli, then the results suggest that these functions may be disturbed in schizophrenic patients. Moreover, there is some evidence that P300 amplitude is inversely correlated with the degree of psychopathology, as measured by various standard clinical assessment instruments (Roth et al 1979, 1980a, Josiassen et al 1981). Roth et al (1981) and Brecher & Begleiter (1983) did not, however, observe significant correlations between indexes of psychopathology and P300 amplitude.

Although most ERP studies have compared symptomatic schizophrenic patients with normal controls, some studies have used depressed patients as an additional control group (Levit et al 1973, Roth et al 1981, Pfefferbaum et al 1984, Shagass et al 1978, Steinhauer & Zubin 1982). The P300s of the depressed patients were found to be either similar to or slightly smaller than those of the normal controls but still tended to be larger than those of schizophrenic patients.

Whereas most studies have not reported differences in P300 latency between schizophrenic patients and normal controls, data from two studies (Roth et al 1979, Pfefferbaum et al 1984) indicated that schizophrenic patients have late P300s, suggesting slowed stimulus processing. These recent reports suggest that small but significant differences in P300 latency between schizophrenic patients and normal controls may have been overlooked in earlier work.

Dichotic listening tasks have been used recently to assess attentional deficit in schizophrenia as suggested by Hink & Hillyard (1978) (Baribeau-Braun et al 1983, Hiramatsu et al 1983, Saitoh et al 1983). Whereas Saitoh et al and Hiramatsu et al found no evidence in the schizophrenic patients of changes in either N100[5] or P300 according to the allocation of attention, Baribeau-Braun et al reported that schizophrenic patients had enhanced N100s to stimuli in attended ears, but only at a fast rate of stimulation.[6] This modulation of N100 amplitude by attention indicates integrity of early stimulus selection. Despite

---

[4]It is interesting that most of the paradigms used to study ERPs in schizophrenic patients are based on behavioral measures of attention that were developed in the 1960s or earlier. Only recently have ERP paradigms derived from current models of attention and information processing been applied to schizophrenia.

[5]We use the term "N100" to refer to the early attention effect that yields an apparent enhancement of the N100 peak.

[6]At a slow rate of stimulation, however, Baribeau-Braun et al reported the same results as Saitoh and coworkers.

this early selectivity, the schizophrenic patients performed poorly on the target detection task. Moreover, even when they detected targets accurately, their P300s were smaller than in the control subjects. A similar reduction in P300 amplitude was reported in studies (reviewed above) that did not assess attention effects on N100. Baribeau-Braun et al concluded that the schizophrenic attentional disorder stems not from general slowness or absence of selectivity but from an inability to control and maintain a selective processing strategy (cf Shakow 1962, Gjerde 1983). We believe that additional studies of this type, which test specific hypotheses concerning attention or information processing, will be most fruitful. Otherwise, we run the risk of simply reifying the finding of "impaired attention" in schizophrenia.

STUDIES OF SUBJECTS AT RISK FOR SCHIZOPHRENIA   Given that P300 differentiates schizophrenic patients and normal controls, then these differences may be present in vulnerable persons as well. Friedman et al (1982) used two oddball paradigms to elicit ERPs in high-risk and normal children. Based on a preliminary analysis, they reported that the high-risk children exhibited smaller P300s to target tones than did matched, normal control children. These findings are consistent with those obtained in symptomatic, adult schizophrenic patients, thus suggesting a deficit in information processing capacity in genetically defined high-risk children.

Recently, however, following additional analyses, D. Friedman (personal communication 1985) indicated that the group mean P300s of the high-risk and control children do not appear to differ significantly. It will be crucial to see the data analyzed fully and presented completely; nevertheless, if the P300 decrement is not observed in the high-risk children, there are methodological differences between the cross-sectional and high-risk studies that could account for this difference.

One difference is that the sample studied by Friedman et al (1982) was restricted to intact families, and, presumably, parents with less severe schizophrenic disorders. A second issue in interpreting high-risk data is that only a relatively small percentage of the offspring of schizophrenics is expected to develop the disorder. This would be consistent with the view that reduced P300 amplitude is an early sign of impending disorder rather than merely an index of potential (i.e. genetic) vulnerability. Therefore, comparison of group means may be a weak method of detecting vulnerability markers of schizophrenic disorder in a sample of high-risk children (Nuechterlein 1982). A more appropriate strategy would be to test for the existence of a disproportionately large, extreme-scoring subset of high-risk subjects with abnormalities (Dawson & Nuechterlein 1984). It is, of course, also possible that reduced P300 is an episode or state marker rather than a vulnerability or trait marker of schizophrenia and thus would not be apparent in high-risk children.

An approach related to the study of offspring of schizophrenic patients is the study of their siblings, known to have an increased predisposition to schizophrenia (Kety et al 1968). Saitoh et al (1984) used a dichotic listening task to elicit ERPs in siblings of schizophrenic probands with no history of psychiatric or neurological disorder. Whereas the siblings and normal controls showed an enhanced N100 wave according to the allocation of attention between two ears (channels), the siblings failed to exhibit augmentation of P300 to detected targets in the attended ear. In an earlier study using the same paradigm, schizophrenic patients showed neither the channel (N100) nor the target (P300) effect shown by normal controls (Hiramatsu et al 1983). In contrast, Baribeau-Braun et al (1983) found a normal channel (N100) effect in their schizophrenic patients, similar to the siblings studied by Saitoh et al (1984), but no target (P300) effect. The N100 differences between the findings of Baribeau-Braun et al (1983) and those of Saitoh and coworkers may lie in techniques or in patient selection. Nevertheless, if the pattern of sibling results reported by Saitoh et al is found to hold up, this would suggest that reduced P300 is a vulnerability marker of schizophrenia.

Another study supporting the potential usefulness of ERPs as vulnerability markers of schizophrenia is that of Simons (1982), who studied P300 in subjects selected on the basis of a measure of high anhedonia. This trait, according to Chapman et al (1976, 1980), characterizes persons at risk for schizophrenia. Simons' anhedonic subjects had significantly smaller P300s than controls to signals preceding erotic stimuli but normal P300s to neutral stimuli. These results, as well as those derived from the selective attention paradigm, are consistent with the view of P300 as a vulnerability marker of schizophrenia.

STUDIES OF FAMILIAL AND SOCIOENVIRONMENTAL FACTORS

The earlier trend to impugn the parents of a schizophrenic patient (and, in particular, the mother) as being the cause of the disorder (Fromm-Reichmann 1948) has largely ended with the advent of modern biological psychiatry. The concept of a schizophrenogenic mother was weakened substantially by the findings of adoption studies, which showed that the proportion of adopted-away offspring of schizophrenic patients that developed the disorder was about the same as would be expected had those same offspring been raised by their biological parents (Heston 1966, Higgins 1966, Rosenthal et al 1968). Moreover, study of a small number of adopted-away children of normal parents, raised by families that included a schizophrenic parent, failed to reveal higher than normal incidence of schizophrenia (Wender et al 1974).

In the last decade, however, data have begun to accumulate that implicate familial or social factors in the development of schizophrenia or the severity of its expression. There are four sets of data that bear on this point. Before reviewing them, it is well to remember that Singer & Wynne (1966) noted abnormal communication and interaction patterns ("communication deviance" or CD) in the families of schizophrenic patients. These authors suggested that such patterns could influence the cognitive development of the offspring and lead to thought disorder in schizophrenic patients.

Recent work suggests that some of their views may be borne out, i.e. that disturbed communication patterns in families may be associated with psychiatric disorder in the children of such families. A striking example of this effect is seen in the so-called "UCLA family project" (Doane et al 1981, M. Goldstein 1985). The UCLA project is a 15-year follow-up study of the outcome of 64 disturbed adolescents selected from an outpatient clinic to which they had been referred for academic or interpersonal difficulties or conflicts with authorities.

At follow-up, Goldstein (1985) found that several measures of parental behavior were significantly related to psychiatric outcome. The measures were: (a) *Communication Deviance* (CD)—A communication style in which there are difficulties in maintaining a clear focus of attention and meaning (Wynne et al 1976); (b) *Affective Style* (AS)—Verbal behavior that is critical, guilt-inducing, or intrusive (Doane et al 1981); and (c) *Expressed Emotion* (EE)—Negative critical attitudes and/or emotion-laden statements directed to a specific person in the family (Brown et al 1962, 1972). Generally speaking, the more pathological the rating on the parental measure, the more schizophrenia spectrum disorder was seen in the offspring at 30 years of age. Thus, an analysis of 12 low, 30 intermediate, and 21 high CD families yielded, respectively, 8, 17, and 67% of cases with schizophrenia spectrum disorders in the high-risk children or their siblings. Similar results, indicating significant associations between parental behavior and outcome, were found with the AS and EE measures. Although the original cohort of subjects was not selected on the basis of a history of parental psychopathology, a post-hoc analysis of the first-degree relatives of the subjects was undertaken. Preliminary results indicate that there was a fourfold increase in the risk of schizophrenia spectrum disorder if there was a family history of psychiatric disorder. Therefore, the combination of positive family history, high EE, and negative AS may be particularly pernicious.

A study of similar import was conducted by Tienari and coworkers (Tienari et al 1985). Their investigation involved a follow-up of 184 adopted-away offspring of 171 schizophrenic women. Interviews, questionnaires, and rating scales were used to rate the quality of mental health in the adoptive family. Similar data were collected from a matched control group of parents free from psychosis. In an interim description of outcomes (limited to high-risk cases),

Tienari et al reported that in a cohort over 25 years of age, there was a significant association between psychiatric status of the offspring and ratings of family "mental health." In families classified as "healthy" (healthy, mildly disturbed, or neurotic), 93% of the high-risk children were classified as healthy; the remaining 7% were rated as "ill" (character disordered, borderline, or psychotic). In contrast, in the two most disturbed family types (moderately and severely disturbed), the percentages of healthy and ill children were 48 and 52, respectively.

In both the M. Goldstein and Tienari et al studies, the data indicate that the combination of a diathesis for schizophrenia and a stressful environment during development results in a significant increase in the proportion of children who manifest psychiatric disorders. There is, however, little evidence to suggest that a stressful environment alone results in a rate of schizophrenia spectrum disorders that is greater than would be expected in the population at large.

A recently completed, 20-year follow-up study of Israeli children at risk for schizophrenia provides additional support for these suggestions. This study, conceived by Rosenthal (Nagler & Mirsky 1985), contrasted the outcome of two groups of 25 high-risk children, one group that was raised in kibbutz settings, the other in cities and towns in Israel. Two matched control groups were also studied. The kibbutz setting was of special interest, since children are raised in a communal setting ("children's house"), with the major responsibility for rearing assumed by a professional childcare worker. The children's contact with their parents is relatively limited in the kibbutz. It might, therefore, be expected that such a setting would buffer the high-risk subjects against the pernicious effects of high CD, negative AS, and high EE—assuming that one or more of these factors was present in the family setting. In fact, the data indicate that high-risk children who were raised by their own parents in general fared better than high-risk children raised on kibbutzim (Mirsky et al 1985). Twenty-six percent of the kibbutz high-risk cases developed a schizophrenia spectrum disorder by an average age of 25 as compared to 13% of the town-raised, high-risk cases. Moreover, there were 9 cases (39%) of affective disorder among the kibbutz high-risk subjects as compared to one case (4%) in the town high-risk group.[7]

The high incidence of affective disorder was unexpected and raised some question about the original parental diagnoses. Data reported by the authors, however, tended to support the claim that the parents were indeed schizophrenic and provided little evidence that those with affective symptoms sired offspring with affective disorders: There were no differences in manic symptoms between the parents of schizophrenia spectrum as compared to affective offspring.

[7]There were no cases of spectrum disorder in the control groups.

How can the results of this study be squared with those of M. Goldstein (1985) and Tienari et al (1985)? It may be that although the communal rearing in the kibbutz reduced parent-child contact, the kibbutz setting itself served, in effect, as a hypercritical extended family. Kibbutzim are intolerant of deviance, and the high-risk children tended to behave differently from their peers (Ayalon & Merom 1985, Sohlberg & Yaniv 1985). Since the identities of all of the high-risk children were well known on the kibbutz, self-fulfilling prophecies could have led to "like father, like son" expectations for these children (Mirsky & Duncan-Johnson 1984). Thus, the operation of the same critical, hostile, intrusive parental behaviors reflected in AS and EE factors [as identified by M. Goldstein (1985)] could have produced this outcome. On a kibbutz, these factors would have been operating in a larger, community context, as opposed to a family context.

We wish to cite one additional bit of evidence in support of the familial stress-diathesis hypothesis of schizophrenia. In a reanalysis of Rosenthal's adoption data, Lowing and Mirsky (cited in Mirsky & Duncan-Johnson 1984) found that among the 20 subjects with DSM-III diagnoses of schizophrenia spectrum, severity of disorder was positively correlated with reported familial stress. Thus, among the 10 subjects with a diagnosis of schizophrenia or schizotypal personality disorder ("hard spectrum"), there were significantly more reported stressors during childhood than in the 10 cases with diagnoses of schizoid, borderline, or mixed personality disorder ("soft spectrum"). The stressors tended to be those that attributed to parents the following types of behaviors: general harshness, intrusiveness, and restriction of the child's autonomous functioning. Also reported were alienation from parents and chronic arguments. It should be noted that there were no differences in overall reported stressors between subjects with and without disorders; significant differences were seen only within the disordered group.

VULNERABILITY TO SCHIZOPHRENIA: SOME WORKING HYPOTHESES

Table 1 summarizes factors that research over the past 25 years has shown to predispose a person to the development of schizophrenia. It is reasonable to assume that the presence of fewer factors, or their presence in milder forms, might predispose to a less severe disorder (i.e. ranging from schizoid through schizotypal personality). However, we do not know this to be the case; and it may be that there are unique biological and environmental circumstances associated with each spectrum diagnosis. Nevertheless, much of the data reviewed above supports the correlation between severity of stressors and severity of the disorder. We propose the following hypotheses:

Table 1 Summary of Factors Involved in Vulnerability to Schizophrenia

Life Stages	Factors
1. Genetic	Inherited schizophrenic diathesis, including possible brain abnormalities
2. Prenatal	Possible aberrant intrauterine development leading to brain abnormalities
3. Birth	Increased vulnerability to birth trauma; asphyxia leading to brain abnormalities; reduced birth weight
4. Infancy through Adulthood	Pandysmaturation and persistent neurointegrative deficit; attentional deficit; impaired cognitive skills; chaotic family situation with communication deviance; punitive affective style, negative expressed emotion; anhedonia; "different" from peers, troubled, aggressive, reclusive

1. We assume the existence of a genetic diathesis for schizophrenia that is expressed as one or more brain abnormalities that can be exacerbated by intrauterine and birth events. *These schizophrenogenic brain abnormalities or "SBA" are posited to be the underlying biological bases of schizophrenia.*

2. *The hypothesized SBA can arise anew in ontogeny as a genetic mutation in the absence of a family history of the disorder.* Such a mutation would then be subject to the same influences (protective or exacerbating) as a person with a genetic diathesis and could sire offspring who would be at risk for the disorder. We propose that there is no phenotypic expression of schizophrenia that does not include as its key element the SBA.

3. *Sporadic schizophrenia can also develop from the appropriate set of intrauterine and birth complications; in this case, individuals with sporadic schizophrenia could not transmit risk of schizophrenia to their offspring.* Genetic versus sporadic schizophrenia can, at present, only be inferred from family pedigree studies. Walker & Shaye (1982) recently provided data on attentional differences between genetic and sporadic cases, suggesting that markers differentiating these two forms of disorder could be developed.

4. *The first manifestations (during infancy and early childhood) of SBA are the pandysmaturation (PDM) syndrome (Fish 1975); later signs (during childhood and adolescence) comprise a neurointegrative deficit* (NID) (Marcus et al 1985).

5. *Manifestations of PDM/NID depend on the extent to which events during the intrauterine and birth periods exacerbate SBA.* The data provided by Fish (1985) and Marcus et al (1985) suggest that the proportion of high-risk offspring with PDM/NID ranges from 58–68%. Although similar proportions of schizophrenic patients perform poorly on such attentional measures as the CPT (Orzack & Kornetsky 1966) and show evidence of enlarged

ventricles on CT scan (Weinberger et al 1979), it is not known whether these are overlapping groups.

6. *The development of schizophrenia spectrum disorder results from exposure of a person with SBA to environmental stressors.* At high levels of SBA, less environmental stress is needed to produce a schizophrenic disorder. Conversely, at high levels of environmental stress, less SBA is sufficient to produce a disorder. Low levels of SBA or stress result in less severe outcomes. According to our model, schizotypal personality disorder represents the interface of spectrum disorders and schizophrenia. Figure 2 illustrates the hypothesized relation between SBA and environmental stress in the development of schizophrenic disorders.

7. *Sources of environmental stress include the following:*
   (*a*) The clumsiness and feelings of "being different" associated with PDM/ NID;

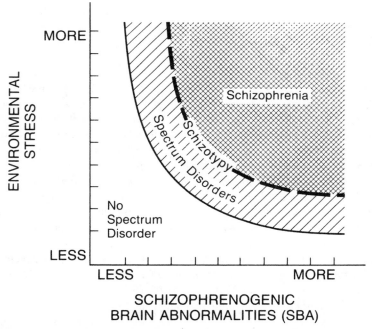

Figure 2   Relation between schizophrenogenic brain abnormalities (SBA) and environmental stress in the development of schizophrenic disorders. Our model proposes that there is no phenotypic expression of schizophrenia that does not include SBA as a key element. At high levels of SBA, less environmental stress is needed to produce a schizophrenic disorder. Conversely, at high levels of environmental stress, less SBA is sufficient to produce a disorder. Low levels of SBA or stress result in less severe outcomes. It is proposed that schizotypal personality disorder (heavy dashed line) represents the interface between spectrum outcomes (striped area) and schizophrenia (cross-hatched area). Note the similarity between our hypothesized relation and that proposed by Zubin & Steinhauer (1981).

(b) The increased dependency on parents occasioned by being different or impaired;

(c) The deficient attentional and cognitive capacities leading to poor academic performance and impaired coping skills;

(d) Stressful family interaction patterns, including high degrees of expressed emotion (EE) and a punitive, affective style (AS) of child rearing;

(e) Communication deviance (CD) in the family leading to difficulties in communication with those outside the family and, therefore, to increased isolation;

(f) Frequent hospitalizations of a parent and/or other family members.

8. *A schizophrenic disorder develops when the combination of diathesis (SBA) and stress exceeds a threshold value.* The stress probably leads to high levels of physiological arousal (Gjerde 1983). The development of the disorder in a vulnerable person may represent an adaptation analagous to the development of the concrete attitude in a brain-injured person to ward off a "catastrophic situation" (K. Goldstein 1951).

9. *CD is correlated with measures of impaired attention [e.g. reaction time (Shakow 1962), CPT (Orzack & Kornetsky 1966)], and impaired information processing [e.g. P300 (Duncan-Johnson 1985)].* We hypothesize that the various characteristics of CD described by Singer & Wynne (1966) (e.g. unclear communication, lack of commitment to ideas, closure problems) are interpersonal expressions of impaired attention and/or information processing. Such impairment in one family member may be sufficient to result in CD; impairment in two or more members would raise the CD level substantially. To our knowledge, there has been no attempt to relate CD and attentional deficit directly in families of schizophrenic or high-risk persons.

CONCLUSION

The next step in achieving a comprehensive assessment of schizophrenic deficit involves a program that "studies diverse types of patients with valid and current diagnoses; uses paradigms that tap different aspects of information processing; assesses the effects of the experimental variables on the full range of event-related potential components; and correlates these components with behavioral responses and measures of brain structure and function" (Duncan-Johnson 1985). We add only that studies of familial environment must also be included in any comprehensive research program in schizophrenia. Such correlational studies can lead to new heuristic subgroupings of schizophrenic patients.

Finally, as Zubin et al (1985) pointed out, "It does little good to continue to find a difference in overall response level between normals and schizophrenics in our electrophysiological, positron emission, biochemical, and behavioral measures unless we use the knowledge to lead to new approaches to classification, treatment, and etiology."

Literature Cited

Andreasen, N. C. 1982. Negative symptoms in schizophrenia: Definition and reliability. *Arch. Gen. Psychiatry* 39:784–88

Andreasen, N. C., Olsen, S. 1982. Negative v positive symptoms in schizophrenia: Definition and validation. *Arch. Gen. Psychiatry* 39:789–94

Andreasen, N. C., Dennert, J. W., Olsen, S. A., Damasio, A. R. 1982a. Hemispheric asymmetries and schizophrenia. *Am. J. Psychiatry* 139:427–30

Andreasen, N. C., Olsen, S. A., Dennert, J. W., Smith, M. R. 1982b. Ventricular enlargement in schizophrenia: Relationship to positive and negative symptoms. *Am. J. Psychiatry* 139:297–302

Andreasen, N. C., Smith, M. R., Jacoby, C. G., Dennert, J. W., Olsen, S. A., 1982c. Ventricular enlargement in schizophrenia: Definition and prevalence. *Am. J. Psychiatry* 139:292–96

Ariel, R. N., Golden, C. J., Berg, R. A., Quaife, M. A., Dirksen, J. W., et al. 1983. Regional cerebral blood flow in schizophrenics. *Arch. Gen. Psychiatry* 40:258–63

Asarnow, R. F., MacCrimmon, D. J. 1978. Residual performance deficit in clinically remitted schizophrenics: A marker of schizophrenia? *J. Abnorm. Psychol.* 87:597–608

Asarnow, R. F., MacCrimmon, D. J. 1982. Attention/information processing, neuropsychological functioning, and thought disorder during the acute and partial recovery phases of schizophrenia: A longitudinal study. *Psychiatry Res.* 7:309–19

Asarnow, R. F., Nuechterlein, K. H., Marder, S. R. 1983. Span of apprehension performance, neuropsychological functioning, and indices of psychosis-proneness. *J. Nerv. Ment. Dis.* 171:662–69

Asarnow, R. F., Steffy, R. A., MacCrimmon, D. J., Cleghorn, J. M. 1977. An attentional assessment of foster children at risk for schizophrenia. *J. Abnorm. Psychol.* 86:267–75

Ayalon, M., Merom, H. 1985. The teacher interview. *Schizophr. Bull.* 11:117–20

Baribeau-Braun, J., Picton, T. W., Gosselin, J.-Y. 1983. Schizophrenia: A neurophysiological evaluation of abnormal information processing. *Science* 219:874–76

Berger, P. A. 1981. Biochemistry and the schizophrenias: Old concepts and new hypotheses. *J. Nerv. Ment. Dis.* 169:90–99

Bleuler, E. 1911. *Dementia Praecox; or, the Group of Schizophrenias.* Transl. H. Zinkin. New York: Int. Univ. Press

Bowers, M. B. Jr. 1980. Biochemical processes in schizophrenia: An update. *Schizophr. Bull.* 6:393–403

Brecher, M., Begleiter, H. 1983. Event-related brain potentials to high-incentive stimuli in unmedicated schizophrenic patients. *Biol. Psychiatry* 18:661–74

Broadbent, D. E. 1971. *Decision and Stress.* New York: Academic

Broen, W. E. 1968. *Schizophrenia Research and Theory.* New York: Academic

Brown, G. W., Birley, J. L., Wing, J. K. 1972. Influence of family life on the course of schizophrenic disorders: A replication. *Br. J. Psychiatry* 121:241–58

Brown, G. W., Monck, E. M., Carstairs, G. M., Wing, J. K. 1962. The influence of family life on the course of schizophrenic illness. *Br. J. Prev. Soc. Med.* 16:55–68

Buchsbaum, M. S. 1977. The middle evoked response components and schizophrenia. *Schizophr. Bull.* 3:93–104

Buchsbaum, M. S., Cappelletti, J., Ball, R., Hazlett, E., King, A. C., et al. 1984a. Positron emission tomographic image measurement in schizophrenia and affective disorders. *Ann. Neurol.* 15:S157–65

Buchsbaum, M. S., DeLisi, L. E., Holcomb, H. H., Cappelletti, J., King, A. C., et al. 1984b. Anteroposterior gradients in cerebral glucose use in schizophrenia and affective disorders. *Arch. Gen. Psychiatry* 41:1159–66

Callaway, E., Naghdi, S. 1982. An information processing model for schizophrenia. *Arch. Gen. Psychiatry* 39:339–47

Callaway, E., Stone, G. 1960. Re-evaluating focus of attention. In *Drugs and Behavior,* ed. L. Uhr, J. G. Muller, pp. 393–98. New York: Wiley

Callaway, E., Tueting, P., Koslow, S. H., eds. 1978. *Event-related Brain Potentials in Man.* New York: Academic

Chapman, L. J., Chapman, J. P., Raulin, M. L. 1976. Scales for physical and social anhedonia. *J. Abnorm. Psychol.* 85:374–82

Chapman, L. J., Edell, W. S., Chapman, J. P. 1980. Physical anhedonia, perceptual aberration, and psychosis proneness. *Schizophr. Bull.* 6:639–53

Cohen, R., Sommer, W., Hermanutz, M. 1981. Auditory event-related potentials in chronic schizophrenics: Effects of electrodermal response type and demands on selective attention. In *Electroneurophysiology and Psychopathology* (Ser: *Adv. Biol. Psychiatry*), ed. C. Perris, D. Kemali, L. Vacca, pp. 180–85. Basel, Switzerland: Karger

Dawson, M. E., Nuechterlein, K. H. 1984. Psychophysiological dysfunctions in the developmental course of schizophrenic disorders. *Schizophr. Bull.* 10:204–32

Doane, J. A., West, K. L., Goldstein, M. J., Rodnick, E. H., Jones, J. E. 1981. Parental communication deviance and affective style: Predictors of subsequent schizophrenia-spectrum disorders in vulnerable adolescents. *Arch. Gen. Psychiatry* 38:679–85

Donchin, E. 1981. Surprise! . . . surprise? *Psychophysiology* 18:493–513

Donchin, E., ed. 1982. *Cognitive Psychophysiology*. Hillsdale, NJ: Erlbaum

Donchin, E., Ritter, W., McCallum, W. C. 1978. Cognitive psychophysiology: The endogenous components of the ERP. See Callaway et al 1978, pp. 349–411

Duncan-Johnson, C. C. 1981. P300 latency: A new metric of information processing. *Psychophysiology* 18:207–15

Duncan-Johnson, C. C. 1985. P300 applications to research on schizophrenia. *Electroencephalogr. Clin. Neurophysiol.* In press

Duncan-Johnson, C. C., Donchin, E. 1977. On quantifying surprise: The variation of event-related potentials with subjective probability. *Psychophysiology* 14:456–67

Duncan-Johnson, C. C., Donchin, E. 1982. The P300 component of the event-related brain potential as an index of information processing. *Biol. Psychol.* 14:1–52

Duncan-Johnson, C. C., Roth, W. T., Callaway, E., Fujii, J. S., Kopell, B. S. 1982. Shift of sensory modality: Effects on P300 and RT. *Psychophysiology* 19:314–15

Duncan-Johnson, C. C., Roth, W. T., Kopell, B. S. 1984. Effects of stimulus sequence on P300 and reaction time in schizophrenics: A preliminary report. In *Brain and Information: Event Related Potentials,* ed. R. Karrer, J. Cohen, P. Tueting, pp. 570–77. New York: New York Acad. Sci.

Erlenmeyer-Kimling, L., Cornblatt, B. 1978. Attentional measures in a study of children at high risk for schizophrenia. See Wynne et al 1978, pp. 359–65

Fish, B. 1975. Biologic antecedents of psychosis in children. In *Biology of the Major Psychoses,* ed. D. X. Freedman. Research Publ., *Assoc. Res. Nerv. Ment. Dis.* 54:44–83

Fish, B. 1977. Neurobiologic antecedents of schizophrenia in children: Evidence for an inherited, congenital neurointegrative defect. *Arch. Gen. Psychiatry* 34:1297–1313

Fish, B. 1985. *Infant predictors of the longitudinal course of schizophrenic development.* Presented at NIMH High-Risk Consortium, San Francisco

Fish, B., Hagin, R. 1973. Visual-motor disorders in infants at risk for schizophrenia. *Arch. Gen. Psychiatry* 28:900–4

Flor-Henry, P. 1983. Hemisyndromes of temporal lobe epilepsy: Review of evidence relating psychopathological manifestations in epilepsy to right- and left-sided epilepsy. See Myslobodsky 1983, pp. 149–74

Frame, C. L., Oltmanns, T. F. 1982. Serial recall by schizophrenic and affective patients during and after psychotic episodes. *J. Abnorm. Psychol.* 91:311–18

Franzen, G., Ingvar, D. H. 1975. Abnormal distribution of cerebral activity in chronic schizophrenia. *J. Psychiatr. Res.* 12:199–214

Friedman, D., Vaughan, H. G. Jr., Erlenmeyer-Kimling, L. 1982. Cognitive brain potentials in children at risk for schizophrenia: Preliminary findings. *Schizophr. Bull.* 8:514–31

Fromm-Reichmann, F. 1948. Notes on the development of treatment of schizophrenics by psychoanalytic psychotherapy. *Psychiatry* 2:263–73

Garmezy, N., Streitman, S. 1974. Children at risk: The search for the antecedents of schizophrenia. Part 1. Conceptual models and research methods. *Schizophr. Bull.* (Exp. Issue No. 8):14–90

Gjerde, P. F. 1983. Attentional capacity dysfunction and arousal in schizophrenia. *Psychol. Bull.* 93:57–72

Golden, C. J., Graber, B., Coffman, J., Berg, R. A., Newlin, D. B., et al. 1981. Structural brain deficits in schizophrenia. *Arch. Gen. Psychiatry* 38:1014–17

Golden, C. J., Moses, J. A., Zelazowski, R., Graber, B., Zatz, L. M., et al. 1980. Cerebral ventricular size and neuropsychological impairment in young chronic schizophrenics. *Arch. Gen. Psychiatry* 37:619–23

Goldstein, K. 1951. *Human Nature in the Light of Psychopathology.* Cambridge, MA: Harvard Univ. Press

Goldstein, M. J. 1985. *The UCLA family project.* Presented at NIMH High-Risk Consortium, San Francisco

Gottesman, I. I., Shields, J. 1982. *Schizophrenia: The Epigenetic Puzzle.* Cambridge: Cambridge Univ. Press

Grant, D. A., Berg, E. A. 1948. A behavioral analysis of degree of reinforcement and ease of shifting to new responses in a Weigl-type card sorting problem. *J. Exp. Psychol.* 38:404–11

Grunebaum, H., Weiss, J. L., Gallant, D., Cohler, B. J. 1974. Attention in young children of psychotic mothers. *Am. J. Psychiatry* 131:887–91

Gur, R. E., Gur, R. C., Skolnick, B. E., Caroff, S., Obrist, W. D., et al. 1985. Brain function in psychiatric disorders. *Arch. Gen. Psychiatry* 42:329–34

Hansen, J. C., Hillyard, S. A. 1980. Endogenous brain potentials associated with selective auditory attention. *Electroencephalogr. Clin. Neurophysiol.* 49:277–90

Hansen, J. C., Hillyard, S. A. 1983. Selective attention to multidimensional auditory stimuli in man. *J. Exp. Psychol: Hum. Percept. Perform.* 9:1–19

Haracz, J. L. 1982. The dopamine hypothesis: An overview of studies with schizophrenic patients. *Schizophr. Bull.* 8:438–69

Harvey, P., Winters, K., Weintraub, S., Neale, J. M. 1981. Distractibility in children vulnerable to psychopathology. *J. Abnorm. Psychol.* 90:298–304

Hemsley, D. R., Richardson, P. H. 1980. Shadowing by context in schizophrenia. *J. Nerv. Ment. Dis.* 168:141–45

Heston, L. L. 1966. Psychiatric disorders in foster home reared children of schizophrenic mothers. *Br. J. Psychiatry* 112:819–25

Higgins, J. 1966. Effects of child rearing by schizophrenic mothers. *J. Psychiatr. Res.* 4:153–67

Hillyard, S. A., Hink, R. F., Schwent, V. L., Picton, T. W. 1973. Electrical signs of selective attention in the human brain. *Science* 182:177–80

Hillyard, S. A., Kutas, M. 1983. Electrophysiology of cognitive processing. *Ann. Rev. Psychol.* 34:33–61

Hillyard, S. A., Picton, T. W., Regan, D. 1978. Sensation, perception and attention: Analysis using ERPs. See Callaway et al 1978, pp. 223–321

Hink, R. F., Hillyard, S. A. 1978. Electrophysiological measures of attentional processes in man as related to the study of schizophrenia. *J. Psychiatr. Res.* 14:155–65

Hiramatsu, K., Kameyama, T., Niwa, S., Saitoh, O., Rymar, K., et al. 1983. Schizophrenic deficits in information processing as reflected in event-related potential abnormalities during syllable discrimination tasks. In *Neurophysiological Correlates of Normal Cognition and Psychopathology* (Series: *Adv. Biol. Psychiatry*), ed. C. Perris, D. Kemali, M. Koukkou-Lehmann, pp. 63–74. Basel: Karger

Huston, P. E., Shakow, D., Riggs, L. A. 1937. Studies of motor function in schizophrenia: II. Reaction time. *J. Gen. Psychol.* 16:39–82

Ingvar, D. H., Franzen, G. 1974. Distribution of cerebral activity in chronic schizophrenia. *Lancet* 2:1484–86

Jernigan, T. L., Zatz, L. M., Moses, J. A. Jr., Berger, P. A. 1982a. Computed tomography in schizophrenics and normal volunteers. I. Fluid volume. *Arch. Gen. Psychiatry* 39:765–70

Jernigan, T. L., Zatz, L. M., Moses, J. A. Jr., Cardellino, J. P. 1982b. Computed tomography in schizophrenics and normal volunteers. II. Cranial asymmetry. *Arch. Gen. Psychiatry* 39:771–73

Johnson, R. E. Jr., Donchin, E. 1978. On how P300 amplitude varies with the utility of the eliciting stimuli. *Electroencephalogr. Clin. Neurophysiol.* 44:424–37

Johnson, R. E. Jr., Donchin, E. 1980. P300 and stimulus categorization: Two plus one is not so different from one plus one. *Psychophysiology* 17:167–78

Johnstone, E. C., Frith, C. D., Crow, T. J., Husband, J., Kreel, L. 1976. Cerebral ventricular size and cognitive impairment in chronic schizophrenia. *Lancet* 2:924–26

Josiassen, R. C., Shagass, C., Roemer, R. A., Straumanis, J. J. 1981. The attention-related somatosensory evoked potential late positive wave in psychiatric patients. *Psychiatry Res.* 5:147–55

Josiassen, R. C., Shagass, C., Straumanis, J. J., Roemer, R. A. 1984. Psychiatric drugs and the somatosensory P400 wave. *Psychiatry Res.* 11:151–62

Kety, S. S. 1980. The syndrome of schizophrenia: Unresolved questions and opportunities for research. *Br. J. Psychiatry* 136:421–36

Kety, S. S., Rosenthal, D., Wender, P. H., Schulsinger, F. 1968. The types and prevalence of mental illness in the biological and adoptive families of adopted schizophrenics. See Rosenthal & Kety 1968, pp. 345–62

Korboot, P. J., Damiani, N. 1976. Auditory processing speed and signal detection in schizophrenics. *J. Abnorm. Psychol.* 85:287–95

Kraepelin, E. 1913. *Dementia Praecox and Paraphrenia.* Transl. R. M. Barclay from 8th German Ed. of "Textbook of Psychiatry. Vol. III, P. 2, on Endogenous Dementias." Edinburgh: Livingstone

Kutas, M., McCarthy, G., Donchin, E. 1977. Augmenting mental chronometry: The P300 as a measure of stimulus evaluation time. *Science* 197:792–95

Lang, P. J. 1959. The effect of aversive stimuli on reaction time in schizophrenia. *J. Abnorm. Soc. Psychol.* 59:263–68

Levit, R. A., Sutton, S., Zubin, J. 1973. Evoked potential correlates of information processing in psychiatric patients. *Psychol. Med.* 3:487–94

Lewis, M. E. 1980. Biochemical aspects of schizophrenia. In *Essays in Neurochemistry and Neuropharmacology*, ed. M. B. H. Youdim, W. Lovenberg, D. F. Sharman, J. R. Lagnado, 4:1–67. New York: Wiley

Luchins, D. J., Weinberger, D. R., Wyatt, R. J. 1979. Schizophrenia: Evidence for a subgroup with reversed cerebral asymmetry. *Arch. Gen. Psychiatry* 36:1309–11

Marcus, J., Auerbach, J., Wilkinson, L., Burack, C. M. 1981. Infants at risk for schizophrenia. *Arch. Gen. Psychiatry* 38:703–13

Marcus, J., Hans, S. L., Lewow, E., Wilkinson, L., Burack, C. M. 1985. Neurological findings in high-risk children: Childhood assessment and 5-year followup. *Schizophr. Bull.* 11:85–100

Matthysse, S. 1978. Missing links. See Wynne et al 1978, pp. 148–50

McCarthy, G., Donchin, E. 1981. A metric for thought: A comparison of P300 latency and reaction time. *Science* 211:77–80

McGhie, A., Chapman, J., Lawson, J. S. 1965. Effect of distraction on schizophrenic performance. (1) Perception and immediate memory. (2) Psychomotor ability. *Br. J. Psychiatry* 111:383–98

McNeil, T. F., Kaij, L. 1978. Obstetric factors in the development of schizophrenia: Complications in the births of preschizophrenics and in reproduction by schizophrenic parents. See Wynne et al 1978, pp. 401–29

McNeil, T. F., Kaij, L. 1985. *Offspring of women with nonorganic psychosis: Early sample characteristics and mental disturbance at six years of age.* Presented at NIMH High-Risk Consortium, San Francisco

Mednick, S. A., McNeil, T. F. 1968. Current methodology in research on the etiology of schizophrenia: Serious difficulties which suggest the use of the high-risk group method. *Psychol. Bull.* 70:681–93

Mednick, S. A., Mura, E., Schulsinger, F., Mednick, B. 1971. Perinatal conditions and infant development in children with schizophrenic mothers. *Soc. Biol.* 18:S103–13

Milner, B. 1963. Effects of different brain lesions on card sorting. *Arch. Neurol.* 9:90–100

Mirsky, A. F. 1969. Neuropsychological bases of schizophrenia. *Ann. Rev. Psychol.* 20:321–48

Mirsky, A. F., Duncan-Johnson, C. C. 1984. Nature versus nurture in schizophrenia—the struggle continues. *Integrative Psychiatry* 2:137–48

Mirsky, A. F., Silberman, E. K., Latz, A., Nagler, S. 1985. Adult outcomes of high-risk children: Differential effects of town and kibbutz rearing. *Schizophr. Bull.* 11:150–54

Morstyn, R., Duffy, F. H., McCarley, R. W. 1983. Altered P300 topography in schizophrenia. *Arch. Gen. Psychiatry* 40:729–34

Myers, R. E. 1972. Two patterns of perinatal brain damage and their conditions of occurrence. *Am. J. Obstet. Gynecol.* 112:246–76

Myslobodsky, M. S., ed. 1983. *Hemisyndromes.* New York: Academic

Myslobodsky, M. S., Mintz, M., Tomer, R. 1983. Neuroleptic effects and the site of abnormality in schizophrenia. See Myslobodsky 1983, pp. 347–88

Näätänen, R. 1982. Processing negativity: An evoked potential reflection of selective attention. *Psychol. Bull.* 92:605–40

Näätänen, R., Gaillard, A. W. K., Mantysalo, S. 1978. Early selective-attention effect on evoked potential reinterpreted. *Acta Psychol.* 42:313–29

Näätänen, R., Michie, P. T. 1979. Early selective-attention effects on the evoked potential: A critical review and reinterpretation. *Biol. Psychol.* 8:81–136

Nagler, S., Mirsky, A. F. 1985. Introduction: The Israeli high-risk study. *Schizophr. Bull.* 11:19–29

Nasrallah, H. A., Jacoby, C. G., McCalley-Whitters, M., Kuperman, S. 1982. Cerebral ventricular enlargement in subtypes of chronic schizophrenia. *Arch. Gen. Psychiatry* 39:774–77

Neale, J. M. 1971. Perceptual span in schizophrenia. *J. Abnorm. Psychol.* 77:196–204

Neale, J. M., Oltmanns, T. F. 1980. *Schizophrenia.* New York: Wiley

Nuechterlein, K. H. 1982. Specificity of deficits to vulnerability to schizophrenic disorders: Compared to whom, what, and when? In *Preventive Intervention in Schizophrenia: Are We Ready?*, pp. 126–30. DHHS Publ. (ADM) 82-1111. Washington, DC: Supt. Doc., GPO

Nuechterlein, K. H. 1983. Signal detection in vigilance tasks and behavioral attributes among offspring of schizophrenic mothers and among hyperactive children. *J. Abnorm. Psychol.* 92:4–28

Nuechterlein, K. H., Dawson, M. E. 1984. Information processing and attentional functioning in the developmental course of schizophrenic disorders. *Schizophr. Bull.* 10:160–203

Okita, T. 1979. Event-related potentials and selective attention to auditory stimuli varying in pitch localization. *Biol. Psychol.* 9:271–84

Okita, T. 1981. Slow negative shifts of the human event-related potential associated with selective information processing. *Biol. Psychol.* 12:63–75

Oltmanns, T. F. 1978. Selective attention in schizophrenic and manic psychoses: The effect of distraction on information processing. *J. Abnorm. Psychol.* 87:212–25

Orzack, M. H., Kornetsky, C. 1966. Attention dysfunction in chronic schizophrenia. *Arch. Gen. Psychiatry* 14:323–26

Pass, H. L., Klorman, R., Salzman, L. F., Klein, R. H., Kaskey, G. B. 1980. The late positive component of the evoked response in acute schizophrenics during a test of sustained attention. *Biol. Psychiatry* 15:9–20

Payne, R. W., Mattussek, P., George, E. I. 1959. An experimental study of schizophrenic thought disorder. *J. Ment. Sci.* 105:627–52

Pfefferbaum, A. 1985. P3 latency and amplitude abnormalities in mental disorders. *Electroencephalogr. Clin. Neurophysiol.* In press

Pfefferbaum, A., Wenegrat, B. G., Ford, J. M., Roth, W. T., Kopell, B. S. 1984. Clinical application of the P3 component of event-related potentials: II. Dementia, depression and schizophrenia. *Electroencephalogr. Clin. Neurophysiol.* 59:104–24

Rieder, R. O., Mann, L. S., Weinberger, D. R., van Kammen, D. P., Post, R. M. 1983. Computed tomographic scans in patients with schizophrenia, schizoaffective, and bipolar affective disorder. *Arch. Gen. Psychiatry* 40:735–39

Rieder, R. O., Rosenthal, D., Wender, P., Blumenthal, H. 1975. The offspring of schizophrenics: Fetal and neonatal deaths. *Arch. Gen. Psychiatry* 32:200–11

Rodnick, E. H., Shakow, D. 1940. Set in the schizophrenic as measured by a composite reaction time index. *Am. J. Psychiatry* 97:214–25

Rosenthal, D. 1970. *Genetic Theory and Abnormal Behavior.* New York: McGraw-Hill

Rosenthal, D., Kety, S. S., eds. 1968. *The Transmission of Schizophrenia.* New York: Pergamon

Rosenthal, D., Wender, P., Kety, S. S., Schulsinger, F., Welner, J., et al. 1968. Schizophrenics' offspring reared in adoptive homes. See Rosenthal & Kety 1968, pp. 377–91

Rosvold, H. E., Mirsky, A. F., Sarason, I., Bransome, E. D. Jr., Beck, L. H. 1956. A continuous performance test of brain damage. *J. Consult. Psychol.* 20:343–50

Roth, W. T. 1977. Late event-related potentials and psychopathology. *Schizophr. Bull.* 3:105–20

Roth, W. T., Cannon, E. H. 1972. Some features of the auditory evoked response in schizophrenics. *Arch. Gen. Psychiatry* 27:466–71

Roth, W. T., Horvath, T. B., Pfefferbaum, A., Kopell, B. S. 1980a. Event-related potentials in schizophrenics. *Electroencephalogr. Clin. Neurophysiol.* 48:127–39

Roth, W. T., Horvath, T. B., Pfefferbaum, A., Tinklenberg, J. R., Mezzich, J., et al. 1979. Late event-related potentials and schizophrenia. In *Evoked Brain Potentials and Behavior. Downstate Series of Research in Psychiatry and Psychology,* ed. H. Begleiter, 2:499–515. New York: Plenum

Roth, W. T., Pfefferbaum, A., Horvath, T. B., Berger, P. A., Kopell, B. S. 1980b. P3 reduction in auditory evoked potentials of schizophrenics. *Electroencephalogr. Clin. Neurophysiol.* 49:497–505

Roth, W. T., Pfefferbaum, A., Kelly, A. F., Berger, P. A., Kopell, B. S. 1981. Auditory event-related potentials in schizophrenia and depression. *Psychiatry Res.* 4:199–212

Rutschmann, J., Cornblatt, B., Erlenmeyer-Kimling, L. 1977. Sustained attention in children at risk for schizophrenia: Report on a continuous performance test. *Arch. Gen. Psychiatry* 34:571–75

Saitoh, O., Hiramatsu, K., Niwa, S., Kameyama, T., Itoh, K. 1983. Abnormal ERP findings in schizophrenics with special regards to dichotic detection tasks. In *Laterality and Psychopathology,* ed. P. Flor-Henry, J. Gruzelier, pp. 379–94. Amsterdam: Elsevier

Saitoh, O., Niwa, S., Hiramatsu, K., Kameyama, T., Rymar, K., et al. 1984. Abnormalities in late positive components of event-related potentials may reflect a genetic predisposition to schizophrenia. *Biol. Psychiatry* 19:293–303

Sameroff, S. J., Zax, M. 1978. Young offspring of schizophrenic women. See Wynne et al 1978, pp. 430–41

Seidman, L. J. 1983. Schizophrenia and brain dysfunction: An integration of recent neurodiagnostic findings. *Psychol. Bull.* 94:195–238

Shagass, C. 1977. Early evoked potentials. *Schizophr. Bull.* 3:80–92

Shagass, C., Roemer, R. A., Straumanis, J. J., Amadeo, M. 1978. Evoked potential correlates of psychosis. *Biol. Psychiatry* 13:163–84

Shagass, C., Straumanis, J. J., Roemer, R. A., Amadeo, M. 1977. Evoked potentials of schizophrenics in several sensory modalities. *Biol. Psychiatry* 12:221–35

Shakow, D. 1962. Segmental set: A theory of the formal psychological deficit in schizophrenia. *Arch. Gen. Psychiatry* 6:17–33

Simons, R. F. 1982. Physical anhedonia and future psychopathology: An electrocortical continuity? *Psychophysiology* 19:433–41

Singer, M. T., Wynne, L. C. 1966. Principles for scoring communication defects and deviances in parents of schizophrenics: Rorschach and TAT scoring manuals. *Psychiatry* 29:260–88

Sohlberg, S. C., Yaniv, S. 1985. Social adjustment and cognitive performance of high-risk children. *Schizophr. Bull.* 11:61–65

Sokoloff, L. 1979. Mapping of local cerebral functional activity by measurement of local cerebral glucose utilization with [^{14}C] deoxyglucose. *Brain* 102:653–68

Sokoloff, L., Kennedy, C., Smith, C. B. 1985. The deoxyglucose method for the measurement of local glucose utilization and the metabolic mapping of functional neural pathways in the central nervous system. In *Research Methods in Neurochemistry,* ed. N. Marks, R. Rodnight, 6:79–116. New York: Plenum

Squires, K. C., Donchin, E., Herning, R. I., McCarthy, G. 1977. On the influence of task relevance and stimulus probability on event-related potential components. *Electroencephalogr. Clin. Neurophysiol.* 42:1–14

Stammeyer, E. C. 1961. *The effects of distraction on performance in schizophrenic, psychoneurotic, and normal individuals.* PhD thesis. Catholic Univ., Washington, DC

Steinhauer, S., Zubin, J. 1982. Vulnerability to schizophrenia: Information processing in the pupil and event-related potential. In *Biological Markers in Psychiatry and Neurology,* ed. E. Usdin, I. Hanin, pp. 371–85. Oxford: Pergamon

Stevens, J. R., Langloss, J. M., Albrecht, P., Yolken, R., Wang, Y.-N. 1984. A search for cytomegalovirus and herpes viral antigen in brains of schizophrenic patients. *Arch. Gen. Psychiatry* 41:795–801

Sutton, S. 1969. The specification of psychological variables in an average evoked potential experiment. In *Average Evoked Potentials: Methods, Results and Evaluations,* ed. E. Donchin, D. B. Lindsley, pp. 237–98. Washington, DC: GPO

Sutton, S., Braren, M., Zubin, J., John, E. R. 1965. Evoked potential correlates of stimulus uncertainty. *Science* 150:1187–88

Sutton, S., Hakerem, G., Zubin, J., Portnoy, M. 1961. The effect of shift of sensory modality on serial reaction-time: A comparison of schizophrenics and normals. *Am. J. Psychol.* 74:224–32

Sutton, S., Tueting, P., Zubin, J., John, E. R. 1967. Information delivery and the sensory evoked potentials. *Science* 155:1436–39

Tienari, P., Sorri, A., Lahti, I., Naarala, M., Wahlberg, K.-E., et al. 1985. *Interaction of genetic and psychosocial factors in schizophrenia: The Finnish adoptive family study.* Presented at NIMH High-Risk Consortium, San Francisco

Torrey, E. F., Peterson, M. R. 1976. The viral hypothesis of schizophrenia. *Schizophr. Bull.* 2:136–46

Tueting, P., Sutton, S., Zubin, J. 1970. Quantitative evoked potential correlates of the probability of events. *Psychophysiology* 7:385–94

Verleger, R., Cohen, R. 1978. Effects of certainty, modality shift and guess outcome on evoked potentials and reaction times in chronic schizophrenics. *Psychol. Med.* 8:81–93

Walker, E., Shaye, J. 1982. Familial schizophrenia: a predictor of neuromotor and attentional abnormalities in schizophrenia. *Arch. Gen. Psychiatry* 39:1153–56

Weinberger, D. R., Bigelow, L. B., Kleinman, J. E., Klein, S. T., Rosenblatt, J. E., et al. 1980. Cerebral ventricular enlargement in chronic schizophrenia. *Arch. Gen. Psychiatry* 37:11–13

Weinberger, D. R., DeLisi, L. E., Perman, G. P., Targum, S., Wyatt, R. J. 1982. Computed tomography in schizophreniform disorder and other acute psychiatric disorders. *Arch. Gen. Psychiatry* 39:778–83

Weinberger, D. R., Torrey, E. F., Neophytides, A. N., Wyatt, R. J. 1979. Lateral cerebral ventricular enlargement in chronic schizophrenia. *Arch. Gen. Psychiatry* 36:735–39

Weinberger, D. R., Wagner, R. L., Wyatt, R. J. 1983. Neuropathological studies of schizophrenia: A selective review. *Schizophr. Bull.* 9:193–212

Wender, P. H., Rosenthal, D., Kety, S. S., Schulsinger, F., Welner, J. 1974. Crossfostering: A research strategy for clarifying the role of genetic and experimental factors in the etiology of schizophrenia. *Arch. Gen. Psychiatry* 30:121–28

Windle, W. F. 1969. Brain damage by asphyxia at birth. *Sci. Am.* 4:76–84

Wohlberg, G. W., Kornetsky, C. 1973. Sustained attention in remitted schizophrenics. *Arch. Gen. Psychiatry* 28:533–37

Wynne, L. C., Cromwell, R. L., Matthysse, S., eds. 1978. *The Nature of Schizophrenia: New Approaches to Research and Treatment.* New York: Wiley

Wynne, L. C., Singer, M., Bartko, J., Toohey, M. 1976. Schizophrenics and their families: Recent research on parental communication. In *Psychiatric Research: The Widening Perspective,* ed. J. M. Tanner, pp. 254–86. New York: Int. Univ. Press

Yates, A. J. 1966. Psychological deficit. *Ann. Rev. Psychol.* 17:111–44

Zahn, T. P. 1985. Psychophysiological approaches to psychophysiology. In *Psychophysiology,* ed. M. G. H. Coles, S. W. Porges, E. Donchin. New York: Guilford. In press

Zahn, T. P., Rosenthal, D., Shakow, D. 1961. Reaction time in schizophrenic and normal subjects in relation to the sequence of series of regular preparatory intervals. *J. Abnorm. Soc. Psychol.* 63:161–68

Zahn, T. P., Rosenthal, D., Shakow, D. 1963. Effects of irregular preparatory intervals on reaction time in schizophrenia. *J. Abnorm. Soc. Psychol.* 67:44–52

Zubin, J., Steinhauer, S. R. 1981. How to break the logjam in schizophrenia: A look beyond genetics. *J. Nerv. Ment. Dis.* 169:477–92

Zubin, J., Steinhauer, S. R., Day, R., von Kammen, D. P. 1985. Schizophrenia at the crossroads: A blueprint for the 80's. *Compr. Psychiatry.* In press

Ann. Rev. Psychol. 1986. 37:321–49

INDIVIDUAL PSYCHOTHERAPY AND BEHAVIOR CHANGE

Morris B. Parloff

Department of Psychology, American University, Washington, D.C. 20016

Perry London

Harvard Graduate School of Education, Harvard University, Cambridge, Massachusetts 02138

Barry Wolfe

Psychosocial Treatments Research Branch, National Institute of Mental Health, Rockville, Maryland 20857

CONTENTS

OVERVIEW.. 321
EFFICACY RESEARCH FINDINGS 324
   Global Outcome Surveys via Meta-analysis...................................... 324
   Treatment of Specific Problems 327
ISSUES AND TRENDS 337
   Manuals of Therapy 337
   Brief Therapies 338
   Clinical Trials 338
   Placebos and Specificity of Effects.. 338
   Theory Development... 339
   Integrations 340
   Koans 342

OVERVIEW

This chapter is limited to a consideration of outcome research published during the period 1980–1984 dealing with the treatment of adults by a range of

The US Government has the right to retain a nonexclusive royalty-free license in and to any copyright covering this paper.

The authors gratefully acknowledge the assistance of Marlene E. Fassberg, Harvard Graduate School of Education, in the preparation of this manuscript.

individual psychosocial therapies. For purposes of continuity we attempt to update some of the outcome issues and findings identified by Phillips & Bierman in Volume 32 (1981) and by Gomes-Schwartz et al, Volume 29 (1978). We highlight recent changes, major findings, and persistent koans. Consistent with current ARP policy, we have undertaken an interpretive critical analysis rather than a comprehensive review of research. References cited are intended to be primarily illustrative rather than exhaustive.

The field of psychotherapy has simultaneously experienced two seemingly incongruent developments: increased conceptual and methodological sophistication, and increased skepticism regarding the scientific merit of the preponderantly positive outcome research findings. Among the methodological and conceptual efforts to enhance the quality and replicability of research we highlight these: (a) application of meta-analysis methods for the synthesis of independent research findings; (b) manualization of "brief" therapies; (c) adaptation of clinical trials research designs to facilitate identification of "interactions" between kinds of interventions and kinds of changes; and (d) integration of theory (cognitive and affective), of process and outcome in research, and of a range of therapeutic strategies. (The emphasis on ecumenism is not intended to dismiss the internecine struggles which persist in a less strident form between behavioral and nonbehavioral therapists.)

Before turning to a consideration of some major issues and trends, we review the evidence and critiques of meta-analytic summaries of treatment outcome studies and present narrative reviews of treatment effects with selected *DSM-III* and *Behavioral Medicine* categories.

Skepticism has been stimulated by the methodologists' reports that through the legerdemain of meta-analytic integrative methods the effects of psychotherapy—globally considered—are now found to be even more powerful than ever previously reported. Indeed, there is ample evidence that psychosocial therapies are associated with therapeutic change in a wide range of patients. However, the evidence fails thus far to detect appreciable differences between the various therapies in the nature or degree of benefits effected.

These positive findings have been received with ambivalence. Practitioners were understandably disappointed that their own preferred brand of therapy was not found to be uniquely effective. Practitioners complain that most efficacy studies sacrifice "external validity" for "internal validity."

The criticism regarding the limited generalizability of research findings refers to the fact that "efficacy" research, in its effort to approximate an ideal set of test conditions, chooses not to represent the conditions under which therapy is actually conducted. Generalizations are further limited because research results are frequently based on data derived from patients, therapists, and techniques that are not representative of actual practice.

Researchers, unaccustomed to uniformly positive results, challenged the findings by raising two major questions: is the meta-analysis approach appropriate for psychotherapy research, and are the positive effects reported attributable to the specific interventions of psychotherapy or to the nonspecific and placebo influences routinely associated with all therapies?

Third-party payers were disappointed that the research failed to identify ineffectual or unsafe treatments and thus offered no independent rationale for restricting reimbursement. Since several hundred brand names of psychosocial treatments have now been identified (Herink 1980), a basis for such restriction seemed urgent. Similarly nonreassuring has been the evidence that even informal psychological interventions may effect sizable "cost-offsets," i.e. reducing number and periods of hospitalization, and reducing use of outpatient medical services (Mumford et al 1982, Schlesinger et al 1983).

Perhaps one of the most important and not fully anticipated consequences of the current pervasively positive research evidence is that investigator and policymaker alike now require considerably more evidence than the mere demonstration that "psychotherapy works." The effects must also be shown to result from the putatively therapeutic intervention and not from placebos. The concept of placebo, derived from the field of medicine, has been reflexively and inappropriately applied to the field of psychotherapy.

In the recent past a prod to outcome research was the federal government's expressed interest in making "scientific" evidence of safety, efficacy, and efficiency prerequisite for its reimbursement of mental health services. Hard research evidence would also guide officials in making wise (i.e. cost-containing) policy decisions relevant to their expanded roles as third-party mediators between mental health care suppliers and consumers, and protectors of consumers. The policymakers' public emphasis on the need for credible evidence signaled to the researcher that an accelerated demand for rigorous and vigorous research was in the offing (Parloff 1980, 1982, Perry 1982).

This appraisal was correctly noted by Phillips & Bierman (1981) in their ARP review. In the interim a change in governance has occurred and with it the seemingly urgent political pressures on researchers have abated. This does not, however, signal that the researcher is no longer obligated to address these public concerns. It merely suggests that for the moment reimbursement issues are considered too important to be left in the hands of researchers (London & Klerman 1982, Andrews 1983, Klerman 1984).

Researchers have continued to test the efficacy of psychosocial therapies although assessment is not an area of high prestige within the scientific community. Researchers much prefer to be seen as basic scientists and theoreticians who are concerned primarily with unraveling the mysteries of the "processes" of change. In part the reason for the popularity of "applied" outcome research is that studies increasingly attempt to combine both outcome and process investigations. Others pursue outcome research on the presumption that only after specifiable and clinically useful effects are reliably associated with replicable interventions will the conduct of meticulous process studies be justified. However, the emphasis on outcome research has largely resulted from the greater availability of federal funding for such research.

EFFICACY RESEARCH FINDINGS

". . . you have no tenderness, nothing but truth, and so you judge unjustly"—Dostoyevsky.

Two distinct approaches to outcome research have been pursued: global outcome surveys, and studies of particular therapies for specific problems and disorders. In recent years the global approach to assessing the efficacy of psychotherapy (including the behavioral therapies) has adopted meta-analytic procedures. This has led some critics to infer that meta-analysis is limited to global assessments. Without subscribing to this error we focus on meta-analysis summaries as providing the most frequently cited evidence for "global" effectiveness.

Global Outcome Surveys via Meta-analysis

SUMMARY OF META-ANALYSIS INTEGRATIONS   During the 1970s, research evidence regarding the effectiveness of the various psychotherapies appeared to be modestly positive and of small magnitude (Luborsky et al 1975, Bergin & Lambert 1978, Frank 1979). By the 1980s, however, with the application of meta-analytic methods to the integration of research findings, the magnitude of the effects of psychosocial therapies was described as positive and large (Smith et al 1980, Shapiro & Shapiro 1982).

The latter conclusions were controversial for two reasons: (a) They were not based on new and better research findings but on a new statistical method (meta-analysis) for integrating old ones. (b) To some scholars, its use yielded suspicious findings from the extant data. For instance, in one meta-analytic survey, psychodynamic, behavioral, and cognitive therapies all emerged as equally effective, and neither duration of therapy nor length of therapist experience was found to be related to treatment's effectiveness (Smith et al 1980). Other integrations found, inconsistently, that the size of benefits at termination of treatment diminished over time (Mash & Terdal 1980, Smith et al 1980, Andrews & Harvey 1981) or that treatment gains were so consistently maintained afterward that the value of doing routine follow-up studies was itself doubtful (Nicholson & Berman 1983).

The two basic methods of meta-analysis involve statistical combinations either of significance levels or of Effect Sizes (ES). The latter, which examines the magnitude of effects across studies, is more commonly used in the meta-analysis of psychotherapy outcome studies (Strube & Hartmann 1983). ES is obtained by dividing the mean difference in outcome scores between the treatment and control groups by the standard deviation (usually) of the control group (Smith et al 1980). The resultant statistic is essentially a difference in standard (z) score means. ES is thus comparable for outcome measures originally expressed in different raw units (Cohen 1981).

The most comprehensive meta-analytic study of psychotherapy outcomes was conducted by Smith et al (1980). To avoid the problem of biased selection—the chief contaminant of previous reviews—the authors sought to include all published and unpublished studies in the English language which had compared at least one treatment group to an untreated or waiting-list control group or to another therapy group.

A corpus of 475 studies was reviewed involving 25,000 patients treated by any of 78 therapies for an average of 16 sessions. A total of 1766 separate outcome comparisons yielded effect sizes averaging .85 standard deviations. Smith et al (1980) interpreted this finding to mean that "the average person who receives therapy is better off at the end of it than 80% of the persons who do not" (p. 87). When instances of "placebo treatment" and "undifferentiated counseling" were removed from the data set, the average effect size increased to .93 standard deviation units. This permitted the inference that the average treated patient was better off at the end of treatment than about 85% of prospective patients who had not been treated. According to Rosenthal & Rubin (1982), the effect sizes attributed to psychotherapy by Smith et al are equivalent to reducing an illness or death rate from 66% to 34%—a clinically substantial feat.

Shapiro & Shapiro (1982) added later literature and used even more rigorous selection criteria than did Smith et al. Only 21 of the 143 studies they found eligible overlapped with those of Smith et al, and their findings were even more supportive of the potency of psychosocial therapies. Mean effect size approached one standard deviation.

Of special relevance are three independent confirmations of the original Smith et al (1980) survey based on reanalyses of subsets of their data: Andrews & Harvey (1981) restricted their reanalysis to "real" patients, i.e. "neurotics" who had sought treatment; Landman & Dawes (1982) limited their sample to studies involving a random assignment of patients to either a treatment or placebo control group; and Prioleau et al (1983) initially confined their meta-analysis to 32 comparisons of psychotherapy vs placebo groups. [Their subsequent dismissal of these findings is not based on the mean ES obtained—which was identical to that reported by Smith et al—but on the failure of the evidence to support the relationships which they had hypothesized should exist between "placebo" and "active" treatment conditions. According to Dawes (1983) and Garfield (1983), the conclusions of Prioleau et al (1983) appear to have depended on the interpretation of statistically nonsignificant trends.]

At a minimum, the meta-analysis evidence suggests that deliberate psychotherapeutic interventions are more useful than their absence, and that the magnitude of their effects—as measured by reasonable standards—is substantial. The reactions to these findings, and particularly to the conclusion that one kind of treatment, judged by its own standards, works about as well as another (Glass & Kliegl 1983), has provoked "religious crusades, minor vendettas, and . . . numerous scholarly bloodbaths" (Wortman 1983, p. 224).

Assertions continue to be made that in contrast to behavior therapy, the nonbehavioral psychotherapies have failed to demonstrate effectiveness beyond that attributable to placebo effects (Rachman & Wilson 1980, Prioleau et al 1983, Wilson & Rachman 1983). Indeed, psychotherapy may be "the major placebo of our time" (Shapiro 1984, p. 106).

CRITIQUE OF META-ANALYSIS METHODOLOGY   The typical criticism of meta-analyses is that in an effort to answer a global question regarding the efficacy of psychotherapy, they have indiscriminately lumped together therapies, problems, patient populations, and measures. As a consequence, potentially useful discriminations and relationships may have been obscured (Kendall 1984).

Even if one assumed that the nearly 500 studies included in the Smith et al 1980 review provided a reasonably representative sample of the population of all assessment studies—a stipulation not conceded by some (Wilson & Rachman 1983)—such studies do not, in fact, provide an adequate representation of the range of problems, patients, therapies, and qualified therapists typically involved in the practice of psychotherapy (Parloff 1982, 1984).

With regard to patients, for example, major categories of problems are systematically underrepresented—e.g. depression and alcoholism—while milder problems such as phobias are overrepresented. Therapists were preponderantly novice psychologists and psychiatric residents, and the therapies were chiefly short-term behavioral approaches.

Smith et al (1980) postulate that measures of change are interchangeable since they all assess some relevant aspect of well-being. In effect, a reduction of "hallucinations" is equated by these methodologists with a reduction in "anxiety" or "avoidance" behaviors. A related criticism is that the assumption of comparability of measures may lead the reviewer arbitrarily to omit from analysis some conceptually critical measures originally included in a study (Paul 1984).

The question " Is psychotherapy effective?" may no longer strike many as worth asking, let alone answering. However, the fact that the question continues to be asked of the field implies an expectation that a common metric exists—one that could provide such an answer. The logic of meta-analysis does offer a common metric. The problem regarding global assessment does not inhere in meta-analysis per se but in the practice of posing the question in terms too general to apply to the whole field of psychotherapy. The methodology cannot be held liable for the lack of sophistication or errant purposes of the researcher. Meta-analytic results could, for example, be more safely interpreted if obtained from a more circumscribed range of conditions treated by a well-specified and narrow range of interventions (Klein & Rabkin 1984).

Meta-analysis has also been attacked for including studies of "inadequate designs." This criticism usually holds that the corpus of studies may include some that suffer serious design flaws, e.g. nonrandom assignment of cases to therapy and to control groups, nonblind assessments, high or differential dropout rates, or poor outcome measurement. The results derived from such studies are given as much weight as those derived from studies having greater internal validity (Strube & Hartmann 1983, Wilson & Rachman 1983).

Glass & Kliegl (1983) remind their critics that no effort was made to preselect studies on the basis of methodological biases regarding good design and "internal validity." The fact that ES failed to correlate significantly with most of the factors identified by methodologists as prerequisite for adequate research (Smith et al 1980) was offered as justification for dismissing this nagging concern.

In our view, it is important to require that a research design offer a high degree of internal validity because only such studies permit a confident inference that the reported outcome is in response to the treatment provided. A poor experiment that shows an effect size equal to that in a "good" study is hard to interpret.

Nor has meta-analysis escaped questioning from statisticians. There is disagreement about the appropriate procedures for deriving, combining, and interpreting effect size estimates (Yeaton & Sechrest 1981, Fiske 1983, Strube & Hartmann 1983, Rosenthal & Rosnow 1984). Statistical criticisms also reflect a growing concern that the homogeneity of effect size estimates must be tested across the sample of experiments; conceivably, variation in ES estimates may not permit the inference that the studies shared an underlying population of effect sizes (Hedges 1983).

Despite their limitations, however, conclusions based on meta-analysis are more objective than those derived from narrative summaries or box scores. Its selection procedures and data analyses are public and replicable, and independent investigators may seek answers to their own questions by selecting and analyzing subsets of data drawn from one another's corpus of studies. This may permit successively more refined and sophisticated analyses.

Treatment of Specific Problems

Potentially more useful to the field than global assessments are answers to such questions as "What therapies for what kinds of problems?" Two criteria were used in selecting a problem for review: its public health significance (number affected and/or its disabling nature), and the amount of research conducted during the period under review.

For sake of clarity and consistency of definitions, the names of problems/disorders reviewed were derived primarily from *DSM-III: The Diagnostic and Statistical Manual (Third Edition)* (American Psychiatric Association 1980). Since we also wish to call attention to "Behavioral Medicine"—a field encompassing physical conditions to which psychological factors are thought to be contributory—treatment research in this area is presented separately.

DSM-III CATEGORIES (AXIS I)   The first set of problems considered here—depression, schizophrenia, anxiety disorders, substance use disorders (alcoholism, drug abuse), and eating disorders (obesity, anorexia nervosa, and bulimia)—are derived from DSM-III, which provides a classification strategy that is descriptive and etiologically neutral.

Depression   Treatment efficacy studies are reported according to comparison of different forms of psychotherapy, comparison of psychotherapy and drugs, and psychotherapy combined with drug therapy. The most frequent comparisons of psychotherapies during the period 1980–1984 involve *cognitive* and *behavioral* treatments. Patients treated by cognitive therapy are reported to improve more rapidly initially, but by the end of treatment no differences are evident (Gardner & Oei 1981, Gallagher & Thompson 1982, Wilson et al 1983).

A comparison of experiential and psychoanalytic therapies in the treatment of depressed patients and impulsive patients led Beutler & Mitchell (1981) to infer a clear superiority for the experiential approach. A subanalysis of psychoanalytic treatment patients found that this approach was more effective with depressed than impulsive patients.

Since 1980 at least five controlled investigations and one meta-analysis survey were reported comparing efficacy of psychotherapy and drugs. Of significance are the findings that drugs and psychological interventions may affect different symptom patterns: e.g. a study contrasting interpersonal therapy and a tricyclic drug showed the drug to be superior in the prevention of relapse and the treatment of such symptoms as sleep disturbance and appetite loss, but interpersonal therapy was somewhat superior to drugs in the relief of suicidal feelings, guilt, loss of interest, and improvement of social and interpersonal functioning (Weissman et al 1981, Weissman 1984). The social functioning improvement became apparent only 6–8 months after treatment began.

Earlier claims regarding the superiority of cognitive therapy over some drugs in the reduction of symptoms of depression (Rush et al 1977) appear to be supported by Kovacs et al (1981), Rush et al (1982), Blackburn et al (1981), and Bellack et al (1981). We note that the Bellack et al findings that social-skills therapy and placebo had a significantly greater effect than amitriptyline alone were not replicated by Hersen et al (1984). Another recent study that failed to find superiority of psychological treatment over drugs in the treatment of depression was that of Murphy et al (1984).

Steinbrueck et al (1983) did a meta-analysis of 56 controlled studies of psychotherapy and drug therapy. The mean effect sizes of psychotherapy were twice those of drug therapy (1.22 and .61 respectively). Even so, the authors are appropriately cautious in interpreting their findings.

A common question arising in comparing psychological and drug treatments of depression is whether the patients are "suitable" candidates for medication, conventionally thought true primarily of "endogenous" depressions. Neither Blackburn et al (1981) nor Kovacs (1980), however, found significant correlations between ratings of endogenicity and responsiveness to either drugs or psychotherapy. Prusoff et al (1980) reported, moreover, that endogenous (noninstitutionalized) depressed patients responded best to drugs and psychotherapy combined, while reactively depressed patients did equally well with drugs, with interpersonal therapy, or with their combination. Thus, the assumption that drugs are the treatment of choice for nonpsychotic patients with endogenous depressions does not find support in recent research.

Most of the studies cited above also included a combined treatment condition, and a few showed that the combination of pharmacological and individual psychotherapy had beneficial additive or interactive effects, e.g. Blackburn et al (1981) and Blackburn & Bishop (1983). These investigators found that cognitive therapy in combination with doctor's choice of tricyclic was superior to either treatment alone. However, this finding obtained only among "hospital outpatients" and not among patients treated in general practice.

Combinations of drugs and psychological treatments such as social skills training (Hersen et al 1984), cognitive therapy (Murphy et al 1984), and Lewinsohn's behavior therapy (Wilson 1982) also failed to produce effects superior to those of either treatment alone.

In summary, psychological therapies appear to be useful for the treatment of depression. However, recent research concerning the effects of combining psychotherapy with drugs has not sustained the earlier evidence of additivity (Weissman 1979). Since current findings are not consistent with either conventional wisdom or growing clinical practice, this area invites further careful and cautious investigation.

Schizophrenia   Research evidence on the treatment of schizophrenia has generally suggested that psychotherapy is at best ancillary to drugs and social interventions (Mosher & Keith 1980, Heinrichs & Carpenter 1981, Keith & Matthews 1984). The major exception has been the study of Karon & Vanden-

Bos (1981), which reported that psychoanalytically oriented therapy, provided by experienced therapists, over a period of 20 months showed significant advantages over a "maintenance milieu" program.

A recent well-controlled outcome study, specifically designed to address criticisms leveled at earlier investigations of psychodynamic treatment of schizophrenics, failed to support the hypothesized advantages of intensive "exploratory insight-oriented psychotherapy" (EIO). EIO was compared with reality-adaptive supportive (RAS) psychotherapy on a sample of 95 nonchronic schizophrenic patients. They were treated by experienced therapists in hospitals that also provided patients with high quality psychopharmacological management. EIO showed no advantage in alleviating global psychopathology and was significantly inferior to RAS in reducing recidivism or improving role performance (Gunderson et al 1984, Stanton et al 1984).

These findings do not encourage the view that intensive psychodynamic psychotherapy will soon reestablish itself as the "treatment of choice" for schizophrenia. It seems apparent, however, that patients in pre- or posthospital status may be benefited by combinations of supportive psychosocial and pharmacological treatment.

Anxiety disorders   Agoraphobia, social phobia, and simple phobias are reviewed here, plus obsessive-compulsive disorder, which is considered an "anxiety state." Two other anxiety states, panic disorder and generalized anxiety disorder, have typically been treated by cognitive and pharmacological therapies. The pertinent treatment evidence regarding these syndromes was deemed insufficient and is therefore omitted from this review. Psychological treatment of a relatively new anxiety disorder, post-traumatic stress disorder, has also had insufficient empirical attention and is thus omitted.

The embattled consensus is that exposure-based therapies represent the "treatment of choice" for agoraphobia (Barlow & Wolfe 1981); moreover, the more direct the exposure (e.g. in vivo as opposed to imaginal) the more effective the treatment (Jansson & Ost 1982, Barlow & Beck 1984, O'Brien & Barlow 1984). Cognitive therapies have recently challenged these conclusions, citing evidence that at six-month follow-up, cognitive treatment effects are comparable to those of exposure (Biran & Wilson 1981, Emmelkamp & Mersch 1982, Williams & Rappaport 1983).

In any event, 30% of agoraphobics treated with exposure do not benefit, 12% drop out of treatment, and many of those who report benefit may be left with substantial residual disturbances (Jansson & Ost 1982, Barlow & Beck 1984).

Earlier findings suggesting that prolonged intensive exposure was more effective than gradual exposure (Rachman & Wilson 1980) have not held up (Barlow & Beck 1984). In fact, a much higher dropout rate was found among patients treated by prolonged in vivo exposure than among those treated by a more gradual self-paced, home treatment program, which also found that the addition of patient's spouse to the treatment efforts was advantageous (Jannoun et al 1980, Barlow et al 1984).

Exposure-based treatments have been combined with other therapies to strengthen their effectiveness. Cognitive therapies have not shown an enhancing effect when combined with exposure, but combinations of exposure and antidepressant treatment were found therapeutically advantageous (Klein et al 1983, Mavissakalian & Michelson 1983, Mavissakalian et al 1983).

Four studies of social phobia (i.e. incapacitating fears and avoidance of social situations) suggest that social skills training and relaxation training are useful treatments (Barlow & Beck 1984). Specific or simple phobias appear to respond well to several variants of exposure treatment including systematic desensitization, flooding, modeling, and reinforced practice (Rachman & Wilson 1980, Barlow & Wolfe 1981, Linden 1981).

For obsessive-compulsive disorder, in vivo exposure combined with response prevention continues to be reported as the most powerful treatment in comparison to either one alone or to other treatments (Foa & Tillmanns 1980, Rachman & Hodgson 1980, Sturgis & Meyer 1981, Emmelkamp 1982, Barlow & Beck 1984, Turner & Michelson 1984). The combination of exposure with drug therapy (usually ciomipramine) appears to add little to the effects of exposure except with depressed obsessive-compulsive patients (Marks et al 1980, Mawson et al 1982).

Imaginal exposure has been used with "checking rituals" in an effort to habituate the "checker" to his/her own catastrophic fears. Foa et al (1980) found that imaginal exposure may be a necessary addition to the treatment regimen in order to prevent relapse in patients suffering checking rituals. Obsessional thoughts have also been usefully treated by prolonged imaginal exposure (Emmelkamp 1982).

Alcoholism   Two contrasting and fiercely debated goals of treatment confront the investigator: "controlled" drinking or "abstinence." The argument reflects contrasting concepts of the nature of the disorder. Although abstinence has long been considered the proper aim of treatment, data from over 100 studies in which abstinence was the goal showed that 5–15% of the treated patients were drinking at "nonproblem" levels (W. R. Miller 1983). This precipitated a series of behavioral treatment studies in the 1970s which aimed to achieve "controlled drinking."

Sobell & Sobell (1973, 1976) reported that a 17-session behavior therapy program successfully taught "gamma" alcoholics to drink moderately and that, in fact, they were functioning better at two-year follow-up than alcoholics treated with the goal of abstinence. Pendery et al (1982), after conducting a 10-year follow-up of only the Sobells' experimental controlled drinking group, attacked the validity, scientific merit, and even the ethics of the Sobells' study. The Sobells (1984) published a point-by-point rebuttal of the inferences drawn by Pendery et al and concluded that the scrutiny given their study by Pendery et al served only to highlight the strength of their original findings.

Other investigators have also claimed success in teaching alcoholics moderate drinking by means of cognitive therapies, social skills training, behavioral self-control, and multimodal approaches, but they appear less successful with "gamma" alcoholics. Some investigators have concluded that controlled drinking is an appropriate goal primarily with carefully selected, socially stable, early stage problem drinkers (Miller & Hester 1980, W. R. Miller 1983, Peele 1984, Sanchez-Craig et al 1984).

Based on the hundreds of evaluation studies of therapies aimed at effecting abstinence, it is now estimated that about 26% of treated alcoholics are still abstinent at one-year follow-up; the abstinence rate of "spontaneous remission," however, is estimated to be 19%! These estimates have served as a rough baseline against which to evaluate the efficacy of particular treatments (Miller & Hester 1980).

Behavioral approaches to the treatment of alcoholics include aversion therapies, cognitive therapies, and behavioral self-control. Of these, nausea-based aversion therapies appear to be particularly useful, consistently producing abstinence rates averaging 60%–70% at one-year follow-up. Controlled studies continue, however, to be rare.

Among the nonbehavioral therapies, hypnosis and insight-oriented treatment have been studied. Reviews of both controlled and uncontrolled research on hypnosis in the treatment of alcoholism fail to show that it enhances or is superior to alternate therapies (Miller & Hester 1980, Wadden & Penrod 1981). Three controlled studies of insight-oriented psychotherapy with alcoholics showed a high dropout rate, and the levels of improvement were either limited or simply equivalent to those in alternate treatments (Miller & Hester 1980). No more recent controlled investigation using psychotherapy as a treatment of alcoholics was found.

Drug abuse   Treatment programs for drug abusers typically employ a combination of modalities, e.g. pharmacotherapy, including narcotic agonists (e.g. methadone) and antagonists (e.g. naltrexone), behavior therapy, psychotherapy, drug counseling, family therapy, and some form of milieu therapy. While there have been many evaluation studies of large-scale comprehensive treatment programs for drug abusers (NIDA 1981) few experimental studies have been conducted evaluating the efficacy of the component therapies.

Controlled investigations of psychotherapy with drug abuse have focused on treating the accompanying psychiatric disorders of addicts who have been stabilized by methadone. Supportive-expressive psychotherapy resulted in greater improvement in psychiatric symptomatology and employment than did cognitive-behavioral psychotherapy (Woody et al 1983). In the only other controlled study of psychotherapy published during the review period, interpersonal therapy was not found to offer additional benefit to the methadone program or to be superior to the low-contact control condition (Rounsaville et al 1983).

Among the behavioral approaches tested with opiate addicts who have been detoxified and maintained on methadone, contingent reinforcement programs improved compliance to the rules of the drug clinic and reduced the use of particular classes of drugs (Stitzer et al 1983).

Following a review of behavioral strategies, Callahan (1980) concluded that these interventions enhance the usefulness of medical approaches, particularly in the treatment of white middle-class addicts or addicts who suffer from no other disability or deficit.

In sum, behavioral approaches, when useful, produce limited effects on a limited range of behaviors in a limited population of addicts. The literature on nonbehavioral approaches remains sparse and therefore does not yet warrant more than respectful attention.

Eating disorders   The eating disorders discussed here include obesity, anorexia nervosa, and bulimia. All involve disturbances in the regulation of food intake and control of body weight. Because these disorders may have serious (and even fatal) medical consequences as well as psychological ones, treatment usually entails a two-phase process: crisis intervention to get the patient's eating under control, and longer term therapy for problems generating the eating disorder. Most outcome research focuses on the first phase.

Behavioral treatments of obesity appear to be more effective than other treatments in effecting short-term weight loss but outcome is highly variable. Results are often not clinically significant (Brownell 1982b) and efforts to identify predictor variables of successful outcome have failed (Wilson & Brownell 1980).

When spouses have been included in behavioral treatment programs, the average weight loss has increased to about 14–19 pounds from the typical loss of 10–11 pounds (Fremouw & Zitter 1980, Rosenthal et al 1980, Brownell & Stunkard 1981, Pearce et al 1981). Behavior therapy when combined with fenfluramine produces substantial weight loss in the short run—as much as 34 pounds—but this result deteriorates over time (Brownell & Stunkard 1981, Craighead 1984).

Behavior therapy in combination with low calorie diets (400–500 kcal daily) has produced weight losses of over 40 pounds in some patients; however, a 22-month follow-up study (Wadden et al 1983) found that 56% of the patients regained more than half of their weight loss. In a later study, Wadden et al

(1984) reported more stable results based on a one-year follow-up of a comparable sample of patients.

For anorexia, treatment typically focuses first on restoring proper weight and nutrition. Many therapies including behavioral modification and family therapy have reported some success (Hsu 1980), but in many cases, positive initial response does not predict long-term sustained improvement (Bellack & Williamson 1982).

Because bulimia—binge eating followed by "purging"—has only recently achieved the status of a distinct disorder, research consists mainly of single case studies treated mostly by cognitive-behavioral and multimodal approaches. In some cases, exposure and response prevention have been successfully combined (Rosen & Leitenberg 1982) and early improvements from cognitive approaches have been sustained for 3–12 months (Linden 1980, Fairburn 1981, Grinc 1982, Long & Cordle 1982, Gandour 1984).

"BEHAVIORAL MEDICINE" CATEGORIES   As knowledge of the psychosocial factors in medical illness increased and as helping methods and theories broadened, so did the definition of behavioral medicine. The field investigated the impact of behavior and attitude on the causes, prevention, and treatment of "physical" illness. Just as physical ailments may have psychological antecedents and concomitants, so may psychological problems have physical antecedents and concomitants. It is plausible to expect that suitable mental health care may have favorable impact on physical as well as emotional health. This expectation is now tempered by the observation that adaptive behavioral changes may be rapidly effected, but the impact on longstanding habits or chronic illnesses is often transitory (Stuart 1982). Increasingly, the task of therapists is to deal with chronicity, i.e. disorders not subject to "cure" but possibly amenable to amelioration.

The treatment of disorders considered here includes the classical problems earlier included in "psychosomatic medicine" as well as problems previously untouched by psychosocially healing hands—e.g. stress and "lifestyles" affecting ills of the cardiovascular system, the gastrointestinal system, and miscellaneous miseries.

Cardiovascular disorders   We discuss here two cardiovascular disorders, hypertension and "coronary prone behavior," on which there is recent research evidence of the effects of psychological treatment.

For hypertension the main psychological approaches are biofeedback, relaxation training, monitoring, rehearsal, stress management, and social support. These procedures are often combined with diet, drug, and exercise regimens. Results are generally statistically significant and clinically favorable for all of these methods (Alderman et al 1980), but compliance is a major problem, especially in relation to diet, drugs, and exercise regimens (Haynes et al 1979, Brownell 1982a, Agras 1984). There is no firm evidence that one psychological technique is better than another or that such interventions can routinely be applied independent of medical and drug management (Shapiro & Goldstein 1982).

"Type A" behavior has been implicated as a psychological factor in some cases of heart attacks. Suinn (1982) reviewed 16 reports of interventions aimed at modifying Type A behaviors. He found that of six controlled studies with healthy persons five achieved significantly greater effects on treatment groups than on controls. The treatments tested were anxiety management training, cognitive behavior therapy plus problem solving, psychotherapy, and relaxation training (including biofeedback).

Five controlled or comparison-group studies were conducted involving patients suffering heart disease. In one, psychotherapy patients in contrast to rehabilitation patients showed significantly reduced tendencies toward urgency and anger. The results were sustained over a four-year follow-up (Rahe et al 1979). Two studies showed that stress management and cognitive therapy conditions reduced Type A behaviors significantly relative to controls, and two studies found behavior therapies, especially multimodal behavior therapy, more effective than "supportive" psychotherapy.

The Recurrent Coronary Prevention Project (862 volunteers recovering from myocardial infarctions) showed, moreover, that subjects receiving a combination of behavioral and cardiologic counseling reduced Type A Behavior Pattern (TABP) and rate of heart infarct recurrence over a three-year period significantly more than did those who received cardiological counseling alone (Thoreson et al 1985).

A meta-analysis of 34 studies showed that when brief psychotherapeutic or educational interventions were used for persons who had recently suffered a heart attack or who were facing surgery, these seemingly minor interventions produced large effects in terms of speeded recovery, lowered requirements for analgesic and sleeping medications, and shortened hospital stays (Mumford et al 1982).

Gastrointestinal disorders   Combinations of assertiveness training and relaxation were found to reduce symptoms of treated ulcer patients relative to untreated controls (Brooks & Richardson 1980). This replicated earlier results of Chappel et al (1936). Short-term dynamic psychotherapy added to medication produced benefits similar to those of medical treatment alone (Sjodin 1983).

Irritable bowel syndrome appears to respond to supportive psychotherapy, biofeedback, systematic desensitization, or stress management (Whitehead & Bosmajian 1982). A comparative treatment study found that the combination of dynamic short-term psychotherapy with medication was significantly more effective than medication alone after three months and still more pronounced after one year, since by that time the medication treatment group had deteriorated (Svedlund 1983).

Miscellaneous   The miscellaneous problems included here include smoking, cancer, compliance with prophylactic regimens, headaches, and insomnia.

Most people who stop smoking do so on their own rather than with professional help. Initial success rates of "quit clinics" run up to 70%, but recidivism rates are also high (N. E. Miller 1983). For professionally aided smokers, as for long-term weight losers, high recurrence rates suggest that clinic populations are skewed toward hard-core cases (Schachter 1982). Some of the techniques found useful are: rapid smoking and multicomponent programs [self-monitoring, substitute behavior, stress management training, nicotine chewing gum, etc (Lichtenstein 1982)].

There has been some evidence that controlled smoking can be taught and maintained for six months or more (Glasgow et al 1983); however, health risk reduction from such programs has not yet been established (Colletti et al 1982).

Although it is estimated that about 25% of cancer patients have significant psychiatric disturbances (Derogatis et al 1982), treatment reports generally concern group therapy. Individual treatment has concentrated chiefly on efforts to reduce nausea and vomiting connected with chemotherapy. A small number of well-designed studies have found that hypnosis, guided imagery, progressive relaxation, desensitization, and EMG biofeedback all produce significant improvements in these conditions (Redd & Andrykowski 1982).

In the area of prophylactic compliance, reviewed by Epstein & Cluss (1982), 15 studies reported that several behavioral methods were effective in evoking and maintaining adherence to medication use. These interventions included drug feedback, reinforcement for using medication or for symptom control, self-regulation of medication use, and tailoring the drug regimen. Self-monitoring of symptoms or of medication was found to be less effective than reinforcement or feedback.

The dominant psychosocial treatments for tension and migraine headaches are relaxation training and biofeedback information about muscle relaxation, thermal changes, or vasomotor activity. Since individual differences in pain threshold, severity, and tolerance make objective assessment difficult, the main outcome measure is the "headache diary," a self-report of improvement (Blanchard & Andrasik 1982).

Meta-analysis of 48 studies of tension headaches found frontalis EMG biofeedback, relaxation training, or the combination thereof to be more effective than drugs, placebos, or merely monitoring symptoms (Blanchard et al 1980). Cognitive coping procedures have thus far been inconclusive (Bakal et al 1981).

Migraine headaches have been treated by a variety of techniques, but thermal biofeedback and autogenic training show the best effects (Adams et al 1980, Blanchard & Andrasik 1982). According to Brown (1984) and Spanos et al (1981), imaging is more effective in the treatment of migraine headaches than placebo.

Insomnia studies suggest that psychosocial treatments benefit two subtypes which account for about 25% of all insomnia cases: (a) "psychophysiological," based on chronic tension, anxiety or negative conditioning, and (b) "subjective," where the only problem is the patient's feeling of insufficient or disturbed sleep. Borkovec's (1982) review of controlled research on relaxation (and biofeedback), stimulus control, and paradoxical intention reports that all three types of treatment proved significantly more effective than placebo controls, averaging 45% to 71% improvement in patients' reports of the time it took to fall asleep.

In summary, psychological interventions are being usefully applied to an expanding array of somatic disorders. In addition, psychosocial procedures are used for the amelioration of lifestyle problems which represent some of today's main killers: stress, failure to comply with prophylactic and treatment regimens, indulgence in life-threatening appetitive habits of diet, substance abuse, etc.

ISSUES AND TRENDS

Manuals of Therapy

Perhaps the single greatest problem facing the psychotherapy researcher is the lack of standardization of the treatments being tested. While there is much debate regarding the critical elements that are presumed to characterize different forms of treatment, the investigator can have little confidence that these elements are adequately represented or that they are provided with sufficient skills to permit an adequate test of each specified treatment. There has been little reason to believe that the variability among therapists within a school of therapy is less than the variability among therapists across different schools.

This problem is increasingly addressed by a proliferation of treatment manuals and of training, supervision, and monitoring programs for guiding therapists' behaviors during treatment. Equally important, trainers are formalizing standards for assessing therapists' clinical skills (Waskow 1984, Elkin et al 1985). Widely used, research-stimulated treatment manuals include both behaviorally oriented (Beck et al 1979, Linehan 1984) and "dynamically" oriented therapies (Strupp & Binder 1982, Luborsky 1984, Klerman et al 1984).

Standardization of procedures does not, of course, imply stagnation, but the changes will require testing, and this implies that any given standardization must be recognized as transitional. The proliferation of manuals for treating particular ills by particular methods reflects the confluence of increased rigor in controlled research and increasing acceptance of brief clinical therapies.

Brief Therapies

While researchers have long preferred to study brief rather than long-term therapies, increasingly the practice of psychotherapy has also become self-consciously briefer in order to meet public policy concerns (Pardes & Pincus 1981). As used here, brief psychotherapies, in contrast to merely truncated treatments, are deliberately planned to meet clients' limited needs in a limited time (Davanloo 1980, Budman 1981, Mann 1981, Sifneos 1981, Horowitz et al 1984). Nevertheless, research findings based on treatment of limited duration are often taken as default models for ideal lengths of treatment.

Research on duration of treatment as a main effect has been relatively sparse, but recent reviews support the conclusions of Butcher & Koss (1978) and Butcher & Kolotkin (1979) that studies using adequate controls and objective criteria show 60–70% rates of improvement among short-term (including crisis intervention) therapy clients.

Johnson & Gelso (1980) summarized: 36 uncontrolled studies of treatment length; 12 uncontrolled studies where treatment time limits were set in advance; and 12 studies of time-limited vs time-unlimited therapy. The authors conclude that when account is taken of the differential effects of different raters, measures, and time of assessment, short-term treatments are valuable; indeed, short and long therapies appear to have equally durable effects.

Clinical Trials

The randomized clinical trials approach, which is successfully used in psychopharmacology efficacy studies, has been adopted and adapted by relatively few efficacy researchers in psychotherapy (Weissman et al 1981, Murphy et al 1984, Gunderson et al 1984, Elkin et al 1985). Most investigators continue to find the less formal forms of systematic observation and small-scale research to be more congenial. The issue of appropriateness of research paradigms continues to be much discussed. The earlier objection to clinical trials research— that it represented merely a "horse race"—has subsided somewhat as it has become apparent that the approach can provide a good opportunity to investigate what kinds of clinical changes are effected by what kinds of interventions with what kinds of patients.

Placebos and Specificity of Effects

In response to the mounting evidence of the efficacy of psychotherapies, critics have renewed their assertions that the evidence does not meet the criterion of "scientific" assessment. According to such writers as Wilson & Rachman (1983) and Prioleau et al (1983), science now requires demonstration that therapeutic effects can be attributed to the specific treatment actually used rather than to the placebo effects known to be associated with all forms of treatment whatever their potency.

The suggestion that placebo control designs represents the sine qua non of scientific research has not gone unchallenged. Placebo control studies, properly conducted, may address questions about *how* a treatment works but do not offer a critical test of *whether* a treatment works (Grünbaum 1981, Cordray & Bootzin 1983).

It is unlikely that psychotherapy research can devise a placebo that satisfies its medically derived definitional requirements: (*a*) omitting the specific therapeutic components hypothesized to be characteristic of the particular therapy to be tested, and (*b*) encouraging the patient to believe that the intervention is potent and potentially an effective treatment for his/her problems.

Placebo control groups do not offer any more illuminating controls of the contribution of events assumed by theory to be specific, active, or characteristic of a given therapy than could be provided by its comparison with a well-specified alternate form of psychotherapy that does not share the same theoretical base. Similarly, the placebo control model does not offer any more circumspect control of the role of nonspecific or incidental elements common to the therapies being compared than could be provided by an alternate, pretested, "active" treatment form. Under these conditions patients can in good conscience be assigned randomly to one or the other treatment condition. Such established therapies have the advantage of appearing plausible to the therapists, who can then present them to patients in a manner that enhances the treatments' credibility (Klein & Rabkin 1984).

Theory Development

Research increasingly supports the speculation that no single process—emotional, cognitive, physiological, or behavioral—can be accorded primacy in understanding etiology and treatment of a disorder (Coyne 1980, Simons et al 1984). By the same token, treatment approaches that alter one element of the patient's functioning may affect the rest of the system. This folksy bit of wisdom has, however, offered justification for single-minded dedication to a favorite theory and its associated interventions, on the assumption that they provide the greatest leverage on the problem.

Since therapies are—or should be—based on theories regarding what needs changing and how such change may best be achieved, modifications in such theories have direct implications for practice. For example, one modification in theory currently being debated in cognitive psychology is the interrelation of affect and cognition in the change process. Some current theoretical positions appear to require modification of an assumption basic to cognitive therapy.

The theory on which the cognitive and rational therapies were originally based holds that cognition—i.e. interpretation of events—precedes affect and that affect and cognition are part of the same system. In contrast, investigators in cognitive psychology have begun to present empirical evidence that affect may be precognitive rather than postcognitive, and that affect and cognition may be partially independent systems that affect each other (Zajonc 1980, Bower 1981). The implication is that the potency of cognitive approaches is attenuated by the loose association between affect and cognition (Zajonc 1980).

The practitioner may be in no immediate danger of having to revise his/her therapy since cognitive theorists do not yet appear to be close to a consensus. For example, Zajonc's views have been criticized for inappropriately equating cognition with rational, conscious, and deliberate appraisal (R. Lazarus 1982). Cognitive behavior theorists have also been chided for treating feelings as "phenomenal artifacts that are to be controlled" and placing "excessive emphasis on the role of rationality in adaptation" (Mahoney 1980, p. 159).

In contrast to assigning primacy to cognition, Greenberg & Safran (1984) would accord this position to emotional experience. From their information-processing perspective they suggest that emotional experience is synthesized from sets of (a) perceptual motor responses, (b) affectively laden schematic memories, and (c) conceptual interpretations of the meaning of the events surrounding the emotional experience. They hypothesize that many clinical problems result from a breakdown in the synthesizing process and that an important element of therapy is the integration of the different levels of processing involved in the construction of affect. This position has been criticized as an oversimplification in that it proposes a hierarchical notion of emotional processing for the more complicated processes occurring in the nervous system (Mahoney 1984).

We deny ourselves the opportunity to score the recent debates between protagonists of contending theories. We wish instead to emphasize that in view of the nascent state of these and related psychological theories it is probably wise for researchers to carry such theses and preferences lightly and to avoid the temptation of prematurely applying "strong" tests to essentially "weak" theories.

Integrations

The trend toward psychotherapeutic integration has accelerated from a latent theme to an area of active interest. Integration has been advocated in theory by serious scholars (Marmor & Woods 1980, Goldfried 1982a, Beutler 1983); accepted in practice by a large minority of psychologist therapists (Norcross & Prochaska 1982, 1983); approved (obliquely) as a legitimate dimension of psychotherapy research by some methodologists (Smith et al 1980, Shapiro &

Shapiro 1982); and organized by The Society for the Exploration of Psychotherapy Integration. The first "fairly comprehensive" bibliography in this area contains some 330 books and articles, about half of which were published since 1980 (Goldfried & Wachtel 1984).

The main focus of current interest in integrating different combinations of treatment orientations is the convergence of behavioral and psychodynamic views. Despite protests that the systems are fundamentally incompatible and that integrationist efforts are misleading metaphors and misinterpretations of outcome research results (Franks 1984), the integrative mood continues to gain impetus as scholars and healers reach for conciliation from both camps. Behavior therapists exploit the language, theory, and techniques of cognitive psychology to elaborate the simplistic models of S-R behaviorism (Goldfried 1982b, Ryle 1982, Sarason 1982) and psychoanalysts embrace learning theory, environmental contingencies, and the language of action (Marmor & Woods 1980).

The most prolific practical efforts in this direction are represented by the variety of "cognitive behavior therapies" (Beck et al 1979, Ellis & Grieger 1977, Meichenbaum 1980) that serve to integrate treatment models by criticizing narrow S-R behavior models as well as dynamic ones. They force attention to the "mind" (or at least to thought) and thereby legitimize, within the framework of functional analysis, the usefulness of insight and understanding. In this manner they participate in the solution of general psychotherapeutic problems (London 1983). In effect, the cognitive behavior therapists have produced programs for producing "corrective emotional experiences" by argument, instruction, demonstration, and practice rather than by attempts to probe the dynamics of people's inner lives (London 1985).

Efforts at integration may focus separately on theories and techniques. Integrations of theory include attempts to understand an alien theory in terms of the concepts of a more familiar and therefore more congenial theory. Evidence of integration does not require that the proponent of one or the other of the different theories alter clinical practices. However, with the clarification of the "actual" bases for the claimed beneficial effects, we may anticipate that some technical adjustments will be made (Garfield 1980).

Advocates of this form of integration may maintain their convictions regarding the specificity if not the uniqueness of their theories and techniques. This contrasts with the "nonspecificity" hypothesis (Frank 1973, 1975, 1982, Marmor & Woods 1980), which stresses commonalities rather than uniqueness. It holds that the effectiveness of all therapies results from a sharing of the same potent elements.

A quite different view of integration is that of "Technical Eclecticism," as formulated by A. Lazarus (1976). It is not preoccupied with reconciling theories but rather with maximizing the effectiveness of practice by integrating into a treatment package those specific techniques believed to be the most effective regardless of their theoretical origins.

The integration of theory and application continues at a somewhat slower pace. Almost all behavior therapists now admit to "the gap between theory and application" (Wilson & Franks 1982, London 1984). Psychodynamic and experiential therapists—decades after Robert Knight and Carl Rogers—now also recognize the value of formal scientific study of outcome and process.

The movement toward integration has not been without opposition. Critics question whether major differences between theories can be bridged semantically or conceptually, whether all techniques can be rationalized by uncongenial theories, whether therapy trainees will be as effective with a medley of methods as with a coherent point of view, and whether clients will be satisfied without a credible rationale for treatment (Kendall 1982, Franks 1984).

Professional affiliations tend to produce resistance to integration (Goldfried 1982a). Research findings showing "equal" effectiveness of different treatments have been cited to justify continued adherence to favorite therapies (Smith et al 1980, Norcross & Prochaska 1983).

Nevertheless, the potential advantages of integration and cooperation seem to be producing a psychotherapeutic *zeitgeist* that shows every sign of increasing in the foreseeable future. We anticipate that conceptual schemes will follow for better understanding opposing theories and explaining seemingly disjunctive techniques.

Koans

Finally, we wish to consider two related unanswered and perhaps unanswerable questions faced by the psychotherapy researcher. These may be the koans of psychotherapy that deal with the sounds made by one hand persistently clapping against "but on the other hand. . . ." They reflect the contrasting belief and value systems to which therapists and researchers are thought to subscribe: symbols vs reality, freedom vs determinism, meanings vs events, intuition vs logic, spontaneity vs standardization, and understanding vs measurement.

The questions are: Should psychotherapy be made more scientific? Can psychotherapy be made more scientific, i.e. can its activities be made more measurable and replicable?

There is no unanimity of opinion that the field will be best advanced by viewing psychotherapy as a science or "technology." The arguments against this position include the notion that the essentials of psychotherapy (as in surgery) do not inhere only in the procedures used but also in the skills of the practitioner in being useful to the patient. The rigorous research design does not place sufficient value on the centrality of the therapeutic alliance—the depth, stability, and benignity of the relationship between therapist and patient. In contrast to the notion of "standardization," the therapist emphasizes spontaneous interactions, subjective experience, and knowledge based on intuition and acceptance.

Investigators who endorse rigorously controlled research are aware of the special problems that make the implementation of "state-of-the-art" research methodologies—such as "randomized clinical trials"—difficult or impossible. Can a psychological intervention ever be as fully specified and be made as "pure" as a pharmacological one? Consider, for example, the problem of establishing that all participating therapists have mastered what have been hypothesized as the critical elements of the treatment being tested, and that all participating therapists consistently implement the procedures at a comparably high level of skill.

It is in the nature of the debate that it will continue. It is in the nature of reviews to characterize such debates as signs that the field is in "ferment." Finally, it is in the nature of reviewers to diagnose such ferment as "healthy."

We shall not oppose nature.

Literature Cited

Adams, H. E., Feuerstein, M., Fowler, J. L. 1980. Migraine headache: Review of parameters, etiology and intervention. *Psychol. Bull.* 87:217–37

Agras, W. S. 1984. The behavioral treatment of somatic disorders. In *Handbook of Behavioral Medicine,* ed. W. D. Gentry, pp. 479–525. New York: Guilford

Alderman, M. H., Green, L. W., Flynn, B. S. 1980. Hypertension control programs in occupational settings. *Public Health Rep.* 95:158–63

American Psychiatric Association. 1980. *Diagnostic and Statistical Manual.* Washington, DC: Am. Psychiatric Assoc. 3rd ed.

Andrews, G. 1983. Psychotherapy outcome: A wider view leads to different conclusions. *Behav. Brain Sci.* 2:285–94

Andrews, G., Harvey, R. 1981. Does psychotherapy benefit neurotic patients? A reanalysis of the Smith, Glass & Miller data. *Arch. Gen. Psychiatry* 38:1203–8

Bakal, D. A., Demjen, S., Kaganov, J. A. 1981. Cognitive behavioral treatment of chronic headache. *Headache* 21:81–86

Barlow, D. H., Beck, J. G. 1984. The psychosocial treatment of anxiety disorders: Current status, future directions. See Williams & Spitzer 1984, pp. 29–66

Barlow, D. H., O'Brien, G. T., Last, C. G. 1984. Couples treatment of agoraphobia. *Behav. Ther.* 15:41–58

Barlow, D. H., Wolfe, B. E. 1981. Behavioral approaches to anxiety disorders: A report on the NIMH-SUNY, Albany research conference. *J. Consult. Clin. Psychol.* 49:448–54

Beck, A. T. 1976. *Cognitive Therapy and the Emotional Disorders.* New York: Int. Univ. Press

Beck, A. T., Rush, A. J., Shaw, B. F., Emery, G. 1979. *Cognitive Therapy of Depression.* New York: Guilford

Bellack, A. S., Hersen, M., Himmelhoch, J. M. 1981. Social skills training compared with pharmacotherapy and psychotherapy in the treatment of unipolar depression. *Am. J. Psychiatry* 138:1562–67

Bellack, A. S., Williamson, D. A. 1982. Obesity and anorexia nervosa. In *Behavioral Medicine: Assessment and Treatment Strategies,* ed. D. M. Doleys, A. R. Ciminero, R. L. Meredith, pp. 295–316. New York: Plenum

Bergin, A. E., Lambert, M. J. 1978. The evaluation of therapeutic outcomes. In *Handbook of Psychotherapy and Behavior Change,* ed. S. Garfield, A. Bergin, pp. 139–89. New York: Wiley. 2nd ed.

Beutler, L. E. 1983. *Eclectic Psychotherapy: A Systematic Approach.* New York: Pergamon

Beutler, L. E., Mitchell, R. 1981. Differential psychotherapy outcome among depressed and impulsive patients as a function of analytic and experiential treatment procedures. *Psychiatry* 44:297–306

Biran, M., Wilson, G. T. 1981. Treatment of phobic disorders using cognitive and exposure methods: A self-efficacy analysis. *J. Consult. Clin. Psychol.* 49:886–99

Blackburn, I. M., Bishop, S. 1983. Changes in cognition with pharmacotherapy and cognitive therapy. *Br. J. Psychiatry* 143:609–17

Blackburn, I. M., Bishop, S., Glen, A. I. M., Whalley, L. J., Christie, J. E. 1981. The efficacy of cognitive therapy in depression: A treatment trial using cognitive therapy and pharmacotherapy, each alone and in combination. *Br. J. Psychiatry* 139:181–89

Blanchard, E. B., Andrasik, F. 1982. Psychological assessment and treatment of headache: Recent developments and emerging issues. *J. Consult. Clin. Psychol.* 50:859–79

Blanchard, E. B., Andrasik, F., Ahles, T. A., Teders, S. J., O'Keefe, D. 1980. Migraine and tension headache: A meta-analytic review. *Behav. Ther.* 11:613–31

Borkovec, T. D. 1982. Insomnia. *J. Consult. Clin. Psychol.* 50:880–95

Bower, G. H. 1981. Mood and memory. *Am. Psychol.* 36:129–48

Brooks, G. R., Richardson, F. C. 1980. Emotional skills training: A treatment program for duodenal ulcer. *Behav. Ther.* 11:198–207

Brown, J. M. 1984. Imagery coping strategies in the treatment of migraine. *Pain* 18:157–67

Brownell, K. D. 1982a. Behavioral medicine. In *Annual Review of Behavioral Medicine,* ed. C. M. Franks, G. T. Wilson, P. C. Kendall, pp. 156–207. New York: Guilford

Brownell, K. D. 1982b. Obesity: Understanding and treating a serious, prevalent, and refractory disorder. *J. Consult. Clin. Psychol.* 50:820–40

Brownell, K. D., Stunkard, A. J. 1981. Couples training, pharmacotherapy, and behavior therapy in the treatment of obesity. *Arch. Gen. Psychiatry* 38:1224–29

Budman, S. H., ed. 1981. *Forms of Brief Therapy.* New York: Guilford

Butcher, J. N., Kolotkin, R. L. 1979. Evaluation of outcome in brief psychotherapy. *Psychiatr. Clinics North Am.* 2:157–69

Butcher, J. N., Koss, M. P. 1978. Research on brief and crisis oriented therapies. See Bergin & Lambert 1978, pp. 725–68.

Callahan, E. J. 1980. Alternative strategies in the treatment of narcotic addiction: A review. In *The Addictive Behaviors,* ed. W. R. Miller, pp. 143–67. New York: Pergamon

Chappel, M. N., Stafano, J. J., Rogerson, J. S., Pike, F. H. 1936. The value of group psychological procedures in the treatment of peptic ulcers. *Am. J. Dig. Dis.* 3:813–17

Cohen, J. 1981. Review of *The Benefits of Psychotherapy,* ed. M. L. Smith, G. V. Glass, T. I. Miller. *Psychiatry* 44:177–81

Colletti, G., Supnick, J., Rizzo, A. 1982. Long-term follow-up (3–4 years) of treatment for smoking reduction. *Addictive Behav.* 7:429–33

Cordray, D. S., Bootzin, R. R. 1983. Placebo control conditions: Tests of theory or of effectiveness? *Behav. Brain Sci.* 2:286–87

Coyne, J. C. 1980. A critique of cognitions as causal entities with particular reference to depression. *Cogn. Ther. Res.* 6:3–13

Craighead, L. W. 1984. Sequencing behavior therapy and pharmacotherapy for obesity. *J. Consult. Clin. Psychol.* 52:190–99

Davanloo, H., ed. 1980. *Short-Term Dynamic Therapy,* Vol. 1. New York: Aronson

Dawes, R. M. 1983. Trends based on cotton candy correlations. *Behav. Brain Sci.* 6:287–88

Derogatis, L., Morrow, G., Fetting, J., Schmale, A., Hendrichs, M., et al. 1982. Problems of psychiatric disturbances among cancer patients: A multi-hospital study. *Proc. Emergent Soc. Clin. Oncol.* 1:48

Elkin, I., Parloff, M. B., Hadley, S. W., Autry, J. H. 1985. NIMH treatment of depression collaborative research program. *Arch. Gen. Psychiatry* 42:305–16

Ellis, A., Grieger, R. 1977. *Handbook of Rational Psychotherapy.* New York: Springer

Emmelkamp, P. M. G. 1982. *Phobic and Obsessive-Compulsive Disorders: Theory, Research and Practice.* New York: Plenum

Emmelkamp, P. M. G., Mersch, P. P. 1982. Cognition and exposure *in vivo* in the treatment of agoraphobia: Short-term and delayed effects. *Cogn. Res. Ther.* 6:77–90

Epstein, L. H., Cluss, P. A. 1982. A behavioral medicine perspective on adherence to long-term medical regimens. *J. Consult. Clin. Psychol.* 50:950–71

Fairburn, C. G. 1981. A cognitive behavioral approach to the treatment of bulimia. *Psychol. Med.* 11:707–11

Fiske, D. W. 1983. The meta-analytic revolution in outcome research. *J. Consult. Clin. Psychol.* 51:65–70

Foa, E. B., Steketee, G. S., Milby, M. B. 1980. Differential effects of exposure and response prevention in obsessive-compulsive washers. *J. Consult. Clin. Psychol.* 48:71–79

Foa, E. B., Tillmanns, A. 1980. The treatment of obsessive-compulsive neurosis. In *Handbook of Behavioral Interventions: A Clinical Guide,* ed. A. Goldstein, E. B. Foa, pp. 416–500. New York: Wiley

Frank, J. D. 1973. *Persuasion and Healing.* Baltimore: Johns Hopkins Univ. Press. 2nd ed.

Frank, J. D. 1975. General psychotherapy: The restoration of morale. In *American Handbook of Psychiatry,* ed. D. X. Freedman, J. Dyrud, 5:117–32. New York: Basic Books. 2nd ed.

Frank, J. D. 1979. The present status of outcome studies. *J. Consult. Clin. Psychol.* 47:310–16

Frank, J. D. 1982. Therapeutic components shared by all psychotherapies. In *Psychotherapy Research and Behavior Change,* ed. J. H. Harvey, M. M. Parks, pp. 5–37. Washington, DC: Am. Psychol. Assoc.

Franks, C. M. 1984. On conceptual and technical integrity in psychoanalysis and behavior therapy: Two fundamentally incompatible systems. In *Psychoanalytic Therapy and Behavior Therapy: Is Integration Possible?,* ed. H. Arkowitz, S. Messer, pp. 223–47. New York: Plenum

Fremouw, W. J., Zitter, R. E. 1980. Individual and couple behavioral contracting for weight reduction and matintenance. *Behav. Ther.* 3:15–16

Gallagher, D. E., Thompson, L. W. 1982. Treatment of major depressive disorder in older adult outpatients with brief psychotherapies. *Psychother. Theory Res. Pract.* 19:482–90

Gandour, M. J. 1984. Bulimia: Clinical description, assessment, etiology, and treatment. *Int. J. Eating Disord.* 3:3–38

Gardner, P., Oei, T. P. 1981. Depression and self-esteem: An investigation that used behavioral and cognitive approaches to the treatment of clinically depressed clients. *J. Clin. Psychol.* 37:128–35

Garfield, S. L. 1980. *Psychotherapy: An Eclectic Approach.* New York: Wiley

Garfield, S. L. 1983. Does psychotherapy work? Yes, no, maybe. *Behav. Brain Sci.* 6:292–93

Glasgow, R. E., Klesges, R. C., Vasey, M. W. 1983. Controlled smoking for chronic smokers: An extension and replication. *Addictive Behav.* 8:143–50

Glass, G. V., Kliegl, R. M. 1983. An apology for research integration in the study of psychotherapy. *J. Consult. Clin. Psychol.* 51:28–41

Goldfried, M. R., ed. 1982a. *Converging Themes in Psychotherapy: Trends in Psychodynamic, Humanistic, and Behavioral Practice.* New York: Springer. 404 pp.

Goldfried, M. R. 1982b. Cognition and experience. See Goldfried 1982a, pp. 365–73

Goldfried, M. R., Wachtel, P. L., eds. 1984. *Soc. Explor. Psychother. Integration Newsl.* 2(1):1–22

Gomes-Schwartz, B., Hadley, S. W., Strupp, H. H. 1978. Individual psychotherapy and behavior therapy. *Ann. Rev. Psychol.* 29:435–71

Greenberg, L. S., Safran, J. D. 1984. Integrating affect and cognition: A perspective on the process of therapeutic change. *Cogn. Ther. Res.* 8:559–78

Grinc, G. A. 1982. A cognitive-behavioral model for the treatment of chronic vomiting. *J. Behav. Med.* 5:135–41

Grünbaum, A. 1981. The placebo concept. *Behav. Res. Ther.* 19:157–67

Gunderson, J. G., Frank, A. F., Katz, H. M., Vannicelli, M. L., Frosch, J. P., et al. 1984. Effects of psychotherapy in schizophrenia: II. Comparative outcome of two forms of treatment. *Schizophr. Bull.* 10:564–98

Haynes, R. B., Taylor, D. W., Sackett, D. L., eds. 1979. *Compliance in Health Care.* Baltimore: Johns Hopkins Univ. Press

Hedges, L. V. 1983. Statistical summaries in research integration. *Behav. Brain Sci.* 2:295–96

Heinrichs, D. W., Carpenter, W. T. 1981. The efficacy of individual psychotherapy: A perspective and review emphasizing controlled outcome studies. In *American Handbook of Psychiatry,* ed. S. Arieti, H. K. Brodie, 3:586–613. New York: Basic Books

Herink, R., ed. 1980. *The Psychotherapy Handbook.* New York: New Am. Libr.

Hersen, M., Bellack, A. S., Himmelhoch, J. M., Thase, M. E. 1984. Effects of social skill training, amitriptyline, and psychotherapy in unipolar depressed women. *Behav. Ther.* 15:21–40

Horowitz, M., Marmar, C., Krupnick, J., Wilner, N., Kaltreider, N., et al. 1984. *Personality Styles and Brief Psychotherapy.* New York: Basic Books

Hsu, L. K. G. 1980. Outcome of anorexia nervosa. *Arch. Gen. Psychiatry* 37:1041–46

Jannoun, L., Munby, M., Catalan, J., Gelder, M. 1980. A home-based treatment program for agoraphobia: Replication and controlled evaluation. *Behav. Ther.* 11:294–305

Jansson, L., Ost, L. G. 1982. Behavioral treatments for agoraphobia: An evaluative review. *Clin. Psychol. Rev.* 2:311–36

Johnson, D. H., Gelso, C. J. 1980. The effectiveness of time limits in counseling and psychotherapy: A critical review. *Couns. Psychol.* 9(1):70–83

Karon, B. P., VandenBos, G. R. 1981. *Psychotherapy of Schizophrenia: The Treatment of Choice.* New York: Aronson

Keith, S. J., Matthews, S. M. 1984. Schizophrenia: A review of psychosocial treatment strategies. See Williams & Spitzer 1984, pp. 70–88

Kendall, P. C. 1982. Integration: Behavior therapy and other schools of thought. *Behav. Ther.* 13:559–71

Kendall, P. C. 1984. Behavioral assessment and methodology. In *Annual Review of Behavior Therapy: Theory and Practice,* ed. G. T. Wilson, C. M. Franks, K. D. Brownell, P. C. Kendall, 9:39–94. New York: Guilford

Klein, D. F., Rabkin, J. G. 1984. Specificity and strategy in psychotherapy research and practice. See Williams & Spitzer 1984, pp. 306–29

Klein, D. F., Zitrin, C. M., Woerner, M. G., Ross, D. C. 1983. II. Behavior therapy and supportive psychotherapy: Are there any specific ingredients? *Arch. Gen. Psychiatry* 40:139–53

Klerman, G. L. 1984. Psychotherapy and public policy: What does the future hold? See Williams & Spitzer 1984, pp. 347–54

Klerman, G. L., Weissman, M. M., Rounsaville, B. J., Chevron, E. S. 1984. *Interpersonal Psychotherapy of Depression.* New York: Basic Books

Kovacs, M. 1980. The efficacy of cognitive and behavior therapies for depression. *Am. J. Psychiatry* 137:1495–1501

Kovacs, M., Rush, A. J., Beck, A. T., Hollon, S. D. 1981. Depressed outpatients treated with cognitive therapy or pharmacotherapy: A one-year follow-up. *Arch. Gen. Psychiatry* 38:33–39

Landman, J. T., Dawes, R. M. 1982. Psychotherapy outcome: Smith & Glass' conclusions stand up under scrutiny. *Am. Psychol.* 37:504–16

Lazarus, A. A. 1976. *Multimodal Behavior Therapy.* New York: Springer

Lazarus, R. S. 1982. Thoughts on the relations between emotion and cognition. *Am. Psychol.* 37:1019–24

Lichtenstein, E. 1982. The smoking problem: A behavioral perspective. *J. Consult. Clin. Psychol.* 50:804–19

Linden, W. 1980. Multicomponent behavior therapy in a case of compulsive binge-eating followed by vomiting. *J. Behav. Ther. Exp. Psychiatry* 11:297–300

Linden, W. 1981. Exposure treatments for focal phobias: A review. *Arch. Gen. Psychiatry* 38:769–75

Linehan, M. M. 1984. *Dialectical Behavior Therapy for Treatment of Parasuicidal Women: Treatment Manual.* Seattle: Psychology Dep., Univ. Washington

London, P. 1983. Science, culture and psychotherapy: The state of the art. In *Perspectives on Behavior Therapies in the Eighties,* ed. M. Rosenbaum, C. M. Franks, Y. Jaffe, pp. 17–32. New York: Springer

London, P. 1984. Behavior therapy grows a belly. *Contemp. Psychol.* 29:376–78

London, P. 1985. *The Modes and Morals of Psychotherapy.* New York: Hemisphere. 2nd ed.

London, P., Klerman, G. L. 1982. Evaluating psychotherapy. *Am. J. Psychiatry* 139:709–17

Long, C. G., Cordle, C. J. 1982. Psychological treatment of binge eating and self-induced vomiting. *Br. J. Med. Psychol.* 55:139–45

Luborsky, L. 1984. *Principles of Psychoanalytic Psychotherapy: A Manual for Suppor-

tive-Expressive Treatment.* New York: Basic Books

Luborsky, Lester, Singer, B., Luborsky, Lisa. 1975. Comparative studies of psychotherapies: Is it true that "everybody has won and all must have prizes"? *Arch. Gen. Psychiatry* 32:995–1008

Mahoney, M. J. 1980. Psychotherapy and the structure of personal revolutions. In *Psychotherapy Process: Current Issues and Future Directions,* ed. M. J. Mahoney, pp. 157–80. New York: Plenum

Mahoney, M. J. 1984. Integrating cognition, affect, and action: A comment. *Cogn. Ther. Res.* 8:585–89

Mann, J. 1981. The core of time-limited psychotherapy: Time and the central issue. See Budman 1981, pp. 25–43

Marks, I. M., Stern, R., Mawson, D., Cobb, J., McDonald, B. 1980. Clomipramine and exposure for obsessive-compulsive rituals: I. *Br. J. Psychiatry* 136:1–25

Marmor, J., Woods, S. 1980. *The Interface Between the Psychodynamic and Behavioral Therapies.* New York: Plenum

Mash, E. J., Terdal, L. J. 1980. Follow-up assessments in behavior therapy. In *Improving the Long-term Effects of Psychotherapy,* ed. P. Karoly, J. Steffen. New York: Gardner

Mavissakalian, M., Michelson, L. 1983. Self-directed in vivo exposure practice in behavioral and pharmacological treatments of agoraphobia. *Behav. Ther.* 14:506–19

Mavissakalian, M., Michelson, L., Greenwald, D., Kornblith, S., Greenwald, M. 1983. Cognitive-behavioral treatment of agoraphobia: Paradoxical intention vs self-statement training. *Behav. Res. Ther.* 21:75–86

Mawson, D., Marks, I. M., Ramm, L. 1982. Clomipramine and exposure for chronic obsessive-compulsive rituals: III. Two year follow-up and further findings. *Br. J. Psychiatry* 140:11–18

Meichenbaum, D. 1980. *Cognitive Behavior Modification.* New York: Plenum

Miller, N. E. 1983. Behavioral medicine: Symbiosis between laboratory and clinic. *Ann. Rev. Psychol.* 34:1–31

Miller, W. R. 1983. Controlled drinking: A history and a critical review. *J. Stud. Alcohol* 44:68–83

Miller, W. R., Hester, R. K. 1980. Treating the problem drinker: Modern approaches. In *The Addictive Behaviors: Treatment of Alcoholism, Drug Abuse, Smoking and Obesity,* ed. W. R. Miller, pp. 11–141. New York: Pergamon

Mosher, L. R., Keith, S. J. 1980. Psychosocial treatment: Individual, group, family, and community support approaches. *Schizophr. Bull.* 6:10–41

Mumford, E., Schlesinger, H. J., Glass, G. V. 1982. The effects of psychological intervention on recovery from surgery and heart attack: An analysis of the literature. *Am. J. Public Health* 72:141–51

Murphy, G. E., Simons, A. D., Wetzel, R. D., Lustman, P. J. 1984. Cognitive therapy and pharmacotherapy: Singly and together in the treatment of depression. *Arch. Gen. Psychiatry* 41:33–41

Nicholson, R. A., Berman, J. S. 1983. Is a follow-up necessary in evaluating psychotherapy? *Psychol. Bull.* 93:261–78

NIDA. 1981. Effectiveness of drug abuse treatment programs. *NIDA Treatment Research Reports.* DHHS Publ. #ADM 85–1143. Washington, DC: GPO

Norcross, J. C., Prochaska, J. O. 1982. A national survey of clinical psychologists: Characteristics and activities. *Clin. Psychol.* 35:1–9

Norcross, J. C., Prochaska, J. O. 1983. Contemporary psychotherapists: A national survey of characteristics, practices, orientations, and attitudes. *Psychother. Theory Res. Prac.* 20:161–73

O'Brien, G. T., Barlow, D. H. 1984. Agoraphobia. In *Behavioral Treatment of Anxiety Disorders*, ed. S. M. Turner, pp. 143–85. New York: Plenum

Pardes, H., Pincus, H. A. 1981. Brief therapy in the context of national mental health issues. See Budman 1981, pp. 7–22

Parloff, M. B. 1980. Psychotherapy and research: An anaclitic depression. *Psychiatry* 43:279–93

Parloff, M. B. 1982. Psychotherapy research evidence and reimbursement decisions: Bambi meets Godzilla. *Am. J. Psychiatry* 139:718–27

Parloff, M. B. 1984. Psychotherapy research and its incredible credibility crisis. *Clin. Psychol. Rev.* 4:95–109

Paul, G. 1984. Can pregnancy be a placebo effect?—Terminology, designs and conclusions in the study of psychosocial and pharmacological treatments of behavioral disorders. In *Placebo: Clinical Phenomena and New Insights*, ed. L. White, B. Tursky, G. F. Schwartz. New York: Guilford

Pearce, J. W., LeBow, M. D., Orchard, J. 1981. The role of spouse involvement in the behavioral treatment of obese women. *J. Consult. Clin. Psychol.* 49:236–44

Peele, S. 1984. The cultural context of psychological approaches to alcoholism: Can we control the effects of alcohol? *Am. Psychol.* 39:1337–51

Pendery, M. L., Maltzman, I. M., West, L. J. 1982. Controlled drinking by alcoholics? New findings and a reevaluation of a major affirmative study. *Science* 217:169–75

Perry, S. 1982. The brief life of the National

Center for Health Care Technology. *N. Engl. J. Med.* 307:1095–1100

Phillips, J. S., Bierman, K. L. 1981. Clinical psychology: Individual methods. *Ann. Rev. Psychol.* 32:405–38

Prioleau, L., Murdock, M., Brody, N. 1983. An analysis of psychotherapy versus placebo studies. *Behav. Brain Sci.* 6:275–85

Prusoff, B. A., Weissman, M. M., Klerman, G. L., Rounsaville, B. J. 1980. Research diagnostic criteria subtypes of depression: Their role as predictors of differential response to psychotherapy and drug treatment. *Arch. Gen. Psychiatry* 37:796–801

Rachman, S. J., Hodgson, R. J. 1980. *Obsessions and Compulsions.* Englewood Cliffs, NJ: Prentice-Hall

Rachman, S. J., Wilson, G. T. 1980. *The Effects of Psychological Therapy.* New York: Pergamon. 2nd ed.

Rahe, R., Ward, H., Haynes, V. 1979. Brief group therapy in myocardial infarction rehabilitation: Three- to four-year follow-up of a controlled trial. *Psychosom. Med.* 41:229–41

Redd, W., Andrykowski, M. A. 1982. Behavioral intervention in cancer treatment: Controlling aversion reaction to chemotherapy. *J. Consult. Clin. Psychol.* 50:1018–29

Rosen, J. C., Leitenberg, H. 1982. Bulimia nervosa: Treatment with exposure and response prevention. *Behav. Ther.* 13:117–24

Rosenthal, B., Allen, G. J., Winter, C. 1980. Husband involvement in the behavioral treatment of overweight women: Initial effects and long-term follow-up. *Int. J. Obesity* 4:165–73

Rosenthal, R., Rosnow, R. L. 1984. *Essentials of Behavioral Research: Methods and Data Analysis.* New York: McGraw-Hill

Rosenthal, R., Rubin, D. B. 1982. A simple, general purpose display of magnitude of experimental effect. *J. Educ. Psychol.* 74:166–69

Rounsaville, B. J., Glazer, W., Wilber, C. H., Weissman, M. M., Kleber, H. D. 1983. Short-term interpersonal psychotherapy in methadone-maintained opiate addicts. *Arch. Gen. Psychiatry* 40:629–36

Rush, A. J., Beck, A. T., Kovacs, M., Hollon, S. D. 1977. Comparative efficacy of cognitive therapy and pharmacotherapy in the treatment of depressed outpatients. *Cogn. Ther. Res.* 1:17–37

Rush, A. J., Beck, A. T., Kovacs, M., Weissenburger, J., Hollon, S. D. 1982. Comparison of the effects of cognitive therapy and pharmacotherapy on hopelessness and self-concept. *Am. J. Psychiatry* 139:862–66

Ryle, A. 1982. A common language for the psychotherapies? See Goldfried 1982a, pp. 337–51

Sanchez-Craig, M., Annis, H. M., Bornet, A. R., MacDonald, K. R. 1984. Random assignment to abstinence and controlled drinking: Evaluation of a cognitive-behavioral program for problem drinkers. *J. Consult. Clin. Psychol.* 52:390–403

Sarason, I. G. 1982. Three lacunae of cognitive therapy. See Goldfried 1982a, pp. 352–64

Schachter, S. 1982. Recidivism and self-cure of smoking and obesity. *Am. Psychol.* 37:436–44

Schlesinger, H. J., Mumford, E., Glass, G. V., Patrick, C., Sharfstein, S. 1983. Mental health treatment and medical care utilization in a fee-for-service system: Outpatient mental health treatment following the onset of a chronic disease. *Am. J. Public Health* 73:422–29

Shapiro, A. K. 1984. Opening comments. See Williams & Spitzer 1984, pp. 106–07

Shapiro, D., Goldstein, I. B. 1982. Biobehavioral perspectives on hypertension. *J. Consult. Clin. Psychol.* 50:841–58

Shapiro, D. A., Shapiro, D. 1982. Meta-analysis of comparative therapy outcome studies: A replication and refinement. *Psychol. Bull.* 92:581–604

Sifneos, P. E. 1981. Short-term anxiety-provoking psychotherapy: Its history, technique, outcome, and instruction. See Budman 1981, pp. 45–81

Simons, A. D., Garfield, S. L., Murphy, G. E. 1984. The process of change in cognitive therapy and pharmacotherapy for depression. *Arch. Gen. Psychiatry* 41:45–51

Sjodin, I. 1983. Psychotherapy in peptic ulcer disease: A controlled outcome study. *Acta Psychiat. Scand.* 6(307):9–90

Smith, M. L., Glass, G. V., Miller, T. I. 1980. *The Benefits of Psychotherapy.* Baltimore: Johns Hopkins Univ. Press

Sobell, M. B., Sobell, L. C. 1973. Alcoholics treated by individualized behavior therapy: One year treatment outcome. *Behav. Res. Ther.* 11:599–618

Sobell, M. B., Sobell, L. C. 1976. Second year treatment outcome of alcoholics treated by individualized behavior therapy: Results. *Behav. Res. Ther.* 14:195–215

Sobell, M. B., Sobell, L. C. 1984. The aftermath of heresy: A response to Pendery et al.'s critique of "individualized behavior therapy for alcoholics." *Behav. Res. Ther.* 22:413–40

Spanos, N. P., Brown, J. M., Jones, B., Horner, D. 1981. Cognitive activity and suggestions for analgesia in reductions of reported pain. *J. Abnorm. Psychol.* 90:554–61

Stanton, A. H., Gunderson, J. G., Knapp, P. H., Frank, A. F., Vannicelli, M. L., et al. 1984. Effects of psychotherapy in schizophrenia: I. Design and implementation of a controlled study. *Schizophr. Bull.* 10:520–63

Steinbrueck, S. M., Maxwell, S. E., Howard, G. S. 1983. A meta-analysis of psychotherapy and drug therapy in the treatment of unipolar depression with adults. *J. Consult. Clin. Psychol.* 51:856–63

Stitzer, M. L., Bigelow, G. E., McCaul, M. E. 1983. Behavioral approaches to drug abuse. In *Progress in Behavior Modification,* ed. M. Hersen, R. M. Eisler, P. M. Miller, 14:49–124. New York: Academic

Strube, M. J., Hartmann, D. P. 1983. Meta-analysis: Techniques, applications, and functions. *J. Consult. Clin. Psychol.* 51:14–27

Strupp, H. H., Binder, J. L. 1982. *Time-limited Dynamic Psychotherapy (TLDP): A Treatment Manual.* Nashville: Vanderbilt Univ.

Stuart, R. B., ed. 1982. *Adherence, Compliance and Generalization in Behavioral Medicine.* New York: Brunner/Mazel

Sturgis, E., Meyer, V. 1981. Obsessive-compulsive disorders. In *Handbook of Clinical Behavior Therapy,* ed. S. M. Turner, K. S. Calhoun, H. E. Adams, pp. 68–102. New York: Wiley

Suinn, R. M. 1982. Intervention with type A behaviors. *J. Consult. Clin. Psychol.* 50:922–32

Svedlund, J. 1983. Psychotherapy in irritable bowel syndrome: A controlled outcome study. *Acta Psychiatr. Scand.* 67(306):7–86

Thoresen, C. E., Friedman, M., Powell, L. H., Gill, J., Ulmer, D. 1985. Altering the type A behavior pattern in post-infarction patients. *J. Cardiac Rehabil.* In press

Turner, S. M., Michelson, L. 1984. Obsessive-compulsive disorders. In *Behavioral Theories and Treatment of Anxiety,* ed. S. M. Turner, pp. 239–77. New York: Plenum

Wadden, T. A., Penrod, J. H. 1981. Hypnosis in the treatment of alcoholism: A review and appraisal. *Am. J. Clin. Hypn.* 24:41–47

Wadden, T. A., Stunkard, A. J., Brownell, K. D. 1983. Very low calorie diets: Their efficacy, safety, and future. *Ann. Intern. Med.* 99:675–84

Wadden, T. A., Stunkard, A. J., Brownell, K. D., Day, S. C. 1984. Treatment of obesity by behavior therapy and very low calorie diet: A pilot investigation. *J. Consult. Clin. Psychol.* 52:692–94

Waskow, I. E. 1984. Specification of the technique variable in the NIMH treatment of depression collaborative research program. See Williams & Spitzer 1984, pp. 150–59

Weissman, M. M. 1979. The psychological treatment of depression: Evidence for the efficacy of psychotherapy alone, in comparison with, and in combination with pharmacotherapy. *Arch. Gen. Psychiatry* 36:1261–69

Weissman, M. M. 1984. The psychological treatment of depression: An update of clinical trials. See Williams & Spitzer 1984, pp. 89–105

Weissman, M. M., Klerman, G. L., Prusoff, B. A., Sholomskas, D., Padian, N. 1981. Depressed outpatients: Results one year after treatment with drugs and/or interpersonal psychotherapy. *Arch. Gen. Psychiatry* 41:51–55

Whitehead, W. E., Bosmajian, L. S. 1982. Behavioral medicine approaches to gastrointestinal disorders. *J. Consult. Clin. Psychol.* 50:972–83

Williams, J. B. W., Spitzer, R. L., eds. 1984. *Psychotherapy Research: Where Are We and Where Should We Go?* New York: Guilford

Williams, S. L., Rappaport, A. 1983. Cognitive treatment in the natural environment for agoraphobics. *Behav. Ther.* 2:299–314

Wilson, G. T., Brownell, K. D. 1980. Behavior therapy for obesity: An evaluation of treatment outcome. *Adv. Behav. Res. Ther.* 3:49–86

Wilson, G. T., Franks, C. M. 1982. *Contem-porary Behavior Therapy: Conceptual and Empirical Foundations.* New York: Guilford

Wilson, G. T., Rachman, S. J. 1983. Meta-analysis and the evaluation of psychotherapy outcome: Limitations and liabilities. *J. Consult. Clin. Psychol.* 51:54–64

Wilson, P. H. 1982. Combined pharmacological and behavioral treatment of depression. *Behav. Res. Ther.* 20:173–84

Wilson, P. H., Goldin, J. C., Charbonneau-Powis, M. 1983. Comparative efficacy of behavioral and cognitive treatments of depression. *Cogn. Ther. Res.* 7:111–24

Woody, G. E., Luborsky, L., McLellan, C. P., O'Brien, C. P. O., Beck, A. T., et al. 1983. Psychotherapy for opiate addicts. *Arch. Gen. Psychiatry* 40:639–45

Wortman, P. M. 1983. Evaluation research: A methodological perspective. *Ann. Rev. Psychol.* 34:223–60

Yeaton, W. H., Sechrest, L. 1981. Meaningful measures of effect. *J. Consult. Clin. Psychol.* 49:766–67

Zajonc, R. B. 1980. Feeling and thinking: Preferences need no inferences. *Am. Psychol.* 35:151–75

Ann. Rev. Psychol. 1986. 37:351–80

PERSONNEL SELECTION AND PLACEMENT

Milton D. Hakel

Department of Psychology, Ohio State University, Columbus, Ohio 43210, and Applied Research Group, 9660 Hillcroft, Houston, Texas 77096[1]

CONTENTS

INTRODUCTION 351
CRITERIA 353
    Models of Performance 353
    Job Analysis 353
    Performance Measurement 355
PREDICTORS 359
    Computerized Testing 361
    Reviews of Predictors 362
    Selected Research 364
    Assessment Centers 366
    Interviews 366
PREDICTION PROCEDURES AND THEIR ADEQUACY 367
    Bias 367
    Selection Statistics and Validation 368
    Validity Generalization 371
    Utility Analysis 372
PUTTING IT ALL TOGETHER 373

INTRODUCTION

Significant advances have occurred during the two years covered by this review. Viewed one at a time, close up, the gains reported by many investigators look small. You will see many such gains in this review, and many more were left out. Viewing the big picture, however, we have made significant progress. In 1960, Nunnally wrote, "We should not feel proud when we see the

---

[1]Present address: Department of Psychology, University of Houston, University Park Campus, Houston, Texas 77004.

0066-4308/86/0201-0351$02.00

psychologist smile and say, 'The correlation is significant beyond the .01 level.' Perhaps that is the most he can say, but he has no reason to smile" (p. 649). A bit later, Dunnette (1966) argued for reporting effect sizes as well as the usual significance tests. Nowadays effect sizes are reported frequently, and meta-analysis technology has emerged as a way of assessing our cumulative results. Moreover, utility analysis has advanced to where the psychologist can point to the dollars-and-cents impact of those cumulative findings and smile.

The progress has been substantial and real, but lest we get carried away with enthusiasm, the rest of this review will address many issues in personnel selection and placement where further research progress is urgently needed. Severe space limits preclude coverage of other critical topics such as job evaluation, which deserves its own chapter, and recruitment.

What accounts for our progress? In the early 1960s, personnel selection was a pragmatic, empirical, and atheoretical field. It appeared to be a mature technology: there was little innovation, and tests were being used with less and less care. Rains Wallace (1965) wrote, "If ever there was a time in which we require conceptual foundations for what we are currently doing, and what we hope to do in the future, it is now." Brent Baxter (1965) wrote, "With our lack of emphasis on a fundamental and broad psychological approach, we have drifted toward becoming technicians and not scientists. We are better known for our techniques than for fundamental insights."

In 1964, Title VII and the rest of the Civil Rights Act became the law of the land. The values so beautifully expressed in the Declaration of Independence found expression in a law which stimulated our innovation and creativity. Our science and technology are vital because of it.

Over the past two decades, we have seen the place of theory become clearly established. We better understand the roles of constructs, and our statistical technology for working with them, in the forms of structural equation models and item response theory, has improved dramatically.

Thorndike (1949) described the ultimate criterion as "multiple and complex in almost every case," but for the most part, the field has foolishly treated it as a single unitary measure. We have reached the point where the "ultimate criterion" should have been consigned to the history books. Our preoccupation with it has limited our thinking and hindered our research.

While we are well on the way to putting the problem of *the* criterion (Dunnette 1963a) behind us, we now face the *criteria* problem. We continue to pour most of our resources and effort into measurement of predictors and into schemes for relating predictor scores to contaminated and deficient but convenient criterion measures. Far too little attention has been given to what it is we are trying to predict: to behavior, its causes, and its evaluation as effective or ineffective.

CRITERIA

Models of Performance

We've progressed beyond behavior = f(person, environment) and performance = motivation × ability. Dunnette's (1963b) modified model for selection research included components for predictors, individuals, job behaviors, situations, and consequences. The trouble with these formulations, of course, is their generality: they contain almost no content. They don't specify *which aspect* of performance, *what factor* of ability, or *which facets* of the situation are important. In recent years, however, we have begun to specify the content. Owens's developmental-integrative theory (Owens & Schoenfeldt 1979, Owens 1984) was one major programmatic effort that hopefully will continue. Borman et al (1984a) developed an 11-dimension behavioral model of soldier effectiveness. Morrison & Cook's (1983) general model of career patterns, intentions, performance, and turnover postulates dynamic interactions among individual, organizational, and environmental factors. The most comprehensive model was presented by Wetrogan et al (1983). A systemic model, it incorporates 95 factors in 13 domains: cognitive, psychomotor, physical proficiency, affective, vocational preference, interest, information processing, objective and phenomenological organizational structure, objective and phenomenological task structure, and objective and phenomenological social structure. One can easily quarrel with the inclusion or exclusion and the relative emphasis or deemphasis on various constructs and the hypothesized causal interrelations in any of these models. But a comprehensive model's usefulness lies in its ability to help us sort the research literature to see what is well established and what deserves further investigation. Especially useful in this regard is the Job/Person characteristic matrix described by Dunnette & Fleishman (1982). The growing use of confirmatory techniques will facilitate work on models in the years to come.

Job Analysis

Fundamental questions abound about how people encode, store, and recall information about job content and how they associate that content with job titles, various job attributes (worth, difficulty, complexity, interdependence), and attributes of incumbents (knowledge, skills, abilities, and other personal characteristics). Wallace (1983) called for taxonomic work and construct validation studies with respect to job analysis and comparable worth. A major development was the book by Fleishman & Quaintance (1984). It deals with conceptual and methodological issues in developing and using taxonomics in job analysis, test development, performance assessment, and generalization of research findings. There is still much work to be done.

No clear basis for choice among the numerous job analysis methods is currently available (Levine et al 1983). The issues involved in matching method to purpose were discussed in an essay by Eyde et al (1983). Lawshe (1984) reported a practitioner's thoughts about job analysis, describing two continua (detailed versus general, unique versus generic) along which job descriptive statements vary. The first continuum conveys the level of aggregation of the job elements while the second continuum conveys the extent to which the job descriptive information is specific to a particular job or position. Lawshe (1985) viewed content validity analysis strategies as appropriate only when the job behavior under scrutiny is directly observable. Abstract concepts involving reference to unobserved cognitive processes or other constructs require other validation strategies. Lawshe's concepts fit well with several recommendations to improve task inventory construction presented by Chatfield & Royle (1983).

Banks et al (1983) reported the development of a job component inventory constructed at a fairly molar level. It focuses on use of tools and equipment, physical and perceptual requirements, mathematical requirements, communication requirements, and decision making and responsibility requirements. Cunningham et al (1983) reported the development of an inventory for use as a taxonomic tool. Consisting of 617 work elements which, in turn, are related to 102 defined human attributes, it should be usable in computer-based occupational exploration and guidance systems as well as traditional applications. A novel use of job analysis information was reported by Robinson (1984), who developed a worker rehabilitation questionnaire that is integrated with the Position Analysis Questionnaire (PAQ). His work has obvious guidance and placement implications.

Cornelius et al (1984a) cautioned against the uncritical acceptance of a shared stereotype explanation for apparent agreement among PAQ descriptions by naive and expert raters. They pointed out that convergence is appropriately estimated by pooling data within rather than across job titles and that the frequency of does-not-apply responses artifactually increases the magnitude of correlations. Silverman et al (1984) found no effects for age or job experience on incumbent responses to a structured task analysis questionnaire for clerical employees. Cain & Green (1983) conducted a generalizability analysis of DOT ratings. Test-retest reliabilities were generally excellent, and ratings for service jobs were generally less reliable than ratings for manufacturing jobs.

Cornelius et al (1984b) compared two approaches for supplying data for validity generalization analysis. The first approach was an elaborate quantitative procedure involving a job inventory and multivariate item analysis. The second procedure involved simple direct judgments of classification membership by supervisors and incumbents. The second approach was as effective as the first but required only a fraction of the time and cost. R. L. Rosse et al (1984, unpublished manuscript) reported their procedures for analyzing the similarity of 111 army occupational specialties. Most interesting is their use of overall similarity judgments as a basis for creating a stratified sampling plan for the selection of occupations to be used in validation research. A tacit but critical assumption underlying the grouping of similar jobs to create a sample large enough to make validation technically feasible is the assumption that all positions with a given job title are similar. Stutzman (1983) investigated this assumption and found substantial differences. Whether these differences are important depends, of course, on the level of aggregation at which one must work and the aims one is seeking to achieve. Nevertheless, the assumption that two positions are similar because they have the same job title remains open.

Performance Measurement

Research on performance measurement has been one of the most active topics during the review period, with ratings getting most of the attention. Some deplore this emphasis, arguing that what others say about a person reflects little more than a reputational bias weakly related to "Performance." But "Performance" is the contemporary incarnation of the ultimate criterion, and we would do well to pay considerable attention to ratings as well as to other measures. Understanding the determinants of what others say about a person would be an important achievement.

Major conceptual statements presented cognitive views of the performance appraisal process. A particularly comprehensive model of the interrelations of the organizational context within which performance appraisal takes place, the appraiser's information processing system, and the behavioral system of the person appraised was developed by Ilgen & Feldman (1983). DeNisi et al (1984) drew heavily on research in cognitive and social psychology and presented a model and 28 research propositions. Doubtless many of these will be explored in the years to come. The single best source book was Landy et al's (1983) *Performance Measurement and Theory*. Its 12 papers and their associated commentaries cover the topic completely and are indispensable. Hobson & Gibson (1983) reviewed policy capturing as an approach to understanding and improving performance appraisal. Finally, Larson & Rimland (1984) and Osborn (1983) discussed issues and strategies for measuring job performance.

Much experimentation has been conducted in laboratories. Murphy et al (1985) reported the detection of contrast effects from previous performance on evaluations of present performance. We can expect to see more studies like this, as the contrast and assimilation effect paradigm lends itself easily to experimental research. Stone et al (1984) found that the order of positive and negative feedback, along with the expertise of the rater, affect perceptions of feedback accuracy. Phillips (1984) found that the accuracy of leadership ratings was affected by the consistency between a leadership label and the presence of label congruent leadership behaviors and also on the time at which the ratings were taken. Murphy et al (1984) reported that the purpose for which ratings are made does not have general effects on either the overall level of ratings or rating accuracy. Purpose does, however, affect the relationship between accuracy in observation and accuracy in rating and may reflect differences in information processing strategies. Veres et al (1983) reported a field study of ratings in which no difference was detected between research and administrative ratings in halo, scale validity, or fairness criteria.

Balzer et al (1983) investigated the reliability of actual and predicted judgments across a two-week period, showing that most individuals had temporally stable judgment policies, though there were large individual differences. Interestingly, subjects who completed the decision task before describing their subjective policies showed significantly higher reliabilities for predictions based upon those subjective policies than did other individuals who described their subjective policies and then made judgments. Not surprisingly, judgments predicted from a regression model of a judge's policy were more reliable than were actual judgments or judgments predicted from the rater's subjective policy, another manifestation of a basic finding from years of clinical prediction research. Fox et al (1983) suggested that the halo effect is not a unitary concept, but rather should be divided into two distinguishable types, one based on covariance, as reflected in intercorrelation and factor analysis methods, and the other based on co-occurrence, as measured by interaction and dispersion methods. Cotton et al (1983) found that the scaling of stimulus cues for individual decision makers resulted in judgment models that were more successful in reproducing the decision makers' responses than models employing the same cue scales for all decision makers.

Nathan & Lord (1983) investigated two models of the cognitive processes underlying performance ratings: a traditional model, in which behaviors are integrated into dimensional schemata, and a cognitive categorization model, in which observations are integrated into global categories of performance and category prototypes are relied on to make ratings. The traditional model is appropriate for describing the rating process, but a large halo effect, despite conditions designed to minimize its likelihood and a tendency to make errors in later recall, provided some support for the cognitive categorization model. Heneman & Wexley (1983) showed that ratings were less accurate when delayed and when only a small sample of information was observed. DeNisi et al (1983) showed that negative peer rating feedback produced significantly lower perceived performance, cohesiveness, and satisfaction. Cleveland & Landy (1983), on the basis of two simulation studies, suggested that when the pattern of performance is inconsistent with the age stereotype of the job, employees receive lower ratings than when behavior is consistent with the job stereotype. Cardy & Kehoe (1984) investigated the information processing characteristics of raters, showing that selective attention ability, as measured by a field dependence-independence test, was associated with rating accuracy.

There were fewer publications dealing with scale formats per se than in previous years, and those that appeared seemed more interesting. Bartlett (1983) described a novel procedure for converting behavioral checklist ratings into measures equivalent to forced choice ratings, an approach that richly deserves further research. Barnes-Farrell & Weiss (1984) reported that the extremity of the scale values of items in a mixed standards scale affected both the level of performance ratings and the proportion of logically inconsistent response patterns. Benson & Dickinson (1983) found that counts of illogical response patterns on mixed standards scales were not related to Cronbach's alpha. They suggested that illogical responses may reflect the nature of the survey, not reliability per se, and urged caution in the use and interpretation of mixed standards scales. Tziner (1984) found that, compared with a graphic scale, a behaviorally anchored rating scale showed less leniency and less halo as well as higher interrater reliability. Cooper (1983) showed that halo could be reduced by using rating categories that did not force raters to rely on their overall evaluation of the ratee or use the same salient observations as the basis for rating performance on multiple categories. These conclusions confirm the traditional advice about using rating categories that are clear, specific, and nonoverlapping. Rumsey (1984) and Distefano et al (1983) described task- and content-oriented procedures for developing criterion rating instruments.

Pulakos (1984) compared rater error training, rater accuracy training, a combined program, and a control group on halo, leniency, and accuracy of performance evaluations. Training content about errors was associated with reduced halo, and training content about accuracy was associated with less leniency. McIntyre et al (1984) studied the accuracy of performance ratings as influenced by rater training and the perceived purpose of the ratings. Frame-of-reference training was superior to rater error training and no training. The effects of purpose were marginal, and heterogeneous variances made interpretation of the findings somewhat problematic.

Meanwhile, Hunter (1983) conducted a meta-analysis to identify the extent to which ratings were a function of on-the-job performance as measured by work sample tests or supervisors' judgments of workers' knowledge. Both of these factors were important, but even after both were considered, there was considerable unaccounted variance. Pulakos & Wexley (1983) found that perceptual similarity accounted for a sizable percentage of performance rating variance and that lower appraisals were found in dyads where there was mutual perceptual dissimilarity between managers and subordinates. The results, however, overstated the importance of the effect because two-thirds of the subjects were dropped from the analysis. Peters et al (1984) followed up earlier research concerning sex bias and managerial evaluations. Although rater sex was a statistically significant source of variance in overall performance ratings, it accounted for only .007 of the variance. Ratee sex and rater sex-ratee sex interaction terms were nonsignificant. This field study is notable for its relatively good controls and high power. Mount (1984) conducted a multitrait, multi-method analysis of supervisor, self, and subordinate ratings, and compared with prior studies, there was less convergence, more discriminant validity, and less halo. Borman et al (1984b) found that supervisory and peer ratings of overall job performance reflected predominantly the ratees' job performance. Other less directly relevant factors were related to overall performance, but at substantially lower levels. Halo continues to be a concern.

Vance et al (1983) conducted a *longitudinal* examination of rater and ratee effects in performance ratings. Reliable variance in mean ratings was partly attributable to ratees but mainly introduced by raters. Reliable halo variance was attributable to the raters, and range restriction in ratings was a product of stable group performance variability within intact groups of ratees. We need more research like this.

Barrett et al (1985) argued that the phenomenon of the dynamic criterion has been overemphasized in the literature, and they concluded that practitioners should focus on removing sources of criterion unreliability. Rambo et al (1983) analyzed the intercorrelations of weekly production data over a three-and-a-half year period for sewing machine operators and folding and packaging workers. Their results describe the upper limit of reliability and are relevant to criterion dynamism. Research on the temporal stability of criterion factors is urgently needed.

Olson & Borman (1984) described the identification of environmental and situational influences that impact job performance and the development of a questionnaire to measure them. This is also a promising direction for further research.

Komaki's (1984) work on creating behavior observation taxonomies, together with observer training procedures that lead to reliable observations, deserves to be emulated.

Linn (1984) wrote,

> The Achilles heel of criterion-related validity is, of course, the criterion. The real concern for a test to be used in selection is with its validity as an indicator of the idealized qualifications. The degree to which it predicts the criterion measure is of concern only to the degree that the criterion measure is in itself a valid indicator of those idealized qualifications. Most attempts at providing operational definitions of the conditions for fair test use are within the criterion-related validity paradigm. They all rest on the strong assumption that the criterion measure is itself valid and fair. This is a critical, but too frequently overlooked, assumption. This assumption is one more link in the chain between the acceptance of a definition of fairness and determination of whether or not a particular use of a test is consistent with that definition (p. 38).

Kraiger & Ford (1985) conducted a meta-analysis of ratee race effects in performance ratings and found substantial race differences, moderated by the setting of the study (laboratory or field). The differences in field studies are not clearly attributable to bias, but their analysis shows the complexity of the issues inherent in analyzing the relevance of ratings as criteria. We have a long way to go in defining performance domains and devising valid and fair measures of them.

We can expect a continuation of laboratory research on performance appraisal and performance rating issues. Indeed, research on this topic should continue and intensify. From time to time, one wonders about whether it is worthwhile because the findings tend to be fragmentary and the research itself is limited in scope and duration. Generalizability questions abound, but they are empirical questions. This field looks not unlike the research on employment interviewing a decade ago. The practical problems are as great, or perhaps greater, and the concerns about generalizability are as great, or perhaps greater, yet we can expect that the array of findings will eventually have important practical implications.

The preceding comments were a nice way of saying that there has been no practical breakthrough coming from the laboratory research, or at least that nothing has yet emerged that can be recognized as a practical breakthrough. What would one look like? That's hard to say, but it would have high reliability and no bias.

PREDICTORS

While a great deal of activity has taken place in the form of developing new predictor measures, studying their interrelationships, and linking them to criterion measures, little of this work has been accompanied by sophisticated conceptual development. What has been missing has been attention to the concepts and theory underlying the measures. For example, we can now confidently say that cognitive ability tests are substantially related to many job performance criteria. Meta-analysis has shown this to be a dependable empirical statement. For the most part, however, we lack strong theoretical accounts of the determinants of the observed empirical regularities. Our traditional approach has been to use factor analysis and other psychometric tools to infer latent factors that are presumed to cause the observed variation in performance. There is an alternative view that is well presented by Hunt (1983). Writing on the nature of intelligence, Hunt argued, "Mental behavior should be explained by identifying the processes involved in problem solving, rather than by producing abstract descriptions of the outcomes of thinking. In other words, intelligence should be defined in terms of individual differences in cognitive acts, rather than in terms of a person's position determined by an abstract set of factors" (p. 142). Hunt described his and others' research on individual differences in cognition as related to differences in problem representations, problem solving strategies, and elementary cognitive operations. He concluded,

> Intelligence is sometimes evoked as an explanation for behavior. From the viewpoint of cognitive scientists, this is not explanation at all. Thinking is to be explained by determining the requirements of the situation and how people use cognitive processes to satisfy these requirements. Analogously there is a large literature on the causes of intelligence. The cognitive science view is that intelligence is an abstraction and does not have a cause. On the other hand, there are individual differences in specific cognitive behaviors, these differences have causes, and the causes merit investigation. Physical influences such as heredity, nutrition, and brain damage must exert their influence through alteration of mechanistic processes. Educational and cultural influences must exert their influence through changes in representations and strategies (p. 146).

Will tests developed in the light of cognitive science findings lead to better testing? Hunt finds no compelling reason to believe that such would be the case because present tests are the results of an extensive search for instruments that meet the pragmatic criteria of prediction. I am more optimistic. As we better understand our constructs and the behavior they represent, we will be better able to develop valid measures. These measures will better reflect the psychological processes that create performance variability, and this will be true for our predictor measures and for the criterion measures that they are intended to predict.

Embretson (1983) distinguished between "construct representation," which is concerned with identifying the theoretical mechanisms that underlie item responses (such as information processes, strategies, and knowledge stores), and "nomothetic span," which is concerned with the network of relationships between a test score and other variables. As two major types of construct validation research, these approaches address different questions, involve different methods, and require different types of data and analysis. This distinction reflects Hunt's point and is useful, at a minimum, in interpreting research results. James & Brett (1984) focused on models used in developing theories. They expanded the definition of mediated relations to include nonadditive and interactive moderator effects and nonlinear and nonrecursive forms. Confirmatory analysis techniques provide the most informative test of mediation models, but omission of significant variables and mis-specification of causal direction present serious problems. We can expect causal analysis techniques to do for correlational studies what analysis of variance has done for experimentation.

In this general context, it is interesting to note that Flynn (1984) found a total gain in mean IQ of 13.8 points over the 46 years he studied. The combination of IQ gains and the widely reported decline in scholastic aptitude test scores seems almost inexplicable. Obsolete norms have acted as an unrecognized confounding factor in hundreds of studies, and IQ gains of this magnitude pose a serious problem of causal explanation. At a minimum, Flynn's work raises many construct validity questions pertinent both to the construct and its measures.

In an interesting paper on cross-level inference, Mossholder & Bedeian

(1983) discussed the practice and limitations of making inferences from one level of analysis to another, for example, from individual to group or from group to organizational levels. They discussed multiple regression and analysis of covariance as procedures for implementing multi-level analysis, an attempt to partition effects at one level of analysis among variables belonging to a separate level. The multilevel perspective they presented may be viewed as a tool for testing whether alternative multilevel explanations are tenable. Leadership, job design, organizational climate and organizational properties, examples they analyzed in their article, are not particularly relevant to this review, but the analytic focus is. The issues they discussed apply to job analysis, employee selection, and many other personnel research contexts.

In the years to come, we can look forward to sharper conceptualizations of our predictors. Will we eventually develop a comprehensive theory for personnel selection? So far we have proved ourselves to be skillful engineers and technologists. It is time to go beyond technique per se, and to begin to identify the elements of a theory.

Computerized Testing

Conventionally administered paper and pencil tests have a number of shortcomings: excessive administration time, poor differentiation among people of extreme ability, limited capacity for measuring some types of abilities (target identification and tracking), cumbersome and error-prone scoring, expensive and time-consuming replacement, and high vulnerability to theft and compromise. Sands & Gade (1983) described the development of the Computerized Adaptive Screening Test and its evaluation as a replacement for the paper and pencil Enlistment Screening Test. A composite of ten word knowledge items and five arithmetic reasoning items correlated .85 with AFQT scores, slightly better than the 48-item EST. Moreno et al (1984) examined the relationships between corresponding ASVAB and computerized adaptive subtests (CAT) and found that CAT achieved the same measurement precision as a conventional test with half the items. CAT subtest scores correlated as well with ASVAB as did a second administration of the ASVAB. Factor analysis showed that CAT subtests loaded on the same factors as corresponding ASVAB subtests, indicating that the same abilities were being measured.

We are certain to see more computerized testing in the future. Test users should be aware of Green et al's (1984) technical guidelines for computerized adaptive tests, covering issues of dimensionality, measurement error, validity, estimation of item parameters, item pool characteristics, human factors, and equating CAT and conventional tests. Eyde & Kowal (1984) discussed the consumer issues arising from the use of computer software for *interpreting* complex diagnostic and pre-employment tests. Computer-based test interpretation offers many possible advantages but also great potential for abuse.

Item response theory is still more a laboratory curiosity than a major analytic tool used daily by researchers and practitioners. However, change is coming, and computerized adaptive testing is going to force us to update our working knowledge of psychological measurement. Hulin et al (1983) have provided a major service by translating mathematical formulations of item response theory into language that can be readily grasped by researchers and practitioners. With its emphasis on application of measurement theory, this book is *must* reading.

Technical advances continue. Since all tests with more than two items are probably multidimensional, the important question is whether responses can be adequately modeled by a unidimensional item response theory model. Drasgow & Parsons (1983) and Drasgow & Lissak (1983) found that under many circumstances departures from unidimensionality are not serious, and modified parallel analysis successfully detects them. Levine & Drasgow (1983) investigated the relation between incorrect choices and estimated ability, finding that high ability examinees working independently were much more likely to have the same wrong answers than would have been expected from a knowledge- or random-guessing model.

Levine & Drasgow (1982) presented a review, critique, and validation studies of appropriateness measurement, a technique for identifying unusual answer patterns to detect examinees for whom a test score might have limited value as an ability measure. Appropriateness measurement is useful in identifying improperly coached examinees who have been shown answers to some items before the exam, examinees with high ability but atypical schooling or low English fluency, exceptionally creative examinees who might discover novel interpretations for some items, examinees who are very conservative in their use of partial information, or examinees who make alignment errors over a block of items. In each of these cases, the test score is not an appropriate measure of ability, and the item-by-item pattern of answers may be recognizably unusual.

We may expect many applications of item response theory in the coming decade. It makes problems tractable that have been impossible to solve by traditional methods, for example, detection of bias against minority groups in psychological tests, equating instrument translations and appropriateness measurement. The theory's use in adaptive testing has already been noted.

Reviews of Predictors

There may have been as many review articles as reports of original research on predictors published during this two-year period. Schmitt et al (1984a) performed a major service for the field by conducting a meta-analysis of validity studies published between 1964 and 1982 in the *Journal of Applied Psychology* and in *Personnel Psychology*. They analyzed 840 validity coefficients, aggregating them into 366 summary coefficients. They found that concurrent validation designs produced validity coefficients roughly equivalent to those obtained in predictive validation designs, and that both of these designs produced higher validity coefficients than did a predictive design that included direct use of the selection instrument. Performance rating criteria generally produced lower validity coefficients than did the use of other, more "objective" criteria. Cognitive ability tests did not surpass other predictors such as assessment centers, work samples, and supervisory/peer evaluations, but personality measures were clearly less valid. Compared with previous work, much unexplained variance in validity coefficients remained after correction for sample size differences. Schmitt et al concluded by noting the deficiencies of research reports, particularly the omission of information about selection rates, standard deviations, reliabilities, and predictor-criterion intercorrelations.

Hunter & Hunter (1984) reported a meta-analysis of research on various predictors of job performance. For entry-level jobs no predictor had a greater validity than that of ability, which had a corrected mean of .53. For selection on the basis of current job performance, work sample tests had a corrected mean validity of .54. Hiring on ability had a utility of $15.61 billion per year but affected minority groups adversely. Hiring on ability by quotas would have decreased utility by only 5%, but using a minimum qualification cutoff score would have decreased utility by 83%. Using other predictors in conjunction with ability tests might improve validity and reduce adverse impact, but there is as yet no data base for studying this possibility.

Kulik et al (1984) conducted a meta-analysis on the effectiveness of coaching for aptitude test performance. In 14 studies on the SAT, coaching raised scores by an average of .15 standard deviations. In 24 studies on other aptitude and intelligence tests, coaching raised scores by an average of .43 standard deviations. Studies that used pretests reported stronger coaching effects than did studies with posttest only designs. One would like to know whether coaching is equally effective throughout the ability continuum.

Olian (1984) evaluated the status of genetic screening devices against testing standards and legal criteria. Genetic screening for employment involves identification of individuals with hypersusceptibility to toxins in the work environment and selective placement of them.

Campion (1983) reviewed both published and unpublished literature on selection for physically demanding jobs, covering the physiological background underlying selection strategies, the assessment of human physical abilities, the measurement of physical requirements of jobs, and validation studies.

Sackett & Harris (1984) reviewed research and other publications concerning paper and pencil predictors of employee theft and honesty. High reliabilities were consistently reported, and test score comparisons by race and sex generally showed no differences. While positive correlations with validation criteria were consistently found, methodological differences among studies made direct comparisons of test validities difficult.

Mumford (1983) noted the striking validity of peer evaluations and found that the theories put forth to account for their validity were deficient. Barge & Hough (1984a,b) reviewed biodata and vocational assessments, and Kamp & Hough (1984) reviewed personality assessment to identify noncognitive predictor constructs worth studying in Project A.

Meritt-Haston & Wexley (1983) summarized the findings of court cases concerning the legality of educational prerequisites for employment. Twelve studies concerning the validity of educational measures yielded an overall correlation of .26. When ratings were used as criteria, the average validity was .15. Bachman (1983) provided another perspective on educational credentials and argued for competency testing and better measurement of employment behavior as means of reducing reliance on credentials.

Selected Research

Much research investigated various predictors, but only the most noteworthy is described here. Hough et al (1983) and Hough (1984) described the development and validation of an accomplishment record and other alternative selection procedures. The accomplishment record is a major new technique and appears to be unrelated to traditional psychological measures such as aptitude tests, grades, and honors, but appears to correlate with job performance and is fair for females, minorities, and white males. Hogan et al (1984) described the development of a measure of "service orientation" intended to be used in practical selection contexts. Their work appears promising, and particularly noteworthy is its derivation from a personality inventory that itself is based on a theory of human performance. Operational use of personality measures still remains problematic, however.

Schmidt et al (1983) compared expert judgment and small sample criterion-related validity studies showing that, given highly trained and experienced judges, expert judgment may provide more accurate estimates of validity for cognitive tests than do local criterion-related validation studies. Wing et al (1984) used expert judgments to link predictor constructs to criterion categories for Project A.

Gordon & Fitzgibbons (1982) found that past performance and interjob similarity predicted future performance in positions to which female sewing machine operators were promoted. Seniority, however, had no validity. Giniger et al (1983) investigated the decremental theory of aging, which maintains that abilities decline as workers age, and therefore performance should decline also. Distinguishing between jobs requiring speed and those demanding skill, they found, contrary to prediction, that older workers surpassed younger ones in both kinds of jobs. Experience had a greater impact than age on performance, and they recommended a longitudinal design to remove the inherent confounding of age and experience.

Davis (1984) conducted a longitudinal analysis of 38 biodata subgroups. This seven-year follow-up showed significant univariate and multivariate differences and supported the validity of Owens & Schoenfeldt's (1979) developmental-integrative model.

Stahl (1983) reported on the development of a job choice exercise as a measure of managerial motivation that would relate to both achievement and power needs. Gough (1984) reported the development of a managerial potential scale for the CPI. Cornelius & Lane (1984) investigated the power motive and McClellan's leadership motive pattern. The results suggest that motivation to influence others may not be critical for success in technical/professional settings.

Rafaeli & Klimoski (1983) found moderate interrater reliability but no evidence of validity for the use of handwriting analysis in predicting sales success.

A novel approach for detecting faking was described by Pannone (1984), who included a nonexistent piece of equipment in a work experience checklist. Respondents who claimed to have worked with this piece of equipment showed a pattern of elevated responses to other items. Excluding fakers led to a higher validity in predicting job knowledge. Anderson et al (1984) also investigated distorted applicant responses. Applicants in 13 occupational classes rated the extent of their training and experience on job-related tasks and on bogus but superficially similar tasks. Inflation bias was prevalent and pervasive. It was negatively associated with external performance measures in five clerical classes. Two correction procedures were offered.

The point was made earlier that we need to pay more attention to the phenomena we are trying to predict. Consider the prediction of complex executive or managerial behavior. In the past two years a great deal of "soft" research has appeared about these populations, but little of it has yet found its way into our concepts and methods or into the mainstream of research. Critical insights have been provided by case studies (Kotter 1982), simulations, and interview studies at the Center for Creative Leadership by McCall, Lombardo, and their associates (Kaplan 1983, Kaplan et al 1983, Kaplan & Mazique 1983, McCall & Lombardo 1983, Lombardo & McCall 1984, McCall & Kaplan 1985) and elsewhere by Isenberg (1984) and Bentz (1983). Assessment research (Bray & Howard 1983, Lyness & Moses 1983, Moses & Lyness 1983) has also provided significant insights. Senior management predictor and validation research seldom encompasses the richness and detail conveyed in these works. We cannot blissfully assume that the concepts and techniques we use successfully for the selection and placement of nonexempt personnel will work effectively for selecting or promoting entry level supervisors. And at the senior management level, the differences are even greater, and the limitations of large-sample methods are even more apparent. Maybe a comprehensive theory for personnel selection is beyond our grasp.

Assessment Centers

Our major need is to learn more about the assessor's judgment process in real time. Borman et al (1983) sought individual differences in the validity of assessor judgments and found none that exceeded chance magnitudes. Sackett & Dreher (1982) identified methods variance associated with exercises, suggesting that the different situations the exercises represent might become specific targets for prediction. With regard to outcome research, Turnage & Muchinsky (1984) investigated the predictive validity of assessment center ratings and several traditional measures in forecasting supervisory job performance, but the authors acknowledge that the results were equivocal in many ways (criterion unreliability, aggregation biases, poorly trained assessors, etc). Ritchie & Moses (1983) found predictions of women managers' potential to be significantly related to career progress seven years later. They concluded that differences in management potential are far more attributable to individual rather than to sex differences. Schmitt et al (1984b) reported positively on the validity of an assessment center as a predictor of performance ratings for school administrators. Note that the criteria were performance measures rather than promotion measures. Lorenzo (1984) showed that experience as an assessor leads to higher proficiency in interviewing others, obtaining relevant information about job candidates, presenting and defending information about others' managerial qualifications, and communicating this information in concise written reports. Training and experience as an assessor is a major developmental intervention.

Interviews

Microanalytic studies continue to dominate interviewing research. Dipboye et al (1984) examined the effects of previewing application forms on interviewers' gathering and recall of information and the reliability and accuracy of their assessments. Reading the application before the interview increased the amount of correct information gathered during the interview, but interviewers in the nonpreview condition made more reliable evaluations of the applicants' fit to the job and performance during the interview. Rasmussen (1984) studied the joint effects of nonverbal behavior, verbal behavior, and credentials in simulated selection interviews, finding that credentials and verbal behavior play relatively larger roles than nonverbal behavior. Zedeck et al (1983) reported a few interesting individual differences among ten interviewers and higher reliability, when compared with pooled results. Parsons & Liden (1984) reported that communication skills were primary influences on judgments of qualifications when considered simultaneously with other nonverbal cues, and demographic differences were systematically related to these nonverbal cues and judgments of qualifications. Herriot & Rothwell (1983) examined the graduate recruitment interviews of 398 applicants conducted by 99 recruiters. Variables describing the conduct and content of the interviews predicted judgments of applicant suitability over and above the initial judgments made on the basis of the application form alone. Taylor & Sniezek (1984) studied the content of and reactions to college recruitment interviews. Stumpf et al (1984) conducted a longitudinal investigation of the impact of career exploration activities and interview readiness on interview results, finding that both were important in generating career opportunities. Latham & Saari (1984) reported significant correlations between what employees said they would do in hypothetical situations and what peers and supervisors observed them doing on the job. We need more outcome research along these lines to test the effectiveness of redesigned interviewing procedures.

PREDICTION PROCEDURES AND THEIR ADEQUACY

Bias

Our research on bias has become more sophisticated, but the biases are as subtle as ever. They seldom account for large amounts of variance, but their effects are still large enough to change decisions. Linn (1984) explored predictive bias in the context of the conceptual model in which predictors and criteria are viewed as fallible indicators of idealized qualifications. His emphasis is fully consistent with a latent trait approach to measurement and validation research. Following Birnbaum (1981), he outlined path models for analysis of bias. With the increasingly widespread availability of the LISREL data analysis programs, and with increasing sophistication in structural equation modeling (here is another topic that we need to embrace quickly; see James et al 1982), it is only a matter of time until we routinely see causal analyses of the relations among predictor and criterion measures.

A surprising finding of the past two decades has been that criterion performance scores for minority group members are overpredicted. The widely held expectation, in keeping with a belief that tests are biased against minority group members, was that predicted criterion performance would be lower than actual performance of minority group members. That is, there would be a bias against minority group members in that their criterion performance would be underestimated. The vast bulk of the evidence, however, shows either no difference or that use of the majority group equation overpredicts minority group performance. Schmidt & Hunter (1981) concluded that cognitive ability tests "are fair to minority group applicants in the sense that they do not underestimate expected job performance of minority groups" (p. 1128). Though this effect is well documented, its explanation is unclear. Linn & Hastings (1984) showed that the degree of overprediction decreases as the predictive accuracy for whites increases, and also that overprediction can be caused by the effects of selection of variables not included explicitly in the prediction system. They offered an adjustment procedure. Drasgow (1984) and Drasgow & Kang (1984) showed the correlation between a test and a criterion to be almost unaffected by the inclusion of culturally biased items (that is, items measuring material familiar only to a majority group). Hence, inclusion of such items on a test leads to biased measurement: a minority group member has a lower expected test score than a majority group member *of equal ability*. Nevertheless, the test criterion correlations will be essentially equal for both groups. Therefore, differential validity studies provide little or no information about measurement bias, and differential prediction studies, long advocated by many, are once again to be preferred.

Rindskopf & Everson (1984) compared multiple-regression analysis, logistic regression, and structural equation modeling as means of detecting bias in admission to graduate and professional schools. They recommended the use of multiple methods for detecting discrimination, suggesting that converging of results among methods yields stronger conclusions than using single methods. Hoover & Kolen (1984) studied the reliability of six item bias indices. The results showed that within-group sample sizes of 200 are not large enough to yield consistent decisions regarding which items are biased. Ironson et al (1984) examined the validity of three item bias techniques for detecting biased math items in which the reading level was so high for a group of students that the items were useless for assessing math knowledge. Linn & Harnisch's (1981) item response theory approach performed effectively.

To evaluate the fairness of personnel selection tests, Lawshe (1983) recommended a simple method. It consists of computing residuals for each relevant group, based on a common regression line, and then using a t-test, with residuals as the dependent variable and groups as the independent variable, to evaluate whether any of the groups are over- or underpredicted. This method is consistent with the Cleary method, but Norborg (1984) identified circumstances where this simple procedure might be misleading (within-groups slopes are different and intersect at or near the overall predictor mean). Raju & Edwards (1984) recommended the use of test characteristic curves in studying adverse impact ratios in selection despite the fact that raw score scale and ability estimates yield similar adverse impact results.

Selection Statistics and Validation

Many diverse contributions are noted in this section. Research in the military continues to lead the technological development of human resource assignment procedures. The Army Research Institute's Project B was described by Schmitz et al (1984). Kroeker & Rafacz (1983) and Kroeker & Folchi (1984) described the development of the Navy's recruit assignment model, the results of simulations of its use, and its extension to include prediction of attrition. Baker et al (1983) described the development of a microcomputer demonstration system for gathering applicant information, including computerized adaptive test scores, to serve as a database management device for assigning recruits optimally to occupational fields and training schools, providing individualized career information to applicants, and improving person-job placement. Baker (1984) described the development of computerized vocational guidance systems and reviewed five civilian and three military systems. Field trials and evaluations for these technologies are yet to come.

Alexander et al (1983) distinguished between two quite different definitions of the term "selection ratio." They recommended that selection ratio be retained as a population parameter representing the proportion of acceptable applicants, or more specifically, the proportion of individuals in the population scoring above some cutting score. The hiring rate refers to the percentage of total applicants actually hired (or promoted or selected for other treatment) and is sample-dependent. When members of an applicant sample are drawn randomly from the population, the hiring rate can be considered an estimate of the selection ratio. In practical circumstances, however, random selection from the applicant population is a questionable assumption.

Kroeck et al (1983) investigated the impact of imposed quotas on recruitment and performance. Their simulation results showed that an imposed quota that slightly exceeds a small subgroup percentage representation of the population may require extensive recruitment. It may also result in substantial performance differences between subgroups selected into the organization. A particularly important contribution regarding age discrimination was reported by Pritchard et al (1984). They offered a simulation model that accounts for the expected negative relationship between age and promotions found in the absence of age discrimination. The model gives an investigator the opportunity to compare the relationship found in actual data with what would be expected in a given situation in the absence of age discrimination.

de Gruijter & Hambleton (1984a,b) and van der Linden (1984) discussed the problems encountered when using decision theory to set cutoff scores, including inaccurate parameter estimates, choice of test model and consequences, choice of subpopulation, optimal cutoff scores on various occasions, and cutoff scores as targets.

Cascio & Zedeck (1983) offered a tutorial on the interrelations of sample size, effect size, and statistical power. Sackett & Wade (1983) extended earlier work on sample size and power, studying indirect range restriction. Contrary to earlier conclusions, the sample sizes needed to detect true validity are substantially smaller when there is indirect range restriction. With indirect range restriction, the average (N=68) validity study has a 75% chance of detecting validity, if it exists, whereas with direct range restriction, power is only 50%. Bobko (1983) analytically derived the properties of correlation coefficients corrected both for attenuation and range restriction. Bobko's results support the computation and use of the double correction and show that uncorrected coefficients grossly underestimate true validity and that the magnitude of the underestimate is inversely related to the selection ratio. Even the double corrected validity coefficients are slight underestimates. Olson & Becker (1983) also investigated corrections for range restriction. Gross & Kagen (1983) described the conditions under which not correcting for range restriction might be advantageous: small sample sizes, extreme selection, and low population correlation. Alexander et al (1984a,b) presented methods for estimating the unrestricted variance of a variable that has been reduced by direct truncation, and for correcting when both X and Y are truncated. Their work was based on Cohen's research (1959) and included a table for correcting means, standard deviations, and correlations with other variables.

Murphy (1983) investigated single-sample cross-validation designs and concluded that formula estimates for shrinkage should be preferred to single-sample cross-validation designs—they are not worth the effort or the loss of degrees of freedom. Murphy (1984) further elaborated the cost and benefit issues in cross-validation and found multiple sample estimates of cross-validity to be strongly preferable to single-sample designs. Cudeck & Browne (1983) described a cross-validation procedure for comparing the suitability of alternative models of covariance matrices. As we begin to use structural equation models in validation research, this issue will become more important. Marsh (1983) recommended conducting a preliminary factor analysis before analyzing multitrait, multimethod data whenever there is doubt about the underlying trait structure. This may help remove doubt about discriminant validity and method/halo effects because differentiating them is difficult when the relationship between observed measures and underlying traits is unclear.

The concept of synthetic validation originated with Henry Link in 1920, but it has found little application in practice. Mossholder & Arvey (1984) reviewed the concept and its history—both the J-coefficient and the job component model. This review, plus Mecham et al's (1984) writing, should stimulate both further research and practical application. Neidig & Neidig (1984) and Sackett & Dreher (1984) discussed the extent to which content validity procedures can be relied upon to show job relatedness of assessment center dimension ratings. Sackett and Dreher specified conditions under which content validity is appropriate, namely that the assessment center be used as a sample of present behavior rather than as a measure of future performance.

Jones et al (1983) presented an empirical comparison of some commonly used methods for evaluating interrater agreement. The various indices behaved differently and yielded different results, especially when there was little variation among ratings. The percent agreement method provided the most accurate measures. James et al (1984), however, showed that percent agreement is insufficient because it does not account for degrees of agreement, and a new variance-based technique was recommended. M. B. Jones (1983) reported the development of a unit-free index of individual consistency. The correlation coefficient gives the average covariance and does not indicate the degree of consistency of particular individuals.

Cohen (1983) described the high cost of dichotomization in data analysis. Assuming bivariate normality with correlation r, dichotomizing one variable at the mean results in reduction in accounted variance to $.647r^2$; dichotomizing both at the mean, to $.405r^2$. These losses result in reduction in statistical power equivalent to discarding 38% and 60% of the cases under representative conditions. As dichotomization departs from the mean, the costs in accounted variance and power are even larger.

Validity Generalization

Power and the limits of generalization are key issues. Osburn et al (1983) found that both the Callender-Osburn procedure and the Schmidt-Hunter procedure for testing the situational specificity hypothesis lack sufficient statistical power to detect low to moderate true validity variance when sample size is below 100. Raju & Burke (1983) presented two new procedures based on less restrictive assumptions than those used by Schmidt and Hunter and Callender and Osburn. Their results showed that, from a practical point of view, estimates from all of the various procedures are quite comparable. Burke (1984) reviewed validity generalization and meta-analysis based on the correlational model, presenting a tutorial on the development and use of validity generalization procedures to supplement the book by Hunter et al (1982).

Dunbar et al (1985) investigated simultaneous estimation procedures for regression functions of final course grades on a relevant set of predictors from the ASVAB. By using a technique for m-group regression, the hypothesis of validity generalization across training courses could be retained only for carefully selected subsets of courses. The findings helped delimit the range of validity generalization. Complete generalization is untenable, as is complete situational specificity; m-group regression helps to identify the limits of generalization. James & Tetrick (1984) reported the development of a multivariate test of homogeneity of regression weights for correlated data. The test involves two or more independent variables measured at a base time period and repeated measurements taken later on the same dependent variable. It will find application in time-series and cross-situational consistency analyses. Gutenberg et al (1983) showed that information processing and decision making requirements of jobs moderate the validities of both cognitive tests and dexterity tests. Cognitive tests are more valid for jobs high on information processing and decision making demands and should be used for employee selection for such jobs. The same types of tests, however, may demonstrate negative or near zero validities for jobs low on information processing and decision making and should, therefore, not be used for employee selection in such cases. Their results give meaning to the word situation, as it appears in the situational specificity hypothesis. Situation is a vague descriptor, and these results indicate that it should be defined in part by the mental demands of the job activities. Schmidt & Hunter (1984) reported a within-setting test of the situational specificity hypothesis and showed that even when the situation was held constant, there was great variability in observed outcomes. Second, they showed that the variation across studies within the same situation was almost exactly the amount predicted by formulas for sampling error. They concluded that both major predictions of the situational specificity hypothesis had been empirically disconfirmed. Finally, Schmidt et al (1985) discussed their answers to a series of questions on validity generalization.

Utility Analysis

Raters' estimates of dollar-valued criterion performance vary greatly. Bobko et al (1983) conducted an empirical test of several procedures for estimating standard deviations. Using archival data from an insurance company, they demonstrated high accuracy and also suggested a modified procedure using consensual feedback to reduce large variation in individual estimates. Burke & Frederick (1984) investigated two modified procedures using consensual feedback for estimating standard deviations. Boudreau (1983a) incorporated the flow of employees into and out of the work force as a variable affecting personnel program utility. Boudreau (1983b) next incorporated variable costs, taxes, and discounting into previously formulated utility equations. The expanded utility equation corrected previous deficiencies and removed the upward bias resulting from prior omissions.

Schmidt et al (1984) examined the utility implications of top down, minimum score cutoff equal to the mean, and minimum score cutoff one standard deviation below the mean selection procedures, finding that employers using the minimum test score cutoff method do so at a substantial economic cost. Schmidt & Hunter (1983) reported cumulated empirical data for estimating standard deviations of employee output as a percentage of mean output for jobs with non-piecework compensation systems. The standard deviation averaged 20% of mean output. For piecerate jobs the average was 15% of mean output. They concluded that their findings supported the use of 40% of salary as a dollar estimate of the standard deviation. Eaton et al (1985) investigated two additional strategies for estimating the value of performance in complex, expensive systems in which dollar values of performance are not easily estimated. Finally,

Ozer (1985) recommended the correlation coefficient rather than its square as an effect-size indicator to avoid gross underestimates of the magnitudes of relationships.

PUTTING IT ALL TOGETHER

The most significant effort in the measurement and interpretation of human differences yet undertaken began late in 1982 and will continue until 1990. It is Project A, sponsored by the Army Research Institute (Human Resources Research Organization et al 1983). Large, diverse samples of men and women from the major ethnic groups in 19 occupational specialties are being studied longitudinally—prior to entrance to the service, throughout training, and throughout their first and second tours of duty. The array of predictors, encompassing even computerized perceptual and psychomotor measures, is more diverse than in any previous research on human differences. A still greater diversity of measures is being used on the criterion side of the research equation to enable a more accurate interpretation of the meaning of those differences. Project A is vast. Millions of data points will be collected and analyzed, but what is attractive about Project A is that it is a comprehensive and coordinated program aimed both at confirming previous findings and also at adding to our scientific understanding of human differences in designing and engineering new solutions to the problems of assessing people and allocating them to positions. Every major issue in the science and practice of making personnel decisions is being addressed.

Project A is not yet well known outside of personnel research and development circles. Several convention presentations and technical reports have already appeared (many were reviewed herein), and we can look forward in the coming years to major integrated contributions to our science, engineering, and technology. But Project A won't have all the answers, and it won't put the rest of us out of business.

In summary, there are many research issues to be addressed further: How do people encode, store, and use information about jobs? What processes and factors determine what others say about a person? How do ratings relate to other measures of the same constructs? What psychological processes underlie responses to standardized prediction instruments? How can biases be neutralized? Which constructs moderate the relationships between predictors and criteria? What are the costs and benefits of systematic selection and placement? Our field is vital and burgeoning, but further research *is* urgently needed.

Literature Cited

Alexander, R. A., Alliger, G. M., Hanges, P. J. 1984a. Correcting for range restriction when the population variance is unknown. *Appl. Psychol. Meas.* 8:431–37

Alexander, R. A., Barrett, G. V., Doverspike, D. 1983. An explication of the selection ratio and its relationship to hiring rate. *J. Appl. Psychol.* 68:342–44

Alexander, R. A., Carson, K. P., Alliger, G. M., Barrett, G. V. 1984b. Correction for restriction of range when both X and Y are truncated. *Appl. Psychol. Meas.* 8:231–41

Anderson, C. D., Warner, J. L., Spencer, C. C. 1984. Inflation bias in self-assessment examinations: Implications for valid employee selection. *J. Appl. Psychol.* 69:574–80

Bachman, J. G. 1983. Schooling as a credential: Some suggestions for change. *Int. Rev. Appl. Psychol.* 32:347–60

Baker, H. G. 1984. Computerized vocational guidance (CVG) systems: Evaluation for use in military recruiting. *NPRDC Tech. Rep. 84-21.* San Diego

Baker, H. G., Rafacz, B. A., Sands, W. A. 1983. Navy personnel accessioning system (NPAS): III. Development of a microcomputer demonstration system. *NPRDC Tech. Rep. SR 83-36.* San Diego

Balzer, W. K., Rohrbaugh, J., Murphy, K. R. 1983. Reliability of actual and predicted judgments across time. *Organ. Behav. Hum. Perform.* 32:109–23

Banks, M. H., Jackson, P. R., Stafford, E. M., Warr, P. B. 1983. The job components inventory and the analysis of jobs requiring limited skill. *Personnel Psychol.* 36:57–66

Barge, B. N., Hough, L. M. 1984a. *Utility of Biographical Data: A Review and Integration of the Literature.* Minneapolis: Personnel Decis. Res. Inst.

Barge, B. N., Hough, L. M. 1984b. *Utility of Vocational Assessment: A Review and Integration of the Literature.* Minneapolis: Personnel Decis. Res. Inst.

Barnes-Farrell, J. L., Weiss, H. M. 1984. Effects of standard extremity on mixed standard scale performance ratings. *Personnel Psychol.* 37:301–16

Barrett, G. V., Caldwell, M. S., Alexander, R. A. 1985. The concept of dynamic criteria: A critical reanalysis. *Personnel Psychol.* 38:41–56

Bartlett, C. J. 1983. What's the difference between valid and invalid halo? Forced-choice measurement without forcing a choice. *J. Appl. Psychol.* 68:218–26

Baxter, B. 1965. *Quo vadis?* President's Address, Div. Ind. Psychol., Am. Psychol. Assoc., Chicago

Benson, P. G., Dickinson, T. L. 1983. Mixed standard scale response inconsistencies as reliability indices. *Educ. Psychol. Meas.* 43:781–89

Bentz, V. J. 1983. *Success, failures and tragic flaws among high level executives: Recent findings.* Presented at VPI Conf. on Pers. and Perform., Blacksburg, VA

Birnbaum, M. H. 1981. Reply to McLaughlin: Proper path models for theoretical partialling. *Am. Psychol.* 36:1193–95

Bobko, P. 1983. An analysis of correlations corrected for attenuation and range restriction. *J. Appl. Psychol.* 68:584–89

Bobko, P., Karren, R., Parkington, J. J. 1983. Estimation of standard deviations in utility analyses: An empirical test. *J. Appl. Psychol.* 68:170–76

Borman, W. C., Eaton, N. K., Bryan, J. D., Rosse, R. L. 1983. Validity of army recruiter behavioral assessment: Does the assessor make a difference? *J. Appl. Psychol.* 68:415–19

Borman, W. C., Motowidlo, S. J., Rose, S. R., Hanser, L. M. 1984a. Development of a model of soldier effectiveness. *Personnel Decis. Res. Inst. Rep. 95.* Minneapolis

Borman, W. C., White, L. A., Gast, I. F. 1984b. *Factors relating to peer and supervisor ratings of job performance.* Presented at Ann. Meet. Am. Psychol. Assoc., 92nd, Toronto

Boudreau, J. W. 1983a. Effects of employee flows on utility analysis of human resource productivity improvement programs. *J. Appl. Psychol.* 68:396–406

Boudreau, J. W. 1983b. Economic considerations in estimating the utility of human resource productivity improvement programs. *Personnel Psychol.* 36:551–76

Bray, D. W., Howard, A. 1983. Personality and the assessment center method. *Adv. Pers. Assess.* 3:1–34

Burke, M. J. 1984. Validity generalization: A review and critique of the correlation model. *Personnel Psychol.* 37:93–115

Burke, M. J., Frederick, J. T. 1984. Two modified procedures for estimating standard deviations in utility analyses. *J. Appl. Psychol.* 69:482–89

Cain, P. S., Green, B. F. 1983. Reliabilities of selected ratings available from the *Dictionary of Occupational Titles. J. Appl. Psychol.* 68:155–65

Campion, M. A. 1983. Personnel selection for physically demanding jobs: Review and recommendations. *Personnel Psychol.* 36:527–50

Cardy, R. L., Kehoe, J. F. 1984. Rater selective attention ability and appraisal effectiveness: The effect of a cognitive style on the accuracy of differentiation among ratees. *J. Appl. Psychol.* 68:155–65

Cascio, W. F., Zedeck, S. 1983. Open a new window in rational research planning: Adjust alpha to maximize statistical power. *Personnel Psychol.* 36:517–26

Chatfield, R. E., Royle, M. H. 1983. Methods to improve task inventory construction. *NPRDC Tech. Rep. TR 83–36.* San Diego

Cleveland, J. N., Landy, F. J. 1983. The effects of person and job stereotypes on two personnel decisions. *J. Appl. Psychol.* 68:609–19

Cohen, A. C. 1959. Simplified estimators for the normal distribution when samples are singly censored or truncated. *Technometrics* 1:217–37

Cohen, J. 1983. The cost of dichotomization. *Appl. Psychol. Meas.* 7:249–53

Cooper, W. H. 1983. Internal homogeneity, descriptiveness, and halo: Resurrecting some answers and questions about the structure of job performance rating categories. *Personnel Psychol.* 36:489–502

Cornelius, E. T. III, DeNisi, A. S., Blencoe, A. G. 1984a. Expert and naive raters using the PAQ: Does it matter? *Personnel Psychol.* 37:453–64

Cornelius, E. T. III, Lane, F. B. 1984. The power motive and managerial success in a professionally oriented service industry organization. *J. Appl. Psychol.* 69:32–39

Cornelius, E. T. III, Schmidt, F. L., Carron, T. J. 1984b. Job classification approaches and the implementation of validity generalization results. *Personnel Psychol.* 37:247–60

Cotton, B., Jacobs, R., Grogan, J. 1983. Use of individually scaled versus normatively scaled predictor cues in policy-capturing research. *Appl. Psychol. Meas.* 7:159–71

Cudeck, R., Browne, M. W. 1983. Cross-validation of covariance structures. *Multivar. Behav. Res.* 18:147–67

Cunningham, J. W., Boese, R. R., Neeb, R. W., Pass, J. J. 1983. Systematically derived work dimensions: Factor analyses of the occupation analysis inventory. *J. Appl. Psychol.* 68:232–52

Davis, K. R. Jr. 1984. A longitudinal analysis of biographical subgroups using Owens' developmental integrative model. *Personnel Psychol.* 37:1–14

de Gruijter, D. N., Hambleton, R. K. 1984a. On problems encountered using decision theory to set cutoff scores. *Appl. Psychol. Meas.* 8:1–8

de Gruijter, D. N., Hambleton, R. K. 1984b. Reply to van der Linden's "Thoughts on the use of decision theory to set cutoff scores." *Appl. Psychol. Meas.* 8:19–20

DeNisi, A. S., Cafferty, T. P., Meglino, B. M. 1984. A cognitive view of the performance appraisal process: A model and research propositions. *Organ. Behav. Hum. Perform.* 33:360–96

DeNisi, A. S., Randolph, W. A., Blencoe, A. G. 1983. Potential problems with peer ratings. *Acad. Manage. J.* 26:457–64

Dipboye, R. L., Fontenelle, G. A., Garner, K. 1984. Effects of previewing the application on interview process and outcomes. *J. Appl. Psychol.* 69:118–28

Distefano, M. K. Jr., Pryer, M. W., Erffmeyer, R. C. 1983. Application of content validity methods to the development of a job-related performance rating criterion. *Personnel Psychol.* 36:621–31

Drasgow, F. 1984. Scrutinizing psychological tests: Measurement equivalence and equivalent relations with external variables are central issues. *Psychol. Bull.* 95:134–35

Drasgow, F., Kang, T. 1984. Statistical power of differential validity and differential prediction analyses for detecting measurement nonequivalence. *J. Appl. Psychol.* 69:498–508

Drasgow, F., Lissak, R. I. 1983. Modified parallel analysis: A procedure for examining the latent dimensionality of dichotomously scored item responses. *J. Appl. Psychol.* 68:363–73

Drasgow, F., Parsons, C. K., 1983. Application of unidimensional item response theory models to multidimensional data. *Appl. Psychol. Meas.* 7:189–99

Dunbar, S. B., Mayekawa, S., Novick, M. R. 1985. Simultaneous estimation of regression functions for marine corps technical training specialties. *ONR Tech. Rep. 85-1.* Cada Res. Group, Univ. Iowa, Iowa City

Dunnette, M. D. 1963a. A note on *the* criterion. *J. Appl. Psychol.* 47:317–23

Dunnette, M. D. 1963b. A modified model for test validation and selection research. *J. Appl. Psychol.* 47:251–54

Dunnette, M. D. 1966. Fads, fashions, and folderol in psychology. *Am. Psychol.* 21:343–52

Dunnette, M. D., Fleishman, E. A., eds. 1982. *Human Performance and Productivity*, Vol. 1: *Human Capability Assessment.* Hillsdale, NJ: Erlbaum

Eaton, N. K., Wing, H., Mitchell, K. J. 1985. Alternate methods of estimating the dollar value of performance. *Personnel Psychol.* 38:27–40

Embretson (Whitely), S. 1983. Construct validity: Construct representation versus nomothetic span. *Psychol. Bull.* 93:179–97

Eyde, L. D., Kowal, D. M. 1984. Ethical and professional concerns regarding computerized test interpretation services and users. Presented at Symp. *The User of Computer-Based Interpretations: Prospects and*

Problems at Ann. Meet. Am. Psychol. Assoc., 92nd, Toronto

Eyde, L. D., Primoff, E. S., Hardt, R. H. 1983. What should the content of content validity be? *OPRD-Rep. 83-5*. US Off. Personnel Res. Dev., Washington, DC

Fleishman, E. A., Quaintance, M. K. 1984. *Taxonomies of Human Performance: The Description of Human Tasks*. Orlando, FL: Academic

Flynn, J. R. 1984. The mean IQ of Americans: Massive gains 1932 to 1978. *Psychol. Bull.* 95:29–51

Fox, S., Bizman, A., Herrmann, E. 1983. The halo effect: Is it a unitary concept? *J. Occup. Psychol.* 56:289–96

Giniger, S., Dispenzieri, A., Eisenberg, J. 1983. Age, experience, and performance on speed and skill jobs in an applied setting. *J. Appl. Psychol.* 68:469–75

Gordon, M. E., Fitzgibbons, W. J. 1982. Empirical test of the validity of seniority as a factor in staffing decisions. *J. Appl. Psychol.* 67:311–19

Gough, H. G. 1984. A managerial potential scale for the California Psychological Inventory. *J. Appl. Psychol.* 69:233–40

Green, B. F., Bock, R. D., Humphreys, L. G., Linn, R. L., Reckase, M. D. 1984. Technical guidelines for assessing computerized adaptive tests. *J. Educ. Meas.* 21:347–60

Gross, A. L., Kagen, E. 1983. Not correcting for restriction of range can be advantageous. *Educ. Psychol. Meas.* 43:389–96

Gutenberg, R. L., Arvey, R. D., Osburn, H. G., Jeanneret, P. R. 1983. Moderating effects of decision-making/information processing job dimensions on test validities. *J. Appl. Psychol.* 68:602–8

Heneman, R. L., Wexley, K. N. 1983. The effects of time delay in rating and amount of information observed on performance rating accuracy. *Acad. Manage. J.* 26:677–86

Herriot, P., Rothwell, C. 1983. Expectations and impressions in the graduate selection interview. *J. Occup. Psychol.* 56:303–14

Hobson, C. J., Gibson, F. W. 1983. Policy capturing as an approach to understanding and improving performance appraisal: A review of the literature. *Acad. Manage. Rev.* 8:640–49

Hogan, J., Hogan, R., Busch, C. M. 1984. How to measure service orientation. *J. Appl. Psychol.* 69:167–73

Hoover, H. D., Kolen, M. J. 1984. The reliability of six item bias indices. *Appl. Psychol. Meas.* 8:173–81

Hough, L. M. 1984. Development and evaluation of the "accomplishment record" method of selecting and promoting professionals. *J. Appl. Psychol.* 69:135–46

Hough, L. M., Keyes, M. A., Dunnette, M. D. 1983. An evaluation of three "alternative"

selection procedures. *Personnel Psychol.* 36:261–76

Hulin, C. L., Drasgow, F., Parsons, C. K. 1983. *Item Response Theory: Application to Psychological Measurement*. Homewood, IL: Dow Jones-Irwin, Dorsey Professional Series

Human Resources Research Organization, American Institutes for Research, Personnel Decisions Research Institute, Army Research Institute. 1983. Improving the selection, classification, and utilization of army enlisted personnel: Annual report. *ARI Res. Rep. 1347*

Hunt, E. 1983. On the nature of intelligence. *Science* 219:141–46

Hunter, J. E. 1983. A causal analysis of cognitive ability, job knowledge, job performance, and supervisor ratings. In *Performance Measurement and Theory*, ed. F. Landy, S. Zedeck, J. Cleveland, pp. 257–66. Hillsdale, NJ: Erlbaum

Hunter, J. E., Hunter, R. F. 1984. Validity and utility of alternative predictors of job performance. *Psychol. Bull.* 96:72–98

Hunter, J. E., Schmidt, F. L., Jackson, G. B. 1982. *Meta-Analysis: Cumulating Research Findings Across Studies*. Beverly Hills, CA: Sage

Ilgen, D. R., Feldman, J. M. 1983. Performance appraisal: A process approach. In *Research in Organizational Behavior*, Vol. 5, ed. B. M. Staw, L. L. Cummings, pp. 141–98. Greenwich, CT: JAI Press

Ironson, G., Homan, S., Willis, R., Singer, B. 1984. The validity of item bias techniques with math word problems. *Appl. Psychol. Meas.* 8:391–96

Isenberg, D. J. 1984. How senior managers think. *Harvard Bus. Rev*, Nov.–Dec: 81–90

James, L. R., Brett, J. M. 1984. Mediators, moderators, and tests for mediation. *J. Appl. Psychol.* 69:307–21

James, L. R., Demaree, R. G., Wolf, G. 1984. Estimating within-group interrater reliability with and without response bias. *J. Appl. Psychol.* 69:85–98

James, L. R., Mulaik, S. A., Brett, J. M. 1982. *Causal Analysis: Assumptions, Models, and Data*. Beverly Hills, CA: Sage

James, L. R., Tetrick, L. E. 1984. A multivariate test of homogeneity of regression weights for correlated data. *Educ. Psychol. Meas.* 44:769–80

Jones, A. P., Johnson, L. A., Butler, M. C., Main, D. S. 1983. Apples and oranges: An empirical comparison of commonly used indices of interrater agreement. *Acad. Manage. J.* 26:507–19

Jones, M. B. 1983. A unit-free index of individual consistency. *Educ. Psychol. Meas.* 43:379–87

Kamp, J. D., Hough, L. M. 1984. *Utility of*

Personality Assessment: A Review and an Integration of the Literature. Minneapolis: Personnel Decis. Res. Inst.

Kaplan, R. E. 1983. Fixing relationships through joint action. *Cent. Creat. Leadership Tech. Rep. 24.* Greensboro, NC

Kaplan, R. E., Lombardo, M. M., Mazique, M. S. 1983. A mirror for managers: Using simulation to develop management teams. *Cent. Creat. Leadership Tech. Rep. 23.* Greensboro, NC

Kaplan, R. E., Mazique, M. S. 1983. Trade routes: The manager's network of relationships. *Cent. Creat. Leadership Tech. Rep. 22.* Greensboro, NC

Komaki, J. L. 1984. Toward effective supervision: An operant analysis and comparison of managers at work. Presented at Symp. *Back to the Basics: Describing Leaders* at Ann. Meet. Am. Psychol. Assoc., 92nd, Toronto

Kotter, J. P. 1982. *The General Manager.* New York: Free Press

Kraiger, K., Ford, J. K. 1985. A meta-analysis of ratee race effects in performance ratings. *J. Appl. Psychol.* 70:56–65

Kroeck, K. G., Barrett, G. V., Alexander, R. A. 1983. Imposed quotas and personnel selection: A computer simulation study. *J. Appl. Psychol.* 68:123–36

Kroeker, L., Folchi, J. 1984. Classification and assignment within pride (CLASP) system: Development and evaluation of an attrition component. *NPRDC Tech. Rep. TR 84-40.* San Diego

Kroeker, L. P., Rafacz, B. A. 1983. Classification and assignment within pride (CLASP): A recruit assignment model. *NPRDC Tech. Rep. TR 84-9.* San Diego

Kulik, J. A., Bangert-Drowns, R. L., Kulik, C-L. C. 1984. Effectiveness of coaching for aptitude tests. *Psychol. Bull* 95:179–88

Landy, F., Zedeck, S., Cleveland, J. 1983. *Performance Measurement and Theory.* Hillsdale, NY: Erlbaum

Larson, G. E., Rimland, B. 1984. Officer performance evaluation systems: Lessons learned from experience. *NPRDC Tech. Rep. TR 85-6.* San Diego

Latham, G. P., Saari, L. M. 1984. Do people do what they say? Further studies on the situational interview. *J. Appl. Psychol.* 69:569–73

Lawshe, C. H. 1983. A simplified approach to the evaluation of fairness in employee selection procedures. *Personnel Psychol.* 36:601–8

Lawshe, C. H. 1984. *A practitioner's thoughts on job analysis.* Presented at Conf. Content Validity III, Bowling Green State Univ., Bowling Green, OH

Lawshe, C. H. 1985. Inferences from personnel tests and their validity. *J. Appl. Psychol.* 70:237–38

Levine, E. L., Ash, R. A., Hall, H., Sistrunk, F. 1983. Evaluation of job analysis methods by experienced job analysts. *Acad. Manage. J.* 26:339–48

Levine, M. V., Drasgow, F. 1982. Appropriateness measurement: Review, critique and validating studies. *Br. J. Math. Stat. Psychol.* 3:42–56

Levine, M. V., Drasgow, F. 1983. The relation between incorrect option choice and estimated ability. *Educ. Psychol. Meas.* 43:675–85

Linn, R. L. 1984. Selection bias: Multiple meanings. *J. Educ. Meas.* 21:33–47

Linn, R. L., Harnisch, D. 1981. Interactions between item content and group membership on achievement test items. *J. Educ. Meas.* 18:109–18

Linn, R. L., Hastings, N. 1984. Group differentiated prediction. *Appl. Psychol. Meas.* 8:165–72

Lombardo, M. M., McCall, M. W. Jr. 1984. Coping with an intolerable boss. *Cent. Creative Leadership Spec. Rep.,* Greensboro, NC

Lorenzo, R. V. 1984. Effects of assessorship on managers' proficiency in acquiring, evaluating, and communicating information about people. *Personnel Psychol.* 37:617–34

Lyness, K. S., Moses, J. L. 1983. *Measurement strategies for studying ambiguity and managerial behavior.* Presented at Ann. Conv. Am. Psychol. Assoc., 91st, Anaheim

Marsh, H. W. 1983. Multitrait-multimethod analysis: Distinguishing between items and traits. *Educ. Psychol. Meas.* 43:351–58

McCall, M. W. Jr., Kaplan, R. E. 1985. *Whatever it Takes: Decision Makers at Work.* Englewood Cliffs, NJ: Prentice-Hall

McCall, M. W. Jr., Lombardo, M. M. 1983. Off the track: Why and how successful executives get derailed. *Cent. Creative Leadership Tech. Rep. 21.* Greensboro, NC

McIntyre, R. M., Smith, D. E., Hassett, C. E. 1984. Accuracy of performance ratings as affected by rater training and perceived purpose of rating. *J. Appl. Psychol.* 69:147–56

Mecham, R. C., McCormick, E. J., Jeanneret, P. R. 1984. Job component validity based on the PAQ: Its conceptual and empirical basis as contrasted with that of situational validity generalization. *PAQ Newsl.,* pp. 192–216

Meritt-Haston, R., Wexley, K. N. 1983. Educational requirements: Legality and validity. *Personnel Psychol.* 36:743–53

Moreno, K. E., Wetzel, C. D., McBride, J. R., Weiss, D. J. 1984. Relationship between corresponding armed services vocational aptitude battery (ASVAB) and computerized adaptive testing (CAT) subtests. *Appl. Psychol. Meas.* 8:155–63

Morrison, R. F., Cook, T. M. 1983. *Military officer career development and decision making: A multiple-cohort longitudinal an-*

alysis. Presented at Ann. Meet. Am. Psychol. Assoc., 91st, Anaheim

Moses, J. L., Lyness, K. S. 1983. *A conceptual model for studying ambiguity and managerial behavior*. Presented at Ann. Meet. Am. Psychol. Assoc., 91st, Anaheim

Mossholder, K. W., Arvey, R. D. 1984. Synthetic validity: A conceptual and comparative review. *J. Appl. Psychol.* 69:322–33

Mossholder, K. W., Bedeian, A. G. 1983. Cross-level inference and organizational research: Perspectives on interpretation and application. *Acad. Manage. Rev.* 8:547–58

Mount, M. K. 1984. Psychometric properties of subordinate ratings of managerial performance. *Personnel Psychol.* 37:687–702

Mumford, M. D. 1983. Social comparison theory and the evaluation of peer evaluations: A review and some applied implications. *Personnel Psychol.* 36:867–81

Murphy, K. R. 1983. Fooling yourself with cross-validation: Single sample designs. *Personnel Psychol.* 36:111–18

Murphy, K. R. 1984. Cost-benefit considerations in choosing among cross-validation methods. *Personnel Psychol.* 37:15–22

Murphy, K. R., Balzer, W. K., Kellam, K. L., Armstrong, J. G. 1984. Effects of the purpose of rating on accuracy in observing teacher behavior and evaluating teaching performance. *J. Educ. Psychol.* 76:45–54

Murphy, K. R., Balzer, W. K., Lockhart, M. C., Eisenman, E. J. 1985. Effects of previous performance on evaluations of present performance. *J. Appl. Psychol.* 70:72–84

Nathan, B. R., Lord, R. G. 1983. Cognitive categorization and dimensional schemata: A process approach to the study of halo in performance ratings. *J. Appl. Psychol.* 68:102–14

Neidig, R. D., Neidig, P. J. 1984. Multiple assessment center exercises and job relatedness. *J. Appl. Psychol.* 69:182–86

Norborg, J. M. 1984. A warning regarding the simplified approach to the evaluation of test fairness in employee selection procedures. *Personnel Psychol.* 37:483–86

Nunnally, J. 1960. The place of statistics in psychology. *Educ. Psychol. Meas.* 20:641–50

Olian, J. D. 1984. Genetic screening for employment purposes. *Personnel Psychol.* 37:423–38

Olson, C. A., Becker, B. E. 1983. A proposed technique for the treatment of restriction of range in selection validation. *Psychol. Bull.* 93:137–48

Olson, D. M., Borman, W. C. 1984. *Relationships between scales on an army work environment questionnaire and measures of performance*. Presented at Ann. Meet. Am. Psychol. Assoc., 92nd, Toronto

Osborn, W. 1983. Issues and strategies in measuring performance in army jobs. Presented at Symp. *Integrated Criterion Measurement for Large Scale Computerized Selection and Classification* at Ann. Meet. Am. Psychol. Assoc., 91st, Anaheim

Osburn, H. G., Callender, J. C., Greener, J. M., Ashworth, S. 1983. Statistical power of tests of the situational specificity hypothesis in validity generalization studies: A cautionary note. *J. Appl. Psychol.* 68:115–22

Owens, W. A. 1984. *A generalized classification of persons—Box within a box*. Presented at Ann. Meet. Am. Psychol. Assoc., 92nd, Toronto

Owens, W. A., Schoenfeldt, L. F. 1979. Toward a classification of persons. *J. Appl. Psychol.* 65:569–607

Ozer, D. J. 1985. Correlation and the coefficient of determination. *Psychol. Bull.* 97:307–15

Pannone, R. D. 1984. Predicting test performance: A content valid approach to screening applicants. *Personnel Psychol.* 37:507–14

Parsons, C. K., Liden, R. C. 1984. Interviewer perceptions of applicant qualifications: A multivariate field study of demographic characteristics and nonverbal cues. *J. Appl. Psychol.* 69:557–68

Peters, L. H., O'Connor, E. J., Weekley, J., Pooyan, A. 1984. Sex bias and managerial evaluations: A replication and extension. *J. Appl. Psychol.* 69:349–52

Phillips, J. S. 1984. The accuracy of leadership ratings: A cognitive categorization perspective. *Organ. Behav. Hum. Perform.* 33:125–38

Pritchard, R. D., Maxwell, S. E., Jordan, W. C. 1984. Interpreting relationships between age and promotion in age-discrimination cases. *J. Appl. Psychol.* 69:199–206

Pulakos, E. D. 1984. A comparison of rater training programs: Error training and accuracy training. *J. Appl. Psychol.* 69:581–88

Pulakos, E. D., Wexley, K. N. 1983. The relationship among perceptual similarity, sex, and performance ratings in manager-subordinate dyads. *Acad. Manage. J.* 26:129–39

Rafaeli, A., Klimoski, R. J. 1983. Predicting sales success through handwriting analysis: An evaluation of the effects of training and handwriting sample content. *J. Appl. Psychol.* 68:212–17

Raju, N. S., Burke, M. J. 1983. Two new procedures for studying validity generalization. *J. Appl. Psychol.* 68:382–95

Raju, N. S., Edwards, J. E. 1984. Note on "Adverse impact from a psychometric perspective." *J. Appl. Psychol.* 69:191–93

Rambo, W. W., Chomiak, A. M., Price, J. M.

1983. Consistency of performance under stable conditions of work. *J. Appl. Psychol.* 68:78–87

Rasmussen, K. G. Jr. 1984. Nonverbal behavior, verbal behavior, resumé credentials, and selection interview outcomes. *J. Appl. Psychol.* 69:551–56

Rindskopf, D., Everson, H. 1984. A comparison of models for detecting discrimination: An example from medical school admissions. *Appl. Psychol. Meas.* 8:89–109

Ritchie, R. J., Moses, J. L. 1983. Assessment center correlates of women's advancement into middle management: A 7-year longitudinal analysis. *J. Appl. Psychol.* 68:227–31

Robinson, D. D. 1984. A flowchart of a computerized system for identifying alternative occupations for rehabilitation clients. *Pain.* Suppl. 2, World Congr. on Pain, 4th Int. Assoc. Study of Pain, Seattle

Rumsey, M. G. 1984. *Building performance measures with occupational survey data.* Presented at Army Occup. Surv. Prog. (AOSP) Users' Conf., Alexandria, VA

Sackett, P. R., Dreher, G. F. 1982. Constructs and assessment center dimensions: Some troubling empirical findings. *J. Appl. Psychol.* 67:401–10

Sackett, P. R., Dreher, G. F. 1984. Situation specificity of behavior and assessment center validation strategies: A rejoinder to Neidig and Neidig. *J. Appl. Psychol.* 69:187–90

Sackett, P. R., Harris, M. M. 1984. Honesty testing for personnel selection: A review and critique. *Personnel Psychol.* 37:221–45

Sackett, P. R., Wade, B. E. 1983. On the feasibility of criterion-related validity: The effects of range restriction assumptions on needed sample size. *J. Appl. Psychol.* 68:374–81

Sands, W. A., Gade, P. A. 1983. An application of computerized adaptive testing in U.S. Army recruiting. *J. Comput.-Based Instr.* 10(3/4):87–89

Schmidt, F. L., Hunter, J. E. 1981. Employment testing: Old theories and new research findings. *Am. Psychol.* 36:1128–37

Schmidt, F. L., Hunter, J. E. 1983. Individual differences in productivity: An empirical test of estimates derived from studies of selection procedure utility. *J. Appl. Psychol.* 68:407–14

Schmidt, F. L., Hunter, J. E. 1984. A within-setting empirical test of the situational specificity hypothesis in personnel selection. *Personnel Psychol.* 37:317–26

Schmidt, F. L., Hunter, J. E., Croll, P. R., McKenzie, R. C. 1983. Estimation of employment test validities by expert judgment. *J. Appl. Psychol.* 68:590–601

Schmidt, F. L., Hunter, J. E., Pearlman, K., Hirsh, H. R. 1985. Forty questions about validity generalization and meta-analysis. *Personnel Psychol.* 38: In press

Schmidt, F. L., Mack, M. J., Hunter, J. E. 1984. Selection utility in the occupation of U.S. park ranger for three modes of test use. *J. Appl. Psychol.* 69:490–97

Schmitt, N., Gooding, R. Z., Noe, R. A., Kirsch, M. 1984a. Metaanalyses of validity studies published between 1964 and 1982 and the investigation of study characteristics. *Personnel Psychol.* 37:407–22

Schmitt, N., Noe, R. A., Meritt, R., Fitzgerald, M. P. 1984b. Validity of assessment center ratings for the prediction of performance ratings and school climate of school administrators. *J. Appl. Psychol.* 69:207–13

Schmitz, E. J., Nord, R., McWhite, R. 1984. Development of the army's personnel allocation system. *ARI Tech. Rep. 647*

Silverman, S. B., Wexley, K. N., Johnson, J. C. 1984. The effects of age and job experience on employee responses to a structured job analysis questionnaire. *Public Personnel Manage. J.* 13:355–59

Stahl, M. J. 1983. Achievement, power, and managerial motivation: Selecting managerial talent with the job choice exercise. *Personnel Psychol.* 36:775–89

Stone, D. L., Gueutal, H. G., McIntosh, B. 1984. The effects of feedback sequence and expertise of the rater on perceived feedback accuracy. *Personnel Psychol.* 37:487–506

Stumpf, S. A., Austin, E. J., Hartman, K. 1984. The impact of career exploration and interview readiness on interview performance and outcomes. *J. Vocat. Behav.* 24:221–35

Stutzman, T. M. 1983. Within classification job differences. *Personnel Psychol.* 36:503–15

Taylor, M. S., Sniezek, J. A. 1984. The college recruitment interview: Topical content and applicant reactions. *J. Occup. Psychol.* 57:157–68

Thorndike, R. L. 1949. *Personnel Selection.* New York: Wiley

Turnage, J. J., Muchinsky, P. M. 1984. A comparison of the predictive validity of assessment center evaluations versus traditional measures in forecasting supervisory job performance: Interpretive implications of criterion distortion for the assessment paradigm. *J. Appl. Psychol.* 69:595–602

Tziner, A. 1984. A fairer examination of rating scales when used for performance appraisal in a real organizational setting. *J. Occup. Behav.* 5:103–12

Vance, R. J., Winne, P. S., Wright, E. S. 1983. A longitudinal examination of rater and ratee effects in performance ratings. *Personnel Psychol.* 36:609–20

van der Linden, W. J. 1984. Some thoughts on the use of decision theory to set cutoff scores:

Comment on de Gruijter and Hambleton. *Appl. Psychol. Meas.* 8:9–17

Veres, J. F., Feild, H. S., Boyles, W. R. 1983. Administrative versus research performance ratings: An empirical test of rating data quality. *Public Personnel Manage.* 12:290–98

Wallace, M. J. Jr. 1983. Methodology, research practice, and progress in personnel and industrial relations. *Acad. Manage. Rev.* 8:6–13

Wallace, S. R. 1965. Criteria for what? *Am. Psychol.* 20:411–17

Wetrogan, L. I., Olson, D. M., Sperling, H. M. 1983. *A systemic model of work performance.* Presented at Ann. Meet. Am. Psychol. Assoc., 91st, Anaheim

Wing, H., Peterson, N. G., Hoffman, R. G. 1984. *Expert judgments of predictor-criterion validity relationships.* Presented at Ann. Meet. Am. Psychol. Assoc., 92nd, Toronto

Zedeck, S., Tziner, A., Middlestadt, S. E. 1983. Interviewer validity and reliability: An individual analysis approach. *Personnel Psychol.* 36:355–70

Ann. Rev. Psychol. 1986. 37:381–407

ENVIRONMENTAL PSYCHOLOGY

Charles J. Holahan

Department of Psychology, University of Texas, Austin, Texas 78712

CONTENTS

ENVIRONMENTAL ASSESSMENT 383
   Theoretically Oriented Work.. 383
   Applied Work 385
   Summary and Critique 387
COGNITIVE MAPPING.. 388
   Theoretically Oriented Work.. 388
   Applied Work 390
   Summary and Critique 391
ENVIRONMENTAL STRESS... 392
   Theoretically Oriented Work.. 392
   Applied Work 394
   Summary and Critique 396
SPATIAL BEHAVIOR... 397
   Theoretically Oriented Work.. 397
   Applied Work 399
   Summary and Critique 400
GENERAL DIRECTIONS FOR FUTURE RESEARCH...................................... 401

Environmental psychology studies the interrelationship between the physical environment and human behavior and experience. It emerged in the later half of the 1960s as a problem-focused discipline, responding to practical questions posed by architects and planners about real-world design decisions. During the 1970s, in addition to continued problem-oriented work, the field took its first steps toward theory development. Initial theories on the effects of crowding, cognitive development, environmental preference, and spatial behavior, while broadly framed and only partially tested, offered organizing foci for programmatic research and intellectual dialogue (see Proshansky & Altman 1979).

Environmental psychology's emergence into the 1980s was hailed as a "coming of age" (Canter & Craik 1981), though pride over past accomplish

0066-4308/86/0201-0381$02.00

ments was balanced by a recognition of future challenges (Stokols 1982). In fact, a measured development has characterized the field during the first half of the 1980s—a coalescing of work around established interests, along with a refinement in conceptual clarity and interpretive precision and some broadening in the investigative scope of traditional concerns. The primary areas of investigation during this period—environmental assessment, cognitive mapping, environmental stress, and spatial behavior—have been represented in each of the previous *Annual Review of Psychology* chapters (Craik 1973, Stokols 1978, Russell & Ward 1982). At the same time, investigative priorities within these areas have shifted in recent years.

Environmental assessment is beginning to receive the kind of conceptual interest it warrants (e.g. Canter 1983a, Russell & Lanius 1984), though the link between the major empirical focus on Perceived Environmental Quality Indices (PEQIs) and emerging conceptual models is weak. Cognitive mapping is seeing refinements in its long-standing interest in the development of environmental cognition (e.g. Biel 1982, Conning & Byrne 1984), though basic knowledge about the nature of spatial cognition that is accruing in the cognitive sciences is only slowly penetrating environmental psychology. Research on environmental stress has matured into comprehensive and testable models of human reactions to environmental stressors (e.g. Baum et al 1982b), and has broadened in scope beyond traditional interests in crowding and noise to encompass technological risk (e.g. Baum et al 1983a). While work on spatial behavior, central to environmental psychology in its early years, is still extensive, primary emphases have continued to be methodological, with the most interesting new work involving a more refined understanding of territoriality and crime (e.g. Taylor et al 1985).

Although a distinction between cognitive and behavioral emphases continues to be useful in describing research in the field (see Stokols 1978), such a dichotomy is somewhat more forced than previously. Cognitive mediators are now routinely offered in explaining behavioral reactions to stressors (Baum et al 1982a), "place" encompasses both cognitive and behavioral referents (Genereaux et al 1983), and work on orientation aids seeks to facilitate behavior by clarifying corresponding spatial images (Levine et al 1984). The bridge between theory and application continues to be crossed less often, though here too there are important exceptions. Especially noteworthy have been attempts to apply and refine conceptual models of environmental stress in examining the human effects of the nuclear accident at Three Mile Island (Baum et al 1983c).

Applied work relating to environmental assessment continues to be principally evident in PEQIs, and has focused on wilderness and natural environments as well as on residential settings. Cognitive mapping work has moved away from earlier emphases on applications at the urban scale to less ambitious and more focused efforts to develop and test orientation aids in architectural settings such as public buildings (Levine et al 1984). Work relating to environmental stress continues to be reflected in long-standing interests in therapeutic environments as well as in high-rise housing, though the tendency of applied work in both of these areas to be atheoretical also continues. In contrast, applications to technological risk have attempted to be socially useful while simultaneously testing and refining basic models of environmental stress (Baum et al 1983c). A mushrooming interest in office environments, while initiated by a broader concern with postoccupancy evaluation, has also provided an opportunity to enhance privacy in the workplace (Sundstrom et al 1982a). Again, however, applied work in offices has been tied only weakly to conceptual models of privacy and spatial behavior.

In this review, work relating to environmental assessment, cognitive mapping, environmental stress, and spatial behavior is discussed sequentially. The first two areas reflect a primarily cognitive emphasis and the later two a primarily behavioral one. In each case, theoretical work will be reviewed before the corresponding, more place-specific applied work. Each of these major sections is followed by a summary and critique. A final section examines general directions for future research in environmental psychology.

ENVIRONMENTAL ASSESSMENT

Theoretically Oriented Work

GENERAL MODELS   Russell & Lanius (1984) hypothesized a link between the theory of adaptation level (Helson 1964) and environmental assessment. After Russell & Pratt (1980), they described affective appraisals of the environment in terms of a circular ordering of affective categories in a two-dimensional space defined by orthogonal pleasure and arousal axes. Using photographs of environmental scenes with college students, they found that changes in assessments of environments' degree of pleasantness and arousal quality, as well as of more categorical affective descriptors (e.g. "sad" or "calm"), were predictable from systematic variations in prior adaptation level. Adaptation level was varied by the affective nature of an earlier scene the students were exposed to. Russell and Lanius's findings show that prior scenes we have adapted to affect our assessments of later scenes, and these changes in assessments can be described in a multivariate way that emphasizes independent dimensions of pleasure and arousal.

Canter (1983a) provided a multivariate and purposive model of "place evaluation" that envisioned place evaluation in terms of the degree to which a place is seen as helping to achieve goals at different levels of interaction with the place. While Russell & Lanius's (1984) model emphasizes the psychophysical dimension, Canter's underscores a cognitive one. He explained that place evaluation can be understood in terms of three facets: the place's social, spatial, and service *referents,* the *level* of interaction with the place, and the degree of specificity or *focus* of the association with the place. The facet approach to theory definition is used to provide a structural framework for converting the multiple classification scheme of referent, level, and focus into a set of related testable hypotheses.

The cognitive component in environmental assessment is also emphasized in the work of S. Kaplan (1982), where environmental preference is viewed in terms of decision making and choice. Kaplan argued that considerable cognitive analysis and calculation precede an affective appraisal, though some cognitive processes such as categorization and inference can occur without conscious awareness. S. Kaplan (1983) proposed a model of person-environment compatibility combining a purposive aspect with an information processing analysis that suggests a broader framework within which environmental assessment might be viewed. He explained that the quality of a person's interaction with the environment is a function of both the actions the individual attempts to carry out and the informational patterns of the environment. A supportive environment is seen as one where the information necessary for making decisions is readily available and interpretable.

ENVIRONMENTAL ATTRIBUTES   Using slides of Pittsburgh streets with community respondents, Nasar (1983) found that people preferred scenes that were ornate, well kept, open, and clear as to their use. He concluded that the visual attributes of ornateness, upkeep, openness, and clarity are linked separately and additively to preference for the visual environment, and that these findings are generalizable across different residential scenes. Consistent with S. Kaplan's (1983) informational view of supportive environments, scenes in which the general use and specific elements (e.g. entry) were clearly delineated were preferred while those with multiple meanings were disliked.

Interestingly, a consistent finding across a range of studies is that people prefer urban environments that have natural features. Herzog et al (1982), using slides of a wide variety of residential, commercial, and public urban scenes, found that the presence of vegetation in the city is highly valued. R. Kaplan (1983), employing a survey and photoquestionnaire with residents of housing projects in Ann Arbor, Michigan, reported that people judge their housing as friendlier, more supportive, and much more attractive when trees and woods are visible nearby. R. Kaplan (1984), extending work by S. Kaplan & Talbot (1983), suggested that the psychologically restorative quality of natural features in the urban environment may be based on the ability of such features to foster a sense of fascination at the same time that they allow for a perception of orderly coherence.

Im (1984), using slides of the Virginia Tech campus with college students, found that the visual quality of an enclosed urban space can be predicted from the linear combination of its ground slope, height ratio, and vegetation coverage. In free response data, vegetation was the feature most frequently referred to. Based on interviews with over 2500 respondents in 42 municipalities, Fried (1982) concluded that residential satisfaction and neighborhood attachment are based primarily on features of the physical environment and much less on relationships in the social environment. The single strongest predictor of residential satisfaction was ease of access to nature. Wohlwill (1982), employing realistic models of coastal-zone strips with college students, reported that architectural features that were in sharper contrast and more obtrusive in relation to their natural settings were consistently judged as inappropriate and disliked.

INDIVIDUAL AND GROUP DIFFERENCES   Zube & Pitt (1981), using scenic slides of the Connecticut River Valley and Virgin Islands coastal landscapes, discovered that not all groups agree that landscapes with built structures are less attractive than natural settings. They found that city-center blacks judged landscapes with pronounced structures more positively than other groups and that Virgin Islanders perceived coastal hotels and apartment buildings less negatively than other groups. Using photographs of natural and built settings with respondents ranging in age from 6 to 70 years, Zube et al (1983) found that both young children and elderly persons, in contrast to young and middle-aged adults, do not judge landscapes as less attractive as the presence of built features increases. Based on over 700 interviews in Wooster, Ohio, households, Galster & Hesser (1981) concluded that certain groups (young individuals, married persons, female headed households, blacks, and people with many children) consistently report less satisfaction for any given residential context because of their unique needs and relative differences in their ability to alter their environment.

Applied Work

The practical aim of environmental assessment is to develop techniques for systematically describing and evaluating environmental settings. Such techniques could be used to identify standards of quality for various settings and to monitor ongoing variations in quality (Craik 1981). Measurement techniques developed for such purposes have been termed Perceived Environmental Quality Indices (PEQIs). A PEQI affords a quantitative measure of the quality of a physical setting as it is subjectively experienced by a particular group of people. Craik (1981) pointed out that such subjective appraisals can tap variations among places that can only be perceived by human judges, and that reflect meaning in a particular sociocultural context. Most applied work with PEQIs has focused on either the natural environment or the residential and neighborhood environment. Zube et al (1982) pointed out that work with PEQIs involving the natural environment has been most strongly motivated by the practical needs of environmental managers and planners. Much of this research is directed toward meeting the requirements of environmental impact legislation. Zube and his associates noted that published reports have involved a wide range of landscape concerns, including forest management, the identification of scenic highways, the management of scenic views, and user preference for various recreational settings.

Carp & Carp (1982a) discussed the development of an age-unbiased PEQI for the neighborhood that taps global perceptions of the neighborhood as well as evaluations of specific environmental qualities, such as aesthetics, safety, privacy, maintenance, and noise from a variety of sources. Based on interview data from over 2500 San Francisco Bay Area residents, and confirming earlier observations that older persons are prone to give positive evaluations to their living environment, they found a positive association between age and each of their evaluative dimensions. The one exception to this pattern involved safety, with older persons and women more concerned about safety than other groups. In a secondary analysis of these data, Carp & Carp (1982b) concluded that adults 25 and older generally share the same concept of a desirable living environment. They noted, for example, that aesthetic qualities of the living environment had consistently high importance across all age groups, even when compared to factors such as access to services and facilities and relationships with other persons.

Weidemann et al (1982), using a questionnaire format with 250 households, assessed factors relating to residential satisfaction in a Decatur, Illinois, public housing site. The strongest predictors of satisfaction were perception of the attractiveness of the facilities, the suitability of recreation for children and teenagers, and perceptions of police concern with safety and security. Second in importance were perceptions of individual apartments in terms of their comfort, space, and economic value. Hourihan (1984), using a questionnaire format with 400 female residents, assessed neighborhood satisfaction as a function of housing type in Cork, Ireland. Overall neighborhood satisfaction, as well as assessments of cleanliness, clutter, and noise, were more negative in public and older street-type housing than in private detached and semidetached homes. Hourihan pointed out that sources of satisfaction differed across housing groups and that an aggregated model tended to present an upper- and middle-class viewpoint.

Moos & Lemke (1983, 1984) have developed a Multiphasic Environmental Assessment Procedure (MEAP) for evaluating a broad range of settings for older persons, from skilled nursing facilities to semi-independent apartments. The MEAP assesses four dimensions of the facility environment: physical features, policies and program, resident and staff characteristics, and social climate. A guiding assumption of the MEAP is that a facility's environment is a system of interrelated factors. The comprehensive and detailed information it affords about facility environments can be utilized in designing and changing facilities, program planning, and postoccupancy evaluation. The MEAP has been applied in comparing pre and postmove settings in an institutional relocation (Lemke & Moos 1984). Results indicated that the postmove environment offered an improvement over the premove one in environmental quality and controllability. In another application in community care settings for older persons, the MEAP revealed that higher levels of policy choice and resident control were linked to more cohesive, organized, independence-oriented social environments and higher resident activity levels (Moos 1981).

Summary and Critique

Although important advances are being made in developing testable theories of environmental assessment (e.g. Canter 1983a, Russell & Lanius 1984), conceptual development is still at an early and general stage. Explicit links between the major conceptual frameworks (e.g. Canter 1983a, S. Kaplan 1982, 1983, Russell & Lanius 1984) are absent, though shared emphases between at least two perspectives include: the importance of place, a purposive or adaptive focus, a multivariate approach, and increasingly more attention devoted to cognitive factors. Work on environmental attributes affords a consistent picture that nature is valued in the urban environment (e.g. Herzog et al 1982, R. Kaplan 1983), but we need to learn more about more creative design solutions to urban nature and about circumstances where nature contributes little to the urban experience. While important first steps have been made in examining the role of cultural (e.g. Zube & Pitt 1981) and developmental (e.g. Zube et al 1983) differences in environmental assessment, individual and group differences remain an especially salient realm for continued investigation and a key test of the generalizability of emerging theories.

Applied work with PEQIs is admirable for its responsiveness to social and legislative concerns. However, work on landscape perception lacks an explicit tie to theory (Zube et al 1982), remains divided into multiple paradigms and publication outlets (Sell et al 1984), and few PEQIs in this area approach the status of standard and reliable measures (Craik 1983). Work in the residential realm also lacks a link to explanatory theory, though impressive steps have been made toward developing integrative comprehensive frameworks (e.g. Moos & Lemke 1983, 1984). The growing sensitivity to differences in patterns of residential satisfaction across the adult life span (e.g. Carp & Carp 1982a) is of major importance, though the picture needs a fuller appreciation of how patterns of satisfaction evolve during childhood. Finally, if, as Hourihan (1984) suggests, conventional predictive models of residential satisfaction show an upper- and middle-class bias, much more needs to be learned about the pattern and sources of residential satisfaction across different socioeconomic and cultural groups.

COGNITIVE MAPPING

Theoretically Oriented Work

GENERAL MODELS   According to Golledge (1986), the process of acquiring, mentally storing, accessing, and using spatial knowledge has been termed "cognitive mapping." Smith et al (1982) explained that recent advances in computer science (particularly work on artificial intelligence) and cognitive psychology have provided concepts and computational techniques that offer new insights into cognitive mapping. "Computational process modeling" (CPM) involves the development of linked computer models that translate cognitive mapping theories into symbolic terms that allow specific cognitive tasks to be programmed and executed by computers (Golledge 1986). Investigative foci within the CPM approach include: identification of different types of spatial knowledge, the way in which such knowledge is represented and organized, the mechanisms that activate it, and the basic and higher level mental processes that operate on stored spatial information to produce new knowledge, inferences, and environment-directed behaviors (Smith et al 1982). Basing his argument on a CPM approach, Kuipers (1982) suggested that cognitive maps consist of a number of distinct representations—metrical, topological, procedural, and sensorimotor—all of which can be implemented as components of a computational model. He noted that the conventional "map in the head" metaphor for a cognitive map is reflected in the functional specifications for the metrical component in such a computational model.

Gärling et al (1984) speculatively linked the CPM approach of Kuipers (1982) and the focus on "plans" and "places" by Russell & Ward (1982) in proposing a model of the cognitive mapping of large-scale everyday environments. They contended that three interrelated elements are represented in cognitive maps: places, the spatial relations between places, and travel plans. They reasoned that the concepts of "action plans" (linking internal processing to spatial behavior) and "travel plans" (integrated parts of action plans that require traveling to different places) allow a conceptual link between cognitive mapping and everyday behaviors in the environment.

Genereux et al (1983) pointed out that the internal representation of a place includes three distinct types of knowledge: information about its objective attributes, about its affective quality, and about the behaviors that occur there. They noted that environmental psychologists know very little about the last type of knowledge—behavior-place associations. Using a paper-and-pencil rating task with college students, they found that behavioral meaning is an important part of the overall meaning that people attribute to molar physical environments. Judgments about places vary depending on whether individuals focus on the behaviors they expect to occur there, the place's suitability for such behaviors, their reasons for going there, or their activities once there.

Focusing on way-finding, Heft (1981) proposed that knowledge of a route involves an invariant sequence of transitions that link successive vistas. Heft (1983) tested this view, using college students who first viewed either complete or edited versions of a route through a residential neighborhood and then attempted to follow the route in situ. Results demonstrated that the sequence of transitions in a route is especially distinctive information that is sufficient to guide way-finding, and that these nested sequences of information are an adequate description of a route through an environment. Foley & Cohen (1984a) suggested that in solving a specific spatial task, people use only a limited subset of the total knowledge they have about an environment. Foley & Cohen (1984b) tested this proposition with college students, who were asked to make distance estimations from their memory of a familiar and complex university building. They found that the imagery relied on to solve a spatial problem depends on the nature of the problem. Three-dimensional imagery was used when the task emphasized the vertical dimension and imagery of the building exterior was drawn on when the task involved the ends of the wings of the building.

ENVIRONMENTAL ATTRIBUTES   Smith (1984) examined the relationship of the pleasingness of landmarks to the accuracy of distance judgments involving those landmarks, using a schematic map with landmarks that varied in pleasingness (e.g. a park and a dentist's premises). Distance estimates by college students revealed that the more pleasant a landmark is for someone, the more accurately they can judge its remembered distance from another landmark. Evans et al (1984), using a highly realistic filmed simulation with college students, found that a grid structure in an environment facilitates route learning but has little effect on memory for place locations or spatial order. The presence of landmarks, in contrast, enhances memory for place locations and sequential order but is minimally related to route learning. Interestingly, the presence of noise stress reduced location accuracy, though improved memory of sequential order in the grid condition—possibly because under stress individuals rely more heavily on more superficial information, such as sequential order.

INDIVIDUAL AND GROUP DIFFERENCES   Heft & Wohlwill (1986) noted that most theoretical views of the development of cognitive mapping abilities have reflected Piaget's (Piaget & Inhelder 1967) constructivist theory. According to Heft and Wohlwill, the two dominant positions within environmental psychology (Hart & Moore 1973, Siegel & White 1975) share a view of cognitive mapping abilities as developing through several stage-like transformations. In general, spatial knowledge is seen as progressing from a more egocentric or landmark-oriented stage to a more fully coordinated or configurational representation. After summarizing an extensive literature on the development of spatial knowledge, Heft and Wohlwill concluded that these stage-linked theories have generaly been supported. At the same time, it appears that too narrow an adherence to stage models has led to an underestimation of children's spatial knowledge in some circumstances. For example, counter to stage-based assumptions, Biel (1982) discovered that distance estimates from an imagined location made by six-year-old Swedish children were internally consistent and tended to be veridical. Similarly, Conning & Byrne (1984), working with children between the ages of three and five in Scotland, found that some of these preschoolers were able to build a Euclidean (vector-map) mental representation of the environment. Euclidean-like knowledge was associated with the familiarity of the environment, expressed first in the home and lastly in novel settings.

In a less studied realm, Bryant (1982) examined the relationship between college students' personalities and their sense of direction and geographical orientation. Capacity for status, sociability, and self-acceptance predicted a significant increment in pointing error (designating specified landmark directions from imagined locations) variance, even after possible mediating factors such as exploration, familiarity, and spatial visualization were controlled. These personality factors were positively associated with pointing accuracy and negatively related to worrying about becoming lost and pointing error.

Applied Work

Evans et al (1982b), extending earlier work by Appleyard (1976), attempted to identify the physical and sociocultural features of downtown buildings in Orange, California, that enhanced their recall for local residents. Consistent with Appleyard, they reported that buildings were better recalled when they have movement around them, sharp contours, large relative size, a complex shape, and high use. In addition, they found that memory for buildings was strengthened by natural features around the building, ease of pedestrian access, overall building complexity, and uniqueness of architectural style. Moreover, memory for the location of downtown buildings depended on different features than did recall of buildings' names or descriptions, with location memory most enhanced by brightness of color, spatial prominence, and high quality building materials. The authors concluded that buildings can be designed and cited to facilitate residents' overall comprehension of the urban environment.

A major emphasis in recent applied work on cognitive mapping has focused on ways to facilitate orientation in large, complex buildings. Canter (1983b) noted that many modern settings, including university buildings, hospitals, public buildings, and shopping malls, tax most users' orientation skills. He suggested that the orientation aids required in such settings be viewed as a problem in environmental simulation, where the aid must provide a representation of key locations and the directional relationships and distances between those locations.

Levine (1982) speculated that users tend to interpret vertical you-are-here maps as having an alignment relationship to the environment where "up" on the map corresponds to forward in the environment. Extending this reasoning, he argued that the alignment of such maps is critical for wayfinding and that contraligned maps may lead users to walk off in the wrong direction. Levine et al (1984) tested these hypotheses with college students in both a laboratory task and a real-world wayfinding task in a university library. Both studies demonstrated that contraligned maps are relatively difficult for people to use, and that they can direct people away from the desired target direction. The authors concluded that planners should choose the location first and then design the map, and that identical maps should not be used on opposite sides of a hallway.

Gärling et al (1983) attempted to learn what factors facilitate orientation in buildings by studying college students on guided tours through a university building in Sweden. They found that familiarity with the building enhanced orientation, but that decreasing visual information by restricting students' sight on the tour reduced the effect of familiarity. However, presenting students with an initial floor plan of the building tended to counteract the negative effects of restricted sight. The investigation concluded that both visual access and a floor plan or scale model provide effective information for orientation.

Summary and Critique

Theoretical work on cognitive mapping has moved away from earlier emphases on measurement and urban legibility toward more formal theoretical concerns involving the nature and structure of cognitive representations of the environment. Especially significant has been emerging work focusing on computational process models (e.g. Kuipers 1982), and it is likely that future theoretical developments will continue to draw on emerging knowledge in cognitive psychology, cognitive science, and artificial intelligence (see Smith et al 1982). As with environmental assessment, place meaning is also likely to play a role in future theoretical work on cognitive mapping (e.g. Genereux et al 1983); especially needed is work on linkages between place meaning and purposive, goal-directed behavior in the environment (see Gärling et al 1984). In addition, the effects of particular environmental attributes on cognitive mapping, especially interactions between attributes under varying task loads, need to be more fully explored (see Evans et al 1984, Holahan & Sorenson 1985). Moreover, emerging work on the development of spatial knowledge (e.g. Biel 1982, Conning & Byrne 1984) suggests the importance of theoretical work directed toward specifying the generalization of stage-based models across various settings and tasks. Finally, though initial steps have been made in learning about personality and cognitive mapping (Bryant 1982), almost nothing is known about the effects on cognitive mapping of individual differences in cognitive style, imagery, or information processing strategies—issues that might be informed by computational process models.

Applied work on cognitive mapping has shifted from its early emphasis on urban design toward a greater concern with enhancing orientation at the architectural scale. Speculative work has been framed in useful terms (e.g. Canter 1983b, Levine 1982), and supporting empirical work with college students in real-world settings has generally achieved a reasonable balance between internal and external validity, though internal validity predominates (e.g. Garling et al 1983, Levine et al 1984). Research on features predicting memory of downtown buildings (Evans et al 1982b) provides a model of work that might bridge earlier emphases on urban legibility and recent work at the architectural level. The chief problem with applied cognitive mapping work is that there is very little of it. The balance between potential usefulness and interpretive precision in recent work (e.g. Evans et al 1982b, Garling et al 1983, Levine et al 1984), however, provides a sound foundation for continued applied work in this area.

ENVIRONMENTAL STRESS

Theoretically Oriented Work

GENERAL MODELS   According to Campbell (1983), *ambient* stressors are chronic and intractable environmental conditions that, although nonurgent, are negatively valued and place adaptive demands on people. Baum et al (1986), building on Lazarus's (1981) general model of psychological stress, emphasized the instrumental role of pychological factors in the initial *appraisal* of environmental events as stressful. They pointed out that a variety of psychological and environmental factors can mediate the stress reaction, including attitudes toward the source of the stress, perception of risks associated with the stressor, and support from other persons in dealing with the stressor. Fleming et al (1984) underscored the especially powerful mediating role of perceptions of control over the stressor and of coping responses directed toward the source of stress or toward managing the emotional response to the stressor.

Cohen and his associates (Cohen et al 1986) emphasized the importance of "secondary" stressor effects that occur as consequences of the coping process. When coping fails, the individual may develop more pervasive feelings of helplessness and a generalized tendency to give up in the face of obstacles (see also Seligman 1975). Moreover, Cohen and his colleagues pointed out that even successful coping may have deleterious effects when it drains an individual's cognitive or physiological energies or when it is overgeneralized to other inappropriate situations.

DENSITY   Most recent research on environmental stressors has involved high density. In a laboratory study, Epstein et al (1981) found that individuals subjected to higher density became more physiologically aroused, reported more negative affect, and were rated by confederates as more tense and uncomfortable than persons who expereinced low density. There was no evidence of habituation to high density over a three-week period. In summarizing findings from field studies of high density, Epstein (1982) noted that psychological effects are more adverse when the level of control and social cooperation in the setting are lower. In general, effects are most negative in prisons, intermediate in dormitories, and least adverse in family residences. Gormley & Aiello (1982) explicitly examined the link between interpersonal relationships and crowding stress in college dormitories. They reported that the highest levels of annoyance from crowding both at the beginning and the end of the semester occurred for students in tripled rooms who also had negative interpersonal relationships with their roommates.

Cognitive mediators of psychological reactions to high density have been expecially important in recent research. Baum & Gatchel (1981) found that student residents on higher density dormitory corridors reported more control-related problems than residents on less dense corridors. Most interesting, as their attributions about the loss of control shifted over ten weeks from personal factors to environmental ones, residents showed progressively more signs of behavior indicative of helplessness. Further research with students on high density dormitory corridors (Baum et al 1982a) revealed that residents who employ a coping style in which social events are structured and ranked by priority adapt more successfully to high density than residents who fail to use such a coping style. Studying students in a college bookstore, Baum et al (1981) discovered that the effectiveness of prior information in reducing crowding stress depends on how well the information addresses the primary concerns of the individuals in the setting. People unfamiliar with the setting and concerned with situational events benefited most from situational information; those familiar with the environment and concerned with emotional aspects of the setting were helped most by emotional information.

Based on a variety of field studies of helping behavior in 55 Australian communities, Amato (1983) reported that people in large cities are generally less helpful toward strangers than are individuals in small towns. The major decline in helping began in communities of more than 20,000. Using survey data, Rohe (1982) found a positive association between even moderate levels of household density (persons per room) and both reduced satisfaction and more negative forms of behavior, but no link between density and health. After conducting a survey interview with over 100 residents of San Francisco's Chinatown, Loo & Ong (1984) concluded, in contrast to popular belief, that these Chinese residents consistently found high density undesirable, harmful, and stressful. Extended exposure to high density (defined as being raised in Hong Kong) was linked to more negative attitudes about crowding.

A new trend in research on density is an interest in the effects of high density on children. Heft (1985) reviewed work on residential density (relating to both crowding and associated noise) and perceptual-cognitive development, and reported an inverse relationship between density and visual and auditory discrimination, object permanence, the development of schemes, and language skills such as verbal imitation and reading. Aiello et al (1985) reviewed research on high density and children's social behavior, and concluded that density in school and playground settings has been linked, in some circumstances, to decreased social involvement, more verbal and physical aggression, increased competition, and more fearful behavior. Saegert (1981) studied children in New York City public housing, and reported that number of persons per room was positively related to more frequent conflicts, more angry reactions to conflicts, and teachers' ratings of lower behavioral adjustment.

OTHER ENVIRONMENTAL STRESSORS   Using an interview format in both a repeated measures and a comparison group design, Weinstein (1982) found that reported disturbance by traffic noise was stable over time, showed no significant adaptation over a one-year period, and that, with passing time, respondents felt more pessimistic about their ability to adapt to the noise. Spacapan & Cohen (1983), studying college students in a laboratory setting, reported that there are effects and aftereffects from the *anticipatory period* before either noise stress or immersing one's hand in ice water that are similar to those produced by actual exposure to the stressor.

Evans et al (1982a) discovered that college students who were long-term residents of the Los Angeles air basin, in contrast to students who were new migrants to the area, were less sensitive to photochemical smog. Long-term residents mentioned smog less frequently as a community problem, were less likely, for low levels of smog, to say that smog was present in visual slides, were more prone to exaggerate their perceived knowledge of smog, and were more inclined to feel that they were relatively immune to the effects of smog. Finally, relying on archival data from Chicago and Houston, Anderson & Anderson (1984) reported a positive linear relationship between ambient temperatures and violent crime, in contrast to the curvilinear relationship predicted from laboratory research (see Baron 1978).

Applied Work

Research on density with an applied orientation has involved high-rise housing and correctional facilities. In interviews with 600 middle-income German residents, Williamson (1981) found that perceptions of crowding were not intrinsic to high-rise living, but were linked to negative features of particular apartments and to unsatisfactory relations with neighbors. Consistent with Michelson (1977), people's needs and their position in the life cycle were central in shaping satisfaction. Churchman & Ginsberg (1984), who interviewed over 300 middle-income women in Israel, reported both advantages and disadvantages in high-rise buildings; residents liked the large number of people they could meet in high-rise settings but disliked the buildings' height. Stage in the life cycle was a powerful predictive factor, with parents of young children most displeased with high-rise living.

Ray and his associates (1982) systematically varied the density levels of dormitories in a juvenile correctional institution and reported increased social disorganization and negative affect with high density. Generalized responses to high density were also apparent in more negative school performance, social interaction, and cooperation with teachers. In an archival analysis of records of over 500 female prisoners, Ruback & Carr (1984) discovered that the size of the population in the institution was linked to the adjusted rate of disciplinary infractions, even after potential confounding variables were controlled. Wener et al (1985) discussed the application of findings from behaviorally based evaluations in several successive designs for correctional facilities. Design recommendations that proved effective and that are relevant to reducing crowding stress included: restricting facility height to as few stories as possible, decentralizing access to indoor and outdoor recreational areas, and providing increased privacy through access to a variety of social spaces from large group spaces to secluded areas.

Shumaker & Reizensenstein (1982) identified four environmental domains in acute care hospitals that can be stressful for patients: wayfinding, physical discomfort, loss of control, and institutional atmosphere. Even as small a factor as having a view of a natural setting from a hospital room has been positively related to speed of recovery from surgery and to the use of fewer potent analgesics during the postoperative period (Ulrich 1984). Lawton et al (1984a), using survey and observational methods, systematically evaluated the effectiveness of a Philadelphia setting for older persons with organic brain impairments. The setting incorporated design features such as color coding and large graphics for orientation and a large central area as a focus for social interactions. In comparison to a traditional nursing home, the setting engendered more programmed and less pathological activity on the part of patients, decreased bedroom use in favor of using the centralized social area, and a doubling in visiting rate. Reizensenstein & Ostrander (1981) evaluated the functioning of a residential setting in Columbus, Ohio, that incorporated design features at every scale to facilitate independent functioning for persons paralyzed from the neck down. Interview and behavioral data suggested that the setting allowed greater independence than residents had previously experienced, and reduced perceptions of stigma. Zimring et al (1982), who employed an observational procedure in a pretest-posttest design, found that the most therapeutically positive living arrangement in a Massachusetts institution for retarded persons was a design where clearly articulated private and semiprivate spaces allowed residents to control their social interactions.

An emerging area for the application of knowledge about environmental stress involves technological catastrophes such as those associated with nuclear energy and toxic substances. Such catastrophes involve predictable and continuing threats where perceived control is often low (Baum et al 1983a). Baum et al (1983c) compared residents living near the damaged Three Mile Island (TMI) nuclear power plant with carefully selected control samples including people living near an undamaged nuclear power plant and near a traditional coal-fired power plant. They discovered that almost 1 1/2 years after the nuclear accident, TMI residents reported more somatic complaints, anxiety, and depression, showed greater stress-related sympathetic arousal, and performed more poorly on tasks requiring concentration and motivation than did residents in the control communities.

Baum and his colleagues (Baum et al 1983b, Collins et al 1983) applied a taxonomy of coping strategies developed by Folkman & Lazarus (1980) to learn how coping efforts might mediate the psychological consequences of the TMI nuclear accident. Because the stress was chronic and the source of stress difficult to change, reappraisal-based emotional management was more effective in moderating adverse psychological reactions than were either the use of denial or problem-oriented modes of coping. Moreover, TMI residents who had moderate or high levels of social support reported less emotional distress and performed better on tasks tapping motivation and concentration than did TMI respondents with little or no social support (Fleming et al 1982).

Summary and Critique

Influenced by Lazarus's (1981) general perspective, theoretical work on environmental stress has emphasized systemic models that incorporate "transactional" cognitive and coping processes as key mediating constructs (see Baum et al 1982b, Evans & Cohen 1986). Theoretically oriented research on density in dormitories (e.g. Baum & Gatchel 1981) and urban areas (e.g. Amato 1983) has generally effectively balanced the requirements of internal and external validity. Moreover, density research has afforded empirical support for the central role accorded cognitive (e.g. Baum et al 1981), coping (e.g. Baum et al 1982a), and social (e.g. Gormley & Aiello 1982) mediating processes in general models of environmental stress. At the same time, conceptual and methodological refinement is needed to clarify the stress-moderating effects of suggested mediating constructs (Cohen et al 1986), and prospective longitudinal designs are essential to disentangle the complex causal picture in models of environmental stress (Evans & Cohen 1986). Research on noise needs to more thoroughly account for the cognitive and social contextual factors that are now more routinely explored in work on density (Cohen & Spacapan 1984). Research on density should better reflect individual and cultural differences (Epstein 1982), and work on density and child development needs to examine the processes through which density affects development, as well as the long-term developmental effects of high density (Heft 1985).

Applied work on density has tended to show negative consequences in correctional facilities where social cohesion and control are low, and minimal or no adverse effects in high-rise housing when social and economic factors are not problematic (see Epstein 1982). Applied work on high-rise housing, correctional facilities, and therapeutic environments has tended to be atheoretical, and links between applied efforts in these areas and emerging general models of environmental stress are particulary needed. Especially impressive has been newly emerging work on technological catastrophes, where the demands of internal and external validity have been admirably balanced (e.g. Baum et al 1983c), and where links to general stress models involving coping processes (Baum et al 1983b, Collins et al 1983) and social support (Fleming et al 1982) have been explicitly examined. While nuclear power has been the focus of recent work, growing concern over the disposal of toxic chemicals suggests an important realm for extending this research. Especially noteworthy, work on environmental stress has been exemplary in bridging the cognition-behavior and theory-application dichotomies that are generally characteristic of research in environmental psychology.

SPATIAL BEHAVIOR

Theoretically Oriented Work

PERSONAL SPACE   According to Hayduk (1978), personal space refers to the area people maintain around themselves into which other persons cannot intrude without arousing discomfort. In an extensive critical review of research on personal space, Hayduk (1983) concluded that projective measures of personal space correlate poorly with real-life behavior. He pointed out that when projective data are excluded, it is evident that there is a gradual increase in the size of personal space between the ages of 3 and 21. Moreover, recent data suggest that traditional assumptions about cultural differences in personal space be viewed more cautiously. Hayduk added that findings relating to sex differences in personal space have been highly inconsistent, and that new aproaches to examining sex differences need to focus on the underlying mechanisms presumed to link gender to spatial behavior.

Patterson (1982) proposed a broader functional model of nonverbal interaction that includes interpersonal spatial behavior. In contrast to theories of nonverbal interaction that emphasize intimacy, Patterson argued that nonverbal exchange serves variable functions and may be viewed as the product of a sequence of related events. He explained that as the particular function the interaction is serving changes, the resulting arousal, cognitions, and behavior patterns will also change. He speculated that less structured and less evaluative interactions generally reflect the intimacy function, while more structured and more evaluative ones generally reflect the social control function.

Hayduk (1981) had college students stop an approaching experimenter at the distances where they became progressively more uncomfortable, and discovered that the personal space zone is characterized by linearly increasing resistance. Knowles & Brickner (1981) observed college students walking in a hallway with a similar or a dissimilar confederate, and found that, for male students, the group space was more protected from a potential spatial invasion under the similar than the dissimilar condition. Measuring chair distances between conversing college students, Sussman & Rosenfeld (1982) reported that Venezuelans sat closer together than did Japanese. However, they discovered that language was an important factor; Venezuelans sat closer when speaking the language of their own high-contact culture than when speaking the language of the lower-contact American culture. Measuring chair distances in a scale model of a room, Gifford (1982) found that aspects of a social situation, such as interpersonal attraction and the cooperativeness of a task, affected distancing much more strongly than did respondents' sex or personality.

TERRITORIALITY   Recent theoretically oriented work on territoriality has focused on the link between the presence of territorial markers and reduced residential crime. In a critical review of the "defensible space" (see Newman 1972) concept, Taylor et al (1980) noted that early work on defensible space assumed that residential design features that conveyed territorial cognitions and behaviors reduce criminal behavior. They noted that more recent work has emphasized the interactive role of social factors relating to local social networks and the perceived homogeneity of the area (see Merry 1981).

Taylor et al (1985), using survey and on-site observational data on Baltimore households and police crime records, concluded that physical defensible space features play a minor, though not insignificant, role in fostering safety and security in comparison to territorial and social variables. Variations in crime and fear were most strongly linked to territorial factors involving a sense of responsibility for what happened near the home and neighborhood identification, and were next most strongly affected by local social ties. Brower et al (1983) had Baltimore residents respond to drawings of residential backyards, and found that barriers (a fence) and territorial markers (planting) are interpreted by residents from a variety of neighborhoods as indicative of stronger residential territorial attitudes and behaviors. However, physical elements alone were less effective as territorial signs in contexts of high perceived threat.

Brown & Altman (1981) speculated that the more highly defined a residential area is by actual (e.g. fences or locks) or symbolic (e.g. decorative mailboxes or flower beds) barriers, the stronger its territorial identification and the less likelihood of a criminal intrusion. Using archival data on residential burglaries in surburban Salt Lake County, Utah, along with on-site observations, Brown & Altman (1983) found that nonburglarized houses were more likely to have a variety of actual and symbolic barriers that communicated a strong sense of territoriality. Burglarized houses, in contrast, tended to lack such barriers, and the areas around them conveyed a sense of public use.

In telephone interviews with older female Chicago residents, Normoyle & Lavrakas (1984) determined that perceived territoriality was a positive function of individual perceptions of predictability and personal control. Perceived territoriality in turn was inversely related to fear of crime. Using household surveys in moderate- and low-income housing sites, Newman & Franck (1982) found that building size has a positive indirect effect on crime and fear of crime, and is mediated by residents' use and control of areas outside of apartments. Greenberg et al (1982) reported, however, that matched high and low crime neighborhoods in Atlanta differed in physical characteristics (e.g. low crime areas had more homogeneous residential land use and fewer major traffic arteries) to a much greater extent than they did in informal territorial control.

PRIVACY   Altman et al (1981) proposed a speculative "dialectic assumption system" to integrate privacy regulation theory (Altman 1975) and social penetration theory (Altman & Taylor 1973) in a unified framework. The authors assume that social interaction functions in accordance with two dialectical processes—openness-closedness and stability-change—as a unified and dynamic system. Each pole of the two oppositions is assumed to be of equal importance in social behavior, and the interplay of these dialectics is assumed not to be directed at achieving an ideal homeostatic state.

Applied Work

The most direct applications of work on spatial behavior have concerned office and, secondarily, classroom design. Wineman (1982) noted that although privacy is an important concern for office workers, evaluative research typically has revealed that both visual and acoustical privacy are unsatisfactory in modern offices. Sundstrom et al (1982a) used a questionnaire format with employees in a large corporation in a pre-post design to assess the effects of a move from a conventional to an open office plan. The investigators reported that the move resulted in a decline in satisfaction with visual and acoustical privacy, particulary among workers who previously occupied walled offices. A chief complaint concerned decreased ability to conduct confidential conversations. In a questionnaire study with 150 office employees, Sundstrom and his associates (1982b) concluded that the number of enclosed sides was the major predictor of the privacy of workspaces, but that privacy is viewed differently by people in different jobs (e.g. secretaries saw privacy in terms of gross control over social contact, while office managers envisioned it in terms of autonomy from supervision).

Marans & Spreckelmeyer (1982) used questionnaire and observational strategies with building users to evaluate the functioning of a new federal office building designed in a primarily open-office arrangement. Workers in conventional, private offices were more satisfied than those in open or pool arrangements, and satisfaction was higher for persons with a greater degree of control over their environment. The most negative evaluations concerned conversational and visual privacy. Becker and his colleagues (1983) conducted questionnaire surveys of faculty and students at three comparable community colleges that differed in faculty office design. Findings revealed more distractions, more impairment of faculty work and faculty-student interaction, and less privacy in open as compared to closed offices.

Ahrentzen & Evans (1984) interviewed 13 teachers and 65 students from five elementary schools reflecting a variety of classroom designs concerning distraction and privacy in the classroom. They found that environmental factors causing distractions were particularly salient for teachers. The amount of structural walls in classrooms was positively related to satisfaction with the classroom, reduced teacher distraction, and less restriction in potentially distracting classroom activities. At the same time, teachers were effective at managing their curricula to prevent distracting other classes, and tended to like open-perimeter space, possibly because it facilitated mutual support among teachers.

Summary and Critique

Theoretical work on personal space continues to be hampered by a variety of methodological concerns. The validity of projective measures that have been heavily relied on is questionable, and very little is known about correlations among different indices of real-life behavior (Hayduk 1983). Theoretical precision, as well as practical utility, would profit from knowledge of how the size, shape, and permeability of personal space vary across different settings (Hayduk 1981). Moreover, further theoretical development is dependent on an understanding of the social psychological processes that link specified determinants with observed personal space behaviors (Hayduk 1983). Theoretical work on territoriality and crime is progressing at an exciting rate; however, the causal picture is much more complex than originally envisioned. Recent findings underscore the need for more research documenting the relative importance of defensible space in preventing crime compared to other environmental factors (e.g. Greenberg et al 1982), as well as to demographic and sociocultural variables (e.g. Merry 1981, Taylor et al 1985). Also, surprisingly little is known about how defensible space and territorial control vary across different environmental contexts (Taylor et al 1980). Recent theoretical work on privacy (Altman et al 1981) has strengthened the appreciation of privacy management as a dynamic, vital, and fluid process; however, the absence of corresponding empirical investigations to match conceptual advances remains a crucial limitation in the privacy area. Salient topics for empirical work include individual and group differences in privacy needs and regulation, as well as changes in privacy regulation as a function of relationship development and crises in social relationships (Altman et al 1981).

In the applied realm, work on office environments is noteworthy for its use of converging behavioral and self-report measures (e.g. Marans & Spreckelmeyer 1982) and its growing sensitivity to privacy requirements as a function of job demands (e.g. Sundstrom et al 1982b). At the same time, work in this area is almost totally without a theoretical foundation in either the environmental or organizational spheres, and while privacy is discussed in general terms, the related constructs of territoriality, personal space, and crowding are rarely explicitly examined. Moreover, comparisons between open and conventional office plans are now less useful than detailed information about the interactive effects on morale and productivity of specific design features, job levels, and task requirements. In addition, longitudinal approaches are needed to examine adaptation to contrasting design features over the longer periods of time that characterize the work experience. In addition to a general need for more empirical data on the educational effects of classroom design, specific research is needed on coping strategies used by teachers and students in the classroom (see Ahrentzen & Evans 1984), the interactive role of individual differences in distractability and learning style, and underlying theoretical issues derived from the environmental, social psychological, and educational spheres.

GENERAL DIRECTIONS FOR FUTURE RESEARCH

Among the most significant recent developments in environmental psychology is work that has promise of broadening the scope of inquiry in the field. Such work cuts across all four theoretical topics reviewed here, and has the capacity to enrich the character of inquiry in the field more broadly. Four such general areas may be highlighted as suggesting especially fruitful realms for future research.

CULTURE   Rapoport (1983) has underscored the importance of cultural variables in environmental psychology and the need for environmental design to be culture-specific. Salient topics for future research include: comparative cross-national research encompassing developing countries as well as the developed nations (Canter 1983); work on the links between culture-specific social, economic, and governing processes and corresponding supportive features in the built environment (Rapoport 1983); and studies relating the design, use, and modification of the home environment to various aspects of the cultural system (Gauvain et al 1983).

DEVELOPMENT   Wohlwill (1983) pointed out that in contrast to what is known about development and the social environment, very little is known about the role of the physical environment in development. Key areas for future research are: longitudinal analyses of how children adapt to adverse environmental conditions (Wohlwill & Heft 1986); process-oriented research on the behaviors through which children develop environmental competencies and relative control over the environment (Wohlwill 1983, Wohlwill & Heft 1986); analyses of the contextual conditions that interact with major developmental transitions (Wapner et al 1983); and investigations of coping strategies used by competent, community-resident elderly persons (Carp 1986).

TEMPORAL PROCESS   Altman & Rogoff (1986) contended that an appreciation of the dynamic nature of environmental psychology requires knowledge about the process and flow of people's transactions with the environment. Prospective issues for future research include: studies of groups' temporal orientations in terms of the functional and symbolic meanings of associated places and objects (Stokols & Jacobi 1984); analyses of the processes whereby environments are built, organized, become differentiated, achieve stability, and decline (Wicker 1986); and systematic analyses of the process of acceptance and utilization of environmental design research (Kantrowitz 1985).

SOCIAL POLICY   Craik (1986) and Stokols (1983) have suggested the potential relevance of environment and behavior knowledge to the formulation of social policy. Potential topics for future research are: studies of individuals' perceptions of and attitudes toward nuclear power (Saegert 1986) and evaluations of the social and psychological effects of housing policies involving age segregation (Lawton et al 1984b) and exclusionary rental policies (Colten & Marans 1982).

After nearly two decades environmental psychology has achieved a coherent self-identity and organizational and institutional legitimacy. At the same time, it continues to reach toward new investigative frontiers involving cultural and developmental influences, the richness of temporal process, and the prospect of influencing social policy. The intellectual vitality that has characterized the field in the past remains strong as environmental psychology advances into its third decade.

Literature Cited

Ahrentzen, S., Evans, G. W. 1984. Distraction, privacy, and classroom design. *Environ. Behav.* 16:437–54

Aiello, J. R., Thompson, D. E., Baum, A. 1985. Children, crowding, and control: Effects of environmental stress on social behavior. See Wohlwill & van Vliet 1985, pp. 97–124

Altman, I. 1975. *The Environment and Social Behavior.* Monterey, CA: Brooks/Cole

Altman, I., Rogoff, B. 1986. World views in psychology and environmental psychology: Trait, interactional, organismic, and transactional perspectives. See Stokols & Altman 1986

Altman, I., Taylor, D. A. 1973. *Social Penetration: The Development of Interpersonal Relationships.* New York: Holt

Altman, I., Vinsel, A., Brown, B. B. 1981. Dialectic conceptions in social psychology: An application to social penetration and privacy regulation. *Adv. Exp. Soc. Psychol.* 14:107–60

Altman, I., Wohlwill, J. F. 1983. *Behavior and the Natural Environment.* New York: Plenum

Amato, P. R. 1983. Helping behavior in urban and rural environments: Field studies based on a taxonomic organization of helping episodes. *J. Pers. Soc. Psychol.* 45:571–86

Anderson, C. A., Anderson, D. C. 1984. Ambient temperature and violent crime: Tests of the linear and curvilinear hypotheses. *J. Pers. Soc. Psychol.* 46:91–97

Appleyard, D. 1976. *Planning a Pluralistic City.* Cambridge, MA: MIT Press

Baron, R. A. 1978. Aggression and heat: The "long hot summer" revisited. In *Advances in Environmental Psychology,* ed. A. Baum, J. E. Singer, S. Valins, 1:57–84. Hillsdale, NJ: Erlbaum

Baum, A., Calesick, L. E., Davis, G. E., Gatchel, R. J. 1982a. Individual differences in coping with crowding: Stimulus screening and social overload. *J. Pers. Soc. Psychol.* 43:821–30

Baum, A., Fisher, J. D., Solomon, S. K. 1981. Type of information, familiarity, and the reduction of crowding stress. *J. Pers. Soc. Psychol.* 40:11–23

Baum, A., Fleming, R., Davidson, L. M. 1983a. Natural disaster and technological catastrophe. *Environ. Behav.* 15:333–54

Baum, A., Fleming, R., Singer, J. E. 1983b. Coping with victimization by technological disaster. *J. Soc. Issues* 39:117–38

Baum, A., Gatchel, R. J. 1981. Cognitive determinants of reaction to uncontrollable events: Development of reactance and learned helplessness. *J. Pers. Soc. Psychol.* 40:1078–89

Baum, A., Gatchel, R. J., Schaeffer, M. A. 1983c. Emotional, behavioral, and physiological effects of chronic stress at Three Mile Island. *J. Consult. Clin. Psychol.* 51:565–72

Baum, A., Singer, J. E., Baum, C. S. 1982b. Stress and the environment. See Evans 1982, pp. 15–44

Becker, F. D., Gield, B., Gaylin, K., Sayer, S. 1983. Office design in a community college: Effect on work and communication patterns. *Environ. Behav.* 15:699–726

Biel, A. 1982. Children's spatial representation of their neighborhood: A step towards a general spatial competence. *J. Environ. Psychol.* 2:193–200

Brower, S., Dockett, K., Taylor, R. B. 1983. Residents' perception of territorial features and perceived local threat. *Environ. Behav.* 15:419–37

Brown, B. B., Altman, I. 1981. Territoriality and residential crime: A conceptual framework. In *Environmental Criminology,* ed. P. J. Bratingham, P. L. Bratingham, pp. 55–76. Beverly Hills, CA: Sage

Brown, B. B., Altman, I. 1983. Territoriality, defensible space and residential burglary: An environmental analysis. *J. Environ. Psychol.* 3:203–20

Bryant, K. J. 1982. Personality correlates of sense of direction and geographical orientation. *J. Pers. Soc. Psychol.* 43:1318–24

Campbell, J. M. 1983. Ambient stressors. *Environ. Behav.* 15:355–80

Canter, D. 1983a. The purposive evaluation of places: A facet approach. *Environ. Behav.* 15:659–98

Canter, D. 1983b. Way-finding and signposting: Penance or prosthesis? In *Information Design: The Design and Evaluation of Signs and Printed Material,* ed. R. Easterby, pp. 245–64. Chichester, UK: Wiley

Canter, D., Craik, K. H. 1981. Environmental psychology. *J. Environ. Psychol.* 1:1–11

Canter, D., Craik, K. H., Griffiths, I. 1983. Editorial. *J. Environ. Psychol.* 3:1–3

Carp, F. M. 1986. Environment and aging. See Stokols & Altman 1986.

Carp, F. M., Carp, A. 1982a. Perceived environmental quality of neighborhoods: Development of assessment scales and their relation to age and gender. *J. Environ. Psychol.* 2:295–312

Carp, F. M., Carp, A. 1982b. The ideal residential area. *Res. Aging* 4:411–39

Churchman, A., Ginsberg, Y. 1984. The image and experience of high rise housing in Israel. *J. Environ. Psychol.* 4:27–41

Cohen, S., Evans, G. W., Stokols, D., Krantz, D. S., eds. 1986. *Behavior, Health, and*

Environmental Stress. New York: Plenum. In press

Cohen, S., Spacapan, S. 1984. The social psychology of noise. In *Noise and Society*, ed. D. M. Jones, A. J. Chapman, pp. 221–45. New York: Wiley

Collins, D. L., Baum, A., Singer, J. E. 1983. Coping with chronic stress at the Three Mile Island: Psychological and biochemical evidence. *Health Psychol.* 2:149–66

Colten, M. E., Marans, R. W. 1982. Restrictive rental practices and their impact on families. *Popul. Res. Policy Rev.* 1:43–58

Conning, A. M., Byrne, R. W. 1984. Pointing to preschool children's spatial competence: A study in natural settings. *J. Environ. Psychol.* 4:165–75

Craik, K. H. 1973. Environmental psychology. *Ann. Rev. Psychol.* 24:403–22

Craik, K. H. 1981. Environmental assessment and situational analysis. In *Toward a Psychology of Situations*, ed. D. Magnusson, pp. 37–48. Hillsdale, NJ: Erlbaum

Craik, K. H. 1983. The psychology of the large scale environment. In *Environmental Psychology: Directions and Perspectives*, ed. N. R. Feimer, E. S. Geller, pp. 67–105. New York: Praeger

Craik, K. H. 1986. Psychological perspectives on technology as societal option, source of hazard and generator of environmental impacts. In *Technology Assessment, Environmental Impact Assessment and Risk Analysis: Contributions from the Psychological and Decision Sciences*, ed. V. Covello, J. Mumpower. New York: Springer-Verlag. In press

Epstein, Y. M. 1982. Crowding stress and human behavior. See Evans 1982, pp. 133–48

Epstein, Y. M., Woolfolk, R. L., Lehrer, P. M. 1981. Physiological, cognitive, and nonverbal responses to repeated exposure to crowding. *J. Appl. Soc. Psychol.* 11:1–13

Evans, G. W., ed. 1982. *Environmental Stress*. Cambridge, UK: Cambridge Univ. Press

Evans, G. W., Cohen, S. 1986. Environmental stress. See Stokols & Altman 1986

Evans, G. W., Jacobs, S. V., Frager, N. B. 1982a. Behavioral responses to air pollution. In *Advances in Environmental Psychology*, ed. A. Baum, J. E. Singer, pp. 237–69. Hillsdale, NJ: Erlbaum

Evans, G. W., Skorpanich, M. A., Gärling, T., Bryant, K., Bresolin, B. 1984. The effects of pathway configuration, landmarks, and stress on environmental cognition. *J. Environ. Psychol.* 4:323–35

Evans, G. W., Smith, C., Pezdek, K. 1982b. Cognitive maps and urban form. *Am. Plann. Assoc. J.* 48:232–44

Feimer, N. R., Geller, E. S. 1983. *Environmental Psychology: Directions and Perspectives*. New York: Praeger

Fleming, R., Baum, A., Gisriel, M. M., Gatchel, R. J. 1982. Mediating influences of social support on stress at Three Mile Island. *J. Hum. Stress* 14–22

Fleming, R., Baum, A., Singer, J. E. 1984. Toward an integrative approach to the study of stress. *J. Pers. Soc. Psychol.* 46:939–49

Foley, J. E., Cohen, A. J. 1984a. Mental mapping of a megastructure. *Can. J. Psychol.* 38:440–53

Foley, J. E., Cohen, A. J. 1984b. Working mental representations of the environment. *Environ. Behav.* 16:713–29

Folkman, S., Lazarus, R. S. 1980. An analysis of coping in a middle-aged community sample. *J. Health Soc. Behav.* 21:219–39

Fried, M. 1982. Residential attachment: Sources of residential and community satisfaction. *J. Soc. Issues* 38:107–19

Galster, G. C., Hesser, G. W. 1981. Residential satisfaction: Compositional and contextual correlates. *Environ. Behav.* 13:735–58

Gärling, T., Book, A., Lindberg, E. 1984. Cognitive mapping of large-scale environments: The interrelationship of action plans, acquisitions, and orientation. *Environ. Behav.* 16:3–34

Gärling, T., Lindberg, E., Mantyla, T. 1983. Orientation in buildings: Effects of familiarity, visual access, and orientation aids. *J. Appl. Psychol.* 68:177–86

Gauvain, M., Altman, I., Fahim, H. 1983. Homes and social change: A cross-cultural analysis. See Feimer & Geller 1983, pp. 180–218

Genereux, R. L., Ward, L. M., Russell, J. A. 1983. The behavioral component in the meaning of places. *J. Environ. Psychol.* 3:43–55

Gifford, R. 1982. Projected interpersonal distance and orientation choices: Personality, sex, and social situation. *Psychol. Q.* 45:145–52

Golledge, R. G. 1986. Environmental cognition. See Stokols & Altman 1986

Gormley, F. P., Aiello, J. R. 1982. Social density, interpersonal relationships, and residential crowding stress. *J. Appl. Psychol.* 12:222–36

Greenberg, S. W., Rohe, W. M., Williams, J. R. 1982. Safety in urban neighborhoods: A comparison of physical characteristics and informal territorial control in high and low crime neighborhoods. *Popul. Environ.* 5:141–64

Hart, R. A., Moore, G. T. 1973. The development of spatial cognition: A review. In *Image and Environment: Cognitive Mapping and Spatial Behavior*, ed. R. M. Downs, D. Stea, pp. 246–88. Chicago: Aldine

Hayduk, L. A. 1978. Personal space: An evaluative and orienting overview. *Psychol. Bull.* 85:117–34

Hayduk, L. A. 1981. The permeability of personal space. *Behav. Sci.* 13:274–87

Hayduk, L. A. 1983. Personal space: Where we now stand. *Psychol. Bull.* 94:293–335

Heft, H. 1981. An examination of constructivist and Gibsonian approaches to environmental psychology. *Popul. Environ.* 4:227–45

Heft, H. 1983. Way-finding as the perception of information over time. *Popul. Environ.* 6:133–50

Heft, H. 1985. High residential density and perceptual-cognitive development: An examination of the effects of crowding and noise in the home. See Wohlwill & van Vliet 1985, pp. 39–76

Heft, H., Wohlwill, J. F. 1986. Environmental cognition in children. See Stokols & Altman 1986

Helson, H. 1964. *Adaptation Level Theory.* New York: Harper & Row

Herzog, T. R., Kaplan, S., Kaplan, R. 1982. The prediction of preference for unfamiliar urban places. *Popul. Environ.* 5:43–59

Holahan, C. J., Sorenson, P. E. 1985. The role of figural organization in city imageability: An information processing analysis. *J. Environ. Psychol.* In press

Hourihan, K. 1984. Context-dependent models of residential satisfaction: An analysis of housing groups in Cork, Ireland. *Environ. Behav.* 16:369–93

Im, S. 1984. Visual preferences in enclosed urban spaces: An exploration of a scientific approach to environmental design. *Environ. Behav.* 16:235–62

Kantrowitz, M. 1985. Has environment and behavior research "made a difference"? *Environ. Behav.* 17:25–46

Kaplan, R. 1983. The role of nature in the urban context. See Altman & Wohlwill 1983, pp. 127–61

Kaplan, R. 1984. The impact of urban nature: A theoretical analysis. *Urban Ecol.* 8:189–97

Kaplan, S. 1982. Where cognition and affect meet: A theoretical analysis of preference. In *Knowledge for Design,* ed. P. Bart, A. Chen, G. Francescato, pp. 183–88. Washington, DC: EDRA

Kaplan, S. 1983. A model of person-environment compatibility. *Environ. Behav.* 15:311–32

Kaplan, S., Talbot, J. F. 1983. Psychological benefits of a wilderness experience. See Altman & Wohlwill 1983, pp. 163–203

Knowles, E. S., Brickner, M. A. 1981. Social cohesion effects on spatial cohesion. *Pers. Soc. Psychol. Bull.* 7:309–13

Kuipers, B. 1982. The "map in the head" metaphor. *Environ. Behav.* 14:202–20

Lawton, M. P., Fulcomer, M., Kleban, M. H. 1984a. Architecture for the mentally impaired elderly. *Environ. Behav.* 16:730–57

Lawton, M. P., Moss, M., Moles, E. 1984b. The suprapersonal neighorhood context of older people: Age heterogeneity and well-being. *Environ. Behav.* 16:89–109

Lazarus, R. S. 1981. The stress and coping paradigm. In *Models for Clinical Psychopathology,* ed. C. Eisdorfer, D. Cohen, A. Kleinman, P. Maxim, pp. 177–214. New York: Spectrum

Lemke, S., Moos, R. H. 1984. Coping with an intra-institutional relocation: Behavioral change as a function of residents' personal resources. *J. Environ. Psychol.* 4:137–51

Levine, M. 1982. You-are-here maps: Psychological considerations. *Environ. Behav.* 14:221–37

Levine, M., Marchon, I., Hanley, G. 1984. The placement and misplacement of you-are-here maps. *Environ. Behav.* 16:139–57

Loo, C., Ong, P. 1984. Crowding perceptions, attitudes, and consequences among the Chinese. *Environ. Behav.* 16:55–87

Marans, R. W., Spreckelmeyer, K. F. 1982. Evaluating open and conventional office design. *Environ. Behav.* 14:333–51

Merry, S. E. 1981. Defensible space undefended: Social factors in crime control through environmental design. *Urban Aff. Q.* 16:397–422

Michelson, W. 1977. *Environmental Choice, Human Behavior, and Residential Satisfaction.* New York: Oxford Univ. Press

Moos, R. H. 1981. Environmental choice and control in community care settings for older people. *J. Appl. Soc. Psychol.* 11:23–43

Moos, R. H., Lemke, S. 1983. Specialized living environments for older people. In *Handbook of the Psychology of Aging,* ed. J. E. Birren, K. W. Schaie, pp. 864–89. New York: Van Nostrand Reinhold. 2nd ed.

Moos, R. H., Lemke, S. 1984. Supportive residential settings for older people. In *Elderly People and the Environment,* ed. I. Altman, M. P. Lawton, pp. 159–90. New York: Plenum

Nasar, J. L. 1983. Adult viewers' preference in residential scenes: A study of the relationship of environmental attributes to preference. *Environ. Behav.* 15:589–614

Newman, O. 1972. *Defensible space: Crime Prevention Through Urban Design.* New York: Macmillan

Newman, O., Franck, K. A. 1982. The effects of building size on personal crime and fear of crime. *Popul. Environ.* 5:203–20

Normoyle, J., Lavrakas, P. J. 1984. Fear of crime in elderly women: Perceptions of control, predictability, and territoriality. *Pers. Soc. Psychol. Bull.* 10:191–202

Patterson, M. L. 1982. A sequential functional

model of nonverbal exchange. *Psychol. Rev.* 89:231–49

Piaget, J., Inhelder, B. 1967. *The Child's Conception of Space.* New York: Norton

Proshansky, H. M., Altman, I. 1979. Overview of the field. In *Resources in Environment and Behavior,* ed. W. P. White, pp. 3–36. Washington, DC: *Am. Psychol. Assoc.*

Rapoport, A. 1983. Development, culture change and supportive design. *Habitat Int.* 7:249–68

Ray, D. W., Wandersman, A., Ellisor, J., Huntington, D. E. 1982. The effects of high density in a juvenile correctional institution. *Basic Appl. Soc. Psychol.* 3:95–108

Reizensenstein, J. E., Ostrander, E. R. 1981. Design for independence: Housing for the severely disabled. *Environ. Behav.* 13:633–39

Rohe, W. M. 1982. The response to density in residential settings: The mediating effects of social and personal variables. *J. Appl. Soc. Psychol.* 12:292–303

Ruback, R. B., Carr, T. S. 1984. Crowding in a women's prison: Attitudinal and behavioral effects. *J. Appl. Soc. Psychol.* 14:57–68

Russell, J. A., Lanius, U. F. 1984. Adaptation level and the affective appraisal of environments. *J. Environ. Psychol.* 4:119–35

Russell, J. A., Pratt, G. 1980. A description of the affective quality attributed to environments. *J. Pers. Soc. Psychol.* 38:31–22

Russell, J. A., Ward, L. M. 1982. Environmental psychology. *Ann. Rev. Psychol.* 33:651–88

Saegert, S. 1981. Environment and children's mental health: Residential density and low income children. In *Handbook of Psychology and Health,* ed. A. Baum, J. E. Singer, 2:247–71. Hillsdale, NJ: Erlbaum

Saegert, S. 1986. Environmental psychology and social change. See Stokols & Altman 1986

Seligman, M. E. P. 1975. *Helplessness.* San Francisco: Freeman

Sell, J. L., Taylor, J. G., Zube, E. H. 1984. Toward a theoretical framework for landscape perception. In *Environmental Perception and Behavior: An Inventory and Prospect,* ed. T. F. Saarinen, D. Seamon, J. L. Sell, pp. 61–83. Chicago: Univ. Chicago Dep. Geogr.

Shumaker, S. A., Reizensenstein, J. E. 1982. Environmental factors affecting inpatient stress in acute care hospitals. See Evans 1982, pp. 179–223

Siegel, A. W., White, S. H. 1975. The development of spatial representations of large-scale environments. In *Advances in Child Development and Behavior,* ed. H. W. Reese, 10:9–55. New York: Academic

Smith, C. D. 1984. The relationship between the pleasingness of landmarks and the judg-

ment of distance in cognitive maps. *J. Environ. Psychol.* 4:229–34

Smith, T. R., Pellegrino, J. W., Golledge, R. G. 1982. Computational process modeling of spatial cognition and behavior. *Geogr. Anal.* 14:305–25

Spacapan, S., Cohen, S. 1983. Effects and aftereffects of stressor expectations. *J. Pers. Soc. Psychol.* 45:1243–54

Stokols, D. 1978. Environmental psychology. *Ann. Rev. Psychol.* 29:253–95

Stokols, D. 1982. Environmental psychology: A coming of age. In *The G. Stanley Hall Lecture Series,* ed. A. G. Kraut, 2:155–205. Washington, DC: Am. Psychol. Assoc.

Stokols, D. 1983. *Scientific and policy challenges of a contextually-oriented psychology.* Presidential addr. to Div. Popul. Environ. Psychol. Am. Psychol. Assoc., Anaheim, CA.

Stokols, D., Altman, I., eds. 1986. *Handbook of Environmental Psychology.* New York: Wiley. In press

Stokols, D., Jacobi, M. 1984. Traditional, present oriented, and futuristic modes of group-environment relations. In *Historical Social Psychology,* ed. K. Gergen, M. Gergen, pp. 303–24. Hillsdale, NJ: Erlbaum

Sundstrom, E., Herbert, R. K., Brown, D. W. 1982a. Privacy and communication in an open-plan office: A case study. *Environ. Behav.* 14:379–92

Sundstrom, E., Town, J. P., Brown, D. W., Forman, A., McGee, C. 1982b. Physical enclosure, type of job, and privacy in the office. *Environ. Behav.* 14:543–59

Sussman, N. M., Rosenfeld, H. M. 1982. Influence of culture, language, and sex on conversational distance. *J. Pers. Soc. Psychol.* 42:66–74

Taylor, R. B., Gottfredson, S. D., Brower, S. 1980. The defensibility of defensible space: A critical review and a synthetic framework for future research. In *Understanding Crime,* ed. T. Hirschi, M. Gottfredson, pp. 53–71. Beverly Hills, CA: Sage

Taylor, R. B., Gottfredson, S. D., Brower, S. 1985. *J. Res. Crime Delinquency.* In press

Ulrich, R. S. 1984. View through a window may influence recovery from surgery. *Science* 224:420–21

Wapner, S., Ciottone, R. A., Hornstein, G. A., McNeil, O. V., Pacheco, A. M. 1983. An examination of studies of critical transitions through the life cycle. In *Toward a Holistic Developmental Psychology,* ed. S. Wapner, B. Kaplan, pp. 111–32. Hillsdale, NJ: Erlbaum

Weidemann, S., Anderson, J. R., Butterfield, D. I., O'Donnell, P. M. 1982. Residents' perceptions of satisfaction and safety: A basis for change in multifamily housing. *Environ. Behav.* 14:695–724

Weinstein, N. D. 1982. Community noise problems: Evidence against adaptation. *J. Environ. Psychol.* 2:87–97

Wener, R., Frazier, W., Farbstein, J. 1985. Three generations of evaluation and design of correctional facilities. *Environ. Behav.* 17:71–95

Wicker, A. W. 1986. Behavior settings reconsidered: Temporal stages, resources, internal dynamics, context. See Stokols & Altman 1986

Williamson, R. C. 1981. Adjustment to the highrise: Variables in a German sample. *Environ. Behav.* 13:289–310

Wineman, J. D. 1982. Office design and evaluation: An overview. *Environ. Behav.* 14:271–98

Wohlwill, J. F. 1982. The visual impact of development in coastal zone areas. *Coastal Zone Manage. J.* 9:225–48

Wohlwill, J. F. 1983. Physical and social environment as factors in development. In *Human Development: An Interactional Perspective,* ed. D. Magnusson, V. L. Allen, pp. 111–29. New York: Academic

Wohlwill, J. F., Heft, H. 1986. The physical environment and the development of the child. See Stokols & Altman 1986

Wohlwill, J. F., van Vliet, W., eds. 1985. *Habitats for Children: The Impacts of Density.* Hillsdale, NJ: Erlbaum

Zimring, C. M., Weitzer, W., Knight, R. C. 1982. Opportunity for control and the designed environment: The case of an institution for the developmentally disabled. In *Advances in Environmental Psychology: Environment and Health,* ed. A. Baum, J. E. Singer, 4:171–210. Hillsdale, NJ: Erlbaum

Zube, E. H., Pitt, D. G. 1981. Cross-cultural perceptions of scenic and heritage landscapes. *Landscape Plann.* 8:69–87

Zube, E. H., Pitt, D. G., Evans, G. W. 1983. A lifespan developmental study of landscape assessment. *J. Environ. Psychol.* 3:115–28

Zube, E. H., Sell, J. L., Taylor, J. G. 1982. Landscape perception: Research, application, and theory. *Landscape Plann.* 9:1–33

Ann. Rev. Psychol. 1986. 37:409–32

DIAGNOSIS AND CLINICAL ASSESSMENT: The Current State of Psychiatric Diagnosis

Lee N. Robins and John E. Helzer

Department of Psychiatry, Washington University School of Medicine, 4940 Audubon Avenue, St. Louis, Missouri 63110

CONTENTS

THE NEW ENTHUSIASM FOR PSYCHIATRIC DIAGNOSIS IN THE UNITED STATES 410
HOW THE CHANGE TOOK PLACE 412
REMAINING CONFLICTS 414
THE STRUCTURE AND CONTENT OF DSM-III 414
MORE BASIS ISSUES: CATEGORIES vs DIMENSIONS 418
THE ORGANIZATION OF THE NOMENCLATURE 420
MEASURING HOW SATISFACTORY A DIAGNOSTIC SYSTEM IS 422
CONCLUSIONS 429

This chapter reviews the historical shift from an anti- to a pro-diagnostic stance among members of the psychiatric community, while noting the pockets of resistance to the idea of categorical diagnoses that still remain among both social scientists and psychodynamic psychiatrists. It reviews the state of psychiatric diagnosis as expressed in the official diagnostic system adopted by the American Psychiatric Association (1980), and the changes about to be incorporated into a revision of that system. It discusses the influence of the American system on the psychiatric nomenclature in the rest of the world, as reflected in usage and in projected revisions of the International Classification of Disorders (World Health Organization 1977).

9966-4308/86/0201-0409$02.00

Given the divisive attitudes toward diagnosis, the biases of the authors should be clear at the beginning. Although keenly aware of the contradictions among the various goals for which psychiatric nomenclatures are used, and the fact that current practices are often based on tradition and politics rather than scientific evidence, the authors believe that diagnoses are indispensable to communication among clinicians and researchers. They also believe that despite the obvious shortcomings of the current system, agreement as to the broad outlines of important categories across nations and time is not entirely the result of psychiatric imperialism, but rather springs from a correspondence between these categories and phenomena in the real world that have parallels to physical diseases. The fact that no one has yet defined psychiatric disorder in a way that settles the membership of every possible case or prevents the inclusion in diagnostic systems of some "disorders" that seem ludicrous to the common man does not mean that there is not broad agreement on major categories, at least for the more severe disorders and for those few disorders for which physical etiological factors have been identified.

THE NEW ENTHUSIASM FOR PSYCHIATRIC DIAGNOSIS IN THE UNITED STATES

In the 1940s and 1950s, psychiatric diagnosis was unpopular. The chief criticisms leveled against it were that it ignored individual variation and that it was somehow dehumanizing. That viewpoint has been heard less frequently since approximately the early 1960s, when the domination of American psychiatry by psychoanalysis began to wane, and what has been called the "neo-Kraepelinian" school began to gain acceptance (Klerman 1983). The term "neo-Kraepelinian" meant both a reawakening of interest in psychiatric classification and a view that classification should arise out of the observation of phenomenology and course of illness rather than out of unproved etiological theories.

A focus on diagnosis had never entirely disappeared in the United States even during the period when it was at low ebb. In particular, the Department of Psychiatry at Washington University emphasized phenomenological description by diagnostic category achieved by systematic interviewing of consecutive or randomly selected series of patients and control subjects and verified by demonstrating the stability of the symptom picture through long-term follow-up studies. Considered a maverick in the 1940s and 1950s, that department found its allies chiefly in England and in Scandinavia.

Attention to descriptive psychiatry at Washington University stemmed from the belief that current etiological theories were not based on evidence that could stand scientific scrutiny. Careful description of phenomenologically uniform groups, it was postulated, should be the first step in selecting groups that would also be found to share a common etiology. It was anticipated that a common etiology would in turn suggest diagnosis-specific treatment. It was this conviction that symptoms and etiology were closely linked that marked Washington University's divergence from the psychoanalytic school. Psychoanalysts believed that diametrically opposite symptom patterns (e.g. internalizing and externalizing disorders) often had a common etiology. If this was so, and if treatment addressed the etiological factors, diagnosis based on symptom description had little relevance to either understanding causes or designing treatments.

Not only was diagnosis emphasized at Washington University, but the pattern of diagnoses used differed considerably from that of other American psychiatric centers. For example, because members of the department were convinced by empirical research showing that electroconvulsive therapy was a successful treatment method for depressive disorder they felt it was important that depressive disorder not be missed. As a result, there was a striking bias toward this diagnosis and against the diagnosis of schizophrenia in patients with both affective and psychotic symptoms. This diagnostic style largely explained the sympathy with which the department was viewed by British psychiatry, which had the same bias. The department also limited itself to a few well-described diagnoses, finding no use for terms such as adjustment disorder and most of the personality disorders because they were felt to be too imprecise and ill described, or for the categories of psychosomatic disorders, because the evidence that these illnesses had a psychogenic basis was unconvincing.

An important part of the diagnostic system, however, was an "undiagnosed psychiatric illness" category for atypical cases, representing the belief that the categories used were not exhaustive, and that it might be possible through further studies to identify more disorders. Another feature of the Washington University approach was that it tended toward "clumping" rather than "splitting." At a time when other psychiatrists were breaking diagnoses into subcategories such as endogenous and reactive depressions and psychotic vs neurotic depressions, it used the term "manic-depressive disorder" to encompass all types and degrees of depression. The basis of this view was a study of the course of that disorder over time which had shown that the same patient could have an episode at one point that was very mild and a second that was very severe—some episodes with and some without psychotic features.

Early in its history, the Washington University department shared the general view in American psychiatry, and specified in DSM-I (American Psychiatric Association 1952), that each patient was to get only a single diagnosis. In the late 1960s, a method for allowing multiple diagnoses was proposed, in which the diagnosis with the earlier onset was always to be considered the primary diagnosis (Robins & Guze 1972).

It is worth dwelling on the philosophy of the psychiatry department at

Washington University because its views, long an anathema to the psychiatric establishment, now play a dominant role in American psychiatry. But there is still considerable doubt among some psychiatrists and psychologists as to the wisdom of this new enthusiasm for diagnosis. The claim that the interest in diagnosis is etiologically neutral has been doubted by some, and instead is thought to hide a belief that all psychiatric illness has some biological error as its cause. In turn, the belief in biological causes has been said to lead to therapeutic nihilism and a lack of interest in the "whole" patient.

The charge that an interest in diagnosis implies a belief in a biological etiology probably stems from the historical concurrence of an interest in diagnosis and an absence at Washington University of the antibiological stance that modern psychoanalysis has taken. In fact, clinical, social, genetic, and biochemical research into etiological factors coexisted harmoniously there. All comers were welcome so long as the research produced results that could be replicated and empirically tested.

The charge that physicians who diagnose lack interest in the patient as a person was seen by Washington University physicians as a negative view of what they regarded as proper modesty with respect to their area of expertise. They noted that as medical advances have resulted in disorder-specific effective therapies, the physician now can offer more than authority, kindliness, and human concern, which are humanistic but not necessarily curative. Diagnosis in psychiatry was viewed as a way of achieving the same advances for psychiatric disorders that it had for medical disorders. As Guze (1977) put it, "Whether the diagnosis is . . . mania, schizophrenia, or obsessional neurosis . . . is more important in treatment, course or outcome than whether the individual is male or female, black or white, educated or ignorant, married or divorced, well adjusted or not, religious or not, etc." He would advocate rapid categorization of disorder as the most humane behavior possible by a physician, because it leads most directly to selecting the treatment that will relieve the patient's distress.

HOW THE CHANGE TOOK PLACE

It is never easy to explain historical changes, and the rising star of diagnosis in the United States is no exception. Those interested in diagnosis have published prolifically, and this has no doubt made a big difference. Another reason was that biochemical hypotheses about possible metabolic defects in the central nervous system that had long been resistant to testing in the complex structures of the brain became testable with the development of microtechniques that could identify activity in specific brain areas. Developments in brain imaging have also increased the potential for identifying functional abnormalities. Studies of adoptees in Scandinavia (Rosenthal & Kety 1968) suggested crossfostering as a method for genetic studies that could separate nature and nurture as effectively as had the elegant studies of identical twins reared apart for which appropriate cases were always too scarce. These opportunities for precise biochemical measurement and family studies prompted the need for homogeneous samples and pure control groups. In turn, these studies promised to furnish the data necessary to criticize and improve current diagnostic categories.

A critical event for the change was the coincidence of Dr. Robert Spitzer's simultaneous roles as one of a small group assigned to define the areas of concern and diagnostic tools to be used in the NIMH Collaborative Depression Study and as head of the task force to produce the new official diagnostic manual DSM-III (American Psychiatric Association 1980). In the first of these roles, he worked closely with Dr. Eli Robins of Washington University, learning his diagnostic views and the operational criteria that had been developed for making diagnoses at Washington University and published as the "Feighner criteria" (Feighner et al 1972). His previous experience with the US-UK project, which found that the high rates of schizophrenia in U.S. in-patients as compared with British patients was a matter of diagnostic tradition rather than a difference in the patients' symptoms (Cooper et al 1972), had prepared him for a sympathetic view toward the Washington University pro-depression bias. He hoped that implementing similar atheoretical operational criteria for DSM-III would make possible uniform diagnostic practices even in the absence of shared etiological theories among the various psychiatric schools in the U.S., and perhaps eventually lead to data that would permit resolution of some of these conflicts.

The decision to prepare diagnostic criteria for DSM-III similar to those used at Washington University was made several years before the actual publication of that volume. Those years were filled with review by many panels of experts, much rewriting, and much arguing of positions. It is perhaps remarkable that as much remains of the original vision as there is. The stamp of the Washington University approach is still clear, although there have indeed been many changes. The most dramatic difference is the expansion of the list of diagnoses. There has been subtyping and splitting of diagnoses, in part on the basis of new empirical data, but often because the volume needed to accommodate the categories traditionally used by clinicians with very differing views. Thus DSM-III contains more than 200 diagnoses instead of the original 20 or less used at Washington University. Also, many of the names have been altered, in part because the old names were sometimes being used with different meanings by different groups, but more often because they had become associated with one or another adversarial group, and a new term was intended to be politically neutral.

Despite the controversy and compromise that DSM-III represents, it has succeeded in giving much of academic psychiatry a new interest in diagnostic issues, and has committed the field to the use of clearly stated criteria that are to be combined in some quantitative fashion. It has also fostered the twin principles that the value of any diagnostic scheme can be tested empirically and that the current diagnostic scheme is only a set of hypotheses about reality, subject to change and development based on empirical research.

As Spitzer et al (1975) put it:

Premature closure (of a diagnostic scheme) can be avoided only by the recognition that any classification system and its criteria should be regarded with varying degrees of tentativeness and should be subject to continued revision according to new knowledge . . . The specified criteria would facilitate rather than discourage future research because they would provide explicit definitions for the categories, which would enable investigators to better study the comparative validity of alternative criteria. . . . Perhaps the true value of the suggested criteria will be demonstrated not by how long they remain unchanged but by the rapidity with which they facilitate research that results in their modification and improvement.

REMAINING CONFLICTS

As the battle over whether or not diagnosis should occur at all has subsided, the current form of psychiatric diagnosis continues to be challenged. Among the current issues are dimensional vs categorical diagnosis, the function of diagnostic axes, the broad groupings into which diagnoses are assembled, the use of diagnostic hierarchies, the degree of specificity with which criteria are designated and their empirical basis, and the validity of cultural variation. Crosscutting these issues are questions about the competitive needs of researchers, clinicians, and administrators, who have differing requirements, particularly in terms of narrowness and precision.

Some of these criticisms can be discussed in the context of DSM-III and its organization. Others challenge the very concept of a manual of categorical diagnoses like DSM-III. We will begin with those that are less sweeping indictments of the current system.

THE STRUCTURE AND CONTENT OF DSM-III

(a) *The axes.* The *Manual* is organized around five axes. Axis I contains the clinical syndromes, Axis II the personality disorders and specific developmental disorders, and Axis III the pertinent physical disorders and/or conditions. These three constitute the official diagnostic assessment. Axis IV provides a 7-point scale for the rating of any psychosocial stressors that may be considered pertinent to the present illness, and Axis V provides a 7-point scale for rating the highest level of adaptive functioning that the patient has achieved over the preceding year. Each point on these two scales is defined and examples are given for both adults and children. The use of these axes is considered to be experimental. Only the first two are required for statistical reporting, and only they represent areas in which much current research is going on. For the purposes of this chapter, we will consider only Axes I and II.

(b) *Major categories on Axes I and II*. The organization of diagnoses in DSM-III is in part constrained by the need to be compatible with the International Classification of Diseases (ICD-9-CM), for purposes of international reporting. However, there is no need to use the same grouping of diagnoses, nor is there any restriction on adding new diagnoses or subdividing those that appear in ICD-9.

On Axis I, there are two major divisions, into Disorders Usually First Evident in Infancy, Childhood, or Adolescence and other disorders. While this division is roughly that between child and adult psychiatry, included among the "child" disorders are the eating disorders, anorexia nervosa and bulimia, disorders treated at least as frequently in adults, and among the disorders appearing *after* the "childhood" section is Gender Identity Disorder of Childhood.

The adult section of Axis I varies in the breadth of its subcategories. Large groups include the Organic Mental Disorders, the Substance Abuse Disorders, the Affective Disorders, the Anxiety Disorders, and the Psychosexual Disorders. There are also "V" codes to accommodate conditions treated by psychiatrists that are not considered to be mental disorders. These include malingering, antisocial behavior, bereavement, school and job problems, marital problems, etc. Finally, there is the opportunity for deferring diagnosis, denying the presence of any diagnosis or treatable condition, or saying that the picture fits none of the categories provided.

Axis II has only two sections: Specific Developmental Disorders and Personality Disorders. Diagnoses may also be deferred for Axis II or absence of an Axis II diagnosis noted.

There have been criticisms of the structure of DSM-III. One would expect that there should be resemblance among syndromes within the major groups on an axis. Yet empirical studies have found that antisocial personality, on Axis II, is more highly correlated with the substance abuse disorders than they are among themselves, even though they are within a single group on a different axis (Robins et al 1986). Similarly, panic disorder, which is in Axis I Anxiety Disorders, is more closely associated with depression, which is in Axis I Affective Disorders, than it is with other disorders in the Anxiety Disorder group.

There are also logical problems. Axis II is supposed to cover those diagnoses that are present from birth and especially long lasting. Yet mental retardation and pervasive developmental disorders, which both begin early and are irreversible, are included on Axis I.

(*c*) *The coverage.* As noted above, DSM-III contains approximately 205 diagnoses. Many clinicians use only a small proportion of those listed, even when they see a broad range of patients. This is in part because the plethora of diagnoses makes it difficult for a clinician to keep all the alternatives in mind when making diagnostic decisions, and in part because the great number reflects compromises between factions, so that the same set of symptoms can actually be subsumed under different diagnostic rubrics.

(*d*) *The text.* The text of DSM-III is long compared with that of previous editions of the *Manual.* It comes close to being a textbook of psychiatry. It provides a description of each illness category as well as material on what is known regarding the age of onset, clinical course, associated features, degree of impairment, complications, predisposing factors, illness prevalence, sex ratio, familial pattern, and differential diagnosis. The criteria sections specify the symptoms related to each disorder, the minimum number of symptoms required, sometimes a minimum or maximum age of onset, rarely the number of months over which the disorder develops, and disorders that may preempt this diagnosis. As an example of the preemptions, a patient who has symptoms of schizophrenia is not given the diagnosis of schizophrenia if there is simultaneous onset of symptoms of organic brain dysfunction, since the latter is considered a likely cause of the psychotic symptoms. The typical exclusion criterion is: "Not due to another mental disorder, such as . . ." with a listing of a few examples.

The elaborate text is generally seen as a large step forward. However, psychodynamic psychiatrists have complained that it is based too exclusively on statistical studies and overlooks some important clinical research (Bayer & Spitzer 1985).

(*e*) *Hierarchies.* Although DSM-I (American Psychiatric Association 1952) allowed only a single diagnosis per patient, DSM-II (American Psychiatric Association 1968) allowed multiple diagnoses "when appropriate" and mandated them if organic brain syndrome or mental retardation was the result of a specific physical condition (Freedman et al 1972). Yet there remained rules under which only a single diagnosis should be identified. If a set of symptoms that occurring alone would warrant a diagnosis appeared in a given patient only when another diagnosis was in an active phase, this embedded diagnosis should be considered a symptom of the disorder in which it was embedded. Common examples are panic attacks, bouts of problem drinking, and hypochondriacal concerns that appear only during depressive episodes. The problem with this rule is that clear-cut instances for its application can be found only if the presumed major disorder is episodic or goes into remission. That is, if an alcohol abuser becomes depressed, one cannot know whether the depression is only a side effect of his alcohol abuse unless he stops drinking so that it can be observed whether the depression lifts.

One sees in DSM-II the roots of the DSM-III concept of multiple diagnoses combined with diagnostic hierarchies and the reason that it has been difficult to operationalize the hierarchical rules. DSM-III also allows and indeed recommends multiple diagnoses in certain circumstances. It suggests that if multiple diagnoses are given, the diagnoses that occasioned seeking care be designated the principal diagnosis. (This does not help, of course, in epidemiological studies, where the identified case may not be seeking care.)

DSM-III also has diagnostic hierarchies that require excluding one diagnosis if another has caused it. Decisions seem to have been made on a disorder-by-disorder basis as to whether a particular diagnosis should be preempted by another and what the preempting diagnoses should be. The only general principle offered is that Axis II (specific developmental disorders and the personality disorders) diagnoses should not be made if their symptoms are present only when some Axis I disorder is active.

As specific as criteria are in most of DSM-III, there are no decision rules for ascertaining whether a disorder that is a possible excluder of a second diagnosis is causative or merely coincident with the second diagnosis. In addition, the list of preempting diagnoses is often incomplete. A typical statement is "not due to another mental disorder, such as a Depressive Disorder or Schizophrenia." It is not clear what disorders other than depressive disorder or schizophrenia could also preempt the disorder of interest.

The DSM-III approach to diagnostic hierarchies has recently been called into question (Boyd et al 1984) on empirical grounds. A large epidemiological study, the Epidemiological Catchment Area project, which made diagnoses with and without the DSM-III hierarchies, found that the strong correlations between pairs of diagnoses implied by making one preempt the other were not always present, and that in fact correlations were sometimes stronger between pairs of diagnoses for which no preemptions were specified. In response to this criticism, hierarchies will largely disappear in the revision of DSM-III now being prepared.

Multiple diagnoses will therefore become even more abundant than they now are. This may increase discrepancies between American and international systems, since ICD-9 is hierarchical, choosing organic disorders over functional ones, psychoses over neuroses, and neuroses over personality disorders and other disorders.

(f) *Rigidity of criteria*. DSM-III often provides very specific rules for minimum number of symptoms, minimum number of times a symptom was manifested, maximum ages of onset, and minimum ages at which a diagnosis can be made. These cutoff points have rarely been empirically tested to find out whether they are optimal or even necessary. We do not know, for example, that persons with many panic attacks, but never more than two in a three-week period (and who therefore do not meet DSM-III criteria for Panic Disorder) are different in their outcomes or associated symptoms from people who have had three attacks in three weeks, nor whether infantile autism, which must begin before 30 months, differs in its consequences for a child's future from the similar pattern of symptoms called Childhood Onset Pervasive Developmental Disorder, which begins between 30 months and 12 years of age.

Symptoms are often assorted into groups, with the requirement that a minimum number of groups be represented. The purpose of this requirement, which has been termed the "Chinese menu system" (Klerman 1978), is to assure that the whole syndrome is present.

These often arbitrary cutoffs should reduce the variation in cases across settings and across studies, so that research results from one site have a better chance of being replicated across sites. However, they often dismay clinicians because they seem to interdict giving diagnoses they "know in their bones" to be correct, because the case does not quite meet these specific criteria. When precise criteria are not met, clinicians are given several options. When patients come close to meeting criteria, they may be assigned the diagnosis the clinician believes is present as a "provisional" diagnosis; given somewhat more uncertainty, the clinician can give an "atypical" diagnosis within the category he believes applies. He may also designate a patient simply as having some unidentified psychotic or some unidentified nonpsychotic disorder.

While the false precision implied by these numeric criteria is galling, it is hard to see how this rigidity can be entirely dispensed with and still maintain the goal of uniformity of diagnosis across settings. Early drafts for the revision of DSM-III, responding to these objections, replace some of the numeric criteria with words like "often" and "sometimes." The danger is that such words are likely to be translated into numbers, and into different numbers by different users.

The revision will also drop most of the symptom groups, and it will cover the issue of a case's being sufficiently representative of the total syndrome by requiring enough individual symptoms so that a narrow or monosymptomatic picture would not qualify.

MORE BASIC ISSUES: CATEGORIES VS DIMENSIONS

There are many psychologists who would say that any solution to these criticisms of DSM-III's structure and content would merely patch over the more serious issue, which is that categorical diagnoses inevitably lead to unresolvable problems because they force the selection of cutting points that have no empirical or practical basis. They would recommend abandoning diagnostic criteria in favor of a dimensional approach.

Argument in favor of a dimensional approach to psychiatric diagnosis is possible because there are as yet no definitive tests for the presence of a disorder. While many psychiatrists and others believe that there will someday be such tests because some biochemical abnormality will turn out to be a necessary precondition of the clinical picture, they would agree that at present diagnosis depends on the degree of similarity between a person's signs and symptoms and some ideal picture of the phenomenology of the disorder. At present, then, there is no need to argue over whether or not the underlying structure on which diagnosis is based is truly dimensional, since the only available method for making a diagnosis at present is a dimensional one. Psychiatrists using DSM-III count signs and symptoms to decide, within the limits laid out by DSM-III, whether or not the individual has enough of these signs and symptoms to warrant the diagnosis. The argument rests on whether or not dimensions should be translated into categories by setting a cut point beyond which a symptom or disorder is considered present and below which it is considered absent, as DSM-III does.

There is no question that some of DSM-III's problems outlined above would disappear if categorical diagnosis were abandoned. It would not, for example, be necessary to have provisional diagnoses or "atypical" diagnoses to handle cases that almost meet criteria. In a dimensional system, a numerical value would indicate what proportion of the set of diagnostic items in a dimension of disorder a given case has experienced. Hierarchies would presumably not be used, since each dimension could have a separate value in multidimensional space. Axes would have no a priori meaning, but groupings of dimensions into superdimensions could occur on the basis of their empirical correlations.

In principle, the problem of cutoff points for symptoms could also disappear, since the diagnostic dimension could be created by a grouping of symptom-level dimensions. However, this would create a very complex scale, each symptom having a different weight, which might well frustrate studies of the relative importance of a dimension's elements.

If these problems could be solved by a dimensional system, why not use one? The obvious attraction of a cut point is that it simplifies decision making. As an example, a primary care physician who must decide whether or not to refer patients to a mental health specialist welcomes a cut point that eliminates most of his patients from the need for such a decision by declaring them to be free of disorder.

The simplicity of categorical diagnoses has its drawbacks as well as its advantages, however. As pointed out by Finn (1982), choosing the best cutoff point along a dimension to use in defining disorders as categories requires knowing the relative costs for those improperly assigned in terms of whatever action will be taken as a result of their assignment. If the action is treatment, for example, lowering the cut point so that more of the people who could benefit from treatment will get it inevitably increases the number who will get treatment without benefiting from it. One would like to choose the cut point that selects the best cost-benefit ratio of false negatives to false positives. The problem with categorical diagnoses is that the cut point is fixed ahead of time, and the best cutoff point with respect to making one decision is not necessarily the best with respect to another decision.

Recent developments in decision theory (Sackett et al 1985, Ch. 4), which estimate whether benefits are likely to exceed costs for a given action, seem to provide a solution to this dilemma by allowing a maximum-likelihood approach to categorical diagnosis. If one assumes that in the presence of a disorder treatment is desirable, the fact that its presence is discerned with varying certainty permits applying dimensional principles. Instead of simply reporting a diagnosis as present or absent, the diagnostician reports the number of positive criteria met. The resulting score is then applied to a chart of cost-benefits that is specific to the particular intervention contemplated to see whether that degree of similarity to definitely being a case warrants applying the particular strategy being considered.

This clinical decision-making strategy can serve other purposes, such as seeking correlates of disorder or studying natural history by follow-up. In such studies, each individual is weighted in the data analysis on the basis of his resemblance to an undoubted case. The great advantage of this approach is that it makes studies across sites and populations much more comparable than they now are, because it amounts to standardizing the sample's diagnostic composition. Previous failures to replicate results across studies often resulted from the fact that the distributions of cases by the severity of their disorder differ across studies as does the distribution of control cases with respect to their freedom from symptoms of the disorder (Helzer & Coryell 1983).

In brief, the categorical cutting points in diagnostic systems are convenient for simplifying decisions under known conditions, but they may not be optimal under other conditions and for other populations. However, the choice need not be made between the simplicity of the categorical system vs the loss of information that choosing a single category implies. Analytic techniques can do much to preserve the easy shorthand that categories provide without forfeiting all precision.

THE ORGANIZATION OF THE NOMENCLATURE

The ideal after which a psychiatric diagnostic system strains is a set of categories that have mutually exclusive criteria, are qualitatively different, and are jointly exhaustive. These categories should then be organized into families of diagnoses in such a way that within-family correlations are greater than between-family correlations. However, national and international classification systems are the products of lobbying and compromise. Such a history does not make for logic or elegance. ICD-9 and DSM-III both fall far short of the ideal with respect to their organization. For example, ICD-9, as a result of bowing to multiple viewpoints, has 19 different diagnostic categories that include depression as a major or significant feature. This accommodation of overlapping categories has meant that the "participation of most governments and national associations has been assured and life has been made easier for record clerks, but in the process all coherence and unity have been lost" (Kendell 1973).

Nonetheless, as Kendell also points out, "the advantages of being able to communicate freely and reasonably accurately with other workers throughout the world are so great that it is worth tolerating a classification that falls short of our personal aspirations."

We have noted above that in DSM-III, the goal of stronger correlations within than between groups of diagnoses has not been met in all cases. There are also instances in which different diagnoses have overlapping criteria, as for example alcohol abuse and alcohol dependence. Thus both systems fall short of meeting the criteria for a rational system, though they represent improvements over earlier systems.

ICD-9 and DSM-III are only the latest of many efforts in psychiatric history to rationalize the nomenclature; some of them have been successful, and others have foundered on the politics of psychiatry. The most famous successful example was Emil Kraepelin's (1974) bringing together several nineteenth century syndromes that involved severe intellectual and personality deterioration under one rubric which he labeled dementia praecox (and for which Eugen Bleuler shortly thereafter introduced the term schizophrenia.) Kraepelin also differentiated this group from what he called manic-depressive insanity in which the typical clinical picture was an episodic illness with prominent affective changes and interepisode recovery rather than chronic deterioration.

The task force responsible for constructing DSM-III also tried to overturn the traditional organization of the nomenclature as exemplified by DSM-II and ICD-9 by dropping the term "neurosis" as a major classifier. This change was prompted by studies discussed above which found that episodes which on a cross-sectional basis could be called "depressive neurosis" and "psychotic depressive episodes" occurred as part of a single illness in many individuals studied longitudinally, and did not even seem to represent progression of the illness (i.e. a "neurotic" episode could follow a "psychotic" one). In the end, this effort was successful only in part because of constraints to remain consistent with ICD-9, and more importantly because of enormous opposition from the psychoanalytic and psychodynamic branches of American psychiatry (Bayer & Spitzer 1985). They fought for the term "neurotic" because it had come to symbolize the etiologic theory of the psychodynamic school that certain disorders were the product of intrapsychic conflict. The outcry from psychodynamic psychiatrists and their threats to scuttle the whole enterprise finally resulted in a compromise. A new diagnosis, "Dysthymia," was created to fulfill the role previously filled by depressive neurosis, and for Dysthymia, Panic Disorder, and Obsessive Compulsive Disorder, a parenthetical phrase allowing the use of the term neurosis was included.

The coming revision of DSM-III promises to continue the progress toward a more rational system. For example, there are plans to combine Alcohol Abuse and Dependence into a single diagnosis, removing the overlap between their categories. But approaches to rationality will continue to be a gradual process. Not only must consensus be achieved by committees made up of representatives of a variety of psychiatric schools, but there is also a vast inertia when it comes to making major changes, both because of the need for the American system to be compatible with the international nomenclature and because changes disrupt the ability of a nomenclature to function as a shorthand form of communication. Each time a major change occurs, a new language must be learned, and the relevance of the existing body of literature based on the former nomenclature is called into question.

MEASURING HOW SATISFACTORY A DIAGNOSTIC SYSTEM IS

DSM-III, which was published in 1980, is now in the process of revision only five years later. The changes will not cause a major departure from its design, which was itself a radical shift from the previous *Manual,* because there has been general acceptance of the idea of providing specific diagnostic criteria. The revision will attempt to improve those areas that have caused dissatisfaction among clinicians and researchers.

The history of diagnostic systems is a history of change, and noting that changes are about to occur in DSM-III does not mean that most of the problems being addressed by these changes have been solved permanently. It may be useful, as this revision is taking place, to review some recent thinking about the desiderata of a diagnostic system, and how one could evaluate whether changes are likely to be improvements.

Diagnostic systems serve many purposes, and it is unlikely that any one system will be the best for each of these purposes. They are used by administrators of hospitals, by departments of health for annual reports and budget requests to state legislatures, by doctors and patients making insurance claims, and of most interest to the writers and readers of this chapter, as a tool for developing new knowledge about adequate treatment and about the nature of disorder itself.

Blashfield & Draguns (1976a) offer five purposes of classification: communication, information retrieval (i.e. ability to use existing relevant literature), descriptive value, prediction, and as a source of concepts for scientific theory. They also offer four criteria by which a psychiatric classification can be judged (1976b): reliability, coverage, descriptive validity, and predictive validity. Each influences the degree to which the purposes will be met.

1. *Reliability*. Reliability increases as the elements of the diagnostic system become more specific and the rules for combining them become more explicit. Another important factor is the degree to which its definitions and rules fit the training and beliefs of those applying the system. While carefully defined criteria and explicit diagnostic algorithms clearly reduce the range of interpretation possible, no system is or ever can be so explicit that it cannot be bent to accommodate the diagnostician's own views. Thus the degree to which the users agree on diagnostic concepts will influence the reliability of their diagnostic practice.

An attempt by Ward et al (1962) to distinguish between the contributions of the system and way in which it was applied, at a time when the official diagnostic system was much less detailed than it is at present, found that the system itself accounted for about 60% of the disagreements and 30% was attributable to the diagnosticians. The remaining 10% resulted from clinical change in the patient and other miscellaneous events. It would be expected that this 2-to-1 ratio of system to clinician responsibility would have decreased with the increase in specificity represented by DSM-III.

There probably is a limit to how much reliability should be sought. Maximizing reliability may produce undesirable results with respect to validity, for example. Also, too much attention to reliability can actually be self-defeating. The more explicit the criteria, the more likely they are not to fit a particular case. The only way to combine specificity with completeness is to lengthen the list of specific criteria. This is one reason why DSM-III is so much larger than its predecessors. However, long lists of criteria are hard to remember, and it is tedious to compare a presenting patient's complaints against them. The risk, then, is that the criteria will be applied erratically or ignored, producing less reliable results than if more realistic reliability goals had been set.

The use of structured interviews for gathering diagnostically relevant clinical information is a methodology that has become increasingly popular in the last few years. It allows uniform application of lengthy criterion lists and so improves the consistency of diagnosis. A structured or standardized interview has been defined as an interview in which "standard questions are asked in a predetermined order, and the set of available responses is often fixed" (Tsuang et al 1980). However, the terms "structured" and "standardized" are applied to instruments that range widely in the amount of structure imposed. The least structured is simply a fixed list of topics to be covered in whatever way and in whatever order the interviewer sees fit. At the other end there may be a completely specified procedure that includes defined questions to open each topic and specified follow-up branches according to the answers to the initial question, fixed scoring choices, and automatic (generally by computer) combination of scores according to the system's algorithms to produce diagnoses (Helzer 1983). The most recent trend is to go still farther by having the interview computer-presented, so that even the variation caused by different interviewers' ways of reading standardized questions to the respondent is eliminated.

One of the principal ways in which standardized interviews increase reliability is by making uniform the amount of information obtained. When diagnosticians use a free-form investigative technique, they usually choose a likely diagnosis within the first few minutes and spend the remainder of the time trying to confirm it. This approach is by no means unique to psychiatric diagnosis. Often in medicine the provisional diagnosis is made on the basis of a first glance at the patient, in which a characteristic gait or skin condition is recognized (Sackett 1978). In psychiatric diagnosis, grooming and the mood revealed by facial expression serve as similar provocation to instantaneous pattern recognition and early diagnostic judgment (Grossman et al 1971). This rapid homing in on a diagnosis wreaks least havoc with reliability when there is agreement that only a single diagnosis is to be selected, because skilled clinicians are likely to agree on what the chief presenting problem is, even when they vary enormously on the amount of additional information they choose to elicit if they are not required to follow a checklist of topics or more formal interview structure. For example, Climent et al (1975) found that even striking symptoms such as suicidal thoughts were reported three times more frequently when a checklist was used rather than a free-form interview. When the goal is to elicit all diagnoses that apply to a patient, clinicians in free-form interviews vary greatly in the completeness of their coverage. A standardized interview scrupulously applied guarantees that premature closure will not occur.

The literature provides evidence that clinicians omit collecting data even on topics they themselves believe to be essential in making a diagnosis. For example, Weitzel et al (1973) developed a structured checklist of 15 mental status items which a group of experts agreed should be routinely recorded for all patients. They then compared free-form and checklist examinations of the same patients. They found that patients responded similarly to the same items in the two interview situations, but in the free-form examinations, there were numerous omissions. Comments were recorded about all 15 items for only 4 of 49 patients examined. Meikle and colleagues (1970) also found that when a checklist was substituted for a free-form narrative, the mean number of descriptive items per patient increased.

Improvements in reliability resulting from structured interviewing should be greater as the interview's structure becomes more rigid. The lowest level of structure—a list of topics to be pursued—guarantees that each item will be attended to, but not that each will be given equal attention. When the level of structure is increased to specify questions to be asked, along with specified follow-up questions, the amount of information obtained for each item becomes more uniform. However, there can still be variation in what the diagnostician records, and consequently in how much of what the respondent said will enter into the diagnostic formulation. Interviews that provide a limited list of coding categories make the recording uniform, and computerization of the diagnostic algorithms guarantees that all the relevant items will enter into the diagnostic decision.

The fact that the reliability of a psychiatric diagnostic system varies with the interviewing method used to ascertain whether criteria are present, as well as with explicitness of criteria and of algorithms, underscores the fact that one cannot talk about the reliability of a diagnostic system per se apart from the operations that constitute its implementation. An instrument that does not match the diagnostic system well may lead to misjudging its value—in either direction. Since clinicians are highly variable in the degree to which they follow any system when left to their own devices, evaluating a system requires constructing a structured interview to serve it and seeing that the interview is used conscientiously.

There are now a few structured interviews available that could be used to compare all or parts of DSM-III with other diagnostic systems. These include the NIMH Diagnostic Interview Schedule (DIS) (Robins et al 1981), which provides 43 DSM-III diagnoses, all the Feighner (1972) diagnoses, and almost all of the Research Diagnostic Criteria (RDC) diagnoses (Spitzer et al 1978). The SADS and SADS-L (Spitzer & Endicott 1977) was originally constructed to assess RDC diagnoses. It has been modified to cover DSM-III diagnoses as well (Myers & Weissman 1981). The PDI (Othmer et al 1981), originally designed to make Feighner diagnoses, has been modified to make DSM-III diagnoses as well. The DIS has been combined with the Present State Examination (PSE) (Wing et al 1974) to create the Composite International Diagnostic Interview (CIDI) (Robins et al 1983), and this composite instrument will allow comparing DSM-III and PSE syndromes. Finally, there is a semistructured interview, the Structured Psychiatric Examination (SPE) (Romanoski & Chahal 1981) which was based on the PSE and modified to allow evaluation of the whole of DSM-III, and is designed to allow comparing DSM-III with the ICD-9. Spitzer is creating a new instrument, the SCID, in the same format as the SADS, which will make diagnoses according to the revision of DSM-III now being written. It can be compared with the SADS-L modified to conform to DSM-III criteria.

These multisystem interviews allow simultaneous assessment of multiple diagnostic systems in the same sample with the same interview format and the same interviewer, avoiding a number of possible confounders that would have to be taken into account if different instruments were used on successive occasions. By repeating the interview within a short time, the reliability of the systems can be compared.

2. *Coverage*. The two systems in greatest use today, ICD-9 and DSM-III, have as their goal complete coverage of the population of persons who present to psychiatrists. The need for this breadth is an administrative one. Statistics must be prepared into which each patient will fit. For this reason, provision must be made for people who consult psychiatrists but do not have a psychiatric disorder. For some psychiatrists, counseling with regard to problems in living or conducting psychoanalyses with essentially healthy patients may be a major part of their clinical practice. DSM-III copes with this problem through its "V" codes, described above.

Not all of the patients whom the man on the street would say have no mental disorder are given a "V" code. Among these are patients who receive diagnoses of adjustment disorder, which is a reaction to a stress or adverse event so excessive that it impairs functioning; tobacco use disorder, criteria for which have been met at some time by about two-thirds of the general population who have ever been heavy smokers; and many of the personality disorders, such as narcissistic and histrionic.

Also of dubious value are the monosymptomatic diagnoses. Examples are psychogenic amnesia, psychogenic fugue, multiple personality, psychogenic pain disorder, kleptomania. Although they may serve administrative purposes, they do not justify their existence on the basis of communicating a large amount of information in a few words. They merely name a symptom without implying anything about the history, course, or associated symptoms. Nor are they unique symptoms; instead they can be symptoms of other disorders. Somatization disorder includes amnesia as well as pain on no known physical basis among its symptoms; antisocial personality includes stealing, and therefore kleptomania. If these monosymptomatic diseases share the destiny of erstwhile medical monosymptomatic "disorders" like fever and catalepsy, they will soon disappear when they are recognized as being part of various syndromes.

The Feighner diagnoses (Feighner et al 1972), and the Research Diagnostic Criteria (Spitzer et al 1978) have not aimed for complete coverage, but these systems have been used mainly for research studies, not for administrative purposes. As research tools, they have been designed with strict criteria that should select homogeneous groups of cases with definite disorders, rather than attempting to assign questionable cases. To take care of monosymptomatic pictures and other atypical patterns, the residual categories of "undiagnosed disorder" and "uncertain if psychiatrically ill" were provided.

Assuming that the goal is research rather than administration, so that an incomplete system is acceptable even though it will always include a residual group of undiagnosed subjects, how does one decide which diagnoses shall be included? Two criteria suggested by Blashfield & Draguns (1976b), valid description and prediction, to be discussed below, make a diagnosis worth incorporating.

3. *Valid descriptions of affected persons*. The validity of a diagnosis can be assessed both in terms of its internal structure—i.e. its symptoms, response to treatment, and course—and in terms of its association with possible etiological factors. At this stage in our understanding of most psychiatric disorders, validity cannot be ascertained in any absolute way. However, if a disorder has the same pattern of symptoms across cases and over time and is associated with known precursors, leads to predictable degrees of impairment if untreated, and responds to specific treatments, the chances that it is a valid diagnosis are greatly increased.

The structured diagnostic interviews described under "Reliability" above can serve for comparing the relative validity of the same diagnoses within the same system. However, to serve as assessments of validity, these interviews must be expanded to date the respondent's experience of first symptoms and to date his exposure to possible risk factors, to record his subsequent symptomatic and symptom-free periods, his use of treatment facilities, treatments received and his treatment response, disorders in his family members, and level of social impairment. These questions allow comparing diagnoses with respect to their association with genetic and environmental risk factors and the stability of their courses and consequences. By repeating the interview after a considerable follow-up interval, the validity criteria of stability of symptoms, failure of the disorder to develop into another disorder that might have explained the earlier symptoms, and prediction of course can be established more definitively.

With the data from such studies it is possible to learn whether symptoms are consistent across cases and have a coherent structure in terms of their intercorrelations and time sequence of appearance. Symptoms may form a set of dimensions, as in the alcohol disorders, where social consequences of excessive drinking form one subscale while medical complications form a different subscale, or they may have a fixed order of onset and consequently a fixed relative frequency. Obviously, such assessment of symptom structures requires multisymptomatic diagnoses. It is for this reason that the monosymptomatic diagnoses discussed above are unsatisfactory—it is difficult to decide whether or not they are valid.

The studies suggested also allow ascertaining whether the disorder shows a standard course and standard risk factors. If studies are based on unbiased samples of persons with a disorder, they also provide the necessary epidemiological data that allow applying Bayesian methods to decide whether future cases do or do not have the same diagnosis. As Feinstein (1973) describes the process:

> The purpose of the (diagnostic) reasoning is to provide satisfactory explanations for the observed evidence; and the format consists of a branching series of logical decisions, each of

which produces intermediate conclusions during the progressive transformation of input to output. . . . In the Bayesian approach, the input depends on the patient's symptoms, signs, or other medical data . . . A statistical formula is used to calculate, as output, the likelihood that a particular disease is present. . . . (A) Bayesian calculation depends on quantitative data that are seldom available: the rates with which certain symptoms, signs, and diseases occur in the pertinent population. . . . The Bayesian strategy provides only the computation of a diagnostic probability.

This statement shows the dependence of diagnostic decisions on epidemiologic studies. Epidemiologic studies provide the data that allow the calculation of a likelihood estimate of the presence of the disorder based on similarity to cases identified in such studies. This approach to diagnosis is necessary when the etiology of the disorder of interest is not yet known and when there are no definitive physical tests for its presence. This stage in all of medicine usually precedes the discovery of etiology. It is only after a group homogeneous with respect to cross-sectional picture, history, and course is identified that it becomes possible to find risk factors external to the disorder that may give clues to etiology. Of course, once an etiological factor is found, it often leads to refining the description, i.e. dissecting away cases with a superficial resemblance to the group that has the common etiology and perhaps linking the described group with another on the basis of common etiology despite some phenomenological differences.

4. *Prediction.* When diagnoses are based on associations among features of the course and symptoms that are not themselves necessarily interdependent (e.g. insomnia plus weight loss is a much more powerful pair of associated symptoms for depression than weight loss and lack of appetite or insomnia and fatigue, because one member of the pair is not a necessary corollary of the other), the chances that a true disorder exists is strong *just because there is no a priori reason to expect such correlations to exist.* These nontrivial correlations repeated in many individuals are an important form of prediction.

The single symptom diagnosis is not a good basis for descriptive psychiatry because it does not put diagnosis to this test. We have discussed intercorrelations among symptoms in the context of categorical diagnoses. Analogous conclusions are valid for a dimensional approach to diagnosis. It is more problematic to claim validity for a single dimension diagnosis than for a diagnosis based on multiple dimensions.

The ability to predict course from knowing the cross-sectional picture also provides strong evidence for a valid diagnosis. However, alone it is not definitive. The obvious analogy from medical disorders is that not all fatal diseases are the same disease.

In order to test the prediction of course by a diagnosis, course must, obviously, not be used to make the diagnosis. Otherwise the prediction is circular. However, once the association between symptoms and course has been observed repeatedly, it is tempting to integrate course into the diagnostic description. The problem is that the association between symptoms and course may be statistically powerful but is rarely perfect. As a result, the diagnosis then excludes individuals who meet every other criterion except, for example, age of onset, frequency of attacks, or duration of symptoms. What then are these deviant cases to be called?

Outcome has traditionally been incorporated into diagnostic criteria for schizophrenia, mental retardation, alcoholism, and pervasive developmental disorders (autism). In some cases the inclusion of prognosis in diagnosis is obvious in DSM-III as in the description of schizophrenia: "Continuous sign of the illness for at least 6 months . . . with some signs of illness at present." In other cases, it is more subtle. For example, a DSM-III criterion for anorexia nervosa is "Weight loss of at least 25% of original body weight." A difficulty is that if an effective treatment is found, the diagnosis that used bad prognosis as a criterion becomes nonsense. Does schizophrenia disappear if a treatment that allows total remission is found? What of the anorexic patient who comes to a physician before that much weight loss has occurred and whose treatment is so successful that a weight loss of that magnitude never occurs? Were such patients never ill?

Not only is there the problem of what to do with the occasional person who seems to recover entirely from disorders that are supposed to be permanent, or too soon from a disorder that is thought to lead to a specified level of disability, but the use of prognosis is impractical as well. Prognosis cannot be used to diagnose current patients because one does not know the eventual outcome.

Prediction outside of the symptoms of the disorder itself and their course is also valuable evidence for the validity of diagnosis. Evidence often used includes the presence of similar disorders in the families of respondents. This evidence has sometimes been misinterpreted as demonstrating a biological basis for the disorder. While it is true that families share genes, they also share almost every other possible predictor. Consequently, if we can identify *any* predictor of a disorder, an elevated rate in family members is likely to be found. If it is not, this suggests that the disorder is caused by nonfamilial environmental factors such as disasters or military exposure, is extremely transitory, or perhaps the diagnostic category is invalid.

CONCLUSIONS

Diagnostic issues have reached a new level of concern in the psychiatric community, stimulated in part by the publication of DSM-III and in part by the fact that the Mental Health Division of the World Health Organization is beginning to prepare for publication of the next edition of the International Classification of Diseases, ICD-10. DSM-III has played a part in this revival of diagnostic interest by providing for general use such specific criteria that the ordinary clinician and the researcher for the first time know whether or not their methods conform to the published criteria. In the days before DSM-III, it was possible for those using very disparate definitions all to claim to be making diagnoses according to the official nomenclature.

DSM-III has had remarkable popularity in countries in which it has no official support, as well as in this country (Spitzer et al 1983). It has set the pace for the revision of the International Classification of Diseases, ICD-10. There has been agreement that ICD-10 will follow the same pattern of well-specified criteria and will adopt many of the substantive changes that appeared in DSM-III and will appear in DSM-III-Revised.

The interest in diagnosis that has captured the research community is being further stimulated by the tying of insurance company and government reimbursements to diagnostic decisions. We seem to have entered an era in which categorical diagnosis cannot be ignored because it will be the basis for deciding how many hospital days constitute appropriate treatment for a patient. Despite the advances recently made in studying course and treatability, this step seems a bit beyond what research data can currently support!

At best, diagnoses are imperfect descriptions of reality. They do not fully express the uniqueness of the individual, and they use arbitrary cut points that exclude some people who require treatment and include others who do not. But diagnoses from a well-structured system provide a useful way of succinctly communicating a good deal, but by no means everything, about a patient's history and likely future. Without diagnoses, scientific advances would come much more slowly, because we would be bereft of the simplifying assumptions that make rapid advances possible. Those advances in turn change the substance of the diagnoses that we make, selecting and adding elements that are predictive and dropping those that are not, with the goal of gradually developing a diagnostic system that increasingly divides all of psychiatric disorders into nonoverlapping categories that can be reliably assessed, that have a common etiology, and that allow predicting course.

ACKNOWLEDGMENTS

This research was supported by the Epidemiological Catchment Area Program (ECA). The ECA is a series of five epidemiologic research studies performed by independent research teams in collaboration with staff of the Division of Biometry and Epidemiology (DBE) of the National Institute of Mental Health (NIMH). The NIMH Principal Collaborators are Darrel A. Regier, Ben Z. Locke, and Jack D. Burke, Jr.; the NIMH Project Officer is Carl A. Taube. The Principal Investigators and Co-Investigators from the five sites are: Yale University, U01 MH 34224—Jerome K. Myers, Myrna M. Weissman, and Gary L. Tischler; The Johns Hopkins University, U01 MH 33870—Morton Kramer and Sam Shapiro; Washington University, St. Louis, U01 MH

33883—Lee N. Robins and John E. Helzer; Duke University, U01 MH 35386—Dan Blazer and Linda George; University of California, Los Angeles, U01 MH 35865—Marvin Karno, Richard L. Hough, Javier I. Escobar, M. Audrey Burnam, and Dianne M. Timbers. This work acknowledges support of this program as well as Research Scientist Award MH 00334, Clinical Research Center MH 31302, and NIMH Training Grant MH 17104.

Literature Cited

American Psychiatric Association. 1952. *Diagnostic and Statistical Manual of Mental Disorders*. Washington, DC: Am. Psychiatric Assoc. 132 pp.

American Psychiatric Association. 1968. *Diagnostic and Statistical Manual of Mental Disorders*. Washington, DC: Am. Psychiatric Assoc. 134 pp. 2nd ed.

American Psychiatric Association. 1980. *Diagnostic and Statistical Manual of Mental Disorders*. Washington, DC: Am. Psychiatric Assoc. 494 pp. 3rd ed.

Bayer, R., Spitzer, R. L. 1985. Neurosis, psychodynamics, and DSM-III. *Arch. Gen. Psychiatry* 42:187–96

Blashfield, R. K., Draguns, J. G. 1976a. Evaluative criteria for psychiatric classification. *J. Abnorm. Psychol.* 85:140–50

Blashfield, R. K., Draguns, J. G. 1976b. Toward a taxonomy of psychopathology. *Br. J. Psychiatry* 42:574–83

Boyd, J. H., Burke, J. D. Jr., Gruenberg, E., Hozer, C. A. III, Rae, D. S., et al. 1984. Exclusion criteria of DSM-III. *Arch. Gen. Psychiatry* 41:983–89

Climent, C. E., Plutchik, R., Estrada, H., Gaviria, L. F., Arevalo, W. 1975. A comparison of traditional and symptom-checklist-based histories. *Am. J. Psychiatry* 132:450–53

Cooper, J. E., Kendell, R. E., Gurland, B. J. 1972. *Psychiatric Diagnosis in New York and London*. Maudsley Monogr. No. 20. London: Oxford Univ. Press

Feighner, J. P., Robins, E., Guze, S. B., Woodruff, R. A., Winokur, G., Munoz, R. 1972. Diagnostic criteria for use in psychiatric research. *Arch. Gen. Psychiatry* 26:57–63

Feinstein, A. R. 1973. An analysis of diagnostic reasoning. 1. The domains and disorders of clinical macrobiology. *Yale J. Biol. Med.* 46:212–32

Finn, S. E. 1982. Base, rates, utilities, and DSM-III: Shortcomings of fixed-rule systems of psychodiagnosis. *J. Abnorm. Psychol.* 91:294–302

Freedman, A. M., Kaplan, H. I., Sadock, B. J. 1972. *Modern Synopsis of Comprehensive Textbook of Psychiatry*, pp. 202–24. Baltimore: Williams & Wilkins

Grossman, J. H., Barnett, G. O., McGuire, M. T. 1971. Evaluation of computer acquired patient histories. *J. Am. Med. Assoc.* 215:1286–91

Guze, S. B. 1977. The future of psychiatry: Medicine or social science? *J. Nerv. Ment. Dis.* 165:225–30

Helzer, J. E. 1983. Standardized interviews in psychiatry. *Psychiatr. Dev.* 2:161–78

Helzer, J. E., Coryell, W. 1983. More on DSM-III: How consistent are precise criteria? *Biol. Psychiatry* 18:1201–3

Kendell, R. E. 1973. Psychiatric diagnoses: A study of how they are made. *Br. J. Psychiatry* 122:437–43

Kendell, R. E. 1974. The stability of psychiatric diagnoses. *Br. J. Psychiatry* 124:352–56

Klerman, G. L. 1978. The evolution of a scientific nosology. In *Schizophrenia: Science and Practice*, ed. J. C. Shershow. Cambridge, MA: Harvard Univ. Press

Klerman, G. L. 1983. The significance of DSM-III in American psychiatry. See Spitzer et al 1983, pp. 3–25

Kraepelin, E. 1974. Comparative psychiatry. In *Themes and Variations in European Psychiatry*, ed. S. R. Hirsch, M. Shepherd. Charlottesville: Univ. Virginia Press

Meikle, S., Gerritse, R. A. 1970. A comparison of psychiatric symptom frequency under narrative and check-list conditions. *Am. J. Psychiatry* 127:379–82

Myers, J. K., Weissman, M. 1981. *Yale Greater New Haven Health Survey Validity Interview*. New Haven: Yale Univ.

Othmer, E., Penick, E. C., Powell, B. J. 1981. *Psychiatric Diagnostic Interview (PDI)*. Los Angeles: West. Psychol. Serv.

Robins, E., Guze, S. B. 1972. Classification of affective disorders: The primary-secondary, the endogenous-reactive, and the neurotic-psychotic concepts. In *Recent Advances in the Psychobiology of the Depressive Illnesses*, ed. T. A. Williams, M. M. Katz, J. A. Shield, pp. 283–93. Washington, DC: GPO

Robins, L. N., Helzer, J. E., Croughan, J. L., Williams, J. B. W., Spitzer, R. L. 1981. *The NIMH Diagnostic Interview Schedule: Version III*. Washington, DC: Public Health Serv. (HSS) ADM-T-42-3 (5/81, 8/81)

Robins, L. N., Helzer, J. E., Przybeck, T. 1986. Substance abuse in the general population. In *Mental Disorder in the Community: Progress and Challenge,* ed. J. Barrett. New York: Guilford. In press

Robins, L. N., Wing, J., Helzer, J. E. 1983. *The Composite International Diagnostic Interview (CIDI).* Geneva: World Health Organ.

Romanoski, A., Chahal, R. 1981. *The Standardized Psychiatric Examination Intercalated Interview.* Baltimore: Johns Hopkins Univ.

Rosenthal, D., Kety, S. S. 1968. *The Transmission of Schizophrenia.* London: Pergamon

Sackett, D. L. 1978. Clinical diagnosis and the clinical laboratory. *Clin. Invest. Med.* 1:37–43

Sackett, D. L., Haynes, R. B., Tugwell, P. 1985. *Clinical Epidemiology: A Basic Science for Clinical Medicine.* Boston/Toronto: Little, Brown

Spitzer, R. L., Endicott, J. 1977. *Schedule for Affective Disorders and Schizophrenia.* New York: New York State Psychiatric Inst.

Spitzer, R. L., Endicott, J., Robins, E. 1975. Clinical criteria for psychiatric diagnosis and DSM-III. *Am. J. Psychiatry* 132:1187–92

Spitzer, R. L., Endicott, J., Robins, E. 1978. Research diagnostic criteria: Rationale and reliability. *Arch. Gen. Psychiatry* 35:773–82

Spitzer, R. L., Williams, J. B. W., Skodol, A. E. 1983. *International Perspectives on DSM-III.* Washington, DC: Am. Psychiatric Press. 413 pp.

Tsuang, M. T., Woolson, R. F., Simpson, J. C. 1980. The Iowas structured psychiatric interview. *Acta Psychiatr. Scand. Suppl.* 62: 1–38

Ward, C. H., Beck, A. T., Mendelson, M., Robinson, J. A. 1962. The psychiatric nomenclature. *Arch. Gen Psychiatry* 7:198–205

Weitzel, W. D., Morgan, D. W., Guyden, T. E., Mock, J. E., Erbaugh, J. K. 1973. Toward a more efficient mental status examination. *Arch. Gen. Psychiatry* 28:215–18

Wing, J. K., Cooper, J. E., Sartorius, N. 1974. *Measurement and Classification of Psychiatric Symptoms.* London: Cambridge Univ. Press

World Health Organization. 1977, 1978. *Manual of the International Statistical Classification of Diseases, Injuries, and Causes of Death,* Vols. 1, 2. Geneva: WHO. 9th (1975) revision

Ann. Rev. Psychol. 1986. 37:433–93

UNDERSTANDING THE CELLULAR BASIS OF MEMORY AND LEARNING

C. D. Woody

Departments of Anatomy and Psychiatry, Mental Retardation Research Center, Brain Research Institute, UCLA Medical Center, Los Angeles, California 90024

CONTENTS

LOCALIZATION OF THE ENGRAM.. 434
    Older Studies 435
    Recent Studies 438
    Circuitry Involved in Simple Conditioning 440
ASSOCIATIVELY ACQUIRED BEHAVIOR... 443
    Random Stimulus Paradigm.. 444
    Overlap versus Trace Presentations 445
    Alpha Conditioning versus Long-Latency Conditioning 447
    The Role of Nonassociative As Well As Associative Cellular Processes in the Induction
        of Learned Behavior 448
THE ROLE OF THE NEURON IN INTEGRATION 457
    Cable Properties 457
    Ionic Conductances 460
    Second Messengers 466
ACCELERATION OF RATES OF CONDITIONING 469
SOME EXPERIMENTAL TECHNOLOGIC FRONTIERS................................... 471
    Neuroanatomy 471
    Electrophysiology 473

There is broad agreement among experimentalists and many theoreticians that an improved understanding of memory and learning must proceed from an improved understanding of the cellular basis of these phenomena. Previous understandings and conceptualizations drawn mainly from behavioral observation have begun to give way in light of knowledge of cellular mechanisms supporting learned behavior. As a result, new concepts are emerging. Localization of engrams may be seen as a matter of defining physical-chemical interactions at the level of nerve membranes—not simply areas of the brain in which such changes occur. Engram formation may be seen to derive from temporal and spatial relationships between electrical and chemical neural events, as opposed to contingencies between extrinsic stimuli alone, and these fundamental, subcellular processes may be recognized as coequals with the neural circuitry in determining the behavioral outcomes of engram functions— a view somewhat novel to more traditional psychophysiological considerations. Although comprehensive surveys of the newest, relevant experimental results in psychophysiology, neurobiology, and biophysics have recently appeared (Kandel & Schwartz 1982, Woody 1982a,c, Thompson et al 1983a, Hille 1984, Alkon & Woody 1985, Farley & Alkon 1985), they have not been in agreement with respect to their underlying conceptualizations, including those concerning what constitute the more useful techniques and approaches for experimental research. This review assumes a knowledge of experimental results derived from the aforementioned reviews and focuses on those conceptual and technological frontiers that are either being reexamined or created by means of these new findings.

LOCALIZATION OF THE ENGRAM

Despite half a century's research efforts (cf Lashley 1929, Kluver & Bucy 1939, Denny-Brown 1951, Ojemann 1966, Woody & Black-Cleworth 1973, Woody et al 1974, Alkon 1979), some have continued to search for *the* "engram" (cf Thompson et al 1983b). Historically, the search has been based on two predicates: one that physicalistic representations of mnemonic processes (engrams) must be found within the neural circuitry, and second that there must be "localization" of such processes to a focal region of the brain. The first premise has been validated by a wealth of experimentation, particularly that of the past two decades. The latter premise may be fallacious if it assumes but a single mechanism of learning or a single locus of representation within the brain. This is because experimental studies over the past 50 years have provided ample evidence that memory and learning are represented over many neurons, the latter distributed over broad portions of the nervous system (Woody 1982c, Squire & Butters 1984; also see Tables 11–1 and 11–5 in Woody 1984a). In vertebrates, evidence has been found for at least two separate cellular mechanisms supporting associative conditioning in three different regions of the brain (Woody & Black-Cleworth 1973, Woody et al 1976, Brons & Woody 1980, Matsumura & Woody 1982). In *Hermissenda,* there is evidence that changes in at least two different ionic conductances can occur in the type B photoreceptors to support associative conditioning—a fast, potassium "A" current and a slower, calcium-dependent potassium current (Alkon 1979; see further details below) and that changes in prephotoreceptor substances and in other type A photoreceptors may also contribute (Farley 1985, Farley & Alkon 1985).

Interestingly, the antithetical view of Lashley (see Beach et al 1960), that all neural elements have equipotentiality for mnemonic change and equal representation for support of learned behavior, is equally unsupported by available evidence. Thus, one can see how memory or a specific kind of memory could have been thought to be localized to the hippocampus (cf Penfield & Milner 1958, Victor et al 1971) or to the cerebellum or even the subcerebellar nuclei (Thompson et al 1983b; cf Goldman-Rakic 1984).

Older Studies

What is the evidence in favor of broadly distributed engrams? Human neuropathological studies have long disclosed surprising preservation of function despite extensive loss of brain tissue [e.g. motor function in human anencephalics (see Gamper 1926 and Figure 19 in Jung & Hassler 1960); posttraumatic recovery of function (Brodal 1969)]. In animals, Lashley (1929) found that it required removal of more than 90 percent of the involved cellular elements (or at least of those in the visual cortex that he imagined were involved) before a visually mediated, learned behavior could be disrupted. The number of elements removed seemed to count almost as much as the selectivity of which elements were removed, though this was largely due to an inability, using gross ablation techniques, to remove only those neurons that served a single function (see Eccles 1977). How ablation may lead to variable degrees of dysfunction in broadly distributed networks is illustrated by the example of information processing using simple adaptive elements shown in Figure 1.

When comprehensive studies of the activity of single units in relation to conditioning were begun, Jasper et al (1960) found correlates of operantly conditioned behavior over broad regions of the cortex, just as Pavlov (1927) had predicted. Jasper and colleagues did not conclude that the learned behavior had an equipotential representation, but instead noted differences in latency and functional representation from region to region. Thus, activity evoked by a cue CS at the sensory cortex preceded activity evoked at the motor cortex, and activity at the motor cortex preceded performance of the learned movement. In addition, in the sensory receptive regions, many units responded to the CS with a decreased firing, whereas in the motor areas almost all of the neurons responded initially with an increased rate of discharge.

The observations of Jasper and associates were confirmed and extended to other forms of conditioning (Evarts 1966, Woody et al 1970, Thach 1978). In the cat, the widespread distribution of the elements involved in conditioning was demonstrated directly, using Asanuma and associates' (1968) micro-

Receptors

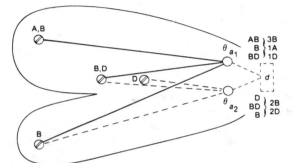

$\theta_{a_1} = 3; \theta_{a_2} = 3$:

Discriminates B, but not A, D

$\theta_{a_1} = 2; \theta_{a_2} = 2$:

Discriminates A, B, D and survives ablation of any 1 of 3 inputs to a_1

$\theta_{a_1} = 2; \theta_{a_2} = 1$:

Discriminates A, B, D and survives ablation of any 1 of 3 inputs to a_1 and/or a_2

Figure 1   A model of a broadly distributed network that could support aspects of learned behavior. The task is to learn to discriminate between different letters. A simple set of receptive elements is shown at the upper left. The uppermost of the four elements is receptive to (and intersected by) the letters A and B but not D. The lowest element is receptive to B only. The receptivity of the remaining two elements is as indicated. Assigning these elements and their second-order projections to different regions of a "brain" has some interesting consequences for message processing. Changing θ, the number of inputs required to fire the second-order elements a_1 and a_2, changes the discriminative property d of the network as summarized in the diagram to the right. Redundancy permits ablation to produce disfunction *or lack thereof* as described in that diagram (after Woody 1982a).

stimulation technique[1] to identify the extent of the cortical motor regions that were involved. Identification of the interneuronal projection of each stimulated unit area was accomplished by averaging the EMG activity elicited at target and nontarget musculature (Woody et al 1970, Woody & Engel 1972). In such comparisons, about a quarter of the stimulated unit areas was found to project to target muscles involved with production of the CR, a quarter to nontarget muscles, a quarter to both muscles, and a quarter to neither (Table 1). The percentage of CR-projective units increased with conditioning to favor production of the CR. These findings, based on extracellular stimulation of 5–25 units (cf Stoney et al 1968), were later confirmed in intracellularly stimulated units (Table 1; Woody & Black-Cleworth 1973), and the ability to detect the peripheral motor projections of single cortical units reliably was itself subsequently confirmed in the monkey (Fetz & Finocchio 1975).

[1]See below (p. 473ff) for a more detailed discussion of use of this and other techniques to measure neural excitability.

Table 1 Polysynaptic projections of units of the motor cortex of cats to peripheral muculature as a function of learned behavioral response.[a]

Type of response conditioned	Muscle Groups				
	Eye	Nose	Both	O/Other	Total (n)
EC (unit-areas)					
Eye conditioned	**47%**[b]	18%	35%	—	92[c]
Both conditioned	25%	25%	50%	—	87[c]
Nose conditioned	14%	**47%**	39%	—	169[c]
IC (single units)					
Naive	25%	20%	22%	33%	176[e]
Eye conditioned	**34%**	13%	21%	32%	221[d]
Both conditioned	20%	17%	**36%**	27%	149[e]

[a]Numbers of units tested (n) and percentages found to project (stimulation produced a distinguishable EMG response) to different muscle groups are shown as functions of different conditioned movements. EC = extracellularly stimulated, IC = intracellularly stimulated; Eye = orbicularis oculis muscle, Nose = levator oris muscle, Both = both eye and nose muscles; O/Other = nonprojective or projecting elsewhere (not tested EC).
[b]Percentages in boldface increased after conditioning.
[c]Woody & Engel 1972.
[d]Woody & Black-Cleworth 1973.
[e]Brons & Woody 1980.

Interestingly, at the motor cortex the increases in CS-evoked unit discharge after conditioning did not necessarily exceed levels of discharge found in response to other stimuli of comparable intensity (see Engel & Woody 1972). Thus, mean levels of evoked discharge per se did not provide the basis for the CS to elicit the needed response at rostral, motor areas. Mean levels of evoked discharge *times* the numbers of units activated provided this basis. In contrast, at more caudal association areas (Woody et al 1976, Woody 1977), levels of activity evoked by the CS after conditioning were comparatively greater in responding units than were levels of activity evoked by equally loud but behaviorally neutral auditory stimuli. This evidence confirmed the involvement of an extensive cortical circuitry with differently coded patterns of unit activation supporting discriminatively elicited conditioned behavior and behavior resulting in performance of a particular conditioned motor response.

A number of other observations were made that were consistent with Lashley's observations and with widespread representation of first predicate, physicalistic representations of learning and memory. These observations also showed that while the pathways and neural elements supporting production of the CR were broadly distributed, they were nonetheless quite specific in their function.

For example, in eyeblink conditioned cats:

1. the cells *that projected to the proper target musculature* were those in which increased activity in response to the CS was found (Woody et al 1970,

Woody & Engel 1972, Woody & Black-Cleworth 1973, Brons & Woody 1980);

2. the excitability of these cells was increased whereas that of other cells in the immediate surround was not (Woody et al 1970, Woody & Engel 1972, Woody & Black-Cleworth 1973, Brons & Woody 1980);

3. the change in unit discharge elicited by the click CS reflected a momentary change in the probability of firing which, when expressed across the ensemble of CR projective neurons, produced a magnitude and latency of discharge sufficient to initiate production of the learned movement (see Figure 4 of Woody et al 1970);

4. these populations of cells could be repeatedly sampled in separate experiments with comparable results with F-test significance by cell and by cat (Brons & Woody 1980);

5. ablation of sufficient numbers of these cells (or suppression of their function by means of topical application of 25%[2] KCl) suppressed acquisition (or performance) of the blink CR but not performance of the unconditioned eyeblink response (Woody & Brozek 1969b, Gutman et al 1972, Woody et al 1974); and

6. introduction of an electrical CS to the motor cortex, when paired with the usual tap US used to produce conditioning, produced a comparable blink CR (Woody & Yarowsky 1972).

Although engrams supporting performance of the CR were thought to have been found (Woody 1982a), localization of *the* engram was not claimed. This was because of the widespread representation of these cellular changes, the inability to localize the exact location of the changes within each penetrated nerve cell, and also because evidence was found that *additional* engrams supporting discriminative and associative aspects of the conditioning were located elsewhere (Woody et al 1976).

Recent Studies

Recent "localization" studies (McCormick et al 1982a,b,c) of another type of classically conditioned facial reflex, the nictitating membrane response (NMR), led Goldman-Rakic (1984) to conclude that the critical site for learning resided in the dentate-interpositus nuclei, whereas the investigators themselves considered the "primary engram" for the delay CR and for producing discrete adaptive motor responses to have been found in the cerebellum (Thompson 1983, Thompson et al 1983b). The results in question were as follows. Stereotactic lesions of only the medial dentate-lateral interpositus nuclei or their output pathway could abolish the learned (NMR) response without affecting the unconditioned response. In contrast, removal of large areas of the cerebellar

---

[2]weight per volume

cortex or other subcortical areas frequently did not abolish the learned response (see Goldman-Rakic 1984). Bilateral destruction of the critical dentate/interpositus nuclear region did not prevent learning of a conditioned heart-rate response, whereas unilateral ablation of the lateral cerebellum could abolish both ipsilateral NMR and hindpaw-flexion CRs (Lincoln et al 1982, Thompson 1983).

Although these findings appeared to be inconsistent, careful examination showed that lesion of either cerebellum or interpositus nuclei could disrupt NMR conditioning. Nonetheless, disagreement continued as to which areas of the cerebellum or brainstem were critical. While massive aspirations of the cerebellar cortex as well as other deep nuclear regions sometimes failed to abolish eyelid CRs (McCormick & Thompson 1984), Yeo et al (1984) described a small portion of the hemisphere (lobulus simplex) of the cerebellar cortex that, when removed, prevented the CR. Llinas et al (1975) had shown earlier that the inferior olive system was necessary for acquisition and retention of some forms of motor learning, while the cerebellum itself was not. [Brooks and colleagues reported that lesions of the cerebellum interfered with tracking and with performance of intentional movements in animals (Brooks et al 1973, Brooks 1979).] Others found additional areas that were sensitive to lesion with respect to mediation of NMR or long latency eyeblink conditioning, including regions of the pons (Lavond et al 1981, Desmond & Moore 1982), the red nucleus (Rosenfeld & Moore 1983), the superior cerebellar peduncle and brainstem reticular system (Desmond & Moore 1982, Moore et al 1982), and supratrigeminal areas (Desmond & Moore 1983).

Earlier experiments in human, monkey, cat, dog, rat, and pigeon had indicated that some forms of conditioned behavior (including long-latency conditioning of this type) could be acquired and retained not only following lesion of the motor cortex (Trendelenberg 1915, Franz & Lashley 1917, Lashley 1921, Jellinek & Koppanyi 1923, Lashley 1924, Pavlov 1927, Foerster 1936, Harlow & Bromer 1942) or pyramidal tract (Starlinger 1895, Rothman 1907), but after functional removal of the entire cortex by decortication (Culler & Mettler 1934, Ten Cate 1934a,b, Girden et al 1936, Poltyrew 1936, Bromiley 1947, Norman et al 1974) and following diencephalic or mesencephalic decerebration (Treves & Aggazzotti 1901, Head & Riddoch 1917, Rogers 1922, Poltyrew & Zeliony 1929, 1930, Bard & Macht 1958, Gastault 1958, Galambos & Sheatz 1962, Markel & Adam 1969, Markel et al 1969, Norman et al 1977). Yet other studies (Bures & Buresova 1960, Doty 1974) had provided convincing evidence that engrams could be shuttled about interhemispherically as well as subcortically during the consolidation phase of learning, and Oakley and Russell (1977) had shown that if an animal was initially trained with its cortex intact, decortication resulted in little retention loss of the CR, but if animals were initially trained as hemidecorticates, subsequent removal of remaining tissue abolished the CR. Still others (Papsdorf et al 1965) provided evidence that some conditioned NMR responses could be selectively and reversibly abolished by producing spreading depression of the contralateral motor cortex.

Chronic unit recordings obtained from the dentate-interpositus complex (McCormick & Thompson 1984) showed activity related to performance of the conditioned NMR, but as Farley & Alkon (1985) pointed out, the degree to which the training correlates in unit activity were pairing-specific was not reported, and no attempts were made to study these units intracellularly or determine the nature and location of any local cellular changes.

In retrospect, the results of the NMR lesion experiments are interpretable either in terms of a distributed engram analogous to that supported by Lashley's original experiments or with the possibility (Ito 1985) that alterations of summated PSPs along potentiated startle circuitry could result in altered motor performance. Both the fact that distributed engrams may give the appearance of moving their locus within the cerebellum and brainstem (or elsewhere, cf Woody 1982a, Merzenich et al 1983) and the fact that lesion effects may be variable, such as those described above, could result from the probabilistic nature of the neuronal ensemble's normal operation (e.g. Figure 1). This subject has been treated in greater depth elsewhere (see Woody 1982a).

Circuitry Involved in Simple Conditioning

What these and other experimental studies show is that even the simplest forms of learned behavior are supported by extensive neural circuitry of which more than one portion may be necessary for different latencies of response and various other aspects of sensory discrimination and learned motor performance. Even the degree to which tissue above the level of the thalamus is or is not involved is not determined by the ablational studies of NMR conditioning since, as Thompson and colleagues point out (1983a), if destruction of a structure does not impair the particular form of learning that induces the neuronal change, it does not mean that the structure plays no role in that form of learning; it means only that its role is not essential. When tested, virtually every region of the brain whose neurons show learning-induced changes has been found by the lesion method to play some role in learning, at least under some conditions (Thompson et al 1983a).

How then may one define the circuits primarily involved in mediating simple learned behavior? As might be expected, short-latency CRs greatly facilitate elucidation of the neural pathways that underlie such functions. Although knowledge of the circuitry underlying conditioned blink responses elicited at short, 20 ms onset latencies by click-CS is still incomplete, a great deal is known or can be inferred about this circuitry and its involvement in discriminative, associatively conditioned behavior.

The latencies of performance of the short latency eyeblink CR in response to associative pairing of a one msec click CS with glabella tap-US are sufficiently brief that the motor pathways for its initiation have been almost completely elucidated (Woody & Brozek 1969a,b, Woody et al 1970, Sakai & Woody 1980, Woody 1984b). The efferent pathway for mediation of the short-latency conditioned blink reflex runs from the motor cortex (onset 13 ms after click-CS), by a possible interneuron, to the facial nucleus (17 ms onset), and finally to the orbicularis oculi muscles (20 ms onset of CR). Conduction time plus synaptic delay between the motor cortex and the periphery corresponds to the latencies between activation of the cortical units, activation of the facial motoneurons plus or minus an intervening interneuron, and performance of the CR. It has not yet been possible to confirm or exclude the presence of an interneuron[3] between cortex and motoneuron, to explain the significance of the "extra" 2 ms delay seen with use of the electrical CS delivered to the motor cortex (Woody & Yarowsky 1972), or to circumvent the variance of 2–3 ms in latency of mean unit activation, which is still ten times longer than the delay of 0.3–0.5 ms in neural transmission at each chemical synapse in the circuit.

The afferent limb of the CR is likely to be mediated through the cochlear nucleus and its immediate acoustic relay nuclei and then by nonspecific acoustic nuclei such as the lateral lemniscal and paralemniscal nuclei, regions of the auditory system at which specific startle and conditioning-related neural transmissions are thought to interact (Davis et al 1982a,b, Tischler & Davis 1983). The adjacent, lateral tegmental nuclei have been linked by recordings of multiple unit activity to the support of discriminatively elicited CRs to auditory stimuli (Birt et al 1979, Birt & Olds 1981, 1982). Other studies (Gabriel et al 1976, Ryugo & Weinberger 1978, Disterhoft et al 1982, Weinberger 1982b) suggest that the "adjunct lemniscal" system (cf Morest 1964, 1965, Aitkin et al 1970, Jones & Powell 1971, Graybiel 1972, 1973, Harrison & Howe 1974, Edwards 1975, Webster & Aitken 1975, Edwards & DeOlmos 1976, Glendenning et al 1981, Kudo 1981, Henkel 1983, Imig & Morel 1983) as opposed to the more direct, "classical" auditory pathways (Diamond & Neff 1957, Rose & Woolsey 1958, Thompson 1960) has a prepotential for adaptation during conditioning, including projections through the magnocellular portion of the medial geniculate nucleus (Weinberger 1982b) to the adjacent posterior thalamic nuclei as well as to neurons in the deep layers of the superior colliculus and underlying tegmentum. The auditory association cortex is also likely to be involved (Woody et al 1976) but is not necessary for elaboration and performance of the CR (Woody et al 1974). The roles of the cingulate cortex and hippocampus in production of this reflex are still unknown. Although there

---

[3]Interneurons may play a significant role in conditioning (Spencer et al 1966a,b,c, Durkovic 1983).

are a number of learning paradigms for which an intact hippocampus has been shown to be essential (Weisz et al 1980, Berger & Orr 1982), the hippocampus and cingulate cortex are unnecessary for at least some types of eyeblink conditioning (Solomon & Moore 1975, Weisz et al 1980), and the latencies of activation of these areas have been found to be longer than those for initiation of the short latency blink CR (Berger & Orr 1982, Gabriel et al 1982, Thompson et al 1982). The cerebellum and its related circuitry may play an important role in conditioning, but not necessarily in initiation of the learned motor response since activation of units therein may not be rapid enough to support initiation of short latency blink responses.

How useful are the latencies of the conditioned nictitating membrane response and the long latency blink CR in elucidating the underlying circuitry? Neuronal unit responses in the cerebellar nuclei may precede some long latency blink or NMR CRs by as much as 50 ms or more, and the onset latencies for these CRs vary from 80 to over 300 ms. Some cerebellar pathways are among the fastest conducting known (Grundfest & Campbell 1942). Given conduction times of 7 ms along longer and much more slowly conducting pathways from cortex to facial periphery, cerebellar response latencies could allow several round trips between cortex and periphery, much less between the anatomically closer cerebellum and the motoneurons supporting eyelid closure or the NMR.

Use of a long-lasting CS, as commonly practiced in overlap conditioning (see p. 445 and Figure 3), can also pose a problem in tracing pathways. This is because of ambiguities that arise concerning which portion of the stimulus activates the response. Among some of the more extensively studied conditioning preparations, the CS durations are: 1 ms click (short, 20 ms latency blink CR), 350 ms tone (long, 80 − >300 ms latency blink CR and NMR), 9 intracellular depolarizing pulses (Walters & Byrne 1983) or a 500 ms shock (Carew et al 1983) (*Aplysia* analogs of conditioning), 6 sec light [avian cardiac conditioning with 1 sec CR and 100–400 ms latency motoneuron responses (Cohen & Durkovic 1966, Cohen 1974, 1984)], and 30 sec light (*Hermissenda* conditioning).

Experimental studies of learning are frequently pursued in invertebrates because it is assumed that the circuitry of invertebrate systems is more easily understood than that of vertebrates. This assumption also merits scrutiny. Tracing circuits in invertebrate preparations is difficult because they have much slower conduction times, action potentials, and "transmission" latencies than do vertebrate preparations. Even in invertebrate circuits with fewer than 150 neurons, there may be great functional variability. For example, in studies of 50 pairs of Type A and Type B photoreceptors in *Hermissenda,* Alkon & Fuortes (1972) found highly varied interactions: reciprocal inhibition in 22 pairs; inhibition of A upon B in 10 pairs; inhibition of B upon A in 12 pairs; and no interactions in 6 pairs of photoreceptors. More detailed knowledge concerning secondary circuit connections is available in mammalian than in invertebrate species (Ranson 1959, Truex & Carpenter 1969). Finally, while complex problems of sensorimotor integration may appear to be more easily solved in simpler, invertebrate preparations, the solutions may be inapplicable to the more complex circuitry of the mammalian brain. Nonetheless, as will be seen, each preparation offers its own advantages and disadvantages, and comparative studies of the cellular mechanisms that support simple learning in invertebrates may be very useful.

ASSOCIATIVELY ACQUIRED BEHAVIOR

Associative conditioning implies conditioned behavior that derives from a particular temporal association between variables such as CS and US or response and reward or punishment. In the case of instrumental or operant conditioning, the motor activity of the organism is instrumental in bringing about the presentation of rewarding stimuli (or cessation of presentation of aversive stimuli), and some temporal relationship between these variables is important for the development of the learned behavior just as in classical conditioning. Some view these temporal relationships with regard to contingency or causal factors related to the production of the learned behavior (Thorndike 1911, cf Rescorla 1969, Farley 1985, Farley & Alkon 1985). Others view these relationships in the context of evolution of the cellular mechanisms that support adaptive behavior (Woody 1982a).

> Causality implies a necessity of response and, according to Russell (1964), "simple rules of the form 'A causes B' are never to be admitted in science, except as crude suggestions in early stages. The causal laws . . . are all, obviously, elaborate inferences from the observed course of nature." Modern quantum theory reinforces the above conclusion. "So far as the physical sciences are concerned, such propositions as 'A causes B' are never to be accepted, and our inclination to accept them is to be explained by the laws of habit and association. These laws themselves, in their accurate form, will be elaborate statements as to nervous tissue— primarily its physiology, then its chemistry, and ultimately its physics." Contingency, which is ambiguous and may mean either touching (temporally), dependent, or related, is better left to more precise mathematical expressions of relationships between variables including those of correlation and conditional probability (see Woody 1982a).

Although the exact relationships are still unknown, the dynamics of associative behavior are believed by many investigators to reflect the dynamics of chemical reactions involved in long-lasting macromolecular changes (Schmitt 1962) that can persistently influence neural integration and transmission. Figure 2 compares the frequency dependence of calcium conductance across the neural membrane on repetitive depolarizing stimulation with the frequency dependence of classically conditioned behavior on the interstimulus interval (ISI) between CS and US presentation.

**Effects of Interstimulus Interval on Conditioning (Left)
and on Neuronal Calcium Conductance (Right)**

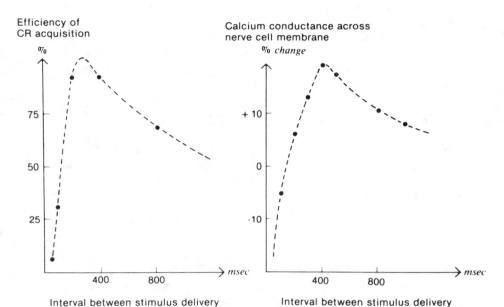

Figure 2   Note the similarities between the curves on the left and right and their abscissas. The ordinate of the graph to the left reflects conditioned reflex behavior, whereas that to the right reflects a molecular process involving a change in conductance of ions across a nerve cell membrane to be described further below (from Woody 1982a).

Before considering the cellular changes in more detail, several aspects of experimentally studied associative processes merit consideration. The first is use of a "random" stimulus paradigm as a control for associative processes. The second is use of overlap instead of trace pairings to produce conditioning. The third is the relation of alpha conditioning to longer latency conditioning. The fourth is the extent to which nonassociatively controlled cellular mechanisms support associative conditioning.

Random Stimulus Paradigm

How should one test for the dependence of learned behavior and cellular change on an associative temporal relationship? One means for doing so is to evaluate behavioral (and cellular) effects of presenting stimuli such as CSs and USs in other than the appropriate temporal relationship for inducing learned behavior.

Rescorla (1969) suggested that by randomly presenting CS and US, one might reduce the likelihood that either positive or negative contingencies between CS and US could occur. As a result, many investigators have adopted a "random" paradigm as a standard control procedure in establishing "associatively" obtained responses (e.g. Alkon 1982, Thompson 1983). Unfortunately, there are several limitations to this control procedure.

First, the unpaired, randomization control approach is not random in the proper statistical sense since it involves a limited number of presentations (see Woody 1982a). Second, simultaneous, overlap, and 100–400 ms ISI forward order pairings are sometimes excluded from this approach and sometimes not. The validity of either choice is problematic. Third, the precise series given is usually "tailored" and too complex to publish in entirety. Thus, the experiments may not be readily repeatable by other investigators.

The alternative to the "random" control is an unpaired or explicitly un-paired control. By unpaired is meant separate, serial presentations of the associated stimuli. By explicitly un-paired is meant backwards pairing of US and CS or pairing at a specific order or interval that is not likely (from Figure 2) to produce conditioning. The explicitly un-paired approach suffers when "backwards" conditioning is successful, as can happen in some instances (Dostalek & Krasa 1972, Spetch et al 1981) or when conditioned inhibition results (see Rescorla 1969). Usually, however, backwards pairing fails to produce a conditioned response and therefore represents a useful behavioral control procedure. The procedure is straightforward and easily repeated by other investigators. Moreover, it tests a specific temporal aspect of the relationship shown in Figure 2. (The more aspects tested, the better.)

Results of forwards and backwards pairing also need to be compared with those of extinction studies and with results in naive animals and animals given serial presentations of CSs or USs alone because a number of studies have shown that serial or interspersed presentations of extra USs or CSs can lead to inhibition (or facilitation) of conditioned behavioral performance (Pavlov 1927, Kimble & Dufort 1956, Kamin 1957, Rescorla 1969; for further details see Woody 1982a,b). It is not yet known whether this occurs (a) by inhibition of the conditioning mechanisms, (b) by intervening habituatory processes, or (c) by facilitation of reciprocal reflex pathways.

These limitations reflect the complexities of mammalian learning and the fact that we do not as yet understand the cellular bases of these complexities. By instituting a variety of "controls," one can learn more about the nature of associative conditioning and have a broader data base upon which disagreements about optimal control paradigms can be resolved.

Overlap versus Trace Presentations

Parametric differences between the use of trace (temporally separated) and overlap stimulus presentations (Figure 3) to produce conditioning have been discussed in detail elsewhere (e.g. Woody 1982a). Overlap presentations are often used because they are more effective in producing conditioned behavior (Gormezano 1974). This may be because of the cumulatively increased inten-

(A) Overlap paradigm

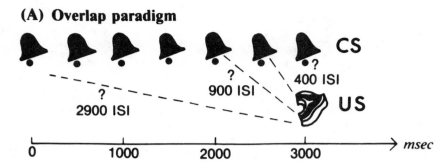

(B) Trace paradigm

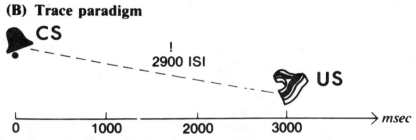

Figure 3   Different interstimulus intervals (ISIs) arising from overlap (A) and trace (B) associative paradigms (from Woody 1982a).

sity of the stimuli or because of the ability of these hit and miss kinds of presentations to "hit" more often on the optimal interstimulus interval for producing cellular change (see Figures 2 and 3).

Overlap presentations are problematic in that the overlap between stimuli can create ambiguities with respect to their order and intervals, aspects of presentation that are fundamental to the development of associative behavior described above. Because of these ambiguities and those posed in calculating onset latencies, no primary circuit supporting associatively conditioned behavior can be properly defined with overlap CS-US presentations. The possibility also cannot be excluded that nonassociative potentiation may be facilitated by the overlap situation (Bliss & Gardner-Medwin 1973, Bliss & Lomo 1973, Brown & McAfee 1982, Lnenicka & Atwood 1985) as may habituation—either occurring as a consequence of the long-lasting CS. Despite these limitations, overlap conditioning has been used in most eyelid and NMR conditioning (short-latency blink conditioning excepted), in avian cardiac conditioning, and in *Hermissenda* conditioning, though not in producing analogs of conditioning in *Aplysia*.

In *Hermissenda,* a nudibranch mollusk, it is unclear whether aversive conditioning produced by pairing a light CS with a rotational US will develop as effectively when trace pairings are used in place of overlap stimuli (Farley 1985). The training paradigm preferentially involves *simultaneous* presentations of a 30 sec CS and a 30 sec US. Grover & Farley (1983) point out that forward pairings "produce no appreciable neural or behavioral change," although Alkon (1985) notes that some behavioral changes occur with forward pairing at certain ISIs. Under these circumstances, random stimulus presentations must, by definition, be less effective than overlap pairings. Thus, using random pairings, one cannot be certain that an appropriate control for associative effects has been provided.

Alpha Conditioning versus Long Latency Conditioning

When appropriately used, the term alpha conditioning refers to conditioned responses of short onset latencies (e.g. Table 3.2 in Woody 1982a). As noted above, short onset latencies greatly facilitate elucidation of underlying neural circuitry. Early investigations by Grant & Norris (1947) found conditioned response components of several different latencies, among which the shortest latency components represented sensitized responses. Since Grant and Norris's studies, it has been possible to demonstrate conditioned responses of alpha (12–115 ms) latencies, including 20 ms onset latency conditioned blink responses, that meet all of the associative criteria of longer latency CRs (Woody et al 1976). It is inadvisable, therefore, to use latency as a substitute for more accurate criteria of associative vs nonassociative responses.

Sometimes the term alpha conditioning has been used with reference to the presence or absence of an initial response to the CS before conditioning (Hull 1934, Kandel & Spencer 1968, Thompson 1979, Thompson 1983, Farley & Alkon 1985), but as Carew and associates point out (1984) both phenomena represent but a single process (Woody & Brozek 1969b, Young et al 1976, Harvey & Gormezano 1981). As Rescorla (1969) noted, selection of the response to be studied makes the principal difference in whether a CS will or will not elicit a conspicuous motor response prior to conditioning. In NMR conditioning in rabbits, 85 db tones are said not to produce behavioral responses prior to conditioning, whereas in short latency eyeblink conditioning in cats, 65–70 db clicks may or may not, depending on the particular animal used. Click (and presumably tone) stimuli of 65–70 db intensity are capable of producing *neural* responses at the level of motor neurons (Woody & Brozek 1969b). In *Hermissenda,* there is normally a strong phototropic response to light. When a photophobic response is produced by aversive conditioning, there is no initial photophobic response to the CS, but there is a phototropic response.

Pavlov and other behaviorists recognized that it would be possible to use CSs which produced a slight salivatory response initially to produce copious salivatory CRs when paired with presentations of appropriate USs. Now, as then, the presence or absence of a weak initial response to the CS is a poor guide to whether or not an associatively conditioned response can be developed, the presence of a preexisting response depending on the sensitivity of response detection by the experimenter and how the response is defined.

The possibility arises that certain types of conditioning might result from the formation of de novo pathways involving new growth and new connections. Tsukahara and associates' (1981, 1982, 1983) findings of changes in PSPs at the level of the red nucleus with conditioning provide the best likelihood for demonstrating such an effect (see review by Farley & Alkon 1985). [Synaptic growth can, of course, occur developmentally to support newly acquired behavior (cf Cragg 1967, Hubel & Wiesel 1970, Truman & Reiss 1976, Rosenzweig & Bennett 1977).] With completely new growth during condition-ing, an initial motor response to the CS might not be expected to be present, and distinctions based on the presence or absence of a response to the CS prior to conditioning might therefore be thought useful; however, because of parallel, polysensory and polymotor pathways, a small response to the CS could still be found prior to conditioning for which new neural connections were responsible.

Some evidence exists in invertebrates for a role of growth in sensitization and habituation (Bailey & Chen 1983), but some investigators believe that the time required for new growth of cell processes is too long for this to be a major means for rapid mammalian learning (Alkon 1980a). The growth of new cells also appears unlikely as a basis for such learning. In mammals such as primates, evidence is now available that all neurons of the brain are generated during prenatal and early postnatal life (Rakic 1985).

Theoretically, new growth could pose problems for long-lasting information handling (Woody 1962, 1982a). Growth of a completely new pathway represents a change in circuitry that could beneficially or adversely affect all prior, dependent circuitry operations, particularly the line-labeling of those pathways (see Bullock & Horridge 1965, Mountcastle 1974, Woody 1982a for further discussion).

The Role of Nonassociative As Well As Associative Cellular Processes in the Induction of Learned Behavior

Although classical associative processes play a key role in the development of learned behavior, it now seems likely that an equally important role is played by nonassociative processes and by additional associative processes besides that (those) illustrated on the left of Figure 2. First, there are the earlier mentioned demonstrations of successful backward conditioning and pseudoconditioning, which may be as or more robust than conditioning itself (Harris 1941, Woody 1982a, Berthier & Woody 1984). Second, there is the unavoidable production of cellular changes, during pairing, by nonassociative processes such as habituation, sensitization, latent facilitation, and latent inhibition as discussed below. Third, there are unavoidable commonalities in relationships underlying different associative processes. As a result, more than one associative process may be activated by pairing stimuli. Fourth, much of the present evidence from cellular studies of acquired behavior is indicative of nonassociative versus associative processes in its induction.

HABITUATION AND SENSITIZATION   Cellular changes produced by habituation or sensitization could complicate analysis of cellular changes supporting associative conditioning. Habituation typically involves a decrease in the magnitude and frequency of a response following repetitive presentation of a single stimulus. Thompson & Spencer (1966) noted nine features of habituation in vertebrates, including spontaneous response restoration over time, dishabituation by presenting a novel stimulus, and generalization of habituation to other stimuli. Most, but not all, of these features have been found in studying habituation in other phyla (see Woody 1982a). Sensitization involves an increased responsiveness to a stimulus as a consequence of nonrepetitive, totally separated presentation of another stimulus or variations thereof. A distinguishing feature of sensitization is the broad degree of generalization both for stimuli to which the response is enhanced and for the response itself.

Much of the evidence for the cellular basis of habituation and sensitization is derived from work of Kandel and associates in *Aplysia*. This research has recently been reviewed in detail (Kandel 1976, 1979, Kandel & Schwartz 1982, Camardo et al 1984; cf Farley & Alkon 1985). Kandel postulates that changes occur at presynaptic terminals which alter the quanta of transmitter released at the synapses, much as hypothesized by Hebb (1949).[4] Evidence for this possibility, though indirect, is extensive and corresponds to that found in crustacea (Krasne 1969, Wine & Krasne 1972, Krasne & Bryan 1973, Kennedy et al 1974) as well as in mammals and other vertebrates (Spencer et al 1966a,b,c, Farel 1974). The major limitation is lack of direct evidence for localization at the terminals. In *Aplysia,* current passed at somatic locations, where the critical measurements are made, can influence events at the terminals. Yet there is insufficient evidence to indicate whether the cable properties of the processes allow results of voltage clamping at the soma to be referred to distant terminal loci or even whether spike generation occurs in the presynaptic terminals, both important points (see Woody 1982a). Other gaps in our knowledge of the cellular basis of habituation and sensitization have been discussed recently by Farley & Alkon (1985). Kandel and colleagues (e.g. Klein & Kandel 1980) suggest that with habituation, calcium conductance and internal calcium concentrations are reduced at the presynaptic terminal, and that with sensitization intracellular calcium is increased secondary to a change

---

[4] But not as a consequence of postsynaptic generation of an action potential (see Carew et al 1984).

in a potassium conductance. A modulation involving changes in intracellular calcium concentration at nerve terminals would resemble the mechanism thought to potentiate transmission at the neuromuscular junction (Katz & Miledi 1968, McGraw et al 1982).

Farley & Alkon (1985) indicate that sensitization and habituation are virtually absent from their model of conditioning in *Hermissenda*. This is not the case in most other models of conditioning in vertebrates and invertebrates. As Pavlov (1927) noted, sensitization would be expected to result from the presentation of any novel stimulus and habituation from any repeated stimulation. Both conditions occur during CS-US pairing.

LATENT FACILITATION AND INHIBITION   The physiological basis of latent facilitation and inhibition can be traced to early work of Graham-Brown & Sherrington (1912) and Ukhtomsky (1926, 1950). In their studies, electrical stimulation of the cortex produced long-lasting changes in responsiveness to subsequently applied stimuli. This finding has been confirmed and extended by more recent studies using either direct or indirect means of cortical stimulation (Loucks 1933, 1935, Tchilingaryan 1963, Wagner et al 1967, Doty 1974, Bindman et al 1979, Woody 1982d) and electrophysiological as well as behavioral means of testing cortical neural excitability (Woody et al 1970, Woody & Engel 1972). The changes in neural excitability are long lasting and latent, unless specifically elicited or detected, and can arise from serial presentations of stimuli such as USs (Brons & Woody 1980, Brons et al 1982). They are likely to form the basis of behavioral phenomena such as pseudoconditioning and blocking (Kamin 1957). Reciprocal organization of facilitatory and inhibitory motor pathways suggests that both facilitatory and inhibitory mechanisms might be found at the cellular as well as the behavioral level (see Woody 1982a). Detailed evidence is offered elsewhere (Berthier & Woody 1984) that such phenomena contribute to associative conditioning. Recent evidence that inhibitory as well as facilitatory mechanisms can be found may be summarized as follows.

Brons et al (1982) found decreases in excitability to weak (nanoampere) extracellular electrical stimulation of neurons of the motor cortex after serial presentations of USs. These changes affected all motor projective cells, irrespective of whether or not they projected (interneuronally) to muscles involved in producing the UR. Behavioral effects were later found that were attributable to such changes and were comparable to those of latent inhibition. These effects were manifest as a reduction in initial levels of performance during subsequent conditioning using the same US.

Evidence for a separate, facilitatory cortical mechanism supporting the motor specificity of learned facial movements was found earlier in comparable regions of the feline cortex (Woody & Black-Cleworth 1973, Brons & Woody

1980). That mechanism was induced nonassociatively by serial presentations of the US, and expression of the neural changes was latent, behaviorally, except when manifest as a facilitation of the rate of subsequent conditioning in which the same US was employed. Excitability increases occurred in neurons supporting movements similar to the UR. Cells of the facial nuclei as well as neurons of the motor cortex underwent changes in excitability (Woody & Black-Cleworth 1973, Jordan et al 1976, Brons & Woody 1980, Matsumura & Woody 1982). In the absence of associative presentations of CS and US, these excitability increases lasted no more than a month. With associative presentations of CSs and USs, the increases lasted longer, supporting behavior that endured for over a year.

Mechanisms of this type may be dissimilar from those supporting "potentiation" since the typical stimulus parameters for their induction are not the same. (When stimuli applied to neural tissue are intense and their presentation sufficiently rapid, a "potentiation" of neuronal transmission may result.) However, the parameters of stimulation required for the induction of potentiation are not uniform, and this phenomenon is not found at every synaptic connection or in every neuron (Lloyd 1949, Beswick & Conroy 1965, Lomo 1971, Bliss & Lomo 1973, Andersen et al 1980, Brown & McAfee 1982, Swanson et al 1982, Barrionuevo & Brown 1983, Levy & Steward 1983, Voronin 1983). That in the hippocampus following tetanic or high rates of stimulation may, at least in part, be attributable to postsynaptic neuronal changes (Lynch & Baudry 1984).

Whether such potentiation more closely resembles sensitization or latent facilitation is open to question. Parametrically speaking, it resembles neither. Sensitization commonly follows presentation of a single stimulus; latent facilitation, the slow presentation of repeated stimulation; and potentiation, the rapid presentation of repeated stimuli. Generally speaking, it is these and other parameters of stimulus presentation that appear to govern the pre-, intra-, or postsynaptic locations of the resulting neurocellular changes (Woody 1982a). The opportunity to distinguish such changes physiologically promises the best separation of the phenomenon of sensitization from those of potentiation and latent facilitation, as well as the various features of habituation from latent inhibition (cf Woody 1982a).

SENSORY PRECONDITIONING AND OTHER VARIATIONS OF ASSOCIATION   Sensory preconditioning is an associative process in which the association is between two CSs rather than between a CS and a US (Brogden 1939). [Presumably, any liminal stimulus will do, since USs can themselves function effectively as CSs (Gormezano & Tait 1976).] The formation of the association is tested by subsequently forming a conditioned reflex to one of the two stimuli that were originally paired. Without further training the other stimulus is capable of eliciting the conditioned response.

The optimal ISI for producing sensory preconditioning differs from that for producing classical associative conditioning (Hoffeld et al 1958). This is shown in Figure 4. Comparison of overlap between effective temporal parameters herein and those in Figure 2 indicates that associative processes besides those identified with *Pavlovian* conditioning can potentially occur during *associative* conditioning and complicate cellular analysis of the learned behavior. Differences in the optimal ISIs for their development provide an excellent opportunity for separating the underlying cellular changes. Recent electrophysiological studies have found cellular correlates of sensory preconditioning in vertebrates. Buchhalter et al (1978) showed increased excitability to weak extracellular stimulation in neurons of the motor cortex of cats given pairings similar to those used to produce sensory preconditioning. This was a different excitability change than that found to support latent facilitation in neurons of the same cortical region after conditioning since it was disclosed by weak (nA) extracellular stimulation.

Other parameters of association are revealed in food aversion conditioning (Garcia et al 1974, Palmerino et al 1980; also see Figure 3.12 in Woody 1982a) or other, more complex forms of conditioning such as chain reflexes and second-order conditioning (see Pavlov 1927, Woody 1982a, Sahley et al 1984,

Optimal ISIs for Sensory Preconditioning

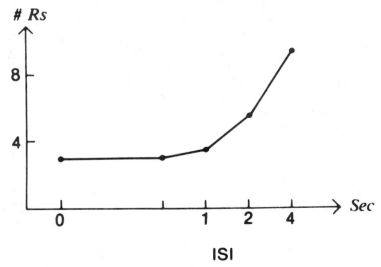

Figure 4   Effectiveness of different ISIs in producing sensory preconditioning (after Hoffeld et al 1958 in Woody 1982a).

Farley & Alkon 1985). Some of the differences in association are manifested by differences in extinction (Rizley & Rescorla 1972) or in closure and consolidation of conditioning (Bures & Buresova 1979, Buresova & Bures 1979).

CONDITIONING   Though early speculations favored presynaptic hypotheses (Hebb 1949, Kandel 1976), present evidence favors the view that changes in postsynaptic ionic conductances occur during conditioning to support the development of learned motor tasks. Woody & Black-Cleworth (1973) studied neurons of the motor cortex of awake cats and found direct evidence for a change in cable properties reflected by an increased excitability to intracellularly injected current pulses after conditioning. Rall (1970, 1974) and Woody & Black-Cleworth (1973) postulated that postsynaptic conductance changes might alter the input resistance of dendritic cables and thereby influence integration of postsynaptic potentials. Further supporting evidence for a postsynaptic change was found in later studies (Brons & Woody 1980). Other evidence was found in locust neurons that input resistance could be increased or decreased with operant conditioning depending on the aspect of behavior that was reinforced (Woolacott & Hoyle 1976, 1977). Then, studies by Alkon and associates (Alkon 1979, Crow & Alkon 1978) provided evidence that membrane resistance could change postsynaptically in the type B photoreceptor of *Hermissenda* after associative conditioning of an aversive response to light.

In the absence of cable analysis, some of the conditioning results in *Aplysia* (Walters et al 1982, Walters & Byrne 1983, Carew et al 1983, Hawkins et al 1983, Byrne et al 1985) could be interpreted as indicative of a postsynaptic rather than a presynaptic change. Alkon (1984) has recently advanced a specific model for the mechanism by which postsynaptic resistance changes can increase neuronal excitability. Formulation of a more detailed mammalian model of the effects of postsynaptic change has awaited cable analysis of cortical pyramidal cells of known geometry, introduction of known ionic conductances into the model, and measurements of ionic currents in these cells in vivo—phenomena that are just now being investigated experimentally (Holmes & Woody 1984, Woody et al 1985).

More than one mechanism is involved in conditioning. Mammalian studies disclosed a different mechanism involved in increasing unit excitability at caudal regions of the cerebral cortex following conditioning than that found rostrally at the motor cortex. At caudal, association cortex areas, increases in excitability were found on injecting weak nA currents *extracellularly* (EC) but not on injecting intracellular currents (Woody et al 1976). Thus, they differed in character from the postsynaptic increases in neural excitability to intracellularly applied currents that were found in the motor cortex[5] to support latent facilita-

---

[5]Also from the less specific *decreases* in excitability that appeared to support latent inhibition (see p. 450).

tion of the learned motor response (Woody & Black-Cleworth 1973). The caudal increases in cortical cellular excitability to weak extracellular current were isomorphic with increases in activity of units of the same cortical region in response to the CS after conditioning (Woody et al 1976). These changes in excitability may contribute to the ability of the CS to evoke the learned response selectively after conditioning since the magnitude of the change is greatest in CS-receptive neurons. Although the caudal cortical regions that contain these associatively produced changes are unnecessary for conditioning to occur (Woody et al 1974, Woody & Yarowsky 1972), removal of these areas has been shown to reduce discriminability between CSs and other stimuli (Diamond & Neff 1957).

Multiple subcellular mechanisms are involved in invertebrate conditioning. Alkon (1979) directly demonstrated decreases in potassium and calcium conductance by voltage clamping the type B photoreceptor. Decreases in K^+ conductance produced an increase in input resistance and augmented PSPs in these cells, thus supporting performance of the CR. The changes lasted for days and have since been studied extensively, with great care and ingenuity, to give the most comprehensive picture of cellular changes with conditioning presently available (see Farley & Alkon 1985).

Three variables appear to change in the type B photoreceptor of *Hermissenda* to support conditioning: a fast, 4-aminopyridine-sensitive potassium conductance (gK^+_A), the internal concentration of calcium, $[Ca^{2+}]_i$, and a calcium-dependent potassium conductance ($gK^+_{Ca^{2+}}$). [The light-induced sodium conductance and classical, voltage-dependent potassium conductance (delayed rectifier) in these cells are unaffected by this training paradigm (Farley & Alkon 1985).] Phosphorylations of $20,000-25,000$ dalton proteins are associated with the changes in conductance (Neary et al 1981, Neary & Alkon 1983). There are likely to be changes in other parts of the circuitry as well. The type A photoreceptor also undergoes changes in excitability after conditioning (Alkon 1984), and extracts of optic ganglia (prephotoreceptor substances) can produce increases in the input resistance of the type B photoreceptors, the latter suggesting possible contributions of additional mechanisms to the earlier described postsynaptic changes.

In *Hermissenda,* the nature of the association used in conditioning is such that the type B photoreceptor receives depolarization from application of both a light CS and a rotational US (Alkon 1980b, Crow & Alkon 1980, Farley et al 1983). Although different synapses are involved, there may not be a true heterosynaptic effect arising from application of the CS and US (see Woody 1982a). Instead, these two different inputs produce the same cellular event (depolarization) postsynaptically. Influx of Ca^{2+} during depolarization appears to activate a Ca^{2+}/ calmodulin-dependent protein kinase with concomitant facilitation of the production of long-lasting conductance changes (Acosta-

Urquidi et al 1984, Connor & Alkon 1984). Repeated injections of positive current paired with presentation of light can produce a comparable Ca^{2+}-mediated decrease in potassium conductance (Alkon 1984). The degree of depolarization produced by the two events (light and rotation) in combination permits the cell to reach but not exceed a range in which useful adaptations can occur. Too little depolarization will not produce a lasting membrane change. Too much (as with too intense a light CS) negates any change.

Another important feature is that the light CS-induced currents shunt inhibitory inputs to the type B photoreceptor arising from the hair cells' response to the rotational US. It is, therefore, the temporal relationship between light and rotation that determines whether or not long-lasting postsynaptic conductance changes will occur during conditioning of this type. The timing involves overlap between depolarization, early shunting, and later, increased input resistance produced by the light CS and by the rotational US. It is this overlap that results in a potentiated response to the paired as opposed to the separated stimuli.

It is unclear whether this relationship supports a phenomenon analogous to latent facilitation, potentiation, or classical associative conditioning. Farley & Alkon (1985) characterize their paradigm as demonstrating a virtual absence of nonassociative learning processes, yet some of their evidence suggests otherwise. Enhancement of long-lasting depolarization responses does not occur when light is separated from rotation by 10 or more sec (Alkon 1983) or when the 30 sec period of rotation immediately follows the 30 sec period of light (Farley 1985). The optimal ISI for light-rotation aversive conditioning in *Hermissenda* does not resemble that found for associative conditioning in vertebrate preparations (Farley 1985). Simultaneous presentations are far more effective than forward presentations, which are even less effective than backward presentations (Farley 1985). Farley and Alkon suggest that a lag in reaching peak acceleration may provide a significant delay in the timing of the rotational stimulus, but it is unclear, partly because of use of the overlap paradigm, whether onset or peak acceleration is the critical factor resulting from application of the US. Maximal g is reached from 500 msec to 15 sec after onset, depending on the apparatus used (Alkon 1976, Farley & Alkon 1985).

Other nonassociative effects can be found in the activity of the type A photoreceptor, which exhibits alterations in firing rate in response to the first few presentations of light in a manner resembling sensitization and/or habituation (Figure 2 of Alkon 1976). In addition, unpaired presentations of light and rotation can lead to some cumulative depolarization of the type B photoreceptor (Farley 1985). Also of note is the observation that after extinction, the preparation fails to exhibit spontaneous recovery or disinhibition of the CR over time, although some learning savings can be demonstrated with subsequent conditioning (Farley & Alkon 1985). Finally, reduction of training-produced differences in the contribution of gK^+_A to the conductance changes in the type B cell augments rather than diminishes the pairing-specific differences in response (Farley et al 1983, Farley & Alkon 1985).

Two important conclusions can be drawn from these results. The first is that unambiguous interpretations of results relatable to mammalian learning are unlikely to emerge from invertebrate conditioning studies because of differences in timing and slowness of neural events in these preparations (making explicit comparisons impossible). Consider, for example, two alternative interpretations of the *Hermissenda* results: (*a*) *Hermissenda* conditioning and its underlying changes are nonassociative because simultaneous rather than forward pairing produces optimal learning and the random control is inadequate; (*b*) *Hermissenda* conditioning and its changes are associative (because the peak of acceleration is delayed) and meet most associative tests.

The second conclusion is that while questionably causal or classically associative, the *Hermissenda* conditioning example meets many of our present definitions of associative phenomena and provides an objective, directly observed, physicalistic example of a mechanism by which resulting associative or causal-appearing behavior might be supported. Specifically, "the synaptic relations of the visual-statocyst network determine the pairing specificity of the network's response" (Alkon 1983). This finding is of considerable significance because it suggests that objective, cellular definitions of associative or causal behavior may be found that are preferable to or scientifically more precise than present behavioral definitions.

There are still other recent experimental results that are difficult to categorize, but are of potential relevance to the subject of associatively induced cellular change. There is, for example, the transient increase in input resistance produced in cortical neurons by extracellular application of acetylcholine (ACh) or intracellular application of cyclic GMP (Krnjevic et al 1971, Woody et al 1978, Swartz & Woody 1979). This increase can be made to persist when depolarization-induced discharge is associated, yet this "association" is also atypical in that it coincides with rather than follows application of ACh or cGMP. There is also the potentiation and disfacilitation of postsynaptic potentials by nucleotide actions described by Libet et al (1975) and Kobayashi et al (1978); cf Libet (1984). In those studies a slow EPSP (excitatory postsynaptic potential) produced by application of acetyl-B-methylcholine in the superior cervical ganglion can be enhanced by coapplication of cyclic AMP, dopamine, or by conditioning stimulation of the SIF interneuron to these cells (Libet et al 1975, Kobayashi et al 1978, Libet 1979, 1984). This enhancement can be disrupted by addition of cyclic GMP during or within 10 min of the coapplication period. As will be seen later, interpretation of these results is complicated by uncertainty concerning the mechanisms of cyclic nucleotide action in sympathetic ganglia (see Briggs & McAfee 1982, Woody 1982a) and by the inability to demonstrate well-defined slow synaptic potentials in some preparations (Briggs & McAfee 1982). Finally, there are the data of O'Brien et al (1977), Voronin (1980, 1983), and Bindman et al (1982) that represent nonassociatively rather than associatively produced effects of pyramidal tract or direct cortical stimulation on neural excitability.

To summarize the present review of research on associative phenomena, a surprising amount of evidence implicates a substantial role for "nonassociative" processes in associative learning. First, there are the "classical" nonassociative processes such as habituation, sensitization, and potentiation for which some evidence of cellular changes has been obtained. In each case, these cellular changes could be produced nonassociatively by aspects of the associative paradigms used for conditioning. Second, there are the atypical associative or unrecognized nonassociative processes such as those exhibited by conditioning in *Hermissenda*. Next, there are the "neoclassical" nonassociative processes with behavioral changes as or more robust than those produced associatively. These processes include pseudoconditioning, latent facilitation, latent inhibition, reflex learning, and the like (Woody 1982a,b). Evidence in mammals (see earlier) indicates that cellular changes that underlie these processes can be produced nonassociatively by serial presentations of unconditioned (and sometimes conditioned) stimuli. Finally, both invertebrate and mammalian results force consideration of the likelihood that *more than one mechanism is involved* in conditioning.

THE ROLE OF THE NEURON IN INTEGRATION

The neuron is elegantly designed to handle the integration of multiple message transmissions and to undergo the adaptations that alter the weightings of these transmissions. Those postsynaptic changes that have been found experimentally to support simple learning do so by altering the integrative properties of neurons. The classical Sherringtonian view that spatial and temporal integration reflect the convergence of afferents on a pool of neurons has been greatly expanded by our increased knowledge of the cable properties of single neurons and of the ionic conductances that influence integration and serve message transmission. The next sections will review the neuronal cable properties and ionic conductances and also the second messengers of neurotransmission.

Cable Properties

Postsynaptic integration involves the summation of large numbers of synaptic inputs over the cable space of the cell. Given the electrotonic nature of current flow in dendrites, the effect of a synapse on a target cell will be a function of the distance of that synapse from the site of action potential generation in the soma.

The decrement of the signal conducted through the dendrite can be quantified in model neurons with use of the cable equation:

$$V + r_m c_m \, \partial v / \partial t = (r_m / r_i) \, \partial^2 v / \partial^2 x$$

where: V = deviation of the membrane potential from resting level; r_m = resistance across an area of resting membrane ($\Omega \cdot$ cm); c_m = capacitance of an area of membrane (F/cm); r_i = resistivity of the cytoplasm (Ω/cm); t = time (sec); x = distance along conductor axis (cm). The quantity $r_m c_m$ is equal to the time constant of the membrane τ, which reflects the time at which the membrane potential will have fallen to $1/e$ of its previous value. The quantity $\sqrt{r_m / r_i}$ is known as the space constant λ, which denotes the distance over which the signal must travel to drop to $1/e$ of its previous value in a cable of infinite length. The cable equation may be rewritten as:

$$V = \lambda^2 \, \partial^2 v / \partial x^2 - \tau \, \partial v / \partial t$$

showing how the change in membrane voltage from rest is a function of both time and distance (cf Rall 1962, 1970, 1974, 1977, Jack 1979, Jack et al 1983). *These physical laws govern the spatiotemporal relationships between electrical neural events.*

CELL MORPHOLOGY   The morphology of the cell is well worth considering in applying the cable equation to models of cell function. Recent studies have found significant effects of dendritic geometry on the cable properties of hippocampal neurons and neocortical pyramidal cells (Turner & Schwartzkroin 1980, Holmes & Woody 1983, Turner 1984) that would be undetected were equivalent cylinder assumptions (Rall 1962) substituted for the actual anatomy.

Lorente de Nó & Condouris (1959) and Eccles (1964) postulated that the distal dendrites on some cells with extensive dendritic arborizations were at a distance of several space constants from the cell body, rendering synapses at those sites ineffective in altering the potential of the soma. Dendrites capable of supporting active spikes (Spencer & Kandel 1961, Nicholson & Llinas 1971, Traub & Llinas 1979, Llinas & Sugimori 1980b) could provide a means for circumventing this problem. Recent evidence suggests that most distal dendrites are but one to two space constants distant from the soma (Turner & Schwartzkroin 1980, T. H. Brown et al 1981). This means that local changes in specific ionic conductances, though elicited at or near synapses anatomically distant from sites of spike initiation, are likely to exert some effect on the potential at the soma and that the postulates of Lorente and Eccles may not hold for many central neurons.

MEMBRANE RESISTANCE   Changes in ionic conductance (g) will alter neuronal membrane resistance (conductance being the electrical inverse of resistance) and thereby alter the integrative properties of the postsynaptic cables. In general, all such changes will influence λ, and λ will affect the weighting of PSPs conducted between their point of origin in the dendrites and the locus of spike initiation in or near the soma. The resulting changes in weighting of synaptic inputs will have attributes resembling those of perceptron-like automata (see Woody 1982a). Knowledge of the geometry of the cell, which will affect λ and τ, along with estimation of appropriate values for conductance and magnitude and duration of the postsynaptic potential, can allow one to use the cable equation to estimate what effect a given set of inputs will have on the cell in question (cf Brown & Johnston 1983, Johnston & Brown 1983, Lev-tov et al 1983). When cable equations are carefully applied with appropriate consideration of λ and r_m, one outcome (Holmes 1985) suggests that swelling of the spine heads alone is not likely to alter the efficacy of synaptic inputs delivered at these regions, thus weighing theoretically against the hypothesis that swelling of spine heads (Van Harreveld & Fifkova 1975, Fifkova & Van Harreveld 1977, Fifkova et al 1982) is a mechanism for adult learning. (Other "growth" changes such as increases in synaptic contact area could conceivably occur at the terminals and cause synaptic inputs to become operative, inoperative, or more or less efficacious in generating or shunting currents.)

More than 20,000 synapses are estimated to impinge on some cortical neurons (Diamond et al 1970), and the duration of synaptic activation of ionic conductance changes may vary from <1 to >>200 msec (Hille 1984). Assuming that cortical neurons have spontaneous discharge rates of 5 to 10 per sec (Woody 1977), one might expect far more than 100 synaptic inputs to be active during any given msec. These inputs, consisting of excitatory and inhibitory postsynaptic potentials (PSPs), may arise from other means besides the classical increases in ionic conductances accompanied by decreases in membrane resistance. Recent studies have shown that some PSPs can be produced by momentarily *decreasing* tonically activated conductances and increasing resistance (Godfraind et al 1970, Engberg & Marshall 1971, Krnjevic et al 1971, Siggins et al 1971, Weight & Votava 1971, Brown et al 1982, Cole & Nicoll 1983, Woody et al 1985).

The integral of this ongoing temporal and spatial summation of activity will have a resistance as well as a voltage component. Each component will influence the probability of discharge of the unit. The integral of PSP activity will itself be influenced by the time constant of the cell membrane, by the duration of the PSPs, by changes in λ, by the numbers of different processes that converge, and by where along the cable those processes terminate. This is exclusive of electrical contacts between cells (Bennett & Goodenough 1978), which will also contribute as will any effects of metabolic processes such as electrogenic pumps (Boulpaep & Sackin 1979).

NONUNIFORM CONDUCTANCES   In dendrites without spike propagation, such as those of neocortical pyramidal cells, the effectiveness of synaptic inputs depends significantly on the nature of the ionic conductances and their equilibrium potentials along the cable (Holmes & Woody 1984). The equilibrium potentials of ionic conductances along the cell membrane depend on the identities of each ionic channel. Recent studies indicate that the assumption of a fixed r_m in applying the cable equation will not provide a satisfactory approximation of what occurs in real neurons. Fleshman et al (1983) suggested that results obtained in spinal neurons might best be explained by assuming different values of r_m for soma and dendrites. By introducing nonuniform postsynaptic conductances into the cable equation and considering the equilibrium potential of each local conductance in relation to the resting potential, Holmes & Woody (1984) found effects resembling those of inserting different values of effective R_m all along the cable length. When such conductances were active, equipotentiality no longer held throughout the cable space of the neuron. Certain distributions of activated ionic conductances significantly influenced local resting potentials and caused the "resting potential" to vary over different portions of the cell. Further consequences of changes in transmembrane potential on the conductances themselves are discussed below under the heading VOLTAGE DEPENDENCY.

In summary, integration within the cell is a complex and attractively interdependent matter (attractive with regard to the possibilities for modulation of probabilistic operations involving numerically large inputs whose weighting can be changed by postsynaptic conductance mechanisms). To understand the possible relationship between ISI and Δg depicted earlier in Figure 2, one must understand the anatomical nature of dendritic cables, the location of postsynaptic conductances along the cables, the equilibrium potentials of these conductances, and their sensitivities to change as a consequence of chemical and voltage inputs.

Ionic Conductances

Since long-lasting changes in membrane properties supporting learning are likely to arise from long-lasting changes in ionic conductances, it behooves us to consider which of these conductances might be best suited to these purposes. The ionic channels that are known to contribute to conductance across the plasma membrane of most nerve cells are those of Na^+, Ca^{2+}, K^+, and Cl^-. Recent research has disclosed a number of variations among these four ionic species with regards to their sensitivities to change as a consequence of electrical or chemical events (cf Catterall 1980, 1984, Hagiwara 1983, Hille 1984). Which of the various conductances are most likely to be involved in mechanisms supporting learning is discussed below, together with the physical variables or stimulus senitivities by which long-lasting conductance changes might be brought about.[6]

SODIUM   Two types of sodium conductances are presently recognized, each distinguished by the blocking action (or lack thereof) of the puffer fish poison, tetrodotoxin (TTX). One arises from a TTX-sensitive fast sodium channel responsible for spiking, the other is TTX-insensitive (Hodgkin & Huxley 1939, 1952, Cole & Curtis 1940, Cole 1968, Baker et al 1971). The electrical and chemical sensitivities of the TTX-sensitive sodium channel, beyond those originally described by Hodgkin and Huxley, are actively being investigated (see Catterall 1980, Armstrong 1981) as is the nature of the nicotinic, cholinergic receptor that appears to be closely related to the channel itself (Raftery et al 1980, Conti-Tronconi & Raftery 1982, Anholt et al 1984). It is not yet established if sodium channels are present in the plasma membrane of dendrites of central neurons (see Llinas & Sugimori 1980b), but there are evidently insufficient numbers of sodium channels in the dendrites of most cortical neurons to support sodium spike propagation (Woody et al 1984). The slower, Na-dependent generator potentials characteristic of sensory receptors have been shown to be TTX-insensitive in Pacinian corpuscles, crayfish stretch receptors, and in retinal photoreceptors (Hagins & Yoshikami 1975, Loewenstein 1963). (It is the slower, nonspike-generating conductances that are most likely to contribute to long-lasting conductance changes.) In neurons, sodium conductances may contribute to anomalous rectification together with potassium conductances (Mayer & Westbrook 1983, Stafstrom et al 1984). Sodium pump mechanisms (cf Baker et al 1971, Baker 1972, Rasmussen & Goodman 1977) may alter the membrane potentials of nerve cells in ways reflecting nonresistive (electrogenic) effects of different ionic concentration gradients across the membrane (Boulpaep & Sackin 1979).

CHLORIDE   Chloride conductances exist across the plasma membrane and are thought to be major mediators of inhibitory postsynaptic potentials in the mammalian central nervous system (Roberts et al 1976), but relatively little is known about them, in part because chloride ions equilibrate so rapidly across the cell membrane. Hille (1984) describes three categories of Cl^- channel: one, weakly voltage dependent (in muscle) could be mistaken for a linear current leak; a second, steeply voltage dependent, was obtained from single channel recordings in *Torpedo;* and a third (synaptic) was neurotransmitter operated. The latter is thought to be present in central neurons. GABA (gamma-aminobutyric acid) is thought to exert its inhibitory action by increasing Cl^- conductance through these channels in crayfish neuromuscular junctions, both

---

[6]Since new developments are occurring so rapidly in this field, the present review will likely need significant updating in the near future.

presynaptically (Takeuchi & Takeuchi 1966) and postsynaptically (Takeuchi & Takeuchi 1967), and in mammalian nerve cells (Adams & Brown 1975, Harris & Allan 1985).

CALCIUM   Of the calcium conductances, several different aspects are described which need not reflect mutually exclusive channels but rather different properties or variations thereof. One is a fast calcium conductance that is blocked by magnesium, cobalt, and manganese, but not by TTX (Fatt & Ginsborg 1958, Hagiwara & Naka 1964, Kostyuk 1980, Tsien 1983; cf Hagiwara 1983). This channel probably mediates transmitter release at the presynaptic terminal and may support calcium spiking. (A second calcium-dependent conductance is described that is blocked by TTX and may represent simply the ability of some calcium to pass through normal sodium channels.) A slower calcium conductance is recognized in *Helix* and other invertebrate preparations (Baker et al 1971, Meech 1974, Hagiwara 1975, Eckert & Lux 1976, Heyer & Lux 1976a,b) which is insensitive to TEA and TTX and whose magnitude can be altered by hyperpolarizing and depolarizing currents. Its properties resemble those of the fast, vertebrate calcium conductance. While some relatively slow and prolonged changes in calcium conductances have been reported in invertebrates, none have been as long lasting as those reported in potassium conductance (Alkon 1984), changes in which may be controlled by changes in intracellular calcium concentration. Thus, the changes in gCa^{2+} in Figure 2 could act indirectly to produce long lasting changes in nerve membrane properties. As Rasmussen (1979) and Hille (1984) point out, changes in calcium concentrations can also control contraction, secretion, gating, and calmodulin-kinase and a number of other important second messenger actions (see below and Woody 1982a) and impart a voltage dependence secondary to the voltage dependence of calcium entry into the cell.

Llinas and colleagues classify calcium-dependent currents as a function of their thresholds of activation, studied in vitro in cerebellar (Purkinje), olivary, and thalamic neurons (Llinas & Sugimori 1980a,b, Llinas & Yarom 1981a,b, Jahnsen & Llinas 1984a,b). One current is activated at low threshold at about the same region of depolarization (about -40 mV) as the slow calcium conductance in *Helix*. The other is found at a "higher" threshold, at more hyperpolarizing levels of the transmembrane potential. That current could represent an inactivated state of the slow calcium channel or a separate channel with separate activation properties or, conceivably, calcium-dependent electrical couplings between cells (Loewenstein 1973, 1975, Nahvi et al 1980, Ribak et al 1980). Hagiwara (1983) also distinguishes between high and low threshold Ca^{2+} channels, and notes that many conductances across neuronal membranes resemble those across muscle or egg-cell membranes.

Calcium channels are thought to be inactivated by accumulation of sufficient levels of intracellular free calcium (Hagiwara 1983, Eckert & Chad 1984, 1985). This is important because changes in internal calcium concentration have been implicated in three different types of cellular adaptation: the muscle end plate potentiation of Katz & Miledi (1968); also see Llinas & Heuser 1977), changes in presynaptic terminals thought to support habituation and sensitization (Kandel & Schwartz 1982) and changes in the type B photoreceptor of *Hermissenda* that supports conditioning (Alkon 1979, Connor & Alkon 1984). Depolarization, which activates calcium channels, can also contribute to their inactivation either directly or indirectly by inducing calcium entry (Connor & Stevens 1971, Hagiwara 1983).

POTASSIUM   A surprising number of different potassium conductances have recently been recognized (S. H. Thompson 1977, D. J. Adams et al 1980, P. R. Adams et al 1982a,b, Hagiwara 1983, Hille 1984). Of those recognized earlier, the voltage-dependent, "delayed rectifier" represents the fast, calcium-insensitive potassium conductance that is blocked by tetraethylammonium (TEA) and causes the repolarization of nerve membranes that follows spike discharge. Delayed rectifier channels of axons can vary considerably among different genera and even within the same axon with respect to the extracellular TEA concentrations required to block the channels (Hille 1984).

Another rapid, voltage-dependent potassium conductance, gK^+_A, is the A-current, which has been characterized in invertebrate preparations by Connor & Stevens (1971), Neher (1971), and Alkon et al (1982a), in vertebrate spinal motoneurons by Barrett & Crill (1972), and in hippocampal pyramidal cells by Johnston & Hablitz (1979) and Gustaffson et al (1982). The A-current is usually blocked or reduced by 4-aminopyridine. It can be rapidly inactivated (to some degree) by depolarization and potentiated by hyperpolarization.

A third potassium conductance, $gK^+_{Ca^{2+}}$, is the slow, calcium-dependent potassium current. It can be activated by increasing $[Ca^{2+}]_i$ or by a positive-going shift in membrane polarization (Meech & Standen 1975, Heyer & Lux 1976a,b, Hagiwara 1983; cf Barrett et al 1982). Its initial activation may be primarily voltage dependent, i.e. secondary to a depolarization accompanied by an increased calcium conductance. Hyperpolarization reduces Ca^{2+} entry and thereby decreases $gK_{Ca^{2+}}$. In some preparations, a larger depolarization can also inactivate $gK^+_{Ca^{2+}}$, presumably secondary to a voltage–Ca^{2+} dependent inactivation of $gK_{Ca^{2+}}$ (Heyer & Lux 1976a). The calcium-dependent potassium channel can be blocked in mammals by apamin, a peptide found in bee venom (Hugues et al 1982a,b).

A fourth potassium current is the M-current which can be influenced by levels of polarization of the plasma membrane (D. A. Brown et al 1981, Adams et al 1982a). It is a current that is tonically activated at normal levels of resting potential and is inactivated by the muscarinic cholinergic agonist muscarine, hence the name "M" or muscarinic current (Adams et al 1982b). Atropine, a muscarinic antagonist, blocks this inactivation. [Although atropine can impair recall in some memory-learning experiments (cf Woody 1982a), it has not been established if this action is direct or indirect or related in any way to its effects on this particular channel.]

A fifth potassium current, the anomalous or inward rectifier, is termed such because of a difference in outward versus inward electrical current passed across the membrane. It is rapidly activated by negative-going changes in membrane potential and by shifts in K^+ concentration which alter the cell's electrochemical potential (Hagiwara 1983). It can be blocked by cesium or sodium applied extracellularly. The most detailed descriptions of this currently come from studies in muscle and egg-cell membranes (Katz 1949, Hagiwara & Takahashi 1974, Hagiwara 1983).

The Q-current is still another current that can contribute to the resting membrane conductance and to anomalous rectification as described by Halliwell & Adams (1982); it is sensitive to cesium but not to TTX or to calcium blockers. This current and some other leakage currents may also reflect potassium channels but little is presently known about these channels.

Another potassium current, the S-current, appears to be unique to *Aplysia*. Klein & Kandel (1980) describe a potassium current found in *Aplysia* sensory neurons that is sensitive to the presence of extracellular serotonin. Dopamine may act similarly (Deterre et al 1982). Investigation of the K^+ channels responsible for this "S"-current indicates that they are usually open at the resting potential of these cells. Addition of 30–60 μM of 5-hydroxytryptamine (5-HT) is thought to act to close these channels reversibly through the following cascade of reactions: serotonin activates an adenylate cyclase and the formed cAMP dependent protein kinase phosphorylates some protein controlling the K^+ channel (S-channel). This action results in a slow EPSP that is thought to underly the process of sensitization reported in these sensory neurons. I-V plots for this K^+ current indicate a slight outward rectification and voltage dependence (Siegelbaum et al 1982).

In contrast, Drummond et al (1980) report a 5-HT sensitive K^+ current in the *Aplysia* R-15 neuron, which *increases* in the presence of low (0.1–10 μM) 5-HT. Unlike the facilitation described by Siegelbaum and colleagues, this acts to inhibit the cell through hyperpolarization. The 5-HT induced increase in gK^+ is also mediated by a cAMP-dependent protein kinase (cf Adams & Levitan 1982, Benson & Levitan 1983); however, its voltage dependence is characterized by inward rather than outward rectification. An interesting similarity between the effects of 5-HT reported by Siegelbaum et al (1982) and Drummond et al (1980) is that at high concentrations of 5-HT (20–50 μM), the latter group reports excitatory effects on R-15 neurons. Some suggest that this dose-dependent result might reflect two entirely different mechanisms of 5-HT action, the low dose involving K^+ conductances and the high dose involving possible Na^+ or Ca^{2+} conductance changes. It should also be noted that two types of serotonin receptors (Peroutka et al 1981) may be present and may be coupled to different effector mechanisms.

Which of these potassium currents may be responsible for the membrane changes supporting conditioning in vertebrate preparations is not yet established, but some are likely to be involved since potassium ions are the major current carriers across nerve membranes. Potassium channels have the capacity to undergo long-lasting modifications, changes in the A-current and in $gK_{Ca^{2+}}$ having been linked to conditioning in *Hermissenda* and changes in potassium currents being thought to mediate long-lasting, cholinergic-induced increases in resistance in the same cortical neurons that were shown to have excitability increases after conditioning (see earlier discussion). The A-current is interesting since it can be potentiated by a preceding hyperpolarization, inhibited by strong depolarization or increases in internal concentration of calcium, and maintained at different steady levels over long periods of time (Alkon 1979, Alkon et al 1982b). The M-current is interesting because it is demonstrably sensitive to cholinergic agents and is also a steady-state current that can be modulated up or down by neurotransmission. The calcium-dependent potassium current is interesting because it is sensitive to calcium, which can be altered by different frequencies (and polarities) of stimulation (Figure 2). Because it involves both calcium and potassium in the effects, this current can potentially undergo long-lasting changes without causing much change in resting potential (thus providing primarily a resistive change in postsynaptic integration).

Despite these attractive possibilities for ionic channels supporting learning, it is clear that many of these channels can act differently from species to species and from cell to cell. Evidence specifically relatable to learning and memory requires analysis of cells established as being directly involved in these processes and experiments performed on these cells in their natural states.

VOLTAGE DEPENDENCY   Nearly all of the above ionic currents are sensitive to different levels of polarization of the plasma membrane. Magnitudes of voltage-dependent conductance change can be as great as that of sodium conductance in association with the sodium spike. In that case, the input resistance of the cell may fall to as little as 10% of its resting value at the peak of the action potential (Frank & Fuortes 1956). As a result, the integral of PSP activity within the cell may be effectively reset by virtue of current shunting across the cell membrane.

Because of this voltage dependence,[7] PSPs that reflect extrinsic, stimulus-activated neurotransmission potentially can influence other conductances within the neurons in which they arise. Thus, not only do the longer-lasting PSPs form "traces" of the stimuli by which they are initiated, but they also cause secondary changes in local conductance (and therefore resistance) within the cell.

One may ask if there is a linear or nearly linear region of change in current with potential within nerve cells. Such a region of the current-voltage relationship could be useful for well-controlled summation of PSPs leading to spike generation. Evidence exists in in vivo mammalian preparations that such a range occurs near the resting potential of some cortical neurons (Lux & Pollen 1966, Krnjevic et al 1971, Woody & Gruen 1978). However, in vitro experimentation in similar neurons with hyperpolarized resting potentials discloses variable but significant degrees of nonlinear, anomalous rectification in both depolarizing and hyperpolarizing directions relative to the resting potential (Stafstrom et al 1984; cf Llinas & Sugimori 1980a,b for studies of other central neurons). Further studies are needed to resolve this question.

Second Messengers

Second messengers are ions or chemicals that are released intracellularly (in the cytosol, in the microsomes, and even within the plasma membrane of the cell) consequential to extracellular neurotransmitter or hormonal action (Sutherland 1972). They function to carry the message of neurotransmission within nerve cells so that a change in regulation of protein synthesis, intermediary metabolism, ionic conductance, or some other appropriate internal chemical change can take place. Temporal and spatial-concentrational relationships between these agents and their byproducts are likely to influence chemical reactions controlling engram formation and expression within nerve cells.

The significance of the message carried by a particular messenger can vary from cell to cell and from time to time—e.g. direct relay of immediate neurotransmission, formation of a delayed message trace, signalization of a contingency required for engram production, or generation of a regulatory input to the postsynaptic cell—and must be determined experimentally for each characterizable, repeatable circumstance. The rapid transport of any soluble (nonmembrane-bound) second messengers of neuronal transmission may also influence postsynaptic integration (Horwitz 1981, 1983), especially in spinous processes, by direct flow as opposed to electrical cable effects.

The principal second messenger agents are Ca^{2+}, cyclic AMP, cyclic GMP, and the products of hydrolysis of phosphatidylinositols. Detailed reviews are available concerning the proposed role of each of these second messengers in

---

[7]Also calcium dependence since calcium entry is voltage dependent.

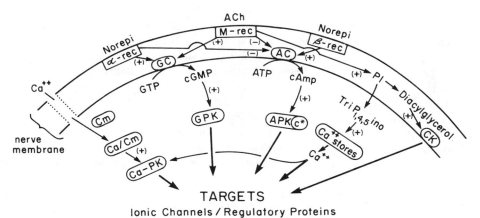

Figure 5   A general model of some second messenger effects. Drawn from presently available but still limited evidence, this model could require modification for different types of cells. ACh = acetylcholine; M-rec = muscarinic cholinergic receptor; Norepi = norepinephrine; α-rec and β-rec = alpha and beta noradrenergic receptors, respectively; GC = guanylate cyclase; AC = adenylate cyclase; GTP = guanosine triphosphate; ATP = adenosine triphosphate; cGMP = cyclic guanosine 3'5' monophosphate; cAMP = cyclic adenosine 3'5' monophosphate; CM = calmodulin; Ca-PK = calcium-activated, calmodulin-dependent protein kinase; GPK = cGMP-activated protein kinase; APK = CAMP-activated protein kinase; C* = catalytic subunit of APK; PI = phosphoinositol; CK = C-kinase; Tri P$_{1,4,5}$ ino = triphosphoinositol; + = facilitates (production of); − = inhibits (production of).

neurotransmission (Rasmussen & Goodman 1977, Greengard 1978, 1979, Bartfai 1980, Briggs & McAfee 1982, Cheung 1982, Woody 1982a, Drummond 1983, Berridge 1984, Nestler & Greengard 1984, Rasmussen & Barrett 1984).

Each second messenger is associated with activation of one or more protein kinases (Figure 5). Calcium activates calcium-calmodulin-dependent protein kinases; cyclic AMP activates cyclic-AMP-dependent protein kinases; cyclic GMP activates a cyclic-GMP-dependent protein kinase; and diacylglycerol (and the phorbol esters) activate C-kinases. These effects are by no means independent of each other. Thus, the phosphodiesterases that hydrolize the phosphatidylinositols to yield diacylglycerol and triphosphoinositol also promote the mobilization of intracellular calcium, and diacylglycerol itself produces the release of arachidonic acid, the activation of guanylate cyclase, and the formation of cyclic GMP (Berridge 1984). Ca^{2+} can also affect calcium-dependent steps related to other kinase actions or kinase precursors, and cAMP and cGMP have secondary interactions of their own (see Figures 5.9 and 5.12 in Woody 1982a). The interdependence is, in fact, quite remarkable and probably serves regulatory effects that are necessary complements to conductance changes.

The assumption is made increasingly that a conformational or structural change in a protein macromolecule (Schmitt 1962) can persistently change ionic conductance in the plasma membrane in such a way as to persistently influence postsynaptic integrative properties and thereby mediate certain forms of learned behavior.[8] Since the end stage of many second messenger-activated protein kinase effects is a protein phosphorylation or dephosphorylation (Greengard 1979), it is likely that some proteins involved are those that alter the conductance of ion channels. Thus, experimental knowledge of second messenger action is essential to an understanding of the cellular basis of learned behavior. Present evidence now hints at some of the potentially relevant reaction pathways.

Intracellularly administered cyclic GMP or cyclic GMP activated protein kinase (Woody et al 1978, Bartfai et al 1985) can mimic the excitability changes seen in mammalian cortical cells after conditioning. In these cells, these effects appear to be a consequence of muscarinic cholinergic neurotransmission (Swartz & Woody 1979, 1984). Nonetheless, extensive attempts to relate the fast EPSP, slow IPSP, and slow EPSP in neurons of the sympathetic ganglia to the actions of calcium, cAMP, and cGMP have not proved confirmatory of the original second messenger hypotheses (see Hartzell 1981, Briggs & McAfee 1982, Woody 1982a). To satisfy these hypotheses would require satisfaction of at least the following criteria: 1. evidence should be provided that binding of transmitter at a membrane receptor results in activation of an appropriate enzyme (adenylate cyclase or guanylate cyclase, respectively) for production of cyclic AMP or cyclic GMP; 2. synaptic activity should increase intracellular levels of cAMP or cGMP in the same neurons as well as increase the phosphorylation of appropriate protein substrates prior to the alteration of membrane conductance (as should inhibitors of phosphodiesterase activity, which breaks down cAMP and cGMP); 3. a similar alteration of membrane conductance should be produced by intracellular injection of the cyclic nucleotide or its activated protein kinase. It has not yet been possible to satisfy all these criteria in neurons of the central nervous system, nor has consistent evidence for these criteria been found in other neuronal systems. For example, cyclic AMP was thought to alter membrane conductance as a consequence of norepinephrine/dopamine release in sympathetic ganglia, and cyclic GMP was thought to alter membrane conductance as a consequence of acetylcholine binding to the muscarinic receptors of similar cells (Greengard & Kebabian 1974), but as Briggs and McAfee (1982) point out, although some of these criteria were satisfied, including characterization of a synaptic phosphorylation itself (Greengard 1982, Nestler & Greengard 1984), exogenous dopamine only

---

[8]Since actin filaments have been demonstrated in dendritic spines of central neurons (Katsumaru et al 1982), changes that might influence neuronal integrative properties by means other than changes in ionic conductance must also be considered.

slightly raised levels of cAMP in some preparations, cyclic cAMP sometimes degraded to a hyperpolarizing adenosine receptor agonist, and the more powerful intracellular techniques failed to demonstrate well-defined, slow PSPs. In addition, the expected conductance changes in response to cAMP and cGMP were not found or were found inconsistently in many preparations (see Woody 1982a), and the contribution of an electrogenic sodium pump to the generation of the slow PSPs also became a matter of some uncertainty (Nishi & Koketsu 1968, Koketsu & Nakamura 1975, Smith & Weight 1977, Libet 1984). Given these results and those in other central neurons (Krnjevic et al 1976, Woody et al 1978, Benardo & Prince 1982), one infers that different concentrations of calcium and cyclic nucleotides can influence different modulatory processes by different actions in different cells (cf Rasmussen 1979, Bartfai 1980, Woody 1982a).

In invertebrates, evidence was found that calcium/calmodulin-dependent protein kinase might decrease the A-current postsynaptically in the type B photoreceptor of *Hermissenda* (Acosta-Urquidi et al 1982, Neary & Alkon 1983, Acosta-Urquidi et al 1984; also see DeLorenzo 1980, Grab et al 1981) and increase the release of transmitter, presynaptically, by phosphorylating a protein in the squid giant synapse (Llinas et al 1985) and that a cyclic AMP-dependent protein kinase might decrease delayed K^+ and gK^+_A currents in *Hermissenda* and *Aplysia* neurons (Castellucci et al 1980, Kaczmarek et al 1980, Castellucci et al 1982, Alkon et al 1983, Kaczmarek & Strumwasser 1984; cf Cedar et al 1972, Cedar & Schwartz 1972); however, others' studies of *Aplysia* neurons indicated that cyclic AMP-dependent protein kinase could *increase* potassium conductance (W. B. Adams et al 1980, Triestman 1981, Lemos et al 1984) and also calcium conductance (Castellucci et al 1980, cf Hockberger & Connor 1983). Phosphorylation of sodium channels was also reported to be cyclic AMP dependent (Catterall 1984). As a result, considerable caution must be exercised in applying general hypotheses of second messenger actions to specific cell examples or to specific ionic conductances.

ACCELERATION OF RATES OF CONDITIONING

Given the complexities of cellular substrates of learning described above, a most surprising recent finding is that rates of acquisition of classically conditioned responses can be accelerated in mammals by adding electrical stimulation of the hypothalamus (HS), associatively, to presentations of conventional CSs and USs (Voronin et al 1975, Kim et al 1983, Woody et al 1983). A forward order of CS-US-HS presentation (as opposed to a backward order) is necessary for accelerated conditioning to occur, suggesting that this is not simply a potentiation, arousal, or sensitization-like effect, but instead is an acceleration of one or more of the fundamental processes supporting conditioning.

Earlier studies showed that hypothalamic stimulation given simultaneously with or just before stimulation of the motor cortex facilitated the production of stimulation-induced limb movements (Murphy & Gellhorn 1945). Later studies (Voronin 1974, Voronin et al 1975) found that development of nondiscriminatively elicited foreleg CRs could be accelerated by pairing an auditory CS and an electrical US with hypothalamic stimulation. Finally, the rate of acquiring discriminative eyeblink CRs was found to be accelerated by Kim et al (1983) after pairing hypothalamic stimulation with the same click-CS and tap-US that had been used previously to produce blink CRs at slower rates of acquisition. The number of CS-US pairings needed to produce eyeblink conditioning was reduced from 1000 (Woody et al 1974) to less than 20 by adding electrical stimulation of the lateral region of the hypothalamus (HS) 580 ms after the CS (and 240 ms after the US). The CRs were produced discriminatively to the click CS and not to a hiss discriminative stimulus (DS) of comparable intensity and were associative, their emergence depending on the order of CS, US, and HS presentations. Discriminative eyeblink CRs did not develop in explicitly un-paired, "backward HS" sessions in which HS was given 2.5 sec before each CS-HS pairing. Repeated pairings of the CS and HS (without tap US) failed to produce acquisition of an eyeblink CR within 100 pairings. The latency of the rapidly produced CR was long, >100 msec. During conditioning, increases in CS-evoked unit responses occurred in neurons of the motor cortex at latencies 100 msec or more after onset of the click CS. This corresponded with the behavioral observation that the majority of eyeblink CRs occurred with onset latencies longer than 100 msec. Recently, by changing the ISI, it has been found possible to produce a short-latency CR equally rapidly.

Theories that propose a two-stage model of conditioning based on fear and association (Weinberger 1982a) do not seem likely to explain this effect (but cf Rescorla & Solomon 1967). This is because the fear component of that model is the more rapid of the two stages. Accelerating its rapidity alone would not be likely to help accelerate the overall rate of acquisition, since the slower, associative process would remain. Also, while enhanced fearfulness can enhance the rate of learning, this is a sensitizing-like effect that is not tightly linked to associative stimulus presentations.

Another possible explanation lies in acceleration of one of the two different mechanisms thought to support the cellular basis of short-latency eyeblink conditioning. In this case, either the associative or the nonassociative mechanisms might be sped up by hypothalamic stimulation.

Short-latency activation of cortical cells by HS is predictive of loci of hypothalamic stimulation that will accelerate conditioning (Woody et al 1983). This activation resembles the depolarization-induced discharge given during applications of ACh or cGMP to transform transient increases in input resistance in neurons of the motor cortex into persistent increases. Studies currently in progress suggest that hypothalamic stimulation produces a comparable increase in input resistance in the same cells. This supports the possibility that the process of latent facilitation (see earlier discussion concerning mechanisms supporting the motor stage of this type of learning) is accelerated.

SOME EXPERIMENTAL TECHNOLOGIC FRONTIERS

Experimental findings are only as reliable as the methodologies by which they have been obtained. The following material is provided to assist the reader in evaluating the merits and pitfalls of some methodologies of relevance to behavioral neuroscience.

Neuroanatomy

IDENTIFICATION OF ELECTROPHYSIOLOGICALLY STUDIED NEURONS   In the past, studies of single cell neurophysiology in the central nervous system have depended largely on antidromic activation of the studied unit for cell identification. Now it is possible to inject the studied unit with horseradish peroxidase (HRP) or a fluorescent dye on completion of in vivo or in vitro intracellular physiological studies (e.g. Kitai et al 1976, Jankowska et al 1976, Snow et al 1976, Christensen & Ebner 1978, Sakai et al 1978a). Using this technique, one can confirm the possibility of studying, electrophysiologically, every commonly found neuroanatomical cell type in the cat motor cortex (Sakai et al 1978b). Within 48 hours of injection, some HRP is likely to remain in soluble form, and the soma and dendritic processes of the studied neuron may be disclosed by diaminobenzidine (DAB) reaction. After about 48 hours, the reaction product of HRP may be found by use of the DAB method, and with cobalt intensification procedures (Adams 1977), the soma and axonal projections of the unit may be preferentially disclosed. Either iontophoretic procedures or pressure injection may be used to apply the marking agent (Curtis 1964, Remler et al 1968, Koike et al 1974, Zieglgansberger et al 1974, McCaman et al 1977, Sakai et al 1978a, Woody et al 1981).

RECONSTRUCTION OF CELL MORPHOLOGY   Injection with HRP greatly simplifies identification of the cell's processes and reconstruction of serial sections of brain tissue to give a three-dimensional view of the cell. Morphologic features that might otherwise be difficult to detect may be made conspicuous by this means (e.g. Murakami et al 1982, 1984). Fine detail such as investiture of incoming presynaptic terminals by dendritic spines can be more easily defined by electron microscopic examination of serial sections of the cell following injection of HRP (Figure 6, left). Another example (Figure 6, right) shows a beaded dendritic process. The enlargement defined by the HRP contains a mitochondrion. Consequently, it is possible to compare changes in electro-

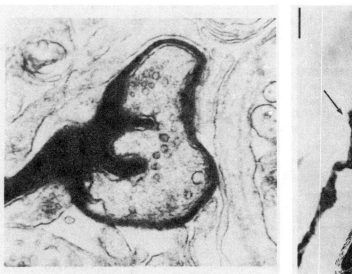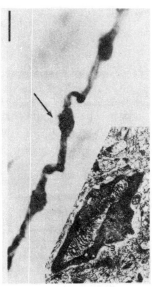

Figure 6 (Left)   An HRP-filled dendritic spine enveloping a presynaptic terminal. (Right) A beaded dendrite of an HRP-filled neuron. The calibration bar is 5 μm. The bead with the arrow contains a mitochondrion—lower right enlargement. I thank Drs. G. Vrensen and C. Ribak for preparing electron photomicrographs of these HRP injected cells.

physiological properties of central neurons studied in vivo with possible changes in morphology.

FIXATION AND THE EXTRACELLULAR SPACE   One unresolved frontier of neuroanatomical research concerns disclosure of the actual in vivo morphology of the extracellular space. Studies by Cragg (1980) show that the extent of the extracellular space disclosed postmortem is very much a function of the fixation procedure used. Many neuroanatomists accept close approximations between cell membranes as representative of the proper fixation and, presumably, the accurate extent of the extracellular space (cf Peters & Jones 1984); however, other studies (Levin et al 1970, Van Harreveld & Steiner 1970) suggest that a more enlarged space may provide a more accurate reflection of the actual in vivo condition. Given these uncertainties plus the variability of fixation by present perfusion of immersion procedures, delineation of changes in spines or synaptic junctions attributable to other than fixation variability can prove difficult, although in vitro studies with careful evaluation of artifactually produced effects suggest that alterations in synaptic morphology can occur that reflect differences in some synaptic physiological properties (e.g. Fields & Ellisman 1985).

Electrophysiology

EVALUATION OF POSSIBLE INJURY CAUSED BY INTRACELLULAR PENETRA-
TION   Electrophysiologists have long suspected that penetration of cells by
recording electrodes could produce significant injury, not simply of the type
associated with a rapid and progressive decline in spike amplitude followed by
cessation of discharge but of a type associated with a stable but reduced spike
amplitude. This possibility has led a number of investigators to reject data from
cells with small spike amplitudes or resting potentials even though such recordings might form a majority of the data obtained (cf Kandel et al 1961, Llinas &
Sugimori 1980a).

Recent studies suggest that many stable penetrations associated with "small"
spike amplitudes need not reflect injury but may instead reflect penetration of
dendritic cables remote from sites of active spike initiation and/or propagation
(Woody et al 1984). Reversible increases in spike amplitude during intracellular pressure injection of fluid volumes provide further support for this
possibility as do intracellular injections showing HRP confined to dendritic
processes (Houchin 1973, Woody et al 1984) and in vitro demonstrations of
directly visualized dendritic penetration (Llinas & Sugimori 1980b).

Comparisons of poststimulus time histograms of in vivo spike activity
elicited by weak auditory stimuli from intracellularly penetrated units, including some with spike amplitudes as small as 30 mV, with those of recordings and
histograms obtained from comparable, extracellularly recorded units show no
deterioration in the ability of the units to respond to these stimuli (Woody et al
1984). This provides objective evidence that normal information transfer properties of cells can be operative in the face of penetration.

To permit normal operations after cell penetration, the cell membrane would
have to seal tightly about the penetrating electrode. That this occurs is supported by results of patch-clamp studies indicating that avulsed membranes can
reseal, provided appropriate levels of calcium concentration are maintained
(Sakmann & Neher 1983). Also, injection of ramp depolarizing currents into
penetrated neurons can disclose few minimal gradient responses (Koike et al
1968a,b, Richter et al 1974; cf Woody & Gruen 1978), weighing further against
the likelihood of signficant leakage injury being present. Recent voltage clamp
data (Llinas et al 1985) indicate that the presynaptic terminals of the squid can
be penetrated and sometimes pressure injected with little or no leakage injury.

MEASUREMENT OF NEURAL EXCITABILITY   Three different means or levels
have been found by which neural excitability can be assessed in vivo in relation
to different behavioral states. The first is by injection of microamp current
pulses, extracellularly, through metal electrodes (Asanuma et al 1968, Stoney
et al 1968, Woody et al 1970, Asanuma & Rosen 1973). The second is by
injection of nanoamp current pulses, intracellularly, through micropipettes

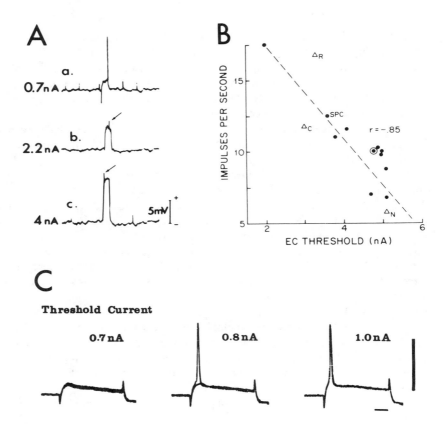

Figure 7 A. Illustration of extracellular "threshold" current required to produce unit discharge within a 10 msec current pulse. Current level was increased between a and c from 0.7nA to 2.2nA threshold and then to 4nA. Trailing edge stimulus artifact has been removed from b and c so that the spike may be easily seen. The voltage calibration is shown to the right of "c". Note that the latency of spike discharge (arrows) is shorter with higher current level than at threshold. Data are from Woody et al 1976. B. A plot of mean baseline rate of spontaneous unit discharge versus mean thresholds to extracellular (EC) nA stimulation obtained from cells of the motor cortex in naive cats (no CS or US given), and in cats given CS only, CS-US, and US-CS presentations. (These values are shown as unlabeled dots. Circled dot indicates overlap of two means.) Triangles refer to data drawn from other studies employing extracellular nA stimulation and obtained from the posterior association cortex in cats that received CS trials only (N), conditioning pairs of CS and US trials (C), or pseudorandomly presented CS and US trials (R). SPC refers to a data point obtained from cats presented with 10 consecutive pairs of CS (click) and DS (hiss) trials in a sensory preconditioning type of paradigm. The data support an inverse linear relationship ($r = -.85$) between spontaneous firing rate and threshold (from Brons, Woody, & Allon 1982). C. The method is shown for determining the threshold current for spike elicitation by a 10 ms, intracellularly applied depolarizing current pulse. The voltage calibration is 40 mV. The time calibration is 2 ms.

(Woody & Black-Cleworth 1973 and Figure 7C). The third is by injection of 10 msec current pulses of from 0.2 to 100 nA magnitude, extracellularly, through fluid-filled, $\leq$ 1 μm tipped, glass microelectrodes (Woody et al 1976 and Figure 7A). Using K^+-sensitive compound electrodes (cf Wong & Woody 1978) to insure that micropipette tips were correctly positioned in the proper tissue compartments, extracellular loci of stimulation have been confirmed for currents as low as 2nA. With less bulky, single electrodes, some thresholds as low as 0.2nA were found (Woody et al 1976).

The first two methods appear to measure much the same index of neural excitability (reflecting postsynaptic excitability changes such as those that support learned motor performance) while the third method appears to measure a different index or locus of excitability.

Tasaki (1959) showed long ago that extracellularly applied currents cross vertebrate neuronal membranes. This has been supported by results in central mammalian neurons (Raabe & Lux 1973) and also by indirect evidence from some other investigations (Rusinov 1953, Morrell 1961, Gustafsson & Jankowska 1976). Extracellular delivery of 4 *micro*amp currents through metal electrodes (Asanuma & Rosen 1973) has been found to produce intracellularly recordable PSPs, monosynaptically or even polysynaptically, depending on the cortical layer at which microstimulation was performed. Evidence from these and other studies indicates that extracellularly applied *micro*amp currents excite by crossing the membrane, either of the postsynaptic cell via its recurrent collaterals or of the terminals of the presynaptic neurons. However, the observation that more cortical cells are excited by positive than by negative extracellularly applied *nano*amp current suggests that such current may not cross the membrane in sufficient amount to excite by depolarizing to critical firing threshold. In fact, many cells can be excited by weak extracellularly applied current of either polarity (cf Tables 2 and 3; also cf Woody et al 1976, Woody 1977, Woody & Gruen 1977). Interestingly, in in vivo mammalian experiments, it is only the excitability changes detected by extracellular nA stimulation that have been shown to be induced associatively.

Changes in unit excitability measured by the above means are reproducible and are well correlated with changes in the probability of spike discharge elicited by CSs before and after conditioning and with various other behavioral states (cf Woody & Black-Cleworth 1973, Woody et al 1976, Woody 1977, Buchhalter et al 1978, Brons 1979, Brons & Woody 1980, Brons et al 1982). In addition, it has been possible to demonstrate a consistent relationship between thresholds of extracellularly applied, nA stimulation, and the rate of spontaneous discharge of studied units (see Figure 7B).

MEASUREMENT OF INPUT RESISTANCE   Purves (1981) has recently reviewed the various approaches used to measure input resistance in single, in-

Table 2 Percentage of extracellular units in conditioned animals[a]

Polarity[b]	Click(%)	Hiss(%)	Both(%)	$\overline{0}$(%)
+	50(1.6)	42(2.3)	39(2.8)	41(2.2)
−	5	0	5	0
=	45(3.0)	58(4.9)	56(4.7)	59(5.2)

[a]Source: Woody et al 1976.

[b]+, responding preferentially to positive-going electrical current pulse; −, responding preferentially to negative-going pulse; and =, without polarity preference. Units divided into click-responsive (click), hiss-responsive (hiss), click- and hiss-responsive (both), and unresponsive (0) units. Mean threshold response currents, in nA, are shown in parentheses for + and = data.

Table 3 Percentage of 0.2-nA electrical stimuli eliciting a discharge[a]

Latency[b]	During Stimulus Pulse	Immediately after Stimulus Pulse	20 ms after Stimulus Pulse
+V	50	32	10
+C	20	2	2
−V	20	26	12
−C	12	6	0

[a]Source: Woody et al 1976.

[b]V, percentage of stimulus deliveries (0.2 nA) eliciting discharges of any variable latency within the 10 ms; C, percentage of stimulus deliveries (0.2 nA) eliciting discharges varing no more than 1 ms in latency during the 10-ms period; +, positive-going current; −, negative-going current. Data are from 1 extracellular unit.

tracellularly penetrated cells. In general, use of electrodes with time constants capable of separating the cell's input resistance from the resistance of the penetrating electrode is advisable, and continuous rebalancing of voltage displacements produced by injecting constant current pulses into the cells may also be worthwhile (Woody et al 1984). In awake animals useful measurements of resistance change may be obtained by balancing prior to cell penetration and using averaging techniques to reduce noise reflected by nonsystematic fluctuations of electrode resistance after penetration (Woody et al 1978). One goal of such studies is to determine if changes in input resistance comparable to those found in invertebrate preparations occur in vertebrates after conditioning.

One must be cautious lest applications of sizable currents, particularly in the depolarizing direction, produce undesired changes in the input resistances of some cells. Besides effects of voltage-dependent rectification, described earlier, long-lasting changes in membrane properties reflected by alterations in excitability may occur following prolonged applications of polarizing currents (Rusinov 1953, Morrell 1961, Bindman et al 1979).

IN VITRO VERSUS IN VIVO TECHNIQUES   The use of in vitro tissue slice recording techniques by Li & McIlwain (1957), Andersen et al (1977), and others has led to widespread adoption of this in method for investigating central nervous tissue (Dingledine 1984). Virtually all of the techniques involve making a slice of tissue sufficiently thin (200–500 μm) to permit oxygenation via the medium in which the slice is immersed. Slicing can result in significant deafferentation of inputs to the cells studied in addition to possible anoxic damage (cf Kass & Lipton 1982) and unavoidable injury to the surround, with release of potassium and other chemicals consequential to tissue destruction.

Virtually all slice techniques require a period of oxygenation of approximately one hour at temperatures well below those occurring in situ before recordings approaching those found in vivo can be obtained from the preparation. Many attribute this to recovery from diaschesis, a spinal shock or concussive-like phenomena. The possibility that spreading depression has occurred in the interim also has not been ruled out. Following rest and, one hopes, recovery, the preparation's advantages lie in the ability to record activity resembling that found in vivo with great stability (for hours) and the ability to change the surrounding fluid medium easily and rapidly. The latter permits the addition of chemicals, the cellular response to which can then be tested. (Tissue culture approaches that avoid the slicing procedure by no means guarantee the provision of normal cells.)

Recent findings (Stafstrom et al 1984) suggest that resting potentials considerably hyperpolarized to those found in awake (in vivo) preparations may occur in vitro. Since the ionic conductances mentioned earlier are voltage dependent, it could be inadvisable to relate results of in vitro studies to less hyperpolarized states without introducing sufficient steady depolarizing current to alter the overall level of transmembrane potential. In cells with extensive processes (the majority perhaps of those encountered in the central nervous system), it may not be possible to introduce sufficient current to accomplish this due to limitations in the cell's cable properties.

MEASUREMENT OF IONIC CURRENTS   It is useful to measure ionic currents with voltage clamp techniques (Hodgkin & Huxley 1952, Cole 1968). An example of the application of this approach to studies of ionic conductances supporting conditioned behavior may be found in the work of Alkon (1979) and colleagues (Farley & Alkon 1985). Quantitative measurements of ionic currents as a function of voltage depend on maintenance of an applied voltage level throughout the cable space of the studied cell (Cole 1968). In squid axon this may be accomplished by inserting a tubular electrode along the entire axon length. This is not possible in cells or processes of more complex geometry in which sometimes a clamp of but 1–10% of a space constant can be achieved. In the latter instance useful results may still be obtained, provided that these limitations are recognized when interpretations are made.

Recent technical advances (Sakmann & Neher 1983) have permitted the use of patch clamp techniques to measure membrane currents generated by single ion channels. Those studies, too, have their limitations—often, the need to clean the cell membrane (e.g. with a digestive enzyme) to secure a high resistance, electrode-to-cell coupling and sometimes the avulsion of the membrane itself, with or without subsequent resealing (Hamill et al 1981). Nonetheless, the current measurement approaches are providing increasingly detailed knowledge concerning channel kinetics (Corey & Hudspeth 1979, Lux et al 1981) and their sensitivities to pharmacologic agents (Quandt & Narahashi 1982), and both patch and voltage clamp approaches are receiving widespread application (see Hille 1984 for recent general review), including recent in vitro (Alkon 1979, Siegelbaum et al 1982, Brown & Johnston 1983, Johnston & Brown 1983, Barrionuevo & Brown 1983) and in vivo (Woody et al 1985) applications to preparations used to investigate learning.

ACKNOWLEDGMENTS

I thank T. Bartfai, W. Holmes, R. Pay, and J. Strecker for invaluable assistance in preparing portions of this manuscript, and I also thank them and S. Aou, D. Birt, and J. Garcia for constructive review of the manuscript. Preparation of this review was supported in part by AFOSR and NINCHDS as were some of the research studies of Woody and colleagues.

Literature Cited

Acosta-Urquidi, J., Alkon, D. L., Neary, J. T. 1984. Intrasomatic injection of a Ca^{2+} calmodulin dependent protein kinase simulates biophysical effects of associative learning in a *Hermissenda* photoreceptor. *Science* 224:1254–57

Acosta-Urquidi, J., Neary, J. T., Alkon, D. L. 1982. Ca^{2+}-dependent protein kinase regulation of K^+ (V)-currents: A possible biochemical step in associative learning of *Hermissenda*. *Soc. Neurosci. Abstr.* 8:825

Adams, D. J., Smith, S. J., Thompson, S. H. 1980. Ionic currents in molluscan soma. *Ann. Rev. Neurosci.* 3:141–67

Adams, J. C. 1977. Technical considerations on the use of horseradish peroxidase as a neuronal marker. *Neuroscience* 2:141–45

Adams, P. R., Brown, D. A. 1975. Actions of gamma-aminobutyric acid on sympathetic ganglion cells. *J. Physiol.* 250:85–120

Adams, P. R., Brown, D. A., Constanti, A. 1982a. M-currents and other potassium currents in bullfrog sympathetic neurons. *J. Physiol.* 330:537–72

Adams, P. R., Brown, D. A., Constanti, A. 1982b. Pharmacological inhibition of the M-current. *J. Physiol.* 332:223–62

Adams, W. B., Levitan, I. B. 1982. Intracellular injection of protein kinase inhibitor blocks the serotonin induced increase in K^+ conductance in *Aplysia* neuron R15. *Proc. Natl. Acad. Sci. USA* 79:3877–80

Adams, W. B., Parnas, I., Levitan, I. B. 1980. Mechanism of long-lasting synaptic inhibition in *Aplysia* neuron R15. *J. Neurophysiol.* 44:1148–60

Aitken, L. M., Anderson, D. J., Brugge, J. F. 1970. Tonotopic organization and discharge characteristics of single neurons in nuclei of the lateral lemniscus of the cat. *J. Neurophysiol.* 33:421–40

Alkon, D. L. 1976. Neural modification by paired sensory stimuli. *J. Gen. Physiol.* 68:341–58

Alkon, D. L. 1979. Voltage-dependent calcium and potassium ion conductances: A contingency mechanism for an associative learning model. *Science* 205:810–16

Alkon, D. L. 1980a. Cellular analysis of a gastropod (*Hermissenda crassicornis*) model of associative learning. *Biol. Bull.* 159:505–60

Alkon, D. L. 1980b. Membrane depolarization accumulates during acquisition of an associative behavioral change. *Science* 210:1375–76

Alkon, D. L. 1982. A biophysical basis for molluscan associative learning. See Woody 1982b, pp. 147–70

Alkon, D. L. 1983. Intersensory convergence: A prerequisite for primary changes of molluscan associative learning. *Fortschr. Zool.* 28:355–68

Alkon, D. L. 1984. Calcium-mediated reduction of ionic currents: A biophysical memory trace. *Science* 226:1037–45

Alkon, D. L. 1985. Changes of membrane currents and calcium-calmodulin-dependent phosphorylation of specific proteins during associative learning. See Alkon & Woody 1985, pp. 3–17

Alkon, D. L., Acosta-Urquidi, J., Olds, J., Kuzma, G., Neary, J. T. 1983. Protein kinase injection reduces voltage-dependent potassium currents. *Science* 219:303–6

Alkon, D. L., Fuortes, M. G. F. 1972. Responses of photoreceptors in *Hermissenda*. *J. Gen. Physiol.* 60:631–49

Alkon, D. L., Lederhendler, I., Shoukimas, J. J. 1982a. Primary changes of membrane currents during retention of associative learning. *Science* 215:693–95

Alkon, D. L., Shoukimas, J. J., Heldman, B. 1982b. Calcium-mediated decrease of a voltage-dependent potassium current. *Biophys. J.* 40:245–50

Alkon, D. L., Woody, C. D., eds. 1985. *Neural Mechanisms of Conditioning*. New York: Plenum

Andersen, P., Sundberg, S. H., Sveen, O., Wigstrom, H. 1977. Specific long-lasting potentiation of synaptic transmission in hippocampal slices. *Nature* 266:736–37

Andersen, P., Sundberg, S. H., Sveen, O., Swann, J. W., Wigstrom, H. 1980. Possible mechanisms for long-lasting potentiation of synaptic transmission in hippocampal slices from guinea pigs. *J. Physiol.* 302:463–82

Anholt, R., Lindstrom, J., Montal, M. 1984. The molecular basis of neurotransmission: Structure and function of the nicotinic acetylcholine receptor. In *Enzymes of Biological Membranes*, ed. A. Martonosi, 3:335–401. New York: Plenum

Armstrong, C. M. 1981. Sodium channels and gating currents. *Physiol. Rev.* 61:644–83

Asanuma, H., Rosen, I. 1973. Spread of mono- and polysynaptic connections within cat motor cortex. *Exp. Brain Res.* 16:507–20

Asanuma, H., Stoney, S. D. Jr., Abzug, C. 1968. Relationship between afferent input

and motor outflow in cat motorsensory cortex. *J. Neurophysiol.* 31:670–81

Bailey, C. H., Chen, M. 1983. Morphological basis of long-term habituation and sensitization in *Aplysia*. *Science* 220:91–93

Baker, P. F. 1972. Transport and metabolism of calcium ions in nerve. *Prog. Biophys. Mol. Biol.* 24:177–223

Baker, P. F., Hodgkin, A. L., Ridgway, E. B. 1971. Depolarization and calcium entry in squid giant axons. *J. Physiol.* 218:709–55

Bard, P., Macht, M. B. 1958. The behavior of chronically decerebrate cats. In *Ciba Foundation Symposium on the Neurological Basis of Behavior*, ed. G. E. W. Wolstenholme, C. M. O'Connor, pp. 55–75. Boston: Little, Brown

Barrett, J. N., Crill, W. E. 1972. Voltage clamp analysis of conductances underlying cat motoneuron action potentials. *Fed. Proc.* 31:305

Barrett, J. N., Magleby, K. L., Pallotta, B. S. 1982. Properties of single calcium-activated potassium channels in cultured rat muscle. *J. Physiol.* 331:211–30

Barrionuevo, G., Brown, T. H. 1983. Associative long-term potentiation in hippocampal slices. *Proc. Natl. Acad. Sci. USA* 80:7347–51

Bartfai, T. 1980. Cyclic nucleotides in the central nervous system. *Curr. Top. Cell. Regul.* 16:226–63

Bartfai, T., Woody, C. D., Gruen, E., Nairn, A., Greengard, P. 1985. Intracellular injection of cGMP-dependent protein kinase results in increased input resistance in neurons of the mammalian motor cortex. *Soc. Neurosci. Abstr.* 11:1093

Beach, F. A., Hebb, D. O., Morgan, C. T., Nissen, H. W. 1960. *The Neuropsychology of Lashley*. New York: McGraw-Hill. 564 pp.

Benardo, L. S., Prince, D. A. 1982. Long term modulation of intrinsic membrane properties of hippocampal neurons. See Woody 1982b, pp. 13–35

Bennett, M. V. L., Goodenough, D. A. 1978. Gap junctions, electotonic coupling, and intercellular communication. *Neurosci. Res. Program Bull.* 162:373

Benson, J. A., Levitan, I. B. 1983. Serotonin increases an anomalously rectifying K$^+$ current in the *Aplysia* neuron R15. *Proc. Natl. Acad. Sci. USA* 80:3522–25

Berger, T. W., Orr, W. B. 1982. Role of the hippocampus in reversal learning of the rabbit nictitating membrane response. See Woody 1982b, pp. 1–12

Berridge, M. J. 1984. Inositol triphosphate and diacylglycerol as second messengers. *Biochem. J.* 220:345–60

Berthier, N. E., Woody, C. D. 1984. An essay on latent learning. In *The Neurophysiology of Learning,* ed. N. Butters, L. Squire, pp. 504–12. New York: Guilford

Beswick, F. B., Conroy, R. T. W. L. 1965. Optimal tetanic conditioning of heteronymous monosynaptic reflexes. *J. Physiol.* 180:134–46

Bindman, L. J., Lippold, C. J., Milne, A. R. 1979. Prolonged changes in excitability of pyramidal tract neurones in the cat: A postsynaptic mechanism. *J. Physiol.* 286:457–77

Bindman, L. J., Lippold, C. J., Milne, A. R. 1982. A postsynaptic mechanism underlying long-lasting changes in the excitability of pyramidal tract neurones in the anaesthetized cat. See Woody 1982b, pp. 171–78

Birt, D., Nienhuis, R., Olds, M. 1979. Separation of associative from non-associative short latency changes in medial geniculate and inferior colliculus during differential conditioning and reversal in rats. *Brain Res.* 167:129–38

Birt, D., Olds, M. 1981. Associative response changes in lateral midbrain tegmentum and medial geniculate during differential appetitive conditioning. *J. Neurophysiol.* 46:1039–55

Birt, D., Olds, M. 1982. Auditory response enhancement during differential conditioning in behaving rats. See Woody 1982b, pp. 483–501

Bliss, T. V. P., Gardner-Medwin, A. R. 1973. Long-lasting potentiation of synaptic transmission in the dentate area of the unanesthetized rabbit following stimulation of the perforant path. *J. Physiol.* 232:357–74

Bliss, T. V. P., Lomo, T. 1973. Long-lasting potentiation of synaptic transmission in the dentate area of the anaesthetized rabbit following stimulation of the perforant pathway. *J. Physiol.* 232:331–56

Boulpaep, E. L., Sackin, H. 1979. Equivalent electrical circuit analysis and rheogenic pumps in epithelia. *Fed. Proc.* 38:2030–36

Briggs, C. A., McAfee, D. A. 1982. Proving a role for cyclic AMP in synaptic transmission. *Trends Pharmacol. Sci.* 3:241–44

Brodal, A. 1969. *Neurological Anatomy: In Relation to Clinical Medicine.* New York: Oxford Univ. Press. 2nd ed.

Brogden, W. J. 1939. The effect of frequency of reinforcement upon the level of conditioning. *J. Exp. Psychol.* 24:419–31

Bromiley, R. B. 1947. Conditioned responses in a dog after removal of neocortex. *J. Comp. Physiol. Psychol.* 41:102–10

Brons, J. F. 1979. *Differences in excitability and activity in cortical neurons after Pavlovian conditioning, extinction, and prevention of US alone.* PhD thesis. Univ. Calif., Los Angeles

Brons, J. F., Woody, C. D. 1980. Long-term changes in excitability of cortical neurons after Pavlovian conditioning and extinction. *J. Neurophysiol.* 44:605–15

Brons, J. F., Woody, C. D., Allon, N. 1982. Changes in the excitability to weak intensity extracellular electrical stimulation of units of the pericruciate cortex in cats. *J. Neurophysiol.* 47:377–88

Brooks, V. B. 1979. Control of the intended limb movements by the lateral and intermediate cerebellum. In *Integration in the Nervous System,* ed. H. Asanuma, V. J. Wilson, pp. 321–56. New York: Igaku-Shoin

Brooks, V. B., Kozlovskaya, I. B., Atkin, A., Horvath, F. E., Uno, M. 1973. Effects of cooling the dentate nucleus on tracking-task performance in monkeys. *J. Neurophysiol.* 36:974–95

Brown, A. M., Camerer, H., Kunze, D. L., Lux, H. D. 1982. Similarity of unitary Ca^{2+} currents in three different species. *Nature* 299:156–58

Brown, D. A., Constanti, A., Adams, P. R. 1981. Slow cholinergic and peptidergic transmission in sympathetic ganglia. *Fed. Proc.* 40:2625–30

Brown, T. H., Fricke, R. A., Perkel, D. H. 1981. Passive electrical constants in three classes of hippocampal neurons. *J. Neurophysiol.* 46:812–27

Brown, T. H., Johnston, D. 1983. Voltage-clamp analysis of mossy fiber synaptic input to hippocampal neurons. *J. Neurophysiol.* 50:487–507

Brown, T. H., McAfee, D. A. 1982. Long-term synaptic potentiation in the superior cervical ganglion. *Science* 215:1411–13

Buchhalter, J., Brons, J., Woody, C. D. 1978. Changes in cortical excitability after presentations of a compound auditory stimulus. *Brain Res.* 156:162–67

Bullock, T. H., Horridge, G. A. 1965. *Structure and Function in the Nervous Systems of Invertebrates,* Vol. 1. San Francisco: Freeman

Bures, J., Buresova, O. 1960. The use of Leao's spreading depression in the study of interhemispheric transfer of memory traces. *J. Comp. Physiol. Psychol.* 53:558–63

Bures, J., Buresova, O. 1979. Neurophysiological analysis of conditioned taste aversion. In *Brain Mechanisms in Memory and Learning,* ed. M. A. B. Brazier, pp. 127–38. New York: Raven

Buresova, O., Bures, J. 1979. The anterograde effect of ECS on the acquisition retrieval and extinction of conditioned taste aversion. *Physiol. Behav.* 22:641–45

Byrne, J. H., Ocorr, K. A., Walsh, J. P., Walters, E. T. 1985. Analysis of associative and nonassociative neuronal modifications in *Aplysia* sensory neurons. See Alkon & Woody 1985, pp. 55–73

Camardo, J. S., Siegelbaum, A. S., Kandel, E.

R. 1984. In *Primary Neural Substrates of Learning and Behavior*, ed. D. L. Alkon, J. Farley, pp. 185–203. New York: Cambridge Univ. Press

Carew, T. J., Abrams, T. W., Hawkins, R. D., Kandel, E. R. 1984. See Camardo et al 1984, pp. 169–83

Carew, T. J., Hawkins, R. D., Kandel, E. R. 1983. Differential classical conditioning of a defensive withdrawal reflex in *Aplysia californica*. *Science* 219:397–400

Castellucci, V. F., Kandel, E. R., Schwartz, J. H., Wilson, F. D., Nairn, A. C., Greengard, P. 1980. Intracellular injection of the catalytic subunit of cyclic AMP-dependent protein kinase simulates facilitation of transmitter release underlying behavioral sensitization in *Aplysia*. *Proc. Natl. Acad. Sci. USA* 77:7492–96

Castellucci, V. F., Nairn, A. L., Greengard, P., Schwartz, J. H., Kandel, E. R. 1982. Inhibitor of adenosine 3', 5' monophosphate dependent protein kinase blocks presynaptic facilitation in *Aplysia*. *J. Neurosci.* 2:1673–81

Catterall, W. A. 1980. Neurotoxins that act on voltage-sensitive sodium channels in excitable membranes. *Ann. Rev. Pharmacol. Toxicol.* 20:15–43

Catterall, W. A. 1984. The molecular basis of neuronal excitability. *Science* 223:653–61

Cedar, H., Kandel, E. R., Schwartz, J. H. 1972. Cyclic adenosine monophosphate in the nervous system of *Aplysia californica*. I. Increased synthesis in response to synaptic stimulation. *J. Gen. Physiol.* 60:558–69

Cedar, H., Schwartz, J. H. 1972. Cyclic adenosine monophosphate in the nervous system of *Aplysia californica*. II. Effect of serotonin and dopamine. *J. Gen. Physiol.* 60:570–87

Cheung, W. Y. 1982. Calmodulin: An overview. *Fed. Proc.* 41:2253–57

Christensen, B. N., Ebner, F. F. 1978. The synaptic architecture of neurons in opossum somatic sensory-motor cortex: A combined anatomical and physiological study. *J. Neurocytol.* 7:39–60

Cohen, D. H. 1974. Neural pathways mediating a conditioned autonomic response. In *Limbic and Autonomic Nervous Systems Research*, ed. L. DiCara, pp. 223–75. New York: Plenum

Cohen, D. H. 1984. Identification of vertebrate neurons modified during learning: Analysis of sensory pathways. See Camardo et al 1984, pp. 129–54

Cohen, D. H., Durkovic, R. G. 1966. Cardiac and respiratory conditioning, differentiation, and extinction in the pigeon. *J. Exp. Anal. Behav.* 9:681–88

Cole, A. E., Nicoll, R. A. 1983. Acetylcholine mediates a slow synaptic potential in hippocampal pyramidal cells. *Science* 221:1299–1301

Cole, K. S. 1968. *Membranes, Ions, and Impulses.* Berkeley: Univ. Calif. Press

Cole, K. S., Curtis, H. J. 1940. Membrane action potentials from the squid giant axon. *J. Cell. Comp. Physiol.* 15:147–57

Connor, J. A., Alkon, D. L. 1984. Light- and voltage-dependent increases of calcium ion concentration in molluscan photoreceptors. *J. Neurophysiol.* 51:745–52

Connor, J. A., Stevens, C. F. 1971. Voltage-clamp studies of a transient outward membrane current in gastropod neural somata. *J. Physiol.* 213:21–30

Conti-Tronconi, B. M., Raftery, M. A. 1982. The nicotinic cholinergic receptor: Correlation of molecular structure with functional properties. *Ann. Rev. Biochem.* 51:491–530

Corey, D. P., Hudspeth, A. J. 1979. Ionic basis of the receptor potential in a vertebrate hair cell. *Nature* 281:675–77

Cragg, B. G. 1967. Changes in visual cortex on first exposure of rats to light. *Nature* 215:251–53

Cragg, B. 1980. Preservation of extracellular space during fixation of the brain for electron microscopy. *Tissue Cell* 12:63–72

Crow, T. J., Alkon, D. L. 1978. Retention of an associative behavioral change in *Hermissenda*. *Science* 201:1239–41

Crow, T. J., Alkon, D. L. 1980. Associative behavioral modification in *Hermissenda*: Cellular correlates. *Science* 209:412–14

Culler, E., Mettler, F. A. 1934. Conditioned behavior in a decorticate dog. *J. Comp. Psychol.* 18:291–303

Curtis, D. R. 1964. Microelectrophoresis. In *Physiological Techniques in Biological Research*, ed. W. L. Nastuk, 5A:144. New York: Academic

Davis, M., Gendelman, D. S., Tischler, M. D., Gendelman, P. M. 1982a. A primary acoustic startle circuit: lesion and stimulation studies. *J. Neurosci.* 2:791–805

Davis, M., Parisi, T., Gendelman, D. S., Tischler, M., Kehne, J. H. 1982b. Habituation and sensitization of startle reflexes elicited electrically from the brainstem. *Science* 218:688–90

DeLorenzo, R. J. 1980. Postsynaptic densities: Calmodulin and calcium-dependent phosphorylation. *Trans Am. Soc. Neurochem.* 11:81

Denny-Brown, D. 1951. Frontal lobes and their functions. In *Modern Trends in Neurology*, ed. A. Feiling, pp. 13–89. New York: Harper

Desmond, J. E., Moore, J. W. 1982. A brain stem region essential for classically conditioned but not unconditioned nictitating membrane response. *Physiol. Behav.* 28:1029–33

Desmond, J. E., Moore, J. W. 1983. A supra-trigeminal region implicated in the classically conditioned nictating membrane response. *Brain Res. Bull.* 10:765–73

Deterre, P., Paupardin-Tritsch, D., Bockaert, J., Gerschenfeld, H. M. 1982. cAMP-mediated decrease in K^+ conductance evoked by serotonin and dopamine in the same neuron: A biochemical and physiological single-cell study. *Proc. Natl. Acad. Sci. USA* 79:7934–38

Diamond, I. T., Neff, W. D. 1957. Ablation of temporal cortex and discrimination of auditory patterns. *J. Neurophysiol.* 20:300–15

Diamond, J., Gray, E. G., Yasargil, G. M. 1970. The function of the dendritic spine: An hypothesis. In *Excitatory Synaptic Mechanisms. Proc. 5th Int. Meet. Neurobiol., 1969*, pp. 213–22. Oslo: Scandanavia Univ. Books

Dingledine, R., ed. 1984. *Brain Slices.* New York/London: Plenum. 442 pp.

Disterhoft, J. F., Shipley, M. T., Kraus, N. 1982. Analyzing the rabbit NM conditioned reflex arc. See Woody 1982c, pp. 433–49

Dostalek, C., Krasa, H. 1972. Backward conditioning: One session vs. ten-session experiment. *Activ. Nerv. Super.* 14:58–59

Doty, W. R. 1974. Interhemispheric transfer and manipulation of engrams. In *Cellular Mechanisms Subserving Changes in Neuronal Activity*, ed. C. D. Woody, K. A. Brown, T. Crow, F. D. Knispel, pp. 153–59. Brain Inform. Serv. Univ. Calif., Los Angeles

Drummond, A. H., Benson, J. A., Levitan, I. B. 1980. Serotonin-induced hyperpolarization of an identified *Aplysia* neuron is mediated by cyclic AMP. *Proc. Natl. Acad. Sci. USA* 77:5013–17

Drummond, G. I. 1983. Cyclic nucleotides in the nervous system. *Adv. Cyclic Nucleotide Res.* 15:373–494

Durkovic, R. G. 1983. Classical conditioning of the flexion reflex in spinal cat: Features of the reflex circuitry. *Neurosci. Lett.* 39:155–60

Eccles, J. C. 1964. *The Physiology of Synapses.* New York: Springer–Verlag

Eccles, J. C. 1977. Stages in reconstitution of the visual image. In *The Self and Its Brain: An Argument for Interactionism*, ed. K. R. Popper, J. C. Eccles, pp. 264–69. New York: Springer Int.

Eckert, R., Chad, J. E. 1984. Inactivation of Ca channels. *Prog. Biophys. Mol. Biol.* 44:215–67

Eckert, R., Chad, J. E. 1985. Calcium-dependent regulation of Ca channel inactivation. See Alkon & Woody 1985, pp. 261–82

Eckert, R., Lux, H. D. 1976. A voltage-sensitive persistent calcium conductance in neuronal somata of Helix. *J. Physiol.* 254:129–51

Edwards, S. B. 1975. Autoradiographic studies of the projections of the midbrain reticular formation: Descending projections of nucleus cuneiformis. *J. Comp. Neurol.* 161:341–58

Edwards, S. B., DeOlmos, J. S. 1976. Autoradiographic studies of the projection of the midbrain reticular formation: Ascending projections of nucleus cuneiformis. *J. Comp. Neurol.* 165:417–32

Engberg, I., Marshall, K. C. 1971. Mechanism of noradrenaline hyperpolarization in spinal cord motoneurones of the cat. *Acta Physiol. Scand.* 83:142–44

Engel, J. Jr., Woody, C. D. 1972. Effects of character and significance of stimulus on unit activity at coronal–pericruciate cortex of cat during performance of conditioned motor response. *J. Neurophysiol.* 35:220–29

Evarts, E. V. 1966. Pyramidal tract activity associated with a conditioned hand movement in the monkey. *J. Neurophysiol.* 29:1011–27

Farel, P. B. 1974. Habituation and persistent PTP of a monosynaptic response. See Doty 1974, pp. 45–56

Farley, J. 1985. Cellular mechanisms of causal detection in a mollusc. See Alkon & Woody 1985, pp. 19–54

Farley, J., Alkon, D. L. 1985. Cellular mechanisms of learning, memory, and information storage. *Ann. Rev. Psychol.* 36:419–94

Farley, J., Richards, W. G., Ling, L. J., Liman, E., Alkon, D. L. 1983. Membrane changes in a single photoreceptor cause associative learning in *Hermissenda*. *Science* 221:1201–3

Fatt, P., Ginsborg, B. L. 1958. The ionic requirements for the production of action potentials in crustacean muscle fibres. *J. Physiol.* 142:516–43

Fetz, E. E., Finocchio, D. V. 1975. Correlation between activity of motor cortex cells and arm muscle during operantly conditioned response patterns. *Exp. Brain Res.* 23:217–40

Fields, R. D., Ellisman, M. H. 1985. Synaptic morphology and differences in sensitivity. *Science* 228:197–99

Fifkova, E., Anderson, C. L., Young, S. J., Van Harreveld, A. 1982. Effect of anisomycin on stimulation-induced changes in dendritic spines of the dentate granule cells. *J. Neurocytol.* 11:183–210

Fifkova, E., Van Harreveld, A. 1977. Long-lasting morphological changes in dendritic spines of dentate granular cells following stimulation of the entorhinal area. *J. Neurocytol.* 6:211–30

Fleshman, J. W., Segev, I., Cullheim, S., Burke, R. E. 1983. Matching electrophysiological with morphological measurements in cat alpha-motoneurones. *Soc. Neurosci. Abstr.* 9:341

Foerster, O. 1936. Motorische Felder und Bahnen. In *Handbuch der Neurologie,* ed. O. Bumke, O. Foerster, 6:1–357. Berlin: Springer–Verlag

Frank, K., Fuortes, M. G. F. 1956. Stimulation of spinal motoneurons with intracellular electrodes. *J. Physiol.* 134:451–70

Franz, S. I., Lashley, K. S. 1917. The retention of habits by the rat after destruction of frontal portions of the cerebrum. *Psychobiology* 1:3–18

Gabriel, M., Miller, J. D., Saltwick, S. E. 1976. Multiple unit activity of the rabbit medial geniculate nucleus in conditioning, extinction, and reversal. *Physiol. Psychol.* 4:124–34

Gabriel, M., Orona, E., Foster, K., Lambert, R. W. 1982. Mechanism and generality of stimulus significance coding in a mammalian model system. See Woody 1982c, pp. 535–65

Galambos, R., Sheatz, G. C. 1962. An electroencephalograph study of classical conditioning. *Am. J. Physiol.* 203:173–84

Gamper, E. 1926. Bau und Leistungen eines menschlichen Mittelhirnwesens (Arhinencephalie mit Encephalocele), zugleich ein Beitrag zur Teratologie und Fasersystematik. *Z. Gesamte Neurol. Psychiatr.* 104: 49–120

Garcia, J., Hankins, W. G., Rusiniak, K. W. 1974. Behavioral regulation of the milieu interne in man and rat. *Science* 185:824–31

Gastault, H. 1958. The role of the reticular formation in establishing conditioned reactions. In *The Reticular Formation of the Brain,* ed. H. H. Jasper, L. D. Proctor, R. S. Knighton, W. D. Noshay, R. T. Costello, pp. 561–89. Boston: Little, Brown

Girden, E., Mettler, F. A., Finch, G., Culler, E. 1936. Conditioned responses in a decorticate dog to acoustic, thermal, and tactile stimulation. *J. Comp. Psychol.* 21:367–85

Glendenning, K. K., Brunso-Bechtold, J. K., Thompson, G. C., Masterton, R. B. 1981. Ascending auditory afferents to the nuclei of the lateral lemniscus. *J. Comp. Neurol.* 197:673–703

Godfraind, J. M., Krnjevic, K., Pumain, R. 1970. Unexpected features of the action of dinitrophenol on cortical neurones. *Nature* 228:562–64

Goldman-Rakic, P. S. 1984. 1984 Donald B. Lindsley Prize in Behavioral Neuroscience. *Soc. Neurosci. Newsl.* 15:1–2

Gormezano, I. 1974. The interstimulus interval and mechanisms for CS-CR functions in classical conditioning. See Doty 1974, pp. 97–110

Gormezano, I., Tait, R. W. 1976. The Pavlovian analysis of instrumental conditioning. *Pavlovian J. Biol. Sci.* 11:37–55

Grab, D. J., Carlin, R. K., Siekevitz, P. 1981. Function of calmodulin in postsynaptic densities II. Presence of a calmodulin-activatable protein kinase activity. *J. Cell Biol.* 89:440–48

Graham-Brown, T., Sherrington, C. S. 1912. On the instability of a cortical point. *Proc. R. Soc. London Ser. B* 85:250–77

Grant, D. A., Norris, E. B. 1947. Eyelid conditioning as influenced by the presence of sensitized beta-responses. *J. Exp. Psychol.* 37:423–33

Graybiel, A. M. 1972. Some fiber pathways related to the posterior thalamic region in the cat. *Brain Behav. Evol.* 6:363–93

Graybiel, A. M. 1973. The thalamo-cortical projection of the so-called posterior nuclear group: A study with anterograde degeneration methods in the cat. *Brain Res.* 49:229–44

Greengard, P. 1978. *Cyclic Nucleotides, Phosphorylated Proteins, and Neuronal Function.* New York: Raven

Greengard, P. 1979. Cyclic nucleotides, phosphorylated proteins, and the nervous system. *Fed. Proc.* 38:2208–17

Greengard, P. 1982. Intracellular signals in the brain. *Harvey Lect.* 75:277–331

Greengard, P., Kebabian, J. W. 1974. Role of cyclic AMP in synaptic transmission in the mammalian peripheral nervous system. *Fed. Proc.* 33:1059–67

Grover, L., Farley, J. 1983. Temporal order sensitivity of associative learning in *Hermissenda. Soc. Neurosci. Abstr.* 9:915

Grundfest, H., Campbell, B. 1942. Origin, conduction, and termination of impulses in the dorsal spino-cerebellar tract of cats. *J. Neurophysiol.* 5:275–94

Gustafsson, B., Galvan, M., Grafe, P., Wigstrom, H. 1982. A transient outward current in a mammalian central neurone blocked by 4-amino pyridine. *Nature* 299:252–54

Gustafsson, B., Jankowska, E. 1976. Direct and indirect activation of nerve cells by electrical pulses applied extracellularly. *J. Neurophysiol.* 258:33–61

Gutman, W., Brozek, G., Bures, J. 1972. Cortical representation of conditioned eyeblink in the rabbit studied by a functional ablation technique. *Brain Res.* 40:203–13

Hagins, W. A., Yoshikami, S. 1975. Ionic mechanisms in excitation of photoreceptors. *Ann. NY Acad. Sci.* 264:314–25

Hagiwara, S. 1975. Ca-dependent action potential. In *Membranes and Ionic Conductors,* ed. G. Eisenman, 3:359–81. New York: Dekker

Hagiwara, S. 1983. *Membrane Potential-Dependent Ion Channels in Cell Membrane:*

Phylogenetic and Developmental Approaches. New York: Raven

Hagiwara, S., Naka, K. I. 1964. The initiation of spike potential in barnacle muscle fibers under low intracellular Ca^{++}. *J. Gen. Physiol.* 48:141–61

Hagiwara, S., Takahashi, K. 1974. The anomalous rectification and cation selectivity of the membrane of a starfish egg cell. *J. Membr. Biol.* 18:61–80

Halliwell, J. V., Adams, P. R. 1982. Voltage-clamp analysis of muscarinic excitation in hippocampal neurons. *Brain Res.* 250:71–92

Hamill, O., Marty, A., Neher, E., Sakmann, B., Sigworth, F. J. 1981. Improved patch-clamp techniques for high-resolution current recording from cells and cell-free membrane patches. *Pflügers Arch.* 391:85–100

Harlow, H. F., Bromer, J. A. 1942. Acquisition of new responses during inactivation of the motor, premotor, and somesthetic cortex in the monkey. *J. Gen. Psychol.* 26:299–313

Harris, J. D. 1941. Forward conditioning, backward conditioning, pseudo-conditioning, and adaptation to the conditioned stimulus. *J. Exp. Psychol.* 28:491–502

Harris, R. A., Allan, A. M. 1985. Functional coupling of γ-aminobutyric acid receptors to chloride channels in brain membranes. *Science* 228:1108–10

Harrison, J. M., Howe, M. E. 1974. Anatomy of the afferent auditory nervous system of mammals. In *Handbook of Sensory Physiology*, ed. W. D. Keidel, W. D. Neff, Vol. 5(1): New York: Springer-Verlag

Hartzell, H. C. 1981. Mechanisms of slow postsynaptic potentials. *Nature* 291:539–44

Harvey, J., Gormezano, I. 1981. Effects of haloperidol and pimozide on classical conditioning of the rabbit nictitating membrane response. *J. Pharmacol. Exp. Ther.* 218:712–19

Hawkins, R. D., Abrams, T. W., Carew, T. J., Kandel, E. R. 1983. A cellular mechanism of classical conditioning in *Aplysia*: Activity-dependent amplification of presynaptic facilitation. *Science* 219:400–5

Head, H., Riddoch, G. 1917. The automatic bladder, excessive sweating and some other reflex conditions in gross injuries of the spinal cord. *Brain* 40:188–223

Hebb, D. O. 1949. *The Organization of Behavior: A Neuropsychological Theory.* New York: Wiley

Henkel, G. K. 1983. Evidence of sub-collicular auditory projections to the medial geniculate nucleus in the cat: An autoradiographic and horseradish peroxidase study. *Brain Res.* 259:21–30

Heyer, C. B., Lux, H. D. 1976a. Properties of a facilitating calcium current in pace-maker neurones of the snail, *Helix pomatia. J. Physiol.* 262:319–48

Heyer, C. B., Lux, H. D. 1976b. Control of the delayed outward potassium currents in bursting pace-maker neurones of the snail, *Helix pomatia. J. Physiol.* 262:349–82

Hille, B. 1984. *Ionic Channels of Excitable Membranes.* Sunderland, MA: Sinauer

Hockberger, P. E., Connor, J. A. 1983. Intracellular calcium measurements with Arsenazo III during cyclic AMP injections into molluscan neurons. *Science* 219:869–71

Hodgkin, A. L., Huxley, A. F. 1939. Action potentials recorded from inside a nerve fibre. *Nature* 144:710–11

Hodgkin, A. L., Huxley, A. F. 1952. Currents carried by sodium and potassium ions through the membrane of the giant axon of *Loligo. J. Physiol.* 116:449–72

Hoffeld, D. R., Thompson, R. F., Brogden, W. J. 1958. Effect of stimuli-time relations during preconditioning training upon the magnitude of sensory preconditioning. *J. Exp. Psychol.* 56:437–42

Holmes, W. R. 1985. *Cable theory modeling of the effectiveness of synaptic inputs in cortical neurons.* PhD thesis. Univ. Calif., Los Angeles

Holmes, W. R., Woody, C. D. 1983. Effects of input currents of local increases in membrane resistance in cortical pyramidal cell dendrites explored using a passive cable model for determining the transient potential in a dendritic tree of known geometry. *Soc. Neurosci. Abstr.* 9:603

Holmes, W. R., Woody, C. D. 1984. Some effects of tonic afferent activity on input from individual synapses as modeled in a cortical pyramidal cell of known morphology. *Soc. Neurosci. Abstr.* 10:1073

Horwitz, B. 1981. An analytical method for investigating transient potentials in neurons with branching dendritic trees. *Biophys. J.* 36:155–92

Horwitz, B. 1983. Unequal diameters and their effects on time-varying voltages in branched neurons. *Biophys. J.* 41:51–66

Houchin, J. 1973. Procion yellow electrodes for intracellular recording and staining of neurones in the somato-sensory cortex of the rat. *J. Physiol.* 232:67–69

Hubel, D. H., Wiesel, T. N. 1970. The period of susceptibility to the physiological effects of unilateral eye closure in kittens. *J. Physiol.* 206:419–36

Hugues, M., Duval, D., Kitabgi, P., Lazdunski, M., Vincent, J. P. 1982a. Preparation of a pure monoiodo derivative of the bee venom neurotoxin apamin and its binding properties to rat brain synaptosomes. *J. Biol. Chem.* 257:2762–69

Hugues, M., Romey, G., Duval, D., Vincent, J. P., Lazdunski, M. 1982b. Apamin as a selective blocker of the calcium dependent potassium channel in neuroblastoma cells: Voltage-clamp and biochemical characterization of the toxin receptor. *Proc. Natl. Acad. Sci. USA* 79:1308–12

Hull, C. L. 1934. Learning II. The factor of the conditioned reflex. In *A Handbook of General Experimental Psychology*, ed. D. Murchison, pp. 392–455. Worcester, MA: Clark Univ. Press

Imig, T. J., Morel, A. 1983. Organization of the thalamocortical auditory system in the cat. *Ann. Rev. Neurosci.* 6:95–120

Ito, M. 1985. How can the cerebellar neuronal network mediate a classical conditioned reflex? See Alkon & Woody 1985, pp. 221–22

Jack, J. J. B. 1979. An introduction to cable theory. In *The Neurosciences: Fourth Study Program*, ed. F. O. Schmitt, F. G. Worden, pp. 423–38. Cambridge, MA: MIT Press

Jack, J. J. B., Noble, D., Tsien, R. W. 1983. *Electric Current Flow in Excitable Cells.* London: Oxford Univ. Press

Jahnsen, H., Llinas, R. 1984a. Electrophysiological properties of guinea-pig thalamic neurones: An in vitro study. *J. Physiol.* 349:205–26

Jahnsen, H., Llinas, R. 1984b. Ionic basis for the electroresponsiveness and oscillatory properties of guinea-pig thalamic neurones in vitro. *J. Physiol.* 349:227–47

Jankowska, E., Rastad, J., Westman, J. 1976. Intracellular application of horseradish peroxidase and its light and electron microscopical appearance in spinocervical tract cells. *Brain Res.* 105:557

Jasper, H., Ricci, G., Doane, B. 1960. Microelectrode analysis of cortical cell discharge during avoidance conditioning in the monkey. *Electroencephalogr. Clin. Neurophysiol. Suppl.* 13:137–55

Jellinek, A., Koppanyi, T. 1923. Lernfahigheit gehirnverlitzter Ratten. *Anz. Akad. Wiss. Wien Math-Naturwiss. Kl.* 17:130

Johnston, D., Brown, T. H. 1983. Interpretation of voltage-clamp measurements in hippocampal neurons. *J. Neurophysiol.* 50:464–86

Johnston, D., Hablitz, J. 1979. Voltage clamp analysis of CA3 neurons in hippocampal slices. *Soc. Neurosci. Abstr.* 5:292

Jones, E. G., Powell, T. P. S. 1971. An analysis of the posterior group of thalamic nuclei on the basis of its afferent connections. *J. Comp. Neurol.* 143:185–216

Jordan, S. E., Jordon, J., Brozek, G., Woody, C. D. 1976. Intracellular recordings of antidromically identified facial motoneurons and unidentified brain stem interneurons of awake, blink conditioned cats. *Physiologist* 19:245

Jung, R., Hassler, R. 1960. The extrapyramidal motor system. In *Handb. Phys-*

iol. Sect. 1, Vol. 2: *Neurophysiology*, ed. J. Field, H. W. Magoun, V. E. Hall, p. 863 ff. Washington, DC: Am. Physiol. Soc.

Kaczmarek, L. K., Jennings, K. R., Strumwasser, F., Nairn, A. C., Walter, U., et al. 1980. Microinjection of catalytic subunit of cyclic AMP-dependent protein kinase enhances calcium action potentials of bag cell neurons in cell culture. *Proc. Natl. Acad. Sci. USA* 77:7487–91

Kaczmarek, L. K., Strumwasser, F. 1984. A voltage-clamp analysis of currents underlying cyclic AMP-induced membrane modulation in isolated peptidergic neurons of *Aplysia. J. Neurophysiol.* 52:340–49

Kamin, L. J. 1957. The retention of an incompletely learned avoidance response. *J. Comp. Psychol.* 50:457–60

Kandel, E. R. 1976. *Cellular Basis of Behavior.* San Francisco: Freeman

Kandel, E. R. 1979. Cellular insights into behavior and learning. *Harvey Lect.* 73:29–92

Kandel, E. R., Schwartz, J. H. 1982. Molecular biology of learning: Modulation of transmitter release. *Science* 218:433–43

Kandel, E. R., Spencer, W. A. 1968. Cellular neurophysiological approaches in the study of learning. *Physiol. Rev.* 48:65–134

Kandel, E. R., Spencer, W. A., Brinley, F. J. Jr. 1961. Electrophysiology of hippocampal neurons. 1. Sequential invasion and synaptic organization. *J. Neurophysiol.* 24:225–42

Kass, I. S., Lipton, P. 1982. Mechanisms involved in irreversible anoxic damage to the in vitro rat hippocampal slice. *J. Physiol.* 332:459–72

Katsumaru, H., Murakami, F., Tsukahara, N. 1982. Actin filaments in dendritic spines of red nucleus neurons demonstrated by immunoferritin localization and heavy meromyosin binding. *Biomed. Res.* 3:337–40

Katz, B. 1949. Les constantes electriques de la membrane du muscle. *Arch. Sci. Physiol.* 2:285–99

Katz, B., Miledi, R. 1968. The role in calcium of neuromuscular facilitation. *J. Physiol.* 195:481–92

Kennedy, D., Calabrese, R., Wine, J. J. 1974. Presynaptic inhibition: Primary afferent depolarization in crayfish neurons. *Science* 186:451–54

Kim, E. H. -J., Woody, C. D., Berthier, N. E. 1983. Rapid acquisition of conditioned eye blink responses in cats following pairing of an auditory CS with glabella tap US and hypothalamic stimulation. *J. Neurophysiol.* 49:767–79

Kimble, G. A., Dufort, R. H. 1956. The associative factor in eyelid conditioning. *J. Exp. Psychol.* 52:386–91

Kitai, S. T., Kocsis, J. D., Preston, R. J., Sugimori, M. 1976. Monosynaptic inputs to caudate neurons identified by intracellular injection of horseradish peroxidase. *Brain Res.* 109:601–6

Klein, M., Kandel, E. R. 1980. Mechanism of calcium current modulation underlying presynaptic facilitation and behavioral sensitization in *Aplysia*. *Proc. Natl. Acad. Sci. USA* 77:6912–16

Kluver, H., Bucy, P. 1939. Preliminary analysis of functions of the temporal lobes in monkeys. *Arch. Neurol. Psychiatry* 42:979–1000

Kobayashi, H., Hashiguchi, T., Ushiyama, N. 1978. Postsynaptic modulation by cyclic AMP, intra- or extracellularly applied, or by stimulation of preganglionic nerve, in mammalian sympathetic ganglion cells. *Nature* 271:268–70

Koike, H., Kandel, E. R., Schwartz, J. H. 1974. Synaptic release of radioactivity after intrasomatic injection of choline-³H into an identified cholinergic interneuron in abdominal ganglion of *Aplysia Californica*. *J. Neurophysiol.* 37:815

Koike, H., Okada, Y., Oshima, T., Takahashi, K. 1968a. Accommodative behavior of cat pyramidal tract cell investigated with intracellular injection of currents. *Exp. Brain Res.* 5:173–88

Koike, H., Okada, Y., Oshima, T. 1968b. Accommodative properties of fast and slow pyramidal tract cells and their modification by different levels of their membrane potential. *Exp. Brain Res.* 5:189–201

Koketsu, K., Nakamura, M. 1975. Some analyses of the slow inhibitory postsynaptic potential in bullfrog sympathetic ganglia. *Kurume Med. J.* 22:5–11

Kostyuk, P. G. 1980. Calcium ionic channels in electrically excitable membrane. *Neuroscience* 5:945–59

Krasne, F. B. 1969. Excitation and habituation of the crayfish escape reflex: The depolarizing response in lateral giant fibers of the isolated abdomen. *J. Exp. Biol.* 50:29–46

Krasne, F. B., Bryan, J. S. 1973. Habituation: Regulation through presynaptic inhibition. *Science* 182:590–92

Krnjevic, K., Puil, E., Werman, R. 1976. Is cyclic guanosine monophosphate the internal "second messenger" for cholinergic actions on cortical neurons? *Can. J. Physiol. Pharmacol.* 54:172–76

Krnjevic, K., Pumain, R., Renaud, L. 1971. The mechanism of excitation by acetylcholine in the cerebral cortex. *J. Physiol.* 215:247–68

Kudo, M. 1981. Projections of the nuclei of the lateral lemniscus in the cat: An autoradiographic study. *Brain Res.* 221:57–69

Lashley, K. S. 1921. Studies of cerebral function in learning. III. The motor areas. *Brain* 44:255–85

Lashley, K. S. 1924. Studies of cerebral function in learning. V. The retention of motor habits after destruction of the so-called motor areas in primates. *Arch. Neurol. Psychiatry* 12:249–76

Lashley, K. S. 1929. *Brain Mechanisms and Intelligence: A Quantitative Study of Injuries to the Brain*. Chicago: Chicago Univ. Press

Lavond, D. G., McCormick, D. A., Clark, G. A., Holmes, D. T., Thompson, R. F. 1981. Effects of ipsilateral rostral pontine reticular lesions on retention of classically conditioned nictitating membrane and eyelid responses. *Physiol. Psychol.* 9(4):335–39

Lemos, J. R., Novak-Hofer, I., Levitan, I. B. 1984. Phosphoproteins associated with the regulation of a K⁺ conductance in *Aplysia* cell R15. *Soc. Neurosci.* 10:5 (Abstr.)

Levin, V. A., Fenstermacher, J. D., Patlak, C. S. 1970. Sucrose and inulin space measurements of cerebral cortex in four mammalian species. *Am. J. Physiol.* 219:1528–33

Lev-tov, A., Miller, J. P., Burke, R. E., Rall, W. 1983. Factors that control amplitude of EPSPs in dendritic neurons. *J. Neurophysiol.* 50:399–412

Levy, W. B., Steward, O. 1983. Temporal contiguity requirements for long-term associative potentiation/depression in the hippocampus. *Neuroscience* 8:791–97

Li, C.-L., McIlwain, H. 1957. Maintenance of resting membrane potentials in slices of mammalian cerebral cortex and other tissues in vitro. *J. Physiol.* 139:178–90

Libet, B. 1979. Which postsynaptic action of dopamine is mediated by cyclic AMP? *Life Sci.* 24:1043–58

Libet, B. 1984. Heterosynaptic interaction at a sympathetic neuron as a model for induction and storage of a postsynaptic memory trace. In *Neurobiology of Learning and Memory*, ed. G. Lynch, J. L. McGaugh, N. M. Weinberger, pp. 405–30. New York: Guilford

Libet, B., Kobayashi, H., Tanaka, T. 1975. Synaptic coupling into the production and storage of a neuronal memory trace. *Nature* 258:155–57

Lincoln, J. S., McCormick, D. A., Thompson, R. F. 1982. Ipsilateral cerebellar lesions prevent learning of the classically conditioned nictitating membrane/eyelid response. *Brain Res.* 242:190–93

Llinas, R., Heuser, J. E., eds. 1977. Depolarization-release coupling systems in neurons. *Neurosci. Res. Program Bull.* 15:555–687

Llinas, R., McGuinness, T. L., Leonard, C. S., Sugimori, M., Greengard, P. 1985. Intraterminal injection of synapsin I or calcium/calmodulin-dependent protein kinase II alters neurotransmitter release at the squid giant synapse. *Proc. Natl. Acad. Sci. USA* 82:3035–39

Llinas, R., Sugimori, M. 1980a. Electrophysiological properties of in vitro purkinje cell somata in mammalian cerebellar slices. *J. Physiol.* 305:171–95

Llinas, R., Sugimori, M. 1980b. Electrophysiological properties of in vitro purkinje cell dendrites in mammalian cerebellar slices. *J. Physiol.* 305:197–213

Llinas, R., Walton, K., Hillman, E. D., Sotelo, C. 1975. Inferior olive: Its role in motor learning. *Science* 190:1230–31

Llinas, R., Yarom, Y. 1981a. Electrophysiology of mammalian inferior olivary neurones in vitro. Different types of voltage-dependent ionic conductances. *J. Physiol.* 315:549–67

Llinas, R., Yarom, Y. 1981b. Properties and distribution of ionic conductances generating electroresponsiveness of mammalian inferior olivary neurones in vitro. *J. Physiol.* 315:569–84

Lloyd, D. P. C. 1949. Post-tetanic potentiation of response in monosynaptic reflex pathways of the spinal cord. *J. Gen. Physiol.* 33:147–70

Lnenicka, G. A., Atwood, H. L. 1985. Long-term facilitation and long-term adaptation at synapses of a crayfish phasic motoneuron. *J. Neurobiol.* 16:97–110

Loewenstein, W. R. 1963. Separation of transducer and impulse-generating processes in sensory receptors. *Science* 142:1180–81

Loewenstein, W. R. 1973. Membrane junctions in growth and differentiation. *Fed. Proc.* 32:60–64

Loewenstein, W. R. 1975. Permeable junctions. *Cold Spring Harbor Symp. Quant. Biol.* 40:49–63

Lomo, T. 1971. Potentiation of monosynaptic EPSPs in the perforant path-dentated granule cell synapse. *Exp. Brain Res.* 12:46–63

Lorente de Nó, R., Condouris, G. A. 1959. Decremental conduction in peripheral nerve: Integration of stimuli in the neuron. *Proc. Natl. Acad. Sci. USA* 45:592–617

Loucks, R. B. 1933. Preliminary report of a technique for stimulation or destruction of tissues beneath the integument and the establishing of a conditioned reaction with faradization of the cerebral cortex. *J. Comp. Psychol.* 16:439–44

Loucks, R. B. 1935. The experimental delimitation of neural structures essential for learning: The attempt to condition striped muscle responses with faradization of the sigmoid gyri. *J. Psychol.* 1:5–44

Lux, H. D., Neher, E., Marty, A. 1981. Single channel activity associated with the calcium dependent outward current in *Helix pomatia*. *Pflügers Arch.* 389:293–95

Lux, H. D., Pollen, D. A. 1966. Electrical constants of neurons in the motor cortex of the cat. *J. Neurophysiol.* 29:207–20

Lynch, G., Baudry, M. 1984. The biochemistry of memory: A new and specific hypothesis. *Science* 224:1057–63

Markel, E., Adam, G. 1969. Learning phenomena in mesencephalic rats. *Acta Physiol. Acad. Sci. Hung.* 36:265–70

Markel, E., Anda, E., Juhasz, G., Adam, G. 1969. Discriminative learning in mesencephalic rats. *Acta Physiol. Acad. Sci. Hung.* 36:271–76

Matsumura, M., Woody, C. D. 1982. Excitability changes of facial motoneurons of cats related to conditioned and unconditioned facial motor responses. See Woody 1982c, pp. 451–58

Mayer, M. L., Westbrook, G. L. 1983. A voltage-clamp analysis of inward (anomalous) rectification in mouse spinal sensory ganglion neurones. *J. Physiol.* 340:19–45

McCaman, R. E., McKenna, D. G., Ono, J. K. 1977. A pressure system for intracellular and extracellular ejections of picoliter volumes. *Brain Res.* 136:141

McCormick, D. A., Clark, G. A., Lavond, D. G., Thompson, R. F. 1982a. Initial localization of the memory trace for a basic form of learning. *Proc. Natl. Acad. Sci. USA* 79:2731–35

McCormick, D. A., Guyer, P. E., Thompson, R. F. 1982b. Superior cerebellar peduncle lesions selectively abolish the ipsilateral classically conditioned nictitating membrane/eyelid response of the rabbit. *Brain Res.* 244:347–50

McCormick, D. A., Lavond, D. G., Thompson, R. F. 1982c. Concomitant classical conditioning of the rabbit nictitating membrane and eyelid response: Correlations and implications. *Physiol. Behav.* 28:769–75

McCormick, D. A., Thompson, R. F. 1984. Cerebellum: essential involvement in the classically conditioned eyelid response. *Science* 223:296–99

McGraw, C. F., Nachshen, D. A., Blaustein, M. P. 1982. Calcium involvement and regulation of presynaptic nerve terminals. In *Calcium and Cell Function*, ed. W. Y. Cheung, 2:81–110. New York: Academic

Meech, R. W. 1974. The sensitivity of *Helix aspersa* neurons to injected calcium ions. *J. Physiol.* 237:259–77

Meech, R. W., Standen, N. B. 1975. Potassium activation in *Helix aspersa* under voltage clamp: A component mediated by calcium influx. *J. Physiol.* 249:211–39

Merzenich, M. M., Kaas, J. H., Wall, J. T., Sur, M., Nelson, R. J., et al. 1983. Progression of change following median nerve section in the cortical representation of the hand in areas 3b and 1 in adult owl and squirrel monkeys. *Neuroscience* 10:639–65

Moore, J. W., Desmond, J. E., Berthier, N. E. 1982. The metencephalic basis of the conditioned nictitating membrane response. See Woody 1982c, pp. 459–82

Morest, D. K. 1964. The neuronal architecture of the medial geniculate body of the cat. *J. Anat.* 98:611–30

Morest, D. K. 1965. The lateral tegmental system of the midbrain and the medial geniculate body: Study with Golgi and Nauta methods in cat. *J. Anat.* 99:611–34

Morrell, F. 1961. Effects of anodal polarization on the firing pattern of single cortical cells. *Ann. NY Acad. Sci.* 92:860–76

Mountcastle, V. B., ed. 1974. *Medical Physiology,* Vol. 1. St. Louis: Mosby. 13th ed.

Murakami, F., Katsumaru, H., Maeda, J., Tsukahara, N. 1984. Reorganization of corticorubral synapses following cross-innervation of flexor and extensor nerves of adult cat: A quantitative electron microscopic study. *Brain Res.* 306:299–306

Murakami, F., Katsumaru, H., Saito, K., Tsukahara, N. 1982. A quantitative study of synaptic reorganization in red nucleus neurons after lesion of the nucleus interpositus of the cat: An electron microscopic study involving intracellular injection of horseradish peroxidase. *Brain Res.* 242:41–53

Murphy, J. P., Gellhorn, E. 1945. The influence of hypothalamic stimulation on cortically induced movements and on action potentials of the cortex. *J. Neurophysiol.* 8:341–64

Nahvi, M. J., Woody, C. D., Tzebelikos, E., Ribak, C. E. 1980. Electrophysiologic characterization of morphologically identified neurons in the cerebellar cortex of awake cats. *Exp. Neurol.* 67:368–76

Neary, J. T., Alkon, D. L. 1983. Protein phosphorylation/dephosphorylation and the transient, voltage-dependent potassium conductance in *Hermissenda crassicornis.* *J. Biol. Chem.* 258:8979–83

Neary, J. T., Crow, T., Alkon, D. L. 1981. Change in a specific phosphoprotein band following associative learning. *Nature* 293:658–70

Neher, E. 1971. Two fast transient current components during voltage clamp on snail neurons. *J. Gen. Physiol.* 58:36–53

Nestler, E. J., Greengard, P. 1982. Distribution of Protein I and regulation of its state of phosphorylation in the rabbit superior cervical ganglion. *J. Neurosci.* 2:1011–23

Nestler, E. J., Greengard, P. 1984. *Protein Phosphorylation in the Nervous System.* New York: Wiley

Nicholson, C., Llinas, R. 1971. Field potentials in the alligator cerebellum and theory of their relationship of Purkinje cell dendritic spikes. *J. Neurophysiol.* 34:509–13

Nishi, S., Koketsu, K. 1968. Early and late after-discharges of amphibian sympathetic ganglion cells. *J. Neurophysiol.* 31:109–21

Norman, R. J., Buchwald, J. S., Villablanca, J. R. 1977. Classical conditioning with auditory discrimination of the eyeblink in decerebrate cats. *Science* 196:551–53

Norman, R. J., Villablanca, J. R., Brown, K. A., Schwafel, J. A., Buchwald, J. S. 1974. Classical eyeblink in the bilaterally hemispherectomized cat. *Exp. Neurol.* 44:363–80

Oakley, D. A., Russell, I. S. 1977. Subcortical storage of Pavlovian conditioning in the rabbit. *Physiol. Behav.* 18:931–37

O'Brien, J. H., Wilder, M. B., Stevens, C. D. 1977. Conditioning of cortical neurons in cat with antidromic activation as the unconditioned stimulus. *J. Comp. Physiol. Psychol.* 91:918–29

Ojemann, R. G. 1966. A critical survey of the literature. *Neurosci. Res. Program Bull.* 4:1–70

Palmerino, C. C., Rusiniak, K. W., Garcia, J. 1980. Flavor-illness aversions: The peculiar roles of odor and taste in memory for poison. *Science* 208:753–55

Papsdorf, J. D., Longman, D., Gormezano, I. 1965. Spreading depression: Effects of applying KCl to the dura of the rabbit on the conditioned nictitating membrane response. *Psychon. Sci.* 2:125–26

Pavlov, I. P. 1927. *Conditioned Reflexes,* transl. and ed. G. V. Anrep. London: Oxford Univ. Press

Penfield, W., Milner, B. 1958. Memory deficit produced by bilateral lesions in the hippocampal zone. *AMA Arch. Neurol. Psychiatry* 79:475–97

Peroutka, S. J., Lebovitz, R. M., Snyder, S. H. 1981. Two distinct central serotonin receptors with different physiological functions. *Science* 212:827–29

Peters, A., Jones, E. G., eds. 1984. *Cerebral Cortex,* Vol. 1, *Cellular Components of the Cerebral Cortex.* New York: Plenum

Poltyrew, S. S. 1936. Verborgene assoziationen des grosshirns bei hunden. *Z. Biol.* 97:306–7

Poltyrew, S. S., Zeliony, G. P. 1929. Der hund ohne grosshirn. *Am. J. Physiol.* 90:475–76

Poltyrew, S. S., Zeliony, G. P. 1930. Grosshirnrinde und Assoziationsfunktion. *Z. Biol.* 90:160–64

Purves, R. D. 1981. *Microelectrode Methods for Intracellular Recording and Iontophoresis.* London: Academic

Quandt, F. N., Narahashi, T. 1982. Modification of single Na^+ channels by batrachotoxin. *Proc. Natl. Acad. Sci. USA* 79:6732–36

Raabe, D. H., Lux, H. D. 1973. Hyperpolarizing synaptic inhibition in cat neocortex. *Brain Res.* 52:389–93

Raftery, M. A., Hunkapiller, M. W., Strader, C. D., Hood, L. E. 1980. Acetylcholine receptor: Complex of homologous subunits. *Science* 208:1454–57

Rakic, P. 1985. Limits of neurogenesis in primates. *Science* 227:1054–56

Rall, W. 1962. Electrophysiology of a dendritic neuron model. *Biophys. J. Suppl.* 2:145–67

Rall, W. 1970. Cable properties of dendrites and effects of synaptic location. In *Excitatory Synaptic Mechanisms*, ed. P. Andersen, J. K. S. Jensen, pp. 175–87. Oslo: Universitats Forlaget

Rall, W. 1974. Dendritic spines, synaptic potency, and neuronal plasticity. See Doty 1974, pp. 13–21

Rall, W. 1977. Core conductor theory and cable properties of neurons. *Handb. Physiol.* Sect. 1, *The Nervous System I. Cellular Biology of Neurons*, ed. E. R. Kandel, pp. 39–97. Bethesda, MD: Am. Physiol. Soc.

Ranson, S. W. 1959. *The Anatomy of the Nervous System*. Revised by S. L. Clark. New York: Saunders. 10th ed.

Rasmussen, H. 1979. *Calcium and cAMP as Synarchic Messengers*. New York: Wiley

Rasmussen, H., Barrett, P. Q. 1984. Calcium messenger system: An integrative view. *Physiol. Rev.* 64:938–84

Rasmussen, H., Goodman, D. B. P. 1977. Relationships between calcium and cyclic nucleotides in cell activation. *Physiol. Rev.* 57:421–509

Remler, M. P., Selverston, A. I., Kennedy, D. 1968. Lateral giant fibers of crayfish: Location of somata by dye injection. *Science* 162:281

Rescorla, R. A. 1969. Pavlovian conditioned inhibition. *Psychol. Bull.* 72(2):77–94

Rescorla, R. A., Solomon, R. L. 1967. Two-process learning theory: Relationships between Pavlovian conditioning and instrumental learning. *Psychol. Rev.* 74(3):151–82

Ribak, C., Woody, C. D., Nahvi, M. J., Tzebelikos, E. 1980. Ultrastructural identification of physiologically recorded neurons in the cat cerebellum. *Exp. Neurol.* 67:377–390

Richter, D. W., Schlue, W. R., Mauritz, K. H., Nacimiento, A. C. 1974. Comparison of membrane properties of the cell body and the initial part of the axon of phasic motor neurones in the spinal cord of the cat. *Exp. Brain Res.* 20:193–206

Rizley, R. C., Rescorla, R. A. 1972. Associations in second order conditioning and sensory preconditioning. *J. Comp. Physiol. Psychol.* 81:1–11

Roberts, E., Chase, T. N., Tower, D. B., eds. 1976. *GABA in Nervous System Function*. New York: Raven

Rogers, F. T. 1922. Studies of the brain stem VI. An experimental study of the corpus striatum of the pigeon as related to various instinctive types of behavior. *J. Comp. Neurol.* 35:21

Rose, J. E., Woolsey, C. N. 1958. Cortical connections and functional organization of the thalamic auditory system of cat. In *Biological and Biochemical Bases of Behavior*, ed. H. F. Harlow, C. N. Woolsey, pp. 127–50. Madison: Univ. Wis. Press

Rosenfeld, M. E., Moore, J. W. 1983. Red nucleus lesions disrupt the classically conditioned nictitating membrane response in rabbits. *Behav. Brain Res.* 10:393–98

Rosenzweig, M. R., Bennett, E. L. 1977. Effects of environmental enrichment or impoverishment on learning and on brain values in rodents. In *Genetics, Environment, and Intelligence*, ed. A. Oliverio, pp. 163–95. Amsterdam: Elsevier

Rothman, M. 1907. Uber die physiologische wertung der corticospinalen (pyramiden-) bahn. *Arch. Anat. Physiol. Physiol. Abt.*, pp. 217–75

Rusinov, V. S. 1953. An electrophysiological analysis of the connecting function in the cerebral cortex in the presence of a dominant area. *Proc. Int. Union Physiol. Sci.* 19:147–56

Russell, D. F. 1964. *A History of Western Philosophy*. New York: Simon & Schuster

Ryugo, D. K., Weinberger, N. M. 1978. Differential plasticity of morphologically distinct neuron populations in the medial geniculate body of the cat during classical conditioning. *Behav. Biol.* 22:275–301

Sahley, C. L., Rudy, J. W., Gelperin, A. 1984. Associative learning in a mollusk: A comparative analysis. See Comardo et al 1984, pp. 243–58

Sakai, M., Sakai, H., Woody, C. D. 1978a. Intracellular staining of cortical neurons by pressure microinjection of horseradish peroxidase and recovery by core biopsy. *Exp. Neurol.* 58:138–44

Sakai, M., Sakai, H., Woody, C. D. 1978b. Sampling distribution of morphologically identified neurons of the coronal-pericruciate cortex of awake cats following intracellular injection of HRP. *Brain Res.* 152:329–33

Sakai, H., Woody, C. D. 1980. Identification of auditory responsive cells in coronal-pericruciate cortex of awake cats. *J. Neurophysiol.* 44:223–31

Sakmann, B., Neher, E., eds. 1983. *Single Channel Recording*. New York: Plenum. 503 pp.

Schmitt, F. O. 1962. *Macromolecular Specificity of Biological Memory*. Cambridge, MA: MIT Press

Siegelbaum, S. A., Camardo, J. S., Kandel, E.

R. 1982. Serotonin and cyclic AMP close single K⁺ channels in *Aplysia* sensory neurones. *Nature* 299:413–17

Siggins, G. R., Oliver, A. P., Hoffer, B. J., Bloom, F. E. 1971. Cyclic adenosine monophosphate and norepinephrine: Effects on transmembrane properties of cerebellar Purkinje cells. *Science* 171:192–94

Smith, P. A., Weight, F. F. 1977. Role of electrogenic sodium pump in slow synaptic inhibition is re-evaluated. *Nature* 267:68–70

Snow, P. J., Rose, P. K., Brown, A. G. 1976. Tracing axons and axon collaterals of spinal neurons using intracellular injection of horseradish peroxidase. *Science* 191:312–13

Solomon, P. R., Moore, J. W. 1975. Latent inhibition and stimulus generalization for the classically conditioned nictitating membrane response in rabbits *(Oryctolagus cuniculus)* following dorsal hippocampal ablation. *J. Comp. Physiol. Psychol.* 89:1192–1203

Spencer, W. A., Kandel, E. R. 1961. Electrophysiology of hippocampal neurons. IV. Fast prepotentials. *J. Neurophysiol.* 24:272–85

Spencer, W. A., Thompson, R. F., Neilson, D. R. Jr. 1966a. Alterations in responsiveness of ascending and reflex pathways activated by iterated cutaneous afferent volleys. *J. Neurophysiol.* 29:240–52

Spencer, W. A., Thompson, R. F., Neilson, D. R. Jr. 1966b. Decrement of ventral root electrotonus and intracellularly recorded PSPs produced by iterated cutaneous afferent volleys. *J. Neurophysiol.* 29:253–74

Spencer, W. A., Thompson, R. F., Neilson, D. R. Jr. 1966c. Response decrement of the flexion reflex in the acute spinal cat and transient restoration by strong stimuli. *J. Neurophysiol.* 29:221–39

Spetch, M. L., Wilkie, D. M., Pinel, J. P. J. 1981. Backward conditioning: A reevaluation of the empirical evidence. *Psychol. Bull.* 89:163–75

Squire, L. R., Butters, N., eds. 1984. *Neuropsychology of Memory.* New York: Guilford

Stafstrom, C. E., Schwindt, P. C., Crill, W. E. 1984. Cable properties of layer V neurons from cat sensorimotor cortex in vitro. *J. Neurophysiol.* 52:278–89

Starlinger, J. 1895. Die durchschneidung beider pyramiden beim hunde. *Neurol. Zentralbl.* 14:390–94

Stoney, S. D. Jr., Thompson, W. D., Asanuma, H. 1968. Excitation of pyramidal tract cells by intracortical microstimulation: Effective extent of stimulating current. *J. Neurophysiol.* 31:659–69

Sutherland, E. W. 1972. Studies on the mechanisms of hormone action. *Science* 177:401–8

Swanson, L. W., Teyler, T. J., Thompson, R. F. 1982. Hippocampal long-term potentiation mechanisms and implications for memory. *Neurosci. Res. Program Bull.* 20:613–69

Swartz, B. E., Woody, C. D. 1979. Correlated effects of acetylcholine and cyclic guanosine monophosphate on membrane properties of mammalian neocortical neurons. *J. Neurobiol.* 10:465–88

Swartz, B. E., Woody, C. D. 1984. Effects of intracellular antibodies to cGMP on responses of cortical neurons of awake cats to extracellular application of muscarinic agonists. *Exp. Neurol.* 86:388–404

Takeuchi, A., Takeuchi, N. 1966. On the permeability of the presynaptic terminal of the crayfish neuromuscular junction during synaptic inhibition and the action of gamma-aminobutyric acid. *J. Physiol.* 183:433–49

Takeuchi, A., Takeuchi, N. 1967. Anion permeability of the postsynaptic membrane of the crayfish neuromuscular junction. *J. Physiol.* 191:575–90

Tasaki, I. 1959. Conduction of the nerve impulse. *Handb. Physiol.,* Sect. 1: *Neurophysiology,* ed. J. Field, pp. 75–121. Washington, DC: Am. Physiol. Soc.

Tchilingaryan, L. I. 1963. Changes in excitability of the motor area of the cerebral cortex during extinction of a conditioned reflex elaborated to direct electrical stimulation of that area. In *Central and Peripheral Mechanisms of Motor Functions,* ed. E. Gutman, P. Hnik, pp. 167–75. Prague: Publ. House Czeck. Acad. Sci.

Ten Cate, J. 1934a. Akustische und optische reaktionen der katzen nach teilweisen und totalen exstirpationen des neopalliums. *Arch. Neerl. Physiol.* 19:191–264

Ten Cate, J. 1934b. Konnen die bedingten reaktionen such auch ausserhalb der grosshirnrinde bilden? *Arch. Neerl. Physiol.* 19:469–81

Thach, W. T. 1978. Correlation of neural discharge with patterns and force of muscular activity, joint position, and direction of intended next movement in motor cortex and cerebellum. *J. Neurophysiol.* 41:654–76

Thompson, R. F. 1960. Function of auditory cortex of cat in frequency discrimination. *J. Neurophysiol.* 23:321–34

Thompson, R. F. 1979. Associative ("alpha") conditioning in an isolated mammalian system: The cat spinal cord. *Neurosci. Res. Program Bull.* 17:570–71

Thompson, R. F. 1983. Neuronal substrates of simple associative learning: Classical conditioning. *Trends Neurosci.* 6(7):270–75

Thompson, R. F., Berger, T. W., Berry, S. D., Clark, G. A., Kettner, R. E., et al. 1982. Neuronal substrates of learning and memory:

Hippocampus and other structures. See Woody 1982c, pp. 115–29

Thompson, R. F., Berger, T. W., Madden, J. IV. 1983a. Cellular processes of learning and memory in the mammalian CNS. *Ann. Rev. Neurosci.* 6:447–91

Thompson, R. F., McCormick, D. A., Lavond, D. G., Clark, G. A., Kettner, R. E., et al. 1983b. The engram found? Initial localization of the memory trace for a basic form of associative learning. *Prog. Psychobiol. Physiol. Psychol.* 10:167–96

Thompson, R. F., Spencer, W. A. 1966. Habituation: A model phenomenon for the study of neuronal substrates of behavior. *Psychol. Rev.* 173:16–43

Thompson, S. H. 1977. Three pharmacologically distinct potassium channels in molluscan neurones. *J. Physiol.* 265:465–88

Thorndike, E. L. 1911. *Animal Intelligence*. New York: Macmillan

Tischler, M. D., Davis, M. 1983. A visual pathway that mediates fear conditioned enhancement of acoustic startle. *Brain Res.* 276:55–71

Traub, R. D., Llinas, R. 1979. Hippocampal pyramidal cells: Significance of dendritic ionic conductances for neuronal function and epileptogenesis. *J. Neurophysiol.* 42:476–96

Trendelenburg, W. 1915. Untersuchungen uber den ausgleich der bewegungsstorungen nach rindenausschaltungen am affengrosshirn. *Z. Biol.* 65:103–38

Treves, Z., Aggazzotti, A. 1901. Essai d'education du pigeon prive des hemispheres cerebraux. *Arch. Ital. Biol.* 36:189–91

Triestman, S. N. 1981. Effect of adenosine 3', 5'-monophosphate on neuronal pacemaker activity: A voltage clamp analysis. *Science* 211:59–61

Truex, R. C., Carpenter, M. B. 1969. *Human Neuroanatomy*. Baltimore: Williams & Wilkins. 6th ed.

Truman, J. W., Reiss, S. E. 1976. Dendritic reorganization of an identified motoneuron during metamorphosis of the tobacco hornworm moth. *Science* 192:477–79

Tsien, R. W. 1983. Calcium channels in excitable cell membranes. *Ann. Rev. Physiol.* 45:341–58

Tsukahara, N., Fujito, Y., Kubota, M. 1983. Specificity of the newly-firmed corticorubral synapses in the kitten red nucleus. *Exp. Brain Res.* 51:45–56

Tsukahara, N., Fujito, Y., Oda, Y., Maeda, J. 1982. Formation of functional synapses in the adult cat red nucleus from the cerebrum following cross-innervation of forelimb flexor and extensor nerves: I. Appearance of new synaptic potentials. *Exp. Brain Res.* 45:1–12

Tsukahara, N., Oda, Y., Notsu, T. 1981.

Classical conditioning mediated by the red nucleus in the cat. *J. Neurosci.* 1:72–79

Turner, D. A. 1984. Segmental cable evaluation of somatic transients in hippocampal neurons (CA1, CA3, and Dentate). *Biophys. J.* 46:73–84

Turner, D. A., Schwartzkroin, P. A. 1980. Steady-state electronic analysis of intracellularly stained hippocampal neurons. *J. Neurophysiol.* 44:184–99

Ukhtomsky, A. A. 1926. Concerning the condition of excitation in dominance. *Nov. Refl. Fiziol. Nerv. Sist.* 2:3–15; also see Ukhtomsky, A. A. 1927. *Psychol. Abstr.* 1:581

Ukhtomsky, A. A. 1950. *Parabiosis and the Dominant*. Collected works, Vol. 1. Leningrad: Lzd. LGU (In Russian).; also see Ukhtomsky, A. A. 1911. *On the dependence of cortical motor reactions upon central associated influences*. Moscow (In Russian)

Van Harreveld, A., Fifkova, E. 1975. Swelling of dendritic spines in the fascia dentata after stimulation of the perforant fibers as a mechanism of post-tetanic potentiation. *Exp. Neurol.* 49:736–49

Van Harreveld, A., Steiner, I. 1970. The magnitude of the extracellular space in electron micrography of superficial and deep regions of the cerebral cortex. *J. Cell. Sci.* 6:793–805

Victor, M., Adams, R. D., Collins, G. H. 1971. *Wernicke-Korsakoff Syndrome*. Philadelphia: Davis

Voronin, L. L. 1974. A study of neurophysiological mechanisms of learning on a simple behavioral model. *Proc. Int. Congr. Physiol. Sci., 26th, New Delhi* 10:79–80

Voronin, L. L. 1980. Microelectrode analysis of the cellular mechanisms of conditioned reflex in rabbits. *Acta Neurobiol. Exp.* 40:335–70

Voronin, L. L. 1983. Long-term potentiation in the hippocampus. *Neuroscience* 10:1051–69

Voronin, L. L., Gerstein, G., Kudriashov, I. E., Ioffe, S. V. 1975. Elaboration of a conditioned reflex in a single experiment with simultaneous recording of neural activity. *Brain Res.* 92:385–403

Wagner, A. R., Thomas, E., Norton, T. 1967. Conditioning with electrical stimulation of motor cortex: Evidence of a possible source of motivation. *J. Comp. Physiol. Psychol.* 64:191–99

Walters, E. T., Byrne, J. H. 1983. Associative conditioning of single sensory neurons suggests a cellular mechanism for learning. *Science* 219:405–8

Walters, E. T., Carew, T. J., Hawkins, R. D., Kandel, E. R. 1982. Classical conditioning in *Aplysia:* Neuronal circuits involved in associative learning. See Woody 1982c, pp. 677–95

Webster, W. R., Aitken, L. M. 1975. Central auditory processing. In *Handbook of Psychobiology*, ed. M. S. Gazzaniga, C. Blakemore, pp. 325–65. New York: Academic

Weight, F. F., Votava, J. 1971. Slow synaptic excitation in sympathetic ganglion cells: Evidence for synaptic inactivation of potassium conductance. *Science* 170:755–58

Weinberger, N. M. 1982a. Effects of conditioned arousal on the auditory nervous system. In *The Neural Basis of Behavior*, ed. A. L. Beckman. Jamaica, NY: Spectrum

Weinberger, N. M. 1982b. Sensory plasticity and learning: The magnocellular medial geniculate nucleus of the auditory system. See Woody 1982c, pp. 697–710

Weisz, D. J., Solomon, P. R., Thompson, R. F. 1980. The hippocampus appears necessary for trace conditioning. *Bull. Psychon. Soc. Abstr.* 193:244

Wine, J. J., Krasne, F. B. 1972. The organization of escape behaviour in the crayfish. *J. Exp. Biol.* 56:1–18

Wong, B., Woody, C. D. 1978. Recording intracellularly with potassium ion sensitive electrodes from single cortical neurons in awake cats. *Exp. Neurol.* 61:219–25

Woody, C. D. 1962. *Some aspects of information processing in the CNS.* Honors thesis. Harvard Med. Sch., Boston, MA

Woody, C. D. 1977. Changes in activity and excitability of cortical auditory receptive units of the cat as a function of different behavioral states. *Ann. NY Acad. Sci.* 290:180–99

Woody, C. D. 1982a. *Memory, Learning, and Higher Function: A Cellular View.* New York: Springer-Verlag

Woody, C. D. 1982b. Neurophysiologic correlates of latent facilitation. See Woody 1982c, pp. 233–48

Woody, C. D., ed. 1982c. *Conditioning: Representation of Involved Neural Functions.* New York: Plenum

Woody, C. D. 1982d. Acquisition of conditioned facial reflexes in the cat: Cortical control of different facial movements. *Fed. Proc.* 41:2160–68

Woody, C. D. 1984a. Studies of Pavlovian eyeblink conditioning in awake cats. In *Neurobiology of Learning and Memory*, ed. G. Lynch, J. L. McGaugh, N. M. Weinberger, pp. 181–96. New York: Guilford

Woody, C. D. 1984b. The electrical excitability of nerve cells as an index of learned behavior. See Camardo et al 1984, pp. 101–27

Woody, C. D., Alkon, D. L., Hay, B. 1984. Depolarization-induced effects of intracellularly applied calcium-calmodulin dependent protein kinase in neurons of the motor cortex of cats. *Brain Res.* 321:192–97

Woody, C. D., Black-Cleworth, P. 1973. Differences in excitability of cortical neurons as a function of motor projection in conditioned cats. *J. Neurophysiol.* 36:1104–16

Woody, C. D., Brozek, G. 1969a. Gross potential from facial nucleus of cat as an index of neural activity in response to glabella tap. *J. Neurophysiol.* 32:704–16

Woody, C. D., Brozek, G. 1969b. Changes in evoked responses from facial nucleus of cat with conditioning and extinction of eye blink. *J. Neurophysiol.* 32:717–26

Woody, C. D., Engel, J. Jr. 1972. Changes in unit activity and thresholds to electrical microstimulation at coronal–pericruciate cortex of cat with classical conditioning of different facial movements. *J. Neurophysiol.* 35:230–41

Woody, C. D., Gruen, E. 1977. Comparison of excitation of single cortical neurons in awake cats by extracellularly and intracellularly delivered current. *Soc. Neurosci. Abstr.* 3:1667

Woody, C. D., Gruen, E. 1978. Characterization of electrophysiological properties of intracellularly recorded neurons in the neocortex of awake cats: A comparison of the response to injected current in spike overshoot and undershoot neurons. *Brain Res.* 158:343–57

Woody, C. D., Kim, E. H.-J., Berthier, N. E. 1983. Effects of hypothalamic stimulation on unit responses recorded from neurons of sensorimotor cortex of awake cats during conditioning. *J. Neurophysiol.* 49:780–91

Woody, C. D., Knispel, J. D., Crow, T. J., Black-Cleworth, P. 1976. Activity and excitability to electrical current of cortical auditory receptive neurons of awake cats as affected by stimulus association. *J. Neurophysiol.* 39:1045–61

Woody, C. D., Nenov, V., Gruen, E., Donley, P., Vivian, M., et al. 1985. A voltage-dependent, 4-aminopyridine sensitive, outward current studied *in vivo* in cortical neurons of awake cats by voltage squeeze techniques. *Soc. Neurosci. Abstr.* 11:955

Woody, C. D., Ribak, C. E., Sakai, M., Sakai, H., Swartz, B. 1981. Pressure microinjection for the purposes of cell identification and subsequent ultramicroscopic analysis. In *Current Trends in Morphological Techniques*, ed. J. E. Johnson Jr., 2:219–40. Boca Raton, FL: CRC Press

Woody, C. D., Swartz, B. E., Gruen, E. 1978. Effects of acetylcholine and cyclic GMP on input resistance of cortical neurons in awake cats. *Brain Res.* 158:373–95

Woody, C. D., Vassilevsky, N. N., Engel, J. Jr. 1970. Conditioned eye blink: Unit activity at coronal–precruciate cortex of the cat. *J. Neurophysiol.* 33:851–64

Woody, C. D., Yarowsky, P. J. 1972. Conditioned eye blink using electrical stimulation of coronal–precruciate cortex as conditional stimulus. *J. Neurophysiol.* 35:242–52

Woody, C. D., Yarowsky, P. J., Owens, J., Black-Cleworth, P., Crow, T. 1974. Effect of lesions of cortical motor areas on acquisition of eyeblink in the cat. *J. Neurophysiol.* 37:385–94

Woolacott, M. H., Hoyle, G. 1976. Membrane resistance changes associated with single, identified neuron learning. *Soc. Neurosci. Abstr.* 2:339

Woolacott, M. H., Hoyle, G. 1977. Neural events underlying learning: Changes in pacemaker. *Proc. R. Soc. London Ser. B* 195:395–415

Yeo, C. H., Hardiman, M. J., Glickstein, M. 1984. Discrete lesions of the cerebellar cortex abolish the classically conditioned nictitating membrane response of the rabbit. *Behav. Brain Res.* 13:261–66

Young, R. A., Cegavske, C. F., Thompson, R. F. 1976. Tone-induced changes in excitability of abducens motor neurons and of the reflex path of nictitating membrane response in rabbit. *J. Comp. Physiol. Psychol.* 90:424–34

Zieglgansberger, W., Sothmann, G., Herz, A. 1974. Iontophoretic release of substances from micropipettes in vitro. *Neuropharmacology* 13:417

Ann. Rev. Psychol. 1986. 37:495–521
Copyright © 1986 by Annual Reviews Inc. All rights reserved

VISUAL SENSITIVITY

T. E. Cohn and D. J. Lasley

School of Optometry, University of California, Berkeley, California 94720

CONTENTS

INTRODUCTION 495
   Theoretical Framework 497
   The Normative Model 498
   Outline 499
   Measuring Sensitivity 499
NOISE LIMITS 501
   Role of Noise in Visual Sensitivity 501
   Noise and Physiological Mechanisms 502
   Limiting Mechanisms 502
   Absolute Threshold 503
SUMMATION 506
   Summation and Uncertainty 506
   Summation and Postreceptor Mechanisms 507
   Luminance Change Detection: Interocular Interactions 508
   Color Mechanisms 510
   Acuity 511
UNCERTAINTY 512
   Psychometric Functions 514
DISCRIMINATION 516
CONCLUSIONS 517

INTRODUCTION

"Cogito, ergo sum." In his *Meditations on the First Philosophy in which the existence of God and the real distinction between the soul and the body of man are demonstrated,* Descartes (Sutcliffe 1968) states: "It is some time ago now since I perceived that, from my earliest years, I had accepted many false opinions as being true, and that what I had since based on such insecure principles could only be most doubtful and uncertain; so that I had to undertake seriously once in my life to rid myself of all the opinions I had adopted up to

495

then, and begin afresh from the foundations, if I wished to establish something firm and constant in the sciences."

Descartes' aim in his meditations was to establish a firm foundation for Science. Unfortunately, the bedrock he found with his method of doubt was a distinction that we all still accept uncritically to greater or lesser extent (Ryle 1949). It is, that there is a fundamental distinction between the domain of the "thinking" substance ("the soul") and all that remains ("the body of man"). In Descartes' view, only the latter was the legitimate object of scientific (empirical) inquiry, as opposed to the "revealed truth" of religion. Logic and a few "indisputable" assumptions could suffice to construct a way of viewing mental activity that was, in some sense, complete. With this we agree with Descartes, provided the assumptions are carefully chosen. The assumptions Descartes chose were the principle of Causality and the notion that the idea of a perfect being (God) implies a cause by a perfect agent (God). We undertake a more modest goal and adopt more limited assumptions. We assume that the brain strives for optimal performance in a given task. We also assume that the visual system possesses intrinsic noise, whose presence can be demonstrated readily and whose effect controls in large measure what we term visual sensitivity.

The latter of these is an assumption that many have doubted, and even now it is frequently given only lip service. Many years ago, Hecht et al (1942), Tanner & Swets (1954), and Barlow (1956) paid explicit attention to the existence of noise and argued that the *optimal* discrimination of visual signals from noise could explain certain human visual behavior. In the years since, this approach and model of visual detection has been accorded only limited acceptance. Use of the term "threshold" is a good example of a different sort of thinking. Prior to the 1940s, a "threshold" was regarded as a barrier never exceeded by noise alone (Hecht et al 1942, Sakitt 1972). As negative evidence accumulated, the threshold theory was modified to permit two state thresholds, and then multistate thresholds. Even now a popular formulation of probability summation (see below) in current use explicitly precludes any but the concept of the threshold in its purest (and most improbable) form. The resistance to the signal/noise approach may be, in part, a holdover from the 19th century, something which Ryle (1949) has contemptuously called the "ghost in the machine" which is an expression he used to describe Cartesian dualism. Noise such as random fluctuations in membrane potential could not possibly sully the psychic domain. Perhaps the problem is simply that we as visual scientists come to grips with the primary objects of our science long before we are taught its methods. Consequently, the eminent vision scientist who once confided that "he had never seen any target-like visual noise" seemed unaware of the flawed antecedents of such a conclusion. No one has ever seen an atom either, but we know that it exists. The evidence for noise is no less compelling.

Eight years have passed since the publication of the last review of visual sensitivity by Macleod (1978). While the physiological diversity and its psychophysical manifestations so elegantly explained in the prior review continue to grow unabated, the beginnings of a rather general understanding also may be emerging. The major components of the thesis of the present paper are as follows: 1. Noise, either intrinsic to visual stimuli or to the observer, provides an irreducible limit on visual behavior. 2. Information-losing neural transformations such as the mathematically simple operations of addition and subtraction among parallel channels, combined with the assumption of optimal detection of noise-obscured signals, can go a long way toward explaining what appear to be rather diverse phenomena of visual sensitivity, spatial and temporal vision, color vision, and binocular vision.

Our materials have been drawn mainly from *Science, Nature, Vision Research, Journal of the Optical Society of America* (Series A as of 1984), *Journal of Physiology, Journal of General Physiology, Perception and Psychophysics*, and *Biological Cybernetics*. Abstracts have only rarely been cited. Results from spatial vision or color vision, ordinarily treated in different chapters of the *Annual Review of Psychology*, have been included insofar as they shed light on sensitivity and because of the increasingly blurred distinctions among those subjects. Citations are intended to be illustrative and reflect work with which we are most familiar. Many appropriate ones are therefore not included because of space limitations. In many cases the work cited was aimed at answering substantive questions other than those that we address. However, the work cited will supply the reader with useful references for specialized areas of the literature not treated in depth here.

Inasmuch as our approach rests on the Theory of Signal Detectability (TSD), we answer the question "Can you recommend a good signal detection reference?" as follows: A general compendium of early articles (Swets 1964), good texts (Green & Swets 1974, Egan 1975), and the only comprehensive review of the methods as applied in vision (Nachmias 1972) are all well worth consulting.

Before outlining the subject matter of the review, we first state our basic theoretical framework and then describe the normative model of the ideal photon detector.

Theoretical Framework

The essence of our approach is an elaboration of how vision ideally ought to occur (the normative theory) in an arbitrarily chosen task (detection) and then a comparison of theory to the results of experiments showing how vision really occurs (the data), the important step being the listing of discrepancies between the two (inferred degradations of the ideal).

This approach is rooted in physical theory, which is necessary, for ultimately it is a physicophysiological theory of visual sensitivity that is sought. The approach is best exemplified by an example provided by its earliest practitioners, Hecht, Shlaer & Pirenne (1942). In that study, the authors pitted the human eye, on the one hand, against the physically ideal eye (perfect photon counter) on the other. Quite aside from the substance of their results, they showed that the virtue of this comparative process was the production of viable physiological hypotheses. For example, in their study it proved necessary to hypothesize a 90% attenuation in the number of light quanta incident at the cornea to match observed performance. Other physical measurements supported such an idea, and to this day the idea of an attenuating filter [within 3 db of their estimate (see Barlow 1977)] is well accepted. This was an early use of a normative theory in the study of vision and serves as the starting point for the present work because it utilized for the first time the normative theory of the ideal photon counter.

The work of three other authors has helped to shape both the field of visual sensitivity and our approach. Tanner & Swets (1954) applied TSD to the field of vision research in an often cited paper. That theory was coupled to a analytical framework known as Receiver Operating Characteristic (ROC) Analysis which allowed the computation of ideal detection for an unlimited array of stimulus situations involving stimuli obscured by noise (as for example the absolute threshold experiment of Hecht et al 1942). It also provided methodological tools, including objective measures of sensitivity and efficiency, that removed the confounding of criterial and sensitivity influences by explicitly accounting for (and measuring) the performance of the decision mechanism.

The other major contributor to the basic structure of this field is H. B. Barlow. In an early paper (1956) he introduced the concept of the ideal detector with an internal degradation. He hypothesized and showed evidence for events in the dark ("dark light") indistinguishable from events caused by light, a concept for which evidence continues to accumulate. In addition to a long history of significant contributions in this area, he has published valuable reviews and tutorials (Barlow 1964b, 1981).

The Normative Model

The model of the ideal photon detector contains elements that have appeared separately in a number of places. One component is the ideal photon counter of Hecht et al (1942), which is a device that reports the quantal count in a fixed space-time frame. The other component, whose configuration depends upon the task assigned it, is the ideal decison maker of Tanner & Swets (1954). In the signal detection (yes/no) task employed by Hecht et al, it utilizes the count by computing a likelihood ratio (a decision variable that can be shown to be monotonic with quantal count) which is then compared to a cutoff. The cutoff is chosen to maximize the expected value of the observer's decisions based upon the costs and values of the various outcomes and the probability of stimulus. Receiver operating characteristic (ROC) analysis (Peterson et al 1954) both assists one to compute performance predicted of the ideal device, given the task, and also allows one to examine the performance of a real detector. With

ROC analysis, differences between real and ideal performance can be quantified. Despite the simplicity of this model, it provides a useful starting point for examining the complexities of the visual system.

A note on TSD is warranted. When introduced 30 years ago, TSD was successful in initial tests of certain of its predictions (Tanner & Swets 1954), but soon thereafter, negative results for other predictions emerged and that list continued to grow. This apparent failure of the ideal detector should not be considered grounds for dismissing TSD, but rather the basis for adopting explicit degradations to the ideal detector in order to model real eyes. The list of failures is in fact part of the list of degradations that we shall offer as the beginnings of an explanation of visual sensitivity.

Outline

Having argued for the value of a normative theory of visual sensitivity, we now outline the subject matter of this review. The review treats topics of traditional interest to the visual scientist such as limits on sensitivity, adaptation, and summation, and dwells as well on less traditional areas such as the effects of noise, visual uncertainty, and the relation between visual identification and visual detection. The review emphasizes results, mostly of the past eight years, that bear on either similarities between human sensitivity and ideal sensitivity as defined in the normative model or degradations of the model that are needed to explain departures from attainable (ideal) sensitivity. The degradations fall into several categories. First we consider noise in its various guises and how it lowers sensitivity. Then we discuss information-losing neural transformations and how, coupled with noise, these influence sensitivity. (Response nonlinearities are not emphasized in this review. As we point out below, many types of nonlinearities need not affect sensitivity). Then we discuss the potent effects of "uncertainty" upon sensitivity, which can arise in the presence of noise. Uncertainty can, in turn, lead to "transducer-like" behavioral nonlinearities. Finally, we explore some new results at the interface between detection and identification, tending to suggest that the whole of visual threshold behavior can be approached through the auspices of a single normative sensitivity model. In the interest of examining physiological phenomena that bear on visual sensitivity and to circumvent the near-absence of data from early retinal elements of mammalian models, we will step from one species to the next as if no differences existed.

Measuring Sensitivity

The concept of visual sensitivity has evolved dramatically in the past several decades. Prior to the 1950s, sensitivity was measured as the increase of the threshold energy or energy of a stimulus that was "just seen." The introduction of TSD (Tanner & Swets 1954) focused attention upon performance apart from threshold and independent of criterion factors (see Green & Swets 1974, p.

126). Readers will no doubt be quite familiar with the measure of sensitivity, detectability (d'), its nonparametric cousin probability correct, $P(C)$, and the method of obtaining and utilizing ROC curves to find these and related measures. An unfortunate overemphasis has been placed upon the existence of the criterion-free sensitivity measure, resulting in neglect of the normative model provided by TSD.

While detectability (d') has come to be a familiar parameter to many in the field, the major emphasis of much methodological progress of recent years has been upon the development of fixed performance level (threshold) seeking algorithms usually called staircases. Staircases were introduced in vision by Cornsweet (1962) for the purpose of rapidly converging on a constant stimulus level, termed the "threshold." If performance was too good, the stimulus could be lowered in energy, if too poor it could be raised. The implicit assumption is that such a set of rules would lead to convergence and this is so, provided the observer does not change his cutoff midway through a determination. Recent contributions to the methods of staircases have emphasized speed and accuracy of determination. Quest (Watson & Pelli 1983) optimally uses prior trials to estimate the sought-after level. Each variant on the staircase theme has implicit within it a performance level upon which the process converges in well-defined situations. The art (or architecture) of staircase design is to optimize a variety of parameters. These may include the starting stimulus level, the step size and rules for altering it, and the stopping rules. Coupling the staircase to two-alternative forced choice techniques solves the wandering criterion problem. One result is that we can now measure "thresholds" more precisely than ever before, at a time when finally many doubt both their existence and their utility in model making.

PHYSIOLOGICAL SENSITIVITY   Sensory scientists have long tried to compare sensitivity determined psychophysically with that determined physiologically. Traditional sensitivity measures, being measures of stimulus energy to achieve a defined endpoint, lent some confidence because they were specified in the same units, but that is only a necessary condition for success. When one analyzes the basis for the two measures they are very different. In the former case we have the stimulus that the observer says he just sees. In the latter case we have, for example, the stimulus whose neural response an experimenter just detects. Even if observer and experimenter are one and the same person, which often is the case, imagine the stringency of assumptions required to bring these measurables into line! On the other hand, ROC analysis can serve as a basis for both types of measurement. A number of laboratories have employed these techniques to get physiological estimates of sensitivity for single cells ranging from photoreceptors (Cohn 1983) to ganglion cells (Levick et al 1983) to cortical neurons (Tolhurst et al 1983, Bradley et al 1985). Riggs (1983) predicts increased use of these tools in vision.

NOISE LIMITS

Noise is defined as a stochastic disturbance that obscures information of interest. A large diversity of types of noise has been identified in the visual system. Noise may arise externally, as in the quantum character of light (Hecht et al 1942, Cohn 1976, Geisler 1984, Geisler & Davila 1985), or in the statistics intrinsic to non-Poisson sources (Teich & Saleh 1981). Stochastic fluctuations of eye position, accommodation, and pupil size obviously can contribute noise to the internal correlates of visual stimuli.

Photoreceptors themselves contribute noise to visual signals. The noise falls into at least two categories. Quantum bumps were described for invertebrate photoreceptors (Yeandle 1958) and later for vertebrate rods by Baylor et al (1979) and for mammalian cones by Nunn et al (1984). These are discrete, stereotyped, transient excursions from the baseline membrane current or potential. The bumps themselves can be of variable amplitude and time of occurrence that can lead to a multiplicative noise (Lillywhite 1981). Second, the membrane potential in rods (Schwartz 1977) and in cones (Simon et al 1975) and membrane current (Baylor et al 1980) exhibits a light-dependent variability. It is in the nature of membranes to be noisy. The spectral quality of this noise places some of it outside of physiological limits, it being filtered out at the first synapse (Schwartz 1977, Ashmore & Copenhagen 1980, Ashmore & Falk 1977, 1980).

Each subsequent neural stage presumably can introduce its own contribution to this array, owing to 1. the irreducible physical necessity for stochastic behavior of synapses mediated by molecular events (Falk & Fatt 1974) resulting in doubly stochastic processes (Teich et al 1982), 2. the thermal fluctuations of membrane potential due to resistivity, and 3. to the action of finite numbers of pores and of ionic visitors to and from the cell. This list is quite long and one needs some guideposts to sort out which if any of the sources of stochastic behavior bears on performance in a given task. In this regard, use of the engineering approach of "referring noise to the input" is promising (Ahumada & Watson 1985).

Role of Noise in Visual Sensitivity

Tasks involving sensitivity by definition are those in which errors are made, and errors arise only if there is noise. Noise then has the status of an obligatory entity in visual models. It is not optional. One senior vision scientist is fond of saying that he doesn't care to consider noise until he has understood the "signals." Unfortunately, the two go together. One has no choice but to consider noise, for along with the stimulus, it is a co-equal determinant of sensitivity. The field of visual sensitivity has shown a remarkable and rapid evolution in this regard. A decade ago, most vision models that included noise did so only implicitly. Now the model maker cannot present a formulation without being asked how he/she has accounted for noise in the model.

The three works cited above, upon which the present analysis is based, each dealt with noise in a revolutionary way. Hecht et al (1942) examined the noise inherent in their stimuli. That was a first. They also examined and rejected (erroneously, Cohn 1981) the possibility of a decision criterion noise of internal origin. Tanner & Swets (1954) showed the descriptive value of a noise-based theory of visual sensitivity. Their contributions centered on the importance of events that occurred in the absence of the stimulus. Chief among these was the false alarm, an erroneous report of detection whose theoretical importance is now known to equal that of the frequency-of-seen, the basis for the traditional measure of visual sensitivity. Tanner and Swets were able to show that visual performance had to be specified upon at least two dimensions—one dealing with sensitivity, and the other dealing with the decision criterion. Measuring only the frequency-of-seeing function confounded these two. Finally, Barlow's (1956) contribution was to advance the hypothesis that the noise responsible for setting the sensitivity limit (known as the absolute threshold) could be quantified, localized, and identified with a precision that only now we can begin to appreciate. In Barlow's view, "dark noise" results from the spontaneous decomposition of visual photopigment. This step marked the beginning of efforts to find internal limitations on visual sensitivity.

Noise and Physiological Mechanisms

A given source of noise might or might not affect performance depending on its magnitude in comparison to other sources of noise in the chain of events. But the matter is made far more complex by the parallel organization at each level beyond the photoreceptors (Lennie 1980, Nelson et al 1981). Additional complicating factors are nonlinearities of processing that occur in each level of organization and inefficiencies of the decision process (Burgess et al 1981).

The present view is that one or several mechanisms in the parallel array most nearly "tuned" in its response properties to the given stimulus is the one that has the largest response to the stimulus and which therefore determines the sensitivity to it (Teller 1980, Watson et al 1983). If all mechanisms were equally noisy, this view would be correct, but if one cannot justify an equal noisiness assumption, then a more general proposition must be entertained. It is that in a given parallel array the mechanisms of maximum signal-to-noise ratio (SNR) are those whose properties are most strongly manifest in behavior.

Limiting Mechanisms

Leaving aside consideration of decision process inefficiencies, the question of which mechanism (channel, feature detector) limits performance is another way of asking which one is manifest in performance. Consider the cascade of elements in which the mechanisms with the maximum SNR appear. The least sensitive element of that chain is the one whose properties are manifest in behavior (Teller 1980). This leads to a final subtlety. Behavior is uninfluenced by nonlinearities after the site of the limiting noise ("Birdsall's theorem" stated and proved in Lasley & Cohn 1981b).

There have been a number of recent attempts to examine the variability of responses of neural elements at several levels of neural processing such as the photoreceptor (Baylor et al 1980), the bipolar (Ashmore & Falk 1977), and retinal ganglion cells (Cohn et al 1975, Levick et al 1983, Frishman & Levine 1983). The nature of the variability can itself supply insights as to the underlying mechanisms. For example, Mastronarde (1983) reports correlated noise in the spontaneous activity of neighboring retinal ganglion cells and concludes that this results from a distal source of noise. That accords well with the conclusions of Levick et al (1983), who show that the high quantum efficiency of these cells requires that their noisiness comes exclusively from the stimulus, something that neighboring cells would certainly share provided they heard from the same photoreceptors.

Response properties and the beginnings of quantification of response variability are known for other elements in the chain including the neurons in the primary cortical receiving area for vision (Dean 1981, Tolhurst et al 1983, Bradley et al 1985). Unfortunately, there is not now enough information in hand to know under given conditions which element is limiting and thus which is manifest in behavior (e.g. which is being studied in a psychophysical task).

Absolute Threshold

Under conditions of absolute threshold, or even for weak adapting lights, the circumstances are noisiest but ironically easiest to understand. Under these conditions two sources of noise predominate in behavior. These are "dark noise," the photon-like events that occur in the dark, and quantal noise, the fluctuation in the arriving photon stream. In the case of quantal noise the marked influence is traceable to simple mathematics. The variability of a photon stream (expressed as the standard deviation of the arriving photon count in a given interval divided by the mean) is highest for weakest lights. In fact, under conditions that are "physiological," in the sense that measurable responses can be obtained, this ratio can lie near unity. This must swamp the influence of all other sources of noise and may be the reason why a number of studies have reported quantum limited absolute or increment thresholds (Cohn 1976, Krauskopf & Reeves 1980, Levick et al 1983). In the dark, the dark noise is quite obvious in both single cell recordings (cited above) and in psychophysical data (Barlow 1956). What makes this so is less plain, however. To understand this, one must digress into the subject of the gain of physiological mechanisms, a subject matter intimately tied to light adaptation and its effects, and one sometimes utilized as a proxy for sensitivity. If we idealize the visual system in a given task as a cascade of nervous elements, commencing with the photoreceptor and ending with decision center neurons, it can be appreciated that, in addition to the noise they introduce, each nervous element can be characterized by the gain with which it passes signals on to the next stage.

Nervous elements act as if they possess an adjustable gain so as to maintain the responses to likely stimuli in an acceptable physiological range (Normann & Werblin 1974, Barlow 1981, Laughlin 1981, Ohzawa et al 1982), for it is well known that nervous elements function effectively over a far narrower range than the stimuli that they must signal.

Now consider the condition of no ambient illumination. Signals correlated with light are especially valuable in a biological sense, and so the gain in each successive element is likely to be at its highest possible setting. Consequently, distal sources of noise benefit disproportionately in comparison to proximal sources. On the other hand, when ambient illumination is ample, gains must all be reduced and so dark noise events suffer greatly with each successive stage of attenuation. There is ample evidence consistent with this story, that dark noise has a measurable influence on sensitivity, but only at or near absolute threshold (Barlow 1956, Sakitt 1972, Levick et al 1983). Physiological estimates of the magnitude of dark light of about 0.01 isomerizations per sec per rod (Barlow 1977) are very close to those obtained psychophysically (Baylor et al 1980).

The story presented by Hecht et al (1942) some four decades ago has changed very little in the intervening period. The sensitivity of the eye in the dark seems limited by the stochastic nature of light. A single photon that isomerizes a molecule of photopigment is signaled up the neural chain under conditions where it is unlikely that the photoreceptor can have caught any other quanta. Nonetheless, there are two "buts" to this story. The first is that some photoreceptors are coupled electrically at absolute threshold in such a way that if one receives a quantum, many signal it. The second "but" arises in the quantitative consideration of just how much light is available to perform the task in question compared to how much the observer appears to use. The formalism used for this comparison is the so-called detective quantum efficiency (Rose 1948), a scalar quantity that estimates the fraction of available photons actually used in the task by the observer on the implicit assumption of no other noise. Recent estimates (Barlow 1977, van Meeteren & Barlow 1981, Teich et al 1982, Kersten & Barlow 1985) place this value at roughly 0.5. In other words, when media and photopigment losses have been taken into account, it appears that only one in two quanta signaled is used by the observer in the task. Of course, the model underlying this computation is not secure, and few think that the problem is simply one of lost light. A variety of experiments aimed at uncovering the nature of this inefficiency are converging on the conclusion that the source of it is central, possibly in the decision process (Burgess et al 1981, van Meeteren & Barlow 1981). Others (Lillywhite 1981, Teich et al 1982) place the problem in or near the transducer, arising from multiplicative noise effects. A third possibility (Cohn 1981) is that uncertainty for the parameters of the stimulus to be detected leads to a performance decrement (the uncertainty effect). Critical experiments capable of rejecting even one of these alternatives have not yet been performed.

LIGHT ADAPTATION AND DARK ADAPTATION   The defining characteristic of the phenomenon termed adaptation is sensitivity change. The need for this is as apparent to the photographer as it is to the physiologist. Visual neurons, like photographic film, work well over a narrow range. In the case of developed film, a range of transmissivity of 100:1 is uncommonly large. The range of signaling depends on both the maximum and minimum values possible. Ganglion cells might signal responses with as many as 100 action potentials per second. Photoreceptors are constrained to maximum polarization of perhaps 70 mV. One action potential is a practical minimum in terms of both speed of response and in terms of the variability of the spontaneous discharge against which interpolated spikes are to be detected. Likewise, slow potentials exhibit a noisy baseline ranging as high as one to several millivolts. Such constraints impose limits in a single cell of roughly a two decade range of signaling. Thus the purpose of adaptation, to keep nervous elements operating in their useful range, is clear. What is not so clear is why sensitivity is such a complex function of the adapting or background level.

At the time of the last review of visual sensitivity (Macleod 1978), the view prevailed that nonlinearities that could keep cells behaving properly could nonetheless not serve as an explanation for the entire sensitivity change. In this review, we can report the addition of noise to the picture. One of the most interesting findings has been produced with the very powerful technique of suction electrode recording in which a photoreceptor outer segment is partially ingested by the recording electrode. On this plan one measures current generated in the outer segment. Baylor & Lamb (1982) showed that a light sufficient to bleach about 5% of the photopigment caused a change in responsivity over the length of the outer segment. Further tests showed that the change induced by light is localized to parts of the outer segment, produces there a noise whose power declines over time (Lamb 1981), and this accords with a prediction made some time ago by Barlow (1964a).

Adaptation by steady light has been shown to occur both in receptor and in the postreceptoral network, although rods show less of a change than cones (Hayhoe 1979, Cicerone & Green 1980a, Green & Powers 1982, Copenhagen & Green 1985). Dark adaptation is likewise both receptoral and more proximal (Cicerone & Green 1980b). Moreover, the coupling between receptors that may be an information-losing interaction (Torre et al 1983), and which has been best demonstrated at absolute threshold, appears to persist under light-adapted conditions (Green 1985).

In addition to multiple adaptation sites, there is evidence for more than one type of adaptation. Adelson (1979), for example, has argued for a rapid multiplicative followed by a slower subtractive adaptation process, the latter having been shown by Enroth-Cugell et al (1975).

SUMMATION

A topic traditionally included in a review of sensitivity is that of summation. In classic studies of vision, sensitivity, measured as the inverse of visual threshold ΔI, was found for various values of a physical parameter such as stimulus area. The largest value of this parameter for which the inverse relation $\Delta I = KA$ was found to hold is called the summation area. It was presumed to be the area of visual space over which photons could be physically or physiologically summed. Barlow (1964b) has pointed out, however, that this inference depends on two critical implicit assumptions: (a) that nonquantal noise limits sensitivity and (b) that the detector sums quanta only over the area of the target. If the first assumption is false, then the summing area is the largest value for which the square root relation (Piper's law) holds. In their experiment, Hecht et al (1942) chose a stimulus area considerably smaller than the actual summing area, thereby not optimizing the stimulus as they had set out to do. This and a comparable error for stimulus duration may have led to an underestimate of quantum efficiency.

Ideal photon detectors should exhibit Piper's law as should any quantum fluctuation limited detector. At high adaptation levels, where summation areas are said to be lower, internal noise should limit and then Ricco's law should hold. One can see that the summation area inferred from area-threshold data depends upon how sensitivity limits are modeled. It may be that summation effects attributed to basic physiological processes may be caused instead by mismanagement of the applicable models. For example, summation area has long been thought to change with adaptation level, but this conclusion is based upon implicit and untested assumptions about the nature of the limiting noise, as well as the assumption that the noise is a stationary process. Additionally, stimulus uncertainty may produce summation mediated by decision processes rather than distal physiological elements.

Summation and Uncertainty

While we devote an extensive section below to the notion of stimulus uncertainty and its effect on visual sensitivity, we point out here that uncertainty can be confounded with large summation area (or time), which is a little-known effect that may prove to be important in interpretation of the abnormally large summation that occurs in infants (Hamer & Schneck 1984), in ocular deficiencies such as amblyopia (Miller 1955), in the periphery and in the dark. The uncertain observer processes information from any spatial locus that could contain the stimulus (Nolte & Jaarsma 1967). It has been shown that near threshold the processing of the uncertain but otherwise optimal observer is asymptotic to that of a device that summed the information from all such loci (Cohn 1978). Hence, one cannot easily distinguish an uncertain observer from one with an abnormally large summation area based upon the data obtained from varying area and intensity (Ricco's Law paradigm). This dictum applies as well to any condition in which changes in summation area are of interest, including adaptation varying effects upon spatial summation. The traditional explanation for that effect—a pooling neuron whose connectivity changes— must be juxtaposed with that of an uncertain decision mechanism whose uncertainty is governed by the variable under study. There has been little experimental work as yet to unravel such possibilities.

Summation and Postreceptor Mechanisms

Barlow (1964b) has pointed out that summation is antithetical to good seeing. The latter requires sorting of incoming light into categories with spatial, temporal, and chromatic labels. A plausible first stage of sorting, and one which is easy to imagine in terms of simple physiological mechanisms, is the computation of differences. If two photoreceptors act oppositely on a subsequent bipolar cell (one inhibits and the other excites), then that bipolar carries information as to spatial contrast. Saleh & Cohn (1978) have shown that such a computation markedly lowers sensitivity, and Gottshalk & Buchsbaum 1983 have demonstrated that, combined with mechanisms for signaling the sum of receptor outputs, such computations retain maximal information concerning pattern.

These principles supply some guidance as to how to view the implications of parallel structures of the visual pathway upon sensitivity. At each level beyond the receptors there is an opportunity for further loss of information (in the sense of absolute sensitivity) on computations, presumably to extract biologically important features. These affect absolute sensitivity only if noise in the elements performing the computations is limiting.

Thus it is somewhat surprising that much psychophysical data as developed below converge to the view that first-level postreceptor structures are sensitivity limiting. This could be viewed as a sign that first-level noise is relatively the most important. It could also result from an arbitrary choice either of tasks or stimuli. Possibly such questions can be resolved by the time of the next review of visual sensitivity. For the present, it is important to remember that sensitivity effects that mirror the properties of cortical neurons (De Valois et al 1974) may provide clues as to circumstances where the noise of those neurons was limiting. In all, the possibility that each level can, under the proper conditions of stimulation, be limiting leaves the visual scientist with great leeway for the construction of composite models that exhibit the appropriate diversity of behavior. Size tuning, for example, is quite compatible with spatial frequency tuning. Helmholtzian trichromacy is likewise compatible with Hering-type opponent colors theory: which is operative depends upon which elements contain the limiting noise.

Luminance Change Detection: Interocular Interactions

The binocular interaction whereby two eyes can be shown to be more sensitive than one provides a useful example of the influence of first-level postreceptor mechanisms and how these can be formulated. The earliest attempts to characterize binocular luminance interactions at threshold involved "probability summation" (Pirenne 1943). This term was used because the early research showed a slight facilitation when identical luminance stimuli were presented to both eyes compared to either eye alone. Guth (1971), however, has shown that "probability summation" is at best a misnomer. The facilitation was clearly less than that predicted by a simple energy summation model (Pirenne 1943). Cohn & Lasley (1976) examined the question of what accounted for binocular improvement using a paradigm exploited earlier by Rashbass (1970). Rashbass studied the interactions between brief increment and decrement flash pairs separated in time. When he covaried the luminance changes of the increment-decrement pair, Rashbass found an iso-sensitivity contour with an elliptical shape. The major axis of the ellipse usually fell along either the positive or negative diagonals in the Cartesian coordinate system, where the axes are the magnitudes respectively of the first and second pulses. The inclination of the major axis was dependent upon the interstimulus interval of the two pulses. Rashbass proposed a model that included a linear (temporal) filter followed by a quadratic operator and an integrator. Such a formulation produces a conic section. It is not difficult to show for the limiting cases of perfect summation between stimulus pairs, as well as for perfect differencing, the asymptotic form of the conic sections are pairs of parallel lines. For perfect summation the two lines are parallel to the negative diagonal, while for perfect differencing they parallel the positive diagonal. Rashbass took pains to point out that his model was only the simplest, but by no means unique, mathematical description of the interaction between temporally separated pulses. In a related theoretical development, Cohn & Lasley (1975, 1976) showed that when the ideal observer combines the outputs of perfect differencing and summing channels that are differentially weighted, the iso-sensitivity contour is elliptical. In their formulation the quadratic nonlinearity arises from the properties of the decision mechanism. We have already seen that when the ideal observer is faced with uncertainty, the psychometric function reflects a nonlinearity which on average (i.e. the average of various estimates of the exponent is about two) could be described as quadratic [see for example Carlson & Cohen (1980), who propose a square law detector].

Cohn & Lasley (1976) also used the Rashbass paradigm to investigate the interaction between increment and decrement pairs where each member of the pair was presented independently to the foveae of the two eyes. They too found an elliptical iso-sensitivity contour, with the major axis along the negative diagonal. They concluded that the two eyes exhibit both summing and differencing, with the summing channels dominant.

Cohn et al (1981) used both a correlated/anticorrelated noise paradigm and a recognition paradigm as a further test of the summing-differencing model. Correlated noise to the two eyes should primarily depress the sensitivity of the summing channels, making the differencing channels relatively more sensitive, leading to an ellipse with the major axis along the positive diagonal. Anti-correlated noise should increase the sensitivity of the summing channels, relative to the differencing channels, so increasing the length of the major axis along the positive diagonal. These predictions were borne out qualitatively, but the iso-threshold contours were in all cases enlarged by the noise as well, indicating both types of noise affected both types of channels. Recognition experiments showed that the like-signed stimuli were processed by different channels than those for opposite signed stimuli.

Legge (1984) examined interocular interactions by using grating stimuli. Sinusoidal gratings were presented to one or both eyes, and increment contrast thresholds were determined monocularly and binocularly with in-phase gratings. The resulting increment contrast versus background contrast (on double log coordinates) threshold functions indicated both a facilitative (pedestal) effect for low contrast background gratings and then a monotonic rising leg with a slope of about .6. Legge adopted a model similar to Rashbass's, but with the addition of a compressive nonlinearity following the integrator and both distal and central sources of additive noise.

Legge's formulation provides a convenient framework within which to examine the general issue of binocular summation. A number of studies in this area begin with the premise that there is a monolithic relationship between monocular and binocular sensitivities. The existence of this premise accounts in part for the surprise that has greeted estimates of binocular improvement that have ranged from just under $\sqrt{2}$ to over 2.0. It should be clear, though, that Legge's distal noise and central noise would affect summation in different ways. For example, summing and differencing mechanisms would be manifest in behavior only if noise arising in them limited performance. A given estimate of improvement depends upon which noise limits. Adaptation level seems to be one promising variable to manipulate in that regard.

Color Mechanisms

The appreciation of color provides strong subjective evidence that signals from various receptors are not simply summed. Models utilizing simply first-level post-receptor mechanisms have proved very effective in describing certain color phenomena. Guth et al (1980) presented a vector model of color vision. This model is essentially a Hering zone theory, where the three receptor primaries feed two opponent chromatic channels and a nonopponent luminance channel. The chromatic channels are modeled as differencing channels (Blue-Red and Red-Green) while the luminance channel is a summing channel (Red+Green). The iso-sensitivity contours of this model, when the task is to detect the presence of a luminance change of a composite of two colored lights added algebraically, could consequently be conic sections such as ellipses. For example, the interested reader could plot the data of Boynton et al (1964), using the method of Rashbass (1970) or Cohn & Lasley (1976; also see Interocular Interactions section) with the normalized magnitude of one colored stimulus on one axis and the other colored light on the remaining axis of a Cartesian coordinate system. Positive increments would be above or to the right of the origin and negative increments below or to the left of the origin. Only two quadrants can be plotted (since one light was the background preventing the other from being a decrement), but one would find elliptical threshold contours. When the wavelengths of the two colors were close together, the points could be fitted by summing ellipses, while differencing ellipses would be found for stimuli with dissimilar wavelengths. Their results would be consistent with the model of Guth et al if it is assumed that the detection task of Boynton et al involved information from mechanisms of both luminance and hue change (vector summing and differencing respectively). The required quadratic nonlinearity would be a consequence of optimal combining of likelihood ratio from the two types of channels (Massof & Starr 1980) and explains the nature of "cardinal directions" of color space as revealed in experiments of Krauskopf et al (1982).

Wandell (1985) has provided experimental evidence that makes an interpretation of a mixed strategy plausible by showing that a 540 nm and a 650 nm test light interact differently depending upon whether the lights are allowed to flicker or not. Unlike Boynton et al (1964), Wandell shaped the temporal envelope of his stimuli with a Gaussian weighting function in an effort to isolate the two mechanisms on the basis of a differential sensitivity to temporal frequency. In the case of increment-decrement pairs in the non-flicker case, the increments and decrements were temporally smoothed with the appropriately signed Gaussian function. In the case of stimuli that activate flicker sensitive mechanisms, the sinusoidal flicker was smoothed by a Gaussian window function (Gabor function). When the stimulus was flickered, the increment-decrement analog was produced by out-of-phase sinusoids (180° shift) while the increment-increment analog was created with two in-phase sinusoids. Wandell also found elliptical iso-sensitivity contours with his paradigm. The major axis of the ellipse either inclined along the positive (differencing) diagonal or the negative (summing) diagonal, depending upon whether the two test lights were flickered or not. Wandell emphasizes that some failures of line element theories could have occurred because observers were discriminating between colored stimuli with extended temporal presentations, which allowed eye-movement-induced temporal changes to excite luminance channels, thereby contaminating the discrimination task.

Acuity

Sensitivity to pattern is proving to be especially influenced by features of the array of photoreceptors, a possibility that might once have been considered unlikely. For example, punctate sensitivity has recently been shown for a small violet target, presumably because of the sparseness of "blue cones," by Williams et al (1981). The cone mosaic has been analyzed by Miller & Bernard (1983) and by Hirsch & Hylton (1984). Regularities of the foveal receptor array that interact with the stimulus enable one to see repeating patterns of spatial detail that are ordinarily too fine to be seen (Williams 1985).

Photoreceptor spacing also affects visual acuity. Acuity, or the resolution of spatial detail, may be related to sensitivity. In one sense (Barlow 1964b), good acuity that rests on comparison of luminance at nearby loci may require poor sensitivity, since sensitivity is increased by summation. Alternatively, acuity judgments are enhanced by increment sensitivity (Westheimer 1972). Acuity tasks usually involve identification ("was it an 'E' or some other letter?"). We discuss below the theoretical links between detection and identification tasks. Because of these links it might be expected that formulations of acuity (or of any type of identification) will need to take noise, among other factors, into account. It is therefore encouraging to see sound theoretical work in this direction. Geisler (1984) has developed predictions for the performance of the ideal detector (suitably degraded to reflect human idiosyncrasies) in both acuity and hyperacuity tasks. Geisler & Davila (1985) show that those predictions are consistent with measured human performance. Normative models of ideal detectors for acuity tasks provide a basis to define a measure of efficiency which permits quantitative comparisons between real and ideal observers. Application of such measures has led to surprisingly high values of efficiency (cited above), provided the noise in the task is also generated by the experimenter. For example, Kersten (1984), Burgess et al (1981) report values as high as 30% and 83% respectively. What is important about efficiency this high is that it falls close to the factor that would be computed solely on the basis of the stimulus. If so, the range of physiological degradations that can be inserted is very small. Similar conclusions were reached by Levick et al (1983) for cat retinal ganglion cells.

UNCERTAINTY

Uncertainty is a topic that is relatively new to the vision sensitivity literature, although there are important antecedents elsewhere (Green 1960). However, it is a significant topic because (a) uncertainty is ubiquitous in normal viewing, (b) uncertainty effects can be large (Cohn & Wardlaw 1985), (c) the observer often exhibits intrinsic uncertainty (Tanner 1961, Pelli 1985), and (d) uncertainty has theoretical importance, both in terms of modern mixed task paradigms (Klein 1985) and as a bridge (Benzschawel & Cohn 1985) between signal detection (Green & Birdsall 1978, Starr et al 1975) and identification. Perhaps the most compelling reason to emphasize uncertainty is because its effects spring from situations involving independent parallel channels, and it therefore strongly influences performance in situations that utilize those channels. Since visual uncertainty has not been reviewed in the past, we present summaries of the field going back to early studies.

The ideal observer must have exact knowledge of all signal parameters. Lacking this knowledge, the ideal observer must sample a larger than necessary set of channels to ensure the inclusion of the signal-bearing channels. Uncorrelated noise in the nonsignal-bearing channels leads to a number of predictions for the ideal observer. These predictions can then be compared to the performance of human observers. The optimal observer lacking knowledge of signal parameters is predicted to suffer a deficit in sensitivity. We assume that the ideal observer is capable of monitoring all the relevant channels.

In an early study, Mertens (1956) found that a visual stimulus presented randomly at any one of four different spatial locations was slightly easier to see than one presented at a known location. Cohn & Lasley (1974) replicated Mertens' experiment with experimental conditions designed to increase the probability of finding an uncertainty effect. They found that randomly presenting a target at one of four foveal locations depressed sensitivity, approximately by a factor of two. Cohn & Lasley (1974) concluded that the discrepancy between their results and Mertens' could be traced to a large amount of uncertainty that Mertens probably, unwittingly, introduced into his experiment. Peterson et al (1954), who elaborated the model of the ideal observer degraded-by-uncertainty, showed that the effect of uncertainty upon detectability is highly nonlinear. The greatest effect of an increment of uncertainty is when the initial uncertainty is small. More recently, Pelli (1985) has shown evidence for a large intrinsic spatial uncertainty outside the fovea. This alone could account for Mertens' negative finding.

Lasley & Cohn (1981a) showed that temporal uncertainty also diminishes detectability, which supports the explanation of Cohn & Lasley (1974) for Mertens' results. In addition, the result of this experiment was inconsistent with an explanation of attentional deficit, since only one spatial locus (or channel) was involved, which was sampled at successive intervals in time.

Other dimensions that specify a stimulus include color and motion, and these might be expected to produce uncertainty effects. Rollman & Nachmias (1972) investigated the effects of chromatic uncertainty on the detection of red and green flashes. They found that depriving subjects of prior knowledge of the color of the test flash had a small effect on sensitivity. Greenhouse & Cohn (1978), who also investigated the effects of chromatic uncertainty, found that a shift in the hue of a yellow target either in the direction of red or green (without any change in the overall brightness) resulted in a decline in sensitivity. Motion uncertainty effects were investigated by Sekuler & Ball (1977). They found uncertainty effects for the direction of motion albeit larger than predicted (see Green 1960 for a psychoacoustic example).

Phase and contrast were investigated in addition to spatial frequency effects for sinusoidal gratings by Davis et al (1983). They found frequency and phase uncertainty depressed sensitivity but not contrast uncertainty, the latter being a check on a widely held but mostly untested assumption about mixed stimulus amplitudes.

Davis et al (1983) tested cueing as a means of reversing the uncertainty effect. An auditory cue 750 msec before the stimulus proved to be helpful in reducing the effect of temporal uncertainty although delaying its presentation as long as 500 msec after the end of the trial had some effect in reducing uncertainty. Parametric studies might be useful in this area.

When the ideal observer is uncertain about signal parameters, the signal and noise distributions are no longer equal variance Gaussian probability density functions (pdf), which provides an additional testable prediction of the uncertainty hypothesis. The distributions can be approximated by unequal variance Gaussian pdfs (Peterson et al 1954), with the signal variance greater than the noise variance. This yields the further prediction of the effect of uncertainty on the ideal observer: uncertainty will depress the slope of the ROC curve when plotted on normal deviate coordinates. Cohn & Lasley (1974) and Lasley & Cohn (1981a) found results consistent with this prediction.

Peterson et al (1954) derived an approximation for the functional relationship between d', signal amplitude, noise variance, and M the uncertainty parameter. Nolte & Jaarsma (1967) gave results for these parameters derived from numerical methods showing that the approximation given by Peterson et al is not entirely adequate. By slightly modifying the decision rule for the uncertain observer, Pelli (1985) has shown that more tractable equations can be used to predict the behavior of the ideal observer degraded by uncertainty. A fourth prediction for the ideal observer faced with uncertainty specifies that the psychometric function will become nonlinear. This prediction is discussed in the next section.

Psychometric Functions

The variation of probability of seeing a stimulus as a function of the stimulus magnitude defines the "frequency of seeing" curve or psychometric function. The parameters of the fitted function have often been used to draw inference about the underlying mechanisms of seeing.

Given the extraordinary sensitivity of the visual system, an insight largely derived from carefully reasoned conclusions from the shape of the psychometric function (Hecht et al 1942), it will probably surprise everyone except the aficionado that one pocket of contentiousness revolves around the question of whether the psychometric function is also the "transducer" function. As already mentioned, for the ideal observer, the functional relationship between the detectability of a signal and its amplitude is linear (Green & Swets 1974). Such a function can also legitimately be called a psychometric function. The linearity requires that the noise be Poisson or Gaussian and additive (Green & Swets 1974). As we remarked above, it is unlikely that the intrinsic noise of the visual system is conveniently found in a single locus, since neural signals undoubtably experience both additive and possibly multiplicative noise at multiple sites.

Early measurements of the detectability (d') showed that the psychometric function was nonlinear for luminance change (Tanner & Swets 1954, Nachmias & Kocher 1970). The usual finding was that d' was a function of signal magnitude raised to a positive power, generally varying between 1 and 4, depending upon the subject, the investigator, and probably a host of other unidentified factors. As will be evident, one of these factors is uncertainty, which depends upon both the subject, including his motivation, degree of training, and also the experimental design. Nachmias & Sansbury (1974) showed that the same effect occurs for contrast detection of sinusoidal gratings. They proposed that their results could be explained by a nonlinear transducer followed by a source of additive Gaussian noise. This model has subsequently been adopted as the "nonlinear transducer" model and the implication is that when the independent variable is d' the psychometric function is simply a reflection of the transducer function.

One could argue that the model is nothing more than a description of a result. However, the model becomes more compelling because it appears to explain a rather puzzling phenomenon termed the "pedestal effect," namely, that the threshold contrast of a grating, (or of a luminance increment), is diminished when the grating is superimposed upon a low contrast pattern of the same spatial frequency(s) and phase(s) (Nachmias & Sansbury 1974).

One problem with the nonlinear transducer theory is the large range of values of the exponent of the putative power law transducer that many have found. A hardwired nonlinearity would not be likely to provide such a plethora of estimates. In addition, Lasley & Cohn (1981b) have shown that by experimentally changing physical uncertainty, the value of the exponent can be changed in a direction predicted by the uncertainty hypothesis. Moreover Cohn & Lasley (1985a) have shown that the pedestal effect, which is a mainstay of the nonlinear transducer theory, is obtained for a dichoptically presented pedestal. This requires that the nonlinearity be located in or more proximal to the lateral geniculate (Cohn & Lasley 1985a). Finally, Lasley & Cohn (1981b) showed that by introducing sufficient target noise (so that it swamps any internal noise) the fitted exponent of the psychometric function remains unchanged. Since Birdsall's theorem (Lasley & Cohn 1981b) requires that a transducer nonlinearity to be "invisible" (in the psychometric function) when external noise is dominant, the experimental result is inconsistent with a simple distal transducer nonlinearity. All of this research makes the idea of a distal, hardwired nonlinear transducer less and less attractive.

Such a conclusion requires an explanation for the pedestal effect. Cohn et al (1974) originally explained the effect in vision as an uncertainty reduction effect by analogy to pedestal effects in psychoacoustics discussed by Green (1960). The pedestal provides subjects with information about the temporal parameters of the stimulus. The problem with this explanation, as pointed out by Foley & Legge (1981), is that the optimum pedestal is generally a "threshold" stimulus (i.e. its detectability is finite). Thus it is not clear how a noise-limited signal can contribute much information about signal parameters. However, it must be pointed out that ability of observers to rate the visibility of "unseen stimuli" [a concept that is a holdover from the threshold dogma (Green & Swets 1974)] in an ordinal fashion suggest that it is possible for such a pedestal to give the observer some information about the stimulus. In addition, due regard is not given to learning effects that are possible when feedback is provided (as it was in Cohn et al 1974), which may asymptote sooner with larger (but not too large) pedestals. On the other hand, the best available answer may be provided by Foley & Legge (1981) and Pelli (1985). This is the idea that d' additivity (or z additivity) explains the effect, i.e. the nonlinear combination of the decision variables from the multiple channels gives rise to a nonlinear "transducer like" nonlinearity which combined with d' additivity explains the pedestal effect. This is essentially the same explanation as the nonlinear transducer theory described above. The explanation for d' additivity, to the extent that it is true, is a linear operation on the decision axis of the likelihood ratio distributions under signal and no-signal conditions. The main difference is in the site and cause of the nonlinearity. In any event, the best evidence now indicates that the nonlinearity does not result from a hardwired signal transduction scheme including, but not limited to, Carlson & Cohen's energy detector (1980), but rather results from nonlinearities in the decision processes of the uncertain observer.

PROBABILITY SUMMATION MODELS   The Gaussian cumulative distribution function (cdf) has proved inconvenient for probability summation models. The function recently adopted for this purpose has been described by Weibull (1951) for reliability studies. It has been used to model a device with many independent components, and where failure of only one component leads to failure of the whole device. The same argument was applied by Quick (1974) to model multiple, independent channels when the probability of seeing the stimulus is the probability that at least one channel "sees" the stimulus. Quick's model requires the assumption of a fixed high threshold, which is never exceeded by physiological noise, i.e. there are no false alarms of a sensory origin. False alarms that do occur are explained by the propensity of the subject to guess.

   The high threshold theory has been subjected to countless tests (see Green & Swets 1974 for a review), but virtually none of them have supported the high threshold theory. Most recently, Nachmias (1981) subjected the Quick model to a number of tests. He found that after adjusting the guessing parameter, psychometric functions for different guessing rates could not be superimposed, as predicted by the theory. Additionally, forced choice psychometric functions could not be predicted from psychometric functions derived from Yes/No data. Wilson (1980), taking note of the problems of the high threshold assumption, derives a probability summation model consistent with both the Weibull function and TSD. Finally, an explicit model of visual detection has been proposed that provides a rigorous deductive justification for the Weibull distribution. Maloney & Wandell (1984) present a model of a detection device that gives rise to Poisson statistics because of the manner in which the device samples the internal response. With a number of explicit assumptions, they prove the cdf must be Weibull. The model does require the high threshold assumption. However, the model has been subjected to tests with some success (Casson & Wandell 1984).

DISCRIMINATION

In recent years many investigators have sought to relate the ability of the observer to detect simple stimuli to the observer's ability to discriminate among stimuli. Thomas (1985) has proposed a principle that underlies the modern conception of the relationship between detection and discrimination, namely that the two tasks represent different uses of the same sensory information. Tanner (1956) was the first to derive the relationship between detection and recognition for the ideal observer. This model, despite its elegance and comprehensiveness, is seldom cited by vision researchers. The recent review by Thomas (1985), together with Tanner's formulation, provide a comprehensive treatment of recognition/detection paradigm applied to vision research.

An important issue is the relationship between detection and recognition performance levels, which is dealt with by both Thomas (1985) and Tanner (1956). An early example is provided by Rollman & Nachmias (1972), who show that subjects can identify stimuli they cannot see. Thomas (1985) discusses this apparent paradox. Here we will note that in some cases it is the result of measuring the detectability of a target using forced choice techniques that traditionally result in lower thresholds compared to the Yes/No paradigms (See Green & Swets 1974). In some cases this phenomenon occurs because the two stimuli reciprocally activate the same channel (See Cohn & Lasley 1985b and below). Expressing one's data in terms of recognition angle, a quantity introduced by Tanner (1956), can readily distinguish between these possibilities.

A detection/recognition paradigm is clearly applicable to a number of different problems in vision, most notably to situations where performance may be mediated by parallel channels. Lasley (1985) used the paradigm to investigate both fine stereo mechanisms and Richards' (1970) theory of stereoanomaly. Olzak & Thomas (1986) can be consulted for the discrimination of spatial patterns.

Cohn & Lasley (1985b) have exploited the model to investigate the encoding of increments and decrements. It has been noted that thresholds for increments and decrements are not the same. Kelly & Savoie (1978) suggested an asymmetric (full wave) rectifier. Other plausible models for increment/decrement encoding include separate channels for each or just one channel with reciprocal action (e.g. polarization or depolarization of receptor potential). Cohn (1976) suggested that the latter model with quantum fluctuations could explain greater sensitivity to decrements. Cohn & Lasley (1985b) found that at a high level of foveal adaptation, the detection/recognition results supported the hypothesis of rectifying channels. At a lower level of foveal adaptation, results were consistent with the idea that increments and decrements were encoded by a linear channel with reciprocal action. Kelly (1981), on the basis of quite different experimental methods, has also suggested a similar model.

CONCLUSIONS

Contemporary research in visual processing has been enhanced by rejecting ad hoc models of decision processes. Probability summation is a typical example. In addition, nonlinearities in decision processes should not be confounded with nonlinearities of sensory processes (e.g. energy detectors versus uncertainty). Much effort is expended in trying to find the physiological or mechanistic transduction process that causes a nonlinearity, while ignoring the possibility of a contribution from decision processes which by their nature are nonlinear. It would be preferable to experimentally reject decision process nonlinearities before considering transducer nonlinearities.

The concept of noise and the explicit rejection of the hypothesis that noise has no effect upon human behavior in the absence of a stimulus has enriched vision science. First, it permitted the elaboration of the ideal observer as a normative model, which sets forth an upper limit for performance. Then by modifying the ideal observer with quantum inefficiency, by a variety of internal noise sources, and by uncertainty, comparisons can be made between the model and actual human behavior. If there is a match, then no further degradations in the model are required. There is now substantial evidence that there is at least a qualitative agreement between the normative model, degraded in these ways, and actual behavior of human subjects. More quantitative studies might suggest further degradations. Extending this normative model to incorporate recognition behavior will undoubtably yield new insights about human visual sensitivity as it focuses new attention on how the parallel channels, noise sources, and information transformations combine their effects.

ACKNOWLEDGMENTS

We thank many of our colleagues for their helpful discussions, and particularly thank J. Thomas, T. Benzschawel, and G. Legge for their comments on an earlier version of this manuscript.

Literature Cited

Adelson, E. H. 1979. The kinetics of decay of saturated rod afterimages. *Invest. Ophthalmol. Vis. Sci.* 18:29 (Suppl.)

Ahumada, A. J., Watson, A. B. 1985. Equivalent-noise model for contrast detection and discrimination. *J. Opt. Soc. Am. Ser. A* 2:1133–39

Ashmore, J. F., Copenhagen, D. R. 1980. Different postsynaptic events in two types of retinal bipolar cell. *Nature* 288:84–86

Ashmore, J. F., Falk, G. 1977. Dark noise in retinal bipolar cells and the stability of rhodopsin in rods. *Nature* 270:69–71

Ashmore, J. F., Falk, G. 1980. Responses of rod bipolar cells in the dark-adapted retina of the dogfish, *Scyliorhinus canicula. J. Physiol.* 300:115–50

Barlow, H. B. 1956. Intrinsic noise of cones. *Proc. Natl. Phys. Lab. Symp. No. 8 on Visual Problems of Colour*, pp. 617–30. London: H. M. Stationary Off.

Barlow, H. B. 1964a. Dark adaptation: a new hypothesis. *Vision Res.* 4:47–58

Barlow, H. B. 1964b. The physical limits of visual discrimination. In *Photophysiology*, ed. A. C. Giese, pp. 163–202. New York: Academic

Barlow, H. B. 1977. Retinal and central factors in human vision limited by noise. In *Vertebrate Photoreception*, ed. H. B. Barlow, P. Fatt. New York: Academic

Barlow, H. B. 1981. The Ferrier lecture, 1980: Critical limiting factors in the design of the eye and visual cortex. *Proc. R. Soc. London Ser. B* 212:1–34

Baylor, D. A., Lamb, T. D. 1982. Local effects of bleaching in retinal rods of the toad. *J. Physiol.* 328:49–71

Baylor, D. A., Lamb, T. D., Yau, K. W. 1979. The membrane current of single rod outer segments. *J. Physiol.* 288:589–611

Baylor, D. A., Matthews, G., Yau, K. W. 1980. Two components of electrical dark noise in toad retinal rod outer segments. *J. Physiol.* 309:591–621

Benzschawel, T., Cohn, T. E. 1985. Detection and recognition of visual targets. *J. Opt. Soc. Am. Ser. A* 2:1543–50

Boynton, R. M., Ikeda, M., Stiles, W. S. 1964. Interactions among chromatic mechanisms as inferred from positive and negative increment thresholds. *Vision Res.* 4:87–117

Bradley, A., Skottun, B. C., Ohzawa, I., Sclar, G., Freeman, R. D. 1985. A neurophysiological evaluation of the differential response model for orientation and spatial frequency discrimination. *J. Opt. Soc. Am. Ser. A* 2:1607–10

Burgess, A. E., Barlow, H. B., Jennings, R. J., Wagner, R. F. 1981. Efficiency of human visual signal discrimination. *Science* 214: 93–94

Carlson, C. R., Cohen, R. W. 1980. A simple psychophysical model for predicting the visibility of display information. *Proc. Soc. Inf. Disp.* 21:229–47

Casson, E. J., Wandell, B. A. 1984. Duration discrimination between weak test lights. *Vision Res.* 24:641–45

Cicerone, C. M., Green, D. G. 1980a. Light adaptation within the receptive field centre of rat retinal ganglion cells. *J. Physiol.* 301:517–34

Cicerone, C. M., Green, D. G. 1980b. Dark adaptation within the receptive field centre of rat retinal ganglion cells. *J. Physiol.* 301:535–48

Cohn, T. E. 1976. Quantum fluctuation limit in foveal vision. *Vision Res.* 16:573–79

Cohn, T. E. 1978. Detection of 1-of-M orthogonal signals: Asymptotic equivalence of likelihood ratio and multiband models. *Opt. Lett.* 3:22–23

Cohn, T. E. 1981. Absolute threshold: Analysis in terms of uncertainty. *J. Opt. Soc. Am.* 71:783–85

Cohn, T. E. 1983. Receiver operating characteristic analysis of photoreceptor sensitivity. *IEEE Trans. Syst. Man Cybern.* SMC-13:873–82

Cohn, T. E., Green, D. G., Tanner, W. P., 1975. Receiver operating characteristic analysis. Application to the study of quantum fluctuation effects in optic nerve of *Rana pipiens*. *J. Gen. Physiol.* 66:583–616

Cohn, T. E., Lasley, D. J. 1974. Detectability of a luminance increment: The effect of spatial uncertainty. *J. Opt. Soc. Am.* 64:1715–19

Cohn, T. E., Lasley, D. J. 1975. Spatial summation of foveal increments and decrements. *Vision Res.* 15:389–99

Cohn, T. E., Lasley, D. J. 1976. Binocular vision: Two possible central interactions between signals from two eyes. *Science* 192:561–63

Cohn, T. E., Lasley, D. J. 1985a. Site of the accelerating nonlinearity underlying luminance change detection. *J. Opt. Soc. Am. Ser. A* 2:202–5

Cohn, T. E., Lasley, D. J. 1985b. Discrimination of luminance increments and decrements. *J. Opt. Soc. Am. Ser. A* 2:404–7

Cohn, T. E., Leong, H., Lasley, D. J. 1981. Binocular luminance detection: Availability of more than one central interaction. *Vision Res.* 21:1017–23

Cohn, T. E., Thibos, L. N., Kleinstein, R. N.

1974. Detectability of a luminance increment. *J. Opt. Soc. Am.* 64:1321–27

Cohn, T. E., Wardlaw, J. C. 1985. Effect of large spatial uncertainty on foveal luminance increment detectability. *J. Opt. Soc. Am. Ser. A* 2:820–25

Copenhagen, D. R., Green, D. G. 1985. The absence of spread of adaptation between rod photoreceptors in turtle retina. *J. Physiol.*

Cornsweet, T. N. 1962. The staircase-method in psychophysics. *Am. J. Psychol.* 75:485–91

Davis, E. T., Kramer, P., Graham, N. 1983. Uncertainty about spatial frequency, spatial position, or contrast of visual patterns. *Percept. Psychophys.* 33:20–28

Dean, A. F. 1981. The variability of discharge of simple cells in the cat striate cortex. *Exp. Brain Res.* 44:437–40

De Valois, R. L., Morgan, H., Snodderly, D. M. 1974. Psychophysical studies of monkey vision. III. Spatial luminance contrast sensitivity tests of Macaque and human observers. *Vision Res.* 14:75–81

Egan, J. P. 1975. *Signal Detection Theory and ROC Analysis.* New York: Academic

Enroth-Cugel, C., Lennie, P., Shapely, R. M., 1975. Surround contribution to light adaptation in cat retinal ganglion cells. *J. Physiol.* 247:579–88

Falk, G., Fatt, P. 1974. Limitations to single-photon sensitivity in vision. In *Lecture Notes in Biomathematics, Physics and Mathematics of the Nervous System,* ed. M. Conrad, W. Guttinger, M. Dal Cin, 4:171–204. Berlin: Springer-Verlag

Foley, J. M., Legge, G. E. 1981. Contrast detection and near-threshold discrimination in human vision. *Vision Res.* 21:1041–53

Frishman, L. J., Levine, M. W. 1983. Statistics of the maintained discharge of cat retinal ganglion cells. *J. Physiol.* 339:475–94

Geisler, W. S. 1984. Physical limits of acuity and hyperacuity. *J. Opt. Soc. Am. Ser. A* 1:775–82

Geisler, W. S., Davila, K. D. 1985. Ideal discriminators in spatial vision: Two point stimuli. *J. Opt. Soc. Am. Ser. A* 2:1483–97

Gottschalk, A., Buchsbaum, G. 1983. Information theoretic aspects of color signal processing in the visual system. *IEEE Trans. Syst. Man Cybern.* SMC-13:864–72

Green, D. G. 1985. Rod interactions in turtle photoreceptors: Disenhancement or local adaptation. *Invest. Ophthalmol. Vis. Sci.* 26:193 (Suppl.)

Green, D. G., Powers, M. K. 1982. Mechanisms of light adaptation in rat retina. *Vision Res.* 22:209–16

Green, D. M. 1960. Psychoacoustics and detection theory. *J. Acoust. Soc. Am.* 32:1139–1203

Green, D. M., Birdsall, T. G. 1978. Detection and recognition. *Psychol. Rev.* 85:192–206

Green, D. M., Swets, J. A. 1974. *Signal Detectability Theory and Psychophysics,* New York: Krieger

Greenhouse, D. S., Cohn, T. E. 1978. Effect of chromatic uncertainty on detectability of a visual stimulus. *J. Opt. Soc. Am.* 68:266–67

Guth, S. L. 1971. On probability summation. *Vision Res.* 11:747–50

Guth, S. L., Massof, R. W., Benzschawel, T. 1980. Vector model for normal and dichromatic color vision. *J. Opt. Soc. Am.* 70:197–212

Hamer, R. D., Schneck, M. E. 1984. Spatial summation in dark-adapted human infants. *Vision Res.* 24:77–85

Hayhoe, M. M. 1979. After-effects of small adapting fields. *J. Physiol.* 296:141–58

Hecht, S., Schlaer, S., Pirenne, M. P. 1942. Energy, quanta, and vision. *J. Gen. Physiol.* 25:819–40

Hirsch, J., Hylton, R. 1984. Quality of the primate photoreceptor lattice and limits of spatial vision. *Vision Res.* 24:347–56

Kelly, D. H. 1981. Nonlinear visual responses to flickering sinusoidal gratings. *J. Opt. Soc. Am.* 71:1051–55

Kelly, D. H., Savoie, R. E. 1978. Theory of flicker and transient responses. III. An essential nonlinearity. *J. Opt. Soc. Am.* 68:1481–90

Kersten, D. 1984. Spatial summation in visual noise. *Vision Res.* 24:1977–90

Kersten, D., Barlow, H. B. 1985. Why are contrast thresholds so high. *Invest. Ophthalmol. Vis. Sci.* 26:140 (Suppl.)

Klein, S. A. 1985. Double judgement psychophysics: Problems and solutions. *J. Opt. Soc. Am. Ser. A* 2:1560–85

Krauskopf, J., Reeves, A. 1980. Measurement of the effect of photon noise on detection. *Vision Res.* 20:193–96

Krauskopf, J., Williams, D. R., Heeley, D. W. 1982. Cardinal directions of color space. *Vision Res.* 22:1123–32

Lamb, T. D. 1981. The involvement of rod photoreceptors in dark adaptation. *Vision Res.* 21:1773–82

Lasley, D. J. 1985. Discrimination between crossed and uncrossed disparities. *J. Opt. Soc. Am. Ser. A* 2:399–403

Lasley, D. J., Cohn, T. E. 1981a. Detection of a luminance increment: Effect of temporal uncertainty. *J. Opt. Soc. Am.* 71:845–50

Lasley, D. J., Cohn, T. E. 1981b. Why luminance discrimination may be better than detection. *Vision Res.* 21:273–78

Laughlin, S. 1981. A simple coding procedure enhances a neuron's information capacity. *Z. Naturforsch. Teil C* 36:910–12

Legge, G. E. 1984. Binocular contrast summation-I. Detection and discrimination. *Vision Res.* 24:373–83

Lennie, P. 1980. Parallel visual pathways. *Vision Res.* 20:561–95

Levick, W. R., Thibos, L. N., Cohn, T. E., Catanzaro, D., Barlow, H. B. 1983. Performance of cat retinal ganglion cells at low light levels. *J. Gen. Physiol.* 82:405–26

Lillywhite, P. G. 1981. Multiplicative intrinsic noise and the limits to visual performance. *Vision Res.* 21:291–96

Macleod, D. 1978. Visual sensitivity. *Ann. Rev. Psychol.* 29:613–45

Maloney, L. T., Wandell, B. A. 1984. A model of a single visual channel's response to weak test lights. *Vision Res.* 24:633–40

Massof, R. W., Starr, S. J. 1980. Vector magnitude operation in color vision models: Derivation from signal detection models. *J. Opt. Soc. Am.* 70:870–72

Mastronarde, D. N. 1983. Correlated firing of cat retinal ganglion cells. I. Spontaneously active inputs to X- and Y-cells. *J. Neurophysiol.* 49:303–24

Mertens, J. 1956. Influence of knowledge of target location upon the probability of observation of peripheral observable test flashes. *J. Opt. Soc. Am.* 45:1069–70

Miller, E. F. 1955. Investigation of the nature and the cause of impaired acuity in amblyopia. *Am. J. Optom. Physiol. Optics* 32:10–29

Miller, W. H., Bernard, G. D. 1983. Averaging over the foveal receptor aperture curtails aliasing. *Vision Res.* 23:1365–69

Nachmias, J. 1972. Signal detection theory and its application to problems in vision. In *Handbook of Sensory Physiology,* ed. D. Jameson, L. Hurvich, 7(4):56–78. Berlin: Springer-Verlag

Nachmias, J. 1981. On the psychometric function for contrast detection. *Vision Res.* 21:215–24

Nachmias, J., Kocher, E. C. 1970. Visual detection and discrimination of luminance increment. *J. Opt. Soc. Am.* 60:382–89

Nachmias, J., Sansbury, R. V. 1974. Grating contrast: Discrimination may be better than detection. *Vision Res.* 14:1039–42

Nelson, R., Kolb, H., Robinson, M. M., Marian, A. P. 1981. Neural circuitry of the retina, cone pathways to ganglion cells. *Vision Res.* 21:1527–37

Nolte, L. W., Jaarsma, D. 1967. More on the detection of one of M orthogonal signals. *J. Acoust. Soc. Am.* 41:497–505

Normann, R., Werblin, F. S. 1974. Control of retinal sensitivity. I. Light and dark adaptation of vertebrate rods. *J. Gen. Physiol.* 63:34–61

Nunn, P. J., Schnapf, J. L., Baylor, D. A. 1984. Spectral sensitivity of single cones in the retina of Macaca fascicularis. *Nature* 309:264–66

Ohzawa, I., Sclar, G., Freeman, R. D. 1982.

Contrast gain in the cat visual cortex. *Nature* 298:266–68

Olzak, L. A., Thomas, J. P. 1986. Seeing spatial patterns. In *Handbook of Perception and Human Performance*, ed. K. Boff, L. Kaufman, J. Thomas. New York: Wiley

Pelli, D. G. 1985. Uncertainty explains many aspects of visual contrast detection and discrimination. *J. Opt. Soc. Am. Ser. A* 2:1508–32

Peterson, W. W., Birdsall, T. G., Fox, W. C. 1954. The theory of signal detectability. *IRE Trans. Inf. Theory* 4:171–212

Pirenne, M. 1943. Binocular and uniocular threshold of vision. *Nature* 152:698–99

Quick, R. F. 1974. A vector-magnitude model of contrast detection. *Kybernetik* 16:65–67

Rashbass, C. 1970. The visibility of transient changes of luminance. *J. Physiol.* 210:165–86

Richards, W. 1970. Anomalous stereoscopic depth perception. *J. Opt. Soc. Am.* 61:410–14

Riggs, L. 1983. Optics, the eye, and the brain. *J. Opt. Soc. Am.* 73:736–50

Rollman, G. B., Nachmias, J. 1972. Simultaneous detection and recognition of chromatic flashes. *Percept. Psychophys.* 12:309–14

Rose, A. 1948. The sensitivity of the human eye on an absolute scale. *J. Opt. Soc. Am.* 38:196–208

Ryle, G. 1949. *The Concept of Mind.* Chicago: Univ. Chicago Press

Sakitt, B. 1972. Counting every quantum. *J. Physiol.* 233:131–50

Saleh, B. E. A., Cohn, T. E. 1978. Reduction of the human detective quantum efficiency due to lateral neural interactions. *Biol. Cybern.* 28:137–41

Schwartz, E. A. 1977. Voltage noise observed in the rods of the turtle retina. *J. Physiol.* 272:217–46

Sekuler, R., Ball, K. 1977. Mental set alters visibility of moving targets. *Science* 198:60–62

Simon, E. J., Lamb, T. D., Hodgkin, A. L. 1975. Spontaneous voltage fluctuations in retinal cones and bipolar cells. *Nature* 286:661–62

Starr, S. J., Metz, C. E., Lusted, L. B., Goodenough, D. J. 1975. Visual detection and localization of radiographic images. *Radiology* 116:533–38

Sutcliffe, F. E., transl. 1968. *Descartes' Discourse on Method and the Meditations.* New York: Penguin

Swets, J. A., ed. 1964. *Signal Detection and Recognition by Human Observers.* New York: Wiley

Tanner, W. P. 1956. Theory of recognition. *J. Acoust. Soc. Am.* 28:882–88

Tanner, W. P. 1961. Physiological implications of psychophysical data. *Ann. NY Acad. Sci.* 89:752–65

Tanner, W. P., Swets, J. A. 1954. A decision-making theory of visual detection. *Psychol. Rev.* 61:401–9

Teich, M. C., Prucnal, P. R., Vannucci, G., Breton, M. E., McGill, W. J. 1982. Multiplication noise in the human visual system at threshold: 1. Quantum fluctuations and minimum detectable energy. *J. Opt. Soc. Am.* 72:419–31

Teich, M. C., Saleh, B. E. A. 1981. Interevent-time statistics for shot-noise-driven self-exciting point processes in photon detection. *J. Opt. Soc. Am.* 71:771–76

Teller, D. 1980. Locus questions in visual science. *In Visual Coding and Adaptability*, ed. C. S. Harris. Hillsdale, NJ: Erlbaum

Thomas, J. P. 1985. Detection and identification: how are they related. *J. Opt. Soc. Am. Ser. A* 2:1457–67

Tolhurst, D. J., Movshon, J. A., Dean, A. F. 1983. The statistical reliability of signals in single neurons in cat and monkey visual cortex. *Vision Res.* 23:775–86

Torre, V., Owen, W. G., Sandini, G. 1983. The dynamics of electrically interacting cells. *IEEE Trans. Syst. Man Cybern.* 13:757–65

van Meeteren, A., Barlow, H. B. 1981. The statistical efficiency for detecting sinusoidal modulation of average dot density in random figures. *Vision Res.* 21:765–77

Wandell, B. A. 1985. Color measurement and discrimination. *J. Opt. Soc. Am. Ser. A* 2:62–71

Watson, A. B., Pelli, D. G. 1983. QUEST: A Bayesian adaptive psychometric method. *Percept. Psychophys.* 33:113–20

Watson, A. B., Robson, J. G., Barlow, H. B. 1983. What the eye sees best. *Nature* 302:419–22

Weibull, W. 1951. A statistical distribution function of wide applicability. *J. Appl. Mech.* 18:293–97

Westheimer, G. 1972. Visual acuity and spatial modulation thresholds. In *Handbook of Sensory Physiology*, ed. D. Jameson, L. Hurvich, 7(4):170–87. Berlin: Springer-Verlag

Williams, D. R. 1985. Aliasing in human foveal vision. *Vision Res.* 25:195–205

Williams, D. R., MacLeod, D. I. A., Hayhoe, M. M. 1981. Puctuate sensitivity of the blue-sensitive mechanism. *Vision Res.* 21:1357–75

Wilson, H. R. 1980. A transducer function for threshold and suprathreshold human vision. *Biol. Cybern.* 38:171–78

Yeandle, S. 1958. Evidence of quantized slow potentials in the eye of Limulus. *Am. J. Ophthalmol.* 46:82–87

Ann. Rev. Psychol. 1986. 37:523–64

CULTURE AND BEHAVIOR: PSYCHOLOGY IN GLOBAL PERSPECTIVE

Marshall H. Segall

Social and Political Psychology, The Maxwell School, Syracuse University, Syracuse, New York 13210

CONTENTS

INTRODUCTION 524
  Kinds of Literature Covered 524
  Time Period Covered.. 526
  Why Culture and Behavior: What is Culture Anyway?..................... 526
  More Concrete Methodological Efforts 528
THE HANDBOOKS: A COMING OF AGE.. 529
  The Handbook of Cross-Cultural Psychology............................... 529
  The Handbook of Cross-Cultural Human Development 530
CULTURE IN PSYCHOLOGY AND PSYCHOLOGY
    IN OTHER CULTURES 531
  Teaching Cross-Cultural Psychology.. 531
  The Impact of Psychology in Other Cultures 532
SUBSTANTIVE AREAS OF CROSS-CULTURAL
    RESEARCH 534
  Perception... 534
  Cognition.. 535
  Socialization and Personality Development 539
  Values, Beliefs, and Motives.. 541
  Sex Differences 548
  Sex Roles and Identity.. 549
  Sex Identity Conflict 551
  Aggression.. 552
  Ethnocentric Attribution 552
CULTURAL CONTACT 553
  Modernization 553
  Consequences of Urbanization.. 554
  Bilingualism.. 555
CONCLUDING REMARKS 555

0066-4308/86/0201-0523$02.00

INTRODUCTION

The domain of this review is research relating individual behavior to its cultural context. While all behavior occurs in cultural contexts, only a small portion of behavioral research attends to this. Despite the steady growth in acceptance by mainstream psychologists of "cross-cultural psychology," the preponderance of contemporary psychological research is still designed, conducted, and interpreted as if culture did not matter. Other chapters in this volume describe mostly studies that ignore cultural variables, but monocultural studies will be mentioned here only when they relate to cross-cultural research, as when, for example, cross-cultural psychologists are inspired by a report of monocultural findings to test their generality in other settings.

There is also an anthropological literature in which cultural variables per se compromise the focus, with little or no attention paid to behavior of the individuals who are the carriers of culture. The preponderance of anthropological research deals with culture as if behavior did not matter. Anthropological studies will be reviewed here only when they have induced cross-culturalists to explore behavioral implications. That psychologists should attend more to anthropology is the message of an excellent historical analysis of anthropology's relationship to psychology (Jahoda 1982). In latent form, there is a close relationship even when anthropologists employ their traditional macrolevel approach.

Our focus, however, is on research that attends simultaneously to culture *and* behavior. When psychologists do such research, they usually call it "cross-cultural psychology"; when anthropologists do it, they frequently call it "psychological anthropology." As both labels indicate, there is a domain where the central concerns of anthropology and psychology overlap and there this chapter is located.

Kinds of Literature Covered

The best examplars of this overlapping domain are studies in which comparable behavioral observations are made in several cultural settings, with obtained behavioral differences related systematically to particular features of the settings in a manner consistent with theory-based predictions. Such studies have the potential for enhancing our understanding of human behavior and its development.

In my undergraduate course in cross-cultural psychology I often use the following examination item: "A minimally acceptable theory-testing cross-cultural study involves collection of data in: (*a*) an avuncular society, (*b*) at least 2 societies, (*c*) at least 3 societies, (*d*) laboratories, where extraneous variables can be filtered out." Noting Campbell's warning that studies which consist solely of single-pair comparisons are uninterpretable, because "there are many dimensions of differences which constitute potential rival explanations and which we have no means of ruling out" (Campbell 1961, p. 344), I argue that c is the best answer. The ideal cross-cultural study would have a large number of pairs of groups.

In many respects, such bona fide cross-cultural studies in psychology are models of what cross-cultural psychology ought to be, but more often prescribed than achieved. Within the domain covered here, these model studies constitute a minority. Most fall short of the ideal.

Some were conducted in a single setting, different from the one in which earlier research had established a finding, about which the generality seemed suspect to some cross-culturalists. Others are simply monocultural studies done in non-North American settings, with findings suggesting that cultural variables are relevant. Many studies of this kind are now being done in Europe. They will be reviewed when particularly germane. A growing number of monocultural studies are being conducted in non-Western settings (some highly susceptible to Western cultural influences, some considerably less so) and a number of these studies will also be covered.

Since culture is not co-terminous with society (since, in other words, some societies are multiethnic and hence multicultural), we will also attend to cross-ethnic studies. As asserted by Berry in his recent (1984a) presidential address to the International Association of Cross-Cultural Psychology, a complete cross-cultural psychology is one that includes cross-ethnic studies.

While most of the studies reviewed here contain psychological data in the form of individual responses to stimulus material provided by the researcher to one or more samples of respondents, others *indirectly* test psychological theory by reexamining relations between sets of observations of prevalent aggregate behaviors, such as customs, norms, beliefs, and other practices that have been attributed to particular human groups. Such observations comprise ethnographies that are subject to systematic quantitative comparisons of a theory-testing nature by scholars engaged in "hologeistic research," an enterprise defined by Naroll et al (1980). "A hologeistic (whole earth) study . . . tests theories by correlational analyses using data from worldwide samples of entire societies or all cultures" (Naroll et al 1980, p. 480). Most hologeistic studies employ data consisting of numerical codes derived from ethnographic descriptions (of mostly smaller but widely dispersed "cultures") contained in the Human Relations Area Files. An excellent description of the Files, with instructions for use and examples thereof, may be found in Barry (1980). Comparing smaller cultural units (once popularly but rather ethnocentrically called tribes), studies like these are best described as holocultural studies.

Doing holocultural studies has become easier as standard samples of societies coded on diverse variables become available. Recently, for example, Barry & Schlegel (1982, 1984) have published coded measures of women's contributions to subsistence activities and of adolescent sexual behavior. Using previously published codes on adolescent initiation ceremonies (Schlegel & Barry 1979), the same authors (1980) found evolutionary significance in changes in the importance of gender in ceremonies in different societies.

Since cross-cultural research is replete with methodological difficulties, some of them inherent in the enterprise of comparing behaviors across cultures, efforts to deal with these difficulties continue to attract attention of cross-culturalists. Necessarily, then, contributions of a predominantly methodological nature are also reviewed.

Time Period Covered

Brislin, in his *Annual Review* chapter (1983), reached 1981 in his coverage but the amount of publication near the turn of the decade was "massive" (Brislin 1983, p. 363) and some later, important works could not be thoroughly described. One is the *Handbook of Cross-Cultural Psychology* (Triandis et al 1980); another is the *Handbook of Cross-Cultural Human Development* (R. H. Munroe et al 1981). These were landmark events in the field's history, and it is necessary to provide somewhat more discussion of their contents. So this review covers 1980 through 1985. When earlier references help to explain the findings of a current study, they are also cited.

Since the focal period marks the beginning of the post-Handbook era in cross-cultural psychology, we might now ask whether the field is finally taking off. The present review provides a tentative answer. A caveat is in order, however. This review cannot *cover* the field. Still one of the smaller specialties, cross-cultural psychology nonetheless produces many hundreds of research reports presented in dozens of sources. Actual coverage is a nonrandom sample. Selection reflects judgment; judgment reflects the reviewer's interest and imperfect knowledge.

Why Culture and Behavior: What is Culture Anyway?

If cross-cultural psychology is a strategy whereby we search for generalizations about behavior and its pan-cultural antecedents, we had better know what we mean by culture. Many contributors to the post-Handbook literature seem to follow R. L. Munroe & Munroe (1980), who think of culture as composed of numerous separable (albeit often correlated) contextual factors, including subsistence patterns; social and political institutions; languages; rules governing interpersonal relations; divisions of labor by sex, age, or ethnicity; population density; dwelling styles; and more . . . in effect, the independent variables of cross-cultural psychology. Since explaining differences in behavior across cultures (the dependent variable) requires a search for the relevant independent variables, culture unpackaged, so to speak, Segall (1983a) suggested that the global concept culture was superfluous. Earlier, the anthropologist Whiting had also worried about the "packaged variable" (Whiting 1976).

However, two eminent cross-culturalists argued that the concept of culture is both necessary and in need of better definition. Rohner (1984), after reviewing diverse definitions of culture in the anthropological literature, proposed that "it" be defined as "the totality of equivalent and complimentary learned meanings maintained by a human population, or by identifiable segments of a population, and transmitted from one generation to another" (Rohner 1984, pp. 119–20). Urging that cross-cultural psychologists not use a "loose" concept of culture, Rohner concluded that we need a shared "sentiment" about what "culture" means. In short, cross-cultural psychologists need one of those learned meanings, shared and transmitted! Rohner's essay elucidates problems inherent in the concept culture, but his preferred definition has its own problems, since "culture" includes more than meanings.

Jahoda (1984) also thought Rohner's stress on "meanings" was an unnecessary restriction, but rejected Segall's (1983a) assertion that "culture is nothing more than a set of independent variables" and hence not needing a definition. On the other hand, Jahoda agreed with Segall (1983a) that we have no means of handling "culture" in ways that would render it empirically useful. Then Jahoda departed from Segall and allied himself with Rohner in urging that we should try to find an empirically useful definition.

Subsequently, after considering both Rohner's and Jahoda's contribution to the search for an adequate definition of culture, Segall (1984) concluded that the search was fruitless. Indeed, in the review of the literature that led up to the present chapter, it once again became clear that culture per se is not a variable. Hardly any contempory research reports explain a behavior as a product of "culture."

EMICS AND ETICS   If by 1985 psychologists are still fretting over what culture means, have they come any closer to resolving the emic-etic controversy? Partly a methodological issue (are concepts and instruments generally valid [etic] or only valid in particular cultures [emic]?) and partly an epistemological one (how does one ever determine the cognitive contents of persons from a culture other than one's own—the "emic" classification scheme?), discussions of emics and etics became de rigeur in recent publications. Berry (1984b) redefined the emic/etic distinction as "the tension between the culturally relative and the culturally universal" (p. 337) and opined that cross-cultural comparison is plagued by this tension. Seemingly, cross-cultural psychology is also plagued by continuing debate on how to resolve the dilemma, whether it has a resolution, and whether it is a real dilemma! Discussions that seem to score a few clarity points, yet leave the matter still quite cloudy, include those by Starr & Wilson (1980), Jahoda (1983a) in Deregowski et al (1983), and Starr (1985). A related issue, whether universality or generalizability should be sought, was discussed by van de Vijver & Poortinga (1982) and Poortinga & van de Vijver (1984).

So we still worry about what is emic and what is etic, and we still worry about what culture is, but our empirical research is quite untouched by these metaconceptual, metamethodological musings. If the research is done in diverse ecocultural settings, and if it involves comparable behaviors, it is bona fide cross-cultural research, provided, of course, that the validity of psychological concepts and instruments, when they have been invented in one place and are transported to another, has been empirically ascertained.

More Concrete Methodological Efforts

Many recent studies report the use of tests in settings other than the ones in which they were originally standardized, in a deliberate attempt to assess their validity in the new setting. One such example was reported by Weiss (1980), who administered both a person-drawing test and another "culture-fair" intelligence test to 33 fourth-grade pupils, predominantly Peruvian Indians in the highlands of Eastern Peru. Largely because this sample scored moderately high on one test (the Goodenough-Harris Draw-A-Person), but very low on the other, the author concluded that only the former was usable for such a sample. Similar examples abound. Forty-five papers dealing with assessment problems in diverse cultural settings were presented in a volume (Irvine & Berry 1983) that emerged from a NATO conference held in Kingston, Ontario in August 1981. More such papers were presented at a 1984 conference in Athens (e.g. Poortinga 1984). These papers reveal a consciousness of the need to revalidate tasks in each setting in which we attempt to use them, but nobody has uncovered striking new evidence of universal applicability. There has been no evidence of a culture-free test, nor has anyone demonstrated that we *can't* use any instrument in our armamentarium, provided we interpret scores obtained on it with great caution. Of course, in some of the substantive studies reviewed below, the appropriate caution was present to varying degrees. So this ever-present issue of cross-cultural applicability of concepts and tasks has not been laid to rest.

META-ANALYSIS   In one very important methodological contribution, Strube (1981) argued for the application of meta-analytic techniques (Glass 1976, Rosenthal 1978) to studies done cross-culturally. To illustrate how the use of meta-analysis in conjunction with cross-cultural comparison might provide a means of theory advancement "of great potential," Strube applied it to several studies that reported sex differences in cooperation/competition (e.g. Madsen & Shapira 1977, Kagan et al 1977). The results of the meta-analysis indicated an overall tendency for males to be more competitive than females, though not universally. The prevailing difference was well established for Anglo-American children but less so for others, with an opposite trend for Israeli children. Of course, as Strube noted, the original hypothesis must be validly tested in all the cultures for the meta-analysis to be valid. Moreover, the meta-analysis can inflate convergence of findings if the research method used is identical (and, therefore, possesses similar demand characteristics) everywhere or if the investigators tend to be the same people who just happen to work in a wide range of places, as tends to be the case with research in competitiveness. Nonetheless, by using it, we can become sensitized to the very problems (e.g. shared demand characteristics) that constitute warnings against overinterpreting the meta-analysis. An imperfect method for reviewing accumulated studies, it is surely an advance over the discursive approach of the present review!

THE HANDBOOKS: A COMING OF AGE

The Handbook of Cross-Cultural Psychology

Noted briefly by Brislin (1983), the 6-volume *Handbook of Cross-Cultural Psychology* (Triandis et al 1980) comprised a landmark publication in this field. The second through sixth volumes each had a particular focus; respectively *methodology, basic processes* (perception, cognition, learning, and motivation), *developmental psychology, social psychology,* and *psychopathology.* Reviews that appear in the *Journal of Cross-Cultural Psychology* provide a good indication of their contents. The review of the methodology volume (Malpass 1981) notes that it is the largest of the six; not surprising, he says, since "cross-cultural psychology is primarily a methodological strategy" (p. 493). "A fascinating, if at times bewildering diversity" is noted by Goodnow (1981, p. 499) in her review of the volume on basic processes. A similar assessment of the volume on developmental psychology is provided by Finley (1981). Not comprehensive, he says, but varied, with chapters on infancy, language (including bilingualism), memory and other kinds of cognitive development, and play. The volume on social psychology, according to Argyle (1981), contains many instances of differences in social behavior between cultures, but "only one chapter on the origins and causes of cultural differences" (p. 503), that by Berry (1980a) on social and cultural change. Argyle also deplores the absence of a chapter on intercultural communication, but another multivolume work, that by Landis & Brislin (1983), has since appeared to give this rapidly growing application of cross-cultural psychology a thorough airing. Sundberg (1981) reviews the volume on psychopathology, noting that psychology has long been interested not only in deviance per se, but has also long wondered "about the universality of Western disorders and [has had] a curiosity about uniqueness of aberrations discovered in other cultures" (p. 504). Sundberg views this volume, with references to over 600 scholars, as an attempt to impose order on what is known about disorder. Dragun's chapter on the severe disorders (Draguns 1980) is considered a well-organized review and critique demonstrating that evidence now exists that no disorder is immune to cultural shaping, the neuroses and affective psychoses more so than the schizophrenias.

The first volume in the set, co-edited by Triandis and Lambert, was reviewed by the present writer (Segall 1981a); a summary follows. Lambert introduced the volume by considering the "broad, shifting, flexible" models, paradigms, and frameworks that constitute the "perspectives" of cross-cultural psychology. He noted emerging convergence and mutually corroborative findings from diverse theoretical approaches. Lambert's claim is given substance by Jahoda, who reviewed several of the best-known approaches, including culture and personality, subjective culture, comparative psychometrics, Piagetian and Witkinian cognitive development, and Cole's ethnographic psychology.

Munroe and Munroe emphasized contextual variables and the need to study human behavior comparatively. They gave attention to biological matters, with a focus on adaptive solutions to problems of human existence, while backing away from the tiresome biological vs cultural argument that has for so long cluttered the field.

Contemporary biology looms large in Thompson's chapter, which demonstrated how neo-Darwinian biology can guide cross-cultural psychology. Thompson showed how the insights of contemporary biology offer promising conceptual schemes. Klineberg provided a thoughtful account of the early days (up to 1960) of our enterprise, noting that an interest in social evolution was a part of cross-cultural psychology from its beginning. Lonner's chapter was a review of findings suggesting that where one stands with respect to relativism may influence what one finds, and that universals are to be found if we look for them.

Warwick covered the politics and ethics of cross-cultural research, documenting the genuine risks that confront even the most well-meaning researcher who might nevertheless produce invalid findings and cause harm to her host-country subjects and colleagues.

Volume I of the *Handbook* leads to a positive assessment of cross-cultural psychology, showing it to be rich in questions worth asking, in efforts to devise workable ways to answer them, and in motivation to extract understanding from a dazzling array of facts about a marvelous variety of behaviors. The volume marks a coming of age of an endeavor to internationalize what was once a narrow, scientistic, Euro-American discipline.

The Handbook of Cross-Cultural Human Development

An encyclopedic review of the literature on cultural differences in child development (R. H. Munroe et al 1981), the purpose of which is to indicate future research directions, contains 26 contributions organized into four categories: Perspectives (papers dealing with evolution, universals, psychoanalytic theory, ethnography, and multiethnic societies); early experience and growth (infancy, infant care, ethnic differences in physical growth, and stress); cognitive and moral development; and socialization and outcomes. The editors noted that these contributions demonstrate a decline of interest in the effects of "culture" on "personality" (treated as monolithic entities) and a rise of interest in the effects of particular cultural practices on both developmental processes and personality.

The volume also demonstrates a continuing emphasis on the importance of early experience and an increased tolerance for the search for general relationships—"a modulated nomothetic viewpoint" instead of a position of extreme cultural relativism. There is much evidence in the various chapters that there are laws governing human development and that it is via systematic testing of hypotheses within and across cultures that these laws are most likely to be discovered.

CULTURE IN PSYCHOLOGY AND PSYCHOLOGY IN OTHER CULTURES

Teaching Cross-Cultural Psychology

At the beginning of the post-Handbook era, very few undergraduate curricula included a course in cross-cultural psychology, despite some improvement over the recent past and several calls for such courses (Segall 1980, Cole 1984, Triandis & Brislin 1984) to help remedy ethnocentric attitudes and parochial knowledge (Barrows et al 1981). Even the distribution of selective course syllabi by the APA (1983) has not resulted in a proliferation of courses. That the slow growth in the internationalization of psychology is not due to a dearth of teaching materials was demonstrated by Torney-Purta (1984), who provided an extensive annotated bibliography, including some supplementary texts for courses in developmental psychology (e.g. Dasen & Heron 1980, Morsbach 1980, Tapp 1980, Edwards 1981, Seymour 1981, Young & Ferguson 1981, Dasen 1982, Hartup et al 1982, Kay 1982, Super & Harkness 1982, Wagner & Stevenson 1982, Tallman et al 1983) and for courses in social psychology (e.g. Segall 1979, Coehlo & Ahmed 1980, Brislin 1981, Samovar & Porter 1982, Tajfel 1982, Goldstein & Segall 1983, Landis & Brislin 1983, Naroll 1983, Plath 1983) and many others, described in toto as "a surprising amount of recently published material . . . suitable for infusing an international dimension into undergraduate psychology courses" (Torney-Purta 1984, p. 1042). Russell (1984) pointed out that unless that dimension is introduced, American psychology may remain blind to its culture-bound assumptions and limitations, a point also made by Berry (1983), who warned that "the discipline is so culture-bound and culture-blind that, as it stands now, it should not be employed as is" in cultures outside the United States, not even in Canada (Berry 1983, p. 449). His warnings were echoed by Kennedy et al (1984) and Sexton & Misiak (1984), who traced the roots and consequences of the isolationism of American Psychology and who agreed that the needed consciousness raising would best begin at the undergraduate level. Clearly, the felt need to expand the teaching of cross-cultural psychology is spreading. Whether that will produce a real expansion of cross-cultural courses for either undergraduate or graduate students remains to be seen.

The Impact of Psychology in Other Cultures

Meanwhile, as cross-cultural courses are slowly being added to the curriculum in the United States, as a hoped-for remedy to the parochialism of US-derived psychology, it spreads rapidly into other societies. A special issue of the *International Journal of Psychology* (Sinha & Holtzman 1984) discussed the impact of Western psychology in China (Ching 1984), Turkey (Kağitçibaşi 1984), the Philippines (Lagmay 1984), several Arab nations (Melikian 1984), Venezuela (Salazar 1984), and Africa (Serpell 1984). Throughout is a consistent concern for relevance to national interests and some doubt that Western psychology is well suited to address them. A more hopeful assessment of the applications of cross-cultural child development research to international development emerged from the 1982 AAAS meetings (Wagner 1983). Seeley & Wagner (1983) reviewed this symposium.

APPLICATIONS TO SOCIAL ISSUES   If mainstream Western psychology is less relevant than non-Westerners want it to be, is cross-cultural psychology better able to address social issues in the diverse forms in which they exist throughout the world? Some provocative efforts to respond to this felt need appeared recently. Stating that "to transform the moral and social and political culture of mankind" is "the chief task of the social sciences," Naroll (1983) contributed the first of a projected three-volume work in which he distilled ethnographic data from all parts of the world and extracted from them a provocative set of hypotheses about human values that can provide guidelines in the search for a healthy and happier human condition. Assessing strengths and weaknesses of the world's many cultures against potentially universal values, Naroll showed how a cross-cultural analysis (employing a holocultural research strategy) can provide a theoretically sound and potentially applicable understanding of the social psychological forces that impinge on worldwide problems, such as crime, mental illness, divorce, alcoholism, child abuse, and others.

A volume on the applications of psychology to development projects appeared in England, an outgrowth of a conference held at Lancaster University in 1980 (Blackler 1983), and a group of cross-cultural psychologists prepared a methods manual for field workers engaged in various kinds of development projects (Lonner & Berry 1985). Many of the same group are at work on a WHO-sponsored volume on the applications of cross-cultural psychology to the search for healthier human development (Dasen et al 1986).

To promote healthy human development is to seek ways to minimize human suffering. Alas, suffering cannot be eliminated, and all populations will include persons who live their lives with some handicap. American clinical psychology and allied helping professions have developed an arsenal of techniques, programs, and institutions to help handicapped persons, and U.S. models of programs rooted in a helping profession are a popular American export. That they ought *not* be was suggested in an analysis (Aptekar 1983) of the needs of handicapped persons in Latin America, where the urban poor have little access to professional help and have developed many ingenious self-helping mechanisms, while the rich and powerful readily advocate state-provided services that are available mostly to members of the small, privileged upper classes. Aptekar's accounts of the failures of many helping agencies, contrasted with his accounts of successful efforts by handicapped persons themselves, such as street-corner begging, comprise a thought-provoking discussion of well-intentioned, but nonetheless ethnocentric, efforts to solve Third World problems by transferring U.S. or European models.

MENTAL HEALTH   Many publications dealing with cultural aspects of mental health care, of counseling, and of other kinds of helping systems appeared (e.g. Pedersen et al 1981, Marsella & Pedersen 1981, Gaw 1982, Marsella & White 1982), all of which argue that Western techniques ought not be exported "as is" to non-Western cultures, nor employed without modification for non-core-cultural persons wherever they reside.

Fruitful studies of mental health involve migrants and refugees, partly because of the convenience of studying people of different origins in the same place, and partly because such people are, by nature of their recent experience, under stress. There are numerous examples (e.g. Carpenter & Brockington 1980, Cochrane 1980, Cochrane & Stopes-Roe 1981, Lombardo 1981, Smither 1981, Cheung & Dobkin de Rios 1982, Nguyen 1982, Scott & Scott 1982, Baker 1983). Smither (1981) has produced a good review of the literature on acculturative stress.

Alcoholism in particular was studied by Barry (1982), who found that frequent drunkenness tends to occur in nontechnologically advanced societies, especially ones that rely heavily on hunting, fishing, or gathering. In technologically advanced societies, differences in drinking were influenced more by cultural variations in social control.

INTERCULTURAL CONTACTS   The field of intercultural communications has grown very rapidly in the past five years, with that growth marked by the *International Journal of Intercultural Relations* (now in its seventh year) and a Handbook (Landis & Brislin 1983) with numerous articles in which cross-cultural psychological principles are applied to efforts to reduce intercultural misunderstanding. In a world in which cross-cultural contacts are now common, practical lessons derived from research are becoming available (e.g. Bochner 1982). Much of the research reported in that volume was expressly designed to understand phenomena inherent in contact situations per se.

It appears that mainstream psychology, inherently Western in conception, is gradually being infused with concern for cultural variables and thus readied for application wherever psychological insights might be useful. But, clearly, until the infusion proceeds further, extreme caution is needed. We turn now to some substantive research areas that comprise the core of cross-cultural psychology.

SUBSTANTIVE AREAS OF CROSS-CULTURAL RESEARCH

Much of cross-cultural psychology consists of empirical studies of behavior, ranging from basic processes such as perception and cognition, through the development and change of attitudes, values, and beliefs, to behaviors that reflect contact between culture and culture change.

Perception

An early emphasis of substantive research, basic perception was not an active concern during the 1980s. Some reviews of research on visual perception appeared (e.g. Deregowski 1980, Gillam 1980, Segall 1981b), but there were few new empirical studies. One old issue, the role of fundus pigmentation (as measured by skin color) in color perception, was raised in a study done at three latitudes in Nigeria, Saint Kitts, and Los Angeles (Gaines & Powell 1981); the findings cast doubt on the importance of pigmentation. The influence of experience remains the most tenable explanation of differences in perception.

If few new studies deal with basic theoretical issues in perception, somewhat more are concerned with practical questions such as the comprehension of pictures. Modiano et al (1982) showed colored illustrations (paintings and photographs of familiar objects) to 76 6-year-olds from six Mexican-Indian groups and found no medium difference, but some objects were more readily seen. Boys recognized more objects and there were some ethnic group differences which, unfortunately, went unexplained, beyond a tantalizing comment, "Children with different experiences perceive differently" (Modiano et al 1982, p. 494).

Orientation problems among African children is an issue that remains interesting to a few researchers. Osuji (1982), working with 64 6-year-old Igbo children in Nigeria, found age trends in ability to construct patterns of geometric stimuli of varying complexity with a model present, but a previously noted tendency (in earlier studies) to rotate designs was not evident in this sample.

Another perceptual issue that received attention was color, but the emphasis is more on color lexicons than on perception. An excellent review of this topic, coupled with a report of an empirical study done in Nepal on salience of colors, was provided by Bolton et al (1980). Their data supported the Berlin & Kay (1969) evolutionary hypothesis.

Cognition

In contrast to a dearth of studies on perception, there is a plethora of studies on cognitive behaviors. They are varied in approach and content. The following potpourri reflects well what was found scattered through numerous journals.

Spencer & Darvizeh (1983) compared knowledge of local neighborhoods of 3- and 4-year-olds in Britain and Iran and found no differences in accuracy but distinct stylistic differences in reporting—more pictorial in Iran, more directional in Britain. Rogoff & Waddell (1982) investigated reconstruction by 9-year-old Mayan and U.S. children of an organized three-dimensional miniature scene and found no difference on that task (despite well-documented differences on standard memory tasks), suggesting that if information is organized by a meaningful context, children of any culture may display memory skills equally well. Another memory study (Klich & Davidson 1983) done in Australia found aboriginal children remembering visual experiences better than rural white children.

Posner (1982) investigated the development of mathematical concepts among children, both schooled and unschooled, from an agricultural society and a merchant society (Baoulé and Dioula, respectively, both West African) and found that schooling mattered for the Baoulé but not for the Dioula, but only on tasks involving other than perceptual strategies. Posner concluded that experiences involved both in schooling and being reared in a merchant culture were relevant. The effect of a merchant culture was also studied by Jahoda (1983b), to be mentioned later.

Focusing on language learning, Bates et al (1984) compared sentence interpretation strategies employed by 2- to 5-year-old American and Italian children and found the former relying on word order, the latter on semantic cues. A study of cross-language speech perception (Werker & Tees 1984) involving English infants as well as adult English and adult Salish subjects responding to a Salish speech contrasts showed that infants can discriminate non-native speech contrast without relevant experience, but that this ability declines with age, most dramatically within the first year of life.

How mothers and infants (ranging from 6–36 months) in two cultures (USA and Kenya) interact in teaching tasks was the focus of Dixon et al (1984), who found both differences and similarities across cultures (e.g. the Kenyan mothers were more directive and less reinforcing, but both groups displayed affectively positive interactions). Dasen (1984) studied intelligence among the

Baoulé in the light of Piagetian theory, and in one of many studies dealing with Piagetian conservation (Shea et al 1983) found differences among cultural groups (Madang, North Salomons, and Southern Highlanders of Papua New Guinea) when primary school children were tested for conservation of number, length, quantity, and area. In the same country, a predominantly methodological study (Robin & Shea 1983) reported differences in scores on a visual motor test between Highlanders and Australian children.

Zepp (1983), studying the acquisition of logical concepts among Adjukru children and adults in Ivory Coast (where formal education occurs in French) in order to compare this performance with Kpelle people from Liberia (education in English) who had earlier been studied by Gay & Cole (1967), found that the Adjukru performed far less well than the Kpelle, despite the fact that both groups have similar languages, in which great precision is possible with respect to disjunction. Zepp's (1983) finding led him to conclude that the Gay & Cole (1967) hypothesis that concept acquisition is facilitated by its ease of linguistic expression was not tenable and suggested that features of the formal education system were implicated. One feature of Quranic schools, rote memorization, and some of its positive sociocultural implications were described by Wagner & Lotfi (1983). The effects of schooling on conservation was the concern of Rogan & Macdonald (1983) in a study done in the Ciskei in Southern Africa.

School performance was the dependent variable in an Australian study (Clark & Halford 1983) that asked whether cognitive style accounts for differences between aboriginal and Anglo-Australian children; it did not, but tested intelligence did. In a study in which intelligence test score was the dependent variable, R. L. Munroe & Munroe (1983), with data from 1413 male Abuluya (Kenya) secondary school students, found birth order to be associated with intellectual performance on three different tests (earlier borns performing better), but there was no association with family size. They explained their findings in terms of declining quality in caretaking available to lower birth orders, and linked their study with ideas expressed earlier by Zajonc & Markus (1975).

This baker's dozen of studies illustrates the diversity of topics pursued by psychologists interested in cognition (memory, concept acquisition, conservation, schooling as a contributor, school performances as a consequence, and more). Throughout the panoply of studies pertaining to cognition there lurks continuing concern with cognitive competence of culturally distinct groups. In the next section we examine in some depth recent developments in thinking about cognitive competence.

COGNITIVE COMPETENCE   Rooted in the history of European contact with non-European cultures has been a need on the part of Europeans to discover both how and how well non-Europeans think. Jahoda (1983b) found that

African children in Zimbabwe, with family experience in trading, understood the profit concept in advance of British children of the same age range. This was a noteworthy departure from most early examples of cross-cultural research which seem to have been motivated by an intent to test the facile and obviously ethnocentric proposition that "they" don't think as rationally as we do. Of course, the sin of ethnocentrism was not borne solely by cross-cultural psychology; as Gould (1981) so aptly demonstrated, biological determinism permeated Western science generally, and psychometrics particularly, almost unchallenged up to World War II. Indeed, for decades, cross-cultural research has provided powerful challenges to biological theories of racial differences in intelligence, but recent excitement over sociobiology, much of it well founded, has had the unfortunate side effect of resurrecting such theories.

Increasingly it is recognized that the matter of biological determinism (and not only in the domain of cognitive behavior) is a complex matter. Biological evolution tends to be adaptive, but so does cultural change. So, plausibly arguing that a group's behavior is adaptive to its setting says nothing about the roots of the adaptiveness. Responding to insights inherent in Campbellian epistemology (Campbell 1975), several cross-cultural psychologists in the 1980s argued the parallelism of biological evolution, individual learning, and cultural evolution (e.g. Berry 1980b, 1981, Segall 1981b). In a work that deals with culture and the evolutionary process, R. Boyd and P. J. Richersen (book in preparation) derive a model that explains culturally determined components of the human behavioral phenotype essentially in the same way as genetically inherited adaptations of other organisms are explained. Arguing that we need to understand how the structural features of human cultural transmission interact with environmental contingencies to create the forces of cultural evolution, they assert that some cultural evolutionary forces, like natural selection, have essentially the same character in both the cultural and genetic system.

The dominant emphasis in cross-cultural psychology accordingly has become ecological, whereby cultural recipes for behaviors are seen as cumulatively selected for their adaptive character and transmitted intergenerationally by social means as well as by genetic adaptation (both processes, social and biological, are blind and nonprescient). So, "a cross-cultural difference in behavior ought not to be taken, in itself, as evidence against [nor *for*] a biologically based, genetically influenced behavioral tendency," Segall (1981b, p. 378) argued. The same argument was applied to cross-cultural variations in sex differences by Ember (1981), who showed how distributional evidence says nothing about cause. Berry (1984b), in an essay on cognitive competence, stated

> . . . the question becomes not *whether* biologically-or culturally-rooted differences exist in a particular behavior, but their role, their extent, their interaction, etc. While we have available for study groups which are racially similar but culturally different, there are no groups which

are culturally similar but racially different. Thus we are in a position to explore the contribution of cultural variation to cognitive competence, but not of racial variation independent of culture . . . hence the specific roles of biological or cultural factors cannot be identified (Berry 1984b, p. 335).

In the same essay, Berry reviewed the literature on folk concepts of cognitive competence, an important literature, given the possibility that the Euro-American psychologists' very concept of intelligence may be an in-appropriately imposed etic. Recent examples of emic definitions of competence include Putnam & Kilbride (1980), who did content analyses of school-boys' essays on "intelligence," collected in Mali and Kenya, and found an emphasis on social skills. Working also in Kenya, Super (1980, 1983) found that Kipsigis adults cited verbal cognitive skills useful in modern Kenya. Similar studies have been done in Asia (e.g. Gill & Keats 1980, Chen et al 1982, Keats 1982) and in the U.S. (Sternberg et al 1981). Berry's summary of these and earlier studies is that "they have identified novel qualities or dimensions which have not traditionally been represented in the assessment of cognitive competence" and while something like general intelligence is supportable in the face of these findings, "it is likely to be a general intelligence construct which differs substantially from our present, culture-bound, construct" (Berry 1984b, p. 355).

In any case, it appears that within groups there are measurable and popularly recognized individual differences in competence; across groups, the picture remains clouded.

"RACIAL" DIFFERENCES IN COMPETENCE   Research and polemics on so-called racial differences in intelligence have long been salient features of American history, sociology, and psychology. The controversy, centering mostly on black/white-American mean differences in performance on tests and on school grades, has international implications, since the world's cultural groups also vary in race. Cultures and race are not only confounded worldwide, they are confounded in the U.S. Hence, the issue of race differences is a legitimate concern in this review. The Australian psychologist Mackenzie (1980a,b) produced some telling arguments against genetic explanations such as those that continue to be defended by Jensen (1978, 1980, 1981). Other important discussions, several of them book length, also appeared (Flynn 1980, Taylor 1980, Blau 1981, Scarr 1981). Mackenzie, in a more recent paper (1984), exposed as "the hereditarian fallacy" the notion that high within-race heritability and the inability of particular environmental explanations to account completely for mean performance differences are relevant to a genetic explanation. Instead, he argued,

The choice between a genetic and an environmental account of race differences is most properly based on "jointly genetic/environmental designs," which control for both genetic and environmental differences in a behavior genetic framework. The available evidence from such designs tends to support an environmental over a genetic account, although the evidence is not presently sufficient and gives little insight into what the relevant environmental differences might be (Mackenzie 1984, p. 1214).

As an example of the kind of behavior genetic studies that could be pursued, Mackenzie suggested comparisons of children in Asian countries fathered by American soldiers of different races.

Achievement differences   In a related arena of much current concern in the U.S., consistent reductions in the size of average school achievement score differences between whites and blacks were discussed by Jones (1984) as the likely result of certain societal changes (for example, increased early enrollment in high school mathematics courses) producing increases in black achievement levels.

COGNITIVE DEVELOPMENT   When differences across cultures on tasks relating to ontogenetic developmental theories are found, there is a risk of ethnocentric interpretation. Berry et al (1982) in Adler (1982b) argued that such theories (e.g. Witkinian cognitive style and Piagetian genetic epistemology) are not inherently ethnocentric, but must be accompanied by concern for functional adaptiveness of behavior in cultural and ecological context. Rogoff (1982) also argued the importance of context. Her argument is applied specifically to memory development in a later paper (B. Rogoff & J. Mistry, "Memory Development in Cultural Context," in preparation). Other issues pertaining to cognitive development were contained in more comprehensive reviews of developmental psychology (e.g. Adler 1982a).

Socialization and Personality Development

Child-rearing variations are the concern of several studies. Gibson et al (1984) observed contact stimulation provided to young children in Greece, USA, and USSR. Ispa (1984) compared 63 American-born and Soviet immigrant women in the U.S.; the Americans enjoyed more child-care contributions from their husbands, the Russian women turned more to medical personnel for child-rearing advice. In Uganda, Opolot (1982) surveyed child-rearing practices among 240 mothers from four ethnic groups (Baganda, Iteso, Acholi, Lugbara). Considerable uniformity was found in some respects (discouragement of aggression, expectations of obedience, high level of body contact) and in other respects Baganda stood out (independence training and a permissiveness regarding rearing and toilet training). Rather than asking mothers about their practices, Bell & Miller (1982) interviewed teenage school children in a Bavarian village and found a sex difference in their views of where to get information on how to rear children. A step beyond these monocultural studies is one by Ryback et al (1980) that involves six cultures, but it, too, relies on student reports. Several steps beyond is one by R. H. Munroe & Munroe (1980), who reviewed earlier coded ethnographies from 84 societies and found that they could offer a cross-cultural generalization relating parental permissiveness to household structure; namely, the greater the number of families occupying a single dwelling, the more permissive was the society. Permissiveness was noted by McSwain (1981) among adults in both East Timor and Papua New Guinea, but in the former it is combined with "insensitivity" and physical restriction, while in the latter, permissiveness combines with parental awareness and encouragement of dependence. McSwain saw these rearing differences as related to infant behavioral differences, with the New Guinean babies displaying less irritation and aggression than the East-Timores. Zern (1980) employed the holocultural strategy to uncover a relationship between "disequilibrating" or challenging child-rearing practices and cultural complexity, and interpreted such practices as facilitating cognitive development.

Turning to emic notions of how to raise children, Keller et al (1984) compared pregnant women in a highly industrialized, nuclear-family society (Germany) with a sample from a nonindustrialized, developing country (Costa Rica). The German mothers-to-be expected earlier cognitive development and anticipated acting earlier to stimulate cognitive growth. If the world becomes increasingly industrialized, such differences may well diminish, as is suggested below when modernization research is considered.

MORAL DEVELOPMENT   Piaget (1932) and Kohlberg (1969) both claimed to have uncovered culturally universal sequences of moral development. Over the years there have been many cross-cultural applications or tests of their respective models. Edwards (1981) provided a thorough review of research on objective versus subjective responsibility and imminent justice versus naturalistic justice in studies based on Piaget's notions. She also reviewed studies based on Kohlberg's approach and found it cross-culturally valid. The reviewed research suggested to Edwards that the major stimulus for moral development is any kind of role-taking opportunity that leads us to expect differences in moral judgment by members of societies varying in complexity of social structure. Subsequent research confirms this. To cite one recent study (Bouhmama 1984), 20 secondary school pupils from each of two societies, Algeria and Britain, produced significant differences in scores of moral maturity, related by the author to cultural and religious values. Another study (Marín 1981) found differences in perceived justice in Colombia and USA.

Future orientation and time perspectives   Future planning may be done by adolescents everywhere, but Sundberg et al (1983) found differences between 15-year-olds of both sexes from small towns in India, the U.S., and Australia in time spans. How time is allocated to activities was studied in two Bantu-speaking Kenyan groups, a Quechua-speaking Peruvian group, and an upper-middle class American group by R. H. Munroe et al (1983), who found regularities and differences. In all four groups, food preparation by adult females consumed 12 to 19% of their time. Within USA, Gonzalez & Zimbardo (1985) reported different time frames for social classes and occupations.

Values, Beliefs, and Motives

At the very heart of the concept culture is the expectation that different peoples will possess different values, beliefs, and motives reflected in numerous behaviors. Travelers to foreign lands detect them quickly, sensing that they are viewing not only different lifestyles but also different attitudes toward life itself.

To delineate such differences is one of the enterprises of cross-cultural psychology. Developing techniques for inferring such dispositions from observable behavior, linking the inferred dispositions to ecological and cultural forces which might be their antecedents, and examining the changes in such dispositions as the culture changes are all part of this enterprise.

Excellent surveys of the pre-1980 work in this field can be found in the *Handbook of Cross-Cultural Psychology,* particularly in Volume 5 (Triandis & Brislin 1980). Zavalloni (1980) noted the preponderance of descriptive research on values and reviewed several influential approaches to the measurement of values in diverse settings. The early efforts set forth a number of value dimensions along which societies were believed to vary [familiar ones being Dionysian/Appolonean (Benedict 1934) and the multiclustered dichotomies of C. Kluckhohn (1956) and of F. Kluckhohn & Strodtbeck (1961) among others]. Zavalloni's (1980) review rightly points out that most earlier research on values yielded static, descriptive data and provided little information on either their determinants or consequents. This assessment is still valid.

Davidson & Thomson (1980) argued that the study of attitudes cross-culturally had not yielded many substantive findings (at least they chose to present few, in favor of discussing methodological issues). Nonetheless, they concluded that prior to 1980, substantive findings revealed that the "basic cognitive processes [underlying attitude acquisition] such as information and cue utilization are relatively invariant across cultures. What does vary from culture to culture is the belief content of these processes" (Davidson & Thomson 1980, p. 62). Insofar as they described attitudinal content, they dealt mostly with such arenas as managerial attitudes, intergroup attitudes, and various attitudes that might plausibly be linked with technological change of the kind Western psychologists often dub "modernity." Berry's (1980a) review of studies of social and cultural change contains several that deal with attitudes relating to marginality, cultural pluralism, assimilation, and modernism per se.

Here, too, can be found a good review of research on attitudes toward achievement, or achievement motivation, which has long been an interest of students of dynamics of cultural change.

Brislin's (1983) chapter in the *Annual Review of Psychology* contained an update (to 1981) of studies of achievement motivation, attitudes toward success, Machiavellianism, locus of control, authoritarianism, and moral values; his emphasis, however, was on methodological issues inherent in efforts to study these cross-culturally.

If, as many American social scientists (e.g. Heilbroner 1974) suggest, the stressed values of an industrial civilization are hard work, efficiency, environmental exploitation, material (as opposed to spiritual) achievement, autonomy, competitiveness, and perhaps most importantly, concern with self and self improvement, to what extent are such values shared by other societies? What other values are more salient in other societies?

Focusing on work-related values, Hofstede (1980) administered questionnaires to employees of a multinational firm with units both in highly industrialized nations (e.g. U.S.A., Australia, and Great Britain) and in others where industry is a younger, less pervasive feature (e.g. Pakistan). Several of his items can be construed as measures of individualism (confirmed by a factor analysis), and this value was found to be less characteristic of the less industrialized nations.

INDIVIDUALISM   But what is "individualism" and with what opposing value is it to be contrasted? Triandis and colleagues are endeavoring to define operationally a dimension labeled *individualism/collectivism* and note in several reports (e.g. Hui & Triandis 1985) that "collectivism" is not well understood. To define it, they gave 49 cultural psychologists and anthropologists a questionnaire requiring responses "as if" one were an individualist or collectivist. The items concerned seven categories (e.g. considering effects on others of own's behavior, feeling of involvement with others) with respect to ten target groups (e.g. spouse, co-workers, neighbors). The two role-play perspectives yielded differences: "individualists" and "collectivists" were differentially concerned with other people, but more so for some targets than others. And some of the seven behavioral categories yielded clearer differences than others. The two most salient were considering implications of one's decisions and sharing of material resources. This methodological effort showed that within the research community, collectivism is a concept with verisimilitude. It can be defined as having relatively high concern for others. It remains to be seen if this concept has cross-cultural usefulness (i.e. is a derived *etic*) with "real people" as well as social scientists. If so, it can incorporate such dimensions as "allocentric-idiocentric" which Triandis (1983) found to be a dimension along which Hispanic U.S. Navy recruits differed from "mainstream" Americans. Hispanics, manifesting allocentrism, valued good interpersonal relations, harmony, and loyalty more than did the non-Hispanics. Hsu (1981) found that the individualism-collectivism dimension describes a salient difference between Americans and Chinese. The concept as developed in the Illinois laboratory has been translated into a test, the INDCOL scale, which Hui (1984) has subjected to numerous validation studies. He, like Hsu, showed that collectivism was more likely to be valued by Chinese than by Americans, at least among college students. That the individualism-collectivism construct bears on behaviors other than responding to questionnaire items was shown in a scenario study, conducted both in Hong Kong and Illinois, wherein students allocated money to themselves and partners. The Chinese were more equality oriented and more other-serving than their American counterparts (Hui & Triandis 1984). This finding is compatible with other recent oriental/Western comparisons of reward or resource allocation (e.g. Mahler et al 1981, Bond et al 1982, Leung & Bond 1984, and Murphy-Berman et al 1984) as well as in Brazil (Rodriques 1982).

Returning to Illinois, Triandis et al (1985) investigated individual differences in individualism-collectivism (employing the term allocentric vs idiocentric to specify that they are operating at the "psychological level") and found that allocentrism correlated with other values such as cooperation, equality, and honesty, while idiocentrism correlated with individualistic values such as "comfortable life," pleasure, need for achievement, alienation, anomie, and loneliness. This carefully constructed and pretested INDCOL measure will likely be used extensively in future cross-cultural research. If, as there is reason to believe, the values of industrial society are spreading to developing nations, a good measure of individualism-collectivism may be as attractive to students of "modernization" as were McClelland's measures of achievement motivation in recent decades.

ACHIEVEMENT   Allied with individualism in industrial society is concern for personal achievement. Since McClelland (1971) argued that achievement motivation was a necessary precursor of economic development, there was hope that its facilitation among non-Western peoples could speed their economic development. By 1980, however, confronted by evidence that psychology probably accounts for a very small proportion of the variance in macroeconomic wellbeing, by warnings that the encouragement of entrepreneurship in settings where the opportunity structure is deficient may produce frustration and domestic or international turmoil, and by evidence that in some societies achievement is defined explicitly in terms of group norms rather than individual accomplishment, interest in studying achievement motivation cross-culturally waned. During the period surveyed, few studies focused on achievement motivation.

One of the few used projective techniques with a sample of adult Korean immigrants. A veteran psychoanalytically oriented anthropologist (DeVos 1983) interpreted the protocols as showing that these migrants arrive in the USA with very strong "internalized need," greater than what DeVos had found a generation ago for a Japanese sample. But, as Maehr (1980) suggested, most scholars appear ready to abandon achievement motivation because the concept has different cultural connotations.

ACHIEVEMENT ATTRIBUTION   Recently, beliefs about achievement have come into cross-cultural focus. Do individuals believe they *can* succeed? Is striving linked with success in all cultural settings? A number of studies [e.g. Betancourt & Weiner (1982)] deal with perception of ability to achieve, a concept that derives from Rotter's (1966) IE-Scale approach to the measurement of locus of control.

The Rotter Scale has frequently been administered to several samples in a single study because the authors had reason to believe those samples would differ on it in ways that reflect cultural values. Thus, Reimanis & Posen (1980) used the scale with samples of university students in Nigeria, Rhodesia, Zimbabwe, and the United States and tested a set of hypotheses linking "powerlessness" (externality) with alienation, believed by the authors to be a characteristic in (white) Rhodesia and (black) Zimbabwe when the data were collected. They found that while personal control did not differ between pairs of culturally similar groups (whites in the USA and Rhodesia, blacks in Nigeria and Zimbabwe) "Control Ideology" and "System Control" scores were different across the two Black African samples.

A preliminary step in cross-cultural research on attribution of achievement has been to examine the usefulness of the Rotter Scale for this purpose. In Sri Lanka, employing 23 items translated into Sinhala and Tamil, Niles (1981) obtained responses from 192 14- to 16-year-old school children in the city of Colombo and subjected them to a factor analysis. He found two factors, a finding that earlier studies had obtained in Western settings. But in Sri Lanka, the loadings in the two factors were different, leading the author to label them "Fatalism" and "Powerlessness." The first is not different from the West, but the second is. Apparently in this poor developing country, success is attributed not only to self effort versus external factors (the "Fatalism" dimension), but to one's own ability vs the power of other persons (the "Powerlessness" dimension). That internality-externality is multidimensional and perhaps differentially so in different societies was also suggested by Munro (1979), who, after criticizing the use of generalized locus of control scales of the Rotter variety, constructed his own questionnaire for use among blacks and whites in Africa. Also, an important effort in Canada by a team of researchers (Lefcourt et al 1979) resulted in an essentially new version of a success attribution scale. Lefcourt and colleagues, arguing that internality/externality a la Rotter (1966) should be independent of stability (one's own ability and the inherent difficulty of a task are stable causes, while one's effort or luck are unstable causes, with, of course, ability and effort internal while task difficulty and luck are external) produced a multiattributional scale that could measure causality in terms of these two dimensions. They also constructed it to measure two "contexts"—one being achievement, the other affiliation, and, in a balanced way, two outcomes—success and failure. This more complex instrument for the measurement of attributional causality has received its most thorough cross-cultural use in work by Chandler and colleagues in a five-country study.

Chandler et al (1981, 1983) administered the 48-item multidimensional-multiattributional causality scale to a total of 684 university students in India, Japan, South Africa, Yugoslavia, and the United States. (314 were male, 370 female, majoring in education, social science, and physical science. We are told nothing about their ethnicity. One wonders, for example, whether the South African sample was black or white.) With this questionnaire, respondents could have indicated whether *ability, effort, task* (called "context" in the 1981 report) or *luck* were the determinants of various successes and failures in the domains of task achievement and affiliation (the latter domain ignored in the 1981 report). The results permitted the claim that "by not limiting cross-cultural comparisons to the internal-external dimension of locus of control within the achievements domain, this study provided more possibilities for comprehending the complexity of causal attribution" (Chandler et al 1981, p. 218). This was justified by the finding that across the five samples, achievement was most often seen as the result of *effort,* an unstable, but internal factor. But there were differences across the societies that were complex enough that they would not have been detected with a less complex measuring instrument. For example, the Japanese students were most internal in causal attribution for failures and least internal in causal attribution for success, while the Indian students were *least* internal for failure and *most* internal for success. There were other differences across the country samples for ability, context, and levels and for the stability composite (ability and context minus effort and luck), but not for effort or overall internality (ability and effort minus context and luck).

Sex differences and data relating to attribution of success in affiliation are discussed in a second report (Chandler et al 1983). Studying male and female attribution for success and failure in two domains in several cultural settings provides a useful means for seeking associations between gender differences in success attribution and cultural variations. First, however, they found a general sex difference—pooling over the five country samples. Females attributed achievement less to task factors; the females were thus significantly more internal. But on closer examination this general finding turned out to be heavily determined by the data from India. The Indian females most consistently outscored males in attributing achievement to internal factors. In the other samples, there were more similarities than differences between the sexes. The Indian females attributed their achievement successes less to task factors, but this was less so for failures. Also, the sex differences were stronger in the affiliation domain than in the achievement domain. Together, the Chandler et al papers (1981, 1983) should set the stage for work in a wider variety of settings (different countries, samples other than university students) with this instrument that appears appropriately sensitive to the multidimensionality of culturally influenced beliefs about the determinants of success and failure.

Since societies today have very different opportunity and reward structures that are different for various subgroups within them, we should expect both intercultural and intergroup differences in locus of control and achievement attribution. In addition to the studies reviewed above, we find reports of such findings. A study done with German, Japanese, and USA university students of both sexes was briefly reported (Krampen & Wieberg 1981). Using an instrument designed to yield scores of three dimensions of control—chance, powerful others, and internality—the authors found both intercultural and between-sex differences. For example, the Germans and Americans were more internal than the Japanese; the Americans were less likely than the other two groups to attribute success to powerful others; the Germans more than either group acknowledged their felt powerlessness; and females were more external, particularly with respect to chance.

A study done in Fiji (Kishor 1983) compared two ethnic groups (Fijians and Fiji-Indians) of differing academic achievement in 9th grade on the Nowicki & Strickland (1973) children's locus of control scale and found higher internality for the higher achieving group, the Fiji-Indian. Kishor concluded, "culturally conditioned motivational patterns rather than socioeconomic factors underlie the ethnic discrepancies in their academic performance" (Kishor 1983, p. 306). Other recent cross-cultural studies of linkages between locus of control and academic achievement have been reported from Israel (Bar-Tal & Bar-Zahar 1977), Sri Lanka (Faustman & Mathews 1980), and Hungary (Rupp & Nowicki 1978).

The literature lacks experiments that bear directly on ways to stimulate achievement-oriented behavior or to modify perception of success determinants, but it contains at least one attempt to modify behavior in a classroom. Working in a rural Lebanese school with 22 11- to 12-year-old boys and girls, Saigh (1980) used Skinnerian techniques successfully to suppress unwanted distracting behaviors. Token awards (checkmarks on the blackboard) for every 10-minute trouble-free period, with the marks to be traded for opportunities to swim, resulted in predictable declines in the target behaviors. It would be well if more research on achievement-related behaviors focused on what can be done to the environment to shape behavior, rather than on presumed-to-exist states of the organism such as motives. Whereas some of the favorite concepts of

American psychologists, like achievement motivation, are culture-bound, basic principals of behavior modification, and the premise that behavior is shaped by its contingent consequences, promise to be universally valid.

SOCIAL PERCEPTION   When exploring how persons in different cultures understand their world, we must not impose etic dimensions of social perception. Bond (1983) warns that when doing research on social perceptions among non-Western peoples, "we must be careful to refrain from creating their world in the image of our own" (Bond 1983, p. 157). He questions whether all peoples even make attributions regarding either their own or other persons' behavior. It would be ironic indeed if we continued to do research on how attributions are made in cultures where they aren't made at all! Arguing that "the concept of the separate person is central to all theories of attribution" (p. 146), Bond argues that the concept of attribution may be bound to cultures that have political and social philosophies of individualism. In cultures where behavior is largely routine enactment of social roles, lay persons may have little need to formulate theories to explain individual variations in behavior. Perhaps, then, a good tactic is to test the ecological validity of the concept, which can best be done by collecting open-ended responses to viewed behavior episodes. Bond's provocative question has also been raised by other cross-cultural psychologists (e.g. Pepitone 1981). The Chandler et al studies (1981, 1983) reviewed above can, in the light of the Bond and Pepitone essays, be viewed either as showing that cultural variations influence the size of the self-serving bias in success attribution or as evidence that the comparisons are invalid because of differential relevance of the "ability, effort, task, and luck" response categories employed in those studies. Thus, we are left with the disquieting possibility that studies of cultural differences in achievement attribution may be no less ambiguous than were studies in achievement motivation and need to be approached with methodological and conceptual sophistication.

Sophistication is not the hallmark of recent studies of values, many of which involve questionnaire responses provided by university students in different countries. Thus, Reynolds (1984), using the Rokeach Value Survey found some differences and some similarities between Germans and Americans. Pushing the matter a step further, Hogan (1980) found that students both in Germany and the USA earned Rokeach scores that correlated with authoritarianism and self-estimated intelligence. Dealing only with South African female nursing students rather than general university students in this notoriously authoritarian and racist society, Furnham (1984) compared 54 "Africans," 25 "Indians," and 44 "Europeans" on terminal and instrumental values of the Rokeach (1956) scale and on the 5-item Srole (1956) Anomie Scale (no measure of authoritarianism was employed). Reflecting the hierarchy of political power and status that prevails in South Africa, Indians scored intermediate between whites and blacks on most measures. Contrasting white and black scores, the author found large significant differences between them on anomie, but only low correlation between it and either the instrumental or terminal values. The African and Europeans, not surprisingly, differed on some values; for example, the Africans emphasized the sociopolitical concerns of equality and peace, while the Europeans valued the individualistic notions of friendship and love.

There were other such descriptive studies that tell us nothing about why persons in different societies respond the way they do to values inventories. Still, as part of an historical record of attitude change in rapidly developing countries, such studies might be useful. If we could know on a continuing basis how well-defined Chinese populations respond to well-validated measures during an era when American-made television programs interspersed with commercials for American-made products are coming to fill the screens across China, we might trace some of the psychological consequences of the seemingly unrelenting spread of industrial society.

Sex Differences

Cross-cultural research is a promising strategy for understanding why males and females behave differently. When sex differences are shown to vary across cultures, we seem close to demonstrating that nurture and not nature is their "cause." However, in a very thoughtful review of findings on sex differences, Ember (1981) persuasively argued that "the available evidence does not warrant any strong conclusions" (p. 531), this because so little cross-cultural research has been designed to test causal theories and because sex (biological) and differences in relevant experiences are always confounded. Because they are confounded in different ways across cultures gives an exciting theory-testing potential to cross-cultural research, but that potential has not yet been realized. Most studies still merely describe sex differences. A demonstration of how the available facts fail to support either a nature or nurture conclusion, despite the frequency with which their respective advocates cite them, is a highlight of Ember's (1981) review.

Still, distributional evidence on sex differences is provocative, and we should keep track of accumulating evidence that while males and females differ in some ways everywhere, they differ in different ways and to different degrees. By adding plausible theories that predict differential sex differences, we could understand better both sex differences and the particular behaviors for which there are both sex differences and cultural differences. Thus, an analysis of (a) sex differences in aggressive behavior, (b) cultural differences in aggressive behavior, and (c) cultural variation in sex differences in aggressive behavior, all taken together, should illuminate both the reasons for differences between the sexes and the causes of aggression per se. Ember's (1981) review reveals that we are not yet at this millennium, although we already know much about the cross-cultural distribution of sex differences in some behaviors (e.g. aggression, conformity, playmate selection, nurturance, and dominance) but not for many others (e.g. linguistic skills, self-concept, and general differences in the behavior patterns of newborns and infants). However, to put all this together, theory-testing research is needed. Since Ember's (1981) review, have we advanced in this direction?

The question is not easily answered; sometimes an intriguing fact about a sex difference in one or another culture is imbedded in a study with another focus. For example, a study done in a region of South Africa known as the Ciskei (Rogan & Macdonald 1983) was undertaken to determine whether a special teaching program that stressed "physical and mental interaction" would result in better Piagetian conservation performance among African high school students. The study compared scores in a Science Reasoning Task (Shayer & Whary 1973) earned by 359 students who received the program with scores earned by 243 students in control schools. The major finding was a positive evaluation of the program; the program produced better performance in the experimental group, but the program worked far better for boys. During the program most of the actual object manipulation was done by the boys, and when the students worked in groups the boys were most often the leaders. Was this encouraged by the teachers? Were the teachers mostly male? Among Ciskei teenagers, what are the cultural influences that might have contributed to their different behaviors and thence to the differential outcome of the training program? We don't know; these are questions that need attention.

Some recent cross-cultural studies have sex differences as their focus. A holocultural study by Barry & Schlegel (1982) found females contributing most to subsistence more in root crop societies than in those with grain crops. Other consistencies and variations were noted. A monocultural study done in a non-Western (but Western-influenced) setting, namely, a Nigerian University (Adejumo 1981), found the familiar sex difference in assertiveness, but not for law students.

Sex Roles and Identity

Interest in sex-role orientation has been spurred by Bem's (1974) Sex-Role Inventory. Recent studies done in the United States (e.g. Downing 1979, Pedhazur & Tetenbaum 1979) have inspired cross-cultural use. Maloney et al (1981) compared American (USA) and Israeli university students and found that while the two female samples earned very similar scores, Israeli men were less sex-typed than the American men, but at the same time fewer Israelis were androgynous. Assuming the Bem Scale to be applicable in Israel, these findings suggest that Israeli culture contains experiences that shape male identities differently than in the U.S. But is the scale culture free? Kaschak & Sharratt

(1983), doubting its applicability in Latin America, developed their own instrument, one in Spanish language for use in Costa Rica and perhaps in other Latin American countries. A carefully done instrument development effort, it yielded some interesting incidental findings. At an early stage, when many items were available as candidates for inclusion, item selectors could readily agree that many items were clearly male or female. Thus, for 60 "M" and 49 "F" items, at least 85% of the judges concurred. However, among both male and female judges, there was far more agreement with respect to male than female characteristics, suggesting that in this Latin American society, maleness is a more clearly defined concept (stereotype?) than is femaleness. Ironically, half or more of the 20 "M" and 20 "F" items in the final "new" scale were identical to items on the Bem (1974) scale. Still, the new scale, dubbed LASRI, is now available for further use in Latin America. Other recent Latin American studies include Diaz-Loving et al (1981), Kranau et al (1982), and Soto & Shaver (1982).

A similar scale, the CPI Fe Scale (Gough 1966), has already been used in Korea (Gough et al 1968), in Israel (Levin & Karni 1971), and in Japan (Nishiyama 1975). Subsequently, Pitariu (1981) administered a translation of the 30-item scale to 570 males and 300 females in Romanian schools and colleges and found that 31 of the items differentiated the two groups significantly. While three items actually differentiated the sexes in the wrong direction, the overall results confirmed earlier cross-cultural validation studies.

In Australia, where popular stereotype has it that sex roles are sharply defined, Callan & Liddy (1982), studying young children (3-, 4- and 5-year-olds), 50 of them Euro-Australians, 100 of them aboriginal (of whom 50 were urban and 50 rural), obtained scores that were similar to those typically found in the West. However, the urban aboriginal children (but not the rural ones) had lower sex preference scores, which the authors attributed to lack of experience with traditional sex-role behaviors. Another finding is that with increasing age (from three to five years) boys had increasingly higher scores than girls on sex preferences.

A related issue is the popular perception of behavioral traits of the sexes. Since the mid-1970s, Best and Williams, with a diversity of colleagues, have presented adjective check lists and other tasks designed to identify behavior that could be attributed to one or the other sex to samples of children and adults in many nations (e.g. Best et al 1977, Williams et al 1977, Williams et al 1979). A later study (Williams et al 1981) demonstrates how the research program has proceeded and provides a typical set of findings. 428 5-year-old and 8-year-old children in five European countries (France, Germany, Norway, the Netherlands, and Italy) were read 32 stories, each containing a particular trait, 16 of each judged to be stereotypically male and female. By selecting male or female silhouettes, the subjects mostly revealed similarities in sex stereotypes in this set of countries. And, except in Norway and Germany, children of each sex knew their own sex stereotype better than the other sex. Also, stereotypes were better known by 8-year-olds than by 5-year-olds. The authors concluded, "there are general similarities in the patterns of traits differentially ascribed to men and women in all Western countries" (Williams et al 1981, p. 344). More recently, the two senior authors (Williams & Best 1982) put all their team's work together in a comprehensive volume reporting findings on both children and adults from 30 nations, some non-Western (e.g. Malaysia, Nigeria, Peru). The pancultural nature of sex stereotypes is the outstanding finding of this comprehensive research program.

Will sex stereotypes persist? The movement for equality of the sexes is flourishing in most industrial nations and has at least been noticed worldwide. In 1985, to celebrate the end of the United Nations' Decade of Women, an international conference occurred in Nairobi; delegates attended from many nations, both industrial and developing. As sexual equality grows, behavioral differences may diminish and so may the sex stereotypes. Is there evidence that the ideology of sexual equality is spreading? It probably is, but there is as yet little systematic evidence. But we now have an instrument to measure sex-role ideology (Kalin et al 1982), the cross-cultural equivalence of which has been at least minimally established in three English-speaking samples of University students in Canada, England, and Ireland. Psychometrically, the Kalin et al (1982) SRI (sex role ideology) scale is similar in the three countries. Also, of both methodological and substantive interest is the preliminary finding that females were more feminist than the males in all three countries.

Another scale that can measure changes in beliefs about equality of the sexes, first developed in the United States (Jacobson et al 1976), has been employed by Scher et al (1979) in a Hebrew language version with a sample composed of 136 males and 110 females. These Israeli respondents generally were more egalitarian than U.S. respondents; Israeli males in particular were more so than American males; within Israel, the females were more egalitarian than the men.

Sex Identity Conflict

R. L. Munroe & Munroe (1981), pursuing an issue they focused on a decade ago (1971), collected more data on male pregnancy symptoms as an index of sex-identity conflict. This time their data came from Nepal, with findings in line with those from earlier research (e.g. level of symptomatology correlated with preference for the mother role) and from American Samoa, a Polynesian locale where sex-role differentiation is quite weak, with findings running counter to the prevailing ones. In Samoa, male pregnancy, as assessed from both husband and wife reports of the phenomenon, was correlated with male preference for the *male* role. As is so often the case in cross-cultural research, when avidly stirred, the plot thickens!

Aggression

Mounting attention has been given to the study of cultural similarities and differences in aggression behavior, including a compilation of reports from several nations (Goldstein & Segall 1983), several studies derived from a "motivation theory" of aggression developed by Kornadt (1983, 1984a,b), and a focus on children with data from the Six Culture Study (Lambert 1981, 1985a,b). Recent approaches tend increasingly to be biosocial, as illustrated by the work of Bolton (1981, 1984), relating cultural factors, hypoglycemia, folk illness, and hostile behavior. Evidence is mounting that most aggressive acts everywhere are committed by male adolescents (Segall 1983b), and why this is so appears to involve both cultural and biological factors, with the latter having to do more with competition and social dominance (Keating et al 1981). More exclusively cultural hypotheses also continue to be tested, as in a study of intergroup aggression involving Hindus and Moslems in India (Kanekar & Merchant 1982) and Jews and Arabs in Israel (Jaffe et al 1981, Nevo 1984). Two studies compared attitudes toward rape and factors affecting attributions of responsibility to rape victims in India and USA (L'Armand et al 1981, Kanekar & Kolsawalla 1981).

Ethnocentric Attribution

Relations between groups in multiethnic societies can be explored in a variety of ways. With ideas about ethnocentric behavior derived from the turn-of-the-century theorizing of Sumner (1906), neatly codified many years later by LeVine & Campbell (1972), we are armed with numerous testable propositions. Many concern the development of ethnic attitudes and were recently reviewed (Aboud & Skerry 1984). When Taylor & Jaggi (1974) merged thinking about ethnocentricism with Kelley's (1973) principle of attribution, they could predict and find that members of one ethnic group (Hindus) would make internal attributions for ingroup members performing socially desirable acts and external attributions for the performance of undesirable acts, and that they would do the reverse if the same acts were performed by outgroup members (Muslims in this case). In this study, however, no data were collected from the Muslims.

Hewstone & Ward (1985) obtained responses from two groups, Chinese and Malays. Hewstone & Ward worked in two different settings, both involving Chinese and Malay university students, but possessing very different political circumstances, so that relations between the two groups were different in each place. In Malaysia, with a nationalistic government ideology, where Chinese people are a threatened outgroup, only the Malays behaved in accord with the ethnocentric attribution hypothesis. There, the Chinese appeared to favor the Malays, making more internal attributions for positive behaviors performed by Malays than by Chinese. In Malaysia, the Chinese revealed other indices of self-denigration. For example, they refrained from negatively stereotyping the Malays but applied some negative stereotypes to themselves. In Singapore, on the other hand, where the Chinese are not a political minority group, while they still did not make attributions in the manner suggested by the hypotheses, neither did they derogate themselves nor did they show favoritism to the Malays. The Malays in Singapore again attributed internal causes to the positive behaviors of their own group more than to negative behaviors, but here they did not denigrate the Chinese outgroup. Thus, by conducting essentially identical experiments in two different settings, Hewstone & Ward (1985) not only demonstrated that ethnocentric attribution is a nonuniversal tendency; they provided evidence for putative mechanisms whereby sociostructural and cultural influences impinge on the phenomenon. A praiseworthy study, it employs a sophisticated research design (a multifactorial experiment) and the experiment is repeated in two cultural settings where the experimenters had reasonable expectations of different outcomes, with their expectations grounded in theory. That the study was reported in an APA journal that features rigorously refereed social psychology experiments is a sign that cross-cultural psychology in the post-Handbook era has not only come of age; it is entering the mainstream of psychology. In their discussion of ethnocentric attribution, Hewstone & Ward (1985) called their readers' attention to a number of related studies done during this period, some likely to be known to mainstream psychologists, but others not so readily accessible (Clammer 1982, 1983, Hewstone et al 1983, Hewstone & Jaspars 1982, 1984). We have here an encouraging example of good theorizing, sophisticated design, and sensitivity to cultural variables leading to new insights in an area of concern that is both theoretical and applied.

CULTURAL CONTACT

Cultures do not exist in isolation. Aspects of one penetrate others. Humans, metaphorically and in a very real sense, carry culture from place to place, and sometimes they return to their culture of origin and face reentry problems (Adler 1981, Martin 1984). Further, the contents of culture are transmitted by the media, mass and otherwise. Hence, a large portion of the cross-cultural literature deals with products of cultural contact, most of which are understandable as "modernization."

Modernization

Nowhere are cultures static. Everywhere a process known variously as modernization, westernization or acculturation is proceeding, sometimes so rapidly that its psychological concomitants are an urgent topic of study. Many studies reviewed in earlier sections could as well have been placed under the modernization rubric, for no matter what behavior cross-cultural psychologists study today, it is behavior that is changing as cultures change, via cultural contact, migration, the spread of communication, and other facts that make the picture of distinct and separate cultures obsolete. Many studies that focus on changing values and behaviors, with explicit attention to changing cultural forces, have appeared in the period under review. Examples include a study of conflict resolution style among Mexican children (Kagan et al 1981) which showed effects of urbanization, and one that focuses on Mexico-U.S. differences in attitudes toward sexual permissiveness, which are changing in both societies (LaBeff & Dodder 1982). Other evidence of consequences of modernization may be found in Rogoff (1980) and Jahoda (1981), both of which deal with cognitive consequences of schooling, a potent modernizing agent. The issue of acculturative stress received continuing attention. A good discussion of this issue was provided by Dyal and Dyal (1981). One issue that has received even more attention is the influence of urban living, which, as nations modernize, is an increasingly frequent experience.

Consequences of Urbanization

In much of the world, the modernization process includes urban migration. As more and more people come to live in cities, how does their behavior change? A research tradition in both sociology and psychology provides one view of urbanites that focuses on diminished helpfulness as a characteristic behavior, but diverse views exist regarding its underlying mechanism, and competing evidence for the very existence of the phenomenon clouds the picture. Amato (1983) found 18 field studies conducted in six countries (USA, Australia, Canada, Israel, Turkey, and the Netherlands); in nine of the studies, urbanites were found to be less helpful than people in small towns; in five, no difference was found; and in four, *higher* rates of helping behavior were found for urbanites under certain conditions. The diverse findings were not correlated with country; thus, in some countries both lower and higher rates of helping behavior were found for urbanites. The studies referred to included several cross-cultural ones; Amato (1981) in Australia and the U.S., Korte & Ayvalioglu (1981) in Turkey, and Yinon et al (1981) in Israel. Observing that many of the prior studies did not adequately sample either communities or helping behaviors, Amato (1983) employed six different kinds of helping behaviors in a randomly selected sample of 55 cities and towns in eastern Australia and found that population size was negatively associated with helping on four kinds of behavior (naming a favorite color to a student working on a class project, correcting an inaccurate direction, assisting someone with a hurt leg, and donating to a charity). For the dropped envelope measure, helping rates were low and did not vary with community size. The sixth situation involved nonresponse rates to a recent Australian census, and it was found that larger communities had a lower nonresponse rate. Relating his findings to several classic studies and theories of urban life (e.g. Latané & Darley 1970, Milgram 1970) and to a recent discussion of differences in various forms of helping such as "giving" and "doing" (Smithson et al 1983), Amato favored a social inhibition perspective (Latané & Darley 1970) but qualified his conclusion by noting that "explanations for urban unhelpfulness must take into account the nature of the helping" (Amato 1983, p. 585).

Bilingualism

Many questions regarding the cognitive effects of bilingualism have been examined in earlier years. More recently, questions of behavioral style and perceived status of self and other that come to the fore when bilinguals interact with co-nationals and foreigners were investigated in Hong Kong by Pierson & Bond (1982), who found that the Chinese university students majoring in English behaved differently when being interviewed either in Cantonese or English by Chinese or American interviewers.

CONCLUDING REMARKS

What we have seen in this chapter is a small sample of what has appeared in a 5-year span in the continuing development of cross-cultural psychology. Post-Handbook publications in cross-cultural psychology have been so numerous that by this reviewer's reckoning more than half of those encountered have not been cited here, primarily because of space constraints. Some whole topics have not even been touched upon. For some other topics, the output was so prolific (as for example on cognitive behaviors) that space allowed only a sampling designed to indicate the general tenor of the research. Clearly, this means that cross-cultural psychology is now richer and more diverse than the literature that *was* discussed indicates. The obvious conclusion? The field denoted by the phrase *culture and behavior* is now so large that in the future several chapters in the *Annual Review of Psychology* should be devoted to separate parts of the total endeavor. The field of cross-cultural psychology defies coverage as a whole. It is no longer a novelty for students of behavior to collect comparable data in diverse settings, nor is the comparative research strategy limited to just a few topics. Whatever the class of behavior studied by psychologists, some of their studies will include concern for cultural variables. It is hoped that what has been covered here will serve to demonstrate that such concern is essential.

ACKNOWLEDGMENTS

Graduate students in the Maxwell School specializing in cross-cultural research helped to assemble the literature in this field, a literature that is no longer found only in journals that specialize in it. Especially assiduous and successful in this task were Françoise Knaack, Liz Hanahan, and Lora Roeckle. Ms. Knaack also made substantive contributions to the assessment of the materials reviewed, and she shepherded the several drafts of this chapter through the word processor. The students share my pleasure that we found so much, and my regrets that we could describe so little.

Literature Cited

Aboud, F. E., Skerry, S. A. 1984. The development of ethnic attitudes: A critical review. *J. Cross-Cult. Psychol.* 15:3–34

Adejumo, D. 1981. Sex differences in assertiveness among university students in Nigeria. *J. Soc. Psychol.* 113:139–40

Adler, L. L. 1982a. Cross-cultural research and theory. In *Handbook of Developmental Psychology*, ed. B. B. Wolman, pp. 76–90. Englewood Cliffs, NJ: Prentice-Hall. 1040 pp.

Adler, L. L., ed. 1982b. *Cross-Cultural Research at Issue.* New York: Academic. 400 pp.

Adler, N. 1981. Reentry: Managing cross-cultural transitions. *Group Organ. Stud.* 6:341–56

Amato, P. 1981. Urban-rural differences in helping behavior in Australia and the United States. *J. Soc. Psychol.* 114:289–90

Amato, P. 1983. Helping behavior in urban and rural environments: Field studies based on a taxonomic organization of helping episodes. *J. Pers. Soc. Psychol.* 45:571–86

American Psychological Association. 1983. *The Undergraduate Psychology Curriculum from an Intercultural Perspective: Selected Courses.* Washington, DC: APA

Aptekar, L. S. 1983. Suggestions for providing services to the handicapped in Latin America. *World Dev.* 11:995–1004

Argyle, M. 1981. Review of *Handbook of Cross-Cultural Psychology*, Vol. 5, *Social Psychology*, ed. H. C. Triandis, R. W. Brislin. *J. Cross-Cult. Psychol.* 12:501–4

Baker, R. 1983. *The Psychological Problems of Refugees.* London: British Refugee Council. 142 pp.

Barrows, T. S., Klein, S. F., Clark, J. L. D. 1981. *What College Students Know and Believe About Their World.* New Rochelle, NY: Change Magazine Press. 56 pp.

Barry, H. 1980. Description and uses of the Human Relations Area Files. See Triandis & Berry 1980, pp. 445–78

Barry, H. 1982. Cultural variations in alcohol abuse. In *Culture and Psychopathology*, ed. I. Al-Issa, pp. 309–38. Baltimore: Univ. Park Press

Barry, H., Schlegel, A. 1982. Cross-cultural codes on contributions by women to subsistence. *Ethnology* 21:165–88

Barry, H., Schlegel, A. 1984. Measurements of adolescent sexual behavior in the standard sample of societies. *Ethnology* 23:315–29

Bar-Tal, D., Bar-Zahar, Y. 1977. The relationship between perception of locus of control and academic achievement. *Contemp. Educ. Psychol.* 2:181–99

Bates, E., MacWhinney, B., Caselli, C., Devescovi, A., Natale, F., Venza, V. 1984. A cross-linguistic study of the development of sentence interpretation strategies. *Child Dev.* 55:341–54

Bell, B., Miller, W. 1982. Child-rearing practices reported by school children in Bavaria. *J. Soc. Psychol.* 117:13–18

Bem, S. L. 1974. The measurement of psychological androgyny. *J. Consult. Clin. Psychol.* 42:155–62

Benedict, R. 1934. *Patterns of Culture.* Boston: Houghton Mifflin. 290 pp.

Berlin, B., Kay, P. 1969. *Basic Color Terms: Their Universality and Evolution.* Berkeley: Univ. Calif, Press. 178 pp.

Berry, J. W. 1980a. Social and cultural change. See Triandis & Brislin 1980, pp. 211–79

Berry, J. W. 1980b. Ecological analyses for cross-cultural psychology. In *Studies in Cross-Cultural Psychology*, ed. N. Warren, 2:157–89. London: Academic. 357 pp.

Berry, J. W. 1981. Cultural systems and cognitive styles. In *Intelligence and Learning*, ed. M. Friedman, J. Das, N. O'Conner, pp. 395–405. New York: Plenum. 622 pp.

Berry, J. W. 1983. The sociogenesis of social sciences: An analysis of the cultural relativity of social psychology. In *The Sociogenesis of Language and Human Conduct*, ed. B. Bain, pp. 449–54. New York: Plenum. 580 pp.

Berry, J. W. 1984a. *Presidential address.* Presented at Int. Assoc. Cross-Cult. Psychol. Conf., 7th, Acapulco

Berry, J. W. 1984b. Towards a universal psychology of cognitive competence. *Int. J. Psychol.* 19:335–61

Berry, J. W., Dasen, P. R., Witkin, H. A. 1982. Developmental theories in cross-cultural perspective. See Adler 1982b, pp. 13–21

Best, D. L., William, J. E., Cloud, J. M., Davis, S. W., Robertson, L. S., et al. 1977.

Development of sex-trait stereotypes among young children in the United States, England, and Ireland. *Child Dev.* 48:1375–84

Betancourt, H., Weiner, B. 1982. Attributions for achievement-related events, expectancy, and sentiments: A study of success and failure in Chile and the United States. *J. Cross-Cult. Psychol.* 12:362–74

Blackler, F., ed. 1983. *Social Psychology and Developing Countries*. Chichester, Engl.: Wiley. 297 pp.

Blau, Z. S. 1981. *Black Children-White Children: Competence Socialization, and Social Structure*. New York: Free Press. 283 pp.

Bochner, S. 1982. *Cultures in Contact: Studies in Cross-Cultural Interaction*. Oxford: Pergamon. 246 pp.

Bolton, R. 1981. Susto, hostility, and hypoglycemia. *Ethnology* 20:261–76

Bolton, R. 1984. The hypoglycemia-aggression hypothesis: debate versus research. *Curr. Anthropol.* 25:1–53

Bolton, R., Curtis, A. T., Thomas, L. L. 1980. Nepali color terms: Salience on a listing task. *J. Steward Anthropol. Soc.* 12:309–22

Bond, M. H. 1983. A proposal for cross-cultural studies in attribution. In *Attribution Theory: Social and Functional Extensions*, ed. M. Hewstone, pp. 144–57. Oxford: Blackwell. 409 pp.

Bond, M. H., Leung, K., Wan, K. C. 1982. How does cultural collectivism operate? The impact of task and maintenance contribution on reward distribution. *J. Cross-Cult. Psychol.* 13:186–200

Bouhmama, D. 1984. Assessment of Kohlberg's stages of moral development in two cultures. *J. Moral Educ.* 13:124–30

Brislin, R. W. 1981. *Cross-Cultural Encounters: Face-to-Face Interaction*. New York: Pergamon. 350 pp.

Brislin, R. W. 1983. Cross-cultural research in psychology. *Ann. Rev. Psychol.* 34:363–400

Callan, V. J., Liddy, L. 1982. Sex-role preference in Australian Aboriginal and white children. *J. Soc. Psychol.* 117:147–48

Campbell, D. T. 1961. The mutual methodological relevance of anthropology and psychology. In *Psychological Anthropology*, ed. F. Hsu, pp. 333–52. Homewood, IL: Dorsey. 520 pp.

Campbell, D. T. 1975. On the conflicts between biological and social evolution and between psychology and moral tradition. *Am. Psychol.* 30:1103–26

Carpenter, L., Brockington, I. F. 1980. A study of mental illness in Asians, West Indians, and Africans living in Manchester. *Br. J. Psychiatry* 137:201–5

Chandler, T. A., Shama, D. D., Wolf, F. M., Blanchard, S. K. 1981. Multi-attributional causality for achievement across five-cross-national samples. *J. Cross-Cult. Psychol.* 12:207–21

Chandler, T. A., Shama, D. D., Wolf, F. M. 1983. Gender differences in achievement and affiliation attributions. *J. Cross-Cult. Psychol.* 14:241–56

Chen, M., Braithwaite, V., Jong, T. 1982. Attributes of intelligent behavior: Perceived relevance and difficulty by Australian and Chinese students. *J. Cross-Cult. Psychol.* 13:139–56

Cheung, F., Dobkin de Rios, M. F. 1982. Recent trends in the study of the mental health of Chinese immigrants to the United States. *Res. Race Ethnic Relat.* 3:145–63

Ching, C. C. 1984. Psychology and the four modernizations in China. *Int. J. Psychol.* 19:57–65

Clammer, J. 1982. The institutionalization of ethnicity: The culture of ethnicity in Singapore. *Ethnic Racial Stud.* 5:127–39

Clammer, J. 1983. Chinese ethnicity and political culture in Singapore. In *The Chinese in Southeast Asia*, Vol. 2, *Identity, Culture, and Politics*, ed. P. Gosling, L. Lim, pp. 266–84. Ann Arbor, MI: Cent. South and Southeast Asian Stud. 284 pp.

Clark, L. A., Halford, G. S. 1983. Does cognitive style account for cultural differences in scholastic achievement? *J. Cross-Cult. Psychol.* 14:279–96

Cochrane, R. 1980. Mental illness in England, in Scotland and in Scots living in England. *Soc. Psychiatry* 15:9–15

Cochrane, R., Stopes-Roe M. 1981. Psychological symptom levels in Indian immigrants to England—a comparison with native English. *Psychol. Med.* 11:319–27

Coehlo, G. V., Ahmed, P. I. 1980. *Uprooting and Development: Dilemmas of Coping with Modernization*. New York: Plenum. 556 pp.

Cole, M. 1984. The world beyond our borders. What might our students need to know about it? *Am. Psychol.* 39:998–1005

Dasen, P. R. 1982. Cross-cultural aspects of Piaget's theory: The competence-performance model. See Adler 1982a, pp. 163–70

Dasen, P. R. 1984. The cross-cultural study of intelligence: Piaget and the Baoulé. *Int. J. Psychol.* 19:407–34

Dasen, P. R., Berry, J. W., Sartorius, N., eds. 1986. *Healthy Human Development: Applications from Cross-Cultural Psychology*. Beverly Hills: Sage. In press

Dasen, P. R., Heron, A. 1980. Cross-cultural study of Piaget's theory. See Triandis & Heron 1980, pp. 295–342

Davidson, A. R., Thomson, E. 1980. Cross-cultural studies of attitudes and beliefs. See Triandis & Brislin 1980, pp. 25–71

Deregowski, J. B. 1980. Perception. See Triandis & Lonner 1980, pp. 21–115

Deregowski, J. B., Dziurawiec, S., Annis, R. C., eds. 1983. *Explications in Cross-Cultural Psychology*. Amsterdam: Swets & Zeistlinger. 455 pp.

DeVos, G. A. 1983. Achievement motivation and intra-family attitudes in immigrant Koreans. *J. Psychoanal. Anthropol.* 6:25–71

Diaz-Loving, R., Diaz-Guerrero, R., Helmreich, R. L., Spence, J. T. 1981. Cross-cultural comparison and psychometric analysis of masculine (instrumental) and feminine (expressive) traits. *Rev. Asoc. Latinam. Psicol. Soc.* 1:3–37 (In Spanish)

Dixon, S. D., LeVine, R. A., Richman, A., Brazelton, T. B. 1984. Mother-child interaction around a teaching task: An African-American comparison. *Child Dev.* 55:1252–64

Downing, N. E. 1979. Theoretical and operational conceptualizations of psychological androgyne: Implications for measurement. *Psychol. Women Q.* 3:284–92

Draguns, J. 1980. Psychological disorders of clinical severity. See Triandis & Draguns 1980, pp. 99–174

Dyal, J. A., Dyal, R. Y. 1981. Acculturation, stress and coping. *Int. J. Intercult. Relat.* 5:301–28

Edwards, C. P. 1981. The comparative study of the development of moral reasoning and judgment. See R. H. Munroe et al 1981, pp. 501–30

Ember, C. R. 1981. A cross-cultural perspective on sex differences. See R. H. Munroe et al 1981, pp. 531–80

Faustman, W. D., Mathews, W. M. 1980. Perception of personal control and academic achievement in Sri Lanka: Cross-cultural generality of American research. *J. Cross-Cult. Psychol.* 11:245–52

Finley, G. E. 1981. Review of *Handbook of Cross-Cultural Psychology*, Vol. 4, *Developmental Psychology*, ed. H. C. Triandis, A. Heron. *J. Cross-Cult. Psychol.* 12:499–501

Flynn, J. R. 1980. *Race, IQ and Jensen*. London: Routledge & Kegan Paul. 320 pp.

Furnham, A. 1984. Value systems and anomie in three cultures. *Int. J. Psychol.* 19:565–79

Gaines, R., Powell, G. J. 1981. Children's color perception in relation to habitat and skin color. *Child Dev.* 52:914–20

Gaw, A., ed. 1982. *Cross-Cultural Psychiatry*. Boston: Wright/PSG. 366 pp.

Gay, J., Cole, M. 1967. *The New Mathematics and An Old Culture*. New York: Holt, Rinehart & Winston. 100 pp.

Gibson, J. T., Wurst, K. K., Cannonito, M. 1984. Observations on contact stimulation provided young children in selected areas of Greece, USA, USSR. *Int. J. Psychol.* 19:233–43

Gill, R., Keats, D. 1980. Elements of intellectual competence: Judgements by Australian and Malay university students. *J. Cross-Cult. Psychol.* 11:233–43

Gillam, B. 1980. Geometrical illusions. *Sci. Am.* 242(1):102–11

Glass, G. V. 1976. Primary, secondary, and meta-analysis research. *Educ. Res.* 5:3–8

Goldstein, A. P., Segall, M. H. 1983. *Aggression in Global Perspective*. Elmsford, NY: Pergamon. 475 pp.

Gonzalez, A., Zimbardo, P. G. 1985. Time in perspective. *Psychol. Today* 19:20–26

Goodnow, J. J. 1981. Review of *Handbook of Cross-Cultural Psychology*, Vol. 3, *Basic Processes*, ed. H. C. Triandis, W. J. Lonner, *J. Cross-Cult. Psychol.* 12:496–99

Gough, H. G. 1966. A cross-cultural analysis of the CPI femininity scale. *J. Consult. Psychol.* 3:136–41

Gough, H. G., Chun, K., Chung, Y.-E. 1968. Validation of the CPI femininity scale in Korea. *Psychol. Rep.* 22:155–60

Gould, S. J. 1981. *The Mismeasure of Man*. New York: Norton. 352 pp.

Hartup, W. W., Ahammer, I. M., Pick, H. L., eds. 1982. *Review of Child Development Research*, Vol. 6. Chicago: Univ. Chicago Press. 774 pp.

Heilbroner, R. L. 1974. *An Inquiry into the Human Prospect*. New York: Norton. 150 pp.

Hewstone, M., Bond, M., Wan, K. C. 1983. Social facts and social attributions: The explanation of intergroup differences in Hong Kong. *Soc. Cognit.* 2:140–55

Hewstone, M., Jaspars, J. 1982. Intergroup relations and attribution processes. In *Social Identity and Intergroup Relations*, ed. H. Tajfel, pp. 99–133. Cambridge: Cambridge Univ. Press. 608 pp.

Hewstone, M., Jaspars, J. 1984. Social dimensions of attribution. In *The Social Dimension: European Developments in Social Psychology*, ed. H. Tajfel, 2:379–404. Cambridge: Cambridge Univ. Press. 715 pp.

Hewstone, M., Ward, C. 1985. Ethnocentrism and causal attribution in Southeast Asia. *J. Pers. Soc. Psychol.* 48:614–23

Hofstede, G. 1980. *Culture's Consequences: International Differences in Work-Related Values*. Beverly Hills, CA: Sage. 475 pp.

Hogan, H. W. 1980. German and American authoritarianism, self-estimated intelligence and value priorities. *J. Soc. Psychol.* 111:145–46

Hsu, F. L. K. 1981. *Americans and Chinese: Passages to Differences*. Honolulu: Univ. Hawaii Press. 562 pp. 3rd ed.

Hui, C. H. 1984. *Development and Validation of an Individualism-Collective Scale. ONR Tech. Rep. 31.* Dep. Psychol., Univ. Ill., Champaign. 53 pp.

Hui, C. H., Triandis, H. C. 1984. *The Effects of Partner Relationships, Resource Availability, Culture, and Collectivist Tendency on Reward Allocation. ONR Tech. Rep. 32.* Dep. Psychol., Univ. Ill., Champaign. 33 pp.

Hui, C. H., Triandis, H. C. 1985. Individualism-collectivism: A study of cross-cultural researchers. *J. Cross-Cult. Psychol.* In press

Irvine, S. H., Berry, J. W., eds. 1983. *Human Assessment and Cultural Factors.* New York: Plenum. 671 pp.

Ispa, J. 1984. A comparison of Soviet and American women's perceptions of the postpartum period. *J. Comp. Fam. Stud.* 15:95–108

Jacobson, L., Anderson, C., Berletich, M., Berdahl, K. 1976 Construction and initial validation of a scale measuring equal rights for men and women. *Educ. Psychol. Meas.* 36:913–18

Jaffe, Y., Shapir, N., Yinon, Y. 1981. Aggression and its escalation. *J. Cross-Cult. Psychol.* 12:21–36

Jahoda, G. 1981. The influence of schooling on adult recall of familiar stimuli: A study in Ghana. *Int. J. Psychol.* 16:59–71

Jahoda, G. 1982. *Psychology and Anthropology: A Psychological Perspective.* New York: Academic. 305 pp.

Jahoda, G. 1983a. The cross-cultural emperor's new clothes: The emic-etic issue revisited. See Deregowski et al 1983, pp. 19–37

Jahoda, G. 1983b. European 'lag' in the development of an economic concept: A study in Zimbabwe. *Br. J. Dev. Psychol.* 1:113–20

Jahoda, G. 1984. Do we need a concept of culture? *J. Cross-Cult. Psychol.* 15:139–51

Jensen, A. R. 1978. The current status of the IQ controversy. *Aust. Psychol.* 13:7–28

Jensen, A. R. 1980. *Bias in Mental Testing.* New York: Free Press. 786 pp.

Jensen, A. R. 1981. *Straight Talk About Mental Tests.* London: Methuen 269 pp.

Jones, L. 1984. White-Black achievement differences. The narrowing group. *Am. Psychol.* 39:207–13

Kagan, S., Knight, G. P., Martinez, S., Santana, P. E. 1981. Conflict resolution style among Mexican children. *J. Cross-Cult Psychol.* 12:222–32

Kagan, S., Zahn, G., Gealy, J. 1977. Competition and school achievement among Anglo-American and Mexican-American children. *J. Educ. Psychol.* 69:432–41

Kağitçibaşi, C. 1984. Socialization in traditional society: A challenge to psychology. *Int. J. Psychol.* 19:145–57

Kalin, R., Heusser, C., Edmonds, J. 1982. Cross-national equivalence of a sex-role ideology scale. *J. Soc. Psychol.* 116:141–42

Kanekar, S., Kolsawalla, M. B. 1981. Factors affecting responsibility attributed to a rape victim. *J. Soc. Psychol.* 113:285–86

Kanekar, S., Merchant, S. M. 1982. Aggression, retaliation, and religious affiliation. *J. Soc. Psychol.* 117:295–96

Kaschak, E., Sharratt, S. 1983. A Latin American sex role inventory. *Cross-Cult. Psychol. Bull.* 18(1):3–6

Kay, M. A., ed. 1982. *Anthropology of Human Birth.* Philadelphia: Davis. 445 pp.

Keating, C. F., Mazur, A., Segall, M. H. 1981. Culture and the perception of social dominance from facial expression. *J. Pers. Soc. Psychol.* 40:615–26

Keats, D. 1982. Cultural bases of concepts of intelligence. A Chinese versus Australian comparison. *Proc. Asian Workshop Child Adolesc. Dev., 2nd, Bangkok,* pp. 67–75

Keller, H., Miranda, D., Gauda, G. 1984. The naive theory of the infant and some maternal attitudes: A two-country study. *J. Cross-Cult. Psychol.* 15:165–79

Kelley, H. 1973. The processes of causal attribution. *Am. Psychol.* 28:107–28

Kennedy, S., Scheirer, J., Rogers, A. 1984. The price of success: Our monocultural science. *Am. Psychol.* 39:996–97

Kishor, N. 1983. Locus of control and academic achievement: Ethnic discrepancies among Fijians. *J. Cross-Cult. Psychol.* 14:297–308

Klich, L. Z., Davidson, G. R. 1983. A cultural difference in visual memory: on le voit, on ne le voit plus. *Int. J. Psychol.* 18:189–201

Kluckhohn, C. 1956. Toward a comparison of value emphases in different cultures. In *The State of the Social Sciences,* ed. L. D. White, pp. 116–32. Chicago: Univ. Chicago Press. 504 pp.

Kluckhohn, F. R., Strodtbeck, F. L. 1961. *Variations in Value Orientations.* Evanston, IL: Row, Peterson. 437 pp.

Kohlberg, L. 1969. Stage and sequence: The cognitive developmental approach to socialization. In *Handbook of Socialization Theory and Research,* ed. D. A. Goslin, pp. 347–480. New York: Rand-McNally. 1182 pp.

Kornadt, H.-J. 1983. A cross-cultural analysis of the development of aggression. See Deregowski et al 1983, pp. 285–97

Kornadt, H.-J. 1984a. Motivation theory of aggression and its relation to social psychological approaches. In *Social Psychology of Aggression: From Individual Behavior to Social Interaction,* ed. A. Mummendey, pp. 21–31. Berlin/New York: Springer-Verlag. 176 pp.

Kornadt, H.-J. 1984b. Development of aggressiveness: A motivation theory perspective. In *Aggression in Children and Youth,* ed. R. M. Kaplan, V. J. Konecni, R. W. Novaco, pp. 73–87. The Hague: Nijhoff. 367 pp.

Korte, C., Ayvalioglu, N. 1981. Helpfulness in Turkey: Cities, towns and urban villages. *J. Cross-Cult. Psychol.* 12:123–41

Krampen, G., Wieberg, H.-J. W. 1981. Three aspects of locus of control in German, American, and Japanese university students. *J. Soc. Psychol.* 113:133–34

Kranau, E. J., Green, V., Valencia-Weber, G. 1982. Acculturation and the Hispanic woman: Attitudes toward women sex-role attribution, sex-role behavior, and demographics. *Hisp. J. Behav. Sci.* 4:21–40

LaBeff, E. E., Dodder, R. A. 1982. Attitudes toward sexual permissiveness in Mexico and the United States. *J. Soc. Psychol.* 116:285–86

Lagmay, A. V. 1984. Western psychology in the Philippines: Impact and response. *Int. J. Psychol.* 19:31–44

Lambert, W. W. 1981. Toward an integrative theory of children's aggression *Ital. J. Psychol.* 8:153–64

Lambert, W. W. 1985a. Some strong strategies in the aggression of children in six cultures. In *The Content of Culture: Constants and Variants*, ed. R. Bolton. New Haven: HRAF Press. In press

Lambert, W. W. 1985b. What happens to children when they act aggressively in six cultures. In *Affect, Conditioning and Cognition: Essays on the Determinants of Behavior*, ed. F. R. Brush, J. B. Overmier. Hillsdale, NJ: Erlbaum. In press

Landis, D., Brislin, R. 1983. *Handbook of Intercultural Training*. New York: Pergamon. 950 pp. 3 vols.

L'Armand, K., Pepitone, A., Shanmugam, T. E. 1981. Attitudes toward rape. A comparison of the role of chastity in India and the United States. *J. Cross-Cult. Psychol.* 12:284–303

Latané, B., Darley, J. 1970. *The Unresponsive Bystander: Why Doesn't He Help?* New York: Appleton-Century-Crofts. 131 pp.

Lefcourt, H. M., von Baeyer, C. L., Ware, E. E., Cox, D. J. 1979. The multi-dimensional–multiattributional causality scale: The development of a good specific locus of control scale. *Can. J. Behav. Sci.* 11:286–304

Leung, K., Bond, M. H. 1984. The impact of cultural collectivism on reward allocation. *J. Pers. Soc. Psychol.* 47:793–804

Levin, J., Karni, E. S. 1971. A comparative study of the CPI femininity scale: validation in Israel. *J. Cross-Cult. Psychol.* 2:387–91

LeVine, R. A., Campbell, D. T. 1972. *Ethnocentrism: Theories of Conflict, Ethnic Attitudes and Group Behavior*. New York: Wiley. 310 pp.

Lombardo, A. G. G. E. 1981. Moroccan emigrants in the Netherlands and the Dutch mental health care. *Psychopathol. Afr.* 17:422–25

Lonner, W. J., Berry, J. W., eds. 1985. *Field Methods in Cross-Cultural Research*. Beverly Hills, CA: Sage. 325 pp.

Mackenzie, B. 1980a. Hypothesized genetic racial differences in IQ: A criticism of three proposed lines of evidence. *Behav. Genet.* 10:225–34

Mackenzie, B. 1980b. Fallacious use of regression effects in the I. Q. controversy. *Aust. Psychol.* 15:369–84

Mackenzie, B. 1984. Explaining race differences in IQ: The logic, the methodology, and the evidence. *Am. Psychol.* 39:1214–33

Madsen, M., Shapira, A. 1977. Cooperation and challenge in four cultures. *J. Soc. Psychol.* 102:189–95

Maehr, M. L. 1980. *Culture and achievement motivation: Beyond Weber and McClelland.* Presented at Ann. Meet. Am. Educ. Res. Assoc., Boston

Mahler, I., Greenberg, L., Hayoski, H. 1981. A comparative study of rules of justice: Japanese versus American. *Psychologia* 24:1–8

Maloney, P., Wilkof, J., Dambrot, F. 1981. Androgeny across two cultures: United States and Israel. *J. Cross-Cult. Psychol.* 12:95–102

Malpass, R. 1981. Review of *Handbook of Cross-Cult. Psychology*, Vol. 2, *Methodology*, ed. H. C. Triandis, J. Berry. *J. Cross-Cult. Psychol.* 12:493–96

Marin, G. 1981. Perceived justice across cultures. Equity vs equality in Colombia and in the United States. *Int. J. Psychol.* 16:153–59

Marsella, A. J., Pedersen, P., eds. 1981. *Cross-Cultural Counseling and Psychotherapy*. Elmsford, NY: Pergamon. 358 pp.

Marsella, A. J., White, G. M., eds. 1982. *Cultural Conceptions of Mental Health and Therapy*. Dordrecht: Reidel. 414 pp.

Martin, J. N. 1984. The intercultural reentry: Conceptualization and directions for future research. *Int. J. Intercult. Relat.* 8:115–34

McClelland, D. C. 1971. *Motivational Trends in Society*. New York: General Learning Press. 24 pp.

McSwain, R. 1981. Care and conflict in infant development: An East Timorese and Papua New Guinean comparison. *Inf. Behav. Dev.* 4:225–46

Melikian, L. H. 1984. The transfer of psychological knowledge to the Third World countries and its impact on development: The case of five Arab Gulf oil-producing states. *Int. J. Psychol.* 19:65–77

Milgram, S. 1970. The experience of living in cities. *Science* 167:1461–68

Modiano, N., Maldonado, P., Luz, M., Villasana B., S. 1982. Accurate perception of colored illustration: Rates of comprehension in Mexican-Indian children. *J. Cross-Cult. Psychol.* 13:490–95

Morsbach, H. 1980. Major psychological factors influencing Japanese interpersonal relations. In *Studies in Cross-Cultural Psychology*, ed. N. Warren, 2:317–42. London: Academic. 357 pp.

Munro, D. 1979. Locus-of-control attribution: Factors among blacks and whites in Africa. *J. Cross-Cult. Psychol.* 10:157–72

Munroe, R. H., Koel, A., Munroe, R. L., Bolton, R., Michelson, C., Bolton, C. 1983. Time allocation in four societies. *Ethnology* 22:355–70

Munroe, R. H., Munroe, R. L. 1980. Household structure and socialization practices. *J. Soc. Psychol.* 111:293–94

Munroe, R. H., Munroe, R. L., Whiting, B. B., eds. 1981. *Handbook of Cross-Cultural Human Development*. New York: Garland. 900 pp.

Munroe, R. L., Munroe, R. H. 1971. Male pregnancy symptoms and cross-sex identity in three societies. *J. Soc. Psychol.* 84:11–25

Munroe, R. L., Munroe, R. H. 1980. Perspectives suggested by anthropological data. See Triandis & Lambert 1980, pp. 253–318

Munroe, R. L., Munroe, R. H. 1981. Male pregnancy symptoms and sex-identity conflict in Nepal and Samoa. *J. Soc. Psychol.* 115:133–34

Munroe, R. L., Munroe, R. H. 1983. Birth order and intellectual performance in East Africa. *J. Cross-Cult. Psychol.* 14:3–16

Murphy-Berman, V., Berman, J., Singh, P., Pachuri, A., Kumar, P. 1984. Factors affecting allocation to needy and meritorious recipients: A cross-cultural comparison. *J. Pers. Soc. Psychol.* 46:1267–72

Naroll, R. 1983. *The Moral Order: An Introduction to the Human Situation*. Beverly Hills, CA: Sage. 497 pp.

Naroll, R., Michik, G., Naroll, F. 1980. Holocultural research methods. See Triandis & Berry 1980, pp. 479–521

Nevo, O. 1984. Appreciation and production of humor as an expression of aggression. A study of Jews and Arabs in Israel. *J. Cross-Cult. Psychol.* 15:181–98

Nguyen, S. D. 1982. The psycho-social adjustment and the mental health needs of Southeast Asian refugees. *Psychiatr. J. Univ. Ottawa* 7:26–35

Niles, F. S. 1981. Dimensionality of Rotter's I-E Scale in Sri Lanka. *J. Cross-Cult. Psychol.* 12:473–79

Nishiyama, T. 1975. Validation of the CPI femininity scale in Japan. *J. Cross-Cult. Psychol.* 5:482–89

Nowicki, S., Strickland, B. 1973. A locus of control scale for children. *J. Consult. Clin. Psychol.* 40:148–55

Opolot, J. A. 1982. Ethnicity and child-rearing practices in Uganda. *J. Soc. Psychol.* 116:155–62

Osuji, O. N. 1982. Constructing complex geometric patterns: A study of age and ability among Igbo children of eastern Nigeria. *J. Cross-Cult. Psychol.* 13:481–89

Pedersen, P., Draguns, J., Lonner, W., Trimble, J., eds. 1981. *Counseling Across Cultures*. Honolulu: Univ. Press Hawaii. 370 pp.

Pedhazur, E. J., Tetenbaum, T. J. 1979. Bem sex-role inventory: A theoretical and methodological critique. *J. Pers. Soc. Psychol.* 37:996–1016

Pepitone, A. 1981. Lessons from the history of social psychology. *Am. Psychol.* 36:972–85

Piaget, J. 1932. *The Moral Judgment of the Child*. London: Routledge & Kegan Paul. 418 pp.

Pierson, H. D., Bond, M. H. 1982. How do Chinese bilinguals respond to variations of interviewer language and ethnicity? *J. Lang. Soc. Psychol.* 1:123–39

Pitariu, H. 1981. Validation of the CPI femininity scale in Romania. *J. Cross-Cult. Psychol.* 12:111–17

Plath, D., ed. 1983. *Work and Lifecourse in Japan*. Albany, NY: State Univ. NY Press. 280 pp.

Poortinga, Y. H. 1984. *Conceptual Implications of Item Bias*. Presented at Adv. Stud. Inst. Conf. Human Assessment, Athens, Greece

Poortinga, Y. H., van de Vijver, F. R. J. 1984. *Generalizability Theory as a Framework for the Interpretation of Cross-Cultural Differences*. Wassenaar, Netherlands: NIAS. 17 pp.

Posner, J. K. 1982. The development of mathematical knowledge in two West African societies. *Child Dev.* 53:200–8

Putnam, D., Kilbride, P. 1980. *A relativistic understanding of intelligence: Social intelligence among the Singhay of Mali and the Samia of Kenya*. Presented at Ann. Meet. Soc. Cross-Cult. Res., Philadelphia

Reimanis, G., Posen, C. 1980. Locus of control in Western and African Cultures. *J. Soc. Psychol.* 112:181–89

Reynolds, B. K. 1984. A cross-cultural study of values of Germans and Americans. *Int. J. Intercult. Relat.* 8:269–78

Robin, R. W., Shea, J. D. C. 1983. The Bender Gestalt Visual Motor Test in Papua New Guinea. *Int. J. Psychol.* 18:263–70

Rodriques, A. 1982. Replication: A neglected type of research in social psychology. *Interam. J. Psychol.* 16:91–109

Rogan, J. M., Macdonald, M. A. 1983. The effect of schooling on conservation skills: An intervention in the Ciskei. *J. Cross-Cult. Psychol.* 14:309–22

Rogoff, B. 1980. Schooling and the development of cognitive skills. See Triandis & Heron 1980, pp. 233–94

Rogoff, B. 1982. Integrating context and cognitive development. In *Advances in Developmental Psychology*, ed. M. E. Lamb, L. Brown, 2:125–70. Hillsdale, NJ: Erlbaum. 213 pp.

Rogoff, B., Waddell, K. J. 1982. Memory for information organization a scene by children from two cultures. *Child Dev.* 53:1224–28

Rohner, R. 1984. Toward a conception of culture for cross-cultural psychology. *J. Cross-Cult. Psychol.* 15:111–38

Rokeach, M. 1956. Political and religious dogmatism; an alternative to the authoritarian personality. *Psychol. Monogr.* 70:1–43

Rosenthal, R. 1978. Combining results of independent studies. *Psychol. Bull.* 85:185–93

Rotter, J. 1966. Generalized expectancies for internal versus external control of reinforcement. *Psychol. Monogr.* 80:1–28

Rupp, M., Nowicki, S. 1978. Locus of control among Hungarian children: Sex, age, school achievement, and teacher's ratings of developmental competence. *J. Cross-Cult. Psychol.* 9:359–65

Russell, R. 1984. Psychology in its world context. *Am. Psychol.* 39:1017–25

Ryback, D., Sanders, A. L., Lorentz, J., Koestenblatt, M. 1980. Child-rearing practices reported by students in six cultures. *J. Soc. Psychol.* 110:153–62

Saigh, P. A. 1980. The effects of positive group reinforcement on the behavior of Lebanese school children. *J. Soc. Psychol.* 110:287–88

Salazar, J. M. 1984. The use and impact of psychology in Venezuela: Two examples. *Int. J. Psychol.* 19:113–22

Samovar, L. A., Porter, R. E., eds. 1982. *Intercultural Communication: A Reader*. Belmont, CA: Wadsworth. 423 pp. 3rd ed.

Scarr, S. 1981. *Race, Social Class, and Individual Differences in I.Q.* Hillsdale, NJ: Erlbaum. 560 pp.

Scher, D., Nevo, B., Beit-Hallahmi, B. 1979. Beliefs about equal rights for men and women among Israel and American students. *J. Soc. Psychol.* 109:11–15

Schlegel, A., Barry, H. 1979. Adolescent initiation ceremonies: Cross-cultural codes. *Ethnology* 18:199–210

Schlegel, A., Barry, H. 1980. The evolutionary significance of adolescent initiation ceremonies. *Am. Ethnol.* 7:696–715

Scott, W. A., Scott, R. 1982. Ethnicity, interpersonal relations, and adaptation among families of European migrants to Australia. *Aust. Psychol.* 17:165–80

Seeley, K. M., Wagner, D. A. 1983. Research-policy issues for childhood programs in the third world. *Hum. Dev.* 26:55–60

Segall, M. H. 1979. *Cross-Cultural Psychology: Human Behavior in Global Perspective*. Monterey, CA: Brooks/Cole. 269 pp. Reprinted 1984, Syracuse, NY: Orange Student Bookstore

Segall, M. H. 1980. On the teaching of cross-cultural psychology. *J. Cross-Cult. Psychol.* 11:89–99

Segall, M. H. 1981a. Review of *Handbook of Cross-Cultural Psychology*, Vol. 1, *Perspectives*, ed. H. C. Triandis, W. W. Lambert. *J. Cross-Cult. Psychol.* 12:490–93

Segall, M. H. 1981b. Cross-cultural research on visual perception. In *Scientific Inquiry and the Social Sciences*, ed. M. Brewer, B. Collins, pp. 361–84. San Francisco: Jossey-Bass. 523 pp.

Segall, M. H. 1983a. On the search for the independent variable in cross-cultural psychology. In *Human Assessment and Cultural Factors*, ed. S. H. Irvine, J. W. Berry, pp. 122–37. New York: Plenum. 671 pp.

Segall, M. H. 1983b. Aggression in global perspective: A research strategy. See Goldstein & Segall 1983, pp. 1–43

Segall, M. H. 1984. More than we need to know about culture but are afraid not to ask. *J. Cross-Cult. Psychol.* 15:153–62

Serpell, R. 1984. Commentary: The impact of psychology on Third World development. *Int. J. Psychol.* 19:179–92

Sexton, V. S., Misiak, H. 1984. American psychologists and psychology abroad. *Am. Psychol.* 39:1026–31

Seymour, S. 1981. Cooperation and competition. See R. H. Munroe et al 1981. pp. 717–38

Shayer, M., Whary, D. 1973. Piaget in the classroom. Testing a whole class at the same time. *Sch. Sci. Rev.* 54:447–57

Shea, J. D., Ogaiea, M., Bagara, B. 1983. Conservation in community school children from Madang, Southern Highlands, and North Solomons provinces of Papua New Guinea. *Int. J. Psychol.* 18:203–14

Sinha, D., Holtzman, W. H., eds. 1984. The impact of psychology on Third World development. *Int. J. Psychol.* 19:3–192 (Special issue).

Smither, R. 1981. Psychological study of refugee acculturation: A review of the literature. *J. Refugee Resettlement* 1:58–63

Smithson, M., Amato, P., Pierce, P. 1983. *Dimensions of Helping Behavior*. Oxford: Pergamon. 165 pp.

Soto, E., Shaver, P. 1982. Sex-role traditionalism assertiveness, and symptoms of Puerto Rican women living in the United States. *Hisp. J. Behav. Sci.* 4:1–19

Spencer, D., Darvizeh, Z. 1983. Young children's place-descriptions, maps and route-finding: A comparison of nursery school children in Iran and Britain. *Int. J. Early Childhood* 15:26–31

Srole, L. 1956. Social integration and certain corollaries. *Am. Soc. Rev.* 21:709–16

Starr, B. J. 1985. *Measurement issues and the emic-etic distinctions.* Presented at 14th Soc. Cross-Cult. Res. Conf., San Juan, Puerto Rico

Starr, B. J., Wilson, S. 1980. Some epistemological and methodological issues in the design of cross-cultural research. In *Research in Culture Learning: Language and Conceptual Studies,* ed. M. P. Hamnett, R. W. Brislin, pp. 143–53. Honolulu: Univ. Press Hawaii. 195 pp.

Sternberg, R., Conway, B., Ketron, J., Bernstein, M. 1981. People's conceptions of intelligence. *J. Pers. Soc. Psychol.* 41:37–55

Strube, M. 1981. Meta-analysis and cross-cultural comparison. Sex differences in child competitiveness. *J. Cross-Cult. Psychol.* 12:3–20

Sumner, G. 1906. *Folkways.* Boston: Ginn. 692 pp.

Sundberg, N. D. 1981. Review of *Handbook of Cross-Cultural Psychology,* Vol. 6, *Psychopathology,* ed. H. C. Triandis, J. Draguns. *J. Cross-Cult. Psychol.* 12:504–7

Sundberg, N. D., Poole, M. E., Tyler, L. E. 1983. Adolescent expectations of future events—A cross-cultural study of Australians, Americans, and Indians. *Int. J. Psychol.* 18:415–27

Super, C. M. 1980. Cross-cultural research on infancy. See Triandis & Heron 1980, pp. 17–54

Super, C. M. 1983. Cultural variation in the meaning and uses of children's "intelligence." See Deregowski et al 1983, pp. 199–212

Super, C. M., Harkness, S. 1982. The infant's niche in rural Kenya and metropolitan America. See Adler 1982b, pp. 47–55

Tajfel, H., ed. 1982. *Social Identity and Intergroup Relations.* London: Academic. 528 pp.

Tallman, I., Marotz-Baden, R., Pindas, P. 1983. *Adolescent Socialization in Cross-Cultural Perspective.* New York: Academic. 325 pp.

Tapp, J. 1980. Studying personality development. See Triandis & Heron 1980, pp. 343–424

Taylor, D., Jaggi, V. 1974. Ethnocentrism and causal attribution in a South Indian context. *J. Cross-Cult. Psychol.* 5:162–71

Taylor, H. F. 1980. *The IQ Game: A Methodological Study into the Heredity-Environment Controversy.* London: Harvester

Torney-Purta, J. 1984. Annotated bibliography of materials for adding an international dimension to undergraduate courses in development and social psychology. *Am. Psychol.* 39:1032–42

Triandis, H. C. 1983. *Allocentric vs. Idiocentric Social Behavior: A Major Cultural Difference Between Hispanics and the Mainstream.* ONR Tech. Rep. 16. Dep. Psychol., Univ. Ill. Champaign

Triandis, H. C., Berry, J., eds. 1980. *Handbook of Cross-Cultural Psychology,* Vol. 2, *Methodology.* Boston: Allyn & Bacon. 546 pp.

Triandis, H. C., Brislin, R. W., eds. 1980. *Handbook of Cross-Cultural Psychology,* Vol. 5, *Social Psychology.* Boston: Allyn & Bacon. 414 pp.

Triandis, H. C., Brislin, R. W. 1984. Cross-cultural psychology. *Am. Psychol.* 39:1006–16

Triandis, H. C., Draguns, J., eds. 1980. *Handbook of Cross-Cultural Psychology,* Vol. 6, *Psychopathology.* Boston: Allyn & Bacon. 370 pp.

Triandis, H. C., Heron, A., eds. 1980. *Handbook of Cross-Cultural Psychology,* Vol. 4, *Developmental Psychology.* Boston: Allyn & Bacon. 492 pp.

Triandis, H. C., Lambert, W. W., eds. 1980. *Handbook of Cross-Cultural Psychology,* Vol. 1, *Perspectives.* Boston: Allyn & Bacon. 392 pp.

Triandis, H. C., Lambert, W. W., Berry, J. W., Lonner, W., Heron, A., et al., eds. 1980. *Handbook of Cross-Cultural Psychology.* Boston: Allyn & Bacon. 2507 pp. 6 vols.

Triandis, H. C., Leung, K., Villareal, M. J., Clark, F. L. 1985. *Allocentric vs. Idiocentric Tendencies: Convergent and Discriminant Validation.* Univ. of Ill. 39 pp. (Mimeo.)

Triandis, H. C., Lonner, W. J., eds. 1980. *Handbook of Cross-Cultural Psychology,* Vol. 3, *Basic Processes.* Boston: Allyn & Bacon. 383 pp.

van de Vijver, F. J. R., Poortinga, Y. H. 1982. Cross-cultural generalization and universality. *J. Cross-Cult. Psychol.* 13:387–408

Wagner, D. A., ed. 1983. *Child Development and International Development: Research-Policy Interfaces.* San Francisco: Jossey-Bass. 123 pp.

Wagner, D. A., Lotfi, A. 1983. Learning to read by 'rote.' *Int. J. Soc. Lang.* 42:111–21

Wagner, D. A., Stevenson, H. W., eds. 1982. *Cultural Perspectives on Child Development.* San Francisco: Freeman. 315 pp.

Weiss, S. 1980. Culture-fair intelligence test and Draw-A-Person scores from a rural Peruvian sample. *J. Soc. Psychol.* 111:147–48

Werker, J. F., Tees, R. C. 1984. Cross-language speech perception: Evidence for perceptual reorganization during the first year of life. *Infant Behav. Dev.* 7:49–63

Whiting, B. 1976. The problem of the packaged variable. In *The Developing Individual in a Changing World*, ed. K. Riegel, J. Meachem, 1:303–9. Chicago: Aldine. 409 pp.

Williams, J. E., Best, D. L. 1982. *Measuring Sex Stereotypes: A Thirty Nation Study*. Beverly Hills, CA: Sage. 368 pp.

Williams, J. E., Best, D. L., Tilquin, C., Keller, H., Voss, H.-G., et al. 1981. Traits associated with men and women: Attribution by young children in France, Germany, Norway, the Netherlands and Italy. *J. Cross-Cult Psychol.* 12:327–46

Williams, J. E., Daws, J. T., Best, D. L., Tilquin, C., Wesley, F., Bjerke, T. 1979. Sex-trait stereotypes in France, Germany, and Norway. *J. Cross-Cult. Psychol.* 10:133–56

Williams, J. E., Giles, H., Edwards, J. R., Best, D. L., Daws, J. T. 1977. Sex-trait stereotypes in England, Ireland, and the United States. *Br. J. Soc. Clin. Psychol.* 16:303–9

Yinon, Y., Sharon, I., Azgad, Z., Barshir, I. 1981. Helping behavior of of urbanites, Moshavniks, and Kibbutzniks. *J. Soc. Psychol.* 113:143–44

Young, H. B., Ferguson, L. R. 1981. *Puberty to Manhood in Italy and America*. New York: Academic. 294 pp.

Zajonc, R. B., Markus, G. B. 1975. Birth order and intellectual development. *Psychol. Rev.* 82:74–88

Zavalloni, M. 1980. Values. See Triandis & Brislin 1980, pp. 73–120

Zern, D. S. 1980. Child-rearing practices and societal complexity: Effect of disequilibrium on cognitive development. *J. Soc. Psychol.* 110:171–75

Zepp, R. 1983. A West African replication of the four card problem. *J. Cross-Cult. Psychol.* 14:323–27

Ann. Rev. Psychol. 1986. 37:565–610

EMOTION: TODAY'S PROBLEMS

Howard Leventhal and Andrew J. Tomarken

Department of Psychology, University of Wisconsin, Madison, Wisconsin 53706

CONTENTS

INTRODUCTION 565
COGNITION-AROUSAL THEORY 567
   Empirical Tests of Cognition-Arousal Theory 567
   Other Relevant Evidence 570
   General Summary 574
EMOTION AND EXPRESSIVE BEHAVIOR 575
   The Link Between Expression and Feeling: Alternative Hypotheses 576
   The Facial Feedback Hypothesis 577
   Peripheral versus Central Linkage of Feeling to Expression 582
LATERALIZATION AND EMOTION 583
   Lateralized Perceptual Processing of Emotional Stimuli 583
   Lateralization of Autonomic Feedback and Body Symptoms 584
   Lateralization of Expressive Behavior 585
   Lateralization of Emotional States 586
   Additional Methodological and Conceptual Issues 590
EMOTION AND MEMORY 591
   Mood State-Dependent Memory 591
   Mood Congruity Effects 592
   Bower's Network Model of Emotional Memory 594
   Mood Effects on Cognitive Processes 595
   Additional Methodological and Conceptual Issues 596
CONCLUSION 598
   The Biological Basis of Emotion 598
   Emotion and Interpersonal Communication 599
   Emotional Development 600

INTRODUCTION

For the past 100 years, four types of theory have dominated thought and research on emotion: (*a*) Darwinian-evolutionary theory, which assumes the existence of multiple emotions and focuses on their form (expressive response patterns), functions, and evolutionary history (Darwin 1904, McDougall 1921,

0066-4308/86/0201-0565$02.00

Izard 1971, Plutchik 1980); (b) body reaction theory, which assumes different emotions are a product of different patterns of autonomic response (James 1950, Schachter 1957); (c) central neural theories, which seek to identify the neural structures involved in emotional expression, feeling and behavior; and (d) cognition-arousal theory, which attempts to define emotion as the integration of thought and/or perceptions with arousal (Sully 1902, Russell 1960, Schachter & Singer 1962, Schachter 1964). The diversity of theoretical perspectives virtually insures views that are neither exclusive nor complementary.

The result is confusion and cries that emotion is undefined (Lazarus 1984), and yet this diversity is necessary. Each of these often vague, yet different theoretical approaches provides its own view of emotions; together they define the phenomena, suggest specific mechanisms underlying them, and frame the questions we should address.

Given the above history, reviewing the current status of emotion research is no easy task. Our efforts have been duly compensated, however, by the opportunity to share in the intellectual excitement, the open atmosphere, and the promise of new theoretical integrations that pervade the field (see Izard et al 1984, Scherer & Ekman 1984). We have come to believe that much of the conflict and confusion in this area stems from an unwillingness to grant independent conceptual status to emotion. This "begrudging" attitude has three components: (a) the behavioristic legacy and its suspicion of subjective concepts; (b) the traditional cognitive hold on our thinking in which emotion is a combination of arousal and cognition (Schachter 1964, Cofer 1972); and (c) the reluctance of cognitively oriented scientists to view an emotion as anything more complex than a "stop" or interrupt rule in a simulation of mental operations (Simon 1982). Admitting a richer concept of emotion to the lexicon could generate major upheavals in cognitive theory as emotions theory addresses the growing theoretical and empirical knowledge in neuroscience and molecular biology.

Our review aims to cover a wide range of perspectives, although the limitations of space dictate a restricted range of content and the exclusion of many valuable contributions. We first focus on cognition-arousal theory. This work is important both for its quantity and as an illustration of the problems that emerge when one argues that the quality of emotions (i.e. emotion categories as subjective or expressive events) can be reduced to cognitions. We turn then to studies of expressive behavior, which generally view categories of emotion (subjective and cognitive) as emerging (in different ways) from innate motor programs.

Following this, we review the rapidly growing area of research on lateralization of emotional processing before turning to emotion and memory. In the conclusion, we briefly discuss some common themes emerging from these disparate areas of research and their implications for emotion theory. In the process we suggest the need for a more complex, hierarchical view of emotional processing, one that is compatible with the developmental stages of an organism that both thinks and feels.

COGNITION-AROUSAL THEORY

We begin our review with an emotion theory that has dominated social-psychological research for the past 20 years, cognition-arousal theory (Schachter & Singer 1962, Schachter 1964). According to Schachter and his colleagues (Schachter & Singer 1962, Schachter 1964), an emotional state is the product of an interaction between two components, physiological arousal (characterized as heightened sympathetic activation) and a cognition about the cause of that arousal. Since arousal is perceived as emotionally non-specific, it determines only the intensity of emotional states, while cognitions determine their quality. A core assumption here is that both arousal and cognitions are *necessary* components for emotional experience. However, they are not jointly sufficient since the perception or attribution of a causal connection between the two is additionally necessary for emotional experience to arise.

A further set of postulates pertains to the consequences of "unexplained arousal," and these have been the subject of most of the empirical tests of Schachter's theory. Specifically, it is held that the individual engages in an epistemic search designed to explain this state. If the cause unearthed by this process is a likely emotional stimulus, emotional experience will occur.

We will first concentrate upon studies that were conducted to directly test various predictions derived from cognition-arousal theory. Then we will discuss findings from other sources relevant to an evaluation of Schachter's theory.

Empirical Tests of Cognition-Arousal Theory

MISATTRIBUTION OF AROUSAL TO EMOTIONAL CUES   Beginning with the original Schachter & Singer (1962) study, numerous investigations have tested the prediction that the particular combination of drug-induced arousal and either misinformation or no information about the source of that arousal heightens responsivity to emotionally relevant contextual cues. In turn, this heightened responsivity is expected to result in intensified emotional experience relative to that found in subjects that were similarly drugged but correctly informed or subjects not drugged. Across studies a variety of sympathomimetic drugs (e.g. epinephrine, isoprenaline, ephedrine) have been combined with cues for emotions as diverse as humor, fear, anger, and elation. Overall, these investigations would appear to fall into one of two categories: those that clearly fail to support Schachter's theory (e.g. Rogers & Deckner 1975, Marshall & Zimbardo 1979, Maslach 1979) and those that provide limited support, with some, but not all, findings consistent with predictions (e.g. Erdmann & Janke 1978, Gerdes 1979, Schachter & Wheeler 1962; for more complete reviews, see Cotton 1981, Reisenzein 1983). However, even among studies in the latter category, the great majority have failed to provide support for the specific prediction that increased arousal heightens self-reported emotional experience relative to that found in placebo conditions. Indeed, to our knowledge the sole exception to this general conclusion is the study by Gerdes (1979), which found effects for males only. Additionally, in contrast to Schachter's claim that arousal is affectively neutral, several studies have found that unexplained arousal induces heightened negative affect (Rogers & Deckner 1975, Marshall & Zimbardo 1979, Maslach 1979).

In sum, the evidence for Schachter's position from investigations manipulating arousal via drugs is generally weak. However, this conclusion must be tempered by the methodological flaws of various studies. In particular, as Reisenzein (1983) has noted, several studies have failed to demonstrate that drugs produced significantly greater reported arousal than placebo manipulations (e.g. O'Neal & Kaufman 1972, Erdmann & Janke 1978). In addition, subjects in drug-informed conditions have frequently attributed their arousal to the emotional cues present, while uninformed subjects have often failed to attribute arousal to emotional cues (e.g. Gerdes 1979, Marshall & Zimbardo 1979, Maslach 1979). The importance of these manipulation failures is demonstrated by Gerdes's (1979) results showing that the attributions to emotional cues made by females in the drug-informed condition at least partially accounted for the differential sex effects on affect measures. Although it is unclear exactly why subjects have often not made the predicted attributions, some have suggested that these effects may result from imprecise synchrony between the occurrence of drug-induced arousal and exposure to contextual cues (Gerdes 1979, Schachter & Singer 1979). However, these and other methodological criticisms that could be offered in defense of cognition-arousal theory additionally serve to emphasize the highly restrictive conditions required for the emergence of the predicted effects.

MISATTRIBUTION OF AROUSAL TO NEUTRAL CUES   While the previous section reviewed research testing the prediction that misattribution effects can intensify emotional experience, this section focuses upon studies testing the converse hypothesis that the misattribution of emotional arousal to nonemotional sources can attenuate emotional experience. Nisbett & Schachter (1966) first demonstrated this phenomenon by showing that low-fear subjects who expected that an inert placebo would arouse them subsequently tolerated more intense shocks and rated their shocks as less painful. Over the years, a number of subsequent investigations have attempted to manipulate subjects' attributions by similar information about the putative effects of pills, or by other means such as exposure to background noise described as an arousing stimulus. In many cases, the predicted misattribution effects have emerged. For example, it has been shown that experimental manipulations designed to produce misattribution of arousal to neutral cues can produce reduced fear of shock on both self-report (e.g. Ross et al 1969) and physiological (e.g. Loftis & Ross 1974a,b) indices, less anxiety in testing situations (e.g. Weiner & Samuel 1975), and declines in aggressive behavior after provocation (Harris & Huang 1974). Similarly, the prediction that misattribution of arousal to neutral cues reduces anxiety is supported by the evidence that subjects led to attribute arousal to a pill subsequently demonstrate increased cheating (e.g. Dienstbier & Munter 1971) and decreased dissonance in a forced compliance paradigm (e.g. Zanna & Cooper 1974).

At first glance, this wealth of evidence appears to offer impressive support for the misattribution hypothesis. Unfortunately, other findings indicate several key limitations. One of these concerns the generality of the misattribution phenomenon. Some laboratory studies have found that misattribution effects fail to occur under high-fear (Nisbett & Schachter 1966) or high-stress (Dienstbier 1972) conditions. Similarly, despite promising initial results (Storms & Nisbett 1970, Barefoot & Girodo 1972), later attempts in clinical contexts to manipulate attributions concerning anxiety or other negative emotional states have generally failed (e.g. Bootzin et al 1976, Chambliss & Murray 1979, Cotton et al 1980; for a review see Ross & Olson 1981). Most clients probably have an obvious and relatively immutable explanation for their arousal, and their highly salient emotional reactions may themselves become the focus of attention (Dienstbier 1979). Therefore, these negative findings do not necessarily contradict Schachter's theory, according to which a state of uncertainty about the source of arousal and an opportunity for information search are necessary for misattribution effects to occur. However, these results do indicate that the misattribution phenomenon may arise only in contexts that are novel, associated with mild levels of negative affect, or in other respects conducive to ambiguity concerning the source of symptoms (Cotton 1981, Ross & Olson 1981). Finally, we should note that, once again, some failures to produce misattribution effects appear to result from imprecise synchrony between the onset of expected placebo effects and emotional reactions (Ross & Olson 1981).

Perhaps more damaging to Schachter's formulation is the evidence that studies which do find predicted effects on self-report and behavioral indexes of affect often fail to find predicted differences on attribution measures (e.g. Nisbett & Schachter 1966, Loftis & Ross 1974a,b, Calvert-Boyanowsky & Leventhal 1975). Moreover, there are alternative mediational formulations capable of accounting for reductions in affect. Calvert-Boyanowsky & Leventhal (1975) have proposed that results consistent with misattribution hypotheses may actually be traceable to reductions in uncertainty afforded by accurate information about symptoms. Both their study and Rodin's (1976) have supported this view by showing that differences in prior information about symptoms, but not differences in attributional cues, affected emotional behavior. Although it is unclear whether the preparatory information hypothesis can account for all findings in this literature (Dienstbier 1979), these two studies indicate that in many cases it may provide a better account than the original attributional one.

Other Relevant Evidence

In this section, we briefly review findings from related areas relevant to cognition-arousal theory.

EXCITATION TRANSFER   While research designed explicitly to test Schachter's misattribution predictions has often failed to support hypotheses, studies of the related phenomenon of excitation transfer (Zillmann 1971) have generally provided results consistent with the basic thrust of cognition-arousal theory. As formulated by Zillmann, the major premises of excitation transfer theory are that: (a) sympathetic activity does not terminate abruptly, but dissipates slowly; and (b) individuals often fail to attribute sympathetic activation accurately to more than one cause. On this basis, the theory predicts that, in certain circumstances, residual arousal from a prior situation will inseparably combine with the arousal induced in a subsequent situation and thereby intensify both emotional experience and emotional behavior in the latter context. It is further proposed that for this effect to occur, the individual must mistakenly attribute *all* the arousal experienced in the second context to the emotional stimuli present there.

A number of studies by Zillmann and his colleagues have supported these basic predictions. For example, they have shown that residual excitation from physical exertion can intensify feelings of anger and aggressive behavior (e.g. Zillmann et al 1972) and heighten sexual excitement (Cantor et al 1975); that residual sexual arousal can promote aggression (e.g. Zillmann 1971) and the enjoyment of music (Cantor & Zillmann 1973); and that residual excitation from humor can enhance aggression (Mueller & Donnerstein 1977; for more complete reviews see Zillmann 1978, 1983, Reisenzein 1983).

Several studies have also tested mediational assumptions concerning the importance of inaccurate linkage of arousal to inducers. These have shown that excitation transfer will occur only if the individual is placed in a second situation after obvious arousal cues linked to the original context have declined, but before the more subtle residual excitation has dissipated (e.g. Cantor et al 1975). Other investigations have demonstrated that transfer effects are attenuated when a causal linkage between an inducing condition and an excitatory reaction is merely suggested (Younger & Doob 1978) or when the salience of prior arousal is heightened by a manipulation of attentional focus (Reisenzein & Gattinger 1982).

Finally, alternative mediational hypotheses have been ruled out. For example, two sets of findings are inconsistent with a simple drive interpretation, according to which the heightened drive associated with sympathetic activity, rather than intensified emotional experience in the transfer phase, accounts for observed effects. The first is the evidence noted above that transfer effects fail to occur if individuals are placed in an emotional situation immediately after excitation (when drive levels would be expected to be maximal). The second is the observation that residual excitation transferred to an annoyance context can induce heightened aggression even when the actual opportunity to aggress occurs at a later point in time, well after residual activation has subsided (Zillmann & Bryant 1974, Bryant & Zillmann 1979).

In sum, there is a wealth of evidence demonstrating the excitation transfer phenomenon and supporting Zillmann's mediational interpretation of it. Given the evident similarities between excitation-transfer theory and cognition-arousal theory, one might argue that the high level of corroboration for the former offers support for the latter. However, this position overlooks some important differences between the two perspectives. Even though both theories assume a process of misattribution, excitation transfer theory does not propose that this is the culmination of an "epistemic search" designed to reduce uncertainty about the sources of arousal. On the contrary, it presupposes a more careless organism whose misattributions occur, in Reisenzein's (1983) terms, almost "by default" (p. 258), simply because certain veridical causal factors lack salience. Moreover, although cognition-arousal theory emphasizes that the perception of increased physiological arousal precedes emotional experience, transfer effects are most likely to occur precisely when individuals are becoming *less aware* of residual excitation. In short, it appears that excitation-transfer theory places less emphasis on conscious, volitional processes than does cognition-arousal theory.

BOGUS PHYSIOLOGICAL FEEDBACK   According to cognition-arousal theory, the interoception of actual physiological arousal is a necessary condition for emotional experience to arise. Valins (1966) challenged this assumption by asserting that the belief that one is aroused, independent of actual changes in activation, may be sufficient for emotional experience. His original studies demonstrating the effects of false heart rate feedback on ratings of sexual attractiveness (Valins 1966) and approach behavior in a fearful context (Valins & Ray 1967) supported this view. Over the years, a number of subsequent experiments have replicated this basic effect by showing that bogus feedback about internal states can affect evaluations of and responses to a variety of affective stimuli (for reviews see Liebhart 1979, Hirschman & Clark 1983).

However, there have also been a number of failures to produce false feedback effects. In particular, it has often been difficult to replicate Valins & Ray's (1967) finding that bogus feedback of autonomic quiescence can reduce anxiety (e.g. Sushinsky & Bootzin 1970, Kent et al 1972). These negative results would appear attributable to more stringent subject selection criteria in later experiments, since there is evidence that feedback is particularly ineffective for individuals experiencing high levels of fear (e.g. Borkovec & Glasgow 1973, Conger et al 1976) or anxiety (Koenig 1973). In turn, these results suggest that bogus feedback may only affect individuals experiencing mild to moderate levels of arousal and lacking substantial prior experience in the feedback context.

Liebhart (1979) has attempted to account for this varied pattern of results across studies by proposing a cognitive model that specifies the necessary conditions for feedback effects to occur. These include uncertainty, information seeking, the availability of explanatory contextual features, and the presence of feedback consistent with expectations or preexistent schemas.

In contrast to Liebhart, others have asserted that actual physiological changes mediate feedback effects. That physiological differences between feedback and control groups have sometimes been found lends credence to this position (for reviews see Harris & Katkin 1975, Hirschman & Clark 1983). However, only two studies have shown that autonomic responses were actually related to emotional behavior (Gaupp et al 1972, Detweiler & Zanna 1976). Furthermore, the fact that feedback groups showed heart rate deceleration in both these cases indicates that physiological activity may actually reflect the attentional processes emphasized by Valins (1966) and Liebhart (1979) (see e.g. Lacey & Lacey 1970).

More damaging to traditional interpretations of feedback results is the evidence that attentiveness to external cues per se may be sufficient to elicit similar effects. Most studies have compared feedback groups to a control group told simply that sounds are "extraneous." For this reason, these investigations have confounded differences in meaning attached to sounds with differences in attention paid to them. Most importantly, two of the three studies that have experimentally disentangled these two factors have found that subjects attending to sounds believed to reflect autonomic activity do not differ significantly from those attending to sounds of no given significance (Stern et al 1972, Parkinson & Manstead 1981; but see Botto et al 1974). Although it is presently unclear why attention to sounds alone is sufficient to produce these effects (see Parkinson & Manstead 1981 for some preliminary speculations), the mere demonstration of its importance strongly calls into question traditional interpretations of the bogus feedback phenomenon.

AUTONOMIC SPECIFICITY OF EMOTIONS   Another issue of relevance to an evaluation of cognition-arousal theory is that of autonomic specificity for different emotions. As noted above, according to cognition-arousal theory (e.g. Schachter 1964) and related formulations (e.g. Zillmann 1983), arousal is nonspecific in that it determines the intensity but not the quality of emotional experience. Although there is evidence for nonspecificity in some contexts (Zillmann 1983), other studies have found evidence of emotion-specific autonomic patterns. For example, Weerts & Roberts (1976) have replicated the earlier findings of Ax (1953) and J. Schachter (1957) by showing that diastolic blood pressure increased more during anger than fear imagery while heart rate and systolic blood pressure increased equally. Recent studies have extended these findings. For example, Schwartz et al (1981) have shown reliable cardiovascular differentiation between imagery-induced states of happiness, sadness, anger, fear, and relaxation. Similarly, Ekman et al (1983) found that directions to adopt emotion-prototypic facial expressions, and, to a lesser extent, instructions to relive past emotional experiences, resulted in autonomic patterns that discriminated among several negative emotions (e.g. disgust and anger from each other and from fear and sadness) as well as between positive and negative emotions.

Previous criticisms of Schachter's failure to account for autonomic specificity (e.g. Lang 1971) have been rebutted with the evidence of interoceptive insensitivity to what would appear to be relatively subtle differences (e.g. Schachter & Singer 1962, 1979, Zillmann 1978, 1983). However, a study by Erdmann & van Lindern (1980) suggests that even if these patterns are indiscriminable, their measurable differences may still affect the nature of emotional experience. Specifically, using a traditional misattribution paradigm, these authors found that drug-induced arousal failed to intensify reported anger among subjects exposed to an anger-provoking context, but *did* intensify *anxiety*. Importantly, this effect occurred despite the fact that placebo subjects exposed to identical contextual cues repc.ted increased anger but not anxiety. The authors explain the surprising results in the drug-arousal condition by noting that: (*a*) according to psychophysiological assessments, the drug (orciprenaline) induced circulatory patterns more consistent with those normally associated with anxiety than anger (see e.g. Weerts & Roberts 1976); and (*b*) the situational cues might logically have provoked anxiety as well as anger. While these results may be partially attributed to the effects of unexplained arousal (e.g. Marshall & Zimbardo 1979, Maslach 1979), the authors' interpretation clearly implies that the specific match between contextual cues and autonomic activity (or possibly central activity, see below) can have an important impact on emotional experience. Given the evidence for perceptual insensitivity to fine-grained autonomic differences, these findings in turn highlight the limitations attendant upon an emotion theory that focuses solely upon *perceived* arousal.

THE ROLE OF AUTONOMIC ACTIVITY IN EMOTIONAL EXPERIENCE   According to cognition-arousal theory, heightened activity in the sympathetic branch of the autonomic nervous system is a *necessary* condition for emotional experience to arise. As noted above, this position is weakened by the evidence from misattribution studies that increased peripheral arousal generally fails to intensify self-reported emotional experience. Other findings from related sources similarly suggest that autonomic activity may often play only a limited role in the genesis of emotional experience. However, the issues here are sufficiently complex to prevent precise delineation of the conditions under which this conclusion holds. For example, in his original critique of the James-Lange theory of emotion, Cannon (1927, 1931) noted evidence that sympathectomized animals show no diminution of emotional behavior. However, others have argued that these behaviors are almost always well learned (e.g. Mandler 1962, Schachter 1964). This is an important observation given the evidence for progressive dissociation between at least some affective states and behaviors as the latter become well learned (e.g. fear and avoidance; for a review see Mineka 1979). In addition, Cannon's critics have cited other findings indicating that animals deprived of visceral innervation are slower to *acquire* emotional responses. Human studies assessing the emotional sequalae of spinal cord injuries are also relevant. Unfortunately, their results are inconsistent and weakened by methodological confounds (for a review see Reisenzein 1983).

More clear-cut support for the notion that autonomic activity may often be only a weak determinant of emotional experience comes from studies assessing the effects of beta-adrenergic blockers, which act to reduce peripheral arousal: these drugs typically fail to attenuate emotional reactions (e.g. Gottschalk et al 1974, Erdmann & van Lindern 1980; but see Frankenhauser 1975). Furthermore, there is an additional piece of evidence pointing to the conclusion that visceral input may often be a relatively minor factor. This is the often-noted discrepancy between the slow reactivity of the autonomic nervous system and the rapidity with which emotional reactions normally occur (see Cannon 1927, Grossman 1967).

General Summary

Overall, research testing predictions derived from cognition-arousal theory has yielded disappointing results. Studies on misattribution of drug-induced arousal to emotional cues have only rarely corroborated Schachter's theory. Particularly lacking is unambiguous support for the specific prediction that increases in arousal intensify emotional experience under constant contextual cues. This assertion is also weakened by the evidence that false physiological feedback alters self-reports of affect. However, it should be noted that the bogus feedback phenomenon itself is subject to interpretive difficulties. Although research on misattribution of emotional arousal to neutral cues has yielded results more favorable to cognition-arousal theory, there is compelling evidence that nonattributional processes may mediate these effects. Finally, excitation-transfer studies have consistently supported Zillmann's theory. However, excitation-transfer theory differs from cognition-arousal theory in several important respects.

Despite some notable differences, there would appear to be one characteristic shared by the phenomena of misattribution of drug-induced arousal to emotional cues, misattribution of emotional arousal to neutral cues, and affective change induced by false feedback. They all occur only under relatively delimited conditions. In each case, effects appear dependent on precise timing between the onset of either veridical or perceived arousal and the occurrence of attributional cues. Additionally, both misattribution and false feedback effects may be limited to novel contexts eliciting low to moderate levels of autonomic activity (Cotton 1981). Viewed from the perspective of the perceptual-motor model that we have presented previously (see e.g. Leventhal 1984), this latter boundary condition makes good sense. Novel, moderately arousing contexts would appear least likely to elicit rapid and reflexive processing of both situational and physiological cues. Instead, these contexts may require the more deliberate conceptual processing presupposed by Schachter's theory and cognitive interpretations of false feedback effects (e.g. Liebhart 1979).

Even under these conditions, however, it is important once again to note the evidence that peripheral feedback often has only weak effects on emotional experience. This point suggests that the misattribution effects that do occur may be due to different mediational processes than those proposed by cognition-arousal theory. In particular, the effects of experimental manipulations may frequently be mediated by changes in *central* nervous system activity. In this vein, it is important to point out that investigations yielding misattribution effects (e.g. excitation transfer studies and studies in which subjects ingest drugs known to have central effects such as amphetamines or ephedrine) typically fail to rule out the possibility that central-neural rather than peripheral-autonomic mechanisms account for the observed findings.

EMOTION AND EXPRESSIVE BEHAVIOR

In sharp contrast to the environmental definition of emotion quality in cognition-arousal theory, traditional research on expressive behavior operates under the nativist assumption that a pattern of expressive behavior creates or reflects an underlying, specific emotional state. At least three types of data are consistent with the hypothesis of innate expressive reactions: (a) The universality of emotional expressions as seen in the ability of adults to match expressions from a different culture to the generating situation (Ekman et al 1982); (b) The appearance of discriminable expressions of smiling, anger, disgust, etc, soon after birth (Hiatt et al 1979, Ekman & Oster 1982, Sternberg et al 1983) in response to physical stimuli such as tastes (Ganchow et al 1983) and social stimuli (Meltzoff & Moore 1977, Field et al 1982); and (c) The differentiation and elaboration of expressions at approximately the same rate by both blind and sighted children (Goodenough 1932).

The Link Between Expression and Feeling: Alternative Hypotheses

While these findings support a nativist explanation of expressive behavior, they do not bear directly on the hypothesis that subjective feelings are caused by expression, nor do they show that subjective feelings are parallel to expressive reactions and innately differentiated. For example, expressive reactions or displays can also be understood as basic reactions to interpersonal stimuli rather than as expressions of internal feeling states (Bekoff 1981, Redican 1982). Infant data provide strong evidence of the power of interpersonal cues in eliciting expressions. Newborns turn toward high pitched vocalizations, show cycling arm movements when looking at an adult (Brazelton et al 1974), smile and display open-eyed surprise and glum brow-knitting reactions to the same reactions in a female experimenter (Field et al 1982), and at 11 to 21 days of age are interested in and will imitate the lip and tongue protrusions and hand motions of an adult model (Meltzoff & Moore 1977). While these infant expressions could reflect feelings induced by the adult model, they may be orienting and communicative responses (I am listening, I see you, talk to me) designed to encourage, integrate, and regulate social interaction (Trevarthan 1984).

Even if expressive reactions and subjective emotions are linked, this association could take various forms. First, both expressive behavior and subjective emotion could be products of a central neural process. Second, they could be directly and causally connected, with either or both acting as cause. Third, expression and feeling could influence one another, but to a degree mediated by an underlying, central mechanism. In this latter case, the influence of expression on feeling and feeling on expression may be asymmetrical (e.g. feelings may have a greater impact on expression than vice versa). Given the empirical evidence and the elaboration of theoretical models arguing that motor behavior is the product of central motor templates interacting with lower level loops (e.g. Kennedy 1971, Merton 1972), it is surprising to note that the emotion literature has focused on a simple feedback model in which expressions are assumed to give rise to subjective feelings. We will return to this issue after reviewing the facial feedback work.

The Facial Feedback Hypothesis

The hypothesis that facial feedback is the source of subjective emotion, originally rejected by James (1890), was revived by Tomkins (1962) and Izard's (1971) stimulating analyses of emotional processes in personality. Both authors observed that many of the properties of facial musculature are consistent with the feedback hypothesis. Facial muscles are (a) numerous and complex (Izard 1971) and can contract in part as well as in whole (Tomkins 1962); (b) have sensory nerves that go to the hypothalamic region of the brain (Gellhorn 1964); and (c) do not habituate with repeated firing. While these observations and the previously cited cross-cultural and developmental data add to the plausibility of the hypothesis, they do not directly test it.

Two different methods of manipulating expressive reactions have been used to show that feedback can shape subjective feelings: (a) direct manipulation of facial muscles, and (b) indirect manipulation by instructions to express or hide expression, or by use of contextual cues such as canned laughter to intensify expression. Both types have been successful in varying expression while holding stimulus attributes constant (e.g. electric shocks, cartoons, odors).

DIRECT MANIPULATIONS OF FACIAL EXPRESSION   In an early test of the hypothesis that expressive responses directly control subjective feeling, Nina Bull (Bull 1951, Pasquarelli & Bull 1951) demonstrated that subjects could not experience hypnotically instructed emotions when these emotions were inconsistent with prior expressions into which the subject had been hypnotically "locked." The subject was led to adopt an expression by the experimenter lightly touching specific facial muscles and instructing the subject to contract them.

More recently, Laird and his associates (Laird 1984) have conducted a series of studies using the same method of altering expressions. In the initial study, a frown increased reports of aggressive feelings in response to pictures of children at play or pictures of Klansmen, while a smile increased reports of positive feeling in response to pictures of the children at play (Laird 1974).

Subsequent studies showed that this effect was most pronounced for a subset of subjects assumed to be more sensitive to internal or self-produced cues in general (for a review see Laird 1984). Laird attempted to validate this assumption by demonstrating that subjects more responsive to facial manipulation are also less susceptible to placebo effects (Duncan & Laird 1980) and less sensitive to external food cues (McArthur et al 1980). The generality of Laird's results are unclear, however, given his reliance on nonsalient contextual stimuli. It may be that even high self-perceivers are relatively impervious to facial manipulations when their attention is captured by the external environment, as is likely in natural contexts giving rise to emotions. Additionally, Laird has claimed that the processes that underlie the self-perception effects may be the same as those mediating facial-feedback effects. However, the parallel between these two theories is unclear, since facial-feedback theorists have not proposed that self-perception or self-observation is necessary to the feedback process.

A challenging study by Tourangeau & Ellsworth (1979) forcefully argued that expressive reactions were neither necessary nor sufficient for emotional experience. Their manipulations of facial reactions produced substantial changes in expression but had absolutely no effect on reports of fear or sadness or the autonomic reactions recorded while subjects were observing movies that were fearful, sad, or neutral.

We have no way of determining precisely why Tourangeau and Ellsworth's results differed from Laird's, but offer the following suggestions. First, Tourangeau & Ellsworth's subjects may have held their expressions for too long a period (2 minutes), thus disrupting emotional experience other than distress. Second, Laird's procedures and his use of within-subject designs resulted in approximately 20% of his subjects identifying the purpose of the experiment during the debriefing. To Buck (1980), this suggests demand characteristics. None of Tourangeau and Ellsworth's subjects, on the other hand, realized their study was investigating the effects of expression on feeling. Thus, Laird's subjects may have altered their judgments because they were aware of the "emotional" meaning of their expressions. Finally, the intensity of the manipulated expressions generated by Tourangeau and Ellsworth may not have matched the intensity of feeling aroused by the stimulus, and so disrupted the possible feedback effect. If the manipulated facial expressions were much stronger or weaker than those "naturally" associated with the stimulus, the feedback might have been "discounted."

INSTRUCTIONS AND CONTEXTUAL MANIPULATIONS OF EXPRESSION   To avoid the artificiality and possible demand characteristics associated with direct manipulation of the face, several investigators have varied instructions or contextual cues to alter expressions, examining the impact of this independent manipulation upon stimulus judgments. The effects found have been of small size, restricted to subsamples of subjects, sometimes opposite to the effect predicted by the facial feedback hypothesis, and influenced by the social context.

For example, Leventhal & Mace (1970, studies 1 and 2) have shown that instructing grade school children to laugh, ostensibly for a tape of their reactions, led to more intense expressive reactions and more favorable evaluations of a slapstick movie. College students were also found to evaluate cartoons more favorably when a contextual cue of canned laughter was present (Cupchik & Leventhal 1974, study 1). However, these results held *only* for female subjects; in all three studies males showed a negative relationship between expression and judgment (both between and within conditions).

Leventhal & Mace (1970) noticed that the inverse relationship of expression and judgment for first- and second-grade males appeared to be related to excessively strong, and possibly voluntary and forced, expressive reactions. Cupchik & Leventhal (1974) tested the hypothesis that voluntary, exaggerated expressions would be unrelated to judgments by having female subjects pay attention to and rate the intensity of their expressive reactions prior to making judgments of cartoon stimuli. It was expected that the attentional manipulation would enhance the degree of volitional control over expressive reaction. The results showed that for female subjects attention to expressions increased their intensity, lowered the rated funniness of good cartoons, and led to a breakdown in discrimination between good and bad cartoons (see also Leventhal & Cupchik 1975). Alternative interpretations of these effects are that attention to a component of an emotional state reduces the intensity of the state by disrupting the spontaneity of the response, or by forewarning subjects of their emotional reactions.

Lanzetta & Kleck (1970) exposed subjects to a series of electric shocks of varying intensity under instructions to: (a) express their feelings so that someone watching them on video tape could guess the intensity of the shock, or (b) hide their feelings so the observer would be unable to judge the shock intensity. Facial reactions, autonomic responses (not obtained with the studies so far mentioned), and subjective reports of shock painfulness were recorded for both "practice" and "observation" (on camera) trials.

Their five studies showed the following: First, instructions produced robust differences in expressiveness between conditions. Subjects told to show their feelings produced more distinctive, differentiated facial expressions in response to the shocks than did subjects told to hide their feelings. Second, hide instructions reduced autonomic response and express instructions strengthened autonomic response. These effects were very small during "practice" trials when subjects were varying expressions but not expecting to be filmed, but they were substantial during on camera "observation" trials (Lanzetta et al 1976). A pair of studies showed that observation itself suppresses both expression and autonomic response (Kleck et al 1976).

Third, judgments of a shock's painfulness were not closely linked to changes in expression and autonomic response. No effects were reported in one study, and very small, though statistically reliable, differences were reported in two others (e.g. hide less painful than express). The differences in reported pain between express and hide conditions were at low shock levels in one study and at high levels in another.

Lanzetta and associates believe their manipulation of facial reactions altered emotional reactions. Other contradictory conclusions, however, are equally plausible. For example, it could be argued that emotion was irrelevant to the findings because any increase in motor behavior, facial or otherwise, might increase autonomic response (Obrist 1976). Second, it is possible that both facial and autonomic changes are reactions to feelings of self-consciousness at being observed, since the autonomic effects are only clear for on-camera trials. This latter interpretation would argue against direct feedback from facial action to autonomic response. Third, the inconsistent and weak effect of expressive manipulation on stimulus judgments could be taken to support hypotheses arguing that feedback did *not* alter emotion. On the other hand, unlike a judgment of subjective feeling, judgments of shock painfulness may be tightly linked to the properties of the stimulus and be a poor indicator of subjective state.

In sum, on the basis of our review, we tend to agree with Laird's assessment that expressive changes can alter subjective states. The effect, however, is of very small magnitude and not proportional to the manipulated change in expression. Still unanswered is the question of the mechanism responsible for these effects.

SPONTANEITY OF ACTION, SOCIAL COMMUNICATION, AND FACIAL FEED-BACK   The facial feedback hypothesis is exceptionally difficult to test. It does not adequately specify the conditions under which feedback effects should or should not occur, nor does it take into account the many possible mechanisms that might produce effects similar to those predicted by a feedback hypothesis. Thus, the existence of a feedback effect will remain in doubt until we can specify its mechanisms and necessary and sufficient conditions.

Two possible conditions concern the differences between spontaneous and voluntary motor reactions, and between expressive reactions in a highly social versus nonsocial context. With respect to the first, there appears to be a stronger association between expressive reactions and subjective feelings under conditions that favor spontaneous rather than controlled or voluntary response. In addition to the studies already reviewed, Kraut (1982) examined expressions and judgments in response to a series of 12 odors that were smelled in two trials: a spontaneous trial and a communication trial in which subjects were asked to adopt poses to communicate the quality of the odors. The two conditions were crossed with an alone or together factor. Kraut found that efforts to communicate led to more distinct and exaggerated facial changes and to statistically significant, but very small increases (1/15 the size of the expression changes) in judgments of the odors. The effect was stronger for the pleasant than the unpleasant odors. Most importantly, the association of expression and judgment was substantial ($r=.54$ and $r=.43$) in the spontaneous as compared to the posed conditions ($r=.10$ and $r=.16$ for alone and together respectively).

In addition, we should note the evidence for separate neural control of voluntary and spontaneous facial movements (Crosby & DeJonge 1963, Evarts 1973, Sackeim & Gur 1983), and increasing data that volitional and spontaneous (emotional) expressive reactions differ in appearance. Volitional are more strongly expressed on the left side of the face, while spontaneous responses are either more symmetrical (Ekman et al 1981, Hager & Ekman 1983) or lateralized according to affective valence (Sackeim & Gur 1983; see also the section on lateralization of emotion below). Factors that disrupt spontaneity, such as focusing attention on specific aspects of motor response or "faking" emotion, may reduce the association between expression and emotion (See Zuckerman et al 1981).

As suggested earlier, expressive reactions are highly responsive to social cues. Indeed, as observed by Kraut & Johnston (1979), expressions may be more responsive to social cues than to internal feeling states. They found that bowlers, hockey fans, and strollers smiled in response to people rather than to the nonsocial stimuli that would evoke strong, positive, internal, emotional states (strikes for bowlers, goals by the home team for hockey fans, and sunny weather for strollers). The studies from Lanzetta's laboratory suggested that social context alters the relationship between expressive, autonomic, and subjective indicators: the changes in autonomic response to varied expression occurred under conditions of observation only. The positive association of expression and judgment for female subjects seen in Leventhal's laboratory also appeared in group settings or in response to canned laughter, and the effect dissipated when attention was turned away from the group and focused on the self.

However, interpersonal situations do not always strengthen the relationship between expressive behavior and emotional experience. For example, Kraut (1982) found no effect of social context on the association between expression and judgment of odors, while Laird's research has consistently found feedback effects for subjects sensitive to internal but not external (i.e. social) cues (for a review see Laird 1984).

Moreover, several studies have found an *inverse* relationship between facial expressiveness and autonomic activity, particularly in stressful interpersonal contexts (e.g. Notarius & Levenson 1979, Notarius et al 1982; for a review see Buck 1980). In accounting for these findings, Buck (1980) and Lanzetta & Kleck (1970) have suggested that individuals who inhibit their expressive displays have a social learning history characterized by punishment or rebuke for free emotional expression. The threat of punishment and other aversive consequences of interpersonal conflict in turn elicit heightened autonomic activity. As a result, over time, inhibitory expressions occurring during interpersonal stress have become conditioned stimuli for heightened physiological responding.

Another moderator variable is suggested by the evidence that facial expressions may have little or no impact on experience if they occur during the course of conversation (Ekman 1982, Kraut & Johnston 1979). Thus, social contexts that encourage an active interchange among people may reduce the association between expression and other emotional indicators (but see Levenson & Gottman 1983).

In sum, depending upon individual differences, specific contextual factors, and other moderators that remain to be elucidated, social situations may either facilitate or inhibit expressive reactions, and in so doing they enhance or disrupt the degree of association between these and various indicators of autonomic and subjective response. In this regard, it is also important to note the evidence that self-awareness has powerful effects on emotional responses (e.g. Carver & Scheier 1981, 1982). Indeed, the experience of some subjective emotions may require the prior formation and activation of the self-schema (Lewis & Brooks 1978, Kagan 1984). When taken with the sensitivity of expressive reactions to social factors, the increased salience of the self-schema in social contexts suggests that we are dealing with a complex, emotion-mediating system. This will further complicate tests of any "simple" hypothesis such as that postulating that facial feedback causes subjective feelings.

Peripheral versus Central Linkage of Feeling to Expression

Feedback hypotheses, whether in the autonomic or facial domain, are hard to dismiss. The model of a peripheral to central mechanism for feelings is strongly supported by everyday intuition and introspection (Cannon 1931). James (1950) could not "imagine" emotion without body feedback, and neither can Mandler (1975). Add to this the difficulty of truly disconfirming the hypothesis, and it not surprising to find efforts at reviving the theory. For example, Tomkins (1980) has recently suggested that patterns of facial blood flow generate subjective emotion, and Zajonc (1985) has revived Waynbaum's theory that facial muscle contractions regulate blood flow to and from the brain. Given the rich arterial blood supply to the brain unaffected by facial muscle activity, the burden of proof lies on this theory's advocates to show that facial expressions alter blood supply enough to change brain activity and emotional experience.

Belief in a peripheral feedback mechanism also seems to be strengthened by evidence that spontaneous expressions have a greater impact on subjective states, and that the action of only a specified subset of muscles, for example the zygomatic muscles used in smiling, correlates with subjective feeling (Ekman et al 1982). That these very same muscles generate smiles in infants further supports the argument (Hiatt et al 1979, Sternberg et al 1983).

None of this evidence, however, gives more support to a feedback model of a peripheral to central mechanism than to alternative central models that postulate that feeling and expression are both constructed by a central motor mechanism.

Moreover, feedback effects could be mediated by a central mechanism. For example, Izard (1971) has suggested that feedback may arouse subjective emotion by activating central emotion memories formed over a history of emotional experience. The effects of feedback on subjective experience, therefore, would be indirect.

It is our judgment that feedback effects in emotion will not be understood fully until we develop an effective model of the central motor processes that construct emotion. Leventhal (1984) provides a recent example of one such model. Emotion is postulated to arise from a central motor program involving parallel voluntary and autonomic (or spontaneous) systems. The interaction of the two systems' output generates either an emotional experience or the sensation of movement. For example, voluntary anticipation of a spontaneous movement is likely to cancel the experience of emotion. Such a system would be responsive to social stimuli as well as facial feedback, but the degree to which it would be influenced by feedback would depend upon the degree to which the context alters the interaction of the two motor systems. Elaboration of models of this sort will be essential to a satisfactory interpretation of the feedback studies.

LATERALIZATION AND EMOTION

In reviewing the evidence for the lateralization of emotion, we focus upon several related but distinct areas of research. These include studies of hemispheric differences in the perceptual processing of external emotional cues and autonomic activity, in expressive behavior, and in both chronic and phasic emotional states.

Although this growing area of inquiry has exciting implications for a number of issues central to the study of the emotions (e.g. cognition-emotion interactions, biological substrates of emotion, emotional disorders), there are numerous inconsistencies in findings. Moreover, several fundamental conceptual and methodological issues have yet to be resolved. Unfortunately, space constraints dictate that the present review highlight only the most consistent findings and focus upon those interpretive strategies and methodological approaches that have attained a general consensus among researchers. We will, however, discuss major methodological and conceptual difficulties at appropriate points below.

Lateralized Perceptual Processing of Emotional Stimuli

There is a wealth of evidence suggesting that the perceptual processing of emotional stimuli is primarily under the control of the right hemisphere. Strong support for this notion comes from neuropsychological studies showing that right hemisphere lesions impair the ability to detect the emotional mood of a speaker. No such impairments were found in left-lesioned patients or in the ability of either group to accurately judge the emotional content of spoken passages (Heilman et al 1975, Tucker et al 1976). This latter finding suggests that lesions may specifically impair the ability to decode nonverbal affective cues.

Studies using normal subjects also support the linkage between the right hemisphere and the processing of emotional stimuli. Consistent with findings obtained in clinical contexts, several studies have shown right hemisphere superiority for judgments of the emotional tone of speech in both adults (e.g. Safer & Leventhal 1977, Bryden et al 1982), and children (Saxby & Bryden 1984). Other experiments have shown that adults (e.g. Suberi & McKeever 1977, Ley & Bryden 1979, Safer 1981) and children (Saxby & Bryden 1985) are right hemisphere dominant for the visual recognition of facial expressions of emotion.

Despite the apparent wealth of evidence demonstrating right hemisphere superiority in the decoding of emotional cues, such a conclusion should be qualified. In certain cases, the magnitude of differences appears conditional upon the emotional valence of stimuli. For example, two studies of facial recognition have shown that sad faces produce the greatest right hemisphere advantage and happy faces the least (e.g. Suberi & McKeever 1977, Ley & Bryden 1979). Moreover, at least two studies have shown a *left* hemisphere superiority in response to happy facial expressions (Reuter-Lorenz & Davidson 1981, Reuter-Lorenz et al 1983). Further research is necessary to clarify whether these findings are attributable to an actual left hemisphere advantage in the decoding of specific positively toned cues or to other factors. Given the evidence to be reviewed below indicating a linkage between the left hemisphere and the experience of positive emotions and between the right hemisphere and the experience of negative emotions, one such factor could be actual changes in emotional experience elicited by stimuli (Davidson 1984).

In addition, further research is necessary to clarify the specific cognitive and neural processes responsible for hemispheric differences. For example, several commentators have suggested that the right hemisphere may be especially suited to the processing of emotional stimuli because of its demonstrated superiority in holistic and parallel processing and in integrating analog data arising from several sources (e.g. Safer & Leventhal 1977, Tucker 1981). However, this account leaves unclear whether the right hemisphere advantage is due to its greater ability to structure or decode stimuli, its superior retention or retrieval of attribute patterns and prototypes, or other cognitive processes.

Lateralization of Autonomic Feedback and Body Symptoms

Consistent with the right hemisphere's superiority in decoding emotional stimuli is its close linkage with autonomic and other bodily processes. Davidson et al (1981) have shown that subjects can more readily tap their left hand (which is controlled by the right hemisphere) in synchrony with their heart rates than their right hand. Similarly, there is evidence that individuals who are right hemisphere dominant are better at detecting whether a series of stimuli is contingent upon their heart rates (Hantas et al 1984, Montgomery & Jones 1984).

Clinical studies also suggest hemispheric differences in the processing of bodily cues in general. For example, patients more frequently report conversion and other psychosomatic symptoms on the left side of the body (Galin et al 1977).

Lateralization of Expressive Behavior

Paralleling the evidence for right hemispheric dominance in the *decoding* of emotional and autonomic or other bodily stimuli are findings demonstrating right hemisphere superiority in the transmission or *encoding* of nonverbal cues. Two studies have shown that right, but not left, hemisphere damage is associated with an impaired ability to express or communicate emotion through tone of voice (Tucker et al 1976, Ross & Mesulam 1979). Importantly, this deficit does not appear to be caused by any impairment in the subjective *experience* of emotion (Ross & Mesulam 1979).

The majority of research on hemispheric differences in expressive behavior has focused upon facial expressiveness. Although there have been a number of studies on this subject, progress has been hindered by several of the methodological and conceptual problems noted in the previous section on expressive behavior (Sackeim & Gur 1983). These difficulties include the failure to distinguish between static asymmetries, slow changes, and more rapid facial movements, or between voluntary and spontaneous facial expressions. In addition, some studies have failed to assess the primary functions served by facial expressions; for example, they may be designed to communicate feelings or regulate social interactions (Hager 1982, Sackeim & Gur 1983). Sackeim and Gur (1983) have also pointed out the need to separate actual lateralized differences in expressiveness from a sidedness bias in the observer. As noted above, there is strong evidence of right hemisphere dominance in the perception of emotional facial cues. Such a bias may contribute to the perception of greater emotionality on the left side of the face unless appropriate precautions are taken, such as the use of right- and left-side facial composites (photographs displaying one side of the face and its mirror image). The use of composites also serves to accentuate what may otherwise be undetectable asymmetries in facial expression.

Although it is unfortunate that a number of studies on sidedness biases in facial expressiveness have ignored these conceptual and methodological issues, there are a few relatively firm conclusions that can be drawn concerning voluntary expressions of right-handers. Consistent with the evidence of right hemisphere control over the communication of affective tone, these expressions are typically more pronounced on the left side of the face (controlled by the right hemisphere) than on the right side (controlled by the left hemisphere) (Borod & Caron 1979 1980, Ekman et al 1981, Heller & Levy 1981). However, the left-sided bias is clearer for negative than positive emotions. Indeed, there is some evidence that the voluntary expression of positive emotions may at least sometimes be associated with a right-sided facial bias (e.g. Borod et al 1983, Borod & Koff 1984). In contrast to right-handers, left-handers show no consistent dominance (Sackeim & Gur 1983).

It has been argued that spontaneous emotional expressions are either more symmetrical (Ekman et al 1981, Hager & Ekman 1983) or lateralized according to affective valence (Sackeim & Gur 1983). In the latter view, negative emotions are more likely to be spontaneously expressed on the left side of the face, while positive emotions are more likely to be spontaneously expressed on the right side. However, both hypotheses lack firm support at the present time because of the inconsistent findings and frequent methodological weaknesses of studies testing them. These latter problems include failure to demonstrate that expressions are actually spontaneous, low inter-rater reliabilities and insensitive and potentially biased measurement of facial activity (for a review see Sackeim & Gur 1983).

Lateralization of Emotional States

At one time, the apparent right hemisphere superiority in the processing of emotional stimuli led some theorists to characterize the right hemisphere as the source of emotional experience. Conversely, the left hemisphere was viewed as "nonemotional" (for a review see Tucker 1981). More recent findings indicate, however, that *both* hemispheres contribute to emotional experience. Unfortunately, the relationship between specific patterns of cortical activity and specific emotional states is as yet unclear, as is the nature of the interaction between different regions of the brain.

Perhaps the most consistent pattern of results is one indicating a heightened right hemisphere contribution to negative affective states, particularly depression, and a heightened left hemisphere contribution to positive affective states. Evidence supporting this conclusion comes from studies assessing the effects of selective dampening of hemispheric activity and of selective brain damage, both of which are presumed to disinhibit the emotional tendencies of the contralateral hemisphere (e.g. Sackeim et al 1982). Although not unanimous (Gruzelier 1981), these investigations have generally shown that left hemisphere sedation or damage results in excessive worry, pessimism, and crying, and that right hemisphere sedation or damage results in inappropriate euphoria, indifference, or laughing (see reviews by Gainotti 1972, Tucker 1981, Sackeim et al 1982). More recent lesion studies have shown that these emotional reactions are particularly associated with damage to frontal regions (Kolb & Milner 1981, Robinson & Benson 1981). This selective localization is not surprising, given the extensive anatomical reciprocity of the frontal lobes with the limbic system, as well as other evidence of the frontal lobes' importance in affective regulation (Davidson 1984).

Studies indicating hemispheric asymmetries in clinically depressed populations are also suggestive. Electrophysiological investigations assessing resting EEG have, with some exceptions (see Tucker 1981), found that depressives show heightened right hemisphere activation relative to controls (Abrams & Taylor 1979, Flor-Henry et al 1979, Schaffer et al 1983). Consistent with studies of brain damage effects, these depressed/nondepressed differences appear to occur primarily in the frontal and central, but not parietal, regions of the right hemisphere (Perris & Monakhov 1979, Schaffer et al 1983).

However, depressives frequently show deficits on spatial cognitive tasks requiring involvement of the posterior right hemisphere (e.g. Flor-Henry et al 1983, Taylor et al 1981). A recent study demonstrating a negative correlation between right frontal and right parietal activity in depressives (Davidson et al 1985) suggests that suppression of parietal activity by frontal regions may underlie these cognitive impairments. Conversely, declines in frontal activity may underlie the observed reversal of these cognitive deficits concomitant with improvements in mood (e.g. Kronfol et al 1978; for a review see Tucker 1981).

A third source of evidence concerning lateralization of affective experience comes from studies using normal adults. While there have been exceptions (e.g. Harman & Ray 1977), electrophysiological findings have generally paralleled results obtained with clinical populations by showing heightened right frontal activation during depressed moods and heightened left frontal activation during positive affective states (e.g. Davidson et al 1979, Tucker et al 1981). Indeed, in one recent study, frontal EEG asymmetry accounted for approximately 50% of the variance in self-reported happiness (Davidson et al 1985).

Right-handed normals also report more negative affect in response to information presented initially to the right hemisphere and somewhat more positive affect in response to information presented to the left hemisphere (noted in Dimond et al 1976, Dimond & Farrington 1977, Davidson 1984, Davidson et al 1985). Notably, these effects occur independently of the emotional valence of stimuli; they are found whether stimuli are positive or negative. Additionally, these studies have consistently failed to find hemispheric differences in *recognition* of emotional cues (Davidson 1984). Thus, the obtained differences in self-reports of emotional *experience* do not appear confounded by asymmetrical decoding processes.

Recent investigations by Davidson and Fox have extended the evidence for asymmetries in emotional experience to infants. In one study, 10-month-olds were exposed to a videotape of an actress generating either a happy or sad facial expression. Although there were no asymmetries associated with sad expressions, happy expressions elicited greater left-sided activation (Davidson & Fox 1982). In a second study, neonates tasting a sweet sucrose or bitter citric acid solution showed greater left frontal activation after ingestion of the former and greater right frontal activation after ingestion of the latter. Correspondingly, facial expressions, scored with Izard's MAX system, showed substantially greater "interest" expressions to sucrose and greater "disgust" reactions to citric acid (cited in Fox & Davidson 1984). Once again, no parietal asymmetries were observed in either study.

On the basis of their infant studies and the other evidence reviewed above linking hemispheric asymmetry and positive and negative affective states, Fox & Davidson (1984) have proposed a developmental model of the hemispheric substrates of emotion. This model postulates that the left and right frontal regions of the brain are the anatomical substrates of "approach" and "avoidance" or "withdrawal" tendencies, which are said to be the fundamental basis for positive and negative emotions respectively. It is further proposed that approach and withdrawal are present and asymmetrically organized at birth, at which time they are manifest experientially as interest and disgust. With increased interhemispheric communication and related changes occurring during maturation (e.g. the onset of locomotion), other emotions (e.g. fear and sadness) arise which reflect the joint interaction or "blending" of the two hemispheres.

As have other theorists (e.g. Bakan 1969, Tucker 1981), Fox & Davidson (1984) also suggest that with enhanced commissural transfer, the left hemisphere develops the capacity to inhibit or attenuate the negative responses of the right frontal regions. Although there is a surprising paucity of research explicitly testing this important prediction, it is consistent with the observed relationship between verbal ability (reflecting increased functional activity of the left hemisphere) and the ability to inhibit negative affect in young children (for a review see Fox & Davidson 1984). In addition, there is some evidence that verbal and analytic strategies are particularly effective at inhibiting emotional arousal in adults (Tucker & Newman 1981).

While Fox & Davidson (1984) postulate that hemispheric asymmetries reflect primarily a positive-negative or approach-withdrawal distinction, Tucker & Williamson (1984) have recently proposed a very different model of hemispheric specialization. Building upon previous formulations by Pribram & McGuinness (1975, McGuinness & Pribram 1980), these authors propose two major cortical regulatory systems, *arousal* and *activation*. The arousal system underlies responsivity to input from the external environment. Its activity is said to increase with novel external input (i.e. orienting) and to decline with repetitive input (i.e. habituation). In contrast, the activation system reflects the internal control of behavior and is associated with a vigilant, highly focused attentional style and a "redundancy bias" that facilitates the tight, sequential control of motor activity. The two systems also differ in their anatomical loci and neurochemical regulation. The arousal system is located primarily in the right hemisphere and parietal regions and is controlled by noradrenergic neurotransmission. In contrast, the activation system is left-lateralized and frontal, and subserved by dopaminergic neurotransmission.

Of primary interest in the present context is Tucker and Williamson's specification of the affective features of these two systems. They propose that anxiety is the primary subjective correlate of the left-lateralized activation system. Several findings support this linkage, including evidence that high trait- and state-anxious individuals, obsessive-compulsives, and paranoids have an analytic perceptual style reflecting heightened left-hemisphere activity (e.g. Shapiro 1965). Additionally, in some studies, the task performance of high-anxious subjects has indicated left-hemisphere dominance (e.g. Tucker et al 1978). Conversely, psychopaths and hysterics, both of whom are presumed low in anxiety, tend to show deficits on left hemisphere neuropsychological tasks (e.g. Flor-Henry 1974; for a review see Tucker 1981).

On the other hand, not all data are supportive. For example, one study failed to find effects from trait or state anxiety on left hemisphere tasks (Tyler & Tucker 1982), while others have failed to show that an obsessive-compulsive personality style is consistently associated with a left-sided bias (e.g. Smokler & Shevrin 1979).

More crucial conceptual limitations of a strict linkage of the left hemisphere, the activation system, and anxiety also exist. These are best shown by the striking contrast between Tucker and Williamson's model and another neuro-psychological model of anxiety, that of Gray (for reviews see Gray 1982a,b). While Tucker and Williamson's anxiety system promotes the execution of well-learned motor behavior, Gray's anxiety system, which he calls the behavioral inhibition system (BIS), inhibits or restrains motor behavior. Moreover, in two key respects (heightened responsivity to novel environmental stimuli and innervation by noradrenergic neurotransmission), Gray's anxiety system closely resembles Tucker and Williamson's right-lateralized *arousal* system. This contrast suggests that in actuality both hemispheres may interact to generate different components of anxiety, with left-sided control over a motor output system (i.e. active avoidance) and right-sided control over a perceptual-processing and motor-inhibition system.

In discussing the affective correlates of the right-lateralized arousal system, Tucker and Williamson propose that increased activity in this system is associated with improvements in mood along a euphoriant-optimistic dimension. In support of this claim, they cite evidence that euphoric mood states associated with either manic-depressive illness or the ingestion of stimulant drugs or alcohol are accompanied by increased noradrenergic activity, heightened activation of the right hemisphere, and a more global, expansive cognitive style (e.g. Goldstein & Stolzfus 1973, Schildkraut et al 1978; but see Kelley & Stinus 1984 for the effects of stimulant drugs on dopaminergic systems).

While this evidence of an association between right hemisphere activity and euphoric and manic states appears discrepant with the evidence cited previously indicating that increased right hemisphere activity is linked to depressive mood states, it is necessary to call attention to one important distinction. While Fox and Davidson's depressogenic withdrawal system is linked to activation of the right frontal lobes, Tucker and Williamson's perceptually based arousal system is linked primarily to right parietal activity. In this regard, we should once again note the evidence that in at least some cases (e.g. clinical depression), right frontal lobe activity appears to vary inversely with right parietal activity (Davidson et al 1985). In these instances, a more complete reconciliation between the two models could possibly be reached. Heightened activity in the left frontal "approach" region may act to inhibit right frontal activity. In turn, right frontal inhibition may occasion heightened activity in the right parietal arousal system. We should add that although this scenario may serve as a useful heuristic for resolving an apparent contradiction between two models of affective asymmetry, future research will undoubtedly reveal it to be an oversimplification of cortical realities.

Additional Methodological and Conceptual Issues

We trust that this review has convinced the reader that the study of lateralization of emotion is associated with a number of theoretical and interpretive complexities. In fact, however, several major methodological and conceptual problems have been omitted from the preceding discussion because of space constraints. Some of these problems involve measurement. For example, a commonly used index of hemispheric asymmetry, lateral eye movements (LEMs), has questionable validity at best (Ehrlichman & Weinberger 1978), while another index, the right-left difference score on task performance (or its variants), is often confounded with factors that affect performance independent of an actual hemispheric advantage (see e.g. Stone 1980). Similarly, emotional states have often been conceptualized and operationalized in overly global terms (e.g. "negative affect"), while studies using clinical populations have typically ignored the wealth of evidence indicating marked heterogeneity and distinct subtypes occurring within diagnostic categories (for reviews see Depue 1979, Maser & Tuma 1985).

The major interpretive and conceptual problems in this area arise from our limited understanding of underlying neural processes and their relationship to electrophysiological, neuropsychological, and other indexes. For example, it is often unclear whether brain lesions disinhibit the activity of the contralateral hemisphere or ipsalateral subcortical processes (Tucker 1981). Similar ambiguities surround the interpretation of performance on neuropsychological tests (e.g. does poor performance reflect hemispheric over- or under-activation?) and of EEG data, which may reflect any number of possible patterns of excitation and inhibition involving a number of cortical regions.

In short, researchers studying lateralization of emotion must grapple with highly complex and challenging methodological and theoretical issues. Yet we hope this review also has made evident the genuine progress that has been made in recent years in the face of these difficulties. This fact justifies continued work in this area, as does its clear importance in promoting greater understanding of the psychobiological substrates of emotions and emotional disorder.

EMOTION AND MEMORY

We begin our discussion of emotion and memory by reviewing the evidence for mood state-dependent and mood-congruent memory, and the network model of emotion proposed by Bower and his colleagues to underlie both of these phenomena. We then briefly review additional effects of positive affect and depression on cognitive processes, after which we discuss some methodological and conceptual problems raised by these four areas of research. In the process, we briefly consider prepared conditioning to fear-relevant stimuli and the mere exposure effect, which are of interest because they both may exemplify automatic processing of affective cues.

Mood State-Dependent Memory

Research on memory has shown that retrieval is highly dependent upon the overlap of cues available at the time of learning with those available at recall (see e.g. Tulving & Thomson 1973). These cues may include features of the learner's immediate environment [e.g. neat room/sloppy room (Smith et al 1978)] or internal state [e.g. drugged/not drugged (Eich et al 1975; for a review see Eich 1980)]. Recent studies have extended this evidence to the affective domain by showing that congruence of emotional states at learning and recall can facilitate retrieval. This effect, denoted mood state-dependent retrieval, has been demonstrated in normal adults (e.g. Bower et al 1978, Mecklenbrauker & Hager 1984) and children (Bartlett & Santrock 1979, Bartlett et al 1982), as well as in manic-depressives cycling through euphoric, normal, and dysphoric mood states (e.g. Weingartner et al 1977; for reviews see Bower 1981, Gilligan & Bower 1984).

However, a number of studies have failed to find state-dependent effects (e.g. Isen et al 1978, Laird et al 1982, Nasby & Yando 1982, Bower & Mayer 1985; for a review see Isen 1984). The overall pattern of results indicates that state-dependent memory is a delimited phenomenon more likely to occur when learned material is less accesible (Leight & Ellis 1981). For example, effects are much more likely when: (a) free recall rather than cued recall or recognition tasks are used (e.g. Bartlett & Santrock 1979; Gellerman & Bower, cited in Gilligan & Bower 1984); (b) subjects are administered multiple lists of words rather than single lists (e.g. Bower et al 1978, Bartlett et al 1982); (c) subjects are asked to recall nonsense syllables rather than meaningful material (Leight & Ellis 1981); and (d) low-imagery words are used (Weingartner 1976; for a more extensive review, see Isen 1984). Interestingly, the first of these boundary conditions directly parallels those operative in studies of drug-induced state-dependent retrieval (Eich 1980).

Another restriction may be the nature of the emotional state. Although there have been exceptions (e.g. Bower et al 1978), several studies have found that sad moods produce markedly weaker state-dependent effects than happy moods (e.g. Bartlett & Santrock 1979, Leight & Ellis 1981, Bartlett et al 1982). While the sources of this asymmetry are as yet unclear, two possible causes are the detrimental effects of depressive mood states on encoding and other memorial processes (e.g. Ellis et al 1984; see also the section below on this topic), and subjects' use of remedial self-control strategies designed to attenuate the effects of negative mood induction (e.g. Mischel et al 1976, Isen et al 1978; Barden et al 1981).

When state-dependent effects *do* occur, the relative contribution of the different components of emotion (e.g. affective valence, expressive-motor behavior) is almost always unclear. Clark and her associates have suggested that arousal levels associated with affective states may be the prime retrieval cue. Their study supported this claim by showing that congruence between arousal levels at learning and recall facilitated retrieval even when the sources of arousal differed at the two times (Clark et al 1983). Clearly, however, further research addressing this important issue is necessary.

Mood-Congruity Effects

Emotional states may also selectively facilitate the processing of information with a similar affective tone. For example, in a study showing mood-congruent learning or encoding, Bower et al (1981) found that subjects who read a narrative subsequently recalled more happy incidents if previously induced to adopt a happy mood, and more sad incidents if previously induced to adopt a sad mood. A number of other recent studies have similarly found that mood state at the time of retrieval facilitates recall of mood-congruent information in normal adults (e.g. Isen et al 1978, Teasdale & Fogarty 1979, Laird et al 1982, Natale & Hantas 1982) and children (Nasby & Yando 1982), and in clinically depressed subjects (e.g. Lloyd & Lishman 1975, Clark & Teasdale 1982). Still other investigations have demonstrated mood-congruity effects on related processes such as attention, perceptions of risk, and judgments of various kinds (e.g. Mischel et al 1973, Isen et al 1978, Roth & Rehm 1980, Barden et al 1981, Johnson & Tversky 1983; for reviews see, e.g. Bower 1981, Gilligan & Bower 1984, Isen 1984).

However, not all findings have been supportive. While positive affective states have consistently been associated with selective facilitation of positive material, a number of studies have found that negative affective states, in particular depression, produced weaker, or even nonsignificant, selective effects on memory (e.g. Mischel et al 1976, Hasher et al 1985, Nasby & Yando 1982) and related processes (e.g. Mischel et al 1973, Isen et al 1978). These failures to find robust mood-congruity effects may be due to the possible causes noted above for the complementary failure to find consistent state-dependent learning with negative affective states: depression-induced encoding deficits and subjects' use of remediation strategies. In addition, as Isen (1984) has suggested, these findings may result from the poorer integration of depressed moods into the associative networks of normal subjects known to be generally optimistic (Weinstein 1980), attributionally self-serving (e.g. Zuckerman 1979), or otherwise possessed of a robust positive "illusory glow" (e.g. Alloy & Abramson 1979).

Another issue is the relative potency and proper interpretation of mood-congruent encoding and mood-congruent retrieval effects. Bower and his colleagues have found evidence suggesting that mood states affect encoding rather than retrieval processes (Gilligan & Bower 1984). In turn, they have suggested that what appear to be mood-congruent retrieval effects are actually examples of state-dependent memory (Bower et al 1981). This alternative hypothesis is credible when applied to studies that require subjects to recall personal experiences likely to have been associated with positive or negative mood states when they originally occurred (e.g. Isen et al 1978, Teasdale & Fogarty 1979).

However, state-dependent memory clearly fails to account for all effects observed at retrieval. For example, Nasby & Yando (1982) found that mood at retrieval affected memory for mood-congruent information independent of any possible state-dependent effects. Similarly, Isen et al (1978) and Teasdale & Russell (1983) found that mood at retrieval facilitated recall of material originally learned in a neutral affective state.

An important issue for future research is clarifying the underlying mechanisms responsible for selective encoding and retrieval. Isen et al (1978) have suggested that mood-congruent retrieval occurs because emotional states serve to "prime," or render more accessible, material in memory with a similar affective tone. However, this argument may be more descriptive than explanatory. On the basis of their findings, Bower and his colleagues speculate that two mechanisms may underly mood-congruity effects attributable to selective encoding (e.g. Gilligan & Bower 1984). The first of these, greater elaboration (i.e. thinking about or imaging) of congruent material, occurs because of the greater accessibility of mood-related information and associations such as personal experiences that serve as a basis for elaboration (see e.g. Stevenson 1981). The second mechanism is mood intensity, which is said to increase when mood-congruent material is processed and, by this means, facilitates learning. This position is supported by recent studies by Bower and his associates indicating that increases in the intensity of positive moods (but not negative moods, see below) are associated with better recall of mood-congruent information (for a review see Gilligan & Bower 1984).

Bower's Network Model of Emotional Memory

Bower and his colleagues have also formulated a model of emotional memory that accommodates the evidence for state-dependent learning and for mood-congruent processing, as well as the hypothesized mechanisms responsible for these effects (Bower 1981, Bower & Cohen 1982, Gilligan & Bower 1984). According to this model, emotions are represented in memory as nodes. These are embedded in an elaborate associative network and are connected to other nodes representing expressive behaviors, autonomic activity, verbal labels, eliciting stimuli, and events. Consistent with standard theories of retrieval in cognitive psychology (e.g. Collins & Loftus 1975), it is further proposed that activation of a node above a threshold level is necessary for retrieval. Nodes can become activated directly or indirectly, in the latter case by a process of spreading activation determined by the specific associative connections between nodes.

This model accounts for state-dependent learning by specifying that: (a) mood during encoding becomes associatively linked with target items; and (b) reinstatement of the same mood during retrieval serves to reactivate both the mood unit in memory and its associated linkages, thus facilitating retrieval. Bower and his associates also account for the evidence that state-dependent learning may require that nonmood-related retrieval cues be weak by assuming that mood-related activation is weaker and less direct than alternative paths (e.g. between paired associates in cued recall tasks). Similarly, Bower et al use this model to account for mood-congruency effects and their underlying mechanisms. They assert that moods facilitate elaboration of mood-congruent material by providing access to stored information in memory dominated by mood-related themes, and that heightened intensity produces increased activation of mood nodes and their associates.

However, there may be certain findings that this model, as currently formulated, does not integrate. These include: (a) Bower et al's own failure to find that mood states occurring at the time of retrieval facilitate mood-congruent processing, and (b) the weaker effects of negative than positive moods on both state-dependent retrieval and mood-congruent processing. It should be noted, however, that the latter findings possibly could be attributed to the detrimental effects of sad moods on elaboration (e.g. Ellis et al 1984), and thus accommodated by Bower's model. In addition, Johnson & Tversky (1983) found that mood states produced by newspaper reports of tragic events altered estimates of personal risk independent of the similarity between the story and risks. As they noted, the absence of any local effects determined by degree of association seems inconsistent with a spreading activation framework. Also, as noted by Isen (1984) and by Gilligan & Bower (1984) emotion nodes may have innumerable links; if so, the small amount of activation that could be distributed to any one branch would appear insufficient to facilitate retrieval significantly. This point suggests the need for a more complex model specifying more discrete context-bound emotion units and/or a mechanism for directive activation of particular branches. Finally, as currently formulated, the network model does not address those effects of mood states on memory and other cognitive processes that occur irrespective of the content of the material to be learned or of state-dependent learning. The following section will review the evidence for such effects. For additional criticisms of the associative network model and a discussion of potential alternative models, see the excellent discussion by Isen (1984).

Mood Effects on Cognitive Processes

A number of studies have shown that both experimentally induced (e.g. Masters et al 1979, Leight & Ellis 1981) and naturally occurring (e.g. Henry et al 1973, Cohen et al 1982) states of depression are associated with impaired learning and memory. Furthermore, it appears that these impairments grow in magnitude with increases in the intensity of depression (Gilligan & Bower 1984). Recent investigations attempting to delineate the specific deficits responsible for these effects have indicated that depression may particularly impair the ability to allocate the resources necessary for effortful processing of information (Cohen et al 1982, Ellis et al 1984). This conclusion is consistent with the evidence that depressed moods are associated with greater deficits in: (a) free relative to cued recall (e.g. Henry et al 1973), (b) recall after long relative to short delays (Cohen et al 1982), (c) recall for poorly clustered relative to well-organized material (Weingartner et al 1981), and (d) recall for information requiring high relative to low elaboration (Ellis et al 1984). In the case of bipolar depression, Henry et al (1973) have additionally implicated a specific problem transferring information from short- to long-term memory. This deficit is thought to be caused by depleted catecholamine levels, a position supported by the evidence that treatment with L-dopa can reverse memory impairments.

One major question for future research is the degree to which these cognitive deficits reflect the motivational deficits normally associated with depression

(Cohen et al 1982). In addition, future studies would benefit from methodological refinements. In particular, studies assessing differential deficits associated with depression should match memory tasks on discriminating ability. Otherwise, as Chapman & Chapman (1978) have shown, results may be confounded by psychometric artifacts.

In contrast to depression, positive moods often appear to facilitate cognitive processing. For example, positive affect has been shown to produce better discrimination learning in children (Masters et al 1979) and quicker and more efficient decisional strategies on a complex task (Isen & Means 1983). Positive effect also has been associated with greater use of intuitive rather than analytic-logical heuristics when problem solving, a result that can either facilitate or impair performance depending on task demands (Isen et al 1982). Another effect of positive moods is the development of more inclusive categorization strategies. This is evidenced by a heightened tendency to rate low-prototypic exemplars as members of a category (Isen & Daubman 1984) and by more frequent hits and false alarms on recognition tasks (Bartlett & Santrock 1979). Isen and her associates have suggested that these categorization effects may occur because positive moods bring to mind a greater amount of stored information or because they prime an affective dimension of material that serves to heighten associative bonds (Isen et al 1982, Isen & Daubman 1984).

Another potentially fruitful approach for uncovering the mechanisms that underlie the effects of both positive affect and depression would be to integrate this evidence with findings reviewed above delineating the hemispheric substrates of emotion. For example, it is tempting to speculate that positive affect leads to more inclusive categories because of its association with heightened right parietal activity, which in turn has been related to a more global, expansive cognitive style (for a review see Tucker & Williamson 1984).

Additional Methodological and Conceptual Issues

The induction of mood states is perhaps the major methodological problem faced by studies in each of the four areas of mood and memory research reviewed above. Many studies have induced moods by having subjects read self-statements developed by Velten (1968). Unfortunately, this procedure appears sensitive to demand characteristics (e.g. Polivy & Doyle 1980, Buchwald et al 1981) and may have only weak (e.g. Teasdale & Fogarty 1979) and short-lived (Frost & Green 1982, Isen & Gorgoglione 1983) effects on many subjects. Furthermore, as Mathews & Bradley (1983) have noted, the effects of the Velten statements may not be attributable to changes in mood per se but to semantic priming of memory.

An alternative mood-induction method used by Bower (e.g. Bower et al 1981) and others (e.g. Natale & Hantas 1982) is hypnosis. However, depending on the test used, only 15% to 45% of subjects are highly susceptible. Moreover, there is evidence that subjects who are hypnotizable may be extremely sensitive to subtle demand characteristics (Radtke & Spanos 1981). Other studies have exposed subjects to actual positive or negative experiences, such as success or failure on a prior task (e.g. Mischel et al 1976) or receipt of a gift (e.g. Isen et al 1978). While these procedures appear potent and less sensitive to demand characteristics, studies typically have not assessed their actual effects on emotional states. Although the use of converging operations in the form of diverse stimuli evoking affect helps rule out alternative interpretations of the effects of positive mood inductions (Isen 1984), actual assessments of mood states may be necessary to clarify why depressed moods often fail to produce effects. In the absence of such assessments it is unclear whether null findings are attributable to the failure to induce depressed moods in the first place, the inability of subjects to maintain them over a sufficient duration of time, or the weak effects of depressed moods on cognitive processes per se.

From a more conceptual perspective, there appear to be two major limitations associated with extant research on emotion and memory. First, as we have noted at several points above, the great majority of studies have failed to assess exactly what dimensions of emotion affect memory and other cognitive processes. Particularly lacking is research examining the relationship between the autonomic or expressive components of emotion and memory processes (Zajonc & Markus 1984). This omission is surprising given that Bower's model of emotion (e.g. Gilligan & Bower 1984) and other models (e.g. Lang 1984, Leventhal 1984), specify that motor components of affect are encoded in memory.

A second limitation is the frequent reliance on verbal materials (e.g. word lists, story narratives) having little relationship to the interpersonal and other stimuli that most frequently elicit emotional reactions in naturalistic contexts. While methodological considerations may often necessitate neutral materials (e.g. when mood-congruity effects might confound results), their use may ultimately retard the study of mood-memory interactions. In particular, as several commentators have noted recently (e.g. Clark & Isen 1982, Gilligan & Bower 1984), relative to neutral stimuli, truly affective stimuli may well be processed in a more reflexive, automatic manner (Posner & Snyder 1975, Shiffrin & Schneider 1977) requiring less awareness and intentionality, and interfering less with other ongoing cognitive activity. Alternatively, it may be that automaticity takes the form of a reflexive call for allocation of attentional capacity to affectively significant stimuli (see Dawson & Schell 1985).

However, not all programs of research relevant to the study of emotional memory share these limitations. For example, studies by Zajonc and his colleagues have shown that repeated exposure to stimuli affects likes and dislikes independent of awareness or recognition (for reviews see Zajonc 1980, 1984). Interestingly, Zajonc & Markus (1984) have recently suggested that the development of a "hard" motor memory, in contrast to a "soft" verbal or cognitive memory, may underlie repetition effects.

Automatic processing is similarly important in recent investigations of responses to fear-relevant stimuli. Testing predictions derived from Seligman's (1971) preparedness theory of phobias, Ohman and his colleagues have shown that conditioned electrodermal responses to common phobic stimuli (slides of snakes and spiders) previously paired with shock extinguish much more slowly than responses to neutral stimuli that are rarely the objects of phobias (for reviews see Ohman 1979, Ohman et al 1985). Recent studies have extended these results to interpersonal cues by showing slower extinction to angry (e.g. Ohman & Dimberg 1978) and fearful (e.g. Orr & Lanzetta 1980) faces relative to happy or neutral faces (for a review see Ohman et al 1985).

Consistent with Seligman's original preparedness hypothesis, Ohman has suggested that these findings may reflect automatic processing of fear-relevant stimuli. Supporting this position is the evidence that conditioned electrodermal responses to snake and spider slides are resistant to instructional manipulations (Hugdahl & Ohman 1977, Hugdahl 1978). However, there have been several failures to replicate this finding (e.g. McNally 1981). Moreover, "automatic processing" is a multifaceted construct that has elsewhere proved difficult to validate conclusively in conditioning and related paradigms (for a review see Dawson & Schell 1985). Still, this line of research, and other recent approaches to the structure of phobic fears (e.g. Lang 1979, 1984), likely will prove to be a valuable avenue for elucidating the mechanisms by which at least some affectively relevant stimuli are processed.

CONCLUSION

We have focused on the central themes and problems in four major areas of emotion research: cognition-arousal theory, expressive behavior, lateralization of emotion, and memory. While each area was discussed on its own terms, the selection of these areas and of specific topics within them was designed to resolve major theoretical disputes in the conceptualization of emotional processes, point to common themes in multiple areas, and suggest new directions for emotion research. We can accomplish these goals by summarizing the implications of the reviewed data for the following three issues: (a) the biological basis of emotion; (b) emotion and interpersonal communication; and (c) emotional development.

The Biological Basis of Emotion

The conceptual and empirical developments in both the study of expressive behavior and lateralization provide a dramatic picture of social-emotional competency at birth and in early infancy. The infant possesses a wide array of nonemotional responses (fixation on faces, head turning, imitation of tongue and finger movements, etc), as well as emotional-expressive responses (imitation of smiles, frowns, surprise, etc) to specific, interpersonal cues. The EEG data suggest that positive and negative emotional responses are differentially lateralized in right and left frontal regions respectively, while emotional detection is right parietal. It also suggests that these differences appear in the first year of life. Refinements in existent technology such as the use of short half-life radioisotopes in conjunction with positron emission tomography indicate that in time we will be able to define more precisely the neural patterns involved in the generation of perception, cognition, and specific types of emotion and memory processes (Phelps & Mazziotta 1985). When we can visualize the specialized machinery underlying the construction of emotion, hypotheses that emotional experience requires both autonomic arousal and a cognitive label to generate feeling quality should fade gracefully from the scene.

New technology may show us that specific brain centers or patterns of cortical activity are involved in the generation of emotion. Still to be answered, however, are questions concerning the nature of these innate mechanisms. For example, innate sensory motor programs may be dimensional rather than categorical in nature (Scherer 1984) or, as we think more likely, they may generate both dimensional and categorical determinants of emotion. Other issues to be addressed are the differential role played by these programs in the infant and the adult and the extent to which they operate as reflexes connecting stimulus perceptions to specific responses.

Emotion and Interpersonal Communication

One cannot overemphasize the interpersonal aspect of emotion: emotional behaviors are, above all, a key system for interpersonal communication. The social nature of emotion is visible in every area we have reviewed. It is reflected in the social expressive behaviors of the stooge in the cognition-arousal studies, in the accurate reading of expressive displays across cultures, and in the elicitation of right or left frontal lobe activity in 10-month-old infants by the videotaped expressions of an actress. As noted extensively above, interpersonal factors have also played a crucial moderating role in studies of the relationship between facial expressions and emotional experience. Finally, social communication may also pervade the study of emotion and memory. The elicitors of emotion are likely to be memories of prior social events, and social stimuli (e.g. stories about others, pictures of faces, etc) may be most effective in demonstrating emotional effects on memory. This is seen most clearly in the potency of the face as a conditioned stimulus in studies of preparedness.

Emotional Development

Our reading of the evidence on the universality of expressive behavior and the lateralization of emotional processing suggests an innate, central-motor system for constructing expressions and feelings, with the critical function of cementing interpersonal relationships. Further support comes from the ability to detect these processes during the first year and even the first days of life. It is a system that thrives on social contexts, able to react to social stimuli as well as provoke them. Common sense and the data showing links between emotion and memory suggest that the emotion system undergoes elaborate development over the individual life span. In turn, the power of social cues in eliciting and responding to emotional expression suggests that such emotional development occurs primarily in social interactions. It is in these same social contexts that the infant becomes aware of the distinction between self and other, and that the child elaborates distinctive self-attributes and develops a sense of self-esteem and effectance. Emotion and self-concept are intimately bound in memory (Lewis & Brooks 1978).

Elsewhere we have suggested that the mechanisms responsible for the construction of emotional expressions and experience should be conceptualized as a hierarchical system of three levels: sensory-motor, schematic, and conceptual (Leventhal 1979, 1980, 1984). The sensory-motor level refers to the neonate's and infant's innate readiness to perceive and respond to social stimuli. These structures initiate the emotional conversation that binds the social unit (Trevarthen 1984). When sensory-motor processes are activated by social cues, a memory structure or schema is formed of the emotional episode. This schematic record integrates traces of the sensory-motor activity with those of the perceived attributes of the eliciting situation and of other motor reactions made during the episode. It is a nonverbal (i.e. not semantic) memory with perceptual and motor components (Leventhal 1979, 1984). The schema is also crucial to the differentiation of self from other, and integrates a multitude of social environmental cues.

A review of expressive mimicry suggests that schema construction can begin in the first days, if not the very first hours of life. Indeed, Blass et al (1984) observed emotional distress (angry faces, crying, and whimpering) in 2-day-old infants when a sweet tasting unconditioned stimulus was omitted in extinction trials (CS = a light stroke of the forehead). These data show the appearance of an emotional response to the violation of a previously learned expectation. Evidence on the right hemispheric lateralization of autonomic feedback indicates that autonomic responses may likely become part of these expectancies or schemata. The facial and vocal expressive stimuli that elicit attentional reactions and mimicry are most efficiently decoded in the right parietal and right temporal lobe. The possibility of an intimate connection of the sensory and autonomic systems in right hemisphere processing suggests that specific autonomic patterns may be evoked by expressive displays (Ekman et al 1983) and can be conditioned to them. Thus, socialization may modulate the strength and pattern of the autonomic reactions that are part of different emotion schemata. For example, interactive play between infant and adult could elicit and condition high or low levels of autonomic response to the schema of an emotion episode, depending on whether the play is active or quiet.

As stated earlier, social interaction stimulates emotion and defines higher level cognitive attributes of the self schema (Lewis & Brooks 1978). These attributes create the context that gives meaning to new social situations and within which new emotional episodes are constructed and experienced. Thus, the preverbal 9-month-old has sufficiently well-structured concepts of self and other to be able to use the mother's facial expression in evaluating the safety of an environment (Sroufe & Waters 1976, Feinman & Lewis 1983, Sorce et al 1985).

As the individual matures and becomes increasingly verbal and self-reflective, his or her self-schema reflects the semantic rules of the social environment. Given that schematic structuring begins at birth and is well advanced prior to the development of complex verbal skills, we are not convinced it is reasonable to represent both schematic and verbal cognitive process in a common conceptual network. Thus, it may be in error to describe verbal, perceptual, subjective experiential, autonomic, and expressive events as structurally similar nodes linked by a common type of associative bond (Bower 1981). Substantial differences may exist between schematic and verbal memory in the organization and neurochemical binding of these various nodes, as well as in the makeup of the associative links (Kandel 1983). Further differences in the structure and bonds for verbal and schematic systems may be important determinants of the difficulties people have in controlling emotion (See Leventhal & Mosbach 1983).

The hypothesis that emotions are integrated with the self-concept to a degree that varies as a function of social context and emotional valence suggests the possibility of rich rewards in the study of emotion and personality. The differential effects of positive and negative mood on memory, and the differences in encoding and retrieval by normal and depressed subjects, are simple, indeed trivial, examples of the intimate association of emotion and cognition over the life span. A survey of both the range and the depth of these issues has been provided us by Tomkins (1963). Given another decade of investigation, we may be ready to mine his ore. At this point it seems safe to say that the study of emotion from its various perspectives promises to greatly enrich our understanding of human behavior.

ACKNOWLEDGMENT

The authors gratefully thank Richard Davidson, Alice M. Isen, and Susan Mineka for their extremely helpful comments on earlier versions of the manuscript. In addition, grateful appreciation is extended to Andrea Straus for her extraordinary editorial assistance and Jennifer Soule for typing and administrative assistance.

Literature Cited

Abrams, R., Taylor, M. A. 1979. Differential EEG patterns in affective disorder and schizophrenia. *Arch. Gen. Psychiatry* 36: 1355–58

Alloy, L. B., Abramson, L. Y. 1979. Judgment of contingency in depressed and nondepressed students: Sadder, but wiser? *J. Exp. Psychol: Gen.* 109:441–85

Ax, A. F. 1953. The physiological differentiation between fear and anger in humans. *Psychosom. Med.* 15:433–42

Bakan, P. 1969. Hypnotizability, laterality of eye-movements, and functional brain asymmetry. *Percept. Mot. Skills* 28:927–32

Barden, R. C., Garber, J., Duncan, S. W., Masters, J. C. 1981. Cumulative effects of induced affective states in children: Accentuation, innoculation, and remediation. *J. Pers. Soc. Psychol.* 40:750–60

Barefoot, J. C., Girodo, M. 1972. The misattribution of smoking cessation symptoms. *Can. J. Behav. Sci.* 4:358–63

Bartlett, J. C., Burleson, G., Santrock, J. W. 1982. Emotional mood and memory in young children. *J. Exp. Child Psychol.* 34: 59–76

Bartlett, J. C., Santrock, J. W. 1979. Affect-dependent episodic memory in young children. *Child Dev.* 50:513–18

Bekoff, M. 1981. Development of agonistic behaviour: Ethological and ecological aspects. In *Multidisciplinary Approaches to Aggression Research,* ed. P. F. Brain, D. Benton. New York: Elsevier/North-Holland Biomedical Press

Blass, E. M., Ganchrow, J. R., Steiner, J. E. 1984. Classical conditioning in newborn humans 2-48 hours of age. *Infant Behav. Dev.* 7:223–35

Bootzin, R. R., Herman, C. P., Nicassio, P. 1976. The power of suggestion: Another examination of misattribution and insomnia. *J. Pers. Soc. Psychol.* 34:673–79

Borkovec, T. D., Glasgow, R. E. 1973. Boundary conditions of false heart-rate feedback effects on avoidance behavior: A resolution of discrepant results. *Behav. Res. Ther.* 11:171–77

Borod, J. C., Caron, H. S. 1979. *Facial asymmetry during emotional experience.* Presented at Int. Neuropsychol. Soc. Meet., New York

Borod, J. C., Caron, H. S. 1980. Facedness and emotion related to lateral dominance, sex, and expression type. *Neuropsychologia* 18:237–42

Borod, J. C., Koff, E. 1984. Asymmetries in affective facial expression. See Fox & Davidson 1984, pp. 293–324

Borod, J. C., Koff, E., Caron, H. S. 1983. Right hemispheric specialization for the expression and appreciation of emotion: A focus on the face. In *Cognitive Processing in the Right Hemisphere,* ed. E. Plerecman, pp. 83–110. New York: Academic

Botto, R. W., Galbraith, G. G., Stern, R. M. 1974. Effects of false heart rate feedback and sex-guilt upon attitude toward sexual stimuli. *Psychol. Rep.* 35:267–74

Bower, G. H. 1981. Mood and memory. *Am. Psychol.* 31:129–48

Bower, G. H., Cohen, P. R. 1982. Emotional influences on learning and cognition. See Clark & Fiske 1982, pp. 263–89

Bower, G. H., Gilligan, S. G., Monteiro, K. P. 1981. Selectivity of learning caused by affective states. *J. Exp. Psychol: Gen.* 110: 451–73

Bower, G. H., Mayer, J. D. 1985. Failure to replicate mood-dependent retrieval. *Bull. Psychon. Soc.* 23:39–42

Bower, G. H., Monteiro, K. P., Gilligan, S. G. 1978. Emotional mood as a context for learning and recall. *J. Verb. Learn. Verb. Behav.* 17:573–87

Brazelton, T. B., Koslowski, B., Main, M. 1974. The origins of reciprocity: The early mother-infant interaction. In *The Effect of the Infant on its Caregiver,* ed. M. Lewis, L. A. Rosenblum, pp. 49–76. New York: Wiley

Bryant, J., Zillmann, D. 1979. Effect of intensification of annoyance through unrelated residual excitation on substantially delayed hostile behavior. *J. Exp. Soc. Psychol.* 15:470–80

Bryden, M. P., Ley, R. G., Sugarman, J. M. 1982. A left-ear advantage for identifying the emotional quality of tonal sequences. *Neuropsychologia* 20:83–87

Buchwald, A. M., Strack, S., Coyne, J. C. 1981. Demand characteristics and the Velten mood induction procedure. *J. Consult. Clin. Psychol.* 49:478–79

Buck, R. 1980. Nonverbal behavior and the theory of emotion: The facial feedback hypothesis. *J. Pers. Soc. Psychol.* 38:811–24

Bull, N. 1951. The attitude theory of emotion. *J. Nerv. Ment. Dis. Monogr. 81,* New York

Cacioppo, J. T., Petty, R. 1983. *Social Psychophysiology: A Sourcebook.* New York: Guilford

Calvert-Boyanowsky, J., Leventhal, H. 1975. The role of information in attenuating behavioral responses to stress: A reinterpretation of the misattribution phenomenon. *J. Pers. Soc. Psychol.* 32:214–21

Cannon, W. B. 1927. The James-Lange theory

of emotions: A critical examination and an alternative theory. *Am. J. Psychol.* 34:106–24

Cannon, W. B. 1931. Again the James-Lange and the thalamic theories of emotion. *Psychol. Rev.* 38:281–95

Cantor, J. R., Zillmann, D. 1973. The effect of affective state and emotional arousal on music appreciation. *J. Gen. Psychol.* 89:97–108

Cantor, J. R., Zillmann, D., Bryant, J. 1975. Enhancement of experienced sexual arousal in response to erotic stimuli through misattribution of unrelated residual excitation. *J. Pers. Soc. Psychol.* 32:69–75

Carver, C. S., Scheier, M. F. 1981. *Attention and Self-regulation: A Control-Theory Approach to Human Behavior.* New York: Springer-Verlag

Carver, C. S., Scheier, M. F. 1982. Control theory: A useful conceptual framework for personality-social, clinical, and health psychology. *Psychol. Bull.* 92:111–35

Chambliss, C., Murray, E. J. 1979. Cognitive procedures for smoking reduction: Symptom attribution versus efficacy attribution. *Cognit. Ther. Res.* 3:91–95

Chapman, L. J. A., Chapman, J. P. 1978. The measurement of differential deficit. *J. Psychiatr. Res.* 14:303–11

Clark, D. M., Teasdale, J. D. 1982. Diurnal variation in clinical depression and accessibility of memories of positive and negative experiences. *J. Abnorm. Psychol.* 91:87–95

Clark, M.S., Fiske, S. J. 1982. *Affect and Cognition.* Hillsdale, NJ: Erlbaum

Clark, M. S., Isen, A. M. 1982. The relationship between feeling states and behavior. In *Cognitive Social Psychology,* ed. A. H. Hastorf, A. M. Isen. New York: Elsevier/North-Holland

Clark, M. S., Milberg, S., Ross, J. 1983. Arousal cues arousal-related material in memory: Implications for understanding effects of mood on memory. *J. Verb. Learn. Verb. Behav.* 22:633–49

Cofer, C. 1972. *Motivation and Emotion.* New York: Scott, Foresman

Cohen, R. M., Weingartner, H., Smallberg, S. A., Pickar, D., Murphy, D. L. 1982. Effort and cognition in depression. *Arch. Gen. Psychiatry* 39:593–97

Collins, A. M., Loftus, E. F. 1975. A spreading-activation theory of semantic processing. *Psychol. Rev.* 82:407–28

Conger, J. C., Conger, A. C., Brehm, S. S. 1976. Fear level as a moderator of false feedback effects in snake phobics. *J. Consult. Clin. Psychol.* 44:135–41

Cotton, J. L. 1981. A review of research on Schachter's theory of emotion and the mis-attribution of arousal. *Eur. J. Soc. Psychol.* 11:365–97

Cotton, J. L., Baron, R. S., Borkovec, T. D. 1980. Caffein ingestion, misattribution therapy, and speech anxiety. *J. Res. Pers.* 14:196–206

Crosby, E. C., DeJonge, B. R. 1963. Experimental and clinical studies of the central connections and central relation of the facial nerve. *Ann. Otol. Rhinol. Laryngol.* 72:735–55

Cupchik, G. C., Leventhal, H. 1974. Consistency between expressive behavior and the evaluation of humorous stimuli: The role of sex and self observation. *J. Pers. Soc. Psychol.* 30:429–42

Darwin, C. 1904. *The Expression of the Emotions in Man and Animals.* London: Murray (Original work published 1872)

Davidson, R. J. 1984. Hemispheric asymmetry and emotion. See Scherer & Ekman 1984, pp. 39–57

Davidson, R. J., Fox, N. A. 1982. Asymmetrical brain activity discriminates between positive versus negative affective stimuli in human infants. *Science* 218:1235–37

Davidson, R. J., Horowitz, M. E., Schwartz, G. E., Goodman, D. M. 1981. Lateral differences in the latency between finger tapping and the heartbeat. *Psychophysiology* 18:36–41

Davidson, R. J., Schaffer, C. E., Saron, C. 1985. Effects of lateralized presentations of faces on self-reports of emotion and EEG asymmetry in depressed and normal subjects. *Psychophysiology* 22:353–64

Davidson, R. J., Schwartz, G. E., Saron, C., Bennett, J., Goleman, D. 1979. Frontal vs. parietal EEG asymmetry during positive and negative affect. *Psychophysiology* 16:202–3

Dawson, M. E., Schell, A. M. 1985. Information processing and human autonomic classical conditioning. In *Advances in Psychophysiology,* Vol. 1, ed. P. K. Ackles, J. R. Jennings, M. G. H. Coles. Greenwich, Conn: JAI. In press

Depue, R. A. 1979. *The Psychobiology of the Depressive Disorders: Implications for the Effects of Stress.* New York: Academic

Detweiler, R. A., Zanna, M. P. 1976. Physiological mediation of attitudinal responses. *J. Pers. Soc. Psychol.* 33:107–16

Dienstbier, R. A. 1972. The role of anxiety and arousal attribution in cheating. *J. Exp. Soc. Psychol.* 8:168–79

Dienstbier, R. A. 1979. Emotion-attribution theory: Establishing roots and exploring future perspectives. *Nebr. Symp. Motiv.* 26:237–306

Dienstbier, R. A., Munter, P. S. 1971. Cheating as a function of the labeling of natural arousal. *J. Pers. Soc. Psychol.* 17:208–13

Dimond, S. J., Farrington, L. 1977. Emotional responses to films shown to the right or the left hemisphere by heart rate. *Acta Psychol.* 41:255–60

Dimond, S. J., Farrington, L., Johnson, P. 1976. Differing emotional response from right and left hemispheres. *Nature* 261:690–92

Duncan, J. W., Laird, J. D. 1980. Positive and reverse placebo effects as a function of differences in cues used in self-perception. *J. Pers. Soc. Psychol.* 39:1024–36

Ehrlichman, H., Weinberger, A. 1978. Lateral eye movements and hemispheric assymmetry: A critical review. *Psychol. Bull.* 85:1080–1101

Eich, J. E. 1980. The cue-dependent nature of state-dependent retrieval. *Mem. Cognit.* 8:157–73

Eich, J. E., Weingartner, H., Stillman, R. C., Gillin, J. C. 1975. State dependent accessibility of retrieval cues in the retention of a categorized list. *J. Verb. Learn. Verb. Behav.* 14:408–17

Ekman, P. 1982. *Emotion in the Human Face.* New York: Cambridge Univ. Press

Ekman, P., Friesen, W. V., Ellsworth, P. 1982. Conceptual ambiguities. See Ekman 1982

Ekman, P., Hager, J. C., Friesen, W. V. 1981. The symmetry of emotional and deliberate facial actions. *Psychophysiology* 18:101–6

Ekman, P., Levenson, R. W., Friesen, W. V. 1983. Autonomic nervous system activity distinguishes among emotions. *Science* 221:1208–10

Ekman, P., Oster, H. 1982. Review of research, 1970–1980. See Ekman 1982

Ellis, H. C., Thomas, R. L., Rodriguez, I. A. 1984. Emotional mood states and memory: Elaborative encoding, semantic processing, and cognitive effort. *J. Exp. Psychol: Learn. Mem. Cognit.* 10:470–82

Erdmann, G., Janke, W. 1978. Interaction between physiological and cognitive determinants of emotion: Experimental studies on Schachter's theory of emotion. *Biol. Psychol.* 6:61–74

Erdmann, G., van Lindern, P. 1980. The effects of beta-adrenergic stimulation and beta-adrenergic blockade on emotional reactions. *Psychophysiology* 17:332–38

Evarts, E. V. 1973. Brain mechanisms in movement. *Sci. Am.* 229:96–103

Feinman, S., Lewis, M. 1983. Social referencing at ten months: A second-order effect on infants' responses to strangers. *Child Dev.* 54:878–87

Field, T. M., Woodson, R., Greenberg, R., Cohen, D. 1982. Discrimination and imitation of facial expression by neonates. *Science* 218:179–81

Flor-Henry, P. 1974. Psychosis, neurosis, and epilepsy: Developmental and gender-related effects and their aetiological contributions *Br. J. Psychiatry* 124:144–50

Flor-Henry, P., Fromm-Auch, D., Schopflocher, S. 1983. Neuropsychological dimensions in psychopathology. In *Laterality and Psychopathology*, ed. P. Flor-Henry, J. Gruzelier. Amsterdam: Elsevier

Flor-Henry, P., Koles, Z. J., Howarth, B. G., Burton, L. 1979. Neuropsychological studies of schizophrenia, mania, and depression. In *Hemisphere Asymmetries of Function in Psychopathology*, ed. J. M. Gruzelier, P. Flor-Henry, pp. 21–34. Amsterdam: Elsevier/North-Holland Biomedical Press

Fox, N. A., Davidson, R. J. 1984. Hemispheric substrates of affect: A developmental model. In *The Psychology of Affective Development*, ed. N. A. Fox, R. J. Davidson, pp. 353–81. Hillsdale, NJ: Erlbaum

Frankenhauser, M. 1975. Experimental approaches to the study of catecholamines and emotion. In *Emotions: Their Parameters and Measurement*, ed. L. Levi. New York: Raven

Frost, R. F., Green, M. L. 1982. Duration and post-experimental removal of Velten Mood Induction procedure effects. *Pers. Soc. Psychol. Bull.* 8:341–42

Gainotti, G. 1972. Emotional behavior and hemispheric side of the lesion. *Cortex* 8:41–55

Galin, D., Diamond, R., Braff, D. 1977. Lateralization of conversion symptoms: More frequent on the left. *Am. J. Psychiatry* 134:578–80

Ganchrow, J. R., Steiner, J. E., Daher, M. 1983. Neonatal facial expressions in response to different qualities and intensities of gustatory stimuli. *Infant Behav. Dev.* 6:189–200

Gaupp, L. A., Stern, R. M., Galbraith, G. G. 1972. False heart-rate feedback and reciprocal inhibition by aversion relief in the treatment of snake avoidance behavior. *Behav. Ther.* 3:7–20

Gellhorn, E. 1964. Motion and emotion: The role of proprioception in the physiology and pathology of the emotions. *Psychol. Rev.* 71:457–72

Gerdes, E. P. 1979. Autonomic arousal as a cognitive cue in stressful situations. *J. Pers.* 47:677–711

Gilligan, S. G., Bower, G. H. 1984. Cognitive consequences of emotional arousal. See Izard et al 1984, pp. 547–88

Goldstein, L., Stolzfus, N. W. 1973. Psychoactive drug-induced changes of interhemispheric EEG amplitude relationships. *Agents and Actions* 3:124–32

Goodenough, F. L. 1932. Expression of the emotions in a blind-deaf child. *J. Abnorm. Soc. Psychol.* 27:328–33

Gottschalk, L. A., Stone, W. N., Gleier, G. C. 1974. Peripheral versus central mechanisms accounting for antianxiety effects of propanolol. *Psychosom. Med.* 36:47–56

Gray, J. A. 1982a. *The Neuropsychology of Anxiety: An Enquiry into the Functions of the Septo-Hippocampal System.* Oxford: Oxford Univ. Press

Gray, J.A. 1982b. Precis of *The Neuropsychology of Anxiety: An Enquiry into the Functions of the Septo-hippocampal System.* *Behav. Brain Sci.* 5:469–534

Grossman, S. P. 1967. *A Textbook of Physiological Psychology.* New York: Wiley

Gruzelier, J. H. 1981. Cerebral laterality and psychopathology: Fact and fiction. *Psychol. Med.* 11:219–27

Hager, J. C. 1982. Asymmetries in facial expression. See Ekman 1982

Hager, J. C., Ekman, P. 1983. The inner and outer meanings of facial expressions. See Cacioppo & Petty 1983, pp. 287–306

Hantas, M. N., Katkin, E. S., Reed, S. D. 1984. Cerebral lateralization and heartbeat discrimination. *Psychophysiology* 21:274–78

Harman, D. W., Ray, W. J. 1977. Hemispheric activity during affective verbal stimuli: An EEG study. *Neuropsychologia* 15:457–60

Harris, M. B., Huang, L. C. 1974. Aggression and the attribution process. *J. Soc. Psychol.* 92:209–16

Harris, V. A., Katkin, E. S. 1975. Primary and secondary emotional behavior: An analysis of the role of autonomic feedback on affect, arousal and attribution. *Psychol. Bull.* 82:904–16

Hasher, L., Rose, K. C., Zacks, R. T., Sanft, H., Doren, B. 1985. Mood, recall, and selectivity effects in normal college students. *J. Exp. Psychol: Gen.* 114:104–18

Heilman, K. M., Scholes, R., Watson, R. T. 1975. Auditory affective agnosia: Disturbed comprehension of affective speech. *J. Neurol. Neurosurg. Psychiatry* 38:69–72

Heller, W., Levy, J. 1981. Perception and expression of emotion in right-handers and left-handers. *Neuropsychologia* 19:263–72

Henry, G. M., Weingartner, H., Murphy, D. L. 1973. Influence of affective state and psychoactive drugs on verbal learning and memory. *Am. J. Psychiatry* 130:966–71

Hiatt, S. W., Campos, J. J., Emde, R. N. 1979. Facial patterning and infant emotional expression: Happiness, surprise, and fear. *Child Dev.* 50:1020–35

Hirschman, R. 1975. Cross-modal effects of anticipatory bogus heart-rate feedback in a negative emotional context. *J. Pers. Soc. Psychol.* 31:13–19

Hirschman, R., Clark, M. 1983. Bogus physiological feedback. See Cacioppo & Petty 1983, pp. 177–214

Hugdahl, K. 1978. Electrodermal conditioning to potentially phobic stimuli: Effects of instructed extinction. *Behav. Res. Ther.* 16:315–21

Hugdahl, K., Ohman, A. 1977. Effects of instruction on acquisition and extinction of electrodermal responses to fear relevant stimuli. *J. Exp. Psychol: Hum. Learn. Motiv.* 3:606–18

Isen, A. M. 1984. Toward understanding the role of affect in cognition. In *Handbook of Social Cognition,* ed. R. S. Wyer, T. K. Srull, 3:179–236. Hillsdale, NJ: Erlbaum

Isen, A. M., Daubman, K. A. 1984. The influence of positive affect on decision-making strategy. *Soc. Cognit.* 2:18–31

Isen, A. M., Gorgoglione, J. M. 1983. Some specific effects of four affect-induction procedures. *Pers. Soc. Psychol. Bull.* 9:136–43

Isen, A. M., Means, B. 1983. The influence of positive affect on decision-making strategy. *Soc. Cognit.* 2:18–31

Isen, A. M., Means, B., Patrick, R., Nowicki, G. 1982. Some factors influencing decision-making strategy and risk taking. See Clark & Fiske 1982, pp. 213–61

Isen, A. M., Shalker, T., Clark, M., Karp, L. 1978. Affect, accessibility of material in memory and behavior: A cognitive loop? *J. Pers. Soc. Psychol.* 36:1–12

Izard, C. E. 1971. *The Face of Emotion.* New York: Appleton

Izard, C. E., Kagan, J., Zajonc, R. B., eds. 1984. *Emotions, Cognition, and Behavior.* New York: Cambridge Univ. Press

James, W. 1950. *The Principles of Psychology,* Vol. 2. New York: Dover. (Original work published 1890)

Johnson, E. J., Tversky, A. 1983. Affect, generalization, and the perception of risk. *J. Pers. Soc. Psychol.* 45:20–31

Kagan, J. 1984. The idea of emotion in human development. See Izard et al 1984, pp. 38–72

Kandel, E. R. 1983. From metapsychology to molecular biology: Explorations into the nature of anxiety. *Am. J. Psychiatry* 140:1277–93

Kelley, A. E., Stinus, L. 1984. Neuroanatomical and neuroanatomical substrates of behavior. In *The Psychobiology of Affective Development,* ed. N. A. Fox, R. J. Davidson, pp. 1–75. Hilldale, NJ: Erlbaum

Kennedy, D. 1971. Nerve cells and behavior. *Am. Sci.* 59:36–42

Kent, R. N., Wilson, G. J., Nelson, R. 1972. Effects of false heart-rate feedback on avoidance behavior: An investigation of 'cognitive desensitization'. *Behav. Ther.* 3:1–6

Kleck, R. E., Vaughan, R. C., Cartwright-Smith, J., Vaughan, K., Colby, C. Z., Lanzetta, J. T. 1976. Effects of being observed on expressive, subjective and physiological responses to painful stimuli. *J. Pers. Soc. Psychol.* 34:1211–18

Koenig, K. P. 1973. False emotional feedback and the modification of anxiety. *Behav. Ther.* 4:193–202

Kolb, B., Milner, B. 1981. Observations on spontaneous facial expression after focal cerebral excisions and after intracarotid injection of sodium amytal. *Neuropsychologia* 19:505–14

Kraut, R. E. 1982. Social presence, facial feedback, and emotion. *J. Pers. Soc. Psychol.* 42:853–63

Kraut, R. E., Johnston, R. E. 1979. Social and emotional messages of smiling: An ethological approach. *J. Pers. Soc. Psychol.* 37:1539–53

Kronfol, Z., Hamsher, K. deS., Digre, K., Waziri, R. 1978. Depression and hemispheric functions: Changes associated with unilateral ECT. *Br. J. Psychiatry* 132:560–67

Lacey, J. J., Lacey, B. C. 1970. Some autonomic-central nervous system interrelationships. In *Physiological Correlates of Emotion*, ed. P. Black, pp. 205–27. New York: Academic

Laird, J. D. 1974. Self-attribution of emotion: The effects of expressive behavior on the quality of emotional experience. *J. Pers. Soc. Psychol.* 29:475–86

Laird, J. D. 1984. The real role of facial response in the experience of emotion: A reply to Tourangeau and Ellsworth, and others. *J. Pers. Soc. Psychol.* 47:909–17

Laird, J. D., Wagener, J. J., Halal, M., Szegda, M. 1982. Remembering what you feel: Effects of emotion on memory. *J. Pers. Soc. Psychol.* 42:646–57

Lang, P. J. 1971. The application of psychophysiological methods to the study of psychotherapy and behavior change. In *Handbook of Psychotherapy and Behavior Change*, ed. A. E. Gergin, S. L. Garfield. New York: Wiley

Lang, P. J. 1979. A bio-informational theory of emotional imagery. *Psychophysiology* 16:495–512

Lang, P. J. 1984. Cognition in emotion: Concept and action. See Izard et al 1984, pp. 192–226

Lanzetta, J. T., Cartwright-Smith, J., Kleck, R. E. 1976. Effects of nonverbal dissimulation on emotional experience and autonomic arousal. *J. Pers. Soc. Psychol.* 33:354–70

Lanzetta, J. T., Kleck, R. E. 1970. Encoding and decoding of non-verbal affect in humans. *J. Pers. Soc. Psychol.* 16:12–19

Lazarus, R. S. 1984. On the primacy of cognition. *Am. Psychol.* 39:124–29

Leight, K. A., Ellis, H. C. 1981. Emotional mood states, strategies, and state-dependency in memory. *J. Verb. Learn. Verb. Behav.* 20:251–66

Levenson, R. W., Gottman, J. M. 1983. Marital interaction: Physiological linkage and affective exchange. *J. Pers. Soc. Psychol.* 45:587–97

Leventhal, H. 1979. A perceptual-motor processing model of emotion. In *Perception of Emotion in Self and Others*, ed. P. Pliner, K. Blankenstein, I. M. Spigel, 5:1–46. New York: Plenum

Leventhal, H. 1980. Toward a comprehensive theory of emotion. *Adv. Exp. Soc. Psychol.* 13:139–207

Leventhal, H. 1984. A perceptual-motor theory of emotion. *Adv. Exp. Soc. Psychol.* 17:117–82

Leventhal, H., Cupchik, G. 1975. The informational and facilitative affects of an audience upon expression and the evaluation of humorous stimuli. *J. Exp. Soc. Psychol.* 11:363–80

Leventhal, H., Mace, W. 1970. The effect of laughter on evaluation of a slapstick movie. *J. Pers.* 38:16–30

Leventhal, H., Mosbach, P. 1983. A perceptual-motor theory of emotion. See Cacioppo & Petty 1983, pp. 353–89

Lewis, M., Brooks, J. 1978. Self-knowledge and emotional development. In *The Development of Affect*, ed. M. L. Lewis, L. A. Rosenblum, pp. 205–26. New York: Plenum

Ley, R. G., Bryden, M. P. 1979. Hemispheric differences in processing emotions and faces. *Brain Lang.* 7:127–38

Liebhart, E. H. 1979. Information search and attribution: Cognitive processes mediating the effect of false autonomic feedback. *Eur. J. Soc. Psychol.* 9:19–37

Lloyd, G. C., Lishman, W. A. 1975. Effect of depression on the speed of recall of pleasant and unpleasant experiences. *Psychol. Med.* 5:173–80

Loftis, J., Ross, L. 1974a. Effects of misattribution of arousal upon the acquisition and extinction of a conditioned emotional response. *J. Pers. Soc. Psychol.* 30:673–82

Loftis, J., Ross, L. 1974b. Retrospective misattribution of a conditioned emotional response. *J. Pers. Soc. Psychol.* 30:683–87

Lynn, J. G., Lynn, D. R. 1938. Face-hand laterality in relation to personality. *J. Abnorm. Soc. Psychol.* 33:201–322

Lynn, J. G., Lynn, D. R. 1943. Smile and hand dominance in relation to basic modes of adaptation. *J. Abnorm. Soc. Psychol.* 44:553–55

Mandler, G. 1962. Emotion. In *New Directions in Psychology*, ed. R. Brown. New York: Holt, Rinehart & Winston

Mandler, G. 1975. *Mind and Emotion*. New York: Wiley

Marshall, G. D., Zimbardo, P. G. 1979. Affective consequences of inadequately explained physiological arousal. *J. Pers. Soc. Psychol.* 37:970–85

Maser, J., Tuma, A. M. 1985. *Anxiety and Anxiety Disorders*. Hillsdale, NJ: Erlbaum. In press

Maslach, C. 1979. Negative emotional biasing of unexplained arousal. *J. Pers. Soc. Psychol.* 37:953–69

Masters, J. C., Barden, R. C., Ford, M. E. 1979. Affective state, expressive behavior, and learning in children. *J. Pers. Soc. Psychol.* 37:380–90

Mathews, A. M., Bradley, B. 1983. Mood and the self-reference bias in recall. *Behav. Res. Ther.* 21:223–29

McArthur, L. A., Solomon, M. R., Jaffe, R. M. 1980. Weight and sex differences in emotional responsiveness to propioceptive and pictoral stimuli. *J. Pers. Soc. Psychol.* 39:308–19

McDougall, W. 1921. *An Introduction to Social Psychology*. Boston: Luce

McGuinness, D., Pribram, K. H. 1980. The neuropsychology of attention: Emotional and motivational controls. In *The Brain and Psychology*, ed. M. C. Wittrock. New York: Academic

McNally, R. J. 1981. Phobias and preparedness: Instructional reversal of electrodermal conditioning to fear-relevant stimuli. *Psychol. Rep.* 48:175–80

Mecklenbrauker, S., Hager, W. 1984. Effects of mood on memory: Experimental tests of a mood-state-dependency retrieval hypothesis and of a mood-congruity hypothesis. *Psychol. Res.* 46:355–76

Meltzoff, A. N., Moore, M. K. 1977. Imitation of facial and manual gestures by human neonates. *Science* 75–78

Merton, P. A. 1972. How we control the contraction of our muscles. *Sci. Am.* 226:30–37

Mineka, S. 1979. The role of fear in theories of avoidance learning, flooding, and extinction. *Psychol. Bull.* 86:985–1010

Mischel, W., Ebbesen, E. B., Zeiss, A. 1973. Selective attention to the self: Situational and dispositional determinants. *J. Pers. Soc. Psychol.* 27:129–42

Mischel, W., Ebbesen, E. B., Zeiss, A. M. 1976. Determinants of selective memory about the self. *J. Consult. Clin. Psychol.* 44:92–103

Montgomery, W. A., Jones, G. E. 1984. Laterality, emotionality, and heartbeat perception. *Psychophysiology* 21:459–65

Mueller, C. W., Donnerstein, E. 1977. The effects of humor-induced arousal upon aggressive behavior. *J. Res. Pers.* 11:73–82

Nasby, W., Yando, R. 1982. Selective encoding and retrieval of affectively valent information. *J. Pers. Soc. Psychol.* 43:1244–55

Natale, M., Hantas, M. 1982. Effect of temporary mood states on selective memory about the self. *J. Pers. Soc. Psychol.* 42:927–34

Nisbett, R. E., Schachter, S. 1966. Cognitive manipulation of pain. *J. Exp. Soc. Psychol.* 2:227–36

Notarius, C. I., Levenson, R. W. 1979. Expressive tendencies and physiological response to stress. *J. Pers. Soc. Psychol.* 39:1135–48

Notarius, C. I., Wemple, C., Ingraham, L. J., Burns, T. J., Kollar, E. 1982. Multichannel responses to an interpersonal stressor: Interrelationships among facial display, heart rate, self-report of emotion, and threat appraisal. *J. Pers. Soc. Psychol.* 43:400–8

Obrist, P. A. 1976. The cardiovascular-behavioral interaction—As it appears today. *Psychophysiology* 13:95–107

Ohman, A. 1979. Fear relevance, autonomic conditioning, and phobias: A laboratory model. In *Trends in Behavior Therapy*, ed. P. Sjoden, S. Bates, W. W. Dockens III, pp. 107–33. New York: Academic

Ohman, A., Dimberg, U. 1978. Facial expressions as conditioned stimuli for electrodermal responses: A case of "preparedness"? *J. Pers. Soc. Psychol.* 36:1251–58

Ohman, A., Dimberg, U., Ost, L. G. 1985. Animal and social phobias: Biological constraints on learned responses. In *Theoretical Issues in Behavior Therapy*, ed. S. Reiss, R. Bootzin. New York: Academic. In press

O'Neal, E., Kaufman, L. 1972. The influence of attack, arousal, and information about one's arousal upon interpersonal aggression. *Psychon. Sci.* 26:211–14

Orr, S. P., Lanzetta, J. T. 1980. Facial expressions of emotion as conditioned stimuli for human autonomic responses. *J. Pers. Soc. Psychol.* 38:278–82

Parkinson, B., Manstead, A. S. R. 1981. An examination of the roles played by meaning of feedback and attention to feedback in the 'Valins effect.' *J. Pers. Soc. Psychol.* 40:239–45

Pasquarelli, B., Bull, N. 1951. Experimental investigations of the body-mind continuum in affective states. *J. Nerv. Ment. Dis.* 113:512–21

Perris, C., Monakhov, K. 1979. Depressive symptomatology and systematic structural analysis of the EEG. In *Hemisphere Asymmetries of Function and Psychopathology*, ed. J. H. Gruzelier, P. Flor-Henry. Amsterdam: Elsevier/North-Holland

Phelps, M. E., Mazziotta, J. C. 1985. Positron emission tomography: Human brain function and biochemistry. *Science* 228:799–809

Plutchik, R. 1980. *Emotion: A Psychoevolutionary Synthesis*. New York: Harper & Row

Polivy, J., Doyle, C. 1980. Laboratory induction of mood states through the reading of self-referent mood statements: Affective changes or demand characteristics? *J. Abnorm. Psychol.* 89:286–90

Posner, M. I., Snyder, R. R. 1975. Attention and cognitive control. In *Information Processing and Cognition: The Loyola Symposium,* ed. R. Solso. Hillsdale, NJ: Erlbaum

Pribram, K. H., McGuinness, D. 1975. Arousal, activation and effort in the control of attention. *Psychol. Rev.* 82:116–49

Radtke, H. L., Spanos, N. P. 1981. Temporal sequencing during posthypnotic amnesia: A methodological critique. *J. Abnorm. Psychol.* 90:476–85

Redican, W. K. 1982. An evolutionary perspective on human facial displays. See Ekman 1982, pp. 212–80

Reisenzein, R. 1983. The Schachter theory of emotion: Two decades later. *Psychol. Bull.* 94:239–64

Reisenzein, R., Gattinger, E. 1982. Salience of arousal as a mediator of misattribution of transferred excitation. *Motiv. Emotion* 6:315–28

Reuter-Lorenz, P., Davidson, R. J. 1981. Differential contributions of the two cerebral hemispheres for perception of happy and sad faces. *Neuropsychologia* 19:609–14

Reuter-Lorenz, P., Givis, R. P., Moscovitch, M. 1983. Hemispheric specialization and the perception of emotion: Evidence from right-handers and from inverted and non-inverted left-handers. *Neuropsychologia* 21:687–92

Robinson, R. G., Benson, D. F. 1981. Depression in aphasic patients: Frequency, severity, and clinical-pathological correlations. *Brain Lang.* 14:282–91

Rodin, J. 1976. Menstruation, reattribution, and competence. *J. Pers. Soc. Psychol.* 33:345–53

Rogers, R. W., Deckner, C. 1975. Effects of fear appeals and physiological arousal upon emotions, attitudes, and cigarette smoking. *J. Pers. Soc. Psychol.* 32:222–30

Ross, E. D., Mesulam, M. M. 1979. Dominant language functions of the right hemisphere. *Arch. Neurol.* 36:144–48

Ross, L., Rodin, J., Zimbardo, P. G. 1969. Toward an attribution therapy: The reduction of fear through induced cognitive-emotional misattribution. *J. Pers. Soc. Psychol.* 12:279–88

Ross, M., Olson, J. M. 1981. An expectancy-attribution model of the effect of placebos. *Psychol. Rev.* 88:408–37

Roth, D., Rehm, L. P. 1980. Relationships among self-monitoring processes, memory, and depression. *Cognit. Ther. Res.* 2:149–57

Russell, B. 1960. *An Outline of Philosophy.* New York: Meridian Books (Original work published 1927)

Sackeim, H. A., Gur, R. C. 1983. Facial asymmetry and the communication of emotion. See Caccioppo & Petty 1983, pp. 307–52

Sackeim, H. A., Weinman, A. L., Gur, R. C., Greenberg, M., Hungerbuhler, J. P., et al. 1982. Pathological laughing and crying: Functional brain asymmetry in the expression of positive and negative emotions. *Arch. Neurol.* 39:210–18

Safer, M. A. 1981. Sex and hemisphere differences in access to codes for processing emotional expressions and faces. *J. Exp. Psychol: Gen.* 110:86–100

Safer, M. A., Leventhal, H. 1977. Ear differences in evaluating emotional tones of voice and verbal content. *J. Exp. Psychol: Hum. Percept. Perform.* 3:75–82

Saxby, L., Bryden, M. P. 1984. Left-ear superiority in children for processing auditory emotional material. *Dev. Psychol.* 21:72–80

Saxby, L., Bryden, M. P. 1985. Left visual-field advantage in children for processing visual emotional stimuli. *Dev. Psychol.* 21(2):253–61

Schachter, J. 1957. Pain, fear, and anger in hypertensives and normotensives. *Psychosom. Med.* 19:17–29

Schachter, S. 1964. The interaction of cognitive and physiological determinants of emotional state. *Adv. Exp. Soc. Psychol.* 1:49–80

Schachter, S., Singer, J. 1962. Cognitive, social, and physiological determinants of emotional state. *Psychol. Rev.* 69:379–99

Schachter, S., Singer, J. 1979. Comments on the Maslach and Marshall-Zimbardo experiments. *J. Pers. Soc. Psychol.* 37:989–95

Schachter, S., Wheeler, L. 1962. Epinephrine, chlorpromazine, and amusement. *J. Abnorm. Soc. Psychol.* 65:121–28

Schaffer, C. E., Davidson, R. J., Saron, C. 1983. Frontal and parietal electroencephalogram asymmetry in depressed and nondepressed subjects. *Biol. Psychiatry* 18:753–62

Scherer, K. R. 1984. On the nature and function of emotion: A component process approach. See Scherer & Ekman 1984, pp. 293–317

Scherer, K. R., Ekman, P., eds. 1984. *Approaches to Emotion.* Hillsdale, NJ: Erlbaum

Schildkraut, J. J., Orsulak, P. J., Schatzberg, A. F., Gudeman, J. E., Cole, J. D., et al. 1978. Toward a biochemical classification of depressive disorders. *Arch. Gen. Psychiatry* 35:1427

Schwartz, G. E., Weinberger, D. A., Singer, J. A. 1981. Cardiovascular differentiation of happiness, sadness, anger, and fear following imagery and exercise. *Psychosom. Med.* 43:343–64

Seligman, M. E. P. 1971. Phobias and preparedness. *Behav. Ther.* 2:307–21

Shapiro, D. 1965. *Neurotic Styles.* New York: Basic Books

Shiffrin, R. M., Schneider, W. 1977. Controlled and automatic human information processing: II. Perceptual learning, automatic attending, and a general theory. *Psychol. Rev.* 84:129–90

Simon, H. A. 1982. Affect and cognition: Comments. See Clark & Fiske 1982, pp. 333–42

Smith, S. M., Glenberg, A., Bjork, R. A. 1978. Environmental context and human memory. *Mem. Cognit.* 6:342–53

Smokler, I. A., Shevrin, I. 1979. Cerebral lateralization and personality style. *Arch. Gen. Psychiatry* 36:949–54

Sorce, J. F., Emde, R. N., Campos, J., Klinnert, M. D. 1985. Maternal emotional signaling: Its effect on the visual cliff behavior of 1-year-olds. *Dev. Psychol.* 21:195–200

Sroufe, L. A., Waters, E. 1976. The ontogenesis of smiling and laughter: A perspective on the organization of a development in infancy. *Psychol. Rev.* 83:173–89

Stern, R. M., Botto, R. W., Herrick, C. D. 1972. Behavioral and physiological effects of false heart rate feedback: A relication and extension. *Psychophysiology* 9:21–29

Sternberg, C. R., Campos, J. J., Emde, R. N. 1983. The facial expression of anger in seven-month-old infants. *Child Dev.* 54:178–84

Stevenson, R. J. 1981. Depth of comprehension, effective elaboration, and memory for sentences. *Mem. Cognit.* 9:169–76

Stone, M. A. 1980. Measures of laterality and spurious correlation. *Neuropsychologia* 18:339–45

Storms, M. D., Nisbett, R. E. 1970. Insomnia and the attribution process. *J. Pers. Soc. Psychol.* 16:319–28

Suberi, M., McKeever, W. F. 1977. Differential right hemispheric memory storage of emotional and non-emotional faces. *Neuropsychologia* 15:757–68

Sully, J. 1902. *An Essay on Laughter.* London: Longmans, Green

Sushinsky, L. W., Bootzin, R. R. 1970. Cognitive desensitization as a model of systematic desensitization. *Behav. Res. Ther.* 8:29–33

Taylor, M. A., Redfield, J., Abrams, R. 1981. Neuropsychological dysfunction compared in schizophrenia, affective disorder and coarse brain disease. *Biol. Psychiatry* 16:467–78

Teasdale, J. D., Fogarty, S. 1979. Differential effects of induced mood on retrieval of pleasant and unpleasant events from episodic memory. *J. Abnorm. Psychol.* 88:248–57

Teasdale, J. D., Russell, M. L. 1983. Differential effects of induced mood on the recall of positive, negative and neutral words. *Br. J. Clin. Psychol.* 22:163–72

Tomkins, S. S. 1962. *Affect, Imagery, Consciousness* 1: *The Positive Affects.* New York: Springer-Verlag

Tomkins, S. S. 1963. *Affect, Imagery, Consciousness* 2: *The Negative Affects.* New York: Springer-Verlag

Tomkins, S. S. 1980. Affect as amplification: Some modifications in theory. In *Emotion: Theory, Research, and Experience,* ed. R. Plutchik, H. Kellerman, Vol. 1. New York: Academic

Tourangeau, R., Ellsworth, P. C. 1979. The role of facial response in the experience of emotion. *J. Pers. Soc. Psychol.* 37:1519–31

Trevarthen, C. 1984. Emotions in infancy: Regulators of contact and relationships with persons. See Scherer & Ekman, pp. 129–57

Tucker, D. M. 1981. Lateral brain function, emotion, and conceptualization. *Psychol. Bull.* 89:19–46

Tucker, D. M., Antes, J. R., Stenslie, C. E., Barnhardt, T. N. 1978. Anxiety and lateral cerebral function. *J. Abnorm. Psychol.* 87:380–83

Tucker, D. M., Newman, J. P. 1981. Verbal versus imaginal cognitive strategies in the inhibition of emotional arousal. *Cognit. Ther. Res.* 5:197–202

Tucker, D. M., Stenslie, C. E., Roth, R. S., Shearer, S. L. 1981. Right frontal lobe activation and right hemisphere performance decrement during a depressed mood. *Arch. Gen. Psychiatry* 38:169–74

Tucker, D. M., Watson, R. G., Heilman, K. M. 1976. Affective discrimination and evocation in patients with right parietal disease. *Neurology* 26:354

Tucker, D. M., Williamson, P. A. 1984. Asymmetric neural control in human self-regulation. *Psychol. Rev.* 91:185–215

Tulving, F., Thomson, D. M. 1973. Encoding specificity and retrieval processes in episodic memory. *Psychol. Rev.* 80:352–73

Tyler, S. K., Tucker, D. M. 1982. Anxiety and perceptual structure: Individual differences in neuropsychological function. *J. Abnorm. Psychol.* 91:210–20

Valins, S. 1966. Cognitive effects of false heart-rate feedback. *J. Pers. Soc. Psychol.* 4:400–8

Valins, S., Ray, A. A. 1967. Effects of cognitive desensitization on avoidance behavior. *J. Pers. Soc. Psychol.* 7:345–50

Velten, E. 1968. A laboratory task for the induction of mood states. *Behav. Res. Ther.* 6:473–82

Weerts, T. C., Roberts, R. 1976. The physiological effects of imagining anger-provoking and fear-provoking scenes. *Psychophysiology* 13:74 (Abstr.)

Weiner, M. J., Samuel, W. 1975. The effect of attributing internal arousal to an external source upon test anxiety and performance. *J. Soc. Psychol.* 96:255–65

Weingartner, H., Cohen, R. M., Murphy, D. L., Martello, J., Gerdt, C. 1981. Cognitive processes in depression. *Arch. Gen. Psychiatry* 38:42–47

Weingartner, H., Hall, B., Murphy, D. L., Weinstein, W. 1976. Imagery, affective arousal, and memory consolidation. *Nature* 263:311–12

Weingartner, H., Miller, H., Murphy, D. L. 1977. Mood-state-dependent retrieval of verbal associations. *J. Abnorm. Psychol.* 86:276–84

Weinstein, N. 1980. Unrealistic optimism about future life events. *J. Pers. Soc. Psychol.* 39:806–20

Younger, J. C., Doob, A. N. 1978. Attribution and aggression: The misattribution of anger. *J. Res. Pers.* 12:164–71

Zajonc, R. B. 1980. Feeling and thinking: Preferences need no inferences. *Am. Psychol.* 35:151–75

Zajonc, R. B. 1984. On the primacy of affect. *Am. Psychol.* 39:117–23

Zajonc, R. B. 1985. Emotion and facial efference: A theory reclaimed. *Science* 228:15–21

Zajonc, R. B., Markus, H. 1984. Affect and cognition: The hand interface. See Izard et al 1984, pp. 73–102

Zanna, M., Cooper, J. 1974. Dissonance and the pill: An attribution approach to studying the arousal properties of dissonance. *J. Pers. Soc. Psychol.* 29:703–9

Zillmann, D. 1971. Excitation transfer in communication-mediated aggressive behavior. *J. Exp. Soc. Psychol.* 7:419–34

Zillmann, D. 1978. Attribution and misattribution of excitatory reactions. In *New Directions in Attribution Research*, ed. J. H. Harvey, W. J. Ickes, R. F. Kidd, 2:335–68. Hillsdale, NJ: Erlbaum

Zillmann, D. 1983. Transfer of excitation in emotional behavior. See Cacioppo & Petty 1983, pp. 215–40

Zillmann, D., Bryant, J. 1974. Effect of residual excitation on the emotional response to provocation and delayed aggressive behavior. *J. Pers. Soc. Psychol.* 30:782–91

Zillmann, D., Katcher, A. H., Milavsky, B. 1972. Excitation transfer from physical exercise to subsequent aggressive behavior. *J. Exp. Soc. Psychol.* 8:247–59

Zuckerman, M. 1979. Attribution of success and failure revisited, or: The motivational bias is alive and well in attribution theory. *J. Pers. Psychol.* 47:245–87

Zuckerman, M., DePaulo, B. M., Rosenthal, R. 1981. Verbal and nonverbal communication of deception. *Adv. Exp. Soc. Psychol.* 14:1–59

Ann. Rev. Psychol. 1986. 37:611–51

INSTRUCTIONAL PSYCHOLOGY

Paul R. Pintrich

School of Education, University of Michigan, Ann Arbor, MI 48109

David R. Cross

Combined Program in Education and Psychology, University of Michigan, Ann Arbor, MI 48109

Robert B. Kozma

CRLT,* University of Michigan, Ann Arbor, MI 48109

Wilbert J. McKeachie

CRLT,* University of Michigan, Ann Arbor, MI 48109

CONTENTS

INTRODUCTION 612
LEARNER CHARACTERISTICS 612
    Intelligence 613
    Motivation 614
INSTRUCTIONAL PROCESSES 617
    Media and Technology 618
    Instructional Design 620
    Classroom Instruction and Teaching 622
    Testing and Instruction 624
TASKS, CONTENT, AND OUTCOMES 627
    Reading 627
    Writing 630
    Mathematics 633
    Science 635
    Generalizable Skills and Strategies 637
FINAL THOUGHTS 641

*Center for Research on Learning and Teaching

0066-4308/86/0201-0611$02.00

INTRODUCTION

The term "instructional psychology" was originally used to refer to topics emphasized in instructional design, such as programmed learning, behavioral objectives, and modularized instruction with frequent testing. As behaviorism's influence waned, the term "instructional psychology" began to broaden, becoming virtually synonymous with "educational psychology." Current instructional psychology carries over from its behaviorist beginnings a tough-minded empirical approach to education, but it differs from its behavioristic salad days in a stronger emphasis upon theory, a move from external situational variables to internal cognitive variables, closer connections with cognitive theories of motivation, a focus on school tasks, and greater emphasis upon individual differences. In the behavioristic heyday of instructional psychology, individualization was primarily in terms of time spent in achieving goals. Today instructional psychology thinks of individualization in terms of attribute-treatment interactions—teaching methods that interact with student characteristics. Abilities and dominant motives formerly regarded as fixed are now regarded as potential targets for education. Instructional psychology aims for the development of motivation, cognitive structures, and a repertoire of skills and strategies for learning and problem solving.

The four authors of this chapter complement each other in their areas of specialization but exemplify the trend toward cognitive approaches described by Menges & Gerard (1985) in their review of previous *Annual Review* chapters on instructional psychology. Since the 1983 chapter by Gagne & Dick covered the major instructional theories, we have not attempted to review them here. This chapter reflects the dynamic growth of instructional psychology: the increasing interest in the interaction of cognition and motivation, the movement from hardware-oriented technology to issues of technology grounded in instructional theory, and the trend from static variables toward process variables. We begin with the learner—cognitive and motivational characteristics learners bring to instructional situations. We then deal with instructional processes. Finally, we survey research on the tasks and content of instruction.

LEARNER CHARACTERISTICS

The importance of individual differences in the ability to learn and benefit from instruction has long been a theme of educational psychology (Corno & Snow 1986). Rather than static traits, current research emphasizes a more dynamic process-oriented approach to learner characteristics (e.g. Brown et al 1983, Snow & Lohman 1984). Whereas early instructional psychology dealt primarily with instructional designs involving matters of manipulating presentation and pacing of instructional material, it has become clear that learners seek to learn; they transform what they receive from instruction and create and construct knowledge in their own minds. Thus what the learner brings to the instructional situation in prior knowledge and cognitive skills is of crucial importance. Although there is a variety of learner characteristics that influence learning and instruction (cf Corno & Snow 1986), two of the most important are intelligence and motivation.

Intelligence

The classic area of intelligence has probably shown more signs of change in the last decade than in any period since Thurstone and Spearman introduced factorial studies of intelligence. Recent research on intelligence has been revitalized by cognitive approaches. As Gagne & Dick (1983) pointed out in the last *Annual Review* chapter on Instructional Psychology, intelligence tests predict performance in conventional schools and intelligence interacts with instructional methods to affect educational outcomes. But what is intelligence? Undheim (1981a,b,c,d) has made a persuasive case for the proposition that intelligence is achievement—the result of past learning as well as a predictor of future learning. Psychometric theories of intelligence have attempted to define intelligence by focusing on the number of factors or latent traits of individuals that explain performance and the geometric relationships among these factors (Sternberg 1985). Guilford (1982) proposed that there are 150 factors underlying intelligence, while recent adaptions of general *g* theories focus on crystallized abilities, fluid or analytic abilities, and spatial-visualization abilities (Snow & Lohman 1984). Balke-Aurell (1982) has shown that general or fluid intelligence as well as crystallized intelligence and spatial visualization ability are influenced by educational experience. Learners who are involved in educational programs and in work that demands verbal functioning develop verbal, or crystallized, ability, while participation in activities demanding spatial-visual functioning results in greater development of this somewhat more specialized ability. Snow & Lohman (1984) suggest that crystallized abilities are evoked by familiar tasks and environments, and that novel tasks or unusual instructional techniques that require analysis or decontextualization recruit fluid abilities. These differences can result in attribute treatment interactions (ATIs) between instruction and learners.

Information processing approaches to intelligence have stressed the dynamic processes involved in intelligence rather than static traits of individuals. Sternberg (1985) has related four general information processing paradigms to intelligence. The cognitive-correlates approach has focused on performance of simple tasks (e.g. letter matching) in an attempt to uncover the basic cognitive processes involved such as speed of response and speed of lexical access. In contrast, the cognitive-components approach has utilized more complex tasks such as analogical reasoning to explore the higher-level components involved in performance, for example, inference, application, and executive control. The third approach has attempted to train cognitive processes to demonstrate their existence and importance (e.g. Campione et al 1982). Finally, the cognitive-content approach has examined how differences in the structure and content of individuals' knowledge base influence their performance. For example, Anderson (1983) has proposed that individual differences in performance are a function of the flow of information in the mind, with individuals differing in their declarative knowledge (knowing what something is) and their procedural knowledge (knowing how to do something).

Sternberg (1985) has proposed an ambitious triarchic theory of intelligence that attempts to integrate and synthesize most of the research on intelligence. There are three subtheories in his overall theory. The componential subtheory specifies the components of intelligent performance which include: (*a*) meta-components that exert executive control, (*b*) performance components that execute the plans constructed by the metacomponents, and (*c*) knowledge acquisition components that select, encode, and combine information to create new knowledge. The contextual subtheory deals with how individuals adapt or accommodate to their environment. The third subtheory relates intelligence to experience with a variety of tasks. Regardless of whether this triarchic theory is borne out by future research, it is sure to generate research and provoke discussion.

In contrast to Sternberg's (1985) information processing view, Gardner (1983) suggests that intelligence varies across different domains or symbol systems such as language, music, mathematics, or physical coordination (kinesthetics). He proposes examining the profile of a learner's intelligences in relation to educational goals and matching students with subject matters and teaching methods to develop further intellectual strength. This approach highlights the fact that components measured in traditional intelligence tests emphasize the symbol systems used in schools, which are largely verbal. The current progress in analysis of intellectual functions contributes to an evaluation both of educational goals and educational media. Do we need to be more systematic in facilitating development of aspects of cognition that have been relatively neglected? For example, there is renewed emphasis on the teaching of general problem-solving skills (Frederiksen 1984a) and intellectual skills training (Sternberg 1983) which can be seen partially as a result of the new or cognitive approaches to intelligence. Besides new goals for education, Gardner's (1983) multifaceted approach to intelligence suggests that we reexamine our media of instruction to use other symbol systems.

Motivation

Previous reviews (e.g. Resnick 1981, Gagne & Dick, 1983) have not had separate sections on motivation. In recent years, however, cognitive reformulations of achievement motivation theory (e.g. Weiner 1979, Dweck & Elliott 1983) have revitalized motivational research and suggested productive relationships between research programs in cognition and motivation. The following section focuses on the interactions between motivational characteristics of the learner and cognition and instruction.

ATTRIBUTIONAL MODELS   Cognitive approaches to motivation have been strongly influenced by attribution theory (Weiner 1979). Attributional models stress the importance of the role of perceived ability and effort in achievement dynamics. For example, attribution theory and cognitive reformulations of learned helplessness theory (e.g. Weiner 1979, Peterson & Seligman 1984) suggest that individuals who attribute failure to stable internal causes show passivity in learning, anxiety, and lowered self-esteem. There is, however, controversy over the causal nature of attributions for performance (cf Covington & Omelich 1979, 1984, Wong & Weiner 1981, Weiner 1983, Brown & Weiner 1984). In addition, questions have been raised about the ecological validity of attribution theory for classrooms (Blumenfeld et al 1982, Brophy 1983, Eccles 1983), since much of the attribution research has been done in the laboratory. In contrast to a static view of attributional style, Bandura (1982) has suggested a more dynamic construct of self-efficacy, concerning individuals' beliefs about their ability to achieve goals by their actions in specific situations. Harter (1985) also suggests a more differentiated view of the locus of control issue, proposing a concept of beneffectance (accepting internal control for success and external control for failure). These more dynamic and differentiated constructs suggest promising linkages between motivational and cognitive variables to be explored in future research.

A number of studies have found developmental differences in children's understanding of attributional constructs such as ability and effort with younger children having more undifferentiated concepts of ability and effort and, in fact, defining ability in terms of effort or improvement in learning (e.g. Nicholls 1978, Nicholls & Miller 1983, Blumenfeld et al 1985). Both Nicholls (1984) and Dweck & Elliott (1983) propose that students approach instructional tasks differently depending on their concepts of ability. Students who believe ability can change and improve with learning will approach the task with an orientation to learn and focus on the process of how to do the task. In contrast, students who conceive of ability as capacity will focus on comparative performance and outcome.

Covington's self-worth model (Covington & Beery 1976, Covington 1983, 1984) proposes that individuals are motivated to maintain a high self-perception of ability. Effortful strategic behavior may increase the potential for success; however, if failure occurs, these students must conclude that they lack ability. Hence, effort is a double-edged sword (Covington & Omelich 1979) and students may avoid the dilemma by not trying. Covington suggested that changes in instructional methods such as decreasing competition, giving fewer norm-referenced tests, and individualizing instruction would not threaten students' self-worth as much and might lead to more effortful and strategic behavior.

EXPECTANCY-VALUE MODELS   Expectancy-value models are derived from Atkinson's (1964) need achievement theory. The expectancy component is directly linked to attributions and self-concept whereas the value component is more affective. Task value has not been included in most attributional models, but has been shown by Eccles (1983) to be an important determinant of achievement behavior. Eccles's (1983) model details relationships among socializers (i.e. family, school, and peer influences) and students' goals, self-concepts, expectancies, attributions, and achievement behavior. Dweck & Elliott (1983) also have proposed an expectancy-value model that stresses the dynamic relationships among students' goals, expectancies, values, and performance. Both the Dweck & Elliott (1983) and Eccles (1983) models are important for their emphasis on task value. This new interest in task value complements the recent emphasis on classroom tasks in process-product research (e.g. Doyle 1983) and the concern for context and relevant tasks in cognitive development research (e.g. Paris & Cross 1983).

TEST ANXIETY   Although it is well documented that anxiety often interferes with performance, the mechanisms responsible for this relationship are not yet clear. Morris et al (1981) reviewed the literature on anxiety and found that the more cognitive "worry" component of anxiety seemed to be more highly predictive of performance decrements than the "emotionality" component. Similarly, Wine (1980) suggests that anxiety interferes with performance by inducing self-focused thoughts rather than task-focused thoughts. Information processing approaches (e.g. Benjamin et al 1981, McKeachie 1984) suggest that performance deficits of anxious students may result from problems in encoding the material (i.e. reading the material), in organizing the material (i.e. when studying or reviewing), or in retrieving the information during an exam. McKeachie et al (1985) found support for this view by demonstrating that students high in test anxiety benefited more than other students from a course on learning strategies. Paulman & Kennelly (1984) found that test anxiety and exam-taking skills have separate and interactive effects on performance. This information processing approach incorporates the ideas from both the cognitive-attentional interference model (Wine 1980) and the learning skills deficit model (Culler & Holahan 1980). Clearly, more research is needed on the cognitive and affective interactions among anxiety, learning strategies, and performance.

In contrast to the focus on individuals' cognitive skills or affect, other researchers have focused on the external testing or classroom conditions that foster anxiety. Hill & Wigfield (1984) suggest a number of ways instructional practices could be changed to lessen anxiety including changing reporting practices, decreasing time pressure, preventing continued failure by modifying test difficulty to match skill levels, and changing testing instructions to lessen anxiety and optimize performance. These recommendations parallel those of Covington's (1984) for reducing threats to students' self-worth.

CONCLUSION   The future of research on the interactions between motivation, cognition, and instruction is bright. Researchers will begin to integrate motivational and cognitive variables in their work, although they will have to address the methodological issues involved in measuring dynamic motivational and cognitive constructs with essentially static instruments and designs. Affect and task value are likely to play a larger role in future research. Finally, the ecological validity of these models must be improved. As Brophy (1983) aptly points out, "Classrooms are work settings in which students must cope with activities that are compulsory and subject to public evaluation" (p. 201). This is in contrast to play or laboratory settings, where the student has a choice over activities or where the task and evaluation criteria are clearly defined. More research is needed on how students perceive and value classroom tasks and how classroom instruction interacts with students' motivation and cognition.

INSTRUCTIONAL PROCESSES

Perhaps the most significant contribution made by cognitive theory is the common language it provides for a wide range of educational phenomena. Not only are most experimental, motivational, and differential psychologists now using the same paradigm, but so are researchers on educational media, instructional design, and classroom teaching. For researchers on classroom teaching and tasks, cognitive science has introduced theory to an area that has largely been atheoretical; for instructional designers, it has provided a shift from examination of instructional stimuli, learners' overt responses, and reinforcement to concerns about the instructional effects on cognitive structures and strategies; for media researchers, it has resulted in redefinition of media as activities that correspond to required mental operations and as attributes that support these activities. Conceptions of the learner, the task, the medium, and instruction are being reformulated as parallel interacting processes grounded in cognition (e.g. Glaser 1980, Shuell 1980). In this section we examine the impact of information processing theory on media, instructional design, classroom instruction, and testing, leaving educational tasks for the following section.

Media and Technology

Historically, research on media (e.g. radio, TV, computers) has progressed in waves corresponding to the introduction of new technologies. Each wave has compared the impact of the latest technology to some previous one (Saettler 1968), with accumulated studies culminating in a review attempting to make some summary judgment about the value of the medium. Contemporary examples of these reviews include those by Levie & Dickie (1973), Jamison et al (1974), McKeachie (1974), Berliner & Gage (1976), and Schramm (1977). A typical conclusion of these reviews is that for most tests of achievement one medium is about as good as another.

Recent applications of meta-analytic techniques have uncovered significant findings undetected by the less sensitive box-score summaries. The Kuliks and their colleagues at the University of Michigan have systematically analyzed hundreds of studies and have drawn conclusions more favorable to new technologies but varying by content and level. They found a moderate positive impact of individualized instruction on achievement in college courses (Kulik et al 1979) but not in precollege science and mathematics courses (Kulik & Bangert-Drowns 1983). For computer-assisted instruction, however, a moderate positive impact on achievement and attitudes was found for high school and junior high school students (Bangert-Drowns et al 1985) and elementary school students (Kulik et al 1985), but smaller differences for college students (Kulik & Kulik 1985). Small but significant findings also favored programmed instruction (Kulik et al 1980) and visually based instruction (Cohen et al 1981) in college courses. The medium of instruction and method of instruction are often confounded in research (Clark 1983, 1985), but the continued use of meta-analysis may encourage a standard for reporting of experimental procedures in original studies that permits the subsequent statistical disentanglement of media and methods across studies.

A more important concern is media and methods conceptual disentanglement; how media are defined, distinguished from each other, and from method. Salomon (1978, 1979) observes that various media have much in common. As a new technology is developed, it draws heavily from previous media as early film did from theater. Such commonality diminishes any differences between media in effects on learning. However, media do differ in important ways; each is composed of a distinctive but nonfixed set of elements or attributes (e.g. realism, interactivity, etc) and may employ different symbol systems (e.g. iconic, linguistic, etc). Some features of a medium may be imposed (such as the viewing of a film in large groups in a darkened hall) rather than inherent. But even the inherent attributes are capabilities that may or may not be employed. Thus a television presentation not using the more distinctive features of the medium may look more like a lecture than another application of television which does. These different clusters of attributes and symbol systems interact with the message, the task, and the learner. For example, certain attributes of a medium (e.g. a video cut to closeup, to draw on Salomon's 1979 study) may evoke mental operations required by a certain task (e.g. recalling visual details of a story) for learners of certain aptitudes (e.g. those facile at relating details to conceptual wholes) while other attributes (e.g. video zoom) serve to supplant this operation for those less adept. Exposure to this isomorphic operation may result in the acquisition of the corresponding mental skills, as was the case in the Salomon study. This conceptualization of media emphasizes their psychological effects rather than their comparative effectiveness.

Rather than comparing the overall effectiveness of radio versus television, Beagles-Roos & Gat (1983) examined the differences and outcomes. They found that when children were exposed to a television and radio story with the soundtrack in common, those in the television group were better at picture sequencing, recall of details from the story, and making inferences based on actions. Those in the radio group were better at recognizing expressive language, at making inferences based on verbal sources, and on knowledge unrelated to the story (see also Meringoff 1980).

Contemporary media research is also examining attributes of a single medium and their corresponding cognitive effects. For example, Kozma (1985) reviews studies of educational television and the effects of pacing, cueing, modeling, and transformation. Johnston & Ettema (1985) examined research to determine what characteristics of television might make it effective for prosocial learning. Similarly, Tennyson and colleagues (Tennyson 1980, 1981, Tennyson & Buttrey 1980, Johansen & Tennyson 1983) studied attributes of computer-based instruction. One group of students was given control of the amount and sequence of instruction, continuing reports on their progress, and instructional advisement; a second group's instruction was computer controlled; a third group had control of their instruction but no progress reports. The group with personal control and progress reports performed better than the group without progress reports and saved time while performing as well as the computer controlled group.

Lepper (1985) describes the ability of computer games to evoke challenge, curiosity, and personal control in learners, potentially increasing learning. If motivational enhancements result in mindful engagement in the task, learning will be facilitated. Comparison of television and print showed that learners who perceive a medium as "hard" invest more mental effort in processing its messages (Salomon 1974, 1983). Krendl & Watkins (1983) found that learners who were told that a subsequent televised presentation was educational were more able to make inferences and generalizations about the story (i.e. learn at a deeper level) on posttests than viewers who were told the same presentation was for entertainment. Baker et al (1981) found a negative correlation between the use of instructional games and basic skills achievement in reading and mathematics. Some motivational enhancements in computers and other media may actually depress the use of effective cognitive strategies or reduce time on the learning task.

A related question is the presumption that learning to program computers can transfer to higher cognitive skills. Whereas Clements & Gullo (1984) found that children taught computer programming for 12 weeks scored higher on measures of reflectivity and divergent thinking than students taking computer-based instruction in reading and mathematics, Pea & Kurland's (1984) review found little support for this contention. The transfer of programming skills may depend on extensive practice, on explicit efforts to decontextualize them, and on motivation for their transfer (Salomon 1984). Thus the question becomes not whether transfer will take place, but under what conditions are learners likely to transfer what kinds of programming skill.

Instructional Design

Instructional design has taken on a new aura of respectability as the result of a call for a "science of the artificial" (Simon 1981) and a renewed call for the development of a "linking science" between psychology and instructional practice (Glaser 1982b). The design of instruction that fosters the acquisition of performance based on our knowledge of how learning occurs is central to a theory of instruction (Glaser 1982b). Between the previous review in this series (Gagne & Dick 1983) and a recent book (Reigeluth 1983), 14 different instructional design models have been described. Though as many as seven of these models share a common notion that instruction must support the learner's cognitive processing, the models tend to be idiosyncratic in terminology. Clearly, integration is needed (Reigeluth 1983).

A dominant model seems to be emerging from information processing theory. This theory is already strongly reflected in the design of complex human-computer systems (Schneiderman 1980, Card et al 1983, Rubenstein & Hersh 1984) and is debuting in instructional design literature (Brezin 1980, Bovy 1981, Winn 1982, Bruning 1983, Kozma 1985). From information processing constructs such as perception, limitations of short-term memory, organization of long-term memory, and metacognition, these authors draw implications, though not yet design principles, related to stimulus cuing, the use of images and visuals, schemata modification, and cognitive monitoring. Similarly, measures of individual differences are shifting to a description of variation in learners' present knowledge and schema structure, in cognitive strategies or styles, and in basic cognitive processes (e.g. channel capacity, reaction time, etc). Correspondingly, adaptive instruction (Shuell 1980) builds on learners' strengths (capitalization), performs functions the learners are unable to perform (compensation), or provides them with cognitive skills or knowledge needed to learn (remediation).

While research on aptitude-treatment interactions has failed to identify the number of consistent relationships one would need to construct an extensive set of design principles (Cronbach & Snow 1977), this research has shown that those learners scoring high in general ability and prior knowledge do especially well under instruction that is significantly incomplete, because it affords opportunities for them to elaborate and organize learning themselves (Snow & Lohman 1984). On the other hand, less able students benefit from explicit, structured instruction. Simultaneously, these students should also receive instruction aimed at developing their learning strategies and skills. These conclusions parallel those of Tobias (1982) and complement the antagonistic relationship between effective and enjoyable instructional treatments described by Clark (1982). These recommendations, however, amount to design heuristics rather than the specific principles initially anticipated from this line of research. They suggest additional research and development on computer-based instruction with learner-control and advisement along the lines of Tennyson's work (Johansen & Tennyson 1983).

CONCLUSION: MEDIA AND METHODS   Clark (1983, 1984, 1985) contends that research on media attributes and effects continues to confound media and method. Zooming, for example, is a method of directing attention that may be performed just as well in other ways, such as by using static arrows in photographs. Attributes and symbol systems are only correlated with media and should not be considered media variables. Clark (1983) concludes that "media are mere vehicles that deliver instruction but do not influence student achievement any more than the truck that delivers our groceries causes changes in our nutrition," (p. 445). He recommends that researchers refrain from producing additional studies exploring the relationship between media and learning.

We contend that research on media variables is still important. Each medium is composed of a characteristic, flexible cluster of attributes (some of which are shared with other media, some not) and this cluster may, but need not be, employed to create a presentation other media are incapable of creating. To the extent that this presentation supports (i.e. cues, supplants, etc) cognitive processes necessary or sufficient for learning a particular task, the medium makes a unique contribution to learning. As Salomon & Gardner (1984) point out, researchers need to study the effects media can be made to have, rather than those they may typically have. The trend in technology development is toward an integrated media form that draws together the most distinctive attributes of various media (i.e. computer-based interactive video). While this integrated medium makes comparative studies less meaningful, it increases the importance of attribute studies. We need to decide which attributes we want in this new, synthesized medium, how they interact with methods, and when they will be most useful. This warrants continued research on the relationship between media and learning. Research on technology not only can help us understand the role of media and methods in learning but increase our understanding of learning processes (Greeno 1985).

Classroom Instruction and Teaching

The previous section focused on instructional design as a link between cognitive psychology and instruction. The current section adds ecological validity to the discussion by reviewing central themes regarding actual instruction in classrooms. The best source for a review of this area is the forthcoming third edition of *The Handbook of Research on Teaching* (Wittrock 1986). Although there is a variety of research programs on teaching (Shulman 1986), three of the most central for instructional psychology are the process-product, the classroom management, and student cognition programs.

PROCESS-PRODUCT RESEARCH PROGRAM   The process-product program has been the most popular and productive paradigm in research on teaching in the 1970s and into the 1980s (Shulman 1986). The program has focused on correlational relationships between teacher classroom behavior and student achievement (Brophy & Good 1986), highlighting the importance of engaging and maintaining student involvement with school tasks. The concepts of student time-on-task, academic learning time, and other variations of the time variables are seen as mediators between teacher behavior and achievement (Shulman 1986). A recent edited volume (Fisher & Berliner 1985) provides a comprehensive history and review of instructional time. Process-product research also stresses the importance of an active, direct instructional role for the teacher. Although the findings are probably most generalizable to basic skills instruction in the elementary grades, they also have relevance for instructional practice in general.

For example, Rosenshine (1983, Rosenshine & Stevens 1986) has described six teaching functions that are important for effective instruction. These functions include: 1. daily review and checking previous day's work with reteaching if necessary; 2. presenting new content or skills, proceeding in small steps but at a rapid pace; 3. providing initial student practice with the teacher monitoring student understanding; 4. providing instructional feedback and corrections to students; 5. providing independent student practice with a high rate of success (90–100%); and 6. weekly or monthly review.

Besides these general teaching functions, Brophy & Good (1986) summarize the research on teacher behaviors during a lesson by breaking them into categories of (*a*) giving information, (*b*) asking questions, and (*c*) providing feedback. Structuring the material by using overviews or advance organizers is important in introducing a topic (Mayer 1979, Luiten et al 1980), and although clarity of instruction is important, other positive teacher presentation behaviors (i.e. challenge, enthusiasm) do not seem to be related to student engagement (Brophy et al 1983). The effect of asking questions depends upon the level of difficulty or lesson context (Winne 1979, Brophy & Good 1986). In terms of feedback, Brophy (1981, Brophy & Good 1986) suggested that to be effective, praise should be contingent, specific, and informative for the student, including acknowledging correct and incorrect responses as such but not involving personal praise or criticism of the student.

The process-product tradition has generated a corpus of knowledge about classrooms, teachers, and students that describes the reality of classroom instruction and serves as the foundation for teacher preservice and inservice programs. However, interest in the strictly correlational studies has waned, replaced by experimental studies of teacher behavior and student achievement (e.g. Good & Grouws 1979) and an interest in the context effects of task content, classroom structure, and student characteristics.

CLASSROOM ORGANIZATION AND MANAGEMENT RESEARCH PROGRAMS   The classroom management program of research is closely related to process-product research but has a distinctly ecological flavor (Doyle 1986, Shulman 1986). The central assumption of this approach is that classrooms are characterized by certain features of group settings regardless of the particular teachers and students. These features (such as the publicness of events, multiple events occurring simultaneously, the immediacy and unpredictability of events, and the fact of a shared history) create pressures and demands (the environmental press) to which both teachers and students must respond (Doyle 1986). A key component of classroom organization is activity structure. Activities such as group lectures, small groups, or seatwork have different functions, rules, and norms that can prescribe both teacher and student behavior (Berliner 1983). For example, presenting a lesson in a recitation instead of using a small group or seatwork requires the teacher to control student behavior more to maintain the lecture or discussion and limits student-student interaction (Bossert 1979, Doyle 1986). Another important component of structure is the nature of the academic tasks students confront in the classroom (Doyle 1983, Blumenfeld et al 1985). For example, filling in a worksheet on Christopher Columbus makes very different cognitive demands on students than writing a report requiring library research. This focus on the nature and use of classroom tasks currently is a major area of interest for classroom researchers and links them to developments in cognitive psychology and curriculum developers' concern with content (Doyle 1983, 1986).

THE STUDENT COGNITION RESEARCH PROGRAM   The student mediating or cognition program of research is a fairly recent development. Partially in reaction to the simple correlational strategies of the process-product tradition and their treatment of the student as an empty black box, many researchers have attempted to examine how students process, interpret, and make sense out of all the information presented to them in the classroom (Shulman 1986). Researchers interested in academic outcomes of schooling have attempted to move beyond simple notions of time-on-task to explore student information processing while they are engaged in actual school work (e.g. Corno & Mandinach 1983). For example, using a stimulated recall technique, Peterson et al (1982) found that, independent of student ability, students who used specific cognitive strategies (e.g. relating information being taught to prior knowledge) performed better on an achievement test. Peterson et al (1984) also found that student self-reports of attention, understanding, and affect mediated the relationship between instruction and achievement and that these student cognitions were better predictors of student learning than observers' ratings of time-on-task. Obviously, time-on-task is a necessary condition for learning, but it is not sufficient; it depends on the cognitive and motivational processes engaged in by the student during task performance.

Besides this "technical" socialization, other researchers have examined how student perceptions mediate social outcomes of schooling (Blumenfeld et al 1983, Weinstein 1983). For example, Brattesani et al (1984) found that teacher expectancy effects were mediated by students' perceptions of differential treatment by the teacher. Although this program of research must struggle with problems in measuring student cognitions, it promises to be one of the most active and exciting areas in research on teaching and learning over the next several years.

CONCLUSION   Classroom research provides the context for the application of cognitive psychology to instruction. As Glaser (1982a) points out, researchers in the substantive domains of reading, math, science, and writing are examining the micro processes of learning and instruction while classroom researchers are exploring the macro processes or general principles of teaching and learning relevant to classroom ecology. These general principles of classroom instruction and management may be seen as necessary, but not sufficient, conditions for improved instruction. Obviously, we need collaborative research on both the micro and macro processes of learning and instruction. The interest in student mediating cognitions and academic tasks by classroom researchers and the current interest in school tasks by cognitive psychologists suggest that much useful research will emerge in the future on how to both manage a classroom and teach the content of the curriculum that will improve student learning in all areas.

Testing and Instruction

Testing issues that have recently captured public attention include debates about bias in testing, the role of minimum competency testing, and the decline of scores on standardized achievement tests (Glaser & Bond 1981, Haney 1984). Although the outcomes of these debates will certainly affect educational practice, they tend not to inform instructional design. On the other hand, there is a quiet revolution going on in the field of testing that shows considerable promise for linking testing and instruction (Tyler & White 1979, Burstein 1983). The twin goals of this revolution are to enhance (a) the validity of educational tests, and (b) the sensitivity of these tests to the processes and outcomes of learning. Interest in instructionally relevant testing has been fueled by the inadequacies of traditional achievement tests as instructional instruments (see Koslin et al 1979, Tyler 1979, Frederiksen 1984b, Johnston 1984). In this section we review several developments that should benefit the design and assessment of instruction.

TEACHER-MADE TESTS   An important source of information about how to measure learning processes and outcomes is the testing practices of teachers. The strength of teacher-made tests is that they are closely related to the realities and needs of teaching. "These methods—quizzes, essay tests, discussions, exercises, lab problems, etc.—may not always be 'scientific,' but they often have a great deal to recommend them" (Calfee 1985, p. 3). On the other hand, teachers may overlook sound principles of test construction. Calfee (1985) describes how teachers and researchers working together were able to develop a computer-based assessment procedure for writing instruction that informed classroom practice, met state-mandated minimum competency requirements, and was technically sound. Schwartz & Taylor (1978, 1979) discuss a similar effort where researchers and teachers worked together to develop valid measures of quantitative skills such as measurement of length. They validated their measures in part by demonstrating convergence between an ecologically valid measure and a test-like measure (e.g. performance in a game and performance on a test) of the same quantitative skill, and in part by asking teachers to assess the similarity between the measures and the skills actually taught in classrooms.

COGNITIVE PSYCHOLOGY AND TESTING   Cognitive psychology has proved to be a valuable resource not only for improved formulations of thinking and learning but also for methods for assessing these processes (Glaser 1981, Schoenfeld 1982, Messick 1984a). For example, Curtis & Glaser (1983) discuss how recent advances in reading theory can inform the assessment of reading achievement in four areas: decoding, accessing semantic word information, sentence processing, and discourse analysis. Although reading is seen as an interactive process involving all of these components, Curtis and Glaser point out that current instructional and testing practices address only the lower level processes at the expense of the higher order processes and the interactions between them. The authors offer concrete suggestions for modifying reading achievement tests.

Another example of the impact of cognitive psychology is found in the work of Brown & VanLehn (1980, 1982). They describe a computer-based system for diagnosing the faulty rules—or "bugs"—that produce children's arithmetic errors. A major feature of this work is the finding that most errors do not result from ignorance, but from use of systematic rules that are partially correct. Once a bug has been accurately diagnosed, an instructional prescription follows naturally. Similarly, Glaser (1981) reviews research by Bartholomae (1980) which shows how to analyze writing samples for systematic errors, thereby providing information about the "bugs" students have in their "intermediate system" for producing the meaning and intent of the writer through the written code.

DYNAMIC ASSESSMENT   Testing is and should be an integral part of instruction. Nevertheless, traditional psychometric practices do not directly address the dynamic nature of the testing, teaching, and learning cycle (Feuerstein et al 1981). However, dynamic assessment procedures based upon the work of Vygotsky (1978) should prove valuable in this regard. Two features of Vygotsky's theory are relevant to dynamic assessment. First, Vygotsky recognized that learning and development occur in a social context, with students receiving guidance and feedback about their performance. This view adds another dimension to learning, for learning is measured not only by the amount of knowledge gained, but also by the extent to which mastery can be demonstrated independently of social support. Second, based upon this "scaffolding" view of learning and development, Vygotsky advocated assessing students' propensity for learning by measuring their "zone of proximal development." This zone is defined as the difference between a student's current level of performance—what he or she can achieve independently—and potential level of performance—what he or she can achieve with support.

Brown and her colleagues (Brown & French 1979, Brown & Ferrara 1985) have begun to investigate the utility of dynamic assessment procedures. In one study (Campione et al 1984), learning efficiency and near- and far-transfer were assessed in addition to static predictors of learning (i.e. IQ). Learning efficiency was measured by the number of hints required for successful performance, an indicator of the amount of "scaffolding" required by the learner from an adult assistant. The dynamic measures were better predictors of the children's gains between pre- and post-test than were the static measures.

CONTEXTUAL ASSESSMENT   The role of context in assessment has received extensive treatment recently (Scarr 1981, Messick 1983, 1984b), and these considerations have important implications for the validity of educational testing. The current emphasis on cognitive measurement at the expense of metacognitive, motivational, and attitudinal measurement provides researchers and teachers with an incomplete educational profile (Paris et al 1985). Messick (1983) discusses treating the child as context, so that rational choices can be made among variables (i.e. cognitive, personal/social, and health/physical) that are theoretically important determinants of learning. Messick also discusses measurement of characteristics of the researcher, teacher, classroom, school, peers, family, and the larger cultural community in which they are imbedded as illustrated in Mercer's (1979) System of Multicultural Pluralistic Assessment (SOMPA), which systematically utilizes physical, personal/social, and cultural information in the assessment of child characteristics.

EDUMETRICS   If testing is going to inform instruction, there must be a testing technology that parallels the technology available for measuring stable individual differences. Carver (1974) has provided a felicitous term for this new technology—"edumetrics." The goal of edumetrics is to provide instructionally useful information about students: their educationally relevant characteristics, their potential for learning, and a sensitive evaluation of what they have learned or failed to learn. A fundamental difference between traditional psychometrics and the upstart "edumetrics" is the latter's emphasis on the measurement of change.

A major goal of this section was to show that the edumetric technology is already substantial, including collaborations between teachers and researchers (Schwartz & Taylor 1978, Calfee 1985), the tasks of cognitive psychologists (Glaser 1981, Schoenfeld 1982), the principles of learning research used in dynamic assessment (Brown & Campione 1985), and the assessment of context (Messick 1983). Furthermore, many useful ideas—such as using criterion groups to select items that are maximally sensitive to learning—can be found in other papers by Bereiter (1962), Hambleton et al (1978), and Lipsey (1983).

TASKS, CONTENT, AND OUTCOMES

In this final section of the review we turn our attention to the tasks, content, and outcomes of instruction. In the first part we review instructional research in the major content areas: reading, writing, mathematics, and science. The second part is devoted to research on the instruction of generalizable problem solving skills and learning strategies.

Reading

As befits the centrality of reading to functioning in a literate society, there continues to be an enormous research effort devoted to the processes of reading and their instruction. The most direct entrance to the voluminous literature on reading is via edited volumes (e.g. Anderson et al 1984, Mandl et al 1984, Waller & MacKinnon 1984, Whitehurst 1984, Besner et al 1985, Carr 1985,

Orasanu 1985), although there are other recent works of special note. Among these are the *Handbook of Reading Research*, edited by Pearson (1984a), which has sections on methodological issues in the study of reading as well as sections on basic processes and instructional practices. In addition, there is a chapter on reading by Calfee & Drum (1986) in the new *Handbook of Research on Teaching*. Finally, a lacuna in the reading literature has been filled by a new graduate level text (Downing & Leong 1982).

Resnick (1981) concentrated her review on comprehension, because comprehension research was the focal topic of the 1970s; in this review we take a step up the ladder of cognitive processes to research on reading strategies and their instruction, reflecting a major interest of researchers during the past five years (Paris et al 1983, Pressley & Levin 1983a,b, Baker & Brown 1984).

STRATEGIC READING   Reading is not a linear process proceeding from written text to comprehension, but is rather a series of complex interactions between the reader, text, and context of reading. These interactions require strategies such as rereading in response to comprehension failure (Garner et al 1983, 1984), skimming ahead to establish an organizational scheme, using context to process unfamiliar words (Potter 1982), and summarizing text to ensure understanding and remembering (Brown et al 1983, Winograd 1984).

Comprehension monitoring (Wagoner 1983) has received substantial attention because this metacognitive skill is essential for competent reading. According to Paris & Myers (1981), "Reading comprehension involves many perceptual and cognitive skills, but a major component is the ability to monitor one's level of understanding while reading. This kind of mental pulse-taking is important because it is a measure of progress toward a reading goal and a signal for comprehension failures. Checking comprehension thus provides a link between the reader's purposes, progress, and behavior" (p. 5).

What do we know about the development of comprehension monitoring? First, we know that mature readers monitor their comprehension as they read, although there are substantial intra- and interindividual differences in the actual strategies used (Baker & Anderson 1982). Second, we know that better and/or older readers monitor their comprehension more effectively than poor and/or younger readers (Harris et al 1981, Paris & Myers 1981).

Other research has attempted to refine these basic findings. For example, Markman & Gorin (1981) found that 8- and 10-year-old children performed better when they were provided exemplars of the problem types (i.e. falsehoods or inconsistencies) than when they were provided with no information other than "some of the essays have problems with them." Furthermore, Markman & Gorin found that these children were able to adjust their standard of evaluation according to the instructional set. In a related study, Baker (1984) found that children 5, 7, 9, and 11 years old were able to use multiple standards of evaluation (i.e. lexical, internal consistency, and external consistency) when instructed to "find the mistakes." Although the older children in Baker's study outperformed the younger ones, all of her children performed better than same-aged children in uninstructed studies. In addition to age differences, Baker found task differences: the internal consistency standard was used least effectively, although even the youngest children were able to use it. In summary, these studies show that (a) school-aged children can effectively monitor their comprehension when instructed to do so, (b) they can adjust their standards for comprehension monitoring, and (c) they can use multiple standards simultaneously.

READING INSTRUCTION   Corresponding to the growing knowledge base about reading are efforts to translate this knowledge into a model of instruction (Pearson & Tierney 1983, Duffy et al 1984, Beck 1985). Ideally, these models should be based not only on knowledge about basic processes but also on information gained from process analyses of learning and instruction (e.g. Calfee & Piontkowski 1981, Omanson et al 1984), as well as the evaluation of instructional programs (Mezynski 1983, Johnson & Baumann 1984, Tierney & Cunningham 1984). Here we review two instructional approaches, direct instruction and reciprocal teaching, that reflect emerging trends in the design and implementation of reading instruction. Again, our emphasis on strategic reading will be apparent.

An effective model of direct instruction was discussed earlier in this review (see Classroom Instruction and Teaching). Research on teaching reading has also shown that students learn to read most efficiently when they receive direct, systematic instruction from their teachers (Pearson 1984b, Rosenshine & Stevens 1984). For example, Hansen (1981, Hansen & Pearson 1983) has successfully implemented and evaluated a program designed to increase children's inferential comprehension skills through direct instruction. The major features of this program were pre- and postreading group discussions that emphasized inferential comprehension. Before reading, the discussions focused on making predictions based on the children's prior knowledge about the topic, and after reading the teachers asked questions requiring inferences (e.g. after reading "Charlotte's Web," the teacher asked: "What kind of person do you think Templeton (the rat) would be if he were human?").

Paris (Paris et al 1984, Paris & Jacobs 1984) has implemented a similar but more ambitious program—Informed Strategies for Learning (ISL)—for direct instruction of strategic reading skills. The training included lessons designed to increase children's awareness of reading goals, plans, and strategies, as well as instruction about comprehension skills (i.e. kinds of meaning, inferential and critical reading, summarizing) and how to evaluate and monitor one's own comprehension. The classrooms receiving ISL showed greater gains than control classrooms on a variety of reading tasks.

Reciprocal teaching methods, although embodying the principles of direct instruction, in addition explicitly adopt a Vygotskian (1978) perspective on instruction. Teachers scaffold budding reading skills through prompts and examples and then foster individual control of reading by gradually removing social supports (Au & Kawakami 1984a, Brown et al 1984). Au & Kawakami (1984b) proposed a model of comprehension instruction with two major phases: a scriptal phase where teachers and students access background knowledge and specify initial predictions, and a text phase where teachers and students evaluate their predictions, clarify text ideas, and make inferences among text ideas. Au and Kawakami's results show that whereas first grade discussion groups spent most of their time in the scriptal phase, third grade groups spent most of their time in the text phase. Furthermore, the third grade groups spent less time in teacher-initiated, teacher-cued discussion than did the first grade groups. Hence, there was a developmental progression toward greater student control and higher-level processing of the text.

Pallincsar & Brown (1984) discuss a reciprocal teaching program where seventh grade poor comprehenders were taught comprehension-fostering and comprehension-monitoring activities (i.e. summarizing, questioning, clarifying, and predicting). As was the case in the Au and Kawakami study, a major goal of the instruction was to foster self-regulated comprehension, in this case by having the students take turns in leading a dialogue centered on pertinent features of the text. The program was more successful than typical classroom practice using both tutors and small group discussions, as indicated by measures of gain, transfer, and generalization.

Finally, Pearson (1985, Pearson & Gallagher 1983) outlines an approach to reading instruction that provides explicit steps for the release of task responsibility from the teacher to the student. Instruction proceeds through three phases: (*a*) modeling, where the teacher is solely responsible for task performance; (*b*) guided practice, where the student performs the task with help from the teacher; and (*c*) application, where the student performs independently of the teacher. According to Pearson, this approach meshes well with direct instruction emphasizing the processes of reading, where teachers model reading strategies such as predicting or summarizing and then pass responsibility for these activities on to their students. The research on reading instruction reviewed in this section provides many exemplars of this process-oriented approach to direct instruction and parallels recent developments in writing, mathematics, and science instruction.

Writing

In her 1981 review, Resnick pointed out that psychologists were just beginning research on written composition. Since then there has been a surge of interest in this area. A new journal, *Written Communication,* has been started, and the *Handbook of Research on Teaching* has a chapter on written composition

(Scardamalia & Bereiter 1986). In addition, there have been a number of recent books on research in written composition (e.g. Frederiksen & Dominic 1982, Whiteman 1982, Mosenthal et al 1983, Beach & Birdwell 1984). Reflecting the interest in writing by several disciplines, there are multiple paradigms employed by writing researchers (Bereiter & Scardamalia 1983, Mosenthal 1983). However, with increased attention from psychologists, research in this area is focusing on the cognitive processes involved in producing text, in contrast to the finished product (cf Resnick 1981, Bertram et al 1982). The psychological models (e.g. Sommers 1980, Flower & Hayes 1981a, 1984) have departed from the classical rhetorical linear model (planning, composing, and editing) to suggest a more interactive and recursive writing process. This section focuses on: 1. the cognitive processes of the writer as a producer of text and 2. writing instruction and technology.

COGNITIVE PROCESSES OF THE WRITER   Although recent psychological models of the composition process argue against the mapping of a single linear model onto the cognitive processes of the writer, the categories of planning, composing, or translating, and reviewing or editing are useful divisions for summarizing research in this area (e.g. Hume 1983; cf Scardamalia & Bereiter 1986, however). Cognitive models of writing suggest that planning includes the cognitive processes of accessing knowledge in long-term memory or from external sources, drawing inferences, organizing the information, and setting goals (Flower & Hayes 1981a, 1984). Research shows that good writers, in comparison to poor writers, produce better, more elaborate goals and spend more time in planning, especially in global planning in contrast to sentence-level planning (Hume 1983). In addition, research on in-process planning, which examines the pauses made during a writing session for evidence of planning, shows that good writers spend more time in long planning pauses and pause more to consider substantive thematic issues than sentence-level, grammatical issues (Flower & Hayes 1981b, Hume 1983).

A central issue in writing research concerns the nature of the planning process and how plans are translated into text. Or, more colloquially, how do ideas become prose? Flower & Hayes (1984) proposed a multiple representation thesis to clarify the relationship between planning and composing. They suggested that writers create a variety of internal and external representations of meaning (e.g. images, schemas, propositions, notes, drafts) which are then instantiated in text. Scardamalia & Bereiter (1982) suggest that plans are instantiated by assimilating them to knowledge-telling strategies for novices and young children and reflective-planning strategies for experts. Flower & Hayes (1984) also suggest that finding analogies and accommodating general problem-solving skills to prose constraints are used in translating plans to text. Hume (1983) summarized the research on translating or composing by noting that this subprocess creates a large cognitive demand as the writer copes with the global issues of instantiating goals and plans, as well as with organization, clarity, grammar, spelling, punctuation, handwriting, etc. As some of these skills (i.e. handwriting and spelling) become automatized through practice and experience, the writer can spend more time on substantive issues. More research is needed on this process of translating in general, and in particular, on how certain skills become automatized in young or novice writers.

The subprocesses of reviewing and revising have received somewhat more empirical attention than translating. Novice writers, even children, do review their texts, but they often focus on surface level issues such as spelling, grammar, and punctuation rather than on global issues such as style or purpose (Hume 1983). Novice writers often make only minor corrections, not substantive changes, in revisions (Bridwell 1980, Sommers 1980, Faigley & Witte 1981). Thus, as in the planning process, we see the problems of limited processing capacity, lack of knowledge, and executive control preventing sufficient allocation to substance.

WRITING INSTRUCTION AND TECHNOLOGY   Just as there are a number of writing research paradigms, programs in writing instruction are even more diverse (Scardamalia & Bereiter 1986). Rhetoric theory has evolved from stressing Aristotle's topoi as strategies for generating text to emphasizing the topoi as exemplars for a finished product (Applebee 1984b). Surveys of writing instruction in public schools suggest that instruction does not occur often, tends to focus on word and sentence level skills, and involves mainly recitation of previously learned material (Graves 1978, Applebee 1984a). However, with the popularity of the cognitive process movement, writing instruction is beginning to focus on how to teach students cognitive strategies for planning, organizing, translating, reviewing, and revising their text. Scardamalia & Bereiter (1986) summarize the various direct instruction approaches to teaching strategies for writing as well as procedural facilitation methods where the teacher supports the students' efforts in a collaborative manner. As in reading instruction, these developments focus on explicit instruction and process-oriented approaches.

Another aspect of writing instruction and research concerns the impact of the microcomputer and of word processing programs. There have been numerous articles in the popular press about the transformations and improvements this technology will have on writing. Unfortunately, the research necessary to support this enthusiasm is lacking (Bridwell et al 1984). Several developments, however, are worthy of note. Frase (1984) describes three modes of computer intervention (advisory, emulation, tutorial) and elaborates on an advisory system, *Writer's Workbench,* that was developed to provide writers with a detailed analysis of their compositions. Providing writers with information on word use, readability, and complexity, as well as spelling and punctuation, the program leaves the revision decision in the writer's hands. In an evaluative study of this system, Kiefer & Smith (1983) found that students who used *Writer's Workbench* for a semester improved their editing skills, compared to students who used word processing without *Writer's Workbench*. In evaluating the effectiveness of word processing programs, we are reminded of Clark's (1985) warning against confounding media and method effects. While *Writer's Workbench* is focused on analysis and revision of the writing process, other computer-based writing programs focus on structure and argument. Programs such as WANDA, QUILL, SEEN, and PREWRITE are designed to facilitate the early, invention phase of the process. Although the verdict is still out on the effects of these programs, it is encouraging to see the development of software based on cognitive process models.

Mathematics

Research interest in the psychology of mathematics has remained strong since Resnick's (1981) Instructional Psychology chapter, as is evident by the number of new edited books in this area (Brainerd 1982, Carpenter et al 1982, Ginsburg 1983, Lesh & Landau 1983). In addition, there are the published proceedings of a major conference on mathematical education (Zweng et al 1983) and a chapter in *The Handbook of Research on Teaching* (Romberg & Carpenter 1986). Finally, Resnick & Ford's (1981) integrative review still provides a contemporary view of psychological thinking about mathematics learning and instruction. The major themes of the current instructional psychology of mathematics are reflected in several recent papers devoted exclusively to mathematics instruction. These themes emphasize in turn models of teaching, research, cognitive processes, and development.

Shavelson (1981) outlines an approach to teaching mathematics that links psychological knowledge about (*a*) subject-matter structure, (*b*) student cognitive structure, (*c*) teacher decision making, and (*d*) instructional context. Shavelson's integration of information from diverse fields of inquiry is facilitated by his consistently cognitive approach to the problem of mathematics education.

In a novel paper that emphasizes the close relationship between teaching and researching, Cobb & Steffe (1983) introduce the notion of the teaching experiment. Teaching experiments have two critical features: first, teaching experiments consist of either long-term or short-term instructional interactions between teachers and students (macroschemes or microschemes); the goal is to observe the learner's dynamic passage from one state of knowledge to another. The second feature of teaching experiments is that the teacher's actions are guided by explicit models of the students' mathematical knowledge: "From this perspective, the activity of teaching involves a dialectic between modeling and practice" (Cobb & Steffe 1983, p. 86).

In an application of cognitive learning theory to the process of doing mathematics, Gagne (1983) divides the problem-solving task into three phases: (*a*) translating from a verbal problem statement to a mathematical expression, (*b*) carrying out an operation on the expression, and (*c*) validating the solution. Although there is little controversy about his performance model, the instructional implications Gagne draws require clarification (Wachsmuth 1983) or rebuttal (Steffe & Blake 1983).

Whereas Gagne (1983) presents an adult performance model of mathematical problem solving, Resnick (1983) presents a developmental model of number understanding tracing the development of number concepts and skills through three periods of development: (*a*) the preschool period, during which counting and quantity comparison abilities emerge; (*b*) the early primary period, during which children invent mental procedures for addition and subtraction and master simple story problems; and (*c*) the later primary period, during which children acquire the structure and notation of the decimal system. In a later paper, Resnick (1985) discusses the processes by which children construct mathematical knowledge and thereby pass through these three developmental periods. Taking this work a step further, Resnick (1982, Resnick & Omanson 1985) investigates instructional procedures that specifically build on knowledge of children's constructive processes.

In the remainder of this section we review empirical research on mathematics learning and instruction. This brief review reflects researchers' current interest in the mathematical accomplishments of young children.

Gelman (1980, Gelman & Gallistel 1978, Starkey & Gelman 1982) has documented the impressive quantitative accomplishments of preschoolers, which include the numerical representation of small arrays, arithmetic reasoning about numbers they can accurately represent, and some knowledge about infinity. In a related effort, Fuson (Fuson et al 1982, Fuson & Hall 1983) reviews research on preschoolers' acquisition of the number word sequence as the linguistic counterpart to their numerical skill. Although early number word sequences are merely rote strings, these soon develop into flexible and meaningful sequences that can be applied to concrete problems. These early skills—numerical and linguistic—form the foundation for later arithmetic and problem-solving learning in school.

The development of addition is being worked out in some detail. Houlihan & Ginsburg (1981) reported that the first graders in their study used only counting procedures such as counting-all and counting-on; however, the second graders used both counting and noncounting methods (e.g. addition by place value). If the older children used a counting procedure at all, it was the more efficient counting-on procedure. Secada et al (1983) were able to identify a set of three subskills that appeared to account for the transition from counting-all to counting-on. Third grade, according to Ashcraft (1982, Ashcraft & Fierman 1982), is the time when children begin retrieving arithmetic facts from memory, with the transition from a counting model to a retrieval model being mostly complete by the fourth grade. However, the representation of the factual memory store is still being debated, with Ashcraft favoring semantic-based storage (1983, Ashcraft et al 1984) and Baroody (1983, 1984) favoring stored procedural knowledge. Finally, Brainerd (1983) suggests that a major facilitator of development in addition is improvement in short-term memory functioning.

Carpenter & Moser (1982, 1983) have studied the informal problem-solving abilities of first graders and found that they were able to analyze and represent the structure of simple word problems in order to solve them. Building on this work and the work of others (e.g. Nesher 1982, Vergnaud 1982), Briars & Larkin (1984), and Riley et al (1983) have constructed formal models of children's skill in solving elementary word problems.

Kintsch & Greeno (1985) have taken these efforts one step further by combining principles from a theory of text processing (van Dijk & Kintsch 1983) with hypotheses based on the Riley et al (1983) model for understanding word problems, in an integrated model of problem comprehension. Kintsch and Greeno report that model predictions based on processing requirements for different problems are generally consistent with existing results.

Studying performance on multiplication and division word problems, Fischbein et al (1985) found that primitive intuitive models (e.g. repetitive addition in the case of multiplication) seemed to influence the choice of a numerical procedure even after children have had formal algorithmic training. Since these intuitive models correspond to the way in which the corresponding concept (e.g. multiplication) is usually taught, teachers face the dilemma of introducing a concept through a method that will later conflict with the formal concepts that are ultimately the goal.

Science

Science research is similar to research in mathematics because of the forceful impact that cognitive psychology has had on the methods and focus of research. However, unlike the field of mathematics instruction, and certainly unlike reading, there has yet to appear an edited volume devoted entirely to science. Nevertheless, there are several book chapters and journal articles that are useful entries into the literature on science learning and instruction.

An excellent starting point is White & Tisher's (1986) *Handbook of Research on Teaching* chapter on Natural Science which reviews most of the science education research of the 1970s. The hallmarks of their chapter are emphases on learning and the dynamic aspects of acquiring knowledge on the one hand, and the affective (e.g. student attitudes) and contextual (e.g. classroom management) aspects of instruction on the other. Another major reference is a special issue of the *Journal of Research in Science Teaching* devoted to a set of meta-analyses directed toward science education research questions (see Anderson et al 1983). The questions addressed by this multi-institutional effort include the effects of curricular programs, instructional systems, teaching techniques, and teacher and student behaviors on outcomes in science.

Other trends in science instruction research parallel those mentioned elsewhere in this review. For example, Maehr (1983) provides a motivational analysis of lagging science achievement that suggests a different set of policy prescriptions than do traditional cognitive analyses of this national problem (e.g. more time on task). Maehr's major conclusion is that science instruction should be designed to foster continuing self-guided achievement.

Based on a large-scale naturalistic study of elementary and secondary science classrooms, Hacker (1984) describes profiles of intellectual skills actually practiced by students in science lessons. The science teachers in Hacker's sample had definite preferences for teaching strategies, and their instructional behaviors were matched to changes in the student profiles. The importance of teacher behavior in science education is further underscored by Walberg et al's (1982) secondary analysis of the National Assessment of Educational Progress data. Walberg et al found that the quality of instruction and the social psychological climate of the classroom were the only unequivocal and potentially manipulable causes of science learning. Other variables, such as socioeconomic status or amount of homework, were found not to be causal agents of science achievement. As a final example of this sort, research by White (1984), who has designed a computer microworld for learning Newtonian mechanics, demonstrates the power of technology as an instructional tool.

Arguably the strongest influence of psychology on research in science instruction has been the influence of cognitive or information processing psychology (Gentner & Stevens 1983, Larkin & Rainard 1984). As was the case at the time of Resnick's (1981) chapter, physics has received most of the attention from psychologists, in part because the instructional difficulties are most persistent in the case of physics learning (Champagne et al 1982). Nevertheless, the impact of cognitive psychology can now be seen in diverse areas of science instruction, including elementary science (Ross & Maynes 1983), biology (Brumby 1982), chemistry (Gabel et al 1984), genetics (Smith & Good 1984), and geology (Champagne et al 1981).

In the case of physics, research can be divided into three areas: descriptive, prescriptive, and instructional. Descriptive research on physics knowledge has been either developmental (e.g. Siegler 1981, Wilkening 1981, Acredolo et al 1984) or has compared experts and novices (e.g. Chi et al 1981, McClosky & Kohl 1983, Anzai & Yokoyama 1984). The developmental research has focused on the ability of children to integrate information about different variables (e.g. distance and weight in a balance scale task), whereas the research with adults has focused on differences in the knowledge representations and problem solving strategies of experts and novices. A major conclusion of this research is that novices are not merely "empty headed," i.e. they lack information, but that they are "wrong headed," i.e. they have already formed preconceptions (e.g. heavier objects fall faster than lighter objects) that interfere with the learning of truly scientific concepts (Champagne et al 1982).

Reif & Heller (1982) have attempted to improve on the performance of experts by prescribing the kinds of knowledge and procedures that are conducive to effective problem solving in physics. Their formal model of problem solving includes components for (a) describing and analyzing a problem so as to facilitate its subsequent solution, (b) decomposing a problem into manageable subparts and searching for a solution, and (c) assessing the correctness and optimality of the resulting solution. In later work, Heller & Reif (1984) have shown that their formal model can be used to guide accurate problem representations in controlled learning situations, improving the problem solving performance of students who have already taken a physics course. In contrast to the carefully controlled conditions of the Heller & Reif (1984) study, Hewson & Hewson (1983) have implemented a conceptual change model in a more realistic instructional context that deals directly with students' "wrong headedness." Hewson and Hewson's model prescribes instructional strategies for replacing or differentiating the alternative conceptions that students have prior to formal instruction.

Space limitations prevent us from discussing research on other subject areas. However, the cognitive revolution is having an impact in the areas of geography (e.g. MacKenzie & White 1982), social studies (e.g. Armento 1986, Voss et al 1985), art (e.g. Jones & McFee 1986), music (Whitener 1983), motor skills (e.g. Shapiro & Schmidt 1982, MacKenzie & Marteniuk 1985), and military training (e.g. Kyllonen & Alluisi 1985, O'Neil et al 1986).

Generalizable Skills and Strategies

Current cognitive and instructional research stresses the role of prior knowledge in learning. The previous sections on reading, writing, mathematics, and science reflect current interest in the relationship of knowledge to learning and thinking. Although content knowledge is important, it may not be sufficient for effective problem solving. Educators at all levels have been increasingly concerned about generalizable cognitive skills such as problem solving, reasoning, and learning strategies. The following review focuses on research on teaching problem solving and learning strategies.

PROBLEM SOLVING   Research on problem solving and general thinking skills has a long history in psychology. There are several recent books and articles that provide good entry points to the current issues in the field. Chipman et al (1985) and Segal et al (1985) edited volumes that address both thinking and learning skills. Frederiksen (1984a) provided an overview of theories of cognitive psychology related to instruction in problem solving. Glaser (1984) highlighted the problems in applying current knowledge-based structural cognitive theories to the teaching of general problem solving and learning skills. Finally, the entire Winter 1984 issue of *Review of Educational Research* was oriented to issues in the teaching and learning of reasoning skills.

Sternberg (1983) has suggested that general intellectual skills training programs should satisfy the following eight criteria: 1. be based on an information processing theory, 2. be culturally relevant for the individuals involved, 3. provide direct instruction in the desired skills, 4. give attention to motivational components and individual differences, 5. have relevance to real-world behavior, 6. show empirical evidence of its effectiveness, 7. be particularly durable, and 8. transfer. Although most current instructional programs in problem solving cannot meet all of these criteria, several are worthy of note. Venezuela's Project Intelligence was designed to enhance the thinking skills of seventh graders. Evaluation data showed that the experimental group, in contrast to the control group, performed better on the specific thinking skills taught in the course, general intelligence tests, and realistic problem-solving tasks (Herrnstein et al 1983, Adams 1984). Feurstein's Instrumental Enrichment Program (Feuerstein et al 1980) also has shown positive results after two years of training in general intellectual skills for mentally impaired children (Narrol et al 1982). Other studies (e.g. Graham 1981, Haywood & Arbitman-Smith 1981, Yitzhak 1981) have shown less positive results but have involved much less training time than Feurstein's original program. Savell et al (1984) provided a review of the research on Feurstein's program, highlighting the gains on tests of nonverbal intelligence, but concluded that there is little evidence to support changes in self-concept, transfer to general school achievement, or nonschool cognitive tasks. A variety of other training programs, such as de Bono's (1985) CoRT program, Whimbey & Lockhead's (1980) course in analytical reasoning, and Wales's Guided Design (Wales & Stager 1977), attempt to teach general thinking or problem solving skills for college students or adults, but more research that follows Sternberg's (1983) suggestions is needed in order to determine their effectiveness.

The content and procedures of all of these programs differ, yet some commonality emerges. Most programs use a variety of concrete problems or exercises that are assumed to foster higher-order cognitive skills. They also attempt to engage students in discussion of the concepts and principles involved so that thought processes are made explicit. This focus on discussion parallels Glaser's (1984) recommendation of the Socratic method as a means of effective instruction. Collins & Stevens (1982) and Gal'perin (1982) both have found that interactive inquiry methods are effective in teaching general thinking skills. As Glaser (1984) points out, there seems to be little doubt that there is no substitute for extensive experience and knowledge in the problem solving domain in which a problem lies. A problem which is ill defined and difficult to comprehend for the novice may require no creativity from the expert who recognizes several possible approaches to a solution. Nevertheless, two individuals with comparable amounts of experience in problem solving may still differ in their ability to transfer problem solving skills to new problems. Educators can probably facilitate transfer by directly teaching general executive and metacognitive strategies as well as the specific procedures and knowledge involved in solving a set of problems.

LEARNING STRATEGIES AND STUDY SKILLS   Tobias (1982) has defined learning strategies as macroprocesses such as reviewing, note-taking, and comprehension monitoring that complement the more microscopic processes of intelligence. As in the problem solving area, there is controversy about whether or not learning strategies can be taught at a general level. Here, however, the research provides more convincing evidence that learning strategies generalize beyond the context in which they were taught. For example, courses designed to enhance study skills have long been successful (Kulik et al 1983). In addition, as we saw in our section on reading research, extensive studies of learning strategies have dealt with teaching reading to children. This research is well represented in the volumes edited by Pressley & Levin (1983a,b). Weinstein & Mayer (1986) provide a review of research on learning strategies. In this section we focus primarily on university level courses attempting to teach generalizable skills in learning along with metacognitive strategies for the use of those skills.

Weinstein & Underwood (1985) included both basic concepts of cognition and specific training in such strategies as elaboration and self-monitoring in a training course for college students. The most striking result from their research was an increase in reading comprehension; reported use of effective learning strategies increased, anxiety was reduced, and grades in later courses also improved. McKeachie et al (1985) compared gains of students in their "Learning to Learn" course with those of students in other introductory psychology courses and obtained results similar to those of Weinstein. The McKeachie and Pintrich course was developed with an underlying premise that skills would be more likely to be used effectively and transferred if students understood the cognitive theories about why particular strategies work. This parallels Paris et al's (1983) idea that students need not only declarative and procedural knowledge, but also conditional knowledge or an understanding of why a strategy works. This conditional knowledge should result in more motivated used of strategies.

A number of researchers have used Marton & Säljö's (1976) distinction between deep and surface processing to develop their courses. Biggs & Rihn

(1984) evaluated a course, "Effective Learning Skills," which attempted to teach students to take a deep, rather than surface, processing approach to study, resulting in the desired achievement gains plus an increase in intrinsic motivation for learning. Casteñeda et al (1984), however, found that hierarchial elaboration strategies imposed demands beyond the capacities of students and were less effective than linking, grouping, and repetition strategies. For technical, well-structured text and students lacking prior knowledge, the strategies of deeper processing involving constructing hierarchies of constructs or paraphrasing were less effective than strategies of repetition or grouping concepts. This highlights the interaction between the learner and the task and reinforces the notion that strategies are only strategic for some individuals and some tasks.

Dansereau's (1985) interactive learning strategy system makes distinctions between strategies that have a direct primary impact on information (i.e. elaboration) versus support strategies (i.e. reviewing). Strategies can be either algorithmic or heuristic, for a specific or for a general purpose, and either large or small in scope. Dansereau (1985) reported that his course in learning strategies produced improved academic performance and self-reported changes in strategies. More recently, he and his colleagues have found that cooperative learning of strategies carries over to more effective learning individually (Larson et al 1984, Yager et al 1985).

Learning and problem solving strategies are of no avail if the learner is not motivated to use them. As we have already seen, the apparently obvious positive effects of increased competence on motivation turn out not to be obvious. Motivation and self-concept are influenced by many variables outside an instructional program in learning and problem solving. Thus, instructional strategies need to deal explicitly with motivational retraining as well as cognitive skills and strategies. McCombs (1984) has developed programs to enhance student motivation through teaching self-awareness, personal control, and positive self-evaluation. Attribution retraining programs (e.g. Dweck & Licht 1980) also may be useful, but only as part of a larger program that focuses on skill training. Changing attributions without changing actual skill and performance may be misleading by convincing students they have needed abilities when in fact they do not.

CONCLUSION   One of the hopes of educators has been to adapt instruction to individual learners; learning strategy research suggests that we may also improve learning by adapting learners to teaching and the tasks. At elementary, secondary, and post-secondary levels, training in learning strategies and problem solving seems to be effective. Students change from the beginning to the end of a course, and in some cases transfer their learning beyond the training situation. Unfortunately, random assignment, appropriate controls, follow-up to determine long-term transfer of skills, and analysis of which components of the training are of most value—these desirable features of research—are difficult to achieve and provide ample scope for further research. Future research needs to address which strategies are effective for whom in what situations. In teaching both learning strategies and problem solving, there seem to be no quick, cheap, cure-alls. Explicit attention to these skills and strategies through direct extensive training and practice is needed for improved performance. Moreover, motivational and cognitive training components need to be synthesized in these programs.

FINAL THOUGHTS

It is over a decade since McKeachie's (1974) chapter on instructional psychology. What changes have occurred! The growth and progress of the field in just a decade is quite impressive. Despite the fact that educational research in 1974 was relatively much better supported by the government and foundations, today there are more journals, more articles, and more fields of research. Particularly noteworthy is the greater internationalization of the field. As our citations indicate, European, Asian, Australian, Latin American, and other researchers are making interesting and substantial contributions.

Substantively, local and middle-range theories and an overall cognitive approach give the field a much richer conceptual flavor. We now have a substantial corpus of ongoing research on the learning and teaching of school subjects, particularly reading and mathematics. Similar efforts are now going forward in writing, science, social science, music, physical education, and other fields. Product-oriented research oriented primarily to input and outcomes has merged into process-product research which in turn is beginning to be integrated with content-knowledge research. This offers hope for greater use by educators by providing them with the knowledge of how to teach content as well as how to run and manage a classroom. As research becomes more useful to teachers, they in turn are more likely to become teacher-researchers, creating local theories and testing the validity of concepts in their own day to day teaching.

As the field develops, global constructs are being looked at more analytically. Static conceptions of learners are evolving into more dynamic process-oriented theories. For example, "intelligence" and "motivation" are giving way to more componential, process descriptions of learners. Similarly, general principles of instructional design such as "Minimize learner errors," are yielding to more complex analyses of a learner's prior experience, strategies, information processing characteristics, the task demands, and a consideration of the levels of outcome.

What is the relationship of instructional psychology to instructional practice?

Some of the older prescriptions such as active learning are even more clearly indicated. A new one—direct teaching for metacognitive understanding of procedures, skills, and strategies—is emerging. At the same time, the increased complexity of analyses makes it more and more difficult to come up with simple prescriptions. Rather, the theories and results of instructional research form the schemata that will help teachers to interact effectively with unique students in unique classroom settings.

ACKNOWLEDGMENTS

We thank Allan Wigfield, Karen Wixson, and Phyllis Blumenfeld for comments on earlier drafts. Thanks also to Maria Huntley for typing the manuscript and to Diane Puhl and Rick Hensley for bibliographic assistance.

Literature Cited

Acredolo, C., Adams, A., Schmid, J. 1984. On the understanding of the relationships between speed, duration, and distance. *Child Dev.* 55:2151–59

Adams, M. J. 1984. Project intelligence. *Hum. Intell.* 5(4):8–9

Anderson, J. R. 1983. *The Architecture of Cognition*. Cambridge, MA: Harvard Univ. Press

Anderson, R., Kahl, S., Glass, G., Smith, M. 1983. Science education: A meta-analysis of major questions. *J. Res. Sci. Teach.* 20:379–85

Anderson, R., Osborn, J., Tierney, R. 1984. *Learning to Read in American Schools: Basal Readers and Content Texts*. Hillsdale, NJ: Erlbaum

Anzai, Y., Yokoyama, T. 1984. Internal models in physics problem solving. *Cognit. Instr.* 1:397–450

Applebee, A. N. 1984a. *Contexts for Learning to Write: Studies of Secondary School Instruction*. Norwood, NJ: Ablex

Applebee, A. N. 1984b. Writing and reasoning. *Rev. Educ. Res.* 54:577–96

Armento, B. 1986. Research on teaching social studies. See Wittrock 1986

Ashcraft, M. 1982. The development of mental arithmetic: A chronometric approach. *Dev. Rev.* 2:213–36

Ashcraft, M. 1983. Procedural knowledge versus fact retrieval in mental arithmetic: A reply to Baroody. *Dev. Rev.* 3:231–35

Ashcraft, M., Fierman, B. 1982. Mental addition in third, fourth, and sixth graders. *J. Exp. Child Psychol.* 33:216–34

Ashcraft, M., Fierman, B., Bartolotta, R. 1984. The production and verification tasks in mental addition: An empirical comparison. *Dev. Rev.* 4:157–70

Atkinson, J. W. 1964. *An Introduction to Motivation*. New York: Van Nostrand

Au, K., Kawakami, A. 1984a. Vygotskian perspectives on discussion processes in small group reading lessons. In *The Social Context of Instruction: Group Organization and Group Processes*, ed. P. Peterson, L. Wilkinson, M. Hallinan. New York: Academic

Au, K., Kawakami, A. 1984b. A conceptual framework for studying the long-term effects of comprehension instruction. *Q. Newsl. Lab. Comp. Hum. Cognit.* 6:95–100

Baker, E., Herman, J., Yeh, J. 1981. Fun and games: Their contribution to basic skills instruction in elementary school. *Am. Educ. Res. J.* 18(1):83–92

Baker, L. 1984. Children's effective use of multiple standards for evaluating their comprehension. *J. Educ. Psychol.* 76:588–97

Baker, L., Anderson, R. 1982. Effects of inconsistent information on text processing: Evidence for comprehension monitoring. *Read. Res. Q.* 17:281–94

Baker, L., Brown, A. 1984. Metacognitive skills and reading. See Pearson 1984a, pp. 353–94

Balke-Aurell, G. 1982. Changes in ability as related to educational and occupational experience. *Göteborg Studies in Educational Science*, No. 40. Göteborg, Sweden: Acta Univ. Göthoburgensis

Bandura, A. 1982. Self-efficacy mechanism in human agency. *Am. Psychol.* 37(2):122–47

Bangert-Drowns, R. L., Kulik, J. A., Kulik, C.-L. C. 1985. Effectiveness of computer-based education in secondary school. *J. Comp. Instr.* In press

Baroody, A. 1983. The development of procedural knowledge: An alternative explanation for chronometric trends of mental arithmetic. *Dev. Rev.* 3:225–30

Baroody, A. 1984. A reexamination of mental arithmetic models and data: A reply to Ashcraft. *Dev. Rev.* 4:148–56

Bartholomae, D. 1980. The study of error. *Coll. Compos. Commun.* 31:253–69

Beach, R., Bridwell, L. S. 1984. *New Directions in Composition Research.* New York: Guilford

Beagles-Roos, J., Gat, I. 1983. Specific impact of radio and television on children's story comprehension. *J. Educ. Psychol.* 75:(1)128–37

Beck, I. 1985. Comprehension instruction in the primary grades. In *Research Foundation for a Literate America,* ed. R. Anderson, J. Osborn, R. Tierney. Lexington, MA: Heath

Benjamin, M., McKeachie, W. J., Lin, Y., Holinger, D. P. 1981. Test anxiety: Deficits in information processing. *J. Educ. Psychol.* 73(6):816–24

Bereiter, C. 1962. Using tests to measure change. *Personnel Guid. J.* 20:6–11

Bereiter, C., Scardamalia, M. 1983. Levels of inquiry in writing research. See Mosenthal et al 1983, pp. 3–25

Berliner, D. 1983. Developing conceptions of classroom environments: Some light on the T in classroom studies of ATI. *Educ. Psychol.* 18:1–13

Berliner, D., Gage, N. 1976. The psychology of teaching methods. In *The Psychology of Teaching Methods.* Chicago: Univ. Chicago Press

Bertram, B., Collins, A., Rubin, A. D., Gentner, D. 1982. Three perspectives on writing. *Educ. Psychol.* 17(3):131–45

Besner, D., Waller, T., MacKinnon, E., eds. 1985. *Reading Research: Advances in Theory and Practice,* Vol. 5. New York: Academic

Biggs, J. B., Rihn, B. A. 1984. The effects of intervention on deep and surface approaches to learning. In *Cognitive Strategies and Educational Performance,* ed. J. Kirby. Orlando, FL: Academic

Blumenfeld, P. C., Hamilton, V. L., Bossert, S. T., Wessels, K., Meece, J. 1983. Teacher talk and student thought: Socialization into the student role. In *Teacher and Student Perceptions: Implications for Learning,* ed. J. Levine, M. Wang, pp. 143–92. Hillsdale, NJ: Erlbaum

Blumenfeld, P. C., Pintrich, P. R., Hamilton, V. L. 1985. Children's concepts of ability, effort and conduct. *Am. Educ. Res. J.* In press

Blumenfeld, P. C., Pintrich, P. R., Meece, J., Wessels, K. 1982. The formation and role of self perceptions of ability in elementary classrooms. *Elem. Sch. J.* 82(5):401–20

Blumenfeld, P. C., Mergendollar, J., Swarthout, D. 1985. Task as heuristics for understanding student learning and motivation. *J. Curr. Issues.* In press

Bossert, S. T. 1979. *Tasks and Social Relationships in Classrooms.* New York: Cambridge Univ. Press

Bovy, R. C. 1981. ECTJ/ERIC-IR Young Scholar Paper: Successful instructional methods: A cognitive information processing approach. *Educ. Commun. Technol. J.* 29:(4)203–18

Brainerd, C., ed. 1982. *Children's Logical and Mathematical Cognition.* New York: Springer-Verlag

Brainerd, C. 1983. Young children's mental arithmetic errors: A working-memory analysis. *Child Dev.* 54:812–30

Brattesani, K., Weinstein, R., Marshall, H. 1984. Student perceptions of differential teacher treatment as moderators of teacher expectation effects. *J. Educ. Psychol.* 76:236–47

Brezin, M. J. 1980. ECTJ/ERIC-IR Young Scholar Paper: Cognitive monitoring: From learning theory to instructional applications. *Educ. Commun. Technol. J.* 28:(4)243–66

Briars, D., Larkin, J. 1984. An integrated model of skill in solving elementary word problems. *Cognit. Instr.* 1:245–96

Bridwell, L. S. 1980. Revising strategies in twelfth grade students' transactional writing. *Res. Teach. Engl.* 14:197–222

Bridwell, L. S., Nancarrow, P. R., Ross, D. 1984. The writing process and the writing machine: Current research on word processors relevant to the teaching of composition. See Beach & Bridwell 1984, pp. 381–98

Brophy, J. 1981. Teacher praise: A functional analysis. *Rev. Educ. Res.* 51(1):5–32

Brophy, J. 1983. Conceptualizing student motivation. *Educ. Psychol.* 18(3):200–15

Brophy, J., Good, T. 1986. Teacher behavior and student achievement. See Wittrock 1986

Brophy, J., Rohrkemper, M., Rashid, H., Goldberger, M. 1983. Relationships between teachers' presentations of classroom tasks and students' engagement in those tasks. *J. Educ. Psychol.* 75(4):544–52

Brown, A. L., Bransford, J. D., Ferrara, R. A., Campione, J. C. 1983. Learning, remembering, and understanding. In *Handbook of Child Psychology,* ed. P. H. Mussen, 3:77–166. New York: Wiley. 4th ed.

Brown, A. L., Campione, J. C. 1985. Three faces of transfer: Implications for early competence, individual differences, and transfer. *Adv. Dev. Psychol.* 3:

Brown, A. L., Day, J., Jones, R. 1983. The development of plans for summarizing text. *Child Dev.* 54:968–79

Brown, A. L., Ferrara, R. 1985. Diagnosing zones of proximal development. In *Culture, Communication, and Cognition: Vygotskian Perspectives,* ed. J. Wertsch. New York: Cambridge Univ. Press

Brown, A. L., French, L. 1979. The zone of

potential development: Implications for intelligence testing in the year 2000. *Intelligence* 3:255–73

Brown, A. L., Pallincsar, A., Armbruster, B. 1984. Instructing comprehension-fostering activities in interactive learning situations. See Mandl et al 1984, pp. 255–86

Brown, J., VanLehn, K. 1980. Repair theory: A generative theory of bugs in procedural skills. *Cognit. Sci.* 4:379–426

Brown, J., VanLehn, K. 1982. Towards a generative theory of "bugs." See Carpenter et al 1982, pp. 117–35

Brown, J., Weiner, B. 1984. Affective consequences of ability vs. effort ascriptions: Controversies, resolutions, and quandaries. *J. Educ. Psychol.* 76(1):146–58

Brumby, M. 1982. Consistent differences in cognitive styles shown for qualitative biological problem-solving. *Br. J. Educ. Psychol.* 52:244–57

Bruning, I. L. 1983. ECTJ/ERIC-IR Young Scholar Paper: An information processing approach to a theory of instruction. *Educ. Commun. Technol. J.* 31:(2)91–102

Burstein, L., ed. 1983. Linking testing and instruction. *J. Educ. Meas.* 20(2):99–101 (Special issue)

Calfee, R. 1985. Home-grown tests have virtues, too. *Update: The Study of Stanford and the Schools* 2(1):3

Calfee, R., Drum, P. 1986. Research on teaching reading. See Wittrock 1986

Calfee, R., Piontkowski, D. 1981. The reading diary: Acquisition of decoding. *Read. Res. Q.* 16:346–73

Campione, J. C., Brown, A. L., Ferrara, R. A. 1982. Mental retardation and intelligence. In *Handbook of Human Intelligence*, ed. R. J. Sternberg, pp. 392–490. Cambridge: Cambridge Univ. Press

Campione, J. C., Brown, A., Ferrara, R., Bryant, N. 1984. The zone of proximal development: Implications for individual differences and learning. In *Children's learning in the "zone of proximal development"*, ed. B. Rogoff, J. Wertsch. *New Directions for Child Development*, No. 23, pp. 77–91. San Francisco: Jossey-Bass

Card, S. K., Moran, T. P., Newell, A. 1983. *The Psychology of Human-computer Interaction.* Hillsdale, NJ: Erlbaum

Carpenter, T., Moser, J. 1982. The development of addition and subtraction problem-solving skills. See Carpenter et al 1982, pp. 9–24

Carpenter, T., Moser, J. 1983. The acquisition of addition and subtraction concepts. See Lesh & Landau 1983, pp. 7–44

Carpenter, T., Moser, J., Romberg, T., eds. 1982. *Addition and Subtraction: A Cognitive Perspective.* Hillsdale, NJ: Erlbaum

Carr, T., ed. 1985. The development of reading skills. *New Directions in Child Development*, No. 27. San Francisco: Jossey-Bass

Carver, R. 1974. Two dimensions of tests: Psychometric and edumetric. *Am. Psychol.* 29:512–18

Casteñada, S., López, M., Romero, M. 1984. *Understanding the role of five induced learning strategies in scientific text comprehension.* Presented at Int. Congr. Psychol., Acapulco, Mexico

Champagne, A., Klopfer, L., Desena, A., Squires, D. 1981. Structural representations of students' knowledge before and after science instruction. *J. Res. Sci. Teach.* 18:97–111

Champagne, A., Klopfer, L., Gunstone, R. 1982. Cognitive research and design of science instruction. *Educ. Psychol.* 17:31–53

Chi, M., Feltovich, P., Glaser, R. 1981. Categorization and representation of physics problems by experts and novices. *Cognit. Sci.* 5:121–52

Chipman, S. F., Segal, J. W., Glaser, R., eds. 1985. *Thinking and Learning Skills: Current Research and Open Questions.* Hillsdale, NJ: Erlbaum

Clark, R. E. 1982. Antagonism between achievement and enjoyment in ATI studies. *Educ. Psychol.* 13:(2)92–101

Clark, R. E. 1983. Reconsidering research on learning from media. *Rev. Educ. Res.* 53:(4)445–59

Clark, R. E. 1984. "Where's the Beef?": A reply to Heinich. *Educ. Commun. Technol. J.* 32:(4)229–32

Clark, R. E. 1985. Confounding in educational computing research. *J. Educ. Comp. Res.* 1:(2)129–40

Clements, D. H., Gullo, D. F. 1984. Effects of computer programming on young children's cognition. *J. Educ. Psychol.* 76:(6)1051–64

Cobb, P., Steffe, L. 1983. The constructivist researcher as teacher and model builder. *J. Res. Math. Educ.* 14:83–94

Cohen, P. A., Ebeling, B. J., Kulik, J. A. 1981. A meta-analysis of outcome studies of visual-based instruction. *Educ. Commun. Technol. J.* 29:(1)26–36

Collins, A., Stevens, A. L. 1982. Goals and strategies of inquiry teachers. In *Advances in Instructional Psychology*, ed. R. Glaser, 2:65–119. Hillsdale, NJ: Erlbaum

Corno, L., Mandinach, E. 1983. The role of cognitive engagement in classroom learning and motivation. *Educ. Psychol.* 18:88–100

Corno, L., Snow, R. E. 1986. Adapting teaching to individual differences among learners. See Wittrock 1986

Covington, M. V. 1983. Motivated cognitions. In *Learning and Motivation in the Classroom*, ed. S. Paris, G. Olson, M. Stevenson, pp. 139–64. Hillsdale, NJ: Erlbaum

Covington, M. V. 1984. The self-worth theory

of achievement motivation: Findings and implications. *Elem. Sch. J.* 85:5–20

Covington, M. V., Beery, R. 1976. *Self-worth and School Learning.* New York: Holt, Rinehart & Winston

Covington, M. V., Omelich, C. L. 1979. Are causal attributions causal? A path analysis of the cognitive model of achievement motivation. *J. Pers. Soc. Psychol.* 37:1487–1504

Covington, M. V., Omelich, C. L. 1984. Controversies or consistencies? A reply to Brown and Weiner. *J. Educ. Psychol.* 76(1):159–68

Cronbach, L. J., Snow, R. E. 1977. *Aptitudes and Instructional Methods: A Handbook for Research on Interactions.* New York: Irvington

Culler, R. E., Holahan, C. J. 1980. Test anxiety and academic performance: The effects of study related behaviors. *J. Educ. Psychol.* 72:16–20

Curtis, M., Glaser, R. 1983. Reading theory and the assessment of reading achievement. *J. Educ. Meas.* 20:133–47

Dansereau, D. F. 1985. Learning strategy research. In *Thinking and Learning Skills: Relating Instruction to Basic Research,* ed. J. Segal, S. Chipman, R. Glaser, 1:209–40. Hillsdale, NJ: Erlbaum

de Bono, E. 1985. The CoRT thinking program. See Dansereau 1985, pp. 363–88

Downing, J., Leong, C. 1982. *Psychology of Reading.* New York: Macmillan

Doyle, W. 1983. Academic work. *Rev. Educ. Res.* 53(2):159–200

Doyle, W. 1986. Classroom organization and management. See Wittrock 1986

Duffy, G., Roehler, L., Mason, J. 1984. *Comprehension Instruction: Perspectives and Suggestions.* New York: Longman

Dweck, C. S., Elliott, E. S. 1983. Achievement motivation. In *Handbook of Child Psychology,* ed. P. H. Mussen, 4:643–91. New York: Wiley

Dweck, C. S., Licht, B. G. 1980. Learned helplessness and intellectual achievement. In *Human Helplessness: Theory and Applications,* ed. J. Garber, M. Seligman, pp. 197–211. New York: Academic

Eccles, J. 1983. Expectancies, values and academic behaviors. In *Achievement and Achievement Motives,* ed. J. T. Spence, pp. 75–146. San Francisco: Freeman

Faigley, L., Witte, S. 1981. Analyzing revision. *Coll. Compos. Commun.* 32:400–14

Feuerstein, R., Miller, R., Rand, Y., Jensen, M. 1981. Can evolving techniques better measure cognitive change? *J. Spec. Educ.* 15:201–19

Feuerstein, R., Rand, Y., Hoffman, M. B., Miller, R. 1980. *Instrumental Enrichment.* Baltimore: Univ. Park Press

Fischbein, E., Deri, M., Nello, M., Marino, M. 1985. The role of implicit models in solving verbal problems in multiplication and division. *J. Res. Math. Educ.* 16:3–17

Fisher, C., Berliner, D., eds. 1985. *Perspectives on Instructional Time.* New York: Longman

Flower, L., Hayes, J. R. 1981a. A cognitive process theory of writing. *Coll. Compos. Commun.* 32:365–87

Flower, L., Hayes, J. R. 1981b. The pregnant pause: An inquiry into the nature of planning. *Res. Teach. Engl.* 15:229–43

Flower, L., Hayes, J. R. 1984. Images, plans, and prose: The representation of meaning in writing. *Writ. Commun.* 1(1):120–60

Frase, L. T. 1984. Knowledge, information and action: Requirements for automated writing instruction. *J. Comput.-Based Instr.* 11:55–59

Frederiksen, C. H., Dominic, J. F. 1982. *Writing: The Nature, Development, and Teaching of Written Communication,* Vol. 2. Hillsdale, NJ: Erlbaum

Frederiksen, N. 1984a. Implications of cognitive theory for instruction in problem-solving. *Rev. Educ. Res.* 54:363–407

Frederiksen, N. 1984b. The real test bias: Influences of testing on teaching and learning. *Am. Psychol.* 39:193–202

Fuson, K., Hall, J. 1983. The acquisition of early number word meanings: A conceptual analysis and review. See Ginsburg 1983, pp. 50–109

Fuson, K., Richards, J., Briars, D. 1982. The acquisition and elaboration of the number word sequence. In *Children's Logical and Mathematical Cognition: Progress in Cognitive Developmental Research.* New York: Springer-Verlag

Gabel, D., Sherwood, R., Enochs, L. 1984. Problem-solving skills of high school chemistry students. *J. Res. Sci. Teach.* 21:221–33

Gagne, R. M. 1983. Some issues in the psychology of mathematics instruction. *J. Res. Math. Educ.* 14:7–18

Gagne, R. M., Dick, W. 1983. Instructional psychology. *Ann. Rev. Psychol.* 34:261–95

Gal'perin, P. Y. 1982. Intellectual capabilities among older preschool children: On the problem of training and mental development. In *Review of Child Development Research,* ed. W. Hartup, 6:526–46. Chicago: Univ. Chicago Press

Gardner, H. 1983. *Frames of Mind: The Theory of Multiple Intelligences.* New York: Basic Books

Garner, R., Macready, G., Wagoner, S. 1984. Readers' acquisition of the components of the text-lookback strategy. *J. Educ. Psychol.* 76:300–9

Garner, R., Wagoner, S., Smith, T. 1983. Externalizing question-answering strategies of good and poor comprehenders. *Read. Res. Q.* 18:439–47

Gelman, R. 1980. What young children know about numbers. *Educ. Psychol.* 15:54–68

Gelman, R., Gallistel, C. 1978. *The Child's Understanding of Number*. Cambridge, MA: Harvard Univ. Press

Gentner, D., Stevens, A. 1983. *Mental Models*. Hillsdale, NJ: Erlbaum

Ginsburg, H., ed. 1983. *The Development of Children's Mathematical Thinking*. New York: Academic

Glaser, R. 1980. General discussion: Relationships between aptitude, learning and instruction. In *Aptitude, Learning and Instruction*, Vol. 2, ed. R. Snow, P. Federico, W. Montague. Hillsdale, NJ: Erlbaum

Glaser, R. 1981. The future of testing: A research agenda for cognitive psychology and psychometrics. *Am. Psychol.* 36:923–36

Glaser, R. 1982a. The future of educational research. *Educ. Res.* 11(8):16–17

Glaser, R. 1982b. Instructional psychology: Past, present, and future. *Am. Psychol.* 37:(3)292–305

Glaser, R. 1984. Education and thinking—the role of knowledge. *Am. Psychol.* 39:93–104

Glaser, R., Bond, L., eds. 1981. Testing: Concepts, policy, practice, and research. *Am. Psychol.* 36(10):997–1000

Good, T., Grouws, D. 1979. The Missouri mathematics effectiveness project: An experimental study in fourth grade classrooms. *J. Educ. Psychol.* 71:355–62

Graham, E. E. 1981. Feuerstein's instrumental enrichment used to change cognitive and verbal behavior in a city-core, multi-ethnic Toronto Secondary School. *Diss. Abstr. Int.* 43-02-A:428. Toronto: Univ. Toronto

Graves, R. 1978. *Balance the Basics: Let Them Write*. New York: Ford Found.

Greeno, J. 1985. *Advancing cognitive science through instructional development of advanced systems*. Presented at AERA, Chicago

Guilford, J. P. 1982. Cognitive psychology's ambiguities: Some suggested remedies. *Psychol. Rev.* 89:48–59

Hacker, R. 1984. A hierarchy of intellectual development in science. *Br. J. Educ. Psychol.* 54:137–51

Hambleton, R., Swaminathan, H., Algina, J., Coulson, D. 1978. Criterion-referenced testing: A review of technical issues and developments. *Rev. Educ. Res.* 48:1–47

Haney, W. 1984. Testing reasoning and reasoning about testing. *Rev. Educ. Res.* 54:597–654

Hansen, J. 1981. The effects of inference training and practice on young children's reading comprehension. *Read. Res. Q.* 16:391–417

Hansen, J., Pearson, D. 1983. An instructional study: Improving the inferential comprehension of good and poor fourth-grade readers. *J. Educ. Psychol.* 75:821–29

Harris, P., Kruithoff, A., Terwogt, M., Visser, T. 1981. Children's detection and awareness of textual anomaly. *J. Exp. Child Psychol.* 31:212–30

Harter, S. 1985. Competence as a dimension of self-evaluation: Toward a comprehensive model of self-worth. In *The Development of the Self*, ed. R. Leahy. New York: Academic

Haywood, H. C., Arbitman-Smith, R. 1981. Modification of cognitive functions in slow-learning adolescents. In *Frontiers of Knowledge in Mental Retardation: Social, Educational, and Behavioral Aspects*, ed. P. Mittler, 1:129–40. Baltimore: Univ. Park Press

Heller, J., Reif, F. 1984. Prescribing effective human problem-solving processes: Problem description in physics. *Cognit. Instr.* 1:177–216

Herrnstein, R. J., Nickerson, R. S., de Sanchez, M., Swets, J. A., eds. 1983. *Project Intelligence: The Development of Procedures to Enhance Thinking Skills*. Final rep. to Minister for Development of Human Intelligence, The Republic of Venezuela. Harvard Univ. and Bolt, Beranek & Newman

Hewson, M., Hewson, P. 1983. Effects of instruction using students' prior knowledge and conceptual change strategies on science learning. *J. Res. Sci. Teach.* 20:731–43

Hill, K. T., Wigfield, A. 1984. Test anxiety: A major educational problem and what can be done about it. *Elem. Sch. J.* 85:105–26

Houlihan, D., Ginsburg, H. 1981. The addition methods of first- and second-grade children. *J. Res. Math. Educ.* 12:95–106

Hume, J. 1983. Research on the composing process. *Rev. Educ. Res.* 53(2):201–16

Jamison, D., Suppes, P., Wells, S. 1974. The effectiveness of alternative instructional media: A survey. *Rev. Educ. Res.* 44(1):1–67

Johansen, K. J., Tennyson, R. D. 1983. Effect of Adaptive Advisement on Perception in learner-controlled, computer-based instruction using a rule-learning task. *Educ. Commun. Technol. J.* 31:(4)226–36

Johnson, D., Baumann, J. 1984. Word identification. See D. Pearson 1984a, pp. 583–608

Johnston, J., Ettema, J. 1985. Using television to best advantage: Research for prosocial television. In *Perspectives on Media Effects*, ed. J. Bryant, D. Zillman. Hillsdale, NJ: Erlbaum

Johnston, P. 1984. Assessment in reading. See Pearson 1984a, pp. 147–84

Jones, B., McFee, J. 1986. Research on teaching art and aesthetics. See Wittrock 1986

Kiefer, K. E., Smith, C. R. 1983. Textual analysis with computers: Tests of Bell Laboratories' computer software. *Res. Teach. Engl.* 17:201–14

Kintsch, W., Greeno, J. 1985. Understanding and solving word arithmetic problems. *Psychol. Rev.* 92:109–29

Koslin, B., Koslin, S., Zeno, S. 1979. Towards an effectiveness measure in reading. In *Testing, teaching, and learning: Report of a conference on research on testing*, chair. R. Tyler, S. White. Washington, DC: NIE

Kozma, R. 1985. The implications of instructional psychology for the design of educational broadcast television. *Educ. Commun. Technol. J.* In press

Krendl, K. A., Watkins, B. 1983. Understanding television: An exploratory inquiry into the reconstruction of narrative content. *Educ. Commun. Technol. J.* 31:(4)201–12

Kulik, C.-L. C., Kulik, J. A. 1985. *Effectiveness of Computer-based Education in College*. Ann Arbor: Cent. Res. Learn. Teach.

Kulik, C.-L. C., Kulik, J. A., Shwalb, B. J. 1983. College programs for high-risk and disadvantaged students: A meta-analysis of findings. *Rev. Educ. Res.* 53:397–414

Kulik, J. A., Bangert-Drowns, R. L. 1983. Effectiveness of technology in precollege mathematics and science teaching. *J. Educ. Tech. Syst.* 12:(2)137–58

Kulik, J. A., Cohen, P. A., Ebeling, B. J. 1980. Effectiveness of programmed instruction in higher education: A meta-analysis of findings. *Educ. Eval. Policy Anal.* 2:(6)51–64

Kulik, J. A., Kulik, C-L. C., Bangert-Drowns, R. L. 1985. Effectiveness of computer-based education in elementary schools. *Comp. Hum. Behav.* In press

Kulik, J. A., Kulik, C.-L. C., Cohen, P. A. 1979. A meta-analysis of outcome studies of Keller's Personalized System of Instruction. *Am. Psychol.* 34:(4)307–18

Kyllonen, P. C., Alluisi, E. A. 1985. Learning and forgetting facts and skills. In *Handbook of Human Factors/Ergonomics*, ed. G. Salvendy. New York: Wiley. In press

Larkin, J., Rainard, B. 1984. A research methodology for studying how people think. *J. Res. Sci. Teach.* 21:235–54

Larson, C. O., Dansereau, D. F., O'Donnell, A., Hythecker, V., Lambiotte, J. G., Rocklin, T. 1984. Verbal ability and cooperative learning: Transfer effects. *J. Read. Behav.* 16:(4)289–95

Lepper, M. 1985. Microcomputers in education: Motivational and social issues. *Am. Psychol.* 40:(1)1–18

Lesh, R., Landau, M., eds. 1983. *Acquisition of Mathematics Concepts and Processes*. London: Academic

Levie, W., Dickie, K. 1973. The analysis and application of media. In *Second Handbook of Research on Teaching*, ed. R. Travers. Chicago: Rand McNally

Lipsey, M. 1983. A scheme for assessing measurement sensitivity in program evaluation and other applied research. *Psychol. Bull.* 94:152–65

Luiten, J., Ames, W., Ackerson, G. 1980. A meta-analysis of the effects of advance organizers on learning and retention. *Am. Educ. Res. J.* 17:211–18

MacKenzie, C. L., Marteniuk, R. G. 1985. Motor skill. *Can. J. Psychol.* In press

MacKenzie, A. A., White, R. T. 1982. Fieldwork in geography and long-term memory structures. *Am. Educ. Res. J.* 19:623–32

Maehr, M. 1983. On doing well in science: Why Johnny no longer excels; why Sarah never did. In *Learning and Motivation in the Classroom*, ed. S. Paris, G. Olson, H. Stevenson, pp. 179–210. Hillsdale, NJ: Erlbaum

Mandl, H., Stein, N., Trabasso, T., eds. 1984. *Learning and Comprehension of Text*. Hillsdale, NJ: Erlbaum

Markman, E., Gorin, L. 1981. Children's ability to adjust their standards for evaluating comprehension. *J. Educ. Psychol.* 73:320–25

Marton, F., Säljö, R. 1976. On qualitative differences in learning: I. Outcome and process. *Br. J. Educ. Psychol.* 46:4–11

Mayer, R. 1979. Can advance organizers influence meaningful learning? *Rev. Educ. Res.* 49:371–83

McCloskey, M., Kohl, D. 1983. Naive physics: The curvilinear impetus principle and its role in interactions with moving objects. *J. Exp. Psychol: Learn. Mem. Cognit.* 9:146–56

McCombs, B. L. 1984. *Metacognitive and cognitive components of motivation: Teaching self-awareness and self-management via a problem-solving approach*. Presented at AERA, New Orleans

McKeachie, W. J. 1974. Instructional psychology. *Ann. Rev. Psychol.* 26:161–93

McKeachie, W. J. 1984. Does anxiety disrupt information processing or does poor information processing lead to anxiety? *Int. Rev. Appl. Psychol.* 33:187–203

McKeachie, W. J., Pintrich, P. R., Lin, Y-G. 1985. Learning to learn. In *Cognition, Information Processing and Motivation*, ed. G. d'Ydwelle, pp. 601–18. Amsterdam: Elsevier

Menges, R. J., Girard, D. L. 1985. Development of a research specialty: Instructional psychology portrayed in *The Annual Review of Psychology*. *Instr. Sci.* 12:83–98

Mercer, J. 1979. *System of Multicultural Pluralistic Assessment (SOMPA) Technical Manual*. New York: Psychol. Corp.

Meringoff, L. K. 1980. Influence of the medium on children's story apprehension. *J. Educ. Psychol.* 72:(2)240–49

Messick, S. 1983. Assessment of children. In *Handbook of Child Psychology*, ed. P. H. Mussen, 1:477–526. New York: Wiley. 4th ed.

Messick, S. 1984a. Abilities and knowledge in educational achievement testing: The assessment of dynamic cognitive structures. In *Social and Technical Issues in Testing: Implications for Test Construction and Usage*, ed. B. Plake. Hillsdale, NJ: Erlbaum

Messick, S. 1984b. The psychology of educational assessment. *J. Educ. Meas.* 21:215–37

Mezynski, K. 1983. Issues concerning the acquisition of knowledge: Effects of vocabulary training on reading comprehension. *Rev. Educ. Res.* 53:253–79

Morris, L. W., Davis, M., Hutchings, C. 1981. Cognitive and emotional components of anxiety: Literature review and a revised worry-emotionality scale. *J. Educ. Psychol.* 73:541–55

Mosenthal, P. 1983. Describing classroom writing competence: A paradigmatic perspective. *Rev. Educ. Res.* 53(2):217–51

Mosenthal, P., Tamor, L., Walmsley, S. 1983. *Research on Writing: Principles and Methods*. New York: Longman

Narrol, H., Silverman, H., Waksman, M. 1982. Developing cognitive potential in vocational high school students. *J. Educ. Res.* 76(2):107–12

Nesher, P. 1982. Levels of description in the analysis of addition and subtraction word problems. See Carpenter et al 1982, pp. 25–38

Nicholls, J. G. 1978. The development of the concepts of effort and ability, perception of academic attainment and the understanding that difficult tasks require more ability. *Child. Dev.* 49:800–14

Nicholls, J. G. 1984. Achievement motivation: Conceptions of ability, subjective experience, task choice, and performance. *Psychol. Rev.* 91:328–46

Nicholls, J. G., Miller, A. T. 1983. The differentiation of the concepts of difficulty and ability. *Child Dev.* 54:951–59

Omanson, R., Beck, I., Voss, J., McKeown, M. 1984. The effects of reading lessons on comprehension: A processing description. *Cognit. Instr.* 1:45–68

O'Neil, H. F., Anderson, C. L., Freeman, J. A. 1986. Research in teaching in the armed forces. See Wittrock 1986

Orasanu, J., ed. 1985. *A Decade of Reading Research: Implications for Practice*. Hillsdale, NJ: Erlbaum. In press

Pallincsar, A., Brown, A. 1984. Reciprocal teaching of comprehension-fostering and comprehension-monitoring activities. *Cognit. Instr.* 1:117–76

Paris, S. G., Cross, D. R. 1983. Ordinary

learning: Pragmatic connections among children's beliefs, motives and actions. In *Learning in Children: Progress in Cognitive Development Research*, ed. J. Bisanz, G. Bisanz, R. Kail. New York: Springer-Verlag

Paris, S., Cross, D., Lipson, M. 1984. Informed strategies for learning: A program to improve children's reading awareness and comprehension. *J. Educ. Psychol.* 76:1239–52

Paris, S., Jacobs, J. 1984. The benefits of informed instruction for children's reading awareness and comprehension skills. *Child Dev.* 55:2083–93

Paris, S., Jacobs, J., Cross, D. 1985. Toward an individualistic psychology of exceptional children. In *Intelligence and Cognition in Special Children: Perspectives on Mental Retardation, Learning Disabilities, and Giftedness*, ed. J. Borkowski, J. Day. New York: Ablex. In press

Paris, S., Lipson, M., Wixson, K. 1983. Becoming a strategic reader. *Contemp. Educ. Psychol.* 8:293–316

Paris, S., Myers, M. 1981. Comprehension monitoring, memory, and study strategies of good and poor readers. *J. Read. Behav.* 13:5–22

Paulman, R. G., Kennelly, K. J. 1984. Test anxiety and ineffective test taking: Different names, same construct? *J. Educ. Psychol.* 76(2):279–88

Pea, R. D., Kurland, D. M. 1984. On the cognitive effects of learning computer programming. *New Ideas Psychol.* 2:(2)137–68

Pearson, D., ed. 1984a. *Handbook of Reading Research*. New York: Longman

Pearson, D. 1984b. Direct explicit instruction of reading comprehension. See Duffy et al 1984

Pearson, D. 1985. Reading comprehension instruction: Six necessary changes. *Read. Teach.* 38:724–38

Pearson, D., Gallagher, M. 1983. The instruction of reading comprehension. *Contemp. Educ. Psychol.* 8:317–44

Pearson, D., Tierney, R. 1983. In search of a model of instructional research in reading. In *Learning and Motivation in the Classroom* ed. S. Paris, G. Olson, H. Stevenson, pp. 39–60. Hillsdale, NJ: Erlbaum

Peterson, C., Seligman, M. 1984. Causal explanations as a risk factor for depression: Theory and evidence. *Psychol. Rev.* 91 (3):347–74

Peterson, P. L., Swing, S. R., Braverman, M. T., Buss, R. 1982. Students' aptitudes and their reports of cognitive processes during direct instruction. *J. Educ. Psychol.* 74(4):535–47

Peterson, P. L., Swing, S. R., Stark, K. D., Waas, G. A. 1984. Students' cognitions and time on task during mathematics instructions. *Am. Educ. Res. J.* 21(3):487–516

Potter, F. 1982. The use of linguistic context: Do good and poor readers use different strategies? *Br. J. Educ. Psychol.* 52:16–23

Pressley, M., Levin, J. 1983a. *Cognitive Strategy Research: Educational Applications.* New York: Springer-Verlag

Pressley, M., Levin, J. 1983b. *Cognitive Strategy Research: Psychological Foundations.* New York: Springer-Verlag

Reif, F., Heller, J. 1982. Knowledge structures and problem solving in physics. *Educ. Psychol.* 17:102–27

Reigeluth, C. M., ed. 1983. *Instructional-design Theories and Models: An Overview of Their Current Status.* Hillsdale, NJ: Erlbaum

Resnick, L. B. 1981. Instructional psychology. *Ann. Rev. Psychol.* 32:659–704

Resnick, L. B. 1982. Syntax and semantics in learning to subtract. See Carpenter et al 1982

Resnick, L. B. 1983. A developmental theory of number understanding. See Ginsburg 1983, pp. 110–52

Resnick, L. B. 1985. Constructing knowledge in school. In *Development and Learning: Conflict or Congruence?,* ed. L. Liben, D. Feldman. Hillsdale, NJ: Erlbaum. In press

Resnick, L., Ford, W. 1981. *The Psychology of Mathematics for Instruction.* Hillsdale, NJ: Erlbaum

Resnick, L., Omanson, S. 1985. Learning to understand arithmetic. In *Advances in Instructional Psychology,* Vol. 3, ed. R. Glaser. Hillsdale, NJ: Erlbaum. In press

Riley, M., Greeno, J., Heller, J. 1983. Development of children's problem-solving ability in arithmetic. See Ginsburg 1983

Romberg, T., Carpenter, T. 1986. Research on teaching and learning mathematics: Two disciplines of scientific enquiry. See Wittrock 1986

Rosenshine, B. 1983. Teaching functions in instructional programs. *Elem. Sch. J.* 83: 335–51

Rosenshine, B., Stevens, R. 1984. Classroom instruction in reading. See Pearson 1984a, pp. 745–98

Rosenshine, B., Stevens, R. 1986. Teaching functions. See Wittrock 1986

Ross, J., Maynes, F. 1983. Experimental problem solving: An instructional field experiment. *J. Res. Sci. Teach.* 20:543–56

Rubenstein, R., Hersh, H. 1984. *The Human Factor—Designing Computer Systems for People.* Burlington: Digital Press

Saettler, P. 1968. *A History of Instructional Technology.* New York: McGraw-Hill

Salomon, G. 1974. What is learned and how it is taught: The interaction between media, message, task, and learner. In *Media and Symbols,* ed. D. Olson. Chicago: Univ. Chicago Press

Salomon, G. 1978. On the future of media research. *Educ. Commun. Technol. J.* 26: (1)37–46

Salomon, G. 1979. *Interaction of Media, Cognition, and Learning.* San Francisco: Jossey-Bass

Salomon, G. 1983. The differential investment of mental effort in learning from different sources. *Educ. Psychol.* 18:(1)42–50

Salomon, G. 1984. On ability development and far transfer: reflections on Pea and Kurland's paper. *New Ideas Psychol.* 2:169–76

Salomon, G., Gardner, H. 1984. The computer as educator: Lessons from television research. Cambridge: Project Zero, Harvard Univ.

Savell, J. M., Rachford, D. L., Twohig, P. T. 1984. *Empirical Status of Feurstein's "Instrumental Enrichment" (FIE) Technique as a Method of Teaching Thinking Skills.* Washington, DC: US Army Res. Inst.

Scardamalia, M., Bereiter, C. 1982. Assimilative processes in composition planning. *Educ. Psychol.* 17(3):165–71

Scardamalia, M., Bereiter, C. 1986. Written composition. See Wittrock 1986

Scarr, S. 1981. Testing *for* children: Assessment and the many determinants of intellectual competence. *Am. Psychol.* 36:1159–66

Schneiderman, B. 1980. *Software Psychology: Human Factors in Computer and Information Systems.* Boston: Little, Brown

Schoenfeld, A. H. 1982. Measures of problem-solving performance and of problem-solving instruction. *J. Res. Math. Educ.* 13:31–49

Schramm, W. 1977. *Big Media, Little Media.* Beverly Hills: Sage

Schwartz, J., Taylor, E. 1978. Valid assessment of complete behavior: The TORQUE approach. *Q. News. Inst. Comp. Hum. Dev.* 2:54–58

Schwartz, J., Taylor, E. 1979. Project TORQUE. In *Testing, Teaching, and Learning: Report of a conference on research on testing.* Washington, DC: NIE

Secada, W., Fuson, K., Hall, J. 1983. The transition from counting-all to counting-on in addition. *J. Res. Math. Educ.* 14:47–57

Segal, J., Chipman, S., Glaser, R., eds. 1985. *Thinking and Learning Skills: Relating Instruction to Basic Research,* Vol. 1. Hillsdale, NJ: Erlbaum

Shapiro, D. C., Schmidt, R. A. 1982. The schema theory: Recent evidence and developmental implications. In *The Development of Motor Control and Coordination,* ed. J. Kelso, J. Clark, pp. 113–50. New York: Wiley

Shavelson, R. 1981. Teaching mathematics: Contributions of cognitive research. *Educ. Psychol.* 16:23–44

Shuell, T. J. 1980. Learning theory, instructional theory and adaption. In *Aptitude, Learning and Instruction*, Vol. 2, ed. R. Snow, P. Federico, W. Montague. Hillsdale, NJ: Erlbaum

Shulman, L. S. 1986. Paradigms and research programs in the study of teaching: A contemporary perspective. See Wittrock 1986

Siegler, R. 1981. Developmental sequences within and between concepts. *Monogr. Soc. Res. Child. Dev.* 46:(2, 189)

Simon, H. A. 1981. *The Sciences of the Artificial*. Cambridge: MIT Press. 2nd ed.

Smith, M., Good, R. 1984. Problem solving and classical genetics: Successful versus unsuccessful performance. *J. Res. Sci. Teach.* 21:895–912

Snow, R. E., Lohman, D. F. 1984. Toward a theory of cognitive aptitude for learning from instruction. *J. Educ. Psychol.* 76(3):347–76

Sommers, N. 1980. Revision strategies of student writers and experienced adult writers. *Coll. Compos. Commun.* 31:378–88

Starkey, P., Gelman, R. 1982. The development of addition and subtraction abilities prior to formal schooling in arithmetic. See Carpenter et al 1982

Steffe, L., Blake, R. 1983. Seeking meaning in mathematics instruction: A response to Gagne. *J. Res. Math. Educ.* 14:210–13

Sternberg, R. J. 1983. Criteria for intellectual skills training. *Educ. Res.* 12:6–12

Sternberg, R. J. 1985. *Beyond IQ*. Cambridge: Cambridge Univ. Press

Tennyson, R. 1980. Instructional control strategies and content structure as design variables in concept acquisition using computer-based instruction. *J. Educ. Psychol.* 72(4):525–32

Tennyson, R. D. 1981. Use of adaptive information for advisement in learning concepts and rules using computer-assisted instruction. *Am. Educ. Res. J.* 18:(4)425–38

Tennyson, R. D., Buttrey, T. 1980. Advisement and management strategies as design variables in computer-assisted instruction. *Educ. Commun. Technol. J.* 28:(3)169–76

Tierney, R., Cunningham, J. 1984. Research on teaching reading comprehension. See Pearson 1984a, pp. 609–56

Tobias, S. 1982. When do instructional methods make a difference? *Educ. Res.* 11:(4)4–10

Tyler, R. 1979. Educational objectives and educational testing: Problems now faced. See Tyler & White 1979

Tyler, R., White, S., chair. 1979. *Testing, teaching, and learning: Report of a conference on research on testing*. Washington, DC: NIE

Undheim, J. O. 1981a. On intelligence I: Broad ability factors in 15-year-old children and Cattell's theory of fluid and crystallized intelligence. *Scand. J. Psychol.* 22:171–79

Undheim, J. O. 1981b. On intelligence II: A neo-spearman model to replace Cattell's theory of fluid and crystallized intelligence. *Scand. J. Psychol.* 22:181–87

Undheim, J. O. 1981c. On intelligence III: Examining developmental implications of Cattell's broad ability theory and of an alternative neo-spearman model. *Scand. J. Psychol.* 22:243–49

Undheim, J. O. 1981d. On intelligence IV: Toward a restoration of general intelligence. *Scand. J. Psychol.* 22:251–56

van Dijk, T., Kintsch, W. 1983. *Strategies of Discourse Comprehension*. New York: Academic

Vergnaud, G. 1982. Cognitive and developmental psychology and research in mathematics education: Some theoretical and methodological issues. *For. Learn. Math.* 3:(2)31–41

Voss, J. F., Greene, T. R., Post, T. A., Penner, B. C. 1985. Problem solving skill in the social sciences. In *The Psychology of Learning and Motivation: Advances in Research and Theory*, ed. G. Bower. New York: Academic

Vygotsky, L. 1978. *Mind in Society: The Development of Higher Psychological Processes*, ed. and transl. M. Cole, V. John-Steiner, S. Scribner, E. Souberman. Cambridge, MA: Harvard Univ. Press

Wachsmuth, I. 1983. Skill automaticity in mathematics instruction: A response to Gagne. *J. Res. Math. Educ.* 14:204–9

Wagoner, S. 1983. Comprehension monitoring: What it is and what we know about it. *Read. Res. Q.* 18:328–46

Walberg, H., Pascarella, E., Haertel, G., Junker, L., Boulanger, D. 1982. Probing a model of educational productivity in high school science with national assessment samples. *J. Educ. Psychol.* 74:295–307

Wales, C. E., Stager, R. A. 1977. *Guided Design*. Morgantown, WV: Cent. Guided Design, Univ. West Virginia

Waller, T., MacKinnon, E., eds. 1984. *Reading Research: Advances in Theory and Practice*, Vol. 4. New York: Academic

Weiner, B. 1979. A theory of motivation for some classroom experiences. *J. Educ. Psychol.* 71:3–25

Weiner, B. 1983. Some methodological pitfalls in attributional research. *J. Educ. Psychol.* 75(4):530–43

Weinstein, C. E., Mayer, R. E. 1986. The teaching of learning strategies. See Wittrock 1986

Weinstein, C. E., Underwood, V. L. 1985. Learning strategies: The *how* of learning. In *Thinking and Learning Skills: Relating In-*

struction to Basic Research, ed. J. Segal, S. Chipman, R. Glaser. Hillsdale, NJ: Erlbaum

Weinstein, R. 1983. Student perceptions of schooling. *Elem. Sch. J.* 83:287–312

Whimbey, A., Lockhead, J. 1980. *Problem Solving and Comprehension.* Philadelphia: Franklin Inst. Press

White, B. 1984. Designing computer games to help physics students understand Newton's laws of motion. *Cognit. Instr.* 1:69–108

White, R., Tisher, R. 1986. Natural science. See Wittrock 1986

Whitehurst, G., ed. 1984. The development of reading. *Dev. Rev.* 4(1) (Special issue)

Whiteman, M. F. 1982. *Writing: The Nature, Development and Teaching of Written Communication,* Vol. 1. Hillsdale, NJ: Erlbaum

Whitener, W. T. 1983. Comparison of two approaches to teaching band. *J. Res. Music Educ.* 31:5–13

Wilkening, F. 1981. Integrating velocity, time, and distance information: A developmental study. *Cognit. Psychol.* 13:231–47

Wine, J. D. 1980. Cognitive-attentional theory of test anxiety. In *Test Anxiety: Theory Research and Applications,* ed. I. Sarason. Hillsdale, NJ: Erlbaum

Winn, W. 1982. Visualization in learning and instruction: A cognitive approach. *Educ. Commun. Technol. J.* 30:(1)3–25

Winne, P. 1979. Experiments relating teachers' use of higher cognitive questions to student achievement. *Rev. Educ. Res.* 49:13–50

Winograd, P. 1984. Strategic difficulties in summarizing texts. *Read. Res. Q.* 19:404–25

Wittrock, M., ed. 1986. *The Handbook of Research on Teaching.* New York: Macmillan. In press. 3rd ed.

Wong, P., Weiner, B. 1981. When people ask "why" questions and the heuristics of attributional search. *J. Pers. Soc. Psychol.* 40:650–63

Yager, S., Johnson, D. W., Johnson, R. T. 1985. Oral discussion, group-to-individual transfer, and achievement in cooperative learning groups. *J. Educ. Psychol.* 77(1):60–66

Yitzhak, V. 1981. The effect of Feuerstein's instrumental enrichment program on the cognitive reasoning of retarded performers as measured by Piaget's conservation tasks. *Diss. Abstr. Int.* 42-10A:4407. Toronto: Univ. Toronto

Zweng, M., Green, T., Kilpatrick, J., Pollack, H., Suydam, M., eds. 1983. *Proc. 4th Int. Congr. Math. Educ.* Boston: Birkhauser

AUTHOR INDEX

(Names appearing in capital letters indicate authors of chapters in this volume.)

A

Aboud, F. E., 552
Abrams, R., 587
Abrams, T. W., 447, 449
Abramson, L. Y., 593
Abzug, C., 435, 473
Acker, S. R., 5
Ackerson, G., 622
Acosta-Urquidi, J., 454, 469
Acredolo, C., 636
Acredolo, L. P., 154
Adam, G., 439
Adams, A., 154, 636
Adams, D. J., 463
Adams, J. C., 471
Adams, M. J., 638
Adams, P. R., 462-64
Adams, R. D., 435
Adams, W. B., 464, 469
Adejumo, D., 549
Adler, L. L., 539
Adler, N., 553
Aggazzotti, A., 439
Aghajanian, G. K., 90
Agras, W. S., 335
Ahammer, I. M., 531
Ahles, T. A., 336
Ahlström, K. G., 5
Ahmed, P. I., 531
Ahrentzen, S., 400, 401
Ahumada, A. J., 501
Aiello, J. R., 393, 394, 396
Aine, C. J., 45
Ainsworth, M. D. S., 144, 147
Aitken, L. M., 441
Ajzen, I., 268
Akil, H., 96
Alba, J. W., 258, 259, 282
Albaum, G. S., 260
Albert, L. H., 94
Albrecht, P., 298
Alderman, M. H., 334
Alesandrini, K. L., 277
Alexander, R. A., 358, 369, 370
Algina, J., 627
Alho, H., 96
Alkon, D. L., 434, 435, 440, 442, 443, 445, 447-50, 453-56, 462, 463, 465, 469, 477
Allan, A. M., 462
Allen, G. J., 333
Allen, J. G., 236, 244
Alliger, G. M., 370
Allon, N., 450, 474, 475
Alloy, L. B., 593

Alluisi, E. A., 637
Altman, I., 381, 399, 401, 402
Amadeo, M., 304, 305
Amato, P. R., 393, 396
Ambron, S. R., 203, 207, 216, 219
American Psychological Association, 531
Ames, E. W., 139, 142
Ames, W., 622
AMIR, Y., 17-41
Ammons, W. S., 95
ANASTASI, A., 1-15; 3, 9, 10
Anda, E., 439
Andersen, P., 451, 477
Anderson, A. E., 126
Anderson, A. H., 153
Anderson, A. M., 172-74
Anderson, C. A., 394
Anderson, C. D., 279, 365
Anderson, C. J., 150
Anderson, C. L., 459, 637
Anderson, D. C., 394
Anderson, D. J., 441
Anderson, J. R., 282, 386, 614
Anderson, R., 627, 628, 636
Andrade, R., 90
Andrasik, F., 336, 337
Andreasen, N. C., 296, 297
Andrews, G., 323-25
Andrykowski, M. A., 336
Anholt, R., 461
Anisfeld, E., 149
Anisman, H., 85, 88, 90
Annis, H. M., 332
Annis, R. C., 527
Antelman, S. M., 89-91
Antes, J. R., 589
Anthony, A., 153
Anthony, B. J., 45, 46
Anton, W. E., 10
Antonucci, T. C., 147
Anttonen, R. G., 235
Anzai, Y., 636
Apfelbaum, M., 114
Applebee, A. N., 632
Appleton, H., 216
Appleyard, D., 390
Aptekar, L. S., 533
Arbitman-Smith, R., 638
Arevalo, W., 424
Argyle, M., 529
Ariel, R. N., 295
Armbruster, B., 630
Armento, B., 637
Armitage, G., 121
Armstrong, C. M., 461

Armstrong, J. G., 356
Arnold, M. A., 95
Arnt, J., 92
Arvey, R. D., 12, 370, 371
Asanuma, H., 435, 473, 475
Asarnow, R. F., 301
Ash, R. A., 354
Ashcraft, M., 634, 635
Ashmore, J. F., 501, 503
Ashmore, R. D., 233
Ashworth, S., 371
Aslin, R. N., 151
Assimacopoulos-Jeannet, F., 127
Aston-Jones, G., 88
Atkin, A., 439
Atkinson, J. W., 616
Atwood, H. L., 446
Au, K., 630
Auerbach, J., 300
Austin, E. J., 367
Autry, J. H., 337, 338
Ax, A. F., 573
Ayalon, M., 310
Ayvalioglu, N., 554
Azgad, Z., 554
Azmitia, E. C., 87, 96

B

Babad, E. Y., 240
Babtista, L. F., 177
Bachman, J. G., 364
Bagara, B., 536
Bagozzi, R. P., 268, 272, 274
Bahn, K. D., 278
Baile, C. A., 93
Bailey, C. H., 448
Bakal, D. A., 336
Bakan, P., 588
Baker, E., 619
Baker, H. G., 369
Baker, L., 628
Baker, P. F., 461, 462
Baker, R., 533
Balke-Aurell, G., 613
Ball, K., 513
Ball, R., 298
Balota, D. A., 52, 60
Balzer, W. K., 355, 356
Bandura, A., 8, 141, 615
Bangert-Drowns, R. L., 363, 618
Banks, M. H., 354
Banks, M. S., 139
Banks, W. P., 56
Bar-Tal, D., 30, 546
Bar-Zahar, Y., 546

653

Baran, K. W., 144
Barber, T. X., 235
Bard, E. G., 153
Bard, P., 439
Barden, R. C., 592, 593, 595, 596
Barefoot, J. C., 569
Barge, B. N., 364
Bargh, J. A., 47, 62, 64
Baribeau-Braun, J., 304, 305, 307
Barlow, D. H., 330, 331
Barlow, H. B., 496, 498, 500, 502-7, 511, 512
Barnes-Farrell, J. L., 357
Barnett, G. O., 424
Barnhardt, T. N., 589
Baron, R. A., 394
Baron, R. S., 569
Baroody, A., 635
Barrett, D. E., 150
Barrett, G. V., 358, 369, 370
Barrett, J. N., 463
Barrett, P. Q., 467
Barrionuevo, G., 451, 478
Barrows, T. S., 531
Barry, H., 525, 526, 533, 549
Barshir, I., 554
Bartfai, T., 467-69
Bartholomae, D., 626
Bartko, J., 308
Bartlett, C. J., 357
Bartlett, F. C., 47
Bartlett, J. C., 591, 592, 596
Bartolotta, R., 635
Bartus, R. T., 87
Bates, E., 535
Bateson, P., 151
Batra, R., 271, 274
Baudry, M., 98
Bauer, R. A., 260
Baum, A., 382, 383, 392-94, 396, 397
Baum, C. S., 382, 392, 396
Baumann, J., 629
Baumeister, A. A., 92
Baxter, B., 352
Bayer, R., 416, 421
Baylor, D. A., 501, 503-5
Beach, F. A., 435
Beach, R., 631
Beagles-Roos, J., 619
Beales, H., 275
Bearden, W. O., 280
Beattie, A. E., 265
Beck, A. T., 328, 333, 337, 341, 423
Beck, I., 629
Beck, J. G., 330, 331
Beck, L. H., 301
Becker, B. E., 370
Becker, F. D., 400
Becker, H., 252

Becklen, R., 58, 59, 63
Bedeian, A. G., 361
Bedell, J., 10
Beeghly, M., 140, 144
Beer, B., 87
Beery, R., 615
Beez, W., 235
Begleiter, H., 305
Beit-Hallahmi, B., 33
Bekoff, M., 576
Belch, G. E., 275
Belk, R. W., 278
Bell, B., 539
Bellack, A. S., 329, 334
Bellington, C. J., 125
Belluzzi, J. D., 88
Belsky, J., 147
Bem, D. J., 248, 249
Bem, S. L., 239, 245, 246
BEN-ARI, R., 17-41; 40
Benardo, L. S., 469
Benedict, R., 541
Benjamin, M., 616
Bennett, E. L., 448
Bennett, G. K., 10, 11
Bennett, J., 587
Bennett, M. V. L., 459
Benson, C. E., 274
Benson, D. F., 587
Benson, J. A., 464
Benson, P. G., 357
Bent, R., 206
Bentler, P. M., 268
Bentz, V. J., 365
Benzschawel, T., 510, 512
Berdahl, K., 551
Bereiter, C., 627, 631, 632
Bereiter, D. A., 95
Berg, E. A., 296
Berg, R. A., 295, 296
Berger, P. A., 87, 293, 296, 297, 304, 305
Berger, T. W., 442
Bergin, A. E., 324
Berglass, S., 249
Berletich, M., 551
Berlin, B., 535
Berliner, D., 618, 622, 623
Berman, J. S., 324
Bernard, C., 110
Bernard, G. D., 511
Bernstein, M., 538
Berridge, M. J., 467
Berrios, N., 91
Berry, J. W., 525-29, 531, 532, 537-39, 541
Berry, S. D., 442
Berscheid, E., 236, 239, 244, 252
Berthier, N. E., 448, 450
Bertram, B., 631
Besner, D., 627
Best, D. L., 550, 551

Beswick, F. B., 451
Betancourt, H., 544
BETTMAN, J. R., 257-89; 259, 261, 263-65, 273, 277
Beutler, L. E., 328, 340
Biederman, I., 47
Biegon, A., 96
Biehal, G., 263, 264
Biehal, G. J., 261
Biel, A., 382, 390, 391
Bierley, C., 278
Bierman, K. L., 322, 323
Bigelow, G. E., 333
Bigelow, L. B., 296, 297
Biggs, J. B., 639
Bignami, G., 85
Binder, J. L., 337
Bindman, L. J., 450, 457, 476
Binet, A., 1, 6
Biran, M., 330
Birdsall, T. G., 498, 512, 513
Birkhead, T. R., 170
Birley, J. L., 308
Birnbaum, M. H., 367
Birt, D., 441
Bishop, P., 78, 81, 83, 96, 97
Bishop, S., 328, 329
Bisserbe, J.-C., 78
Bizman, A., 356
Bjerke, T., 550
Bjork, E. L., 142
Bjork, R. A., 591
Björklund, A., 96
Black, J. B., 47
Blackburn, I. M., 328, 329
Black-Cleworth, P., 434, 436-38, 441, 447, 450, 451, 453, 454, 470, 474-76
Blackler, F., 532
Blair, E., 261
Blake, R., 61, 634
Blanc, G., 91
Blanchard, D. C., 85
Blanchard, E. B., 336, 337
Blanchard, R. J., 85
Blanchard, S. K., 545-47
Blashfield, R. K., 422, 426
Blasi, J., 33
Blass, E. M., 600
Blau, Z. S., 538
Blaustein, M. P., 450
Blehar, M., 144, 147
Blencoe, A. G., 354, 356
Bleuler, E., 294
Bliss, T. V. P., 446, 451
Bloem, W., 54
Bloom, F. E., 84, 88, 90, 95
Bloom, S., 88
Blumenfeld, P. C., 615, 623, 624
Blumenthal, H., 300
Blundell, J. E., 83
Bobko, P., 370, 372

Bobrow, D. B., 44
Bochner, S., 534
Bock, R. D., 361
Bockaert, J., 464
Boeckmann, M. E., 227
Boesch, C., 181
Boesch, H., 181
Boese, R. R., 354
Bogdany, F. J., 174
Boies, S. W., 44
Bolen, D., 250
Bolles, R. C., 181, 184, 185
Bolton, C., 541
Bolton, R., 535, 541, 552
Bond, L., 625
Bond, M., 238, 246
Bond, M. H., 543, 547, 555
Bonner, J. T., 176, 181
Book, A., 388, 391
Booth, D. A., 89
Bootzin, R. R., 339
Borkovec, T. D., 337
Borman, W. C., 353, 358, 366
Bornet, A. R., 332
Bornstein, M. H., 142
Borod, J. C., 586
Boruch, R. F., 202, 203, 207, 208, 221, 229
Bosmajian, L. S., 335
Bossert, S. T., 623, 624
Bostsarron, J., 114
Botto, R. W., 572
Boudreau, J. W., 372
Bouhmama, D., 540
Boulanger, D., 636
Boulpaep, E. L., 459, 461
Bousfield, D., 86
Bovy, R. C., 620
Bowden, D. M., 89, 98
Bower, G. H., 47, 64, 340
Bowers, K. S., 235
Bowers, M. B. Jr., 293
Bowers, W. J., 90
Boyd, J. H., 417
Boyle, P. C., 114, 127
Boyles, W. R., 356
Boynton, R. M., 510
Bozarth, M. A., 90, 95
Bozinoff, L., 259
Bradley, A., 500, 503
Bradley, B., 596
Bradley, R. H., 149
Bradley, R. J., 86
Braestrup, C., 92
Braff, D., 585
Brainerd, C. J., 9, 633, 635
Braithwaite, V., 538
Bransford, J. D., 612
Bransome, E. D. Jr., 301
Braren, M., 303
Brattesani, K., 624
Braun, C., 236

Braverman, M. T., 624
Bray, D. W., 365
Bray, G. A., 119, 127
Brazelton, T. B., 535, 576
Brecher, M., 305
Bregman, A. S., 56
Brehm, S. S., 572
Bresolin, B., 389, 391
Bretherton, I., 140, 144
Breton, M. E., 501, 504
Brett, J. M., 360, 367
Brewer, M. B., 248
Brezin, M. J., 620
Briand, K., 46
Briars, D., 634, 635
Brickman, P., 250
Brickner, M. A., 398
Bridwell, L. S., 631, 632
Briggs, C. A., 457, 467, 468
Brines, M., 180
Brinley, F. J. Jr., 473
Brislin, R. W., 526, 529, 531, 533, 542
Britton, D. R., 94
Britton, K. T., 84
Broadbent, D., 45, 47-49, 66-68
Broadbent, D. E., 304
Brobeck, J. R., 112, 123
Brock, T. C., 270
Brockington, I. F., 533
Brodal, A., 435
Brody, N., 325, 326, 338
Broen, W. E., 301
Broerse, J., 142
Brogden, W. J., 451
Bromer, J. A., 439
Bromiley, R. B., 439
Brons, J. F., 434, 437, 438, 450-53, 474, 475
Bronson, G. W., 151
Brooks, G. R., 335
Brooks, J., 582, 600, 601
Brooks, V. B., 439
Brooks-Gunn, J., 145
Brophy, J. E., 236, 615, 617, 622, 623
Brower, S., 392, 398, 401
Brown, A. G., 471, 626, 628
Brown, A. L., 142, 612, 614, 626-28, 630
Brown, A. M., 451, 459
Brown, B. B., 399, 401
Brown, D. A., 462-64
Brown, D. W., 383, 399-401
Brown, G. W., 308
Brown, J. M., 337, 615, 626
Brown, K. A., 439
Brown, T. H., 446, 451, 458, 478
Browne, M. W., 370
Brownell, K. D., 333, 335
Brownstein, M. J., 82, 85, 92

Brozek, G., 438
Brozek, J., 114
Brucks, M., 261, 265
Brudzyński, S. M., 87
Brugge, J. F., 441
Brumby, M., 636
Bruner, J. S., 145
Bruning, I. L., 620
Bruno, K. J., 277
Brunso-Bechtold, J. K., 441
Brush, F. R., 93
Bryan, J. D., 366
Bryan, J. S., 449
Bryant, J., 570, 571
Bryant, K. J., 389-92
Bryant, N., 626
Bryden, M. P., 584
Bryk, A. S., 197, 211
Brzoska, J., 167
Buchanan, A., 87
Buchhalter, J., 452, 475
Buchsbaum, G., 507
Buchsbaum, M. S., 298, 304
Buchwald, A. M., 596
Buchwald, J. S., 439
Buck, R., 578, 581
Bucy, P., 434
Budman, S. H., 338
Buijs, R. M., 79
Bull, D., 142
Bull, N., 577
Bullen, B., 95
Bullock, T. H., 448
Bunker, J. P., 206
Bunney, B. S., 90
Burack, C. M., 300, 311
Bures, J., 438, 439, 453
Buresova, O., 439, 453
Burgess, A. E., 502, 504, 511
Burgess, J. W., 152
Burghardt, G. M., 176
Burke, J. D. Jr., 417
Burke, M. C., 275
Burke, M. J., 371, 372
Burke, R. E., 460
Burkell, J., 53, 57, 58, 67
Burleson, G., 591, 592
Burnkrant, R. E., 269
Burns, T. J., 581
Burstein, L., 625
Burton, L., 587
Burtt, E. H., 170
Busch, C. M., 364
Buss, R., 624
Butcher, J. N., 338
Butcher, L. L., 89
Butler, M. C., 370
Butterfield, D. I., 386
Butters, N., 434
Butterworth, G., 138
Buttrey, T., 619
Byrne, J. H., 453
Byrne, R. W., 382, 390, 391

C

Cabanac, M., 95
Cacioppo, J. T., 270, 273-75
Cadotte, E. R., 281
Cafferty, T. P., 355
Caggiula, A. R., 89, 91
Cain, P. S., 354
Calabrese, R., 449
Calcich, S., 261
Calder, B. J., 271, 272, 280
Caldwell, M. S., 358
Calesick, L. E., 382, 393, 396
Calfee, R., 625, 627-29
Callahan, E. J., 333
Callan, V. J., 550
Callaway, E., 301, 304
Callender, J. C., 371
Calvert-Boyanowsky, J., 569
Camardo, J. S., 449
Camerer, H., 451, 459
Campbell, B., 442
Campbell, D. T., 198, 207, 212, 213, 215, 217, 218, 221-23, 225
Campbell, J. M., 392
Campion, M. A., 363
Campione, J. C., 612, 614, 626, 627
Campos, J. J., 136, 140
Cannon, E. H., 304
Cannon, J. T., 96
Cannon, W. B., 110, 111
Cannonito, M., 539
Canter, D., 382, 383, 387, 390, 392, 402
Cantor, J. R., 570
Cantor, N., 239
Cantril, H., 246
Capon, N., 261
Cappelletti, J., 298
Card, S. K., 620
Cardellino, J. P., 296, 297
Cardy, R. L., 356
Carew, T. J., 442, 447, 449
Carlin, R. K., 469
Carlson, C. R., 509, 516
Carlson, V., 142
Carney, R. M., 123
Caroff, S., 295
Caron, H. S., 586
Carota, N., 235
Carp, A., 386, 387
Carp, F. M., 386, 387, 402
Carpenter, L., 533
Carpenter, M. B., 443
Carpenter, T., 633, 635
Carpenter, W. T., 329
Carr, D., 95
Carr, T. H., 47, 60, 61, 627
Carr, T. S., 395
Carron, T. J., 354
Carson, K. P., 370

Carstairs, G. M., 308
Carter, R. C., 56
Cartwright, B. A., 174
Cartwright-Smith, J., 579
Caruso, T. P., 97
Carver, C. S., 582
Carver, R., 627
Cary, S., 169
Cascio, W. F., 369
Caselli, C., 535
Cassidy, D. J., 142
Casson, E. J., 516
Castellano, C., 94
Castellucci, V. F., 469
Casteñada, S., 640
Catalan, J., 331
Catanzaro, D., 500, 503, 504, 512
Catterall, W. A., 460, 461, 469
Cecire, S., 141
Cedar, H., 469
Cegavske, C. F., 447
Cervone, D., 58
Chad, J. E., 463
Chahal, R., 425
Chajczyk, D., 53
Chakravarti, D., 263, 264
Chambliss, C., 569
Champagne, A., 636, 637
Chandler, S. H., 91
Chandler, T. A., 545-47
Chan-Palay, V., 78
Chapman, J. P., 301, 307
Chapman, L. J., 307
Chapman, L. J. A., 596
Chappel, M. N., 335
Charbonneau-Powis, M., 328
Chase, T. N., 461
Chatfield, R. E., 354
Cheal, M., 86
Cheesman, J., 61
Chen, H., 211, 214, 226
Chen, M., 203, 448
Cheney, D. L., 79, 178
Cheng, L., 125
Cherry, E. C., 45
Chestnut, R. W., 274
Cheung, F., 533
Cheung, W. Y., 467
Chevron, E. S., 337
Chi, M. T. H., 265, 636
Childers, T. L., 276
Ching, C. C., 532
Chiodo, L. A., 90, 91
Chipman, S. F., 637
Chmiel, N. R. J., 53, 54, 59, 60
Chomiak, A. M., 358
Chomsky, N., 182
Christensen, A. V., 92
Christensen, B. N., 471
Christensen, D., 236, 244
Christie, J. E., 328, 329
Chromiak, W., 151

Chun, K., 550
Chung, Y.-E., 550
Churchill, G. A., 280, 281
Churchill, L., 78
Churchman, A., 395
Cicerone, C. M., 505
Ciottone, R. A., 402
Claiborn, W., 235
Clammer, J., 553
Clark, D. M., 592
Clark, F. L., 543
Clark, G. A., 434, 435, 438, 439, 442
Clark, J. L. D., 531
Clark, J. T., 86
Clark, L. A., 536
Clark, M. S., 264, 274
Clark, R. D. III, 140
Clark, R. E., 618, 621, 633
Clarke, C., 146
Clarke-Stewart, A., 149
Claxton, J. D., 279
Cleghorn, J. M., 301
Clements, D. H., 620
Cleveland, J. N., 355, 356
Climent, C. E., 424
Cloud, J. M., 550
Cluss, P. A., 336
Cobb, J., 331
Cobb, P., 633
Cochrane, R., 533
Cody, J. J., 235
Coehlo, G. V., 531
Cofer, C., 566
Coffman, J., 296
Cogenza-Murphy, D., 96
Cohen, A. C., 370
Cohen, A. J., 389
Cohen, D., 140
Cohen, D. H., 442
Cohen, D. K., 200, 219
Cohen, J. B., 268, 269, 272, 325, 371
Cohen, L. B., 139, 142, 151
Cohen, P. A., 618
Cohen, P. R., 594
Cohen, R. M., 96, 304
Cohen, R. W., 509, 516
Cohen, S., 392, 394, 396, 397
Cohen, Y., 51
Cohler, B. J., 301
Cohn, J. F., 140
COHN, T. E., 495-521; 500-5, 507-10, 512, 513, 515, 517
Colby, C. Z., 579
Cole, A. E., 459
Cole, J. D., 590
Cole, K. S., 461, 477
Cole, M., 531, 536
Coleman, D. L., 117, 118
Coleman, L., 277
Collett, T. S., 174
Colletti, G., 336

Collias, E. C., 166
Collias, N. E., 166
Collins, A. M., 594, 631, 638
Collins, D. L., 396
Collins, G. H., 435
Colombo, J., 153
Colt, W. D., 95
Colten, M. E., 402
Coltheart, M., 49
Combs, B., 260
Comrey, A. L., 3, 7
Condouris, G. A., 458
Conger, A. C., 572
Conger, J. C., 572
Conn, L. K., 235
Conner, R. F., 216
Conning, A. M., 382, 390, 391
Connor, J. A., 455, 463
Conover, J. N., 261
Conrad, C., 47
Conroy, R. T. W. L., 451
Constanti, A., 463, 464
Conti-Tronconi, B., 96
Conti-Tronconi, B. M., 461
Conway, B., 538
Conway, M., 249
Cook, F. L., 199
Cook, J. M., 96
COOK, T. D., 193-232; 201-4,
    206, 216, 219, 221, 222,
    224, 228, 229
Cook, T. M., 353
Cooper, B. R., 92
Cooper, H., 236
Cooper, J., 235, 245, 246, 272
Cooper, J. E., 413, 425
Cooper, W. H., 357
Copenhagen, D. R., 501, 505
Coppella, J. W., 241
Corbett, D., 89
Corbett, S. W., 113-15, 118,
    121, 128
Cordle, C. J., 334
Cordray, D. S., 339
Corey, D. P., 478
Cornblatt, B., 301
Cornelius, E. T. III, 354, 365
Cornell, E. H., 142
Cornish, E. R., 115
Corno, L., 612, 613, 624
Cornsweet, T. N., 500
Corrigan, J. G., 37
Corrigan, R., 142
Corteen, R. S., 48
Coryell, W., 420
Coss, R. G., 152
Costa, E., 79, 86, 93, 96
Cotton, B., 356
Cotton, J. L., 568, 569, 575
Coulson, D., 627
Covington, M. V., 615, 617
Cox, D. J., 544
Cox, J. E., 118, 125, 127

Coyle, J. T., 87, 97
Coyne, J. C., 274, 339
Cragg, B. G., 448, 472
Craighead, L. W., 333
Craik, K. H., 382, 385, 387,
    402
Crano, W. D., 235, 236
Crassini, B., 142
Crill, W. E., 463
Crisp, A. H., 126
Crocker, J., 47, 259, 277
Croll, P. R., 364
Cronbach, L., 199
Cronbach, L. J., 199, 203, 207,
    214, 216, 218, 219, 222-
    24, 226, 621
Crosby, E. C., 581
Crosby, L. A., 279
CROSS, D. R., 611-51; 616,
    627, 629
Croughan, J. L., 425
Crow, T. J., 296, 297, 453, 454
Crowne, D. P., 235
Croyle, R. T., 272
Cruce, J. A. F., 118
Crum, R., 260
Cruse, H., 173
Crutcher, M. D., 91
Cudeck, R., 370
Cullen, E., 171
Culler, E., 439
Culler, R. E., 616
Cullheim, S., 460
Cumming, D. C., 126
Cummings, E. M., 142, 149
Cunningham, J. W., 354, 629
Cupchik, G. C., 578, 579
Cureton, E. E., 6
Cureton, K. J., 122
Curio, E., 169, 178
Currie, M. G., 93
Curry, D. J., 266
Curtin, T. R., 201
Curtis, A. T., 535
Curtis, D. R., 471
Curtis, H. J., 461
Curtis, M., 625

D

Daher, M., 576
Dallas, M., 46, 47
Damasio, A. R., 297
Dambrot, F., 549
Damiani, N., 301
Dannemiller, J. L., 139
Dannenbring, G. L., 46
Dansereau, D. F., 640
DARK, V. J., 43-75; 46, 47,
    49, 54
Darley, J. M., 234, 243-47, 249
Darveniza, P., 98
Darvizeh, Z., 535

Darwin, C., 565
Dasen, P. R., 531, 532, 535,
    539
Daubman, K. A., 596
Daumer, K., 172
Davanloo, H., 338
David, J. L., 201
Davidson, A. R., 541
Davidson, B. J., 49, 51, 56
Davidson, G. R., 535
Davidson, J. M., 86
Davidson, L. M., 382, 396
Davidson, R. J., 584, 587-90
Davies, D. R., 44, 45, 50, 63,
    67
Davies, R. F., 89, 99
Davila, K. D., 501, 511
Davis, E. T., 513
Davis, F., 242
Davis, G. E., 382, 393, 396
Davis, J. W., 88
Davis, K. L., 87
Davis, K. R. Jr., 365
Davis, M., 85, 140, 441, 616
Davis, R., 261
Davis, S. W., 550
Dawes, R. M., 251, 325
Daws, J. T., 550
Dawson, M. E., 293, 301, 306
Day, J., 628
Day, R., 292, 293, 313
Day, S. C., 333
Dean, A. F., 500, 503
Dean, R. L., 87
DeCasper, A. J., 139
Deckner, C., 567, 568
DeEskinazi, F. G., 83, 96
DeFrance, J. F., 82
de Gruijter, D. N., 369
Deighton, J., 271, 272
DeJonge, B. R., 581
Del Boca, F. K., 233
Delini-Stula, A., 97
DeLisi, L. E., 298, 296
DeLoache, J. S., 142
DeLong, M. R., 87, 91
DeLorenzo, R. J., 469
Deluca, J., 151
Demaree, R. G., 371
Demarest, J., 154
Demjen, S., 336
DeNisi, A. S., 354-56
Dennert, J. W., 296, 297
Denny-Brown, D., 434
DeOlmos, J. S., 441
DePaulis, A., 83, 92
DePaulo, B. M., 581
Depoortere, H., 92
Depue, R. A., 590
Deregowski, J. B., 527, 534
Deri, M., 635
Derogatis, L., 336
DeRuiter, L., 124

de Sanchez, M., 638
Desena, A., 636
Desmond, J. E., 439
Deterre, P., 464
Detweiler, R. A., 572
Deutsch, D., 47
Deutsch, J. A., 47, 86
De Valois, R. L., 507
Devescovi, A., 535
De Vito, W. J., 93
DeVos, G. A., 544
DeVries, G. J., 79
De Wied, D., 94
Diamond, A., 151
Diamond, I. T., 441, 454
Diamond, J., 459
Diamond, R., 585
Diaz-Guerrero, R., 550
Diaz-Loving, R., 550
Dick, W., 613, 614, 620
Dickie, K., 618
Dickinson, T. L., 357
Dienstbier, R. A., 569, 570
Digre, K., 587
DiMascio, A., 86
Dimberg, U., 598
Dimond, S. J., 587
Dingledine, R., 477
Dipboye, R. L., 366
Dirksen, J. W., 295
Dispenzieri, A., 364
Distefano, M. K. Jr., 357
Disterhoft, J. F., 441
Dixon, S. D., 143
Doane, B., 435
Doane, J. A., 308
Dobkin de Rios, M. F., 533
Dockett, K., 398
Dodder, R. A., 554
Dollinger, J., 169
Dominic, J. F., 631
Donahoe, C. P., 122
Donchin, E., 302, 303
Donley, P., 453, 459, 478
Donnerstein, E., 570
Doob, A. N., 571
Dooley, D. J., 97
Doren, B., 593
Dornbusch, S. M., 203, 207, 216, 219
Dornic, S., 47, 62, 66, 67
Dossett, D. L., 268
Dostalek, C., 445
Doty, W. R., 439, 450
Doverspike, D., 369
Dowler, J. K., 148
Downing, J., 628
Downing, N. E., 549
Doyle, C., 596
Doyle, W., 616, 623
Draguns, J. G., 422, 426
Drasgow, F., 362, 368
Dreher, G. F., 366, 370

Driscoll, A., 278
Drucker-Colin, R. R., 78, 86, 88
Drum, P., 628
Drummond, A. H., 464
Drummond, G. I., 467
Dubitsky, T. M., 277
Dudley, C. A., 93
Duffy, F. H., 304
Duffy, G., 629
Dufort, R. H., 445
Dumais, S. T., 63, 67
Dunbar, S. B., 371
DUNCAN, C. C., 291-319
Duncan, C. P., 261
Duncan, J., 55, 58, 67
Duncan, J. W., 577
Duncan, S. L., 246
Duncan, S. W., 592, 593
Duncan-Johnson, C. C., 302-4, 310, 313
Dunn, A. J., 92
Dunn, J., 144
Dunn, W., 218
Dunnett, S. B., 96
Dunnette, M. D., 352, 353, 364
Durkovic, R. G., 441, 442
Dusek, J. B., 235, 236
Dustman, R. E., 45
Dutton, D. G., 240
Duval, D., 463
Dweck, C. S., 615, 616, 640
Dyal, J. A., 554
Dyal, R. Y., 554
Dyer, F. C., 167, 179
Dziurawiec, S., 527

E

Eagle, T. C., 266
Earle, D. C., 139
Easley, J. A., 223, 227
Eaton, N. K., 366, 372
Ebbesen, E. B., 592, 593, 597
Ebeling, B. J., 618
Ebner, F. F., 471
Eccles, J. C., 435, 458, 615, 616
Eckersdorf, B., 87
Eckert, R., 462, 463
Edell, J. A., 275, 276
Edell, W. S., 307
Eden, D., 235
Edmonds, J., 551
Edwards, C. N., 235
Edwards, C. P., 531, 540
Edwards, J. E., 368
Edwards, J. R., 550
Edwards, S. B., 441
Edwards, W., 211, 215
Effrein, E. A., 249
Egan, J. P., 497
Egeth, H. E., 55, 53

Egly, R., 51, 52
Ehrlich, S., 52, 55
Ehrlichman, H., 590
Eibl-Eibesfeldt, I., 166, 186
Eich, E., 55
Eich, J. E., 591, 592
Eimas, P. D., 182
Einhorn, H. J., 264
Eisenberg, J., 364
Eisenman, E. J., 355
Ekman, P., 566, 573, 575, 576, 581, 582, 586, 600
Elardo, R., 149
Elashoff, J. D., 236
Elkin, I., 337, 338
Elliott, E. S., 615, 616
Ellis, A., 341
Ellis, H. C., 592, 595
Ellisman, M. H., 472
Ellisor, J., 395
Ellsworth, P., 575, 582
Ellsworth, P. C., 578
Elmore-Yalch, R., 270
Ely, R. J., 242
Ember, C. R., 537, 548, 549
Embretson (Whitely), S., 360
Emde, R. N., 140, 145
Emery, G., 337, 341
Emlen, S., 181
Emmelkamp, P. M. G., 330, 331
Emson, P. C., 78
Endicott, J., 414, 425, 426
Engberg, I., 459
Engel, E., 58
Engel, J. Jr., 435-38, 441, 450, 473
Engle, J., 92
Enochs, L., 636
Enroth-Cugel, C., 506
Epstein, A. N., 86, 127
Epstein, H. T., 151
Epstein, L. H., 336
Epstein, S., 9
Epstein, Y. M., 393, 397
Erbaugh, J. K., 424
Erber, J., 173
Erdmann, G., 568, 573, 574
Erffmeyer, R. C., 357
Eriksen, B. A., 52, 53
Eriksen, C. W., 52, 53, 57
Erlenmeyer-Kimling, L., 301, 306
Estes, W. K., 52
Estrada, H., 424
Ettema, J., 619
Evans, G. W., 385, 387, 389-92, 394, 396, 397, 400, 401
Evans, M., 247
Evarts, E. V., 435
Everitt, B. J., 89, 90
Everson, H., 368

Evett, L. J., 60
Ewer, R. F., 166, 186
Ewert, J-P., 164
Eyde, L. D., 8, 354, 361

F

Faber, M. D., 265
Faden, A. I., 95
Fagan, J. F. III, 146, 147
Fagen, J. W., 141
Fahim, H., 402
Faigley, L., 632
Fairburn, C. G., 334
Fairweather, G. W., 199
Falender, V. J., 249
Falk, G., 501, 503
Farah, M. J., 54
Farbstein, J., 395
Farel, P. B., 449
Fariello, R. G., 92
Farina, A., 236, 238, 241, 244-48
Faris, P. L., 93
Farley, J., 434, 435, 440, 443, 447-50, 453-56, 477
Farran, D. C., 149
Farrington, L., 587
Fatt, P., 462
Faucheux, C., 241
Faust, I. M., 124
Faustman, W. D., 546
Fazio, R. H., 234, 246, 247, 249, 272
Feeley, M. M., 201
Feighner, J. P., 413, 425, 426
Feild, H. S., 356
Fein, G. G., 148
Feinman, S., 140
Feinstein, A. R., 427
Feiring, C., 144, 147
Feldman, J. M., 355
Feldman, R. S., 86, 244
Felson, R. B., 248
Feltovich, P., 636
Fenemore, J., 86
Fenstermacher, J. D., 472
Ferguson, L. R., 531
Ferguson, N. B. L., 119
Fernald, A., 154
Ferrara, R. A., 612, 614, 626
Ferrero, P., 96
Fetting, J., 336
Fetz, E. E., 436
Feuerstein, G., 95
Feuerstein, R., 626, 638
Feustel, T. C., 46, 47
Field, T. M., 140, 148
Fields, R. D., 472
Fierman, B., 634, 635
Fifkova, E., 459
Finch, G., 439
Fink, S. I., 58, 59

Finley, G. E., 529
Finn, S. E., 419
Finocchio, D. V., 436
Fischbein, E., 635
Fischer, K. W., 150
Fischhoff, B., 260
Fish, B., 299, 311
Fishbein, M., 268
Fisher, A., 97
Fisher, C., 622
Fisher, J. D., 393
Fisher, K. C., 117
Fishler, I., 60
Fisk, A. D., 63
Fiske, D. W., 327
Fiske, S. T., 264, 274
Fitzgerald, M. P., 366
Fitzgibbons, W. J., 364
Flanagan, J. C., 7
Flanders, J. P., 235
Flay, B. R., 221, 224
Fleishman, E. A., 8, 353
Fleming, E. S., 235
Fleming, J. H., 240
Fleming, R., 382, 392, 396, 397
Fleshman, J. W., 460
Fletcher, G., 249
Florez, J., 95
Flor-Henry, P., 296, 299
Flower, L., 631
Flynn, B. S., 334
Flynn, J. R., 360
Foa, E. B., 331
Fode, K. L., 234, 235, 244
Foerster, O., 439
Fogarty, S., 592, 593, 596
Folchi, J., 369
Foley, J. E., 389
Foley, J. M., 515
Folkes, V. S., 281
Folkman, S., 396
Follett, B. K., 167
Fontenelle, G. A., 366
Foote, S., 88
Forbes, G. B., 123
Ford, G. T., 280
Ford, J. K., 358
Ford, J. M., 304, 305
Ford, M. E., 595, 596
Ford, W., 633
Forman, A., 400, 401
Formisano, R. A., 267
Forse, D. D., 184
Foster, K., 442
Fournier, V., 92
Fowler, C. A., 59
Fox, N. A., 588
Fox, S., 356
Fox, W. C., 498, 512, 513
Frager, N. B., 394
Frame, C. L., 301
Franck, K. A., 399
Francolini, C. M., 53

Frank, A. F., 330, 338
Frank, J. D., 324, 341
Frank, K., 465
Frankenhauser, M., 574
Frankfurt, M., 96
Franks, C. M., 341, 342
Frantz, A., 95
Franz, S. I., 439
Franzen, G., 295
Frase, L. T., 632
Fray, P. J., 96
Frazier, W., 395
Frederick, J. T., 372
Frederickson, W. T., 139
Frederiksen, C. H., 631
Frederiksen, N., 614, 625, 638
Fredricks, A. J., 268
Freed, W. J., 96
Freedman, A. M., 416
Freeman, H. E., 205, 218, 219
Freeman, J. A., 637
Freeman, R. D., 500, 503, 504
Fremouw, W. J., 333
French, L., 626
Frey, K. A., 78
Fricke, R. A., 458
Fried, M., 385
Friedman, A., 47
Friedman, D., 306
Friedman, M., 335
Friedrich, F. J., 45
Friesen, W. V., 573, 575, 581, 582, 586, 600
Frisch, R. E., 126
Frishman, L. J., 503
Frith, C. D., 296, 297
Frodi, A. M., 149
Frodj, M., 149
Fromm-Auch, D., 587
Fromm-Reichmann, F., 292, 307
Frosch, J. P., 330, 338
Frost, R. F., 596
Frye, G. D., 92
Fryklund, I., 57
Fujii, J. S., 304
Fujimoto, M., 96
Fujito, Y., 448
Fulcomer, M., 395
Fulero, S., 247
Fullan, M., 199
Fuortes, M. G. F., 442, 465
Furnham, A., 547
Furse, D. J., 261
Fuson, K., 634
Fuxe, K., 97

G

Gabel, D., 636
Gabriel, M., 441, 442
Gade, P. A., 361
Gage, F. H., 96
Gage, N., 618

Gagne, R. M., 613, 614, 620, 634
Gaidis, W. C., 278
Gaillard, A. W. K., 303
Gaines, R., 534
Gainotti, G., 586
Galambos, R., 439
Galbraith, G. G., 572
Galin, D., 585
Gallager, D. W., 92
Gallagher, D. E., 328
Gallagher, M., 630
Gallant, D., 301
Galler, J. R., 154
Gallistel, C., 634
Gallup, G. G., 178
Gal'perin, P. Y., 638
Galster, G. C., 385
Galvan, M., 463
Gamper, E., 435
Ganchrow, J. R., 576, 600
Gandour, M. J., 334
Gann, D. S., 95
Gannon, P. J., 87
Garattini, S., 89
Garbart, H., 55
Garber, J., 592, 593
Garcia, J., 452
Garcia-Coll, C., 146
Gardner, H., 614, 621
Gardner, M. P., 262, 273
Gardner, P., 328
Gardner-Medwin, A. R., 446, 451
Garfield, S. L., 325, 339, 341
Garling, T., 388, 389, 391, 392
Garmezy, N., 294
Garner, K., 366
Garner, R., 628
Garrow, J. S., 116, 119
Gash, D. M., 96
Gast, I. F., 358
Gastault, H., 439
Gast-Rosenberg, L., 11
Gat, I., 619
Gatchel, R. J., 382, 383, 393, 396, 397
Gattinger, E., 571
Gauda, G., 540
Gauger, L. L., 88
Gaupp, L. A., 572
Gauvain, M., 402
Gaviria, L. F., 424
Gaw, A., 533
Gay, J., 536
Gaylin, K., 400
Gazzaniga, M. S., 50
Gealy, J., 528
Geffen, G., 48
Geisler, W. S., 501, 511
Gekoski, M. J., 141
Gelade, G., 55, 67
Gelder, M., 331

Gelfand, D. L., 178
Geller, D. M., 93
Geller, V., 64
Gellhorn, E., 470, 577
Gelman, R., 634
Gelperin, A., 85
Gelso, C. J., 338
Gendelman, D. S., 441
Gendelman, P. M., 441
Genereux, R. L., 382, 388, 391
Gentner, D., 631, 636
George, E. I., 301
Georgopoulos, A. P., 91
Gerard, H. B., 246
Gerdes, E. P., 568
Gerdt, C., 595
German, D. C., 89, 91, 98
Gerritse, R. A., 424
Gerschenfeld, H. M., 464
Gershon, E. S., 87
Gershon, M. D., 93
Gerstein, G., 469, 470
Ghiselli, E. E., 10
Gibbons, B. N., 242
Gibbons, F. X., 242
Gibson, E. J., 142
Gibson, F. W., 355
Gibson, J. J., 138
Gibson, J. T., 539
Gield, B., 400
Gifford, R., 398
Giles, H., 550
Gill, J. L., 120, 335
Gill, R., 538
Gillam, B., 534
Gillessen, D., 93
Gilligan, S. G., 591-97
Gillin, J. C., 591
Gilovich, T., 272
Giniger, S., 364
Ginsberg, Y., 395
Ginsborg, B. L., 462
Ginsburg, H., 633, 634
Girard, D. L., 612
Girardier, L., 127
Girden, E., 439
Girodo, M., 569
Gisriel, M. M., 396, 397
Givis, R. P., 584
Gjerde, P. F., 293, 301, 306, 313
Glanville, N. T., 125
Glaser, R., 617, 620, 624-27, 636-38
Glasgow, R. E., 336
Glass, A. L., 47
Glass, G. V., 215, 323-27, 335, 340, 342, 636
Glassman, A. H., 84
Glazer, R., 333
Gleier, G. C., 574
Gleitman, L. C., 182, 189
Glen, A. I. M., 328, 329

Glenberg, A., 591
Glendenning, K. K., 441
Glick, S. D., 89
Glickstein, M., 439
Glowinski, J., 91
Godfraind, J. M., 459
Gold, M. S., 84
Goldberg, A. M., 86
Goldberg, A. P., 123
Goldberg, L. J., 91
Goldberger, M., 623
Golden, C. J., 295-97
Goldfried, M. R., 8, 340-42
Goldin, J. C., 328
Goldman, J. M., 86
Goldman-Rakic, P. S., 151, 435, 438, 439
Goldschmid, M., 235, 236
Goldsmith, H. H., 147
Goldstein, A., 94
Goldstein, A. P., 531, 552
Goldstein, E. B., 58, 59
Goldstein, I. B., 335
Goldstein, K., 313
Goldstein, L., 590
Goldstein, M., 78
Goldstein, M. J., 308, 310
Goleman, D., 587
Golinkoff, R. M., 142
Golledge, R. G., 388, 391
Gomes-Schwartz, B., 322
Gonzalez, A., 541
Gonzalez-Lima, F., 97
Good, R., 636
Good, T., 236, 622, 623
Goodenough, D. A., 459
Goodenough, D. J., 512
Goodenough, F. L., 576
Gooding, R. Z., 362
Goodman, D. B. P., 461, 467
Goodman, D. M., 584
Goodman, G. D., 60
Goodman, R. R., 78
Goodnow, J. J., 529
Goodwyn, S. W., 154
Gopher, D., 44
Gopnik, A., 144
Gordon, J., 169
Gordon, M. E., 364
Gorgoglione, J. M., 596
Gorin, L., 628
Gormezano, I., 445, 451
Gormley, F. P., 393, 396
Gosnell, B. A., 125
Gosselin, J.-Y., 304, 305, 307
Gottesman, I. I., 293, 294
Gottfredson, S. D., 392, 398, 401
Gottlieb, G., 150, 152
Gottman, J. M., 582
Gottschalk, A., 507
Gottschalk, L. A., 574
Gough, H. G., 365

Gould, C. G., 172, 182
GOULD, J. L., 163-92; 164, 166, 167, 169, 172-74, 176, 179, 180, 182, 185-88
Gould, S. J., 537
Grab, D. J., 469
Graber, B., 296, 297
Grafe, E., 115
Grafe, P., 463
Graham, D., 115
Graham, E. E., 638
Graham, F. K., 46
Graham, N., 513
Graham-Brown, T., 450
Granbois, D. H., 267
Grandison, L., 92
Grandmaison, L. J., 91
Grant, D. A., 296, 447
Gratton, A., 99
Graves, R., 632
Gray, E. G., 459
Gray, J. A., 589
Gray, J. M., 123
Graybiel, A. M., 441
Graziano, W. G., 237
Green, B. F. Jr., 9, 354, 361
Green, D. G., 503, 505
Green, D. M., 497, 499, 512-17
Green, J. A., 153
Green, L. W., 334
Green, M. L., 596
Green, T., 633
Green, V., 550
Greenamyre, J. T., 78, 98
Greenbaum, C. W., 40
Greenberg, J. R., 144
Greenberg, L. S., 340
Greenberg, M., 586
Greenberg, R., 140
Greenberg, S. W., 399, 401
Greene, T. R., 637
Greener, J. M., 371
Greenfield, P. M., 235
Greengard, P., 86, 468, 469
Greenhouse, D. S., 513
Greenleaf, E. A., 274
Greeno, J., 622, 635
Greenwald, A. G., 272
Greenwald, D., 331
Greenwald, M., 331
Greenwood, M. R. C., 118
Greitz, T., 97
Grether, D., 267
Grevert, P., 94
Grieger, R., 341
Griffin, D. R., 188
Griffiths, I., 402
Grill, H. H., 85
Grillner, S., 166
Grinc, G. A., 334
Grogan, J., 356
Gross, A. L., 370
Gross, R. H., 246

Grossman, J. H., 424
Grossman, S. P., 79
Grouws, D., 623
Grover, L., 447
Gruen, E., 468
Gruenberg, E., 417
Grünbaum, A., 339
Grundfest, H., 442
Grunebaum, H., 301
Grunwald, G. B., 98
Gruzelier, J. H., 586
Guba, E. G., 203, 211, 218, 219, 227
Gudeman, J. E., 590
Gueutal, H. G., 355
Guidotti, A., 92, 96
Guilford, J. P., 613
Guion, R. M., 3, 11
Gulick, A., 115
Gullo, D. F., 620
Gumbel, E., 40
Gummow, L., 45
Gunderson, J. G., 330, 338
Gunnar, M. R., 140, 145
Gunstone, R., 636, 637
Gur, R. C., 295
Gur, R. E., 295
Gurland, B. J., 413
Gurll, N. J., 95
Gurwitz, S. B., 250
Gustafson, G. E., 143, 153
Gustafsson, B., 463, 475
Gutenberg, R. L., 12, 371
Guth, S. L., 508, 510
Gutman, D., 58, 59
Gutman, W., 438
Guttentag, M., 211, 215
Guyden, T. E., 424
Guyer, P. E., 438

H

Habermas, J., 218
Hablitz, J., 463
Hacker, R., 636
Hadjiconstantinou, M., 93
Hadley, S. W., 322, 337, 338
Haertel, G., 636
Hagenaar, R., 54
Hager, J. C., 581, 585, 586
Hager, W., 591
Hagin, R., 299
Hagins, W. A., 461
Hagiwara, S., 460, 462-64
Hahn, M. E., 151
Hailman, J., 165
Haith, M. M., 136
HAKEL, M. D., 351-80
Hakerem, G., 303
Halal, M., 591, 592
Halford, G. S., 536
Hall, B., 592
Hall, H., 354

Hall, J., 634
Hall, V. C., 236
Halliwell, J. V., 464
Halpain, S. C., 78
Hambleton, R. K., 369, 627
Hamer, R. D., 506
Hamill, O., 478
Hamilton, D. L., 247
Hamilton, V. L., 615, 623, 624
Hammer, R. P. Jr., 96
Hamsher, K. deS., 587
Haney, W., 625
Hanges, P. J., 370
Hanin, I., 86, 97
Hankins, W. G., 452
Hanley, G., 382, 383, 391, 392
Hannah, D. B., 271
Hans, S. L., 300, 311
Hansen, J. C., 50, 303, 629
Hanser, L. M., 353
Hantas, M. N., 585, 592, 596
Haracz, J. L., 293
Hardiman, M. J., 439
Harding, C. F., 167
Harding, C. G., 142
Hardt, R. H., 8, 354
Harik, S. I., 89
Harkness, S., 531
Harlow, H. F., 439
Harman, D. W., 587
Harnisch, D., 368
Harper, A. E., 114
Harris, C. W., 5
Harris, J. D., 448
Harris, M. B., 569
Harris, M. M., 363
Harris, P., 628
Harris, R. A., 462
Harris, R. J., 274, 277
Harris, R. S., 124
Harris, V. A., 572
Harrison, J. M., 441
Hart, R. A., 389
Harter, M. R., 45
Harter, S., 615
Hartman, J., 151
Hartman, K., 367
Hartmann, D. P., 324, 327
Hartup, W. W., 145
Hartwick, J., 269
Hartzell, H. C., 468
Harvey, J., 447
Harvey, P., 301
Harvey, R., 324, 325
Hasher, L., 258, 259, 282
Hashiguchi, T., 456
Hassett, C. E., 357
Hassler, R., 435
Hastak, M., 260
Hastie, R., 262
Hastings, N., 368
Hastorf, A., 246
Hastorf, A. H., 241, 247, 248

Hawkins, R. D., 442, 447, 449
Hay, B., 461, 473, 476
HAY, D. F., 135-61; 140, 141, 144, 145, 154
Hayduk, L. A., 397, 398, 400
Hayes, J. R., 631
Hayes, L. A., 140
Hayes-Roth, B., 263
Hayhoe, M. M., 505, 511
Haynes, R. B., 335, 420
Haynes, V., 335
Hayoski, H., 543
Haywood, H. C., 638
Hazlett, E., 298
Head, H., 439
Hearst, E., 185
Heath, R. G., 87
Hebb, D. O., 435
Hecht, S., 496-98, 501, 502, 504, 506, 514
Heckman, J. J., 221
Hede, A. J., 638
Hedges, L. V., 327
Heeley, D. W., 510
Heft, H., 389, 394, 397, 402
Heilbroner, R. L., 542
Heiligenberg, W., 168
Heilman, K. M., 584, 585
Heim, T., 126
Heinrich, B., 176, 184
Heinrichs, D. W., 329
Heinz, S. P., 44, 48
Heisenberg, W., 68
Heldman, B., 465
Heller, J., 635, 637
Heller, W., 586
Helmreich, R. L., 550
Helson, H., 56, 383
HELZER, J. E., 409-32; 415, 420, 424, 425
Hemmingsen, A. M., 113
Hemsley, D. R., 301
Hendrichs, M., 336
Heneman, R. L., 356
Henik, A., 53
Henkel, G. K., 441
Hennessey, M. J., 143
Hennigan, K. M., 224
Henry, G. M., 595
Henry, J. L., 94
Henschel, A., 114
Herbert, R. K., 383, 399
Herink, R., 323
Herkenham, M., 78, 96
Herman, B. H., 94
Herman, C. P., 569
Herman, J., 619
Hermanutz, M., 304
Hernandez, D. E., 94
Herning, R. I., 303
Heron, A., 526, 529, 531
Herrick, C. D., 572
Herriot, P., 367

Herrmann, E., 356
Herrnstein, R. J., 638
Hersen, M., 329
Hersh, H., 620
Hertz, M., 172
Herve, D., 91
Hervey, G., 121
Hervey, G. R., 124
Herz, A., 471
Herzog, T. R., 384, 387
Hess, E. H., 167, 176
Hess, R. D., 203, 207, 216, 219
Hesser, G. W., 385
Hester, R. K., 332
Heston, L. L., 307
Hetherington, A. W., 127
Heuser, J. E., 463
Heusser, C., 551
Hewson, M., 637
Hewson, P., 637
Hewstone, M., 552, 553
Heyer, C. B., 462, 463
Heym, J., 87, 88, 90
Hiatt, S. W., 576, 582
Higgins, E. T., 47
Higgins, J., 307
Hildebrandt, K. A., 148
Hill, K. T., 617
Hille, B., 434, 459-63, 478
Hillman, E. D., 439
Hillyard, S. A., 45, 46, 50, 303-5
Hilton, J. L., 239, 243-47
Himmelhoch, J. M., 329
Himms-Hagen, J., 127
Hinde, R. A., 151, 181
Hink, R. F., 303, 305
Hiramatsu, K., 304, 305, 307
Hirsch, J., 119, 124
Hirschman, E. C., 274
Hirschman, J., 572
Hirsh, H. R., 372
Hirsh-Pasek, K., 153
Hirvonen, M. D., 128
Hobson, C. J., 355
Hoch, S. J., 277
Hochberg, J. E., 69
Hockberger, P. E., 469
Hodgkin, A. L., 461, 462
Hodgson, R. J., 331
Hoehn-Saric, R., 92
Hoffeld, D. R., 452
Hoffer, B. J., 459
Hoffman, J. E., 50, 52, 55, 57, 63, 67
Hoffman, M. B., 638
Hoffman, R. G., 364
Hofstede, G., 542
Hogan, H. W., 547
Hogan, J., 364
Hogan, R., 364
Hogarth, R. M., 264
Hökfelt, T., 78

Holaday, J. W., 95
HOLAHAN, C. J., 381-407; 391, 616
Holbrook, M. B., 274, 277
Holcomb, H. H., 298
Holender, D., 45, 54, 61, 62
Holinger, D. P., 616
Hollis, K. L., 183
Hollister, L. E., 87
Hollon, S. D., 328
Holloway, W. R. Jr., 87
Holmes, D. L., 148
Holmes, D. T., 439
Holmes, J. G., 243, 248
Holmes, W. R., 453, 458-60
Holtzman, J. D., 50
Holtzman, W. H., 532
Homa, D., 51, 52
Homan, S., 368
Hood, L. E., 461
Hoover, H. D., 368
Horner, D., 337
Horner, T. M., 140
Hornik, R. C., 203, 207, 216, 219
Hornstein, G. A., 402
Horowitz, B. A., 126
Horowitz, F. D., 140
Horowitz, M., 338
Horowitz, M. E., 584
Horridge, G. A., 448
Horton, E. S., 115
Horvath, F. E., 439
Horvath, T. B., 304, 305
Horwitz, B., 466
Houchin, J., 473
Houck, M. R., 50, 63
Hough, L. M., 364
Houlihan, D., 634
Hourihan, K., 386, 387
House, E. R., 209
Houston, M. J., 276
Howard, A., 365
Howard, G. S., 329
Howard, J. L., 92
Howarth, B. G., 587
Howe, M. E., 441
Hoyer, W. D., 280
Hoyle, G., 453
Hozer, C. A. III, 417
Hsu, F. L. K., 543
Hsu, L. K. G., 334
Huang, L. C., 569
Huang, Y. H., 90
Hubel, D. H., 448
Huber, J., 265, 266
Hudspeth, A. J., 478
Huebner, D. K., 154
Hugdahl, K., 598
Hughes, E. F. X., 203, 207
Hugues, M., 463
Hui, C. H., 542, 543
Hulin, C. L., 362

Hull, C. L., 7
Hume, A., 631, 632
Humphreys, G. W., 52, 60
Humphreys, L., 242
Humphreys, L. G., 361
Hungerbuhler, J. P., 586
Hunkapiller, M. W., 461
Hunn, C., 97
Hunt, E., 359
Hunt, S. P., 78, 79
Hunter, J. E., 11, 357, 363, 364, 367, 371, 372
Hunter, M. A., 139, 142
Hunter, R. F., 363
Huntington, D. E., 395
Husband, J., 296, 297
Huston, J. P., 99
Huston, P. E., 301
Hutchings, C., 616
Hutchinson, J. W., 262, 265, 275
Hutchinson, R. R., 85
Huxley, A. F., 461, 477
Hwang, C-P., 149
Hylton, R., 511
Hythecker, V., 640

I

Iacino, R., 150
Ickes, W., 238, 239, 246, 247
Ignatovitch, G. S., 153
Ihrig, L. H., 142
Ikeda, M., 510
Ilgen, D. R., 355
Im, S., 385
Imig, T. J., 441
Immelmann, K., 169, 176
Inbar, J., 240
Ingold, K., 92
Ingraham, L. J., 581
Ingvar, D. H., 97, 295
Inhelder, B., 261, 389
Inhoff, A. W., 52
Innis, R. B., 78
Insel, T. M., 96
Ioffe, S. V., 469, 470
Ironson, G., 368
Irvine, S. H., 528
Isen, A. M., 262, 267
Isenberg, D. J., 365
Ispa, J., 145
Ito, M., 440
Itoh, K., 304, 305
Iversen, L. L., 86, 92
Iversen, S. D., 86, 92, 96
Iwasaki, S., 53
Izard, C. E., 566, 577, 583

J

Jaarsma, D., 507, 513
Jack, J. J. B., 458

Jacklin, C. N., 144
Jackson, D. N., 3, 7
Jackson, G. B., 371
Jackson, J. L., 78
Jackson, P. R., 354
Jackson, W. K., 84
Jacobi, M., 402
Jacobs, B. L., 84, 87, 88, 90
Jacobs, J., 627, 629
Jacobs, R., 356
Jacobs, S. V., 394
Jacobson, J. L., 148
Jacobson, L., 235, 244, 246
Jacobson, S. W., 148
Jacoby, C. G., 296, 297
Jacoby, J., 278, 280
Jacoby, L. L., 46, 47
Jaffe, R. M., 577
Jaffe, Y., 552
Jagacinski, C. J., 265
Jaggi, V., 552
Jahnsen, H., 462
Jahoda, G., 524, 527, 535, 536, 554
Jain, A. K., 266
Jalowiec, J., 83, 96
Jalowiec, J. E., 89
James, L. R., 360, 367, 371
James, W., 44, 50, 62, 68-70
James, W. P. T., 126
Jamison, D., 618
Janke, W., 568
Jankowska, E., 475
Jannoun, L., 331
Jansson, L., 330
Jarvie, G. J., 122
Jaskir, J., 147
Jaspars, J., 553
Jasper, H., 435
Jeanneret, P. R., 8, 12, 370, 371
Jeanrenaud, B., 127
Jellinek, A., 439
Jenkins, H. M., 170, 185
Jenkins, R. L., 281
Jennings, K. R., 469
Jennings, R. J., 502, 504, 511
Jensen, A. R., 236
Jensen, M., 626
Jensen, R. A., 94
Jernigan, T. L., 296, 297
Jiang, J. B., 97
Johansen, K. J., 619, 621
Johansson, O., 78
Johansson, P., 85
John, D., 259, 277
John, E. R., 303
John, G., 259
Johnson, D. H., 338, 629
Johnson, D. W., 640
Johnson, E. J., 260-62, 264, 266, 267
Johnson, J. C., 354

Johnson, L. A., 370
Johnson, M. D., 267
Johnson, P. R., 118, 124
Johnson, R. D., 266
Johnson, R. E. Jr., 303
Johnson, R. T., 640
Johnston, D., 459, 463, 478
Johnston, J., 619
Johnston, P., 625
Johnston, R. E., 581, 582
Johnston, T. D., 150
JOHNSTON, W. A., 43-75; 44, 46-49, 54, 64
Johnstone, E. C., 296, 297
Jolles, J., 94
Jones, A. P., 370
Jones, B., 337, 637
Jones, E. E., 239, 241, 247-49
Jones, E. G., 441, 472
Jones, G. E., 585
Jones, J. E., 308
Jones, L. S., 88
Jones, M. B., 371
Jones, R. A., 234, 628
Jones, S. C., 245, 246
Jong, T., 538
Jordan, S. E., 451
Jordan, W. C., 369
Jordon, J., 451
Jose, J., 235
Josefsson, J.-O., 85
Josiassen, R. C., 304, 305
Jouvet, M., 87
Juhasz, G., 439
Jung, R., 435
Junker, L., 636
Jusczyk, P. W., 151, 189

K

Kaas, J. H., 440
Kaczmarek, L. K., 469
Kagan, J., 146
Kagan, S., 528, 554
Kaganov, J. A., 336
Kagel, J. H., 258
Kagen, E., 370
Kağitçibaşi, C., 532
Kahl, S., 636
Kahneman, D., 44, 45, 48, 53, 57, 58, 66, 67, 260, 281
Kaij, L., 300
Kaiser, D., 277
Kalin, R., 551
Kaltreider, N., 338
Kameyama, T., 304, 305, 307
Kamin, L. J., 445, 450
Kamp, J. D., 364
Kandel, E. R., 178, 182, 442, 447, 449, 469
Kanekar, S., 552
Kang, T., 368
Kantrowitz, M., 402

Kanwar, R., 265
Kaplan, H. I., 416
Kaplan, R. E., 365, 384, 387
Kaplan, S., 384, 387
Karni, E. S., 550
Karon, B. P., 329
Karp, L., 591-93, 597
Karpiak, S. E., 97
Karren, R., 372
Kaschak, E., 549
Kaskey, G. B., 304
Kass, I. S., 477
Kastin, A. J., 94
Katcher, A. H., 570
Katkin, E. S., 572, 585
Katsumaru, H., 469, 471
Katz, B., 450, 463, 464
Katz, H. M., 330, 338
Katz, S., 138
Kaufman, A. S., 3
Kaufman, L. N., 128
Kaufman, N. L., 3
Kavas, A., 260, 268, 269
Kawakami, A., 630
Kay, M. A., 531
Kay, P., 535
Keating, C. F., 552
Keats, D., 538
Kebabian, J. W., 468
KEESEY, R. E., 109-33; 113-
    15, 118, 119, 121, 122,
    125, 127, 128
Kehne, J. H., 441
Kehoe, J. F., 356
Kehret-Ward, T., 279
Keith, S. J., 329
Kellam, K. L., 356
Keller, H., 540, 550, 551
Kellerman, H., 84
Kelley, A. E., 590
Kelley, H. H., 237, 239, 244
Kelly, A. F., 304, 305
Kelly, D. H., 517
Kelly, P. A. T., 96
Kemnitz, J. W., 127
Kempley, S. T., 46
Kendall, P. C., 326, 342
Kendell, R. E., 413, 421
Kendrick, C., 144
Kennedy, C., 297
Kennedy, D., 449, 471, 576
Kennedy, S., 531
Kennell, J. H., 153
Kennelly, K. J., 616
Kent, R. N., 8
Keren, G., 48
Kernan, J. B., 274
Kersten, D., 504, 511
Kertzman, C., 154
Ketron, J., 538
Kettner, R. E., 434, 435, 438,
    442
Kety, S. S., 292, 294, 307, 412

Keyes, M. A., 364
Keys, A., 114
Khachaturian, H., 96
Khutzian, S. S., 153
Kiefer, K. E., 633
Kiel, G. C., 261
Kilbride, P., 538
Killam, K. F., 86
Kilpatrick, J., 633
Kim, E. H.-J., 469, 470
Kimble, G. A., 445
Kinchla, R. A., 57
King, A. C., 298
King, A. P., 152
King, A. S., 235
King, J. E., 154
Kintsch, W., 277, 635
Kirsch, M., 362
Kirschenbaum, D. S., 122
Kirsner, K., 46
Kishor, N., 546
Kisielius, J., 270-73, 276
Kitabgi, P., 463
Kitai, S. T., 471
Kjerulff, K., 9
Klaus, M. H., 153
Kleban, M. H., 395
Klebanoff, L. B., 206
Kleber, H. D., 84, 333
Kleck, R. E., 247
Kleiber, M., 113, 116
Klein, D. F., 327, 331, 339
Klein, M., 449, 464
Klein, R. E., 150
Klein, R. H., 304
Klein, R. P., 145
Klein, S. A., 512
Klein, S. F., 531
Klein, S. T., 296, 297
Kleinman, J. E., 296, 297
Kleinstein, R. N., 515
Klerman, G. L., 323, 328, 329,
    337, 338, 410, 418
Klesges, R. C., 336
Klich, L. Z., 535
Kliegl, R. M., 326, 327
Klimoski, R. J., 365
Klinghammer, E., 167
Klinnert, M. D., 601
Klopfer, L., 636, 637
Klorman, R., 304
Kluckhohn, C., 541
Kluckhohn, F. R., 541
Kluge, L., 119
Kluver, H., 434
Knapp, P. H., 330
Knehans, A. W., 127
Knight, G. P., 554
Knight, R. C., 396
Knispel, J. D., 434, 437, 438,
    441, 447, 453, 454, 474-76
Knoell, D. M., 5
Knowles, E. S., 398

Kobayashi, H., 456
Kocher, E. C., 514
Kocsis, J. D., 471
Koel, A., 541
Koenig, K. P., 572
Koestenblatt, M., 540
Koff, E., 586
Kofman, O., 87, 99
Kofod, H., 91
Kohl, D., 636
Kohlberg, L., 540
Kohn, P., 235
Kohout, F. J., 278
Koike, H., 471, 473
Koketsu, K., 469
Kokkinidis, L., 90
Kolb, B., 587
Kolb, H., 502
Kolen, M. J., 368
Koles, Z. J., 587
Kollar, E., 581
Kolotkin, R. L., 338
Kolsawalla, M. B., 552
Koltermann, R., 174
Komaki, J. L., 358
Komisaruk, B. R., 93
Konishi, M., 166, 177
Koob, G. F., 84, 94, 95
Kopell, B. S., 304, 305
Kopin, I. J., 95
Kopp, C. B., 145
Koppanyi, T., 439
Korboot, P. J., 301
Kornadt, H.-J., 552
Kornblith, S., 331
Kornetsky, C., 301, 311, 313
Korte, C., 554
Koslin, B., 625
Koslin, S., 625
Koslowski, B., 576
Koss, M. P., 338
Kostyuk, P. G., 462
Kotter, J. P., 365
Kourilsky, M., 279
Kovacs, M., 328, 329
Kowal, D. M., 361
Koyama, S., 95
Kozlovskaya, I. B., 439
KOZMA, R. B., 611-51; 619,
    620
Kraepelin, E., 294, 421
Kraiger, K., 358
Kramer, P., 513
Krampen, G., 546
Kranau, E. J., 550
Krantz, D. S., 392, 396
Krasa, H., 445
Krasne, F. B., 449
Kraus, N., 441
Kraus, V., 38
Krauskopf, J., 503, 510
Kraut, R. E., 250
Kreel, L., 296, 297

Krendl, K. A., 619
Krieger, D. T., 82, 85, 92
Krinar, G., 95
Krinsky, S. J., 142
Krnjevic, K., 459
Kroeck, K. G., 369
Kroeker, L., 369
Kroeker, L. P., 369
Krogsgaard-Larsen, P., 91
Kronfol, Z., 587
Kruithoff, A., 628
Krupnick, J., 338
Kubota, M., 448
Kudo, M., 441
Kudriashov, I. E., 469, 470
Kugelmass, S., 40
Kuhar, M. J., 78
Kuhn, T. S., 217
Kuipers, B., 388, 391
Kulik, C.-L. C., 363, 618, 639
Kulik, J. A., 363, 618, 639
Kumar, P., 543
Kunze, D. L., 451, 459
Kuperman, S., 296
Kurland, D. M., 620
Kurtz, A. K., 6
Kutas, M., 45, 46, 303, 304
Kuzma, G., 469
Kyllonen, P. C., 637

L

LaBarbera, P. A., 280
LaBeff, E. E., 554
LaBerge, D., 50, 62, 66, 67
Lacatis, D., 114
Lacey, B. C., 572
Lacey, J. J., 572
Lagakos, S. W., 266
Lagmay, A. V., 532
Lahey, B. B., 122
Lahti, I., 308, 310
Laird, J. D., 577, 581, 591, 592
Lajtha, A., 78, 82, 86, 92
Lalonde, R. J., 221
Lamb, M. E., 149
Lamb, T. D., 501, 505
Lambert, M. J., 324
Lambert, R. W., 442
Lambert, W. W., 526, 529, 552
Lambiotte, J. G., 640
Landau, M., 633
Landis, D., 529, 531, 533
Landman, J. T., 325
Landsberg, L., 120, 125, 126
Landy, F. J., 355, 356
Lane, F. B., 365
Lane, J. D., 94
Lang, P. J., 301
Langer, S., 135
Langloss, J. M., 298
Lanius, U. F., 382, 383, 387

Lanzetta, J. T., 579, 581, 598
Larkin, J., 635, 636
Larson, C. O., 640
Larson, D. L., 97
Larson, G. E., 355
Lashley, K. S., 169, 439
LASLEY, D. J., 495-521; 503,
    508-10, 512, 513, 515, 517
Last, C. G., 331
Latané, B., 555
Latham, C. J., 83
Latham, G. P., 367
LaTour, S. A., 281
Latz, A., 294, 300, 309
Laughhunn, D. J., 260
Laughlin, S., 504
Lavond, D. G., 434, 435, 438,
    439
Lavooy, J., 151
Lavrakas, P. J., 399
Lawshe, C. H., 354, 368
Lawson, J. S., 301
Lawson, R., 234
Lawton, M. P., 395, 402
Layman, M., 260
Layton, R. A., 261
Lazarus, A. A., 341
Lazarus, R. S., 273, 274, 340,
    392, 396
Lazdunski, M., 463
Lea, S. E. G., 169, 188
Leavitt, C., 272
Lebovitz, R. M., 465
LeBow, M. D., 333
Lederhendler, I., 463
Lefcourt, H. M., 544
Leger, D. W., 178
Legge, G. E., 509, 515
Lehrer, P. M., 393
Leibel, R. L., 119
Leibowitz, S. F., 89
Leigh, T. W., 259
Leight, K. A., 592, 595
Leighton, K., 140
Leitenberg, H., 334
Leith, C. R., 45
Le Magnen, J., 125
Lemke, S., 386, 387
LeMoal, M., 94, 95
Lemos, J. R., 469
Lennie, P., 502, 506
Leonard, C. S., 469, 473
Leong, C., 628
Leong, H., 509
Lepper, M., 272, 619
Le Roith, D., 85
Lesh, R., 633
Leung, K., 543
Levenson, R. W., 573, 581,
    582, 600
LEVENTHAL, H., 565-610;
    569, 575, 578, 579, 583,
    584, 597, 600, 601

Levick, W. R., 500, 503, 504,
    512
Levie, W., 618
Levin, H. M., 215
Levin, I. P., 266
Levin, J., 9, 628, 639
Levin, V. A., 472
Levine, A. S., 85, 89, 94, 125
Levine, E. L., 354
Levine, M. P., 144, 151, 382,
    383, 391, 392
Levine, M. V., 362
Levine, M. W., 503
LeVine, R. A., 535, 552
Levine, S., 140
Levit, R. A., 304, 305
Levitan, I. B., 464, 469
Leviton, L. C., 202-4, 206-8,
    228, 229
Levitsky, D. A., 122
Levitt, M. J., 147
Lev-tov, A., 459
Levy, J., 586
Levy, W. B., 451
Lewis, J., 48
Lewis, J. W., 96
Lewis, M. E., 96, 144, 145,
    147, 293
Lewis, T. L., 151
Lewow, E., 300, 311
Ley, R. G., 584
Li, C.-L., 477
Li, E. T. S., 125
Libet, B., 456, 469
Licht, B. G., 640
Lichtenstein, E., 336
Lichtenstein, M., 273
Lichtenstein, S., 260
Liddy, L., 550
Liebeskind, J. C., 96
Liebhart, E. H., 572, 575
Light, R. J., 213, 214
Lillywhite, P. G., 501, 504
Liman, E., 454, 456
Lin, D. H., 122
Lin, Y., 616
Lin, Y-G., 616, 639
Lincoln, J. S., 439
Lincoln, Y. S., 203, 211, 218,
    219, 227
Linda, G., 280
Lindauer, M., 168, 179
Lindberg, E., 388, 391, 392
Lindblom, C. E., 195, 200, 219
Linden, W., 331, 334
Lindstrom, J., 461
Lineberry, C. G., 91
Linehan, M. M., 337
Ling, L. J., 454, 456
Ling, M., 95
Linn, R. L., 358, 361, 367, 368
Lippa, A. S., 87
Lippold, C. J., 450, 457, 476

Lipsey, M., 627
Lipson, M., 628, 629, 639
Lipton, M. A., 86
Lipton, P., 477
Lishman, W. A., 592
Lisoprawski, A., 91
Lissak, R. I., 362
Llinas, R., 439, 458, 461-63, 466, 469, 473
Lloyd, D. P. C., 451
Lloyd, G. C., 592
Lloyd, I. H., 168
Lloyd, K. G., 92
Lnenicka, G. A., 446
Lockhart, M. C., 355
Lockhead, J., 638
Loewenstein, W. R., 461, 462
Loftis, J., 569
Loftus, E. F., 594
Logan, G. D., 49, 63, 57
Lohman, D. F., 612, 613, 621
LoLordo, V. M., 184
Lombardi, W., 47
Lombardo, A. G. G. E., 533
Lombardo, M. M., 365
Lomo, T., 446
LONDON, P., 321-49; 323, 341, 342
Long, C. G., 334
Longman, D., 440
Lonner, W. J., 35, 38
Loo, C., 394
López, M., 640
Lord, C., 272
Lord, R. G., 356
Lorente de Nó, R., 458
Lorentz, J., 540
Lorenz, K. Z., 164, 165
Lorenzo, R. V., 366
Loriaux, M. D., 126
Lotfi, A., 536
Loucks, R. B., 450
Lovinger, D. M., 98
Lowe, D. G., 53
Lowy, M. T., 85, 94
Luborsky, L., 333, 337
Luborsky, Lester, 324
Luborsky, Lisa, 324
Lucas, D. B., 274
Luchins, D. J., 297
Luine, V. N., 96
Luiten, J., 622
Lundh, L. G., 66
Lupoli, J., 122
Lusted, L. B., 512
Lustman, P. J., 329, 338
Luttinger, D., 94
Lutz, R. J., 267, 275
Lux, H. D., 451, 459, 462
Luz, M., 534
Lyall, K. C., 199

Lynch, G., 98
Lynch, J. G., 263, 266
Lyness, K. S., 365

M

Maccoby, E. E., 144
MacCrimmon, D. J., 301
MacDonald, K., 147
MacDonald, K. R., 332
Macdonald, M. A., 536, 549
Mace, W., 578, 579
Macht, M. B., 439
Mack, M. J., 372
MacKay, D. G., 48
MacKenzie, A. A., 637
Mackenzie, B., 538, 539
MacKenzie, C. L., 637
MacKenzie, S. B., 275
MacKinnon, E., 627
Macleod, D., 496, 505
MacLeod, D. I. A., 511
Macready, G., 628
MacTurk, R. H., 145
MacWhinney, B., 535
Madden, J. IV, 434, 440
Madsen, M., 528
Maeda, J., 448, 471
Maehr, M. L., 544, 636
Magelund, G., 92
Maggio, J. E., 78
Magleby, K. L., 463
Mahadik, S. P., 97
Mahler, I., 543
Mahoney, M. J., 340
Main, D. S., 370
Main, M., 576
Maldonado, P., 534
Malhotra, N. K., 266
Maloney, L. T., 516
Maloney, P., 549
Malpass, R., 529
Maltzman, I. M., 331
Mandinach, E., 624
Mandl, H., 627
Mandler, G., 274
Mann, J., 338
Mann, L. S., 296, 297
Manning, J. W., 95
Manstead, A. S. R., 572
Mantyh, P. W., 78, 79
Mantyla, T., 391, 392
Mantysalo, S., 303
Manugian, V., 95
Marangos, P. J., 78
Marans, R. W., 400-2
Marcel, A. J., 60, 66, 67
Marchak, F., 61
Marchon, I., 382, 383, 391, 392
Marcus, J., 300, 311
Marder, S. R., 301
Margolis, R., 169
Marian, A. P., 502

Marin, G., 540
Marin, O. S. M., 49, 53, 54, 59, 60
Marino, M., 635
Mariscal, S., 169
Markel, E., 439
Markman, E., 628
Marks, I. M., 331
Marks, L. J., 265
Markus, G. B., 536
Markus, H., 241, 247, 248, 267, 273
Marler, P., 168, 169, 176-78, 186, 187
Marmar, C., 338
Marmor, J., 340, 341
Marotz-Baden, R., 531
Marsden, C. D., 84, 97
Marsella, A. J., 533
Marsh, H. W., 370
Marshall, G. D., 567, 568, 573
Marshall, H., 624
Marshall, J. F., 91
Marshall, K. C., 459
Marshall, P. G., 86
Martello, J., 595
Marteniuk, R. G., 637
Martin, G. B., 140
Martin, J. A., 144
Martin, J. B., 82, 85, 92
Martin, J. N., 553
Martin, M. M., 57
Martin, R., 124
Martinez, J. L., 94
Martinez, S., 554
Marton, F., 639
Marty, A., 478
Marx, J. L., 96
Maser, J., 590
Mash, E. J., 324
Maslach, C., 567, 568, 573
Mason, J., 629
Mason, S. T., 88
Mason, W. A., 166, 186
Massof, R. W., 510
Masters, J., 155
Masters, J. C., 592, 593, 595, 596
Masterton, R. B., 441
Mastronarde, D. N., 503
Mathews, A. M., 596
Mathews, W. M., 546
Matsumura, M., 434, 451
Matthews, G., 501, 503, 504
Matthews, S. M., 329
Matthysse, S., 300
Mattussek, P., 301
Maurer, D., 151
Mauritz, K. H., 473
Mavissakalian, M., 331
Mawson, D., 331
Maxwell, R. A., 92

Maxwell, S. E., 329, 369
Mayekawa, S., 371
Mayer, J. D., 591
Mayer, M. L., 461
Mayer, R. E., 639
Mayer, R. N., 278, 622
Maynard Smith, J., 172
Maynes, F., 636
Mayr, E., 152
Mazique, M. S., 365
Mazis, M. B., 275
Mazur, A., 552
Mazursky, D., 280
Mazziotta, J. C., 599
McAfee, D. A., 446, 457, 467,
   468
McArthur, L. A., 577
McBride, J. R., 361
McCall, M. W. Jr., 365
McCall, R. B., 146, 151
McCalley-Whitters, M., 296
McCallum, W. C., 303
McCaman, R. E., 471
McCann, J., 265
McCarley, R. W., 304
McCarthy, G., 303
McCarthy, M. E., 145
McCarthy, W., 8
McCaul, M. E., 333
McCauley, C., 47, 60, 61
McClelland, D. C., 543
McClelland, J. J., 52
McCloskey, M., 636
McCluskey, K. A., 155
McCombs, B. L., 640
McConkie, G. W., 52, 55
McCormick, D. A., 434, 435,
   438-40
McCormick, E. J., 8, 370
McCracken, K. J., 121
McCulloch, J., 97
McCune-Nicholich, L., 144
McDonald, B., 331
McDonough, J. H., 78
McDougall, W., 565
McFarland, D. J., 168
McFee, J., 637
McGaugh, J. L., 94
McGaw, B., 215
McGee, C., 400, 401
McGhie, A., 301
McGill, W. J., 501, 504
McGillis, D., 248
McGinty, D. J., 86, 88
McGraw, C. F., 450
McGrew, W. C., 181
McGuffog, C., 147
McGuinness, D., 588
McGuinness, B. L., 469, 473
McGuire, M. T., 424
McIlwain, H., 477
McIntosh, B., 355
McIntyre, R. M., 357

MCKEACHIE, W. J., 611-51;
   616, 618, 639, 641
McKeever, W. F., 584
McKenna, D. G., 471
McKenzie, R. C., 364
McKeown, M., 629
McKnew, D. H., 149
McLaughlin, C. L., 93
McLaughlin, M. W., 197, 206,
   207
McLaughlin, P. J., 95
McLellan, C. P., 333
McNally, R. J., 598
McNeil, O. V., 402
McNeil, T. F., 294, 300
McNiven, M. A., 121
McSwain, R., 540
McSweeney, F. K., 278
McWhite, R., 369
Means, B., 596
Mecham, R. C., 8, 370
Mecklenbrauker, S., 591
Mednick, B., 300
Mednick, S. A., 294, 300
Meece, J., 615, 624
Meech, R. W., 462, 463
Meeker, R. B., 92
Meglino, B. M., 355
Meichenbaum, D. H., 235, 341
Meikle, S., 424
Melikian, L. H., 532
Mellon, P. M., 235, 236
Meltzoff, A. N., 140, 141
Menasco, M. B., 266
Mendels, G. E., 235
Mendelson, M. J., 139, 423
Menges, R. J., 612
Menne, J. W., 8
Menten, T. G., 139
Menzel, R., 172, 173
Mercer, J., 627
Merchant, S. M., 552
Merikle, P., 61
Merikle, P. M., 57
Meringoff, L. K., 619
Meritt, R., 366
Meritt-Haston, R., 364
Merom, H., 310
Merry, S. E., 398, 401
Mersch, P. P., 330
Mertens, J., 512
Merton, P. A., 576
Merton, R. K., 234, 251
Merzenich, M. M., 440
Messick, S., 4, 625-27
Messing, R. B., 94
Mestyán, J., 126
Mesulam, M. M., 585
Metcalf, B. L., 279, 280
Mettler, F. A., 439
Metz, C. E., 512
Meyer, D. E., 47
Meyer, R. J., 261, 266, 265

Meyer, V., 331
Meyers, E. D. Jr., 151
Mezynski, K., 629
Mezzich, J., 304, 305
Michelson, C., 541
Michelson, L., 331
Michelson, W., 395
Michie, P. T., 303
Michik, G., 525
Mickelsen, O., 120
Middlestadt, S. E., 366
Midgley, D. F., 261
Mielke, K. W., 203
Milavsky, B., 570
Milberg, S., 592
Milby, M. B., 331
Miledi, R., 450, 463
Milgram, S., 555
Miller, A. T., 615
Miller, D. B., 152
Miller, D. S., 115
MILLER, D. T., 233-56; 241,
   243, 247, 248
Miller, E. F., 507
Miller, H., 591
Miller, J. D., 91, 441
Miller, J. P., 459
Miller, L., 40
Miller, N. E., 78, 336
Miller, P., 45
Miller, R. L., 250, 626, 638
Miller, T. I., 324-27, 340, 342
Miller, W. H., 511, 539
Miller, W. R., 331, 332
Millis-Wright, M., 57
Millon, T., 3, 7
Milne, A. R., 450, 457, 476
Milner, B., 296
Miloy, S., 89
Mineka, S., 574
Miniard, P. W., 268, 269
Minor, M. W., 235
Mintz, M., 299
Miranda, D., 540
MIRSKY, A. F., 291-319; 291,
   292, 294, 300, 301, 309,
   310
Mischel, W., 8, 9
Mishkin, M., 185
Misiak, H., 531
Mitchel, J. S., 127
Mitchell, A. A., 265, 272, 274,
   275
Mitchell, K. J., 372
Mitchell, R., 328
Mitchell, S. A., 144
Mitterer, J. O., 53
Mizerski, R. W., 280
Mock, J. E., 424
Modiano, N., 534
Mogenson, G. J., 91
Mogilnicka, E., 97
Mohler, H., 93

Moles, E., 402
Monaco, G. E., 277
Monakhov, K., 587
Monck, E. M., 308
Montal, M., 461
Monteiro, K. P., 591, 592, 596
Montgomery, W. A., 585
Moody, T. W., 78
Moore, D. L., 275
Moore, G. T., 389
Moore, J. W., 439, 442
Moore, M. K., 140
Moore, R. Y., 88, 90
Moos, R. H., 386, 387
Morales, A., 86
Moran, T. P., 620
Moray, N., 48
Morel, A., 441
Moreno, K. E., 361
Morest, D. K., 441
Morgan, C. T., 435
Morgan, D. W., 424
Morgan, H., 507
Morgane, P. J., 85, 89
Morison, V., 139
Morley, J. E., 85, 89, 94, 125
Morrell, F., 475, 476
Morris, L. W., 616
Morrison, F., 60
Morrison, R. F., 353
Morrongiello, B. A., 141
Morrow, G., 336
Morsbach, H., 531
Morselli, P. L., 92
Morstyn, R., 304
Morton, J., 46
Mosbach, P., 601
Moscovici, S., 241
Moscovitch, M., 584
Mosenthal, P., 631
Moser, J., 633, 635
Moses, J. A., 296, 297
Moses, J. A. Jr., 296, 297
Moses, J. L., 365, 366
Mosher, L. R., 329
Moskal, J. R., 98
Moss, M., 402
Moss, R. L., 93
Mossholder, K. W., 361, 370
Motowidlo, S. J., 353
Mount, M. K., 358
Mountcastle, V. B., 45
Movshon, J. A., 500, 503
Mrosovsky, N., 115, 117
Muchinsky, P. M., 366
Mueller, C. W., 570
Mulaik, S. A., 367
Muller, T. E., 279
Mumford, E., 323, 335
Mumford, M. D., 364
Mumford, P., 115
Munby, M., 331
Munoz, R., 413, 425, 426

Munro, D., 544
Munroe, R. H., 526, 530, 536, 540, 541, 551
Munroe, R. L., 526, 530, 536, 540, 541, 551
Munter, P. S., 569
Mura, E., 300
Murakami, F., 469, 471
Murchison, C., 135
Murdock, M., 325, 326, 338
Murnane, R. J., 221
Murphy, D. L., 591, 592, 595
Murphy, G. E., 329, 338, 339
Murphy, J. P., 470
Murphy, K. R., 355, 356, 370
Murphy-Berman, V., 543
Murray, E. J., 569
Murray, P., 141
Murray, T., 279
Mussen, P. H., 136, 138
Musser, L. M., 237
Myers, B. J., 153
Myers, J. K., 425
Myers, R. D., 78, 87
Myers, R. E., 300
Myles-Worsley, M., 54
Myslobodsky, M. S., 299

N

Naarala, M., 308, 310
Näätänen, R., 46, 303
Nachmias, J., 497, 513, 514, 516, 517
Nachshen, D. A., 450
Nacimiento, A. C., 473
Nadi, N., 87
Naghdi, S., 301
Nagler, S., 294, 300, 309
Nagy, J. N., 148
Nahvi, M. J., 462
Nairn, A., 468
Nairn, A. C., 469
Naka, R. Y., 462
Nakamura, M., 469
Nancarrow, P. R., 632
Narahashi, T., 478
Narin, F., 37
Naroll, F., 525
Naroll, R., 525, 531, 532
Narrol, H., 638
Nasar, J. L., 384
Nasby, W., 591-93
Nash, A., 140, 141
Nasrallah, H. A., 296
Natale, F., 535
Natale, M., 592, 596
Nathan, B. R., 356
Navon, D., 44, 57
Neale, J. M., 301
Neary, J. T., 454, 469
Neeb, R. W., 354

Needleman, P., 93
Neff, W. D., 441, 454
Neger, W. J., 236
Neher, E., 463, 473, 478
Neidig, P. J., 370
Neidig, R. D., 370
Neilson, D. R. Jr., 441, 449
Neisser, U., 44, 57-59, 63, 69
Nelson, C. A., 140
Nelson, G., 50, 63
Nelson, M. C., 280
Nelson, R. J., 440, 502, 572
Nelson, S. R., 78
Nemeroff, C. B., 92, 94
Nemeth, C., 241
Nenov, V., 453, 459, 478
Neophytides, A. N., 296, 312
Nesher, P., 635
Nestler, E. J., 467, 468
Nevo, B., 551
Nevo, O., 552
Newell, A., 620
Nello, M., 635
Newlin, D. B., 296
Newman, J. P., 588
Newman, O., 398, 399
Newsome, S. L., 52
Newstead, S., 221
Nguyen, S. D., 533
Nicassio, P., 569
Nicholls, J. G., 615
Nicholson, C., 458
Nicholson, R. A., 324
Nickerson, R. S., 638
Nicolaides, S., 124
Nicoll, R. A., 459
Nielsen, L. L., 64
Nienhuis, R., 441
Niles, F. S., 544
Ninan, P. T., 96
Ninio, A., 48
Nirenberg, M., 98
Nisbett, R. E., 568, 569
Nishi, S., 469
Nishiyama, T., 550
Nishizawa, Y., 127
Nissen, H. W., 435
Nissen, M. J., 49
Niwa, S., 304, 305, 307
Noble, D., 458
Noe, R. A., 362, 366
Nolan, C., 279
Nolte, L. W., 507, 513
Norborg, J. M., 368
Norcross, J. C., 340, 342
Nord, R., 369
Nord, W. R., 278
Norgren, R., 85
Norman, D. A., 44
Norman, J., 40
Norman, R. J., 439
Normann, R., 504
Normansell, L., 87, 97

Normansell, L. A., 83, 85, 87, 94
Normoyle, J., 399
Norris, E. B., 447
Norton, T., 450
Norton-Griffiths, M. N., 186
Notarius, C. I., 581
Notsu, T., 448
Nottebohm, F., 166
Novak-Hofer, I., 469
Novick, M. R., 371
Nowicki, G., 596
Nowicki, S., 546
Nozick, R., 209
Nuechterlein, K. H., 293, 301, 306
Nunn, P. J., 501
Nunnally, J., 351
Nurenberger, J., 87

O

Oakley, D. A., 439
Oatman, L. C., 46
Obermiller, C., 269
Obert, H-J., 167
O'Brien, C. P. O., 333
O'Brien, G. T., 330, 331
O'Brien, J. H., 457
Obrist, P. A., 580
Obrist, W. D., 295
O'Connell, E. J., 235
O'Connor, J., 357
Ocorr, K. A., 453
Oda, Y., 448
O'Donnell, A., 640
O'Donnell, P. M., 386
O'Donohue, T. L., 78
Oei, T. P., 328
Ofir, C., 266
Ogaiea, M., 536
Ohman, A., 598
Ohzawa, I., 500, 503, 504
Ojemann, R. G., 434
Okada, Y., 473
O'Keefe, D., 336
Okita, T., 303
Olds, J., 469
Olds, M., 441
Olian, J. D., 363
Oliva, T. A., 274
Oliver, A. P., 459
Oliver, R. L., 280
Oliverio, A., 94
Olney, J. W., 93
Olsen, R. J., 221
Olsen, S. A., 296, 297
Olshavsky, R. W., 261, 267
Olson, C. A., 370
Olson, D. M., 353, 358
Olson, G. A., 94
Olson, J. C., 265, 275
Olson, J. M., 569

Olson, R. D., 94
Oltmanns, T. F., 301
Olton, D. S., 188
Olzak, L. A., 517
Omanson, R., 629
Omanson, S., 634
Omelich, C. L., 615
O'Neal, E., 568
O'Neil, H. F., 637
Ong, P., 394
Ono, J. K., 471
Opfinger, E., 172, 174
Opolot, J. A., 539
Oppenheim, R. W., 151
Opsahl, C. A., 127
Orasanu, J., 628
Orchard, J., 333
O'Regan, J. K., 52
Orona, E., 442
Orr, S. P., 598
Orr, W. B., 442
Orsulak, P. J., 590
Orzack, M. H., 301, 311, 313
Osborn, J., 627
Osborn, W., 355
Osburn, H. G., 12, 371
Oshima, T., 473
Ossowska, K., 92
Ost, L. G., 330
Oster, H., 576
Ostrander, E. R., 395
Osuji, O. N., 534
Othmer, E., 425
Owen, W. G., 505
Owens, J., 434, 438, 441, 454, 470
Owens, W. A., 353, 365
Owings, D. H., 178
Ozer, D. J., 373

P

Paap, K. R., 52
Pacheco, A. M., 402
Pacht, A. R., 206
Pachuri, A., 543
Pack, S. J., 242
Padian, N., 328, 338
Page, T. J., 269
Palardy, J., 235
Palay, S. L., 78
Palgi, P., 40
Pallincsar, A., 630
Pallotta, B. S., 463
Palmer, S. E., 47
Palmerino, C. C., 452
Pan, H. S., 78
Panitch, D., 245, 246
PANKSEPP, J., 77-107; 78, 81, 83-85, 87, 89, 91, 92, 94-97, 99
Pannone, R. D., 365
Panula, P., 79, 93

Papsdorf, J. D., 440
Parameswaran, S. V., 124
Parasuraman, R., 44, 45, 50, 63, 67
Pardes, H., 338
Paris, S. G., 616, 627-29, 639
Parisi, T., 441
Park, C. W., 261, 264, 265, 275, 278
Parkington, J. J., 372
Parkinson, B., 572
PARLOFF, M. B., 321-49; 323, 326, 337, 338
Parmelee, C. M., 47, 60, 61
Parnas, I., 469
Parsons, C. K., 362
Pascarella, E., 636
Pasquarelli, B., 577
Pass, H. L., 304
Pass, J. J., 354
Patel, J., 78
Patlak, C. S., 472
Patrick, C., 323
Patrick, R., 596
Patterson, M. L., 238, 239, 246, 247, 397
Patton, M. L., 95
Patton, M. Q., 203, 218, 219, 227
Paul, G., 326
Paul, S. M., 96
Paulman, R. G., 616
Paupardin-Tritsch, D., 464
Pavelchak, M. A., 264, 274
Pavlov, I., 183, 187
Pavlov, I. P., 435, 439, 445, 450, 452
Payne, J. W., 260, 266, 267
Payne, R. W., 301
Pazdernik, T. L., 78
Pazos, A., 95
Pea, R. D., 144, 620
Peake, P. K., 9
Pearce, J. W., 333
Pearlman, K., 8, 11, 372
Pearson, D., 628-30
Peat, N. C., 281
Pedersen, J., 140
Pedersen, P., 533
Pedhazur, E. J., 549
Peele, S., 332
Peleaux, R., 140
Pellegrino, J. W., 388, 391
Pelli, D. G., 500, 512, 513, 515
Pendery, M. L., 331
Penfield, W., 435
Penick, E. C., 425
Penner, B. C., 637
Penney, J. B., 78, 98
Penney, J. B. Jr., 78
Penrod, J. H., 332
Pepitone, A., 547, 552
Percy, L., 227, 274, 276

Perkel, D. H., 458
Perkins, N., 127
Perlson, M. R., 5
Perman, G. P., 296
Peroutka, S. J., 465
Perris, C., 587
Perry, S., 323
Pert, A., 96, 97
Pert, C. B., 78, 96, 97
Peter, J. P., 278
Peters, A., 472
Peters, L. H., 357
Peters, S., 177
Peterson, C., 615
Peterson, D., 9
Peterson, M. R., 189, 298
Peterson, N. G., 364
Peterson, P. L., 624
Peterson, R. E., 122
Peterson, W. W., 498, 512, 513
Petrinovich, L., 177
Petty, R. E., 270, 273-75
Pezdek, K., 390, 392
Pfaff, D. W., 85
Pfefferbaum, A., 304, 305
Pfeifer, S., 147
Pfeiffer, A., 95
Phelps, M. E., 599
Phillips, J. S., 322, 323, 355
Phillips, M. A., 198, 214
Phillips, M. I., 93
Philpott, A., 60
Piaget, J., 261, 389
Pick, H. L., 531
Pickar, D., 595, 596
Pickert, R., 177
Picton, T. W., 303-5, 307
Pierce, L., 50, 52
Pierce, P., 555
Pierson, H. D., 555
Pietromonaco, P., 62
Pike, F. H., 335
Pillemer, D. B., 214
Pincus, H. A., 338
Pindas, P., 531
Pinel, J. P. J., 445
PINTRICH, P. R., 611-51; 615,
    616, 623, 639
Piontkowski, D., 629
Pirenne, M. P., 496-98, 501,
    502, 504, 506, 508, 514
Pisoni, D. B., 151
Pitariu, H., 550
Pitt, D. G., 385, 387
Plath, D., 531
Platt, G., 251
Plomin, R., 152
Plotsky, P. M., 95
Plutchik, R., 84, 424
Podgorny, P., 51
Polivy, J., 596
Pollack, H., 633
Pollen, D. A., 466

Poltyrew, S. S., 439
Pomerantz, J. R., 57
Poole, M. E., 540
Poortinga, Y. H., 527, 528
Pooyan, A., 357
Porte, J. D., 124
Porter, R. E., 531
Portnoy, M., 303
Portoghese, P. S., 97
Posen, C., 544
Posner, J. K., 535
Posner, M. I., 44, 45, 47-49,
    51, 53, 54, 56, 59, 60, 62,
    66, 67
Post, R. M., 296, 297
Post, T. A., 637
Potter, F., 628
Powell, B. J., 425
Powell, G. J., 534
Powell, L. H., 335
Powell, T. P. S., 441
Powers, M. K., 505
POWLEY, T. L., 109-33; 117-
    19, 121, 125, 127
Prange, A. J. Jr., 94
Pratt, G., 383
Prescott, P. A., 139
Pressley, M., 9, 628, 639
Presson, C. C., 142
Preston, R. J., 471
Preussler, D. W., 90, 91
Pribram, K. H., 588
Price, D. L., 87
Price, J. M., 358
Primoff, E. S., 6, 8, 354
Prince, D. A., 469
Prinz, S. M., 148
Prinzmetal, W., 56, 57
Prioleau, L., 325, 326, 338
Pritchard, R. D., 369
Prochaska, J. O., 340, 342
Prohaska, T., 244
Proshansky, H. M., 381
Prucnal, P. R., 501, 504
Prusoff, B. A., 328, 329, 338
Pryer, M. W., 357
Przybeck, T., 415
Puglisi-Allegra, S., 94
Puil, E., 469
Pujol, J. F., 89
Pulakos, E. D., 357
Pumain, R., 459
Punj, G. N., 261, 266
Purcell, G., 61
Purves, R. D., 475
Putnam, D., 538
Puto, C., 266
Pye, C., 153

Q

Quaife, M. A., 295
Quaintance, M. K., 353

Quandt, F. N., 478
Quartermain, D., 89, 118
Quenzer, L. F., 86
Quesney, L. F., 92
Quick, R. F., 516
Quinn, W. G., 182, 183, 187
Quirion, R., 96

R

Raabe, D. H., 475
Rabbitt, P. M. A., 46, 47, 62,
    66, 67
Rabin, A. L., 33
Rabkin, J. G., 327, 339
Rachford, D. L., 638
Rachman, S. J., 326, 327, 330,
    331, 338
Radke-Yarrow, M., 149, 150
Radtke, H. L., 597
Rae, D. S., 417
Rafacz, B. A., 369
Rafaeli, A., 365
Rafal, R. D., 45
Raftery, M. A., 461
Rahe, R., 335
Rainard, B., 636
Rainbow, T. C., 78, 96
Rajecki, D. W., 238, 239, 246,
    247
Raju, N. S., 368, 371
Rakic, P., 448
Rall, W., 453, 458, 459
Rambo, W. W., 358
Ramey, C. T., 149, 150
Ramm, L., 331
Rand, Y., 626, 638
Randolph, W. A., 356
Ranson, S. W., 127, 443
Rapoport, A., 401, 402
Rappaport, A., 330
Rappaport, E. B., 125
Rapport, M. M., 97
Rashbass, C., 508, 510
Rashid, M., 623
Rasmussen, H., 461, 462, 467,
    469
Rasmussen, K. G. Jr., 366
Rastad, J., 471
Ratner, N. B., 153
Raulin, M. L., 307
Raviv, A., 30, 40
Rawls, J., 209
Ray, A. A., 571, 572
Ray, D. W., 395
Ray, M. L., 271, 274
Ray, W. J., 587
Rayner, K., 52, 52, 55
Read, S. J., 242
Rebar, R. W., 126
Reckase, M. D., 361
Redd, W., 336
Redfield, J., 587

Redican, W. K., 576
Redmond, D. E., 84
Redmond, D. E. Jr., 90
Redner, R., 198, 214
Reed, S. D., 585
Reeder, G. D., 248
Reeves, A., 50
Regan, D., 303
Rehavi, M., 96
Rehm, L. P., 593
Reichardt, L. F., 97
Reif, F., 637
Reigeluth, C. M., 620
Reilly, M. D., 261
Reimanis, G., 544
Rein, M., 200
Reina, J. C., 123
Reinis, S., 86
Reisenzein, R., 568, 570, 571, 574
Reiss, S. E., 448
Reizensenstein, J. E., 395
Remington, R., 50, 52
Remler, M. P., 471
Renaud, L., 456, 459, 466
Renfrew, J. W., 85
Renner, K. J., 96
Rescorla, R. A., 443-45, 447, 453, 470
Resnick, L. B., 614, 628, 631, 633, 634, 636
Rethans, A. J., 259, 260
Reuter-Lorenz, P., 584
Revuelta, A. V., 79
Revusky, S., 176, 184, 185
Reynolds, B. K., 547
Reynolds, D. G., 95
Reynolds, T. J., 265
Reznick, S., 146
Rheingold, H. L., 139, 141, 144, 148
Rhodewalt, F., 249
Ribak, C. E., 462, 471
Ricci, G., 435
Richards, J. G., 93, 634
Richards, W. G., 454, 456
Richardson, F. C., 335
Richardson, G. A., 155
Richardson, P. H., 301
Richins, M. L., 281
Richman, A., 535
Richter, D. W., 473
Riddoch, G., 439
Ridgway, E. B., 461, 462
Rieder, R. O., 296, 297, 300
Riggs, L. A., 301
Rigter, H., 94
Rihn, B. A., 639
Riley, D. A., 45
Riley, J. G. A., 48
Riley, M., 635
Rimland, B., 355
Rindskopf, D., 368

Ring, K., 238, 245, 246
Riordan, E., 126
Ritchie, R. J., 366
Ritter, W., 303
Rivier, J., 94
Rizley, R. C., 453
Rizzo, A., 336
Robbins, T. W., 89, 90
Roberts, D. C. S., 88
Roberts, E., 91
Roberts, P., 97
Roberts, R., 573
Roberts, W. W., 97
Robertson, L. S., 550
Robin, R. W., 536
Robins, E., 411, 413, 414, 425, 426
ROBINS, L. N., 409-32; 415, 425
Robinson, D. D., 354
Robinson, J. A., 423
Robinson, M. M., 502
Robinson, R. G., 587
Robinson, T. E., 85, 100
Robson, J. G., 502
Roche, A. F., 151
Rock, I., 58, 59
Rocklin, T., 640
Rodgers, D. A., 206
Rodgers, R. J., 83, 92
Rodin, J., 569, 570
Rodnick, E. H., 301, 308
Rodriques, A., 543
Rodriguez, I. A., 592, 595
Roedder, D. L., 272, 280
Roehler, L., 629
Roemer, R. A., 304, 305
Rogan, J. M., 536, 549
Rogers, A., 531
Rogers, C., 236
Rogers, F. T., 439
Rogers, R. W., 567, 568
Rogerson, J. S., 335
Rogoff, B., 402
Rohe, W. M., 393, 399, 401
Rohner, R., 527
Rohner-Jeanrenaud, F., 127
Rohrbaugh, J., 356
Rohrkemper, M., 623
Rokeach, M., 547
Rollman, G. B., 513, 517
Rolls, B. J., 121
Romanoski, A., 425
Romberg, T., 633
Romero, M., 640
Romsos, D. R., 127
Roose, S. P., 84
Rose, A., 504
Rose, D., 139
Rose, J. E., 441
Rose, K. C., 593
Rose, P. K., 471
Rose, S. R., 353

Rosen, I., 473, 475
Rosen, J. C., 334
Rosenbaum, M., 40
Rosenblatt, J. E., 296, 297
Rosenblatt, M., 95
Rosenfeld, B., 84
Rosenfeld, H. M., 398
Rosenfeld, M. E., 439
Rosenhan, D. L., 246
Rosenshine, B., 622, 629
Rosenthal, B., 333
Rosenthal, D., 294, 300, 301, 307, 412
Rosenthal, R., 234-37, 240, 244, 246, 325, 327
Rosenzweig, M. R., 18
Rosnow, R. L., 327
Ross, D. C., 331, 632
Ross, E. D., 585
Ross, H. S., 139, 142, 144
Ross, I., 260
Ross, J., 592, 636
Ross, L., 272
Ross, M., 247, 249
Ross, R. R., 235
Rosse, R. L., 366
Rossi, J. III, 84, 89, 99
Rossi, P. H., 199, 205, 211, 214, 218, 219, 226
Rossiter, J. R., 276
Rosvold, H. E., 301
Roth, D., 593
Roth, J., 85
Roth, R. S., 587
Roth, V. J., 259
Roth, W. T., 304, 305
Rothbart, M., 247, 248
Rothman, M., 439
Rothschild, M. L., 277, 278
Rothstein, S. I., 170
Rothwell, C., 367
Rothwell, N. J., 115, 121, 126, 127
Rotter, J., 544
Rounsaville, B. J., 329, 333, 337
Routtenberg, A., 98
Rovee-Collier, C., 141
Rovee-Collier, C. K., 141
Rovine, M., 147
Rowe, E. A., 121
Royle, M. H., 354
Ruback, R. B., 395
Rubenstein, R., 620
Rubin, A. D., 631
Rubin, D. B., 235, 236, 325
Rudd, J., 278
Ruddy, M. G., 47
Rudnicky, A. I., 56
Rudy, J. W., 452
Rumsey, M. G., 357
Rupp, M., 546
Rush, A. J., 328, 337, 341

Rushton, J. P., 9
Rusiniak, K. W., 452
Rusinov, V. S., 475, 476
Russell, B., 566
Russell, D. F., 443
Russell, G. J., 279
Russell, I. S., 439
Russell, J. A., 382, 383, 387, 388, 391
Russell, M. L., 593
Russell, R., 531
Russo, J. E., 261, 262, 264, 279, 280
Rutschmann, J., 301
Rutter, M., 147
Ryan, M. J., 269
Ryback, D., 540
Ryle, A., 341
Ryle, G., 496
Rymar, K., 304, 305, 307

S

Saari, L. M., 367
Sackeim, H. A., 581, 585, 586
Sackett, D. L., 335, 420, 424
Sackett, G. A., 139
Sackett, G. P., 181
Sackett, P. R., 363, 366, 369, 370
Sackin, H., 459, 461
Sadock, B. J., 416
Saegert, S., 394, 402
Saettler, P., 618
Safer, M. A., 584
Safran, J. D., 340
Sahley, C. L., 452
Sahley, T. L., 84
Saigh, P. A., 546
Saito, K., 471
Saitoh, O., 304, 305, 307
Sakai, H., 441, 471
Sakai, M., 471
Sakitt, B., 496, 504
Sakmann, B., 473, 478
Salancik, G. R., 249
Salasoo, A., 46, 47
Salazar, J. M., 532
Saleh, B. E. A., 501, 507
Säljö, R., 639
Salomon, G., 618-21
Salop, S. C., 275
Saltwick, S. E., 441
Saltzer, E. B., 268
Salzman, L. F., 304
Samainin, R., 89
Sameroff, S. J., 300
Samovar, L. A., 531
Samson, F. E., 78
Samuel, W., 569
Samuel, Y., 38
Samuels, H. R., 145
Sanchez-Craig, M., 332

Sandberg, K., 97
Sanders, A. L., 540
Sandini, G., 505
Sands, W. A., 361, 369
Sanft, H., 593
Sanghera, M. K., 91
Sansbury, R. V., 514
Santana, P. E., 554
Santiesteban, H. L., 95
Santrock, J. W., 591, 592, 596
Sanua, V. D., 40
Saper, C. B., 93
Sarason, I. G., 10, 64, 301, 341
Sarat, A. D., 201
Sarne, Y., 96
Saron, C., 587, 590
Sartorius, N., 425
Sarvey, J. M., 98
Saul, B. B., 236, 244
Savell, J. M., 638
Saville, E., 126
Savoie, R. E., 517
Sawchenko, P. E., 94
Sawin, D. B., 150
Sawin, L. S., 242
Sawyer, S., 91
Saxby, L., 584
Sayer, S., 400
Scardamalia, M., 631, 632
Scarr, S., 538, 626
Schachter, J., 566, 573
Schachter, S., 110, 336
Schaeffer, M. A., 382, 383, 396
Schaffer, C. E., 587, 590
Schaffner, A. E., 98
Schaninger, C. M., 261
Schatzberg, A. F., 590
Scheel-Krüger, J., 91, 92
Scheich, H., 97
Scheier, M. F., 582
Scheirer, J., 531
Schell, A. M., 597, 598
Schemmel, R., 120
Scher, D., 551
Scherer, K. R., 566, 599
Schiepers, C., 52
Schildkraut, J. J., 590
Schlaer, S., 496-98, 501, 502, 504, 506, 514
Schlegel, A., 525, 526, 549
Schlesinger, H. J., 323, 335
Schlue, W. R., 473
Schmale, A., 336
Schmid, J., 636
Schmidt, F. L., 11, 354, 364, 367, 371, 372
Schmidt, H., 55
Schmidt, R. A., 637
Schmitt, F. O., 443, 468
Schmitt, N., 362, 366
Schmitz, E. J., 369
Schnapf, J. L., 501
Schneck, M. E., 506

Schneider, W., 44, 48, 62, 63, 66, 67
Schneiderman, B., 620
Schoenfeld, A. H., 625, 627
Schoenfeldt, B. B., 5
Schoenfeldt, L. F., 5, 353, 365
Scholes, R., 584
Schopflocher, S., 587
Schramm, W., 618
Schulsinger, F., 294, 300, 307
Schumann, D., 270, 273, 275
Schur, E. M., 252
Schvaneveldt, R. W., 47
Schwafel, J. A., 439
Schwarcz, R., 97
Schwartz, B., 126, 185, 187
Schwartz, D., 93
Schwartz, E. A., 501
Schwartz, G. E., 573, 584, 587
Schwartz, J., 84, 625, 627
Schwartz, J. H., 469
Schwartz, P. M., 148
Schwartzkroin, P. A., 458
Schwent, V. L., 303
Schwindt, P. C., 461, 466, 477
Sciglimpaglia, D., 261
Sclafani, A., 119, 120
Sclar, G., 500, 503, 504
Scott, C. A., 259, 272, 277
Scott, R. A., 241, 247, 248, 252
Scott, W. A., 533
Scriven, M. S., 203, 207-9, 211, 212, 215, 225
Seashore, H. G., 10, 11
Seaver, W. B., 235
Secada, W., 634
Sechrest, L., 198, 214, 327
Seefeld, M. D., 122
Seeger, T. F., 96, 97
Seeley, K. M., 532
Segal, J. W., 637
SEGALL, M. H., 523-64; 526, 527, 530, 531, 534, 537, 552
Segev, I., 460
Seidman, L. J., 293
Sekuler, R., 513
Seligman, M. E. P., 392, 615
Sell, J. L., 386, 387
Selverston, A. I., 471
Selye, M., 126
Senior, K., 145
Serpell, R., 532
Sexton, V. S., 531
Seydoux, J., 126, 127
Seyfarth, R. M., 178
Seymour, S., 531
Sforzo, G. A., 96, 97
SHADISH, W. R., JR., 193-232; 195, 197, 200, 201, 204, 206, 228
Shaffer, A., 216

Shagass, C., 304, 305
Shakow, D., 301, 306, 313
Shalker, T., 591-93, 597
Shama, D. D., 545-47
Shanan, J., 40
Shane, G. S., 11
Shani, A. B., 235
Shanmugam, T. E., 552
Shapely, R. M., 506
Shapir, N., 552
Shapira, A., 528
Shapiro, A. K., 326
Shapiro, D., 324, 325, 335, 340
Shapiro, D. A., 324, 325, 340
Shapiro, D. C., 637
Sharfstein, S., 323
Sharon, I., 554
Sharratt, S., 549
Shatz, M., 154
Shavelson, R., 633
Shaver, P., 64
Shavit, Y., 96
Shavitt, S., 270
Shaw, B. F., 337, 341
Shaw, C., 235, 245
Shaw, M., 51
Shaw, P., 51
Shaye, J., 301, 311
Shayer, M., 549
Shea, J. D. C., 536
Shearer, S. L., 587
Sheatz, G. C., 439
Sheimann, I. M., 153
Shepard, R. N., 51
Sheppard, B. H., 269
Sheras, P. L., 235, 245
Sherk, D. L., 242
Sherrington, C. S., 450
Sherwood, R., 636
Shettleworth, S. J., 171
Shevrin, I., 589
Shields, J., 293, 294
Shiffrin, R. M., 44-49, 62, 63, 66-68
Shiloach, J., 85
Shimp, T. A., 260, 268, 269, 275
Shinkfield, A. J., 229
Shipley, M. T., 441
Sholomskas, D., 328, 338
Short, E. J., 150
Shoukimas, J. J., 463, 465
Shoulson, I., 98
Showers, C., 239
Shuell, T. J., 617, 620
Shulman, L. S., 622-24
Shumaker, S. A., 395
Shur, S., 33
Shwalb, B. J., 639
Sidtis, J. J., 50
Siegel, A. W., 389
Siegelbaum, A. S., 449
Siegelbaum, S. A., 464, 478

Siegler, R., 636
Siekevitz, P., 469
Sifneos, P. E., 338
Siggins, G. R., 459
Sigworth, F. J., 478
Silberman, E. K., 294, 300, 309
Silk, A. J., 274
Silver, M. J., 235
Silverman, H., 638
Silverman, S. B., 354
Simon, E. J., 501
Simon, H., 91
Simon, H. A., 566, 620
Simon, S. R., 143
Simon, Th., 1
Simons, A. D., 329, 338, 339
Simons, R. F., 307
Simpson, J. C., 424
Sims, E. A. H., 115
Sims, L. S., 265
Singer, B., 324, 368
Singer, J. A., 573
Singer, J. E., 382, 392, 396, 397
Singer, L. T., 146, 147
Singer, M. T., 308, 313
Singh, P., 543
Sinha, D., 532
Sistrunk, F., 354
Siviy, S., 87, 97
Siviy, S. M., 83, 85, 87, 94, 96
Sjodin, I., 335
Skelton, J. A., 249
Skelton, J. M., 57
Skerry, S. A., 552
Skodol, A. E., 430
Skolnick, B. E., 295
Skolnick, P., 96
Skorpanich, M. A., 389, 391
Skottun, B. C., 500, 503
Skrypnek, B. J., 237
Skuse, D. H., 154, 155
Slade, A., 59
Sladek, J. R., 96
Slater, A., 139
Slaughter, D. T., 150
Slaymaker, F., 148
Slovic, P., 260
Smallberg, S. A., 595, 596
Smith, A. W., 166
Smith, C. B., 297, 390, 392
Smith, C. D., 389
Smith, C. R., 633
Smith, D. E., 357
Smith, E. R., 86
Smith, G. P., 93
Smith, J. E., 94
Smith, M. C., 46, 636
Smith, M. L., 215, 324-27, 340, 342
Smith, M. R., 296, 297
Smith, P. A., 469
Smith, R. E., 272

Smith, S. J., 463
Smith, S. M., 178
Smith, T. R., 388, 391, 628
Smither, R., 533
Smithson, M., 555
Smokler, I. A., 589
Smolak, L., 144, 151
Smythies, J. R., 86
Snapper, K., 211, 215
Snidman, N., 146
Sniezek, J. A., 367
Snodderly, D. M., 507
Snow, P. J., 471
Snow, R. E., 236, 612, 613, 621
Snyder, C. R. R., 47-49, 51, 56, 62, 66, 67
Snyder, M., 47, 234, 236-40, 244, 246, 249, 252
Snyder, R., 277
Snyder, R. R., 597
Snyder, S. H., 78, 82, 86, 92, 96
Sobell, L. C., 331, 332
Sobell, M. B., 331, 332
Sohlberg, S. C., 310
Sokoloff, L., 97, 297
Solomon, M. R., 279
Solomon, P. R., 442
Solomon, R. L., 470
Solomon, S. K., 393
Sommer, W., 304
Sommers, N., 631, 632
Sophian, C., 141
Sorce, J. F., 145
Sorenson, P. E., 391
Soroko, F., 92
Sorri, A., 308, 310
Sosnowski, R. J., 148
Sotelo, C., 439
Sothmann, G., 471
Soto, E., 550
Spacapan, S., 394, 397
Spanos, N. P., 337
Speckart, G., 268
Spence, J. T., 550
Spencer, C. C., 365
Spencer, D., 535
Spencer, W. A., 441, 447, 449, 458, 473
Sperber, R. D., 47, 60, 61
Sperling, G., 50
Sperling, H. M., 353
Spetch, M. L., 445
Spielberger, C. D., 10
Spiro, R. L., 278
Spitzer, R. L., 414, 416, 421, 425, 430
Sprague, J. M., 86
Spreckelmeyer, K. F., 400, 401
Springer, D., 119, 120
Squire, L. R., 185
Squires, D., 636

Squires, K. C., 303
Srole, L., 547
Sroufe, L. A., 147
Srull, T. K., 261-63, 273
Stacy, E., 47
Staddon, J. E. R., 185
Staelin, R., 261, 266, 275, 276, 279
Stafano, J. J., 335
Stafford, E. M., 354
Stafstrom, C. E., 461, 466, 477
Stager, R. A., 638
Stahelski, A. J., 237, 239, 244
Stahl, M. J., 365
Stake, R. E., 223, 227
Stalley, S., 116
Stammeyer, E. C., 301
Standaert, D. G., 93
Standen, N. B., 463
Stanovich, K. E., 61
Stanton, A. H., 330
Stanton, P. K., 98
Stark, K. D., 624
Starkey, P., 634
Starlinger, J., 439
Starr, B. J., 527
Starr, S. J., 510, 512
Stäubli, U., 99
Steele, C. M., 250
Steffe, L., 633, 634
Steffens, A. B., 124
Steffy, R. A., 301
Stein, L., 88
Stein, N., 627
Steinbrueck, S. M., 329
Steiner, I., 472
Steiner, J. E., 576, 600
Steinfels, G. F., 87, 88, 90
Steinhauer, S., 304, 305
Steinhauer, S. R., 292, 293, 312, 313
Steketee, G. S., 331
Stenberg, C. R., 140
Stenevi, U., 96
Stenslie, C. E., 587, 589
Stephens, D., 279, 280
Stern, J. S., 118, 121, 126
Stern, M., 148
Stern, R., 331
Stern, R. M., 572
Stern, W. C., 89
Sternberg, C. R., 576, 582
Sternberg, R., 538
Sternberg, R. J., 613, 614, 638
Sternthal, B., 270-73, 276, 280
Stevens, A. L., 636, 638
Stevens, C. D., 457
Stevens, C. F., 463
Stevens, J. R., 298
Stevens, R., 622, 629
Stevenson, H. W., 531
Stevenson, R. J., 594
Steward, O., 98

Stewart, D. W., 261, 266
Stewart, L., 61
Sticht, T. C., 5
Stiles, W. S., 510
Stillman, R. C., 591
Stinus, L., 95
Stitzer, M. L., 333
Stock, M. J., 115, 121, 126, 127
Stokols, D., 382, 392, 396, 402
Stolzfus, N. W., 590
Stone, D. L., 355
Stone, E. A., 88
Stone, G., 301
Stone, M. A., 590
Stone, T. W., 127
Stone, W. N., 574
Stonehill, D., 126
Stoney, S. D. Jr., 435, 473
Stopes-Roe M., 533
Storlien, L. H., 114
Storms, M. D., 569
Strack, S., 596
Strader, C. D., 461
Strange, P. G., 78
Straumanis, J. J., 304, 305
Strecker, R. E., 90
Streitman, S., 294
Strenta, A. C., 247
Strickland, B., 546
Strodtbeck, F. L., 541
Stroop, J. R., 53
Strube, M. J., 324, 327
Strumwasser, F., 469
Strupp, B. J., 122
Strupp, H. H., 322, 337
Stuart, R. B., 334
Stufflebeam, D. L., 229
Stumpf, S. A., 367
Stunkard, A. J., 122, 333
Sturgis, J., 331
Stutzman, T. M., 355
Suberi, M., 584
Suchman, E., 195, 200, 217, 218, 223
Sugarman, J. M., 584
Sugimori, M., 458, 461, 462, 466, 469, 471, 473
Suinn, R. M., 335
Sujan, M., 264, 274
Sullivan, A. C., 125
Sully, J., 566
Sumner, G., 552
Sundberg, N. D., 529, 540
Sundberg, S. H., 451, 477
Sundstrom, E., 383, 399-401
Super, C. M., 531, 538
Supnick, J., 336
Suppes, P., 618
Sur, M., 440
Surprenant, C., 280, 281
Surridge, D. H., 86
Sushinsky, L. W., 572

Sussman, N. M., 398
Sutcliffe, F. E., 495
Sutherland, A., 235, 236
Sutherland, E. W., 466
Sutton, R. E., 94
Sutton, S., 295, 298, 303-5
Suydam, M., 633
Svedlund, J., 336
Sveen, O., 451, 477
Svensson, T., 84
Swaminathan, H., 627
Swann, J. W., 451
Swann, W. B. Jr., 47, 237, 238, 240, 242, 246, 249
Swanson, L. W., 94
Swartz, B. E., 456, 468, 469, 471, 476
Swets, J. A., 496-99, 502, 514, 638
Swing, S. R., 624
Swinyard, W. R., 272
Szegda, M., 591, 592

T

Tait, R. W., 451
Tajfel, H., 531
Takahashi, K., 464
Takahashi, L. T., 85
Takemori, A. E., 97
Takeuchi, A., 462
Takeuchi, N., 462
Talbot, J. F., 384
Tallman, I., 531
Tallman, J. F., 92
Tamkin, G., 216
Tamor, L., 631
Tanaka, T., 456
Tanford, S., 238, 239, 246, 247
Tanke, E. D., 236, 239, 244, 252
Tannenbaum, G. S., 94
Tanner, W. P., 496, 498, 499, 502, 503, 512, 514, 516, 517
Tapp, J., 531
Tapp, S., 267
Targum, S., 296
Tasaki, I., 475
Tassin, J. P., 91
Tassinary, L., 59
Taylor, D. A., 399
Taylor, D. G., 147
Taylor, D. W., 335
Taylor, E., 625, 627
Taylor, H. F., 538
Taylor, J. G., 386, 387
Taylor, J. R., 279
Taylor, M. A., 587
Taylor, M. C., 235
Taylor, M. S., 367
Taylor, R. B., 392, 398, 401
Taylor, S. E., 47

Tchilingaryan, L. I., 450
Teasdale, J. D., 592, 593, 596
Teders, S. J., 336
Teel, J. E., 280
Tees, R. C., 535
Teich, M. C., 501, 504
Teitelbaum, P., 127
Teller, D., 502, 503
Ten Cate, J., 439
Tennyson, R. D., 619, 621
Terdal, L. J., 324
Terman, G. W., 96
Terrace, H. S., 182
Terwogt, M., 628
Tetenbaum, T. J., 549
Tetrick, L. E., 371
Teyler, T. J., 451
Thach, W. T., 435
Thaler, R., 260
Thase, M. E., 329
Thelen, E., 143, 152
Thibaut, J. W., 239
Thibos, L. N., 500, 503, 504,
    512, 515
Thomas, E., 450
Thomas, J. P., 516, 517
Thomas, L. L., 535
Thomas, R. L., 592, 595
Thompson, D. E., 394
Thompson, G. C., 441
Thompson, H. K., 79
Thompson, J. K., 122
Thompson, L. W., 328
Thompson, R. F., 434, 435,
    438-42, 445, 447, 449,
    451, 452
Thompson, R. H., 126
Thompson, S. H., 463
Thompson, W. D., 436, 473
Thomson, D. M., 591
Thomson, E., 541
Thor, D. H., 87
Thoresen, C. E., 335
Thorndike, E. L., 184
Thorndike, R. L., 236, 352
Thorpe, L. A., 142
Thorpe, W., 187
Thorson, E., 277
Thurlby, P. L., 126
Tienari, P., 308, 310
Tierney, R., 627, 629
Tillmanns, A., 331
Tilquin, C., 550, 551
Tinbergen, N., 163, 164, 170
Tinklenberg, J. R., 304, 305
Tipper, S. P., 53, 54, 59, 60
Tischler, M. D., 441
Tisher, R., 635
Tobias, S., 621, 639
Tobin, G., 121
Tolhurst, D. J., 500, 503
TOMARKEN, A. J., 565-610
Tombaugh, T. N., 91

Tomer, R., 299
Tomic, T., 153
Tomkins, S. S., 577, 582,
    601
Toohey, M., 308
Topol, B., 250
Tordy, G. R., 8
Torney-Purta, J., 531
Torre, V., 505
Torrey, E. F., 296, 298,
    312
Tourangeau, R., 578
Tower, D. B., 461
Town, J. P., 400, 401
Trabasso, T., 627
Traub, R. D., 458
Trayhurn, P., 126
Trehub, S. E., 142
Treiber, F., 142
Treiman, R., 153
Treisman, A., 45, 53, 58, 67
Treisman, A. M., 48, 55-58, 67
Trend, M. G., 224
Trendelenberg, W., 439
Trevarthen, C., 576, 600
Treves, Z., 439
Triandafillou, J., 127
Triandis, H. C., 526, 529, 531,
    541-43
Triestman, S. N., 469
Trimble, J., 533
Triscari, J., 125
Trisler, G. D., 98
Tronick, E. Z., 140
Truex, R. C., 443
Trulson, M. E., 90, 91
Truman, J. W., 448
Tryon, G. S., 10
Trzeciak, A., 93
Tsal, Y., 50, 52
Tsien, R. W., 458, 462
Tsuang, M. T., 424
Tsukahara, N., 448, 469, 471
Tucker, D. M., 584-89, 591,
    596
Tucker, L. R., 9
Tueting, P., 303
Tugwell, P., 420
Tukey, J. W., 223
Tulving, F., 591
Tuma, A. M., 590
Turnage, J. J., 366
TURNBULL, W., 233-56
Turner, D. A., 458
Turner, R. C., 121
Turner, S. M., 331
Turner, T. J., 47
Tutin, C. E. G., 181
Tversky, A., 260, 281
Twohig, P. T., 638
Tybout, A. M., 271, 272
Tyler, L. E., 540
Tyler, R., 625

Tyler, S. K., 589
Tzebelikos, E., 462
Tziner, A., 357, 366

U

Uhr, J. W., 97
Ukhtomsky, A. A., 450
Ullman, S., 138
Ulmer, D., 335
Ulrich, R. S., 395
Underwood, G. L., 47, 53
Underwood, V. L., 639
Undheim, J. O., 613
Unger, L. S., 274
Ungerstedt, U., 90
Uno, M., 439
Uranowitz, S. W., 47
Urry, V. W., 11
Ushiyama, N., 456
Uzgiris, I. C., 142

V

Vale, W., 94
Vale, W. W., 94
Valencia-Weber, G., 550
Valentino, K. L., 97
Valins, S., 571, 572
Vance, R. J., 358
VandenBos, G. R., 329
Van der Heijden, A. H. C., 54
van der Linden, W. J., 369
Vandersteel, M., 262
Vander Tuig, J. G., 127
van de Vijver, F. J. R., 527
Van Dijk, A., 93
van Dijk, T., 635
van Dijk, T. A., 277
Van Harreveld, A., 459
van Kammen, D. P., 296, 297
VanLehn, K., 626
van Lindern, P., 573, 574
van Meeteren, A., 504
Vannicelli, M. L., 330, 338
Vannucci, G., 501, 504
Vargish, T., 95
Vasey, M. W., 336
Vassilevsky, N. N., 435-38,
    441, 450, 473
Vaughan, H. G. Jr., 306
Vaughan, K., 579
Vaughan, R. C., 579
Vaughn, J., 55
Vavra, T. G., 274
Velten, E., 596
Ventura, I., 96
Venza, V., 535
Veres, J. F., 356
Vergnaud, G., 635
Verleger, R., 304
Victor, M., 435
Vieth, W., 169, 178

Vietze, P. M., 145
Vigersky, R. A., 126
Vilberg, T. R., 115, 119, 125, 127
Villablanca, J. R., 439
Villareal, M. J., 543
Villasana B., S., 534
Vincent, J. P., 463
Vincent, L., 126
Vinsel, A., 401
Virzi, R. A., 55
Visser, T., 628
Vitetta, E. S., 97
Vivian, M., 453, 459, 478
Vogt, M., 87
Volpe, B. T., 50
von Baeyer, C. L., 242, 544
von Frisch, K., 163, 168, 172-74
von Kammen, D. P., 292, 293, 313
von Wright, J. M., 49
Voronin, L. L., 451, 457, 469, 470
Voss, H.-G., 550, 551
Voss, J., 629
Voss, J. F., 637
Votava, J., 459
Vyas, S., 46
Vygotsky, L., 626, 630

W

Waas, G. A., 624
Wachsmuth, I., 634
Wachtel, P. L., 341
Waddell, K. J., 535
Wadden, T. A., 332, 333
Wade, B. E., 369
Wade, G. N., 123
Wagener, J. J., 591, 592
Wagner, A. R., 450
Wagner, D. A., 531, 532, 536
Wagner, R. F., 502, 504, 511
Wagner, R. L., 298
Wagoner, S., 628
Wahlberg, K.-E., 308, 310
Waksman, M., 638
Walberg, H., 636
Wales, C. E., 638
Walgren, M. C., 121
Walker, A. S., 142
Walker, E., 301, 311
Walker, J. A., 45
Walker, J. M., 96
Walker, P., 59
Wall, J. T., 440
Wall, S., 144, 147
Wallace, M. J. Jr., 353
Wallace, S. R., 352
Waller, T., 627
Walmsley, S., 631
Walsh, B. T., 84
Walsh, J. P., 453

Walter, U., 469
Walters, E. T., 453
Walters, J. K., 151
Walters, R. H., 8, 141
Walton, K., 439
Wamsley, J. K., 78
Wan, K. C., 543, 553
Wandell, B. A., 510, 516
Wandersman, A., 395
Wang, Y.-N., 298
Wapner, S., 402
Warburton, D. M., 86
Ward, C. H., 423
Ward, H., 335
Ward, L. M., 57, 382, 388, 391
Wardlaw, J. C., 512
Wardlaw, S., 95
Ware, E. E., 544
Warner, J. L., 365
Warnock, G. J., 209
Warr, P. B., 354
Warren, J. M., 153
Warshaw, P. R., 269
Warwick, P. M., 119
Waskow, I. E., 337
Waters, D. H., 89
Waters, E., 144, 147
Watkins, B., 619
Watson, A. B., 500-2
Watson, J. S., 140
Watson, R. G., 584, 585
Watson, R. T., 584
Watson, S. J., 96
Waziri, R., 587
Weber, S. J., 216
Webster, W. R., 441
Wedzony, K., 92
Weekley, J., 357
Weerts, T. C., 573
Wehner, R., 180
Weibull, W., 516
Weidemann, S., 386
Weight, F. F., 459, 469
Weinberger, A., 590
Weinberger, D. A., 573
Weinberger, D. R., 296-98, 312
Weinberger, N. M., 441, 470
Weiner, B., 281, 615
Weiner, M. J., 569
Weingarten, H. P., 127
Weingartner, H., 591, 592, 595, 596
Weinman, A. L., 586
Weinstein, C. E., 639
Weinstein, N. D., 394
Weinstein, R., 624
Weinstein, W., 592
Weintraub, S., 301
Weisberg, R. W., 151
Weiss, A. A., 40
Weiss, C. H., 197, 202, 211, 226
Weiss, D. J., 361
Weiss, H. M., 357

Weiss, J. L., 301
Weiss, R. S., 200
Weiss, S., 528
Weissenburger, J., 328
Weissman, M. M., 328, 329, 333, 337, 338, 425
Weisz, D. J., 442
Weitzel, W. D., 424
Weitzer, W., 396
Wells, G. L., 270
Wells, S., 618
Welner, J., 294, 307
Wemple, C., 581
Wender, P. H., 294, 300, 307
Wenegrat, B. G., 304, 305
Wener, R., 395
Werblin, F. S., 504
Werker, J. F., 535
Werman, R., 469
Wesley, F., 550
Wesman, A. G., 10, 11
Wessels, K., 615, 624
West, K. L., 308
West, L. J., 331
West, M. J., 152
West, S. G., 198, 214
Westbrook, G. L., 461
Westheimer, G., 511
Westman, J., 471
Wetrogan, L. I., 353
Wetzel, C. D., 361
Wetzel, R. D., 329, 338
Wexley, K. N., 354, 356, 357, 364
Whalley, L. J., 328, 329
Whary, D., 549
Wheeler, L., 568
Wheeler, R. J., 235
Whimbey, A., 638
White, B., 636
White, G. M., 533
White, H., 56
White, H. L., 92
White, K., 97
White, L. A., 358
White, R. T., 635, 637
White, S. H., 389, 625
Whitehead, W. E., 335
Whitehurst, G., 627
Whiteman, M. F., 631
Whitener, W. T., 637
Whiting, B. B., 526, 530
Whitney, J. C., 259
Wholey, J. S., 197, 203, 204, 207, 211, 227
Wickens, C. D., 44
Wicker, A. W., 402
Wickler, S. J., 126
Widen, L., 97
Widmayer, S. M., 148
Wieberg, H.-J. W., 546
Wieczorek, C. M., 78
Wieland, S. J., 85
Wiesel, T. N., 448

Wiesner, E., 30
Wigfield, A., 617
Wiggins, N. H., 9
Wigstrom, H., 451, 463, 477
Wilber, C. H., 333
Wilcox, S., 138, 142
Wilde, L., 267
Wilder, M. B., 457
Wilding, J., 60
Wilkening, F., 636
Wilkie, D. M., 445
Wilkinson, L., 300, 311
Wilkof, J., 549
William, J. E., 550
Williams, D. R., 510, 511
Williams, J. B. W., 425, 430
Williams, J. E., 550, 551
Williams, J. R., 399, 401
Williams, S. L., 330
Williams, W., 199
Williamson, D. A., 334
Williamson, P. A., 588, 596
Williamson, R. C., 395
Willis, R., 368
Wilner, N., 338
Wilson, D. H., 50
Wilson, F. D., 469
Wilson, G. J., 572
Wilson, G. T., 326, 327, 330-
    33, 338, 342
Wilson, H. R., 516
Wilson, P. H., 328, 329
Wilson, S., 527
Wilterdink, E. J., 128
Windle, W. F., 300
Wine, J. D., 616
Wine, J. J., 449
Wineman, J. D., 399
Winett, R. A., 258
Wing, H., 372, 364
Wing, J. K., 308, 425
Winn, R. L., 368
Winn, W., 620
Winne, P. S., 358, 623
Winnik, H. Z., 24, 40
Winograd, P., 628
Winokur, G., 413, 425, 426
Winter, C., 333
Winter, J., 97
Winters, K., 301
Wise, D., 88
Wise, R. A., 89-91, 95, 99
Witherspoon, D., 46
Witkin, H. A., 261
Witte, S., 632
Wittrock, M., 622
Wixson, K., 628, 639
Woerner, M. G., 331
Wohlberg, G. W., 301
Wohlwill, J. F., 385, 389, 402
Wolf, F. M., 545-47
Wolf, G., 371
Wolf, S. S., 78
Wolf, T. H., 6

Wolfarth, S., 92
WOLFE, B., 321-49
Wolfe, B. E., 330, 331
Wolfe, J. M., 57
Wolford, G., 59-61
Wong, B., 475
Wong, P., 615
Wood, B., 48
Woodruff, R. A., 413, 425, 426
Woodruff, R. B., 281
Woods, D. L., 50
Woods, S. C., 124, 340, 341
Woodside, A. G., 274
Woodson, R., 140
WOODY, C. D., 433-93; 434-
    38, 440, 441, 443-54, 456-
    62, 464, 466-71, 473-76,
    478
Woody, G. E., 333
Woolacott, M. H., 453
Woolfolk, R. L., 393
Woolsey, C. N., 441
Woolson, R. F., 424
Word, C. O., 246
World Health Organization, 409
Wortman, P. M., 326
Wright, E. S., 358
Wu, J. Y., 79
Wurst, K. K., 539
Wyatt, R. J., 296-98, 312
Wynne, L. C., 308, 313
Wyshak, G., 126

Y

Yager, S., 640
Yalch, R., 279, 280
Yalch, R. F., 270
Yando, R., 591-93
Yang, C. R., 91
Yang, H.-Y. T., 93
Yaniv, S., 310
Yarom, Y., 462
Yarowsky, P. J., 434, 438, 441,
    454, 470
Yarrow, L. J., 145
Yasargil, G. M., 459
Yates, A. J., 301
Yates, J. F., 265
Yau, K. W., 501, 503, 504
Yeandle, S., 501
Yeates, K. O., 150
Yeaton, W., 198, 214
Yeaton, W. H., 327
Yeh, J., 619
Yen, S. S. C., 126
Yeo, C. H., 439
Yeomans, J. S., 87, 99
Yim, G. K., 85, 94
Yin, R. K., 221, 223
Yinon, Y., 552, 554
Yitzhak, V., 638
Yokoyama, T., 636
Yolken, R., 298

York, D. A., 127
Yoshikami, S., 461
Young, A. B., 78, 98
Young, E., 96
Young, H. B., 531
Young, J. B., 120, 125, 126
Young, R. A., 447
Young, S. J., 459
Young, S. M., 275
Young, W. S. III, 78
Younger, B. A., 142, 151
Younger, J. C., 571
Yuchtman-Yaar, E., 38

Z

Zacharko, R. M., 90
Zacks, R. T., 593
Zadny, J., 246
Zagon, I. S., 95
Zahn, G., 528
Zahn, T. P., 293, 301
Zahn-Waxler, C., 149
Zajonc, R. B., 258, 267, 271,
    273, 340
Zanna, M. P., 235, 242, 245,
    246, 272
Zarbin, M. A., 78
Zatz, L. M., 296, 297
Zavalloni, M., 541
Zax, M., 300
Zedeck, S., 355, 366, 369
Zegers, R. A., 235
Zeiss, A., 593
Zeiss, A. M., 592, 593, 597
Zeithaml, V. A., 262, 279
Zelazo, P., 143
Zelazowski, R., 296, 297
Zeliony, G. P., 439
Zeno, S., 625
Zepp, R., 536
Zerbe, R. L., 95
Zern, D. S., 540
Zerweck, C., 153
Zeskind, P. S., 150, 153
Zieglgänsberger, W., 94, 471
Zillmann, D., 570, 571, 573
Zimba, L. D., 61
Zimbardo, P. G., 541, 567-69,
    573
Zimmer, M. R., 278
Zimring, C. M., 396
Zito, K. A., 91
Zitrin, C. M., 331
Zitter, R. E., 333
Zivkovic, B., 92
Zolovick, A. J., 87, 89, 99
Zube, E. H., 385-87
Zubin, J., 292, 293, 303-5, 312,
    313
Zucker, L. M., 118
Zucker, T. F., 118
Zuckerman, M., 90

SUJECT INDEX

A

Ability
  of communication recipients
    consumer psychology, 270
  and personal selection, 353
Ability measure
  and computerized testing, 362
Abortion
  euthenic
    schizophrenic mothers, 294
Academic anxiety
  and standardized testing, 9
Accommodation
  and infant attachment, 148
Accuracy training
  of raters
    and personnel selection, 357
Acetylcholine
  in memory and learning, 456
  and neurochemistry of be-
    havior, 78
Acetylcholine synapses
  and reward circuits, 99
Achievement
  attitudes
    and instructional psycholo-
      gy, 618
    cross-cultural studies, 543
    racial differences, 539
Achievement attribution
  cross-cultural focus, 544
Achievement dynamics
  in instructional psychology,
    615
Acquired behavior
  memory and learning, 443
Acquisition
  in infancy, 142
Acronyms
  in selective attention, 57
Action
  spontaneity of, 580
Active schemata
  and selective attention, 65
Acuity
  in visual sensitivity, 511
Adaptation
  and visual sensitivity, 499
Adaptive behavior
  memory and learning, 443
Adaptive functioning
  and the DSM-III, 414
Adenosine
  and neurochemistry of be-
    havior, 78
Adenosine receptor agonist
  in memory and learning, 469
Adipose stores

and body weight regulation,
  120
Adipose tissue
  and body weight regulation,
    111
Adjunctive behavior
  and learning, 185
Adjustment disorder
  and the DSM-III, 426
Administration
  education of
    and program evaluation,
      207
Adolescence
  in the DSM-III, 415
  future planning, 540
  sexual behavior
    in different societies, 526
Adoption
  availability of infants for, 149
Adoption studies
  in diagnosis of schizophrenia,
    293
Adult life span
  environmental impact on, 387
Adulthood
  infant as eventual, 137
Advertising
  deception in, 279
  processing of, 274-77
Advertising stimuli
  mood and memory, 262
Affect
  and cognition
    loose association between,
      340
  in consumer psychology, 273
Affective disorder
  in children raised on kibbut-
    zim, 309
Affective experience
  lateralization of, 587
Affective interactions
  in instructional psychology,
    616
Affective precedence
  in consumer psychology, 273
Affective states
  and processing of information,
    593
Affective style (AS)
  and schizophrenia, 308
Age
  and promotion
    expected negative relation-
      ship of, 369
Age differentiation criterion
  and standardized testing, 1
Age discrimination

and personnel selection, 369
Aggregation biases
  and personnel selection, 366
Aggression
  and consumer behavior, 281
  cross-cultural studies, 552-53
  and neurochemistry, 85
  and research on destiny, 394
  and situational specificity, 10
Aggressive behavior
  and cognition arousal theory
    emotion study, 569
Aging
  and body weight regulation,
    123
Agoraphobia
  and individual psychotherapy,
    330
Aid to families with dependent
  children (AFDC)
  and program evaluation, 195
Alcohol abuse
  and the DSM-III, 416
Alcoholism
  goals of treatment, 331-32
  and individual psychotherapy
    studies, 326
Alliances
  and biology of learning, 181
Alpha conditioning
  and biology of learning, 187
  in memory and learning, 444
Amblyopia
  and visual sensitivity, 507
Amenorrhea
  body weight regulation, 126
Amino acids
  as inhibitory transmitter in the
    brain, 91
Analysis
  and consumer psychology,
    261
Anhedonia
  and etiology of schizophrenia,
    307
Annual rhythm
  and body weight regulation, 117
Anomalies
  in trial and error learning, 185
Anorectic drugs
  and body weight regulation,
    122
Anorexia nervosa
  and body weight regulation,
    126
  DSM-III criterion for, 429
  in the DSM-III, 415
  and individual psychotherapy,
    333

Anterograde tracing techniques
and neurochemistry of be-
havior, 99
Antigens
and schizophrenia studies, 297
Anxiety
attachment relationships
in infancy, 147
and benzodiazepine receptors,
96
and the left lateralized activation system, 589
and neurochemistry of be-
havior, 88
and selective attention, 64
Anxiety disorders
in the DSM-III, 415
and individual psychotherapy,
330
Anxiety management training
and Type A behavior, 335
Aplysia
and biology of learning, 182
cellular basis of habituation
in, 449
Appetite loss
and individual psychotherapy,
328
Appetite suppressants
and body weight regulation,
122
Aptitude treatment interaction
instructional psychology, 621
Architectural style
uniqueness of
in environmental psychology, 390
Arguments
chronic in family life, 310
Army Research Institute
and personnel selection, 373
Arousal
muscimol affecting, 92
Artificial intelligence
and environmental assessment,
391
Asphyxia neonatorum
and pregnancy and birth complications (PBC), 300
Assertiveness training
as treatment for gastrointestinal disorders, 335
Assessment
covariation
in consumer psychology,
259
environmental
research, 382
Assessment centers
and personnel selection, 366
Assessment procedure (MEAP)
evaluating environmental impact, 386

Assimilation
and infant attachment, 148
Assimilation effect paradigm
in personnel selection and
placement, 355
Association
in memory and learning, 451
Associative learning
and biology of learning, 187
and inductive abstraction, 169
Associative temporal relationship
in memory and learning, 444
Assumption
and program evaluation, 219
Attachment
in infancy, 147
Attachment formation
normative processes underlying, 145
Attention
and consumer psychology,
258-59
and infant perception, 139
and motivation
in learning, 168
and PET studies in schizophrenia, 297
and studies of schizophrenia,
295
Attention control
as construct in test validation, 7
Attention spans
and neurochemistry of be-
havior, 82
Attentional deficit
and schizophrenia, 300-1
Attentional disturbances
and genetic risk for schizophrenia, 299
Attentional phenomena
see Selective attention
Attentional spotlight
and spatial perception
in selective attention, 51
Attitude behavior consistency
and consumer psychology,
280
Attitude behavior relations
in consumer psychology, 272
Attitudes
and achievement
and instructional psychology, 618
and behavior influencing
consumer psychology, 267-
68
effect of
toward advertisement, 274-
75
Attribute
in consumer psychology, 263
environmental assessment of,
384

job
and personal selection, 353
Attribution theory
in instructional psychology,
615
Attrition
prediction of
and personnel selection, 369
Auditory discrimination
and research on density, 394
Auditory stimuli
and perceptual organization,
56
Authority
and situational specifity, 10
Automatic attention
and selection, 62-63
see also Selective attention
Automatic responses
and evidence for late selection, 48
Automobile industry
and program evaluation, 209
Autonomic activity
emotional experience, 574
and facial expressiveness, 581
Autonomic feedback
and body systems, 584-85
Autonomic nervous system
and body weight regulation,
125
Availability valence model
in consumer psychology, 270
Aversion
and biology of learning, 178
Aversion therapy
treatment of alcoholics, 332

B

Backwards pairing
and conditioned response, 445
Balance regulation
and neurochemistry, 93
Basal metabolism
and regulation of body weight,
110
Bees
directional cues in, 167
see also Honey bees
Behavior
attitudes influencing
consumer psychology, 268
and visual sensitivity, 503
see also Culture and behavior
Behavior observation taxonomies
and personnel selection, 358
Behavior therapy
and eating disorders, 333
in treatment of drug abuse,
332
trends in Israel, 29
Behavioral medicine

and individual psychotherapy
    research, 322
Behavioral nonlinearities
    and visual sensitivity, 499
Behavioral self control
    and alcoholism, 332
Behavioral units
    and biology of learning, 166
Beliefs
    and consumer psychology,
        258
    culture and behavior, 541
Benefit cost analysis
    and program evaluation, 215
Benzodiazepine receptor system
    and neurochemistry of be-
        havior, 92
Benzodiazepines
    and neurochemistry of be-
        havior, 88
Bias
    and personnel selection, 367
    in testing, 624
    in trial and error learning, 185
Biased selection
    in individual psychotherapy
        studies, 325
Bilingualism
    culture and behavior, 555
Binge eating
    behavioral therapy for, 334
Biodata
    and personnel selection, 364
Biofeedback
    as treatment for hypertension,
        334
Biofeedback techniques
    trends in Israel, 29
Biological predisposition
    and schizophrenia research,
        292
Biological risk
    studies of
        in infancy, 148
Biology of learning
    cognitive trial and error, 187-
        89
    conclusion, 189-90
    introduction, 163-64
    learning in the field, 171-82
    learning in the lab, 182-87
    see also Learning
Bird navigation
    and learning, 180
Birdsall's theorem
    and visual sensitivity, 515
Birth process
    and schizophrenic brain dam-
        age diathesis, 300
Biting reflexes
    and neurochemistry of be-
        havior, 85
Blood pressure

and body weight regulation,
    117
Body core temperature
    regulation of, 112
Body energy homeostasis
    and body weight regulation,
        11
Body energy stores
    functional significance of,
        116-18
Body fat
    and intraspecies weight varia-
        tion, 116
Body reaction theory
    emotion research, 566
Body symptoms
    and autonomic feedback, 584-
        85
Body weight
    control of
        and eating disorders, 333
Bombesin
    and neurochemistry of be-
        havior, 78
Bonding hypothesis
    and timing of experience
        infancy, 153
Borderline
    in the schizophrenia spectrum,
        293
Bower's network model
    of emotional memory, 594-95
Brain
    and engrams
        in memory and learning,
            434-40
    see also Neurochemistry of
        behavior
Brain disease
    in schizophrenia, 294
Brain foraging circuits
    and neurochemistry of be-
        havior, 98
Brain imaging
    and diagnosis, 412
Brain imaging techniques
    and schizophrenia research,
        292
Brain opioids
    general functions of, 94
Brain stimulation techniques
    neurochemistry of behavior,
        97
Brand
    and memory
        in consumer psychology,
            263
Brazelton neonatal assessment
    mother-infant interaction, 150
Breathing rhythms
    and opioid system, 95
Brief therapies
    research findings on, 338

Broadbent
    on selective attention, 67
Brown adipose tissue
    thermogenesis
        body weight regulation, 126
Budget shifts
    and program evaluation, 198
Building complexity
    in environmental psychology,
        390
Bulimia
    in the DSM-III, 415
    and individual psychotherapy,
        333

C

Cable properties
    memory and learning, 457
Caesarian delivery
    as risk factor
        infancy studies, 148
Calcium conductance
    memory and learning, 443
cAMP
    in memory and learning, 469
Cancer
    psychotherapy for, 336
Cardiovascular disorders
    in treatment for hypertension,
        334
Cardiovascular tone
    and opioid systems, 95
Case history data
    and standardized testing, 2
Catecholamines
    and body weight regulation,
        125
Categories
    and the DSM-III, 418
Category verbalizations
    and consumer psychology,
        265
Causal analysis
    and program evaluation, 217
Causal explanation
    and program evaluation, 207
Causal mechanism
    and attention, 66
Cell morphology
    memory and learning, 458
    reconstruction of, 471
Cell suface architecture
    and neurochemistry of be-
        havior, 98
Cellular basis of memory and
    learning
    associatively acquired be-
        havior, 443
    experimental technologic
        frontiers, 471-78
    localization of the engram,
        434-40

rates of conditioning, 469-71
role of the neuron in integration, 457-69
Central nervous system disease
role in the etiology of schizophrenia, 294
Central neural theories
emotion research, 566
Central vision
use of by newborns, 151
Cerebellum
in memory and learning, 435
Change
and program evaluation, 198
Channel kinetics
and learning, 478
Chemoarchitecture
of the brain
and behavior, 78
Chemotherapy
psychotherapy for, 336
Child development
kibbutz, 21
Child guidance
in the kibbutz populations, 33
Childhood
in the DSM-III, 415
Childhood psychopathology
antecedents of, 147
Childrearing
and environment
infancy studies, 148
Children
choices as consumer, 272
and consumer psychology, 280
and consumption symbolism, 278
Kaufman assessment
battery for children, 3
mentally impaired
training in general intellectual skills for, 638
prenatal disturbance
and schizophrenia, 295
recreation for
and environmental psychology, 386
and spatial knowledge, 390
Chilling
and color learning, 173
Chinese menu system
in the DSM-III, 418
Chloride conductances
memory and learning, 461
Choice
interactions with memory
in consumer psychology, 264
Cholecystokinin
and neurochemistry of behavior, 78

Chromatic uncertainty
visual sensitivity, 513
Chronicity
and studies of schizophrenia, 296
Classical conditioning
biology of learning, 183
Classification
and standardized testing, 7
Classification decisions
and standardized testing, 11
Classroom design
and spatial behavior, 399
Classroom instruction
cognitive psychology and instruction, 622
Classroom organization
in instructional psychology, 623
Classroom teaching
and instuctional psychology, 617
Client groups
and program evaluation, 201
Clinical assessment
see Diagnosis and clinical assessment, 409
Clinical psychology
in Israel, 29
Clinical syndrome
and the DSM-III, 414
Clinical trials
of possible future practices, 207
research findings on, 338
Clonidine
withdrawal symptoms
behavioral neurochemistry, 84
CO_2
color learning, 173
Coding
modality and sematic
and selective attention, 46
Cognition
and affect
loose association between, 340
culture and behavior, 535
relationship between
in consumer psychology, 273
Cognition arousal theory
emotion research, 566
emotional state product of, 567-75
Cognitive categorization model
and performance ratings
personnel selection, 356
Cognitive competence
in other cultures, 536-37
Cognitive coping procedures
and tension headaches, 336

Cognitive development
and environment, 381-402
in other cultures, 539
Cognitive frameworks
and program evaluation, 202
Cognitive mapping
and environment, 382
in environmental psychology, 388
Cognitive maps
and learning, 188
Cognitive mediators
and reactions to stressors, 382
Cognitive message reactions
in consumer psychology, 269
Cognitive processes
in mood effects, 595-96
instructional psychology, 614
underlying performance ratings
personnel placement, 356
of the writer, 631
Cognitive psychology
and testing, 625
Cognitive psychophysiological studies
and schizophrenia, 300-7
and schizophrenia research, 292
Cognitive science
and environmental assessment, 391
Cognitive therapies
and exposure
effect of combining, 331
Collective education
in Israel, 21
Color
and selective attention, 64
Color learning
in the honey bee, 172-73
Color phenomena
and post-receptor mechanisms, 510
Communal rearing
and incidence of affective disorder, 310
Communication
and biology of learning, 180-82
high pressure
in consumer psychology, 274
and infancy, 143-44
and use of the DSM-III, 422
Communication deviance
in the families of schizophrenic patients, 308
Community mental health
and program evaluation, 201
Comparison skills
and consumer psychology, 280

Compensatory choice
in consumer psychology, 266
Compensatory equalization
and program evaluation, 221
Competence
racial differences in, 538
Competency testing
instructional psychology, 624
Complaint behavior
and consumer relations, 281
Complex partial epilepsy
suffering from, 299
Complexity
and personnel selection, 353
Comprehension
as construct in test validation,
7
Comprehension monitoring
and reading, 628
Computational accuracy
as constructs
in standardized testing, 8
Computer games
instructional psychology, 619
Computerized Adaptive Screening Tests
and personnel selection, 361-
69
Computerized axial tomography
(CT)
and schizophrenia research,
292
Computerized testing
and personnel selection, 361
Comrey Personality Scales
and test validity, 3
Concepts
and biology of learning, 189
Conceptual models
in environmental psychology,
382
Conditioned behavior
in memory and learning, 439
Conditioning
acceleration of rates of
memory and learning, 469
effects of interstimulus interval on, 444
presynaptic hypotheses of, 453
simple
circuitry involved in, 440
Confirmatory analysis techniques
and personnel selection, 360
Consciousness
and learning, 188
Consequence
and attention, 66
Consistent matching (CM)
and selective attention, 63
Construct validation
in standardized testing, 3-4
Construct validity
and personnel selection, 360

Constructs
in test validation, 4-8
Consumer education
and policy issues, 279
Consumer memory
and mood effects, 262
Consumer psychology
conclusion, 281
group and social influences,
278
individual decision making,
258-78
introduction, 257
policy issues, 279
Consumers
and program evaluation, 209
Consumption symbolism
and consumer psychology,
278
Content
and instructional psychology,
627
Context effects
in consumer psychology, 266
Contextual assessment
in instructional psychology,
626
Contingency research
and decision processes
in consumer psychology,
266
Contingent reinforcement programs
in drug abuse programs, 333
Continuity
and development in infancy,
137
and social relations, 147
Continuous performance
in schizophrenia, 301
Control
in personal environment, 400
instructional psychology, 614
Control group standards
and program evaluation, 212
Controlled attention
and selection, 62-63
Controlled drinking
as goal of treatment
in alcoholism, 331
Cooperation
and studies of schizophrenia,
295
Cooperativeness
in task
and environmental psychology, 398
Cooperatives
in Israel, 19
Coping
modes of
and environmental psychology, 396

Coronary prone behavior
and treatment for hypertension, 334
Correctional facilities
density research, 397
Cortical atrophy
alterations in
patients with schizophrenia,
296
in schizophrenia, 294
Cost benefit
and consumer psychology,
261
Cost effectiveness analysis
and program evaluation, 215
Coupon usage
and consumer psychology,
268
Covariation
assessment of
in consumer psychology,
259
CR-protective units
in memory and learning, 436
Crime
environmental psychology,
382
and temperatures
linear relationship between,
394
and territoriality, 400
Criteria
in program evaluation, 209
Criteria problem
in personnel selection, 352
Criterion related validation
standardized testing, 3
Criterion unreliability
and personnel selection, 366
Cross-cultural psychology
the handbook of, 529-30
teaching, 531
Cross-cultural studies
culture and behavior, 525
in Israel, 37
Cross validation
of standardized testing, 3
Crowding
effect of on development
nonhuman studies, 150
and environment, 381-402
Crowding stress
and interpersonal rela-
tionships, 393
Crying
absence of
and genetic risk for schizophrenia, 299
and deep despondency
neurochemistry of behavior,
87
Cue hierarchies
in learning, 174

Cue recognition
and biology of learning, 164-
65
Cultural contact
and modernization, 553
Culture
and biology of learning, 180
and consumer psychology,
257-58
influences of on childrearing,
149
variables in environmental
psychology, 401-2
Culture and behavior
psychology in global perspective, 523
a coming of age, 529-31
concluding remarks, 555
cross-cultural research, 534-
53
cultural contact, 553-55
culture in psychology, 531-
34
introduction, 524-29
Cyclic GMP
in memory and learning, 456
Cytomegalovirus antigens
and schizophrenia studies, 297

D

Daily energy requirements
and relationship to body mass,
113
Danger avoidance system
and biology of learning, 184
Dark adaptation
and visual sensitivity, 505
Darwinian evolutionary theory
in research on emotion, 565-
66
Data collection
and program evaluation, 209
Database management device
and personnel selection, 369
Davidson's depressogenic withdrawal system
and hemispheric asymmetry,
590
Daycare
impact on childrearing, 149
Deception
in advertising, 279
Decimal system
acquiring the structure and
notation of, 634
Decision making
and consumer psychology,
258
and program evaluation, 202
Decision making model
and social programming, 197
Decision processes

and contingency research
in consumer psychology,
266
Decortication
in memory and learning, 439
Defensive behavior
and biology of learning, 182
Deficient neurointegration
etiology of schizophrenia, 295
and schizophrenia, 299
Democratic process
and program evaluation, 211
Demonstration projects
as strategy of social change,
199
Denate interpositus complex
in memory and learning, 440
Density
in environmental psychology,
393
Dependent variables
and program evaluation, 209
Dependence
and revision of DSM-III, 422
and situational specificity, 10
Depression
and cognitive processing, 596
and individual psychotherapy,
326-28
see also NIMH collaborative
depression study, 413
Depressive disorder
in diagnosis and clinical
assessment, 411
Depressive neurosis
in the DSM-III, 421
Depressive syndrome complex
brain normalities in, 299
Deprivation
effect of on development
nonhuman studies, 150
and motivation
in learning, 168
Developing societies
see also Psychology in Israel
Development
emotional, 599-600
process of
in infancy, 137
reversibility of
infant studies, 154-55
and social environment, 402
stages and shifts in, 150
theories of
in human infancy, 136
Developmental
and social environment, 402
Diacylglycerol
memory and learning, 467
Diagnosis and clinical assessment
current state of psychiatric diagnosis, 409

basis issues, 418-20
conclusions, 429-30
how the change took place,
412-14
measuring, 422-29
new enthusiasm for, 410-12
remaining conflicts, 414
structure and content of
DSM-III, 414-18
Diagnostic utility
and concurrent validation
in standardized testing, 4
Dichotic listening task
assessing attentional deficit
in schizophrenia, 304-5
and selective attention, 47
Diet
and body weight regulation,
120
Dietary obesity
and body weight regulation,
120
Differential conditionability
and learning, 185
Difficulty
and personnel selection, 353
Diffusion
and program evaluation, 221
Digger wasps
and food acquisition, 171
Dimensions
and the DSM-III, 418
Displaced letter
and selective attention, 51
Direct thinking
as construct in test validation,
7
Disadvantaged groups
and mass immigration
in Israel, 25
Disconfirmation
and level of performance
in advertising, 281
Discontinuance
and program evaluation, 200
Discontinuity
and development in infancy,
137
Discrimination
and infant perception, 139
and visual sensitivity, 516
Disorder-specific effective
therapies
and diagnosis, 412
Displacement activity
and motivation
in learning, 168
Display position
in selective attention, 50
Disruption
and spontaneity of the response
emotion studies, 579

Distance judgments
    and relationship of pleasing-
        ness of landmarks, 389
Distancing
    and environmental psycholo-
        gy, 398
Distress vocalizations (DVs)
    and neurochemistry of be-
        havior, 84
Divergent thinking
    in instructional psychology,
        620
Doctoral studies
    in Israel, 34
Dominance orders
    and biology of learning, 181
Dopamine
    and feeding programs, 85
    in memory and learning, 456
    and neurochemistry of be-
        havior, 90-91
Dose response curves
    neurochemistry of behavior,
        83
Drug abuse
    treatment programs for, 332
Drugs
    and body weight regulation,
        123
    neurochemistry of behavior,
        83
DSM-III catagories
    and individual psychotherapy,
        328
Durables
    and consumer psychology
        in advertising, 281
Dynamic assessment
    in testing
        instructional psychology,
            629
Dynamics
    and social programs, 196
Dynorfins
    and neurochemistry of be-
        havior, 94
Dysthymia
    in the DSM-III, 421

E

Early selection
    and attention, 47-49
Early selection effect
    and schizophrenia, 303
Eating disorders
    in the DSM-III, 415
    and individual psychotherapy,
        333
Economics
    and development of psycholo-
        gy in Israel, 18

Education
    and the Israeli state, 19, 30
    and program evaluation, 203
Educational ideology
    kibbutz, 21
Educational psychology
    and instructional psychology,
        612
    in Israel, 22
Edumetrics
    instructional psychology, 627
Effects
    and semantic interference, 54
Effect sizes(ES)
    in individual psychotherapy,
        324
    in personnel selection, 352
Effect theories
    of selective attention, 68
Effector organization
    and biology of learning, 165-
        67
Efferent feedback
    and selective attention, 46
Egg retrieval behavior
    and cue recognition, 164
Egg rolling
    and biology of learning, 167
Eitingon, Max
    as Freudian disciple, 20
Elaboration likelihood model
    (ELM)
    in consumer psychology, 270
Electroconvulsive shock
    and color learning, 173
Electroconvulsive therapy
    in depressive disorders, 411
Embedded diagnosis
    and the DSM-III, 416
Emics and etics
    culture and behavior, 527
Emotion
    autonomic specificity of, 573
    and expressive behavior, 575-
        83
    and infants' attention, 139
    and lateralization, 583-91
    and memory, 591-98
    today's problems, 565-600
        cognition arousal theory,
            567-75
        conclusion, 598-600
        emotion and expressive be-
            havior, 575-83
        emotion and memory, 591-
            98
        introduction, 565-67
        lateralization and emotion,
            583-91
Emotional cues
    misattribution of arousal to,
        567
Emotional distress

and environmental psycholo-
    gy, 396
Emotional experience
    in autonomic activity, 574
Emotional memory
    Bower's network model, 594-
        95
Emotional states
    lateralization of, 586-90
Emotional stimuli
    of lateralized perceptual pro-
        cessing, 583-84
Emotionality
    high pressure
        in consumer psychology,
            274
Empirical tests
    of cognition arousal theory
        emotion studies, 567
Empiricism
    and standardized testing, 7
Endogenicity
    in individual psychotherapy,
        329
Endogenous motivation
    and learning, 167-68
Endorphins
    and neurochemistry of be-
        havior, 94
Enemy learning
    and selective learning, 183
Energy excess
    metabolic adaptations to, 115
Energy expenditure
    and body weight regulation,
        113
    and energy status, 115
Energy regulation
    and body weight, 110
Energy status
    and energy expenditure, 115
Engram
    localization of
        in memory and learning,
            434-40
Enkephaline
    and neurochemistry of be-
        havior, 79, 94
    and program evaluation, 202
Enlistment Screening Test
    and personnel selection, 361
Enrichment
    effect of on development
        nonhuman studies, 150
Entrenchment
    and social programs, 196
Entrepreneurship
    cross-cultural studies, 543
Environment
    bidirectional influences of
        in infancy, 152
    infant as part of, 137
    and infant motivation, 145

rearing
  infancy studies, 148
  and the schizophrenic, 292
Environmental assessment
  general models of, 383
Environmental contingencies
  and models of S-R behavior-
    ism, 341
Environmental psychology
  assessment, 383-88
  cognitive mapping, 388-92
  future research, 401-2
  spatial behavior, 397-401
Environmental stressors
  adaptation research, 394
  and neurochemistry of be-
    havior, 88
  and schizophrenic brain dis-
    orders, 312
  theoretically oriented work,
    392
Epidemiological catchment area
    project
  and the DSM-III hierarchies,
    417
Epilepsy
  psychotic manifestation in
    patients, 299
Equipotential representation
  and learned behavior, 435
Error
  and biology of learning, 187
Escape
  and biology of learning, 177
Ethnic relations
  studies of
    in Israel, 35
Ethnicity
  and mass immigration
    in Israel, 25
Ethnics
  for criteria selection
    program evaluation, 209
Ethnocentric attribution
  cross-cultural studies, 552-53
Etiology
  diagnosis and clinical assess-
    ment, 411
  see also Learning
Euthenic abortion
  and schizophrenic women,
    293
Evaluative judgments
  and the relationship of cogni-
    tion to effect
    in consumer psychology,
      273
Evaluation practice
  theories of, 224-30
Evaluation theorists
  and program evaluation, 218
Evaluation usage
  knowledge base about, 200-8

Evaluator partisanship
  in program evaluation, 210
Event related brain potentials
    (ERPs)
  and schizophrenic research,
    292
Evolving concepts of test valida-
    tion
  constructs in test validation, 4-
    8
  summary, 12-13
  traits and situations, 8-10
  validity generalization, 10-12
  validity in the test construction
    process, 2-4
Excitation transfer
  and cognition arousal theory,
    570
Excitatory postsynaptic potential
  in memory and learning, 456
Exercise
  and opioid systems, 95
  and weight loss, 122
Expectancies and interpersonal
    process
  behavioral influences, 234-38
  conclusion, 250-52
  introduction, 233-34
  meditation links, 238-44
  processing target behavior,
    244-48
  self-concept change, 248-50
Expectancy effects
  teacher
    instructional psychology,
      624
Expectancy value model
  in instructional psychology,
    616
Expectation
  and consumer psychology,
    258
  level of performance
    in advertising, 281
Experience
  as component of temperament,
    147
  early infancy
    reversibility of, 152
  and environment, 381-402
  timing of
    effects during infancy, 152
Experiments
  and program evaluation, 221
Expertise
  effects of
    and consumer psychology,
      265
Exploration
  in environmental psychology,
    390
  in infancy, 141-42
Exploratory insight oriented psy-

chotherapy (EIO)
  outcome studies, 330
Exploratory sniffing
  and neurochemistry of be-
    havior, 85
Exposure
  and cognitive therapies
    effect of combining, 331
Expressed emotion (EE)
  and schizophrenia, 308
Expression
  feeling
    central linkage of, 582
  and feeling
    link between, 576
  instructions and contextual
    manipulations of, 578
Expressive behavior
  and emotion, 575
  lateralization of, 585-86
Expressive mimicry
  in human infant, 600
Eye fixations
  and attentional spotlight, 50

F

Face validity
  and standardized testing, 2
Facial expression
  direct manipulations of
    emotion studies, 577
  and infant recognition, 139
  and learning, 181
Facial feedback hypothesis
  and subjective emotion, 577
Facial motoneurons
  in memory and learning, 441
Facilitation
  and associative cellular pro-
    cesses
    in induction of learned be-
      havior, 448
Factor analysis
  and personnel selection, 356
  and standardized testing, 12
Factor analytic models
  and program evaluation, 223
Failure
  and standardized testing, 9
Familial environment
  and diagnosis and clinical
    assessment, 429
Familial factors
  in schizophrenia, 307-10
Familiarity
  in environmental psychology,
    390
Family
  hypercritical extended
    and incidence of affection
      disorder, 310
Family decision making

and consumer psychology, 278
Family therapy
  in treatment of drug abuse, 332
  trends in Israel, 29
Fat cell morphology
  and body weight regulation, 124
Fear anxiety
  and neurochemistry of behavior, 88
Fear relevant stimuli
  and phobic stimuli, 598
Feature detector
  and learning performance, 169
  and visual sensitivity, 502
Feature integration
  and partial attention, 55
  in selective attention, 54
Federal reform programs
  assessment of, 195
Feedback
  in program evaluation, 201
Feedback accuracy
  in personnel selection and placement, 355
Feedback matching
  and biology of learning, 177
Feeding behavior
  and regulation of body weight, 109
Feeding programs
  dopamine
    neurochemistry of behavior, 85
Feeding research
  neurochemistry of behavior, 83
Feeling and expression
  link between, 576
Feelings
  expression
    central linkage of, 582
Fenfluramine
  and behavior therapy for obesity, 333
Fishbein Ajzen models
  in consumer psychology, 267
Fixation
  and the extracellular space, 472
Flower handling
  and associative tasks
    learning in honey bees, 175
Food acquisition
  and selective learning, 171
Food avoidance learning
  and imprinting, 176
Food deprivation
  and neurochemistry of behavior, 89
Food intake

and changes in body energy stores, 110
Food reinforcement
  in selective learning, 169
Food supply
  variation in
    stability of body weight, 115
Foot shock
  and neurochemistry of behavior, 85
Foraging
  and learning behavior, 186
Form discrimination
  and biology of learning, 169
Foveal adaptation
  visual sensitivity, 517
Freud's theory
  in kibbutz life, 25
Functional demature
  and neurochemistry of behavior, 82
Functional literacy
  and test validation, 5
Funding
  program evaluation, 211

G

GABA
  as inhibitory transmitter in the brain, 91
  and neurochemistry of behavior, 82
Gabor function
  and visual sensitivity, 510
Gamma alcoholics
  success with multimodal approaches, 332
Gastrointestinal disorders
  psychological treatment for, 335
Gender identity disorder of childhood
  in the DSM-III, 415
General Aptitude Test Battery
  and classification decisions, 11
Genes
  bidirectional influences of
    in infancy, 152
Genetic constraints
  in learning, 170
Genetic diathesis
  for schizophrenia, 311
Genetic epistemology
  and the infant as information processor, 138
Genetic obesity
  and body weight metabolism, 118
Genetic screening device
  and personnel selection, 363

Genetic susceptibility
  to neurointegrative deficit (NID)
    and schizophrenia, 300
Genetics
  in schizophrenia, 292
Gestalt
  trends in Israel, 29
Global concept culture
  and behavior, 626
Global outcome surveys
  via meta analysis, 324
Glucose metabolism
  abnormalities in, 297
  etiology of schizophrenia, 295
Glutamate
  and neurochemistry of behavior, 78, 98
Glycogen
  and body weight regulation, 111
Goal-directed behavior
  in environment, 391
Goal specification
  and program evaluation, 211
Gonadal hormones
  and body weight metabolism, 123
Group differences
  environmental psychology, 385
Growth
  and locomotion
    in childhood, 143
Guilt
  and individual psychotherapy, 328

H

Habit
  and automatic processing, 62
Habituation
  and associative cellular processes
    in induction of learned behavior, 448
  and biology of learning, 182, 187
  cellular changes produced by, 449
  to high density, 393
  and infancy, 141
Hadassah Vocational Guidance Institute
  and Israeli psychology, 36
Hallucination
  and neurochemistry of behavior, 88
Headaches
  psychotherapy for, 336
Health
  link between density and health, 393

Health psychology
  in Israel, 27
Helmholtzian trichromacy
  and visual sensitivity, 508
Hemispheric asymmetries
  in clinically depressed pop-
    ulations, 587
  and infant studies, 588
Hemispheric function
  etiology of schizophrenic, 295
Henrietta Szold Institute
  and Israeli psychology, 36
Herpes antigens
  and schizophrenia studies,
    298
Hibernation
  weight regulation process, 117
Hierarchies
  in the DSM-III system, 416-
    17
High fat diet
  and body weight regulation,
    121
Hippocampus
  in memory and learning, 435
Hiring
  on ability
    personnel selection, 363
Histrionic
  and the DSM-III, 426
Hologeistic research
  culture and behavior, 525
Home buying
  and family decision making,
    278
Home range
  honey bees and learning, 180
Home treatment program
  individual psychotherapy, 331
Homeostasis
  and regulation of body weight,
    110
Homeostatic regulation
  and neurochemistry of be-
    havior, 78
Homophone
  and evidence for late selection
    in selective attention, 48
Honesty
  and situational specificity, 10
Honey
  directional cues in, 167
Honey bees
  and food sources
    role in selective learning,
      171
  and hive temperature, 168
Hospitalization
  as risk factor
    infancy studies, 148
Hostility
  and selective attention, 64
Human abilities

and constructs
  in standardized testing, 7
Human behavioral phenotype
  in other cultures, 537
Human development
  cross-cultural
    handbook of, 530
Human experimentation
  and the Israel Psychological
    Association, 28
Human reactions
  to environmental stressors,
    382
Hyperphagia
  and body weight regulation,
    120
Hypertension
  and body weight regulation,
    118
  one effect of psychological
    treatment, 334
  and sodium
    body weight regulation, 118
Hypnosis
  nonbehavioral therapies, 332
Hypochondriacal concerns
  and the DSM-III, 416
Hypothalamic motivational sys-
    tems
  and brain stimulation tech-
    niques
    neurochemistry of behavior,
      97
Hypothalamus
  neurochemistry of behavior,
    79
  ventromedial
    body weight regulation, 127
Hypotonia
  and genetic risk for schizo-
    phrenia, 299

I

Identity
  and priming effects, 46
  and sex roles, 549-50
Identity priming
  and selective attention, 46, 54
Ideology
  and development of psycholo-
    gy in Israel, 18
Illusory conjunctions
  in selective attention, 57
Imagery
  in environmental psychology,
    392
Imitation
  in infancy, 140
Immigration
  into Israel
    and the need for psycholog-
      ical help, 21

Implementation
  and program evaluation, 214
Imprinting
  battery rolling goose
    and learning, 170
  and selective learning, 168-70
  and song
    in learning, 186
Improvement
  and program evaluation, 204-5
Indirect range restrictions
  in personnel selection, 369
Individual differences
  and consumer psychology,
    261
Individual psychotherapy
  and behavior change, 321
  efficacy research findings,
    324-37
  issues and trends, 337-42
  overview, 321-24
Individualism
  cross-cultural studies, 542
Inductive reasoning
  biology of learning, 183
Inductive synapses
  and neurochemistry, 77
Industrial psychology
  in Israel, 23
Industry
  practice of psychology in
    Israel, 31
Infancy
  adolescent psychiatry
    conclusion, 155-56
  infant as developing system,
    150-55
  infant as eventual adult,
    145-50
  infant as part of the natural
    world, 142-45
  in the DSM-III, 415
  expressive behavior and
    lateralization, 598
Infant-mother attachment
  and theory of object relations,
    144
Infant studies
  and hemispheric asymmetry,
    588
Infants
  and genetic risk for schizo-
    phrenia, 299
  and visual sensitivity, 506
Inference
  and consumer psychology,
    265
  instructional psychology, 614
Information
  and selective attention, 44
  storage and learning, 180
Information acquisition
  in consumer psychology, 260

Information processing
  and consumer psychology,
    257-50
  development in infancy, 144
  and schizophrenia, 300
Information processing strategies
  in environmental psychology,
    392
Information processor
  infant as, 137
Information provision
  and policy issues, 279
Information retrieval
  and the use of the DSM-III,
    422
Information transformation
  and visual sensitivity, 518
Informed Strategies for Learning
    (ISL)
  and instruction of strategic
    reading skills, 629
Ingested energy
  and body weight regulation,
    112
Inhibition
  and associative cellular pro-
    cesses
    in induction of learned be-
      havior, 448
  physiological basis of
    memory and learning, 450
Innate motor programs
  and biology of learning, 166
Innate recognition
  in the biology of learning, 165
  and learning, 181
Innovation
  and social programs
    program evaluation, 199
Input resistance
  measurement of
    memory and learning, 475
In service training
  and program evaluation, 203
Insomnia
  psychotherapy for, 336
Instruction
  and instructional psychology,
    618
  reading
    implementation of, 629
Instructional psychology
  final thoughts, 641-42
  instructional processes, 617-27
  introduction, 612
  learner characteristics, 612-17
  tasks, content, outcomes, 627-
    41
Insulin
  and body weight regulation,
    124
Integration
  in program evaluation, 229

role of neuron in, 457
  studies of
    in Israel, 35
Integration techniques
  in program evaluation, 216
Integrations
  and individual psychotherapy,
    340
Intellectual ability
  and infancy, 146
Intelligence
  evoked as an explanation for
    behavior, 360
  instructional psychology, 613
Intelligence tests
  evolution of, 1-13
Intentions
  effects on behavior
    in consumer psychology,
      268
Intercultural communication
  culture and behavior, 533
Interdependence
  and personnel selection, 353
Interference
  semantic
    in selective attention, 53
Intergroup behavior
  studies of
    in Israel, 35
Interjob similarity
  and past performances
    predicting future perfor-
      mance, 364
International classification of dis-
    orders
  see Diagnosis and clinical
    assessment
International Psychoanalytical
    Association
  and accreditation of Israeli
    teaching institutes, 20
Interocular interactions
  and visual sensitivity, 508
Interpersonal communication
  and emotion, 599
Interstimulus intervals (ISIs)
  arising from overlap, 446
Interventions
  and program evaluation, 213
Interviewing
  in diagnosis and clinical
    assessment, 424
  and personnel selection, 359
  and program evaluation, 223
Intracellular penetration
  cells by recording electrodes,
    473
Intragastric feeding
  and body weight regulation,
    121
Intrapsychic conflict
  disorders as the product of, 421

Inventing
  infant as information pro-
    cessor, 138
Invertebrate conditioning studies
  and mammalian learning, 456
Ionic conductance
  memory and learning, 458
  supporting learning, 460
Ionic currents
  measurement of, 477
IQ
  prediction of from recognition
    abilities, 146
IQ gains
  and scholastic aptitude test
    scores, 360
Irritable bowel syndrome
  supportive psychotherapy for,
    335
Israel Defense Forces
  practice of psychology in, 31
Israel Institute for Applied Social
    Research
  and Israeli psychology, 36
Israel Psychological Association
  organizational aspects of, 25-
    27
Item response theory
  in personnel selection, 352

J

James, William
  and the role of sensory and
    semantic priming, 68-69
  and selective attention, 44
Jewish people
  development of psychology in
    Israel, 18
Job analysis
  in personnel selection, 353
  and standardized testing, 7
Job corps
  and program evaluation, 195
Job knowledge
  and personnel selection, 365
Job performance
  environmental influences that
    impact, 358
Judgment
  as construct in test validation,
    7

K

Kamin effect
  and learning, 174
Kaufman Assessment Battery for
    Children
  and test validity, 3
Kibbutz life
  and incidence of schizophre-
    nia, 309

in Israel, 19
psychological work in, 32
Kleiber's formula
and expenditure of energy
body weight regulation, 114
Knowledge
and consumer psychology,
257
and personnel selection, 353
and selective attention, 44
Knowledge decision process
in consumer psychology, 281
Koan
in psychotherapy research,
342-43

L

Landmark memory
in hunting wasps, 164
Landmark navigation
and biology of learning, 179
Landscape
environmental psychology,
385
Language
and attention, 44
and biology of learning, 189
in infancy, 142
Language of action
and models of S-R behaviorism, 341
Late selection
and attention, 47-49
Latency conditioning
in memory and learning, 444
Latent facilitation
physiological basis of
memory and learning, 450
Lateral hypothalamus
and body weight regulation,
127
Lateralization
and emotion, 583-91
Lateralized perceptual processing
of emotional stimuli, 583
Law
of psychologists
in Israel, 27, 39
Learned behavior
nonassociative/associative
cellular processes
in the induction, 448
see also Cellular basis of
memory and learning
Learned characteristics
and educational psychology,
612
Learned helplessness
and learning, 185
Learned meanings
culture and behavior, 527
Learned sequences

and adaptation, 176
Learning
consolidation phase of, 439
and consumer behavior, 277
and the newborn, 140
and PET studies in schizophrenia, 298
and validity of educational
tests, 625
see also Cellular basis of
memory and learning
Learning abilities
genetic constraints to, 170
Learning disabilities
in the kibbutz population, 33
Learning strategies
and study skill, 639
Learning theory
and models of S-R behaviorism, 341
Lifestyle problems
amelioration of, 337
Light
phototropic response to, 447
Light adaptation
and visual sensitivity, 505
Linearity
and visual sensitivity, 514
Linguistic structure
effects of
on advertising, 277
LISREL
data analysis programs, 365
and program evaluation, 223
Locomotion
in infancy, 143
Localization
in selective attention, 52
Logic
and performance ranking, 212
Logical positivism
and program evaluation, 217
Logical validity
and standard testing, 2
Logistic regression
and personnel selection, 368
Long latency conditioning
in memory and learning, 447
Loss of interest
and individual psychotherapy,
328
Luminance
and visual sensitivity, 514
Luminance change detection
and visual sensitivity, 508

M

MA degree
in Israel, 21, 34
Male pregnancy symptoms
and sex identity conflict, 551

Management
education of
and program evaluation,
207
Management research programs
in instructional psychology,
623
Managerial motivation
and personnel selection, 365
Manic depressive illness
and noradrenergic activity,
589-90
Manipulable solutions
in program evaluation, 225
Manipulanda
in program evaluation, 218
Manual dexterity
as constructs
in standardized testing, 8
Marxism
and the Jewish state of Israel,
18
Math knowledge
for assessing, 368
Mathematics
psychology of, 633
Measurement
and visual sensitivity, 499
Media
instructional psychology, 618
Melodic patterns
perception of visual sym-
metry, 142
Membrane potential
and noise, 496
Membrane resistance
memory and learning, 458
Memory
and consumer psychology,
259, 261
and distance estimations, 389
emotion and self-concept, 600
and emotion, 591-98
link with learning cues, 174-
75
and the newborn, 140
and PET studies in schizophrenia, 298
and the relationship of cognition to affect
in consumer psychology,
273
and selective attention, 44
and vasporessin
neurochemistry of behavior,
93
see also Cellular basis of
memory and learning;
Emotional memory; Mood
state dependent
memory
Memory arrays
and biology of learning, 180

Memory structure
  and production systems analysis, 282
Men
  and insecure attachment in infancy, 147
Mental health
  culture and behavior, 533
  in Israel, 29
Mental health care
  impact on physical health, 334
Mental retardation
  in the DSM-III, 415
Meta analysis
  in culture and behavior, 528
  in program evaluation, 216
Meta analysis methodology
  critique of, 326
Meta analysis methods
  and individual psychotherapy research, 322
Metabolic defects
  in the central nervous system, 412
Metabolism
  adaptation to energy deficit, 114-15
Metabolites
  and body weight regulation, 123-25
Metacognition
  and instructional design, 620
Meta-evaluation
  and program evaluation, 224
Methadone
  in treatment of drug abuse, 332
Method trade-offs
  in program evaluation, 220
Middle class bias
  in environmental psychology, 388
Migration
  urban
    cross-cultural studies, 554
Milieu therapy
  in treatment of drug abuse, 332
Military
  and psychological work
    in Israel, 31
Millon Clinical Multiaxial Inventory
  and test validity, 3
Mobility
  impact on child bearing, 149
Modality
  and priming effects, 46
Modality priming
  and selective attention, 46
Modernization
  culture and behavior, 553
Modularized instruction

and instructional psychology, 612
Monitoring
  as treatment for hypertension, 334
Monoclonal technology
  in neuroscience, 97
Mood
  in consumer psychology, 260
  and infants' response to environment, 146
Mood congruity effects
  and the processing of information, 592-93
Mood effects
  on cognitive processing, 595-96
Mood state dependent memory
  and emotion, 591-92
Moral development
  universal sequences of, 540
Morphine
  neurochemistry of behavior, 83
Mother-infant interactions
  Brazelton neonatal assessment, 150
Motion uncertainty effects
  visual sensitivity, 513
Motivation
  of communication recipients
    consumer psychology, 270
  instructional psychology, 614
  and studies of schizophrenia, 295
Motives
  culture and behavior, 541
Motor learning
  acquisition and retention of, 439
Motor strategy
  and biology of learning, 166
Multiethnic population
  psychological
    in Israeli army, 32
Multiphasic environmental assessment procedure
  evaluating environmental impact, 386
Multiple regression analysis
  and personnel selection, 368
Multiple value positions
  program evaluation, 216
Muscarinic cholinergic neurotransmission
  in memory and learning, 468
Muscimol
  and neurochemistry of behavior, 92
Musculature(R)
  in cellular basis of memory and learning, 437
Mutilation

muscimol affecting, 92
Myocardial infarctions
  counseling of Type A behavior, 335

N

Narcissism
  and the DSM-III, 426
Narcotic agonists
  in treatment of drug abuse, 332
Navigation
  and biology of learning, 179
Negative conditioning
  and individual psychotherapy, 337
Negative feedback
  in personnel selection and placement, 355
Negativity
  processing
    and schizophrenia, 304
Neighborhood environment
  requirements of environmental legislation, 386
Neonatal jaundice
  as risk factor
    infancy studies, 148
Nerve membranes
  physical-chemical interactions, 433-34
Nervous system development
  psychological ability
    human infancy, 151
Nervous system maturation
  and schizophrenia, 299
Neural circuitry
  and engrams, 434
Neural dysfunctions
  neurochemistry of behavior, 79
Neural excitability
  measurement of
    and behavioral states, 473
Neural transformations
  and visual sensitivity, 497
Neural transplant techniques
  and behavioral analysis, 96
Neuroanatomy
  in memory of learning, 471
Neurobiological factors
  in schizophrenia, 292
Neurochemistry of behavior
  closing remarks, 98-100
  functions of major neurochemistry systems, 86-96
  new storehouse of
    neuroscientific knowledge, 77-83
  promise of new techniques, 96-98

quest for meaningful results in psychopharmacology, 83-86
Neurointegrative deficit (NID) and schizophrenic brain abnormalities, 311
Neuroleptics and behavior, 90
Neurological damage in schizophrenia, 294
Neuron role of integration, 457
Neuronal calcium conductance effect of interstimulus interval, 444
Neurotoxins and neurochemistry of behavior, 99
Neutral cues misattribution of arousal to, 568-69
Nicotinic neuromuscular junction and neurochemistry of behavior, 86-87
Nictitating membrane response in memory and learning, 438
NIMH collaborative depression study diagnosis and clinical assessment, 413
Noise controlling visual sensitivity, 496
and physiological mechanisms, 502
Noise limits in visual sensitivity, 501
Nonassociative learning and biology of learning, 182
Noncognitive predictor constructs and personnel selection, 364
Nonopioid peptides and neurochemistry of behavior, 92-94
Nonquantal noise and visual sensitivity, 506
Nonreported primes and subliminal semantic analysis in selective attention, 60
Nonsemantic processing in selective attention, 54
Nonuniform conductances supportive learning, 460-66
Nonwords in selective attention, 57
Norepinephrine autoregulatory functions neurochemistry of behavior, 88
and neurochemistry of behavior, 82

Norepinephrine turnover and body weight regulation, 120
Nuclear energy and environmental psychology, 396
Nucleotide actions in memory and learning, 456

O

Obesity and body weight regulation, 118
and individual psychotherapy, 333
and regulation of body weight, 109
Object-based attention and selective attention, 45
and selective processing, 56
Object permanence and research on density, 394
Object permanence task in infancy, 141
Object relations and theory of, 144
Observation and program evaluation, 223
Observational learning and the newborn, 140
Obsessive compulsive disorder and individual psychotherapy, 330
Obstetrical practices and mother-infant bonding, 153
Ocular deficiencies and visual sensitivity, 506
Odor learning and honey bees, 173
Office design and spacial behavior, 400
Office environments and environmental stress, 383
Olfactory coding and biology of learning, 165
Operant conditioning in memory and learning, 453
Opiate addicts behavioral approaches tested with, 333
Opiates addictive properties of, 95
Opioid receptor system and neurochemistry of behavior, 78
Outcomes in program evaluation, 218
Overeating and body weight regulation, 120
Overlap in memory and learning, 445

Overlapping objects in selective attention, 58

P

P300 component and schizophrenia, 303
Pain and opioid systems, 96
Pairing relationship in associative learning, 173
Pairing specificity in memory and learning, 456
Pairings and biology of learning, 181
Palestine Psychoanalytical Society and acceptation of Israeli teaching institutes, 20
Pandysmaturation (PDM) and genetic risk for schizophrenia, 299
and schizophrenic brain abnormalities, 311
Panic disorder in the DSM-III, 415
Parafoveal attention and sensory priming effects, 52
Paranoid disorders in the schizophrenic spectrum, 293
Parental age as risk factor infancy studies, 148
Parental care and biology of learning, 177
Parental psychopathology influences of on childrearing, 149
Parkinson's disease role of dopamine, 90
Past performance and interjob similarity predicting future performance, 364
Pattern sensitivity to vision, 511
Pavlovian conditioning in memory and learning, 452
Pedestal effect and visual sensitivity, 514
Peers development in infancy, 144
Peptide neurobiology and behavior, 92
Peptide systems and neurochemistry of behavior, 82
Perceived ability in instructional psychology, 615

Perceived Environmental Quality
  Indices (PEQIs)
  and environmental psycholo-
    gy, 382
  requirements of environmental
    legislation, 386
Perceived threat
  environmental psychology,
    399
Perceiving
  infant as information pro-
    cessor, 138
Percent agreement method
  personnel selection and place-
    ment, 371
Perception
  and consumer psychology,
    258
  in cross-cultural research, 534
  and instructional design, 620
Perceptual organization
  in selective attention, 56
Perceptual segregation
  in selective attention, 57
Performance
  brain task, 496
  and program evaluation, 208
  selecting standards of
    in program evaluation, 214
  strategies for estimating the
    value of, 372
  and test anxiety, 616
Performance assessment
  and program evaluation, 215
Performance measurement
  research on
    and personnel selection,
      355-59
Personal space
  and environmental psycholo-
    gy, 397
Personality
  and the DSM-III, 426
Personality development
  in other cultures, 539
Personality disorder
  in the DSM-III, 415
  in the schizophrenic spectrum,
    293
Personality theories
  and constructs
    in standardized testing, 7
Personnel assessment
  in standardized testing, 10
Personnel selection
  and placement
    criteria, 353-59
    introduction, 351-53
    prediction procedures, 367-
      73
    predictors, 359-67
  and standardized testing, 7
Persuasion

in consumer psychology, 267,
  270
Persuasion processes
  contingency approaches to
    consumer psychology, 271
Pharmacotherapy
  in treatment of drug abuse,
    332
Phenothiazine
  psychotic disorders, 198
Phobias
  and individual psychotherapy,
    330
  systematic desensitization, 198
Phobic stimuli
  and fear-relevant stimuli, 598
Photon detector
  and visual sensitivity, 498
Photoreceptors
  contributing noise to visual
    levels, 501
Physical disorders
  and the DSM-III, 414
Physical features
  and spatial attention, 55
Physical illness
  producing psychological prob-
    lems
    in Israel, 29
Physiological feedback
  in cognition arousal theory,
    571
Physiological sensitivity
  and vision, 500
Piaget's theory
  and biology of learning, 189
  and the infant as information
    processor, 138
Picrotoxin
  neurochemistry of behavior,
    83
Placebo controls
  in program evaluation, 214
Placebo effects
  and opioid systems, 95
Placebo influences
  and individual psychotherapy,
    323
Placebos
  and deficiency of psy-
    chotherapies, 33-39
Plasma membrane
  memory and learning, 461
Pleasure
  neurochemistry of behavior,
    87
  and opioid systems, 95
Policy issues
  in consumer psychology, 279
Political impactedness
  and social programs, 196
Polyclonal antibodies
  in neuroscience, 97

Population growth
  and human behavior and
    adjustment
    in Israel, 19
Position Analysis Questionnaire
  (PAQ)
  behavioral constructs in, 12
  and personnel selection, 354
Positron emission transaxial
  tomography (PET)
  and schizophrenia, 292
Postoccupancy evaluation
  in environmental psychology,
    383
Postreceptor mechanisms
  and visual sensitivity, 507
Postsynaptic integration
  memory and learning, 457
Postsynaptic neuronal changes
  and sensitization
    in memory and learning,
      451
Post-traumatic stress disorder
  and individual psychotherapy,
    330
Potassium conductances
  in memory and learning, 463
Potassium conductant
  and conditioning
    memory and learning, 454
Potential
  in memory and learning, 456
Power
  and indirect range restriction
    in personnel selection, 369
Powerlessness
  and research on attribution of
    achievement, 544
Precursors
  in infant development, 151
Prediction
  and the DSM-III, 422, 428
Prediction procedures
  and personnel selection, 367
Predictive utility
  and concurrent validation
    in standardized testing, 4
Predictor measures
  and personnel selection, 359
Preevaluative tasks
  and program evaluation, 215
Preference
  and infant perception, 139
Prenatal teratogens
  as risk factor
    infancy studies, 148
Prestige
  and Israeli psychology, 40
Price
  and consumer psychology,
    259
Primary eating disorder
  obesity as, 110

Priming effects
  and selective attention, 45
  and sematic interference, 54
  and top down control of selec-
    tive processing, 46
Priming stimuli
  and biology of learning, 167
Prior knowledge
  role of
    in learning, 637
Prioritizing
  procedures for
    and program evaluation,
      211
Privacy
  in environmental psychology,
    399
  in the workplace, 383
Privacy management
  and environmental psycholo-
    gy, 401
Problem drinking
  and the DSM-III, 416
Problem solving
  elementry school mathematics,
    635
  in instructional psychology,
    637
Problem solving skills
  instructional psychology, 614
  and the writer, 631
Processing
  in consumer psychology, 264
Processing capacity
  and selective attention, 44
Processing dissociation
  of split-brain patients, 50
Product
  and consumer psychology,
    257-58
  and misleading advertising,
    280
Product performance
  in consumer psychology, 260
Professional guides
  and program evaluation, 201
Professional training
  and program evaluation, 203
Program evaluation
  conclusion, 230
  constructing valid knowledge,
    217-24
  evaluating usage, 200-8
  introduction, 193-95
  theories of evaluation practice,
    224-30
  valuing, 208-17
Program managers
  and program evaluations, 217
Program planning
  and environmental psycholo-
    gy, 387
Programmed learning

and instructional psychology,
  612
Programs
  and industrial psychology
    in Israel, 23
Project A
  measuring and interpretation
    of human differences
    and personnel selection, 373
Project level
  and program evaluation, 206
Project turnover
  and program evaluation, 197
Promotion
  and age
    expected negative relation-
      ship, 369
Prophylactic regimens
  psychotherapy for, 336
Proprioceptive feedback
  and biology of learning, 165-
    66
Provocation
  and cognition-arousal theory
    emotion study, 569
Psychiatric diagnoses
  and personality tests, 2
  see also Diagnosis and clinical
    assessment
Psychiatric disorder
  see Diagnosis and clinical
    assessment
Psychoanalysis
  in Israel, 20
Psychobehavioral taxonomy
  working hypotheses, 84
Psychological adjustment
  in the kibbutz population, 33
Psychological research
  on infants, 135-61
Psychology ability
  and nervous system develop-
    ment, 151
Psychology in Israel
  development of, 19-25
  historical background, 18-19
  in society, 37-40
  organizational aspects, 25-29
  psychologists at work, 29-33
  research, 34-37
  state of, 37-40
  training, 33-34
Psychometric functions
  and visual sensitivity, 514
Psychomotor measures
  measurement and interpreta-
    tion of human differences
    and personnel selection, 373
Psychopathology
  and infancy, 146
Psychosis
  and ventricular enlargement,
    296

Psychosocial factors
  in schizophrenia, 292
Psychotic depressive episodes
  in the DSM-III, 421
Psychotic disorders
  phenothiazine, 198
Psychotic symptoms
  and diagnosis and clinical
    assessment, 411
Public health
  and individual psychotherapy,
    327
Purchase
  and consumer psychology,
    257-58
Purging
  behavioral therapy for, 334

Q

Quality
  and consumer psychology,
    259

R

Radio
  in instructional psychology,
    619
Random stimulus paradigm
  in memory and learning, 444
Rater error training
  of raters
    and personnel selection, 357
Reaction times
  in schizophrenic patients, 301
  in selective attention, 50
Reactivity
  and infants' response to en-
    vironment, 146
Reading
  and instructional psychology,
    627
Reading ability
  and test validation, 5
Realism
  and program evaluation, 219
Reality adaptive supportive
  (RAS) psychotherapy
    outcome studies, 330
Recall
  brand items, 276
Receiver operating characteris-
  tics(ROC) analysis
    and visual sensitivity, 498
Recognition abilities
  and measure of IQ
    in infancy, 146
Recognition memory
  and infancy, 141
Recovery

from surgery
and environmental psychology, 395
Recurrent coronary prevention project
counseling of Type A behavior, 335
Reflectivity
in instructional psychology, 620
Reflex evaluation
and consumer psychology, 279
Regional cerebral blood flow
and schizophrenia, 295
Regression model
and personnel selection, 356
Regulated energy
factors altering the level of, 120
Regulation of body weight
body weight-a homeostatic perspective, 111-12
energy expenditure, 112-16
mechanisms of, 123-28
summary and conclusions, 128-30
variation in, 116-23
Rehabilitation psychology
in Israel, 22, 30
Relationship development
privacy regulation as a function of, 401
Relaxation
as treatment for gastrointestinal disorders, 335
Relaxation training
as treatment for hypertension, 334
Reliability
in the DSM-III, 423
Reproduction
recognition and motor behavior, 176
Reproductive activity
and body weight regulation, 118
Research
psychological
in Israel, 34
Respiratory illness
as infancy studies, 148
Response
effect of visual stimuli on, 276
Response biases
and learning, 185
Response mode
in consumer psychology, 266
Responsiveness
in individual psychotherapy, 329
Resting oxygen consumption

and body weight regulation, 119
Resting rate
energy expenditure
and balance, 114
Retardation
in the kibbutz population, 33
Retarded children
in Israel, 21
Ricin
and neurochemistry of behavior, 99
Rigidity
and situational specificity, 10
Risk
perceptions of
in consumer psychology, 260
Role evaluators
in program evaluation, 226

S

Sampling strategies
and program evaluation, 222
Satisfaction
consumer research on, 280-81
Schema based attention
and selection, 63-64
selective attention, 45
Schema theory
and consumer psychology, 259
and selective attention, 69
Schematic
and priming effects, 46
Schematic analysis
and selective attention, 44
Schematic inquiry
in consumer psychology, 272
Schematic priming
and selective attention, 47
Schizoid
in the schizophrenia spectrum, 293
Schizophrenia
diagnosis and clinical assessment, 411
etiology and expression of, 291-313
cognitive psychophysiological studies, 300-7
conclusion, 313
familial and socioenvironmental factors, 307-10
introduction, 291-94
neurological and neuroanatomical studies, 294-300
vulnerability to, 310-13
research evidence on the treatment of, 329

Schizophrenic disorders
role of dopamine, 90
Scholastic aptitude test scores
and IQ gains, 360
School lunch programs
evaluation, 205
Science
and instructional psychology, 635
social goals
in Israel, 24
Scripts
and consumer psychology, 259
Search
in consumer psychology, 260
Second messengers
within the plasma membrane
memory and learning, 466
Security
and environmental psychology, 386
Selection statistics
and personnel selection, 368-71
Selective attention
conclusion, 70
introduction, 43-45
review of empirical literature, 45-65
review of theories, 65-70
Selective learning
and imprinting, 168-70
Self-control
and toilet training, 145
Self-esteem
and emotion and memory, 600
Self-evaluation
and program evaluation, 201
Self-guided achievement
instructional psychology, 636
Self schemata
effect of
on selective attention, 64
Self-stimulation behavior
and depletion of norepinephrine, 99
Self-worth
in instructional psychology, 615
Semantic priming
and nonselected objects, 59-60
and selective attention, 47
Semantic processing
of nonselected objects, 59
in selective attention, 53
Semantics
and priming effects, 46
Semantic selection
and attention, 48
Senior management predictor
and personnel selection, 365
Sensitivity

visual, 499
Sensitization
and associative cellular processes
induction of learned behavior, 448
and biology of learning, 187
cellular changes produced by, 449
Sensory biases
and selective attention, 67
Sensory modalities
in infancy, 142
Sensory preconditioning
effectiveness of different ISIs, 452
in memory and learning, 451
Sensory processing
and cue recognition, 164
Sensory selection
and attention, 48
Separation distress
and opioid systems, 95
Septal syndrome
and neurochemistry of behavior, 82
Serial processing
and detection of feature conjunctions, 55
Serial recall task
in schizophrenia, 301
Serotonin
and neurochemistry of behavior, 82, 87
Service deliverers
and program evaluation, 203
Services
and consumer psychology, 257-58
Sex
significance of in raters
personnel evaluation, 357
Sex differences
attribution of success in
affiliation, 545
cross-cultural research, 548-49
Sex identity conflict
culture and behavior, 551
Sex roles
and identity, 549
Sexual behavior
and neurochemistry, 93
Sexual identity
see Gender identity disorder of childhood
Shape learning
and honey bees, 173
Shrinkage
formula estimates for
and personnel selection, 370
Siblings
development in infancy, 144
Sign stimuli

and motivation
in learning, 168
and selective learning, 183
Sign stimulus strategy
and biology of learning, 165
Signal detection
and visual sensitivity, 497
Single sample cross-validation
designs
and personnel selection, 370
Situational specificity
and standardized testing, 8-10
Size
and indirect range restrictions
in personnel selection, 369
Size estimates
and program evaluation, 215
Skill training
in instructional psychology, 640
Skills
and personnel selection, 353
Sleep disturbance
and individual psychotherapy, 328
Smoking
and body weight regulation, 123
psychotherapy for, 336
Social behavior
and biology of learning, 180-82
Social class
influences of on childrearing, 149
and mass immigration
in Israel, 25
Social cognition
in consumer psychology, 272
Social communication
and facial feedback, 580
Social competence
and infancy, 146
Social conformity
and situational specificity, 10
Social forces
and development of psychology in Israel, 18
Social functioning
and individual psychotherapy, 328
Social goals
in Israel, 24
Social imprinting
and learning, 181
Social issues
and psychology in other cultures, 532
Social milieu
and the Israeli state, 19
Social penetration theory
in environmental psychology, 399

Social perception
cross-cultural studies, 547
Social phobia
and individual psychotherapy, 330
Social policy
and relevance of environment, 402
Social problems
and time bound relationships, 205
Social programming methods
and evaluation, 198
Social relations
in infancy, 142-44
Social skills training
and individual psychotherapy, 329
Social support
as treatment for hypertension, 334
Socialization
and personality development, 539
Society
state of psychology in
Israel, 37-40
Socioenvironmental factors
in schizophrenia, 307-10
Sodium
and hypertension
and body weight regulation, 121
Sodium conductances
memory and learning, 461
Somatic disorders
psychological interventions
for, 337
Somatic pain
control of
neurochemistry of behavior, 83
Somatosensory selection task
and schizophrenia, 304
Somatostatin
neurochemistry of behavior, 79
Song
and biology of learning, 177
Soup
bidirectional influences of genetic heritage, 152
Space
importance of
and selective attention, 49
Spatial attention
and accuracy of stimulus processing, 56
and processing priority
and selective attention, 45-49
Spatial behavior
and environment, 381-402

Spatial cues
  selection on the basis of, 65
Spatial knowledge
  in environmental psychology,
    388
Spatial locus
  and visual sensitivity, 507
Spatial patterns
  visual sensitivity, 517
Spatial task
  and studies of schizophrenia,
    296
Spatial visual functioning
  instructional psychology, 613
Spatial visualization
  as constructs
    in standardized testing, 8
  in environmental psychology,
    390
Species identification
  in infancy, 139
Species recognition
  and biology of learning, 169
Specificity of effects
  and efficacy of psychothera-
    pies, 338-39
Speech
  adult to infant, 153
  and infancy, 143
Spelling ability
  and test validation, 5
Spinal cord
  neurochemistry of behavior,
    79
Sporadic schizophrenia
  in diagnosis of schizophrenia,
    293
  and intrauterine and birth
    complications, 311
Stability
  and regulation of body weight,
    110
Stake holder service
  in program evaluation, 228
Standard
  choice of
    in program evaluation, 214
  and program evaluation, 208
Stanford Binet test
  evolution of, 1
Starvation
  and neurochemistry of be-
    havior, 89
Status
  of psychology
    in Israel, 39
Stereoanomaly
  and visual sensitivity, 517
Stereotypes
  in consumer psychology, 278
Stimulant drugs
  and noradrenergic activity,
    589-90

Stimulation
  and development in infancy,
    154
Stimuli
  concurrent
    and selective attention, 44
Stimulus encoding
  and selective attention, 66
Stimulus response "reflex"
  biology of learning, 183
Strategic reading
  comprehension monitoring,
    628
Stress
  and neurochemistry of be-
    havior, 82
  and opioid systems
    effect of behavior on, 95
  see also Environmental stress-
    ors
Stress induced analgesia
  and opioid systems, 96
Stress management
  as treatment for hypertension,
    334
Structural equation models
  in personnel selection, 352
Structured interview
  and the DSM-III, 425
Student Cognition Research Program
  in instructional psychology,
    623
Study skills
  and learning strategies, 639
Substance P
  and neurochemistry of be-
    havior, 78
Substrates
  and body weight regulation,
    123-25
Summation
  in visual sensitivity, 506
Sun orientation
  and biology of learning, 179
Swaddling
  as standard of infant care, 149
Symptom patterns
  and diagnosis and clinical
    assessment, 414
Symptoms
  stability of
    and the DSM-III, 427
Synthetic validation
  concept of
    and personnel selection, 370
System of Multicultural Pluralistic Assessment (SOMPA)
  and instructional psychology,
    627
Systematic desensitization
  and phobias
    program evaluation, 198

T

Targeting
  and program evaluation, 204-
    05
Task (detection)
  visual sensitivity, 497
Task comprehension
  and studies of schizophrenia,
    295
Task demands
  and studies of schizophrenia,
    269
Task effect
  in consumer psychology, 266
Task strategies
  and personnel placement, 354
Tasks
  and instructional psychology,
    627
Taste detection
  and neurochemistry of be-
    havior, 89
TCDD (2,3,7,8-
    Tetracholorodibenzo-p-
    dioxin)
  effect of on weight, 122
Teacher made tests
  instructional psychology, 625
Teacher presentation behaviors
  and classroom teaching, 622
Teaching
  cognitive psychology and in-
    struction, 622
  cross-cultural psychology, 531
Teaching masks
  in other cultures, 535
Technical eclecticism
  and individual psychotherapy,
    341
Technological catastrophes
  and environmental psycholo-
    gy, 396
Technology
  and industrial psychology
    in Israel, 23
  and media, 618
  and writing instruction, 632-
    33
Television
  in instructional psychology,
    619
Temperament
  and infancy, 146-47
  and infants' response to en-
    vironment, 146
Temperatures
  and crime
    linear relationship between,
      394
Temporal process
  and environmental psycholo-
    gy, 402

Tension
  psychosocial treatments for,
    336
Territoriality
  and crime, 400
  and environmental psycholo-
    gy, 382
Test anxiety
  and performance, 616
Test construction process
  place of validity in, 2-4
Test validation
  see Evolving concepts of test
    validation
Testing
  cognitive psychology, 625
  instructional psychology, 612,
    624
Tests and scales
  Comrey Personality Scales
    and test validity, 3
  Kaufman Assessment Battery
    for Children
    and test validation, 3
  Millon Clinical Multiaxial In-
    ventory
    and test validation, 3
  Multiphasic Environmental
    Assessment Procedure
    evaluating environmental
      impact, 386
  Perceived Environmental
    Quality Indices
    environmental psychology,
      382
  Personality Research Form
    and test validity, 3
  Position Analysis Questionaire
    (PAQ)
    behavioral constructs in, 12
    and personnel selection, 354
  Stanford Binet
    and age differentiation crite-
      rion, 1
  System of Multicultural
    Pluralistic Assessment
    instructional psychology,
      627
  Wisconsin card sorting test
    use of in schizophrenia, 296
Thalamic somatic axis
  and neurochemistry, 93
Theoretical empiricism
  in test development, 12
Theory development
  in individual psychotherapy,
    339-40
Theory of signal detectability
  (TSD)
  and visual sensitivity, 497
Therapist experience
  and treatment effectiveness,
    324

Thermogenesis
  and body weight regulation,
    126
Thought disorder
  in schizophrenia patients
    and familial communica-
      tion deviance, 308
Threats
  selective learning of, 178
Threshold primes
  and selective attention, 59-60
Threshold theory
  and multistate thresholds
    visual sensitivity, 496
Time
  link with learning cues, 174-
    75
Time bound relationships
  social problems, 205
Time learning
  and honey bees, 173
Time sharing
  and motivation
    in learning, 168
Tobacco use disorder
  and the DSM-III, 426
Toxic substances
  and environmental psycholo-
    gy, 396
Toxins
  effect of on weight, 122
Trace presentation
  in memory and learning,
    445
Training
  of psychologists
    in Israel, 33-34
Trait constructs
  and standardized testing, 8
Tranquilizers
  and neurochemistry of be-
    havior, 88
Transducer function
  and visual sensitivity, 514
Transmission latencies
  in memory and learning, 442
Transmitters
  degradative pathways for
    and neurochemistry of be-
      havior, 78
Treatment effect
  and program evaluation, 217
Treatment programs
  evaluation of, 213
Trees
  and environmental psycholo-
    gy, 384
Trial and error learning
  distinguished from classical
    conditioning, 184
Triphosphoinositol
  memory and learning, 467
Twin studies

  in diagnosis of schizophrenia,
    293
Type A behavior
  in cases of heart attacks, 335
Type A photoreceptors
  in memory and learning, 435

U

Uncertainty effects
  and vision sensitivity, 512-14
Unconditioned response
  and cellular basis of memory
    and learning, 438
Underactivity
  and genetic risk for schizo-
    phrenia, 299
Undifferentiated counseling
  and effect sizes, 325
Union owned enterprises
  in Israel, 19
Urbanization
  consequences of, 554-55
  impact on childrearing, 149
Usage
  of program evaluation
    methods to stimulate, 204
Usage behavior
  and consumer psychology,
    258
Utility analysis
  and personnel selection, 372

V

Valid knowledge
  knowledge base about con-
    structing, 217
Validation
  and personnel selection, 368-
    71
  and standardized testing, 1
Validity coefficients
  and predictors
    personnel selection, 363
Validity generalization
  in standardized testing, 10-12
Validity shrinkage
  in cross validation, 13
Validity threats
  and program evaluation, 219
Value analysis
  and program evaluation, 230
Values
  culture and behavior, 541
Valuing
  knowledge base about, 208
Variable matching (VM)
  and selective attention, 63
Vasoactive intestinal peptide
  neurochemistry of behavior,
    79
Vasopressin

and memory
  neurochemistry of behavior,
    93
Vegetation
  environmental psychology,
    385
Ventricular size
  alterations in
    patients with schizophrenia,
      296
Ventromedial hypothalamic
  (VMH) syndrome
  and energy expenditure, 110
Ventromedial hypothalamus
  and body weight regulation,
    127
Vigilance tasks
  in schizophrenia, 301
Viral brain infections
  etiology of schizophrenic,
    295-98
Visual abilities
  at age two months, 151
Visual sensitivity
  conclusions, 517-18
  discrimination, 516-17
  introduction, 495-501
  noise limits, 501-6
  summation, 506-12
  uncertainty, 512-16
Visual stimuli

processing of
  in advertising, 275
Vocalization
  and biology of learning, 178
Vocational assessments
  and personnel selection, 364
Vocational counseling
  in Israel, 36
Voltage dependancy
  in memory and learning, 465
Vulnerability
  to schizophrenia, 310-13

W

Waking arousal
  and neurochemistry of be-
    havior, 89
Wasting syndrome
  and body weight regulation,
    122
Weaning
  as limit to infancy, 136
Weight
  see Regulation of body weight
Weight loss
  and exercise, 122
  metabolic adaptation to
    and body weight regulation,
      119

Weighting techniques
  and program evaluation, 215
Welfare
  and the Israeli state, 19
Wisconsin Card Scoring Test
  use of in schizophrenia, 296
Withdrawal symptoms
  behavioral neurochemistry, 84
Women
  euthenia abortion, 294
  mother infant interactions, 150
Women-infant children program
  and social programs, 196
World Health Organization
  and international classifica-
    tion, 409
Worth
  in personnel selection, 353
Writing
  and instructional psychology,
    630-33
Writing instruction
  and technology, 632

Z

Zooming
  as media method
    in instructional psychology,
      621

CUMULATIVE INDEXES

CONTRIBUTING AUTHORS, VOLUMES 33–37

A

Achenbach, T. M., 35:227–56
Alkon, D. L., 36:419–93
Amado, G., 33:343–70
Amir, Y., 37:17–41
Anastasi, A., 37:1–15
Ardila, R., 33:103–22
Asher, S. R., 34:465–509

B

Baum, A., 36:349–83
Ben–Ari, R., 37:17–41
Bettman, J. R., 37:257–89
Birren, J. E., 34:543–75
Bolles, R. C., 33:87–101
Borgen, F. H., 35:579–604
Brewer, M. B., 36:219–43
Brislin, R. W., 34:363–400
Browne, M. A., 35:605–25
Brugge, J. F., 36:245–74
Buchsbaum, M. S., 34:401–30

C

Cairns, R. B., 35:553–77
Cantor, N., 36:275–305
Cascio, W. F., 35:461–518
Clark, E. V., 34:325–49
Cohn, T. E., 37:495–521
Cook, T. D., 37:193–232
Cooper, J., 35:395–426
Cotman, C. W., 33:371–401
Cross, D. R., 37:611–51
Croyle, R. T., 35:395–426
Cummings, L. L., 33:541–79
Cunningham, W. R., 34:543–75

D

Darian-Smith, I., 33:155–94
Dark, V. J., 37:43–75
Deaux, K., 36:49–81
Diaz-Guerrero, R., 35:83–112
Dick, W., 34:261–95
Duncan, C. C., 37:291–319

E

Edelbrock, C. S., 35:227–56
Eron, L. D., 33:231–64
Eysenck, H. J., 34:167–93

F

Fanselow, M. S., 33:87–101
Farley, J., 36:419–93
Faucheux, C., 33:343–70
Feder, H. H., 35:165–200
Finkelstein, P., 33:515–39
Fischer, K. W., 36:613–48
Fraisse, P., 35:1–36
Friedman, A. F., 34:167–93

G

Gagné, R. M., 34:261–95
Gould, J. L., 37:163–92
Green, B. F., 35:37–53
Grunberg, N. E., 36:349–83

H

Haier, R. J., 34:401–30
Hakel, M. D., 37:351–80
Hall, J. A., 35:37–53
Harris, L. C., 35:333–60
Harvey, J. H., 35:427–59
Hastie, R., 34:511–42
Hay, D. F., 37:135–61
Haywood, H. C., 33:309–42
Hecht, B. F., 34:325–49
Helzer, J. E., 37:409–32
Hendersen, R. W., 36:495–529
Henderson, N. D., 33:403–40
Hillyard, S. A. 34:33–61
Holahan, C. J., 37:381–407
Holland, P. C., 33:265–308
Honzik, M. P., 35:309–31
Horton, D. L., 35:361–94

I

Iscoe, I., 35:333–60

J

Johnston, W. A., 37:43–75

K

Kamil, A. C., 36:141–69
Kassarjian, H. H., 33:619–49
Keesey, R. E., 37:109–33
Kessler, R. C., 36:531–72
Kihlstrom, J. F., 36:385–418

Klaber, M., 36:115–40
Knoll, E., 34:195–222
Kolers, P. A., 34:129–66
Kozma, R. B., 37:611–51
Kramer, A., 36:307–48
Kramer, R. M., 36:219–43
Krantz, D. S., 36:349–83
Kravitz, D. A., 33:195–230
Kutas, M., 34:33–61

L

Lam, Y. R., 36:19–48
Lanyon, R. I., 35:667–701
Lasley, D. J., 37:495–521
Laurent, A., 33:343–70
Leventhal, H., 37:565–610
Loevinger, J., 34:195–222
Loftus, E. F., 33:441–75
London, P., 37:321–49

M

Mahoney, M. J., 35:605–25
Marshall, J. F., 35:277–308
McFadden, D., 34:95–128
McGaugh, J. L., 34:297–323
McGrath, J. E., 33:195–230
McKeachie, W. J., 37:611–51
McLeod, P., 33:477–514
Medin, D. L., 35:113–38
Meyers, C. E., 33:309–42
Miller, D. T., 37:233–56
Miller, N. E., 34:1–31
Mills, C. B., 35:361–94
Mineka, S., 36:495–529
Mirsky, A. F., 37:291–319
Mollon, J. D., 33:441–75
Monahan, J., 33:441–75

N

Nieto-Sampedro, M., 33:371–401

O

Oeltjen, P. D., 33:581–618

P

Panksepp, J., 37:77–107
Parke, R. D., 34:465–509

Parloff, M. B., 37:321–49
Pervin, L. A., 36:83–114
Peterson, R. A., 33:231–64
Phillips, D. P., 36:245–74
Pintrich, P. R., 37:611–51
Pitz, G. F., 35:139–63
Posner, M. I., 33:477–514
Powley, T. L., 37:109–33
Premack, D., 34:351–62
Price, R. H., 36:531–72

R

Rescorla, R. A., 33:265–308
Reykowski, J., 33:123–54
Rheingold, H. L., 36:1–17
Robins, L. N., 37:409–32
Roitblat, H. L., 36:141–69
Rorer, L. G., 34:431–63
Russell, J. A., 33:651–88

S

Sachs, N. J., 35:139–63
Sarason, S. B., 36:115–40
Schneider, B., 36:573–611

Segall, M. H., 37:523–64
Shadish, W. R., Jr., 37:193–232
Showers, C., 36:275–305
Silvern, L., 36:613–48
Simon, N. G., 35:257–76
Smith, E. E., 35:113–38
Snowdon, C. T., 34:63–94
Staw, B. M., 35:627–66
Switzky, H. N., 33:309–42

T

Tajfel, H., 33:1–39
Tenopyr, M. L., 33:581–618
Tomarken, A. J., 37:565–610
Traub, R. E., 36:19–48
Turnbull, W., 37:233–56

V

Valsiner, J., 35:553–77
Van Sluyters, R. C., 32:477–522

W

Wakefield, J. A. Jr., 34:167–93
Ward, L. M., 33:651–88

Weary, G., 35:427–59
Wenegrat, B., 33:515–39
Westheimer, G., 35:201–26
Wexley, K. N., 35:519–51
Whalen, R. E., 35:257–76
Wickens, C. D., 36:307–48
Widiger, T. A., 34:431–63
Wightman, F. L., 34:95–128
Wimer, C. C., 36:171–218
Wimer, R. E., 36:171–218
Wolfe, B., 37:321–49
Woody, C. D., 37:433–93
Wortman, C. B., 36:531–72
Wortman, P. M., 34:223–60

Y

Yalom, I., 33:515–39
Yamamoto, K., 34:543–75
Young, F. W., 35:55–81

Z

Zedeck, S., 35:461–518

CHAPTER TITLES, VOLUMES 33–37

PREFATORY CHAPTER
Behavioral Medicine: Symbiosis Between
    Laboratory and Clinic N. E. Miller 34:1–31
Perception and Estimation of Time P. Fraisse 35:1–36
Development as the Acquisition of Familiarity H. L. Rheingold 36:1–17
Evolving Concepts of Test Validation A. Anastasi 37:1–15

ATTENTION
Selective Attention W. A. Johnston, V. J. Dark 37:43–75

BIOLOGICAL PSYCHOLOGY
Brain Function, Synapse Renewal, and
    Plasticity C. W. Cotman, M. Nieto-Sampedro 33:371–401
Human Behavior Genetics N. D. Henderson 33:403–40
Electrophysiology of Cognitive Processing S. A. Hillyard, M. Kutas 34:33–61
Hormones and Sexual Behavior H. H. Feder 35:165–200
Brain Function: Neural Adaptations and
    Recovery from Injury J. F. Marshall 35:277–308
Animal Behavior Genetics: A Search for the
    Biological Foundations of Behavior R. E. Wimer, C. C. Wimer 36:171–218
Cellular Mechanisms of Learning, Memory,
    and Information Storage J. Farley, D. L. Alkon 36:419–93
The Neurochemistry of Behavior J. Panksepp 37:77–107

CHEMICAL SENSES
See SENSORY PROCESSES

CLINICAL AND COMMUNITY PSYCHOLOGY
Large Group Awareness Training P. Finkelstein, B. Wenegrat, I.
    Yalom 33:515–39
Diagnosis and Clinical Assessment: The
    DSM-III H. J. Eysenck, J. A. Wakefield Jr.,
    A. F. Friedman 34:167–93
Social and Community Interventions I. Iscoe, L. C. Harris 35:333–60
Individual Psychotherapy and Behavior
    Change M. B. Parloff, P. London, B. Wolfe 37:321–49
Diagnosis and Clinical Assessment: The
    Current State of Psychiatric Diagnosis L. N. Robins, J. E. Helzer 37:409–32
See also PSYCHOPATHOLOGY

COGNITIVE PROCESSES
Comprehension, Production, and Language
    Acquisition E. V. Clark, B. F. Hecht 34:325–49
Animal Cognition D. Premack 34:351–62
Concepts and Concept Formation D. L. Medin, E. E. Smith 35:113–38
Judgment and Decision: Theory and
    Application G. F. Pitz, N. J. Sachs 35:139–63

COMPARATIVE PSYCHOLOGY, ETHOLOGY, AND ANIMAL BEHAVIOR
Ethology, Comparative Psychology, and
    Animal Behavior C. T. Snowdon 34:63–94
The Biology of Learning J. L. Gould 37:163–92

COUNSELING
　　See EDUCATION AND COUNSELING

DEVELOPMENTAL PSYCHOLOGY
　　Social and Personality Development　　　　R. D. Parke, S. R. Asher　　　　34:465–509
　　Psychology of Adult Development　　　　　J. E. Birren, W. Cunningham, K.
　　　　　　　　　　　　　　　　　　　　　Yamamoto　　　　　　　　　　34:543–75
　　Life-Span Development　　　　　　　　　M. P. Honzik　　　　　　　　　35:309–31
　　Child Psychology　　　　　　　　　　　R. B. Cairns, J. Valsiner　　　　35:553–77
　　Stages and Individual Differences in Cognitive
　　　　Development　　　　　　　　　　　K. W. Fischer, L. Silvern　　　　36:613–48
　　Infancy　　　　　　　　　　　　　　　D. F. Hay　　　　　　　　　　37:135–61

EDUCATION AND COUNSELING
　　Instructional Psychology　　　　　　　　R. M. Gagné, W. Dick　　　　　34:261–95
　　Counseling Psychology　　　　　　　　　F. H. Borgen　　　　　　　　　35:579–604
　　The School as a Social Situation　　　　　S. B. Sarason, M. Klaber　　　　36:115–40
　　Instructional Psychology　　　　　　　　P. R. Pintrich, D. R. Cross, R. B.
　　　　　　　　　　　　　　　　　　　　　Kozma, W. J. McKeachie　　　37:611–51

EMOTION
　　Emotion: Today's Problems　　　　　　　H. Levanthal, A. J. Tomarken　　37:565–610

ENVIRONMENTAL PSYCHOLOGY
　　Environmental Psychology　　　　　　　　J. A. Russell, L. M. Ward　　　33:651–88
　　Environmental Psychology　　　　　　　　C. J. Holahan　　　　　　　　37:381–407

GENETICS OF BEHAVIOR
　　See BIOLOGICAL PSYCHOLOGY

GERONTOLOGY (MATURITY AND AGING)
　　See DEVELOPMENTAL PSYCHOLOGY

HEARING
　　See SENSORY PROCESSES

HYPNOSIS
　　Hypnosis　　　　　　　　　　　　　　J. F. Kihlstrom　　　　　　　　36:385–418

INDUSTRIAL PSYCHOLOGY
　　See PERSONNEL-ORGANIZATIONAL
　　　　PSYCHOLOGY

LEARNING AND MEMORY
　　Behavioral Studies of Associative Learning in
　　　　Animals　　　　　　　　　　　　R. A. Rescorla, P. C. Holland　　33:265–308
　　Hormonal Influences on Memory　　　　　J. L. McGaugh　　　　　　　　34:297–323
　　Human Learning and Memory　　　　　　D. L. Horton, C. B. Mills　　　35:361–94
　　The Ecology of Foraging Behavior:
　　　　Implications for Animal Learning and
　　　　Memory　　　　　　　　　　　　A. C. Kamil, H. L. Roitblat　　　36:141–69
　　Understanding the Cellular Basis of Memory
　　　　and Learning　　　　　　　　　　C. D. Woody　　　　　　　　　37:433–93

MENTAL RETARDATION
　　Mental Retardation　　　　　　　　　　H. C. Haywood, C. E. Meyers, H.
　　　　　　　　　　　　　　　　　　　　　N. Switsky　　　　　　　　　33:309–42

MOTIVATION
　　Social Motivation　　　　　　　　　　　J. Reykowski　　　　　　　　　33:123–54
　　Biological Motivation　　　　　　　　　R. E. Whalen, N. G. Simon　　　35:257–76
　　Controllability and Predictability in Acquired
　　　　Motivation　　　　　　　　　　　S. Mineka, R. W. Hendersen　　36:495–529
　　The Regulation of Body Weight　　　　　R. E. Keesey, T. L. Powley　　　37:109–33

PERCEPTION
Perception and Representation   P. A. Kolers   34:129–66

PERSONALITY
Personality: Stages, Traits, and the Self   J. Loevinger, E. Knoll   34:195–222
Personality Structure and Assessment   L. G. Rorer, T. A. Widiger   34:431–63
Personality Assessment   R. I. Lanyon   35:667–701
Personality: Current Controversies, Issues, and
Directions   L. A. Pervin   36:83–114

PERSONNEL-ORGANIZATIONAL PSYCHOLOGY
Organizational Development and Change   C. Faucheux, G. Amado, A. Laurent   33:343–70
Organizationl Behavior   L. L. Cummings   33:541–79
Personnel Selection and Classification   M. L. Tenopyr, P. D. Oeltjen   33:581–618
Consumer Psychology   H. H. Kassarjian   33:619–49
Psychological Issues in Personnel Decisions   S. Zedeck, W. F. Cascio   35:461–518
Personnel Training   K. N. Wexley   35:519–51
Organizational Behavior: A Review and
Reformulation of the Field's Outcome
Variables   B. M. Staw   35:627–66
Engineering Psychology   C. D. Wickens, A. Kramer   36:307–48
Organizational Behavior   B. Schneider   36:573–611
Consumer Psychology   J. R. Bettman   37:257–89
Personnel Selection and Placement   M. D. Hakel   37:351–80

PSYCHOLINGUISTICS
See COGNITIVE PROCESSES

PSYCHOLOGY AND CULTURE
Cross-Cultural Research in Psychology   R. W. Brislin   34:363–400
Culture and Behavior: Psychology in Global
Perspective   M. H. Segall   37:523–64

PSYCHOLOGY AND LAW
The Psychology of Law   J. Monahan, E. F. Loftus   33:441–75

PSYCHOLOGY IN OTHER COUNTRIES
Psychology in Latin America Today   R. Ardila   33:103–22
Contemporary Psychology in Mexico   R. Diaz-Guerrero   35:83–112
Psychology in a Developing Society: The Case
of Israel   R. Ben–Ari, Y. Amir   37:17–41

PSYCHOPATHOLOGY
Abnormal Behavior: Social Approaches   L. D. Eron, R. A. Peterson   33:231–64
Psychopathology: Biological Approaches   M. S. Buchsbaum, R. J. Haier   34:401–30
Psychopathology of Childhood   T. M. Achenbach, C. S. Edelbrock   35:227–76
Social Factors in Psychopathology: Stress,
Social Support, and Coping Processes   R. C. Kessler, R. H. Price, C. B.
Wortman   36:531–72
Etiology and Expression of Schizophrenia:
Neurobiological and Psychosocial Factors   A. F. Mirsky, C. C. Duncan   37:291–319
See also CLINICAL AND COMMUNITY
PSYCHOLOGY

PSYCHOPHARMACOLOGY
See BIOLOGICAL PSYCHOLOGY

RESEARCH METHODOLOGY
Test Theory and Methods   D. J. Weiss, M. L. Davison   33:629–58
Information Processing Models—In Search of
Elementary Operations   M. I. Posner, P. McLeod   33:477–514
Evaluation Research: A Methodological
Perspective   P. M. Wortman   34:223–60

704   CHAPTER TITLES

Quantitative Methods for Literature Reviews   B. F. Green, J. A. Hall   35:37–53
Scaling   F. W. Young   35:55–81
Latent Structure and Item Sampling Models
    for Testing   R. E. Traub, Y. R. Lam   36:19–48
Program Evaluation: The Worldly Science   T. D. Cook, W. R. Shadish, Jr.   37:193–232

SENSORY PROCESSES
    Color Vision   J. D. Mollon   33:41–85
    Touch in Primates   I. Darian-Smith   33:155–94
    Audition: Some Relations Between Normal
        and Pathological Hearing   D. McFadden, F. L. Wightman   34:95–128
    Spatial Vision   G. Westheimer   35:201–26
    Progress in Neurophysiology of Sound
        Localization   D. P. Phillips, J. F. Brugge   36:245–74
    Visual Sensitivity   T. E. Cohn, D. J. Lasley   37:495–521

SEX ROLES
    Sex and Gender   K. Deaux   36:49–81

SLEEP
    See BIOLOGICAL PSYCHOLOGY

SOCIAL PSYCHOLOGY
    Social Psychology of Intergroup Relations   H. Tajfel   33:1–39
    Group Research   J. E. McGrath, D. A. Kravitz   33:195–230
    Social Inference   R. Hastie   34:511–42
    Attitudes and Attitude Change   J. Cooper, R. T. Croyle   35:395–426
    Current Issues in Attribution Theory and
        Research   J. H. Harvey, G. Weary   35:427–59
    The Psychology of Intergroup Attitudes and
        Behavior   M. B. Brewer, R. M. Kramer   36:219–43
    Social Cognition: A Look at Motivated
        Strategies   C. Showers, N. Cantor   36:275–305
    Expectancies and Interpersonal Processes   D. T. Miller, W. Turnbull   37:233–56

SPECIAL TOPICS
    Endorphins and Behavior   R. C. Bolles, M. S. Fanselow   33:87–101
    Sport Psychology   M. A. Browne, M. J. Mahoney   35:605–25
    Health Psychology   D. S. Krantz, N. E. Grunberg, A.
        Baum   36:349–83

VISION
    See SENSORY PROCESSES

ⒶⓇ Annual Reviews Inc. | ORDER FORM

A NONPROFIT SCIENTIFIC PUBLISHER

4139 El Camino Way, Palo Alto, CA 94306-9981, USA • (415) 493-4400

Annual Reviews Inc. publications are available directly from our office by mail or telephone (paid by credit card or purchase order), through booksellers and subscription agents, worldwide, and through participating professional societies. Prices subject to change without notice.

- **Individuals:** Prepayment required on new accounts by check or money order (in U.S. dollars, check drawn on U.S. bank) or charge to credit card — American Express, VISA, MasterCard.
- **Institutional buyers:** Please include purchase order number.
- **Students:** $10.00 discount from retail price, per volume. Prepayment required. Proof of student status must be provided (photocopy of student I.D. or signature of department secretary is acceptable). Students must send orders direct to Annual Reviews. Orders received through bookstores and institutions requesting student rates will be returned.
- **Professional Society Members:** Members of professional societies that have a contractual arrangement with Annual Reviews may order books through their society at a reduced rate. Check with your society for information.

Regular orders: Please list the volumes you wish to order by volume number.
Standing orders: New volume in the series will be sent to you automatically each year upon publication. Cancellation may be made at any time. Please indicate volume number to begin standing order.
Prepublication orders: Volumes not yet published will be shipped in month and year indicated.
California orders: Add applicable sales tax.
Postage paid (4th class bookrate/surface mail) **by Annual Reviews Inc.** Airmail postage extra.

ANNUAL REVIEWS SERIES		Prices Postpaid per volume USA/elsewhere	Regular Order Please send:	Standing Order Begin with:
			Vol. number	Vol. number
Annual Review of **ANTHROPOLOGY** (Prices of Volumes in brackets effective until 12/31/85)				
[Vols. 1-10	(1972-1981)	**$20.00/$21.00**]		
[Vol. 11	(1982)	**$22.00/$25.00**]		
[Vols. 12-14	(1983-1985)	**$27.00/$30.00**]		
Vols. 1-14	(1972-1985)	**$27.00/$30.00**		
Vol. 15	(avail. Oct. 1986)	**$31.00/$34.00**	Vol(s). _____	Vol. _____
Annual Review of **ASTRONOMY AND ASTROPHYSICS** (Prices of Volumes in brackets effective until 12/31/85)				
[Vols. 1-2, 4-19	(1963-1964; 1966-1981)	**$20.00/$21.00**]		
[Vol. 20	(1982)	**$22.00/$25.00**]		
[Vols. 21-23	(1983-1985)	**$44.00/$47.00**]		
Vols. 1-2, 4-20	(1963-1964; 1966-1982)	**$27.00/$30.00**		
Vols. 21-23	(1983-1985)	**$44.00/$47.00**		
Vol. 24	(avail. Sept. 1986)	**$44.00/$47.00**	Vol(s). _____	Vol. _____
Annual Review of **BIOCHEMISTRY** (Prices of Volumes in brackets effective until 12/31/85)				
[Vols. 30-34, 36-50	(1961-1965; 1967-1981)	**$21.00/$22.00**]		
[Vol. 51	(1982)	**$23.00/$26.00**]		
[Vols. 52-54	(1983-1985)	**$29.00/$32.00**]		
Vols. 30-34, 36-54	(1961-1965; 1967-1985)	**$29.00/$32.00**		
Vol. 55	(avail. July 1986)	**$33.00/$36.00**	Vol(s). _____	Vol. _____
Annual Review of **BIOPHYSICS AND BIOPHYSICAL CHEMISTRY** (Prices of Vols. in brackets effective until 12/31/85)				
(*Formerly* Annual Review of Biophysics and Bioengineering)				
[Vols. 1-10	(1972-1981)	**$20.00/$21.00**]		
[Vol. 11	(1982)	**$22.00/$25.00**]		
[Vols. 12-14	(1983-1985)	**$47.00/$50.00**]		
Vols. 1-11	(1972-1982)	**$27.00/$30.00**		
Vols. 12-14	(1983-1985)	**$47.00/$50.00**		
Vol. 15	(avail. June 1986)	**$47.00/$50.00**	Vol(s). _____	Vol. _____
Annual Review of **CELL BIOLOGY**				
Vol. 1	(1985)	**$27.00/$30.00**		
Vol. 2	(avail. Nov. 1986)	**$31.00/$34.00**	Vol(s). _____	Vol. _____
Annual Review of **COMPUTER SCIENCE**				
Vol. 1	(avail. late 1986)	**Price not yet established**	Vol. _____	Vol. _____
Annual Review of **EARTH AND PLANETARY SCIENCES** (Prices of Volumes in brackets effective until 12/31/85)				
[Vols. 1-9	(1973-1981)	**$20.00/$21.00**]		
[Vol. 10	(1982)	**$22.00/$25.00**]		
[Vols. 11-13	(1983-1985)	**$44.00/$47.00**]		
Vols. 1-10	(1973-1982)	**$27.00/$30.00**		
Vols. 11-13	(1983-1985)	**$44.00/$47.00**		
Vol. 14	(avail. May 1986)	**$44.00/$47.00**	Vol(s). _____/_____	Vol. _____

Annual Review of ECOLOGY AND SYSTEMATICS (Prices of Volumes in brackets effective until 12/31/85)

[Vols. 1-12	(1970-1981) . . . . **$20.00/$21.00**]			
[Vol. 13	(1982) . . . . **$22.00/$25.00**]			
[Vols. 14-16	(1983-1985) . . . . **$27.00/$30.00**]			
Vols. 1-16	(1970-1985) . . . . **$27.00/$30.00**			
Vol. 17	(avail. Nov. 1986) . . . . **$31.00/$34.00**	Vol(s). _____	Vol. _____

Annual Review of ENERGY (Prices of Volumes in brackets effective until 12/31/85)

[Vols. 1-6	(1976-1981) . . . . **$20.00/$21.00**]			
[Vol. 7	(1982) . . . . **$22.00/$25.00**]			
[Vols. 8-10	(1983-1985) . . . . **$56.00/$59.00**]			
Vols. 1-7	(1976-1982) . . . . **$27.00/$30.00**			
Vols. 8-10	(1983-1985) . . . . **$56.00/$59.00**			
Vol. 11	(avail. Oct. 1986) . . . . **$56.00/$59.00**	Vol(s). _____	Vol. _____

Annual Review of ENTOMOLOGY (Prices of Volumes in brackets effective until 12/31/85)

[Vols. 9-16, 18-26	(1964-1971; 1973-1981) . . . . **$20.00/$21.00**]			
[Vol. 27	(1982) . . . . **$22.00/$25.00**]			
[Vols. 28-30	(1983-1985) . . . . **$27.00/$30.00**]			
Vols. 9-16, 18-30	(1964-1971; 1973-1985) . . . . **$27.00/$30.00**			
Vol. 31	(avail. Jan. 1986) . . . . **$31.00/$34.00**	Vol(s). _____	Vol. _____

Annual Review of FLUID MECHANICS (Prices of Volumes in brackets effective until 12/31/85)

[Vols. 1-5, 7-13	(1969-1973; 1975-1981) . . . . **$20.00/$21.00**]			
[Vol. 14	(1982) . . . . **$22.00/$25.00**]			
[Vols. 15-17	(1983-1985) . . . . **$28.00/$31.00**]			
Vols. 1-5, 7-17	(1969-1973; 1975-1985) . . . . **$28.00/$31.00**			
Vol. 18	(avail. Jan. 1986) . . . . **$32.00/$35.00**	Vol(s). _____	Vol. _____

Annual Review of GENETICS (Prices of Volumes in brackets effective until 12/31/85)

[Vols. 1-15	(1967-1981) . . . . **$20.00/$21.00**]			
[Vol. 16	(1982) . . . . **$22.00/$25.00**]			
[Vols. 17-19	(1983-1985) . . . . **$27.00/$30.00**]			
Vols. 1-19	(1967-1985) . . . . **$27.00/$30.00**			
Vol. 20	(avail. Dec. 1986) . . . . **$31.00/$34.00**	Vol(s). _____	Vol. _____

Annual Review of IMMUNOLOGY

Vols. 1-3	(1983-1985) . . . . **$27.00/$30.00**			
Vol. 4	(avail. April 1986) . . . . **$31.00/$34.00**	Vol(s). _____	Vol. _____

Annual Review of MATERIALS SCIENCE (Prices of Volumes in brackets effective until 12/31/85)

[Vols. 1-11	(1971-1981) . . . . **$20.00/$21.00**]			
[Vol. 12	(1982) . . . . **$22.00/$25.00**]			
[Vols. 13-15	(1983-1985) . . . . **$64.00/$67.00**]			
Vols. 1-12	(1971-1982) . . . . **$27.00/$30.00**			
Vols. 13-15	(1983-1985) . . . . **$64.00/$67.00**			
Vol. 16	(avail. August 1986) . . . . **$64.00/$67.00**	Vol(s). _____	Vol. _____

Annual Review of MEDICINE (Prices of Volumes in brackets effective until 12/31/85)

[Vols. 1-3, 5-15, 17-32	(1950-52; 1954-64; 1966-81) . . . . . **$20.00/$21.00**]			
[Vol. 33	(1982) . . . . **$22.00/$25.00**]			
[Vols. 34-36	(1983-1985) . . . . **$27.00/$30.00**]			
Vols. 1-3, 5-15, 17-36	(1950-52; 1954-64; 1966-85) . . . . . **$27.00/$30.00**			
Vol. 37	(avail. April 1986) . . . . **$31.00/$34.00**	Vol(s). _____	Vol. _____

Annual Review of MICROBIOLOGY (Prices of Volumes in brackets effective until 12/31/85)

[Vols. 18-35	(1964-1981) . . . . **$20.00/$21.00**]			
[Vol. 36	(1982) . . . . **$22.00/$25.00**]			
[Vols. 37-39	(1983-1985) . . . . **$27.00/$30.00**]			
Vols. 18-39	(1964-1985) . . . . **$27.00/$30.00**			
Vol. 40	(avail. Oct. 1986) . . . . **$31.00/$34.00**	Vol(s). _____	Vol. _____

Annual Review of NEUROSCIENCE (Prices of Volumes in brackets effective until 12/31/85)

[Vols. 1-4	(1978-1981) . . . . **$20.00/$21.00**]			
[Vol. 5	(1982) . . . . **$22.00/$25.00**]			
[Vols. 6-8	(1983-1985) . . . . **$27.00/$30.00**]			
Vols. 1-8	(1978-1985) . . . . **$27.00/$30.00**			
Vol. 9	(avail. March 1986) . . . . **$31.00/$34.00**	Vol(s). _____	Vol. _____